Don Green SCSO.
4801 Milnor Dr.
Memphis, TN.
38128-4813
Tel. 901-381-5138

POCKET
PARTNER

Compiled by

Dennis H
Thom

F

Sequoia Publishing, Inc.
Littleton, Colorado, U.S.A.

This Pocket Partner Belongs To:

Name:	
Home Address:	
Home Phone:	
Business Address:	
Business Phone:	
In case of accident or serious illness, please notify:	
Name:	
Phone Number:	

Sequoia Publishing, Inc.
  Department 101
  P.O. Box 620820
  Littleton, Colorado 80162
  (303) 932-1400
  Website: http://www.sequoiapublishing.com

Printed in the U.S.A.
Library of Congress Catalog Card Number 00131473
EAN# 978-188507155-2
UPC# 769344-00071-7

ISBN 1-885071-55-8

This book is dedicated to:

-our families and friends-
for their patience, understanding,
and support during the creation
of this book;

-the law enforcement community-
for their relentless pursuit
of the bad guys and the
protection of those they serve;

-our country's Armed Forces-
who have fought for God and country
and preserved the freedoms
we enjoy today.

Thanks to all of you!

Biographies

Dennis "Bones" Evers is a 12-year veteran police officer. He has a degree in Criminology from Grossmont College and has completed dozens of additional specialty courses including EMT, Hazmat, Hostage Negotiation, Explosives, Terrorism, Kidnapping, Extortion, Officer Survival, Kinesic Interview, and Civil Defense. His 12 years of experience include 8 years as a Field Training Officer and Academy Instructor. He was an officer for the Navajo County Sheriffs Dept. for 9 years and Chief of Police, Taylor, Arizona for 3 years. He is currently an author and consultant.

Thomas J. Glover is an author and co-owner of Sequoia Publishing. He has a Masters degree in Geology from the University of Texas and has an extensive background in computers, publishing, marketing and business management. He is the author and owner of the best selling book ***Pocket Ref*** (Sequoia Publishing, 1989-2005) and has also authored or co-authored ***AutoRef, DeskRef, Handyman In-Your-Pocket, Pocket PCRef, TechRef, and Measure for Measure.***

Trish M. Glover is an author, graphic artist, editor, and desk top publishing expert for Sequoia Publishing. She has a degree in History from The Metropolitan State College of Denver, Colorado and has worked for Sequoia for the past twelve years.

Mary E. Miller is an author. She has a degree in Psychology from the University of Colorado, Boulder and has a broad background of finance, education, and business management.

Publishers Note

Sequoia Publishing, Inc. has made a serious effort to provide accurate information in this book. However, the probability exists that there are errors and misprints and that variations in data values may also occur depending on field conditions. Information included in this book should only be considered as a general guide and Sequoia Publishing, Inc. does not represent the information as being exact.

The publishers would appreciate being notified of any errors, omissions, or misprints which may occur in this book. Your suggestions for future editions would also be greatly appreciated.

Errors and omissions which have been identified for all Sequoia Publications have been compiled into an errata sheet, which is available at www.sequoiapublishing.com. (Once on the website, click "site map" on the main menu bar and then look for "Errata sheets.")

Additional Products by Sequoia

Acknowledgments

A Special Thanks to Investigator Kate Battan, for her invaluable feedback and suggestions for the fourth edition. Investigator Battan has been with the Jefferson County Sherriff's Office for over 19 years and has been an instructor at various law enforcement academies for over 10 years.

Tony Aguilar, Captain in the San Diego County Marshal's Dept., for reviewing and editing the manuscript.

Jamie Crippin, Agent, Colorado Bureau of Investigation, for providing the information on EOD resources.

Mary Glover and Becky Tennessen for their help with the difficult process of proofing this book.

Rev. Dr. David Guy, for writing the section on Critical Incident Stress Debriefings especially for this book.

Lieutenant Steve Knoll of the Englewood Police Dept., for his helpful feedback and answers to questions.

Dot Larson, Durango, Colorado, translation consultant on the Spanish Phrases section.

George Last, of Operation Lifesaver, for providing information on railroad stopping distances and emergency telephone numbers.

Americo N. Moscoso, Arvada, Colorado, translation consultant on the Spanish Phrases section.

George Schiro, Forensic Scientist, Louisiana State Police Crime Laboratory, for reviewing and contributing to the information on Crime Scene Response.

Chet Ubowski, Agent-in-Charge/Laboratory of Colorado Bureau of Investigation, for reviewing and editing the manuscript.

Richard Young of Sequoia, who compiled much of the information on weather, natural disasters, and stopping distances.

Also, thanks to the following who provided information for this book: Aerocare, Charles W. Dahlinger, Factory Mutual System, National Insurance Crime Bureau, National Center for Missing and Exploited Children, National Rifle Association, National Law Enforcement Officers Memorial Fund, Hornady Manufacturing Company, Operation Lifesaver, and the American Red Cross

The information in this manual was collected from numerous sources and if not properly acknowledged, Sequoia Publishing, Inc. would like to express its appreciation for those contributions.

Table of Contents

Resources Used · 8

Communications · 9

Crimes Against Children · · · · · · · · · · · · · · · · · · 69

Explosives · 109

First Aid · 127

General Information · 155

Incident Management Systems · · · · · · · · · · · · · · 199

Investigation and Interrogation · · · · · · · · · · · · · 263

Natural Disasters and Weather · · · · · · · · · · · · · 335

Safety and Health of Officers · · · · · · · · · · · · · · 355

Substance Abuse · 369

Terrorism and Countermeasures · · · · · · · · · · · · 461

Transportation · 517

Weapons and Ballistics · · · · · · · · · · · · · · · · · · · 543

HazMat · 603

Phone Directory · 943

Calendars and Time · 1029

Index · 1041

Resources Used

Canadian Centre for Occupational Health and Safety

Centers for Disease Control and Prevention

Chemical, Biological, Radiological Handbook, CIA

Colorado Department of Public Health and Environment

CONPLAN, United States Government Interagency Domestic Terrorism Concept of Operations Plan

Department of Homeland Security

Federal Emergency Management Agency (FEMA)

Bennett, Wayne W. And Hess, Karen M., *Criminal Investigation* (Wadsworth Publishing Co., 1998)

Law Enforcement Academy Student Packet, Arapahoe Community College, (Littleton, CO)

National Institute for Occupational Health and Safety

Police Academy Syllabus, San Diego Community College (CA)

Royal Canadian Mounted Police Online University

State of California Peace Officer Standards & Training Telecourse

Virginia Dept. of Emergency Management.

U.S. Army Field Manuals, especially FM19-20 and FM 21-11

U.S. Department of Justice

U.S. Department of The Treasury

U.S. Department of Transportation

U.S. General Services Administration

U.S. Occupational Safety and Health Administration

WorkSafe Western Australia

COMMUNICATIONS

Spanish Phrase Book · 10

  Commands · 10
  Drug Interrogation · 11
  Drug Related Words · 11
  Miranda Advisement · 12
  Miranda Waiver · 13
  Numbers and Alphabet · 13
  Pat-Down Commands · 14
  Personal Information · 15
  Units of Measure · 15
  Vehicle Stop · 16

Government Electronic Databases · · · · · · · · · · · · · · · 17

SWAT Hand Signals · 25

American Sign Language - Alphabet and Numbers · · 28

Morse Code · 28

Phonetic Alphabet - Military and Law Enforcement · · 29

Semaphore Alphabet · 30

Braille Alphabet · 31

"Ten" Radio Codes · 31

US Amateur Ham Radio Frequencies · · · · · · · · · · · · · 33

Spanish Phrase Book

Do you speak English?......¿Habla usted Inglés?
  Ah-bla oo-sted een-glayce?

Commands

Come with me. .....Venga conmigo. ....**Ven**-gah cone-**me**-go.
Come here...........Venga aquí. ....**Ven**-gah ah-**kee**.
Do it! ....¡Hágalo!...............**Ah**-gah-loh!
Don't talk. ....No hable. ....No **ah**-bleh.
Drop it!.................¡Suéltelo! ....**Swehl**-teh-lo!
Drop the pistol/revolver! ...¡Suelte el revólver!
  Swehl-the el reh-**vohl**-vair!
Drop the knife! .....¡Suelte el cuchillo! .**Swehl**-the el koo-**chee**-yo!
Drop the weapon! ¡Suelte el arma! .....**Swehl**-the el **ahr**-mah!
Follow me. ....Sígame. ....**See**-gah-meh.
Get out of the house. ....Salga de la casa.
  Sahl-ga deh lah cah-sah.
Get out of the apartment....Salga del apartamento.
  Sahl-ga del a-pahr-tah-**mehn**-toh.
Get out of the vehicle.........Salga del vehículo.
  Sahl-ga del veh-**hee**-coo-loh.
Give me the information. ....Deme la información.
  Deh-meh la een-for-**mah**-syohn.
Give me your license. ....Deme su licencia.
  Deh-meh soo lee-**sehn**-sya.
Go over there. ......Vaya para allá. ......**Vah**-yah **pah**-dah ah-**yah**.
Go away................Váyase. ....**Vah**-yah-seh.
Hands behind your head! ..¡Manos detrás de la cabeza!
  Mah-nohs deh-**trahs** deh lah kah-**beh**-sah!
Hurry up! ....¡Apúrese!...............**Ah**-**poo**-reh-seh!
Let's go. ....Vamos. ....**Vah**-mohs.
Listen to me. ....Escúcheme. ....Ehs-**koo**-cheh-meh.
Quickly. ....Rápidamente. ....Rah-peed-ah-**mehn**-the.
Repeat, please. ....Repita, por favor. ....Reh-**peet**-ah, pohr fah-**vohr**.
Sign your name here..........Firme su nombre y apellido aquí.
  Feer-meh soo **nohm**-breh ee ah-pey-yeedoh ah-**kee**.
Sit down. ....Siéntese. ....See-**ehn**-teh-seh.
Speak more slowly............Hable más despacio.
  Ah-bleh mahs deh-**spah**-syoh.
Stay inside. ....Quédese adentro...**Keh**-deh-seh ah-**dain**-troh.
Stay outside.........Quédese afuera......**Keh**-deh-seh ah-**fwehr**-ah.
Stay there. ....Quédese allí. ....**Keh**-deh-seh ah-**yee**.
Stay here. ....Quédese aquí........**Keh**-deh-seh ah-**kee**.

Stand up, or stop.................Párese, or pare.
    Pah-reh-seh, or Pah-reh.
Tell me the truth. ....Dígame la verdad.
    Dee-gah-meh lah vehr-dahd.
Tell me fast...........Dígame rápido.......***Dee****-gah-meh **rah**-peed-oh.*

Drug Interrogation

Have you heard of anyone who sells drugs?
  ¿Ha oído de alguien que venda drogas?
    *Ah oh-**ee**-doh deh **ahl**-ghee-en keh vehn-dah **droh**-gahs?*
Do you know anyone who sells drugs?
  ¿Conoce usted a alguien que venda drogas?
    *Kohn-**oh**-seh oo-**sted** ah **ahl**-ghee-en keh **vehn**-dah **droh**-gas?*
Do you use drugs?.............¿Usa usted drogas?
    Oo*-sah oo-**sted droh**-gahs?*
Do you sell drugs?.............¿Vende usted drogas?
    Vehn*-deh oo-**sted droh**-gahs?*
Have you ever been imprisoned or held in any other institution?
  ¿Ha estado usted alguna vez en la cárcel, o en alguna otra
  institución?
    *Ah ehs-**tah**-doh oo-**sted** ahl-**goo**-nah vace ehn lah **car**-cel*
    *oh ehn ahl-**goo**-nah **oh**-trah een-stee-**too**-syon?*
Where? ....¿Dónde? ....***Dohn****-deh?*
When? ....¿Cuándo? ....***Kwahn****-doh?*
Why? ....¿Por qué?.............*Pohr-**keh**?*

Drug-Related Words

drug(s)..................droga/s ....***droh****-gah/s*
drugged ....drogado ....*droh-**gah**-doh*
drunk ....borracho ....*bo-**rah**-choh*
intoxicated ....intoxicado ....*een-toh-see-**cah**-doh*
glue......................cemento, engrudo, cola
  *seh-**mehn**-toh, ehn-**groo**-doh, coh-lah*
hallucinogenics ...alucinantes ....*ah-loo-see-**nahn**-tehs*
hashish................hachi, chocolate ....***ah****-chee, shoh-coh-**laht**-eh*
heroin ....heroína ....*ehr-oh-**een**-ah*
injection ....inyección ....*een-yek-**syon***
LSD, acid ....LSD, ácido lisérgico, ácido, sello
  *el-eh es-eh deh, **ah**-see-doh lee-**sehr**-hee-koh,*
  *ah-see-doh, **sehl**-yoh*
marijuana plant....planta de marijuana
  plahn*-tah deh mahr-ee-**hwan**-ah*
amphetamines, methedrine, speed ..metadrina, anfetamina
  *meh-tah-**dree**-nah, ahn-feh-tah-**mee**-nah*
morphine..............morfina ....*mor-**fee**-nah*

narcotics	narcóticos	*nar-**coh**-tee-cohs*
needle	aguja	*ah-**goo**-ha*
outfit	estuche, equipo hipodérmico	
	*eh-**stoo**-cheh, eh-**kee**-poh hee-poh-**dair**-mee-koh*	
pills	píldoras	*peel-doh-rahs*
pipa	cachimbo/a	*ka-**cheem**-boh/ah*
rainbows	chochos (Mexican)	*cho-chos*
red devils	diablos rojos	*dee-**ah**-blohs **roh**-hos*
spoon	cuchara	*koo-**chah**-rah*
stimulants	estimulantes	*eh-**steem**-oo-lahn-tehs*
whites	blancas	*blahn-kahs*
yellow jackets	arribas	*ah-**reeb**-ahs*

Miranda Advisement

You have the right to remain silent.

Usted tiene el derecho de permanecer en silencio.

*Oo-**sted** tee-**en**-eh el de-**reh**-cho deh pair-mahn-eh-**sair** en see-**lentz**-eeo.*

If you give up that right, anything you say can and will be used against you in court of law.

Si usted renuncia a este derecho, cualquier cosa que usted diga puede ser y será usado en contra suya en la corta.

*See oo-**sted** reh-**noon**-see-ah ah **ehs**-teh de-**reh**-cho, kwal-kee-air **coh**-sa keh oo-**sted** **deega** pwehdeh sair ee said-**ah** oosahdoh en **cone**-tra **soo**ya en lah **core**-teh.*

You have the right to speak to an attorney and to have them present during questioning.

Usted tiene el derecho de hablar con un abogado y de tenerlo presente durante el interrogatorio.

*Oo-**sted** tee-**en**-eh el deh-**reh**-cho deh ah**blar** cone oon ah-boh-**gah**-do ee deh the-**nair**-lo preh-**sent**-ay du-**rahn**-the el een-teh-roh-gah-**toh**-ryoh.*

If you cannot afford an attorney, one will be appointed for you free of charge.

Si usted no puede pagar por un abogado, se le asignará uno, libre de costo a usted.

*See oo-**sted** noh **pweh**-deh pa-**gahr** por oon ah-boh-**gah**-doh, seh leh ah-seeg-nah-**rah** **oo**noh, **lee**-brah deh **coe**-stoh a oo-**sted**.*

You have the right to stop this interview at anytime.

Usted tiene el derecho de terminar esta entrevista en cualquier momento.

*Oo-**sted** tee-**en**-eh el deh-**reh**-cho deh tehr-mee-**nahr** **eh**-sta ehn-treh-vees-tah en **kwal**-kee-air moh-**men**-toh.*

Miranda Waiver

Do you understand each of these rights that I have just read to you?

¿Comprende usted cada uno de estos derechos que le acabo de leer?

*Kohm-**prehn**-deh oo-**sted** cah-dah **oo**-noh deh eh-stos deh-**reh**-chos keh leh ah-**cah**-boh deh leh-**air**?*

With these rights in mind, do you wish to speak to me?

Con estos derechos en mente, ¿desea usted hablar conmigo?

*Cone eh-stohs deh-**reh**-chos en **men**-teh, des-**say**-ah oo-**sted** ah-**blar** cone-**mee**-goh?*

Miranda Note: *Be sure to check with your department for any special requirements. Typically you do not have to 'explain' miranda rights, only ask if they understand them. If the person does not understand them, you should explain it until they understand and waive their rights or until they invoke their right to remain silent. Typically you are not obligated to ask if they want an attorney, however the phrases below are included if needed:*

Do you want a lawyer? ......¿Quiere un abogado?

*Kee-**ai**-reh oon ah-boh-**gah**-doh?*

Do you want to talk to a lawyer?

¿Quiere usted hablar con un abogado?

*Kee-**air**-eh oo-**sted** ah-**blahr** cone oon ah-boh-**gah**-doh?*

Numbers and Alphabet

zero	cero	**seh**-roh
one	uno	**oo**-noh
two	dos	*dohs*
three	tres	*trehs*
four	cuatro	**quah**-troh
five	cinco	**seen**-koh
six	seis	*sayce*
seven	siete	*see-**eh**-the*
eight	ocho	**oh**-choh
nine	nueve	**nweh**-veh
ten	diez	*dyehs*
eleven	once	**ohn**-seh
twelve	doce	**doh**-seh
thirteen	trece	**treh**-seh
fourteen	catorce	*kah-**tor**-seh*
fifteen	quince	**keen**-seh
sixteen	dieciséis	*dyehs-ee-sayce*
seventeen	diecisiete	*dyehs-ee-**syeh**-the*
eighteen	dieciocho	*dyehs-ee-**oh**-choh*
nineteen	diecinueve	*dyehs-ee-**nweh**-veh*
twenty	veinte	**behn**-the
twenty one	veintiuno	**behn**-teh-**oon**-oh
thirty	treinta	*treh-**een**-tah*
forty	cuarenta	*kwahr-**en**-tah*

fifty	cincuenta	*seen-**kwen**-tah*
sixty	sesenta	*seh-**sehn**-tah*
seventy	setenta	*seh-**tehn**-tah*
eighty	ochenta	*oh-**chen**-tah*
ninety	noventa	*noh-**ven**-tah*
one hundred	cien	*see-**en***
one hundred one	ciento uno	*see-**en**-toh-**oon**-oh*
one thousand	mil	*meehl*
one million	un millón	*oon mee-**lyohn***

A	*ah*	N	***en**-eh*
B	*beh*	Ñ	***en**-yeh*
C	*seh*	O	*oh*
Ch	*cheh*	P	*pay*
D	*deh*	Q	*coo*
E	*eh*	R	***air**-eh*
F	*efeh*	RR	***airrr**-eh*
G	*heh*	S	***es**-eh*
H	***ah**-cheh*	T	*the*
I	*ee*	U	*oo*
J	***ho**-ta*	V	*veh*
K	*kah*	W	***do**-ble-veh*
L	***el**-eh*	X	*ek-eese*
LL	***eh**-yeh*	Y	*e-gree-**eh**-ga*
M	***em**-eh*	Z	***seh**-ta*

Pat Down Commands

Stop! Police! ......¡Pare! ¡Policía!......**Pah**-reh! Poh-lee-**see**-yah!
Hands up!.............Manos arriba! ....**Mah**-nohs ah-**ree**-bah!
Spread your fingers!..........¡Extienda los dedos!
   *Ehs-tee-**ehn**-dah lohs **deh**-dohs!*
Slowly turn around! ....¡Voltéese despacio!
   *Vohl-**teh**-eh-seh deh-**spah**-syoh!*
Kneel down slowly!............¡Arrodíllece despacio!
   *Ah-roh-**dee**-eh-seh deh-**spah**-syoh!*
With your hands in front you, slowly come down to your stomach!
  ¡Con las manos adelante, échese al suelo despacio sobre su estómago!
   *Cone lahs **mah**-nohs ah-deh-**lahn**-the, **eh**-cheh-seh ahl **sweh**-loh deh-**spah**-syoh **soh**-breh soo eh-**stoh**-mah-goh!*
Put your hands behind your back!
  ¡Ponga las manos detrás de la espalda!
   ***Pohn**-gah lahs **mah**-nohs deh-**trahs** deh lah ehs-**pahl**-dah!*
Put your right hand behind your back!
  ¡Ponga la mano derecha detrás de la espalda!
   ***Pohn**-gah lah **mah**-noh deh-**reh**-cha deh-**trahs** deh lah ehs-**pahl**-dah!*

Put your left hand behind your back!
¡Ponga la mano izquierda detrás de la espalda!
Pohn-gah lah **mah**-noh ees-kee-**air**-dah deh-**trahs** deh lah ehs-**pahl**-dah!

Turn your head to the: ......Voltee la cabeza a la:
*Vohl-**teh**-eh lah ca-**beh**-sah ah lah:*

   Left ....Izquierda ....*Ees-kee-**air**-dah*

   Right ....Derecha.................*Deh-**reh**-cha*

Spread your legs................Separe las piernas.
*Seh-**pah**-reh lahs pee-**air**-nahs.*

Cross your fingers. ....Cruce los dedos.
*Kroo-seh lohs **deh**-dohs.*

Relax your fingers..............Relaje los dedos.
*Reh-**lah**-heh lohs deh-dohs.*

Don't move!..........¡No se mueva! ....*Noh seh **mweh**-vah!*

Calm Down...........¡Quieto! ....*Key-**eh**-toh!*

Personal Information

What is your name? ....¿Cómo se llama?
Koh-moh seh yahmah?

What is your birthdate? .....¿Cuál es la fecha de su nacimiento?
*Kwal ehs la **feh**chah deh soo nah-cee-mee-**ehn**-toh?*

Where were you born? ......¿Dónde nació?
Dohn-deh nah-syoh?

Where do you live? ....¿Dónde vive usted?
*Dohn-deh vee-veh oo-**sted**?*

Where do you work?..........¿Dónde trabaja usted?
*Dohn-deh trah-**bah**-ha oo-**sted**?*

Where do you go to school?.......¿Adónde va a la escuela?
*Ah-**dohn**-deh vah ah ah lah ehs-kway-la?*

What is your Social Security number?
¿Cuál es su número de Seguro Social?
*Kwal ehs soo **noo**-meh-roh deh seh-**goo**-roh soh-cee-**ahl**?*

Do you live with anyone? ..¿Vive usted con alguien?
*Vee-veh oo-**sted** cone **ahl**-gyehn?*

Are you married? ....¿Es usted casado/a?
*Ehs oo-**sted** cah-**sah**-doh/dah?*

What is your husband's/wife's name?
¿Cómo se llama su esposo/a?
*Koh-moh seh yah-mah soo eh-**spoh**-soh/sah?*

Units of Measure

balloon ....baluna, globo, bola..*bah-**loon**-ah, **gloh**-boh, **boh**-la*

bindle............paquetito, bolsita ...*pah-keh-**tee**-toh, bohl-**see**-tah*

brick..............ladrillo ....*lah-**dree**-yo*

can ....lata ....*lah*-tah

dime bag	bolsita de a diez	*bohl-**see**-tah deh a **dee**-ehs*
gram	gramo	***grah**-moh*
half gram	medio gramo	***meh**-dee-oh **grah**-moh*
joint	pitillo	*pee-**tee**-yoh*
lid	tapa	***tah**-pah*
nickel bag	bolsita de a cinco	*bohl-**see**-tah deh ah seen-koh*
ounce	una onza	***oo**nah **ohn**-sa*
piece	cacho *or* trozo	***kah**-choh *or* **troh**-zo*
quarter ounce	cuarto de onza	***kwahr**-toh deh **ohn**-sa*
half ounce	media onza	***meh**-dee-ah **ohn**-sa*

Vehicle Stop

Do you have a driver's license?
¿Tiene usted una licencia de manejar?
*Tee-**ehn**-eh oo-**sted** **oon**ah lee-**sehn**-sya de mah-nay-**hawr**?*

Come out with your hands up. ....Salga con las manos arriba.
***Sahl**-gah cone lahs **mah**-nohs ah-**rhee**-bah.*

Driver, slowly turn off the engine with your right hand.
Chofer, apague despacio el motor, con la mano derecha.
***Choh**-fair, ah-**pah**-geh deh-**spah**-syoh el moh-**tor**, cone lah **mah**-noh deh-**reh**-cha.*

Drop the keys outside. ....Tire las llaves afuera.
***Tee**-reh lahs **ya**-vehs ah-**fwair**-ah.*

Face me. ....Voltee. ....*(Vohl-**teh**-eh)*

Lie down on the ground. .....Acuéstese boca abajo.
*Ah-**kweh**-steh-seh **boh**-kah ah-**bah**-hoh.*

Open the car door. ....Abra la puerta del carro.
*Ah-**brah** lah **pwair**-tah del **car**-oh.*

Put your hands on: ....Ponga sus manos en:
***Pohn**-gah soos mahnohs ehn:*

  the dashboard ......el tablero del carro. *.el tah-**ble**-ro del **car**-oh.*
  the steering wheel ......el volante. ....*el voh-**lahn**-the.*
  the door ....la puerta. ....*lah **pwair**-tah.*
  the seat in front of you ....el asiento enfrente de usted.
  *el ah-see-**en**-toh ehn **frehn**-the deh oo-**sted**.*

Passenger/s ....Pasajero/s ....*Pah-sah-**hehr**-oh/s*

Next to (to the right of) the driver ......A la derecha del chofer
*Ah lah deh-**reh**-cha dehl **choh**-fehr*

Front passenger ....pasajero de adelante
*Pah-sah-**hehr**-oh deh ah-deh-**lahn**-the*

Behind the driver .Detrás del chofer ...*Deh-**trahs** dehl **choh**-fehr*

Seated in the rear Sentado atrás ....*Sehn-**tah**-doh ah-**trahs***

Take two steps forward. ....Dé dos pasos hacia adelante.
***Deh** dohs **pah**-sohs ah-**see**-ah ah-deh-**lahn**-the.*

Government Electronic Databases

Unless other contact information is given, the following databases are limited to access via your agency's secure communications system.

CCD - Consular Consolidated Database
Agency: Bureau of Consular Affairs

A database containing all visa and passport applicants' names, identifying features, and fingerprints.

CIS - Central Index System
Agency: U.S. Citizenship and Immigration Service (USCIS) under Dept. of Homeland Security (DHS)

Helps locate files about legal immigrants, naturalized citizens and aliens who were formally excluded or deported. Files usually contain name, date of birth, nationality, date of entry, immigration status and the applicable INS files control office. Name and birthdate or file number are needed to retrieve information.

CLASP - Consular Lost & Stolen Passport
Agency: Department of State

A system used in overseas posts and borders. It is a system that provides centralized information on lost and stolen passports. Phone: (202) 955-0430

CLASS - Consular Lookout And Support System
Agency: Department of State

Automated database containing information about aliens who have been denied visas, those who might be found ineligible should they apply, and those whose visa applications require an opinion from the Department of State prior to issuance.

DCII - Defense Central and Investigations Index
Agency: Department of Defense

An unclassified system operated by the Defense Investigative Service; access limited to federal agencies with investigative, counterintelligence or adjudicative responsibilities. Data consists of an alphabetical list of people who have been subjects, victims, or cross-referenced incidental subjects in DOD personnel security checks or criminal, counterintelligence and fraud investigations. The information is protected by the Privacy Act of 1994.

EPIC - El Paso Intelligence Center
Agencies: Cooperative effort of DEA, USCIS, DHS, Customs, Coast Guard, ATF, FAA, USMS, FBI, IRS, USSS, Dept. of State, Dept. of Interior, CIA, and DOD.

Contains information about illegal traffic in drugs, weapons, currency, and alien smuggling. It's two primary functions are the exchange of time-sensitive tactical intelligence to disrupt the flow of illegal drugs, and use of the intelligence process to support other programs of interest to its participating agencies. State and local law enforcement agencies have access to EPIC through a designated group within their organization, or through a member agency; member agencies have direct access to all EPIC information. Phone: 888-USE-EPIC (888-873-3742) 24/7

EDGAR - Electronic Data Gathering, Analysis & Retrieval
Agency: Securities and Exchange Commission (SEC)

Contains some documents that companies and other entities are required to file with the SEC. Not all documents submitted to the SEC are included for a variety of reasons. Public filings to the SEC are available on the SEC home page within 48 hours after being filed.

FPDC - Federal Procurement Data Center
Agency: U.S. General Services Administration

Contains purchasing information for more than 60 federal agencies dating back to October, 1978. Data includes agency name, contract, order and modification numbers, purchase office and address, award date, product or service, and contractor name and address. A variety of reports are published quarterly. Phone: (703) 872-8621 or (703) 872-8534.
Webpage: http://www.fpdc.gov

FIRS - Fingerprint Identification Records System
Agency: Federal Bureau of Investigation (FBI)

Stores criminal record information and assists in fingerprint identification. Fingerprints available are from people arrested or incarcerated; those fingerprinted for military service, federal employment application, alien registration and naturalization, or who want their fingerprints on file for personal identification purposes. Records on 24 million people are contained in the automated file. Manual files contain about 10 million older records.

Gateway - (Name of system, not an acronym)
Agency: Dept. of the Treasury, FinCEN

State and local LE agencies can research records filed under the Bank Secrecy Act and the Suspicious Activity Reporting System. Alerts the inquiring agency about similar queries on the same subject.

IBIS - Interagency Border Inspection System
Agency: Dept. of Homeland Security and U.S. Customs
Information database with law enforcement data on wanted or missing persons, criminal history, criminal investigation information, terrorists, foreign fugitives, and stolen property.

ICTS - Interpol Case Tracking System
Agency: U.S. National Central Bureau
Contains information about people, property and organizations involved in international crime. Can help determine whether there is an international connection to an investigation, or whether those involved have any previous international criminal activity.

III - Interstate Identification Index
Agency: Federal Bureau of Investigation (FBI)
Criminal records of 24 million people born after 1956; or those born earlier whose first arrest was recorded with the FBI from 1974 on. The database contains people arrested for felonies and serious misdemeanors, and older records for certain fugitives or repeat offenders.

JMIE - Joint Maritime Information Element
Agencies: Combined records from the Office of Naval Intelligence, Military Sealift Command, DEA, Dept. of State, Customs, CIA, Coast Guard, Maritime Admin., Dept. of Energy, Defense Intelligence Agency, USCIS, NSA and the Executive Office of the President's Office of National Drug Control Policy.
Contains data on maritime-related law enforcement and national foreign intelligence, used to interdict narcotics or smuggling, sea and defense zone surveillance, petroleum traffic monitoring, border control and emergency sealift management. At-sea and in-port information about commercial and private vessels from 35 locations, and vessel registration files from Florida, California, Delaware, Puerto Rico and the Virgin Islands.

LESC - Law Enforcement Support Center
Agency: U.S. Immigration & Customs Enforcement (ICE)
Contains data from six databases (ICE database, NCIC, III, SEVIS, US-VISIT, NSEERS) on immigration status, and information on aliens who have been arrested or are being investigated for criminal activities. Responds to requests from federal, state and local law enforcement agencies. Access through the NLETS system only 24/7.

NADDIS - Narcotics & Dangerous Drugs Info. System

Agency: Drug Enforcement Administration (DEA)

Information on cases related to narcotics, and smuggling of other contraband, aliens or funds. Access through EPIC or local DEA offices.

NAILS - National Automated Immigration Lookout System

Agency: Department of Homeland Security

An inter-agency database that provides information on immigration history, immigration file location, immigrant's applications for benefits, detention information, and deportation information. This database also includes information on immigrants who are classified as "lookout" immigrants (Immigrants that have either potential information or confirmed case information that would exclude them from entering the US).

NCIC 2000 - National Crime Information Center

Agency: Federal Bureau of Investigation (FBI)

The NCIC 2000 gives access to the criminal records of 24 million people through the Interstate Identification Index (III). The NCIC 2000 has expanded from it's predecessor (NCIC) to include enhanced name searching, fingerprint identification, mugshots and other identifying features (such as scars and tattoos), missing and unidentified persons, probation and parole records, SENTRY file of currently incarcerated people, deported felons, foreign fugitives, and state control terminal agency manuals. It also includes information about a variety of stolen, missing or wanted goods including guns, vehicles, license plates, boats, financial instruments (stocks, bonds, securities), and generic identifying images for articles such as vehicles and boats. The NCIC 2000 also provides access to the ATF Violent Felon File, the US Secret Service Protection File, the gang and terrorist organizations file, the Index to State Criminal History Records, and Criminal History Records of Federal Offenders; the Originating Agency Identifier file, and the protective order file. Most law enforcement agencies have access to the NCIC 2000.

NLETS - National Law Enforcement Telecom. System

Agencies: State and local agencies include motor vehicle and licensing departments in addition to law enforcement. Federal agencies include Customs, FBI, DOJ, Secret Service, USMS, Dept. of State, Dept. of the Army, Dept. of the Interior, Naval Criminal Investigative Service, and Air Force Office of Special Investigations, Dept. of Homeland Security, and the National Insurance Crime Bureau (NICB).

NLETS links together all criminal justice and law enforcement agencies in the US and Puerto Rico, as well as INTERPOL

Canada. The system provides access to vehicle registration information including cars, trucks, boats, aircraft and snowmobiles. Information about individuals includes driver's license and history, criminal records, sex offender registration, and parole/probation and corrections data. There is a directory of participating organizations, and hazardous material file data. Files available from the Canadian Police Information Centre include wanted individuals, criminal histories, information on stolen vehicles, articles, guns, securities, and stolen boats or motors. Users can send free-form messages to each other individually, or broadcast a message.

NETC - National Explosives Tracing Center

Agency: Bureau of Alcohol, Tobacco, Firearms & Explosives (ATF)
Provides tracking information on explosives from their place of manufacture to purchase. Federal, state, county, local, and foreign law enforcement agencies can request a trace.
During normal business hours (M-F; 7:30am-4:30pm EST) you can request a trace by calling (202) 927-4590 or (800) 461-8441.
For non-emergency requests outside of normal business hours complete the "ATF F 3325.1 - Request for Explosive Tracing' form, and fax to (202) 927-4570 or email to: explosivestracing@atf.gov. The center will do the trace and respond the next business day. The form is available on-line at http://www.atf.gov/aexis2/tracing_new.htm
For after hour emergency assistance, complete the form listed above and contact the EOC (Enforcement Operations Center) at (888) 283-2662.

NW3C or NWCCC - National White Collar Crime Center

Agency: Bureau of Justice Assistance, USDOJ/OJP
Database contains information about people and businesses suspected of economic, computer, and high-tech crimes such as credit card fraud, computer fraud, advanced fee loan schemes, and investment and securities fraud. Phone: 1-800-221-4424 or 804-323-3563. Website: http://www.nw3c.org

NIIS - Nonimmigrant Information System

Agency: Dept. of Justice, and U.S. Citizenship & Immigration Service (USCIS)
Includes information about arrivals and departures of all nonimmigrant aliens (those who enter the US temporarily) except Canadians and Mexicans visiting for pleasure. It is accessible through INS offices.

RISS - Regional Information Sharing System

Agency: Bureau of Justice Assistance, US DOJ/OJP

RISS is a federally-funded program involving more than 7,000 local, state and federal law enforcement agencies in all 50 states, Guam, Puerto Rico, Washington D.C., U.S. Virgin Islands, Canada, Australia, and England. It supports coordination and information sharing among local, state and federal law enforcement agencies, and provides members with criminal intelligence and investigative support services. Six regional projects operate in all 50 US states, the District of Columbia and Canada. The six regions vary in terms of the services they offer and the crimes they choose to target.

Website: http://www.rissinfo.com   Or contact the Bureau of Justice Assistance, 202-616-7829.

RISS Regions:

MAGLOCLEN - Middle-Atlantic-Great Lakes Organized Crime Law Enforcement Network

Serves member agencies in Australia, DC, DE, England, IN, MD, MI, NJ, NY, OH, Ontario, PA, and Quebec. Focuses on organized crime, gangs and violent crime. Phone: 215-504-4910

MOCIC - Mid-States Organized Crime Info. Center

Serves Canada, IL, IA, KS, MN, MO, NE, ND, SD, and WI. Focuses on narcotics trafficking, organized crime, professional traveling criminals, gangs and violent crime. Phone: 417-883-4383.

NESPIN - New England State Police Info. Network

Serves agencies in Canada, CT, ME, MA, NH, RI, and VT. Focuses on narcotics trafficking, organized crime, major criminal activity, gangs and violent crime. Phone: 508-528-8200.

ROCIC - Regional Organized Crime Info. Center

Serves AL, AR, FL, GA, KY, LA, MS, NC, OK, PR, SC, TN, TX, VA, Virgin Islands, and WV. Focuses on narcotics violators, professional traveling criminals, organized crime, gangs, and violent crime.

Phone: 615-871-0013 Website: http://www.rocic.com

RMIN - Rocky Mountain Information Network

Serves members in AZ, CO, ID, MT, NV, NM, UT, WY and Canada. Focuses on narcotics trafficking and associated criminal activity, gangs and violent crime. Phone: 602-351-2320

WSIN - Western States Information Network

Serves member agencies in AK, Australia, CA, Canada, Guam, HI, OR, and WA. Focuses on narcotics trafficking and criminal organizations. Phone: 916-263-1166.

SIC - Securities Information Center

Agency: Securities and Exchange Commission (SEC)
The Center's database contains reports of lost, stolen and counterfeit securities certificates. It was established in 1977 to reduce trafficking in such certificates, and is used primarily by investment professionals.

SENTRY (Name of system, not an acronym)

Agency: Federal Bureau of Prisons, Dept. of Justice
Information on all federal prisoners since 1980, including physical description, profile, place of incarceration or release location, personal history, security designation, custody classification, numerical identifiers, sentencing information, and past and present institution assignments. Currently available to several Dept. of Justice agencies and US Probation Services offices. Phone: 202-307-3065

SEVIS - Student & Exchange Visitor Information System

Agency: Department of Homeland Security, and U.S. Immigration & Customs Enforcement (ICE)
This is a web-based system that maintains information on international students and exchange visitors in the U.S.
Website: http://www.ice.gov/graphics/sevis

SPICIN - South Pacific Islands Criminal Intelligence Network

Agency: South Pacific Chiefs of Police in 21 countries
Promotes the gathering, recording and exchange of information about drug trafficking, mobile criminals, organized/white collar crime, money laundering, terrorism, use of Pacific Island waters and aircraft, and other international crime. Provides assistance to its member countries and other national and international law enforcement agencies concerning criminal history checks, location of suspects, witnesses or fugitives, missing or wanted persons, firearm checks, driver's license or license plate checks, vehicle registration, military checks, and stolen vessels.
Website: http://www.spicin.com

TECS - Treasury Enforcement Communications System

Agency: Dept. of the Treasury, managed by Customs
Designed to interface with several other law enforcement systems, and provide controlled access to information about suspects through several applications:
  • It is the clearing house for IBIS (Inspection/Interagency Border Inspection System) which facilitates passenger processing.

- It has information-sharing capabilities that allow queries, on-line entry and maintenance of records, and access to other external data sources such as NCIC, NLETS and commercial directories.
- On-line entry of enforcement reports, including the capture, storage and display of full narrative text. Reports can be viewed, printed or downloaded by other users.

TSC - Terrorist Screening Center

Agency: FBI, Dept of Justice, Dept of State, Dept of Treasury, and Dept of Homeland Security

This center compiles information from ten different databases to coordinate terrorist screening efforts for local law enforcement, U.S. Customs & Border Protection, and the State Department. Information is there for quick response and access when a known or suspected terrorist is encountered. It assists agencies in keeping terrorists out of the U.S. and locating the ones that are already in the U.S. The ten different databases that contribute information are: Top 10 Fugitive List (Air Force), CLASS (Consular Lookout And Support System), IBIS (Interagency Border Inspection System), Interpol terrorism watch list, NAILS (National Automated Immigration Lookout System), No-Fly (Dept of Defense), Selectee (Dept of Transportation), TTIC (Terrorist Threat Integration Center), VGTOF (Violent Gang & Terrorist Organization File), and Warrant Information.

TTIC - Terrorist Threat Integration Center

Agency: DCI Counterterrorist Center, Department of Defense, FBI Counterterrorism Division, Department of Homeland Security

This center compiles all terrorist threat intelligence and all information on known and suspected terrorists in order to provide law enforcement with accurate information and also to provide comprehensive terrorist threat assessments.

Source: *1997 Investigator's Guide to Information Sources*, published by the General Accounting Office, General Services Administration.

Swat Hand Signals

YES
Nod head.

NO
Turn head from side to side.

SILENCE
Hold index finger straight up over

SEARCH or LEAD
Point to the eyes with index and middle fingers.

ME or I
Point to yourself.

SHIELD
Hold arm horizontal and close to chest.

TIME
Point at watch with index finger.

STOP or STANDBY
Hand straight up, palm forward.

LISTEN
Hand goes behind ear, palm facing forward.

NUMBERS
Ex: "3" - hold up the number desired.

DISREGARD or CANCEL
Cutting motion across throat.

LOOK or SEE
Slightly cup the hand over the eyebrows.

SUSPECT
Grab the forearm.

HOSTAGE
Grab the throat.

STACK UP BEHIND ME
Pat the butt a couple of times.

COVER
Pat the head a couple of times.

WINDOW or ATTIC
Draw a square in the air with both index fingers, starting above the head.

DOOR
Draw a square, but exclude the bottom line.

FLASHBANG
Simulate an underhand toss.

I DON'T KNOW or UNKNOWN
Bring both hands up to the side with palms up.

GET DOWN or TAKE COVER
Palm faces ground; move arm up and down.

REPEAT or I DON'T UNDERSTAND
Turn head from side to side while bringing palms.

DOOR OPENS IN
Pretend to turn a door knob and pull inward.

DOOR OPENS OUT
Pretend to turn a door knob and push it outward.

COME or FOLLOW ME
Palm toward face, bring hand up and down.

GO THERE
Point to the place; move arm back then forward.

AROUND
Make hooking motion in direction desired.

FORCE ENTRY (kick or ram)
Arm horizontal; fist is moved forward and back.

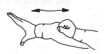

DOUBLE TIME
Extend arm and move fist up and down a few times.

TURN LIGHTS ON/OFF
Close fist, then spread fingers out as arm moves forward; repeat.

ARMED
Move thumb up and down like a hammer or gun.

READY TO GO
Thumb straight up, fingers to palm.

YOU or THAT
Point to the person or object.

OK or SECURE or I UNDERSTAND
Make circle with index finger and thumb, then point the circle.

CRISIS ENTRY
(Dynamic Entry)
Form the letter "C" with fingers and thumb.

TALK
Bring index finger and thumb together a few times.

SIDE of BUILDING
Slide hand up and down with fingers extended.

MIRROR or VIDEO CAMERA
Rotate hand back and forth with palm flat.

Swat hand signals provided courtesy of SWAT Magazine
Phone: 520-775-5902

American Sign Language

A		J		S		2	
B		K		T		3	
C		L		U		4	
D		M		V		5	
E		N		W		6	
F		O		X		7	
G		P		Y		8	
H		Q		Z		9	
I		R		1		10	

Morse Code

A	•—	N	—•	0	—————
B	—•••	O	———	1	•————
C	—•—•	P	•——•	2	••———
D	—••	Q	——•—	3	•••——
E	•	R	•—•	4	••••—
F	••—•	S	•••	5	•••••
G	——•	T	—	6	—••••
H	••••	U	••—	7	——•••
I	••	V	•••—	8	———••
J	•———	W	•——	9	————•
K	—•—	X	—••—		
L	•—••	Y	—•——	Error	••••••••
M	——	Z	——••	Wait	•—•••
				End Message	•—•—•

Phonetic Alphabet

Letter	Law Enforcement	Military
A	Adam	Alpha
B	Boy	Bravo
C	Charles	Charlie
D	David	Delta
E	Edward	Echo
F	Frank	Foxtrot
G	George	Golf
H	Henry	Hotel
I	Ida	India
J	John	Juliet
K	King	Kilo
L	Lincoln	Lima
M	Mary	Mike
N	Nora	November
O	Ocean	Oscar
P	Paul	Papa
Q	Queen	Quebec
R	Robert	Romeo
S	Sam	Sierra
T	Tom	Tango
U	Union	Uniform
V	Victor	Victor
W	William	Whiskey
X	X-ray	X-ray
Y	Young	Yankee
Z	Zebra	Zulu

Semaphore Alphabet

A		M		Y	
B		N		Z	
C		O		1	
D		P		2	
E		Q		3	
F		R		4	
G		S		5	
H		T		6	
I		U		7	
J		V		8	
K		W		9	
L		X		0	

Braille Alphabet

A	⠁	M	⠍	Y	⠽
B	⠃	N	⠝	Z	⠵
C	⠉	O	⠕	1	⠁
D	⠙	P	⠏	2	⠃
E	⠑	Q	⠟	3	⠉
F	⠋	R	⠗	4	⠙
G	⠛	S	⠎	5	⠑
H	⠓	T	⠞	6	⠋
I	⠊	U	⠥	7	⠛
J	⠚	V	⠧	8	⠓
K	⠅	W	⠺	9	⠊
L	⠇	X	⠭	0	⠚

"Ten" Radio Codes

10–1	Receiving poorly, bad signal
10–2	Receiving OK, signal strong
10–3	Stop transmitting
10–4	Message received
10–5	Relay message
10–6	Busy, please stand by
10–7	Out of service
10–8	In service
10–9	Repeat message
10–10	Finished, standing by
10–11	Talk slower
10–12	Visitors present

10–13.............Need weather or road conditions
10–16.............Pickup needed at_____
10–17.............Urgent Business
10–18.............Is there anything for us
10–19.............Nothing for you, return to base
10–20.............My location is_____
10–21.............Use a telephone
10–22.............Report in person to_____
10–23.............Stand by
10–24.............Finished last assignment
10–25.............Can you contact_____?
10–26.............Disregard last information
10–27.............I'm changing to channel_____
10–28.............Identify your station
10–29.............Your time is up for contact
10–30.............Does not conform to FCC rules
10–32.............I'll give you a radio check
10–33.............Emergency traffic at this station
10–34.............Help needed at this station
10–35.............Confidential information
10–36.............The correct time is_____
10-37 ....Wrecker needed at_____
10-38 ....Ambulance needed at_____
10-39 ....Your message has been delivered
10-41 ....Please change to channel_____
10-42 ....Traffic accident at_____
10-43 ....Traffic congestion at_____
10-44 ....I have a message for_____
10-45 ....All units within range please report in
10-50 ....Break channel
10-60 ....What is the next message number
10-62 ....Unable to copy, please call on the phone
10-63 ....Net directed to_____
10-64 ....Net clear
10-65 ....Standing by, awaiting your next message
10-67 ....All units comply
10-70 ....Fire at_____
10-71 ....Proceed with transmission in sequence
10-73 ....Speed trap at_____
10-75 ....Your transmission is causing interference
10-77 ....Negative contact
10-81 ....Reserve hotel room for_____
10-82 ....Reserve room for_____
10-84 ....My telephone number is_____
10-85 ....My address is_____
10-89 ....Radio repairman is needed at_____
10-90 ....I have TVI
10-91 ....Talk closer to the microphone
10-92 ....Your transmitter needs adjustment
10-93 ....Check my frequency on this channel
10-94 ....Please give me a long count
10-95 ....Transmit dead carrier for 5 seconds
10-99 ....Mission completed, all units secure
10-200 ....Police needed at_____

Ham Radio Emergency Frequencies

Net Name (specific coverage area - if not already stated)	Frequency (MHZ)	Local Days	Local Time
Alabama			
Alabama Day Net	146.84-	Su	8:30 pm
Alabama Emergency Net	3.965 7.243	Tu	7:30 pm
Alabama Emergency Net J (Florence, Colbert Co)	146.61-	Daily	6:00 pm
Alabama Emergency Net Q (Covington Co)	146.94-	M	7:30 pm
Alabama Emergency Net S (Marshall Co)	147.20+	Tu	8:00 pm
Alabama Emergency Net U (Tuscaloosa)	147.30-	Tu	8:30 pm
Alabama Emergency Net V (Tallapoosa Co)	145.33-	Th	7:30 pm
Alabama Emergency Net W (Calhoun Co)	147.09+	M	8:00 pm
Alabama Emergency Net Y (Etowah Co)	147.16+	Tu	8:30 pm
Alabama Emergency Net Z (DeKalb Co)	147.27+	M,F	7:30 pm
Alabama Section Net CW	3575	Daily	7:00 pm 10:00pm
Alabama Traffic Net Mike	3965	Daily	6:30 pm
Alabama Traffic Net Mike	3965	Su	8:00 am
Anniston Emergency. Radio Club Net	147.04+	M	7:30 pm
Auburn University Amateur Radio Club Net (Auburn)	147.24+	Su	9:00 pm
Baldwin Co Emergency Net	146.685-	Su	3:00 pm
Bibb Co ARES Net	145.39-	M	7:00 pm
Blount Co ARC Training Net	146.70-	Su	9:00 pm
Boll Weevil Net (Enterprise area)	147.24+	Tu	7:00 pm
Butler Co 2 Meter Net (AL & SE MS)	146.67-	Th	7:00 pm
Calhoun Co RACES Net	146.78-	M	7:00 pm
Clay Co Amateur Radio Society (Clay & Surrounding Counties)	147.255(131.8)	Tu	8:30 pm
Cullman Co RACES/ARES Training Net	145.310 144.710	Su	8:30 pm
Dale Co ARES Net	146.98-	M (1)	7:00 pm
Dale Co SKYWARN Net (SE AL)	145.39-	M (3)	7:00 pm
Deer Stand Hill Net (Pike Co)	146.82-	M	8:30 pm
Dixie ARES Net (Montgomery area)	145.31-	Tu	8:00 pm
East Alabama Two-Meter Net (Auburn, Opelika area)	147.12+	Su	8:00 pm
Etowah Co ARES/RACES Net	146.82-	Th	8:00 pm
Franklin Co ARES Net	147.16+	Daily	9:00 pm
Jackson Co Emergency Net	146.90-	Th	7:00 pm
Jefferson Co Emergency Net (Birmingham area)	146.88-	Tu	9:00 pm
Lawrence Co SKYWARN Net	145.27-	Th	7:45 pm
Limestone Co ARES Net	145.15-	Th	7:00 pm
Madison Co Emergency Net	146.94-	Th	7:30 pm
Marshall Co SKYWARN Net	147.20+	M	8:00 pm
Mercury Amateur Radio Association, Northern Alabama (Huntsville area)	145.29-	Su	8:45 pm
Mobile Co ARES Net	146.94-	Th	7:30 pm
Monroe Co ARES Net	146.82	Tu	8:00 pm
Monroe Co ARES Net	146.67	Tu	8:00 pm
Monroe Co ARES Net	147.160+(167.9)	when needed	
Morgan Co ARES Net	147.00+	Th	7:30 pm

North Alabama SKYWARN Net (Moulton area)	146.96- 147.24+ 147.36+ 146.78-	Th	8:00 pm
Saint Clair Co ARES/RACES Net	146.13-	Tu	8:00 pm
Salem Hill SKYWARN Net (East Central Alabama & West Central Georgia)	146.94-	Tu	7:30 pm
Shelby Co ARES Net	146.98-	Tu	8:00 pm
South Alabama Radio Club 2-Meter Net (South Central Alabama & NW Florida Panhandle)	147.26-(100)	Th (1, 2, 4, 5)	7:30 pm
South Alabama Radio Club Net (Covington Co)	147.26-	Th	7:30 pm
Talladega Co ARES/RACES Net	146.74-	Th	8:00 pm
Walker Co Emergency Net	146.64-	M	8:00 pm
West Alabama ARES Net (Choctaw Co)	147.08+	M	7:30 pm
West Alabama Emergency Net (Tuscaloosa Co & West Central Alabama)	146.82-	Su	8:30 pm
Winston Co Emergency Net	147.36+	Daily	8:00 pm
Wiregrass Amateur Radio Club Net (Dothan area)	145.43-	Th	8:30 pm

Alaska

Alaska CW Net	3.54 7.042 14.05 144.100 CW	Daily	7:00 pm
Alaska Snipers Net (Alaska, Yukon, British Columbia)	3.92	Daily	6:00 pm
Alaska, Pacific Emergency Preparedness Net (Alaska & lower 48 states)	14.292	M-F	8:30 am
Anchorage ARES Net	147.30+	Th	8:00 pm
Earthquake/Tsunami/ARES Net (Alaska)	3.92 14.29	when needed	
Hallicrafters Collectors International Sunday Net (worldwide)	14.293	Su	1:30 pm
HFpack The HF Portable Group (North America, Pacific, Atlantic)	5.3715	Sa, Su	9:45 pm
Juneau ARES Net (Juneau, Haines, Gustavus, and vicinity)	147.30+	Tu	7:00 pm
Kodiak ARES Net (Kodiak Island)	146.88-	when needed	
Motley Group (Alaska & Yukon)	3.933	Daily	9:00 am
Polar Amateur Radio Klub of Alaska (Anchorage, Kenai, Mat-Su Valley, Soldotna)	147.300	Th	9:00 pm

Alberta, Canada (Emergency & National Traffic Nets)

Alberta ARES	3.75	Su	8:30 am 9:00 pm
Alberta Public Service Net (Alberta, British Columbia, Saskatchewan)	3.74	Daily	6:30 pm
Alberta Traffic Net	3.685	Daily	6:00 pm
Calgary ARES	146.85-	Th	8:30 pm

Arizona

Arizona Amateurs on Television (AATV) (Phoenix Area)	146.840-(162.2) Video input: 434.00	W, Su	1:00 am
Arizona RACES Net	3.99	Su	8:00 am
Arizona SKYWARN Net (Central Arizona)	146.74-	Daily	8:00 pm
Arizona SKYWARN Net (S Central Arizona)	442.800+(100)	W	8:00 pm
Arizona State Emergency Net	3.99	Su	7:30 am
Arizona Traffic & Emergency Net	3.992	Daily	7:00 pm
Cochise Co ARES/RACES Net	147.02+(PL162.2)	W (2,4)	8:00 pm
Gila Co RACES	146.74- 449.65-	Th	7:00 pm

Maricopa Co Emergency Resource Net (Phoenix Metro area)	146.82-(PL162.2) 442.6+(PL 100)	Th	8:00 pm
Mohave Co ARES (Northwest Arizona, Southern Nevada, Eastern California)	146.76- 448.25		7:00 am
NWS Phoenix Sector 7 SKYWARN Net (Southwest Arizona, Southeast California)	146.88- (PL152.2)	W	8:00 pm
Pima Co Emergency Net	3.995	Su	8:45 am
Pima Co RACES Net	147.30+	Sa	1:00 pm
Pinal Co Emergency Communications Group	147.200+(162.2)	Tu	7:00 pm
White Mountain Emergency Ham Radio Net (Slow Low, Arizona)	145.31-(110.9)	W (2,4)	7:30 pm

Arkansas

Arkansas ARES Net	3.9875	Su	7:00 am
Arkansas Mockingbird Net	3.928	M-F	4:30 pm
Arkansas Phone Net	3.9875	M-Sa	6:00 am
Arkansas Razorback Net	3.9875	Daily	6:30 pm
Baxter Co Emergency Net	146.88-	M	8:00 pm
Central Arkansas Radio Emergency Net	146.94-	Th	8:00 pm
Cross Co SKYWARN/ARES Net (NE Arkansas)	145.310-	Su	9:00 pm
District 3 SKYWARN Net	147.15+	when needed	
Faulkner Co ARC 10 Meter Net	28.49	Tu	4:00 pm
Fort Smith Salvation Army (SATERN) (West Central Arkansas)	146.94-	W (3)	7:00 pm
Hot Springs Co Emergency Net (S Central AK)	147.36+	F	7:00 pm
Nevada & Hempstead Counties ARES Net (Nevada & Counties in SW Arkansas)	146.685-(114.8)	when needed	12:00am
North Arkansas Amateur Radio Society Emergency Net (50 mile radius from Harrison)	147.000-	M	7:00 pm
Polk Co ARES Net (West Central Arkansas)	146.82-	Th	8:00 pm
Southeast ARS Net	146.58	M	8:00 pm
Tri States Emergency AR Net (SW Arkansas, NE Texas, SE Oklahoma)	147.045	Su	9:02 pm
5YM University WeatherNet (Northwest Arkansas)	147.135+	M	8:00 pm

British Columbia, Canada (Emergency & National Traffic Nets)

British Columbia Emergency Net CW (USA: ID, MT, OR; Canada: AB, BC, MB, SK)	3.652	Daily	7:00 pm
British Columbia Public Service SSB (USA: WA; Canada:AB, BC, MB, NT, SK)	3.729	Daily	5:30 pm
Chilliwack Emergency Roll Call Net (Chilliwack to Vancouver)	147.510 linked to 443.000 +5	M	7:00 pm

California

Alameda Disaster Preparedness Net	146.880-(77)	Th	7:00 pm
Alameda Simplex	146.505	W	7:00 pm
ALERT (Orange Co)	145.16-(PL136.5)	M	9:00 pm
American Red Cross (Orange Co)	145.22-(PL103.5)	W	12:00pm
Anza ARES/RACES Net	145.34-(PL107.2)	Tu	7:30 pm
Arcata ARES Net	146.43	M	7:00 pm
ARES 6 Meter Net (San Diego Co)	52.68-	Sa	8:00 pm
ARES Central District Net (San Diego Central area)	147.48	Su	7:30 pm
ARES Eastern District Net (Eastern San Diego Co)	147.57	Su	7:30 pm
ARES Northern District HF Net (San Diego Co)	3.924	Su	8:15 am
ARES Northern District Net (San Diego Northern district)	146.73-	Su	8:30 am
ARES Northwest District (San Fernando Valley & Los Angeles)	146.58	M	9:00 pm

ARES Response Area 3 (Northern Orange Co)	145.34- (PL136.5)	M	7:15 pm
ARES Response Area 5 (Southern Orange Co)	145.42-	M	7:15 pm
ARES San Diego Section (San Diego & Imperial Valley)	3.905	Su	9:00 am
Boy Scouts of America Net (Riverside, Los Angeles, San Bernardino, & Orange)	145.22-	Sa	7:00 pm
Buena Park RACES	145.565	M	7:15 pm
California Rescue Communications HF Net (West Coast)	7.25	M-F	8:30 am
Central Mountain RACES Net	144.99	M	7:30 pm
Charlie on 10 at 9 (San Jose & San Francisco Bay area)	28.35	W	9:00 pm
Citrus Belt ARC Public Service Net (San Bernardino & Riverside Co)	146.85-	W	7:00 pm
Clairemont Repeater Assoc Club Net (Los Angeles, Orange, San Bernardino & Riverside)	145.22- (PL103.5)	Tu	7:00 pm
Clairemont Repeater Assoc Tech Info (Los Angeles, Orange, San Bernardino, & Riverside)	145.22- (PL103.5)	Th	7:00 pm
Coachella Valley ARC Public Service	146.025+	M,W,F	8:00 am
Coachella Valley ARC, ARES/RACES Net	146.025+(PL157.7)	Th	7:00 pm
Colton RACES Net	147.25+(PL157.7)	M	7:30 pm
Contra Costa RACES/ARES County Wide Net	147.735-(107.2)	Th	7:15 pm
Corona/Norco RACES Net	147.06+(PL146.2)	M	8:00 pm
Costa Mesa RACES	147.06+(PL173.8)	M	7:20 pm
Cupertino Amateur Radio Emergency Service	147.570 simplex	Tu	7:45 pm
Cypress RACES	144.345	M	7:30 pm
Eel River Delta ARES Net (San Francisco section)	146.58	M	7:00 pm
El Dorado County ARES (El Dorado, Nevada, Placer, Amador, Yuba, Sutter, Sacramento Counties)	146.825-(82.5)	M	8:00 pm
Eureka ARES Net	146.46	M	7:00 pm
Fountain Valley RACES (Fountain Valley and adjacent cities)	145.26-(136.5)	M	7:30 pm
Hemet ARES/RACES Net	224.12-	Tu	7:00 am
Hemet Public Service Net, RACES	145.42+PL88.5)	Tu	7:15 pm
Hospital Disaster Support Team (Orange Co)	146.97- (PL136.5)	Tu	7:30 pm
Humboldt Co ARES Net	146.76-(PL103.5) 147.00-(PL103.5)	M	7:30 pm
Humboldt Co Eel River Valley ARES Net	146.580	M	7:00 pm
Humboldt Co Eel River Valley ARES Net	446.000	M	7:15 pm
Huntington Beach CERT	147.485-(PL103.5)	W	7:30 pm
Huntington Beach RACES	145.14-(PL110.9)	M	7:15 pm
Imperial Co District ARES HF Net	3.933	Su	8:30 am
Imperial Valley ARC CW Net (West Coast)	7.05	W	8:30 pm
Imperial Valley ARES VHF Net	147.15+(107.2)	Su	7:30 pm
Indian Wells Valley ARES/RACES Net (Ridgecrest, Inyokern, Trona, Olancha, California City, Bishop)	146.64- 145.34-(100)	M	7:30 pm
Inland Valley Schools ARC (San Barnardino, Riverside Co)	445.90- (PL146.2)	Tu	7:00 pm
Jefferson Noon Net (N CA, S OR)	7.232	Daily	12:00pm
Jefferson Noon Net - VHF (Northern California, Southern Oregon)	146.79- 146.82- 146.91- 147.18+(100)	Daily	12:30pm
Jurupa AREA/RACES Net	146.445	W	8:00 pm
Lake Co ARES Net	146.775-	W (1)	7:30 pm
Livermore RACES/ARES Net (Dublin, Eastern Alameda Co, Livermore, Pleasanton)	147.120+(100) 145.350-(100)	M	7:00 pm

Loma Linda RACES Net	147.24+(PL156.7)	Tu	8:00 pm
Los Gatos ARES (Santa Clara Valley)	147.39+	Tu	7:45 pm
Marin Co RACES Net	147.33+(PL203.5)	Tu	7:30 pm
Milpitas ARES/RACES	114.135 224.72-(100)	Tu	7:15 pm
Morango Basin RACES Net	147.705-(PL123.0)	M	6:30 pm
Moreno Valley ARES/RACES Net	147.645-(PL110.9)	Tu	7:30 am
Mountain View ARES/RACES	146.535	M	8:15 pm
Newberry RACES Net (Springs area)	147.51	M	7:00 pm
Newport Beach RACES	145.160-	M	7:30 pm
Northern Alameda Co ARES/RACES	147.48+ 440.90+	Th	7:15 pm
Northern California Net	3.63	Daily	7:00 pm
Ontario Red Cross Net	147.30-(PL123.0)	Tu	7:30 pm
Orange Co ARC Net, SSB	21.375	W	7:30 pm
Orange Co ARES Public Service	3.965	Su	9:00 am
Orange County RACES	52.62-(PL103.5)	M	7:00 pm
Orange County RACES	146.895-(PL136.5)	M	7:00 pm
Pass (Banning/Beaumont) ARES/RACES Net	147.915-(PL123.0)	W	7:00 pm
Petaluma ARES/ACS Net	146.91-(PL88.5)	M	7:30 pm
Radio Amateur Trans Society ARES/RACES (Coachella Valley)	146.94- (PL107.2)	M	7:00 pm
Radio Inter-Zone Amateur League (Southern California)	1283.675 1284.475	Tu	7:00 pm
Rag Chew Group (Tech/Social) Net (Riverside City area)	145.52	W	8:30 pm
Ramona Outback ARS NVIS Net (San Diego Co)	3.924	W (1, 2, 3, 5)	7:30 pm
Rancho Cucamonga RACES Net	147.30+	M	7:00 pm
Redlands Emergency Communications Group	147.180+(88.5)	Daily	7:00 am
Redlands RACES/ARES Net	147.180+(88.5)	M	7:45 pm
Riverside Co ARA Public Service Net	146.88-(146.2)	M	7:15 pm
Riverside Co RACES/ARES	3.945	Su	8:30 am
Sacramento Valley Noon Net	146.91-	Daily	12:00pm
Sacramento Valley Traffic Net	146.850	Daily	9:00 pm
Salvation Army Team Emergency Net (N CA)	146.06+(100)	Tu	8:00 pm
Salvation Army Team Emergency Net (Imperial)	147.32+(107.2)	Th	8:30 pm
San Bernardino Co RACES Net	146.91-	M	8:00 pm
San Bernardino Co RACES SSB	3.9875	M	7:30 pm
San Diego ARES Eastern District HF Net (San Diego Co)	3.925	Su	8:45 am
San Diego ARES Southern District HF Net (San Diego Co)	3.913	Su	8:45 am
San Francisco ARES Net (San Francisco East & North Bay)	145.150-	W	8:00 pm
San Francisco DPW Net (Greater San Francisco Bay area)	145.150- (114.8)	Th	12:00pm
Sanoma/Mendocino Coast ARES Net	147.825-(PL103.5)	Tu	7:00 pm
Santa Barbara Section ARES HF Net (Ventura, Santa Barbara, San Luis Obispo Counties)	3.86 7.26	M (1)	8:30 pm
Santa Barbara Section VHF Net (Ventura, Santa Barbara, San Luis Obispo Counties)	144.23 USB	M	8:30 pm
Santa Maria ARES 220 Net (North Santa Barbara Co)	223.80-	last M	8:15 pm
Santa Maria ARES VHF Net (North Santa Barbara Co)	145.14-	M	8:00 pm
Santa Rosa ARES Net	146.73-offset (88.5PL) 147.45 simplex	M	7:30 pm

Sebastopol ARES/ACS Net	145.35-(PL88.5)	M	7:30 pm
Seismic Network EarthQuake Net (S California)	147.705-(PL114.8)	M	9:00 pm
Shasta Co ARES VHF Net (Shasta Co & N CA)	146.64-(107)	M	8:00 pm
Siskiyou/Modoc Co ARES	3.987	Th- when needed	7:30 pm
Siskiyou Co Amateur Radio Emergency Volunteers	146.79- 146.82- 146.97- 147.18+(100)	Daily	12:00 pm
Southern Oregon, Northern California, Nevada Regional ARES	3.987	W	7:00 pm
Sojourners (North California, South Oregon)	3.987	M	8:45 pm
Sonoma Valley ARES/ACS Net	146.205+(PL88.5)	M	7:30 pm
Southern Calif. ARA, Club Net (Orange, Los Angeles, San Bernardino, Riverside)	448.775-	Tu	7:00 pm
Southern California Net (Los Angeles, Orange, San Diego, Santa Barbara)	147.00-	Daily	9:00 pm
Southern California Net (Santa Barbara)	3.598	M-F	7:15 pm
Southern California Six Meter Club Tech (Los Angeles, Orange, Santa Barbara, Riverside Ctys)	50.4	Su	10:00am
Southern California Six Meter Club, SSB	50.150 USB	Tu	8:00 pm
Southern California/Santa Barbara Section Net	147.00+(PL131.8)	Daily	9:00 pm
Southern Humboldt Co ARES Net	146.79-(PL103.5)	M	7:00 pm
S OR, N CA, N NV ARES Net	3.987	W	7:00 pm
Southern Peninsula Emergency Communications System (N Santa Clara Co)	145.27-	M	8:00 pm
Southwest Riverside Co ARES/RACES Net	146.805-(PL100.0)	W	7:30 pm
Stanford Amateur Radio Club Weekly Net	440.200+(123)	M	7:30 pm
Sun City ARES/RACES Net	146.58	W (1)	6:30 pm
Sun City PACKET	144.91	W	9:00 am
Sun City Public Service Net	146.58	T	6:30 pm
Upland RACES Net	147.30+(PL123.0)	M	7:00 pm
Valley RACES Net (Valley area)	147.595	M	7:00 pm
Victor Valley RACES Net	146.94-	M	7:00 pm
West Desert RACES Net	147.45	M	7:15 pm
Yucaipa RACES Net	147.57(PL103.5)	M	7:00 pm
Yucaipa Valley Amateur Radio Club (Southern California)	147.18+(88.5) 445.34-(88.5)	M	7:15 pm
Colorado			
Arapahoe Co ARES	146.88-(100)	Su	9:30 am
ARES District 10 (Jackson, Larimer, Weld Ctys)	145.115-	W	9:00 pm
ARES District 11 (Boulder Co & Metro area)	146.76-	M	8:00 pm
ARES District 13 (Denver Co & Metro area)	147.33+	Su	8:00 pm
ARES District 14 (El Paso & Teler Counties)	146.97-(100)	Tu	7:00 pm
ARES District 16 (Pueblo & Huerfano Counties)	145.205-	Tu	8:00 pm
ARES District 23 (Jefferson Co)	146.67-	Th	7:30 pm
ARES District 24 (Jefferson & Elbert Counties)	147.225+	Th	8:00 pm
ARES District 27 (Adams Co)	145.43-	M	7:45 pm
Colorado 2M SSB ARES Net	144.22	M	7:00 pm
Colorado ARES HF	3.928	Su	8:00 am
Colorado ARES VHF Net	145.31-	Su	8:30 am
Longmont Amateur Radio Club Informal Net	147.270+(100) 448.800-(88.5)	Su	8:00 pm
Connecticut			
Area 2 ARES (New Haven & Middlesex Ctys.)	145.29-	M (2)	7:30 pm
ARES Area 3 North (CT)	147.225+(156.7)	W	8:15 pm

Communications

ARES/SKYWARN (Connecticut)	3.965 145.68 52.490	when needed	
Bears of Manchester Emergency Net (Manchester & surrounding towns)	145.11-	M (2)	9:15 pm
Bears of Manchester Traffic Net (CT, Western MA, Eastern MA, RI)	147.345+	Sa	9:15 pm
Bears of Manchester Traffic Net (CT, Western MA, Eastern MA, RI)	145.11-	Su-F	9:15 pm
Connecticut Net	3.64	Daily	7:00 pm
Connecticut Phone Net	3.965	Daily	6:00 pm
Connecticut Phone Net	3.965	Su	10:00am
CT ARES HF Net (CT and surrounding parts of NY, MA, RI)	3.965	Th	6:15 pm
CT RTTY Net (wide area, CT centered)	3.600 (dial-LSB)	Su	7:00 pm
GNARC/ARES Net (Norwalk, Wilton, Westport, Weston Counties)	147.39+	M	8:00 pm
Greater Newington Emergency Net	145.45-	M	8:00 pm
Newington Emergency Net	145.45- 224.84-	Th	7:30 pm
Northern Connecticut Emergency Net (CT, Western MA, RI)	147.347+(77.0)	Sa	9:15 pm
Nutmeg VHF Traffic Net (Central Connecticut)	147.15+ 146.88-	Daily	9:30 pm
SKYWARN, Fairfield Co	147.39+ 146.535	when needed	7:30 pm
SKYWARN, Hartford & Tolland Co	147.00+	Th	9:00 pm
SKYWARN, Litchfield Co - Primary	145.370-(PL77.0)	M	8:00 pm
SKYWARN, Litchfield Co - Backup	146.850-(PL141.3)	M	8:00 pm
SKYWARN, Middlesex Co	145.29-(PL110.0)	M	8:00 pm
SKYWARN, New Haven Co Weather Net	147.505 (input) (PL77.0) 146.505 (output)	Th	7:30 pm
SKYWARN, New London Co	146.73-(PL156.7)	W	8:00 pm
SKYWARN, Windham Co	147.225+(PL156.7)	W	8:00 pm
Southeastern Connecticut ARES Net (New London Co)	146.67- (PL156.7)	M	8:00 pm
Western Connecticut Net	147.18+	Daily	8:30 pm
Delaware			
Delaware Emergency Phone Net	3.905	Sa	6:00 pm
Delaware Traffic Net	3.905	M-F	6:30 pm
Nanticoke Amateur Radio Club (W Sussex Co)	145.21-	M	8:00 pm
Sussex Emergency Net (Lower Delaware)	147.18+	Daily	8:30 pm
Florida			
ALERT ARES/RACES Net (Lee Co)	146.880-	W	7:30 pm
ARES Net (Walton Co)	147.24+	W	7:30 pm
ARES Net (Putnam Co)	146.49	Tu	7:00 pm
ARES Net (Alachua Co)	147.00-(103)	Daily	7:00 pm
ARES Net (Washington Co)	145.37-	W	7:00 pm
ARES Net (Volusia Co)	147.06+	Th	8:30 pm
ARES Net (Levy Co)	146.82-	Th	8:00 pm
ARES Net (Lake Co)	146.745-	M-Sa	6:00 pm
ARES/RACES Net (Monroe Co)	147.06+	Th	8:00 pm
ARES/RACES Net (Manatee Co)	147.03+	Tu	7:00 pm
ARES/RACES Net (Citrus Co)	146.88-	W	7:15 pm
ARES/RACES Net (Orange Co)	147.06+	Su	8:00 pm
ARES/RACES Net (Martin Co)	146.925-	M	7:30 pm
ARES/RACES Net (Collier Co)	146.955-	M	7:00 pm

ARES/RACES Net (Pasco Co)	146.73-	Th	7:00 pm
Broward Co Emergency Preparedness Net	146.91-(110.9)	M	7:15 pm
Capital District ARES Net (Tallahassee area)	146.655-(94.8)	Su	8:00 pm
Clay Co ARES	146.67-	Su	7:30 pm
Collier Co Emergency Net (Collier, Southern Lee, & Hendry Counties)	147.03+ 443.700+	Tu (1, 3, 4, 5)	7:00 pm
Dade Co Emergency Net	147.15+	W	7:45 pm
Eagle Net (West Central Florida)	145.43-(100) 442.29+(100)	Daily	8:30 pm
East Panhandle ARES Net	146.745-	M-Sa	6:00 pm
EECN District ARES Net (Florida)	145.23-	Tu	7:00 pm
Florida Amateur Sideband Traffic Net	3.94		
Florida Crown Emergency Net (Duval Co)	146.76-	W	7:30 pm
Florida Midday Traffic Net	7.242		
Florida Public Operations Net	3.908		
Florida Shrine ARA	7.236		
Glades Co ARES/RACES (Only sometimes on week 4)	147.300-(100)	Tu (1, 2, 3, 4)	8:00 pm
Gold Coast Emergency Net (Broward & Palm Beach Counties)	146.61- 146.82	Th	7:30 pm
Hendry Co Emergency Net (Hendry & Glades Counties)	144.9	M	7:00 pm
Hernando Co ARES/Skywarn Net	146.805-	M	8:00 pm
Highlands Co Emergency Net	147.27+	W	7:30 pm
Hillsborough Co ARES/RACES Net	147.105+(146.2)	W	8:00 pm
Keys Emergency Net (Monroe Co)	146.715-	W	7:15 pm
Lake Co ARES	147.00-(PL103.5)	Daily	7:00 pm
Manatee Co ARES Net	28.45	M	7:00 pm
Northern Florida ARES Net	3.95	M-Sa	8:00 pm
OARC Emergency Net (Okeechobee Co)	147.195+	M	8:00 pm
Okaloosa Co ARES Net	147.360+(100.0) 146.790-	when needed	
Orange Co ARES/RACES (Metro Orlando, Orange, & surrounding Counties)	146.73-(103.5)	Th	7:00 pm
Osceola Co ARES/RACES Net	145.35+	Th	7:00 pm
Palm Beach Co Emergency Net	146.67-	W	8:00 pm
Pensacola Area ARES Net (Escambia & Santa Rosa Counties)	146.70-	M	8:00 pm
Pinellas Co AR Emergency Preparedness Net (ARES/ACS/SKYWARN)	145.170 442.4 442.8 (all 156.7)	Tu	7:30 pm
Pinellas Co AR Emergency Preparedness Net	145.17- 442.4+(156.7)	Tu	7:30 pm
Pinellas Co ARES Net	28.45	Tu	7:00 pm
Pinellas Co ARES Preparedness Net	145.17	Tu	7:30 pm
Pinellas Co ARES and SKYWARN Net	145.210- 146.790- 442.350+ 443.850+ (All 146.2)	Tu	8:00 pm
Polk Co ARES/SKYWARN Net	146.985-(127.3)	Tu	7:30 pm
Polk Co ARES/SKYWARN Net	147.375+(127.3)	Tu	7:30 pm
Pompano Emergency Net (Broward Co)	145.51	Tu	7:30 pm
RACES Net (Marion Co)	147.135+	W	7:00 pm
RACES Net (Brevard Co)	146.61-		
RACES Net (Brevard Co)	147.135+	W	9:00 am
Red Cross ARES/RACES Net (South Florida)	147.000-	W	6:45 pm
Santa Rosa Co ARES Net	147.70+	M	7:00 pm

Sarasota Emergency Radio Club/ARES	146.73-	W	7:30 pm
Saturday Night 6 Pack (Palm Beach Co, Grid EL96)	53.21	Sa	9:00 pm
Seminole Co ARES (Orlando & N Seminole Co)	147.195+	M	8:00 pm
SKYWARN Net (Broward Co)	146.79-	Daily	7:00 pm
South County ARES/RACES Net (Palm Beach Co)	145.290-	W	7:30 pm
South Florida ARES Net	3.94	Sa	8:00 am
St Lucie Co ARES Net	146.755-	Th	8:00 pm
St Lucie Repeater Assoc. Ragchew/Traders Net (St Lucie, Indian River, & Martin Counties)	146.775	Su	8:00 pm
Sumter Co ARES Net	146.925-(123)	M	8:30 pm
The Intercontinental Amateur Traffic Net (worldwide)	14.3	Daily	7:00 am
Treasure Coast Road Show (Port St. Lucie)	146.925-(PL107.2)	F	4:00 pm
Treasure Coast Weather Net (St. Lucie, Indian River, & Martin Counties)	146.775-	Su	9:00 pm
WCFN (West Central Florida Net)	145.43 442.95	Su	7:30 pm
WCFN (West Central Florida Net) - Weeknight	145.43 442.95	M,W,F	9:00 pm
Wednesday Night 69 Net (Palm Beach Co, Grid EL96)	53.21	W	9:00 pm
West Central Florida Section Net	3.911	Su	7:30 pm
West Central Florida SKYWARN Net (NWS Ruskin Central Warning Area)	145.430(100.0) 442.950(100.0) 444.425(103.5) 3.911	when needed	
West Panhandle District Emergency Net (Santa Rosa, Escambia, Okaloosa, & Walton Counties)	146.70-	M	8:00 pm
Georgia			
40 Meter Training Net (Georgia)	7.275	Su	4:30 pm
Albany ARC 2 Meter Net (Southwest Georgia)	146.82-	M	9:00 pm
Albany Metro SKYWARN Net	146.92-	when needed	
Banks Co ARES Net (Banks & Jackson Ctys.)	147.225+(123)	Tu	7:30 pm
Bibb Co ARES Net (Macon metro area)	146.805- 443.075+	Th (2,4)	9:00 pm
Bubba (Northeast Georgia)	28.44	Daily	8:00 pm
Central Georgia UHF Net	443.075 444.425 444.525 444.700	W	8:30 pm
Central Savannah River ARES Net (E Cent. GA)	146.985-	W	8:30 pm
Chattahoochee Valley Emergency Net (Columbus & Western Georgia)	146.61-	W	8:30 pm
Chattooga Co SKYWARN Net	145.535	Tu	8:30 pm
Cherokee Capital Amateur Radio Society (Calhoun & Northwest Georgia)	146.745- 443.675(100)	Tu	9:00 pm
Cherokee Co ARES Net (Metro Atlanta, NW GA)	145.27-	when needed	
Cherokee Co ARES/SKYWARN (Metro Atlanta, Northwest Georgia)	145.37-(100)	M	8:45 pm
Clarke Co ARES Net (Northeast Georgia)	147.045+	Sa	5:30 pm
Clarke Co SKYWARN Net (Northeast Georgia)	146.745-	when needed	
Claxton ARES Net (Claxton & SE Georgia)	147.075+	Tu	8:30 pm
Coastal Amateur Radio Society (SE Coastal GA)	146.70-	Tu	9:00 pm
Cobb Co ARES/SKYWARN	146.88-(100)	W	9:00 pm
Coweta Co ARES Net (Midwest Georgia)	145.13-(156.7)	Su	9:00 pm
Dalton Amateur Radio Club Net (N Central GA)	145.23-	Su	9:30 pm
Dawson Co RACES/ARES (Northern Georgia)	146.835+(100)	M	8:00 pm
DeKalb Co ARES Net (Atlanta)	145.45-	Su	8:00 pm

Fayette Co Repeater Association Weekly VHF Net (Atlanta south metro area, Fayette, & surrounding Counties)	145.210-(131.8)	Tu	9:00 pm
Flint ARC Net, Sunsweet/Chula Tower Net (South Central Georgia)	145.49-	Th, F, Sa	9:00 pm
Four Rivers Amateur Radio Net (SE Georgia)	146.625-	M	8:00 pm
GA SSB Net (Alabama, Florida, Georgia)	3.975	Daily	7:00 pm
Georgia ARES Net	3.975	Su	6:00 pm
Georgia Baptist Ham Net	3.865	Su	4:00 pm
Georgia Traffic & Emergency Net	3.983	Daily	7:15 pm
Gwinnett Co ARES/SKYWARN (Atlanta metro area)	147.075+(PL82.5)	M	9:00 pm
Gwinnett GARS Want Swap Info Net (Gwinnett Co)	147.075+(82.5)	M	8:00 pm
Jackson Co ARES Net (Banks, Hall, & Jackson Counties)	147.225+(123)	Tu	7:30 pm
Lanierland Radio Club Net (NE Georgia)	146.67-	W	8:30 pm
Liberty Co Emergency Comm Association (North Coastal Georgia)	145.47-	Th	8:00 pm
Milledgeville ARC VHF Net (E Central Georgia)	146.70-	Th	8:00 pm
North Fulton ARES (Atlanta)	145.470-	Su	7:30 pm
North Georgia Disaster Relief Team Net (North Central Georgia, Eastern Alabama)	147.015- 224.700- 443.700+	Th	9:00 pm
North Georgia Radio Club Net (N Central GA)	146.955-	Su	7:30 pm
Okefenokee Radio Amateur Club (SE Georgia)	146.64- (PL141.3)	Tu	9:00 pm
Savannah Simplex Net	147.555	M	9:00 pm
Southeast Regional Amateur Emergency Net (Southeast Georgia)	147.00-	Su	8:00 pm
Spalding Co Emergency Service Net (North Central Georgia)	145.39-	Th	8:30 pm
Statesboro Amateur Radio Society (SE Georgia)	147.105+	Tu	8:00 pm
The Northwest Georgia Emergency Net (NW Georgia, Rome, parts of NW Alabama)	146.940-(88.5)	M (1, 2, 3, 4)	9:00 pm
Toccoa Amateur Radio Society (NE Georgia)	147.33+	Th, F, Sa	8:00 pm
Walker Co ARES Net (NW Georgia)	145.35-	Sa	5:45 pm
Waycross Area Repeater Assoc (S Central GA)	146.64-	Tu	9:00 pm
West Georgia Amateur Radio Society Local Net (75 mi. radius from Oak Mountain in Carroll Co)	146.640-(131.8)	M, Th	8:00 pm

Hawaii

Friendly Net (Hawaii)	3.86	Daily	9:00 am
Hawaii Afternoon Net	7.088	Daily	4:00 pm
Hawaii Emergency Net (Hawaii and adjacent waters)	1.888 3.888 7.088	when required	
Pacific ARES Net	3.905 7.08	W (1)	7:30 pm

Idaho

Bonner Co RACES/ARES Net	145.23	Tu	7:00 pm
Boundary Co ARES/RACES Net	146.96	M	7:00 pm
Emmett ID Emergency Simplex (Emmett & part of Treasure Valley)	146.48	Su	7:30 pm
Friendly Amateur Radio Mission Net (Idaho)	3.937		
Idaho-Oregon Boy Scout 2 Meter (SW ID, E OR)	147.24+	W	4:00 pm
IMN - Idaho Montana Net	3.647		
Lewis & Clark Trail Hilltop Dx Society (Treasure Valley)	147.360+(100)	W	7:00 pm
Northwest Traffic Net (Northwest Idaho, Eastern Washington)	146.98- 147.82+		

RACES/ARES Idaho State	3.99	Th	7:30 pm
Southwestern Idaho 2 Meter Net (Boise Valley)	145.44	Su	9:00 pm
SW Idaho RACES/ARES Weekly (SW ID, SE OR)	147.24+	M	8:00 pm

Illinois

Adams Co ARES Net (NE MO)	147.03+(103.5)	W	7:00 pm
Bolingbrook Amateur Radio Society Net (Northwest Illinois)	147.330+ 224.540-	Th	8:00 pm
Clark Co ARES Net (40 mile radius)	146.520	W	9:00 pm
Cook Co ARES Net	146.88-(107.2)	W (4)	9:00 pm
DuPage Co ARES (DuPage & Cook Counties)	145.39-	Tu	8:00 pm
IL ARES Section Net	3.905 7.23	Su (1,3)	4:30 pm
Illinois Emergency Net	3.94	Su	8:00 am
Jacksonville ARS Net (Morgan, Cass, Scott, Green, and Macourin Counties)	146.775-	Su	9:00 pm
Lake Co RACES/ARES	147.18+(PL127.3)	M	8:00 pm
Lamoine Emergency ARC (McDonough Co, Macomb, IL)	147.060+(103.5)	Su	8:00 pm
Macon Co Amateur Radio Emergency Service	442.250-(103.5) 449.250+	W	9:00 pm
McHenry Co RACES/ARES	146.835-(91.5)	M	8:00 pm
Mid Continent Amateur Radio Service (Midwest)	7.258	Daily	7:30 am
Ogle Co ARES	147.045+(67.0)	Tu	9:00 pm
Plainfield RACES (Plainfield, Lockport, Joliet)	146.715-(107.2)	Th (1,3)	7:30 pm
Rockford Area 2 Meter Net	146.61-	M	8:00 pm
Salvation Army Team Emergency Net (Rockford)	146.52	Tu, F	12:00pm
Salvation Army Team Emergency Net (Rockford & Winnebago Counties)	146.61-(114.8)	Th	8:00 pm
Salvation Army Team Emergency Radio Net (Chicago & surrounding suburbs)	146.76-	Tu	8:00 pm
Schaumburg ARC EmComm & ARES Net (Shaumburg, NW Cook, & N DuPage Counties)	145.23-(107.2) 442.275+(114.8)	Th (1)	8:30 pm
St Clair Co ARES/RACES	147.120+	Tu	7:00 pm
Will Co ARES	444.550+(114.8)	Tu	9:00 pm
Winnebago Co ARES & Info Net (N Central IL)	147.195-(114.8)	Th	7:00 pm
Winnebago Co ARES and Info Net (30 Miles around Rockford)	147.195+ (114.8)	Th	7:00 pm

Indiana

Clark Co ARC ARES Net (Clark Co & Louisville, Kentucky)	146.85	W	9:00 pm
Clifty Amateur Radio Society (Jefferson Co)	145.17-	Th	7:30 pm
Dugger ARC (West Central Indiana)	146.775	M	8:00 pm
East Central Indiana Repeater Association	147.000+	Tu	8:00 pm
Evansville Rag Chewers Net (South Indiana)	146.58-	M-F	7:30 am
Fayette Co Repeater Group Net (Union, Fayette, Rush, & part of Wayne Counties)	146.745-	W	8:00 pm
Gibson Co ARC	145.41-	W	9:00 pm
Hamilton Co ARES	147.39+ 444.125+	Su	8:00 pm
Harrison Co ARES Net (Harrison, Crawford, Flyod, & Perry Counties)	146.820-	M	8:30 pm
HCARES (Hamilton Co & surrounding area)	147.39	Su	8:00 pm
Henderson ARC Net (S Indiana, W Kentucky)	145.49-	Th	8:00 pm
Henry Co ARES/RACES Net	147.36+	W	9:00 pm
Huntington Co ARES	146.685-	Tu,Sa	8:00 pm
Illiana SKYWARN (W Central IN, E Central IL)	146.685-(151.4)	as needed	1:00 am
Indiana Code Net	3.705	Daily	6:15 pm

Indiana Section ARES/Emergency Net	3.91	Su(4)&as needed	8:00 am
Indiana Section CW Net (QIN)	3.656 7.062	Daily	9:30 am
Indiana Section CW Net (QIN)	3.656	Daily	7:00 pm
Indiana Traffic Net	3.91	Daily	8:30 am 4:30 pm
Indiana Wet Net	3.91		
Indiana, Michigan & Ohio (IMO) (Fort Wayne)	146.88-	Daily	6:30 pm
Indianapolis/Marion Co ARES Net (Marion Co & surrounding area)	146.700-	W	7:30 pm
Jackson Co Net	145.43-	W	8:00 pm
KB9LDZ Repeater Net (Wabash Co)	147.03+(131.8)	M	8:00 pm
Laughery Valley ARC RACES/ARES Net (Dearborn Co, IN 50 mile radius)	147.285-	M (1)	9:00 pm
Miami Co ARES/RACES Net (Peru)	147.345+	Su	8:30 pm
Mid-State Amateur Radio Club (Johnson & surrounding Counties)	146.835-(151.4)	Su	7:00 pm
Morgan Co ARES Net (Martinville)	147.06	W	8:00 pm
Muncie Area ARC (East Central Indiana)	146.73-	Su	9:00 pm
Old Post Amateur Radio Emergency Net (Knox Co)	146.67-	Th	8:00 pm
Owen Co ARES Net (Spencer)	146.985-	W	7:30 pm
Pike Co ARC Net (Southwest Indiana: Dubois, Pike, Knox, Daviess, Gibson, Warrick)	145.450 147.000	Tu	8:30 pm
Richmond ARA (Wayne & Union Co)	147.18+	Su	8:00 pm
Ripley Co Repeater Association (Southeast Indiana)	146.805- 224.46-	Su	8:00 pm
SMART (Southeast Indiana, North Central Kentucky)	146.745- 146.595	when needed	
South Central Area Net (Bartholomew, Jackson, & Jennings Counties)	146.79-	Tu	8:30 pm
Tri-State Emergency Net (Southwest Indiana, Southeast Illinois, Western Kentucky)	146.79-(88.5)	W & as needed	8:00 pm
Wabash Co Amateur Radio Club Traffic Net	147.03-(131.8)	M	8:00 pm
Wabash Valley Emergency Svcs Net (Vigo Co)	146.685-(151.4)	Su	8:30 am
Whitley Co (ARES Net)	145.27-(PL131.8) 444.55+	W	7:15 pm

Iowa

Calhoun Co Area ARES Net (NW & Central Iowa)	145.49-	Su	8:30 pm
Central Iowa ARES Net (Central & West-Central Iowa)	146.94 147.075	Su	8:00 pm
Hawkeye REACT Net (Linn Co)	146.49	W	9:30 pm
Heartland ARES Net (District 2)	145.29+	M	9:00 pm
Iowa 75 Meter Net	3.97	M-Sa	12:30pm 5:30 pm
Iowa Slow Speed Code Net	3.7	Daily	8:00 pm
Iowa Traffic & Emergency Net	3.97	Su	5:30 pm
Linn Co ARES Net	146.745-	Su	7:00 pm
MID-Land Amateur Radio Club/ Lyon Co ARES 2-Meter Net (SW MN, Extreme NW IA, SE SD)	145.31-(110.9)	Tu	7:15 pm
Polk Co ARES Net	146.94	Tu	7:00 pm
Sac Co ARES Net (30 mile radius of Sac Co)	146.925	Tu, Th	8:30 pm
Taylor Co ARA (Southwest Iowa)	147.135	Su	8:00 pm
Tri-State ARES (Howard Co)	147.075+(103.5)	Su	7:00 pm
West Central Iowa ARES Net	147.09+	M,W,F	8:30 pm

Kansas

Auxiliary Communications Team (Douglas Co)	147.03+	Tu	9:00 pm
BARCBADS ARES Net (Jefferson Co)	146.835-	Th	7:30 pm

Central Kansas 10 Meter Net (Saline & Ottawa Counties)	28.45	M	8:00 pm
Central States Traffic Net (KS & 6 other states)	7.2535	M-Sa	12:30pm
Chanute Area ARC Net	146.745-	Th	7:30 pm
Great Salt Plains ARC Net (South Central Kansas, North Central OK)	147.30+	Su	9:00 pm
Harvey Co RACES (S Central Kansas)	146.61-	M	8:30 pm
Jayhawk ARS & Wyandotte Co ARES Net (Kansas City, Kansas)	147.15+	Th	7:00 pm
Johnson Co ARES CW Net (Kansas City metro - Kansas & Missouri)	3.68	Tu (1,3,4)	6:45 pm
Johnson Co ARES Net	145.29- 147.24-	Tu	7:00 pm
Johnson Co ARES Packet Net (Kansas City metro - Kansas & Missouri)	145.03	Tu (1,3,4)	6:15 pm
Johnson Co Emergency Communications Service (Johnson Co & Kansas City metro)	145.47-	M	7:00 pm
Kansas and W Missouri SATERN HF Net	3.92	Tu	8:30 pm
Kansas ARES Group Alfa 1-2 Meter Net (Shawnee & Wabaunsee Counties)	146.670-	Tu	8:30 pm
Kansas CW Traffic Net	3.61	Daily	7:00 pm 10:00pm
Kansas D-3 SKYWARN Weather Net (Northwestern Kansas)	146.82-(156.7)	Daily	12:00pm
Kansas Emergency Network	144.10 144.15 53.30	Sa (2,4)	7:30 pm
Kansas RACES Net	3.94	Th (1)	7:00 pm
Kansas Sideband Net	3.92	Daily	6:30 pm
Leavenworth Co ARES Training Net	147.00+	Su	7:30 pm
Leavenworth Co ARES Net	147.00+(151.4)	Th (2-5)	7:30 pm
Manhattan Area ARS Net	147.255+	Tu	9:00 pm
Mine Creek ARC/Linn Co ARES (Linn & Miami Counties)	147.285+	Th	8:00 pm
North Central Kansas ARES/RACES Net (North Central Kansas, linked to Lincoln Nebraska)	146.94+ 146.865 149.95 448.85	Su	9:00 pm
Osborne Repeater User's Group (Osb, Rook, Smith, Russ, Mit)	147.375+	W	9:00 pm
Reno Co ARA Net	146.67-	Tu (1,3,4)	8:00 pm
Saline Co ARES Net	146.73-	Th (1)	8:00 pm
South Central ARES Net (Sedgwick, Harvey, Kingman, Reno, & Cowley Counties)	146.820-	M	9:00 pm
South Central Kansas ARES VHF Traffic Net	146.80-	Th	7:15 pm
Southwest Kansas ARES Group, Inc. KS0ECC (Parts of Southwestern Kansas)	443.575+(88.5) 442.025+(103.5) (145.650 simplex echolink node #184850)	F (4)	9:00 pm
Sunflower Amateur Radio Club Emergency Net (Sherman Co)	147.030-	Th	8:00 pm
Trojan ARC ARES Net(ARES Dist. 3, Zone 39)	146.82-	Th	8:30 pm
Wheat State Wireless Assoc (Miami Co)	147.36	Su	7:00 pm
Zone 14A ARES 2 M Net (NE KS)	146.61-	Th	9:00 pm
Zone 24B ARES Net (Sedgwick Co)	146.82-	M	9:00 pm
Zone 38A ARES Net (Phillips & Norton Ctys.)	147.12+	Th	9:00 pm
Zone 9 ARES Net (Lyon, Greenwood, & Morris)	146.985-	Su	9:00 pm
Kentucky			
Area 13 ARES Net (Central Kentucky)	146.865	Sa	9:00 am

Capital ARS Club Net (Central Kentucky)	147.105+(PL107.2)	M	8:30 pm
Christian Co Emergency Net (Christian & Trigg Counties)	147.03+	Tu	8:00 pm
Fayette Co ARES Net (Central Kentucky)	146.760-	Th	9:00 pm
Fourth District ARES Net (IN, KY, TN)	147.33+	Daily	9:00 pm
Henderson Co ARES Net (Henderson Co, KY & Vanderburg Co, IN)	146.520	Su	8:00 pm
Jessamine Co Amateur Wireless Society	145.49	Th	8:30 pm
Kentucky Emergency Net	3.995	Tu	8:00 pm
Kentucky District 7 Amateur Radio Emergency Communications Team Net (N KY, District 7)	147.375+	Th	8:00 pm
LaRue Co ARES Net (Central Kentucky)	146.535	Tu	8:00 pm
Lawrence Co Emergency Net (Lawrence Co & Wayne, WV)	147.39-	Su	9:00 pm
Madison Co Public Service Net (Madison, Rockcastle, Jackson, Fayette Counties)	146.865-(192.8)	M	7:00 pm
Monroe Co ARES (Monroe Co & surrounding Counties)	146.775-	Su	7:30 pm
Mountain Amateur Radio ARES Net (Pineville)	146.835+(PL100.0)	W	9:00 pm
Muhlenberg Co ARES Simplex Net	146.535	Tu	7:30 pm
Purchase Area Emergency Net (Paducah)	147.06-	Su	8:00 pm
Rockcastle Co ARES Simplex Net	147.49	W	8:00 pm
SMART (Northern Kentucky, Southern Indiana)	146.745- 146.595	when needed	
Southeastern Kentucky Emergency Net (Southeastern KY & Perry Co)	146.67-	Su	9:00 pm
Taylor Co ARES Net (Taylor & Green Counties)	146.55	Th	9:00 pm
Tristate 2 Meter Net (KY, OH, WV)	146.94-	Daily	7:30 pm
Wide Area Repeaters Net - WARN (Kentucky areas: 2,3,4,5,6; and Southern Indiana counties along the Ohio River)	146.625- 147.180- 443.350+ 444.400+(151.4)	Su	8:30 pm
Louisiana			
Acadiana ARA Net (South Central Louisiana)	146.820-	M	7:00 pm
Acadiana ARES Net (South Central Louisiana)	145.37-(103)	Tu	7:00 pm
Emergency & Tactical Traffic Net- Daytime (LA, MS, OK, TX)	7.285	when needed	
Emergency & Tactical Traffic Net- Nighttime (LA, MS, OK, TX)	3.873	when needed	
Health & Welfare Traffic Net - Daytime (LA, MS, OK, TX)	7.29	when needed	
Health & Welfare Traffic Net - Nighttime (LA, MS, OK, TX)	3.938	when needed	
Louisiana (Northeast and Central Louisiana, South Arkansas, West Central Mississippi)	147.015 MHZ (occasional 103.5 Hz tone)	M	8:00 pm
Louisiana ARES Net	3.873	Su	7:30 pm
Louisiana CW Net	3.673	Daily	7:00 pm
Southeast Louisiana ARES	145.37-(114.8)	Su	8:00 pm
Maine			
Aroostook Co Emergency Net	146.73-	M	8:00 pm
Cumberland Co Emergency Net (Cumberland Co & South Maine)	147.09+	Sa	7:30 pm
Downeast Info & Emergency Radio (Coastal Hancock Co)	146.595-	W	8:00 pm
Ellsworth Amateur Wireless Association On-Air-Meeting (Down East, ME)	147.030+(100)	W	7:00 pm
Lincoln Co Emergency & Info Net (Lincoln Co & surrounding area)	146.985 28.385	Su	7:00 pm
Maine Emergency Communications Net	3.94	Su	6:30 pm

Maine Public Service Net	3.94	Su	9:00 am
Oxford Co ARES (Central W Maine)	146.88-(100)	M (2-5)	8:00 pm
Pine Tree Net (Maine)	3.596	Daily	7:00 pm
Sea Gull (Northern New England)	3.94	M-Sa	5:00 pm
Sunrise Co ARES Net (Washington Co)	147.33+(118.8)	M	7:00 pm
Tri-County ARES Net (Waldo, Knox, & Kennebec Counties)	146.22+	Su	8:00 pm
Twelve Co Emergency Net (Maine)	146.88- 146.67 146.82 146.85	Su	9:45 am
Waldo Area ARES Net (Waldo & surrounding Counties)	147.27+	W	8:30 pm

Manitoba, Canada

No Emergency or National Traffic Nets listed

Maryland

Alegany Co ARES/RACES Net (ACARN)	146.880-(123,100)	Tu	7:00 pm
Ann Arundel Co ARES Net	146.805	Su	8:00 pm
Baltimore Co ARES/RACES Net	146.67-	Tu (1,2)	7:30 pm
Baltimore Traffic Net (metro)	146.67-	Daily	6:30 pm
Baltimore Traffic Net Backup (Central Maryland)	145.33	Daily	6:30 pm
Carroll Co Amateur Radio Emergency Team	145.41-	Tu	8:30 pm
Delmarva Amateur Radio Enhancement Net (Delmarva Peninsula)	146.82-	M	9:00 pm
Four States Net (Washington Co)	147.09+	Th	7:00 pm
Frederick Co ARES Net	147.06+	M	7:30 pm
Harford Co ARES/RACES Net	146.775-(97.4)	Tu	7:30 pm
Howard Co ARES Net	147.135+	Tu	7:30 pm
Kent ARES/RACES Net (Kent & Queen Anne's Counties)	147.375	Tu (1,2,3,5)	8:00 pm
Maryland - Delaware - DC Net	3.643 7.076	Daily	7:00 pm
Maryland - Delaware - DC Net	3.643 7.076	Daily	10:00pm
Maryland Emergency Phone Net (MD, DC)	3.92	Daily	6:00 pm
Montgomery Co RACES/ARES	146.955-(no PL)	Tu	8:00 pm
Saint Mary's ARES Net (Saint Mary's & Calvert Counties)	146.64-	M	8:00 pm
Tri-State 2 Meter Net (W MD near Cumberland)	146.880-(123)	M	8:00 pm
Washington Co ARES/RACES Net (Washington Co & adjoining counties in PA & Western VA)	146.94+	Tu	7:00 pm

Massachusetts

Cape Cod & Islands 2 Meter Net	146.685+	Daily	7:30 pm
East Massachusetts 2 Meter Net	145.23-(88.5)	Daily	8:00 pm
East Massachusetts/Rhode Island Phone Net	3.918	Daily	5:30 pm
Eastern Massachusetts ARES Section Net	146.61-(146.2) 449.925-(88.5) 53.81-(71.9)	Su (3)	8:00 pm
Franklin Co ARES Net	146.985	Tu	9:00 pm
Massachusetts RACES (Franklin Co)	146.94-	M (1)	7:30 pm
Massachusetts RACES (Hampden & Hampshire Counties)	146.97-(114.8)	M (1)	7:15 pm
Massachusetts RACES (S Worcester Co)	146.91-	M (1)	7:00 pm
Massachusetts RACES (Berkshire Co)	145.37-	M (1)	7:15 pm
Massachusetts RACES (N Worcester Co)	146.985-	M (1)	7:45 pm
Massachusetts RACES 1A (Boston & Western suburbs)	146.64-	M (1)	7:30 pm
Massachusetts RACES 1C (Groton & Westford)	146.955-(74.4)	M (1)	7:30 am

Massachusetts RACES HF	3.943	when needed	
Massachusetts RACES Secondary	448.625-(88.5)	as needed	1:00 am
Massachusetts RACES Sector 2A (Bristol Co)	147.135+	M (1)	7:30 pm
Massachusetts RACES Sector 2B(Plymouth Co)	145.25-	M (1)	8:00 pm
Massachusetts RACES Sector 2C(Cape & Isls.)	146.955-(88.5)	M (1)	8:00 pm
Massachusetts RACES Sector 2D (Norfolk Co)	146.865-(146.2)	M (1)	7:30 pm
Massachusetts Statewide RACES Net	53.31 (71.9)	M (1)	7:00 pm
Massachusetts/Rhode Island Emergency Net	3.937 3.943	when needed	
Montachusett Emergency Net (N Central MA)	145.45-	Su	9:00 am
Natick Emergency Radio Net (Framingham, Natick, Wayland, Weston, Sherborn, & Dover)	147.420 447.675(203.5)	M	8:00 pm
New England Phone Net (MA & New England)	3.945	Su	8:30 am
Salvation Army Team Emergency Net (Boston)	145.23-(88.5)	F	9:00 pm
W Massachusetts Emergency ARES Net - Greenfield (Franklin Co)	146.985-	Tu	9:00 pm
W Massachusetts Emergency ARES Net - Greylock (Berkshire & Franklin Co)	53.23	Su	9:15 am
W Massachusetts Emergency ARES Net- Greylock (Western Massachusetts)	224.1	Su	9:30 am
W Massachusetts Emergency ARES Net- Greylock (Western Massachusetts)	146.91-	Su	9:00 am
W Massachusetts Emergency ARES Net- Montachusett (NE Worcester Co)	145.45-	Su	9:00 am
W Massachusetts Emergency ARES Net- Springfield (Hampden & Hampshire Counties)	146.94-	Su	8:45 am
W Massachusetts Emergency ARES Net- Templeton (NW Worcester Co)	145.37-	Tu	8:30 pm
W Massachusetts Emergency ARES Net - Warren (SW Worcester Co)	147.21+	Su	8:50 am
W Massachusetts Emergency ARES Net - Warren (SE Worcester Co)	147.345+	Su	9:00 am
W Massachusetts Emergency ARES Net - Worcester (Central Worcester Co)	146.97-	Su	9:15 am
W Massachusetts Section Emergency ARES Net (Western MA)	3.937	Su	8:30 am
Whitman AR Emergency Phone Net (SE MA)	147.225	Su	8:30 am
Worcester Emergency Simplex Net (Worcester & surrounding communities)	146.595 146.580 147.585 147.525	M	8:00 am
Michigan			
American Red Cross ARS (St Clair Co)	146.80-	Tu	8:00 pm
ARPSA (St Joseph Co)	145.31-(PL94.8)	M	8:30 pm
Barry Amateur Radio Association 2- Meter Simplex Net (SW Michigan)	146.460	Th	7:00 pm
Calhoun Co RACES/SKYWARN	146.66-	M	7:00 pm
Cascades Amateur Radio Society Thursday Night Net (Jackson, MI)	146.880-	Th	9:00 pm
Copper Country ARES Net (Houghton, Hancock area)	146.88-	W	9:00 pm
Dickinson Co ARES Net (Dickinson & Florence Counties)	146.85-	Tu	6:30 pm
District Three ARPSC	145.31-(131.8)	Su	6:00 pm
Five Co ARES Net (W Central Michigan)	146.74-	Tu	8:30 pm
Hiawatha 2 Meter Emergency Net (Marquette & Alger Counties)	147.27+	Su	7:00 pm
Ionia Co ARES	145.13-(94.8)	M	7:00 pm
Jackson Co ARES/RACES Net (County plus)	146.880-(100.0)	Su	9:00 pm

Lapeer Co ARES	146.62-	M	9:00 pm
Leon Clancy 6 M Memorial Net (N Lower MI)	51.980-(442.8+)	Su	8:00 pm
Leon Clancy Memorial Net (Local repeater)	51.980-offset	Su	8:00 pm
Macomb Co RACES	147.20+	Th	8:00 pm
Michigan Amateur Communications System	3.953	Daily	11:00am 1:00 pm
Michigan Amateur Radio Alliance (Grand Rapids)	145.23-(94.8)	Th	8:00 pm
Michigan ARPSC Net	3.932	Su	5:00 pm
Michigan District 8 ARES RACES Net	3.932	F	7:30 pm
Michigan Net QMN	3.663	Daily	7:30 pm 10:00pm
Michigan Splatter Stick Net	144.210	Tu,Th	8:30 pm
Michigan Third District ARPSC	145.310-(131.8) 147.100+(100.0) 146.96-	Su	8:00 pm
Michigan Traffic Net	3.952	Daily	7:00 pm
Mid Michigan Six Meter Net	Single VHF net 52.525	Su	9:00 pm
Midland Co Public Service Net	147.000+	Th	9:00 pm
Muskegon Co ARES Net	146.82-	Su	7:00 pm
North Branch Amateur Radio Club Net (Thumb area, Bad Axe South to Warren)	443.450 443.550- (107.2 114.8)	Su	8:30 pm
Oakland Co ARPSC	145.250-(100)	Th	8:00 pm
Salvation Army Team Emergency Net (Detroit)	147.18-(100)	M	7:30 pm
Salvation Army Team Emergency Net (Detroit area)	145.33-(100)	M	9:00 pm
SE Michigan Traffic Net (Metropolitan District)	145.33-	Daily	10:15pm
Scanner Enthusiast Net (Oakland & surrounding area)	145.490+(67.0)	Tu	8:00 pm
Straits Area Amateur Radio Club (Northern Michigan, upper peninsula)	146.68-	M	8:00 pm
Tuesday Night SMART Club Net (Local SW MI)	147.040+	Tu	8:00 pm
Two-Meter Plus (Jackson Co)	145.28-	M,W,F	9:00 pm
Upper Peninsula Net (IL, IN, MI, MN, WI)	3.921	Daily	5:00 pm
Upper Peninsula Net (IL, IN, MI, MN, WI)	3.921	Su	12:00pm
Washtenaw Co ARES	145.15-	W	8:15 pm
Washtenaw Co RACES	146.92-	W	8:00 pm
Western Michigan Traffic Net	145.270(PL94.8) Lowell repeater	M, W, F, Su	9:00 pm
Minnesota			
Marshall Emergency Net (Lincoln, Lyon, Redwood, Yellow Medicine)	147.195+	W	9:00 pm
Minnesota ARES HF Net	3.86	Su	6:00 pm
Northeast Minnesota Emergency Service Net	147.39+ 147.24+ 145.37- 147.12+ 145.29-; 145.23- 444.30+(103.5)	Su	8:00 pm
Rochester ARES Net (Southeast Minnesota)	146.82-	Su	
Scott Co ARES Net	146.535	M	7:00 pm
Wright Co Amateur Radio Society (WCARS) (Central Minnesota)	147.00+	F	8:00 pm
Mississippi			
Attala Co ARES	146.85-	Th	8:00 pm
Capitol Area Emergency Net (Jackson metro)	146.76-	Su	8:30 pm
Delta ARA Net (West Delta)	147.18+	M-F	7:00 pm

DeSoto Co Em Training & Info Net (NW MS)	146.91	M	8:30 pm
Emergency & Tactical Traffic Net- Daytime (LA, MS, OK, TX)	7.285	when needed	
Emergency & Tactical Traffic Net- Nighttime (LA, MS, OK, TX)	3.873	when needed	
Hattiesburg Area Emergency Net	146.775-	Su	9:00 pm
Health & Welfare Traffic Net - Daytime (LA, MS, OK, TX)	7.29	when needed	
Jackson ARC Emergency Net	146.94-	Tu	9:00 pm
Jackson Co Emergency Net	145.11-	Daily	8:00 pm
Laurel ARC Net (Jones Co)	146.61-	Tu	7:30 pm
Lowndes Co ARES	146.625-	Tu (1)	7:00 pm
Magnolia Section Net	3.8625	Sa, Su	7:00 am
Magnolia Section Net	3.8625	M-F	6:00 am
Meridian Area Emergency Net	146.70-	Tu	7:00 pm
Metro-Jackson ARES Net	444.00+(100)	Su	8:00 pm
Mississippi Baptist Hams Net	7.26	Su	2:00 pm
Mississippi Coast ARC Net (Gulf Coast)	146.73-	W	8:00 pm
Mississippi Section Phone Net	3.862	Daily	6:00 pm
Mississippi Traffic Net	3.665	Daily	6:45 pm
Mississippi/Louisiana Emergency Net (Vicksburg area)	147.27+	Su	9:00 pm
NE Mississippi SKYWARN Net	147.38+	M	8:00 pm
Pine Belt Repeater Association (Southeast Mississippi)	147.09+ 146.775- 442.2+	Daily	8:00 pm
Stone Co ARES Net	145.27-	Su	8:00 pm
SW Mississippi ARES	146.85-	Th	7:30 pm
West Coastal Mississippi ARES Net (Hancock, Harrison, and Jackson Counties)	146.33-	M,W,F	7:00 pm
Missouri			
Adair Co ARES Net	145.13-	Tu	7:00 pm
Audrain ARES Net (North Central Missouri)	147.255+	Th	9:00 pm
Central Missouri Emergency Net	146.760-	W	12:00pm 9:00 pm
Christian Co ARES Net (Southwest Missouri)	145.23-(162.2)	Tu	7:30 pm
DOERS ARC (East Central Missouri)	146.625-	Tu	8:00 pm
District-I, Amateur Radio Emergency Services Net (Pulaski, Phelps, Maries, Miller, Laclede, & Texas Counties)	145.55 simplex	W	7:00 pm
DOERS (E Central Missouri, W Central Illinois)	146.625-	Tu	8:00 pm
Hambutchers (Missouri & surrounding states)	7.28	M-F	12:05pm
Jackson Co ARES	146.97-	Sa	9:00 am
JARC ARES Net (Southwest Missouri)	147.21+	M	7:30 pm
Lake Ozark ARC (Central Missouri)	146.73-	F	9:00 pm
Lake Ozark ARC (Central Missouri)	28.35	W	9:00 pm
Linn Co ARC Simplex Net (N Central Missouri)	146.565	Su	7:30 pm
Macon Co ARES Net	146.805-	W	8:30 pm
Missouri Emergency Net	144.2 144.25 53.30	Sa (2,4)	7:30 pm
Missouri Emergency Services Net (Missouri & contiguous states)	3.963 7.263	Su	6:15 pm
Missouri Section Net (MON)	3.585	Daily	7:00 pm 9:45 pm
Missouri Sideband Net	3.963	Daily	5:45 pm
Moniteau Co ARES Net (MCAN)	146.575 444.625+(127.3)	W (1,3,5)	8:45 pm
Paul Revere Net (Greater Kansas City area)	146.94-	Sa	12:00am

PCL Net (SW MO, NW AR)	145.010 alt 145.090	M	7:00 pm
PCL Net (Patience and Chicken Lips) (Little Rock, Branson, Springfield, Joplin, Lebanon)	145.010 147.495 145.090	M	7:00 pm
Sedalia-Pettis Amateur Radio Klub Net (75 mile radius of Sedalia)	147.03-(179.9)	Su	8:00 pm
South Side Amateur Radio Club Net (50-70 mile radius of Ramymore)	147.12+	Tu	9:00 pm
Southside ARC Tuesday Night Net (Kansas City metro, E Central KS, W Central MO)	147.1200+	Tu (1, 2, 4, 5)	8:00 pm
Southwest Missouri Regional SKYWARN Net (Southwest Central Missouri)	145.490-(136.5 or DTMF 22) alt 146.910-	M	7:00 pm
SW Missouri SKYWARN Training Net (SW & Central MO, SE KS, NW AR, NE OK)	145.49-(136.5)	Tu	7:00 pm
St Louis Co ARES	146.850 MHZ tone 141.3 Hz	W	7:30 pm
Suburban Radio Club (St Louis City & Co)	146.85-	Tu	8:00 pm
Sullivan ARC Net	146.805-	M	8:00 pm
Taney Co ARES	147.195+	M	9:00 pm
Warrensburg Area Net (50 mile radius of Warrensburg)	146.88-	Sa	8:30 pm
Montana			
Custer Co Amateur Radio Emergency Services	146.92-	Tu	7:30 pm
GFAAR ARES (North Central Montana)	146.73-	Tu	7:00 pm
Idaho Montana Net (Idaho, Montana)	3.647		
Lewis & Clark Co ARES Net (Lewis & Clark, Jefferson, and Silver Counties)	147.82-	Tu	7:30 pm
Missoula Co Emergency VHF Net	147.04+	Th	8:00 pm
Montana RACES	3.947	Su (1,3)	9:00 am
Northern Lights ARES Net (Daniels, Sheridan, & Roosevelt)	147.10+	Su	7:30 pm
Valley Co ARES Net (Valley, Rossevelt, & Phillips Counties)	146.84-	W	7:00 pm
Western Montana ARES Net	3.91	Su (2, 4)	9:00 am
Nebraska			
Dodge Co ARES Net (East Nebraska)	146.67-	W	7:00 pm
Elkhorn Valley ARC Net (Northeast Nebraska)	146.73-	M	9:00 pm
Mid-Nebraska ARES Net (Grand Island vicinity)	146.94-	Daily	7:00 pm
Midlands ARES (Omana area)	146.94-	Su	8:00 pm
Nebraska 40 Meter Net (NE&surrounding states)	7.282	Daily	1:00 pm
Nebraska Cornhusker Net	3.98		
Nebraska Morning Phone Net	3.982	Daily	7:30 am
Nebraska Storm Net (NE & surrounding states)	3.982	Daily	6:30 pm
Saunders Co ARES Net	145.31-	W	8:00 pm
West Nebraska Net (W NE & Western states)	3.95	M-Sa	7:00 am
Nevada			
Clark Co Nevada ARES/RACES Net	147.18+(100) 145.11-(100) 145.22-(100) 447.325-(127.3)	M	7:30 pm
NE Nevada ARES Net (Lander & Humboldt Ctys)	146.91-	W	7:30 pm
NE Nevada ARES Net (Elko Co)	449.75-	W	7:30 pm
Nevada Section ARES Net (Nevada Section, NE California, S Idaho)	3.965 7.28	Sa	8:30 am
Nevada State RACES Net	3.9965	W	7:00 pm
Northern Nevada Amateur Radio Services Net (Northwest Nevada)	146.61-	Th	9:00 pm

Rural Amateur Radio Association (Nevada & Western states)	3.965	Sa	10:00am
Sierra Intermountain Emergency Net (Western Nevada, Eastern California)	3.9965	Th	7:00 pm
Sierra Intermountain Emergency RA (Carson Valley)	147.33+	Th	6:30 pm
TARA Heavenly Valley Net (Tahoe Basin, Carson, and Sacramento Valley)	147.24+	M	7:30 pm
Western Nevada Noon Net (NW Nevada, NE California)	147.21+(123) 147.15+(123)	Daily	12:00pm
New Hampshire			
Balknap Co ARES Net	147.39+	W	9:00 pm
Capital Area ARES Net (Merrimack Co)	146.895-	M	8:00 pm
Carroll Co ARES Net	147.03+	F	7:00 pm
Central New Hampshire ARES Net	147.39+	W	8:00 pm
Granite State Phone Net (NH)	3.943	Daily	6:00 pm
Hillsborough Co Emergency Net	146.73-(PL88.5) 146.73-(PL127.3)	Tu	7:45 pm
Manchester ARES Net	147.330 146.685	Su	8:00 pm
Nashua Area Emergency Net (Hillsborough Co)	147.045+	Tu	8:00 pm
North Country District Emergency Net (Carroll, Coos, & North Grafton Counties)	3.862	when needed	
North Country District Emergency Net (Carroll, Coos, & North Grafton Counties)	146.655-(PL100) 145.43-(PL114.9) 147.57 simplex	Th	8:00 pm
Seacoast Emergency Net (SE NH, NE MA, E Rockingham & Strafford Counties)	146.805- 147.57	Th	9:00 pm
Tristate FM Emergency Net (Cheshire Co, surrounding Vermont & Massachusetts area)	146.805- (PL100.0)	W	7:30 pm
Twin State Emergency Net (Sullivan Co, SW New Hampshire, SE Vermont)	146.76-	Tu	7:30 pm
Western Hillsborough Co ARES Net	443.975-(PL110.9)	Tu	8:15 pm
Western Rockingham Co ARES Net (S NH)	146.85-(PL85.4)W	M	8:00 pm
New Jersey			
Atlantic Co ARES Net	146.745-	Tu (2,4)	8:00 pm
Bergen/Passaic Co SKYWARN Training Net	146.700-(141.3)	M	10:00pm
Bergen/Passaic SKYWARN Net	146.700-	when needed	1:00 am
Burlington Co Emergency Net	147.15 145.47-	W	7:00 pm
Camden Co ARES Net	146.82-	M	7:30 pm
Camden Co OEM	146.895 (192.8)	Th	7:30 pm
Cumberland Co Emergency Net	146.655-	W	7:30 pm
Englewood ARES Net	147.135	W (1,3)	8:00 pm
Gloucester Co Emergency Net	147.18+	Su	8:00 pm
Hudson Co ARES/SKYWARN Simplex Net	146.535	last M	7:00 pm
JSARS Traffic Net (Ocean Co)	146.91-(127.3)	Daily	7:30 pm
Mercer Co Emergency Net	146.67-(131.8)	Tu (4)	7:30 pm
Middlesex Co RACES Net	147.12+	W	7:00 pm
Monmouth Co ARES/RACES	147.045+	Tu	7:30 pm
Morris Co ARES	146.895-	M (2)	8:00 pm
New Jersey VHF Net Late Session (North NJ)	146.700-	Daily	10:30pm
NJ State RACES Net	3.9905	M (4)	8:00 pm
NJ-NY SATERN Net (NJ, E NY, E PA)	449.975-(151.3)	Tu	8:30 pm
NNJ Red Cross Net (Northern New Jersey)	146.895-(151.4)	M (4)	7:15 pm
Northern New Jersey ARES Net	146.895-(151.4)	M (2)	8:00 pm
Ocean Co ARES (Manahawkin)	146.835-	W (3)	8:30 pm

Ocean Co ARES (Toms River)	146.91- 146.835-	W (1, 2,4)	8:30 pm
SKYWARN Tri-County (Northern NJ, Tri-County)		when needed	
South Jersey Traffic Net (Southern New Jersey)	147.15+(127.3) 145.47-(127.3) 448.325-(127.3)	Su, M, W, F	8:00 pm
South Jersey VHF Net (South NJ, East PA)	147.345+	Daily	10:30pm
Southern New Jersey Section Emergency Admin Net	147.345+	Tu (4)	9:00 pm
The Central Jersey Traffic Net (New Jersey)	146.760-(PL156.7)	Daily	8:00 pm
The Marvelous Marvin Net (Central New Jersey)	147.12+	M-F	7:30 am 5:00 pm
Union Co ARES Net (Tri-County area)	449.975-(141.3)	Su	8:30 pm
Union Co ARES Net	146.685-(123)	Su	8:30 pm
Y2K Emergency Preparedness Net (DE, MD, NJ, NY, PA)	53.555	F	7:30 pm
Y2K Emergency Preparedness Net (DE, MD, S NJ, E PA)	147.345+	Tu	9:00 pm

New Mexico

Bernalillo Co ARES	146.900-(67) 146.940-(100) 146.960-(100)	Th	7:00 pm
Deming ARC Thursday Night Net (Luna, Grant, & Dona Ana Counties)	146.820-	Th	7:30 pm
Lincoln Co ARES/RACES Net	146.92-	Su (1, 3)	7:00 pm
MVRC Emergency Team Net (Las Cruces)	146.64-(100)	W	6:45 pm
New Mexico ARES/RACES State Wide Net (New Mexico & surrounding states)	3.939	Su (1,3)	6:30 pm

New York

Albany Co Emergency Services Net	147.12+	Tu	7:30 pm
Allegany Highland ARC/ARES Net (Allegany Co)	145.43- 146.955- 147.21+	Tu (2, 4)	8:30 pm
Big Apple Traffic Net (New York City)	146.43	Daily	8:00 pm
Black River Valley Service Net (Boonville)	146.655-	Daily	9:00 pm
Brookhaven Township ARES/RACES	145.21-	Th	7:30 pm
Broome Co ARES Net	146.73-	M	7:30 pm
Central District ARES Net (Central NY area)	147.00-	M (3)	8:30 pm
Central New York Traffic Net	147.30+	Su,Tu,W, F,Sa	9:15 pm
Central New York Traffic Net	147.00-	M-Th	9:15 pm
Chemung Co ARES Net	147.36+	Su,Th	9:00 pm
Chenango Co ARES Net	146.685-	W	7:30 pm
Columbia-Greene Co Emergency Services Net	147.21+	Tu	7:00 pm
Cortland Co ARES	147.18+	M	7:00 pm
Delaware Co SKYWARN Net	146.955-(127.3) 146.745-	when needed	1:00 am
Dutchess Co ARES Training Net	147.045+(PL100)	M (1)	9:00 pm
Dutchess Co ARES Training Net	146.97-(PL100)	W (3)	7:30 pm
Eastern New York Emergency Services Net (Eastern New York and surrounding sections)	145.25-(PL100) 448.575; 443.60 449.025; 444.75 445.725; 29.680 445.975; 53.19 447.025	Tu (1)	8:00 pm
Eastern Suffolk ARES Net (East Hampton, Riverhead, & Shelter Island)	147.195+	M	7:30 pm
Genesee Co ARES	147.285+ 147.15 (alt)	W (1)	7:00 pm
Herkimer Co ARES/RACES (Central NY state)	145.110-	Tu	7:00 pm

Herkimer Co SKYWARN (Lower Herkimer Co)	147.9	when needed	
Huntington Township ARES/RACES	147.21-	M	8:30 pm
Islip Township ARES/RACES	147.345+	Th	8:30 pm
Jefferson Co Radio Anateur Civil Emergency Service (Lewis, Jefferson, St Lawrence, Oswego, & Onadoga Counties)	147.255+(155.4)	W (2,4)	7:00 pm
Lewis Co RACES/ARES Net	146.955-	Su	6:00 pm
Nassau Co ARES (Nassau Co, Long Island)	146.805-	M	8:00 pm
New York City ARES	147.000-(136.5) 445.825-(156.7)	M	8:00 pm
New York City RACES	147.000-(136.5) 445.825-(156.7)	M (1)	8:45 pm
New York State Co Net	3.677	Su	9:30 am
New York State CW Net - Cycle 4	3.677 1.825	Daily	7:00 pm 10:00pm
New York State Phone Traffic & Emergency Net	3.925	Daily	6:00 pm
New York State RACES Voice Net	3.9935 7.245	Su	9:00 am
Northern District Net (Northeast New York)	145.11-	Daily	7:00 pm
OCTEN (Oneida Co Traffic & Emergency Net) (Oneida & Surrounding Counties)	145.450-	Daily	6:30 pm
Oneida Co Traffic & Emergency Net (Oneida Co & vicinity)	146.88-	Daily	9:30 pm
Oneida Co Traffic & Emergency Net (Oneida Co & vicinity)	146.94-	Daily	6:30 pm
Oneida Co Traffic & Emergency Net-OCTEN (Oneida Co & vicinity)	145.170-	Daily	9:30 pm
Oneida/Madison Emergency Net	145.17-	Tu (1)	7:15 pm
Oneonta ARC Net (Otsego Co)	146.85-	W	6:45 pm
Onondaga Co Radio Emergency Net	147.30+	M (1, 3)	7:30 pm
Ontario Co ARES/RACES Net	146.82-	Sa	8:30 am
Orange Co ARES/RACES/SKYWARN Net (Hudson Valley, New York)	146.76-(100)	M (1,2,3)	8:00 pm
Orleans Co ARC Net	145.27-	Tu	9:00 pm
Otsego Co ARES/RACES	146.85-	Th	7:00 pm
Schenectady Co Emergency Net	224.06-	Su	1:15 pm
Schenectady Co Emergency Net	147.06-	Su	1:30 pm
Schenectady Co Emergency Net	3.953	Su	2:00 pm
Schentady/Utica Equipment, Traffic, and Ragchewers Net	147.440	Daily	7:30 pm
Schoharie Co RACES Net (Montgomery, Schoharie, Fulton, & Schenectady Counties)	146.610-(123.0)	Tu	6:45 pm
SKYWARN New York City District	147.27+	when needed	
SKYWARN Priority Channel, (24 County area of New York & Pennyslvania)	147.075+	when needed	
Staten Island SKYWARN Net	445.825	when needed	
Steuben Co ARES/RACES Net	145.19-	F (4)	8:30 pm
Suffolk Co ARES/RACES Net	145.33-	M	9:00 pm
Tioga Co ARES/RACES Disaster Services Net (TIGARDS)	146.76- 146.73- alt	Su	8:00 pm
Town of Babylon Amateur Radio Emergency Services (Babylon Township,SW Suffolk Co)	146.685-(110.9)	M	8:15 pm
Wayne Co RACES Net	146.685-	Su	7:45 pm
Westchester Co ARES/RACES	147.06	W	9:45 pm
Western Catskill Net (W Catskills of NY & DE)	147.315(PL127.3)	W	7:00 pm
Western Catskill Net (Delaware Co)	146.955-(127.3)	W	7:00 pm
Western District Net (Western Counties of New York)	146.640-	Daily	6:30 pm 9:30 pm
Western District Net - Morning (W Ctys. of NY)	146.64-	Sa, Su	11:00am

Western New York Emergency Net (Western New York, Buffalo, Rochester)	146.670-(107.2) 145.255+ 146.910-	Su	7:00 pm
Western New York Emergency Net (Western District of New York)	146.67-(107.2)	Su	7:00 pm
Western New York Section Coordination	3.955 7.155	when needed	
Western New York SKYWARN Net (Arkwright)	145.31-	Tu	7:00 pm
Western New York SKYWARN Net (Attica)	146.67-	Tu	7:30 pm
Yates Co ARES/RACES Net	145.37-	Th	8:00 pm

Newfoundland-Labrador, Canada (National Traffic Net)

Newfoundland Traffic Net (CW)	3.7	Daily	7:30 pm

North Carolina

7.240 Club (CT, FL, GA, NC, OH, NH, NJ, NY, SC, VA, WV)	7.24	M-Sa	10:00am
Alamance Co ARES Net	147.375+(PL114.8)	Tu	8:00 pm
Alexander Co ARES/RACES Net	441.625+(123)	Su	9:00 pm
Ashe Co ARES Net (Northwest North Carolina)	147.30+(PL103.5)	W	9:00 pm
Carolinas Net (North Carolina, South Carolina)	3.573	Daily	10:00pm
Charlotte (CLT) SKYWARN Net (Charlotte NWS District)	145.35-	when needed	
Forsyth Co ARES Net (Forsyth, Stokes, & Davie Counties)	145.47-(100)	W	8:30 pm
Gaston Co ARES Emergency Training Net	147.120+	Th	7:00 pm
Gaston Co ARES Emergency Training Net	145.230-	Th	7:00 pm
Lincoln Co RACES/ARES	147.015+ 442.35+	Tu	
Metrolina Two-Meter Emergency Net (Mecklenburg Co)	146.94	Daily	9:00 pm
Montgomery Co Amateur Radio Society	147.09+(100)	M	8:30 pm
Moore Co ARS Net (Sandhills of North Carolina)	147.24+	Su, W	8:00 pm
Nash Co ARES Net (Nash Co & Surrounding area)	146.805; 145.29 444.70; 444.50 224.22; 444.975 147.03; 442.125	Tu	8:30 pm
New Hanover Co ARES Net	146.670-(88.5)	W	8:00 pm
North Carolina Evening Net	3.923	Daily	6:30 pm
North Carolina Morning Net	3.927	Daily	7:45 am
North Carolina SSB Net	3.938	Daily	7:30 pm
Orange Co ARES Net	442.15+	Sa	9:30 am
Piedmont Emergency Training Net (Foothills, S Piedmont of North Carolina)	145.35-	Daily	8:00 pm
Pitt Co Emergency Communications Net (Pitt Co & surrounding Counties)	147.09+(131.8)	M	9:00 pm
Rockingham Co ARES Net (North Central North Carolina, South Central Virginia)	146.850-(103.5) 147.345-(103.5) 224.780-	M	9:00 pm
Southeastern North Carolina Traffic Net (Southeast North Carolina, Northeast South Carolina)	147.045+ 147.360+ 146.520	Daily	8:00 pm
Tar Heel Emergency Net (North Carolina ARES)	3.923 7.232	Daily	7:30 pm
Wake Tech College Repeater WB4TOP (Wake Co)	146.61-	Th	8:00 pm
Wilson Co Amateur Radio Association ARES Net	146.76	M	8:30 pm

North Dakota

Forx ARC Monday Night Net (Grand Forks area)	146.94-	M	9:00 pm
Storm Net (North Dakota)	3.937 7.232	during storm events	

Ohio			
147.225 Repeater Group Net (Springfield, Ohio area)	147.225+(123)	Su, W when needed	9:30 pm
20/9 Friday Night Net (Mahoning Valley)	147.315+	F	9:15 pm
ARES Traffic and Training Net (Eastern Ohio)	146.85	Tu	8:15 pm
Buckeye Net (Ohio)	3.577	Daily	6:45 pm 10:00pm
Buckeye Net RTTY (Ohio)	3.605	Daily	6:00 pm
Burning River Traffic Net (North Central Ohio)	147.15+	Daily	9:30 pm
Butler Co Amateur Radio Emergency Services	147.3300	Tu	8:30 pm
Carroll ARS Weekly Net (Franklin, Licking, Fairfield, Pickaway, Madison, Union, Delaware)	147.05+	W	8:00 pm
Crawford Co Net	146.85-	Tu	8:00 pm
Dayton Amateur Radio Association Communications Van Net	146.940-(100)	Su	8:30 pm
Dayton SKYWARN - Miami Valley/W Central Ohio/IN White Water Valley Section Net (15+ Counties in West Central Ohio)	146.64- 146.835-(67.0)	when needed	1:00 am
DeForest ARC Net (South Central Ohio)	147.00+(PL94.8)	Th	9:00 pm
Erie Co FARA Emergency & ARES Net (North Central Ohio)	146.805-(110.9)	Su	8:00 pm
Guernsey Co SKYWARN Wx Training Net (Eastern Ohio)	146.85	Tu	8:00 pm
Guernsey Co ARES and Traffic Net (East Ohio: Guernsey, Muskingum, & Noble Counties)	146.85-(91.5)	Tu	8:15 pm
Hamilton Co ARPSC Training Net	145.37-	Th	9:00 pm
HEARS (Hancock Co)	147.15+	W	8:00 pm
Hanry Co Amateur Radio Net (Northwest Ohio)	147.315+	Su	8:00 pm
Highland Amateur Radio Association Net (South Central & Southwest Ohio)	147.21+(100) 146.685-	M	9:00 pm
Huron Co ARES	146.865	Su	6:30 pm
Huron Co ARES Net	147.48	Su	6:30 pm
Licking Co ARES Net	145.47-1	W (1)	8:30 pm
Lorain Co ARA Sunday Evening ARES Net	147.15+	Su	8:30 pm
Northwest Ohio ARES Traffic Net	146.94-	Daily	6:45 pm
Northern Columbina Co ARES Net (120 mile diameter of Salem)	147.255+(156.7) 444.675+(156.7)	Tu	9:00 pm
OPERATION Team Net (Northeast Ohio, Northwest Pennyslvania)	Single VHF net w/ Offset & PL tone: 147.39+(PL131.8)	Su	6:30 pm
Ohio District 3 ARES Net	145.11-(67.0) 224.16	W, as needed	8:00 pm
Ohio Section ARES Net	3.875	Su	3:00 pm
Ohio Single Sideband Net	3.9725	Daily	10:30am 4:15 pm 6:45 pm
Ohio Valley ARES/RACES Net (Tri-State area: Kentucky, Ohio, West Virginia)	146.715-(103.5) 146.940 146.760 146.610-(103.5)	Th	9:00 pm
Over The Hill Net (Dayton metro)	146.940-(100)	W	11:30am
Pioneer Amateur Radio Fellowship Inc (Akron)	147.135+(110.9)	M	7:00 pm
Portage Co Emergency Net	145.68	Tu	9:00 pm
Portage Co Emergency Net	146.39-	Su	8:30 pm
Queen City Emergency Net (SW OH, N KY)	147.24+	Tu	10:00pm
Richland Co ARES Net (Richland Co & surrounding areas)	146.94+	W	9:00 pm
Sandusky Co ARES Net	146.91-	W	7:45 pm
Sandusky Co ARES Net	146.910-	Su	7:15 pm

Seneca Co ARES Net	145.45-	Su	8:00 pm
Shelby Co ARES (S Lima to N Dayton)	443.20+	Su	7:00 pm
Steubenville (Ohio)-Weirton (West Virginia) ARC	146.94-	Su	8:00 pm
Trumbull Co ARES/RACES Net	28.375	W	8:00 pm
Warren Co RACES/ARES	146.865-	M	8:30 pm
Washington Co Emergency Net (Southeast Ohio, West Central West Virginia)	3.925	Su	12:00pm
West Central Ohio ARES Net (Ohio ARES District 3)	145.110-(67) 224.160-	W	8:00 pm
Wyandot Co ARES Net	146.685-	Su	7:00 pm

Oklahoma

Altus Area Amateur Radio Assoc. (Jackson Co)	146.79-	M	7:30 pm
Arkansas/Oklahoma Salvation Army Net	3.941	Sa (2)	8:00 am
Arkansas/Oklahoma Salvation Army Net	146.82- 145.07 packet	Sa (2)	8:00 am
Bartlesville Area Info & Swap (NE Oklahoma)	146.655-	W	9:00 pm
Bartlesville Rag Chew Net (NE Oklahoma)	444.775+(PL107.2)	W	8:30 pm
Central OK Chapter 63 QCWA	3.855	Su	8:00 am
Central OK VHF Club/Chap 63 QCWA (Oklahoma City area)	145.41-	Th	7:00 pm
Central Oklahoma District Packet ARES (Oklahoma City area)	146.82-	Th	8:00 pm
Central Oklahoma District ARES (OK City area)	145.07-	Th	8:00 pm
Chisholm Trail Amateur RadioClub Net (SW OK)	146.730-	Th	7:00 pm
Chisholm Trail ARC/Stephens Co ARES (Southwest Oklahoma)	146.73-	Tu	9:00 pm
Cleveland Co SKYWARN (50 mile radius of Oklahoma City)	146.06+(141.7)	when needed	
E Oklahoma, W Arkansas SKYWARN	146.88- 443.85+	when needed	
EARS Emergency Service Net (Central OK)	147.135+	Sa (1)	11:00am
Enid ARC Night Net (Garfield Co)	147.15+ 444.40	M	8:00 pm
Great Plain Radio (Woodward)	146.73-	Tu	9:00 pm
Kay Co Area 2 Meter Net	146.91-	M	9:00 pm
Mayes Co ARC Net (Northeast Oklahoma)	147.06+(88.5)	Th	7:00 pm
Muskogee ARC Club Net	146.745-	M	7:00 pm
Northeast Oklahoma ARES VHF Net (NE OK, NW AR, SW MO, SE KS)	147.36+(88.5)	Su	2:00 pm
Northeast Oklahoma Radio Amateur Net	147.36+	Tu	8:00 pm
Oklahoma ARES Training Net	7.26	Su	3:30 pm
Oklahoma Baptist Disaster Relief Net (AR, KS, OK, TX)	7.275	Su	3:30 pm
Oklahoma City Citizen Response Team (metro area)	145.41 144.81	M	7:00 pm
Oklahoma Insomia Net (Southern Oklahoma)	147.075+(131)	Daily	10:30pm
Oklahoma Insomnia Net (Oklahoma)	147.15+(136.5)	Daily	10:30pm
Oklahoma Phone Emergency Net	3.9	Su	8:00 am
Oklahoma Training Net (CW)	7.12065	Daily	5:45 pm
Pottawatomie Co ARC (Lincoln, Pottawatomie, & Cleveland Counties)	145.39-	Th	8:00 pm
Rogers Co Wireless Association	147.09+	Tu	8:00 pm
Southern Oklahoma Amateur Radio Emergency Services (South Central Oklahoma)	147.150+(131.8) 147.315+(151.4) 146.700-(173.8) 147.165+(131.8)	M	8:00 pm
Southwest Oklahoma ARES Net (Comanche Co)	146.91-	Th	7:00 pm
Star Club Insomia Net (Southern Oklahoma)	147.075+(131)	Daily	10:30pm
Stillwater Area Net (Payne Co)	145.35-	Th	8:00 pm

Triple T Net (Northeast quadrant of Oklahoma)	145.11 443.850 442.00 (linked)	F	10:00pm
Tulsa Amateur Radio Thursday Night Net (50,000 square miles)	145.110-(88.5) W5IAS linked system	Th	8:00 pm
Tulsa ARC Net (Northeast quadrant of Oklahoma)	145.11-(88.5) linked	Th	8:00 pm
Tulsa ARC YL Net	145.11	Sa	8:00 pm
Tulsa ARES Net (Eastern Oklahoma)	146.94	Tu	9:00 pm
Tulsa Hospital Disaster Net (Eastern Oklahoma)	146.34- 443.85+	when needed	
Tulsa SKYWARN - Remote Operation (E OK)	444.10+	when needed	
Tulsa SKYWARN - Secondary (Eastern OK)	146.94-	when needed	
Tulsa SKYWARN - wide-area link (Eastern OK)	443.85+	when needed	

Ontario, Canada (Emergency & National Traffic Nets)

Kingsmere Traffic Net (Ottawa Valley & E ON)	147.36+	M,W,F	9:00 pm
Niagara Peninsula 2 Metre Net	147.24+	Daily	6:30 pm
Ontario Phone Net	3.742	Daily	7:00 pm
Ontario Section Net (D, E, and L)	3.667		
Toronto Open Line Net (Greater Toronto & Golden Horseshoe)	147.06+	Daily	6:30 pm
Trans-Provincial Net (Ontario)	7.055		
Twin Soo Mini Net (Sault Ste Marie & vicinity)	146.34+	Daily	9:00 pm

Oregon

ARES Mid Columbia (The Dalles, Oregon and Goldendale, Washington)	146.74-	Th	6:00 pm
ARRL Oregon Section Management Net	3.98	Sa	8:00 am
Benton Co ARES Net	147.16+	Tu	7:45 pm
Central Oregon ARES Net (Deschutes, Jefferson, Crook Co)	147.36+	Su	8:00 pm
Central Oregon Coast ARC (West Lake Co)	146.80-	W	7:00 pm
Clackamas Co ARES	145.21-(PL110.9)	Su	7:00 pm
Clatsop Co ARES	145.88-	M	7:00 pm
Columbia Co ARES	146.88-(114.8) 147.47	Tu	7:00 pm
District 1 ARES Net (Columbia, Clatsop, Clackamas, Multnomah, Tillamook, Washington, and Yamhill Counties)	147.32+	Daily	7:30 pm
District 4 ARES Net (Benton, Lane, Lincoln, Linn, Marion, and Polk Counties)	146.78-	Su, Tu	7:00 pm
Douglas Co ARES	145.43-	M	7:00 pm
Generation X Radio Amateur Youth Net (Northwest Oregon)	145.330-	W	7:00 pm
HEART - Hospital Emergency Amateur Radio Team (East & West sides of Portland, ARES D-1)	145.390-(100) 147.435[-1.035 MHz] (100)	Th	7:00 pm
Hood Rover Co ARES	147.10+(PL100.0)	M	7:30 pm
Hoodview ARC Information Net (Portland metro)	147.28+(167.9)	W	7:30 pm
Jackson Co ARS	146.94-	Su,Tu,F	7:30 PM
Lincoln Co ARS Net	145.37-	Tu	8:00 pm
Linn Co ARES Net	147.200	M	7:00 pm
Marion/Polk Co ARES Net - District 0 (Salem & area)	146.86-	M,Th	7:00 pm
Multnomah Co	147.88-	Tu	7:00 pm
Multnomah Co ARES/RACES (Portland metro)	146.84-	W	7:00 pm
Oregon ARES Traffic Net	3.9935	Daily	5:30 pm
Oregon City ARES/ARES Net (Oregon City & Clackamas Co)	146.56-	Su	7:30 pm

Oregon Emergency Net	3.98	Daily	6:00 pm 7:00 pm
Oregon Section ARES/RACES Net	3.9935	when needed	
Oregon Section EC Roundtable	3.9935	Sa	9:00 am
Oregon Section Net	3.587	Daily	6:30 pm 10:00pm
Southern Oregon FM Net (Josephine Co)	147.30+	M	7:30 pm
Tillamook Co Emergency AR Service	147.22+	W	7:00 pm
UMESRO (Umatilla & Morrow Co)	146.78-(PL67.0)	Th	7:30 pm
Washington Co ARES	146.90-	Tu	7:00 pm
Western Oregon VHF Emergency Net - WOVEN	146.78-(primary) 146.82-(alternate) 146.72(PL100.0) (alternate)	Daily	7:30 pm
Yamhill Co ARES	146.64-	M	7:00 pm
Pennsylvania			
Allegheny Co Public Service Net	147.09+	W	9:00 pm
Allegheny Co SKYWARN	147.09+	W(1, 3)	8:30 pm
ARES/RACES of Delaware Co	147.195+ 447.375-(100.0) 442.250+(131.1)	W	7:30 pm
Armstrong Co Public Service Net	145.41+	M	9:00 pm
Beaver Co Public Service Net	146.85-	M	8:30 pm
Beaver Co Severe Weather Net	146.85-	when needed	
Berwick ARS (Lower Luzerne & Columbia Ctys)	145.13(PL77)	W	7:00 pm
Blair Co ARES Net	146.61-	Tu	8:00 pm
Blair Co ARES Ten Meter Net	28.44	M	8:00 pm
Breakfasteers Net (Beaver Co)	146.85-	M-F	8:45 am
Butler Co Public Service Net	147.30+	Th	9:00 pm
Cambria Co ARES Net	145.21-	M	7:00 pm
Capital Area Traffic Net	145.43-	M	8:30 pm
Carbon Co RACES/ARES Net	147.255	W	9:00 pm
Chester Co ARES/RACES Net (Chester Co, Pennsylvania and adjacent counties including those in New Jersey & Delaware)	146.94-(131.8) 146.985-(100.0) 446.525-(100.0) 446.175-(100.0)	Th	7:30 pm
Clarion Co ARES Net	146.985- 444.425+	Su	7:30 pm
Cumberland Valley ARC Sunday Night Net (Franklin Co)	147.120+	Su	9:00 pm
District 4 ARES (Eastern Pennsylvania)	147.225+(PL203.5)	Tu	7:00 pm
District 6 ARES (Susquehanna, Luzerne, and Lackawana Counties)	147.00+	Tu, Th	8:00 pm
District N-1 ARES Net (Clarion, Erie Crawford, Forest, & Lawrence Counties)	145.23-	Th	8:00 pm
Eastern Pennsylvania CW Net	3.61	Daily	7:00 pm
EPA Emergency Phone/Traffic Net (Eastern Pennsylvania Section)	3.917	Daily	6:00 pm
Erie Co ARES SKYWARN Net	146.61-	Su	9:00 pm
Huntingdon Co ARES Net (Blair, Center, Huntingdon, Mifflin, & Fulton Counties)	146.70- 145.31-	Su	8:30 pm
Lackawanna Co Amateur Radio Emergency Communication Net	146.94-	W	8:00 pm
Luzerne Co ARES Net	145.41-	Su	8:00 pm
McKean Co ARES & SKYWARN Net	147.24-(PL173.8) 147.30+(PL173.8)	Su	9:30 pm
Monroe Co Office of Emergency Services	146.865-	Su	8:00 pm
Northwestern PA 2 Meter Net (Erie & Crawford Counties)	145.13-	Daily	9:00 pm

SATERN of Western Pennsylvania (Greater Pittsburgh area)	146.61- 444.95+ 223.98+ 146.955	Tu	8:00 pm
Schuylkill Co Emergency Services Net	145.37-	Tu	8:00 pm
SE PA Practice & Training Net (Bucks, Montgomery & Lehigh Counties)	145.31-	Su, W	8:00 pm
SW PA District One ARES Net	147.09+	Su	7:30 pm
Wayne Co Amateur Radio Emergency Communications	146.655-	M	8:00 pm
Western PA Phone & Traffic Net	3.983	Daily	6:00 pm
Western Pennsylvania Emergency Net	7.272 3.983	Su (2, 4)	5:30 pm
Westmoreland Co ARES Net	145.150-(131.8)	W	8:00 pm
York Co ARES/RACES Service Net	146.97-	M	8:30 pm
Puerto Rico			
Aguadilla ARES Zone 3 (NW Puerto Rico)	145.54	when needed	
Arecibo ARES Zone 2 (N Central Puerto Rico)	146.58	Th	8:00 pm
Carolina ARES Zone 8 (Northeast Puerto Rico)	146.57	when needed	
Guayama ARES Zone 7 (SE Puerto Rico)	146.47	when needed	
Mayaguez ARES Zone 4 (SW Puerto Rico)	146.56	when needed	
Ponce ARES Zone 5 (S Central Puerto Rico)	146.57	when needed	
Puerto Rico Net - Slow (PR & Virgin Islands)	3.71	when needed	
Red Communications Emergencia Esta Puerto Rico (Eeastern Puerto Rico)	146.65- 146.57	Daily	7:30 pm
San Juan ARES Zone 1 (N Central Puerto Rico)	145.55	when needed	
Quebec, Canada (Emergency & National Traffic Nets)			
Quebec Section Net	3.667	Daily	7:30 pm
VE2RTQ (Quebec via VHF/UHF links)	145.19-	Daily	6:30 pm
Rhode Island			
Eastern Mass/Rhode Island Phone Net	3.915	Daily	5:30 pm
Eastern Mass/Rhode Island Slow Speed Net	3.715	Daily	8:00 pm
Mass/Rhode Isl Emergency Phone Net	3.915	when needed	
Rhode Island SKYWARN/ARES Training and Information Net (Rhode Island, Eastern Massachusetts, Eastern Connecticut)	146.70- 146.76- 147.165+	W	8:30 pm
Rhode Island/Eastern Massachusetts Traffic Net - 2 Meter	147.36+	M-F	7:00 pm
Saskatchewan, Canada (Emergency & National Traffic Nets)			
ARES Net (Saskatchewan)	3.753		
Avonlea Repeater Group (SE Saskatchewan)	147.06-		
Saskatchewan Evening Phone Net	3.744		
Saskatoon 2 Meter	146.64-		
South Carolina			
Anderson Radio Club 2-Meter Net (Northeast SC, Western NC, Northeast GA)	146.79-	Daily	8:30 pm
Beaufort Co ARES	145.31-	Th	8:30 pm
Blue Ridge 2-Meter Net (W SC, NC, N GA)	146.61-	Daily	9:00 pm
Charleston ARES	145.25 146.79-	Su	8:00 pm
Columbia ARC Bi-Weekly Net (Central Midlands of South Carolina)	146.775- 147.33+ 444.20+(156.7) linked	Su,W	8:30 pm
Foothills ARC 2-Meter Net (Pickens Co)	146.70-(107.2)	Th	8:00 pm
Horry Co SKYWARN (Horry, Georgetown, & Marion Counties)	147.12+ 145.11-	when needed	

North Midlands SKYWARN Net (North Midlands of South Carolina)	145.49- 146.925- 146.895- 147.00+ 147.195+	Daily	9:30 pm
Oconee 2 Meter Net (NW SC, NE GA)	147.27+	M-F	8:00 pm
Pickens Co 2 Meter Net (Pickens, Anderson, Greenville & Oconee Counties)	146.70-(107.2)	M	8:00 pm
South Carolina ARES/RACES Net	3.9935	M (1, 3)	6:00 pm
South Carolina Single Sideband Net (South Carolina & surrounding states)	3.915	Daily	7:00 pm
Spartanburg 2 Meter Net	147.315+	M, W, F	8:30 pm
Tri-County ARS Simplex Emergency Net (Northeast South Carolina)	146.535	Tu	8:30 pm
York Co 2 Meter Net (York and surrounding counties of NC & SC)	147.030-	Daily	8:30 pm
South Dakota			
Aberdeen Area 2 Meter Net (75 mile radius of Aberdeen)	147.030+ Tone 146.2	W	9:30 pm
NE South Dakota 2 Meter Net	146.85-	Tu	9:00 pm
NE South Dakota SKYWARN Net	146.67-	M-F	7:00 pm
Sioux Empire ARC Net (Sioux Falls area)	146.895-	Tu	6:45 pm
South Dakota CW Net	3.65	M-F	7:00 pm
South Dakota NEO Evening Net	3.86	Daily	6:00 pm
South Dakota NJQ Noon Net	3.87	Su	1:00 pm
South Dakota NJQ Noon Net	3.87	M-Sa	12:15 pm
South Dakota Sunday Emergency Net	3.96	Su	9:00 am
Tri-State Emergency Weather Net (SW South Dakota, NW Nebraska, E Central Wyoming)	146.850-	Daily	9:00 pm
Walworth Co Net	3.7	Su	12:45pm
Tennessee			
Anderson Co ARES	146.88-	Tu	8:00 pm
Blount Co ARES/RACES Emergency Net (Blount, Knox, Loudon, Sevier, & Anderson Ctys)	146.940	Th	9:00 pm
Chattanooga ARC Emergency Service Net (50 mile radius of Chattanooga)	146.79-	Th	8:00 pm
Chester Co ARES Net (Chester, Madison, McNairy, Hardeman, & Henderson Counties)	147.105+(156.7)	Tu	8:00 pm
Clarksville ARES (Montgomery Co)	147.39+	W	7:00 pm
Cocke Co ARES Simplex Net (E TN, W NC)	147.510	M	7:30 pm
Cookeville Repeater Association Net (Middle TN)	147.21+	Tu	8:30 pm
Cumberland Co Emergency Service Net (5 Counties)	146.895-(118.5)	Su & as needed	8:00 pm
Davidson Co Amateur Radio Emergency Preparedness Net	145.47-	M	7:00 pm
Dickson Co ARES/SKYWARN Net	146.580-(Simp)+ 146.955-(114.8)+ 442.375-(123.0)	Th	7:30 pm
East Tennessee SKYWARN	147.30 224.50 444.575	when needed	
Giles SKYWARN Training Net (Giles Co, Middle TN, Northern AL)	146.775-	F	8:00 pm
Greene Co Emergency Net (East Tennessee)	145.39-	M	9:00 pm
Hardeman Co Emergency Net	147.570	W	8:15 pm
Heart of Tennessee ARES and SKYWARN Training Net (Rutherford and Surrounding Counties)	145.23-(114.8) 145.37-(114.8) 146.955-(114.8) 147.36+(114.8) 147.075(114.8)	Tu	7:30 pm

Lincoln Co Emergency Net (Southern Middle Tennessee, North Central Alabama)	147.03+	M	6:30 pm
Maury Co Repeater Net (Central & South Middle Tennessee)	147.12+	M-F	8:30 pm
McMinn AR 2 Meter Phone Net	145.310-(141.3)	M	8:30 pm
McMinn Co 70 cm Phone Net	442.275+(141.3)	M	8:45 pm
McNairy Co ARES	146.805-	Th	8:00 pm
METERS Training Net (Most of Middle Eastern Tennessee; Knox, Blount, Sevier, Jefferson, Roane, Anderson, and Campbell Counties)	147.300-(100) 224.500-(100) 444.575+(100)	W	8:15 pm
Middle Eastern Tennessee Emergency Radio Service Training Net	147.30 224.50 444.575	W	9:00 pm
Middle Tennessee SKYWARN Homepage/Middle Tennessee Emergency Amateur Radio Society	443.725+(107.2) 443.975+(107.2) 444.450+(107.2) 444.650+(107.2) 444.600+(107.2) 442.225+	Th	8:00 pm
Monday Night Trader Net (Middle Eastern TN)	147.135-(123.0)	M	8:00 pm
Plateau ARC 2 Meter ARES-RACES (Cumberland Co & surrounding Counties)	146.865-	Sa	8:00 pm
Rhea Co ARES/RACES Net (Rhea, Meigs, & Bradley Counties)	147.39+	Sa	9:00 pm
Roane Co Amateur Radio Club Net	147.015+	M	9:00 pm
Saturday Morning Check-in (40 mile radius of Jackson)	442.90+ (PL114.8)	Sa	10:00am
Scenic City Amateur Radio Society Repeater Net (Greater Chattanooga area)	444.15+	Sa	9:30 pm
Sevier Co Amateur Radio Emergency Service (Eastern Tennessee)	146.850-	M	7:30 pm
Shelby Co ARES Net (Western Fayette, Chelby, Memphis, & Tipton Counties)	146.88-	Th	9:00 pm
SKYWARN Training Net (Jackson)	147.21+	W	8:00 pm
Tag SKYWARN (NE AL, NW GA, SE TN)	146.61-	Tu	8:00 pm
Tennessee Section ARES Net (Tennessee & adjoining states)	3.98	M	7:15 pm
Tennessee Section ARES HF Net	3.98	M	6:45 pm
The KARC Sunday Evening Info Net (Sullivan & Adjoining Counties)	146.97-	Su	8:30 pm
Tri-County ARC (Cumberland, White, VanBuren, & Putnam Counties)	147.375-	Tu	7:30 pm
UCARA Information Net (Putnam and surrounding Counties)	145.27-(123.0)	Th	8:30 pm
Unicoi Co ARES Net	147.165+	Th	7:00 pm
West Tennessee Weather Net	146.97-	Daily	8:00 pm
West Tennessee West Kentucky Emergency Net (W TN, W KY, SE MO)	146.700-	Su	9:00 pm
Wilson Co ARC Information Net (Wilson Co & surrounding communities)	147.105+ (PL100 Hz)	Th	7:00 pm
Texas			
ARES Severe Weather Net (Texas)	146.76-	when needed	
Austin/Travis Co ARES Net	147.36-(131.8)	Su	7:30 pm
Austin/Travis Co ARES Net (Packet)	145.73	Su	8:00 pm
Bastrop Co ARES	145.35-(114.8) 443.75+(114.8)	Su	6:45 pm
Big Bend Emergency Net (Big Bend Trans-Pecos area)	3.922	Su	8:30 am
Brazoria Co Emergency Traffic Net (South of Houston)	146.920-(103.5) 443.825+(103.5) linked	M	8:00 pm

Central Texas Emergency Net (Central, Eastern & Southeastern Texas)	3.91	Su	8:00 am
Central Texas Traffic Net	147.14+	Daily	6:30 pm
Central Texas Traffic Net	147.10+	Daily	7:30 pm
Collin Co ARES	147.18+	Su (1, 3)	9:00 pm
Collin Co ARES	146.74-	Su (2, 4)	8:00 pm
Concho Valley (Tom Green, Concho, Irion, & Sutton Counties)	146.94-	M	8:00 pm
Coppell ARES/RACES Net (Coppell, Flower Mound, Carrollton)	444.225	Su (1,3)	7:45 pm
District 32 RACES (Texas)	7.248 3.975	Su (1, 3, 5)	1:30 pm
East Texas Emergency Communication Service - ARES (Smith Co)	147.00-(88.5)	M	7:15 pm
Emergency & Tactical Traffic Net - Daytime (Louisiana, Mississippi, Texas)	7.285	when needed	1:00 am
Emergency & Tactical Traffic Net - Nighttime (Louisiana, Mississippi,Texas)	3.873	when needed	1:00 am
Grayson Co ARES Net	147.00+	Su (2, 4)	9:00 pm
Hays Co ARES Net	147.10+	M	6:45 pm
Health & Welfare Traffic Net - Daytime (Louisiana, Mississippi, Texas)	7.29	when needed	1:00 am
Health & Welfare Traffic Net - Nighttime (Louisiana, Mississippi, Texas)	3.935	when needed	1:00 am
HF pack Net HF Portable Group Central Zone (W5, W0, W4, W8, W9 Regions)	5.3715	F, Sa, Su	8:45 pm
Irving RACES/ARES Net	146.72-	Th (1)	7:30 pm
KARS Net (W Houston, Kathy, Brookshire TX)	147.20+	Tu (1, 2, 4)	8:00 pm
Lone Star Storm Spotters Network Weekly Round Table Net (Texas)	147.080+(100.0)	Th	8:00 pm
McLennan Co ARES (Waco, Central Texas)	145.15-	M	8:00 pm
Mesquite RACES/ARES Net (Dallas & surrounding Counties)	145.31-(162.2)	Tu (2, 4)	8:30 pm
Nacogdoches ARC (Nacogdoches & Angelina Counties)	146.84-	W	8:00 pm
North Texas Section ARES	3.873	M	7:30 pm
North West Harris Co ARES Net	146.72-(123.0)	Su (1)	8:00 pm
North West Harris Co ARES Net	146.76-(103.5)	Su (2)	8:00 pm
North West Harris Co ARES Net	147.30+(151.4)	Su (3)	8:00 pm
North West Harris Co ARES Net	146.49	Su (4)	8:00 pm
North West Harris Co ARES Net	146.45	Su (5)	8:00 pm
Northeast Texas Traffic & Emergency Net	147.16+ 147.52	M-F	6:15 pm 9:00 pm
Northeast Texas Traffic & Emergency Net	147.30+	M-F	6:15 pm
Northwest Texas Emergency Net (Texas Panhandle & Western Texas)	3.95	Su	8:00 am
Pampa Amateur Radio VHF Net (50 mile radius of Pampa)	146.90-	W	8:00 pm
Panhandle Traffic & Emergency Net (NM, KS, Panhandles of TX & OK)	3.933		
Parker Co RACES/ARES (Parker, Wise, Tarrant, Palo Pinto, Johnson, & Hood Counties)	147.040+(110.9)	Tu (2)	7:00 pm
Pearland ARC Weekly Net (Pearland, Friendswood, S Houston, & Clear Lake)	147.220+(167.9)	Su	9:00 pm
Pecos Co Emergency Net	145.37-(88.5)	Su	7:00 pm
Potter-Randall ARES/RACES (TX panhandle)	145.35-	when needed	
Rains Amateur Radio Association Information & ARES Net (Hunt, Wood, Rains, Hopkins, VanZandt, & Counties)	146.92-(88.5)	Tu	7:30 pm

Sabine Valley ARA Info & Traffic Net (Hunt & surrounding North Texas Counties)	146.78-(114.8)	W	9:00 pm
San Antonio Emergency Communication Traning Net	147.18+(103.5)	Su	9:00 pm
Texas Traffic Net (South TX, OK, LA, AR, NM)	3.873	Daily	6:30 pm
Waller Co ARES Net	146.72-(123)	W	7:30 pm
Washington Co Emergency Preparedness Net	145.39-	Su	8:00 pm
West Gulf Region Emergency Net	3.944	Su	8:00 am
Williamson Co ARES	145.13-	Su	8:00 pm

Utah

Box Elder Co ARES Net (Box Elder, Cache, & Weber Counties)	145.43-	W	8:00 pm
Colar Co ARES (Kanab City & adjacent communities)	146.88	M	7:30 pm
Davis Co ARES	147.42+	Th	7:00 pm
Dixie Amateur Radio Club (Washington Co)	146.91-	Su	7:00 pm
New Harmony Valley ARS	145.52	M	6:30 pm
RACES	3.96	Sa (3)	8:00 am
Salt Lake Co ARES	146.88- 449.90-	W	8:00 pm
Santaquin State Emergency Comm Net (Southern Utah Co)	145.52	Su	8:45 pm
Utah Co ARES	147.34+(100)	Tu	9:00 pm
Weber Co ARES	146.90-	Tu	7:30 pm

Vermont

Addison Co ARA Sunday Evening Net (District 7)	147.36+	Su	8:30 pm
Central Vermont Traffic Net (Cent. VT, NH, NY)	146.880-(110.9)	Daily	1:00 pm
Rutland Co ARES Net	147.045-	M	7:30 pm
Tri-State FM Emergency Net (Southeast VT, Southwest NH, Western MA)	146.805-	W	7:30 pm
Twin State Emergency Net (SE VT, SW NH)	146.76-	Tu	7:30 pm
Vermont Phone Emergency Net	3.976	Su	8:00 am
Vermont Phone Traffic Net	3.857	Daily	7:30 pm
Windham Co ARES Net (Southeast VT, Northwest MA, Southwest NH)	147.015+	M (4)	7:30 pm

Virgin Islands

St Croix ARES/RACES (Virgin Isls; St Croix W)	146.91-	Tu	6:30 pm
Virgin Islands ARES Net	146.81-	Tu	6:30 pm
Virgin Islands Net (Virgin Isls, PR, Lesser Antilles)	1.984	Daily	8:01 pm

Virginia

Alexandria Radio Club Net	147.315+ 444.600+(PL107.2)	Th	8:00 pm
Blue Ridge Foothill Emergency Net (Orange, Culpeper, & Madison Counties)	147.12+	Su	8:00 pm
Boone Trail ARES Net (SW VA, E KY)	146.82-	M	8:30 pm
Capital District 6 ARES Net for ECs (Richmond metro area)	146.94-	W (1)	9:00 pm
Chesterfield Co ARES Net	147.36+	Tu	9:00 pm
Classroom on the Air Net (Hampton Road area)	146.85	Sa	7:30 pm
Clinch River Simplex Net (Southwest Virginia)	147.57	F	9:00 pm
District 8 MRX SKYWARN Net (SW VA, NE TN)	146.61-	W	9:30 pm
Eastern Shore ARES Net (District 8, Accomack, Northampton Co)	147.255+ 147.345+	M	8:30 pm
Fairfax Co ARES Net	146.79- 146.91-	W	8:15 pm
Franklin Area Repeater Net (Franklin, Southampton Co)	147.30+	Su	9:00 pm
Goochland Co ARES	147.09+	M	8:00 pm

Hanover Co ARES (East Central Virginia)	145.43-	M (1,2,4)	9:30 pm
Hanover Co ARES (East Central Virginia)	146.715-	M (3)	9:30 pm
Henrico Co ARES Net	146.715-	Th	8:30 pm
Hopewell/Prince George ARES Net	147.39+	W	8:00 pm
Middle Peninsula ARES Net (Gloucester & Mathews Counties)	145.37-	Th	8:00 pm
Montgomery Co ARES/RACES Net (70 mile radius)	147.180+(103.5)	Th	7:30 pm
Mt Vernon ARC ARES Net (Arlington, Alexandria, & Eastern Fairfax Co)	146.655- 28.415	Tu	8:30 pm
National Capital ARES Council Net (Northern Virginia and Washington, D.C.)	146.91 146.79- 146.655-	Su	9:00 pm
Newport News ARES	147.165+	Tu	8:00 pm
Newport News ARES	145.49-	Th	7:30 pm
Northern Piedmont Emergency Net (Virginia ARES District 3)	146.76-	Th	8:00 pm
Northern Virginia Traffic Net	147.30+	Daily	7:30 pm
Old Dominion Emergency Net (Virginia)	3.947	last W	8:45 pm
Old Dominion Emergency Net (Virginia)	7.243	M (2)	6:30 pm
Old Dominion Emergency Net (Virginia)	3.947	M (1, 3)	6:30 pm
Old Dominion Emergency Net (Virginia)	1.9	W (2)	8:45 pm
Pulaski Co ARES Net (New River Valley)	147.18+(PL103.5)	Th	7:30 pm
Richmond City ARES Net	145.11-	Tu	8:00 pm
Russell Co ARES Net	146.835-	M	7:30 pm
Shenandoah Valley Emergency Net (Northwestern Virginia)	146.82-	Daily	7:15 pm
South Tidewater ARES	146.97-	Daily	9:00 pm
Southeast VA Traffic Net	147.197+(100)	Th	7:30 pm
Southwest Virginia District 13 ARES Net (Lynchburg to Wytheville)	146.745- (PL107.2)	Tu	7:30 pm
Tri-County Emergency Net (Fluvanna, Goochland, Louisa Co)	147.27-	M	8:00 pm
Virginia ARES District 13 (Roanoke Valley)	146.745	Tu	7:30 pm
Virginia ARES/RACES Area A Net (Virginia Districts 6, 7, 8, 9, 10)	146.76-	when needed	
Virginia District 2 ARES (Arlington, Fairfax, Prince William Co)	146.415	F	8:30 pm
Virginia Emergency Net Alpha	3.91	when needed	
Virginia Emergency Net Bravo	3.947	when needed	
Virginia Emergency Net Charlie	3.68	when needed	
Virginia Emergency Net Delta	3.62	when needed	
Virginia Emergency Net Echo	145.73	when needed	
Virginia Emergency Net Foxtrot	446.075	when needed	
Virginia Emergency Net Golf	441.05	when needed	
Virginia Emergency Net Hotel	51.28	when needed	
Virginia Fone Net (Virginia & Eastern Coast)	3.947	Daily	4:00 pm 7:30 pm
Virginia RACES District 1 Net (VA, WV, MD)	449.175-(131.8)	Su	7:00 pm
Virginia Tech ARA Net (New River Valley, Blacksburg)	146.715-	Tu	9:00 pm
Virginia Tech Training Net	3.68	Tu	8:00 pm
Western Tidewater Radio Association and ARES Net (Southeast Virginia)	147.195+	W	8:00 pm
Williamsburg Ares ARES (City of Williamsburg and James City Co)	146.76-	W	7:30 pm
York/Poquoson ARES (York Co, City of Poquoson)	146.94-	M	8:00 pm
Washington			
ARES/RACES of King Co Net	146.82-(103.5)	Su	8:00 pm

Clallam Co ARC Net (Northern Olympic Peninsula WA, Southern British Columbia)	146.76-open	Th	7:00 pm
Clallam Co ARES Net	146.76-	Tu	7:00 pm
Clallam Co ARES/RACES Net	146.76-(100)	Tu (2, 3, 4, 5)	7:00 pm
Clark Co ARES & Info Net (Clark Co & Adjacent Counties in Oregon & Washington)	147.24+	Tu	7:00 pm
Combined ARES/RACES Island Co Net	146.860	Sa	8:00 pm
Emergency Radio Communications (ERC) Net-Whatcom Co (Whatcom & Skagit Counties, Southern British Columbia)	145.23-(103.5) Pri simplex 147.42 Sec simplex 146.56	Su	9:00 pm
Emergency Services Coordinating Agency (Snohomish & King Counties)	147.34+	Su	7:45 pm
Evergreen State Traffic System - ESTS (Upper Western Washington, British Columbia)	VHF net:145.190- (tone 127.3)	Daily	5:00 pm
Federal Way ARC Emergency Comm Response Team (South King Co)	147.04+(103.5) 146.76-(103.5)	Su	7:30 pm
King Co Fire Zone 1 ARES Net	147.34+	Su	7:00 pm
Kitsap Co ARES/RACES Simplex Net-VHF	145.430-(179.9)	Su	7:30 pm
Kitsap Co Net (HF)	28.33	Su	7:00 pm
Lake Chelan Radio Club (N Central Washington)	147.10+	W	8:00 pm
Mason Co ARES/RACES	28.35	Su	6:30 pm
Mason Co ARES/RACES	146.72-	Su	9:00 pm
OARS Weekly Information Net (Thurston Co)	147.36+(103.5) 224.46-1.6 441.4+(103.5)	Tu	7:30 pm
Pacific Co Emergency Services Net	147.18 441.675 tone=118.8	Th	7:30 pm
Pierce Co ARES/RACES Net	145.37-(136) 442.45+(103)	Tu	7:00 pm
Seattle Auxiliary Communication Service	146.96-	M	7:00 pm
Skagit Co ARES/RACES Net	145.19-	W	7:00 pm
Snohomish Co ARES Net	146.92-(114.8)	Su	8:30 pm
South King Co ARES Net (King Co Fire Zones 3 & 4)	145.33-	W	7:00 pm
Spokane Co ARES/RACES Net	147.30+	Tu	8:00 pm
Stanwood-Camano ARES Net (Island & Snohomish Counties)	147.57	M	8:00 pm
Thurston Co ARES/RACES Net	147.36+ 224.46- 4441.4+(103.5)	Tu	7:00 pm
Vashon-Maury Island Radio Club and ARES Net (Vashon-Maury Isl. & South Puget Sound)	28.385	Su	7:30 pm
W7AQ 2 Meter Net (Yakima & Lower Yakima Valley)	146.66-(PL123)	M	7:30 pm
Washington Amateur Radio Traffic Systems	3.97	Daily	6:00 pm
Washington Red Cross HF Net	3.993	W	6:30 pm
Washington State Emergency Net	3.985	M	6:30 pm
Washington State Emergency Net	3.985	Sa	9:00 am
Whatcom Co Amateur Emergency Services	147.19+(103.5)alt 146.74-(103.5) 146.50 S	Su	7:00 pm
Yakima Co ARES Net (Yakima & Lower Yakima Valley)	146.66(PL123)	M	7:00 pm
West Virginia			
8 Rivers ARC Net (Pocahontas Co)	145.11-	Su	8:00 pm
8 Rivers ARC Net-Winter (Pocahontas Co)	145.11-	Su	9:00 pm
Barbour Co/Upshur Co ARES/RACES Net (North Central West Virginia)	145.150-(103.5) 146.850-(103.5)	W	8:00 pm 9:00 pm

Cabell Co ARES Net (Eastern Kentucky, Southwest Ohio, Huntington West Virginia)	146.760-(131.8)	Th	9:00 pm
Fayette Co ARES Net	146.79-	Th (2, 4)	8:30 am
Gilmer Co ARES/RACES Net (Central WV)	145.29-	Th	7:00 pm
Ham Talk Weather Net (Kentucky, Maryland, Ohio, Pennsylvania, Virginia, West Virginia)	146.685- 147.285+ 145.29-; 145.27- 444.10+; 444.40+	M	7:00 pm
Harrison Co ARES/RACES (N Central WV)	146.685-	Th	7:00 pm
Kanawha ARC 2 Meter Net (Charleston & Kanawha Counties)	145.35-(91.5)	Su	8:30 pm
Marion Co ARES Net (N Central West Virginia)	145.35-(103.5)	W	8:30 pm
Mountain State Emergency Net (West Virginia)	3.865	Th (2, 4)	6:30 pm
Multi Co ARES/RACES (Northern West Virginia, Western Virginia, Southern Pennsylvania)	146.685- 147.074+ 147.285+	Tu	9:00 pm
Northern West Virginia ARES/RACES	145.30-	W	8:30 pm
Ohio Co ARES Net	146.76-	Su	8:00 pm
Pendleton Co ARES/RACES (E West Virginia)	147.285-	Th	7:00 pm
Pioneer ARA 2 Meter Net (Central West Virginia)	146.835-	Tu	7:00 pm
Plateau Amateur Radio Association 2 Meter Net (South Central West Virginia)	146.79-	Th	8:00 pm
Pocahontas Co ARES Net	145.11-	Tu (2)	8:00 pm
Pocahontas Co ARES Net-Winter	145.11-	Tu (2)	9:00 pm
Raleigh Co ARES/RACES (South West Virginia)	145.370	M	8:30 pm
SAWS ARES/RACES Net (South WV, East KY)	145.33-	Tu	9:00 pm
Steubenville-Weirton ARC (North Panhandle West Virginia, East Central Ohio)	146.94-	Su	8:00 pm
Stonewall Jackson ARA 2 Meter Net (North Central West Virginia)	147.21+	Tu	9:00 pm
Taylor Co ARES Net	28.4	M	8:30 pm
Tri-County ARES Net (West Virginia)	145.15	Su	8:00 pm
Triple States ARES CW Net (Upper WV)	28.48	W	6:46 pm
TSRAC SKYWARN Net (North Panhandle)	146.91-	Tu	7:15 pm
Wayne Co ARES Net (Louisa)	147.39+	M	9:00 pm
West Virginia Fone Net (WV & surr. states)	3.865	Daily	6:00 pm
West Virginia Mid Day Net (WV & surr. states)	7.235	Daily	11:45pm
WVAR ARES/RACES (WV, NE KY, SE OH)	147.27+	Su	9:30 pm
Wisconsin			
ARES & Swap (Central Wisconsin)	146.925-	Su	7:30 pm
Ashland & Bayfield Counties ARES Net (N WI, NE MN, W Upper MI)	146.61- 147.315+	M	8:00 pm
Badger Emergency Net (Wisconsin)	3.985	Daily	12:00pm
Brown Co ARES Net	147.12+ 444.775+	W	8:00 pm
Calumet Co ARES (Northeast Wisconsin)	147.30+	Su	7:30 pm
Dane Co ARES (South Central Wisconsin)	147.150+(123)	W	8:00 pm
Dodge Co ARES (South Central Wisconsin)	146.64-	M	7:30 pm
FCARC Itty Bitty RTTY (Northeast Wisconsin)	146.70-	Tu	7:00 pm
Fox Cities ARES (Northeast Wisconsin)	146.76-	W	9:00 pm
Green Fox ARES (Fox Cities)	146.955	Su	8:00 pm
Green Lake Co Emergency Radio Operators (East Central Wisconsin)	145.21-(123)	M (3)	5:30 pm
Hubertus ARES (Southeast Wisconsin)	145.25-	M	8:00 pm
Jefferson Co ARES Net (Rock, Jefferson, & Walworth Counties)	145.49-	W	8:00 pm
Juneau Co ARES/RACES	146.85-(123)	W (1,3,4)	7:00 pm
MANCORAD (Wisconsin)	146.61-	Su	10:00am

Net	Frequency	Day	Time
Marquette Co ARES (Marquette, Adams, Waushara, & Columbia)	146.595	Sa	10:00am
Milwaukee Emergency Net	146.445-	M	8:00 am
Milwaukee-Waukesha ARES Net (SW WI)	146.67-	M	9:00 pm
North West RACES/ARES (NW Wisconsin)	147.30+	W	8:00 pm
Outagammie Co ARES	146.655-	Su	8:00 pm
Ozaukee Co ARES (Southeast Wisconsin)	147.33+	Th	8:00 pm
Portage Co ARES/RACES (Central Wisconsin)	146.67-(114.8)	Tu	9:00 pm
Price Co ARES (North Central Wisconsin)	147.00	W	9:00 pm
RACES (East Central Wisconsin)	145.13-	M	7:00 pm
RACES/SCVRA (Northwest Wisconsin)	147.33+	M	7:00 pm
Racine/Kenosha Co ARES Net	147.27-	W	8:00 pm
RRRC CW (Southeast Wisconsin)	146.64-	Tu	7:30 pm
Sawyer Co ARES Net (Northwest Wisconsin)	147.255+	Su	7:45 pm
Severe Weather Net (Southeast Wisconsin)	146.91-	when needed	
SEWFARS ARES (Southeast Wisconsin)	146.82	M	7:00 pm
Shawano (North Central Wisconsin)	145.35-	M	8:00 pm
Sheboygan Co ARES (Southeast Wisconsin)	147.255	W	7:00 pm
Sheboygan Co ARES (Northeast Wisconsin)	3.86	Su	10:30am
St Croix Valley RACES Net	145.130-(PL110.9)	M	7:00 pm
Taylor Co ARES Net	147.15+	W	8:30 pm
Tri-County ARC (South Central Wisconsin)	145.49-	Th	8:00 pm
Tri-County Repeater Association Thursday Night Net (Barron, Chippewa, Rusk, Eau Claire, and Taylor Counties)	145.470-	Th	8:00 pm
Waupaca ARES (Central Wisconsin)	146.835	Su	7:30 pm
WI ARES/RACES HF PACTOR Net	3.56	as needed	1:00 am
WI ARES/RACES HF PACTOR Net	7.087	as needed	1:00 am
WI ARES/RACES HF Voice Net	7.25 7.245	Su	7:45 am
WI ARES/RACES HF Voice Net	3.996 3.975	Su	7:45 am
Winnebago Co ARES/RACES (East Central Wisconsin)	147.24+	Su	7:00 pm
Wyoming			
No Emergency Nets Listed			

Local Days Key:
1=1st week of the month
2=2nd week of the month
3=3rd week of the month
4=4th week of the month
5=5th week of the month.

Source: http://www.arrl.org

CRIMES AGAINST CHILDREN

Physical Abuse · **70**

Indicators of Child Abuse · · · · · · · · · · · · · · · · · · · 70
Factors That Increase Risk of Child Abuse · · · · · · · 71
Child Abuse Investigations · · · · · · · · · · · · · · · · · · 71

Injuries Associated with Abuse · · · · · · · · · · · · · · · **79**

Bruises · 79
Burns · 80
Cutaneous (Skin) Injuries · 83
Eye Injuries · 83
Head Injuries · 84
Internal Injuries · 84
Poisoning · 85
Repetitive Accidents · 85

Child Homicides · **86**

Role of Responding Officer · · · · · · · · · · · · · · · · · · · 86
Shaken Baby Syndrome · 87
Munchausen Syndrome by Proxy · · · · · · · · · · · · · · 88
Sudden Infant Death Syndrome (SIDS) · · · · · · · · · · 89

Missing Children · **93**

Initial Response Investigation Checklist · · · · · · · · · · 95
Runaway Case Investigation Checklist · · · · · · · · · · 98
Family Abduction Investigation Checklist · · · · · · · · · 99
Non-Family Abduction Investigation Checklist · · · · · 101
Resources for Missing Children · · · · · · · · · · · · · · · 103
Nt'l Center for Missing & Exploited Children (NCMEC) 103
AMBER Alert Plan · 104
Military Resources · 104
State Clearinghouses for Missing Children · · · · · · · 105

Child Abuse Resources · **108**

Crimes Against Children

Physical Abuse

Introduction

The initial report of child abuse usually comes through a third party – a social worker, teacher, doctor, relative or friend. In many states people who work with children are required to report their suspicions of child abuse. Other times, an officer may observe signs of child abuse while in contact with the family on another matter. It is important to follow up on these suspicions. A child's life may depend on it.

Initial Indicators of Child Abuse

Bruises

- on upper arms, trunk, fronts of thighs, sides of faces, ears and neck, genitalia, stomach and buttocks. (**Accidental bruises** *occur more frequently on the shins, hips, lower arms, foreheads, hands, spines, knees, noses, chin, or elbows.)*
- on an infant, appear especially the face and buttocks.
- in different stages of healing may indicate repeated battering.
- that wrap around, injuring more than one plane of the body.

Burns

- on the buttocks, anogenital region, ankles, wrists, palms or soles of feet.
- with sharply defined edges; may look like a stocking or glove.
- that are symmetrical.
- shaped like the object that caused the burn (an iron, for instance)
- that are uniform in degree, and/or are very deep.
- that cover a large area.
- that are infected or show other signs of neglect.
- varying in age and degree of healing.

Other Visible Injuries

- Welts, fractures, lacerations and abrasions, often in various stages of healing.

Behavioral Indicators

- Wariness of adults, apprehensive when other children cry, extreme aggression or passivity, afraid of his or her parents, afraid to go home.

Factors That Increase Risk Of Child Abuse

Any child may be abused, and child abuse occurs in all levels of society. However, there are some factors that increase a child's risk of abuse.

- Premature birth or low birth weight.
- Being identified as "unusual" or perceived as "different" in physical appearance or temperament.
- Having a disease or congenital abnormality.
- Physical, emotional, or developmental disability (for example: mentally or learning disabled).
- High level of motor activity, fussiness, irritability, or behavior that is different from the parents' expectations.
- Poverty or family unemployment.
- Living in an environment with substance abuse, high crime, and familial or community violence.

The Child Abuse Investigation

Overview

- Attempt to find and interview the complainant.
- Gather information about the injury that led to the report.
- Find out how many children are in the home, and assure their safety.
- Secure the crime scene.
- Notify other departments or agencies as needed.
- Identify and isolate the suspect.
- Identify witnesses, and isolate any who are on scene. Interview anyone who had access to or custody of the child during the time when the injury or injuries allegedly occurred.
- Interview all witnesses separately, especially the parents/caretakers.
  - Victim
  - Care giver(s)
  - Siblings
  - Neighbors or relatives
  - Medical personnel
  - Teachers and other school personnel
  - Emergency service workers
  - Social service workers

- Photograph the victim, the scene and any related evidence as soon as possible. Make sure that medical personnel or the investigating team take and preserve photographs of the victim. (see page 324)
- Thoroughly investigate crime scene and collect physical evidence. (see page 76)
- Obtain copies of all medical records.
- Check police and social service records for previous contact with family.

Interviews

Get the name, address, work and home phone numbers, date of birth and employment info for each party.

Victim (and siblings)

Interview the victim early if death is anticipated.

The victim should be questioned by someone with experience interrogating children. If that is not possible, be sure to use language appropriate to the child's level of development. Make sure that they understand the questions, and have them be very explicit about their answers, since children often do not know the correct definitions of words. Victims of child abuse will usually support the suspect's story to avoid being "disciplined" again, and because they have come to believe that abuse is normal, just punishment for being bad.

- Find out if the child uses special terms or language for the biological parts of the body, using anatomically correct dolls or drawings.
- How did the injury happen? What were the circumstances?
- Who caused it?
- Who was present when it happened?
- Was the non-participating caretaker told of the incident? How and when?
- What instrument did the abuser use, and where is it now?
- Has the object been used for discipline before? When? How often?
- What other methods of punishment were used? Get a detailed description.
- Who administers discipline in the family?
- Is there a past history of abuse or molestation?
- Were children ever left unattended? How often? For how long?

- Are there any "family secrets?"
- Observe the victim for unusual behavior (such as fear or anxiety) in the presence of the suspect.

Suspect (Caretaker, Parent or Guardian)

Abusive caretakers often:
- have no explanation for critical injuries.
- give explanations that do not match the injuries.
- will come up with new explanations once they learn that the original one does not fit the medical evidence.
- give inconsistent explanations of the injuries over time.

Sometimes the changes are apparent from statements abusers have made to others. Additional interviews may be needed to document the changing explanations and to follow up on additional information that the investigation uncovers.

Questions to Ask the Caretaker:

- How did the incident happen?
- What were you doing just before the incident?
- When did you first notice the child was ill or injured, and what exactly did you observe? What do you believe caused the illness or injury?
- If no explanation is given, were there times when the child was unsupervised or in the company of others?
- Who was at home at the time of the incident?
- Who was with the child at the time of the injury or when the child first appeared ill? (Cover as much time as possible up to 5 to 7 days. What is normal, are they normally with a certain person every Saturday, every week night, etc.)
- What was the child's apparent health and activity level for the same period up to the time of the illness? Exactly how did the symptoms develop?
- What is the child's health history since birth?
- Has the child been hospitalized or treated for prior injuries or illnesses? If so, what treatment was needed or what caused those injuries?
- Who normally disciplines the child, and what form of discipline is used?
- What is the health of other children in the family?
- Who is the family doctor or the child's pediatrician?
- Does the child attend school or day care? Who is the child's teacher (or teachers)?

- Has the child shown any recent behavioral changes?
- What is the child's developmental level? Is it consistent with the caretaker's explanation?
- The mother's assessment of her pregnancy, labor, and delivery often provides insight into her attitude about her child, and may indicate whether something about the child is influencing her behavior. Ask questions in an unobtrusive manner:
  - Was this a planned pregnancy?
  - Did you want the baby?
  - Do you like the child?
  - What do you feed the child? How often? Who feeds the child?

Additional parent, stepparent, boyfriend or girlfriend
- Repeat caretaker questions.
- When confronted with evidence of abuse or neglect, what actions did the care giver take?
- Were you aware of past or present abuse?

Neighbors, teachers, relatives & social service workers
- How do you know the victim?
- How do you know about the incident?
- What have you observed: injuries? evidence of neglect? reports of molestation?
- Date and time of observations.
- Did you inform any agencies?
- Is there any documentation of the incident?
- Prior history of abuse, molestation, or neglect?

Paramedics and other emergency personnel
- What time did the call come?
- Who made the call?
- What was the explanation for the call?
- What time did you arrive?
- What was the victim's condition?
- What did you observe?
- What did you do for the victim?
- Who was present at the scene?
- What did the care giver say as you arrived?

Consult With Experts

Identifying experts is as important to the child abuse investigator as identifying and cultivating street informants in other types of investigations. If the investigator does not have a basic knowledge of the causes of young children's injuries, experts may be difficult to identify. Attending training conferences can provide the investigator with a great deal of basic knowledge and help establish a network of experts.

Collect Relevant Information

Medical Information

- Contact and record information on all medical personnel who had contact with the family, such as doctors, nurses, admitting personnel, and emergency room personnel.
- Find out what medical records exist (birth certificates, reports, x-rays, etc.).
- Get the injured child's available medical records, including records of any prior treatment.
  Note: If only one caretaker is suspected of abuse, the nonabusive caretaker may have to sign a release of the records. If both are suspected, most states have provisions that override normal confidentiality rules in the search for evidence of child abuse. Procedures for obtaining these records vary by state.
- What diagnoses were made and what treatments were used? How do you believe the injuries occurred? The attending physician will often be able to express at least an opinion that the caretaker's explanation did not "fit" the severity of the injury. Failure to get an opinion from the attending physician should not end the investigation.
- Speak to any specialists who assisted the attending physician.
- What statements, if any, did the child's parents or caretakers make?
- Is there evidence of old injuries?
- Is there evidence of sexual abuse?
- Does the child's physical condition indicate neglect or failure to thrive?
- Have someone knowledgeable about medical terms translate them into non-medical terms so that the exact nature of the injuries is clear.

- Interview the child's pediatrician about the child's general health since birth and look for a pattern of suspected abusive injuries.

Other Important Sources of Information

- Review EMT records or 911 dispatch tapes. These records are frequently overlooked and can be a valuable source of information. Families with more than one emergency may be abusing children rather than having a long streak of "bad luck."
- Request any police reports and child welfare agency files on the family.
- Collect additional family history concerning domestic violence, substance abuse, and other such connections, even apparently unrelated arrests or charges.

Collect Physical Evidence

- Whatever explanation caretakers offer for the child's injury or injuries, it is vital that the investigator secure physical evidence.
- Gather such evidence immediately after the child's injury is reported, before caretakers have an opportunity to tamper with the scene.
- If the caretakers do not consent to a search of the scene, a search warrant may be necessary. The strongest evidence of the need for such a warrant will be the medical evidence of what probably happened to the child, and the caretakers' inconsistent or absent accounts of the events.
- Caretakers' changing explanations often mean investigators must visit the home or the scene of the injury more than once.
- Be thorough in obtaining photographic evidence of the location where the injury took place.
- Physical evidence and records that must be preserved include:

  - Any object used as a weapon.
  - Piece of furniture from which the child allegedly fell.
  - The child's "environment," including bedding within the bed or crib and other beds in the home.
  - Toys or objects the child allegedly landed upon.
  - In cases involving burns, record any sinks, bathtubs, and pots or pans containing water. Test the temperature of the standing water, water from the water heater and from each tap. Check the temperature

setting of the water heater. This may help disprove an allegation that the child accidentally turned on the hot water. Other sources of heat in the home should be documented, regardless of the caretakers' initial explanation of what burned the child. See water temperature/scald chart on page 83.

- Obtain scrapings from the suspect's and victim's fingernails.
- A complete photographic or videotaped record of the home or other location in which the injuries allegedly occurred. Focus on areas that the caretakers already have identified as the site of the particular trauma (i.e., stairs, bed/crib, or bathtub).
- If the child apparently suffered cigarette burns, collecting cigarette butts found in the home may facilitate analysis of the burn patterns.
- If the case involves a combination of sexual and physical abuse, collecting the child's clothing and bedding may allow identification of what happened and who was involved.
- If the child shows evidence of bite marks, saliva swabbing should be done to allow positive identification of the biter.
- If the child has suffered a depressed skull fracture, any objects the approximate size of the fracture should be seized for appropriate analysis.

Summary: Child Abuse Investigator's Checklist

Consider the following important issues and questions when investigating suspected child abuse:

- ❑ Ask about the child's family history, substance abuse, or other environmental factors in the home; parents' marital status, employment history, or unrealistic expectations of the child.
- ❑ Could the child's behavior or the caretaker's stress have contributed to the crisis?
- ❑ Could the child have done what the caretakers said he did?
- ❑ Is the child a "target" child (one perceived by the parent(s) as having negative characteristics)? Are there other target children present?
- ❑ Was treatment delayed or was hospital "shopping" involved?
- ❑ What are the locations, configurations, and distributions of the injuries?

❑ Do the injuries appear to have been caused by the hands or an instrument? Can you determine what instrument might have been used?

❑ Does the child have multiple injuries in various stages of healing?

❑ Are the injuries within the primary target zone (the back, from the neck to the back of the knees, and including the shoulders and arms) and on more than one leading edge (the outside of an arm or leg) of the body?

❑ Can you determine the positions of the offender and the child during the attack?

❑ Is there any evidence of attempts to hold the child in a certain position or at a certain angle during the attack? Are there control marks on the wrists, forearms or biceps?

❑ Was a careful check made for injuries on the head, mouth, ears and nose?

❑ Examine all other children in the home for possible signs of abuse.

❑ A physical examination of the child must be done and the data recorded precisely.

❑ Obtain laboratory data to support or refute the evidence of abuse.

❑ If the reported history of an injury changes during the course of an investigation, or if the explanations of two adult caretakers conflict, the likelihood of child abuse increases.

❑ Information about a child's birth and neonatal and medical history are critical. Hospital records can confirm or eliminate the existence of birth injuries.

Injuries Associated with Abuse

CAUTION: While the following information may help determine which injuries and illnesses in children are likely to be the result of abuse, it is also very important to work closely with physicians to determine the nature of all injuries.

Bruises

Bruising is the earliest and most visible sign of child abuse. All bruises must be investigated. If the reported cause of an injury is not consistent with the injury seen, investigate further.

- **Bruises on infants**, especially the face and buttocks, are more suspicious than bruises on older children, and should be considered non-accidental until proven otherwise.
- **Bruises on children**, that are likely to be from non-accidental injuries are usually on their upper arms, trunk, fronts of their thighs, sides of their faces, ears and neck, genitalia, stomach, and buttocks.

Bruise Configurations

The configuration of a bruise may help determine whether it was accidental or not, and what type of instrument was used. One of the easiest ways to identify the weapon used to inflict bruises is to ask the caretaker "How were you punished as a child?"

- Rigid objects, such as coat hangers, handles or paddles only strike one plane of the body at a time.
- "Wraparound" objects follow the contours of the body and bruise more than one of the body's planes. Bruises that have parallel lines could be closed-end or looped cords, while bruises that have a single line may be open-end cords.
- Hands can make either rigid or wraparound bruises, depending on the size of the offender's hands and the size of the child.
- The size of bite marks may help determine the biter's approximate age. The shape of the bruise or injury may help identify whose teeth made the marks.

Natural or Normal Bruises

- Bruises on a child's shins, hips, lower arms, forehead, hands, spine, knees, nose, chin or elbows, are likely to be accidental injuries.
- Illnesses such as hemophilia, low blood platelet count, and leukemia may cause children to bruise easily.

- Diseases that cause easy bruising are rare and inflicted bruises are much more common. The medical diagnosis of clotting disorders requires blood tests which must be interpreted by qualified physicians.

- Mongolian Spots, a type of birthmark, resemble bruises, but can be identified by clear cut margins, permanence, and steel gray-blue color. Mongolian spots may be found anywhere on the body, but are typically found on the buttocks and lower back. They are commonly found in African Americans, Asians, and Hispanics. Investigators should await medical reports when investigating such marks.

Burns

Classification of Burns

Burns are classified by the depth of damage.

- **Superficial burn:** Affects only the upper epidermis (the outer layer) of the skin. Symptoms are pain, redness, and swelling.

- **Partial-thickness burn:** Affects the epidermis and the dermis (the second layer) of the skin. Symptoms are intense pain, reddening, blisters, mottled appearance of the skin. This is sometimes referred to as a second-degree burn.

- **Full-thickness burn:** Affects all three layers of the skin, the epidermis, the dermis, and the fat and muscle layer. Symptoms are charred black, brown, or grayish/white areas, and severe pain may be present if the nerves have not been damaged in the affected area. This is sometimes referred to as a third-degree burn.

Skin Conditions That May Look Like Burns

The following conditions are not the result of abuse, but may be confused with abuse-caused burns:

- **Cutaneous (skin) infections:** Impetigo, severe diaper rash, and Scalded Skin Syndrome may resemble a scald injury. A careful history, microbiological tests, and 2-3 weeks observation can usually determine whether these are deliberate burns or just infections.

- **Hypersensitivity Reactions:** Citrus fruits contain a substance which can cause photodermatitis when skin covered with the fruit juice is exposed to sunlight. This reaction may look like a splash burn.

- **Allergic reactions:** Can cause severe local skin irritation that can be mistaken for a burn. Some skin preparations, such as topical antiseptics, can cause a similar burn appearance. Again, exposure history will reveal the presence of such factors.

Folk Remedies That May Look Like Burns

If the cause of a burn is a folk remedy, carefully evaluate all the circumstances surrounding the incident to determine whether the injury needs further investigation.

- **Moxibustion:** An Asian folk remedy that involves putting a hot substance, often burning yarn, on the skin of the abdomen or back. It causes circular lesions that may look like other types of burn injuries.
- **Cupping:** A small amount of flammable substance is put into a cup or glass, then ignited and placed on the skin, and may cause a burn lesion.

Investigator's Checklist for Cases Suspected of Deliberate Burn Injuries in Children

❑ Contact the Emergency Response Team.

❑ Contact the child protective services team.

❑ Review the medical findings with the appropriate medical staff.

❑ Carefully consider the suspicion index findings.

❑ Where was the primary care provider at the time of the incident?

❑ What part of the child's body was burned?

❑ How serious is the burn?

❑ Is the burn a wet contact burn or a dry contact burn?

❑ If from dry contact, what is the shape of the burn? What object does it resemble?

❑ If burn is from a hot liquid, was the child dipped or fully immersed?

❑ What does the line of demarcation look like?

❑ Are any splash burns present?

❑ How symmetrical are lines of immersion if stocking or glove patterns are present?

❑ Is toilet training, soiling or wetting an issue?

❑ Record information about the child's age, height, degree of development and coordination; location of fixtures; temperature and depth of water; weight of burn object, etc.

❑ Compare the burn injury to the uninjured area.

❑ Was the child in a state of flexion (tensed up in resistance to what was happening)?
Examples of flexion include:
  - Folds in the stomach
  - Calf against back of thigh
  - Arms tightened and held firmly against body or folded against body
  - Thighs against abdomen
  - Head against shoulder
  - Legs crossed, held tightly together

Accidental versus Non-Accidental Burns

	Probably Non-Accidental Burns	Probably Accidental Burns
History	• Burns attributed to siblings • Unrelated adult brings child in for care • Accounts of injury differ • Signs of prior "accidents" present • Absence of parental concern • Lesions incompatible with history	• Story is compatible with observed injury
Location	• Buttocks • Anogenital region • Ankles • Wrists • Palms • Soles of feet	• Front of body • Other locations reflecting child's motor activity, level of development, exposure of body to the burning agent
Pattern	• Burns have sharply defined edges; line of immersion may look like a glove or stocking • All layers of the skin (and possibly bone and muscle) are burned • Burns are symmetrical • Burns are older than reported date of injury • Burns are infected or show other signs of neglect • Lesions vary in age • Burn patterns conform to shape of implement used • Degree of burns is uniform • Burns cover a large area	• Burns are of multiple depths interspersed with unburned areas • Usually less severe (i.e., splash burns) • Burns are of partial thickness; only part of the skin has been damaged or destroyed • Burns are asymmetrical • Skin injuries are all the same age

Hot Tap Water Burns

Water Temperature	Time to Produce Serious Burns
120°F	More than 5 minutes
125°F	1.5 to 2 minutes
130°F	About 30 seconds
135°F	About 10 seconds
140°F	Less than 5 seconds
145°F	Less than 3 seconds
150°F	About 1.5 seconds
155°F	About 1 second

Cutaneous (Skin) Injuries

Skin injuries are the most common injuries from abuse. Non-accidental skin injuries differ from accidental ones in location and pattern, presence of multiple injuries of different ages, and the failure of new injuries to appear after hospitalization. Be sure to get a complete history of all injuries from the caretaker.

Eye Injuries

External eye injuries are so common in children that there is seldom clear-cut evidence of abuse. However, it is rare for children under three years old to have retinal hemorrhages, or traumatic damage to the lens, retina or skin around the eye. These should be considered non-accidental injuries and investigated thoroughly.

Signs of Possible Abuse:

- **Two black eyes:** Both eyes are seldom black simultaneously on accidentally injuries.

- **"Raccoon Eyes":** May result from either accidental or non-accidental causes. Non-accidental causes usually create more swelling and skin injury. History will help distinguish between the two.

- **Hyphema:** (the traumatic entry of blood into the front chamber of the eye) May have been caused by striking the eye with a hard object, such as a belt buckle. The child will complain of pain in the eye and have visual problems.

- **Retinal Hemorrhages:** The hallmark of "Shaken Baby Syndrome" and are rarely associated with non-accidental injuries. (See page 87)

Head Injuries

Subdural Hematoma

Subdural hematomas due to child abuse are most common in children less than 24 months old, with peak occurrence at the age of 6 months.

- Signs of subdural hematoma: Classic, specific signs include vomiting, seizures, stupor or coma.
- Non-specific signs include irritability, lethargy, and/or refusal to eat.

Skull Fracture

If a skull fracture is associated with the subdural hematoma, the injury is due to a direct blow to the head, and will usually leave external marks as well. It may result from shaking a baby violently, or throwing a child against a hard object.

Retinal Hemorrhages

Retinal hemorrhages are usually the result of whiplash or violent shaking of a baby or toddler. Therefore, officers must investigate whether these were non-accidental injuries.

Hair Loss or Baldness

Hair loss or baldness may indicate hair pulling as a means of discipline.

Internal Injuries

Internal injuries are second only to head injuries as the most common cause of child abuse deaths. In most instances of abdominal organ injury, there are no external signs of trauma because of the ability of the abdominal wall to absorb a blow without bruising.

Accidental abdominal injuries usually:

- involve a long fall to a flat surface, a motor vehicle accident, or rarely, involvement in contact sports.
- happen to older children, who are brought in for medical attention immediately.
- In school-age children, injuries of the pancreas are quite uncommon, but when they occur they are usually caused by bicycle handlebars or traffic accidents. In children under three, however, the more probable cause is child abuse, because the pancreas is located very deep within the abdomen, and thus is protected from most blows.

Non-accidental internal injuries usually involve:
- areas below the diaphragm.
- younger children.
- delay in seeking medical attention.
- hollow organs, such as the gut and stomach. The liver, spleen and pancreas can all suffer from non-accidental injury as well, but for some reason the kidneys are rarely injured.
- unusual clinical findings which may indicate abuse.

Poisoning

Peak age for accidental poisoning is 2-3 years old. It is rare for accidental poising to occur below the age of 1 or over the age of 6. If the poisoning was non-accidental, the typical history is that it was not observed or the substance was given by a sibling or another child. The history may change over time.

Most frequently used poisons:
Barbiturates, psychoactive drugs, tranquilizers, insulin, ipecac, arsenic, laxatives, salt, water, alcohol, marijuana and opiates.

Symptoms:
Nearly all have major changes in mental status, ranging from irritability, listlessness, lethargy, stupor, convulsions, and coma.

Repetitive Accidents

Multiple bruises, wounds, abrasions, or other skin lesions in varying states of healing may indicate repetitive physical assault. Such repetitive accidents or injuries may indicate that abuse is occurring (Battered Child Syndrome). A careful examination of the circumstances and types of injuries and an assessment of the child and family should be carried out.

Child Homicides

When presented with a child who has died under suspicious circumstances in which there is no obvious sign of abuse, investigators should:

- ask an experienced pediatrician to help locate a specialist whose medical expertise can help make sense of a confusing picture.
- determine if their state requires an autopsy.
  - Most states mandate autopsies when the cause of death of any child under a certain age is undetermined or suspicious.
  - In states without a statutory mandate, ask the medical examiner or the local prosecutor to order an autopsy.

Be aware of the following facts:

- In cases involving strangulation, beating, severe inflicted burns, such as scalding, and the use of a weapon, a child's death is obviously the result of a deliberate abuse.
- The more carefully planned the killing is, the less likely it is that a medical explanation for the death will be found.
- Most infant deaths are related to head injuries, some of which leave no external sign of trauma, and suffocation often leaves no medical sign of the cause of death.
- While caretakers often explain that the child fell off of a piece of furniture or down the stairs, studies show that children do not die in falls from simple household heights; they do not even normally suffer severe head injuries from such falls.

Role of Responding Officer

Even though a child's death may appear to be from natural causes, a thorough investigation is required. The situation must be handled with sensitivity. Be noncommital about the cause of death.

1. Secure the scene.

2. Conduct preliminary interviews with the parents.

- What happened?
- How old is the child?
- When was the last time the child was ill?
- Was the child on any type of medication?
- When did the child last eat?
- What did the child last eat?

- Who is the child's doctor?
- When was the last time the child was seen by the doctor?
- Does the child have any medical problems?
- Is the child allergic to anything that you know of?

3. Collect physical evidence.
- Carefully note the child's:
    - Body position: lying on back, stomach, or side
    - Rigor Mortis: absent, mild or firmly established
    - Liver Mortis: None, posterior, anterior; consistent/inconsistent with body position; whitens to finger pressure?
    - Secretions: mouth or nose; substance - mucus, milk, foam, blood, or food
- What is the room temperature?
- Was the death observed or unobserved?
- Is there any obvious signs of injury?
- Were there any attempts made to revive the child or any medical action taken?
- When was the last time and method of feeding?

When investigating whether a child's death was a homicide, investigators must ask themselves the following questions:

- How do we find out what actually happened to the child?
- How do we make sure we are talking to the right expert about what could have caused the child's death?
- How do we know we have talked to everyone who might be able to shed light on a difficult case?
- Is there a child protection issue for other children present?

Syndromes Related to Child Homicide

Everyone who handles child fatalities must have a basic understanding of the following conditions:

Shaken Baby Syndrome
Symptoms:
- Bleeding in the back of the eyeball, often in both eyes.
- Bleeding inside the head, most often in the upper hemispheres of the brain, caused by the shearing of the blood vessels between the brain and the dura mater or the arachnoid membrane.
- Absence of other external signs of abuse (e.g., bruises), although not always. In most cases of shaken baby

syndrome, there are no skull fractures and no external signs of trauma.

- There are often breathing difficulties, seizures, dilated pupils, lethargy, and unconsciousness. In almost every case, the baby begins to show symptoms within minutes of the injury.

Causes:
- According to studies, retinal bleeding in infants is evidence of Shaken Baby Syndrome, except in the case of:
  - a severe auto accident in which the baby's head either impacted something with severe force or was thrown about wildly without restraint during the crash (external signs are usually present).
  - a fall from several stories onto a hard surface, in which case there are usually other signs of trauma, such as skull fractures, swelling, intracranial collection of blood, and contusions.

Other Identifying Characteristics:
- Often, but not always, when shaking causes death or severe injuries, it has been followed by sudden deceleration caused by throwing the child down onto a surface that may be either soft or hard.
- Shaken Baby Syndrome occurs primarily in children eighteen months of age or younger. It is most often associated with infants less than a year old, because their necks lack muscle control and their heads are heavier than the rest of their bodies.

The shaking necessary to cause death or severe intracranial injury is never unintentional or nonabusive. These injuries are caused by a violent, sustained action in which the infant's head is violently whipped forward and backward, hitting the chest and shoulders. Minor falls and play activities do not involve enough force to cause retinal hemorrhage or the kinds of severe, life-threatening injuries seen in infants who have been shaken.

Munchausen Syndrome By Proxy

Munchausen Syndrome is a psychological disorder in which patients fabricate the symptoms of disease or injury in order to obtain medical attention, and may even intentionally injure or induce illness in themselves. In Munchausen Syndrome by Proxy, a parent or caretaker suffering from Munchausen Syndrome tries to get medical attention by injuring or inducing illness in a child. The parent may try to resuscitate the child or have paramedics or hospital personnel save the child. The following scenarios are common in these cases:

- The child's caretaker repeatedly brings the child for medical care or calls paramedics for alleged problems that cannot be medically documented.
- The child only experiences "seizures" or "respiratory arrest" when the caretaker is there - never in the presence of neutral third parties or in the hospital.
- When the child is hospitalized, the caretaker turns off the life-support equipment, causing the child to stop breathing, and then turns everything back on and summons help.
- The caretaker induces illness by introducing a mild irritant or poison into the child's body.

Investigative Guidelines:
- Consult with all experts possible, including psychologists.
- Exhaust every possible explanation of the cause of the child's illness or death.
- Find out who had exclusive control over the child when the symptoms began or at the time of the child's death.
- Find out if there is a history of abusive conduct toward this child.
- Find out if the nature of the child's illness or injury allows medical professionals to express an opinion that the child's illness or death was neither accidental nor the result of a natural cause or disease.
- In cases of hospitalization, use covert video surveillance to monitor the suspect. Some cases have been solved in this way.
- Determine whether the caretaker had any medical training or a history of seeking medical treatment needlessly. Munchausen Syndrome by Proxy is often a multigenerational condition.

Sudden Infant Death Syndrome

When an unexplained infant death occurs, investigators should be sensitive, but still thorough. Suffocation by accident or with intent can often look like SIDS. Crime scene investigation, interviews, and a thorough medical exam is **critical** in SIDS deaths. Criteria for distinguishing between SIDS and death from child abuse are listed below.

Indicators Consistent with SIDS:
- An apparently healthy infant is fed and put to bed, later found dead. EMS resuscitation is unsuccessful.
- Infant's age is between 1 and 12 months. SIDS occurs most frequently in infants aged 2-4 months, and 90% of cases occur in children under 7 months.
- Bloody, watery, frothy, or mucous nasal discharge. Post-mortem lividity in dependent areas. Marks sometimes found on places where a blood vessel runs near a bone. No skin trauma. Baby apparently well cared for.
- Frequently, mothers used cigarettes during pregnancy. Some victims were premature or had low birth weight. Newborns showed minor defects with regard to their feeding and general temperament. Less height and weight gain after birth. Being a twin or a triplet. Possible history of spitting, gastroesphogeal reflux, thrush, pneumonia, illnesses requiring hospitalization, accelerated breathing or heartbeat, bluish discoloration of the skin due to lack of oxygen in the blood. Usually no signs of difficulty before death.
- Crib or bed in good repair. No dangerous bedclothes, toys, plastic sheets, pacifier strings or pillows stuffed with pellets. No cords, bands or other possible means of entanglement. An accurate description was provided of the child's position, including whether there was head or neck entrapment. Normal room temperature. No toxins or insecticides present. Good ventilation, furnace equipment.
- No previous unexplained or unexpected infant deaths.
- No adequate cause of death found by autopsy.
- Normal skeletal survey, toxicological findings, chemistry studies, microscopic examination, and metabolic screen. Presence of changes in certain organs thought to be more commonly seen in SIDS than in non-SIDS deaths. Occasionally, subtle changes in liver, including fatty change and blood forming in the liver.
- Family has no previous involvement with law enforcement or child protective services.

Indicators Less Consistent with SIDS:
- Infant found not breathing. EMS transports to hospital. Infant lives hours to days.
- History of substance abuse or family illness.
- Infant was 8-12 months of age.

- There are diagnostic signs of a disease process or enlargement of the organs.
- Child has history of recurrent illnesses and/or multiple hospitalizations ("sickly" or "weak" baby). Previous specific diagnosis of organ system disease.
- The death scene includes a defective crib or bed; inappropriate sheets, pillows or sleeping clothes; dangerous toys, plastic sheets, pacifier cords, pellet-stuffed pillows. Evidence exists that the child did not sleep alone. Poor ventilation and heat control. Presence of toxins or insecticides. Unsanitary conditions.
- Family has experienced one previous unexpected or unexplained infant death.
- Autopsy reveals subtle changes in liver, adrenal glands and the heart muscle (myocardium).
- Family has one previous encounter with law enforcement or child protective services.

Signs of Child Abuse (not typically related to SIDS):
- Caretaker gives history that is not typical of SIDS, unclear or inconsistent; indicates a long interval between bedtime and death.
- Child is 12 months of age or older.
- Child has skin and/or traumatic injuries. Signs of malnutrition, neglect, or fractures may also be present.
- Infant was unwanted. Mother received little or no prenatal care, and arrived late at hospital for delivery, or birth occurred outside of hospital. Child has had little or no well-baby care and no immunizations. Mother used cigarettes, drugs, and/or alcohol during and after pregnancy. Child is described as hard to care for or to "discipline." Deviant feeding practices were used.
- Death scene shows chaotic, unsanitary and crowded living conditions. Evidence of drug or alcohol use by caretakers. There are signs of a struggle in crib or other equipment; bloodstained bedclothes. Evidence of hostility, discord, or violence between caretakers. Admission of harm or accusations by caretakers.
- More than one previous unexplained or unexpected infant death has occurred in this family.
- Traumatic cause of death. External bruises, abrasions, burns. Evidence of malnutrition, fractures, or scalp bruises. Abnormal body chemistry values or toxicological findings.

- Family has had two or more previous encounters with law enforcement or child protective services. One or more family members arrested for violent behavior.

Key points about SIDS:
- SIDS is a diagnosis of exclusion following a thorough autopsy, death scene investigation, and comprehensive review of the child and his or her family's case history.
- SIDS is a definite medical entity and is the major cause of death in infants after the first month of life; most deaths occur between the age of 2-4 months.
- SIDS victims appear to be healthy prior to death.
- SIDS cannot be predicted or prevented, even by a physician, at the present time.
- SIDS deaths appear to cause no pain or suffering; death occurs very rapidly, usually during sleep.
- SIDS is not child abuse.
- SIDS is not caused by external suffocation.
- SIDS is not caused by vomiting and choking, or by minor illnesses such as colds or infections.
- SIDS is not caused by diphtheria/pertussis/tetanus (DPT) vaccine, or other immunizations.
- SIDS is not contagious.
- SIDS is not the cause of every unexplained infant death.

SIDS Resources:

American SIDS Institute ·············770-426-8746·········800-232-7437
   http://www.sids.org
National SIDS/Infant Death Resource Center
   http://www.sidscenter.org·······703-821-8955·········866-866-7437
SIDS Alliance
   http://www.sidsalliance.org ····································800-221-7437
Southwest SIDS Research Institute····························800-245-7437
   http://www.swsids.com

Missing Children

Introduction

The purpose of this section is to provide guidance to law enforcement officers in conducting missing child investigations. Included are the recommended steps for each phase of the investigative process for each kind of missing child investigation.

Categories of missing children:

- **Runaway:** This category included those children and youths who have run away from home, as well as "throwaways" (children who have been rejected or abandoned by their families and are homeless.)

- **Family Abductions:** These are cases in which a parent or relative has illegally taken, kept, or concealed the missing child from another parent or legal custodian.

- **Non-Family Abductions:** Commonly referred to as "stranger abductions," these are cases in which the child was taken, kept, or concealed by a person other than his or her parent or legal custodian.

- **Unknown Missing:** These are cases in which the child is missing and the facts of the case are insufficient to determine if the child was abducted, was the victim of an accident, or voluntarily left home.

The rationale for law-enforcement intervention is simple:

Missing child cases often involve a violation of the law and always involve the need to provide protection for the child. Even those youths who voluntarily leave home run the risk of becoming involved in criminal activity or exploitation through involvement in prostitution, child pornography, or with pedophile "protectors." Studies show that 85 percent of exploited children are missing when exploitation occurs.

Each kind of missing child case requires appropriate investigative strategies during each of the following four phases.

Investigative Strategies:

1. **Initial Response:** Regardless of the kind of missing child case, the initial response requires a preliminary investigation to determine the facts of the case and the structure of the subsequent investigation.

2. **Intensive Investigation:** This stage begins once it has been determined that a child is missing and continues until initial lead information is exhausted and further leads have not yet developed.

3. **Sustained Investigation:** The third phase consists of developing leads after the trail grows cold and following whatever leads are generated.
4. **Follow-up and Close-out:** Upon location of the child, or recovery and identification of the child's remains, the final stage includes steps necessary to determine what crimes may have been committed before or during the time the child was missing. It also includes routine steps to close out case files and delete NCIC entries.

Unusual Circumstances

If during the preliminary investigation the patrol officer determines or suspects that any of the following unusual circumstances exists, the police agency must be prepared to take immediate action.

- The missing youth is thirteen years of age or younger.
- The missing youth is believed to be out of the zone of safety for his or her age and developmental stage.
- The missing youth is mentally incapacitated.
- The missing youth is drug dependent, including prescribed medication and/or illegal substances, and the dependency is potentially life threatening.
- The missing youth has been absent from home for more than 24 hours before being reported to the police.
- Based on available information, it is determined that the missing youth is in a life-threatening situation.
- Based on available information, it is believed that the missing child is in the company of adults who could endanger his or her welfare.
- The absence is inconsistent with his or her established patterns of behavior, and the deviation cannot be readily explained.
- Other circumstances are involved in the disappearance that would cause a reasonable person to conclude that the child should be considered "at risk."

Initial Response Investigation Checklist

Administrative

- ❏ Obtain basic facts, details and a brief description of the missing child and abductor.
- ❏ Dispatch officer to scene for preliminary investigation.
- ❏ Search juvenile/incident records for previous incidents related to missing child, and prior police activity in the area, including prowlers, indecent exposure, attempted abductions, etc. Inform responding officer of any pertinent information.
- ❏ Broadcast known details on all police communication channels, to other patrol units, other local and surrounding law enforcement agencies and, if necessary, use NLETS telecommunication network to directly alert agencies in multi-state areas.
- ❏ If necessary, activate established fugitive search plans (prearranged plans among participating police agencies designed to apprehend fleeing fugitives).
- ❏ Maintain records/recordings of telephone communications/messages.
- ❏ Activate established protocols for working with the media.

First Responder

- ❏ Interview parents or person who made initial report.
- ❏ Verify that the child is, in fact, missing.
- ❏ Verify the child's custody status.
- ❏ Identify the circumstances of the disappearance.
- ❏ Determine when, where, and by whom the missing child was last seen.
- ❏ Interview the people who last had contact with the child.
- ❏ Identify the child's zone of safety for his or her age and developmental stage.
- ❏ Based on available information, make an initial determination of the type of incident (non-family abduction, family abduction, runaway, lost, injured or otherwise missing).
- ❏ Obtain a detailed description of missing child, abductor, vehicles, etc.
- ❏ Relay detailed descriptions to communications for broadcast updates.

❑ If your agency has access to K-9 dogs, attempt to track the missing child from their last known location.

❑ Request additional personnel, investigative assistance or supervisory assistance if needed.

❑ Brief and update all additional responding personnel, including supervisors and investigative staff.

❑ Ensure that everyone at the scene is identified and interviewed separately, and that their interview and identifying information is properly recorded. If possible, photograph or videotape images of everyone.

 – Note name, address, home and business telephone numbers of everyone present.
 – Determine each person's relationship to the missing child.
 – Note information that each person may have about the child's disappearance.
 – Determine when and where each one last saw the child.
 – Ask each one, "What do you think happened to the child?"
 – Get the names, addresses and telephone numbers of the child's friends and associates, and of all other relatives and friends of the family.

❑ Interview other family members, friends of the child, friends of the family, and other associates of the child to determine:

 – When each last saw the child
 – What they think happened to the child

❑ Continue to inform the communications unit of all appropriate developing information for broadcast updates.

❑ Obtain and note permission to search home or building where the incident took place.

❑ Search all surrounding areas, including vehicles and other places of concealment.

❑ Treat the area as a crime scene.

❑ Seal & protect the scene and the area of the child's home, including the child's personal articles such as hairbrush, diary, photographs, and items with the child's fingerprints, footprints, and teeth impressions. Be sure that such evidence is not destroyed, and that items which could help in the search or in identifying the child are preserved. If possible, videotape or photograph these areas.
Determine if any of the child's personal items are missing.

- ❑ Evaluate contents and appearance of child's room and residence.
- ❑ Get photographs of the missing child and abductor.
- ❑ Ensure that information about the missing child is entered into the NCIC Missing Person File and that any information on a suspected abductor is entered into the NCIC Wanted Person File.
- ❑ If criteria is established, broadcast an AMBER Alert.
- ❑ Ensure that details of the case have been reported to National Center for Missing and Exploited Children (NCMEC).
- ❑ Prepare and update bulletins for local law enforcement agencies, state missing children's clearinghouse, FBI, and other appropriate agencies.
- ❑ Prepare a flier or bulletin with the child and abductor's photograph and descriptive information. Distribute in appropriate geographic locations.
- ❑ Secure that child's latest medical and dental records.
- ❑ Establish a telephone hotline for tips and leads.
- ❑ Establish a leads management system to prioritize leads and ensure that each one is reviewed and followed up.

Investigative Officer

- ❑ Obtain briefing from first responding officer and other on-scene personnel.
- ❑ Verify the accuracy of all descriptive information and other details developed during preliminary investigation.
- ❑ Obtain a brief recent history of family dynamics.
- ❑ Correct and investigate the reasons for any conflicting information offered by witnesses and other individuals submitting information.
- ❑ Review and evaluate all available information and evidence collected.
- ❑ Develop an investigational plan for follow up.
- ❑ Determine what additional resources and specialized services are required.
- ❑ Execute investigative follow-up plan.

Supervisory Responsibility

- ❑ Get briefing and written reports from first responding officer, investigators and other agency personnel at the scene.
- ❑ Determine whether additional personnel are needed.
- ❑ Determine whether outside help is necessary from
  - – State Police
  - – State Missing Children's Clearinghouse
  - – AMBER Alert
  - – FBI
  - – Specialized Units
  - – Victim Witness Services
  - – NCMEC's Project ALERT
- ❑ Ensure that all the required resources, equipment and assistance necessary to conduct an efficient investigation have been requested and expedite their availability.
- ❑ Establish a command post away from the child's home.
- ❑ Ensure coordination/cooperation among all police personnel involved in the investigation and search effort.
- ❑ Ensure that all required notifications are made.
- ❑ Ensure compliance with all agency policies and procedures.
- ❑ Conduct a criminal history check on all principal suspects and participants in the investigation.
- ❑ Be available to make any decisions or determinations as they develop.
- ❑ Use the media, including radio, TV and newspapers, to help in the search for the missing child, and maintain media relations, per established protocols, throughout the duration of the case.

Runaway Case Investigation Checklist

Initial Investigation

- ❑ Check agency records for recent contact with child (arrests or other activity).
- ❑ Review school record and interview teachers, other school personnel, and classmates.
- ❑ Check contents of school locker.
- ❑ Contact community youth service organizations for information.
- ❑ Check child protective agency records for abuse reports.
- ❑ Use screening procedures to develop an accurate assessment of the child.

❑ Contact the National Runaway Switchboard at 800-621-4000, where parents can leave a message for their child and check to see if their child has left a message for them.

Prolonged Investigation
❑ Update initial NCIC entry by fully loading NCIC Missing Person File with all available information, including medical and dental records.
❑ Consider upgrading investigation to "endangered" if facts warrant.
❑ Re-interview friends, classmates and other info sources.
❑ Help family members prepare/distribute missing child posters.
❑ Provide support for family through nonprofit missing children's organization.
❑ Consider searching NCIC's Unidentified Missing Persons File, using NCIC's Off-line Search capabilities, and notify state medical examiners by providing descriptive information and photograph of missing child.

Recovery/Case Closure
❑ Conduct a thorough interview of the child, document the results of the interview, and involve all appropriate agencies.
  – Why did the child leave?
  – Where did the child go?
  – How did the child survive?
  – Who helped the child during absence?
  – Will the child leave again?
❑ Consider a complete physical examination for the child.
❑ Make the child and family aware of community services to deal with any unresolved issues.
❑ Complete an agency report for the episode that can be promptly accessed and reviewed if the child leaves again.
❑ Cancel alarms and remove the case from NCIC and other information systems.

Family Abduction Investigation Checklist

Initial Investigation
❑ Examine court records if applicable.
❑ Conduct background investigations on both parents.
❑ Provide tasks for left-behind parent.
❑ Interview family and friends of the suspected parent.

❑ Enter info about the child and the suspected parent into NCIC Missing Person File (Involuntary Category).

❑ Obtain and evaluate all information that may indicate a location of the suspected parent.

❑ Coordinate the issuance of an arrest warrant against the suspected parent with prosecutor.

❑ Assure entry of warrant information into NCIC Missing Person File (child) and Wanted Person File (suspect parent).

❑ Consider use of civil procedures such as writ of habeas corpus and writ of assistance.

❑ Provide support for family through nonprofit missing children's organization.

Prolonged Investigation

❑ Secure federal UFAP warrant if facts support issuance.

❑ Identify and "flag" all pertinent sources of information about both the child (school, medical, birth, etc.) and the suspected parent (employment, education, etc.).

❑ Use information sources such as credit bureaus, database systems, motor vehicle bureaus, and the Federal Parent Locator Service (FPLS) to search for the suspected parent through identifiers such as Social Security number, name, date of birth, etc.

❑ Request US Postal Service authorities to provide change of address information and assistance in setting up a mail cover on selected family members or friends of the suspected parent.

❑ Identify and evaluate other information such as employment records, occupational licenses, organization memberships, social interests, hobbies and other lifestyle indicators. This information could provide leads to the suspected parent's whereabouts.

International Abductions

❑ Become familiar with laws of the suspected parent's country concerning custody matters.

❑ Contact U.S. Department of State for assistance in civil aspects of the abduction and potential for return of child through legal and diplomatic channels.

❑ AMBER Alert is international with more and more agencies joining all the time.

❑ Seek information from INTERPOL concerning criminal proceedings against the suspect parent.

Recovery/Case Closure

❑ If possible, arrest the suspected parent away from child.

❑ Notify child protective service workers about possible need for temporary shelter care until the left-behind parent or investigator arrives.

❑ Conduct thorough interview of the child and the abductor, document the results of the interviews, and involve all appropriate agencies.

❑ Provide effective reunification techniques.

❑ Cancel alarms and remove case from NCIC and other information systems.

Non-Family Abduction Investigation Checklist

Initial Investigation

❑ Assign an officer to the victim's residence with the ability to record and "trap and trace" all incoming calls. Consider setting up a separate telephone line or cellular telephone for agency use.

❑ Conduct a neighborhood and vehicle canvass.

❑ Conduct a nearby business canvass to recover any video surveillance that may show the suspect, vehicle, or missing child.

❑ Compile list of known sex offenders in the region.

❑ Develop a profile on possible abductor.

❑ Consider use of polygraph for parents and other key individuals.

❑ In cases of infant abduction, investigate claims of home births made in that area.

❑ Fully load NCIC Missing Person File (involuntary category) with complete descriptive, medical and dental information.

❑ Use NLETS, AMBER Alert, and other information systems to alert local, state, regional and federal law enforcement agencies.

❑ Provide support for family through nonprofit missing children's organization.

Prolonged Investigation

- ❏ Reread all reports and transcripts of interviews.
- ❏ Revisit the crime scene.
- ❏ Review all potential witness and suspect information obtained in the initial investigation, and consider background checks on anyone identified in the investigation.
- ❏ Review all photographs and videotapes.
- ❏ Reexamine all physical evidence collected.
- ❏ Review child protective agency records for reports of abuse on child.
- ❏ Develop timelines and other visual exhibits.
- ❏ Reinterview key individuals.
- ❏ Interview delivery personnel; employees of gas, water, electric and cable companies; taxi drivers; post office personnel; garbage handlers, etc.
- ❏ Critique results of the ongoing investigation with appropriate investigative resources.
- ❏ Arrange for periodic media coverage.
- ❏ Use rewards and crime stopper programs.
- ❏ Contact NCMEC for photo dissemination, age-progression and other case assistance.
- ❏ Update NCIC MPF information as necessary.

Recovery/Case Closure

- ❏ Arrange for a comprehensive physical examination of the victim.
- ❏ Conduct a careful interview of the child, document the results, and involve all appropriate agencies.
- ❏ Provide effective reunification techniques.
- ❏ Cancel alarms and remove case from NCIC and other information systems.
- ❏ Perform constructive post-case critique.

Unknown Missing Cases

Not every case can be readily classified. Cases in which the facts are insufficient to determine the cause of the child's disappearance are called Unknown Missing cases. In many such cases, the only fact apparent is that there is a missing child. Without any facts that indicate otherwise, however, the police agency should assume that the child is endangered and act accordingly, treating it as a Non-Family Abduction.

Resources for Missing Children

National Center for Missing and Exploited Children (NCMEC)

The National Center for Missing and Exploited Children, through its Technical Advisory staff, provides technical assistance to law enforcement agencies handling missing child cases. Technical assistance may include arranging for media display of a missing child's photograph, forwarding lead information obtained from the National Hotline for Missing Children (toll-free: 1-800-843-5678), or providing on-site case review at the request of the investigating law-enforcement agency.

In each kind of missing child case, the investigator should call the National Center's toll-free National Hotline and discuss the case with one of the technical advisors. Each National Center technical advisor is a former law enforcement officer with expertise and field experience with missing child investigations.

The purpose of the National Hotline is to take information on sightings of missing children. The Center can arrange for the nationwide (including Canada) toll-free number, 1-800-843-5678, to be used for sighting information and can include the case in the national missing children's media programs. The 800-operators use a protocol developed by the technical advisors, consisting of about sixty specific questions that are computer supported.

All leads are reviewed by technical advisors and forwarded immediately to the law enforcement agency on record (ORI) in NCIC and the FBI, if involved, by first-class mail, NLETS, or express service. Note that lead information obtained by the National Center is shared only with the law enforcement agencies responsible for the case investigation.

AMBER Alert Plan

The "America's Missing: Broadcast Emergency Response Alert Plan", or AMBER Alert Plan, is a voluntary partnership between law enforcement agencies and broadcasters to activate an urgent bulletin in serious child-abduction cases. The goal is to instantly inform the entire community and to gain community assistance in the search for and safe return of the missing child.

Once law enforcement personnel have been notified about a missing or abducted child, they must first determine if the case meets the criteria for triggering an alert.

AMBER Alert Criteria (recommended by the U.S. Dept. of Justice - http://www.usdoj.gov):
- There is a reasonable belief by law enforcement that an abduction has occurred.
- There is a reasonable belief by law enforcement that the child is in imminent danger of serious bodily injury or death.
- The abducted child is 17 years or younger.
- There is enough descriptive information about the victim and details for the abduction to issue an AMBER Alert.
- The child's name and other critical data (such as the Child Abduction flag) should be entered into the National Crime Information Center (NCIC).

Once the above criteria is met, alert information (such as descriptions, pictures of the child and/or abductor, suspected vehicle, etc) may be gathered for distribution. The information should be faxed to radio stations designated as primary stations under the Emergency Alert System (EAS). The primary station will then forward the information to area radio and television stations and cable systems via the EAS, and will be immediately broadcasted by participating stations.

Military Resources

If the abductor is a member of or employed by a military service, the branch of the military service should be asked to provide, through the Worldwide Locator Service, the most recent duty assignment. The service will need the abductor's full name, Social Security number, date of birth, and last known duty assignment.

If the abductor parent is a member of either the Army or Air National Guard, the State Adjutant General for the state in which the person is a guardsman maintains personnel records.

If the abductor is a retired military or a retired civil service employee and receives a retirement check, a court order should be obtained for examination of records containing personal and address information.

Military Worldwide Locator Services

US Army
Army Worldwide Locator Service
U.S. Army Enlisted Records and Evaluation Center
8899 East 56th St., Indianapolis, IN 46249-5301
(703) 325-3732 (recorded info only)
Requests must be in writing. In an emergency, contact your local Red Cross for assistance in making a request.

US Air Force And Air Force Reserve
AFPC/MSIMDL
550 C Street West, Suite 50
Randolf AFB, TX 78150-4752
(210) 652-5775

US Navy and Naval Reserve
Navy Worldwide Locator Service
Washington, D.C. 20370
(703) 614-5011

US Marine Corps and Marine Corps Reserve
Commandant of the Marine Corps
Headquarters, U.S. Marine Corps (Code MMSB)
Washington, D.C. 20380-1775
(703)784-3942

US Coast Guard
Coast Guard Personnel Command (CGPC-adm-3)
2100 2nd Street, S.W.
Washington, D.C. 20593-0001
Phone: (202) 267-1340   Fax: (202) 267-4985

State Clearinghouses For Missing Children

Many states offer additional support to law enforcement for missing children through state clearinghouses. Contact your state clearinghouse to determine its ability to support missing child case investigations before you need the services.

Alabama Dept. of Public Safety,
Missing Children Bureau ········· 800-228-7688* ······· 334-260-1172
Alaska Dept. of Public Safety ····· 800-478-9333 ·········· 907-269-5497
Arizona Dept. of Public Safety,
Criminal Investigation Research Unit ····················· 602-223-2158
Arkansas Office of the Attorney General,
Missing Children's Services Program ···················· 800-448-3014*
California Dept. of Justice ········· 800-222-3463* ····· 916-227-3290
Colorado Bureau of Investigation,
Missing Children Project ······································ 303-239-4251
Connecticut State Police ·· 800-367-5678
Delaware State Bureau of Identification ···················· 302-739-5883
Florida Dept. of Law Enforc. ······· 888-356-4774 ·········· 904-488-5224
Georgia Bureau of Investigation ·800-282-6564* ······· 404-244-2554
Hawaii Dept. of the Attorney General ······················ 808-586-1449
Idaho Bureau of Criminal Id. ······ 888-777-3922 ·········· 208-884-7136
Illinois Missing Children's Clearinghouse
During business hours ·· 217-785-0631
After business hours ·· 217-786-6677
Indiana Missing Children's
Clearinghouse ·························· 800-831-8953 ·········· 317-232-8310
Iowa Dept. of Public Safety,
Div. of Criminal Investigation ··800-346-5507* ······· 515-281-7958
Kansas Bureau of Investigation··800-572-7463* ······· 785-296-8200
Kentucky State Police,
Missing Child Info Center ········ 800-222-5555* ····· 502-227-8799
Louisiana State Clearinghouse for Missing Children ··504-342-4011
Maine Missing Children
Clearinghouse ·························· 800-483-5678 ·········· 207-287-3987
Maryland Center for Missing Children,
Maryland State Police ············ 800-637-5437 ·········· 410-290-1620
Massachusetts State Police ·· 508-820-2129
Michigan State Police ·· 517-333-4006
Minnesota State Clearinghouse ································ 612-642-0610
Mississippi State Highway Patrol ······························ 601-933-2657
Missouri Division of Drug &
Crime Control ·························· 800-877-3452* ······· 573-751-3452
Montana Department of Justice ································ 406-444-1526
Nebraska State Patrol,
Criminal Records & Identification Division ·············· 402-479-4981
Nevada Office of the Attorney General ···················· 702-486-3539
New Hampshire State Police ···································· 603-271-2663
New Jersey State Police,
Missing Persons ······················ 800-709-7090 ·········· 609-882-2000

New Mexico Department of Public Safety················505-827-3413
New York Division of
  Criminal Justice Services·······800-346-3543··········518-457-6326
North Carolina Division of Victim and
  Justice Services·····················800-522-5437*······919-733-3914
North Dakota Missing Children
  Clearinghouse·····················800-472-2121*······701-328-2121
Ohio Missing Children Clrnghs···800-325-5604··········614-466-5610
Oklahoma State Bureau of Investigation ····················405-848-6724
Oregon Missing Children
  Clearinghouse·············800-282-7155*·····503-378-3720 ext. 4412
Pennsylvania Bureau of Criminal Investigation···········717- 783-5524
Rhode Island State Police, Missing and
  Exploited Children Unit ·········800-546-8066*······401-444-1125
South Carolina Law Enforcement
  Division ·····························800-322-4453··········803-737-9000
South Dakota Attorney General's Office ·····················605-773-3331
Tennessee Bureau of Investigation ··························800-824-3463
Texas Department of Public Safety,
  Missing Persons·················800-346-3243··········512-424-2810
Utah Department of Public Safety,
  Bureau of Criminal Identification·····························801-965-4500
Vermont State Police ··802-773-9101
Virginia State Police···800-822-4453
Washington Missing Children
  Clearinghouse····················800-543-5678··········360-586-0033
West Virginia State Police, Missing
  Children's Clearinghouse·······800-352-0927··········304-558-1467
Wisconsin Department of Justice,
  Crime Information Bureau·······800-843-4673*·······608-261-8126
Wyoming Division of Criminal Investigation,
  Missing Persons ··307-777-7537

*Number can only be dialed within that state.

National Clearinghouses For Missing Children

Canada: Royal Canadian Mounted Police ·················613-993-1525
United States: National Center for Missing and
  Exploited Children ····················800-843-5678··········703-274-3900

Child Abuse Resources

AMA Department of Mental Health
 http://www.ama-assn.org ······· 312-464-5066 ········· 312-464-5000
American Bar Association Center on Children and the Law
 http://www.abanet.org/child/ ································ 202-662-1720
American Humane Association ··························· 303-792-9900
 http://www.americanhumane.org ························ 800-227-4645
American Professional Society on the Abuse of Children (APSAC)
 http://www.apsac.org ···································· 405-271-8202
American Prosecutors Research Institute (APRI)
 http://www.ndaa.org/apri/ ································ 703-739-0321
Childhelp USA/Forester National Child Abuse Hotline
 http://www.childhelpusa.org ······················· 800-422-4453
FBI Child Abduction and Serial Killer Unit & Task Force
 on Missing & Exploited Children ···················· 800-634-4097
Fox Valley Technical College Criminal Justice Dept.,
 Law Enfrcmt Training Programs ···· www.fvtc.edu ···· 800-648-4966
Juvenile Justice Clearinghouse ························ 800-638-8736
Kempe National Center for the Prevention and Treatment of
 Child Abuse and Neglect ·· www.kempecenter.org ··· 303-864-5252
KidsPeace www.kidspeace.org ·· 800-334-4543 ········· 800-257-3223
National Center for Missing and Exploited Children
 http://www.missingkids.com ·· 800-843-5678 ····· 703-274-3900
National Center for the Prosecution of Child Abuse ··· 703-739-0321
 http://www.ndaa-apri.org/apri/programs/ncpca/ncpca_home.html
National Child Safety Council ····· 800-327-5107 ········ 517-764-6070
National Clearinghouse on Child Abuse and Neglect
 http://nccanch.acf.hhs.gov ····························· 703-385-7565
National Committee to Prevent Child Abuse
 http://www.childabuse.org ····························· 312-663-3520
National Network of Children's
 Advocacy Centers ··················· 800-239-9950 ····· 202-639-0597
National SIDS Resource Center
 http://www.sidscenter.org ······················· 703-821-8955, ext. 286
NCJRS Statistics Clearinghouse www.ncjrs.org ········· 800-732-3277
Rape, Abuse and Incest National Network
 http://www.rainn.org ···································· 800-656-4673

Regional Information Sharing Systems

Mid-States Organized Crime Information Center ······· 417-883-4383
Mid-Atlantic/Great Lakes Org. Crime LE Network ····· 215-504-4910
New England State Police Information Network ········· 508-528-8200
Regional Organized Crime Information Center ··········· 615-871-0013
Rocky Mountain Information Network ·················· 602-351-2320
US Dept of Justice, Child Exploitation and Obscenity ·202-514-5780
Western States Information Network ···················· 916-263-1166

EXPLOSIVES

Bomb Threats · 110

   Basic Room Search Technique · · · · · · · · · · · · · · · · 111

   Handling the Media · 114

   Bomb Threat Checklist · 115

   Detecting Letter and Package Bombs · · · · · · · · · · · 116

Regulated Explosive Materials · · · · · · · · · · · · · · · · · · 117

Explosive Ordnance Disposal Units · · · · · · · · · · · · · 122

Vehicle Bomb Explosion Hazards & Evacuation · · · · 126

Explosives

Bomb Threats

Basic DOs and DON'Ts

DO:
- Take every threat seriously.
- Establish incident command.
- Establish a perimeter; most departments have their own guidelines.
- Notify fire dept. and paramedics.
- Ask your supervisor for additional units; one or two officers cannot control a bomb scene properly.
- Take a flashlight.
- Stop, look and listen.
- Make a thorough sweep.
- Try to find out what the item looks like, where it might be, and what type of location it is in.
- Locate witnesses and make them available.
- Get as much information as possible from witnesses and the scene. Have witnesses sign any statement they give you.
- Write down all information; don't trust your memory.
- After talking with initial people on scene, make a rough diagram of what they described to you.
- Make every effort to preserve evidence, but do not risk safety to do so.

DON'T:
- Never search alone.
- Never assume anything.
- Never transmit with your radio or use <u>any</u> device that transmits RF energy within *300 feet* of the site. This includes cell phones, voice tape recorders, video recorders, TV Beta cameras, and two way pagers. If in doubt, don't use it.
- Never touch anything.
- Never turn any switches on or off.
- Never touch, move, or pull anything from the suspect device.
- Never put the suspected object in water.

Bomb threats are delivered in a variety of ways. The majority of threats are called in to the target, occasionally through a third party. Sometimes a threat is written or recorded.

Two reasons for reporting a bomb threat are:
- The caller knows or believes that a bomb has been or will be placed and wants to minimize personal injury or property damage. The caller may be the person who placed the device or someone who is aware of such information.
- The caller wants to disrupt normal activities at the location of the reported bomb.

Initial steps

Contact the person in charge of the building and get his or her assistance in organizing a search. The decision about whether to evacuate the building should be left to the building owner or manager, at least until a suspicious object is found.

- Begin the search outside the building and search all possible hiding places including bushes, doorways, refuse containers, window boxes, etc.
- Determine search responsibility for the entire building.

Basic Room Search Technique

The following basic room search technique uses a two-person search team. Many minor variations are possible when searching a room.

Listen for Clockwork Devices

When the two-person team enters the room to be searched, they should first move to various parts of the room and stand quietly with their eyes closed, listening for a clockwork device, which often can be quickly detected without using special equipment. Even if no clockwork mechanism is detected, the team is now aware of the background noise level within the room itself.

Background noise or transferred sound is always disturbing during a building search, especially a ticking sound that cannot be located. The ticking sound may come from an unbalanced air conditioner fan several floors away or from a dripping sink down the hall. Sound transfers through air-conditioning ducts, along water pipes, and through walls. Buildings heated by steam or hot water are very hard to search because the heating system makes various noises that can be confused with a clockwork device. Background noise may also include outside traffic sounds, rain, and wind.

Divide the Room for Searching

The person in charge of the search team should look around the room and determine how the room is to be divided for searching and to what height the first sweep should extend.

Divide the room into two virtually equal parts based on the number and type of objects in the room to be searched and not on the size of the room. Draw an imaginary line between two objects in the room; e.g., the edge of the window on the North wall to the floor lamp on the South wall.

First Searching Sweep

Determine the average height of most of the items resting on the floor. In a typical room, this height usually includes table or desk tops and chair backs. The first searching height usually covers the items in the room up to hip height.

Second Searching Sweep

The individual in charge again determines the height of the second searching sweep, usually from the hip to the chin or top of the head. Both people return to the starting point and repeat the searching technique at the second selected searching height. This sweep usually covers pictures hanging on walls, built-in bookcases, and tall table lamps.

Third Searching Sweep

The person in charge again determines the next searching height, usually from the chin or the top of the head up to the ceiling. The third sweep is then made. This sweep usually covers high mounted air-conditioning ducts and hanging light fixtures.

Fourth Searching Sweep

If the room has a false or suspended ceiling, the fourth sweep involves investigation of this area. Check flush or ceiling-mounted light fixtures, air conditioning or ventilation ducts, sound or speaker systems, electrical wiring, and structural frame members.

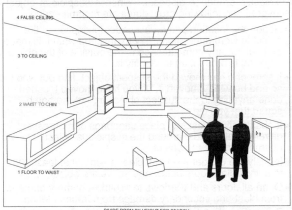

DIVIDE ROOM BY HEIGHT FOR SEARCH

Upon Completion

Post a conspicuous "Search Completed" sign or marker in the area. If a sign is not practical, place a piece of colored scotch tape across the door jamb approximately 2 feet above floor level.

The same basic room search technique can be applied to any enclosed area. Use common sense in searching. For instance, if a guest speaker at a convention has been threatened, common sense dictates searching the speaker's platform and microphones first, but always return to the search technique. Do not rely on random or spot checking of only logical target areas. The bomber may not be a logical person.

In short, the following steps should be taken when searching a room:
- Divide the area and select a search height.
- Start from the bottom and work up.
- Start back-to-back and work toward each other.
- Go around the walls and proceed toward the center of the room.

Suspicious Object Located

The only mission of officers involved in a search is to search for and report suspicious objects. ***Under no circumstances move, jar or touch a suspicious object or anything attached to it.*** Removing or disarming a bomb must be left to the professionals in explosive ordnance disposal. When a suspicious object is discovered, the following procedures are recommended:

- Report the location and an accurate description of the object to Communications. Try to describe what it is made of. Look for any item attached to the outside of the object; if anything is present try to identify it.
- If someone has moved the suspect object, find out who did so and how they moved it. If you have moved touched or done anything to the suspect object, inform the bomb squad that you did.
- If absolutely necessary, place sandbags or mattresses, never metal shields, around the suspicious object. Do not attempt to move the object.
- Identify the danger area and clear a zone of at least 300 feet, including floors below and above the object.
- Open all doors and windows to minimize primary damage from blast and secondary damage from fragmentation.
- Determine whether to evacuate the building. (Usually police have the authority to make this decision once a device has been found; the person in charge of the building is responsible for the decision prior to that time.)
- Do not permit reentry into the building until the device has been removed/disarmed and the building is declared safe.
- Make a visual check for a second device.

Handling The News Media

One appointed person should handle all inquiries from the news media. Everyone else should be instructed not to discuss the situation with outsiders, especially the media. In this way, the news media is provided with accurate information and additional bomb threats are not precipitated by irresponsible statements from uninformed sources.

Source: Dept. Of the Treasury, Bureau of Alcohol, Tobacco and Firearms, *Bomb Threats and Physical Security Planning*

Bomb Threat Checklist

Exact time & date of call: _____
Exact words of caller: _____
_____
_____
_____

Questions to Ask:
1. When is bomb going to explode? _____
2. Where is the bomb? _____
_____
3. What does it look like? _____
_____
4. What kind of bomb is it? _____
_____
5. What will cause it to explode? _____
_____
6. Did you place the bomb? _____
If so, Why? _____
_____
7. Where are you calling from? _____
8. What is your address? _____
_____
9. What is your name? _____
_____

Caller's Voice (circle)

Calm	Disguised	Nasal	Angry	Broken
Stutter	Slow	Sincere	Lisp	Rapid
Giggling	Deep	Crying	Squeaky	Excited
Stressed	Accent	Loud	Slurred	Normal

If voice is familiar, whom did it sound like? _____
_____
Were there any background noises? _____
_____
Remarks: _____
_____
Person receiving call: _____
Telephone number call received at: _____
Report call immediately to: (refer to bomb incident plan) ____

Explosives

Detecting Letter and Package Bombs

REMEMBER: Most bombers set up and deliver the bomb themselves. They do not have to be delivered by a carrier. Bombs can look like almost anything and can be placed or delivered any number of ways. The only common denominator that exists among bombs is that they are designed or intended to explode.

Most bombs are homemade and are limited in their design only by the imagination of, and resources available to, the bomber. When searching for a bomb, suspect anything that looks unusual. Let the trained bomb technician determine what is or is not a bomb.

If Item is Delivered by a Carrier:
- Inspect for lumps, bulges, or protrusions, without applying pressure.
- Balance check if lopsided or heavy sided.

Suspicious Labeling & Addressing:
- Handwritten addresses or labels from companies are improper. Check to see if the company exists and if they sent a package or letter.
- Packages wrapped in string are automatically suspicious, as its need has been eliminated by modern packaging.
- Excess postage on small packages or letters indicates that the object was not weighed by the post office.
- No postage or non-canceled postage.
- No return address or nonsensical return address.
- Any foreign writing, addresses, or postage.
- Handwritten notes, i.e. "To be opened in the privacy of...," "Confidential," "Your Lucky Day is Here," "Prize Enclosed."
- Improper spelling of common names, places, or titles.
- Generic or incorrect titles.

Other Suspicious Characteristics:
- Leaks, stains, or protruding wires, string, tape, etc.
- Packages or letters that are hand delivered or "dropped off for a friend".
- Any letters or packages arriving before or after a phone call from an unknown person asking if the item was received.

If you have a suspicious package or letter, call E.O.D. or Bomb Unit (see page 122)

Source: Dept. Of the Treasury, Bureau of Alcohol, Tobacco and Firearms, Letter and Package Bomb Detection Techniques

Regulated Explosive Materials

2002 List of Explosive Materials Subject to Regulation under 18 United States Code, Chapter 40: Importation, Manufacture, Distribution and Storage of Explosive Materials

This list includes explosives, detonators, and blasting agents, and is intended to include any and all mixtures containing any of the materials on the list. Explosive materials not included on this list may still fall within the coverage of the law if they otherwise meet the statutory definitions in Section 841 of Title 18, United States Code.

Materials are listed alphabetically by their common names, followed by synonyms and chemical names in brackets or parentheses.

The materials listed may only be sold by a licensed dealer. Anyone other than a licensed dealer who wishes to purchase them must obtain a permit. Permits may **not** be issued to:

- Anyone under 21 years of age.
- Anyone convicted in any court of a crime punishable by more than 1 year in prison or under indictment for such a crime.
- Fugitives from justice.
- Anyone who is an unlawful user of or addicted to any controlled substance.
- Anyone who has been adjudicated mentally defective.

The following materials may only be sold within the state in which the dealer is licensed and only sold to residents of that state or a contiguous state which permits the transport, shipment, or receipt of that explosive material.

Acetylides of heavy metals
Aluminum containing polymeric propellant
Aluminum ophorite explosive
Amatex
Amatol
Ammonal
Ammonium nitrate explosive mixtures (cap sensitive)
Ammonium nitrate explosive mixtures (non cap sensitive), (Blasting Agent)
Ammonium perchlorate composite propellant
Ammonium perchlorate explosive mixtures
Ammonium picrate (picrate of ammonia, Explosive D)
Ammonium salt lattice with isomorphously substituted inorganic salts
ANFO (ammonium nitrate-fuel oil) (Blasting Agent)
Aromatic nitro-compound explosive mixtures
Azide explosives
Baratol
Baronol
BEAF [1,2-bis,(2,2-difluoro-2-nitroacetoxyethane)]
Black powder

Black powder based explosive mixtures
Blasting agents, nitro-carbo-nitrates, including non-cap sensitive
  slurry and water gel explosives
Blasting caps
Blasting gelatin
Blasting powder
BTNEC [bis (trinitroethyl)carbonate]
BTNEN [bis (trinitroethyl) nitramine]
BTTN [1,2,4 butanetriol trinitrate]
Bulk salutes
Butyl tetryl
Cellulose hexanitrate explosive mixture
Chlorate explosive mixtures
Composition A and variations
Composition B and variations
Composition C and variations
Copper acetylide
Cyanuric triazide
Cyclonite (RDX)
Cyclotetramethylenetetranitramine (HMX)
Cyclotol
Cyclotrimethylenetrinitramine (RDX)
DATB (diaminotrinitrobenzene)
DDNP (diazodinitrophenol)
DEGDN (diethyleneglycol dinitrate)
Detonating cord
Detonators
Dimethylol dimethyl methane dinitrate composition
Dinitroethyleneurea
Dinitroglycerine (glycerol dinitrate)
Dinitrophenol
Dinitrophenolates
Dinitrophenyl hydrazine
Dinitroresorcinol
Dinitrotoluene-sodium nitrate explosive mixtures
DIPAM (dipicramide; diaminohexanitrobiphenyl)
Dipicryl sulfone
Dipicrylamine
Display fireworks
DNPA (2,2-dinitropropyl acrylate)
DNPD (dinitropentano nitrile)
Dynamite
EDDN (ethylene diamine dinitrate)
EDNA (ethylenedinitramine)
Ednatol
EDNP (ethyl 4,4-dinitropentanoate)
EGDN (ethylene glycol dinitrate)
Erythritol tetranitrate explosives
Esters of nitro-substituted alcohols
Ethyl-tetryl
Explosive conitrates
Explosive gelatins
Explosive liquids
Explosive mixtures containing oxygen-releasing inorganic salts and
  hydrocarbons
Explosive mixtures containing oxygen-releasing inorganic salts and
  nitro bodies

Explosive mixtures containing oxygen-releasing inorganic salts and water insoluble fuels
Explosive mixtures containing sensitized nitromethane
Explosive mixtures containing tetranitromethane (nitroform)
Explosive nitro compounds of aromatic hydrocarbons
Explosive organic nitrate mixtures
Explosive powders
Flash powder
Fulminate of mercury
Fulminate of silver
Fulminating gold
Fulminating mercury
Fulminating platinum
Fulminating silver
Gelatinized nitrocellulose
Gem-dinitro aliphatic explosive mixtures
Guanyl nitrosamino guanyl tetrazene
Guanyl nitrosamino guanylidene hydrazine
Guncotton
Heavy metal azides
Hexanite
Hexanitrodiphenylamine
Hexanitrostilbene
Hexogen (RDX)
Hexogene or octogene and a nitrated N-methylaniline
Hexolites
HMTD (hexamethylenetriperoxidediamine)
HMX (cyclo-1,3,5,7-tetramethylene 2,4,6,8-tetranitramine; Octogen)
Hydrazinium nitrate/hydrazine/aluminum explosive system
Hydrazoic acid
Igniter cord
Igniters
Initiating tube systems
KDNBF (potassium dinitrobenzo-furoxane)
Lead azide
Lead mannite
Lead mononitroresorcinate
Lead picrate
Lead salts, explosive
Lead styphnate (styphnate of lead, lead trinitroresorcinate)
Liquid nitrated polyol and trimethylolethane
Liquid oxygen explosives
Magnesium ophorite explosives
Mannitol hexanitrate
MDNP (methyl 4,4-dinitropentanoate)
MEAN (monoethanolamine nitrate)
Mercuric fulminate
Mercury oxalate
Mercury tartrate
Metriol trinitrate
Minol-2 (40% TNT, 40% ammonium nitrate, 20% aluminum)
MMAN (monomethylamine nitrate); methylamine nitrate
Mononitrotoluene-nitroglycerin mixture
Monopropellants
NIBTN (nitroisobutametriol trinitrate)
Nitrate explosive mixtures

Nitrate sensitized with gelled nitroparaffin
Nitrated carbohydrate explosive
Nitrated glucoside esplosive
Nitrated polyhydric alcohol explosives
Nitric acid and a nitro aromatic compound explosive
Nitric acid and carboxylic fuel explosive
Nitric acid explosive mixtures
Nitro aromatic explosive mixtures
Nitro compounds of furane explosive mixtures
Nitrocellulose explosive
Nitroderivative of urea explosive mixture
Nitrogelatin explosive
Nitrogen trichloride
Nitrogen tri-iodide
Nitroglycerine (NG, RNG, nitro, glyceryl trinitrate, trinitroglycerine)
Nitroglycide
Nitroglycol (ethylene glycol dinitrate, EGDN)
Nitroguanidine explosives
Nitronium perchlorate propellant mixtures
Nitroparaffins Explosive Grade and ammonium nitrate mixtures
Nitrostarch
Nitro-substituted carboxylic acids
Nitrourea
Octogen (HMX)
Octol (75% HMX, 25% TNT)
Organic amine nitrates
Organic nitramines
PBX (plastic bonded explosives)
Pellet powder
Penthrinite composition
Pentolite
Perchlorate explosive mixtures
Peroxide based explosive mixtures
PETN (nitropentaerythrite, pentaerythrite tetranitrate, pentaerythritol
   tetranitrate)
Picramic acid and its salts
Picramide
Picrate explosives
Picrate of potassium explosive mixtures
Picratol
Picric acid (manufactured as an explosive)
Picryl chloride
Picryl fluoride
PLX (95% nitromethane, 5% ethylenediamine)
Polynitro aliphatic compounds
Polyolpolynitrate-nitrocellulose explosive gels
Potassium chlorate and lead sulfocyanate explosive
Potassium nitrate explosive mixtures
Potassium nitroaminotetrazole
Pyrotechnic compositions
PYX (2,6-bis (picrylamino))-3,5-dinitropyridine
RDX (cyclonite, hexogen, T4, cyclo-1,3,5,-trimethylene-2,
   4,6,-trinitramine; hexahydro-1,3,5-trinitro-S-triazine)
Safety fuse
Salts of organic amino sulfonic acid explosive mixture
Salutes (bulk)

Silver acetylide
Silver azide
Silver fulminate
Silver oxalate explosive mixtures
Silver styphnate
Silver tartrate explosive mixtures
Silver tetrazene
Slurried explosive mixtures of water, inorganic oxidizing salt, gelling agent, fuel and sensitizer (cap sensitive)
Smokeless powder
Sodatol
Sodium amatol
Sodium azide explosive mixture
Sodium dinitro-orth-cresolate
Sodium nitrate-potassium nitrate explosive mixture
Sodium picramate
Special fireworks
Squibs
Styphnic acid explosives
Tacot (tetranitro-2,3,5,6-dibenzo-1,3a,4,6a terazapentalene)
TATB (triaminotrinitrobenzene)
TATP (triacetonetriperoxide)
TEGDN (triethylene glycol dinitrate)
Tetranitrocarbazole
Tetrazene [tetracene, tetrazine, 1(5-tetrazolyl)-4-guanyl tetrazene hydrate)]
Tetryl (2,4,6 tetranitro-N-methylaniline)
Tetrytol
Thickened inorganic oxidizer salt slurried explosive mixture
TMETN (trimethylolethane trinitrate)
TNEF (trinitroethyl formal)
TNEOC (trinitroethylorthoformate)
TNEOF (trinitrotoluene, trotyl, trilite, triton)
Torpex
Tridite
Trimethylol ethyl methane trinitrate composition
Trimethylolthane trinitrate-nitrocellulose
Trimonite
Trinitroanisole
Trinitrobenzene
Trinitrobenzoic acid
Trinitrocresol
Trinitro-meta-cresol
Trinitronaphthalene
Trinitrophenetol
Trinitrophloroglucinol
Trinitroresorcinol
Tritonal
Urea nitrate
Water-bearing explosives having salts of oxidizing acids and nitrogen bases, sulfates, or sulfamates (cap sensitive)
Water-in-oil emulsion explosive compositions
Xanthamonas hydrophilic colloid explosive mixture

Source: Dept. Of the Treasury, Bureau of Alcohol Tobacco and Firearms, *Commerce in Explosives; List of Explosive Materials*

Explosives

Explosive Ordnance Disposal Units

Federal Bureau of Investigation ·············· 202-324-2696
  835 Pennsylvania Ave NW, Washington, D.C. 20535-0001
Bureau of Alcohol, Tobacco, Firearms & Explosives 888-283-2662
  650 Massachusetts Ave NW, Room 8290, Washington, D.C. 20226

Alabama
  111st EOD unit ·············· 334-745-0090
  Birmingham Police Dept ·············· 205-254-2107
  Florence Police Dept ·············· 256-760-6500
  Gadsden Police Dept ·············· 256-549-4500
  Huntsville Police Dept ·············· 256-722-7100
  Mobile Police Dept ·············· 251-621-9100
Alaska
  Anchorage Police Dept ·············· 907-786-8900
Arizona
  363rd EOD unit ·············· 602-267-2463
  Arizona DPS ·············· 602-223-2000
  Tucson Police Dept ·············· 520-791-4444
Arkansas
  Little Rock Fire Dept ·············· 501-371-4829
California
  Bakersfield Police Dept ·············· 661-326-3000
  Los Angeles PD EOD ·············· 213-485-7474
  San Francisco Police Dept ·············· 415-671-3169
  Santa Barbara Police Dept ·············· 805-897-2300
  Santa Clara Police Dept ·············· 408-296-2236
  Santa Cruz County Sheriff's Office ·············· 831-471-1121
  Santa Rosa Police Dept ·············· 707-543-3550
  USMC-Camp Pendleton ·············· 760-725-6325
  USN EOD GRP One ·············· 619-437-0727
  USN EOD MU 3 - Sheriff Dispatch ·············· 805-781-4550
  USN EOD MU 7 ·············· 800-873-4127
  Ventura County Sheriff's Dept ·············· 805-654-2311
  Visalia City Police Dept ·············· 559-713-4257
Colorado
  Arapahoe County Sheriff's Office ·············· 303-795-4711
  Colorado Bureau of Investigation ·············· 719-542-1133
  Colorado Springs Metro Explosives Unit ·············· 719-444-7712
  Denver City & County ·············· 303-839-2100
  Douglas County Sheriff's Office ·············· 303-660-7500
  Jefferson County Sheriff's Office ·············· 303-277-0211
Connecticut
  Connecticut State Police ·············· 860-685-8190
  Hartford Police Bomb Squad ·············· 860-527-6300
Delaware
  Delaware State Police HQ ·············· 302-739-5900
  Dover Police Dept ·············· 302-736-7111

Explosives

Florida

221st EOD	904-682-3133
Broward County Sheriff's Office	954-831-8360
Fort Lauderdale Police Dept	954-828-5700
Jacksonville County Sheriff's Office	904-630-2120
Metro-Dade Police Dept	305-476-5423
Monroe County Sheriff's Dept	305-292-7000
Orange County Sheriff's Office	407-836-4071
Tallahassee Police Dept	850-891-4201
USAF-Hurlburt AFB	850-884-6423

Georgia

Atlanta Police Dept	404-853-3434
Cobb County Police Dept	770-499-4182
Georgia Bureau of Investigations	404-244-2600
US Army EOD	404-469-5436
US Army National Guard	770-528-3219

Hawaii

Honolulu Police Dept	808-529-3328

Idaho

Ada County Sheriff's Office	208-377-6790

Illinois

Chicago Police Dept	312-746-7619
Dupage County Sheriff's Office	630-682-7256

Indiana

Evansville Police Dept	812-436-7956
Indiana State Police	317-332-4411
Marion County Sheriff's Office	317-231-8200

Iowa

Des Moines Police Dept	515-283-4800
Iowa State Fire Marshal	515-281-8622

Kansas

Kansas City Police Dept	913-576-6000
Topeka Police Dept	785-368-9551
Wichita Police Dept	316-268-4111

Kentucky

717th EOD Unit	270-798-2312
Kentucky State Police	502-222-0151
Louisville Police Dept	502-574-7010

Louisiana

Louisiana State Police	504-376-8180
New Orleans Police Dept	504-244-4600

Maine

Bangor Police Dept	207-947-7384
Maine State Police	207-624-7068

Maryland

Maryland State Fire Marshall	410-653-8980
Maryland State Police	410-535-1400

Massachusetts

Boston Police Dept Bomb Squad	617-343-4245

Explosives

Massachusetts State Police ·············· 508-820-2300
Springfield Police Dept ················· 413-787-6370
Michigan
  Dearborn Police Dept ················· 313-943-2240
  Grand Rapids Police Dept ··············· 616-456-3400
  Michigan State Police ················· 616-242-6650
Minnesota
  Bloomington Police Dept ··············· 952-563-4900
  Minneapolis Police Dept ··············· 612-673-5705
  St. Paul Police Dept ················· 651-291-1111
Mississippi
  Gulf Port Police Dept ················· 228-868-5959
  Hinds County Sheriff's Office ··············· 601-974-2900
Missouri
  Columbia Police Dept ················· 573-442-6131
  Kansas City Police Dept ··············· 816-482-8170
  Missouri State Police ················· 800-222-6400
  St. Louis Police Dept ················· 314-444-2500
Montana
  Missoula County Sheriff's Office ··············· 406-523-4810
Nebraska
  Lincoln Police Dept ················· 402-441-7204
  Nebraska State Patrol ················· 402-471-9680
  Omaha Police Dept ················· 402-444-5680
Nevada
  Las Vegas Police Dept ················· 702-795-3111
  Reno Police Dept ················· 775-334-2121
New Hampshire
  Nashua Police Dept ················· 603-594-3500
  Rockingham County Sheriff's Office ··············· 603-772-4716
New Jersey
  54th EOD ················· 732-532-7055
  Atlantic City Police Dept ··············· 609-347-5780
  Bergen County Sheriff's Office ··············· 201-599-6210
  Camden County Sheriff's Office ··············· 856-783-1333
  Essex County Sheriff's Office ··············· 973-621-4111
  New Jersey State Police ··············· 609-882-2000
  Union County Police Dept ··············· 908-654-9800
New Mexico
  49th EOD- Holliman AFB ··············· 505-572-5141
  Albuquerque Police Dept ··············· 505-768-2200
  New Mexico State Police ··············· 505-841-9251
New York
  Nassau County Sheriff's Office ··············· 516-573-5550
  New York City Police Dept ··············· 212-741-4835
  Orange County Sheriff's Office ··············· 845-291-4033
North Carolina
  18th EOD Unit ················· 910-396-5801
  Charlotte Police Dept ················· 704-353-1000

Explosives

Gastonia Police Dept	704-866-3300
Greensboro Police Dept	336-373-2216
North Carolina Bureau of Investigation	800-334-3000
Raleigh Police Dept	919-890-3375

North Dakota

Bismarck Police Dept	701-223-1212
Cass County Sheriff's Office	701-241-5858
Grand Forks Police Dept	701-746-2500

Ohio

Cincinnati Fire Division	513-352-2314
Cleveland Police Dept	216-444-8439
Franklin County Sheriff's Office	614-462-3360
Lima Police Dept	419-227-4444
Toledo Police Dept	419-245-3340

Oklahoma

Oklahoma City Police Dept	405-297-1000
Tulsa Police Dept	918-596-9328

Oregon

Oregon State Police	503-378-2110
Portland Police Dept	503-823-3333

Pennsylvania

Allentown Fire Dept.	610-437-7665
Bethlehem Fire Dept.	610-865-7140
Delaware County CID	610-891-4700
Montgomery County Sheriff	610-278-3331
Philadelphia Police Dept	215-335-8013
Pittsburgh Police Dept	412-255-2814
Reading Police Dept	610-376-7481
Scranton Police Dept	570-348-4130

Rhode Island

Fire Marshal Office	401-243-6050
Warwick Police Dept	401-737-2244

South Carolina

Charleston Police Dept	843-577-7074
USN EOD MU12	843-743-0525

South Dakota

Sioux Falls Police Dept	605-367-7230

Tennessee

Chattanooga Police Dept	423-698-9523
Johnson City Police Dept	423-434-6125
Kingsport Police Dept	423-229-9434
Knoxville Police Dept	865-215-7450
Morristown Police Dept	423-585-4683
Nashville	615-862-7740

Texas

Austin Police Dept	512-406-0078
Dallas Police Dept	214-670-3000
Houston Police Dept	713-646-3910
Pasadena Police Dept	713-477-1221

Explosives

San Antonio Police Dept ································· 210-207-7559
Utah
   Utah County Sheriff's Office ··················· 801-343-4130
Vermont
   Vermont State Police ······························· 802-878-7111
Virginia
   Navy EOD MU 2 ···································· 757-462-8452
   Virginia Beach Police Dept···················· 757-427-4141
   Virginia State Police ····························· 804-674-2000
Washington
   Pierce County Sheriff's Office ················· 253-798-7530
   Seattle Police Dept······························· 206-684-8980
   Spokane Police Dept······························ 509-625-4210
   USN EOD MU11 ··································· 360-257-4480
   Washington State Police ························· 425-455-7700
Washington, D.C.
   749th EOD Unit ···································· 202-685-3119
   US Capitol Police ································· 202-228-2800
West Virginia ··· None listed
Wisconsin
   Kenosha Police Dept······························ 262-605-5200
   Milwaukee Police Dept··························· 414-933-4444
Wyoming
   Albany County Sheriff's Office················ 307-721-2526
   Laramie County Sheriff's Office··············· 307-633-4705

Vehicle Bomb Explosion Hazards and Evacuation Distance Tables

Vehicle Description	Maximum Explosives Capacity Pounds (Kilos)	Lethal Air Blast Range Feet (Meters)	Minimum Evacuation Distance Feet (Meters)	Falling Glass Hazard Feet (Meters)
Compact Sedan	500 (227) (in trunk)	100 (30)	1,500 (457)	1,250 (381)
Full Sized Sedan	1,000 (455)	125 (38)	1,750 (534)	1,750 (534)
Van, Passenger or Cargo	4,000 (1,818)	200 (61)	2,750 (838)	2,750 (838)
Small Box Van	10,000 (4,545)	300 (91)	3,750 (1,143)	3,750 (1,143)
Box Van or Fuel/Water Truck	30,000 (13,636)	450 (137)	6,500 (1,982)	6,500 (1,982)
Semi-Trailer	60,000 (27,273)	600 (183)	7,000 (2,134)	7,000 (2,134)

Source: Dept. of the Treasury, Bureau of Alcohol, Firearms and Tobacco, updated 1/14/99.

FIRST AID

Priorities · **128**

CPR · **131**

Heimlich Maneuver · **133**

Mouth to Mouth · **134**

Other First Aid Information

Bites · 135
Bleeding · 136
Broken Bones · 137
Burns · 137
Choking · 140
Diabetic Emergencies · 140
Electric Shock · 141
Eye Injuries · 142
Frostbite · 142
Head and Spine Injuries · 143
Heart Attack · 144
Heat Emergencies · 145
Hypothermia · 145
Nose Injuries · 147
Poisoning · 147
Puncture Wounds to the Torso · · · · · · · · · · · · · · · 150
Seizures · 150
Shock · 151
Stroke · 151
Small Animal Artificial Respiration & CPR · · · · · · · · 152

First Aid

CAUTION

This section is intended for use by personnel who have already been trained in first aid; it is not a substitute for such training, nor for the expert care and advice of a licensed physician. Sequoia Publishing, Inc. does not give medical advice and is not responsible for any use which may be made of this information. Recommended procedures change often as knowledge increases; this section may become outdated.

In each of the states within the United States, a series of laws have been adopted in order to provide immunity to individuals who volunteer assistance in emergency situations. These are called the Good Samaritan Laws. The laws grant immunity from liability if the rescuer acts in good faith within the level of care administered according to his/her level of training. It will not prevent someone from filing a lawsuit against a rescuer; however, it does afford some level of immunity. If gross negligence or violations of the law can be proven, then the rescuer is at risk for judgement.

The most critical emergency procedures are listed in the front for ease of access. Be sure to follow any procedures required by your agency or the priority list below.

Priorities

Assessment of the scene: If approaching a scene where an individual is in need of help, the rescuer should do the following:

1. Make sure the scene is safe

The scene should be safe before getting close to the person in need. This is important ... the rescuer does not want to add to the problem by becoming another victim.

2. Assess the number of persons in need

3. Call for help

Do this as soon as possible, because later you might be so busy with the person in need that it is almost impossible to stop and call. Call for help, even if you think you don't need it; situations can change rapidly.

4. Practice BSI (Body Substance Isolation)

This means keep the person's body fluids away from the rescuer's body. Whenever possible, use personal protective equipment, such as latex gloves, pocket mask, and goggles. A cloth barrier between the rescuer and the injured person is better than no protection. Harmful blood-borne pathogens, as well as other diseases, may be transmitted without protection. If possible, exercise BSI when giving mouth-to-mouth breathing.

5. Assess the nature of the illness

What facts are present to have caused this situation? Is this person a trauma victim or do they have a medical problem? Is the condition obvious or unknown?

6. Assess the person in need by: AVPU

A	Alert	Is the person alert?
V	Verbal	Does the person respond verbally?
P	Pupils equally reactive to light	This can be done quickly if the rescuer is trained. If not trained, mentally note what the eyes look like.
U	Unconscious	Non-responsive to stimuli.

A & V can be ascertained by asking: Are you OK? May I help you? It is imperative to ask a sick person if you can help them, even if they are unconscious. This is called consent and it legally protects the rescuer. In a situation where a child is involved and there is no parent present, the rescuer can proceed without verbal consent. An unconscious person is deemed as implied consent.

7. Perform the ABCs (Airway, Breathing, Circulation)

Perform the ABCs after placing the sick person in a supine position (laying on his/her back). If possible, this should always be done (i.e. not possible if victim has a knife in his/her back).

A: Airway

If the sick person is either conscious or unconscious, check for breathing. Look, listen, feel. Look for the chest to rise, listen to hear any breathing, and feel if there is any air coming from the person's mouth or nose. If there is none, do either a head tilt or jaw thrust (if trauma is suspected). Sometimes the tongue can be the obstruction if the person is unconscious. If there is still no breath, check mouth for any obstruction. Then give two rescue breaths. If airway is obstructed by an object, see Heimlich Manuever on page 133.

B: Breathing

If possible, distressed people should be administered oxygen.
Rescue breaths:

Age	Ventilation Duration	Ventilation Rate
Infant (Birth-1 yr)	1-1.5 seconds	20 breaths/minute
Child (1 yr - 8 yrs)	1-1.5 seconds	20 breaths/minute
8 Years to Adult	2 seconds	10-12 breaths/min.

First Aid

Adequate rates of breathing:
Adult = 12-20 breaths per minute
Child = 15-30 breaths per minute
Infant= 25-50 breaths per minute

C: Circulation

- Check for pulse; use carotid artery for adult and brachial artery for children or infants.

Normal pulse rates at rest: (beats per minute)

Age	Rate
Birth-5 months	120 to 160
6 months-12 months	90 to 140
1 year - 3 years	80 to 130
3 years - 5 years	80 to 120
6 years - 10 years	70 to 110
11 years - 14 years	60 to 105
Adult	60 to 100

If there is no pulse or pulse starts to fall below the above limits, start CPR (page 131).

- Check for external hemorrhage. A quick sweep of the body with hands placed underneath the person and checking all limbs. Signs of external hemorrhage are cool, damp skin, pallor, profuse sweating, fast, weak pulse, thirst, blurred vision, shallow breathing, agitation, and shock.
- Internal hemorrhage has signs of bruising, swelling, pain over vital organs, distortion of extremity, bleeding from body orifice, a tender, rigid, or distended abdomen, dark brown substance vomited, dark tarry stools, excessive thirst, impaired breathing, irregular pulse, and signs of shock.

8. Positioning

If the victim and the rescuer are waiting for additional help, they have done all that is possible within the rescuer's level of training, and the victim is breathing adequately, the rescuer can place the victim on his/her side. This is called the recovery position and is the preferred position for an unconscious person as they may start to vomit. Someone who you suspect may be having a heart problem should be placed in a semi-sitting (Fowler's) position. Someone who is going into shock or who may already be in shock should be placed in the Trendelenburg position (legs elevated and body supine). Person with suspected head or spinal injury should be placed in a supine position and immobilized. If the person has a possible spinal injury, the rescuer should not move the victim, especially if the rescuer is alone, unless the situation itself is life-threatening to the victim. Victims should be placed in a position that is comfortable for them.

9. Document everything

If first aid is administered by an untrained responder, no documentation is required. The responder is covered under Good Samaritan Laws. Professional responders are required to document each incident. If an untrained responder has document the incident, that documentation becomes part of the record. It is advantageous for untrained responders to refrain from documenting.

CPR

Before beginning, see Priorities on page 128.
- Place person on his back and open his mouth.

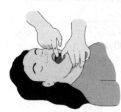

- Sweep your index finger through the person's mouth to dislodge any obstruction, being careful not to force anything farther down the throat. Never do finger sweeps on an infant or small child when you can't see into the throat.

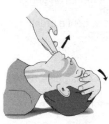

- If nothing is dislodged, put one hand on the victim's forehead and the other under his chin to tilt his head back and open the airway.

- Pinch his nose closed and blow two full breaths into his mouth, pausing in between to take a breath yourself.

First Aid

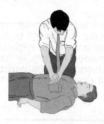

- If victim does not begin to breathe, straddle his thighs or kneel next to him.
- Put the heel of one hand just above the notch at the bottom of the breast bone. Cover that hand with your other hand, fingers interlaced.
- Keeping your elbows straight, shoulders directly above the hands, push sharply inward and upward about 1 ½ inches, 15 times in 10 seconds.
- After 15 compressions, retilt his head, and blow twice into his mouth slowly, with the nose pinched closed, pausing in between to breathe for yourself.
- **If the victim is a child**, the cycle is 5 compressions and 1 breath. Each compression should be about 1½ inches deep and take about 3 seconds, each breath about 1 ½ seconds.
- **If the victim is an infant** (less than 1 year old):

  – Put fingers on the infant's breast bone just below the level of the nipples. Give 5 compressions of about 3 seconds each.
  – Seal the infant's mouth and nose with your mouth.
  – Then give 1 slow, gentle breath for about 1½ seconds.

- Repeat the cycle four times, then check for a pulse.
- When you feel a pulse in the neck, stop compressing, but continue mouth-to-mouth until the person starts breathing on their own.

Continue the cycle of compressions and breaths until:
- The person begins to breathe on their own.
- Another trained person takes over from you.
- You are exhausted and unable to continue.
- The scene becomes unsafe.

Heimlich Maneuver

If the victim is conscious:

- Stand behind the victim.
- Put your arms around the victim's waist.
- Make a fist with one hand and put the thumb against the victim's abdomen, below the breast bone and above the navel - even with their bottom rib.
- Grasp your fist with the other hand and thrust it sharply upward into the victim's abdomen, keeping your elbows out.
- Repeat until the object is expelled. If the victim becomes unconscious, see below.

If the victim is unconscious, call an ambulance, then:

- Lay the victim on their back and open their mouth.
- Sweep your index finger in a hooking motion to remove the object, being careful not to push it farther down the throat. **Never perform blind finger sweeps on an infant or small child.**
- If that doesn't dislodge the object, put one hand on the victim's forehead and the other under their chin to tilt their head back, opening the airway.
- Pinch their nose closed and blow two full breaths into their mouth, pausing in-between to breathe yourself.
- If the victim does not begin to breathe, straddle their thighs. Put the heel of one hand in the center of their abdomen, between the breastbone and the navel. Put your other hand on top of the first one, with fingers interlaced.
- Keep your elbows straight, press the abdomen sharply inward and upward, 6-10 times.
- Check the victim's mouth again to see if the obstruction has been forced out. If so, sweep it out with your finger.
- Repeat these steps until the object comes out or medical help arrives.

To clear a blocked airway in an infant: Give back blows and chest thrusts.

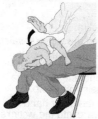

- Hold the infant face down on your forearm, with its face in your hand.
- Strike the infant between the shoulder blades 5 times with your other hand.

- Turn the infant over and put 2 or 3 fingers in the center of its breast bone. Give 5 thrusts with your fingers, each about 1 inch deep.
- Repeat sequence of back blows and chest thrusts as needed.

Mouth to Mouth Breathing

- Open the victim's airway by putting the heel of your hand against their forehand and your fingertips under their jaw. Push the forehead down and lift the jaw until it is pointing straight up.
- Pinch the victim's nose closed and blow two full breaths into their mouth, pausing in-between to breathe yourself.
- If you feel a pulse, but the victim is not breathing, continue with mouth-to-mouth breathing;
  - 1 breath every 5 seconds for an adult.
  - 1 breath every 3 seconds for an infant.

Bites

Animal Bites:
- If the victim is not bleeding heavily, clean the wound thoroughly with soap and water, apply antibiotic, and cover. A severe wound should be cleaned only by trained medical personnel.
- Because of the danger of infection, see a doctor for all bites.

Snake Bites:
- Wash wound with soap and water.
- Keep the bite lower than the heart and don't move it.
- Call for emergency medical help.

Insect Bites (and stings):
Life-threatening allergic reactions are the major danger with insect bites.
Symptoms:
- Seek medical help immediately if any of these signs are present: swelling of throat, pain, itching, hives, redness at the site of the bite, difficult or noisy breathing, and/or decreased consciousness.

Treatment:
- Remove the stinger if there is one.
- Wash the wound with soap and water.
- Use a cold compress to relieve pain and swelling.
- Keep the stung area lower than the heart to slow circulation of the venom.

Spider or Scorpion Stings:
- Wash the wound with soap and water.
- Use a cold compress to relieve pain and swelling.
- Get medical care to receive antivenin.
- If reaction is severe, seek emergency medical help.

First Aid

Bleeding

Bleeding wound:

- Apply pressure directly on the wound with a piece of cloth, or your hand if nothing else is available. Keep the pressure in place; if the victim bleeds through the dressing, just put a new one over it.
- If bleeding continues, elevate the wound above the level of the heart.

Do not elevate a broken arm or leg.

- If the victim is still bleeding, apply pressure at a pressure point.

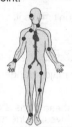

- **Arms** - inside of the wrist (radial artery) or inside of the upper arm (Brachial artery).

- **Legs** - at the crease in the groin (femoral artery).

- Check to be sure you have not impaired the victim's circulation. Ease pressure if pulse rate slows or fingertips or toes turn bluish.

- If bleeding continues, wrap a roll of gauze (or whatever is available) tightly around the dressing. Again, check to be sure the bandage isn't cutting off the victim's circulation.
- If a foreign object is embedded in the wound, don't try to remove it. Removal may increase the bleeding.
  - Hold the edges of the wound together around the object for up to ten minutes.
  - If holding the wound together is ineffective, put a thick "doughnut" of clean cloth, thicker than the object if possible, over the wound. Hold the cloth in place with diagonal strips of bandage that do not go directly over the object.
  - Get the victim to a hospital immediately.

Bleeding from nose, mouth or ear:

- Position the victim so that the bleeding area points downward and blood can flow out. Put a dressing underneath to catch blood, but do not apply pressure. Call an ambulance. If the victim loses consciousness, roll them on their side and monitor for pulse and breathing.

Broken Bones

Fractures, sprains, strains and dislocations are difficult to diagnose and should all be handled as if they were breaks. All such injuries require professional medical attention.

Symptoms:
- Pain, tenderness, swelling, bruising, inability to move the injured part. Victim may feel as though two bones are rubbing together.

Treatment:
- Control bleeding (page 136).
- Treat for shock (page 151).
- Apply cold packs to reduce pain and swelling.
- Splint if necessary and can be done without causing the victim more pain.
- **Do not try to move the victim** unless he is still in danger. If you MUST move a person, stabilize their head and neck first, and keep the spinal cord as still as possible during the process.

Burns

All serious burns (second or third degree burns; burns of the eye, mouth or nose; or burns that cover 15% or more of the body) require professional medical attention. Burn victims under the age of 5 and over the age of 55 are at greater risk.

Burns are normally classified by the depth of damage.

- **Superficial burn:** Affects only the upper epidermis (the outer layer) of the skin. Symptoms are pain, redness, and swelling.
- **Partial-thickness burn:** Affects the epidermis and the dermis (the second layer) of the skin. Symptoms are intense pain, reddening, blisters, mottled appearance of the skin. This is sometimes referred to as a second-degree burn.
- **Full-thickness burn:** Affects all three layers of the skin, the epidermis, the dermis, and the fat and muscle layer. Symptoms are charred black, brown, or grayish/white areas, and severe pain may be present if the nerves have not been damaged in the affected area. This is sometimes referred to as a third-degree burn.

First Aid

Adult	Children less than 5 years
Minor Burn	
• Superficial burns involving less than 50% of body surface • Partial-thickness burn involving less than 15% of the body surface • Full-thickness burn involving less than 2% of the body surface (excluding respiratory tract, face, hands, genitalia or feet)	• A Partial-thickness burn involving less than 10% of the body surface
Moderate Burn	
• Superficial burn involvingmore than 50% of body surface • Partial-thickness burn involving 15% to 30% of the body surface • Full-thickness burn involving 2% to 10% of the body surface (excluding respiratory tract, face, hands, genitalia or feet)	• A Partial-thickness burn of 10% to 20% of the body surface.
Critical Burn	
• Partial-thickness burn involving the respiratory tract, hands, feet, and/or genitalia and covering more than 30% of the body surface • Full-thickness burn involving more than 10% of the body surface • Circumferential burn (a burn that covers all of the way around the patient's arm, neck, fingers, chest or legs) • Any burn involving injuries to the respiratory tract (and other soft tissues) and the musculoskeletal system	• A Full-thickness burn of any extent or partial-thickness burn of more than 20% of the body surface.

Rule of Nine

The Rule of Nine is used for estimating the extent of a burn.

Adult Percentage of Body Surface Area:

Head	9%
Front of Torso (each side is 9%)	18%
Back of Torso (each side is 9%)	18%
Arms (each arm is 9%)	18%
Legs (each leg is 18%)	36%
Perineum (genital region)	1%
Total body	100%

<u>Child Percentage of Body Surface Area:</u>

Head	18%
Front of Torso (each side is 9%)	18%
Back of Torso (each side is 9%)	18%
Arms (each arm is 9%)	18%
Legs (each leg is 14%)	28%
Total body	100%

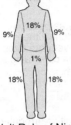

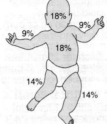

Adult Rule of Nine   Child Rule of Nine

Rule of Palm

The Rule of Palm is used for estimating the extent of a burn. The palm of the patient's hand equals about 1% of their body surface area. To estimate the size of the burn, compare the burned area to their palm to get a percentage.

Treatment for Thermal Burns:

1. Immediately call 911 for help!
2. Stop the burning process! If flame, wet down, smother, then remove clothing. If burning agent is grease, tar, or wax, cool with water and do not remove the agent.
3. Check breathing and airway, especially if burn is in respiratory area.
4. Treat for shock.
5. Try to classify burn as to superficial, partial-thickness, full-thickness and as to minor moderate, or critical.
6. Do not clear any debris from burned body. Remove clothing and jewelry.
7. Wrap with dry sterile dressing or burn sheet.
8. If fingers and toes are burned, make sure jewelry is removed and place sterile gauze pads between the fingers and toes. If eyes are burned, do not open eyelids. Make certain that the burn is a thermal burn, not a chemical burn. Apply sterile gauze pads to both eyes. If burn is chemical, flush with water for 20 minutes.

First Aid

Treatment for Chemical Burns:

1. Immediately call 911 for help!
2. Try to identify the chemical; ask what it is. Do not try to neutralize the chemical with another kind of chemical.
3. Flush the area with water that is a gentle stream for 20 minutes. If a dry chemical is used, brush away as much chemical as possible and then flush the area.
4. Precautions for contamination of wash area and other people should be taken.
5. Apply a sterile dressing or burn sheet.
6. Treat for shock and transport as rapidly as possible.
7. If the eye is affected by the burn, first identify the chemical, flush for 20 minutes, then cover both eyes with sterile moistened pads. If burned victim complains after flushing is stopped, continue to flush.

Treatment for Electrical Burns:

1. Immediately call 911 for help!
2. Treat for shock and respiratory failure.
3. Victim may have a seizure, visual difficulties, irregular heart beat, respiratory distress, irritability, loss of consciousness, shock, and physical injuries.
4. Apply a dry, sterile dressing to burn sites.

Choking

If a person is choking, but can speak or cough forcibly, encourage them to keep coughing and stand by.

If a choking person CANNOT speak or cough, the airway obstruction must be cleared via the Heimlich Maneuver (pg 133).

Diabetic Emergencies

Insulin shock and diabetic coma are two opposite types of emergencies. Insulin shock results from too much insulin in the body; diabetic coma from too much sugar or too little insulin. If a person is unconscious, check for a bracelet identifying the victim as a diabetic.

It can be hard to tell which reaction a person is having.

• ASK "Have you eaten today?" If "yes":
• ASK "Did you take your medication today?"
• Has eaten/no medication = Diabetic Coma
• Has NOT eaten, has taken medication = Insulin Shock

Insulin Shock:
- **Symptoms:** Rapid breathing and pulse, dizziness, weakness, change in level of consciousness, vision difficulties, sweating, headache, numbness in hands or feet, and hunger. May appear to be drunk without the smell of alcohol.

Diabetic Coma:
- **Symptoms:** Develops slowly; preceding symptoms include drowsiness, confusion, deep and fast breathing, thirst, dehydration, fever, sweet or fruity smelling breath, and change in level of consciousness.

Treatment: Always call an ambulance immediately.
- Immediately feed the person something high in sugar (candy, fruit juice, soft drink). **Insulin shock is life threatening,** and sugar can literally be a life saver and won't hurt someone in diabetic coma.

Electric Shock

Do not touch the victim until you have eliminated risk of shock to yourself.
- Unplug appliances or turn off power at the fuse box.
- If you cannot turn off the electricity, use a nonconductive material, such as dry fabric or wood, to move the victim away from the power source.
- Always get professional help for someone who has been shocked, since injuries can be internal and electrical burns can cause electrolyte imbalance, muscle breakdown, and even kidney failure.

High-Voltage:
Electricity from power lines, industrial equipment, railway, subway, or streetcar systems can produce shock up to 20 feet away. **Stay clear and call an ambulance or 911.**
- Perform CPR if unconscious and NOT breathing (page 131).
- If unconscious and breathing, roll on their side and wait for help.
- Treat burns appropriately (page 137).

First Aid

Lightning:
Injuries can range from a minor stun to death, and may cause heart attack, asphyxiation, severe burns, broken bones, and burn or melt clothing and jewelry.
- If the victim's clothes are on fire, extinguish the flames by rolling the victim on the ground, covering with a heavy blanket, or dousing with water.
- Perform CPR if unconscious and NOT breathing (page 131).
- If unconscious and breathing, roll on their side and wait for help.
- Treat burns appropriately (page 137).

Eye Injuries

Eye injuries must be treated very, very gently. Prompt medical help is important to save the person's eyesight.
- If you can see something floating in the eye, try to flush it out with water. If that doesn't work, seek medical attention.
- If something is embedded in the eye, do not try to remove it. Bandage both eyes and go to an emergency room or clinic. Place a paper cup upside down on the injured eye and hold it in place with a bandage.
- Chemical burns: Flush the eye with lots of lukewarm water for 15-30 minutes, then bandage both eyes and get medical attention.

Frostbite

If a person has frostbite, be alert for signs of hypothermia. Call 911 or a doctor for advice on how to handle the frostbite.
Symptoms:
- **Superficial frostbite:** Skin has white or gray patches and feels firm, but not hard. Once frostbite sets in, it is not painful. There will be no tissue loss if it is treated properly.
- **Deep frostbite:** May involve an entire finger, toe, or other body part. The skin feels hard and cold, and affected tissue looks white or gray. Skin does not rebound when pressed. No pulse can be felt in the affected area.

Treatment:
- If possible, take the patient to a hospital while protecting the frozen area from further damage.

First Aid

- **DO NOT:**
    - Rub the frozen tissue.
    - Apply ice or snow to the area.
    - Use cold water or high temperatures to try to thaw the frozen part.
    - Give the victim alcohol or tobacco.
    - Break any blister which may form.
- **Rewarming Tissue:** It is best not to rewarm the tissue in the field, unless there is no alternative.
    - The risk of damage due to improper warming is greater than the risk of delaying treatment.
    - Tissue that is thawed and then refreezes nearly always dies. Frostbitten tissue must be handled extremely gently.
    - If thawing in the field is necessary, use water warmed between 100-106°F in a container large enough for the whole frostbitten area to be submerged without touching the bottom or sides. Water must be maintained at this temperature, so an additional source of water is necessary. Gently circulate the water around the frozen area until the tip becomes flushed.
    - Warmed tissue is extremely painful. Get advice from a physician for pain relief. Pain after rewarming usually indicates that treatment has been successful.
    - Keep rewarmed extremities above heart level if possible.
    - If feet have been frostbitten and rewarmed, do not allow the patient to walk on them unless their life (or yours) depends on it.

Head and Spine Injuries

Symptoms:
- Bleeding, bumps, or depressions on the head, neck or back
- Bruises around eyes or behind ears
- Changes in consciousness
- Inability to move any body part
- Pain in the head, neck, or back
- Numbness or tingling in fingers, toes, hands, or feet
- Seizures
- Persistent headache
- Nausea or vomiting

First Aid

- Loss of balance
- Difficulty seeing or breathing after the injury

Treatment:
- Immobilize the head and neck as much as possible
- Keep airway open
- Monitor breathing, pulse, and consciousness
- Control bleeding (page 136)
- Maintain victim's normal body temperature
- Get professional medical attention

Heart Attack

Symptoms:
- Chest Pain which the victim may describe as pressure, tightness, aching, crushing, fullness, constricting, or heaviness. Many victims think they have heartburn!
  - The pain may be in the center of the chest, one or both shoulders or arms, the neck, jaw or back. Pain does not go away when the victim stops moving.
- Sweating
- Nausea
- Shortness of breath
- Changes in pulse rate
- Pale or bluish skin color

Treatment:
Recognize the symptoms of a heart attack, call 911 immediately. Do not wait to be sure!
- Calm the victim so that fear does not make the problem worse.
- Have the victim stop activity and sit or lie in a comfortable position.
- Loosen clothing as needed to ease circulation and breathing.
- Monitor victim's condition.
- A victim who is unconscious or whose heart has stopped will need CPR (page 131).

First Aid

Heat Emergencies

Heat Cramps:
- **Symptoms:** Heavy exertion results in muscle pain and spasms, usually in leg or abdominal muscles.
- **Treatment:** Get victim to a cool place and give him one-half glass of cool water every 15 minutes.

Heat Exhaustion:
- **Symptoms:** Cool, pale, or moist skin, heavy sweating, dilated pupils, headache, nausea, dizziness, and vomiting. Body temperature appears to be near normal.
- **Treatment:** Move the victim to a cool place and have them lie on their back with feet elevated. Remove or loosen clothing. Apply cold packs, wet towels, or sheets to their body; or fan the victim if these are not available. Give water every 15 minutes, if the victim is conscious.

Heat Stroke:

Heat stroke is life threatening - begin to cool the victim and call for medical help immediately!
- **Symptoms:** Sweat glands shut down so there is no perspiration. Hot, dry, and red skin. Pupils are contracted very small. Body temperature is very high, even up to 105°F. Victim may refuse water, vomit, or lose consciousness.
- **Treatment: ACT IMMEDIATELY!** Cool the victim as soon as possible in any way you can. Place in a bathtub of cool water, wrap in wet sheets, or put in an air conditioned room. Do not wait for help to arrive! Treat for shock (page 151) and do not give anything by mouth.

Hypothermia

Mild:
- **Symptoms:** Shivering, loss of coordination, complains of being cold.
- **Treatment:**
    - Move victim to someplace warm and dry.
    - Add more clothing, or replace wet clothing with dry.
    - Cover the victim's head and neck.
    - Put a barrier between the victim and the ground.

First Aid

- Cover the victim with a space blanket or other vapor barrier.
  - Offer warm nonalcoholic liquids or food.
  - Encourage the victim to move around to generate more heat.
  - Apply heat packs to head, neck, underarms, sides of chest, or groin. Insulate heavily to prevent further heat loss.
  - Warm shower or bath if available and victim is alert.
  - As a last resort, have someone who is NOT hypothermic get into a sleeping bag with the victim. This method may endanger the rescuer. Two people who are hypothermic should not do this.

Moderate:
- **Symptoms:** Listless, confused, does not recognize the problem, shivers uncontrollably, uncoordinated, and speech slurred.
- **Treatment:** Same as mild treatment (above), but cover the victim rather than moving them. Do not allow victim to exercise or move, treat very gently. Check for other injuries, including frostbite (page 142).

Severe:
- **Symptoms:** Internal temperature of 90°F (32.2° C) or less. Unconsciousness, slow pulse and respiration, no shivering, physical collapse, and unresponsive to pain or words.
- **Treatment:** Severe hypothermia is life-threatening. **Call for professional care!** If pulse and respiration are present, treat as above, but don't give oral fluids unless completely conscious. Do not put the person in a warm shower or bath, and be careful to handle the person very gently. Do not rub hands or feet.
- If pulse and respiration are not present, take the above measures to rewarm the person, start CPR (page 131), and get to a medical facility immediately.

Nose Injuries

Most nosebleeds can be controlled by having the victim:

- Sit down and pinch the nose shut.
- Lean forward in order to prevent blood from running into the throat.
- Since walking, talking, or blowing the nose can start the bleeding again, the person should rest quietly until certain that the bleeding has stopped. A severe nosebleed can lead to shock if enough blood is lost.
- If nose bleed occurs in someone who has had a head, neck, or back injury, **DO NOT** attempt to control the bleeding, as it may increase pressure on the injured area. Get medical help immediately.

Poisoning

Poisons cause very different symptoms and require very different treatments. Call a certified Poison Control Center or 911 immediately if you suspect poisoning.

Inhaled Poisons:
Get the victim to fresh air and avoid breathing the fumes yourself. Open doors and windows if it can be done safely. Start CPR (page 131) if the victim is not breathing.

Poison in the Eye:
Rinse the eye with lukewarm water from a pitcher or glass for 15 minutes. Do not force the eyelid open, but have the victim blink as much as possible while rinsing.

Poison on the Skin:
Remove any clothing that has the poison on it. Rinse the skin with running water for 15 minutes.

Swallowed Poisons:
- Remove any remaining substance from the mouth.
- **Chemical or household products:** If the victim is conscious and not having convulsions or is unable to swallow, give one glass of milk or water to drink. Do not force them to drink.
- **Medicines:** Do nothing until instructed by the Poison Control Center.

First Aid

Poison Control Centers (PCCs)

Nationwide Referral Toll-Free Number: 1-800-222-1222
Dialing this number from anywhere in the US will connect you to the nearest local poison control center.

Have the following information available when calling:

❑ Name, age and sex of the victim.

❑ Exact name of the substance involved. If possible, have the container at hand.

❑ Estimate the amount of poison involved.

❑ The time the poisoning occurred.

❑ Any symptoms or preexisting medical conditions.

❑ How the poisoning occurred.

❑ Anything else you think they should know.

Certified Poison Control Centers

Location	Local Emergency Number	Administration
Alabama, Birmingham	800-292-6678	205-939-9201
Tuscaloosa	800-462-0800	205-345-0600
Alaska	800-478-3193	907-261-3193
Arizona, Phoenix	800-362-0101	602-253-3334
Tucson	800-362-0101	520-626-6016
Arkansas	800-376-4766	
California	800-876-4766	
Colorado	800-332-3073	
Denver metro	303-739-1123	
Connecticut	800-343-2722	860-679-3456
Delaware	800-722-7112	215-386-2100
Florida, Jacksonville	800-282-3171	904-549-4480
Miami	800-282-3171	305-585-5253
Tampa	800-282-3171	813-253-4444
Georgia	800-282-5846	404-616-9000
Hawaii		808-941-4411
Idaho	800-860-0620	
Illinois	800-942-5969	309-454-6666
Springfield		217-753-3330
Indiana	800-382-9097	317-929-2323
Iowa, Iowa City	800-272-6477	
Sioux City	800-352-2222	712-277-2222
Kansas	800-332-6633	913-588-6633
Kentucky	800-722-5725	502-589-8222
Louisiana	800-256-9822	318-362-5393
Maine	800-442-6305	207-871-2950
Maryland	800-492-2414	410-706-7701

Massachusetts	800-682-9211	617-232-2120
Michigan, Detroit	800-764-7661	313-745-5711
Marquette	800-764-7661	906-225-3497
Minnesota	800-764-7661	612-347-3141
Mississippi	800-222-1222	601-354-7660
Missouri	800-366-8888	314-772-5200
Montana	800-525-5042	
Nebraska	800-955-9119	402-345-5555
Nevada	800-446-6179	
New Hampshire	800-562-8236	603-650-8000
New Jersey	800-764-7661	
New Mexico	800-432-6866	505-272-2222
New York, Buffalo	800-888-7655	716-878-7654
Hudson Valley	800-336-6997	914-366-3030
Long Island		516-542-2323
New York City	800-210-3985	212-340-4494
Rochester	800-333-0542	716-275-3232
Syracuse	800-252-5655	315-476-4766
North Carolina	800-848-6946	704-355-4000
North Dakota	800-732-2200	701-234-5575
Ohio, Cincinnati	800-872-5111	513-558-5111
Cleveland	888-231-4455	216-231-4455
Columbus	800-682-7625	614-228-1323
Oklahoma	800-764-7661	405-271-5454
Oregon	800-452-7165	503-494-8968
Pennsylvania, Erie	800-822-3232	
Hershey	800-521-6110	717-531-6111
Philadelphia	800-722-7112	215-386-2100
Pittsburgh		412-681-6669
Rhode Island	800-682-9211	401-444-5727
South Carolina	800-922-1117	803-777-1117
South Dakota	800-764-7661	612-347-3141
Tennessee, Memphis	800-288-9999	901-528-6048
Nashville	800-288-9999	615-936-2034
Texas, Galveston	800-764-7661	409-765-1420
Temple	800-764-7661	254-724-7401
Utah	800-456-7707	801-581-2151
Vermont	877-658-3456	802-658-3456
Virginia, Charlotteville	800-451-1428	804-924-5543
Richmond	800-552-6337	804-828-9123
Washington	800-732-6985	206-526-2121
Washington, D.C.		202-625-3333
West Virginia	800-642-3625	
Wisconsin, Madison	800-815-8855	608-262-3702
Milwaukee	800-815-8855	414-266-2222
Wyoming	800-955-9119	402-354-5555

First Aid

Puncture Wound to the Torso

Stab or bullet wounds to the chest or abdomen may create unusual problems:

"Sucking" Chest Wound:

- When a lung or the chest cavity is punctured, air can move in and out through the wound, causing a "sucking" sound and preventing the lungs from functioning properly.
- Cover the wound with a dressing that air cannot pass through and tape it down, leaving one corner loose.

Abdominal Wound:

- A puncture wound to the abdomen may cause organs to protrude outside the body.
- The victim should be placed on their back.
- Do not apply pressure to the protruding organ or try to push it back in.
- Remove any clothing that is near the wound.
- Cover the wound with a sterile, moist dressing.

Seizures

Symptoms:

- Uncontrollable muscle spasms, rigidity, unconsciousness, loss of bladder and bowel control. Breathing may stop temporarily.

Treatment:

- Don't try to restrain the person or put anything in their mouth.
- Move furniture and equipment out of the way and loosen the person's clothes.
- If vomiting occurs, turn the person on their side.
- Stay with the victim until they are fully conscious.

First Aid

Shock

Shock is insufficient blood supply to the heart, lungs, and brain. It can occur with any type of injury, usually within an hour afterward. Always take steps to prevent shock when you encounter an injured person. **Shock can be fatal if it goes untreated!**

Symptoms:
- Restlessness or irritability; confused behavior
- Weak, trembling arms or legs
- Skin looks pale or bluish, feels cool and moist
- Rapid pulse and/or breathing
- Pupils are enlarged

Treatment:
- Victim should lie down, with legs elevated unless there is a broken leg, or injury to the head or neck.
- Help maintain the victim's normal body temperature, but do not overheat.
- Control external bleeding, if any.
- If the victim vomits, lay on their side.
- If the victim has trouble breathing, they should assume a semi-reclining position.
- Do not give the victim anything to eat or drink.
- Get professional medical care.

Stroke

A stroke is an interruption of the brain's blood supply that lasts long enough to damage the brain. Recognize the symptoms and call for professional help.

Symptoms:
- Weakness or numbness in the face, arm, or leg; especially on only one side.
- Difficulty speaking
- Dizziness
- Confusion
- Headache
- Ringing ears
- Mood change
- Unconsciousness

First Aid

- Uneven-sized pupils
- Breathing and swallowing difficulty
- Loss of bowel and bladder control

Treatment:
- Have the victim rest.
- Keep the victim comfortable and calm, but don't let them eat or drink anything.
- If the person vomits, allow the vomit to drain away from the mouth by turning on their side.
- Keep an eye on the victim's breathing and circulation; be prepared to give CPR (page 131) if needed.

Small Animal Artificial Respiration and CPR (Dogs & Cats)

If a dog or cat has become unresponsive (unconscious), check for breathing and heart beat. If it is not breathing, but still has a heart beat, begin artificial respiration (rescue breathing) immediately (see below). If it has no heartbeat, begin CPR (page 153).

Check for Breathing and Pulse:
- **Look** to see if its chest is rising and falling, **listen** for breathing sounds, and **feel** for air coming from the nose for about 5 seconds.
- Check for a heartbeat by putting your hand over the animal's chest cavity where its elbow touches the middle of the chest.

Artificial Respiration:
- Place the animal on its right side on a flat surface.
- Check for a clear airway by opening the animal's mouth and looking inside. If the airway is blocked, pull the tongue outward. If that does not dislodge the blockage, use your fingers, pliers, or tongs to remove any foreign object. You may be able to hold a small dog or cat upside down by its back end and shake it to try to remove the obstruction.
- If the above methods do not work, try the Heimlich Maneuver:
  - Turn the animal upside down with its back against your chest.

- Using both arms, give 5 sharp thrusts to the abdomen.
- Check to see if an object has been dislodged; if it has, remove it.

- With the animal on its side, move its chin to straighten out the throat.

- For large dogs, hold the muzzle closed with one hand, and put your mouth completely over the nose. For small dogs and cats, you may be able to cover the nose and mouth completely with your mouth as you breathe.

- Blow gently into the animal's mouth, 2 times, just enough to move the chest. For cats and small dogs a gentle blow should be enough; for larger dogs, blow harder. Wait for air to leave the lungs before blowing again. If chest does not move, double check for and clear any obstructions.

Number of breaths per minute varies by animal size:
- Over 60 pounds, 10 breaths per minute.
- 11 to 60 pounds, 15 breaths per minute.
- Under 11 pounds, 20 breaths per minute.

- Monitor for heart beat (as described above).

CPR: If the animal's heart stops beating, begin CPR.

For cats and dogs under 30 pounds:
- Lay animal on its right side on a flat surface.

- Put the palm of your hand on the rib cage where the animal's elbow touches the middle of the chest. For puppies and kittens, put your thumb on one side of the rib cage and your fingers on the other side.

- Compress the chest about ½" to 1" at the rate of 80 to 100 compressions per minute.

- Alternate chest compressions with artificial respiration as above, 2 breaths per 15 compressions.

For Dogs over 30 pounds:
- Lay the dog on its right side on a flat surface.

- Put one hand on top of the other on the rib cage where its elbow touches the middle of the chest.

- Keep your arms straight and push down on the rib cage, compressing the chest ¼ of its width at a rate of about 80 compressions per minute.

- Alternate chest compressions with artificial respiration as above, 2 breaths per 15 compressions.

- Continue the cycle of compressions as needed.

First Aid

First Aid Chapter Sources:

American Red Cross, *Community First Aid and Safety,* St. Louis, MO: Mosby-Yearbook, Inc., 1993.

Brown, Robert E., *Emergency/Survival Handbook,* 5th Edition. Bellevue, WA: American Outdoor Safety League, 1990.

Forgey, William W., M.D., *The Basic Essentials of Hypothermia,* Merrillville, IN: ICS Books., Inc., 1991

Limmer, Daniel; O'Keefe, Michael F.; and Dickinson, Edward T. MD, FACEP, *Emergency Care,* 10th Edition, Upper Saddle River, NJ, Pearson Prentice Hall, 2005.

American Heart Association, Heart and Stroke Guide, available http://wwwamhrt.org/Heart_and_Stroke_A_Z_Guide/, May 5, 1998.

Kaiser Permanente, Kaiser Permanente's Health Reference: Cardiopulmonary Resuscitation, available http://www.scl.ncal.kaiperm.org/healthinfo/cpr/

MedicineNet, First Aid, available, www.medicinenet.com/hp.asp?li+MNI, 01/20/98

State of Alaska Cold Injuries and Cold Water Near Drowning Guidelines, (Rev. 01/96), available, http://www.westcst.com/

Dawson, Chad P., U. Of Minn. Sea Grant Program, Survival in cold water: Hypothermia Prevention, available http://www.d.umn.edu/seagr/tourism/hypothermia.html

Adventure Sports Online, Hypothermia, available: www.adventuresports.com/asap/ski/skihypo.htm

Scorpio, Diana, DVM and Nelson, Mico, *Emergency Management: How to Perform Canine CPR,* available: www.vetref.net/articles/_articles/cpr.html

Feldman, Lori H. DVM, *Save A Life, Learn Animal CPR for the EMS Provider,* © 1997 VETEMS Productions

Perform Basic Cardiac Life Support on A Military Working Dog, Soldier's Manual and Trainers Guide, MOS 91T, Animal Care Specialist, Headquarters, Dept. of the Army, August 2002.

First Aid

GENERAL INFORMATION

Geometry Formulas · 156

Trigonometry · 157

Temperature Equivalents · 157

Military Rank· 158

  Air Force · 158
  Navy & Coast Guard · 160
  Army · 162
  Marines · 165

Weights and Measures · 167

North American Area Codes - By State · · · · · · · · · · 172

North American Area Codes - By Code · · · · · · · · · · 178

Social Security Numbering System · · · · · · · · · · · · · 185

General Info

Geometry Formulas

$\pi = 3.14159$

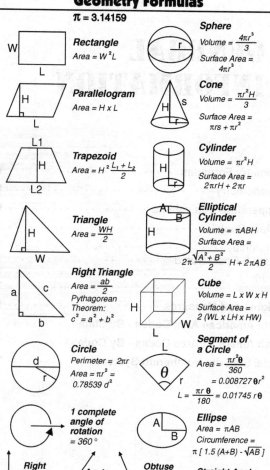

Rectangle
Area = $W^2 L$

Parallelogram
Area = $H \times L$

Trapezoid
Area = $H^2 \dfrac{L_1 + L_2}{2}$

Triangle
Area = $\dfrac{WH}{2}$

Right Triangle
Area = $\dfrac{ab}{2}$
Pythagorean Theorem:
$c^2 = a^2 + b^2$

Circle
Perimeter = $2\pi r$
Area = πr^2 = $0.78539\ d^2$

1 complete angle of rotation
= $360°$

Right Angle = $90°$

Acute Angle < $90°$

Obtuse Angle > $90°$

Straight Angle = $180°$

Sphere
Volume = $\dfrac{4\pi r^3}{3}$
Surface Area = $4\pi r^3$

Cone
Volume = $\dfrac{\pi r^2 H}{3}$
Surface Area = $\pi rs + \pi r^2$

Cylinder
Volume = $\pi r^2 H$
Surface Area = $2\pi rH + 2\pi r$

Elliptical Cylinder
Volume = πABH
Surface Area = $2\pi \dfrac{\sqrt{A^2 + B^2}}{2} H + 2\pi AB$

Cube
Volume = $L \times W \times H$
Surface Area = $2\ (WL \times LH \times HW)$

Segment of a Circle
Area = $\dfrac{\pi r^2 \theta}{360}$ = $0.008727\ \theta r^2$
$L = \dfrac{\pi r \theta}{180} = 0.01745\ r\theta$

Ellipse
Area = πAB
Circumference = $\pi\ [\ 1.5\ (A + B) - \sqrt{AB}\ ]$

Trigonometry

Right Triangle: x, y, z = angles (z=90°)   a, b, c = lengths

$$\sin x = \frac{a}{c}$$

$$\cos x = \frac{b}{c}$$

$$\tan x = \frac{a}{b}$$

$$\tan x = \frac{\sin x}{\cos x}$$

$$\sin x = \cos y$$

$$c = \sqrt{a^2 + b^2}$$

$$b = \sqrt{(c+a)(c-a)}$$

Oblique Triangle: x, y, z = angles   a, b, c = lengths

$$x + y + z = 180°$$

$$\text{Area} = \frac{bc \sin x}{2}$$

$$s = \frac{a+b+c}{2}$$

$$a = \frac{b \sin x}{\sin y}$$

$$a = \frac{c \sin x}{\sin z}$$

$$c = \frac{a \sin z}{\sin x}$$

$$\text{Area} = \sqrt{s(s-a)(s-b)(s-c)}$$

$$\tan x = \frac{a \sin z}{b - (a \cos z)}$$

$$\cos x = \frac{b^2 + c^2 - a^2}{2bc}$$

Temperature Equivalents

F°	C°	F°	C°	F°	C°	F°	C°
-76	-60	22	-5.5	62	17	102	39
-66	-54	24	-4	64	18	104	40
-56	-49	26	-3	66	19	106	41
-46	-43	28	-2	68	20	108	42
-36	-38	30	-1	70	21	110	43
-26	-32	32	0	72	22	112	44
-16	-27	34	1	74	23	114	45.5
-10	-23	36	2	76	24	116	47
-6	-21	38	3	78	25.5	118	48
0	-18	40	4	80	27	120	49
2	-17	42	5.5	82	28	130	54
4	-15	44	7	84	29	140	60
6	-14	46	8	86	30	150	65.5
8	-13	48	9	88	31	160	71
10	-12	50	10	90	32	170	77
12	-11	52	11	92	33	180	82
14	-10	54	12	94	34	190	88
16	-9	56	13	96	35.5	200	93
18	-8	58	14	98	37	212	100
20	-7	60	15.5	100	38		

Celsius temperatures are rounded to the nearest whole degree.

General Info

Military Rank - Air Force

Grade Rank	Insignia
Enlisted (black trim, silver stripes)	
E1 Airman Basic	No insignia
E2 Airman	
E3 Airman 1st Class	
E4 Senior Airman	
E5 Staff Sergeant	
E6 Technical Sergeant	
E7 Master Sergeant	
E7 First Sergeant	
E8 Senior Master Sergeant	
E8 First Sergeant	
E9 Chief Master Sergeant	
E9 First Sergeant	
E9 Command Chief Master	

Grade Rank	Insignia

Enlisted (black trim, silver stripes) cont.

E9 Chief Master Sergeant of Air Force ....

Officer

W1,2,3,4 ....No Warrant Officers

O1 2nd Lieutenant (brass) ....

O2 1st Lieutenant (silver)............

O3 Captain (silver) ....

O4 Major (gold) ....

O5 Lieutenant Colonel (silver) ....

O6 Colonel (silver) ....

O7 Brigadier General (silver) ....

O8 Major General (silver) .... ✭ ✭

O9 Lieutenant General (silver)...................................✭✭✭

O10 General (silver) .... ✭✭✭✭

–   General of the Air Force (silver)...............................
    (Reserved for war time only - 1 person)

Military Rank - Navy & Coast Guard

Grade Rank		Insignia
Enlisted		
E1	Seaman Recruit	No insignia
E2	Seaman Apprentice	
E3	Seaman	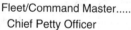
E4	Petty Officer 3rd Class	
E5	Petty Officer 2nd Class	
E6	Petty Officer 1st Class	
E7	Chief Petty Officer	
E8	Sr Chief Petty Officer	
E9	Mst Chief Petty Officer	
E9	Fleet/Command Master Chief Petty Officer	
	Mst Chief Petty Officer of Navy and Coast Guard	

General Info

Grade Rank	Insignia

Officer

W1 Warrant Officer......................No longer in use

W2 Chief Warrant Officer 2 ....

W3 Chief Warrant Officer 3 ....

W4 Chief Warrant Officer 4 ....

W5 Chief Warrant Officer 5 ....None

O1 Ensign (brass)........................

O2 Lieutenant Jr. Grade (silver)..........

O3 Lieutenant (silver) ....

O4 Lieutenant Commander (gold) ....

O5 Commander (silver) ....

O6 Captain (silver) ....

General Info

Military Rank - Navy & Coast Guard Cont.

Grade Rank	Insignia
Officer Cont.	

O7 Rear Admiral (lower half) (silver) ....

O8 Rear Admiral (upper half) ......

O9 Vice Admiral (silver) ....

O10 Admiral (silver) ....

– Fleet Admiral (silver) ....
(Reserved for wartime only)

Military Rank - Army

Grade Rank	Insignia
Enlisted (black trim, orange stripes)	

E1 Private ....No insignia

E2 Private ....

E3 Private 1st Class ....

E4 Corporal or Specialist..

Military Rank - Army Cont.

Grade Rank	Insignia

Enlisted (black trim, orange stripes) Cont.

E4 Specialist......................

E5 Sergeant..

E6 Staff Sergeant......................

E7 Sergeant 1st Class...

E8 Master Sergeant....................

E8 1st Sergeant..

E9 Command Sergeant Major.....

E9 Sergeant Major...

E9 Sergeant Major of the Army...

General Info

Military Rank - Army Cont.

Grade Rank	Insignia
Officer	

W1 Warrant Officer ....

W2 Chief Warrant Officer ....

W3 Chief Warrant Officer ....

W4 Chief Warrant Officer ....

W5 Master Warrant Officer ....

O1 2nd Lieutenant (brass) ....

O2 1st Lieutenant (silver) ....

O3 Captain (silver) ....

O4 Major (gold) ....

O5 Lieutenant Colonel (silver) .....

O6 Colonel (silver) ....

O7 Brigadier General (silver) ....

O8 Major General (silver) ....

O9 Lieutenant General (silver) ....

O10 General-Chief of Staff (silver) ....

— Gen of Army (silver) ....
    (Reserved for wartime only)

Military Rank - Marines

Grade	Rank	Insignia

Enlisted (red base, green stripes)

Grade	Rank	Insignia
E1	Private	No insignia
E2	Private 1st Class	
E3	Lance Corporal	
E4	Corporal	
E5	Sergeant	
E6	Staff Sergeant	
E7	Gunnery Sergeant	
E8	Master Sergeant	
E8	1st Sergeant	
E9	Sergeant Major	
E9	Master Gunnery Sergeant	
E9	Sergeant Major of the Marines	

General Info

Military Rank - Marines

Grade Rank	Insignia
Officer	

W1 Warrant Officer

W2 Chief Warrant Officer 2

W3 Chief Warrant Officer 3

W4 Chief Warrant Officer 4

W5 Master Warrant Officer

O1 2nd Lieutenant (brass)

O2 1st Lieutenant (silver)

O3 Captain (silver)

O4 Major (gold)

O5 Lieutenant Colonel (silver)

O6 Colonel (silver)

O7 Brigadier General (silver)

O8 Major General (silver)

O9 Lieutenant General (silver)

O10 General (silver)

Weights and Measures

1 acre	= 43,560 square foot	area
	= 4,046.86 square meter	
	= 0.00156 square mile	
1 atmosphere (std.)	= 14.696 pounds/square inch	pressure
1 bar	= 0.98692 atmosphere (std)	pressure
1 barrel, US, liquid	= 4.2109 cubic foot	volume
	= 31.5 gallon, US, liquid	
	= 119.24 liter	
1 barrel, US, petroleum	= 1.3333 barrel, US, liquid	volume
	= 42 gallon, US, liquid	
	= 158.99 liter	
1 Btu (intl. table)	= 251.996 calorie (intl. table)	energy
1 bushel, US, dry	= 1.2445 cubic feet	volume
	= 8 gallons, US, dry	
1 caliber	= 0.01 inch	length
	= 0.254 millimeter	
1 calorie (intl. Table)	= 3.088 foot pounds	energy
1 centimeter	= 0.39370 inch	length
	= 0.01 meter	
	= 10 millimeters	
1 cord (wood)	= 128 cubic feet	volume
1 cubic centimeter	= 0.061 cubic inch	volume
1 cubic foot	= 1,728 cubic inches	volume
	= 0.02832 cubic meter	
	= 0.03704 cubic yard	
	= 6.4285 gallons, US, dry	
	= 7.4805 gallons, US, liquid	
	= 28.317 liters	
1 cubic foot/second	= 0.02832 cubic meter/second	flowrate
	= 448.83 gallons/minute US, liquid	
	= 28.317 liters/second	
1 cubic inch	= 16.39 cubic centimeters	volume
	= 0.000579 cubic foot	
	= 0.00372 gallon, US, dry	
	= 0.00433 gallon, US, liquid	
	= 0.01639 liter	
1 cubic meter	= 35.315 cubic feet	volume
	= 1.3079 cubic yards	
	= 227.02 gallons, US, dry	
	= 264.17 gallons, US, liquid	
	= 1,000 liters	
1 cubic meter/second	= 35.315 cubic feet/second	flowrate
	=15,850.3 gallons/minute, US, liquid	
1 cubic yard	= 27 cubic feet	volume
	= 0.76455 cubic meter	
1 cup, US, measuring	= 14.4375 cubic inches	volume
	= 0.0625 gallon, US, liquid	
	= 0.23659 liter	

General Info

1 cup, US, measuring	= 8 ounces, US, liquid	volume
	= 0.5 pint, US, liquid	
	= 0.25 quart, US, liquid	
	= 16 tablespoons, US, measuring	
	= 48 teaspoons, US, measuring	
1 fathom	= 6 feet	length
1 fifth, US, liquid	= 0.75708 liter	volume
	= 25.6 ounces, US, liquid	
1 foot	= 12 inches	length
	= 0.305 meter	
	= 0.000189 mile	
	= 0.3333 yard	
1 foot/second	= 1.0973 kilometer/hour	velocity
	= 0.68182 mile/hour	
1 furlong	= 0.125 mile	length
1 gallon, Imperial	= 1.201 gallons, US, liquid	volume
	= 4.546 liters	
1 gallon, US, Dry	= 0.125 bushel, US, dry	volume
	= 268.80 cubic inch	
	= 0.004405 cubic meter	
	= 8 pint, US, dry	
	= 4 quarts, US, dry	
1 gallon, US, liquid	= 0.13368 cubic foot	volume
	= 231 cubic inches	
	= 16 cups, US, measuring	
	= 0.833 gallon, Imperial	
	= 4 liters	
	= 8 pint, US, liquid	
	= 4 quarts, US, liquid	
1 gallon/minute, US, liquid	= 0.002228 cubic foot/second	flowrate
	= 0.003786 cubic meter/minute	
1 grain	= 0.06480 gram	mass
	= 64.80 milligrams	
	= 0.00229 ounce	
1 gram	= 15.432 grains	mass
	= 1,000 milligrams	
	= 0.03527 ounce	
	= 0.002205 pound	
1 hectare	= 2.4711 acres	volume
1 horsepower	= 0.7457 kilowatt	power
1 hour	= 0.041667 day	time
	= 60 minutes	
	= 3,600 seconds	
1 hundredweight, US	= 45.3592 kilograms	mass
1 inch	= 2.54 centimeter	length
	= 0.0833 foot	
	= 0.0254 meter	
	= 25.4 millimeter	
	= 0.02778 yard	
1 jigger, US, liquid	= 1.5 ounces, US, liquid	volume

1 joule	= 0.73756 foot pound	energy
1 kilogram	= 1,000 grams	mass
	= 35.274 ounces	
	= 2.2046 pounds	
1 kilogram/cubic meter	= 0.06243 pound/cubic foot	density
1 kilometer	= 3,280.84 feet	length
	= 1,000 meter	
	= 0.62137 mile	
	= 1,093.6 yard	
1 kilometer/hour	= 0.91134 foot/second	velocity
	= 0.27778 meter/second	
	= 0.62137 mile/hour	
1 kilowatt	= 1,000 watts	power
1 league	= 3 miles	length
1 liter	= 0.035315 cubic foot	volume
	= 61.024 cubic inch	
	= 0.001 cubic meter	
	= 4.2267 cup, US, measuring	
	= 0.2642 gallon, US, liquid	
	= 33.814 ounce, US, liquid	
	= 2.1134 pint, US, liquid	
	= 1.0567 quart, US, liquid	
	= 33.814 shot, US, liquid	
	= 67.628 tablespoon, US, measuring	
	= 202.88 teaspoon, US, measuring	
1 liter/second	= 0.035315 cubic foot/second	flowrate
	= 15.850 gallon/minute, US, liquid	
1 meter	= 100 centimeters	length
	= 3.2808 feet	
	= 39.37 inches	
	= 0.001 kilometer	
	= 0.0006214 mile	
	= 1,000 millimeters	
	= 1.0936 yards	
1 meter/liter = 0.00235 mile/gallon, intl./US, liquid		fuel consumption
1 meter/second	= 3.2808 feet/second	velocity
	= 3.6 kilometers/hour	
	= 2.2369 mile/hour	
1 mile	= 5,280 feet	length
	= 1.6093 kilometers	
	= 1,609.3 meters	
	= 1,760 yard	
1 mile/gallon	= 425.14 meters/liter	fuel consumption
1 mile/hour	= 1.467 feet/second	velocity
	= 1.61 kilometers/hour	
	= 0.44704 meter/second	
1 milligram	= 0.01543 grain	mass
	= 0.001 gram	
1 millimeter	= 0.1 centimeter	length
	= 0.03937 inch	

General Info

1 millimeter	= 0.001 meter	length
1 minute	= 0.0167 hour	time
1 nautical mile	= 6076.11 feet	length
	= 1.852 kilometers	
1 newton-meter	= 0.73756 foot pound	energy
1 ounce	= 437.5 grains	mass
	= 28.350 grams	
	= 0.02835 kilogram	
	= 28,349.5 milligrams	
	= 0.0625 pound	
1 ounce, troy (gold)	= 0.0833 pound	mass
	= 31.1 grams	
1 ounce, US, liquid	= 1.805 cubic inches	volume
	= 0.125 cup, US, measuring	
	= 0.02957 liter	
	= 0.0625 pint, US, liquid	
	= 0.03125 quart, US, liquid	
	= 2 tablespoon, US, measuring	
	= 6 teaspoon, US, measuring	
1 pascal	= 0.000145 pound/square inch	pressure
1 peck, US, dry	= 0.25 bushel, US, dry	volume
	= 2 gallons, US, dry	
1 pint, US, dry	= 0.015625 bushel, US, dry	volume
	= 33.6 cubic inches	
	= 0.0551 cubic centimeter	
	= 0.125 gallon, US, dry	
	= 0.5 quart, US, dry	
1 pint, US, liquid	= 2 cups, US, measuring	volume
	= 0.125 gallon, US, liquid	
	= 0.47318 liter	
	= 16 ounces, US, liquid	
	= 0.5 quart, US, liquid	
1 pony, US, liquid	= 1 shot, US, liquid	volume
1 pound	= 7,000 grains	mass
	= 453.59 grams	
	= 0.45359 kilogram	
	= 16 ounces	
1 pound/square inch	= 6.895 kilopascals	pressure
1 pound/cubic foot	= 16.0185 kilograms/cubic meter	density
1 quart, US, dry	= 0.03125 bushel, US, dry	volume
	= 67.201 cubic inches	
	= 0.0011 cubic meter	
	= 0.25 gallon, US, dry	
	= 2 pints, US, dry	
1 quart, US, liquid	= 57.75 cubic inches	volume
	= 4 cups, US, measuring	
	= 0.25 gallon, US, liquid	
	= 0.9463 liter	
	= 32 ounces, US, liquid	
	= 2 pints, US, liquid	

1 radian	= 57.296 degrees	angle
1 second	= 0.0167 minute	time
1 shot, US, liquid	= 1 ounce, US, liquid	volume
1 square centimeter	= 0.1550 square inch	area
	= 0.0001 square meter	
1 square foot	= 0.000023 acre	area
	= 144 square inches	
	= 0.0929 square meter	
	= 0.1111 square yard	
1 square inch	= 6.452 square centimeters	area
	= 0.0069 square foot	
	= 0.0006 square meter	
	= 0.0008 square yard	
1 square kilometer	= 247.105 acres	area
	= 1,000,000 square meters	
	= 0.3861 square mile	
1 square meter	= 0.00025 acre	area
	= 0.0001 hectare	
	= 10.764 square feet	
	= 1,550 square inches	
	= 1.196 square yards	
1 square mile	= 640 acres	area
	= 27,878,400 square feet	
	= 2.589 square kilometers	
1 square yard	= 9 square feet	area
	= 1,296 square inches	
	= 0.83613 square meter	
1 tablespoon	= 0.0625 cup	volume
	= 0.0148 liter	
	= 0.5 ounce, US, liquid	
	= 3 teaspoons	
1 teaspoon	= 0.0208 cup, US, measuring	volume
	= 0.0049 liter	
	= 0.1667 ounce, US, liquid	
	= 0.333 tablespoon, US, measuring	
1 ton, long	= 1,016.05 kilograms	mass
	= 2,240 pounds	
	= 1.12 tons, short	
	= 1.01605 metric tons	
1 ton, short	= 907.185 kilograms	mass
	= 2,000 pounds	
	= 0.89286 ton, long	
1 tonne	= 1,000 kilograms or 1 metric ton	mass
1 yard	= 3 feet	length
	= 36 inches	
	= 0.9144 meter	
	= 0.00057 mile	
1 year, leap	= 366 days	time
1 year, normal	= 8,760 hours	time

North American Area Codes - By State

State/Country	City	Area Code
Alabama	Birmingham, Tuscaloosa	205
	Huntsville	256
	Mobile	251
	Montgomery	334
Alaska		907
American Samoa		684
Anguilla		264
Antigua, Barbuda		268
Arizona	Flagstaff, Yuma	928
	Tucson	520
	Phoenix (Central)	602
	Phoenix (East suburbs)	480
	Phoenix (West suburbs)	623
Arkansas	Fayetteville, Ft. Smith	479
	Little Rock, Hot Springs	501
	Jonesboro, Pine Bluff	870
Bahamas		242
Barbados		246
Bermuda		441
British Virgin Islands		284
California	Anaheim, Orange	714
	Bakersfield	661
	Burbank, Glendale	818
	Chico, Yreka	530
	Concord	925
	Del Mar, LaJolla	858
	Eureka, Santa Rosa	707
	Fresno	559
	Long Beach	562
	Los Angeles (Downtown)	213
	Los Angeles (Metro)	323
	Los Angeles, Santa Monica	310
	Modesto, Stockton	209
	Monterey, Santa Cruz	831
	Newport Beach	949
	Oakland, Berkeley	510
	Palm Springs, Barstow	760
	Palo Alto, San Mateo	650
	Pasadena	626
	Riverside	951
	Sacramento	916
	San Bernardino	909
	San Diego	619
	San Francisco	415
	San Jose, Gilroy	408
	Santa Barbara	805
Canada	Alberta, Calgary	403
	Alberta, Edmonton	780

North American Area Codes - By State

State/Country	City	Area Code
Canada (cont.)	British Columbia	250
	British Columbia, Vancouver	604, 778
	Manitoba	204
	New Brunswick	506
	Newfoundland	709
	Nova Scotia, P. Ed. Isl	902
	Ontario, Hamilton	905, 289
	Ontario, Ottawa	613
	Ontario, Sault Ste Marie	705
	Ontario, Thunder Bay	807
	Ontario, Toronto(Metro)	416, 647
	Ontario, Windsor	519
	Quebec, Laval	450
	Quebec, Montreal	514
	Quebec, Quebec City	418
	Quebec, Sherbrooke	819
	Saskatchewan	306
	Yukon, NW Territories	867
Cayman Islands		345
Colorado	Colorado Springs, Pueblo	719
	Denver, Boulder	303, 720
	Grand Junction, Fort Collins	970
Connecticut	Hartford	860
	New Haven, Stamford	203
Delaware		302
Dominica		767
Dominican Republic		809
Florida	Daytona Beach, Lake City	386
	Fort Lauderdale	754, 954
	Gainesville	352
	Jacksonville	904
	Miami	786
	Miami, Key West	305
	Naples	239
	Okeechobee	863
	Orlando	407, 321, 689
	Pensacola, Tallahassee	850
	Saint Petersburg	727
	Sarasota, Ft. Myers	941
	Tampa	813
	Vero Beach	772
	West Palm Beach	561
Georgia	Atlanta (Metro inside I85)	404, 770
	Atlanta (outside I285)	770, 678
	Columbus, Augusta	706
	Macon	478
	Savannah	912
	Valdosta	229

North American Area Codes - By State

State/Country	City	Area Code
Grenada		473
Guam		671
Hawaii		808
Idaho		208
Illinois	Alton	618
	Champaign, Urbana	217
	Chicago	773
	Chicago (Central)	312
	Chicago (Central Suburbs)	630
	Chicago (South Suburbs)	708
	Chicago (N & NW Suburbs)	847, 224
	Peoria	309
	Rockford	815
Indiana	Evansville	812
	Fort Wayne	260
	Gary	219
	Indianapolis (Metro)	317
	Lafayette, Muncie	765
	South Bend	574
Iowa	Cedar Rapids	319
	Council Bluffs	712
	Davenport, Dubuque	563
	Des Moines	515
	Mason City, Ottumwa	641
Jamaica		876
Kansas	Dodge City, Emporia	620
	Kansas City	913
	Topeka, Colby	785
	Wichita	316
Kentucky	Ashland	606
	Bowling Green	270
	Frankfort, Louisville	502
	Lexington	859
Louisiana	Alexandria, Shreveport	318
	Baton Rouge	225
	Hammond, Houma	985
	Lafayette, Lake Charles	337
	New Orleans	504
Maine		207
Mariana Islands (CNMI)		670
Maryland	Baltimore	410, 443
	Silver Spring	301, 240
Massachusetts	Boston (Metro)	617, 857
	Boston (Suburbs)	781, 339
	Cape Cod, Worcester	508, 774
	Lowell, Salem	978, 351
	Springfield	413
Michigan	Ann Arbor	734

North American Area Codes - By State

State/Country	City	Area Code
Michigan (cont.)	Battle Creek	616
	Detroit	313
	Escanaba	906
	Flint	810
	Kalamazoo	269
	Lansing	517
	Muskegon	231
	Pontiac, Troy	248, 947
	Saginaw, Alpena	989
	Warren	586
Minnesota	Bloomington	952
	Brooklyn Park	763
	Duluth	218
	Minneapolis	612
	Rochester	507
	Saint Cloud	320
	Saint Paul	651
Mississippi	Biloxi & Gulf Coast	228
	Jackson, Natchez	601, 769
	Tupelo	662
Missouri	Jefferson City	573
	Kansas City, Saint Joseph	816
	Saint Charles	636
	Saint Louis	314
	Sedalia	660
	Springfield	417
Montana		406
Montserrat		664
Nebraska	Lincoln, Omaha	402
	North Platte, Grand Island	308
Nevada	Las Vegas	702
	Reno, Ely, Elko	775
New Hampshire		603
New Jersey	Camden	856
	Elizabeth, Phillipsburg	908
	Hackensack	201, 551
	New Brunswick	732, 848
	Newark	973, 862
	Trenton, Atlantic City	609
New Mexico		505
New York	Albany	518
	Binghamton, Elmira	607
	Bronx, Brooklyn	718, 347, 917
	Buffalo	716
	Hempstead, Long Island	516
	Hudson Valley	845
	Long Island, Brentwood	631, 516
	Manhattan	212, 646, 917

General Info

North American Area Codes - By State

State/Country	City	Area Code
New York (cont.)	New York City	212, 347, 646, 718, 917
	Queens, Staten Island	718, 347, 917
	Rochester	585
	Syracuse	315
	White Plains, Yonkers	914
North Carolina	Asheville	828
	Charlotte	704, 980
	Fayetteville	910
	Greensboro	336
	Raleigh	919
	Rocky Mount, Greenville	252
North Dakota		701
Ohio	Akron, Canton	330, 234
	Cincinnati	513
	Cleveland (Metro)	216
	Cleveland (Suburbs)	440
	Columbus	614
	Dayton	937
	Marion, Zanesville	740
	Toledo	419, 567
Oklahoma	Lawton	580
	Oklahoma City	405
	Tulsa	918
Oregon	Eugene, Burns	541
	Portland, Salem	503, 971
	Tillamook, Astoria	503
Pennsylvania	Allentown	610, 484
	Altoona	814
	Harrisburg	717
	Philadelphia	215, 267
	Pittsburgh	412, 878
	Pittsburgh (Suburbs)	724, 878
	Scranton, Wilkes-Barre	570
Puerto Rico		787, 939
Rhode Island		401
South Carolina	Charleston	843
	Columbia	803
	Greenville	864
South Dakota		605
St. Kitts, Nevis		869
St. Lucia		758
St. Vincent, Grenadines		784
Tennessee	Celina, Clarksville	931
	Chattanooga, Bristol	423
	Jackson	731
	Knoxville	865
	Memphis	901

North American Area Codes - By State

State/Country	City	Area Code
Tennessee (cont.)	Nashville	615
Texas	Abilene,	325
	Alpine, Midland	432
	Austin	512
	Brownsville	956
	Bryan, College Station	979
	Corpus Christi	361
	Dallas & Suburbs	214, 469, 972
	El Paso	915
	Fort Worth, Arlington	817, 682
	Galveston, Beaumont	409
	Houston	713, 281, 832
	Huntsville	936
	Kerrville	830
	Lubbock, Amarillo	806
	San Antonio	210
	Tyler	430, 903
	Waco	254
	Wichita Falls	940
Trinidad, Tabago		868
Turks and Caicos Islands		649
US Virgin Islands		340
Utah	Logan, St, George	435
	Salt Lake City	801
Vermont		802
Virginia	Arlington	703, 571
	Bristol	276
	Lynchburg	434
	Norfolk	757
	Richmond	804
	Roanoke	540
Washington	Bellevue, Edmonds	425
	Olympia, Vancouver	360
	Seattle	206
	Spokane	509
	Tacoma, Kent	253
Washington, D.C.		202
West Virginia		304
Wisconsin	Eau Claire	715
	Green Bay	920
	Kenosha	262
	Madison	608
	Milwaukee	414
Wyoming		307

General Info

North American Area Codes - By CODE

State/Country	City	Area Code
New Jersey	Hackensach	201
Washington, D.C.		202
Connecticut	New Haven, Stamford	203
Canada	Manitoba	204
Alabama	Birmingham, Tuscaloosa	205
Washington	Seattle	206
Maine		207
Idaho		208
California	Modesto, Stockton	209
Texas	San Antonio	210
New York	Manhattan, NY City	212
California	Los Angeles (Downtown)	213
Texas	Dallas & Suburbs	214
Pennsylvania	Philadelphia	215
Ohio	Cleveland (Metro)	216
Illinois	Champaign, Urbana	217
Minnesota	Duluth	218
Indiana	Gary	219
Illinois	Chicago (N & NW suburbs)	224
Louisiana	Baton Rouge	225
Mississippi	Biloxi & Gulf Coast	228
Georgia	Valdosta	229
Michigan	Muskegon	231
Ohio	Akron, Canton	234
Florida	Naples	239
Maryland	Silver Spring	240
Bahamas		242
Barbados		246
Michigan	Pontiac, Troy	248
Canada	British Columbia	250
Alabama	Mobile	251
North Carolina	Rocky Mount, Greenville	252
Washington	Tacoma, Kent	253
Texas	Waco	254
Alabama	Huntsville	256
Indiana	Ft. Wayne	260
Wisconsin	Kenosha	262
Anguilla		264
Pennsylvania	Philadelphia	267
Antigua, Barbuda		268
Michigan	Kalamazoo	269
Kentucky	Bowling Green	270
Virginia	Bristol	276
Texas	Houston	281
British Virgin Islands		284
Canada	Ontario, Hamilton	289
Maryland	Silver Spring	301
Delaware		302

North American Area Codes - By CODE

State/Country	City	Area Code
Colorado	Denver, Boulder	303
West Virginia		304
Florida	Miami, Key West	305
Canada	Saskatchewan	306
Wyoming		307
Nebraska	North Platte, Grand Island	308
Illinois	Peoria	309
California	Los Angeles, Santa Monica	310
Illinois	Chicago (Central)	312
Michigan	Detroit	313
Missouri	Saint Louis	314
New York	Syracuse	315
Kansas	Wichita	316
Indiana	Indianapolis (Metro)	317
Louisiana	Alexandria, Shreveport	318
Iowa	Cedar Rapids	319
Minnesota	Saint Cloud	320
Florida	Orlando	321
California	Los Angeles (Metro)	323
Texas	Abilene	325
Ohio	Akron, Canton	330
Alabama	Montgomery	334
North Carolina	Greensboro	336
Louisiana	Lafayette, Lake Charles	337
Massachusetts	Boston (Suburbs)	339
US Virgin Islands		340
Cayman Islands		345
New York	Bronx, Brooklyn, NY City	347
Massachusetts	Lowell, Salem	351
Florida	Gainesville	352
Washington	Olympia, Vancouver	360
Texas	Corpus Christi	361
Florida	Daytona Beach, Lake City	386
Rhode Island		401
Nebraska	Lincoln, Omaha	402
Canada	Alberta, Calgary	403
Georgia	Atlanta (Metro inside I285)	404
Oklahoma	Oklahoma City	405
Montana		406
Florida	Orlando	407
California	San Jose	408
Texas	Galveston, Beaumont	409
Maryland	Baltimore	410
Pennsylvania	Pittsburgh	412
Massachusetts	Springfield	413
Wisconsin	Milwaukee	414
California	San Francisco	415
Canada	Ontario, Toronto (Metro)	416

North American Area Codes - By CODE

State/Country	City	Area Code
Missouri	Springfield	417
Canada	Quebec, Quebec City	418
Ohio	Toledo	419
Tennessee	Chattanooga, Bristol	423
Texas	Tyler	430
Texas	Alpine, Midland	432
Washington	Bellevue, Edmonds	425
Virginia	Lynchburg	434
Utah	Logan, Saint George	435
Ohio	Cleveland (Suburbs)	440
Bermuda		441
Maryland	Baltimore	443
Canada	Quebec, Laval	450
Texas	Dallas	469
Grenada		473
Georgia	Macon	478
Arkansas	Fayetteville	479
Arizona	Phoenix (E suburbs)	480
Pennsylvania	Allentown	484
Arkansas	Little Rock, Hot Springs	501
Kentucky	Frankfort, Louisville	502
Oregon	Portland, Salem	503
Oregon	Astoria	503
Louisiana	New Orleans	504
New Mexico		505
Canada	New Brunswick	506
Minnesota	Rochester	507
Massachusetts	Cape Cod, Worcester	508
Washington	Spokane	509
California	Oakland, Berkeley	510
Texas	Austin	512
Ohio	Cincinnati	513
Canada	Quebec, Montreal	514
Iowa	Des Moines	515
New York	Hempstead, Long Island	516
Michigan	Lansing	517
New York	Albany	518
Canada	Ontario, Windsor	519
Arizona	Tucson, Flagstaff	520
California	Chico, Yreka	530
Virginia	Roanoke	540
Oregon	Eugene, Burns	541
New Jersey	Hackensack	551
California	Fresno	559
Florida	West Palm Beach	561
California	Long Beach	562
Iowa	Davenport, Dubuque	563
Ohio	Toledo	567

North American Area Codes - By CODE

State/Country	City	Area Code
Pennsylvania	Scranton, Wilkes-Barre	570
Virginia	Arlington	571
Missouri	Jefferson City	573
Indiana	South Bend	574
Oklahoma	Lawton	580
New York	Rochester	585
Michigan	Warren	586
Mississippi	Jackson, Natchez	601
Arizona	Phoenix (Central)	602
New Hampshire		603
Canada	British Columbia, Vancouver	604
South Dakota		605
Kentucky	Ashland	606
New York	Binghamton, Elmira	607
Wisconsin	Madison	608
New Jersey	Trenton, Atlantic City	609
Pennsylvania	Allentown	610
Minnesota	Minneapolis	612
Canada	Ontario, Ottawa	613
Ohio	Columbus	614
Tennessee	Nashville	615
Michigan	Battle Creek	616
Massachusetts	Boston (Metro)	617
Illinois	Alton	618
California	San Diego	619
Kansas	Dodge City, Emporia	620
Arizona	Phoenix (W suburbs)	623
California	Pasadena	626
Illinois	Chicago (Central subs.)	630
New York	Long Island, Brentwood	631
Missouri	St. Charles	636
Iowa	Ottumwa, Mason City	641
New York	Manhattan, New York City	646
Canada	Ontario, Toronto	647
Turks and Caicos Islands		649
California	Palo Alto, San Mateo	650
Minnesota	Saint Paul	651
Missouri	Sedalia	660
California	Bakersfield	661
Mississippi	Tupelo	662
Montserrat		664
Mariana Islands (CNMI)		670
Guam		671
Georgia	Atlanta (Inside&Outside I285)	678
Texas	Fort Worth, Arlington	682
American Samoa		684
Florida	Orlando	689
North Dakota		701

General Info

State/Country	City	Area Code
Nevada	Las Vegas	702
Virginia	Arlington	703
North Carolina	Charlotte	704
Canada	Ontario, Sault Ste Marie	705
Georgia	Columbus, Augusta	706
California	Eureka, Santa Rosa	707
Illinois	Chicago (South Suburbs)	708
Canada	Newfoundland	709
Iowa	Council Bluffs	712
Texas	Houston	713
California	Anaheim, Orange	714
Wisconsin	Eau Claire	715
New York	Buffalo	716
Pennsylvania	Harrisburg	717
New York	Bronx, Brooklyn	718
New York	Queens, Staten Island	718
New York	New York City	718
Colorado	Colorado Springs, Pueblo	719
Colorado	Denver, Boulder	720
Pennsylvania	Pittsburgh (Suburbs)	724
Florida	Saint Petersburg	727
Tennessee	Jackson	731
New Jersey	New Brunswick	732
Michigan	Ann Arbor	734
Ohio	Marion, Zanesville	740
Florida	Fort Lauderdale	754
Virginia	Norfolk	757
Saint Lucia		758
California	Barstow, Palm Springs	760
Minnesota	Brooklyn Park	763
Indiana	Lafayette, Muncie	765
Dominica		767
Mississippi	Jackson, Natchez	769
Georgia	Atlanta	770
Florida	Vero Beach	772
Illinois	Chicago	773
Massachusetts	Cape Cod, Worcester	774
Nevada	Reno, Ely, Elko	775
Canada	British Columbia, Vancouver	778
Canada	Alberta, Edmonton	780
Massachusetts	Boston (Suburbs)	781
Saint Vincent, The Grenadines		784
Kansas	Topeka, Colby	785
Florida	Miami	786
Puerto Rico		787
Utah	Salt Lake City	801
Vermont		802
South Carolina	Columbia	803

North American Area Codes - By CODE

State/Country	City	Area Code
Virginia	Richmond	804
California	Santa Barbara	805
Texas	Amarillo, Lubbock	806
Canada	Ontario, Thunder Bay	807
Hawaii		808
Dominican Republic		809
Michigan	Flint	810
Indiana	Evansville	812
Florida	Tampa	813
Pennsylvania	Altoona	814
Illinois	Rockford	815
Missouri	Kansas City, Saint Joseph	816
Texas	Fort Worth, Arlington	817
California	Burbank, Glendale	818
Canada	Quebec, Sherbrooke	819
North Carolina	Asheville	828
Texas	Kerrville	830
California	Monterey, Santa Cruz	831
Texas	Houston	832
South Carolina	Charleston	843
New York	Hudson Valley	845
Illinois	Chicago (N, NW subs)	847
New Jersey	New Brunswick	848
Florida	Pensacola, Tallahassee	850
New Jersey	Camden	856
Massachusetts	Boston (Metro)	857
California	Del Mar, La Jolla	858
Kentucky	Lexington	859
Connecticut	Hartford	860
New Jersey	Newark	862
Florida	Okeechobee	863
South Carolina	Greenville	864
Tennessee	Knoxville	865
Canada	Yukon, NW Territories	867
Trinidad, Tobago		868
Saint Kitts, Nevis		869
Arkansas	Jonesboro, Pine Bluff	870
Jamaica		876
Pennsylvania	Pittsburgh	878
Tennessee	Memphis	901
Canada	Nova Scotia, Prince Edward Isl.	902
Texas	Tyler	903
Florida	Jacksonville	904
Canada	Ontario, Hamilton	905
Michigan	Escanaba	906
Alaska		907
New Jersey	Elizabeth, Phillipsburg	908
California	San Bernardino	909

North American Area Codes - By CODE

State/Country	City	Area Code
North Carolina	Fayetteville	910
Georgia	Savannah	912
Kansas	Kansas City	913
New York	White Plains, Yonkers	914
Texas	El Paso	915
California	Sacramento	916
New York	Manhattan, New York City	917
Oklahoma	Tulsa	918
North Carolina	Raleigh	919
Wisconsin	Green Bay	920
California	Concord	925
Arizona	Flagstaff, Yuma	928
Tennessee	Celina, Clarksville	931
Texas	Huntsville	936
Ohio	Dayton	937
Puerto Rico		939
Texas	Wichita Falls	940
Florida	Sarasota, Fort Myers	941
Michigan	Pontiac	947
California	Newport Beach	949
California	Riverside	951
Minnesota	Bloomington	952
Florida	Fort Lauderdale	954
Texas	Brownsville	956
Colorado	Grand Junction, Ft. Collins	970
Oregon	Portland, Salem	971
Texas	Dallas (Suburbs)	972
New Jersey	Newark	973
Massachusetts	Lowell, Salem	978
Texas	Bryan, College Station	979
North Carolina	Charlotte	980
Louisiana	Hammond, Houma	985
Michigan	Alpena, Saginaw	989

General Info

Social Security Numbering

1st 3 Numbers	State Issued	1st 3 Numbers	State Issued
000	Unused	531-539	Washington
001-003	New Hampshire	540-544	Oregon
004-007	Maine	545-573	California
008-009	Vermont	574	Alaska
010-034	Massachusetts	575-576	Hawaii
035-039	Rhode Island	577-579	Washington, DC
040-049	Connecticut	580	Virgin Islands
050-134	New York	580-584	Puerto Rico
135-158	New Jersey	585	New Mexico
159-211	Pennsylvania	586	Pacific Islands
212-220	Maryland	587-588	Mississippi
221-222	Delaware	589-595	Florida
223-231	Virginia	596-599	Puerto Rico
232	North Carolina	600-601	Arizona
232-236	West Virginia	602-626	California
237-246	North Carolina	627-645	Texas
247-251	South Carolina	646-647	Utah
252-260	Georgia	648-649	New Mexico
261-267	Florida	650-653	Colorado
268-302	Ohio	654-658	South Carolina
303-317	Indiana	659-665	Louisiana
318-361	Illinois	667-675	Georgia
362-386	Michigan	676-679	Arkansas
387-399	Wisconsin	680	Nevada
400-407	Kentucky	681-690	North Carolina
408-415	Tennessee	691-699	Virginia*
416-424	Alabama	700-728	Railroad workers through 1963
425-428	Mississippi	729-733	Enumeration at Birth
429-432	Arkansas	734-749	Unassigned - for future use
433-439	Louisiana	750-751	Hawaii*
440-448	Oklahoma	752-755	Mississippi*
449-467	Texas	756-763	Tennessee*
468-477	Minnesota	764-765	Arizona
478-485	Iowa	766-772	Florida
486-500	Missouri	773-899	Unassigned - for future use
501-502	North Dakota	900-999	Not valid - used for program purposes
503-504	South Dakota		
505-508	Nebraska		
509-515	Kansas		
516-517	Montana		
518-519	Idaho		
520	Wyoming		
521-524	Colorado		
525	New Mexico		
526-527	Arizona		
528-529	Utah		
530	Nevada		

* Numbers newly allocated to this area and may not be used yet.

General Info

Acronyms

AAR	Association of American Railroads
AARP	American Association of Retired Persons
AASHTO	American Assoc. of State Highway and Transportation Officials
ABM	Anti-Ballistic Missile
ABO	Agents of Biological Origin
ACDA	United States Arms Control and Disarmament Agency
ACF	Administration for Children and Families
ACP	Area Command Post
ACP	Area Contingency Plan
ACP	Alternate Command Post
ACT FAST	Agent Characteristics Toxicity - First Aid and Special Treatment
ACYF	Administration for Children, Youth, and Families
ADA	Americans with Disabilities Act of 1990
ADAMS	Automated Disaster Assistance Management System
ADASHI	Automated Decision Aid System for Hazardous Incidents
ADD	Administration on Developmental Disabilities
ADDS	Automated Disaster Deployment System
ADRS	Automated Disaster Reporting System
AEC	Atomic Energy Commission
AEC	Agency Emergency Coordinator
AEGL	Acute Exposure Guidelines Level
AF	Air Force
AFB	Air Force Base
AFDC	Aid to Families with Dependent Children
AFEM	Alliance for Fire and Emergency Management
AFGE	American Federation of Government Employees
AFIS	American Forces Information Service
AFNSEP	Air Force National Security Emergency Preparedness
AFOSC	Air Force Operations Support Center
AFRAS	Association For Rescue At Sea
AFRAT	Air Force Radiation Assessment Team
AFRB	Air Force Reserve Base
AFRCC	Air Force Rescue Coordination Center
AFRL	Air Force Research Laboratory
AFRRI	Armed Force Radiobiology Research Institute
AFRTS	Armed Forces Radio and Television Service
AFSPC	Air Force Space Command
AG	Attorney General
AGAR	Alternate Governor's Authorized Representative
AGL	Above Ground Level
AGZ	Actual Ground Zero
AH	Alternate Headquarters
AHCC	Alternate Host Communications Center
AHJ	Agency Having Jurisdiction
AIA	American Insurance Association
AIMS	Arson Information Management System
AIS	Automated Information Systems
ALC	Agency Location Code
ALOHA	Aerial Locations of Hazardous Atmospheres
ALS	Advanced Life Support
ALSM	Airborne Laser Swath Mapping (aka LIDAR)
ALTRETCO	Alternate Regional Emergency Transportation Coordinator
AMA	American Medical Association
AMBUS	Ambulance Bus
AMC	Air Mobility Command
AMES	Ames Laboratory

```
AMPS.........Automated Message Processing System
ANG ...........Air National Guard
ANL ............Argonne National Laboratory
ANRC.........American National Red Cross
ANS ...........Alert and Notification System
ANSI ..........American National Standards Institute
AO .............Area of Operations
AoA ............Administration on Aging
AOC ...........Army Operations Center
AOC ...........Aircraft Operating Center (NOAA)
AOIC ..........Acting Official In Charge
AOR ..........Area of Responsibility
AOV ...........Agency Owned Vehicle
AP ..............Associated Press
APE ...........Area of Potential Effect
APHA.........American Public Health Association
APHIS........Animal and Plant Health Inspection Service
APIC ..........Assoc. for Professionals in Infection Control and Epidemiology
APIS ..........Advanced Passenger Information System
APR ...........Air Purifying Respirator
AQI ............Agricultural Quarantine Inspections
AR..............Army Regulation
ARC...........American Red Cross (also RC)
ARES.........Amateur Radio Emergency Services
ARI.............Acute Respiratory Infection
ARL............Army Research Laboratory
ARNG.........Army National Guard
A-ROC........Alternate Regional Operations Center
ARRL .........American Radio Relay League
ASDAR ......Aircraft-to-Satellite Data Relay
ASDSO........Association of State Dam Safety Officials
ASFPM ......Association of State Floodplain Managers
ASL............American Sign Language
ASLB .........Atomic Safety and Licensing Board
AT ..............Antiterrorism
ATC ...........Air Traffic Control
ATF............Bureau of Alcohol, Tobacco, and Firearms
AT/FP.........Antiterrorism & Force Protection
ATH ...........Air-Transportable Hospital
ATO ...........Air Tasking Order
ATSDR.......Agency for Toxic Substances and Disease Registry
ATV............All Terrain Vehicle
ATWC.........Alaska Tsunami Warning Center (now obsolete - see WCATWC)
AVIP ..........Anthrax Vaccine Immunization Program
AWIS .........Automated Weather Information System

BC..............Branch Chief
BEA ...........Bureau of Economic Analysis
Bent Spear..Nuclear Incident (codeword)
BI ...............Background Investigation
BIA .............Bureau of Indian Affairs
BIDS ..........Biological Integrated Detection System
BIIDB .........Badge Imaging Information Database
BIS .............Bureau of Industry and Security (Commerce)
BJA ............Bureau of Justice Assistance
BLM ...........Bureau of Land Management
BLS ............Bureau of Labor Statistics
BMC...........Bomb Management Center
```

BNA ....Bureau of National Affairs
B-NICE........Biological, Nuclear, Incendiary, Chemical, or Explosive
BoO ....Base of Operations
BOP ....Federal Bureau of Prisons
BOR............Bureau of Reclamation
BPRP ....Bioterrorism Preparedness and Response Program
BRB ....Benefits Review Board
Broken Arrow .....Nuclear Accident (codeword)
BSI...............Border Safety Initiative
BST..............Burn Specialty Team
BTS..............Border and Transportation Security
BTU..............British Thermal Unit
BVA ....Board of Veterans Appeals
BW ....Biological Warfare/Weapons
BY ....Budget Year

C2 ....Command and Control
C3 ....Customs Cybersmuggling Center
C3 ....Command, Control, and Communications
C4 ....Command, Control, Communications, and Computers
C4ISR ....Command, Control, Communications, and Computers,
                Intelligence, Surveillance, and Reconnaissance
CABIN........Chemical And Biological Information Network
CABINET ....Combined Agency Interdiction Network
CAD ....Computer-Assisted (or Aided) Drafting (or Design)
CADD..........Computer-Assisted Drafting and Design
CADW..........Civil Air Defense Warning
CAER..........Community Awareness and Emergency Response
CAGE..........Commercial and Government Entity
CAI..............Chemical Accident/Incident
CAM ....Chemical Agent Monitor
CAMDS......Chemical Agent Munition Disposal System
CAP ....Civil Air Patrol
CAT ....Crisis Action Team
CB ....Chemical Biological
CB ....Cluster Bomb
CBD ....Chemical and Biological Defense
CBER..........Center for Biologics Evaluation and Research
CBIRF........Chemical-Biological Incident Response Force
CBO ....Congressional Budget Office
CBP ....Bureau of Customs and Border Protection (aka BCBP)
CBR ....Chemical, Biological, and/or Radiological
CBRN..........Chemical, Biological, Radiological, or Nuclear
CBRNE ......Chemical, Biological, Radiological, Nuclear, or High-Yield Exposure
CBRT..........Chemical-Biological Response Team
CBRRT ......Chemical & Biological Rapid Response Team
CBT ....Chemical Biological Toxin
CBW ....Chemical and Biological Warfare
CCC............Crisis Coordination Center
CCFP..........National Institute of Justice, Center for Civil Force Protection
CCST..........Chemical Casualty Site Team
CD ....Civil Defense
CDC............Centers for Disease Control
CDCP..........Center for Disease Control and Prevention
CDD............Cross-Disaster Database
CDER..........Center for Drug Evaluation and Research
CDP ....Center for Domestic Preparedness
CDRDB ......Conventional Disaster Resource Database

CEF	Critical Emergency File
CEM	Certified Emergency Manager
CEMIS	Crisis and Emergency Management Information System
CEMO	Canada Emergency Measures Organization
CEMP	Comprehensive Emergency Management Plan
CENL	Chemical Event Notification Level
CEQ	Council on Environmental Quality
CFP	Community and Family Preparedness Program
CFR	Code of Federal Regulations
CG	Coast Guard
CHAWS	Chemical Hazard Warning System
CHEMTREC	Chemical Transportation Emergency Center
CHRIS	Chemical Hazard Response Information System
CIA	Central Intelligence Agency
CIAO	Critical Infrastructure Assurance Office
CIBADS	Canadian Integrated Biochemical Agent Detection System
CICAD	Center for Intelligence Collection Analysis and Dissemination
CID	U.S. Army Criminal Investigation Command
CIF	Central Information File
CIFFC	Canadian Interagency Forest Fire Centre
CINDI	Center for Integration of Natural Disaster Information
CIO	Chief Information Officer
CIS	Bureau of Citizenship and Immigration Services (BCIS)
CJIS	Criminal Justice Information System
CLS	Central Locator System
CM	Countermeasure
CMF	Case Management File
CNR	The Center for National Response
CNWDI	Critical Nuclear Weapons Design Information
CO	Commanding Officer
CO	Communications Officer
COA	Course of Action
COC	Combat Operations Center
COE	U.S. Army Corps of Engineers
COO	Chief Operating Officer
COS	Chief of Staff
CP	Command Post
CPAS	Cellular Priority Access System
CPC	Climate Prediction Center
CPG	Civil Preparedness Guide
CPHC	Central Pacific Hurricane Center
CPTED	Crime Prevention Through Environmental Design
CRC	Contamination Reduction Corridor
CRZ	Contamination Reduction Zone
CS	Chief of Staff
CSAP	Center for Substance Abuse Prevention
CSAT	Center for Substance Abuse Treatment
CSDP	Chemical Stockpile Disposal Program
CSE	Child Support Enforcement
CSEPP	Chemical Stockpile Emergency Preparedness Program
CSI	Center for the Study of Intelligence
CSI	Crime Scene Investigation
CSIRT	Computer Security Incident Response Team
CTC	Counter-Terrorism Center
CTJTF	Counter-Terrorism Joint Task Force
CUSEC	Central United States Earthquake Consortium
CVP	Citizenship Verification Procedures
CW	Chemical Weapons/Warfare

General Info

DA.............Department of the Army
DAR............Designated Agency Representative
DARPA.......Defense Advanced Research Projects Agency
DART.........Disaster Assistance Response Team
DCAA.........Defense Contract Audit Agency
DDC...........Defense Distribution Center
DEA...........Drug Enforcement Administration
DED...........Department of Education
DEFCON......Defense Condition
DESC.........Defense Energy Support Center
DEST.........Domestic Emergency Support Team
DEW..........Distant Early Warning
DFAS.........Defense Finance and Accounting Service
DFC...........Disaster Finance Center
DFO...........Disaster Field Office
DHA...........Disaster Housing Assistance
DHHS.........Department of Health and Human Services
DHP...........Disaster Housing Program
DHS...........Department of Homeland Security
DHUD.........Department of Housing and Urban Development (also HUD)
DIA...........Defense Intelligence Agency
DISA..........Defense Information Systems Agency
DLA...........Defense Logistics Agency
DMV..........Department of Motor Vehicles
DNFSB.......Defense Nuclear Facilities Safety Board
DNS...........Department of Nuclear Safety
DNSC.........Defense National Stockpile Center
DOA...........Dead on Arrival
DOB...........Date of Birth
DOC...........Department of Commerce
DOD...........Department of Defense
DOE...........Department of Energy
DOEd.........Department of Education
DOH...........Department of Health
DOI ....Department of the Interior
DOJ ....Department of Justice
DOL ....Department of Labor
DOM ....Disaster Operations Manual
DOS ....Department of State
DOT ....Department of Transportation
DPL............Denied Persons List
DPMO.........Defense Prisoner of War/Missing Personnel Office
DPRE..........Displaced Persons, Refugees, and Evacuees
DPS ....Department of Public Safety
DPW ....Department of Public Works
DRT ....Disaster Response Team
DSS ....Defense Security Service
DTRA.........Defense Threat Reduction Agency
DVA ....Department of Veterans Affairs
DWR ....Department of Water Resources

EAL............Emergency Action Level
EAM...........Emergency Action Message
EAR...........Emergency Alert Radio
EAS...........Emergency Alert System (formerly EBS)
ECA ....Bureau of Educational and Cultural Affairs
ECP ....Emergency Conservation Program

EDIS ....Emergency Disaster Information System
EDS ....Explosive Detection System
EEGL..........Emergency Exposure Guidance Level
EENET........Emergency Education Network
EEOC..........Equal Employment Opportunity Commission
EET.............Emergency Evacuation Team
EFO.............Emergency Field Office
EHS.............Extremely Hazardous Substance
EICC...........Emergency Information and Coordination Center
EIS..............Epidemic Intelligence Service
EM..............Office of Environmental Management
EMP...........Electromagnetic Pulse
Empty Quiver .....Theft, seizure, or loss of a nuclear weapon or
             component (codeword)
EMRT..........Emergency Medical Response Team
EMT ....Emergency Medical Technician
ENS ....Emergency Notification Service
EO ....Executive Order
EOC............Emergency Operations Center
EP&R..........Emergency Preparedness and Response Directorate
EPA ....Environmental Protection Agency
EPC ....Emergency Preparedness Canada
EPI.............Emergency Public Information
EPOC..........Emergency Point(s) of Contact
EPZ.............Emergency Planning Zone
EQPCE ....Earthquake Preparedness Center of Expertise
ERT ....Emergency Response Team
EUROPOL ..European Police Office

FAA.............Federal Aviation Administration
Faded Giant....Nuclear reactor radiological incident/accident (codeword)
FAO ....Food and Agriculture Organization (UN)
FAR ....Federal Acquisition Regulation
FBI ....Federal Bureau of Investigation
FBIS ....Foreign Broadcast Information Service (see WNC)
FCC ....Federal Communications Commission
FCD ....Financial Crimes Division
FCIC ....Federal Crop Insurance Corporation
FDA ....Food and Drug Administration
FDIC ....Federal Deposit Insurance Corporation
FEB ....Federal Executive Branch
FEC ....Federal Election Commission
FEMA..........Federal Emergency Management Agency
FHA ....Federal Housing Administration
FHML..........Federal Hazardous Material Law
FHWA..........Federal Highway Administration
FINCEN ......Financial Crimes Enforcement Network
FIPS............Federal Information Processing Standard
FJC ....Federal Judicial Center
FLETC ....Federal Law Enforcement Training Center
FMCS..........Federal Mediation and Conciliation Service
FMCSA ....Federal Motor Carrier Safety Administration
FNARS.......FEMA National Radio System
FOB ....Federal Office Building
FOIA ....Freedom of Information Act
FOUO ....For Official Use Only
FPS............Federal Protective Service
FRA ....Federal Railroad Administration

FRB ....Federal Reserve Board
FRS ....Federal Reserve System
FS ....Forest Service
FSIS............Food Safety and Inspection Service
FSM ....Federated States of Micronesia
FSS............Federal Supply Service
FTA ....Federal Transit Administration
FTC............Federal Trade Commission
FTS............Federal Technology Service
FTS............Federal Telephone System
FWS..........United States Fish and Wildlife Service
FY ....Fiscal Year

GAO...........General Accounting Office
GATT ....General Agreement on Tariffs and Trade
GCE ....Government Cost Estimate
GCOS ....Global Climate Observing System
GEMINI ......Global Emergency Management Information Network Initiative
GEMS ....Global Emergency Management System
GILS ....Government Information Locator Service
GIS ....Geographic Information Systems
GIX ....Government Information Xchange
GNIS..........Geographic Names Information System
GPO ....Government Printing Office
GPS ....Global Positioning System
GSA ....General Services Administration
GST ....Ground Support Team
GTA ....Government Travel Authorization
GTS ....Global Telecommunications System

Hazmat ......Hazardous Material(s)
HEAR..........Hospital Emergency Administrative Radio
HERN..........Hospital Emergency Radio Network
HHA ....High Hazard Area
HHS ....Department of Health and Human Services
HIDTA........High Intensity Drug Trafficking Area
HIRA ....Hazard Identification and Risk Assessment
HM ....Hazardous Materials
HMRU ....Hazardous Materials Response Unit
HQ ....Headquarters
HSAS..........Homeland Security Advisory System
HSUS..........The Humane Society of the United States
HUD...........Department of Housing and Urban Development

IAC.............DoD Information Analysis Center
IACP...........International Association of Chiefs of Police
IAEA ....International Atomic Energy Agency
IAF ....Inter-American Foundation
IAIP............Information Analysis and Infrastructure Protection Directorate
IAP ....Incident Action Plan
IC ....Incident Command/Commander
ICAO..........International Civil Aviation Organization
ICAP...........Incident Communications Action Plan
ICBM ....Intercontinental Ballistic Missile
ICC ....Incident Command Center
ICD ....Improvised Chemical Device
ICE ....Bureau of Immigration and Customs Enforcement
ICP..............Incident Command Post

ICS	Incident Command System
IHS	Indian Health Service
ILAB	Bureau of International Labor Affairs
ILO	International Labour Organization
IMF	International Monetary Fund
INF	Intermediate Range Nuclear Forces
INL	Bureau of International Narcotics and Law Enforcement Affairs
INS	Immigration and Naturalization Service (see USCIS)
INTERPOL	International Criminal Police Organization
IOM	International Organization for Migration
IRBM	Intermediate Range Ballistic Missile
IRS	Internal Revenue Service
IRT	Initial Response Team
IRZ	Immediate Response Zone
ISA	Incident Staging Area
ISP	Information Systems Plan
IST	Incident Support Team
IT	Information Technology
ITF	Intelligence Task Force
ITIC	International Tsunami Information Center
IWIN	Interactive Weather Information Network
IWP	Integrated Warning Program
JAG	Judge Advocate General
JCS	Joint Chiefs of Staff
JFC	Joint Force Commander
JFO	Joint Field Office
LANDSAT	Land Satellite
LERN	Law Enforcement Radio Net
LESO	Law Enforcement Security Officer
LETS	Law Enforcement Telecommunications System
LNO	Liaison Officer
LPZ	Low Population Zone
LZ	Landing Zone
MAEC	Mid-America Earthquake Center
MARAD	Maritime Administration
MARS	Military Affiliated Radio System
MC	Marine Corps
MCTL	Militarily Critical Technologies List
MDA	Missile Defense Agency
MO	Medical Officer
MP	Military Police
MPD	Maximum Potential Destruction
MPE	Maximum Permissible Exposure
MPH	Miles Per Hour
NAAK	Nerve Agent Antidote Kit
NACIC	National Counterintelligence Center
NAERG	North American Emergency Response Guidebook
NAFTA	North American Free Trade Agreement
NAICS	North American Industry Classification System
NARFE	National Association of Retired Federal Employees
NARP	Nuclear Accident Response Plan/Procedures
NASA	National Aeronautics and Space Administration
NASAR	National Association for Search and Rescue
NATO	North Atlantic Treaty Organization

General Info

NAWAS	National Alert and Warning System
NBC	Nuclear, Biological, and Chemical
NBII	National Biological Information Infrastructure
NCA	National Cemetery Administration
NCBI	National Center for Biotechnology Information
NCC	National Coordinating Center for Telecommunications
NCCDPHP	National Center for Chronic Disease Prevention and Health Promotion
NCDC	National Climatic Data Center
NCEH	National Center for Environmental Health
NCIC	National Crime Information Center
NCID	National Center for Infectious Diseases
NCIS	Naval Criminal Investigative Service
NCJRS	National Criminal Justice Reference Service
NCO	Non-Commissioned Officer
NCP	National Oil and Hazardous Substances Pollution Contingency Plan (aka National Contingency Plan)
NCR	National Capital Region
NCRR	National Center for Research Resources
NCS	National Communications System
NCTR	National Center for Toxicological Research
NDIC	National Drug Intelligence Center
NDPO	National Domestic Preparedness Office
NDS	National Defense Stockpile
NEC	National Earthquake Center
NEMIS	National Emergency Management Information System
NEMT	National Emergency Management Team
NERSC	National Energy Research Scientific Computing Center
NESDIS	National Environmental Satellite, Data, and Information Service
NETC	National Emergency Training Center
NEXRAD	Next Generation Weather Radar
NFA	National Fire Academy
NFDC	National Fire Data Center
NFP	Not For Profit
NFS	National Forest System
NG	National Guard
NGDC	National Geophysical Data Center
NGO	Non-Governmental Organization
NHC	National Hurricane Center
NHI	National Highway Institute
NHTSA	National Highway Traffic Safety Administration
NIAID	National Institute of Allergy and Infectious Diseases
NIC	National Institute of Corrections
NIDA	National Institute on Drug Abuse
NIFC	National Interagency Fire Center
NIH	National Institutes of Health
NIJ	National Institute of Justice
NIMA	National Imagery and Mapping Agency (replaced by NGA)
NIMH	National Institute of Mental Health
NIOSH	National Institute for Occupational Safety and Health
NIP	National Immunization Program
NIPC	National Infrastructure Protection Center
NIRT	Nuclear Incident Response Team
NIST	National Institute of Standards and Technology
NLETS	National Law Enforcement Telecommunications System
NMB	National Mediation Board
NNSA	National Nuclear Security Administration
NOAA	National Oceanic and Atmospheric Administration

NORTHCOM ......United States Northern Command
NOS............Not Otherwise Specified
NPIN ....CDC National Prevention Information Network
NPS............National Park Service
NPSP..........National Pharmaceutical Stockpile Program
NRAT ....Nuclear Radiological Advisory Team
NRC............United States Nuclear Regulatory Commission
NRCS ....Natural Resources Conservation Service
NRO ....National Reconnaissance Office
NRP ....National Response Plan
NRS ....National Response System
NRT ....National Response Team
NSA/CSS ....National Security Agency/Central Security Service
NSC ....National Security Council
NTIA ....National Telecommunications and Information Administration
NTIS ....National Technical Information Service
NTP ....National Toxicology Program
NTS ....National Traffic System
NTSB ....National Transportation Safety Board
NWC ....National Warning Center
NWCG ....National Wildfire Coordinating Group
NWP ....Neighborhood Watch Program
NWR ....National Weather Radio
NWS ....National Weather Service
NWTRB......Nuclear Waste Technical Review Board

OA ....Office of Administration
OAR ....Office of Oceanic and Atmospheric Research
OAS ....Organization of American States
OC ....Operations Center
OCPM........Office of Crisis Planning and Management
OCRWM ....Office of Civilian Radioactive Waste Management
ODP ....Office of Domestic Preparedness
OEM ....Office of Emergency Management
OER...........Office of Emergency Response
OET ....Office of Emergency Transportation
OHS ....Office of Homeland Security
OI ....Office of Investigations
OIA ....Office of International Affairs (part of DHS)
OIC ....Officer in Charge
OIG ....Office of the Inspector General (USDA)
OJJDP ....Office of Juvenile Justice and Delinquency Prevention
OJP............Office of Justice Programs
ONDCP......Office of National Drug Control Policy
ONP ....Office of National Preparedness
OPS ....Operations
ORD...........Office of Research and Development (EPA)
ORR...........Office of Refugee Resettlement
OSERS ......Office of Special Education and Rehabilitative Services
OSHA........Occupational Safety and Health Administration
OSTI ....Office of Scientific and Technical Information
OTT ....Office of Transportation Technologies
OVC ....Office for Victims of Crime

PACOM......Pacific Command
PAHO..........Pan American Health Organization
PIO ....Public Information Officer
POTUS ......President of the United States

POW/MIA....Prisoner of War/Missing in Action
PPQ...........Plant Protection and Quarantine
PSR...........Personal Service Radio
PTSD.........Post Traumatic Stress Disorder
PTWC........Pacific Tsunami Warning Center

QRT...........Quick Response Team

RACES.......Radio Amateur Civil Emergency Services
RC..............Red Cross (aka ARC)
RCAC.........Red Cross Assistance Center
R&D...........Research & Development
RDT...........Rapid Deployment Team
RECON.......Reconnaissance
RECP.........Regional Emergency Communications Plan
REP...........Regional Evacuation Plan
RF..............Radio Frequency
RFA............Request for Federal Assistance
RFO............Regional Field Office
RMA...........Risk Management Agency
RMI............Republic of the Marshall Islands
RNA............Rapid Needs Assessment
ROTC.........Reserve Officer Training Corps
R&R...........Response & Recovery
RSA............Rehabilitation Services Administration
RSPA..........Research and Special Programs Administration

SAC............Special Agent in Charge
SAMHSA.....Substance Abuse and Mental Health Services Administration
SAT............Satellite
SATCOM....Satellite Communications
SAVE..........Systematic Alien Verification for Entitlement
SBA...........Small Business Administration
SBI............Special Background Investigation
SDWIS.......Safe Drinking Water Information System
SECC.........State Emergency Coordination Center
SECDEF.....Secretary of Defense
SECDHS....Secretary of Homeland Security
SECHHS....Secretary of Health and Human Services
SEER.........Surveillance, Epidemiology, and End Results
SEL............Standardized Equipment List
SEMA.........State Emergency Management Agency
SEMS.........Standardized Emergency Management System
SERT.........State Emergency Response Team
SEVIS........Student and Exchange Visitor Information System
SFO...........State Field Office
SIC............Standard Industrial Classification
SIP............Shelter In Place
SITREP.......Situation Report
SITROOM...Situation Room
SJI............State Justice Institute
Sleeping Dragon....Term used to identify a barrier of protesters who have
                   linked themselves to one another
SNS...........Strategic National Stockpile
SO.............Sheriff's Office
SOB...........Souls on Board
SOC...........State Operations Center
SS.............Secret Service

```
SSA ...........Social Security Administration
SSN ...........Social Security Number
SSS ...........Selective Service System
S&T............Science and Technology Directorate (DHS)
START.......Strategic Arms Reduction Talks
STATREP ...Status Report
STB............State Transportation Board
SWAT ........Special Weapons and Tactics
SWC ..........Severe Weather Center

TADS .........Threat Assessment Database System
TANF .........Temporary Assistance for Needy Families
TAR ...........Tone-Alert Radio(s)
TASC .........Transportation Administrative Service Center
TBA............To Be Announced
TBD ...........To Be Determined
TDY ...........Temporary Duty
TF ..............Task Force
THREATCON.....(Terrorist) Threat Condition
TIPS...........Terrorist Information and Prevention System
Treas..........Department of the Treasury
TRI.............Toxics Release Inventory
TRP ...........Tactical Response Plan
TS..............Top Secret
TSA............Transportation Security Administration
TSI ............Transportation Safety Institute
TVA............Tennessee Valley Authority

UC .............Unified Command
UCP ...........Unified Command Plan
UCT ...........Universal Coordinated Time
UD .............Unified Defense
UN .............United Nations
UNHCR.......United Nations High Commissioner for Refugees Program
UNICEF ......United Nations Children's Fund
UNICOR.....Federal Prison Industries, Inc.
USA ...........United States Army
USACE .......United States Army Corps of Engineers
USAF .........United States Air Force
USAR .........United States Army Reserve
USBR .........Bureau of Reclamation
USC ...........United States Code
USCG .........United States Coast Guard
USCGR.......United States Coast Guard Reserve
USCIS........U.S. Citizenship and Immigration Services
USCS .........United States Customs Service
USDA.........United States Department of Agriculture
USDOI .......United States Department of the Interior
USDOL .......United States Department of Labor
USFA .........United States Fire Administration
USFS .........United States Forest Service
USFW ........United States Fish and Wildlife Service
USG ...........United States Government
USGS .........United States Geological Survey
USIA ..........United States Information Agency (changed to IIP)
USMC .........United States Marine Corps
USMCR......United States Marine Corps Reserve
USML.........United States Munitions List
```

USMRID......United States Army Medical Research of Infectious Diseases
USMS ....United States Marshals Service
USMTF ......United States Message Text Format(ting)
USN ....United States Navy
USNR..........United States Navy Reserve
USNCB ....United States National Central Bureau of INTERPOL
USNORTHCOM.....United States Northern Command
USPACOM..United States Pacific Command
USPHS ....United States Public Health Service
USPS ....United States Postal Service
US&R..........Urban Search & Rescue
USS ....United States Senate
USSC.........United States Sentencing Commission
USSOCOM .United States Special Operations Command
USSOUTHCOM .....United States Southern Command
USSPACECOM .....United States Space Command
USSS ....United States Secret Service
USSTRATCOM......United States Strategic Command
US-Visit.......United States Visitor and Immigrant Status Indicator Technology
USVI ....United States Virgin Islands

VA............Department of Veterans Affairs
VAWO.........Violence Against Women Office
VBA ....Veterans Benefits Administration
VETS ....Veterans' Employment and Training Service
VFD ....Volunteer Fire Department
VI ....Virgin Islands
VIPS ....Volunteers in Police Service
VISTA ....Volunteers in Service to America
VOA ....Voice of America

WAPA ....Western Area Power Administration
WCATWC ...West Coast & Alaska Tsunami Warning Center
WFP............World Food Program (United Nations)
WHMO ....White House Military Office
WHO ....World Health Organization
WHSR........White House Situation Room
WMD ....Weapons of Mass Destruction
WTO ....World Trade Organization

ZIP (Code) ..Zone Improvement Plan
ZULU ....Greenwich Mean Time

Sources:

"The FAAT List" FEMA Acronyms Abbreviations & Terms, US Department of
Homeland Security, Federal Emergency Management Agency, August 2003.

Abbreviation A-Z, The A-Z of Acronyms & Abbreviations on the Net,
http://www.abbreviationz.com/

Abbreviations and Acronyms of the U.S. Government,
http://www.ulib.iupui.edu/subjectareas/gov/docs_abbrev.html

US Links, Federal Government Agencies Database,
http://www.lib.duke.edu/texis/uslinks/uslinks/acronyms.html

INCIDENT MANAGEMENT SYSTEMS

National Incident Management System (NIMS) · · · · **200**

Incident Command System (ICS) · · · · · · · · · · · · · 203
  ICS Command · 206
  ICS Operations · 209
  ICS Planning · 210
  ICS Logistics · 211
  ICS Finance and Administration · · · · · · · · · · · · · 213
  ICS Facilities and Areas · · · · · · · · · · · · · · · · · · · 214
  Incident Action Plan (IAP) · · · · · · · · · · · · · · · · · 214
NIMS Multiagency Coordination Systems · · · · · · · · 220
NIMS Public Information Systems · · · · · · · · · · · · · · 222
NIMS Preparedness · 223
NIMS Resource Management · · · · · · · · · · · · · · · · · 229
NIMS Communications and Information Management 233
NIMS Supporting Technologies · · · · · · · · · · · · · · · 236
NIMS Ongoing Management and Maintenance · · · · · 238
NIMS Resource Typing System · · · · · · · · · · · · · · · 241
NIMS Glossary · 248
NIMS Acronyms · 262

National Incident Management System (NIMS)

On February 23, 2003 the President issued HSPD-5 to develop a new National Incident Management System (NIMS). This system, based on the foundation already laid by pre-existing incident management and emergency response systems, is comprised of a central nationwide template for response for Federal, State, local, and tribal governments during times of domestic incidents (such as terrorism, fires, floods, earthquakes, hurricanes, tornados, typhoons, hazardous material spills, nuclear incidents, aircraft accidents, war-related disasters, etc.) NIMS sets forth a core message of doctrine, concepts, principles, technology, and organization. Under this new system the National Response Plan (NRP) will be developed which will integrate Federal government domestic prevention, preparedness, response, and recovery plans into one all-inclusive, comprehensive plan.

All Federal departments and agencies are required to adopt the NIMS and apply the new system to their individual incident management, emergency prevention, recovery, preparedness, response, and mitigation activities. In addition State and local organizations who want Federal preparedness assistance (such as contracts, grants, etc) will need to adopt NIMS as of FY2005.

NIMS Components

Command and Management

- **ICS - Incident Command System:** Defines the operating characteristics, interactive management components, and structure of incident management and emergency response organizations engaged throughout the life cycle of an incident. (see page 203)

- **Multiagency Coordination Systems:** Defines the operating characteristics, interactive management components, and organizational structure of supporting incident management entities engaged at the Federal, State, local, tribal, and regional levels through mutual-aid agreements and other assistance arrangements. (see pg 220)

- **Public Information Systems:** Refers to the process, procedure and systems needed for communicating timely and accurate information to the public during crisis or emergency situations. (see page 222)

Preparedness

Effective incident management begins with a host of preparedness activities conducted on a "steady-state" basis, well in advance of any potential incident.

- **Planning:** Describe how personnel, equipment, and other resources are used to support incident management and emergency response activities. Plans provide mechanisms and systems for setting priorities, integrating multiple entities and functions, and ensuring that communications and other systems are available and integrated in support of a full spectrum of incident management requirements.

- **Training:** Includes standard courses on multiagency incident command and management, organizational structure, and operational procedures; discipline- specific and agency-specific incident management courses; and courses on the integration and use of supporting technologies.

- **Exercises:** Incident management organizations and personnel must participate in realistic exercises (including multidisciplinary, multijurisdictional, and multisector interaction) to improve integration and interoperability and optimize resource utilization during incident operations.

- **Personnel Qualification and Certification:** Activities are undertaken to identify and publish national-level standards and measure performance to ensure that incident management and emergency responder personnel are appropriately qualified and officially certified to perform NIMS related functions.

- **Equipment Acquisition and Certification:** Incident management organizations and emergency responders at all levels rely on various types of equipment to perform mission essential tasks. A critical component of operational preparedness is the acquisition of equipment that will perform to certain standards, including the capability to be interoperable with similar equipment used by other jurisdictions.

- **Mutual Aid:** Agreements are the means for one jurisdiction to provide resources, facilities, services, and other required support to another jurisdiction during an incident. Each jurisdiction should be party to a mutual-aid agreement with appropriate jurisdictions from which they expect to receive or to which they expect to provide assistance during an incident.

- **Publications Management:** Refers to forms and forms standardization, developing publication materials, administering publications - including establishing naming and numbering conventions, managing the publication and promulgation of documents, and exercising control over sensitive documents and revising publications when necessary.

Resource Management

The NIMS defines standardized mechanisms and establishes requirements for processes to describe, inventory, mobilize, dispatch, track, and recover resources over the life cycle of an incident.

Communications and Information Management

The NIMS identifies the requirement for a standardized framework for communications, information management (collection, analysis, and dissemination), and information-sharing at all levels of incident management.

- **Incident Management Communications:** Ensures that effective, interoperable communications processes, procedures, and systems exist to support a wide variety of incident management activities across agencies and jurisdictions.

- **Information Management:** These processes, procedures, and systems help ensure that information, including communications and data, flows efficiently through a commonly accepted architecture supporting numerous agencies and jurisdictions responsible for managing or directing domestic incidents, those impacted by the incident, and those contributing resources to the incident management effort. Effective information management enhances incident management and response and helps insure that crisis decision making is better informed.

- **Supporting Technologies:** Technology and technological systems provide supporting capabilities essential to implementing and continuously refining the NIMS. These include voice and data communications systems, information management systems (i.e., record keeping and resource tracking), and data display systems. Also included are specialized technologies that facilitate ongoing operations and incident management activities in situations that call for unique technology-based capabilities.

- **Ongoing Management and Maintenance:** Establishes an activity to provide strategic direction for and oversight of the NIMS, supporting both routine review and the continuous refinement of the system and its components over the long term.

Incident Command System (ICS)

"Incident Command System" (ICS) is a management system designed to enable effective and efficient domestic incident management by integrating a combination of facilities, equipment, personnel, procedures, and communications operating within a common organizational structure, designed to enable effective and efficient domestic incident management.

ICS is a highly adaptable system that is used for both near and long-term operations, from small to complex incidents, covers a broad spectrum of emergency situations (both natural and manmade), applicable across disciplines, and is used by all levels of government - Federal, State, local, tribal, the private-sector, and nongovernmental organizations.

ICS Basic Principles

ICS operates according to basic principles to ensure quick and effective resource commitment.

- Most incidents are managed locally.
- The NIMS requires that field command and management function be performed in accordance with a standard set of ICS organizations, doctrine, and procedures.
- ICS is modular and scalable. It is designed to be effective with a single agency or multiple agencies, readily adaptable to new technology, applicable and acceptable to users throughout the country, adaptable to any emergency or incident, and have a scalable organizational structure that is based on the size and complexity of the incident.
- ICS has interactive management components that set the stage for effective and efficient incident management and emergency response.
- ICS establishes common terminology, standards, and procedures that enable diverse organizations to work together effectively.
- ICS incorporates measurable objectives that ensure fulfillment of incident management goals.
- The implementation of ICS should have the least possible disruption on existing systems and processes.
- ICS should be user friendly and be applicable across a wide spectrum of emergency response and incident management disciplines.

ICS Management Characteristics

ICS is based on proven management characteristics, each of which contribute to the strength and overall efficiency of the system.

- Common terminology for organizational functions, resource descriptions, and incident facilities.

- A modular organizational structure that develops in a top-down modular fashion based on the size, hazards, and complexity of the incident.

- Management by objectives, such as establishing overarching objectives, developing and issuing assignments, plans, procedures, and protocols, establishing specific, measurable objectives from various incident activities, and documenting results to measure performance and facilitate corrective action.

- Reliance on an Incident Action Plan (IAP) which provides a coherent means of communicating the overall incident objectives in the contexts of both operational and support activities.

- Manageable span of control, ranging from three to seven subordinates for any individual with incident management supervisory responsibility.

- Predesignated incident locations and facilities for requirements such as decontamination, donated goods processing, mass care, and evacuation. Typical facilities include command posts, bases, camps, staging areas, mass casualty triage areas, etc.

- Comprehensive resource management to maintain an accurate and up-to-date picture of resource utilization.

- Integrated communications which link the operational and support units of the various agencies involved.

- Establishment and transfer of command.

- Chain of command and unity of command, referring to the orderly line of authority within the ranks of the incident management organization and that every individual has a designated supervisor.

- Unified command where multiple jurisdictions can work together effectively without affecting individual agency authority, responsibility, and accountability.

- Accountability at all jurisdictional levels and within individual functional areas during an incident. Accountability includes check-in of all responders, an incident action plan, unity of command, span of control, and resource tracking.

- Deployment ensures that personnel and equipment should respond only when requested or when dispatched by an appropriate authority.
- Information and intelligence is gathered by the incident management organization to establish a process for gathering, sharing, and managing incident-related information.

Five Major Functional Areas of ICS

Command (page 206)
Operations (page 209)
Planning (page 210)
Logistics (page 211)
Finance and Administration (page 213)

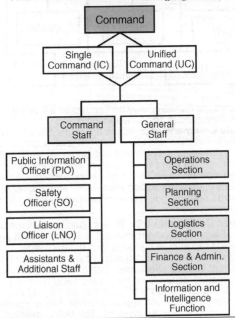

Command

The Command Staff is responsible for overall management of the incident. This includes the single Incident Commander and the Command Staff.

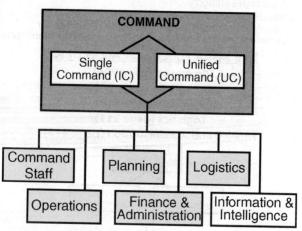

The Command Function may be conducted either with a single Incident Commander or a Unified Command.

- **Single Command - IC:** When an incident occurs within a single jurisdiction and there is no jurisdictional or functional agency overlap, a single Incident Commander (IC) should be designated with overall incident management responsibility. The IC will then develop the incident objectives, Incident Action Plan (IAP), and answer all requests pertaining to the ordering and releasing of incident resources.

- **Unified Command - UC:** This is used in multijurisdictional or multiagency domestic incident management. It provides guidelines to enable agencies with different legal, geographic, and functional responsibilities to coordinate, plan, and interact effectively. The exact composition of the UC structure depends on the location and type of incident. The designated agency officials that participate in the UC represent the different legal authorities and functional areas of responsibility for the incident. The IAP is developed by the Planning Section Chief and is approved by the UC. The Operations Section Chief (usually someone from the agency with the greatest jurisdictional involvement) directs the tactical implementation of the IAP.

- The greatest difference between the two is that in an IC structure there is one commander responsible for establishing the incident management objectives and strategies. In a UC structure, the individuals designated by their jurisdictional authorities must jointly determine objectives, strategies, plans, and priorities and work together to execute integrated incident operations.

- **Area Command:** This is activated only if necessary, depending on the complexity of the incident and incident management span-of-control considerations. It is usually established either to oversee the management of multiple incidents that are each being handled by a separate ICS organization or to oversee the management of a very large incident that involves multiple ICS organizations. Area Command is also used when there are a number of incidents in the same area and of the same type, (such as two or more hazardous material (HAZMAT) or oil spills, and fires) because they would be competing for the same resources to handle the incident.

  An Area Command is responsible for:
  - setting overall incident-related priorities.
  - allocating critical resources according to priorities.
  - ensuring that incidents are properly managed.
  - ensuring that incident management objectives are met and do not conflict with each other or with agency policy.
  - identifying critical resource needs and reporting them to EOCs or multiagency coordination entities.
  - ensuring that short-term emergency recovery is coordinated to assist in the transition to full recovery operations.

- **General staff** under the Command section are responsible for the major functional elements of the ICS including Operations, Planning, Logistics, Finance and Administration, and occasionally Information and Intelligence.

- **Command Staff** positions are established to assign responsibility for key activities not specifically identified in the General Staff functional elements, such as Public Information Officer (PIO), Safety Officer (SO), and Liaison Officer (LNO).

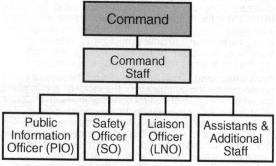

- **Public Information Officer (PIO):** Responsible for interfacing with the public and media regarding the incident's cause, size, current situation, resources committed, and other matters of general interest. Only one PIO should be designated, and the IC must approve the release of all incident-related information.
- **Safety Officer (SO):** Monitors incident operations and advises the IC on all matters relating to operational safety, including the health and safety of emergency responder personnel. The SO has emergency authority to stop and/or prevent unsafe acts during incident operations. Only one SO should be designated.
- **Liaison Officer (LNO):** The point of contact for representatives of other governmental agencies, nongovernmental organizations, and private entities.
- **Assistants to Command Staff and Additional Positions** may become necessary depending on the nature and location of the incident, and specific requirements established by the IC. Additional Position may include Legal Counsel and Medical Advisors.

Operations Section

Responsible for all activities focused on reduction of the immediate hazard, saving lives and property, establishing situational control, and restoration of normal operations.

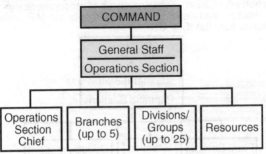

- **The Operations Section Chief** is responsible to the IC or UC for the direct management of all incident-related operational activities. A different chief should be designated for each operational period. Each chief should establish tactical objectives for their period and have direct involvement in the preparation of the IAP for the corresponding period.
- **Branches** may be used in a functional or geographic nature. They are used to divide groups which exceed the recommended span of control (normally a ratio of 1:5, but for large-scale operations, 1:8 or 1:10 is acceptable.)
- **Divisions and Groups** are established when the number of resources exceeds the manageable span of control of the IC and the Operations Section Chief. Divisions divide an incident into a physical or geographical area of operation, and groups divide an incident into functional areas of operation.
- **Resources** refer to the combination of personnel and equipment required to enable incident management operations. Depending on the incident there could be *single resources* (individuals or equipment items), *task forces* (combination of resources to support a specific need or mission with a designated leader), *strike teams* (a set number of resources of the same kind and type with an established minimum number of personnel).

Planning Section

Collects, evaluates, and disseminates incident situation information and intelligence to the IC or UC and incident management personnel, prepares status reports, displays situation information, maintains status of resources assigned to the incident, and develops and documents the IAP based of guidance from the IC or UC.

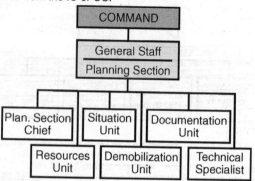

- **The Planning Section Chief** oversees all incident-related data gathering and analysis regarding incident operations and assigned resources, develops alternatives for tactical operations, conducts planning meeting, and prepares the IAP for each operational period.

- **The Resources Unit** makes certain that all assigned personnel and resources have checked in at the incident and is also responsible for keeping track of the current location and status of all assigned resources including personnel, teams, facilities, supplies, and major items of equipment.

- **The Situation Unit** collects, processes, and organizes ongoing situation information, prepares situation summaries, and develops projections and forecasts of future events related to the incident.

- **The Demobilization Unit** develops an Incident Demobilization Plan that has specific instructions for all personnel and resources that will require demobilization.

- **The Documentation Unit** maintains accurate and complete incident files, including all steps taken to resolve the incident. They are responsible for filing, maintaining, and storing incident files for legal, analytical, and historical purposes, and also provide duplication services to incident personnel.
- **Technical Specialists** are activated when needed during an incident. They have special skills and function in a wide variety of incident scenarios requiring technical specialists. They may serve anywhere within the organization.

Logistics Section

Responsible for all support requirements needed to facilitate effective and efficient incident management, including ordering resources from off-incident locations. They also provide facilities, transportation, supplies, equipment maintenance and fuel, food services, communications and information technology support, and emergency responder medical services (such as inoculations).

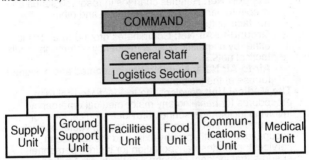

- **The Supply Unit** orders, receives, stores, and processes all incident-related resources, personnel, and supplies.
- **The Ground Support Unit** maintains and services vehicles and mobile equipment at the incident. In addition they maintain a transportation pool to be at the ready for future incidents.
- **The Facilities Unit** sets up, maintains, demobilizes all facilities used in support of incident operations, and provides facility maintenance and security services required to support incident operations.

- **The Food Unit** determines food and water requirements, including planning menus, ordering food, providing cooking facilities, cooking, serving, maintaining food service areas, and managing food security and safety concerns.
- **The Communications Unit** develops the Communications Plan (ICS205) to make the most effective use of the communications equipment and facilities assigned to the incident, installs and tests all equipment, supervises and operates the incident communications center, distributes and recovers communications equipment assigned to incident personnel, and maintains and repairs communications equipment on site. Radio networks for large incidents will normally be organized as follows:
  - **Command Net:** Links together incident command, command staff, section chiefs, branch directors, division, and group supervisors.
  - **Tactical Nets:** Connects agencies, depts, geographical areas, and specific functional units.
  - **Support Net:** Handles changes in resource status and is able to handle logistical requests and other nontactical functions.
  - **Ground-to-Air Net:** Coordinates ground-to-air traffic, either by a specific tactical frequency or through regular tactical nets.
  - **Air-to-Air Nets:** Normally predesignated and assigned for use at the incident.
- **The Medical Unit** develops the Incident Medical Plan, procedures for handling any major medical emergency involving incident personnel, provides medical care for incident personnel (such as vaccinations, vector control, occupational health, prophylaxis, and mental health services), provides transportation for injured personnel, ensures that incident personnel patients are tracked, assists in processing paperwork related to injuries or death of assigned personnel, and coordinates personnel and mortuary affairs for incident personnel.

Finance and Administration Section

When there is a specific need for financial, reimbursement (individual, agency, or department), or administrative services to support incident management activities, a Finance and Administration Section will be established. Not all incidents will need to create this section.

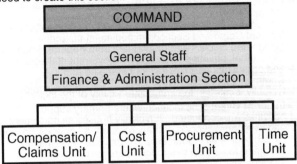

- **The Compensation and Claims Unit** handles injury compensation and claims associated with the incident.
- **The Cost Unit** provides cost analysis data for the incident. They ensure that all equipment and personnel for which payment is required is properly identified, obtain and record all cost data, and analyze and prepare estimates of incident costs.
- **The Procurement Unit** administers all financial matters pertaining to vendor contracts. They coordinate with local jurisdictions to identify sources for equipment, prepares and signs equipment rental agreements, and processes all administrative requirements associated with equipment rental and supply contracts.
- **The Time Unit** is responsible for ensuring proper daily recording of personnel time, and equipment usage time (in the Logistics section or Ground Support Unit).

Information and Intelligence Function

Includes national security and other types of classified information, along with other operational information, such as risk assessments, medical intelligence, surveillance, weather information, geospatial data, structural designs, toxic contaminant levels, and utilities and public works data.

ICS Facilities and Areas

Several kinds and types of facilities may be established in and around the incident area. The requirements of the incident and the desires of the IC will determine the specific kinds of facilities used and their locations.

- **Incident Command Post (ICP):** The location of the tactical-level, on-scene incident command and management organization. It is typically comprised of the Incident Command Section, immediate staff, and other designated officials and responders from Federal, State, local, tribal, private-sector, and nongovernmental agencies and organizations. The Incident Planning and Communications also takes place at this location. It is typically located in the immediate vicinity of the incident.

- **Incident Base:** The location where primary support activities are conducted. It typically houses all equipment and personnel support operations and the Logistics Section (which orders all resources and supplies). It is typically designed to be able to support operations at multiple incident sites.

- **Camps:** They are located in satellite fashion, separate from the Incident Base. They provide certain essential auxiliary forms of support, such as food, sleeping areas, sanitation, and minor maintenance and servicing of equipment. They are mobile and can be relocated to meet changing operational requirements.

- **Mobilization and Staging Areas:** These are established for temporary location of available resources. They are established by the Operations Section Chief to enable positioning of and accounting for resources not immediately assigned. Areas may include temporary feeding, fueling, sanitation services, and temporary housing for personnel, supplies, and equipment.

Incident Action Plan (IAP)

The following represents a template for strategic, operational, and tactical planning that includes all steps an IC and other members of the Command and General Staffs should take to develop and disseminate an Incident Action Plan (IAP). This process may begin with the scheduling of a planned event, the onset of a credible threat, or the initial response to an actual or impending event.

There are five primary phases which must be followed in sequence to ensure a comprehensive IAP.

1. Understand the Situation

The first phase gathers, records, analyzes, and displays situation and resource information in a manner that will ensure a clear picture of the magnitude, complexity, and potential impact of the incident, and the ability to determine the resources required to develop and implement an effective IAP.

2. Establish Incident Objectives and Strategy

The second phase formulates and prioritizes incident objectives and identifies an appropriate strategy. They must conform to the legal obligations and management objectives of all affected agencies. Reasonable strategies that will accomplish overall incident objectives are identified, analyzed, and evaluated to determine the most appropriate strategy for the situation at hand. Evaluation criteria includes public health and safety factors, estimated costs, and various legal, environmental, and political considerations.

3. Develop the Plan

The third phase determines the tactical direction and the specific resources, reserves, and support requirements that will be needed for implementing the selected strategy for one operational period. This phase is usually the responsibility of the IC, who devises a plan that makes the best use of these resources.

4. Prepare and Disseminate the Plan

The fourth phase prepares the plan in a format that is appropriate for the level of complexity of the incident. The initial response may be prepared in an outline for an oral briefing. Incidents spanning over multiple operational periods will then develop plans in writing according to ICS procedures.

5. Evaluate and Revise the Plan

The fifth phase evaluates planned events and checks the accuracy of information used in planning subsequent operational periods. The General Staff should compare planned progress with actual progress, and when deviations occur or new information emerges, the current plan should be modified and redeveloped for the subsequent operational period.

Summation of Planning Responsibilities and Activities
General Responsibilities
- **Planning Section Chief:** Conducts the Planning Meeting and coordinates preparation of the IAP.
- **Incident Commander:** Provides overall control objectives and strategies, establishes procedures for off-incident resource ordering and resource activation, mobilization, and employment, and approves the completed IAP plan by signature.
- **Finance Section Chief:** Provides cost implication of control objectives (as required), evaluates facilities being used and determines if any special arrangements are needed, and ensures that the IAP is within the financial limits established by the IC.
- **Operations Section Chief:** Determines division work assignments and resource requirements.
- **Logistics Section Chief:** Ensures that incident facilities are adequate and that the resource ordering procedure is made known to appropriate agency dispatch centers, develops a transportation system to support operational needs, ensures that the section can logistically support the IAP, and places orders for resources.

Preplanning Steps
The Planning Section Chief should complete the following before the initial Planning Meeting:
- Evaluate the current situation and decide whether the current planning is adequate for the remainder of the operational period.
- Advice the IC and Operations Section Chief of any suggested revisions to the current plan.
- Establish a planning cycle for the IC.
- Determine Planning Meeting attendees in consultation with the IC. Major incidents should include:
  - Incident Commander
  - Command Staff Members
  - General Staff Members
  - Resources Unit Leader
  - Situation Unit Leader
  - Air Operations Branch Director (if established)
  - Communications Unit Leader
  - Technical Specialists (as required)
  - Agency Representatives (as required)

- Establish the location and time for the Planning Meeting.
- Ensure that planning boards and forms are available.
- Notify necessary support staff about the meeting and their assignments.
- Ensure that a current situation and resource briefing will be available for the meeting.
- Obtain an estimate of regional resource availability from agency dispatch for use in planning the next operational period.
- Obtain necessary agency policy, legal, or fiscal constraints for use in the Planning Meeting.

Conducting the Planning Meeting

The Planning Section Chief conducts the Planning Meeting. Every incident must have an action plan (although a written plan is not required at all incidents).

Planning Meeting Checklist:
- The Planning Section gives a briefing on the situation and resource status.
- The IC sets control objectives.
- The Operations Section plots control lines and division boundaries and specifies tactics for each Division or Group.
- The Operations Section and Planning Section specifies resources needed by the Divisions or Groups.
- The Operations, Planning, and Logistics Sections specifies facilities and reports their locations on a map.
- The Logistics Section places and order for resources and overhead personnel.
- The Planning Section and Logistics Section considers communications, medical, and traffic plan requirements.
- The IC, Planning Section, and Operations Section finalizes, approves, and implements the IAP.

Brief on Situation and Resource Status

The Planning Section Chief and/or Resources and Situation Unit Leaders provide an up-to-date briefing on the situation as gathered from the initial IC, the Incident Briefing Form (ICS 201), field observations, operations reports, and regional resources and situation reports.

Set Control Objectives

The IC establishes the general strategy that will be used, states any major policy, legal, or fiscal constraints on accomplishing the objectives, and offers appropriate contingency considerations.

Plot Control Lines and Division Boundaries on a Map

This is normally accomplished by the Operations Section Chief (for the next operational period) and the Planning Section Chief who will determine control line locations, establish division and branch boundaries for geographical division, and determine the need for functional group assignments for the next operational period.

Specify Tactics for Each Division

After determining division geographical assignments, the Operations Section Chief will establish the specific work assignments to be used for each division for the next operational period. Tactics (work assignments) must be within the boundaries set by the IC's general control objectives and should be recorded on the planning matrix.

Specify Resources Needed by Division

After specifying tactics for each division, the Operations Section Chief and the Planning Section Chief will determine the resources needed by division to accomplish the work assignments. Resource needs will be recorded on the planning matrix and should be considered on basis of the type of resources required to accomplish the assignment.

Specify Operations Facilities & Reporting Locations and Plot on a Map

The Operations, Planning, and Logistics Section Chiefs should designate and make available the facilities and reporting locations required to accomplish Operations Section work assignments. The Operations Section Chief should also indicate the reporting time requirements for the resources and any special resource assignments.

Place Resource and Personnel Order

The Planning Section Chief should assess resource needs assessments using the needs indicated by the Operations Section Chief and resources data available from the Planning Section's Resources Unit. The planning matrix will show resource requirements and the resources available to meet those requirements.

Consider Communications, Medical, and Traffic Plan Requirements

The IAP normally consists of the Incident Objectives Form (ICS 202), Organization Chart (ICS 203), Division Assignment List (ICS 204), and a map of the incident area. Larger incidents may require additional forms such as a Communications Plan (ICS 205), a Medical Plan (ICS 206), and a Traffic Plan. The Planning Section Chief determines which forms are needed and prepares them.

Finalize, Approve, and Implement the IAP

The Planning Section is responsible for seeing the IAP is completed, reviewed, and distributed.

Steps for accomplishing the IAP:

- Set the deadline for completing IAP forms.
- Obtain plan forms and review them for completeness and approvals.
- Determine the number of IAPs required.
- Arrange to reproduce the IAP with the Documentation Unit.
- Review the IAP to ensure it is up-to-date and complete prior to the operations briefing and plan distribution.
- Provide the IAP briefing plan, as required, and distribute the plan prior to the beginning of the new operational period.

Examples of ICS Forms

Examples are available from the National Incident Management System document released March 1, 2004 by the Department of Homeland Security.

Number	Purpose
ICS-201 (p. 1)	Incident Briefing
ICS-201 (p. 2)	Summary of Current Actions
ICS-201 (p. 3)	Current Organization
ICS-201 (p. 4)	Resources Summary
ICS-202	Incident Objectives
ICS-203	Organization Assignment List
ICS-204	Assignment List
ICS-205	Incident Radio Communications Plan
ICS-206	Medical Plan
ICS-207	Organizational Chart
ICS-209	Incident Status Summary, with Instructions
ICS-210	Status Change Card
ICS-211	Check-In-List
ICS-213	General Message
ICS-215	Operational Planning Worksheet

NIMS Multiagency Coordination Systems

A multiagency coordination system is a combination of facilities, equipment, personnel, procedures, and communications that are integrated into a common system responsible for coordinating and supporting domestic incidents. This system works to support incident policies and priorities, facilitate logistics support and resource tracking, inform resource allocation decisions using incident management priorities, coordinate incident related information, and coordinate interagency and intergovernmental issues regarding incident management policies, priorities, and strategies. Direct tactical and operational responsibility for conducting incident management activities rests with the Incident Command. The system may contain an Emergency Operation Center (EOC) or Multiagency Coordination Entities.

Emergency Operations Center (EOC)

EOCs represent the physical location where the coordination of information and resources to support incident management takes place. The Incident Command Post (ICP) is located at or near the incident site and is primarily focused on the tactical response. In smaller-scale incidents or in the initial phases of larger incidents, the ICP may perform an EOC type function. EOCs are usually in a more centralized facility and are organized by functional discipline (fire, law enforcement, medical, etc), jurisdiction (city, county, region, etc), or any combination thereof. Typically EOCs are staffed by personnel representing multiple jurisdictions and functions.

Department Operations Centers (DOCs) focus on internal agency incident management and response are physically represented in a higher level EOC. Regardless of the specific organizational structure, EOCs focus on the coordination, communication, resource dispatch and tracking, and information collection, analysis, and dissemination for the incident.

Multiagency Coordination Entities

A multiagency coordination entity (such as an emergency management agency) may be used to facilitate incident management and policy coordination when the incident crosses disciplinary or jurisdictional boundaries. Entities typically consist of people from organizations and agencies with direct incident management responsibility or support, such as action teams, policy committees, incident management groups, executive teams, or other similar teams.

Principle functions include:

- Ensuring that each agency involved in incident management activities is providing appropriate situational awareness and resource status information.
- Establishing priorities between incidents and Area Commands in concert with the IC or UCs involved.
- Acquiring and allocating resources required by incident management personnel in concert with the priorities established by the IC or UC.
- Anticipating and identifying future resource requirements.
- Coordinating and resolving policy issues arising from the incident.
- Providing strategic coordination as required.

NIMS Public Information Systems

Systems and protocols have been set in place to ensure timely and accurate information sharing to the public during times of crisis or emergency situations. The Public Information Office (PIO) works to support and advise Incident command on all public information relating to the management of the incident. It is important to have public information that is timely, accurate, easy-to-understand, and consistent. Therefore, the Joint Information Center (JIC) provides a location to coordinate and integrate information across jurisdictions and functional agencies, including Federal, State, local, tribal, private-sector, and nongovernmental organizations. In UC, the departments, agencies, organizations, and jurisdictions that contribute to joint public information do not lose their individual identities or responsibility for their own programs or policies, but rather each entity contributes to the overall unified message.

Joint Information System (JIS)

The Joint Information System proves an organized, integrated, and coordinated system to deliver understandable, timely, accurate, and consistent information to the public in a crisis. The system works to provide interagency coordination and integration, develops and delivers coordinated messages, supports decision makers, and is flexible, module, and adaptable.

Joint Information Center (JIC)

A Joint Information Center is the physical location where public affairs professionals from all involved agencies can join to obtain critical emergency information, crisis communications, and public affair functions. The JIC provides the organizational structure for coordinating and disseminating official information.

- The JIC must include representatives from each jurisdiction, agency, private-sector, and nongovernmental organization that is involved with incident management activities.
- A single JIC location is preferable, but should be adaptable to have multiple locations if needed.
- Each JIC must have procedures and protocols to communicate and coordinate with other JICs and other appropriate components within the ICS organization.

NIMS Preparedness

Individual Federal, State, local, and tribal jurisdictions are responsible for implementing the preparedness cycle in advance of an incident and appropriately including private-sector and nongovernmental organizations in such implementation.

Concepts and Principles of Preparedness

- **Levels of Capability:** A continuous cycle of planning, training, equipping, exercising, evaluating, and taking action to correct and mitigate. In addition, preparedness focuses on guidelines, protocols, and standards for planning, training, personnel qualification and certification, equipment certification, and publication management.

- **A Unified Approach:** Responses to incidents are handled across functional and jurisdictional lines, as well as between public and private organizations.

- **NIMS Publications:** The NIMS provides or establishes processes for providing guidelines, protocols, standards for planning, training, qualifications, and certification, and publication management.

- **Mitigation:** These activities are important because they provide a critical foundation for prevention, response, and recovery. Mitigation activities include ongoing public education and outreach (designed to reduce loss of life and destruction of property), structural retrofitting (to deter or lessen the effects of incidents and reduce loss of life, destruction of property, and effects on the environment), code enforcement (such as zoning regulation, land management, and building codes), and flood insurance and the buy-out of properties subjected to frequent flooding.

Achieving Preparedness

Individual Federal, State, local, and tribal jurisdictions are responsible for implementing the preparedness cycle in advance of an incident and appropriately including private-sector and nongovernmental organizations. Tools to assist in the implementation are preparedness organizations, personnel qualification and certification, equipment certification, mutual aid, and publication management.

Preparedness Organizations

Preparedness organizations are represented by a wide variety of committees, planning groups, and other organizations that meet regularly and coordinate with one another to ensure an appropriate focus on planning, training, equipping, and fulfilling other requirements within their jurisdiction as well as across other jurisdictions and private organizations.

Preparedness organization at all jurisdictional levels should:

- Establish and coordinate emergency plans and protocols including public communications and awareness.
- Integrate and coordinate the activities of jurisdictions and private organizations.
- Establish standards, guidelines, and protocols that would be necessary to promote interoperability among members.
- Adopt standards, guidelines, and protocols for providing resources to requesting organizations and incident support organizations.
- Set priorities for resources and other requirements.
- Ensure the establishment and maintenance for multiagency coordination, including EOCs, mutual-aid agreements, incident information systems, nongovernmental organization and private-sector outreach, public awareness and information systems, and mechanisms to deal with information and operations security.

Preparedness Programs - Planning

The following plans describe how personnel, equipment, and other governmental and nongovernmental resources will be used to support incident management requirements.

Emergency Operations Plan (EOP)

Each jurisdiction develops an EOP that defines the scope of preparedness and incident management activities necessary for that jurisdiction.

An Emergency Operations Plan (EOP):

- Should describe the purpose of the plan, situation and assumptions, concept of operations, organization and assignment of responsibilities, administration and logistics, plan development and maintenance, and authorities and references.
- Should include organizational structures, roles and responsibilities, policies, and protocols for providing emergency support.
- Should contain functional annexes, hazard-specific appendices, and a glossary.
- Should predesignate jurisdictional and functional area representatives to the IC or UC whenever possible.

- Should include a preincident and postincident plan and protocol for public awareness, education, and communication.
- Facilitates the response and short-term recovery activities (which sets the stage for successful long-term recovery).
- Drives decisions on long-term prevention and mitigation efforts or risk-based preparedness measures directed at specific hazards.
- Should be flexible to use in all emergencies.

Procedures

Each organization involved in the EOP should develop procedures that translate that tasking to that organization into specific action-oriented checklists for use during incidents. Procedures can also include resource listings, maps, charts, other pertinent data, mechanisms for notifying staff, processes for obtaining mutual aid, mechanisms for reporting information or organizational work centers and EOCs, and communications operating instructions.

The four standard levels of procedural documents are:

- **Overview:** A brief concept summary of an incident-related function, team, or capability.
- **Standard Operating Procedure (SOP) or Operational Manual:** A complete reference document that details the procedures for performing a single function or a number of interdependent functions.
- **Field Operations Guide (FOG) or Handbook:** A durable pocket or desk guide that contains essential information required to perform specific assignments or functions.
- **Job Aid:** A checklist or other aid that is useful in performing or training for a job.

Preparedness Plans

Preparedness plans describe the process and schedule for identifying and meeting training needs (based on the EOP) and the process and schedule for developing, conducting, and evaluating exercises and correcting identified deficiencies. In addition it should include arrangements for procuring or obtaining required incident management resources through mutual aid-mechanisms and should develop plans for facilities and equipment that can withstand the effects of hazards that the jurisdiction is more likely to face.

Corrective Action and Mitigation Plans

Corrective Action plans are designed to implement procedures that are based on lessons learned from actual incidents or from training and exercises. Mitigation plans describe activities that can be taken prior to, during, or after an incident to reduce or eliminate risks to persons or property or to lessen the actual or potential effects or consequences of an incident.

Recovery Plans

Recovery plans describe actions beyond rapid damage assessment and those necessary to provide immediate life support for victims. Long-term recovery planning involves identifying strategic priorities for restoration, improvement, and growth.

Preparedness Programs - Training and Exercises

Training and Exercises for all levels of government, private-sector, and nongovernmental organizations is important to improve integration and interoperability. Training involves standard courses to unite all levels so they can function effectively together during an incident (classes range from incident command and management, incident management structure, operational coordination processes and systems, to discipline-specific and agency-specific classes.) ICS training is organized into four courses (Introduction, Basic, Intermediate, and Advanced). To streamline training efforts, the NIMS Integration Center will:

- Facilitate the development of national standards, guidelines, and protocols for incident management training and exercises.
- Facilitate the use of modeling and simulation capabilities for training and exercise programs.
- Facilitate the definition of general training requirements and approved training courses.
- Review and approve discipline-specific requirements and training courses.

Preparedness Programs - Personnel Certification

Personnel Qualification and Certification help ensure that all field personnel in participating agencies and organizations possess a minimum level of knowledge, skills, and experience to executive incident management and activities in a safe and effective manner. Standards typically include training, experience, credentialing, currency, and physical and medical fitness. Personnel that are certified for employment in support of an incident that transcends interstate jurisdictions through the Emergency Management Assistance Compacts System will be required to meet national qualification and certification standards. To enable this qualification and certification function at the national level, the NIMS Integration Center will:

- Facilitate the development and dissemination of national standards, guidelines, and protocols for qualification and certification.
- Review and approve discipline-specific requirements.
- Facilitate the establishment of a data maintenance system to provide incident managers with detailed qualification, experience, and training information needed to find personnel with the proper credentials for the prescribed incident management positions.

Preparedness Programs - Equipment Certification

A critical component of operational preparedness is the acquisition of equipment that will perform to certain standards and be interoperable with other jurisdictions in an incident. To enable national-level equipment certification, the NIMS Integration Center will:

- Coordinate with appropriate Federal agencies, standards-making, certifying, and accrediting organizations, and with appropriate State, local, tribal, private-sector, and nongovernmental organizations to facilitate the development and publication of national standards, guidelines, and protocols for equipment certification.
- Review and approve lists of emergency responder equipment that meet national certification requirements.

Preparedness Programs - Mutual-Aid Agreements

Mutual-aid agreements are the means for one jurisdiction to provide resources, facilities, services, and other support to another jurisdiction during an incident. Each jurisdiction should be party to a mutual-aid agreement, normally including all neighboring or nearby jurisdictions and private-sector and nongovernmental organizations. States should also participate in interstate compacts and look to establish intrastate agreements that encompass all local jurisdictions. Mutual-aid agreements should also be developed with private organizations, such as the American Red Cross, to facilitate the timely delivery of private assistance during an incident. The agreements should be authorized by approved officials from each of the participating jurisdictions.

Mutual-aid agreements should include:

- Roles and responsibilities of individual parties.
- Procedures for requesting and providing assistance.

- Procedures, authorities, and rules for payment, reimbursement, and allocation of costs.
- Notification procedures.
- Protocols for interoperable communications.
- Relationships with other agreements among jurisdictions.
- Workers compensation.
- Treatment of liability and immunity.
- Recognition of qualifications and certifications.
- Sharing agreement, as required.
- Definitions of key terms used in the agreement.

Preparedness Programs - Publication Management

Publication management for the NIMS includes the development of naming and numbering conventions, review and certification of publications, methods for publications control, identification of sources and suppliers for publications and related services, and management of publication distribution.

NIMS Publications can include:
- Qualifications information
- Training course and exercise information
- Task books
- ICS training and forms
- Job aids
- Guides
- Computer programs
- Audio and video resources
- Templates
- "Best Practices"

To enable national-level publication management, the NIMS Integration Center will:
- Facilitate the development, publication, and dissemination of national standards, guidelines, and protocols for a NIMS publication management system.
- Facilitate the development of general publications for all NIMS users as well as their issuance via the NIMS publication management system.
- Review and approve the discipline-specific publication management requirements and training courses submitted by professional organizations and associations.

NIMS Resource Management

Resource management involves coordinating and overseeing the application of tools, processes, and systems that provide incident managers with timely and appropriate resources during an incident. Resources include personnel, teams, facilities, equipment, and supplies.

Resource management has four primary tasks:

- To establish systems for describing, inventorying, requesting, and tracking resources.
- To activate these systems prior to and during an incident.
- To dispatch resources prior to and during an incident.
- To deactivate or recall resources during or after incidents.

Underlying concepts of resource management:

- Providing a uniform method of identifying, acquiring, allocating, and tracking resources.
- Using effective mutual-aid and donor assistance enabled by standardized classification of resources required to support the incident management organization.
- Using a credentialed system tied to uniform training and certification standards to ensure that requested personnel are successfully integrated into ongoing incident operations.
- Encompassing resources that are contributed by private-sector and nongovernmental organizations.
- The EOC, multiagency coordination entities, and specific elements of the ICS are responsible for the coordination of resource management.

Five key principles of effective resource management:

1. **Advance Planning:** Preparedness organizations work together in advance of an incident to develop plans for managing and employing resources in a variety of possible emergency circumstances.
2. **Resource Identification and Ordering:** Resource managers use standardized processes and methodologies to order, identify, mobilize, dispatch, and track the resources required to support incident management activities.
3. **Categorizing Resources:** Resources are categorized by size, capacity, capability, skill, and other characteristics. The NIMS Integration Center will be responsible for

facilitating the development and issuance of national standards for typing resources and certifying personnel.

4. **Use of Agreements:** Formal preincident agreements between parties, both governmental and nongovernmental, are established to ensure the employment of standardized, interoperable equipment, and other incident resources during incident operations.

5. **Effective Management of Resources:** Resource managers use validated practices to perform key resource management tasks systematically and efficiently. Examples include:
   - Acquisition procedures that are used to obtain resources to support operational requirements. Examples include mission tasking, contracting, drawing from existing stocks, and making small purchases.
   - Management information systems that are used to collect, update, and process data, track resources, and display their readiness status. Examples include geographical information systems (GISs), resource tracking systems, transportation tracking systems, inventory management systems, and reporting systems.
   - Ordering, mobilization, dispatching, and demobilization protocols are used to request resources, prioritize requests, activate and dispatch resources to incident, and return resources to normal status. Examples include tracking systems that identify the location and status of mobilized or dispatched resources and procedures to "demobilize" resources and return them to their original locations and status.

Nine processes for managing resources:

1. **Identifying and Typing Resources:** Resource typing entails categorizing by capability the resources that incident managers commonly request, deploy, and employ. The NIMS Integration Center is responsible for defining national resource typing standards so that they may be deployed and used on a national basis.

2. **Certifying and Credentialing Personnel:** Personnel certification entails authoritatively attesting that individuals meet professional standards for the training, experience, and performance required for key incident management functions. Credentialing involves providing documentation that can authenticate and verify the certification and identity of designated incident managers and emergency responders.

3. **Inventorying Resources:** Resource managers use various resource inventory systems to assess the availability of assets provided by public, private, and volunteer organizations. Preparedness organizations enter all resources available for deployment into resource tracking systems maintained at local, State, regional, and national levels. The data is then made available to 911 centers, EOCs, and multiagency coordination entities.

4. **Identifying Resource Requirements:** Resource managers identify, refine, and validate resource requirements throughout the incident life cycle. This process involves accurately identifying what and how much is needed, where and when it is needed, and who will be receiving or using it.

5. **Ordering and Acquiring Resources:** Requests for item that the IC cannot obtain locally are submitted through the local EOC or multiagency coordinating entity using standardized resource-ordering procedures. If the servicing EOC is unable to fill the order locally, the order is forwarded to the next level, generally an adjacent local, State, regional EOC, or multiagency coordination entity.

6. **Mobilizing Resources:** Incident personnel begin mobilizing when notified through established channels. They will be notified of transportation specifics and are required to check in upon arrival. For resource managers, the mobilization process may include equipping, training, and inoculating personnel, designating assembly points that have facilities suitable for logistical support, and obtaining transportation to deliver resources to the incident most quickly. Managers should also prepare and plan for the demobilization process well in advance in order to make the transportation of resources efficient, keep costs low, and the delivery as fast as possible.

7. **Tracking and Reporting Resources:** Resource tracking is a standardized, integrated process conducted throughout the life cycle of an incident by all agencies at all levels. This provides incident managers with a clear picture of where resources are located, helps staff prepare to receive resources, protects the safety of personnel and security of supplies and equipment, and enables the coordination of movement of personnel, equipment, and supplies.

8. **Recovering Resources:** Recovery involves the final disposition of all resources. During this process, resources are rehabilitated, replenished, disposed of, and retrograded.

   - **Nonexpendable Resources** are fully accounted for at the incident site and again when they are returned to the unit that issued them. The issuing unit then restores them to a fully functional capability for the next mobilization. In the case of human resources, such as IMTs, adequate rest and recuperation time and facilities are provided. Important occupational health and mental health issues must also be addressed, including monitoring how such events affect emergency responders over time.

   - **Expendable Resources** are also fully accounted for. The incident management organization bears the costs of expendable resources, as authorized in preplanned financial agreements. Returned resources that are not in restorable condition must be declared as excess. Resources that require special handling and disposition (such as biological waste and contaminated supplies, debris, and equipment) are dealt with according to established regulations and policies.

9. **Reimbursement:** Provides a mechanism to fund critical needs that arise from incident-specific activities. Processes and procedures must be in place to ensure that resource providers are reimbursed in a timely manner.

NIMS Communications and Information Management

Establishing and maintaining a common operating picture and ensuring accessibility and interoperability are principal goals of communications and information management. Prior to an incident, entities responsible for taking appropriate preincident actions use communications and information management processes and systems to inform and guide various critical activities. A common operating picture and systems interoperability provide the framework necessary to:

- Formulate and disseminate indications and warnings.
- Formulate, execute, and communicate operational decisions at an incident site, as well as between incident management entities across jurisdictions and functional agencies.
- Prepare for potential requirements and requests supporting incident management activities.
- Develop and maintain overall awareness and understanding of an incident within and across jurisdictions.

Concepts and Principles
- A common operating picture accessible across jurisdictions and functional agencies.
- Common communications and data standards.

Managing Communications and Information

NIMS communications and info systems enable the essential functions needed to provide a common operating picture and interoperability for incident management at all levels.

- **Incident Management Communications:** Preparedness organizations must ensure that effective communications processes and systems exist to support a complete spectrum of incident management activities.

  - **Individual Jurisdictions** are required to comply with national interoperable communications standards (once they are developed and designated by the NIMS Integration Center).
  - **Incident Communications** will follow the standards called for under the ICS.

- **Information Management:** The NIMS Integration Center is charged with facilitating the definition and maintenance of the information framework required to guide the development of NIMS related information systems.
  - **Policies:**
    * **Preincident information** needs met at the Federal, State, local, and tribal levels in conjunction with the private-sector and nongovernmental organizations, primarily through the preparedness organizations.
    * **The information management** system provides guidance, standards, and tools to enable all entities to integrate their information needs into a common operating picture.
    * **Networks** used by EOCs are established to disseminate critical information, indications, warning, incident notifications, and public communications.
    * **Technology** (such as computers and networks) tie together all command, tactical, and support units involved in incident management. Agencies plan in advance to ensure the effective and efficient use of technologies so that they can share information critical to mission execution and the cataloguing of required corrective actions.
  - **Interoperability Standards:** The NIMS Integration Center will facilitate the development of data standards using the functions and design goals described below:
    * **Incident Notification and Situation Report:** The standardized transmission of data in a common format enables the passing of appropriate notification information to a national system that can handle data queries and information and intelligence assessments and analysis.
    * **Status Reporting:** All levels of government initiate status reports and then disseminate them to other jurisdictions. NIMS will develop a standard set of data elements to facilitate this process.
    * **Analytical Data:** During incidents that involve public health and environmental monitoring, multiple organizations often respond and collect data. Standardization of sampling and data collection enables more reliable laboratory analysis and

improves the quality of assessments provided to decision-makers.

* **Geospatial Information:** Geospatial information is used to integrate assessments, situation reports, and incident notification into a coherent common operating picture. Standards covering geospatial information should be robust enough to enable systems to be used in remote field locations where telecommunications capabilities may not have sufficient bandwidth to handle large images or are limited in terms of computing hardware.

* **Wireless Communications:** The NIMS will include standards to help ensure that wireless communications and computing for all levels of government and involved agencies are interoperable.

* **Identification and Authentication:** Individuals and organizations that access and contribute to the NIMS information must be properly authenticated and certified for security purposes.

* **National Database of Incident Reports:** The NIMS Integration Center and all levels of government will contribute incident reports to a national database that can be used to support incident management efforts.

NIMS Supporting Technologies

Technology and technological systems provide supporting capabilities essential to implementing and continuously refining the NIMS. These include voice and data communications, information, and display systems. The NIMS leverages science and technology to improve capabilities and lower costs.

- **Interoperability and Compatibility:** Systems must be able to work together and should not interfere with one another if the multiple jurisdictions, organizations, and functions that come together under the NIMS are to be effective in domestic incident management. Interoperability and compatibility are achieved through the use of such tools as common communications and data standards, digital data formats, equipment standards, and design standards.

- **Technology Support:** Technology support facilitates incident operations and sustains the research and development programs that underpin the long-term incident management capabilities.

- **Technology Standards:** National standards for key systems may be required to facilitate the interoperability and compatibility of major systems across jurisdictional, geographics, and functional lines.

- **Broad-Based Requirements:** Needs for new technologies, procedures, protocols, and standards to facilitate incident management are identified at both the field and the national levels. Since these needs will most likely exceed available resources, the NIMS provides a mechanism for aggregating and prioritizing them from the local to the national level. These needs will be met across the incident life cycle by coordinating basic, applied, developmental, and demonstration research, testing, and evaluation activities.

- **Strategic Planning for Research & Development:** Identifies future technologies that can improve preparedness, prevention, response, and recovery capabilities or lower the cost of existing capabilities.

Supporting incident management with science & tech:

Supporting technologies enhance incident management capabilities or lower costs through three principal activities: operational scientific support, technology standards support, and research and development support.

- **Operational Scientific Support:** Identifies and mobilizes scientific and technical assets that can be used to support incident management activities.
- **Technical Standards Support:** Enables the development and coordination of technology standards for the NIMS to ensure that personnel, organizations, communications and information systems, and other equipment perform consistently, effectively, and reliably together without disrupting one another. The following principles will be used in defining these standards:
    - **Performance measurement** (collecting hard data on how things work in the real world) is the most reliable basis for standards that ensure the safety and mission effectiveness of emergency responders and incident managers. The performance measurement infrastructure develops guidelines, performance standards, testing protocols, personnel certification, reassessment, and training procedures to help incident management organizations use equipment systems effectively.
    - **A consensus-based** approach to standards builds on existing approaches to standards and takes advantage of SDOs with long-standing interest and expertise. These SDOs include the National Institute of Justice, National Institute for Standards and Technology, National Institute for Occupational Safety and Health, American National Standards Institute, American Society for Testing and Materials, and National Fire Protection Association.
    - **Test and evaluation** will be conducted by private and public sector testing laboratories. They will evaluate equipment against NIMS technical standards.
    - **Technical guidelines** for training emergency responders on equipment use will be developed by vulnerability analysts, equipment developers, users, and standards experts.
- **Research and Development to Solve Operational Problems:** Will be based on the operational needs of the entire range of NIMS users.

NIMS Ongoing Management & Maintenance

HSPD-5 requires the Secretary of Homeland Security to establish a mechanism for ensuring the ongoing management and maintenance of the NIMS. The Secretary will establish a multijurisdictional, multidisciplinary NIMS Integration Center that will provide strategic direction for and oversight of the NIMS. It will include mechanisms for direct participation and consultation from Federal departments and agencies, State, local, and tribal incident management entities, emergency responder and incident management professional organizations, and private-sector and nongovernmental organizations.

The NIMS management and maintenance process relies heavily on lessons learned from actual incidents and domestic incident management training and exercises, as well as recognized best practices across jurisdictions and functional disciplines.

The Secretary of Homeland Security will establish and administer the NIMS Integration Center. Proposed changes to the NIMS will be submitted to the Center for consideration, approval, and publication. The Secretary has the ultimate authority and responsibility for publishing revisions and modifications.

The NIMS Integration Center will be responsible for:
- Developing a national program for NIMS education and awareness.
- Promoting compatibility between national-level standards for the NIMS and those developed by other public, private, and professional groups.
- Facilitating the development and publication of materials and standardized templates to support implementation and continuous refinement of the NIMS.
- Developing assessment criteria for the various components of the NIMS, as well as compliance requirements and time lines for all levels of government regarding NIMS standards and guidelines.
- Facilitating the definition of general training requirements and the development of national-level training standards and course curricula associated with the NIMS. Examples:
  - The use of modeling and simulation capabilities for training and exercise programs.
  - Field-based training, specification of mission-essential tasks, requirements for specialized instruction and

instructor training, and course completion documentation for all NIMS users.
- The review and recommendation of discipline-specific NIMS training courses.
- Facilitating the development of national standards, guidelines, and protocols for incident management training and exercises, including consideration of existing exercise and training programs at all jurisdictional levels.
- Facilitating the establishment and maintenance of a publication management system for documents supporting the NIMS and other NIMS-related publications and materials.
- Reviewing discipline-specific publication management requirements submitted by professional organizations and associations.
- Facilitating the development and publication of national standards, guidelines, and protocols for the qualification and certification of emergency responder and incident management personnel.
- Reviewing and approving the discipline-specific qualification and certification requirements submitted by emergency responder and incident management organizations and associations.
- Facilitating the establishment and maintenance of a documentation and database system related to qualification, certification, and credentialing of incident management personnel and organizations.
- Establishing a data maintenance system to provide incident managers with detailed qualification, experience, and training information needed to credential personnel for prescribed "national" incident management positions.
- Coordination of minimum professional certification standards and facilitation of the design and implementation of a credentialing system that can be used nationwide.
- Facilitating the establishment of standards for the performance, compatibility, and interoperability of incident management equipment and communications systems. Examples:
  - The development and publication of national standards, guidelines, and protocols for equipment certification.
  - Reviewing and approving lists of equipment that meet these established equipment certification requirements.

- Collaborating with organizations responsible for emergency responder equipment evaluation and testing.
- Facilitating the development and issuance of national standards for the typing of resources.
- Facilitating the definition and maintenance of the information framework required to guide the development of NIMS information systems, including the development of data standards for the following: incident notification and situation reports, status reporting, analytical data, geospatial information, wireless communications, identification and authentication, incident reports, and "lessons learned" reports.
- Coordinating the establishment of technical and technology standards for NIMS users.
- Integrating the incident management science and technology needs of departments, agencies, disciplines, private-sector, and nongovernmental organizations operating within the NIMS at all levels.
- Establishing and maintaining a repository and clearinghouse for reports and lessons learned from actual incidents, training, and exercises, as well for best practices, model structures, and model processes for NIMS-related functions.

NIMS Resource Typing System

The NIMS Integration Center is responsible for establishing a national resource typing protocol based on inputs from representatives from various Federal agencies and departments and private organizations, representatives of State and local emergency management, law enforcement, firefighting and emergency medical services, public health, public works, and other entities with assigned responsibilities under the Federal Response Plan and the National Response Plan.

Elements of the National Typing Protocol:

- **Resources:** Consists of personnel, teams, facilities, supplies, and major items of equipment available for assignment or use during incidents.
- **Category:** The function for which a resource would be most useful.
- **Kind:** Broad classes that characterize like resources (i.e. teams, personnel, equipment, supplies, vehicles, and aircraft.)
- **Components:** Resources can comprise of multiple components. An example is an urban search and rescue team may consist of multiple components such as two 31-person teams, four canines, and a comprehensive equipment cache.
- **Metrics:** The measurement standards. The metrics used will differ depending on the kind of resource being typed. The metric must be useful in describing a resource's capability to support the mission. It should also identify the capability and capacity of the resource. An example of an appropriate metric for a hose might be the number of gallons of water per hour that can flow through it.
- **Type:** Refers to the level of resource capability. Typing provides managers with additional information to aid the selection and best use of resources. The type assigned to a resource is based on a minimum level of capability described by the identified metric(s) for that resource. Assigning the Type I label to a resource implies that it has a greater level of capability than a Type II of the same resource.
- **Additional Information:** The protocol will also provide the capability to use additional information that is pertinent to resource decision-making. For example, if a particular set of resources can only be released to support an incident under particular authorities or laws, the protocol should provide the ability for resource managers to understand such limitations.

Important Team Descriptions

Disaster Medical Assistance Team (DMAT)

The below Type descriptions are for a Basic Medical Team. Specialty teams can be assembled based on the needs of the incident. Specialty team examples include burn units, crush injuries, mental health, and pediatric specialties.

Type I
- **Description:** A volunteer group of medical and nonmedical individuals (such as physicians, nurses, nurse practitioners, physician's assistants, pharmacists, EMTs, and other allied health professionals and support staff), usually from the same State or region of the State, that have formed a response team under the guidance of the National Disaster Medical System (NDMS), or similar State or local systems.

- **Human Resources:** Thirty-five deployable personnel who deploy to a site within 24 hours of notification. Staff can function for 72 hours in remote and severe locations without resupply and treat up to 250 victims within 24 hours.

- **Equipment:** A complete set of equipment that can function for 72 hours in remote and severe locations without resupply.

Type II
- **Description:** Same as Type I description (above).

- **Human Resources:** Thirty-five deployable personnel who deploy to a site within 24 hours of notification. Deploy to site within 24 hours of notification with all necessary staff. Function in existing facility using facility's equipment and supplies.

- **Equipment:** Limited to none.

Type III
- **Description:** Same as Type I description (above).

- **Human Resources:** Personnel roster only; may be less than full complement.

- **Equipment:** None.

Disaster Mortuary Operational Response Team (DMORT)

Type I
- **Description:** A volunteer group of medical and forensic personnel (such as medical examiners, coroners, pathologists, forensic anthropologists, medical records technicians, fingerprint technicians, dental assistants, radiologists, funeral directors, mental health professionals, and support personnel), usually from the same geographic

region, that have formed a response team under the guidance of the National Disaster Medical System (NDMS) or State or local systems. The personnel should have specific training and skills in victim identification, mortuary services, forensic pathology, and anthropology methods. DMORTs are mission-tailored on an ad-hoc basis and usually deploy only with personnel and equipment specifically required for that mission. The capability of the team can be expanded to include weapons of mass destruction (WMD) response.

- **Human Resources:** Thirty-one personnel to deploy to a site within 24 hours of notification. They will provide on-site victim identification, morgue operations, and family assistance services.
- **Equipment:** Deployable Portable Morgue Unit (DPMU) add-on available when no local morgue facilities are available.

International Medical Surgical Response Team (IMSuRT)
Type I
- **Description:** A volunteer group of medical and nonmedical individuals, usually from the same State or region of a State, that has formed a response team under the guidance of the National Disaster Medical System (NDMS) and the State Department. The personnel and equipment will be capable of deploying medical and surgical treatment capabilities worldwide. This is the only NDMS team with surgical operating room capability. Currently, a single IMSuRT exists as Type I, being a successor to the previous Incident Support Team specialty DMAT.
- **Human Resources:** Full teams consist of 26 personnel able to begin deployment to outside the continental United States (OCONUS) location within 3 hours of notification. It is a sufficient number of staff for two operating room suites providing emergency surgery, treatment, and stabilization.
- **Equipment:** Usually deploys with all necessary equipment. The teams are fully equipped to provide freestanding surgical capability, but does not usually function in a remote and severe environment without additional support.

Management Support Team (MST)
Type I
- **Description:** A command and control team that provides support and liaison and functions for other National Disaster Medical System (NDMS) teams in the field. A mix of Federal employees from NDMS headquarters, the PHS-2

team, or the CCRF usually staffs MSTs. MSTs do not exist except when deployed in support of a mission. An MST always accompanies an NDMS unit upon deployment and are mission-tailored on an ad-hoc basis and usually deploy only with personnel and equipment specifically required for current support mission.

- **Human Resources:** Deploys to site within 24 hours of notification and provides Federal supervision, coordination, and support on the site of any NDMS team deployment, including ambulatory care (sick call) for Federal personnel.

- **Equipment:** Full complement.

Type II
- **Description:** Same as Type I description (above).

- **Human Resources:** Deploys to site within 24 hours of notification with limited staff and communications equipment, but no tentage.

- **Equipment:** Communication and administrative only.

Urban Search and Rescue (US&R) Task Forces
Type I (Weapons of Mass Destruction - WMD - Level)
- **Description:** Conducts safe and effective search and rescue operations at large or complex Urban Search and Rescue (US&R) operations, including structure collapse incidents involving the collapse or failure of heavy floor, precast concrete, and steel frame construction. The task force performs or provides high-angle rope rescue (including highline systems), confined space rescue (permit required), advanced life support (ALS) intervention, communications, weapons of mass destruction (WMD)/hazardous materials (HazMat) operations, and defensive water rescue. They also conduct safe and effective sustained 24-hour search and rescue operations.

- **Human Resources:** Consists of a 70 person response team. It is a multidisciplinary organization of command, search, rescue, medical, HazMat, logistics, and planning functions. Personnel comply with the National Fire Protection Association (NFPA) 1670 Technician Level requirements for the area of their area of specialty or operations level for support personnel.

- **Equipment:** US&R teams come with a substantial amount of equipment. Rescue equipment includes power tools, electrical equipment, technical rope, and safety equipment. Medical equipment includes antibiotics, medication, canine treatment, incubations, eye care supplies, immobilization and extrication equipment, and personal protective equipment (PPE). Technical equipment includes HazMat equipment, canine search and rescue equipment, and technical specialist equipment. Communications equipment includes radios, charging units, power sources, and computers. Logistical equipment includes water, food, shelter, safety, administrative support, and equipment maintenance.

Type II (Light Level)

- **Description:** Conducts safe and effective search and rescue operations at structure collapse incidents involving the collapse or failure of light frame construction, basic rope rescue operations, ALS interventions, HazMat conditions, communications, and trench and excavation rescue. This team has the ability to conduct safe and effective 12-hour search and rescue operations.

- **Human Resources:** This team is a 28-person response and a multidisciplinary organization with command, search, rescue, medical, HazMat, logistics, and planning functions. Personnel comply with the NFPA 1670 Technical Level requirements for the area of their area of specialty or operations level for support personnel.

- **Equipment:** US&R teams come with a substantial amount of equipment. For a complete description see Type I Equipment list (above).

Urban Search and Rescue (US&R) Incident Support Teams

Type I - US&R Incident Support Team (IST) Full

- **Description:** A fully staffed US&R multifunctional management team activated to provide technical assistance in the acquisition and use of Emergency Support Function (ESF) #9. US&R emergency resources come through advice, Incident Command assistance, incident response planning, management, and coordination of US&R task forces, and obtaining ESF #9 logistical support. The team is organized according to basic Incident Command System (ICS) guidelines, with a command staff and operations, planning, logistics, and finance sections. A Type 1 IST is a full management team providing staffing to fill all necessary ICS functions for the assigned incident. A Type 1 IST can provide 24-hour operations for a minimum of 14 days before requiring personnel rotations and can provide its own administrative and living support as necessary.

- **Human Resources:** The Federal Emergency Management Agency (FEMA) US&R section, based on experience and training qualifications, selects IST members. The team is comprised of qualified National US&R response system personnel, with the ESF #9 assistants and the administration/finance section staffed by FEMA or other Federal agency personnel.

- **Equipment:** ISTs come with all the equipment necessary to perform the assigned task, including administrative and computer supplies. Communication equipment includes microphone, antenna, fax, satellite telephone, radio, and pager. Tools include screwdriver, chisel, drill, hammer, and shovel. Power supply equipment includes power adapter, generator, surge protector, and grounding wire. Logistical equipment includes water, food, shelter, safety, administrative support, and equipment maintenance.

Type II - US&R Incident Support Team (IST) Advance

- **Description:** Activated to provide technical assistance in the acquisition and use of ESF #9, US&R emergency resources through advice, Incident Command assistance, incident response planning, management, and coordination of US&R task forces, and obtaining ESF #9 logistical support. The IST is organized according to basic ICS guidelines, with a command and command staff and operations, planning, logistics, and finance sections. The Type II is an Advance Element of Type 1 IST and will require supplemental IST staffing to maintain 24-hour operations. It can provide its own administrative and living support as necessary.

- **Human Resources:** A 22-person US&R multifunctional management team staffing 14 ICS functions, IST members are selected to the FEMA US&R section based on experience and training qualifications. Twenty of the 22 members filling positions will be qualified National US&R Response System personnel, while the ESF #9 assistants will be FEMA staff.

- **Equipment:** ISTs come with all the equipment necessary to perform the assigned task, including administrative and computer supplies. For a complete listing see Equipment description under Type I (above).

Veterinary Medical Assistance Team (VMAT)

Type I
- **Description:** Volunteer teams of veterinarians, technicians, and support personnel (such as microbiologists, epidemiologists, and veterinary pathologists). These individuals are usually from the same region and have organized a response team under the guidance of the American Veterinary Medical Association and the National Disaster Medical System (NDMS). They also have specific training in responding to animal casualties and animal disease outbreaks during a disaster. VMATs are usually mission-tailored on an ad-hoc basis and usually deploy only with personnel and equipment specifically required for the current mission. All VMATs within the NDMS are considered Type I. Epidemiologic capabilities are limited.

- **Human Resources:** The team consists of sixty personnel plus equipment and will deploy to the site within 24 hours of notification. They provide animal care, treatment, and shelter, food and water testing, and basic epidemiologic capabilities.

- **Equipment:** Full complement.

Type II
- **Description:** Same as Type I description (above).

- **Human Resources:** The team consists of sixty personnel plus equipment. There is some mix of capabilities, and are less than Type I.

- **Equipment:** Limited or none.

Action Plan: *See Incident Action Plan.*

Agency: A division of government, nongovernmental organization, or private organization with a specific function offering a particular kind of assistance. In ICS, agencies are defined as jurisdictional (having statutory responsibility for incident management) or as assisting or cooperating (providing resources or other assistance).

Agency Representative: An individual assigned to an incident by a primary, assisting, or cooperating Federal, State, local, or tribal government agency or private entity that has been delegated the authority to make decisions affecting that agency's participation in incident management activities following appropriate consultation with the leadership of that agency.

Area Command (Unified Area Command): An organization established to oversee the management of multiple incidents that are each being handled by an ICS organization or to oversee the management of a large incident or multiple incidents to which several Incident Management Teams have been assigned. Area Command is responsible for setting overall strategy and priorities, allocating critical resources based on priorities, ensuring that incidents are properly managed, and that objectives are met and strategies followed. Area Command becomes Unified Area Command when incidents are multijurisdictional. Area Command may be established at an emergency operations center facility or at some location other than an incident command post.

Assessment: The evaluation and interpretation of measurements and other information to provide a basis for decision-making.

Assignments: Tasks given to resources to perform within a given operational period that are based on tactical objectives defined in the Incident Action Plan (IAP).

Assistant: Title for subordinates of principal Command Staff positions. The title indicates a level of technical capability, qualifications, and responsibility subordinate to the primary positions. Assistants may also be assigned to unit leaders.

Assisting Agency: An agency or organization providing personnel, services, or other resources to the agency with direct responsibility for incident management.

Available Resources: Resources assigned to an incident, checked in, and available for a mission assignment, normally located in a Staging Area.

Branch: The organizational level having functional or geographic responsibility for major aspects of incident operations. A branch is organizationally between Section and Division/Group in the Operations Section, and between Section and Units in the Logistics Section. Branches are identified by the use of Roman numerals or by functional name (e.g., medical, security, etc.).

Chain of Command: A series of command, control, executive, or management positions in hierarchical order of authority.

Check-in: The process through which resources first report to an incident. Check-in locations include the Incident Command Post, Resources Unit, incident base, camps, staging areas, or directly on the site.

Chief: The ICS title for individuals responsible for management of functional sections: Operations, Planning, Logistics, Finance (Administration), and Intelligence (if established).

Command: The act of directing, ordering, or controlling by virtue of explicit statutory, regulatory, or delegated authority.

Command Post: *See Incident Command Post.*

Command Staff: In an incident management organization, the Command Staff consists of the Incident Command and the special staff position of Public Information Officer, Safety Officer, Liaison Officer, and other positions as required, who report directly to the Incident Commander. They may have an assistant or assistants, as needed.

Common Operating Picture: A broad view of the overall situation as reflected by situation reports, aerial photography, and other information or intelligence.

Communications Unit: An organizational unit in the Logistics Section responsible for providing communication services at an incident or an EOC. A Communications Unit may also be a facility (e.g., a trailer or mobile van) used to support an Incident Communications Center.

Cooperating Agency: An agency supplying assistance other than direct operational or support functions or resources to the incident management effort.

Coordinate: To advance systematically an analysis and exchange of information among principals who have or may have a need to know certain information to carry out specific incident management responsibilities.

Deputy: A fully qualified individual who, in the absence of a superior, can be delegated the authority to manage a functional operation or perform a specific task. In some cases, a Deputy can act as relief for a superior and, therefore, must be fully qualified in the position. Deputies can be assigned to the Incident Commander, General Staff, and Branch Directors.

Dispatch: The ordered movement or a resource or resources to an assigned operational mission or an administrative move from one location to another.

Division: The partition of an incident into geographic areas of operation. Divisions are established when the number of resources exceeds the manageable span of control of the Operations Chief. A division is located within the ICS organization between the branch and resources in the Operations Section.

Emergency: Absent a Presidentially declared emergency, any incident (human caused or natural) that requires responsive action to protect life or property. Under the Robert T. Stafford Disaster Relief and Emergency Assistance Act, an emergency means any occasion or instance for which, in the determination of the President, Federal assistance is needed to supplement State and local efforts and capabilities to save lives and to protect property and public health and safety, or to lessen or avert the threat of a catastrophe in any part of the United States.

Emergency Operations Centers (EOCs): Thy physical location at which the coordination of information and resources to support domestic incident management activities normally takes place. An EOC may be a temporary facility or may be located in a more central or permanently established facility, perhaps at a higher level of organization within a jurisdiction. EOCs may be organized by major functional disciplines (fire, law enforcement, and medical services), by jurisdiction (Federal, State, regional, county, city, tribal), or some combination thereof.

Emergency Operations Plan: The "steady-state" plan maintained by various jurisdictional levels for responding to a wide variety of potential hazards.

Emergency Public Information: Information that is disseminated primarily in anticipation of an emergency or during an emergency. In addition to providing situational information to the public, it also frequently provides directive actions required to be taken by the general public.

Emergency Response Provider: Includes Federal, State, local, and tribal emergency public safety, law enforcement, emergency response, emergency medical (including hospital emergency facilities), and related personnel, agencies, and authorities.

Evacuation: Organized, phased, and supervised withdrawal, dispersal, or removal of civilians from dangerous or potentially dangerous areas, and their reception and care in safe areas.

Event: A planned, nonemergency activity. ICS can be used as the management system for a wide range of events (such as parades, concerts, or sporting events).

Federal: Of or pertaining to the Federal Government of the USA.

Function: In ICS, function refers to the five major activities in the ICS: Command, Operations, Planning, Logistics, and Finance (Administration). The term function is also used when describing the activity involved (such as the planning function). A sixth function, Intelligence, may be established, if required, to meet incident management needs.

General Staff: A group of incident management personnel organized according to function and reporting to the Incident Commander. The General Staff normally consists of the Operations Section Chief, Planning Section Chief, Logistics Section Chief, and the Finance (Administration) Section Chief.

Group: Established to divide the incident management structure into functional areas of operation. Groups are composed of resources assembled to perform a special function not necessarily within a single geographic division. Groups, when activated, are located between branches and resources in the Operations Section. *See Division.*

Hazard: Something that is potentially dangerous or harmful, often the root cause of an unwanted outcome.

Incident: An occurrence or event, natural or human-caused, that requires an emergency response to protect life or property. Incidents can include major disasters, emergencies, terrorist attacks, terrorist threats, wildland and urban fires, floods, hazardous materials spills, nuclear accidents, aircraft accidents, earthquakes, hurricanes, tornadoes, tropical storms, war-related disasters, public health and medical emergencies, and other occurrences requiring an emergency response.

Incident Action Plan (IAP): An oral or written plan containing general objectives reflecting the overall strategy for managing an incident. It may include the identification of operational resources and assignments, as well as attachments that provide direction and important information for management of the incident during one or more operational periods.

Incident Command Post (ICP): The field location at which the primary tactical-level, on-scene incident command functions are performed. The ICP may be collocated with the incident base or other incident facilities and is normally identified by a green rotating or flashing light.

Incident Command System (ICS): A standardized on-scene emergency management construct specifically designed to provide for the adoption of an integrated organizational structure that reflects the complexity and demands of single or multiple incidents, without being hindered by jurisdictional boundaries. ICS is the combination of facilities, equipment, personnel, procedures, and communications operating within a common organizational structure, designed to aid in the management of resources during incidents. It is used for all kinds of emergencies and is applicable to small as well as large and complex incidents. ICS is used by various jurisdictions and functional agencies, both public and private, to organize field-level incident management operations.

Incident Commander (IC): The individual responsible for all incident activities, including the development of strategies and tactics and the ordering and the release of resources. The IC has overall authority and responsibility for conducting incident operations and is responsible for the management of all incident operations at the incident site.

Incident Management Team (IMT): The IC and appropriate Command and General Staff personnel assigned to an incident.

Incident Objectives: Statements of guidance and direction necessary for selecting appropriate strategies and the tactical direction of resources. Incident objectives are based on realistic expectations of what can be accomplished when all allocated resources have been effectively deployed. Incident objectives must be achievable and measurable, yet flexible enough to allow strategic and tactical alternatives.

Initial Action: The actions taken by those responders first to arrive at an incident site.

Initial Response: Resources initially committed to an incident.

Intelligence Officer: The intelligence officer is responsible for managing internal information, intelligence, and operational security requirements supporting incident management activities. These may include information security and operational security activities, as well as the complex task of ensuring that sensitive information of all types (such as classified information, law enforcement sensitive information, proprietary information, or export-controlled information) is handled in a way that not only safeguards the information, but also ensures that it gets to those who need access to it to perform their missions effectively and safely.

Joint Information Center (JIC): A facility established to coordinate all incident-related public information activities. It is the central point of contact for all news media at the scene of the incident. Public information officials from all participating agencies should collocate at the JIC.

Joint Information System (JIS): Integrates incident information and public affairs into a cohesive organization designed to provide consistent, coordinated, timely information during crisis or incident operations. The mission of the JIS is to provide a structure and system for developing and delivering coordinated interagency messages, developing, recommending, and executing public information plans and strategies on behalf of the IC, advising the IC concerning public affairs issues that could affect a response effort, and controlling rumors and inaccurate information that could undermine public confidence in the emergency response effort.

Jurisdiction: A range or sphere of authority. Public agencies have jurisdiction at an incident related to their legal responsibilities and authority. Jurisdictional authority at an incident can be political or geographical (city, county, tribal, State, or Federal boundary lines) or functional (law enforcement, public health).

Liaison: A form of communication for establishing and maintaining mutual understanding and cooperation.

Liaison Officer: A member of the Command Staff responsible for coordinating with representatives from cooperating and assisting agencies.

Local Government: A county, municipality, city, town, township, local public authority, school district, special district, intrastate district, council of governments (regardless of whether the council of governments is incorporated as a nonprofit corporation under State law), regional or interstate government entity, or agency or instrumentality of a local government; an Indian tribe or authorized tribal organization, or in Alaska a Native village or Alaska Regional Native Corporation, a rural community, unincorporated town or village, or other public entity.

Logistics: Providing resources and other services to support incident management.

Logistics Section: The section responsible for providing facilities, services, and material support for the incident.

Major Disaster: As defined under the Robert T. Stafford Disaster Relief and Emergency Assistance Act (42 U.S.C. 5122), a major disaster is: "any natural catastrophe (including any hurricane, tornado, storm, high water, wind-driven water, tidal wave, tsunami, earthquake, volcanic eruption, landslide, mudslide, snowstorm, or drought), or, regardless of cause, any fire, flood, or explosion, in any part of the United States, which in the determination of the President causes damage of sufficient severity and magnitude to warrant major disaster assistance under this Act to supplement the efforts and available resources of States, tribes, local governments, and disaster relief organizations in alleviating the damage, loss, hardship, or suffering caused thereby."

Management By Objective: A management approach that involves a four-step process for achieving the incident goal. The Management by Objectives approach includes the following: establishing overarching objectives; developing and issuing assignments, plans, procedures, and protocols; establishing specific, measurable objectives for various incident management functional activities and directing efforts to fulfill them, in support of defined strategic objectives; and documenting results to measure performance and facilitate corrective action.

Mitigation: The activities designed to reduce or eliminate risks to persons or property or to lessen the actual or potential effects or consequences of an incident. Mitigation measures may be implemented prior to, during, or after an incident. Mitigation measures are often informed by lessons learned from prior incidents. Mitigation involves ongoing actions to reduce exposure to, probability of, or potential loss from hazards. Measures may include zoning and building codes, floodplain buyouts, and analysis of hazard-related data to determine where it is safe to build or locate temporary facilities. Mitigation can include efforts to educate governments, businesses, and the public on measures they can take to reduce loss and injury.

Mobilization: The process and procedures used by all organizations (Federal, State, local, and tribal) for activating, assembling, and transporting all resources that have been requested to respond to or support an incident.

Multiagency Coordination Entity: A multiagency coordination entity functions within a broader multiagency coordination system. It may establish the priorities among incidents and associated resource allocations, deconflict agency policies, and provide strategic guidance and direction to support incident management activities.

Multiagency Coordination Systems: Provides the architecture to support coordination for incident prioritization, critical resource allocation, communications systems integration, and information coordination. The components of multiagency coordination systems include facilities, equipment, emergency operation centers (EOCs), specific multiagency coordination entities, personnel, procedures, and communications. These systems assist agencies and organizations to fully integrate the subsystems of the NIMS.

Multijurisdictional Incident: An incident requiring action from multiple agencies that each have jurisdiction to manage certain aspects of an incident. In ICS, these incidents will be managed under Unified Command.

Mutual-Aid Agreement: Written agreement between agencies and/or jurisdictions in which they agree to assist one another upon request by furnishing personnel, equipment, and expertise in a specified manner.

National: Of a nationwide character, including the Federal, State, local, and tribal aspects of governance and policy.

National Disaster Medical System: A cooperative, asset-sharing partnership between the Department of Health and Human Services, the Department of Veterans Affairs, the Department of Homeland Security, and the Department of Defense. NDMS provides resources for meeting the continuity of care and mental health services requirements of the Emergency Support Function 8 in the Federal Response Plan.

National Interagency Incident Management System (NIMS): A system mandated by HSPD-5 that provides a consistent nationwide approach for Federal, State, local, and tribal governments, the private-sector, and nongovernmental organizations to work effectively and efficiently together to prepare for, respond to, and recover from domestic incidents, regardless of cause, size, or complexity. To provide for interoperability and compatibility among Federal, State, local, and tribal capabilities, the NIMS includes a core set of concepts, principles, and terminology. HSPD-5 identifies these as the ICS; multiagency coordination systems; training; identification and management of resources (including systems for classifying types of resources); qualification and certification; and the collection, tracking, and reporting of incident information and incident resources.

National Response Plan: A plan mandated by HSPD-5 that integrates Federal domestic prevention, preparedness, response, and recovery plans into one all-discipline, all-hazards plan.

Nongovernmental Organization: An entity with an association that is based on interests of its members, individuals, or institutions and that is not created by a government, but may work cooperatively with government. Such organizations serve a public purpose, not a private benefit. Examples of NGOs include faith-based charity organizations and the American Red Cross.

Operational Period: The schedule for executing a given set of operation actions, as specified in the Incident Action Plan. Operational Periods can be of various lengths, although usually not over 24 hours.

Operations Section: The Section responsible for all tactical operations. In ICS, it normally includes subordinate branches, divisions, and groups.

Personnel Accountability: The ability to account for the location and welfare of incident personnel. It is accomplished when supervisors ensure that ICS principles and processes are functional and that personnel are working within established incident management guidelines.

Planning Meeting: A meeting held as needed prior to and throughout the duration of an incident to select specific strategies and tactics for incident control operations and for service and support planning. In larger incidents, the planning meeting is a major element in the development of the Incident Action Plan (IAP).

Planning Section: Responsible for the collection, evaluation, and dissemination of operational information related to the incident, and for the preparation and documentation of the Incident Action Plan (IAP). This section also maintains information on the current and forecasted situation and on the status of resources assigned to the incident.

Preparedness: The range of deliberate, critical tasks and activities necessary to build, sustain, and improve the operational capability to prevent, protect against, respond to, and recover from domestic incidents. Preparedness is a continuous process and involves efforts at all levels of government and between government and private-sector and nongovernmental organizations to identify threats, determine vulnerabilities, and identify required resources. Within the NIMS, preparedness is operationally focused on establishing guidelines, protocols, and standards for planning, training and exercises, personnel qualification and certification, equipment certification, and publication management.

Preparedness Organizations: The groups and fora that provide interagency coordination for domestic incident management activities in a nonemergency context. Preparedness organizations can include all agencies with a role in incident management, for prevention, preparedness, response, or recovery activities. They represent a wide variety of committees, planning groups, and other organizations that meet and coordinate to ensure the proper level of planning, training, equipping, and other preparedness requirements within a jurisdiction or area.

Prevention: Actions to avoid an incident or to intervene to stop an incident from occurring. Prevention involves actions to protect lives and property. It involves applying intelligence and other information to a range of activities that may include such countermeasures as deterrence operations; heightened inspections; improved surveillance and security operations; investigations to determine the full nature and source of the threat; public health and agricultural surveillance and testing processes; immunizations, isolation, or quarantine; and, as appropriate, specific law enforcement operations aimed at deterring, preempting, interdicting, or disrupting illegal activity and apprehending potential perpetrators and bringing them to justice.

Private Sector: Organizations and entities that are not part of any governmental structure. It includes for-profit and not-for-profit organizations, formal and informal structures, commerce and industry, and private voluntary organizations (PVO).

Processes: Systems of operations that incorporate standardized procedures, methodologies, and functions necessary to provide resources effectively and efficiently. These include resource typing, resource ordering and tracking, and coordination.

Public Information Officer: A member of the Command Staff responsible for interfacing with the public and media or with other agencies with incident-related information requirements.

Publications Management: The publications management subsystem includes materials development, publication control, publication supply, and distribution. The development and distribution of NIMS materials is managed through this subsystem. Consistent documentation is critical to success, because it ensures that all responders are familiar with the documentation used in a particular incident regardless of the location or the responding agencies involved.

Qualification and Certification: This subsystem provides recommended qualification and certification standards for emergency responder and incident management personnel. It also allows the development of minimum standards for resources expected to have an interstate application. Standards typically include training, currency, experience, and physical and medical fitness.

Reception Area: This refers to a location separate from staging areas, where resources report in for processing and out-processing. Reception Areas provide accountability, security, situational awareness briefings, safety awareness, distribution of IAPs, supplies and equipment, feeding, and bed down.

Recovery: The development, coordination, and execution of service- and site-restoration plans; the reconstitution of government operations and services; individual, private-sector, nongovernmental, and public-assistance programs to provide housing and to promote restoration; long-term care and treatment of affected persons; additional measures for social, political, environmental, and economic restoration; evaluation of the incident to identify lessons learned; postincident reporting; and development of initiatives to mitigate the effects of future incidents.

Recovery Plan: A plan developed by a State, local, or tribal jurisdiction with assistance from responding Federal agencies to restore the affected area.

Resources: Personnel and major items of equipment, supplies, and facilities available or potentially available for assignment to incident operations and for which status is maintained. Resources are described by kind and type and may be used in operational support or supervisory capacities at an incident or at an EOC.

Resource Management: Efficient incident management requires a system for identifying available resources at all jurisdictional levels to enable timely and unimpeded access to resources needed to prepare for, respond to, or recover from an incident. Resource management under the NIMS includes mutual-aid agreements; the use of special Federal, State, local, and tribal teams; and resource mobilization protocols.

Resources Unit: Functional unit within the Planning Section responsible for recording the status of resources committed to the incident. The unit also evaluates resources currently committed to the incident, the effects additional responding resources will have on the incident, and anticipated resource needs.

Response: Activities that address the short-term, direct effects of an incident. Response includes immediate actions to save lives, protect property, and meet basic human needs. Response also includes the execution of emergency operations plans and of mitigation activities designed to limit the loss of life, personal injury, property damage, and other unfavorable outcomes. As indicated by the situation, response activities include applying intelligence and other information to lessen the effects or consequences of an incident; increased security operations; continuing investigations into the nature and source of the threat; ongoing public health and agricultural surveillance and testing processes; immunizations, isolation, or quarantine; and specific law enforcement operations aimed at preempting, interdicting, or disrupting illegal activity, and apprehending actual perpetrators and bringing them to justice.

Safety Officer: A member of the Command Staff responsible for monitoring and assessing safety hazards or unsafe situations and for developing measures for ensuring personnel safety.

Section: The organizational level with responsibility for a major functional area of incident management (Operations, Planning, Logistics, Finance/Administration, and Intelligence, if established). The Section is organizationally situated between branch and the Incident Command.

Span of Control: The number of individuals a supervisor is responsible for, usually expressed as the ratio of supervisors to individuals. Under the NIMS, an appropriate span of control is between 1:3 and 1:7.

Staging Area: Location established where resources can be placed while awaiting a tactical assignment. The Operations Section manages Staging Areas.

State: When capitalized, refers to any State of the United States, the District of Columbia, the Commonwealth of Puerto Rico, the Virgin Islands, Guam, American Samoa, the Commonwealth of the Northern Mariana Islands, and any possession of the USA.

Strategic: Strategic elements of incident management are characterized by continuous long-term, high-level planning by organizations headed by elected or other senior officials. These elements involve the adoption of long-range goals and objectives, the setting of priorities; the establishment of budgets and other fiscal decisions, policy development, and the application of measures of performance or effectiveness.

Strike Team: A set number of resources of the same kind and type that have an established minimum number of personnel.

Strategy: The general direction selected to accomplish incident objectives set by the IC.

Supporting Technologies: Any technology that may be used to support the NIMS is included in this subsystem. These technologies include orthophoto mapping, remote automatic weather stations, infrared technology, and communications, among various others.

Task Force: Any combination of resources assembled to support a specific mission or operational need. All resource elements within a Task Force must have common communications and a designated leader.

Technical Assistance: Support provided to State, local, and tribal jurisdictions when they have the resources but lack the complete knowledge and skills needed to perform a required activity (such as mobile-home park design and hazardous material assessments).

Terrorism: Under the Homeland Security Act of 2002, terrorism is defined as activity that involves an act dangerous to human life or potentially destructive of critical infrastructure or key resources and is a violation of the criminal laws of the United States or of any State or other subdivision of the United States in which it occurs and is intended to intimidate or coerce the civilian population or influence a government or affect the conduct of a government by mass destruction, assassination, or kidnaping.

Threat: An indication of possible violence, harm, or danger.

Tools: Those instruments and capabilities that allow for the professional performance of tasks, such as information systems, agreements, doctrine, capabilities, and legislative authorities.

Tribal: Any Indian tribe, band, nation, or other organized group or community, including any Alaskan Native Village as defined in or established pursuant to the Alaskan Native Claims Settlement Act, that is recognized as eligible for the special programs and services provided by the United States to Indians because of their status as Indians.

Type: A classification of resources in the ICS that refers to capability. Type I is generally considered to be more capable than Types II, III, or IV, respectively, because of size, power, capacity, or, in the case of incident management teams, experience and qualifications.

Unified Area Command: *See Area Command.*

Unified Command: An application of ICS used when there is more than one agency with incident jurisdiction or when incidents cross political jurisdictions. Agencies work together through the designated members of the UC, often the senior person from agencies and/or disciplines participating in the UC, to establish a common set of objectives and strategies and a single IAP.

Unit: The organizational element having functional responsibility for a specific incident planning, logistics, or finance/administration activity.

Unity of Command: The concept by which each person within an organization reports to one and only one designated person. The purpose of unity of command is to ensure unity of effort under one responsible commander for every objective.

Volunteer: For purposes of the NIMS, a volunteer is any individual accepted to perform services by the lead agency, which has authority to accept volunteer services, when the individual performs services without promise, expectation, or receipt of compensation for services performed.

NIMS Acronyms

ALS	Advanced Life Support
DOC	Department Operations Center
EMAC	Emergency Management Assistance Compact
EOC	Emergency Operations Center
EOP	Emergency Operations Plan
FOG	Field Operations Guide
GIS	Geographic Information System
HAZMAT	Hazardous Material
HSPD-5	Homeland Security Presidential Directive - 5
IAP	Incident Action Plan
IC	Incident Commander
ICP	Incident Command Post
ICS	Incident Command System
IC	Incident Command
IMT	Incident Management Team
JIS	Joint Information System
JIC	Joint Information Center
LNO	Liaison Officer
NDMS	National Disaster Medical System
NGO	Nongovernmental Organizations
NIMS	National Incident Management System
NRP	National Response Plan
PIO	Public Information Officer
POLREP	Pollution Report
PVO	Private Voluntary Organizations
R&D	Research and Development
RESTAT	Resources Status
ROSS	Resource Ordering and Status System
SDO	Standards Development Organizations
SITREP	Situation Report
SO	Safety Officer
SOP	Standard Operating Procedure
UC	Unified Command
US&R	Urban Search and Rescue

Chapter Sources:
National Incident Management System Handbook, March 1, 2004, Dept. of Homeland Security.
Resource Definitions: 120 Resources, September 2004, National Mutual Aid and Resource Management Initiative, Dept. of Homeland Security & FEMA.

INVESTIGATION AND INTERROGATION

Arson and Fire Investigation · 264

Drunk Driving · 267

   Drunk Driving Signs · 269
   Dexterity Testing · 271
   Horizontal Gaze Nystagmus Test · · · · · · · · · · · · · 273
   Walk and Turn Test · 274
   One Leg Stand Test · 275
   Detention of drunk drivers · · · · · · · · · · · · · · · · · 279

Blood Alcohol Content · 282

   Male & Female Blood Alcohol Percentage Tables · · · 283

Motor Vehicle Theft · 284

Crime Scene Response · 286

   Team Member Responsibilities · · · · · · · · · · · · · · 286
   Search Procedures · 288
   Evidence Collection · 293

Post-Mortem Evidence · 308

Investigative Photography · 311

Investigative Tools and Equipment List · · · · · · · · · · 327

Interviewing Victims and Witnesses · · · · · · · · · · · · 329

Search Patterns · 332

Arson and Fire Investigation

Editor's Note: While fire investigations are generally the responsibility of the fire service or a joint law enforcement fire-arson task force, police officers are often first at the scene. The information that you gather will be of assistance to the firefighters in their initial response and the subsequent investigation. In smaller jurisdictions, the investigative responsibility may fall to the patrol officer.

When the Initial Call Is Received, the Responding Officer Should Note:

- Date and time of alarm and how it was transmitted.
- The identity of the person calling. Who discovered and reported the fire, have the person describe the fire.
- Weather conditions in the area. Is it hot, cold, cloudy, or clear? Are conditions in the involved structure appropriate for the weather? For example: if it's cold outside, the windows should be closed; if it's hot, the furnace should be off.
- Are there natural hazards? Is there lightning, heavy snow, ice, flooding or fog? Arsonists have been know to wait for natural conditions that can affect the fire department's response. Lightning strikes can result in multiple fire areas.
- What is the wind direction and speed? The responding officer should contact the local weather station and interview fire fighters on the scene to determine the direction and intensity of the wind. This information will aid investigators in assessing the rate of fire spread and damage.
- Are there obstructions to the scene? Are there barricades, fallen trees, cables, or trash containers obstructing the fire department's access to the scene? Delayed arrival at the fire scene by the fire department could work to an arsonist's advantage, and barricades, both inside and outside of buildings, may be a tool employed by an arsonist.

Key Elements to Note Upon Arrival at a Fire Scene

- Arrival time and the degree and intensity of the fire. A detailed description of the fire in its early stages is essential to a thorough investigation.
- People at the scene. Be sure to note a description of people seen at, near or leaving the scene of the fire.
- Note unusual behavior of people at the scene.

- Are there covered windows and doors. Drawing the shades or covering the windows and doors with blankets are common techniques employed by arsonists to delay discovery of the fire.

- The fire department's method of entry. Were the doors locked or open? Was there any evidence of forced entry before the fire? In the event of an investigation, these facts may aid in determining the identity of the fire setter. Burglars sometimes set fire to a building in order to destroy evidence of the burglary.

- The color of the smoke. Is the smoke an unusual color? This is often the first clue to possible combustibles involved in the fire.

Combustible	Color of Smoke
Acetone	Gray or Black
Benzene	Black
Chlorine*	Yellow green
Cooking Oil	Brown to Black
Iodine*	Violet
Nitric Acid*	Yellow brown

*Not a combustible, but they may contribute to smoke color if present in large quantities.

- The flame color and fire intensity. The color of flame can provide valuable clues to the intensity of the fire.

Flame Color	Temperature	
Faint red	930-1020°F	(500-550°C)
Red	1020-1200°F	(550-650°C)
Orange	1200-1380°F	(650-750°C)
Yellow-orange	1380-1560°F	(750-850°C)
Yellow	1560-1830°F	(850-1000°C)
White-yellow	1830-2190°F	(1000-1200°C)
White	2190°F	(1200°C)

While The Fire Is Being Fought, Be Aware Of:

- Speed of fire spread. Considering the building's structure and occupancy, is the fire spreading unusually fast? Unusually rapid fire spread could indicate the use of an accelerant.

- Separate and seemingly unrelated fires

- Unusual Odors. Some odors are likely to be familiar to fire fighters. These include gasoline, kerosene, paint thinner, lacquer, turpentine, linseed oil, furniture polish, rubber insulation, natural gas, and manufactured gas.

- Reaction of fire to water. Note what happens when water is applied to a flammable liquid fire. Does the liquid float to the top, re-ignite, continue to burn, and spread the fire? Are there rekindles? Is there an increase in burning?
- Obstacles to hinder fire fighting. Has furniture been moved on the premises with the obvious intent to hinder fire fighters?
- Streamers or trailers; combustibles strategically placed to promote fire spread.
- Artificial conditions created to assist fire spread. Arsonists often prop open fire doors or pull down plaster to expose wood. They may also punch holes in ceilings from story to story or punch holes in the walls of different rooms. These actions will enhance fire spread.
- Absence of stock, fixtures, machinery, display cases or records in fires involving industrial or commercial property.
- Absence of clothing, furniture, appliances, personal effects or family pets in dwelling fires.
- Tampering or damage to fire protection facilities. Was the sprinkler system in operable condition? Were the sprinkler valves open and locked into position before the start of the fire? Was the fire alarm in working order?
- Tampering or damage to the burglar alarm.

After The Fire Is Extinguished:

- Begin salvage and overhaul operations. Be careful not to destroy any incendiary devices or other possible evidence. Items near the fire origin should be left undisturbed if possible They will prove valuable after further investigation.

Secure The Scene Until The Investigator Arrives

- Keep unauthorized persons away from the scene. Generally, a fire officer can control the scene until an investigator arrives. If you are reluctant to have the property owner on the premises, be aware of local laws governing this before acting.
- Post a guard with specific instructions. The guard should only permit entrance to persons with authorization, making sure to keep a log of all entrants. The guard should allow nothing to be removed by persons not directly involved in the investigation. Any unusual events should be reported to the assigned investigator immediately.

Excerpted from *A Pocket Guide to Arson and Fire Investigation*, © 1996, Factory Mutual Engineering Corp., reprinted with permission.

Drunk Driving

This section is intended to help street-level officers with their enforcement skills in drunk driving apprehensions and investigations by teaching the "Four Ds" of drunk driving investigations: Detection, Dexterity, Detention and Detailing.

Detection

The detection strategy is used by police officers to look for specific driving behavior that indicates the use of alcohol. A police officer searches for a drunk driver based on common and typical signs. This allows the officer to witness violations first-hand, to establish reasonable suspicion for a traffic stop, and to conduct further investigation which may lead to an arrest.

Officers should be aware of specific times and locations in which there is a high frequency of drunk drivers in the area. A classic example of this would be at 2:00 a.m. on a Friday or Saturday, when liquor establishments are closing (especially in an area that contains four or five such establishments.) An officer may want to patrol within this area, to look for signs of a possible drunk driver.

When investigating a traffic accident, especially during a "prime time" for drunk drivers, officers should look for behavioral signs that may indicate that alcohol was involved, even if the accident was not witnessed by the officer. Upon investigation of the accident it may be difficult to identify the driver, especially if everyone has exited the vehicle, and no one will admit responsibility. This often happens in one-car accidents with several friends in the vehicle. Observe injuries, such as marks caused by the seat belt, and note possible clues as to who may have been driving the vehicle Interview as many witnesses as possible. Interview each person individually, listening for inconsistent statements and clues about who was driving. If the driver is injured, psychophysical exams may not be appropriate. In such cases, note all possible signs of alcohol use, such as quality of speech, color of face, smell of intoxicants, condition of eyes, and statements the driver or passenger(s) may have made regarding drinking. Remember, however, that some signs of intoxication may result from the accident itself and not from the drinking of alcohol.

Drunk drivers are sometimes detected while making routine traffic stops. An officer may not suspect alcohol until face-to-face contact is made. Once an officer suspects the presence of alcohol, he should continue the investigation using the normal procedures as if alcohol was suspected. It is very important to

Investigation

record in detail behavioral signs and results of dexterity tests. Since defense attorneys will bring up the fact that there was very little hazardous driving action, it is very important to have detailed documentation in a police report.

Officers have been taught to look for signs which are common to drunk drivers. The U.S. Dept. of Transportation developed a **Probability Value Guide** for detection of drunk drivers.

With the Probability Value Guide, the percentage following each visual clue is the probability that a driver exhibiting that driving mistake has a blood alcohol level equal to or greater than 0.10%. For example, a wide radius turn indicates a 65% probability that the driver has at least a 0.10% blood alcohol content. In other words, 65 out of 100 drivers who make an excessively wide turn will have a blood alcohol content of 0.10% or more.

The Probability Value Guide figures listed below are for single driving mistakes only and are based on nighttime driving only. Most drunk drivers will make more than one mistake. For instance, a driver who makes an extremely wide turn and is traveling so slowly that it would cause an officer to notice would be making two mistakes. When two or more indicators are seen, add 10% to the value. Thus the driver's score would be 75%, a very high probability that he has a blood alcohol content greater than 0.10%.

Probability Value Guide

Turning with an excessively wide radius	65%
Straddling the center line	65%
Visually seems to be drunk or intoxicated	60%
Almost hitting an object or another vehicle	60%
Weaving	60%
Driving off of roadway (on sidewalk etc)	55%
Swerving	55%
Slow speed (more than 10 mph under the limit)	50%
Stopping without cause in a traffic lane	50%
Drifting	50%
Following too closely to another vehicle	50%
Tires on center or lane line	45%
Erratic braking	45%
Driving into opposing traffic lanes	45%
Signaling inconsistent with driving action	40%
Slow response to a traffic signal	40%
Abrupt or illegal turns	35%
Abrupt or illegal stops	35%
Rapid acceleration or deceleration	30%
Driving with no headlights on	30%

Drunk Driving Signs

In addition to the Probability Value Guide, officers should be aware of and note specific incidents and vehicle signs.

- **Turns:** excessively wide; from a wrong lane or into a wrong lane; cutting corners too sharply; making illegal U-turns; sudden turns; unnecessary lane changes; not using a turn signal; or using the wrong turn signal.
- **Speed:** too fast; too slow; fluctuation of speed; passing without sufficient clearance; or exhibition driving.
- **Driving:** weaving within a lane; crossing the center line; traveling straight along the shoulder of the road; swerving; striking or bumping off the curb; unsafe backing; long and abrupt starts or stops; tailgating; loss of control of the vehicle; driving in the wrong gear or grinding of gears; 'riding' the brakes; or driving with high beams or not having headlights on.
- **Traffic Devices:** disobeying traffic lights or signs; or stopping for a yellow or flashing light.
- **Equipment:** driving on a flat tire; traveling with high beams on or not having headlights on; window open during inclement weather; visibility obstructions (snow, ice, etc.) on windows; unusually loud music; or a dragging muffler.

Personal and Behavioral Signs

Be aware of personal clues or behavioral patterns which can help detect a driver under the influence of intoxicants. Some of these signs can be seen when the driver operates a vehicle; other signs can be observed during face-to-face contact.

- **Posture:** poor; slumped; poor balance; rigid; or leaning.
- **Initial behavior:** averting breath; an immovable stare; silence; examination of documents for a long period of time; emotional display; ignoring the officer; difficulty gathering proper paperwork or removing license from wallet or purse; or window not rolled down all the way during the initial conversation with the officer, as if trying to hide something.
- **Eyes:** red; glazed; bloodshot, the most common sign of alcohol presence; watery; or dilated pupils.
- **Odor of Alcoholic Beverages:** strong, moderate or weak. Note the smell coming from the breath and/or person, but not what type of intoxicant you smell, e.g., "smelled like beer." Defense attorneys will raise the issue of an officer's

ability to smell different kinds of alcoholic beverages. Remember that alcohol itself is odorless.

- **Face:** nose red in color; clammy; lack of eye contact; sleepy; pale; or flushed.
- **Speech:** hesitant or slow; slurred; mumbled; deliberate; repetitive; incoherent; does not start conversation voluntarily; or slow response to questions when asked.
- **Attitude:** angry; hostile; impatient; belligerent; defiant; antagonistic; argumentative; arrogant; aggressive; apologetic; talkative; carefree; polite; cheerful; amused; lack of concentration; sleeping; or accommodating.
- **Documents:** fumbling; dropping; unable to locate the appropriate papers requested by the officer; requesting assistance in finding the paperwork; or selecting wrong documents to give to an officer.
- **Unsuitable Behavior:** crying; giggling; profanity; eating; vomiting; fatigue; hiccups; dizziness; numbness; or attempts to lean on objects such as a vehicle for support and assistance with balance.
- **Unaware of Surroundings:** vehicle still in gear; location of the traffic stop; the time of day; vehicle damage or defect (e.g. driving on a flat tire); or visible injuries.
- **Vehicle:** signs of alcohol containers inside the car; receipts from a bar; or statements from passengers regarding the amount the driver had to drink.
- **Exiting the Vehicle:** using the vehicle for support; not turning the vehicle off or putting the vehicle into gear; leaving the vehicle door open; falling or stumbling when getting out of the vehicle; or stepping out into the lane of traffic.
- **Clothing:** not suitable for the type of weather (e.g. no socks or coat during snow or cold weather); soiled; messy; shirt partially untucked; or shoes untied.
- **Appearing to be Drunk:** eye fixation; tightly gripping the steering wheel; slouching in the seat; gesturing erratically or obscenely; face close to the windshield; drinking in the vehicle; or the driver's head protruding from vehicle.

Signs When Stopping a Suspected Vehicle

The vehicle should be stopped once an officer has observed what he/she believes to be a significant amount of questionable driving and has used the Probability Value Guide to evaluate traffic violations. How the suspect's vehicle stops can also be of value in building a case against a drunk driver.

- Look for a slow or lack of response to the emergency lights and siren.
- Does the driver pull over in a manner that could be considered reckless?
- Do the tires of the vehicle bump into the curb?
- Does the suspect pull off the road, onto the shoulder, then off the shoulder onto a grassy area?
- A suspect may even attempt to flee from the officer.

Motorcycles

Give special attention to motorcycles during the peak hours of drunk driving incidents. Motorcyclists often have additional actions that might indicate drunk driving.

- Drifting in a curve or a turn.
- Difficulty with balance when the motorcycle is stopped.
- Turning problems such as slow braking, improper lean angle, or over corrections.
- Driver is unaware of surroundings.
- Swaying or weaving across or within the lanes.

Dexterity Testing

When a driver is stopped for suspected drunk driving, look for signs of intoxication in two types of behavior: "command behavior" and "voluntary behavior."

Command behavior is the driver's response to a command or instruction given by the officer. This may be as simple as asking the driver to produce a driver's license. Commands given must be clear and concise, using language that is simple and easily understood. The major focus for the officer should be what the suspect did or did not do when commanded. Note what the suspect's response was, and how many times the officer had to repeat or demonstrate the instruction before the suspect responded. Documentation of all behavior is important to help show how an officer developed an opinion as to whether the suspect was under the influence of intoxicants.

Remember that people differ a great deal in their ability to respond to instructions. Some people respond to a uniformed presence with a great deal of nervousness or anxiety. Defense attorneys will attempt to show that their client's behavior was just that: nervous, not intoxicated. Observations of the suspect's voluntary behavior can support the conclusions reached on the basis of the suspect's command behavior.

Voluntary behavior is anything the suspect does or says along with or outside of his command behavior. Examples include asking for a ride home or a nonverbal expression of emotion such as starting to cry. Just as all command behavior should be recorded, all of the suspect's voluntary behavior should also be recorded in the police report.

To assist officers in their drunk driving investigation drivers are put through a series of tests commonly referred to as Field Dexterity Tests, or occasionally as Sobriety Tests. Officers should observe and record the suspect's balance, coordination, vision, reaction time, concentration level, and memory. During this type of testing, an officer should continue to document any voluntary behavior or statements made by the suspect.

Departmental guidelines for the administration of dexterity tests allows all officers to have the same set of fair and objective tests to administer. Such consistency helps officers recognize the same kind of behavior when dealing with intoxicated drivers. This will also aid the prosecuting attorney in preparation for trial, as all dexterity tests within an agency will be the same.

When starting the field dexterity test process, the tests must be explained clearly and demonstrated properly. A suspect should be asked if he or she understands the instructions, and if not, the officer needs to find out which part to explain over again. Maintain a proper stance and distance from the suspect, keeping safety in mind.

The officer should ask the suspect if there is any physical or mental reason that he or she may not be able to perform a certain test that is requested. This question will help eliminate any objection that may be raised in court regarding how the results of a dexterity test were interpreted.

Perform dexterity tests on a flat surface whenever possible. Try to choose a spot that is dry and free of debris. Record the conditions under which the test was performed in the police report, as well as the type of shoes the suspect was wearing. The shoes a suspect wears may have a bearing on the results of tests requiring balance.

During the interview and dexterity testing process, the officer should watch for certain specific behaviors which must be recorded and can be helpful in demonstrating the intoxication of the suspect.

Things to watch for:
- Balance and motor skills
- Coordination
- Odor of intoxicants
- Attention span, concentration level, mental awareness
- Personal factors such as facial expressions, condition of eyes, smell, and speech.
- Mental or physical problems
- Ability to follow instructions
- Attitude, mood swings
- Judgment
- Time perception
- Verbal behavior

The following tests are referred to as the Standardized Field Sobriety Testing Battery. These tests have been recommended by the National Highway Traffic Safety Administration (NHTSA). Use of standardized tests will show that the tests are administered by officers the same way every time. The three recommended tests are the Horizontal Gaze Nystagmus (HGN), Walk and Turn, and the One Leg Stand. When the officer is properly trained and uses all three tests, there is an 83% chance that a suspect who fails the tests has a blood alcohol level higher than 0.10%. It is recommended that officers attend the prescribed training course presented by the NHTSA to learn exactly how to administer the tests.

Horizontal Gaze Nystagmus Test

Nystagmus is the involuntary jerking of the eyes which occurs as the eyes gaze toward the side.

Standardized Procedures
1. Hold index finger 12-15 inches in front of suspect's face - remember to keep your gun side turned away from suspect.
2. Keep the tip of the finger slightly above the suspect's eyes.
3. Move the finger smoothly from side to side.
4. Check for each clue (below) at least twice in each eye.

Standardized Clues
Always check for all three clues in both eyes, in order:
1. lack of smooth pursuit
2. distinct nystagmus at maximum deviation
3. onset of nystagmus prior to 45 degrees.

Note: No clues other than these three are recognized. Officers should not predict a suspect's blood alcohol level.

Standardized Criteria

The maximum number of clues of horizontal gaze nystagmus that a suspect can show is six (all three clues present in both eyes.) If a suspect shows four or more, it should be considered evidence that they are under the influence.

Additional Information regarding HGN testing

Officers need special training in this area, and must pass written tests and demonstrate proficiency. Certification is generally needed for related testimony to be admissible in a court of law. Keep a log book to demonstrate proficiency and use of this test.

Officers should observe pupil size, tracking capability, and vertical/horizontal nystagmus. This test can also be used when testing for drugs. Remember that normal eye movement is smooth, non-jerking tracking of an object. As blood alcohol level increases, eye movement becomes jerky and will often manifest an involuntary oscillation.

Walk and Turn Test

Standardized Procedures

1. Always have the suspect assume the heel-to-toe stance.
2. Confirm that the suspect understands the stance and that he/she should remain in that position while the rest of the instructions are being given.
3. If the suspect breaks out of the stance, stop giving instructions until the stance is resumed.
4. Tell the suspect that he/she will be required to take nine heel-to-toe steps down the line, turn 180° to the left, and take nine heel-to-toe steps up the line.
5. The officer should demonstrate several heel-to-toe steps.
6. The officer should demonstrate a slow turn.
7. Instruct suspects to keep their arms at their sides, to watch their feet, to count the steps out loud, and not to stop walking until the test is finished.
8. Ask the suspect if they understood the instructions. If they don't, ask what part they did not understand, and then re-explain that part.
9. Tell the suspect to begin.
10. If the suspect stops or staggers, allow him to resume from the point where they stopped; do not require the suspect to start over from the beginning.

Standardized Clues

- Loses balance during the instructions
- Starts walking too soon
- Misses heel-to-toe by more than a half inch while walking

- Raises arms more than six inches while walking
- Steps off the line
- Makes and improper turn
- Takes the wrong number of steps

NOTE: There are only eight clues in this test; each should only be counted once, even though it may occur more than one time. Officers can, however, mention in their reports if they see a clue more than once. If the suspect cannot perform or finish the test (e.g., the suspect steps off the line 3 times), they should be considered to have shown nine clues.

Standardized Criteria

If a suspect shows at least two clues on Walk and Turn, it should be considered evidence of being under the influence.

One Leg Stand

Standardized Procedure

1. Tell the suspect to stand with feet together, arms at their side.
2. Tell the suspect not to start the test until the officer says so.
3. Ask if he or she understands how to stand and to wait.
4. Tell the suspect that they will need to stand on one foot, with the other foot held straight about six inches off the ground, toes pointed forward and parallel to the ground.
5. Officer now demonstrates the test.
6. Instruct the suspect that they will need to count from 1001 to 1030.
7. Officer now demonstrates the count (thousand one, thousand two, thousand three, etc.)
8. Ask the suspect if he or she understands all the instructions; if not, re-explain whatever is not understood.
9. Tell the suspect to begin the test.
10. If the suspect stops or puts his or her foot down, allow them to resume at the point of interruption. Do not require the count to begin from the beginning.

Standardized Clues

- Sways
- Puts foot down
- Hops
- Raises arms from side six inches or more

Note: There are only four clues to be considered in this test. If an officer sees additional signs of intoxication during the test, such as slurred speech while counting, they can be recorded in the police report.

Standardized Criteria

If a suspect shows two or more clues on this test, it should be considered evidence that they are under the influence. As with the Walk and Turn test, clues should only be counted once even if they occur more than once during the test.

Other Tests

The following is a list of other dexterity tests officers may wish to use. They do not have the same scientific validation as the three previous tests, but may show additional signs that the suspect is under the influence.

Alphabet Recitation

The suspect is instructed to recite the alphabet aloud starting with the letter D and continuing through the letter P.

- The officer should evaluate the suspect's memory, concentration impairment, speech pattern, hesitation, and the order recited.
- This test will correlate with tests of speech patterns and is very similar to number count and counting sequence tests.
- This test requires a suspect to concentrate.
- This test is not appropriate for use with suspects who are illiterate or have less than a middle school education.
- This test is not appropriate for use when English is not a suspect's primary language.
- The officer administering the test needs a basic, general education as well as the ability to listen closely and demonstrate the test.

Finger Count

The suspect is commanded to count forward and backward to four, while touching the tips of the fingers to the tip of the thumb on the same hand.

- This tests demonstrates whether the suspect can do two simple tasks at the same time.
- This test is easy to perform in any condition or position, (e.g., sitting down).
- This test cannot be used if physical injury has occurred to the suspect's hand or fingers or if the suspect is physically handicapped.
- The only officer training needed is the ability to give the command and demonstrate the test.

Counting Sequence

The suspect is commanded to count; either forward or backward (e.g. 1 to 20; keep the test simple).

- This test evaluates memory and concentration impairment, speech patterns, and hesitation.
- This test is similar to the alphabet test.
- The officer administering the test needs the ability to listen closely for signs such as slurring, rapid speech, lack of accuracy, and memory loss.

Balance

The suspect is commanded to stand erect, feet together, and arms at their side while looking straight ahead.

The suspect is then told to raise and extend the left or right foot forward, without bending the knee. The heel is to be held approximately 6 to 12 inches off the ground for a short period of time (ten seconds).

- This test measures a suspect's balance.
- This test is similar to other tests which require motor skills.
- This test includes the observation of a suspect falling, wobbling, or needing support.
- This test cannot be used if a suspect has an injury or medical problem with their leg.
- This test is best used on a dry, level surface.
- The only officer training needed is the ability to give the command and demonstrate the test.

Romberg Balance

The suspect is commanded to stand at 'attention' with heels and toes together, arms at their side, head tilted back, and eyes closed for approximately 20 seconds.

- This test measures balance. It is similar to the balance test.
- This test is for observation of a suspect's swaying, staggering, or falling.
- This test cannot be used if the suspect has any motor-related medical problems or injuries.
- Like other balance tests, it should be performed on a dry, flat surface.
- The only officer training needed is the ability to give the command and demonstrate the test.

Finger to Nose

This test can be administered two different ways. The second method provides the suspect with additional instructions and allows more precise observations.

Method 1: The suspect is commanded to stand erect with feet together, eyes closed, and arms stretched out to the side at shoulder level with the index finger of each hand extended and the rest of the hand closed in a fist. With the left hand first, the suspect is to touch the tip of the nose with the tip of the finger by swinging the arm in at the elbow. The process is repeated with the right hand.

Method 2: Standing in the same position as in Method 1, the suspect is commanded to swing the right arm at the shoulder, directly in front, as if pointing straight ahead. With their arm extended, they should roll their hand until fisted palm is upward, and then bend their fist backward at the wrist until finger points straight up. The suspect should then bend their arm at the elbow, bring the hand back, and touch the end of the finger to the end of the nose. Then return the hand to the starting position in lock step fashion, by reversing the procedure. Repeat the process a second time, and follow the same procedure with the left hand.

- This test measures a suspect's attention span and their ability to concentrate, while performing motor skills at the same time.
- This test can relate to any test which addresses motor skills.
- This test evaluates a suspect's lack of attention span and loss of balance.
- This test cannot be used if the suspect has any medical motor problems or injuries.
- This test should be used on a dry, level surface.
- The only officer training needed is the ability to give the command and demonstrate the test.

Detention

Waiver of Miranda Rights: Once the suspected drunk driver is read his or her Miranda Rights, agrees to waive those rights, and answers questions for the officer, the officer can ask some questions which may assist in building the case. In the report, the officer should record the time the Miranda Rights were read and the response of the suspect.

Questions officers should ask a drunk driver in custody:

1. Have you been drinking this evening?
   If so, what and how much?
2. When was the last time you ate, and what did you eat?
3. When was the last time you slept, and how much sleep did you get?
4. Do you feel your driving was affected by what you had to drink?
5. What time did you start drinking? What time did you stop drinking?
6. Do you have any physical defects? Are you sick?
7. Have you ever been arrested for drunk driving?
   If so, when?
8. Are you an alcoholic? If so, for how long?
9. How often would you say you drink and drive intoxicated?
10. Where have you been drinking this evening? If they were "bar hopping" try to get the times and amount at each location.
11. Are you on any medication?

Video: As technology improves, officers are using car video cameras more frequently. Video taping allows a jury to witness first-hand the driving and other behavior of the suspect as the officer sees it. Dexterity tests can also be taped for a jury to observe, but for safety reasons, officers may still want to perform the dexterity tests off to the side of the road rather than between the suspect's car and the patrol car. Stepping off to the sidewalk gives more safety and protection from oncoming traffic. Officers should remember that with video tape their actions and statements will also "be on trial" by the defense attorney.

Witnesses: Especially when traffic accidents have injured people, witnesses may be the starting point for the investigation until the parties involved can be interviewed. Keep witnesses apart, and interview them separately. Passengers in the vehicle are important sources of information about the driver. Officers who may have had contact with the suspect for a period of time should be used to help build a better case, as well as paramedics or fire fighters who may have responded to an accident scene.

Photos: Photographs can be very useful for showing the appearance of the driver at the time of the arrest.

Signature: Officers can introduce the signature of the suspect from their fingerprint card or property sheet, and compare it with the signature on their driver's license.

Items Inside the Vehicle: When the vehicle is searched after a suspect's arrest, officers may come upon items such as beer cans or liquor bottles. These items should be taken into evidence. Officers may want to add accurate details to the report. An example would be, "the beer can was half-full and cold on a hot summer night". This would support the idea that the beer was fresh and not left over from some previous time. In the event of a serious alcohol-related accident such evidence may also be protected and saved for fingerprint analysis. As with all evidence, the items taken should be properly marked and tagged as evidence.

Testing Blood Alcohol Content: One test that is initially performed by an officer on the street is a Preliminary Breath Test, which is commonly referred to as a PBT. This testing device will assist officers in assessing subjects whom they believe are near the threshold of the legal alcohol limit. This test should be considered an additional tool, and officers should rely on other observations, such as dexterity testing and driving, in deciding whether to make an arrest. When using either the Preliminary Breath Test or the Breathalyzer, the objective is to get an air sample from the deepest part of the suspect's lungs, which is referred to as alveolar breath.

Blood testing is the most accurate way to measure blood alcohol level. Blood tests can be performed whether suspect is cooperative, uncooperative, or even unconscious (Michigan State Police, Preliminary Blood Testing for O.U.I.L Enforcement, May 1983, P. 10). These test results can be expensive and not readily available, as medical personnel are required to draw the blood samples. Properly storing the blood sample and maintaining a chain of evidence is also an important factor.

Detailing

It is extremely important that the police report is well written and detailed. Make time to write the report as soon as the arrest process is completed, when the facts of the incident are still fresh.

Report Writing

Write a drunk driving report as if there is no chemical test available. A lot of good evidence results from an officer using his five senses: what he or she smelled, saw, heard, touched or tasted. It is important to write the report in chronological order.

By placing certain information under headings, the officer can break the investigation down into neat segments which will assist the officer's memory as he or she writes the report.

Suggested Headings:
- Initial Information
- Initial Observations or Detection
- Arrival at Scene (Accident Cases)
- Contact with Driver
- Dexterity Tests
- Contact with Witnesses
- Contact with Passengers
- Evidence
- Suspect Statements
- Weather and Road Conditions
- Investigation
- Injuries (Accident Cases or Suspect Injured During Arrest)
- Observer's Opinion
- Chemical Test Results
- Vehicle Information (Suspect)
- Additional Information
- Search Warrant

Source: Dahlinger, Charles William, Drunk Driving *Enforcement and Investigations: Learn the Four Ds (Detection, Dexterity, Detention, Detailing),* Copyright 1995, Stipes Publishing, Chicago, IL, used by permission. For more information, call (616) 679-5454.

Investigation

Blood Alcohol Content (BAC)

NOTE: The following information is only a rough guide. The figures used are averages and not accurate enough to be considered legal evidence. Many factors affect how alcohol affects a person's judgment and physical abilities. Individual alcohol tolerance, body weight, gender, rate of consumption, food in the stomach, medication, health, and mood can all cause variations from the average.

Investigation

Effects on Driving

0.02%.....Drivers show mild change; may seem slightly elated.
0.05%.....Drivers hesitant. Alternate from "who cares?" to impulsive aggression. Mild euphoria, decreased inhibitions and control.
0.08%.....Should not drive unless absolutely necessary. Legally considered "under the influence" in all states.
0.10%.....Judgment seriously affected. Comprehension, memory, coordination, and depth perception are impaired. Decreased reaction time.
0.15%.....Unmistakably drunk. All faculties seriously affected. Perception of color, motion, form and distance is disturbed. Poor balance, slurred speech and staggered gait.
0.30%.....Marked lack of muscle coordination, stuporous.
0.40%.....Unconscious; possibly comatose; on verge of death.

Average Drinks

The following are considered an "average drink." Each drink contains about .50 oz pure alcohol.

    1 oz. of 86-proof alcohol*..................43% alcohol
    5 oz. (142 ml) of table wine ....12% alcohol
    12 oz.(341 ml) of beer......................5% alcohol

*Many drinks contain more than 1 oz. of alcohol. A jigger holds 1.5 oz.

International BAC Limits

Canada: According to the Addiction Research Foundation in Canada, the legal standard under the Criminal Code of Canada is 80 mg of alcohol per 100 ml of blood: .08%.

Europe: The Institute of Alcohol Studies (IAS) in the United Kingdom reports that legal limits range from country to country despite efforts to standardize throughout the European Union to 0.05%. Most countries in Europe have a legal limit as 0.05%. Exceptions are Cypres 0.09%; Ireland, Luxembourg, Malta, and the United Kingdom 0.08%; Lithuania 0.04%; Estonia, Poland, and Sweden 0.02%; Czech Republic, Hungary, and Slovakia 0%.

Male Blood Alcohol Percentage-Approximate

Drinks	Body Weight in Pounds								Effect
	100	120	140	160	180	200	220	240	
1	.04	.03	.03	.02	.02	.02	.02	.02	**Rarely Impaired**
2	.08	.06	.05	.05	.04	.04	.03	.03	
3	.11	.09	.08	.07	.06	.06	.05	.05	**Possibly Impaired**
4	.15	.12	.11	.09	.08	.08	.07	.06	
5	.19	.16	.13	.12	.11	.09	.09	.08	**Definitely Impaired - Criminal Penalties in all U.S. states***
6	.23	.19	.16	.14	.13	.11	.10	.09	
7	.26	.22	.19	.16	.15	.13	.12	.11	
8	.30	.25	.21	.19	.17	.15	.14	.13	
9	.34	.28	.24	.21	.19	.17	.15	.14	
10	.38	.31	.27	.23	.21	.19	.17	.16	

Investigation

Female Blood Alcohol Percentage-Approximate

Drinks	Body Weight in Pounds								Effect
	90	100	120	140	160	180	200	220	
1	.05	.05	.04	.03	.03	.03	.02	.02	**Rarely**
2	.10	.09	.08	.07	.06	.05	.05	.04	**Possibly Impaired**
3	.15	.14	.11	.11	.09	.08	.07	.06	
4	.20	.18	.15	.13	.11	.10	.09	.08	**Definitely Impaired Criminal Penalties in all U.S. states***
5	.25	.23	.19	.16	.14	.13	.11	.10	
6	.30	.27	.23	.19	.17	.15	.14	.12	
7	.35	.32	.27	.23	.20	.18	.16	.14	
8	.40	.36	.30	.26	.23	.20	.18	.17	
9	.45	.41	.34	.29	.26	.23	.20	.19	
10	.51	.45	.38	.32	.28	.25	.23	.21	

Subtract .01% for each 40 minutes of drinking.

Drinks referenced in these table represent "average drinks" as described on the previous page.

*All states have passed the ".08 Per Se" law. The final state to put this law into effect is Minnesota; it was effective in August 2005.

Motor Vehicle Theft

According to the National Insurance Crime Bureau (NICB), stolen vehicles that are not recovered are often:

- Shipped overseas or driven across US borders.
- Surgically stripped by chop shops and resold as parts.
- Retagged and resold to unsuspecting consumers.
- Hidden or destroyed by the owner to collect an insurance settlement.

The Top Ten Stolen Vehicles in 2003

1. 2000 Honda Civic
2. 1989 Toyota Camry
3. 1991 Honda Accord
4. 1994 Chevrolet Full Size 1500 Pickup
5. 1994 Dodge Caravan
6. 1997 Ford F150 Series
7. 1986 Toyota Pickup
8. 1995 Acura Integra
9. 1987 Nissan Sentra
10. 1986 Oldsmobile Cutlass

Source: National Insurance Crime Bureau, 02/28/2005
Note: Statistics in this section are based on INSURED vehicles only.

Foreign Hot Spots

Middle East: BMW, Lincoln Town Car, Cadillac
Eastern Europe: Oldsmobile, Harley-Davidson, Mercedes, Jaguar
Australia/Pacific Rim: Porsche, Lexus, Mercedes
Central/South America: Ford Explorer, Nissan Pathfinder

Highest Vehicle Theft Rates

Nearly half of metropolitan statistical areas with the 25 worst theft rates are ports or cities with easy access to the US border.

1. Modesto, CA
2. Phoenix/Mesa, AZ
3. Stockton/Lodi, CA
4. Las Vegas, NV
5. Sacramento, CA
6. Fresno, CA
7. Oakland, CA
8. Miami, FL
9. San Diego, CA
10. Detroit, MI

Source: National Insurance Crime Bureau, 11/15/2004, based on FBI Uniform Crime Reports.

Car Jacking Facts

An FBI study found the following patterns to car jackings:
- Most car jackings occur between 8:00 p.m.-11:00 p.m.
- Friday, Saturday, and Sunday account for nearly half of all car jackings.
- More car jackings (27%) occur in December than in any other month.
- Fifteen metropolitan areas account for 90% of all car jackings.
- Parking lots are the favorite areas for car jackers, followed by city streets, residential driveways, car dealerships, and gas stations.
- Handguns were used in 90% of the cases involving weapons.

Vehicle Theft Fraud Schemes

Owner Give-Up: A vehicle owner orchestrates the destruction of his or her vehicle to collect on an insurance policy. The "stolen" vehicle is usually found completely burned in a secluded area, submerged in a lake, or buried underground.

30-Day Special: Often used by owners of a "lemon" vehicle. They report their vehicle stolen, then hide it for 30 days or just long enough for the insurance claim to be paid. Once paid, the vehicle is often found abandoned.

Export Fraud: A person buys or rents an expensive vehicle, insures it, sells it to an overseas conspirator, and then reports it stolen. The owner not only collects on the insurance policy, he or she may also collect two to three times the vehicle's American value from the overseas sale.

Phantom Vehicles: An individual uses phony title or registration to buy insurance on a nonexistent vehicle. The insured then reports the vehicle stolen before filing a fraudulent insurance claim. Often the fake vehicle will be an antique or luxury model, since the settlement would be greater with a more valuable vehicle.

Scapegoat Theft: Sometimes a person will claim to be the victim of a vehicle theft in order to avoid prosecution for another crime. For instance, someone who has hit a parked car or telephone pole may abandon the vehicle and report it stolen to avoid paying for the damages.

Crime Scene Response

I. Team Member Responsibilities

Team Leader

- Assume control - ensure that team members use appropriate protective equipment and follow standard procedures to protect themselves from health hazards on the scene.
- Gather information for assessment.
- Conduct initial walk through in order to make a preliminary survey. Evaluate potential evidence and prepare a narrative description.
- Assign team members and determine search patterns.
- Establish an off-site command post and facilitate communication between search and investigative personnel.
- Coordinate efforts with other law enforcement agencies.
- Ensure that personnel have access to necessary supplies and equipment.
- Control access to the scene and name someone to log everyone in at the scene. (See Stage 2: Secure & Protect the Crime Scene, page 288)
- Monitor efficiency of search continuously.
- Release scene after final survey and evidence inventory is complete.

Photographer and Photographic Log Recorder

- Photograph the entire area before anyone enters it.
- Photograph crowd, victims, vehicles.
- Photograph the entire scene with close-ups, medium range and long range shots, and use measurement scale as needed.
- Coordinate efforts with Sketch Preparer, Evidence Recorder, and Evidence Recovery team to ensure that all major evidence items are photographed before they are moved.
- Photograph all latent fingerprints and other impression evidence before lifting and casting are done.
- Prepare photographic log and sketch.

Sketch Preparer

- Make a diagram of the area surrounding the scene and orient the diagram with your sketch.
- Include major items of evidence on sketch.
- Designate and label areas to be searched and communicate the information to all other team members.
- Take measurements and double check them, getting appropriate help as needed.
- Make sure all necessary administrative information (i.e., "not drawn to scale") is noted on each sketch.

Evidence Recorder/Custodian

- Make sure all significant evidence is photographed before collection.
- Record on evidence container: Contents (good description) and specific location of recovery (where, what room, address, etc.), initials, date and time.
- Collect and package evidence in such a way as to maintain its integrity.
- Keep the evidence log.
- Be careful to use any needed protection and appropriate methods when working with evidence that could be hazardous, such as blood.

Specialists

Occasionally specialists from outside the agency must be called in when that type of expertise is not available within an agency. When bringing in an outside expert, consider

1. Competence and reliability
2. Ability to work at the scene within LE guidelines and
3. The specialist's role in presenting expert testimony in court.

Be especially aware of which organization has certified the expert; their standards for certification can range from very stringent to none at all. Such specialists might include anthropologists, blood pattern analysts, bomb technicians, criminalists, engineers, entomologists, medical examiners, odontologists, computer crime specialists, or surveyors.

Investigation

II. Search Procedures

Preparation

Before arrival at the scene:
- Discuss the search with the team.
- Select the team leader.
- Be prepared to encounter a dangerous scene or inclement weather. Make sure the team will have the clothing, communication equipment, lighting, shelter, transportation, food, medical assistance, and any other equipment they may need.
- Organize communications with any outside specialists, such as medical examiner, or prosecuting attorney, so that they can help resolve any questions that may arise during the search. Create a command post for major or complicated investigations.

Stage 1: Approach the scene
- Look for discarded evidence, possible approach or escape routes, and signs of forced entry.

Stage 2: Secure and Protect the Crime Scene
- Take control.
- Seal the area. Determine how well the scene has been protected thus far. Whenever possible, use crime scene tape to create an inner and outer perimeter. This will allow space outside the actual scene where criminalists and investigators can brief and plan, while still protected from the media and public. Protect evidence from destruction, tampering, contamination, or removal.
- Document who has been at the scene, and get information from them about its original condition. Begin chain of custody on evidence.
- Take extensive notes - do not rely on memory.
- Begin to record who enters and leaves the scene. Keep out unauthorized people.

Author's Note: Many crime scenes have become tainted and cases lost because unauthorized or unnecessary personnel wanted to "take a look." Regardless of your rank or tenure, if you are in charge of crime scene security, do not allow anyone, including command, onto a scene unless they are there in an official capacity. Log everyone who enters and leaves a crime scene, and if their participation is questionable, tell them you need additional information for use in the event of a subpoena to testify as to why they were there. - **"Bones"**

Stage 3: Plan the Search

- Check the floor with oblique lighting before stepping foot in the scene.
- Cautiously walk through and observe the scene.
- Select an appropriate narrative description technique, take preliminary photos, and establish the extent of the search area.
- Determine what method and procedures are to be used and note special problem areas.
- Assign appropriate personnel and equipment. Identify and protect or collect transient physical evidence.
- Develop a general theory of the crime.
- Document the scene: physical and environmental conditions, assignments, personnel movement, etc.
- Check all doors and windows and document if they are locked or unlocked.
- Note temperature, conditions, and what lights or appliances are on.
- If a corpse is present, examine it visually noting indicators of time of death, post-mortem movement of the body, and any wounds or trauma.
  NOTE: Some jurisdictions give the coroner or medical examiner authority over the body. The officer should do a cursory examination until death investigator declares death.
- When dealing with vehicles, take notes on the VIN, license number, position of key, odometer reading, fuel level, gear shift position, and if the lights were on or off.

Stage 4: Physical Evidence

- Decide what physical evidence is likely to be present.
- Begin with easily accessible and visible areas, and work toward inaccessible, out-of-sight locations looking for things that may have been intentionally hidden.
- Start with the most perishable evidence, and work toward the least perishable.
- Look for indications that items may have been moved accidentally.
- Think about whether the scene appears to have been "faked" or "staged."

Investigation

Stage 5: Narrative description

- Describe conditions at the crime scene in written, audio and/or video form.
- Be aware of what should be present that isn't and what shouldn't be present that is.
- Include conditions such as lights on/off, doors open/closed, heat on/off, drapes open/closed, etc.
- Under most circumstances evidence should <u>not</u> be collected at this point.

Stage 6: Photograph and/or Videotape Scene

- Create a photographic plan first. Take photos as soon as possible and keep a log of them.
- Photograph evidence in its original location before it is collected and packaged.
- Be sure to take overall, medium distance, and close up views of the scene and of each important item.
- To establish scale, take one photo as the scene actually appears and then a photo that includes a recognized scale device such as a ruler or ABFO scale. Coins, pens, etc. are not suitable devices.
- Photograph the area around the scene and all possible entrances and exits.
- Take photos related to statements given by victims, witnesses, and suspects.
- When possible, take photos from eye level to show the scene as it would normally appear to an observer.
- Photograph latent fingerprints at 1:1, or other appropriate scale, before they are lifted.
- Photograph everything; even apparently insignificant things could turn out to be invaluable.
- Shots of dead or injured victims should include close- ups of all visible injuries, hands and fingernails, and anything that might have been used to tie up the victim.
- Instant photographs could be taken for use by investigators. For example, photos of shoe prints could be given to investigators running search warrants; they could look for matching shoe soles.

Stage 7: Diagram/Sketch Scene

- Diagrams and sketches help establish a permanent record of items, conditions, and spatial relationships.

- A rough sketch drawn at the scene, usually not to scale, is later used as the basis for a finished sketch. The rough sketch should include case number, specific location, date and time, preparer's name, weather conditions, lighting conditions, scale or scale disclaimer, compass orientation, evidence, measurements, and a key or legend. Numbered evidence on the sketch can be coordinated with the number designations on the evidence log.

- A systematic method such as coordinates, triangulation, or cross-projection should be used to establish spatial relationships at the scene.

- Sketches should generally be made in the following order:

1. Basic perimeter
2. Large objects, major features
3. Position of evidence
4. Appropriate measurement (double check)
5. Create key/legend, add compass orientation, etc.

Stage 8: Detailed Search

- Remember four basic Ideas:

1. There is only one chance to perform the search properly.
2. The best search is usually the most difficult and time consuming.
3. You cannot "over document" the physical evidence.
4. Search twice, using two different styles:
   - First, cautiously search visible areas, being careful to preserve the evidence.
   - Second, vigorously search hidden or concealed areas.

- Base the search on earlier evaluation of evidence possibilities.

- When feasible, use a specific search pattern, such as a spiral, grid, strip/lane, etc. (see Search Patterns pg 332).

- Make sure everything has been photographed and entered in a photographic log prior to collection.

- Mark all evidence locations on the diagram or sketch.

- Create an evidence log with notations for each item.

- Each item of evidence should be placed in a container and should be initialed by the investigator who collected it. Handle evidence as little as possible and seal containers at the crime scene in such a way that contents cannot fall out; opening the container would obviously change or damage it.

- Label all containers with the information your agency requires.

- Be sure to use the right kind of container for each type of evidence.
- Check entrance and exit areas for potential evidence.
- Collect known standards, such as carpet fibers.
- Continually check all paperwork, recordings of information, and packaging notes for errors that could cause problems later.

Stage 9: Final Survey

- Critically review all aspects of the search. Discuss it with the whole team to be sure that you have been thorough enough, that every essential thing has been documented, and that you've made no assumptions that could pose problems in the future.
- Double check all documentation and make sure all evidence is accounted for before leaving the scene.
- Make sure all the hard-to-access areas and potential hiding spaces have been searched.
- Gather all equipment used in the search.
- Take a final walk-through video (or photos) of the scene to document the condition of the scene at the conclusion of the search.

Stage 10: Release Crime Scene

- Since a warrant may be required to reenter a released scene, have all outside specialists examine the area and complete the final survey before the release is issued.
- Consider having a criminalist and/or an investigator not involved in the scene search and take a "fresh look" at the scene before releasing it.
- Only the person in charge should have the authority to release the scene. Note the time and date of release, to whom the scene was released, and by whom.
- Make sure that any legally required inventory has been given to the person to whom the scene is released.

III. Evidence Collection

Policies vary from one agency to another. Know the policies of your agency, the requirements of your local lab, and check with your supervisor if you have any questions.

Blood Stains

- When dealing with this type of evidence, be very careful to avoid exposure to blood-borne pathogens (see exposure to Blood-Borne Illnesses, page 356).
- If DNA analysis is necessary, take all precautions to avoid contamination; even flakes of dead skin falling into a sample will contaminate it.
- DNA can be destroyed by heat. Do not store specimens at room temperature for more than 1-2 days. Store in a freezer if possible.
- Completely document blood stains before collection. If blood-stain pattern analysis will be done, scaled photos are necessary.
- When collecting blood samples, also collect a "control" near the stain where no blood is visible. This will eliminate anything that is foreign on the scene but not in the blood (cleaning supplies, dirt, etc).

Wet Blood Stains
- Wet blood stains can be quick dried with hair dryer on the cool setting.
- **Small items:** Place item in a paper bag to prevent cross-contamination. Air dry item and bag completely in a secure area. Repackage in paper bag. If using a new bag, send the original bag to the lab as well.
- **Large items:** Absorb stain onto a sterile pre-packaged cotton swab (commonly available to criminalists). *Do not touch the cotton with bare hands.* There are two swabs in the package, one for the stain and one for the control. Put the swab in a paper bag, take to a secure area, and air dry. Repackage in a paper bag to send to lab.

Dried Blood Stains
- **On fabric:** Wrap item in clean paper and place in a brown paper bag or box. Seal and label the container.
- **Small solid objects:** Items may be packaged, labeled, and sent to the lab whole.

- **Large solid objects:** Cover the stain on the large object with clean paper and seal the edges with tape. Send the entire item to the lab.

- **Large unmovable items:** If dried blood is on an object too big to send to the lab, use one of the following techniques:
  - Cut out the bloodstained area of the item and package in a paper envelope. If possible, cut out a negative control sample of the object.
  - Lift the blood stain with fingerprint tape (being careful not to touch the sticky surface with bare hands). Lay the fingerprint tape over the blood stain and surrounding area and rub the non-sticky side with a blunt object to ensure good contact. Lift the blood stain as you would a fingerprint, and place the tape on vinyl acetate backing. Repeat the process several times if needed. Package in separate paper envelopes and label.
  - Scrape the bloodstain into a paper packet using a clean sharp instrument. Blood stains can also be scraped directly onto the sticky side of a piece of fingerprint tape and then placed on vinyl acetate backing.
  - Most criminalists today use pre-packaged cotton swabs, which can be dampened with distilled water. *Do not touch the swab with bare hands.* Air dry any swabs used in a secure area. When dry, place in a paper packet and then in an envelope.

A sample of blood the size of a pin head will usually work as evidence if analysis is to be performed. If you can see it, it is enough to process.

Standard Specimens
- **Live blood samples:** When a sample is drawn for typing or DNA, have it drawn into appropriate stoppered vacutainers. If the victim needs a transfusion, try to get the hospital's pre-transfusion sample. Act quickly, because hospitals do not keep these very long. Bloodstained clothing worn by the person should also be air-dried and frozen for a secondary standard.

- **Buccal swab samples:** Some DNA labs now use buccal (cheek) swabs for standard testing instead of blood draws.
- **Autopsy blood samples:** Ask the pathologist to draw the samples directly from the heart into each vacutainer type so that any type of forensic testing can be done. If no liquid blood is available, typing can be done from a section of deep muscle tissue, liver, or bone. Ask the pathologist to collect and freeze these samples.
- **Types of vacutainers:** Know which type of vacutainer your local lab prefers.
  - **Yellow top:** Suitable for DNA and conventional serological testing.
  - **Purple top:** Suitable for DNA testing, but may interfere with some conventional serological testing.
  - **Red top:** Suitable for conventional serological tests, but not as good for DNA testing. Can be used for pregnancy and HIV tests.
  - **Gray top:** Suitable for toxicological tests; may be suitable for DNA tests; not suitable for conventional serological tests.
  - **Mottled Red top:** Common in emergency room settings; useable if your lab supports it.

Semen Stains

- Look for semen stains on clothes and bedding. Stains should be allowed to air dry, then wrapped in paper, and packaged in paper bags. Do not use plastic.
- Label all clothing and package each piece separately.
- Air dry all fabric completely prior to packaging.
- Handle material as little as possible.
- In sex offense cases, a doctor should always examine and collect evidence from the victim using a Sexual Assault Evidence Collection Kit. Kit instructions must be followed carefully to maximize their usefulness.

To locate semen stains on light clothing or other material, tape a 55mm 47B filter to the end of a 35,000 cp minimum flashlight, such as a Streamlight, and view through amber or orange shooting glasses. Stains will fluoresce.

Other Body Fluid Evidence

Collect ALL evidence that might contain body fluids (i.e., tears, sweat, saliva, etc.). Cigarette butts should be separated by brand and placed in an envelope without ashes.

Handling and Storage of Body Fluid Evidence

Stains & Controls
- Air dry, package in paper, and freeze.
  Note: Stains on plastic or metal should not be frozen, but kept at room temperature and sent to the lab quickly. Condensation from thawing could degrade the evidence.

Liquids (usually standards)
- Blood standards collected in vacutainers should be refrigerated, not frozen, at about 4°C and sent to the lab ASAP.

- Collect saliva on a sterile gauze pad or swabs, allow to air dry, and package in paper. Do not use plastic containers if conventional serology is to be performed; plastic is acceptable for DNA analysis.

Hair
- Human hair may reveal the race of the person from whom it came and the area of the body on which it grew. Microscopic comparison of samples can reveal similar characteristics. The amount of hair recovered and its characteristics will determine the value of the sample. In addition, mitochondrial DNA analysis can now be done on hair; although the results are limited to identifying a person's maternal lineage.

- Collect all hair present, picking it up with fingers or tweezers if possible. Package the hairs in paper wrappers or coin envelopes, fold and seal, and then place in larger evidence envelopes. Label the outer sealed envelope.

- Hair that is attached to something should remain in place. Do not try to remove it, unless there is risk of losing the hair during transport. If the object is small, mark it, wrap it, and seal it in an envelope. If the object is large, wrap the area containing the hair to prevent loss during transport to the lab.

Hair Evidence in Rape Cases
- Comb the victim's pubic region prior to collection of standards. Collect known samples from the victim, the suspect, or any other possible sources for comparison to unknown samples.

- To collect head hairs, have the person lean over a clean sheet of paper and rub their hands through their hair so that loose hairs fall out onto the paper. Pluck 15-20 more hairs from different parts of the head. Do not cut the hair.
- Collect hair from other parts of the body in the same manner. 15-20 pubic hairs are needed.
- Collect hairs from all parts of a suspect's body, even if only head hair is believed to be of interest.

Fibers and Threads

- Fibers and threads are typically found in torn materials, fabric abrasions, or caught on rough sharp surfaces such as damaged screens or broken windows.
- The type or the color of the fiber and sometimes even the type of garment from which it came can usually be determined. Fiber analysis may show similarity to fibers in a suspect's clothing.
- Threads and large fibers usually can be picked up with the fingers and folded in paper and then put in a coin envelope, sealed and marked. Fibers should not be put directly in a mailing envelope since they can fall out. If fiber evidence is scarce or may be easily lost, try to wrap the area or the object containing it in paper and send the whole thing to the lab. Use tape to pick up fibers only if the lab in your area allows it.
- Whenever fiber or thread evidence is recovered, all clothing of those from whom fibers may have come should be sent to the lab.
- Fiber comparisons may help to show contact between two people or between one person and an object (i.e., car seat) and can be useful when it is known that there was no opportunity for that contact other than the offense. Roll each garment into a separate clean sheet of paper and mark the item. If the items come in contact with each other or other objects, comparisons may be valueless.

Handling and Storage of Other Types of Evidence

Glass

- Wrap all objects contaminated with broken glass in paper and send them to the lab for examination.
- Collect all glass found at hit and run scenes. Since headlight glass may fall out at someplace other than the point of impact, do not limit the search to the immediate

area of the collision. Package glass found in different locations separately.

- Small glass fragments should be wrapped in paper, inserted in coin envelopes, pill boxes, or film cans, marked, and sealed.
- Pack large glass fragments in boxes, separate out individual pieces, and cushion them to protect from further damage in shipment. Be wary of trace evidence that may be on the glass. By examining the radial fracture edges, an expert may be able to tell the direction in which the glass was broken.

Standards for Glass Comparison:

- Window Glass: Send small windows in their entirety, or all of the remaining glass to the lab. Take several samples from different parts of a large window. If the evidence glass is big enough to be matched to the remaining glass, the whole broken window is needed.
- Auto glass/headlights: All of the glass left in the shell should be collected. If you think new glass has been installed, remove it and look carefully for small particles left in the shell from the old lens. Submit the new lens to the laboratory along with the remnants of the broken one.
- When investigating an auto accident, it may be necessary to show whether head or taillights were on when the light was broken. All remaining parts, the lamp socket, glass envelope, or sealed beam unit, should be wrapped in paper and saved for the lab. The filaments are quite small and may be hard to locate, but are very important. If recovered, wrap in paper or put in a small pill box sealed with tape.
- Other glass: Collect all glass remnants from broken bottles or other glass objects.

Paint

To effectively recover and preserve paint samples, be sure that each sample is kept in a separate container. Samples can be placed in a small paper bindle, sealed with tape, placed into a coin or mailing envelope, marked, and sealed.

Burglary Paint Samples:

- Look for traces of paint (or plastic, insulation, etc.) on any tools that may have been used to break in. If you find such traces on a tool, wrap the affected end of the tool in clean paper and seal with tape. Never set the tool into any marks or impressions; this would contaminate the evidence and eliminate its usefulness.

- Collect samples of paint from everything at the scene that the tool may have touched, being careful not to destroy the tool mark in the process. Cut around the mark if possible and be sure to include all layers of the paint.
- If the tool itself had paint or other coatings, some may have transferred onto other areas of the scene. Check carefully for these, especially in the tool marks.

Hit and Run Paint Samples:

- Paint may transfer from a vehicle to another vehicle, an object, or to a pedestrian's clothing.
- Whole chips of paint may contain several layers of paint and are potentially more useful in identifying the vehicle. Get samples from all areas of a suspected vehicle that show recent damage, since the paint may vary in type or composition even if the paint is the same color. Flake off the paint by bending the metal slightly, if possible. If not, use a clean metal knife to chip the paint off, being careful to get all layers, down to the metal. Wipe the knife off carefully between each sample and package each one in a separate container.
- When hit and run cases involve more than one vehicle, cross transfer of paint is common. Remove any loose paint chips and place them in a paper bindle. Smeared paint transfers should be flaked or scraped off of the car, including both the transferred layer and the original paint, all the way down to the metal. Keep transfers found on different areas of the car in separate containers. Wrap samples in paper and put them in envelopes. Collect samples of original paint from areas immediately adjacent to each transfer collected. This allows the lab to differentiate between the transferred paint and the vehicle's original paint.
- Check all areas, especially where a garment is torn or where it shows pressure glaze or other signs of contact. Do not try to remove any paint that is found. Instead, mark the garment, carefully roll it in paper, and send it to the lab. It may at least show the color of the part of the vehicle that contacted the victim. It would be rare for this type of evidence to reveal the make and model of the car involved.

Flammable Liquids

- Search the whole arson scene for flammable liquids, since some may have been placed in areas that did not burn. Check any containers at the scene for remaining traces, as well as anything made of porous materials such as mattresses, rugs, upholstery, wood, or drywall, even if the items are partially burned. Check the ground underneath the building for flammable liquids which may have leaked through the floor.

- Pour a small amount of any fluids found in open containers into a clean glass vial (no rubber-lined lids or plastic containers) with an airtight seal.

- Put small samples of soil, wood, or cloth in clean metal cans and seal them immediately to prevent evaporation.

- Samples that are too big to fit into cans should be put in heat-sealed KAPAK plastic. Be sure the lab has a sample of the plastic.

- Mark each package or container and the exhibit itself if possible.

- Submit samples of any flammable fluids normally found at the scene, as well as those found in the possession of a suspect, for comparison with fluids recovered in any partially burned material.

- Submit any materials, clothing, or rags containing suspicious stains or odors that the suspect may have. Package and mark as you would items found at the scene.

Firearms and Ammunition

Firearms:

- Be extremely careful when handling firearms found at a crime scene. Guns should always be unloaded or otherwise rendered harmless before being submitted to the lab. Note the condition of the gun before rendering it safe and write down the steps taken to make it safe.

- Document how many live bullets and/or casings are in the firearm. If possible, place them in styrofoam to show the position they were in the firearm.

- With revolvers, document where the empty casing is positioned in the cylinder and which way the cylinder rotates.

- Do not clean the bore, chamber, or cylinder before submitting a firearm. Never try to fire a gun before the lab examines it.

- Do not pick up a gun by sticking anything in the end of the barrel. It is dangerous and can damage evidence.
- Write down the caliber, make, model, and serial number of the weapon. Mark the gun in an inconspicuous place that won't compromise its value as evidence. Some guns have duplicate serial numbers so your mark is important.
- Pack weapons carefully in heavy cardboard or wooden boxes, making sure they won't move. Leave rifles and shotguns assembled. Label the container "Firearms."
- Label the container "safe" to inform the evidence vault and lab technicians that the firearm has been rendered safe.
- If the gun is to be checked for latent fingerprints, follow instructions on page 305. If there is blood or another substance on the gun, cover it with clean paper and seal it with tape to prevent loss of the sample.

Ammunition:
- Any time firearms are collected, try to recover unused ammunition for comparison as well. It may be found in the weapon, but ammunition kept in the suspect's house or car is likely to be identical to that used in the crime, and identical ammunition may be needed for test purposes. Mark the box the ammunition is in, only if the box doesn't need to be fingerprinted, but never mark the ammunition itself.

Bullets:
- Never attempt to clean bullets before submitting them to the lab.
- Mark bullets on the base.
- Wrap all recovered bullets in paper, seal them in separate pill boxes or envelopes, and submit them to the lab in labeled containers. Not all bullets can be conclusively matched to the gun from which they were fired, so it is important to send all that are found to the lab. Bullets recovered from a body should be air dried and wrapped in paper.

Cartridge Cases and Shotgun Shells:
- Cartridge cases should be wrapped in paper to prevent damage and keep them separate from each other. Place the samples in envelopes or pill boxes, label, and seal.
- Mark cartridges on the outside of the case near the bullet end.
- Mark cartridge cases on the inside by the open end.
- Mark fired shotgun shells either inside or outside of the paper or plastic area.

- Submit the weapon and all unfired ammunition that is found if it is necessary to determine whether a shell or cartridge was fired from a particular weapon. Be sure to submit <u>all</u> evidence cases or shells, since some contain more information than others.

Gunshot Residue:
- Due to extreme fragility, Gunshot Residue (GSR) should be collected as soon as possible: preferably within 3 hours after the crime. Use the GSR kits supplied by your lab and follow directions carefully. Useable results are hard to obtain if the subject is alive and more than six hours have passed, or if the subject has washed his hands. If possible, test a dead body before it is moved, or protect the hands with paper bags.

Powder and Shot Pattern:
- Gun powder residue or shot holes may appear on clothing or other materials which should be submitted to the lab.

- To prevent disturbance of the shot pattern, fold clothing as little as possible and wrap each piece in clean paper. Since microscopic examination and chemical tests will be needed, photos of the pattern are not enough.

- Ammunition identical to that used in the crime (make, type and age) is needed in order to use gunpowder or shot pattern as evidence. The weapon in question must be test fired using identical ammunition in order to establish the distance of the weapon's muzzle from the point of impact.

Serial Number Restoration:
- It may be possible to restore the serial number on a gun if there was not a lot of metal removed in the erasure process. If the original number can be restored, it is usually restamped on the gun. If it cannot be restored, a new number is assigned and stamped thereon by the Dept. of Justice or Numbering Station. Always advise the Dept. of Justice if a gun is to be renumbered after restoring a serial number.

- It is always a good practice to trace all firearms through ATF. They can often trace a firearm all the way back to the original owner.

Tools and Tool Marks
- Tools that come into contact with other things at a crime scene leave striations or impressions that lab comparisons can match back to the tool that made them, and which may be linked back to a suspect.

- Likewise, parts of a broken tool left at a crime scene can sometimes be matched to the rest of the tool in the possession of the suspect.
- It may also be possible to prove that marks on the tools were made by objects which they contacted at the crime scene.

Tool Preservation and Packaging:
- All parts of tools that contain transferred paint, building material, or other contamination should be wrapped in paper and packaged to prevent contact with other surfaces. Never try to fit tools into questioned marks or make any test marks with the tools before the lab examines them, as this will contaminate or destroy the evidence.

Tool Mark Preservation:
- If possible, send the entire item to the lab. Package it to prevent alteration or damage of the mark in shipping. Wrap small objects in clean paper and put into envelopes or boxes. Pack large objects in cartons or crates and protect tool-marked areas with paper.
- If the item cannot be transported to the lab, carefully photograph the mark, with and without a scale, and the space around it. This will help the lab determine how the mark was made and help them make new test marks.
- An expert may be able to make a cast of the tool mark at the scene without damaging it.

Medicines and Drugs
- All such evidence should be sent to the lab in a sealed package. Put each sample in a paper envelope, seal carefully to prevent spills or leakage, and mark it. Certain drugs, such as PCP, should be submitted in heat-sealed KAPAK bags. Substances found in prescription containers should be left inside them, sealed and marked.
- If substances are found in syringes, it is safest if the needles are removed and both parts are packaged in a hazard tube.
- Most controlled substances and common drugs can be identified in the lab by chemical tests, but some can be very hard to analyze unless there are either large quantities to test, or other clues as to what they contain. If prescriptions are involved, contact the pharmacist to confirm what should be in the bottle. This information will help the lab determine whether the contents of the bottle conform to the label or not.

Questioned Documents

- Questioned documents are analyzed for similarities and differences in handwriting, and may be able to match a document back to a suspect. It is important to have as many samples as possible for analysis. Consequently, it is important to submit ALL questioned documents in a given case to the lab, along with enough known samples for comparison.
- Documents may also be analyzed for the presence of fingerprints.
- Documents should be sent to the lab exactly as they are found. Never add notes, markings, alterations, or folds. If absolutely necessary, a personal mark for identification purposes may be made on the back or other area of the document that contains no handwriting or typing.
- Protect all documents by placing them in cellophane, paper, or plastic envelopes, and should be submitted to the lab personally. If it's not possible to deliver them personally, they must be sent by certified or registered mail. Enormous amounts of documents may be shipped by another method, but must be sealed.

Charred Documents

- Carefully avoid any further crumbling of a burned document. Place it on top of loose cotton in a box and deliver it to the lab in person. Further damage is inevitable if a burned document is mailed.

Known Handwriting Samples

- Receipts, promissory notes, credit and employment applications, letters, booking cards, and fingerprint card signatures contain a person's most typical handwriting.
- In many cases, it is important for the known samples to have the same date as the questioned document.
- Ask the suspect for handwriting samples at the first interview, since they may be uncooperative later.

Getting a handwriting sample

- If a new sample of the suspect's handwriting is needed, try to duplicate the materials used in the questioned document as closely as possible. Use the same color and type of paper and writing instrument. For example, ask him to use the same writing style (e.g., cursive handwriting, or printing in block letters). If the questioned document is a check, use blank checks or paper the same size.

Typewritten documents:
- Make several copies of the questioned document on the same type and color of paper using the suspected machine and type with light, medium, and heavy touches.
- Make at least one copy directly on carbon paper: place the carbon paper on top of a piece of paper, with the ribbon removed from the machine or the machine set to "stencil." This method clearly shows disfigurations in typeface, providing a clear-cut example of the machine's typeface.
- If possible, submit the machine, ribbons, and correction tape for analysis.

Other Types of Analysis:
- The lab may be able to perform other types of analysis on questioned documents such as:
    - Matching paper stock, commercially printed material, and checking protectors, rubber stamps, and inks.
    - Identifying raised or indented writing or typing.
    - Restoring or deciphering erased, altered or otherwise obliterated writing.
    - Physical matching of cut or torn paper.
    - Collecting fingerprints.

Latent Fingerprints
- Fingerprints are considered the best evidence for placing a suspect at the crime scene.
- All stationary objects at a crime scene should be tested with powder and 1:1 photographs taken of those which can't be lifted, both with and without identifying marks and scale. Lifted developed prints should be marked, or sealed in marked envelopes.
- Avoid obliterating fingerprints from evidence or adding to those already there. All such evidence should be marked in a distinctive manner.
- Most latent prints will be found on smooth-surfaced objects, such as glass, metal or paper. Touch such items as little as possible and only in areas that are unlikely to hold latent prints. Avoid unnecessary handling, even when using gloves or handkerchiefs, since it may smear or wipe off prints that may be present.
- Using cyanoacrylate ("SuperGlue") fumes and dye stains, prints can be developed and photographed on some textured, non-porous surfaces.
- Paper and documents containing latents should be placed in individual cellophane or manila envelopes, sandwiched

between two sheets of cardboard, wrapped, and placed in a box for mailing.

- Large items containing latents should be placed on heavy cardboard or wood and fastened down with string to prevent movement. If the item is to be examined frequently, use a pegboard and wooden pegs to hold it in place. Bottles and drinking glasses can be shipped by placing them vertically on a piece of wood in the bottom of a box, with the base secured to the wood by nails and the top inserted through a hole in a piece of cardboard fitted into the box.

Computers

- Computer systems are quickly becoming more complex and criminals more adept at using them. The computer you see may be on a network and evidence on a server in a different location. Criminals have many ways of sabotaging attempts to recover computer evidence. In more sophisticated computer-based operations there have even been hidden electromagnetic fields placed around the door, so that when law enforcement removes the computer all data is erased. The safest course is to call in a computer crime specialist to help prepare the affidavit for a search warrant, secure the equipment, and prepare the system for seizure.

Other Evidence

- Bite marks can be matched back to the person who made them using a variety of methods. If the bite has left an impression, a cast can be made from it. If the bite has discolored the skin, it can be photographed using several different techniques.
- Broken Fingernails can also be traced back to a suspect since they have unique striations on them. Collect fingernail fragments in a paper packet, put it in an evidence envelope, and submit it to crime lab for analysis. Get known samples from the suspect and the victim for comparison.
- Shoe prints can be positively matched to a pair of the suspect's shoes. 1:1 photographs should be taken, side lighted by a flash to make the pattern apparent, prior to attempting collection of a shoe print. Casts can also be made and sent to the crime lab after hardening. Other methods include lifting a shoe print from a hard flat surface as you would a fingerprint, or using an electrostatic dust print lifter on dusty shoe prints.

- Tire prints can also be positively matched to the tire which made them. Techniques used are similar to those for shoe prints, above.
- Broken items collected at a crime scene can often be positively matched to fragments found in the suspect's possession by fitting them together like pieces of a puzzle. Put larger fragments in a paper bag or envelope, and smaller pieces in a paper bindle and then an envelope.

Sources for Crime Scene Response:

Forensic Telcourse Committee, California Commission on Peace Officers Standards, "Crime Scene Response Guidelines," 1993, http://police2.ucr.edu/

U.S. Army Field Manual 19-20, Chapters 3 and 9, from http://www.atsc-army.org/cgi-bin/atdl.dll/fm/19-20/

Schiro, George, *Collection and Preservation of Evidence*, http://police2.ucr.edu/evidenc3.htm

National Fish and Wildlife Service, *Evidence Control*, http://toltecs.lab.r1.rws.gov/lab/qaqc/aqac12.htm

Kercheval, Jeffrey C., Mid-Atlantic Association of Forensic Scientists, *Crime Scene Procedures, http://www.gwu.edu/~fors/maafs/crm_scn.htm*

State of Utah Criminalistics Laboratory System, *Evidence Submission Standards, http://www.ps.ex.state.ut.us/cl/evidsu.htm#serdna*

Bennett, Wayne W. And Hess, Kären M., *Criminal Investigation*, fifth edition. Belmont, CA: West Publishing Company, 1998.

National Medicolegal Review Panel, US Dept. Of Justice, *National Guidelines for Death Investigation*, December, 1997

Investigation

Post-Mortem Evidence

Changes that occur over time in a dead body can provide important evidence about how, when, and where the person died. Air temperature at the scene affects nearly all post-mortem evidence, so it is important to document the temperature, and how and when it was measured.

Immediate signs of death

- No breathing or heartbeat.
- Within minutes of death the cornea of the eyes becomes cloudy and the whites look gray.
- Muscles become flaccid.
- Skin becomes pale.

Short-Term signs of death

Algor mortis

Algor mortis is the cooling of the body; under normal circumstances, it cools at about 1.5°F per hour. Many factors can affect the rate of cooling however, such as very high or low air temperatures, the amount of clothing the person was wearing, etc. In addition, if the person was ill, they may have had an internal temperature higher or lower than 98.6°F. In order to establish rate of cooling, the air temperature and the rectal temperature of the corpse should be taken at the crime scene twice; once upon arrival at the crime scene and again just before the body is moved to the coroner's office. Time of death derived just from this measure is very approximate.

Livor mortis

Liver moris is also known as post-mortem lividity or hypostasis. Blood pools in the blood vessels in the lowest areas of the body not supported by a surface. For example, a body lying on its back would show lividity in the small of the back and the neck but not points where it touches the ground.

- 2 hours after death:
  Discolored skin is bluish and blotchy
- 5-6 hours after death:
  Blotches have joined together.
  Skin blanches (turns white) when pressed.
- 10-12 hours after death:
  Skin no longer blanches when pressed.

- The rate at which livor mortis occurs is widely variable. Therefore, livor mortis is not a reliable indicator of time of death.

- However, it is a very useful indicator of whether a body has been moved after death. For instance, if a body is found lying on its back, but lividity is found in its feet rather than the small of the back and the neck, it would be a sign that the body had been moved.

Source for illustrations: U.S. Army Field Manual 19-20, Ch. 19

Rigor Mortis

Rigor mortis is the stiffness found in dead bodies. Immediately after death, the body goes flaccid. Stiffness is first apparent about 2-4 hours after death in the muscles of the eyelids and jaw, and seems to move gradually downward toward the large muscles of the lower body, with the whole body completely stiff in about 12-16 hours. It starts to wear off about 36-48 hours after death and follows the same progression; facial muscles loosening first and working down the body. The rate of rigor mortis progression and disappearance varies depending on air temperature (faster in heat, slower in cold). People killed in intense heat begin to stiffen almost immediately. Likewise, people killed while during vigorous activity stiffen almost immediately. Rigor mortis that is forcibly broken may not return, causing possible confusion in trying to determine time of death.

Longer Term Post-Mortem Changes

Insect Infestation

- Note presence of any insect evidence and collect samples for entomologist.
- Body lice will outlive their host by 3-6 days.
- Blowflies deposit eggs at or near the time of death; larvae hatch within 18-24 hours.
- Insect evidence will give highly variable times of death depending on species, location, season, and temperature.

Plant Life

- If plants were underneath a body, note the fact and collect samples.
- Plants underneath a body will wilt, turn yellow or brown and then die. The rate will vary depending on the type of plant, season, and climate.

Decomposition

- Note the degree of decomposition, including adipocere, putrefaction, mummification, or skeletonization.

Sources for Post-Mortem Evidence:

Giannelli, Paul C. And Imwinkelried, Edward J., *Scientific Evidence*, second edition, Chapter 19, Pathology, section 19-8, "Time of Death," available: http://fws.michie.com/bookstore/reading/nelli/gianch19.html,11/24/97

County of Sacramento, "Emergency Medical Services Policies, Procedures, and Protocols, Policy 2033.01; Determination of Death," revised 9/14/95, available: http://www.co.sacramento.ca.us/ems/2033-01.html, 11/21/97

McFeeley, Patricia J., M.D., Mid-Atlantic Association of Forensic Scientists, "Standards Employed to Determine Time of Death, " available http://www.gwu.edu/~fors/maafs/time_od.htm, 06/19/98.

National Medicolegal Review Panel, US Dept. Of Justice, *National Guidelines for Death Investigation*, December, 1997

Bennett, Wayne W. And Hess, Kären M., *Criminal Investigation*, fifth edition. Belmont, CA: West Publishing Company, 1998.

U.S. Army Field Manual 19-20, Chapter 19: Death

Investigative Photography

General Protocol for Photodocumenting a Crime

- Photograph the entire scene and everything in it that might be evidence before anything is touched or moved.
- Photographs should reproduce as accurately as possible the scene as it would appear to someone standing in the photographer's shoes. Any significant distortion in perspective reduces the photograph's value as evidence. (Photography is inherently distorted because it represents three-dimensional reality as a two-dimensional image; hence the importance of crime scene sketches, notes, and measurements.)
- Photograph the scene as it is found. If something has already been moved, do not try to reconstruct the original situation.
- No one should be working within the crime scene when photographs are taken, and all extraneous objects such as investigative equipment should be excluded.
- Take photographs in progression from general to specific. Take numerous photographs from many angles and at least three ranges:
  - **Long range:** Showing the whole scene or a large portion of it from that angle; full 360 degree coverage of the room or area with clearly identifiable overlapping points
  - **Mid-range:** (10-20 feet from subject) showing a portion of the scene in more detail
  - **Close range:** (5 feet or less) narrowing in on specific items or details that cannot be adequately shown from greater distance
  - **Macro photography:** From as little as a few inches away, may be necessary under some circumstances.
- Take photos both with and without a scale to show size.

General Photography Tips

- Establish a protocol or checklist for photodocumentation.
- Shoot test pictures (or a test roll of film) to make sure the digital chip and batteries are working properly in new camera systems.
- Create a close up to fill the frame as you take the picture rather than enlarging pictures during printing.
- If correct exposure is uncertain, bracket your exposures. That is, take three identical pictures at different f-stops: one above, one at, and one below the expected correct exposure.
- Take many pictures from different angles and distances; more is better than less.
- Review all photos on the computer and after they are developed.
- Label all the files accordingly, and the prints to match after they are developed.
- Keep photographs protected and techniques logged.

Digital Photography

Digital photography has quickly become the standard in most departments. Images can be stored on a computer or CD-ROM and then printed as needed. Each department should establish step-by-step procedures for image processing and equipment. The following information is compiled by the FBI and describes the basic guidelines and procedures for using digital photography for investigative purposes. For more info: see The Scientific Working Group on Imaging Technology (SWGIT) at www.theiai.org/swgit.

Equipment

When documenting crime scenes, it is strongly recommended to use a camera capable of manual override, has interchangeable lenses, off-camera flash, and a tripod mount. The whole idea of photography is to capture an accurate representation of the item or scene; therefore, different cameras may serve different purposes. Consider scene and item characteristics (size, movement, location), lighting, dynamic range of the scene, time constraints, and required end result when selecting a camera.

Equipment should be checked and cleaned regularly for proper performance. If a piece of equipment has fallen outside the specifications and recommendations of either your department or the manufacturer, then it should be taken out of service until updated or corrected.

Image Verification

Anyone who took the original picture or was present at the time the original was taken can verify that is it a true and accurate representation. A processing log should accompany any image that is processed and analyzed. The log should include all development steps (such as dodging, burning, color balancing, contrast adjustment, unsharp masking, multi-image averaging or integration, and Fourier analysis). In addition, any major processing technique should be noted in the case notes.

Preservation of Original Images

The original image, in its native file format, should be stored in an unaltered state. Duplicates or copies should be used as working images. It is recommended that digital files be stored on write-once Compact Disk Recordable (CDR) or Digital Versatile Disk Recordable (DVD-R). It's always a good practice to have additional backups as some of the media listed below has limited shelf-life, write-over capability, or could become corrupted. Original film may be processed if it is a non-destructive process; however, it is recommended to make a duplicate copy of any digital image before processing. In the case of analog video, it is recommended that a copy be made prior to process and analysis, as processing of the original might lead to a degradation of the signal.

Acceptable Photographic Storage Media

- Photographic prints (including instant photography). Note: prints usually do not contain the full resolution and dynamic range available from the original negatives.
- Diskettes
- Magnetic Tape
- Fixed Hard Drives
- Removable Magnetic Media
- Compact Flash Cards
- PC Cards
- Smart Media
- Removable Magneto-Optical Drives
- Write-Once Magneto-Optical Drives

NOT Acceptable Photographic Storage Media

- Inkjet Prints
- Solid Ink Prints
- Thermal Wax Paper Prints
- Dye-Sublimation Prints
- Dry-Silver Prints
- Laser Prints
- Electro-Static Prints

Documentation of Imaging Techniques

Changes to a digital image are acceptable in forensic applications so long as the original image is kept untouched, the steps and techniques used are logged, and the end result enhances the image.

It is normally not necessary to document imaging techniques such as cropping, dodging, burning, color balancing, and contrast adjustment. However, techniques such as unsharp masking, multi-image averaging or integration, and Fourier analysis should be well documented as these steps are usually done to make certain details more visible at the expense of others. Keeping a log of all changes is good practice, because the photo should be able to be reproduced to the same state to be considered as forensic evidence in a court of law.

Software

There are some legal ramifications associated with the software used for image processing. Before purchasing or using any software, be sure to consider the following: Has the software has been accepted by the scientific community? Does it perform as the manufacturer states? Has it been reviewed by the judicial system? Are the features of the software repeatable and reliable?

Image Enhancement

Many digital enhancement techniques have equal counterparts in standard darkrooms. These include brightness and contrast adjustment, color balancing, cropping, dodging, and burning. Many of the nontraditional techniques (those without equal counterparts in the darkroom) may not be acceptable within a forensic environment. These can include color processing, linear filtering, nonlinear contrast adjustments, pattern noise reduction, and random noise reduction. Be sure to check with your departmental guidelines and always keep a copy of the original image.

Image Compression

Original images should never be compressed in any way. It is preferable that working images not be subjected to lossy compression as critical information could be lost as a result of compression. If it is deemed necessary to use lossy compression, the highest quality option is recommended and repeated saving should be avoided due to the loss of image information.

Lossless compression reduces the file size be removing redundant information that can be replaced when the image is reconstructed. Lossless compression does not alter the content of the image. A GIF file is an example of a lossless compression.

Lossy compression reduces the file to a smaller size than a lossless compression, but in the process it removes redundant *and* irrelevant information. Unlike redundant information, the irrelevant information can not be replaced upon reconstruction, and therefore results in a loss of image content. This degradation occurs each time the image is saved, and can, over time, render an image less useful. A JPEG image is an example of lossy compression.

Image Restoration

Images are sometimes degraded by things like defocus or motion blur. Image restoration can often partially restore some of the lost detail by using techniques such as blur removal, color balancing, geometric restoration, grayscale linearization, and warping. Keep in mind that any time an image's noise is adjusted, there is a risk that information will be totally lost and irreplaceable. It's always a good idea to make a copy of the image before attempting to restore it and to keep a detailed log of the steps taken to restore the image.

Digital Photography Glossary

Apple QuickTime™ Movie Format (MOV file): Apple file format for storing and displaying compressed video.

AVI (Audio/Video Interlaced): Microsoft file format for storing and displaying compressed video.

Blur Removal: A process designed to partially or completely remove an image blur caused by defocus and motion blur. The degree to which a blur can be removed is limited by the noise in the image. Often partial deblurring can be successful even when total deblurring is impossible due to lack of information in the original image. This process is often used in restoration techniques.

Brightness Adjustment: The process of making an image brighter by bringing out detail from darkened areas.

Color Balancing: A process where the color components of an image are balanced to accurately reproduce the scene. It is also used when the image lacks contrast and there is a loss of detail in both light and dark areas.

Color Processing: A process were the color space transformations, pseudocoloring, and hues and saturations are adjusted. This can be used to modify the color characteristics of objects. This technique, however, can compromise the color fidelity of the image. Therefore, be sure to check with your departmental standards on if this technique would be acceptable in a forensic environment.

Compression Ratio: The size of a image file before compression, divided by the file size after compression.

Copy Image: A copy of the information contained in a digital image file.

Cropping: The process of removing a portion of the image that is irrelevant or outside of the area of interest.

Deinterlacing: Separating an interlaced frame into two separate fields.

Dodging and Burning: Localized application of making parts of an image brighter or darker during processing.

Fourier Analysis: A method of defining periodic waveforms in terms of trigonometric functions. It is used to enhance video.

Geometric Restoration: A process that removes geometric distortion from an image. It restores the proper spatial relationships among objects in the scene. This process is often used in restoration techniques.

GIF (Graphical Interchange Format): A lossless compression file format.

Grayscale Linearization: The process of adjusting the brightness relationships among objects in the scene. This process is often used in restoration techniques.

Image Analysis: The use of techniques to extract information from an image that was not readily apparent before analysis.

Image Averaging: The process of averaging two similar images together. (For example, sequential video frames might be averaged together to reduce the noise in stationary scenes.)

Image Compression: Reducing the size of a data file.

Image Enhancement: Any process that improves the visual appearance of the image.

Image Processing: Any activity that transforms the image from an input file into an output image.

Image Restoration: Any technique that is applied to an image to remove an undesired effect such as defocus or motion blur.

Image Synthesis: Any process that transforms an actual image (through computer graphic techniques) for illustrative purposes. (For example, age progression, facial reconstruction, accident/crime scene reconstruction.)

Interlaced Scan: Video image format. The video frame consists of two fields, the first being all the odd numbered horizontal lines and the second being all the even numbered lines. All standard TV video signals are in the interlaced format.

Interpolation: A process that increases an image's apparent resolution. Software mathematically averages adjacent pixel densities and places a pixel of that density between the two.

JPEG (Joint Photographic Experts Group): A lossy image compression process. It is recommended to try and avoid compressing photos in a lossy process, see Image Compression section above. For more information see the Image Compression explanation on page 315.

Linear Filtering: This process includes sharpening, deblurring, edge enhancement, and deconvolution. It is commonly used to increase the contrast of small detail within an image. If there is a low degree of linear filtering, the image will be an accurate representation of the scene. However, if a high degree of linear filtering is used, the overall scene may become blurry or have noise (such as grain, snow, or random color dots). The benefit is that although the overall scene may be misrepresented, it may still be useful for interpretation of small details. Be sure to check with your departmental standards on if this technique would be acceptable in a forensic environment.

LZW (Lempel-Ziv-Welch): A lossless compression process used by the TIFF and GIF file formats.

MPEG (Motion Pictures Experts Group): A standard compression algorithm used to compress video and audio files; similar to a JPEG.

Nonlinear Contrast: These processes include gamma correction, grayscale transformation, curves, and look-up tables. Severe adjustments can cause loss of detail, color reversal, and the introduction of artifacts. This technique can be useful to adjust the contrast in selected brightness ranges within the image, such as bringing out details in shaded areas without affecting the highlighted areas. Be sure to check with your departmental standards on if this technique would be acceptable in a forensic environment.

Original Image: An accurate and complete replica of the subject or primary image. Original images should never be altered or adjusted; instead copies should be made and worked on.

Pattern Noise Reduction Filters: A process that identifies repeating patterns in an image and allows the technician to remove them. This is commonly used to remove patterns on fabric, window screens, security patterns, and halftone dots. Overuse of this process might cause selective removal of relevant detail; therefore, be sure to check with your departmental standards on if this technique would be acceptable in a forensic environment.

Primary Image: Refers to the first instance in which an image is recorded or transferred onto any media that is separate from the camera. (For example, flash cards, computers, or a digital image download from the internet.) Primary images should never be worked on; instead a copy should be created to produce a working image.

Progressive Scan (Non-interlaced): Video in which each image frame contains information from all horizontal scan lines (even and odd).

Random Noise Reduction: A process used that applies filters (such as low pass, blurring, median, and despeckling) to images. It reduces the contrast of small detail and suppresses random noise. Overuse might cause loss of relevant detail; therefore, be sure to check with your departmental standards on if this technique would be acceptable in a forensic environment.

Reproducibility: The process to develop images that yields the same results on repeated trials.

Spotting: A technique used during processing to remove dust and scratches from the image. This technique is usually NOT considered acceptable in forensic images.

TIFF (Tagged Image File Format): A image file exchange format that is supported on both Macintosh and PCs. It can be either lossless or lossy.

Warping: A process that changes the spatial relationships among objects in an image. Warping can be used to remove perspective from an image. Used improperly it can distort the natural appearance of the objects in a scene. This process is often used in restoration techniques.

Working Image: Any image that is subject to processing.

Film

If digital photography is not available, film photography can be used. The standard film for use in investigative photography is 35mm color slide film, sometimes called color transparency or color reversal film.

Regardless of the camera equipment used, the following tips will help give consistent results in recording the injury's size, location, color, and pattern.

- Use fine-grain print film with a speed rating of 100 or 200 ISO. This type of daylight film allows for greater sharpness (depth of field) with a minimum of grain and blurriness. Always use a flash when shooting indoors with daylight film. Sixty-second self-developing film is not recommended.
- Keep film and camera equipment in a clean, empty, and dry thermal container or picnic cooler. Do not store film unprotected in a vehicle. Sunlight and extreme temperatures can adversely affect color accuracy, reduce the film's sensitivity to light, and in some cases result in tearing or splitting.
- Store film in the refrigerator or freezer to keep it fresh, but place at room temperature about 2-3 hours before using it (24 hours if film is frozen).
- Process exposed film as soon as possible, to avoid color imbalance or shift.

- To avoid loss of evidence, attach an end flap from the film carton to the back of the camera as a reminder of when the film was loaded, the type of film, and how many exposures the roll contains. Remove rewound film from the camera, and attach an identification sticker to it, or put the film in an evidence bag before sending it in for processing.
- Always have an extra camera and set of batteries.

Crime Scene Considerations

Investigation

Outdoor Crime Scenes
- Approach the crime scene carefully; observe established routes for approach and entry into scene.
- Evidence is vulnerable to destruction.
- Protect crucial evidence from the elements.
- Photograph the crowd at the scene; the perpetrator may be there.
- Include a landmark such as a street sign or address as a point of reference.
- Photograph any paths leading to and from the scene.
- Tire or shoe impressions can be photographed using side lighting to reveal the pattern.
    - The camera lens should be perpendicular to the surface, at a distance which permits the impression to fill the frame.
    - Place a scale on the same plane as the impression and parallel to it in order to indicate size.
    - Set flash at a 20-45 degree angle to the impression. Use a flashlight to find the angle which creates the best contrast.
    - Flash can be shined across the impression in one of three patterns:1) Right to left, left to right, front to back, and back to front; 2) diagonally; or 3) clock coordinates.

Indoor Crime Scenes
- Use available light, plus electronic flash if necessary. Be prepared to discuss lighting technique in court.
- Use a normal lens for most photographs. A wide-angle lens may be used for an overall view of the crime scene.
- Take photos of blood evidence every hour, recording the time and temperature for each set of photos.

- Photograph all fingerprint and foot wear evidence. Since fingerprints can be damaged in the collection process, photograph them before they are collected.
- The height and location of latent prints on porous surfaces must be documented.

Vehicles
- Photograph the vehicle from all angles including the underside. Use an extension pole to photograph the top of the vehicle.
- Be sure to photograph the license plate and registration decal from mid and close ranges.
- Use a macro lens or setting to photograph the VIN.
- Photograph any damaged areas from mid and close range, both with and without scale, to show fracture patterns or tool marks.
- Photograph any relevant items found inside the vehicle.

Photographing Injuries

- Get written permission before photographing injuries. If the injured person is a child, get written consent from parent or guardian.
- Complete an identification sheet and/or take a full-face picture of the person; include his or her name in order to establish the victim's identity.
- If photographs of private areas of a victim's body are required, have a third party present (preferably someone the victim trusts).
- Use a separate roll of film for each case to avoid losing or mixing up evidence.
- In each photo, include an identifying sign including victim's name or initials, birth date, date and time of photographs, case number, and photographer's name. Many 35 mm cameras contain data back attachments that allow the photographer to imprint the time, date and identifying code on each film frame.
- The investigator can also use a medical photography form as a tool for highlighting injury sites, description of injuries, time and date of photographs, the victim's identification or case number, the number of photographs taken, and the photographer's name. The form can then be included in the finished photo envelope as relevant to the chain of custody.

- Avoid taking photographs that might later be alleged to be inflammatory, i.e. unnecessary exposure of sex organs. Take one set of photos in color and one in black and white, as some courts consider color photographs to be more inflammatory.
- Take at least two full-length photographs of the body, at 90 degree angles to each other.
- Take at least one closeup photo of the victim's head and shoulders.
- Take as many closeups of wounds and injuries as needed.
- Decide in advance who will photograph the victim.
- Take two pictures of every view and angle, one for the case file and one for court.
- Compose the picture as the injured area would look normally.
- Photograph the injury with an anatomic landmark, such as an elbow, knee, or belly button to identify the location of the wound.
- Take two photos of each injury: one that includes a "landmark" and one in which the injury fills the frame.
- The film surface, or plane, should be parallel to the injury.
- Take a variety of shots from different angles and distances, since the flash may produce unpredictable reflections. Darker complexions can cause flash reflections and loss of definition. If unsure about the correct exposure, bracket your exposures as described above. This should ensure that at least one of the exposures is correct.
- Include a measuring device, such as an adhesive metric scale directly above or below the injury to accurately represent the injury's size and depth. A standardized color bar may also be placed in the photo for comparison with the color of the injury. This ensures that if color is distorted in the film developing process, adequate color comparisons can still be made.

Methods For Photographing Specific Injuries

Punctures, slashes, rope burns, or pressure injuries

Take photographs straight on or at a slight angle. The straight-on picture gives an overall view of the surface and extent of the injury; shooting from a slight angle shows depth and texture.

Bite Marks

Photograph the same as the wounds above, but be sure to document size, shape, color, depth of indentation, and three dimensional contours. Multiple views from various perspectives are important to document texture and shape. Parallel views best depict shape and size; slanted or indirect views and lighting are used to depict texture.

Bruises

- Since bruises change over time, it may be necessary to photograph them more than once. Some bruises will not be apparent shortly after the injury occurs, but will show up and become more pronounced as time goes on.
- If a second or third series of pictures is required, carefully reproduce the angles and positions used in the first series.
- If a child shows evidence of both old and new bruises, be sure to photograph them all, since this may indicate repeated abuse. Reflective ultraviolet photography can reveal old "healed" injuries.
- Areas of swelling sometimes create a strong reflection because the flash bounces off the rounded, swollen injury site. The reflection may obscure the photograph. To minimize such problems, take photos from several angles and do a follow-up series after the swelling has gone down.

Burns

Photograph burns from ALL angles both before and after treatment. Accidental burns usually have an indistinct or splashed pattern to them, while deliberate burns show distinct lines or well-defined areas of damage.

Facial injuries

If an injury is inside the mouth, keep the mouth open and the wound visible with a plastic or wooden tongue depressor. In the case of an eye injury, use a pocket flashlight (or a toy for a child) so they will look in a different direction and the full extent of the injury can be photographed.

Amputation

Photograph the dismembered body part alone and then in relation to the body as a whole. Take close-ups of the skin's torn edges to help verify the method of amputation in court.

Neglect

Photograph the child's general appearance, including splinters on the soles of the feet, hair loss, extreme diaper rash, wasted buttocks, prominent ribs, or a swollen belly.

Sexually Abused Children

- Make sure the child has a trusted relative or guardian present while you photograph any injuries.
- Let the child know what will be involved in taking the pictures. Tell him or her what body parts will have to be photographed. Do not surprise the child.
- Speak to the child in a manner appropriate to his or her level of development.
- Avoid making quick moves toward the child, as these may be frightening.
- Make eye contact with the child to make him or her more comfortable.
- Keep some toys or coloring books to use as rewards for the child's cooperation.
- Allow the child time to get used to the photographer before taking any pictures.
- Let the child undress himself or herself, or have the relative or guardian help.
- Photograph sexual organs, including overall and close up views of the injury. This may require that the labia be spread apart for closer photography, or that the child kneel down on all four limbs to allow the anus to be photographed.
- Photographing a sexual abuse injury is best done by a medical specialist in the field of child abuse, with appropriate equipment, such as a colposcope.

Crime-Specific Photographs

Accident Scenes

- To prevent distortion of road widths, distances between points, etc., set lenses for normal focal length, except when photographing vehicles.
- Photograph the overall scene from both approaches to the point of impact.
- Show the exact positions of each vehicle, injured and dead victims, any objects directly connected to the accident, and all damaged property.
- Photograph skid marks before and after the vehicle is moved.
- Photograph all points and marks of impact.
- Photograph pavement obstructions and road defects.
- Get close up photos of all damage on every vehicle.
- Photograph any tire tracks, glass, and debris.

Arson

- Photograph the point of origin.
- Photograph incendiary devices.
- If possible, photograph the fire in progress. Use color film to show the color of the smoke, flames, and vapors.
- Photograph everyone at the fire scene.
- Be sure to get exterior shots showing all entrances and exits.
- Show the extent and nature of burn damage.
- Show direction and speed of the fire's spread.
- Get close up shots of rags, papers, gas cans, and other flammable or combustible substances.
- If explosives were used and residue may be present, do not use a flash.

Assaults

- If possible, photograph injuries in color.
- Photograph all weapons.
- Photograph possible signs of the struggle and its intensity.

Burglary, housebreaking, or larceny

- Photograph the exterior of scene, especially points of entry and exit.
- Photograph all damaged areas and objects.

- Get close up and mid-range photos of tool marks. Show enough of the mark and the surface it's on to identify them; photograph with and without scale.
- Take close ups of fingerprints before they are dusted.

Death scenes: homicides and suicides

- Follow procedures in the General Protocol (page 311).
- Get full-length shots of the body, including clothing, all evidence near the body that show the person's height, and the position of the body including all extremities.
- Take close ups of the location of any injuries and post-mortem lividity.
- After the body is moved, photograph the area under it.
- If possible, photograph bloodstains, including their locations, in black and white, and color

Photodocumentation as Court Evidence

- Submit evidence with a form documenting the victim's name, case number, and date and time the photos were taken.
- A remarks section should also be included with the case notes. Outline drawings of the victim's body are helpful to show the specific areas that were photographed.
- Photographs must be properly verified and relevant to the case so that:
  - The photographer or investigator can testify that the pictures accurately portray the findings.
  - The photographer can explain how the photographs were taken.
  - A health professional, not the photographer, who examined the child can verify in court that the photographs accurately represent the findings.

Sources:
Office of Juvenile Justice and Delinquency Programs, U.S. Dept. Of Justice, "Photodocumentation in Child Abuse," 1997.

National Medicolegal Review Panel, US Dept. Of Justice, *National Guidelines for Death Investigation*, December, 1997

Bennett, Wayne W. And Hess, Kären M., *Criminal Investigation*, fifth edition. Belmont, CA: West Publishing Company, 1998.

Sampson, William C., "Crime Scene Photography Techniques," available at: http://www.polaroid.com/at-work/law-enforcement/docs/ infosheet.html, May 18, 1998

Investigative Tools and Equipment List

1. Watch
2. Foul-weather gear (raincoat, umbrella, etc.)
3. Boots for wet conditions, construction sites, etc.
4. Gloves (disposable)
5. Disposable (paper) jumpsuits, hair covers, face shield, etc.
6. Shoe covers
7. Purification mask (disposable)
8. Reflective vest
9. Personal comfort supplies (insect spray, sun screen, etc.)
10. Communications Equipment (cell phone, pager, radio)
11. Important telephone numbers
12. Flashlight
13. Camera - Digital, with extra memory cards & batteries.
14. Camera - 35 mm, with extra batteries, film, etc.
15. Camera - Polaroid, with extra film.
16. Camera - Video, with extra battery
17. Measurement instruments (tape measure, ruler, rolling measuring tape, etc.)
18. Photo placards (signage to ID case in a photo)
19. Tape recorder
20. Writing Implements (pens, pencils, markers)
21. Evidence tape
22. Trace evidence kit (tape, etc.)
23. Latent print kit
24. Gunshot residue analysis kits (SEMS/EDS)
25. Paper bags (for hands, feet, etc.)
26. Paper envelopes
27. Specimen containers for evidence items and toxicology specimens
28. Blood collection tubes (syringes and needles)
29. Presumptive blood test kit

Investigation

30. Clean white linen sheet, stored in plastic bag
31. Body bags (If coroner/medical examiner doesn't provide)
32. Body bag locks (If coroner/medical examiner doesn't provide)
33. Body ID tags (If coroner/medical examiner doesn't provide)
34. Evidence Seal (use with body bags/locks)
35. Disinfectant (Universal Precautions)
36. Waterless hand wash
37. Medical equipment kit (scissors, forceps, tweezers, exposure suit, scalpel handle, blades disposable syringe, large gauge needles, cotton-tipped swabs, etc.)
38. First Aid kit
39. Official identification for yourself
40. Business cards/office cards with phone numbers
41. Departmental scene forms
42. Investigative notebook (for scene notes, etc.)
43. Inventory lists (clothes, drugs, etc.)
44. Crime scene tape
45. Barrier sheeting (to shield body/area from public view)
46. Portable electric area lighting
47. Plastic trash bags
48. Thermometer
49. Hand lens (magnifying glass)
50. Tape or rubber bands
51. Pocket knife
52. Basic hand tools (bolt cutter, screwdrivers, hammer, shovel, trowel, paintbrushes, etc.)
53. Local maps

Source: U.S. Department of Justice, *National Guidelines for Death Investigation*

Interviewing Victims and Witnesses of Crime

Cognitive Interviewing

Both general and specific memory jogging and memory guidance techniques are combined to form the cognitive interview.

This technique is based on two generally accepted principles of memory.

- First, that a memory is composed of a collection of several elements, and the more elements a memory retrieval aid has in common with the memory of the event, the more effective the aid will be.

- Second, a memory has several access routes, so information that is not accessible with one retrieval cue may be accessible with a different cue.

In standard police interviews, victims and witnesses are asked to give a narrative report of what happened in their own words. The investigator then follows up with questions intended to make the report more complete.

The cognitive interview consists of four general methods for jogging memory, plus several specific techniques. The techniques outlined below are explained to the witness before the narrative report. The first two methods attempt to increase the overlap of elements between the stored memory and retrieval cues. The last two methods encourage using multiple retrieval paths.

Primary Techniques

Reconstruct the circumstances

Instruct the witness to reconstruct the incident in general,

"Try to reconstruct in your mind the circumstances that surrounded the incident. Think about what the surrounding environment looked like at the scene, such as rooms, location of furniture, vehicles, the weather, lighting, and any nearby people or objects. Also think about how you were feeling at the time and think about your reactions to the incident."

Mentally reconstructing the circumstances that surrounded a to-be-remembered event has been shown to be a powerful memory aid in numerous laboratory experiments. This technique is certainly easier than physically returning to the scene of a crime, and it may be preferable given that the scene of a crime can change.

Report everything

The investigator explains that some people hold back information because they are not quite sure that the information is important. The witness should be asked not to edit anything, even if things seem unimportant.

Asking the witness to be complete has two positive effects. First, many people do not have a good idea of what information has investigative value. Second, the effort to be complete sometimes leads one to remember an important detail through association with something seemingly unimportant.

Recall the event in a different order

Instruct the witness to recall the event from the end to the beginning,

> "It is natural to go through the incident from beginning to end. However, you also should try to go through the events in reverse order. Or, try starting with the thing that impressed you the most in the incident and then go from there, going both forward and backward in time."

While the events should be recalled initially in the order in which they occurred, recalling the events in reverse order forces the victim or witness to examine the actual memory record looking for benchmarks. When events are recalled in chronological order, some people reconstruct in their minds what must have happened based on prior knowledge of similar crime scenarios. This sometimes leads to incomplete or even inaccurate reports.

Change perspectives

In this method witnesses try to recall the incident from different perspectives that they may have had at the time, or adopt the perspectives of others who were present during the incident. Witnesses may be instructed to place themselves in the role of a prominent character in the incident and think about what he or she must have seen.

Mentally changing perspectives while recalling an event also seems to improve the completeness of reports. In many cases, the witness had a variety of perspectives on the incident, but people tend to report what they remember from one, static perspective.

Additional Techniques

The cognitive interview also uses a series of specific techniques to help an investigator elicit specific items of information following the narrative interview. The investigator might ask witnesses the following:

Physical appearance

"Did the suspect remind you of anyone? If you were reminded of someone, try to think of why. Was there anything unusual about the suspect's physical appearance or clothing?"

Names

"If you think that a name was spoken but you cannot remember what it was, try to think of the first letter of the name by going through the alphabet. Then try to think of the number of syllables."

Numbers

"Was a number involved? Was it high or low? How many digits were in the number? Were there any letters in the sequence?"

Speech characteristics

"Did the voice remind you of someone else's voice? If you were reminded of someone, try to think of why. Was there anything unusual about the voice?"

Conversation

"Think about your reactions to what was said and the reactions of others. Were there any unusual words or phrases used?"

Investigators have been using some of these techniques for years. However, in the mid-1980's, three separate studies carried out by R. Edward Geiselman , Ph.D. And Ronald P. Fisher, Ph.D., found that, when all the techniques are used together, the cognitive interview is effective for enhancing eyewitness memory.

Source: Geiselman, R. Edward and Fisher, Ronald P.,"Interviewing Victims and Witnesses of Crime," US Dept. of Justice *Research in Brief*, December 1985

Search Patterns

- Search for evidence using a specific method or pattern, since a random approach is likely to miss some evidence.
- Searchers should be alert, imaginative, thorough, and bring all of their experience to bear on the search at hand.
- Assume that the evidence collected in the search will be all the evidence there is and will be presented in court. Keep thorough records of everything that is found.
- Seek evidence that can be used to prove
  - that a crime was committed.
  - how the crime it was accomplished.
  - who did it.

Descriptions of Search Patterns

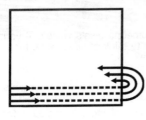

Lane Pattern: Beginning at one end of a rectangular area, searchers walk parallel to each other at the same pace along one edge. Upon reaching the end, searchers turn 180° and walk in the opposite direction, covering new ground.

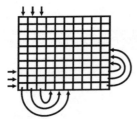

Grid Pattern: The lane pattern described above is repeated a second time, at a 90° angle to the first search so that the whole area is searched twice from different directions.

Investigation

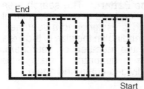

Strip Pattern: The strip pattern is a variant of the Lane Pattern described above. It is used when only one person is available to search an area. The searcher walks from one end of a lane to the other, turns, and walks down the next lane in the opposite direction, repeating until the entire area has been searched.

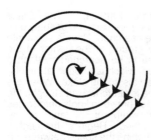

Spiral Pattern: In areas that are more circular, searchers may walk abreast, beginning on the outside of the spiral and walking toward the center along a spiral pattern.

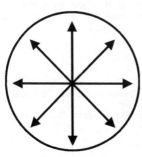

Wheel Pattern: Searchers begin at the center of a circle and walk outward in a spoke pattern toward the perimeter. Repeat the process several times, depending on the size of the search area. A weakness of this pattern is that each area of responsibility for each searcher becomes much wider toward the outside of the circle.

Investigation

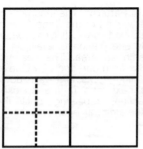

Zone Pattern: The search area is divided into quadrants, each of which is assigned to a searcher. Depending on the size of the area and the number of searchers, each quadrant may be subdivided again and again.

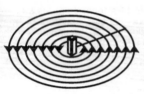

Circle Pattern: The Circle Pattern can also be used by only one searcher. Drive a stake into the ground in the center of the area to be searched. Attach a rope, which is knotted at regular intervals, to the stake. When the rope is stretched out straight, the space between knots determines the width of a lane to be searched. Begin at the center, searching the space between the stake and the first knot by walking in a circle around the stake. As each circle has been completed, move out to the next knot, until the whole area has been covered.

Sources:
Bennett, Wayne W. And Hess, Kären M., *Criminal Investigation*, fifth edition. Belmont, CA: West Publishing Company, 1998.
O'Hara, Charles E., *Fundamentals of Criminal Investigation*, 3rd Edition. Springfield, IL: Bannerstone House, 1973

Investigation

NATURAL DISASTERS AND WEATHER

Emergency Planning & Preparedness · · · · · · · · · · · 336
Emergency Supplies · 338
Emergency Supply Kit Sample Contents· · · · · · · · · 343
Emergency Checklist· 346
Earthquake Intensity Scales · · · · · · · · · · · · · · · · · 348
Heat and Humidity Index · 349
Ice Thickness - Safety · 350
Cold Water Survival Times · · · · · · · · · · · · · · · · · · 350
Wind Chill Temperature Chart · · · · · · · · · · · · · · · 351
Beaufort Wind Speed Scale · · · · · · · · · · · · · · · · · 352
Hurricane Intensity Scale · · · · · · · · · · · · · · · · · · · 353
Fujita-Pearson Tornado Intensity Scale· · · · · · · · · 354

Natural Disasters

Emergency Planning & Preparedness

The following are things each person should know or prepare for in case of an emergency. Being prepared ahead of time will ease the stress and possible hysteria in an emergency.

❑ **Have A Plan!** The most important thing you can do is have a family emergency plan. Assemble and have your supply kit on hand. Have a contact list of family and friends, both inside and outside your immediate area. Have a route set up for evacuation, and have a plan of where to meet if separated. Even if your family is together or evacuating together, make sure each person has a copy of this plan on their person. When developing your family plan, account for things such as:

  – What day it is (i.e. are the kids at school and the parents at work or is it a weekend) and what time of year is it (winter, summer, etc.).
  – Different emergency situations; an evacuation plan might be different for a hurricane versus a fire.
  – Pick two places to meet; one right outside your home in case of a sudden emergency like a fire, the other outside your neighborhood in case you cannot return home or to your neighborhood. Also consider an out of county/state contact if the emergency requires mass evacuation of a very large area.
  – Pick two out-of-town contacts: a primary and an alternate contact. List their full names, phone numbers, addresses, etc. on your plan.
  – Discuss and go over the plan (and all potential variants of it) with all family members.
  – Talk to neighbors and friends and encourage them to create their own plan and be aware of yours.

❑ Learn about and know your community's emergency plans, warning signals, evacuation routes, and locations of emergency shelters.

❑ Learn about options for pets and animals in and on your home and property. Remember most emergency shelters DO NOT accept pets. Have a plan for your animals! The American Red Cross and FEMA have various resources on how to find agencies and shelters in your area that accept animals in emergency situations. Also have contact information for local shelters in case your pet escapes and is rescued in the aftermath.

❑ Post emergency phone numbers at every phone.

❏ Know where the incoming water valve is in your home. You may need to shut it off to stop contaminated water from entering your home.

❏ Have a list on your freezer door of the contents and location of foods. This will minimize the time that the door remains open once the power is out and will extend the life of frozen food without electricity.

❏ Take a basic first aid class. Many injuries are not life threatening and do not require immediate medical attention. Knowing how to treat minor injuries can reduce infection and illness until your area returns to normal.

❏ If you have special medical needs (such as diabetes, etc) talk with your doctor about precautions you should take for emergency situations.

❏ Have a list of medications everyone in your family is on. Periodically rotate medicines to account for expiration dates. It might also be a good idea to have your eye prescription available in case you need to get new glasses or contacts in the aftermath of an emergency.

❏ Rotate contents in your first aid kit. Items such as moist toweletts might dry out over time.

❏ Rotate your food and water stash every six months. Date food boxes, cans, and water bottles, and put newest supplies in the back and older supplies toward the front.

❏ Assemble important family documents (or at least copies of them), such as insurance policies, wills, medical insurance policies and cards, bank records, stocks, birth certificates, identification, licenses, passports, etc, all in one location so that they can easily be assembled in an emergency.

❏ Elderly or disabled people should label all equipment like wheelchairs, canes, and walkers. At least one family member or friend should have a key to their apartment and know where emergency supplies and medications are. Have a plan ahead of time to coordinate how and where you should contact each other.

❏ Inform local authorities about any special needs (i.e. people who are disabled, deaf, elderly, or bedridden).

❏ Have supplies available for disaster aftermath. Protective gear such as hard hats, goggles, heavy work gloves, and watertight boots will aid in cleanup and might not be available (or might have run out) from local stores.

Natural Disasters

Emergency Supplies

Emergency supply kits are invaluable during national emergencies and natural disasters. A kit should be prepared ahead of time and stored in your car, shelter, or at least be available to access quickly in case of an evacuation. The easiest way to start assembling your kit is to think of basic needs such as fresh water, food, clean air, warmth, and shelter. A kit should contain enough to support people for at least three days. Some situations, especially natural disasters that impact evacuation routes or block supply lines, may delay federal help, so if possible, have a kit that could support people in your household for up to two weeks.

Water

An adequate supply of water should be stowed for each person. Amounts for your kit will vary depending on the expected duration and type of emergency, but your kit should include enough water for *at least* three days. The American Red Cross and FEMA recommends storing at least a two-week supply. At the very least stow one gallon per person per day for drinking and sanitation. Children, nursing mothers, and people who are ill require more water per day. Also, if you are in a warm climate, more water per day will be necessary. Store it in clean, washed plastic, glass, fiberglass, or enamel-lined metal containers. If you are in an area that is prone to natural disasters, it might be a good idea to purchase food-grade plastic buckets or drums. Seal the containers tightly, label them with "water" and the date, and store in a cool, dark place. Rotate water every six months. If supplies run low, never ration water. Drink the amount you need and reduce activity and try to stay cool. If a disaster catches you off guard or water is running out, seek out possible hidden water in your home. Use the water in your hot-water tank, pipes, and ice cubes. As a last resort, you can use water in the reservoir tank of your toilet (not the bowl). To use the water in your pipes, let air into the plumbing by turning on a faucet in the house to the highest level. A small amount of water will trickle out, then obtain water from the lowest faucet in the house. To use water in your hot-water tank, be sure the electricity and gas is off, then open and drain at the bottom of the tank. Start the water flowing by turning off the water intake valve and turning on a hot-water faucet. DO NOT turn on the gas or electricity when the tank is empty.

Water Purification

If you need to or are planning to use water for drinking, food preparation, or hygiene outside of the clean stash in your kit, be sure to purify it before drinking it. Contaminated water can contain microorganisms that cause diseases such as dysentery, typhoid, and hepatitis. You can use rainwater, streams, river, or other moving bodies of water, ponds and lakes, and natural springs. Avoid water with floating material, an odor, or a dark color. Use saltwater only if you distill it first. You should not drink flood water. The methods below will help purify your water by killing most microbes, but will not remove other contaminants such as heavy metals, salts, and most other chemicals. Before purifying, let any particles settle to the bottom or strain through layers of paper towel or clean cloth. Also be aware that chlorine tablets, iodine tablets, and liquid bleach will not kill parasitic organisms. If parasites are a concern in your area, consider buying a complete water purification system and pump, available from your local outdoors or camping store.

- **Boiling:** This is the safest method of purifying water. Bring water to a rolling boil for 3-5 minutes. Let cool before drinking. Boiled and stored water will taste better if you put oxygen back into it by pouring it back and forth between two clean containers.

- **Disinfection:** You can use household liquid bleach (that contains 5.25% sodium hypochlorite) to kill microorganisms. Do not use scented bleaches, colorsafe bleaches, or bleaches with added cleaners. Add 16 drops of bleach per gallon of water, stir, and let stand for 30 minutes. If water does not have a slight bleach odor, repeat the dosage and let stand for another 15 minutes. If using other chemicals, such as iodine or water treatment products, they must contain at least 5.25% sodium hypochlorite as the only active ingredient to be effective.

- **Distillation:** This involves boiling water and then collecting the vapor that condenses back to water. The condensed vapor will not include salt and other impurities. If you are going to drink sea water, you need to distill it before drinking it. To distill water, fill a pot halfway with water. Turn the pot's lid upside-down and tie a cup to the handle so that it will dangle right-side-up when the lid is upside-down (make sure the cup is not dangling into the water). Put the lid on the pot and boil for 20 minutes. The water that drips from the lid into the cup is distilled.

Natural Disasters

Food:

Pack non-perishable foods that do not have to be prepared or cooked (i.e. canned goods) and require little or no water in preparation. Remember to include a can opener and, if possible, some dishes and silverware to eat from. If activity is reduced, people can survive on half of their normal food intake for an extended period of time, and often without any food for days. Food, unlike water, can be rationed, except for children and pregnant women. Since water supply will be limited, try to avoid foods that are high in fat, protein, and salt as they will make people thirsty (i.e. if you're packing crackers, pack salt-free crackers). Pack whole grain cereals and canned foods with high liquid content. Try to pack high calorie and nutritious foods. Be sure to include food items for those with special diets and allergies, such as babies, toddlers, and elderly people. Nursing mothers may need liquid formula, in case they are unable to nurse and canned dietetic foods, juices, and soups may be helpful for ill or elderly people. Also be sure to pack nonperishable food for your pets.

For emergency cooking, you can use your fireplace or a grill or camp stove outdoors. You can also heat food with candle warmers, chafing dishes, and fondue pots. Canned foods can e heated and eaten right out of the open can, but be sure to remove the label before placing over an open flame.

If the electricity goes off, you can still use the food in your refrigerator and freezer for a limited time:

- First, use the perishable food from your refrigerator. Your refrigerator will keep foods cool for about 4 hours if unopened. If you add block or dry ice to your refrigerator the food will last even longer.

- Second, use foods from the freezer. Try to reduce the amount of times that the door is opened. Post a list of freezer contents and locations so you know exactly where everything is. A well-insulated freezer will keep foods for at least three days (foods are safe to eat if they still have ice-crystals in their centers). If dry ice is available, 25 pounds of dry ice will keep a ten-cubic-foot freezer below freezing for 3-4 days (use care when handling dry ice, always use dry, heavy gloves).

- Discard any perishable food that has been at temperatures greater than 40°F for more than 2 hours, or if it has an unusual odor, color, or texture.

- Third, begin to eat non-perishable foods and staples that have been stashed.

Shelf-Life of Foods:
- **Use within 6-months:** Powdered milk (boxed); dried fruit; dry, crisp crackers; potatoes.
- **Use within 1 year:** Canned condensed meat and vegetable soups; canned fruits, fruit juices and vegetables; ready-to-eat cereals and uncooked instant cereals; peanut butter; jelly; hard candy and canned nuts; vitamin C.
- **Store indefinitely** (in proper containers and conditions): Wheat; vegetable oils; dried corn; baking powder; soybeans; instant coffee, tea, and cocoa; salt; noncarbonated soft drinks; white rice; bouillon products; dry pasta; powdered milk (in nitrogen-packed cans).

The easiest way to have a stockpile of food in your home is to increase the amount of basic foods that you normally keep on your shelves. Pack foods that your family likes and normally eats. This will increase morale and give a feeling of security. Also, this helps reduce waste of food in non-emergency times, in other words, it isn't just sitting in your shelter until a disaster comes. If you have time to purchase additional food for a disaster, consider the following foods:

- Ready-to-eat canned meats, fruits and vegetables.
- Protein or fruit bars
- Dry cereal or granola
- Peanut butter
- Dried fruit
- Nuts
- Crackers
- Canned juices
- Non-perishable pasteurized milk
- High energy foods
- Vitamins and protein supplements
- Food for infants
- Comfort/stress foods

Food Storage Tips:
- Keep food in a dry, cool, dark area.
- Keep food covered at all times.
- Open food boxes or cans carefully so that you can close them tightly after each use.

- Wrap cookies, crackers, bread, and other grains in plastic bags and seal in tight containers.
- Empty open packages of sugar, dried fruits and nuts into screw-tip jars or air-tight cans to protect them from insects and pests.
- Inspect all food for spoilage before consuming. Avoid eating canned goods that have become swollen, dented, or corroded.
- Use foods before they go bad and rotate them with fresh supplies. Date food items and place new items in the back of the storage area and move older ones to the front. In other words, consume in date order.
- Pack vitamins and protein supplements to assure adequate nutrition.

Clean Air

Potential terrorist attacks could send microscopic "junk" and fine debris into the air. Therefore in such an even, create a barrier between yourself and any contamination. Face masks or dense-weave cotton material, snugly covering your nose and mouth, will help reduce the risk. Make sure each one specifically fits each family member. If you have to improvise, use whatever is on hand to protect your nose, mouth, eyes, and cuts on your skin.

Certain circumstances may require you to stay put in your house, otherwise known as "shelter-in-place", for survival. Use heavyweight plastic garbage bags, plastic sheeting, and duct tape to seal windows, doors, and air vents. Consider precutting and labeling these materials and storing them in your supply kit or shelter. Sealing your space creates a better barrier between you and outside contaminates, but no seal is perfect and some leakage is likely. Consider a portable air purifier with a HEPA (High Efficiency Particulate Air Filtration) filter to remove contaminants from the room. These filters have small sieves that capture very tiny particles, including some biological agents.

Emergency Supply Kit Sample Contents

❑ Water (see page 338).
❑ Water purification tablets containing 5.25% sodium hypochlorite as the only active ingredient.
❑ Food (see page 340) and a can opener.
❑ First aid manual
❑ First aid kit including:
  – 2 pair of Latex gloves (sterile gloves for Latex allergy)
  – Sterile dressings to stop bleeding
  – Cleansing agent/soap and antibiotic towelettes
  – Antibiotic ointment to prevent infection
  – Burn ointment to prevent infection
  – Adhesive bandages in a variety of sizes
  – Wrapping bandages and first aid tape for injuries like sprains
  – Eye wash solution to flush the eyes or as a general decontaminant
  – Thermometer
  – Prescription medications (such as insulin, heart medicine, asthma inhalers, etc.)
  – Prescribed medical supplies (such as glucose and blood pressure monitoring equipment and supplies)
  – Scissors, tweezers, safety pins
  – Tube of petroleum jelly or other lubricant
  – Aspirin or nonaspirin pain reliever
  – Anti-diarrhea medication
  – Antacid (for upset stomach)
  – Laxative
  – Rubbing alcohol
  – Medicine dropper
  – Cotton swabs or cotton balls
  – Hand towels and a plastic tub that can be used for cleaning or for vomiting
❑ Any medications or medical supplies that anyone is taking or might need. Even if help comes within three days, getting refills on prescriptions could be delayed or time consuming, so be sure to stow as much as possible in your kit.
❑ Allergy medication such as an antihistamine and insect itch creams. Also consider insect repellant containing DEET for disaster aftermath. (Standing water is a breeding ground for insects!)

- ❏ If there are infants, be sure to bring formula, diapers, bottles, baby food, powdered milk, medications, moist towelletts, and diaper rash ointment.
- ❏ Elderly people should make sure they have extra water, hearing aid batteries, and other items specifically recommended by their doctor.
- ❏ Pet supplies such as food, water, cages, litter box, newspapers, paper towels, plastic trash bags, grooming items, cleaning supplies, medications, sturdy leashes, harnesses, blankets, bedding, id tags, pet toys, a current phot (if pet escapes), veterinary contact information etc.
- ❏ Hygiene supplies (soap, shampoo, comb, sun screen, feminine supplies, baby wipes, etc)
- ❏ Denture needs
- ❏ Mouthwash (toothpaste may require extra water for rinsing)
- ❏ Household liquid bleach (for sanitation use 9 parts water to one part bleach; to make water safe for drinking, use 16 drops per 1 gallon of water - see water section page 338).
- ❏ Disinfectant
- ❏ Tools and supplies such as a flashlight, batter-operated radio, wrench or pliers (to turn off household gas and water), and a shovel. It is not advisable to include candles or anything that lights with a flame.
- ❏ Extra batteries.
- ❏ Cellular phone, CB radio, prepaid phone card.
- ❏ A whistle to signal for help.
- ❏ Money and matches in a waterproof container.
- ❏ Family documents.
- ❏ Paper, pencils, pens.
- ❏ Personal items such as contact lenses and supplies and glasses.
- ❏ Fire extinguisher
- ❏ Bedding, if you live in a cold climate, pack extra as heat may be out.
- ❏ Clothing, at least one complete change of warm clothing and shoes per person (coat, long pants, long sleeve shirt, sturdy shoes, hat, gloves, change of underwear, blanket). If there is room and time, pack additional items such as t-shirts, shorts, and extra underwear.

- ❑ Rain/snow gear (or other weather-related gear)
- ❑ Needle and thread.
- ❑ Moist toweletts for sanitation.
- ❑ Garbage bags and ties for sanitation.
- ❑ Paper towels
- ❑ Tent, compass, tarps.
- ❑ Matches (in a waterproof container) and candles. Although it is not recommended to have an open flame in your shelter, it might be a last resort if you are stranded for an extended time.
- ❑ Signal flares
- ❑ HEPA filtered masks or fans. If not available, a dusk mask or cotton t-shirt will help filter the air.
- ❑ Plastic sheeting, garbage bags, and duct tape to seal off a room or shelter in case of a terrorist attack, in other words if you are ordered to shelter-in-place (see Clean Air on page 342).
- ❑ List of emergency doctors and family and friends contacts.
- ❑ Maps and evacuation route information.
- ❑ An extra set of keys and extra ids.
- ❑ If there is time, pack some toys or activity books for children, and possibly books or magazines for adults.

Natural Disasters

Emergency Checklist

When an emergency strikes, use the following checklist:
- ❏ Tune to the radio and television for emergency updates.
- ❏ Listen for disaster sirens and warning signals.
- ❏ Assemble your family, friends, and pets.
- ❏ Call your emergency contacts and inform them of your situation and status.
- ❏ Secure any items on your property or in your home that may cause damage in a storm (i.e. bicycles, grills, propane tanks, etc).
- ❏ If you are going to a shelter, remember that they normally do not take pets, make arrangements for your animals at local animal shelters or ask local law enforcement agencies for options.
- ❏ Cover windows and doors with plywood or boards or place large strips of masking tape or adhesive tape on the windows to reduce the risk of breakage and flying glass.
- ❏ Place vehicles under cover, if possible.
- ❏ Lock all windows and doors, even if you are staying home, locking doors may create a tighter seal.
- ❏ Fill sinks and bathtubs with water.
- ❏ Adjust refrigerators and freezers to the coolest possible temperature.
- ❏ Adjust thermostats to the coolest (if in a warm climate) or hottest (if in a cold climate) setting possible.
- ❏ Turn off the incoming water valve to your home.
- ❏ Turn off gas and electricity in your home.
- ❏ Turn off heating, ventilation, and air conditioning systems. Turn off all fans, including the bathroom fan.
- ❏ Close the fireplace or woodstove damper.
- ❏ Fill your car with gas.
- ❏ Water: Stow at least one gallon per person per day, try to get *at least* three days worth, and more if possible. (see water information on page 338)
- ❏ Water purification tablets
- ❏ Food: Stow enough for at least three days of normal eating. Food, unlike water, can be rationed and stretched out longer. Be sure to pack non-perishable food that

requires little or no water for preparation. (See food information on page 340)

❏ Food for pets

❏ Assemble or find your Supply/Survival kit (see page 343)

❏ If you are ordered to evacuate: Take only essential items with you, turn off gas, electricity, and water, disconnect appliances, assemble your emergency kit, follow designated evacuation routes, and expect heavy traffic.

❏ If you are ordered NOT to evacuate: Monitor radio and television for updates, stay indoors until authorities declare the storm is over, do not go outside even if it seems calm (the eye of the storm can pass quickly leaving you exposed when strong winds resume), stay away from windows and exterior doors, seek shelter in a bathroom or basement, a bathtub can provide shelter if you cover yourself with plywood or other materials. If you have a pet, set aside an area that they can relieve themselves as it is not advisable to go outside for any reason. Prepare to evacuate to a shelter if your home is damaged.

❏ If you are in your vehicle: Follow the above instructions (for sheltering-in-place). If you are unable to get indoors quickly and safety, pull to the side of the road and stop your vehicle. Stop under a bridge or shady spot to protect from sun and weather. Close all windows and vents, if possible seat the heating and ventilation. Listen to the radio periodically for advice. Stay where you are until you are told it is safe to get back on the road.

❏ Only if everyone is safe, all supplies are assembled, and there is time should you consider packing things such as photos, mementoes, extra supplies, etc.

Emergency Sources:
Preparing Makes Sense. Get Ready Now, Department of Homeland Security,
READY America, Department of Homeland Security, http://www.ready.gov/
Food and Water in an Emergency, FEMA and The American Red Cross, FEMA-L210, ARC-5055, November 1994
Department of Health and Human Services, Centers for Disease Control and Prevention, http://www.cdc.gov
The American Red Cross, http://www.redcross.org

Natural Disasters

Earthquake Intensity Scales

Mercalli Intensity	Richter Magnitude	Description
I	2	Only detected by instruments
II	2	Detected by instruments, may be felt on top floors of buildings
III	3	Noticeable indoors, like a vibration from a passing vehicle
IV	4	Felt indoors by many, outdoors by a few; dishes & doors disturbed
V	4	Felt by most people, slight damage to dishes, windows, plaster, etc.
VI	5	Felt by all, many frightened, minor to moderate damage
VII	5-6	Much damage to poorly designed buildings; minor damage to well-designed buildings; many people will run outside
VIII	6	Everyone runs outdoors, moderate to major damage; chimneys, columns & walls collapse
IX	7	Major damage to all structures; pipes break, ground cracks
X	7-8	Most masonry & frame structures destroyed, ground badly cracked, landslides
XI	8	Nearly all masonry structures destroyed; large fissures open in ground; land slumps, rails bend greatly
XII	≥8	All construction destroyed. Ground surface waves seen, objects tossed into the air

Mercalli Intensity
Mercalli Intensity is measured by actual observation of resulting damage, not by instruments.

Richter Magnitude
Richter Magnitude is measured by instruments. Each number indicates a 10 fold increase over the previous number (so 8 is not twice as strong as 4; it is 10,000 times as strong). The 1960 earthquake in Chile registered 9.5 on the Richter scale, the strongest earthquake recorded to date.

Heat and Humidity Index

Rel. Hum. %	Air Temperature (°F)														
	70	75	80	85	90	95	100	105	110	115	120	125	130	135	140
0%	64	69	73	78	83	87	91	95	99	103	107	111	117	120	125
5%	64	69	74	79	84	88	93	97	102	107	111	116	122	128	
10%	65	70	75	80	85	90	95	100	105	111	116	123	131		
15%	65	71	76	81	86	91	97	102	108	115	123	131			
20%	66	72	77	82	87	93	99	105	112	120	130	141			
25%	66	72	77	83	88	94	101	109	117	127	139				
30%	67	73	78	84	90	96	104	113	123	135	148				
35%	67	73	79	85	91	98	107	118	130	143					
40%	68	74	79	86	93	101	110	123	137	151					
45%	68	74	80	87	95	104	115	129	143						
50%	69	75	81	88	96	107	120	135	150						
55%	69	75	81	89	98	110	126	142							
60%	70	76	82	90	100	114	132	149							
65%	70	76	83	91	102	119	138								
70%	70	77	85	93	106	124	144								
75%	71	77	86	95	109	130									
80%	71	78	86	97	113	136									
85%	71	78	87	99	117										
90%	71	79	88	102	122										
95%	71	79	89	105											
100%	72	80	91	108											

Category	Apparent Temp.	Dangers
Caution	80°-90°F	Exercise more fatiguing than usual
Extreme Caution	90°-105°F	Heat cramps, exhaustion possible
Danger	105°-130°F	Heat exhaustion likely
Extreme Danger	> 130°F	Heat stroke imminent

Source: National Oceanic and Atmospheric Administration
See page 127 for information on treating heat-related health problems.

Natural Disasters

Ice Thickness - Safety

Safe Loads For Clear Solid Ice

Thickness of Ice	Load or Activity
3 inches	Cross Country Skiers
4 inches	1 person ice fishing
5 inches	1 snowmobile
6 inches	1 ice boat
7 inches	Group activities
8 inches	1 car or truck
9 inches	Several vehicles

Ice thickness may vary within a small area

- New (black) ice is stronger than old (milky) ice
- Ice closer to shore is weaker than ice farther out
- Obstructions i.e., rocks, logs and plants, weaken ice
- Underground springs weaken ice
- Waterfowl and schools of fish prevent ice formation
- Water currents weaken ice
- Ice covered by snow and/or water weakens the ice.

Survival equipment recommended for each person:

- Ice awls
- Life Jacket
- 25 feet of rope
- Whistle

Because ice strength is influenced by so many factors, this information should be used only as a general guide. If you're not sure, stay off the ice.

Cold Water Survival Times

Water Temperature	Exhaustion	Death
80°F (27°C)	indefinite	indefinite
70°-80°F (21°-27°C)	3-12 hrs	3 hrs-indefinite
60°-70°F (16°-21°C)	2-7 hrs	2-40 hrs
50°-60°F (10°-16°C)	1-2 hrs	1-6 hrs
40°-50°F (4°-10°C)	30-60 min	1-3 hrs
32.5°-40°F (0°-4°C)	15-30 min	30-90 min
32.5°F (0°C)	<15 min	15-45 min

Wind Chill Temperature Chart

Air Temp	Wind Speed								
	5	10	15	20	25	30	35	40	45
45	43	34	29	25	23	21	19	18	17
40	37	28	22	18	15	13	11	10	9
35	32	22	16	11	8	6	4	3	2
30	27	16	9	4	1	-3	-5	-6	-7
25	22	10	2	-3	-7	-11	-13	-14	-15
20	16	4	-5	-11	-15	-18	-20	-22	-23
15	11	-3	-12	-18	-22	-26	-28	-30	-31
10	6	-9	-19	-25	-30	-33	-36	-38	-39
5	1	-15	-25	-32	-37	-41	-44	-46	-47
0	-5	-22	-32	-39	-45	-49	-52	-54	-55
-5	-10	-28	-39	-47	-52	-56	-59	-61	-63
-10	-16	-34	-45	-54	-60	-64	-67	-69	-71
-15	-21	-40	-52	-61	-67	-72	-75	-77	-79
-20	-26	-46	-59	-68	-74	-79	-83	-85	-87
-25	-31	-52	-66	-75	-82	-87	-91	-93	-101
-30	-37	-59	-72	-82	-89	-95	-98	-101	-103
-35	-42	-65	-79	-89	-97	-102	-106	-114	-122
-40	-47	-71	-86	-96	-104	-110	-114	-117	-124
-45	-53	-77	-93	-104	-112	-117	-122	-124	-127

Find the outside air temperature in the left column, then read across the row to find the wind speed.

Wind Chill	Possible Effects
30°F or higher	Generally unpleasant
30° to 15 °F	Unpleasant
14° to 0°F	Very unpleasant
1° to - 20°F	Frostbite possible
- 21° to - 60°F	Frostbite likely; outdoor activity dangerous
- 61° or lower	Exposed flesh freezes in 30 sec.

First Aid for Hypothermia, see page 145.
First Aid for Frostbite, see page 142.

Natural Disasters

Beaufort Wind Speed Scale

Beau-fort Scale	Official Descrip.	Knots min	Knots max	Miles/hour min	Miles/hour max	Km/hour min	Km/hour max	Description
0	Calm	0	1	0	1	0	2	Smoke rises vertically; sea is mirror smooth
1	Light air	1	3	1	3	2	6	Smoke shows the direction of the wind but it is not shown by a weather vane.
2	Light breeze	4	6	5	7	7	11	"Wind is felt on the face, leaves rustle in the trees, and a weathervane moves."
3	Gentle breeze	7	10	8	12	13	19	Wind extends a light flag
4	Moderate breeze	11	16	13	18	20	30	"Loose papers blow around," dust raised, and fairly frequent whitecaps occur"
5	Fresh breeze	17	21	20	24	31	39	Small trees sway and crested wavelets appear on inland waters.
6	Strong breeze	22	27	25	31	41	50	"Wind causes whistling in telephone wires some spray on the sea surface, umbrellas difficult to control."
7	Moderate gale	28	33	32	38	52	61	Large trees sway. It is difficult to walking into the wind.
8	Fresh gale	34	40	39	46	63	74	"Twugs breat from trees, long streaks of foam appear on the sea, and moving cars veer on roads."
9	Strong gale	41	47	47	54	76	87	Branches break from trees and some damage may occur to roofing materials.
10	Whole gale	48	55	55	63	89	102	Trees are uprooted; the sea looks white.
11	Storm	56	63	64	72	104	117	Widespread damage.
12	Hurricane	≥64		≥74		≥119		Structural damage on land, storm waves at sea.

Hurricane Intensity Scale - Saffir-Simpson Damage Potential Scale

Category	Central Pressure (in. of Hg)	Wind Speed (mile/hr)	Storm Surge (feet)	Damage Level	Description of Damage
1	≥ 28.94	74-95	4-5	Minimal	Damage to trees, shrubs, foliage and unanchored mobile homes. Well-built structures undamaged. Low-lying coastal roads may flood.
2	28.91-28.50	96-110	6-8	Moderate	Some trees blown down; major damage to mobile homes. Some damage to roofing materials, doors and windows. Major damage to piers. Evacuation of low-lying homes on coast may be required.
3	28.47-27.91	111-130	9-12	Extensive	Leaves torn from trees; some large trees blown down. Mobile homes destroyed; some structural damage to small homes and utility buildings, minor damage to non-load bearing walls. Piers destroyed. Serious flooding near the coast damages structures and structures five feet above sea level may flood as far as 6 miles inland.
4	27.88-27.17	131- 155	13-18	Extreme	Extensive damage to roofing materials and non-load bearing walls. Complete structural failure of roofs on small homes. Major damage to lower floors of structures near the coast. Major erosion of beaches. Land less than 10 ft. above sea level require massive evacuation up to 6 miles inland.
5	≤ 27.15	≥156	>18	Catastrophic	Complete roof structure failure on many buildings. Some complete building failures small buildings blown over or away. Major damage to lower floors of all structures less than 15 ft. above sea level within 500 yards of the coast. Massive evacuation of areas on low ground within 5-10 miles of the coast may be required

Natural Disasters

Fujita-Pearson Tornado Intensity Scale

Scale	Tornado Strength	Tornado Name	Max. Wind Speed (miles/hr)	Path Length (miles)	Avg. Path Length (yards)	Damage	Description of Damages
F0	Weak	Gale	< 73	<1.0	<18	Light	Damage to tree branches, billboards, & chimneys. Some small trees uprooted.
F1	Weak	Moderate	73-112	1.0-3.1	18-55	Moderate	Roofing materials peeled off, mobile homes pushed off foundations or overturned, moving automobiles pushed off road.
F2	Strong	Significant	113-157	3.2-9.9	56-175	Considerable	Roofs torn off wood-frame homes, mobile homes demolished, railroad boxcars pushed over, large trees uprooted or snapped-off.
F3	Strong	Severe	158-206	10-31	176-556	Severe	Roofs and some walls torn off well-built wood-frame homes, locomotives overturned, most trees in forested areas uprooted, automobiles lifted and moved.
F4	Violent	Devastating	207-260	32-99	557-1759	Devastating	Well-built homes leveled, automobiles thrown about, heavy objects become missiles.
F5	Violent	Incredible	261-318	100-315	1760-5456	Incredible	Structures are lifted off foundations and carried away, reinforced concrete structures damaged. Less than 2% of all tornadoes reach this intensity.
F6	-	-	319-380	-	-	-	Not expected to occur on Earth.

SAFETY AND HEALTH OF OFFICERS

Exposure to Blood-Borne Illness · · · · · · · · · · · · · · · 356
Critical Incident Stress Debriefing · · · · · · · · · · · · · · 359
12 Keys to a Longer Career · · · · · · · · · · · · · · · · · · · 362
Health Tips for Shift Workers · · · · · · · · · · · · · · · · · 363
Noise Exposure · 364
Sound Intensities · 365
Personal Protection Equipment (PPE) · · · · · · · · · · · 365
CDC Precaution Guidelines · · · · · · · · · · · · · · · · · · · 367
Law Enforcement Statistics · · · · · · · · · · · · · · · · · · · 368

Safety and Health

Exposure to Blood-Borne Illness

Have You Been Exposed?

Exposure is defined as:
- Injury, by a needle or other object contaminated with blood or certain other bodily fluid, that breaks the skin.
- Blood or certain other bodily fluid that comes in contact with skin if:
    - there is prolonged contact.
    - a large area of skin is involved.
    - the source person is known to have advanced or end-stage AIDS.
    - the skin is broken or a rash is present.
- Blood or certain other bodily fluid that comes in contact with mucous (inside the eyes, lips, or mouth).

Examples of Non-exposure:
- Spattered blood in small amounts on intact skin.
- Breathing in an environment where blood or certain other bodily fluids may have been aerosolized, or in the air.
- Touching a person who may have HIV or AIDS, or simple contact with their possessions.

Body fluids to which this protocol applies:
Blood, any tissue, pleural fluid (lungs), peritoneal fluid (abdomen), cerebrospinal fluid (brain, spine), pericardial fluid (heart), synovial fluid (joints), amniotic fluid (birth), semen, and vaginal secretions.

Body fluids to which this protocol does not apply:
Saliva, feces, vomit, nasal secretions, sputum, sweat, tears, and urine.

HIV is not transmitted by casual contact and dies quickly when it is outside the human body.

If You Have Been Exposed

If you have been exposed as described above, it is critical to follow these steps:

- See a doctor or other health care provider for appropriate medical care.
- In most cases, get a baseline HIV test, regardless of the HIV status of the person to whom you were exposed. Be retested periodically. See your doctor about any illness with fever that you contract within 12 weeks of exposure.

- IMMEDIATELY discuss with your doctor the preventative use of a 2 or 3 drug regimen of anti-HIV drugs (i.e., Zidovudine (AZT) and Epvir (3TC) with or without Crixiavan (Indinivir or IDV). **It is best if these drugs are started within 1-2 hours of exposure**. They are of questionable benefit if started 24-36 hours or more after exposure.

- Be evaluated for immunity to Hepatitis B, regardless of the Hepatitis B status of the person to whom you were exposed. If you are not immune, or if your immune status is unknown, talk to your doctor about the need for preventative medication against Hepatitis B.

Measures to Help Prevent Exposure

The National Institute for Occupational Safety and Health together with the Centers for Disease Control recommend the following safety precautions:

- When blood is present and a suspect or prisoner is combative or threatening, put on gloves as soon as possible. Keep an extra change of clothing available for instances where clothing becomes contaminated with blood.

- Use protective masks or airways when administering CPR, preferably devices with one-way valves which keep the patient's saliva or vomitus from entering the caregiver's mouth.

- During searches:
  - Have suspects empty their own pockets if circumstances permit.
  - Maintain a safe distance from the suspect.
  - Wear protective gloves if exposure to blood is likely and when conducting body cavity searches.
  - Whenever possible, use flashlights and long-handled mirrors to search places that are hidden.
  - Empty the contents of a purse directly onto a table rather than reaching inside.
  - When wearing cotton gloves to collect latent fingerprint evidence, put them on over protective gloves if likely to encounter blood or other body fluids.
  - Use evidence tape instead of staples to seal evidence to avoid tearing or puncturing protective gloves.
  - When a crime scene involves large quantities of blood, wear protective gloves and, if necessary, other protective clothing such as overalls, aprons, and boot

Safety and Health

or shoe covers. Change these items if they become contaminated.
- Do not handle personal items such as combs or pens in situations where they could become contaminated.
- Wear a face mask and eye protection, or a face shield when collecting blood evidence.
- Be alert for sharp objects that could puncture gloves or skin such as hypodermic needles, knives, razors, broken glass, nails, etc.
- When contact with a dead body is required, wear gloves and cover all cuts and abrasions; carefully wash all exposed areas after any contact with blood. The same applies to handling severed body parts.
- When performing or attending an autopsy, wear a protective mask and eyewear, or a face shield, laboratory coat, gloves, and a waterproof apron.
- Forensic laboratories:
  - Keep all blood specimens in a well-constructed, appropriately labeled container with a secure lid. Avoid getting blood on the outside of the container.
  - Wear gloves, a protective mask and eyewear, or a face shield, when processing blood specimens.
  - Use a biological safety cabinet when doing procedures that would have a good chance of generating droplets such as blending, sonicating, or vigorous mixing.
  - Use mechanical pipetting devices to manipulate all liquids in the laboratory.
  - Limit the use of needles and syringes to those situations in which there is no alternative. Do not manipulate used needles by hand, and carefully place them in a puncture-resistant container for disposal or reprocessing.
  - Clean work surfaces of all visible substances, then decontaminate with germicide.
  - Scientific equipment that has been contaminated with blood should be cleaned and then decontaminated before being repaired or transported to the manufacturer.

Sources:
 Colorado Dept. Of Public Health and Environment, *Exposures to Blood or Bodily Fluids in Public Safety Workers*
National Institute for Occupational Safety and Health/Centers for Disease Control, *Guidelines for Prevention of Transmission of HIV and Hep B Virus*

Critical Incident Stress Debriefing

For purposes of this discussion, a "Critical Incident" is defined as an event which is stressful enough to overwhelm the usually effective coping skills of either an individual or a group. In other words, it is an incident that pushes a person beyond his or her normal coping techniques.

Throughout history humans have faced demands that have pushed them further than they were prepared to go. From the Civil War through World War II, stress reactions were diagnosed as "shell shock" and sedation was the course of treatment. The Vietnam War started an era of transition, in which the psychological impact of critical incidents began to be dealt with as a real, treatable issue. It became apparent that there was a need for a quality program that would bring about effective recovery.

A retired firefighter, and later PhD, named Jeffrey Mitchell began studying the effects of stress on firefighters, law enforcement, EMTs, emergency room personnel, and others who are often first on scene or who have to deal with natural disasters or multiple victim situations. Mitchell found common reactions to these critical incidents and developed a strategy to help them recover from high-stress situations. What follows is a brief overview of that process and should not be taken as a cure or long-term strategy for dealing with traumatic situations.

A **typical crisis reaction** includes denial, anger, bargaining, depression, point of resolution, acceptance, new identity, new relationships, and a new scenario. This differs from Critical Incident Stress reactions and must be recognized as a different set of issues. It is possible to get stuck in any one of these steps, and once that is realized it is crucial for that person to seek assistance from friends, family or mental health professionals.

People develop methods in their lives to cope with everyday stress and those who put themselves into intense situations are often confronted with stress factors that may push them beyond their normal coping mechanisms. Critical Incidents are **intense** situations such as natural disasters, accidents, human-induced pain, or mayhem. They elicit strong emotional, physical, and psychological reactions from first responders, rippling out to others involved with lessening effect. Unresolved previous personal trauma or perceived loss may cause a person to react more strongly to such an incident.

Another consideration beyond the **intensity** of the incident is the **duration** of the scene and the frequency of difficult calls and decisions. Each individual has a tolerance for alarm response. The problem is that we are not all aware of how rescues and incidents are going to affect an individual in a specific situation.

Crisis response can bring up issues such as loss of control, immortality (especially around the death of a child), justice, future, one's personal role, and trust in God and others.

People who are susceptible to critical stress are often idealistic, devoted, high energy, goal-oriented, charismatic, or dynamic. One of the key purposes of a Critical Incident Stress Debriefing (CISD) is to remind individuals that they are normal and having normal responses to a bad situation. It is not a departmental critique or discovery tool. CISD is designed to help individuals and groups begin the recovery process needed following a situation that is overwhelming.

Following a critical incident, individuals need to **ventilate** their feelings, **validate** their reactions, and be **educated** about reactions and responses that they, or others on the scene, may experience. They need to learn how to regain the sense of control that the situation may have taken from them. False cures for stress reactions may include denial, alcohol, sex without love, drugs, isolation or anything in done in excess.

Critical Incident Stress Debriefing (CISD) Procedures

A CISD takes 2-2½ hours and should be led by a trained facilitator and peers.

Introduction
Ground rules of confidentiality are presented: no press, no beepers, no one present who was not on the scene or of superior rank (the presence of command personnel may change the freedom of the group).

Facts
Group members introduce themselves, explain how they got involved with the scene, their role on scene, and any details they wish to share.

Thoughts
Group members discuss what they thought about on scene or what they talked about with others. This discussion allows for ventilation of the experience.

Reactions
Discussion centers around reactions that group members may have experienced since the incident occurred and what elements of the incident have been hardest to take.

Symptoms

Information is given about symptom they may experience such as depression, sleep disorders, loss of concentration and decision-making abilities, desire for isolation, increased startle response, survivor's guilt, anxiety, fear, anger, and fear of losing control.

Education

Group leaders confirm that reactions being experienced are normal and present the following suggestions for dealing with the stress:

- Talk to people and tell your story as often as you feel safe doing so.
- Get physical exercise to release the toxins brought on by stress reaction.
- Eat healthy foods and avoid alcohol, caffeine, smoking, high fat foods, and high sugar foods,
- Take vitamins such as C, E, B6, B12, magnesium, and calcium.
- Remain active.
- Set a schedule and follow through with it.
- Be around people you trust.
- Identify emotional responses.
- Journal your thoughts (This will give you have a sense of control and decrease the amount of energy it takes to keep the details fresh).
- Be aware of your methods of dealing with stress.

If a scene or incident causes a marked reaction, seek assistance through available organizations such as your Employee Assistance Program, Peer Counseling, or professional counseling with a medical doctor, psychologist or mental health worker. If physical reactions include chest pain or difficulty breathing, seek medical attention immediately.

This is a brief overview and specific questions can be directed to a local CISD team, a trained Employee Assistance Professional, or mental health worker.

Information courtesy of Rev. Dr. Dave Guy, former chaplain of the Flint, Michigan Police Department for 8 years. Dr. Guy holds a master's degree in Theology, a doctorate in Ministry, and is a licensed, EAP-certified counselor specializing in conflict and stress management.

Safety and Health

12 Keys to a Longer Career

1. **ATTITUDE:** Attitude is everything. If you bring your personal problems to work, or simply fail to remain focused, you, your partner, or a citizen could pay the price.

2. **LIFESTYLE:** Not only is adequate rest important, but overall physical condition as well. If a foot pursuit kills you, get in shape. Mom's right - eat more fruits and vegetables.

3. **EQUIPMENT:** You are only as good as your equipment is functional. Keep a clean weapon, fresh ammo, and know how to use it in high stress situations. Fresh batteries in your flashlight and radio are a must. Maintain and know all of your gear. Wear a vest.

4. **INTUITION:** After working the field you should develop a "sixth sense" that intuitively alerts you to the possibility of danger. If you don't, consider a different line of work. If your inner voice tells you something's not right, don't shrug it off.

5. **FALSE BRAVADO:** If you need backup, call for it. Never be afraid to admit to yourself that a situation is bigger than you are. Denial can hurt.

6. **POSITION IS EVERYTHING:** Never, ever, under any circumstance, let anyone you are questioning get into a better tactical position than you. On traffic stops, take downs, domestics, and life in general, maintain the most advantageous position you can.

7. **DROPPING YOUR GUARD:** Treat all false alarms as real, all domestics as critical, all arrests as hazardous, and no call as routine, and you should finish your shift.

8. **VIGILANCE:** Always watch a suspect's hands and be aware of "suspicious" moves. "Tune in" to the entire scene, ambushes, hidden suspects, and on and on…

9. **HANDCUFF WHEN JUSTIFIED:** Always properly handcuff when appropriate. Love isn't the tie that binds, it's a half pound of cold steel.

10. **SEARCH:** Weapons come in all shapes and sizes. Thoroughly search all suspects and use proper personal protection against needles, razors, etc. A ball point pen stuck through your eyeball can ruin your day.

11. **REACT:** Many cops that have been shot and survived stated they just couldn't believe it was happening to them. Gun, knife, or fist, BELIEVE IT, react immediately, and with appropriate force. Bad guys are called bad for a reason.

12. **THINK COVER:** If all else fails, leave yourself an out. Avoid open spaces. Remember the three "Cs": COVER! COVER! COVER!

By Bones Evers

Health Tips for Shift Workers

Working nights or evenings makes it hard to maintain regular patterns of eating, working, sleeping, and socializing. As a result, shift workers may experience digestive problems, fatigue and related safety problems, and even an increased risk of heart attack.

Diet and Eating Habits

Indigestion, heartburn, stomachache, and loss of appetite are more common among shift workers than among day workers. More serious conditions, such as ulcers, may be more common as well. Eating out of vending machines and the natural decrease in appetite at night result in a lack of healthy, balanced meals. Many rely on caffeine to stay awake through the shift and then can't fall asleep when they get home.

Some scientific studies have indicated that shift workers may be more likely to have heart attacks than day workers, so eating a heart-healthy diet may have important long-term health benefits.

- Keep regular eating patterns as much as possible.
  If possible, eat with your family at regular mealtimes.
- Relax while eating and leave time for digestion.
- Afternoon workers should eat their main meal in the middle of the day, rather than during their work shift. Night workers should eat lightly throughout their shift and have a moderate breakfast after work to minimize digestive discomfort and prevent hunger while sleeping during the day.
- Drink lots of water.
- Eat a balanced diet of vegetables, fruit, lean meat, poultry, fish, dairy products, grains, and bread.
  - Eat crackers and fruit instead of candy bars and pop during work breaks. NO DOUGHNUTS!
  - Minimize salt, caffeine, alcohol, and greasy foods.
  - Avoid excessive use of antacids, tranquilizers, and sleeping pills.

Sleep

Trying to adjust your sleep schedule for shift work can result in a permanent case of jet lag. The human body has a complex set of rhythms and not all of them can be "reset" to accommodate a nocturnal schedule. This disruption in circadian rhythms can cause lack of concentration and motivation, as well as slow reaction time, increasing your risk of accident and injury.

Tips for Getting a "Good Day's Sleep"

- Establish a routine and sleep on a set schedule to make sleep during the day easier.
- Make sure you have a place to sleep that is quiet, comfortable, and dark. If possible, use blackout curtains or tape aluminum foil to the inside of any windows. Also use earplugs if needed to create a quiet space.
- Take time to relax quietly before bed. Learn a relaxation technique you feel comfortable with and use it.
- If you have trouble falling asleep after an hour, read a book or listen to quiet music for awhile. Reschedule sleep time for later in the day if necessary.
- Limit late day commitments to allow for napping.

Other Tips

- Moderate, not strenuous, regular exercise can help your body handle the stress of shift work more easily.
- Learn to recognize and reduce stress through physical fitness, relaxation techniques, and so on.
- Take leisure seriously.

Sources: "Shiftwork and Diet", Applied Ergonomics, Feb. 1996, V. 27, N1, p.17
Canadian Centre for Occupational Health and Safety, "Rotational Shiftwork: A Summary of the Adverse Effects and Improvement Strategies", 1987
Worksafe Western Australia, "Safety and Health in Shiftwork"
Monk, Timothy H., and Folkard, Simon, Making Shiftwork Tolerable (London, Taylor & Francis, 1992

Noise Exposure

The U.S. Dept. of Labor, Occupational Safety and Health Administration (OSHA) Regulation #1910.95 Subpart G Permissible Occupational Noise Exposure requires that sound protection be worn whenever exposure to sound exceeds the levels shown below. Exposure to impulsive or impact noise should not exceed 140 db peak sound pressure level.

Hours per Day	Sound Level (db)
8	90
6	92
4	95
3	97
2	100
1.5	102
1	105
0.5	110
0.25 or less	115

Sound Intensities

Sound Intensities are measured in decibels (db). Normally 1 db is the smallest volume change detectable by the human ear.

db	Degree	Example
0		Absolute Silence
10		Inside a sound proof room
20	Very Faint	Whisper
30		Quiet conversation
40	Faint	Private office noise
45		Needed to awaken a sleeping person
50		Normal office noise
60	Moderate	Normal conversation, close up
70		Normal street noise
80	Loud	Police whistle, inside a high speed auto
90		Truck without a muffler; regular exposure causes damage to hearing
100	Very Loud	Car horn at 15 ft.
110		Nearby train
120		Diesel engine room
130		Threshold of pain/ immediate damage to hearing
140		Artillery Fire
194		50 lbs. of TNT at 10 ft.
225	Deafening	a 12" cannon at 12 ft., above and below

PPE for Biological & Chemical Weapons

PPE Level Definitions

Level A
Maximum protection. Fully encapsulating, chemical resistant suit, gloves and boots with a pressure-demand, self-contained breathing apparatus (SCBA), or a pressure-demand supplied air respirator (air hose) and escape SCBA.

Level B
Used when full respiratory protection is needed but there is less danger to skin. Non-encapsulating splash protective chemical-resistant suit (splash suit) that provides Level A protection against liquids but is not airtight.

Level C
Splash suit with full-faced positive or negative pressure respirator (filter type gas mask) rather than an SCBA or air hose.

Level D
  Coveralls or other work clothes, boots, and gloves.

Source: *Chemical and Biological Terrorism; Personal Protective Equipment*,
National Academy Press, at www.nap.edu/html/terrorism/ch3.html

Respirator & PPE Selection

When using respiratory protection, the type of respirator should
be selected based on the hazard and its airborne concentration.
Current data suggests that SCBA equipment should be used to
enter areas with a potential chemical hazard and that it also
provides protection against biological hazards associated with a
suspected act of bioterrorism.

The CDC's interim recommendations for PPE are as follows:

  • If the type of bioweapon, method of dispersal, level of
    concentration, duration of dispersal is unknown, or if
    airborne dispersal is still occurring, use the highest level of
    protection (i.e. a NIOSH-approved, pressure demand SCBA
    together with a Level A protective suit.)

  • If the suspected biological aerosol is no longer being
    generated, but other conditions may present a splash
    hazard, use a Level B protective suit with an exposed or
    enclosed NIOSH-approved pressure-demand SCBA.

  • If the device did not create high airborne concentration or if
    dissemination was by letter or package that can easily be
    bagged, use a full face-piece respirator with a P100 filter or
    powered air-purifying respirator (PAPR) with high efficiency
    particulate filters.

When bagging letters or packages, avoid creating a puff of air
that could spread the pathogen. Avoid using a large bag and
work very slowly and carefully when putting the object into it.
Wear disposable hooded coveralls, gloves, and foot coverings.

Standard firefighter turnout gear should not be used when
entering areas that may contain biological agents.

Use the decontamination sequence appropriate for the level of
protection employed. Decontaminate equipment with soap and
water, and a solution of 1 part bleach to 10 parts water. Bleach
may damage some types of firefighter turnout gear, which is one
reason that it shouldn't be worn when responding to a biological
incident. After removing gear and protective apparel, shower
with lots of hot water and soap.

Source: *Interim Recommendations for the Selection and Use of Protective
Clothing and Respirators Against Biological Agents* Centers for Disease
Control and Prevention, October 24, 2001.

CDC Precaution Guidelines

The CDC has developed guidelines for handling patients with various types of communicable diseases. When dealing with various bioweapon incidents and their victims, it may be helpful to be aware of terms and precautions. Standard Precautions are considered the minimum standard; all other levels of precaution INCLUDE standard precautions!

Standard Precautions - used with all patients
- Wash hands before and after touching patients regardless of whether gloves are worn.
- Wear gloves when touching blood or body fluids and contaminated items. Change gloves between patients or procedures.
- Wear a mask and eye protection, or a face shield.
- Wear gowns to protect clothing.
- If possible, use needleless devices and safety devices.

Airborne Precautions
Apply to diseases transmitted only by the airborne route, namely tuberculosis, measles, and chickenpox.
- If in a hospital, the responder should be in a negative pressure isolation room. These rooms are not available in the field, so the responder should wear respirators with an –95 filter when handling patients.

Droplet Precautions
Apply to diseases transmitted by close contact with respiratory secretions.
- Wear a surgical mask and gloves.

Contact Precautions
Apply to infections transmitted by direct contact with the infectious substance.
- Wear gloves and change them after each contact with wounds, body fluids, or anything else like to be highly infectious.
- Wash hands immediately after using an antimicrobial agent or waterless antiseptic.
- Wear a gown to cover your clothing.
- Limit movement of patient to only what is essential. Avoid contaminating surfaces and equipment, but if equipment must be shared, be sure to clean and disinfect it between patients.

Sources: *Safe Jobs Now* at www.afscme.org/health/safe07c.htm and *Standard Precautions for Infection Control* at www.cbwinfo.com/Biological/Pathogens/Standard.html

Safety and Health

Law Enforcement Statistics

- Approximately 870,000 sworn law enforcement officers are now serving in the United States, the highest figure ever. About 11.3% of them are female.

- In 2002, there were over 1.4 million violent crimes committed in the U.S. The annual number of violent crimes has declined by 35% since it peaked in 1993 at 4 million.

- 16,810 officers have been killed in the line of duty since the first recorded police death in 1792.

- A total of 1,658 law enforcement officers died in the line of duty during the past 10 years, an average of one death every 53 hours, or 166 per year. 154 officers died in 2004, a 6% increase from the 145 officers who died in 2003.

- On average, more than 58,066 law enforcement officers are assaulted each year, of which 16,494 have been injured.

- The deadliest year in law enforcement history was 1974, when 271 officers were killed. The deadliest decade was the 1970s, when a total of 2,240 officers died, or 224 each year. That figure dropped dramatically in the 1990s to 157 per year.

- The deadliest day in law enforcement history was Sept. 11, 2001 when 72 officers were killed while responding to the terrorist attacks on America.

- New York City has lost more officers in the line of duty than any other department, with 579 deaths. California has lost 1,357 officers, more than any other state. The state with the fewest deaths is Vermont, with 17.

- On the National Law Enforcement Officer's Memorial in Washington D.C. there are 873 federal officers, 445 correctional officers, and 44 military law enforcement officers.

- There are 194 female officers listed on the Memorial, only nine of whom were killed prior to 1970.

- During the last 10 years, more officers were killed feloniously on Wednesdays than any other day of the week. The fewest fatalities occurred on Sundays.

- During the last decade, more officers were killed between 10:00 p.m. and midnight than during any other two hours of the day.

This information courtesy of *National Law Enforcement Officers Memorial Fund*, copyright 1996-2005, used by permission. http://www.nleomf.com/

SUBSTANCE ABUSE

Controlled Substances: Uses and Effects · · · · · · · · **370**

Cannabis · 370
Depressants · 371
Hallucinogens · 373
Inhalants · 375
Narcotics · 376
Steroids · 379
Stimulants · 380

Drug Scheduling · **382**

Schedule I · 383
Schedule II · 386
Schedule III · 388
Schedule IV · 390
Schedule V · 392

Toxicity & Flammability of Chemicals · · · · · · · · · · · **393**

Chemicals Used in Manufacture of Illicit Drugs · · · · **394**

Street Names for Drugs · **398**

Substance Abuse Estimates by State · · · · · · · · · · · **456**

RADAR Network State Centers · · · · · · · · · · · · · · · · · **457**

Substance Abuse Statistics · · · · · · · · · · · · · · · · · · · **459**

Substance Abuse Resources · · · · · · · · · · · · · · · · · · **460**

Substance Abuse

Controlled Substances Uses and Effects

TIP

One of the best ways to identify a drug that you have collected as evidence is to call your local poison control center and describe it to them. See page 148.

Cannabis

Possible Effects:
Disorientation, euphoria, fantasies, hallucinations, image distortion, impaired memory, impaired motor coordination, increased appetite, loss of personal identity, rapidly fluctuating emotions, relaxed inhibitions, unorganized thoughts, and vivid sense of sight, smell, taste, and hearing.

Effects of Overdose:
Fatigue, paranoia, possible psychosis.

Withdrawal Symptoms:
Decreased appetite, hyperactivity, and occasional insomnia.

Hashish and Hashish Oil
Controlled Substances Act Schedule I (see pg. 382)
Trade or Other Names: Gram, Hash, Hash Oil, Quarter Moon
Medical Uses: ....None
Dependence: ....Physical: Unknown
                     Psychological: Moderate
                     Tolerance: Yes
Duration: ....2-4 hours
Usual Method:........Oral, smoked

Marijuana
Controlled Substances Act Schedule I (see pg. 382)
Trade or Other Names: Acapulco Blunts, Bongs, Gold, Grass, Joints, Mary Jane, Reefer, Pot, Sinsemilla, Thai Sticks, Weed
Medical Uses: ....Chronic pain treatment for serious illnesses such as AIDS, cancer, epilepsy, multiple sclerosis. Legal to grow/use with a prescription in Alaska, California, Colorado, Hawaii, Maine, Maryland, Montana, Nevada, Oregon, Vermont, and Washington. Other states have laws that support medical marijuana, but no legal patient protection under the law.
Dependence: ....Physical: Unknown
                     Psychological: Moderate
                     Tolerance: Yes
Duration: ....2-4 hours

Substance Abuse

Usual Method:........Oral, smoked

Tetrahydrocannabinol (THC)
Controlled Substances Act Schedules III (see pg. 382)
Trade or Other Names: Marinol, THC
Medical Uses: ....Control of nausea and vomiting with
chemotherapy patients, and stimulates
appetite in AIDS patients.
Dependence: ....Physical: Unknown
Psychological: Moderate
Tolerance: Yes
Duration: ....2-4 hours
Usual Method:........Oral, smoked

Depressants

Possible Effects:
Confusion, depression, disorientation, dizziness, slurred
speech, drunken behavior without odor of alcohol, headache,
impaired judgment, induced sleep, irritability, loss of motor
coordination, memory impairment, relieve anxiety and stress,
slurred speech.

Effects of Overdose:
Clammy skin, coma, dilated pupils, shallow respiration, weak
or rapid pulse, and possible death.

Withdrawal Symptoms:
Anxiety, convulsions, delirium, insomnia, seizures, tremors,
weakness, and possible death.

Barbiturates
Controlled Substances Act Schedules II, III, IV (see pg. 382)
Trade or Other Names: Alurate, Amobarbital, Amytal,
Aprobarbital, Brevital, Butabarbital,
Butalbital, Butisol, Fiorina, Florinal, Lotusate,
Luminal, Mebaral, Mephobarbital,
Methohexital, Nembutal, Pentobarbital,
Pentothal, Phenobarbital, Secobarbital,
Seconal, Surital, Talbutal, Thiamyl,
Thiopental, Tuinal
Medical Uses: ....Anesthetic, anticonvulsant, hypnotic,
insomnia, pre-operative sedation, sedative,
seizure disorders, veterinary euthanasia.
Dependence: ....Physical: High-Moderate
Psychological: High-Moderate
Tolerance: Yes
Duration: ....1-16 hours (depending on which
classification: ultra short, short,
intermediate, and long lasting)
Usual Method:........Injected, oral

Substance Abuse

Benzodiazepines

Controlled Substances Act Schedule IV (see pg. 382)
Trade or Other Names: Alprazolam, Ambien*, Ativan, Centrax, Chlordiazepoxide, Clonazepam, Clorazepate, Dalmane, Diazepam, Doral, Estazolam, Flunitrazepam (aka Rohypnol, 'date rape drug', rophies, roofies, and roach), Flurazepam, Halazepam, Halcion, Klonopin, Lorzepam, Librium, Midazolam, Oxazepam, Paxipam, Prazepam, ProSom, Quazepam, Restoril, Serax, Sonata*, Tamazepam, Tranxene, Trizolam, Valium, Versed, Verstran, Xanax, Zaleplon*, Zolpidem*
*These drugs have similar properties to benzopdizepines
Medical Uses: ....Antianxiety, anticonvulsant, axiolytic, hypnotic, induce sleep, muscle relaxant, sedative.
Dependence: ....Physical: Moderate
Psychological: Moderate
Tolerance: Yes
Duration: ....1-8 hours
Usual Method:........Injected, oral

Chloral Hydrate

Controlled Substances Act Schedule IV (see pg. 382)
Trade or Other Names: Felsules, Noctec, Somnos
Medical Uses: ....Hypnotic
Dependence: ....Physical: Moderate
Psychological: Moderate
Tolerance: Yes
Duration: ....5-8 hours
Usual Method:........Oral

Gamma Hydroxybutyric Acid (GHB)

Controlled Substances Act Schedules I, III (see pg. 382)
Trade or Other Names: 'Date Rape Drug', GBL, GHB, Liquid X, Sodium Oxybate, Xyrem
Medical Uses: ....None in U.S., anabolic agent, anesthetic, narcolepsy
Dependence: ....Physical: Moderate
Psychological: Moderate
Tolerance: Yes
Duration: ....3-6 hours
Usual Method:........Oral

Glutethimide and Methaqualone

Controlled Substances Act Schedule II (see pg. 382)
Trade or Other Names: Doriden, Quaalude, Sopor

Medical Uses: ....Hypnotic, muscle relaxant, sedative
Dependence: ....Physical: High
                     Psychological: Moderate
                     Tolerance: Yes
Duration: ....4-8 hours
Usual Method:........Oral

Other Depressants

Controlled Substances Act Schedules I, II, III, IV (see pg. 382)
Trade or Other Names: Carisoprodol, Chloral Hydrate, Equanil,
                     Meprobamate, Miltown, Noctec, Noludar,
                     Paral, Paraldehyde, Placidyl, Soma, Valmid
Medical Uses: ....Alcohol withdrawal treatment (Paral;
                     Paraldehyde), antianxiety, hypnotic, sedative
Dependence: ....Physical: Moderate
                     Psychological: Moderate
                     Tolerance: Yes
Duration: ....2-8 hours
Usual Method:........Oral

Hallucinogens

Possible Effects:
  Altered perception of time and distance, dehydration, dilated
  pupils, elevated heart rate, flashbacks, heightened senses,
  increased blood pressure, illusions, hallucinations, perceptual
  distortions, and teeth grinding.
Effects of overdose:
  Cardiac arrest, increased body temperature, electrolyte
  imbalance, longer (or more intense) "trip" episodes, loss of
  memory, psychosis, unable to direct movement, unable to feel
  pain, and possible death.
Withdrawal symptoms:
  Acne, depression, drowsiness, and muscle aches.

Ketamine

Controlled Substances Act Schedule III (see pg. 382)
Trade or Other Names: Ketalar, Ketaset, Special K, Super K
Medical Uses: ....Anesthetic
Dependence: ....Physical: Possible
                     Psychological: High
                     Tolerance: Yes
Duration: ....less than 1 hour
Usual Method:........Injected, oral, smoked, sniffed

Lysergic Acid Diethylamide (LSD)

Controlled Substances Act Schedule I (see pg. 382)
Trade or Other Names: Acid, Boomers, Microdot, Sunshine
Medical Uses: ....None

Substance Abuse

Dependence: ....Physical: None
Psychological: Unknown
Tolerance: Yes
Duration: ....8-12 hours
Usual Method:........Oral

MDMA and Analogs (Amphetamine Variants)
Controlled Substances Act Schedule I (see pg. 382)
Trade or Other Names: Adam, 2C-T-7, 5-MeO-AMT,
5-MeO-DIPT, AMT, DIPT, DOB, DOM, DPT,
Ecstasy, Eve, Love Drug, MBDB, MDA,
MDEA, MDMA, MeO-MIPT, MIPT, NEXUS,
PMA, PMMA, STP, XTC
Medical Uses: ....None
Dependence: ....Physical: None
Psychological: Moderate
Tolerance: Yes
Duration: ....1-6 hours
Usual Method:........Injected (rarely), oral, smoked, sniffed

Mescaline and Peyote
Controlled Substances Act Schedule I (see pg. 382)
Trade or Other Names: Buttons, Cactus, Mescal
Medical Uses: ....None
Dependence: ....Physical: None
Psychological: Unknown
Tolerance: Yes
Duration: ....8-12 hours
Usual Method:........Oral

Phencyclidine and Analogs
Controlled Substances Act Schedules I, II, III (see pg. 382)
Trade or Other Names: Angel Dust, Embalming Fluid, Hog,
Killer Weed, Loveboat, PCE, PCP, PCPy,
Rocket Fuel, Supergrass, TCP, TCPy,
Telazol
Medical Uses: ....None
Dependence: ....Physical: Possible
Psychological: High
Tolerance: Yes
Duration: ....1-12 hours
Usual Method:........Injected, oral, smoked, sniffed

Psilocybin & Psilocyn (and other Tryptamines)
Controlled Substances Act Schedule I (see pg. 382)
Trade or Other Names: Alpha-ethyltryptamine (AET),
Bufotenine, Diethyltryptamine (DET),
Dimethyltryptamine (DMT), "Magic
Mushrooms"
Medical Uses: ....None

Dependence: ....Physical: Unknown
                      Psychological: High
                      Tolerance: Possible
Duration: ....45 minutes-8 hours
Usual Method:........Injected, oral, smoked, sniffed

Inhalants

Possible Effects:
Anxiety, decreased respiration, depression, distortion of time and space, drunken behavior, excitability, fear, flushing, headache, hypotension, impaired memory, loss of motor coordination, low blood pressure, nausea, odor of paint or chemicals on clothes, skin, and breath, organ damage, rash around nose or mouth, red and watery eyes, slurred speech, unpredictable behavior, vitamin deficiency, and wheezing.

Effects of Overdose:
Asphyxiation, aspiration, heart failure, loss of consciousness, methemoglobinemia, respiratory depression, vomiting, and possible death.

Withdrawal Symptoms:
Agitation, anxiety, confusion, convulsions, hallucinations, insomnia, trembling, and vitamin deficiency.

Inhalant General Information

Inhalation of fumes from substances such as adhesives, dry cleaning fluid, gasoline, hair spray, lighter fluid, nail polish remover, paint, paint thinner, rubber glue, spot remover, spray paint, waxes, varnishes.

Chemical Names: Acetone, Amyl Nitrite, Benzene, Butyl Nitrate, Isobutyl Nitrite, Methanol, Methyl Butyl Ketone, Methyl Ethyl Ketone, Methylene Chloride, Nitrous Oxide, Toluene, Trichloroethane, Trichloroethylene

Trade or Other Names: Balloons, Climax, Laughing Gas, Locker Room, Pearls, Poppers, Rush, Snappers, Whippets

Medical Uses: ....Anesthetic (Nitrous Oxide), dilating blood vessels (Amyl Nitrite)

Dependence: ....Physical: Unknown
                      Psychological: Low-High
                      Tolerance: No

Duration: ....30 minutes-2 hours

Usual Method:........Bagged (item placed in a bag, then sniffed), huffed (inhaled from a soaked rag), sniffed

Narcotics

Possible Effects:
Apathy, constipation, constricted pupils, drowsiness, euphoria, flushed face and neck, lack of concentration, lessened physical activity, nausea, passive, relaxed, respiratory depression, and vomiting.

Effects of Overdose:
Clammy skin, coma, confusion, constricted (pinpoint) pupils, convulsions, slow and shallow breathing (respiratory depression), and possible death.

Withdrawal Symptoms:
Chills, cramps, elevated heart rate and blood pressure, irritability, loss of appetite, muscle spasms, nausea, pain (in the bones and muscles of the back and extremities), panic, restlessness, runny nose, severe depression, sweating, tremors, vomiting, watery eyes, and yawning. Most physical symptoms will disappear within seven to ten days.

Codeine

Controlled Substances Act Schedules II, III, V (see pg. 382)

Trade or Other Names: Acetaminophen, APAP with codeine, Coties, Empirin with codeine, Fiorinal with codeine, Fioricet with codeine, Guifenesin with codeine, Promethazine with codeine, Robitussin A©, Tylenol with codeine

Medical Uses: ....Analgesic, antitussive

Dependence: ....Physical: Moderate
Psychological: Moderate
Tolerance: Yes

Duration: ....3-6 hours

Usual Method:........Injected, oral

Fentanyl and Analogs

Controlled Substances Act Schedules I, II (see pg. 382)

Trade or Other Names: Actiq, Alfenta, China Girl, China Town, Dance Fever, Duragesic, Friend, Goodfellas, Great Bear, He-man, Innovar, Jackpot, King Ivory, Murder 8, Sublimaze, Sufenta, Tango & Cash, Wildnil

Medical Uses: ....Analgesic, adjunct to anesthesia, anesthetic

Dependence: ....Physical: High
Psychological: High
Tolerance: Yes

Duration: ....0.10-72 hours

Usual Method:........Injected, smoked, sniffed, transdermal patch, transmucosal absorption

Substance Abuse

Heroin

Controlled Substances Act Schedule I (see pg. 382)
Trade or other Names: Black Tar, Chiva Negra, Diamorphine,
Diacetlymorphine, Horse, Smack
Medical Uses: ....None in U.S., Analgesic, Antitussive
Dependence: ....Physical: High
Psychological: High
Tolerance: Yes
Duration: ....3-6 hours
Usual Method:........Injected, smoked, sniffed

Hydrocodone

Controlled Substances Act Schedules II, III, IV (see pg. 382)
Trade or Other Names: Hycodan, Hycomine, Lorcet, Lortab,
Lortab ASA, Tussionex, Vicodin, Vicoprofen
Medical Uses: ....Analgesic, Antitussive
Dependence: ....Physical: High
Psychological: High
Tolerance: Yes
Duration: ....3-6 Hours
Usual Method:........Oral

Hydromorphone

Controlled Substances Act Schedule II (see pg. 382)
Trade or Other Names: Dilaudid, "Hospital Heroin", Palladone
Medical Uses: ....Analgesic
Dependence: ....Physical: High
Psychological: High
Tolerance: Yes
Duration: ....3-6 hours
Usual Method:........Injected, oral

Methadone, LAAM, and Buprenorphine (Narcotics Treatment Drugs)

Controlled Substances Act Schedule II, III (see pg. 382)
Trade or Other Names: Buprenex, Dolophine, Methadose,
Levo-alpha-acetylmethadol, Levomethadyl
acetate, ORLMM, Suboxone, Subutex
Medical Uses: ....Analgesic, treatment of dependence
Dependence: ....Physical: High
Psychological: High
Tolerance: Yes
Duration: ....12-24 hrs (Methadone); 48-72 hrs (LAAM)
Usual Methods:......Injected, oral

Morphine

Controlled Substances Act Schedule II (see pg. 382)
Trade or Other Names: Dreamer, Duramorph, Emsel, First line,
God's drug, Hows, Kadian, M.S., Miss

Emma, Mister Blue, Morf, Morpho,
MS-Contin, MSIR, Oramorph SR, RMS,
Roxanol, Sweet Morpheus, Unkie
Medical Uses: ....Analgesic
Dependence: ....Physical: High
Psychological: High
Tolerance: Yes
Duration: ....3-12 hours
Usual Method:........Injected, oral, smoked

Opium

Controlled Substances Act Schedule II (see pg. 382)
Trade or Other Names: Hop, Laudanum, Opiates, Paregoric,
Tar
Medical Uses: ....Analgesic, antidiarrheal
Dependence: ....Physical: High-low
Psychological: High-low
Tolerance: Yes
Duration: ....3-6 hours
Usual Method:........Oral, smoked

Oxycodone

Controlled Substances Act Schedule II (see pg. 382)
Trade or Other Names: Encodet, OxyContin, OxyIR, Percocet,
Percodan, Roxicet, Roxicodone, Tylox
Medical Uses: ....Analgesic
Dependence: ....Physical: High
Psychological: High
Tolerance: Yes
Duration: ....3-12 hours
Usual Method:........Injected, oral, sniffed

Other Narcotics

Controlled Substances Act Schedules II, III, IV, V (see pg. 382)
Trade or Other Names: Buprenex, Buprenorphine, Butorphanol,
Darvon, Demerol, Dextropropoxyphene,
Fentanyl, Mepergan, Meperdine,
Methadone, Paregoric, Pentazocine,
Percocet, Percodan, Pethidine, Stadol,
Stadol NS, Talwin, Talwin NX, Thebaine,
Torbugesic, Torbutrol, Tylox
Medical Uses: ....Analgesic, antidiarrheal, antitussive,
pre-anesthesia
Dependence: ....Physical: High-low
Psychological: High-low
Tolerance: Yes
Duration: ....Variable
Usual Method:........Injected, oral, smoked, sniffed

Substance Abuse

Steroids (Anabolic)

Possible Effects:

Acne, aggressive behavior, anger, cardiovascular damage, cerebrovascular toxicity, edema, elevated blood pressure, gynecomastia in males (abnormal breast development), higher cholesterol levels, hostility, improve endurance, increase size and strength of muscles, liver damage, masculinizing effect in women (more body hair, deeper voice, smaller breasts, fewer menstrual cycles), manic episodes, premature balding, reduced sexual function, stunted growth, testicular atrophy, violent behavior, and virilization.

Effects of overdose:

Unknown

Withdrawal Symptoms:

Possible depression

Nandrolone (Decanoate, Phenpropionate)

Controlled Substances Act Schedule III (see pg. 382)
Trade or Other Names: Deca, Deca-Durabolin, Durabolin, Nortestosterone
Medical Uses: ....Anemia, Breast Cancer
Dependence: ....Physical: Unknown
Psychological: Unknown
Tolerance: Unknown
Duration: ....14-21 days
Usual Method:........Injected

Oxymetholone

Controlled Substances Act Schedule III (see pg. 382)
Trade or Other Names: Anadrol-50
Medical Uses: ....Anemia
Dependence: ....Physical: Unknown
Psychological: Unknown
Tolerance: Unknown
Duration: ....24 hours
Usual Method:........Oral

Testosterone (Cypionate, Enanthate)

Controlled Substances Act Schedule III (see pg. 382)
Trade or Other Names: Cypt, Delatestryl, Depo Testosterone, Sten, Sustanon
Medical Uses: ....Hypogonadism
Dependence: ....Physical: Unknown
Psychological: Unknown
Tolerance: Yes
Duration: ....14-28 days
Usual Method:........Injected

Substance Abuse

Stimulants

Possible Effects:
   Enhanced self esteem, euphoria, excitation, exhilaration, increased activity and alertness, increased pulse rate and blood pressure, improved mental and physical performance, insomnia, loss of appetite, prolonged wakefulness, and relieved malaise.

Effects of Overdose:
   Abdominal cramps, aggression, agitation, chest pain with palpitations, convulsions, dizziness, excessive sweating, flushed skin, hallucinations, headache, high fever, hostility, increased body temperature, panic, paranoia, respiratory failure, seizures, suicidal or homicidal tendencies, tremors, vomiting, and possible death.

Withdrawal Symptoms:
   Anxiety, apathy, depression, disorientation, extreme fatigue, irritability, and long periods of sleep.

Amphetamine, Dextroamphetamine, Methamphetamine

Controlled Substances Act Schedule II (see pg. 382)
Trade or Other Names: Adderall, Bennies, Benzedrine, Biphetamine, Crank, Cristal, Desoxyn, Dexedrine, Dextrostat, Ice, Krystal Meth, Methedrine, Obetrol, Speed
Medical Uses: ....Attention Deficit Hyperactivity Disorder (ADHD), Narcolepsy, weight control
Dependence: ....Physical: Possible
Psychological: High
Tolerance: Yes
Duration: ....2-4 hours
Usual Method:........Injected, oral, smoked

Cocaine

Controlled Substances Act Schedule II (see pg. 382)
Trade or Other Names: Blanca, coca, coke, crack, flake, nieve, perico, snow, soda
Medical Uses: ....Local Anesthetic
Dependence: ....Physical: Possible
Psychological: High
Tolerance: Yes
Duration: ....1-2 hours
Usual Method:........Injected, smoked, sniffed

Khat

Controlled Substances Act Schedules I, IV (see pg. 382)
Trade or Other Names: contains cathine and cathinone
Medical Uses: ....Reduces appetite and fatigue (commonly used in East Africa and Arabian Peninsula)

Dependence: ....Physical: Unknown
                   Psychological: Unknown
                   Tolerance: Unknown
Duration: ....Unknown
Usual Method:........Oral

Methcathinone

Controlled Substances Act Schedule I (see pg. 382)
Trade or Other Names: Cat
Medical Uses: Unknown
Dependence: ....Physical: Possible
                   Psychological: High
                   Tolerance: Yes
Duration: ....2-4 hours
Usual Method:........Injected, oral, smoked

Methylphenidate

Controlled Substances Act Schedule II (see pg. 382)
Trade or Other Names: Concerta, Focalin, Ritalin, Metadate,
                   Methylin, West Coast
Medical Uses: ....Attention Deficit Hyperactivity Disorder
                   (ADHD), narcolepsy
Dependence: ....Physical: Possible
                   Psychological: High
                   Tolerance: Yes
Duration: ....2-4 hours
Usual Method:........Injected, oral, smoked, sniffed

Other Stimulants

Controlled Substances Act Schedules III, IV (see pg. 382)
Trade or Other Names: Adipex P, benzphetamine, Bontril,
                   Captagon, Didrex, Diethylproprion, Fastin,
                   Ionamin, Mazanor, Mazindol, Melfiat,
                   Phendimetrazine, Phentermine, Plegine,
                   Prelu-27, Preludin, Provigil, Sanorex,
                   Tenuate, Tepanil
Medical Uses: ....Vasoconstriction, weight control
Dependence: ....Physical: Possible
                   Psychological: Moderate-High
                   Tolerance: Yes
Duration: ....2-4 hours
Usual Method:........Injected, oral

Source: Drugs of Abuse, U.S. Department of Justice, 2005 Edition

Substance Abuse

Drug Scheduling

All substances that require some level of regulation under existing federal law is placed into one of five schedules. Its placement is determined by its medical use, potential for abuse, and safety or dependence liability.

Schedule I Drug & Substance Characteristics

- Has a high potential for abuse.
- Has no current acceptable medical treatment use in the US.
- Lack of accepted safety under medical supervision.
- Examples: heroin, lysergic acid diethylamide (LSD), marijuana, and methaqualone.

Schedule II Drug & Substance Characteristics

- Has a high potential for abuse.
- Has current acceptable medical treatment use in the US with severe restrictions.
- Abuse may lead to severe physical or psychological dependence.
- Examples: morphine, phencyclidine (PCP), cocaine, methadone, and methamphetamine.

Schedule III Drug & Substance Characteristics

- Has less potential for abuse than substances in schedule I and II.
- Has current acceptable medical treatment use in the US.
- Abuse may have moderate or low physical dependence or high psychological dependence.
- Examples: Anabolic steroids, some barbiturates, codeine and hydrocodone with aspirin or Tylenol®.

Schedule IV Drug & Substance Characteristics

- Has low potential for abuse compared to substances in schedule III.
- Has current acceptable medical treatment use in the US.
- Abuse may have limited physical dependence or psychological dependence compared to substances in schedule III.
- Examples: Darvon®, Talwin®, Equanil®, Valium®, and Xanax®.

Schedule V Drug & Substance Characteristics
- Has low potential for abuse relative to substances in schedule IV.
- Has current acceptable medical treatment use in the US.
- Abuse may have limited physical dependence or psychological dependence compared to substances in schedule IV.
- Example: cough medicines with codeine.

Source: Drugs of Abuse, U.S. Department of Justice, 2005 Edition

Schedule I Substances

Substance	DEA Number	Other Names
1-(1-Phenylcyclohexy) pyrrolidine*	7458	PCPy; PHP; rolicyclidine
1-(2-Phenylethyl)-4-phenyl-4-acetoxypiperidine	9663	PEPAP; synthetic heroin
1-[1-(2-Thienyl) cyclohexyl]piperidine*	7470	TCP; tenocyclidine
1-[1-(2-Thienyl) cyclohexyl]pyrrolidine*	7473	TCPy
1-Menthyl-4-phenyl-4-propionoxypiperidine	9661	MPPP; synthetic heroin
2,5-Dimethoxy-4-ethylamphetamine*	7399	DOET
2,5-Dimethoxyamphetamine*	7396	DMA; 2,5-DMA
3,4,5-Trimethoxyamphetamine*	7390	TMA
3,4-Methylenedioxyamphetamine*	7400	MDA; Love Drug
3,4-Methylenedioxy-methamphetamine*	7405	MDMA; Ectasy; XTC
3,4-Methylenedioxy—ethylamphetamine*	7404	N-ethyl MDA; MDE; MDMA
3-Methylfentanyl	9813	China White; fentanyl
3-Methylthiofentanyl	9833	Chine White; fentanyl
4-Bromo-2,5-dimethoxyamphetamine*	7391	DOB; 4-bromo-DMA
4-Bromo-2,5-dimethoxyphenethylamine*	7392	Nexus; 2-CB; has been sold as Ecstacy (MDMA)
4-Methoxyamphetamine*	7411	PMA
4-Methyl-2,5-dimethoxyamphetamine*	7395	DOM; STP
4-Methylaminorex (cis isomer)*	1590	U4Euh; McN-422
5-Methoxy-3,4-methylenedioxyamphetamine*	7401	MMDA
Acetorphine	9319	
Acetyl-alpha-methylfentanyl	9815	
Acetyldihydrocodeine	9051	Acetylcodone

Substance Abuse

Substance	DEA Number	Other Names
Acetylmethadol	9601	Methadyl acetate
Allylprodine	9602	
Alphacetylmethadolexcept levoalphacetylmethadol	9603	
Alpha-ethyltryptamine*	7249	ET; Trip
Alphameprodine	9604	
Alphamethadol	9605	
Alpha-Methylfentanyl	9814	China White; fentanyl
Alpha-Methylthiofentanyl	9832	Chine White; fentanyl
Aminorex*	1585	sold as methamphetamine
Benzethidine	9606	
Benzylmorphine	9052	
Betacetylmethadol	9607	
Beta-Hydroxy-3-methylfentanyl	9831	China White; fentanyl
Beta-Hydroxyfentanyl	9830	China White; fentanyl
Betameprodine	9608	
Betamethadol	9609	
Betaprodine	9611	
Bufotenine*	7433	Mappine; N,N-dimethylserotonin
Cathinone*	1235	Constituent of "Khat" plant
Clonitazene	9612	
Codeine methylbromide	9070	
Codeine-N-oxide	9053	
Cyprenorphine	9054	
Desomorphine	9055	
Dextromoramide	9613	Palfium; Jetrium; Narcolo
Diampromide	9615	
Diethylthiambutene	9616	
Diethyltryptamine*	7434	DET
Difenoxin	9168	Lyspafen
Dihydromorphine	9145	
Dimenoxadol	9617	
Dimepheptanol	9618	
Dimethylthiambutene	9619	
Dimethyltryptamine*	7435	DMT
Dioxaphetyl butyrate	9621	
Dipipanone	9622	Dipipan; phenylpiperone HCl; Diconal; Wellconal
Drotebanol	9335	Metebanyl; oxymethebanol
Ethylmethylthiambutene	9623	
Etonitazene	9624	
Etorphine (except HCl)	9056	
Etoxeridine	9625	

Substance	DEA Number	Other Names
Fenethylline*	1503	Captagon; amfetyline; ethyltheophyline amphetamine
Furethidine	9626	
Gama Hydroxybutyric Acid (GHB)*	2010	GHB; gama hydroxybutyrate sodium oxybate
Heroin	9200	Diacetylmorphine; diamorphine
Hydromorphinol	9301	
Hydroxypethidine	9627	
Ibogaine*	7260	Constituent of "Tabernanthe iboga" plant
Ketobemidone	9628	Cliradon
Levomoramide	9629	
Levophenacylmorphan	9631	
Lysergic acid diethylamide*	7315	LSD; lysergide
Marijuana*	7360	Cannabis; Marijuana
Mecloqualone*	2572	Nubarene
Mescaline*	7381	Constituent of "Peyote" cacti
Methaqualone*	2565	Quaalude; Parest; Opitimil; Somnafac; Mandrax
Methcathinone*	1237	N-Methylcathinone; "Cat"
Methyldesorphine	9302	
Methyldihydromorphine	9304	
Morpheridine	9632	
Morphine methylbromide	9305	
Morphine methylsulfonate	9306	
Morphine-N-oxide	9307	
Myrophine	9308	
N,N-Dimethylamphetamine*	1480	
N-Ethyl-1-phenylcyclohexylamine*	7455	PCE
N-Ethyl-3-piperidyl benzilate*	7482	JB 323
N-Ethylamphetamine*	1475	NEA
N-Hydroxy-3,4-methylenedioxyamphetamine*	7402	N-hydroxy MDA
Nicocodeine	9309	
Nicomorphine	9312	Vilan
N-Methyl-3-piperidyl benzilate*	7484	JB 336
Noracymethadol	9633	
Norlevorphanol	9634	
Normethadone	9635	Phenyldimazone
Normorphine	9313	
Norpipanone	9636	
Para-Flurorfentanyl	9812	China White; fentanyl
Parahexyl*	7374	Synhexyl
Peyote*	7415	Cactus containing mescaline

Substance Abuse

Substance	DEA Number	Other Names
Phenadoxone	9637	
Phenampromide	9638	
Phenomorphan	9647	
Phenoperidine	9641	Operidine; Lealgin
Pholcodine	9314	Copholco; Adaphol; Codisol; Lantuss; Pholcolin
Piritramide	9642	Piridolan
Proheptazine	9643	
Properidine	9644	
Propiram	9649	Algeril
Psilocyn*	7437	Constituent of "Magic Mushrooms"
Psilocyn*	7438	Psilocin; Constituent of "Magic mushrooms"
Racemoramide	9645	
Tetrahydrocannabinols*	7370	THC; Delta-8 THC; Delta-9 THC; others
Thebacon	9315	Acetylhydrocodone; Acedicon; Thebacetyl
Thiofentanyl	9835	China White; fentanyl
Tilidine	9750	Tilidate; Valoron; Kitadol; Lak; Tilsa
Trimeperidine	9646	Promedolum

Schedule II Substances

Substance	DEA Number	Other Names
1-Phenylcyclohexylamine*	7460	Precursor of PCP
1-Piperidinocyclohexanecarbonitrile*	8603	PCC; Precursor of PCP
Alfentanil	9737	Alfenta
Alphaprodine	9010	Nisentil
Amobarbital*	2125	Amytal; Tuinal
Amphetamine*	1100	Dexedrine; Biphetamine
Anileridine	9020	Leritine
Benzoylecgonine	9180	Cocaine metabolite
Bezitramide	9800	Burgodin
Carfentanil	9743	Wildnil
Coca Leaves	9040	
Cocaine	9041	Methyl benzoylecgonine; Crack
Codeine	9050	Morphine methyl ester; Methyl morphine
Dextropropoxyphene, bulk (non-dosage forms)	9273	Propoxyene
Dihydrocodeine	9120	Didrate; Parzone
Diphenoxylate	9170	

Substance	DEA Number	Other Names
Diprenorphine	9058	M50-50
Ecgonine	9180	Cocaine precursor, in Coca leaves
Ethylmorphine	9190	Dionin
Etorphine HCl	9059	M99
Fentanyl	9801	Innovar; Sublimaze; Duragesic
Glutethimide*	2550	Doriden; Dorimide
Hydrocodone	9193	Dihydrocodeinone
Hydromorphone	9150	Dilaudid; Dihydromorphinone
Isomethadone	9226	Isoamidone
Levo-alphacetylmethadol	9648	LAAM; long acting methadone; levomethadyl acetate
Levomethorphan	9210	
Levorphanol	9220	Levo-Dromoran
Meperidine	9230	Demerol; Mepergan; pethidine
Meperidine intermediate-A	9232	Meperidine precursor
Meperidine intermediate-B	9233	Meperidine precursor
Meperidine intermediate-C	9234	Meperidine precursor
Metazocine	9240	
Methadone	9250	Dolophine; Methadose; Amidone
Methadone intermediate	9254	Methadone precursor
Methamphetamine*	1105	Desoxyn; Crank; Speed; D-desoxyephedrine; ICE
Methylphenidate*	1724	Ritalin
Metopon	9260	
Moramide-intermediate	9802	
Morphine	9300	MS Contin; Roxanol; Duramorph; RMS; MSIR
Nabilone*	7379	Cesamet
Opium extracts	9610	
Opium fluid extract	9620	
Opium poppy	9650	Papaver somniferum
Opium tincture	9630	Laudanum
Opium, granulated	9640	Granulated Opium
Opium, powdered	9639	Powdered Opium
Opium, raw	9600	Raw Opium; Gum Opium
Oxycodone	9143	OxyContin; Percocet; Tylox; Roxicodone; Roxicet
Oxymorphone	9652	Numorphan
Pentobarbital*	2270	Nembutal
Phenazocine	9715	Narphen; Prinadol
Phencyclidine*	7471	PCP; Sernylan
Phenmetrazine*	1631	Preludin

Substance Abuse

Substance	DEA Number	Other Names
Phenylacetone*	8501	P2P; phenyl-2-propanone; benzyl methyl ketone
Piminodine	9730	
Poppy Straw	9650	Opium poppy capsules; poppy heads
Poppy Straw Concentrate	9670	Concentrate of Poppy Straw; CPS
Racemethorphan	9732	
Racemorphan	9733	Dromoran
Remifentanil	9739	Ultiva
Secobarbital*	2315	Seconal; Tuinal
Sufentanil	9740	Sufenta
Thebaine	9333	Precursor of many narcotics

Schedule III Substances

Amobarbital & noncontrolled active ingredient*	2126	Amobarbital/ephedrine capsules
Amobarbital suppository dosage form*	2126	
Anabolic steroids*	4000	"Body Building" drugs
Aprobarbital*	2100	Alurate
Barbituric acid derivative*	2100	Barbiturates not spec. listed
Benzphetamine*	1228	Didrex; Inapetyl
Boldenone*	4000	Equipoise; Parenabol; Vebonol; dehydrotestosterone
Buprenorphine	9064	Buprenex; Temgesic
Butabarbital*	2100	Butisol; Butibel
Butalbital*	2100	Fiorinal; Butalbital w/ asprin
Chlorhexadol*	2510	Mechloral; Mecoral; Medodorm; Chloralodol
Chlorotestosterone (same as Clostebol)*	4000	if 4-chlorotestosterone then clostebol
Chlorphentermine*	1645	Pre-Sate; Lucofen; Apsedon; Desopimon
Clortermine*	1647	Voranil
Clostebol*	4000	Alfa-Trofodermin; Clostene; 4-chlorotestosterone
Codeine & isoquinoline alkaloid 90 mg/du	9803	Codeine with papaverine or noscapine
Codeine combination product 90 mg/du	9804	Empirin; Fiorinal; Tylenol; ASA or APAP with Codeine
Dehydrochlormethyltestosterone*	4000	Oral-Turinabol
Dihydrocodeine combination product 90 mg/du	9807	Synalgos-DC; Compal

Substance	DEA Number	Other Names
Dihydrotestosterone*	4000	see stanolone
Dronabinol in sesame oil in soft gelatin capsule*	7369	Marinol; synthetic THC in sesane oil/soft gelatin
Drostanolone*	4000	Drolban; Masterid; Permastril
Ethylestrenol*	4000	Maxibolin; Orabolin; Durabolin-O; Duraboral
Ethylmorphine combination product 15 mg/du	9808	
Fluoxymesterone*	4000	Anadroid-F; Halotestin; Ora-Testryl
Formebolone*	4000	Esiclene; Hubernol
Hydrocodone & Isoquin- oline alkaloid 15 mg/du	9805	Dihydrocodeinone + papaverine or noscapine
Hydrocodone combination product 15 mg/du	9806	Tussionex; Tussend; Lortab; Vicodin;Hycodan;Anexsia++
Ketamine*	7285	Ketaset;Ketalar;Special K;K
Lysergic acid *	7300	LSD precursor
Lysergic acid amide*	7310	LSD precursor
Mesterolone*	4000	Proviron
Methandienone*	4000	(see Methandrostenolone)
Methandranone*	4000	alt. spelling of methandienone
Methandriol*	4000	Sinesex; Stenediol; Troformone
Methandrostenolone*	4000	Dianabol; Metabolina; Nerobol; Perbolin
Methenolone*	4000	Primobolan; Primobolan Depot; Primobolan S
Methyltestosterone*	4000	Android; Oreton; Testred; Virilon
Methyprylon*	2575	Noludar
Mibolerone*	4000	Cheque
Morphine combination product/50 mg/100 ml or gm	9810	
Nalorphine*	9400	Nalline
Nandrolone*	4000	Deca-Durabolin; Durabolin; Durabolin-50
Norethandrolone*	4000	Nilevar; Solevar
Opium combination product 25 mg/du	9809	Paregoric; other combination products
Oxandrolone*	4000	Anavar; Lonavar; Provitar; Vasorome
Oxymesterone*	4000	Anamidol; Balnimax; Oranabol; Oranabol 10
Oxymetholone*	4000	Anadrol-50; Adroyd; Anapolon; Anasteron; Pardroyd

Substance Abuse

Substance	DEA Number	Other Names
Pentobarbital & noncontrolled active ingred.*	2271	FP-3
Pentobarbital suppository dosage form*	2271	WANS
Phendimetrazine*	1615	Plegine; Prelu-2; Bontril; Melfiat; Statobex
Secobarbital & noncontrolled active ingredients*	2316	various
Secobarbital suppository dosage form*	2316	various
Stanolone*	4000	Anabolex; Andractim; Pesomax;dihydrotestosterone
Stanozolol*	4000	Winstrol; Winstrol-V
Stimulant compounds previously excepted*	1405	Mediatric
Sulfondiethylmethane*	2600	
Sulfonethylmethane*	2605	
Sulfonmethane*	2610	
Talbutal*	2100	Lotusate
Testolactone*	4000	Teslac
Testosterone*	4000	Android-T; Androlan; Depotest; Delatestryl
Thiamylal*	2100	Surital
Thiopental*	2100	Pentothal
Tiletamine & Zolazepam combination product	7295	Telazol
Trenbolone*	4000	Finaplix-S; Finajet; Parabolan
Vinbarbital*	2100	Delvinal; vinbarbitone

Schedule IV Substances

Substance	DEA Number	Other Names
Alprazolam*	2882	Xanax
Barbital*	2145	Veronal; Plexonal; barbitone
Bromazepam*	2748	Lexotan; Lexatin; Lexotanil
Butorphanol*	9720	Stadol; Stadol NS; Torbugesic; Torbutrol
Camazepam*	2749	Albego; Limpidon; Paxor
Cathine*	1230	Constituent of "Khat" plant
Chloral betaine*	2460	Beta Chlor
Chloral hydrate*	2465	Noctec
Chlordiazepoxide*	2744	Librium; Libritabs; Limbitrol; SK-Lygen
Clobazam*	2751	Urbadan; Urbanyl
Clonazepam*	2737	Klonopin; Clonopin
Clorazepate*	2768	Tranxene

Substance	DEA Number	Other Names
Clotiazepam*	2752	Trecalmo; Rize
Cloxazolam*	2753	Enadel; Sepazon; Tolestan
Delorazepam*	2754	
Dexfenfluramine*	1670	Redux
Dextropropoxyphene dosage forms	9278	Darvon; propoxyphene; Darvocet; Dolene; Propacet
Diazepam*	2765	Valium; Valrelease
Dichloralphenazone*	2467	Midrin; dichloralantipyrine
Diethylpropion*	1610	Tenuate; Tepanil
Difenoxin 1 mg/25 ug AtSO4/du	9167	Motofen
Estazolam*	2756	ProSom; Domnamid; Eurodin; Nuctalon
Etchlorvynol*	2540	Placidyl
Ethinamate*	2545	Valmid; Valamin
Ethyl loflazepate*	2758	
Fencamfamin*	1760	Reactivan
Fenfluramine*	1670	Pondimin; Ponderal
Fenproporex*	1575	Gacilin; Solvolip
Fludiazepam*	2759	
Flunitrazepam*	2763	Rohypnol; Narcozep; Darkene; Roipnol
Flurazepam*	2767	Dalmane
Halazepam*	2762	Paxipam
Haloxazolam*	2771	
Ketazolam*	2772	Anxon; Loftran; Solatran; Contamex
Loprazolam*	2773	
Lorazepam*	2885	Ativan
Lormetazepam*	2774	Noctamid
Mazindol*	1605	Sanorex; Mazanor
Mebutamate*	2800	Capla
Medazepam*	2836	Nobrium
Mefenorex*	1580	Anorexic; Amexate; Foracil; Pondinil
Meprobamate*	2820	Miltown; Equanil; Deprol; Equagesic; Meprospan
Methohexital*	2264	Brevital
Methylphenobarbita (mephobarbital)*	2250	Mebaral; mephobarbital
Midazolam*	2884	Versed
Modafinil*	1680	Provigil
Nimetazepam*	2837	Erimin
Nitrazepam*	2834	Mogadon
Nordiazepam*	2838	Nordazepam; Demadar; Madar
Oxazepam*	2835	Serax; Serenid-D

Substance Abuse

Substance	DEA Number	Other Names
Oxazolam*	2839	Serenal; Convertal
Paraldehyde*	2585	Paral
Pemoline*	1530	Cylert
Pentazocine*	9709	Talwin; Talwin NX; Talacen; Talwin Compound
Petrichloral*	2591	Pentaerythritol chloral; Periclor
Phenobarbital*	2285	Luminal; Donnatal; Bellergal-S
Phentermine*	1640	Ionamin; Fastin; Adipex-P; Obe-Nix; Zantryl
Pinazepam*	2883	Domar
Pipradrol*	1750	Detaril; Stimolag Fortis
Prazepam*	2764	Centrax
Quazepam*	2881	Doral; Dormalin
Sibutramine*	1675	Meridia
SPA*	1635	1-dimethylamino-1; 2-diphenylethane; Lefetamine
Temazepam*	2925	Restoril
Tetrazepam*	2886	
Triazolam*	2887	Halcion
Zaleplon*	2781	Sonata
Zolpidem*	2783	Ambien; Stilnoct; Ivadal

Schedule V Substances

Codeine preparations - 200 mg/100 ml or 100 gm		Cosanyl; Robitussin A-C; Cheracol Cerose; Pediacof
Difenoxin preparations - 0.5 mg/25 ug AtSO4/du		Motofen
Dihydrocodeine preparations - 10 mg/100 ml or 100 gm		Cophene-S; various others
Diphenoxylate preparations - 2.5 mg/25 ug AtSO4		Lomotil; Logen
Ethylmorphine preparations -100 mg/100 ml or 100 gm		
Opium preparations - 100 mg/100 ml or gm		Parepectolin; Kapectolin PG; Kaolin Pectin P.G.
Pyrovalerone*	1485	Centroton; Thymergix

*Indicates that the substance is a non-narcotic.

Source: U.S Department of Justice, U.S. Drug Enforcement Administration
http://www.usdoj.gov/dea/pubs/scheduling.html

Toxicity & Flammability of Selected Chemicals Used in the Manufacture of Illicit Drugs

Chemical	Acute Toxicity	Flammability	Other Properties
Acetic anhydride	Moderate	Moderate	Irritant, corrosive
Benzene	Moderate/ high	High	Carcinogen, blood disorders
Chloroform	Moderate	Low	Incoordination, probably a carcinogen
Ethanol	Low	High	Incoordination
Hydriodic acid	High	Low	Corrosive, irritant
Hydrochloric acid	High	Low	Corrosive, irritant
Hydrogen cyanide	Extreme	Low	Rapid asphyxiation
Lead acetate	High	Low	Blood disorders
Lithium aluminum hydride	Moderate	High	Water reactive, explosive
Mercury chloride	High	Low	Corrosive, irritant
Methylamine	High	Extreme	Corrosive
Petroleum ether	Low	Extreme	Incoordination
Phenylacetic acid	Low	Low	Irritant
Phosphine	High	Extreme	Rapid asphyxiation
Red phosphorous	Low	Low	Reactive, explosive
Sodium	High	Low	Water reactive, explosive
Thioxyl chloride	High	Low	Water reactive, explosive

Source: Sevick, James R., *Precursor and Essential Chemicals in Illicit Drug Production*, US Dept. Of Justice, October, 1993.

Substance Abuse

Chemicals used in the Manufacture of Illicit Drugs

Chemical	Controlled Substance Produced	Thresholds (in Kilograms) Domestic	Imports & Exports
List I			
N-Acetylanthranilic acid[2]	Methaqulone	40	40
Anthranilic acid[2]	Methaqulone	30	30
Benzaldehyde	Amphetamine; Phenyl-2-propanone	4	4
Benzyl cyanide	Phenyl-2-propanone	1	1
Ephedrine[3,7]	Methamphetamine; Methcathinone	0	0
Ergonovine[1]	LSD	0.010	0.010
Ergotamine[1]	LSD	0.020	0.020
Ethylamine[1]	Ethylamphetamine; MDE	1	1
Gamma-Butyrolactone (GBL)	GHB	0	0
Hydriodic acid	Methamphetamine	1.7	1.7
Hypophosphorous acid[1]	Amphetamine; Methamphetamine	0	0
Isosafrole	MDA; MDE; MDMA	4	4
Methylamine[1]	MDMA; Methamphetamine	1	1
3,4-Methylenedioxyphenyl-2-propanone	MDA; MDE; MDMA	4	4
N-Methylephedrine[3]	N,N-Dimethylamphetamine	1	1
N-Methylpseudoephedrine[3]	N,N-Dimethylamphetamine	1	1
Nitroethane	Amphetamine; MDA; Phenyl-2-propanone	2.5	2.5

Chemical	Controlled Substance Produced	Thresholds (in Kilograms)	
		Domestic	Imports & Exports
Norpseudoephedrine[3]	Amphetamine; 4-Methylaminorex	2.5	2.5
Phenylacetic acid[2]	Phenyl-2-propanone	1	1
Phenylpropanolamine[3&7]	Amphetamine; 4-Methylaminorex	2.5	2.5
Phosphorus (red)	Amphetamine; Methamphetamine	0	0
Phosphorus (white or yellow)	Amphetamine; Methamphetamine	0	0
Piperidine[1]	Phencyclidine (PCP)	0.500	0.500
Piperonal	MDA; MDE; MDMA	4	4
Propionic anhydride	Fentanyl & analogues	0.001	0.001
Pseudoephedrine[3&7]	Methamphetamine; Methcathinone	1	1
Safrole	MDA; MDE; MDMA	4	4
List II			
Acetic anhydride	Heroin; Methaqulone; Phenyl-2-propanone	1,023	1,023
Acetone	Cocaine; Heroin; LSD; MDA; MDE; MDMA; Methamphetamine	150	1,500
Benzyl Chloride	Methamphetamine	1	4
Ethyl ether	Amphetamine; Cocaine; Fentanyl & analogs; Heroin; LSD; MDA; MDE; MDMA; Methamphetamine; Methaqulone; Methcathinone Phencyclidine (PCP); Phenyl-2-propanone	135.8	1,364

Substance Abuse

Chemicals used in the Manufacture of Illicit Drugs (cont.)

Chemical	Controlled Substance Produced	Thresholds (in Kilograms) Domestic	Imports & Exports
Hydrochloric acid[5&6]	Amphetamine; Cocaine; N,N-Dimethylamphetamine; Ethylamphetamine; Fentanyl & analogues; Heroin; LSD; MDA; MDE; MDMA; Methamphetamine; Methaqulone; Methcathinone; Phencyclidine (PCP)	N/C	222.3
Hydrogen chloride gas[5&6]	Amphetamine; Cocaine; N,N-Dimethylamphetamine; Ethylamphetamine; Fentanyl & analogues; Heroin; LSD; MDA; MDE; MDMA; Methamphetamine; Methaqulone; Methcathinone; Phencyclidine (PCP)	0	27
Iodine	Amphetamine; Methamphetamine	0.4	N/C
Methyl ethyl ketone (2-Butanone)	Cocaine; Heroin; MDA; MDE; Methamphetamine	145	1,455
Methyl isobutyl ketone[4]	Cocaine; Heroin; MDA; MDE; Methamphetamine	N/C	1,523
Potassium permanganate	Cocaine	55	500
Sulfuric acid[5&6]	Amphetamine; Cocaine; MDA; MDE; MDMA; Methamphetamine; Phenyl-2-propanone	N/C	347

Chemical	Controlled Substance Produced	Thresholds (in Kilograms)	
		Domestic	Imports & Exports
Toluene	Cocaine; Fentanyl & analogues; Methaqulone; Phencyclidine (PCP); Phenyl-2-propanone	159	1,591

Notes:

1 = and its salts

2 = and its salts and esters

3 = and its salts, optical isomers, and salts of optical isomers

4 = Exports only, to all Western Hemisphere except Canada

5 = Exports to all South American countries & Panama - Domestic for HCl gas

6 = Threshold for HCl acid and sulfuric acid is 50 gallons, the equivalent weight in kilograms is shown

7 = For pseudoephedrine, phenylprropanolamine and combination ephedrine drug products, see 21 USC §§ 802(39)(A)(iv), 802(45) and Historical and Statutory Notes following 21 USC § 802 on Public Law 104-237 § 401(f).

N/C: Not Controlled

All manufacturers, distributors, importers, and exporters are required to register List I chemicals (or precursor chemicals) with the DEA.

Bulk manufacturers of List I (or precursor chemicals) and List II chemicals (or essential chemicals) are required to report the total amount of chemicals produced throughout the year.

Source: <u>Drugs of Abuse</u>, U.S. Department Of Justice, 2005 Edition

Substance Abuse

Street Names & Terms for Drugs

Street Name	Definition	Drug Type
007s	MDMA	hallucinogen
100s	LSD	hallucinogen
151	Crack cocaine	stimulants
2-for-1 sale	A marketing scheme to promote & sell crack	
24-7	Crack cocaine	stimulants
25s	LSD	hallucinogen
2CB	Nexus	hallucinogen
3750	Marijuana cigarette with crack	cann.; stim.
40	OxyContin pill	narcotics
40-bar	OxyContin pill	narcotics
420	Marijuana	cannabis
45 minute psychosis	Dimethyltryptamine	hallucinogen
69s	MDMA	hallucinogen
714s	Methaqualone	depressants
80	OxyContin pill	narcotics
A	LSD; amphetamine	halluc.; stim.
A-bomb	Marijuana cigarette with heroin or opium	cann.; narc.
A-boot	Under the influence of drugs	
Abandominiums	Abandoned row of houses where drugs are used	
Abe	$5 worth of drugs	
Abe's cab	$5 bill	
Abolic	Veterinary steroids	steroids
AC/DC	Codeine cough syrup	narcotics
Acapulco gold	Marijuana (from SW Mexico)	cannabis
Acapulco red	Marijuana	cannabis
Ace	Marijuana cigarette; PCP	cann.; halluc.
Acid	LSD	hallucinogen
Acid cube	Sugar cube containing LSD	hallucinogen
Acid freak	Heavy user of LSD	
Acid head	User of LSD	
Acido	Hallucinogens; LSD	hallucinogen
Ad	PCP; drug addict	hallucinogen
Adam	MDMA	hallucinogen
Aeon flux	LSD	hallucinogen
Afgani indica	Marijuana	cannabis
African	Marijuana	cannabis
African black	Marijuana	cannabis
African bush	Marijuana	cannabis
African woodbine	Marijuana cigarette	cannabis
Agonies	Withdrawal symptoms	
Ah-pen-yen	Opium	narcotics
Aimes	Amyl nitrite	inhalants
Aimies	Amphetamine; amyl nitrite	stim.; inhal.
AIP	Heroin (from Afghanistan, Iran, Pakistan)	narcotics
Air blast	Inhalants	inhalants

Street Name	Definition	Drug Type
Airhead	User of marijuana	
Airplane	Marijuana	cannabis
Al Capone	Heroin	narcotics
Alice B. Toklas	Marijuana brownie	cannabis
All lit up	Under the influence of drugs	
All star	User of multiple drugs	
All-American drug	Cocaine	stimulants
Alpha-ET	Alpha-ethyltryptamine	hallucinogen
Ames	Amyl nitrite	inhalants
Amidone	Methadone	hallucinogen
Amoeba	PCP	hallucinogen
Amp	Amphetamine; marijuana dipped in embalming fluid or formaldehyde, or laced with PCP	stim.; halluc.; cannabis
Amp head	User of LSD	
Amp joint	Marijuana cigarette laced with narcotics	cann.; narc.
Amped	High on amphetamines	
Amped-out	Fatigue after using amphetamines	
Amping	Accelerated heartbeat	
AMT	Dimethyltryptamine	hallucinogen
Amys	Amyl nitrite	inhalants
Anadrol	Oral steroids	steroids
Anatrofin	Injectable steroids	steroids
Anavar	Oral steroids	steroids
Angel	PCP	hallucinogen
Angel Dust	PCP	hallucinogen
Angel hair	PCP	hallucinogen
Angel mist	PCP	hallucinogen
Angel poke	PCP	hallucinogen
Angie	Cocaine	stimulants
Angola	Marijuana	cannabis
Animal	LSD	hallucinogen
Animal trank	PCP	hallucinogen
Animal tranq	PCP	hallucinogen
Animal tranquilizer	PCP	hallucinogen
Antifreeze	Heroin	narcotics
Apple jacks	Crack cocaine	stimulants
Are you anywhere?	Do you use marijuana?	
Aries	Heroin	narcotics
Arnolds	Steroids	steroids
Aroma of men	Isobutyl nitrite	inhalants
Around the turn	Went through a withdrawal period	
Artillery	Equipment for injecting drugs	
Ashes	Marijuana	cannabis
Aspirin	Powder cocaine	stimulants
Assassin of Youth	Marijuana	cannabis
Astro turf	Marijuana	cannabis
Atom bomb	Marijuana mixed with heroin	cann.; narc.

Street Name	Definition	Drug Type
Atshitshi	Marijuana	cannabis
Aunt Hazel	Heroin	narcotics
Aunt Mary	Marijuana	cannabis
Aunt Nora	Cocaine	stimulants
Aunti	Opium	narcotics
Aunti Emma	Opium	narcotics
Aurora borealis	PCP	hallucinogen
Author	Doctor who writes illegal prescriptions	
B	Amount of marijuana to fill a matchbox	cannabis
B-40	Cigar laced with marijuana and dipped in malt liquor	cannabis
B-bombs	Amphetamines; MDMA	stim.; halluc.
B.J.'s	Crack Cocaine	stimulants
Babe	Drug used for detoxification	
Baby	Marijuana	cannabis
Baby bhang	Marijuana	cannabis
Baby habit	Occasional use of drugs	
Baby T	Crack Cocaine	stimulants
Babysit	Guide someone through first drug experience	
Babysitter	Marijuana	cannabis
Back breakers	LSD and strychnine	hallucinogen
Back dex	Amphetamine	stimulants
Back door	Residue left in a pipe	
Back jack	Injecting opium (can also be other drugs)	narcotic
Back to back	Smoking crack after injecting heroin or heroin used after smoking crack	stim.; narc. narc.; stim.
Backtrack	Allow blood to flow back into a needle during injection	
Backup	To prepare a vein for injection	
Backwards	Depressants	depressants
Bad	Crack cocaine	stimulants
Bad bundle	Inferior quality heroin; damaged heroin	narcotic
Bad go	Bad reaction to a drug	
Bad seed	Marijuana; Heroin; peyote	cann.; narc.; halluc.
Badrock	Crack cocaine	stimulants
Bag	Container for drugs (usually marijuana or heroin); a person's favorite drug	
Bag bride	Crack-smoking prostitute	stimulants
Bagging	Using inhalants	inhalants
Baker	Person who smokes marijuana	cannabis
Bale	Marijuana	cannabis
Ball	Crack cocaine; Mexican Black Tar heroin	stim.; narc.
Balling	Vaginally implanted cocaine	stimulants
Balloon	Heroin supplier; a penny balloon that contains narcotics	
Ballot	Heroin	narcotics
Bam	Amphetamine; depressants	stim.; deprs.
Bamba	Marijuana	cannabis
Bambalacha	Marijuana	cannabis

Street Name	Definition	Drug Type
Bambita	Desoxyn or amphetamine derivative	stimulants
Bambs	Depressants	depressants
Bammies	Marijuana, poor quality	cannabis
Bammy	Marijuana	cannabis
Banana split	Combination of 2C-B (Nexus) with other illicit substances, particularly LSD	hallucinogen
Banano	Marijuana or tobacco cigarettes laced with cocaine	cann.; stim.
Bang	Inhalants; to inject a drug	inhalants
Banging	Under the influence of drugs	
Bank bandit pills	Depressants	depressants
Bar	Marijuana	cannabis
Barb	Depressants	depressants
Barbies	Depressants	depressants
Barbs	Cocaine	stimulants
Barr	Codeine cough syrup	narcotics
Barrels	LSD	hallucinogen
Bart Simpson	Heroin	narcotics
Basa	Crack cocaine	stimulants
Base	Cocaine; crack	stimulants
Base crazier	Searching on hands and knees for cocaine/crack	
Base head	A person who bases	
Baseball	Crack cocaine	stimulants
Based out	To have lost control over basing	
Bash	Marijuana	cannabis
Basing	Crack cocaine	stimulants
Basuco	Cocaine; coca paste residue sprinkled on tobacco or marijuana cigarette	stimulants; stim.; cann.
Bathtub crank	Poor quality methamphetamine; methamphetamine produced in bathtubs	stimulants
Bathtub speed	Methcathinone	stimulants
Batman	Cocaine; heroin	stim.; narc.
Batmans	MDMA	hallucinogen
Batt	IV needle; hypodermic needle	
Batted out	Apprehended by law	
Battery acid	LSD	hallucinogen
Batu	Smokable methamphetamine	stimulants
Bazooka	Cocaine; crack; crack and tobacco combined in a joint; coca paste and marijuana	stim.; cann.
Bazulco	Cocaine	stimulants
BC bud	Marijuana from British Columbia or Canada; high-grade marijuana from Canada	cannabis
BDMPEA	Nexus	hallucinogen
Beam	Cocaine	stimulants
Beam me up Scottie (Scotty)	Crack dipped in PCP	stimulants; hallucinogen
Beamer	Crack smoker	stimulants
Beamers	Crack cocaine	stimulants

Street Name	Definition	Drug Type
Bean	A capsule containing drugs; MDMA	hallucinogen
Beannies	Methamphetamine	stimulants
Beans	Crack cocaine; mescaline; amphetamine; depressants	stim.;halluc.; stim.; deprs.
Beast	Heroin; LSD	narc.; halluc.
Beat	Crack cocaine	stimulants
Beat artist	Person selling bogus drugs	
Beat vials	Vials containing sham crack to cheat buyers	
Beautiful boulders	Crack cocaine	stimulants
Beavis & Butthead	LSD	hallucinogen
Bebe	Crack cocaine	stimulants
Bed bugs/ Bedbugs	Fellow addicts	
Beedies	Cigarettes from India (they resemble marijuana joints; vehicle for other drugs)	
Beemers	Crack cocaine	stimulants
Behind the scale	To weigh and sell cocaine	
Beiging	Chemicals altering cocaine to make it look like a higher purity; or to make it look brown	
Belladonna	PCP	hallucinogen
Belt	Effects of drugs	
Belted	Under the influence of drugs	
Belushi	Combination of cocaine and heroin	stim.; narc.
Belyando spruce	Marijuana	cannabis
Bender	Drug party	
Bennie	Amphetamine	stimulants
Bens	Amphetamine; MDMA	stim.; halluc.
Benz	Amphetamine	stimulants
Benzedrine	Amphetamine; MDMA	stim.; halluc.
Benzidrine	Amphetamine	stimulants
Bermuda triangles	MDMA	hallucinogen
Bernice	Cocaine	stimulants
Bernie	Cocaine	stimulants
Bernie's flakes	Cocaine	stimulants
Bernie's gold dust	Cocaine	stimulants
Bhang	Marijuana, Indian term	cannabis
Bibs	MDMA	hallucinogen
Big 8	1/8 kilogram crack	stimulants
Big bag	Heroin	narcotics
Big bloke	Cocaine	stimulants
Big C	Cocaine	stimulants
Big D	LSD	hallucinogen
Big doodig	Heroin	narcotics
Big flake	Cocaine	stimulants
Big H	Heroin	narcotics
Big Harry	Heroin	narcotics
Big man	Drug supplier	

Street Name	Definition	Drug Type
Big O	Opium	narcotics
Big rush	Cocaine	stimulants
Bikers coffee	Methamphetamine and coffee	stimulants
Bill blass	Crack cocaine	stimulants
Billie hoke	Cocaine	stimulants
Bin laden	Heroin (after September 11)	narcotics
Bindle	Small packet of drug powder; heroin	narcotics
Bing	Enough drug for one injection	
Bingers	Crack addicts	
Bingo	To inject a drug	
Bings	Crack cocaine	stimulants
Biphetamine	Amphetamine; MDMA	stim.; halluc.
Bipping	Snorting heroin and cocaine (either together or separately)	narc.; stim.
Birdhead	LSD	hallucinogen
Birdie powder	Cocaine; heroin	stim.; narc.
Biscuit	50 rocks of crack	stimulants
Bite one's lips	To smoke marijuana	cannabis
Biz	Bag or portion of drugs	
Bjs	Crack Cocaine	stimulants
Black	Marijuana; opium; methamphetamine	cann.; narc.; stim.
Black acid	LSD; LSD and PCP	hallucinogen
Black and white	Amphetamine	stimulants
Black bart	Marijuana	cannabis
Black beauties	Amphetamine; depressants	stim.; deprs.
Black beauty	Methamphetamine	stimulants
Black birds	Amphetamine	stimulants
Black bombers	Amphetamine	stimulants
Black cadillacs	Amphetamine	stimulants
Black dust	PCP	hallucinogen
Black eagle	Heroin	narcotics
Black ganga	Marijuana resin	cannabis
Black gold	High potency marijuana	cannabis
Black gungi	Marijuana from India	cannabis
Black gunion	Marijuana	cannabis
Black hash	Opium mixed with hashish	narc.; cann.
Black hole	The high associated with ketamine	depressants
Black mo/ black moat	Highly potent marijuana	cannabis
Black mollies	Amphetamine	stimulants
Black mote	Marijuana mixed with honey	cannabis
Black pearl	Heroin	narcotics
Black pill	Opium pill	narcotics
Black rock	Crack cocaine	stimulants
Black Russian	Opium mixed with hashish	stim.; cann.
Black star	LSD	hallucinogen
Black stuff	Heroin; opium	narcotics
Black sunshine	LSD	hallucinogen

Substance Abuse

Street Name	Definition	Drug Type
Black tabs	LSD	hallucinogen
Black tar	Heroin	narcotics
Black whack	PCP	hallucinogen
Blacks	Amphetamine	stimulants
Blade	Crystal methamphetamine	stimulants
Blanca	Cocaine	stimulants
Blanco	Heroin; cocaine	narc.; stim.
Blank	Container of non-narcotic powder that is sold as heroin	
Blanket	Marijuana cigarette	cannabis
Blanks	Low quality drugs	
Blast	Cocaine; smoke crack; marijuana	stim.; cann.
Blast a joint	To smoke marijuana	cannabis
Blast a roach	To smoke marijuana	cannabis
Blast a stick	To smoke marijuana	cannabis
Blasted	Under the influence of drugs	
Blaxing	Smoking marijuana	cannabis
Blazing	Smoking marijuana	cannabis
Blizzard	A white cloud in a pipe used to smoke cocaine	stimulants
Block	Marijuana	cannabis
Block busters	Depressants	depressants
Blonde	Marijuana	cannabis
Blotter	Crack cocaine; LSD	stim.; halluc.
Blotter acid	LSD; PCP	hallucinogen
Blotter cube	LSD	hallucinogen
Blow	Cocaine; to inhale cocaine; to smoke marijuana	stim.; cann.
Blow a fix/ blow a shot	Injection misses the vein and is wasted in the skin	
Blow a stick	To smoke marijuana	cannabis
Blow blue	To inhale cocaine	stimulants
Blow coke	To inhale cocaine	stimulants
Blow one's roof	To smoke marijuana	cannabis
Blow smoke	To inhale cocaine	stimulants
Blow the vein	To inject a drug	
Blow up	Crack cut with lidocaine to increase size, weight, and street value	stimulants
Blow your mind	To get high on hallucinogens	hallucinogen
Blowcaine	Crack diluted with procaine	stimulants
Blowing smoke	Marijuana	cannabis
Blowout	Crack	stimulants
Blows	Heroin	narcotics
Blue	Crack cocaine; depressants; OxyContin	stim.; deprs.; narc.
Blue acid	LSD	hallucinogen
Blue angels	Depressants	depressants
Blue bag	Heroin	narcotics
Blue barrels	LSD	hallucinogen
Blue birds	Depressants	depressants

Street Name	Definition	Drug Type
Blue boy	Amphetamine	stimulants
Blue bullets	Depressants	depressants
Blue caps	Mescaline	hallucinogen
Blue chairs	LSD	hallucinogen
Blue cheers	LSD	hallucinogen
Blue clouds	Amytal (amobarbital sodium) capsules	depressants
Blue de hue	Marijuana from Vietnam	cannabis
Blue devil	Depressants	depressants
Blue devils	Methamphetamine	stimulants
Blue dolls	Depressants	depressants
Blue heaven	LSD	hallucinogen
Blue heavens	Depressants	depressants
Blue kisses	MDMA	hallucinogen
Blue lips	MDMA	hallucinogen
Blue madman	PCP	hallucinogen
Blue meth	Methamphetamine	stimulants
Blue microdot	LSD	hallucinogen
Blue mist	LSD	hallucinogen
Blue mollies	Amphetamine	stimulants
Blue moons	LSD	hallucinogen
Blue nile	MDMA	hallucinogen
Blue Nitro Vitality	GBL-containing product	depressants
Blue sage	Marijuana	cannabis
Blue sky blond	High potency marijuana from Colombia	cannabis
Blue star	Heroin	narcotics
Blue tips	Depressants	depressants
Blue vials	LSD	hallucinogen
Blunt	Marijuana or cocaine & marijuana inside a cigar	cann.; stim.
Bo	Marijuana	cannabis
Bo-bo	Marijuana	cannabis
Boat	PCP	hallucinogen
Bobo	Crack cocaine	stimulants
Bobo bush	Marijuana	cannabis
Body-packer	Person who ingests wrapped packet of crack or cocaine for transportation of drug	
Body-stuffer	Person who ingests crack vials to avoid prosecution	
Bogart a joint	To salivate on a marijuana cigarette; refuse to share	cannabis
Bohd	Marijuana; PCP	cann.; halluc.
Bolasterone	Injectable steroids	steroids
Bolivian marching powder	Cocaine	stimulants
Bollo	Crack cocaine	stimulants
Bolo	Crack cocaine	stimulants
Bolt	Amphetamine; isobutyl nitrite	stim.; inh.
Bomb	Crack; heroin; large marijuana cigarette; high potency heroin	stim.; narc.; cann.; narc.
Bomb squad	Crack selling crew	

Street Name	Definition	Drug Type
Bomber	Marijuana cigarette	cannabis
Bombido	Heroin; injectable amphetamine; depressants	narc.; stim.; depressants
Bombita	Heroin; amphetamine; depressants	narc.; stim.; depressants
Bombs away	Heroin	narcotics
Bone	Marijuana; $50 piece of crack; high purity heroin	cann.; stim.; narc.
Bonecrusher	Crack cocaine	stimulants
Bones	Crack cocaine	stimulants
Bong	Pipe used to smoke marijuana	cannabis
Bonita	Heroin	narcotics
Boo	Marijuana; methamphetamine	cann.; stim.
Boo boo bama	Marijuana	cannabis
Book	100 dosage units of LSD	hallucinogen
Boom	Marijuana	cannabis
Boomers	Psilocybin/psilocin; LSD	hallucinogen
Boost	Crack cocaine; to steal a drug; to ingest a drug	stimulants
Boost and shoot	Steal to support a habit	
Booster	To inhale cocaine	stimulants
Boot	To inject a drug	
Boot the gong	To smoke marijuana	cannabis
Booted	Under the influence of drugs	
Bopper	Crack cocaine	stimulants
Boppers	Amyl nitrite	Inhalants
Botray	Crack cocaine	stimulants
Bottles	Crack vials; amphetamine	stimulants
Boubou	Crack cocaine	stimulants
Boulder	Crack cocaine; $20 worth of crack	stimulants
Boulya	Crack cocaine	stimulants
Bouncing powder	Cocaine	stimulants
Box labs	Small, mobile, clandestine methamphetamine labs	
Boxed	In jail	
Boy	Cocaine; heroin	stim.; narc.
Bozo	Heroin	narcotics
Brain damage	Heroin	narcotics
Brain pills	Amphetamine	stimulants
Brain ticklers	Amphetamine	stimulants
Brea	Heroin	narcotics
Break night	Staying up all night on a cocaine binge until daybreak	stimulants
Breakdown	$40 of crack cocaine that can be broken down into $20 packages	stimulants
Brewery	Place where drugs are made	
Brick	Crack Cocaine; cocaine; marijuana; 1 kilogram of marijuana	stim.; cann.
Brick gum	Heroin	narcotics
Bridge or bring up	Prepare a vein for injection	

Street Name	Definition	Drug Type
Britton	Peyote	hallucinogen
Broccoli	Marijuana	cannabis
Broja	Heroin	narcotics
Broker	Go-between in a drug deal; heavy drug user	
Bromo	Nexus	hallucinogen
Brown	Marijuana; heroin; methamphetamine	cann.; narc.; stim.
Brown bombers	LSD	hallucinogen
Brown crystal	Heroin	narcotics
Brown dots	LSD	hallucinogen
Brown rhine	Heroin	narcotics
Brown sugar	Heroin	narcotics
Brown tape	Heroin	narcotics
Brownies	Amphetamine	stimulants
Browns	Amphetamine	stimulants
Bubble gum	Cocaine; crack; marijuana from Tennessee	stim.; cann.
Buck	Shoot someone in the head	
Bud	Marijuana	cannabis
Buda	Marijuana; high-grade marijuana joint filled with crack	cann.; stim.
Buddha	Potent marijuana spiked with opium	cann.; narc.
Buffer	A woman who performs oral sex in exchange for crack; crack smoker	stimulants
Bugged	Irritated; covered with sores and abscesses from repeated use of unsterile needles	
Bull	Narcotics agent or police officer	
Bull dog	Heroin	narcotics
Bullet	Isobutyl nitrite; inhalants	inhalants
Bullet bolt	Inhalants	inhalants
Bullia capital	Crack; fake crack	stimulants
Bullion	Crack cocaine	stimulants
Bullyon	Marijuana	cannabis
Bumblebees	Amphetamine	stimulants
Bummer trip	Unsettling and threatening experience from PCP	hallucinogen
Bump	Crack; fake crack; cocaine; boost a high; hit of ketamine ($20)	stimulants
Bumper	Crack cocaine	stimulants
Bumping up	MDMA combined with powder cocaine	halluc.; stim.
Bundle	Heroin	narcotics
Bunk	Fake cocaine; crack cocaine	stimulants
Burese	Cocaine	stimulants
Burn one	To smoke marijuana	cannabis
Burn the main line	To inject a drug	
Burn transaction	Selling a substance as a certain drug	
Burned	Purchase fake drugs	
Burned out	Collapse of veins from repeated injections; permanent impairment from drug abuse	
Burnese	Cocaine	stimulants
Burnie	Marijuana	cannabis

Street Name	Definition	Drug Type
Bush	Marijuana; cocaine; PCP	cann.; stim.; halluc.
Businessman's LSD	Dimethyltryptamine	hallucinogen
Businessman's special	Dimethyltryptamine	hallucinogen
Businessman's trip	Dimethyltryptamine	hallucinogen
Busted	Arrested	
Busters	Depressants	depressants
Busy bee	PCP	hallucinogen
Butler	Crack cocaine	stimulants
Butt naked	PCP	hallucinogen
Butter	Marijuana; crack	cann.; stim.
Butter flower	Marijuana	cannabis
Buttons	Mescaline	hallucinogen
Butu	Heroin	narcotics
Buzz	Under the influence of drugs	
Buzz bomb	Nitrous oxide	inhalants
C	Cocaine	stimulants
C & M	Cocaine and morphine	stim.; narc.
C joing	Place where cocaine is sold	
C-dust	Cocaine	stimulants
C-game	Cocaine	stimulants
C.S.	Marijuana	cannabis
Caballo	Heroin	narcotic
Cabbage head	Person who will use or experiment with any kind of drug	
Cabello	Cocaine	stimulants
Caca	Heroin	narcotics
Cactus	Mescaline	hallucinogen
Cactus buttons	Mescaline	hallucinogen
Cactus head	Mescaline	hallucinogen
Cad/Cadillac	1 ounce	
Cadillac	Cocaine; PCP	stim.; halluc.
Cadillac express	Methcathinone	stimulants
Cafeteria-style use	Using a combination of different club drugs	
Caine	Cocaine; crack	stimulants
Cakes	Round discs of crack	stimulants
Calbo	Heroin	narcotics
California cornflakes	Cocaine	stimulants
California sunshine	LSD	hallucinogen
Cam trip	High potency marijuana	cannabis
Cambodian red/ Cam red	Marijuana from Cambodia	cannabis
Came	Cocaine	stimulants
Can	Marijuana; 1 ounce	cannabis

Street Name	Definition	Drug Type
Canade	Heroin/marijuana combination	narc.; cann.
Canadian black	Marijuana	cannabis
Canamo	Marijuana	cannabis
Canappa	Marijuana	cannabis
Cancelled stick	Marijuana cigarette	cannabis
Candy	Cocaine; crack; amphetamine; depressants	stim.; deprs.
Candy blunt	Blunt (marijuana cigar) dipped in cough syrup	cannabis
Candy C	Cocaine	stimulants
Candy flipping on a string	Combing or sequencing LSD with MDMA; mixing LSD, MDMA, and cocaine	halluc.; stim.
Candy raver	Young people who attend raves; rave attendees who wear candy jewelry	
Candy sugar	Powder cocaine	stimulants
Candy-flipping	LSD mixed with ecstasy	hallucinogen
Candyman	Drug supplier	
Cannabinol	PCP	hallucinogen
Cannabis tea	Marijuana	cannabis
Cap	Crack cocaine; LSD; a capsule of a drug	stim.; halluc.
Cap up	Transfer bulk form drugs to capsules	
Capital H	Heroin	narcotics
Caps	Heroin; psilocybin/psilocin; crack; GHB	narc.; halluc.; stim.; deprs.
Capsula	Crack cocaine	stimulants
Carburetor	Crack stem attachment	stimulants
Care bears	MDMA	hallucinogen
Carga	Heroin	narcotics
Carmabis	Marijuana	cannabis
Carne	Heroin	narcotics
Carnie	Cocaine	stimulants
Carpet patrol	Crack smokers searching the floor for crack	stimulants
Carrie	Cocaine	stimulants
Carrie Nation	Cocaine	stimulants
Carry	To be in possession of drugs	
Cartucho	Package of marijuana cigarettes	cannabis
Cartwheels	Amphetamine	stimulants
Casper	Crack cocaine	stimulants
Casper the ghost	Crack cocaine	stimulants
Cat	Methcathinone	stimulants
Cat in the hats	MDMA	hallucinogen
Cat valium	Ketamine	depressants
Catnip	Marijuana cigarette	cannabis
Caviar	Combination of cocaine and marijuana; crack	stim.; cann.
Cavite all star	Marijuana	cannabis
CDs	Crack	stimulants
Cecil	Cocaine	stimulants
Cest	Marijuana	cannabis
Chalk	Crack; amphetamine; methamphetamine	stimulants
Chalked up	Under the influence of cocaine	stimulants

Street Name	Definition	Drug Type
Chalking	Chemically altering the color of cocaine so it looks white	stimulants
Champagne	Combination of cocaine and marijuana	stim.; cann.
Chandoo/chandu	Opium	narcotics
Channel	Vein into which a drug is injected	
Channel swimmer	Person who injects heroin	narcotics
Chapopote	Heroin	narcotics
Charas	Marijuana from India	cannabis
Charge	Marijuana	cannabis
Charged up	Under the influence of drugs	
Charity	MDMA	hallucinogen
Charley	Heroin	narcotics
Charlie	Cocaine	stimulants
Chase	To smoke cocaine or marijuana	stim.; cann.
Chaser	Compulsive crack user	stimulants
Chasing the dragon	Crack mixed with heroin	stim.; narc.
Chasing the tiger	To smoke heroin	narcotics
Chatarra	Heroin	narcotics
Cheap basing	Crack	stimulants
Check	Personal supply of drugs	
Cheeba	Marijuana	cannabis
Cheeo	Marijuana	cannabis
Cheese	Heroin	narcotics
Chemical	Crack cocaine	stimulants
Chemo	Marijuana	cannabis
Cherry Meth	GHB	depressants
Chewies	Crack cocaine	stimulants
Chiba	Heroin	narcotics
Chiba chiba	High potency marijuana from Colombia	cannabis
Chicago black	Marijuana, term from Chicago	cannabis
Chicago green	Marijuana	cannabis
Chicken feed	Methamphetamine	stimulants
Chicken powder	Amphetamine	stimulants
Chicken scratch	Searching on hand and knees for cocaine	
Chicle	Heroin	narcotics
Chief	LSD; mescaline	hallucinogen
Chiefing	To smoke marijuana	cannabis
Chieva	Heroin	narcotics
Chillum	An object used to smoke opium, hashish, and marijuana	
China cat	High potency heroin	narcotics
China girl	Fentanyl	narcotics
China town	Fentanyl	narcotics
China white	Heroin; fentanyl; synthetic heroin	narcotics
Chinese molasses	Opium	narcotics
Chinese red	Heroin	narcotics
Chinese tobacco	Opium	narcotics

Street Name	Definition	Drug Type
Chip	Heroin	narcotics
Chipper	Occasional drug user; occasional Hispanic user	
Chipping	Uses drugs occasionally	
Chippy	Cocaine	stimulants
Chips	Tobacco or marijuana cigarettes laced with PCP	cann.; halluc.
Chira	Marijuana	cannabis
Chiva/chieva	Heroin	narcotics
Choco-fan	Heroin	narcotics
Chocolate	Marijuana; opium; amphetamine	cann.; narc.; stim.
Chocolate Chip Cookies	MDMA combined with heroin or methadone	halluc.; narc.
Chocolate chips	LSD	hallucinogen
Chocolate ecstasy	Crack made brown by adding chocolate milk during production	stimulants
Chocolate rock	Crack smoked together with heroin	stim.; narc.
Chocolate Thai	Marijuana	cannabis
Choe	Cocaine	stimulants
Cholly	Cocaine	stimulants
Chorals	Depressants	depressants
Christina	Amphetamine	stimulants
Christmas bud	Marijuana	cannabis
Christmas rolls	Depressants	depressants
Christmas tree	Marijuana; amphetamine; methamphetamine; depressant	cann.; stim.; stim.; deprs.
Christmas tree meth	Green methamphetamine produced using Drano crystals	stimulants
Chronic	Marijuana; marijuana mixed with crack	cann.; stim.
Crystal methadrine	MDMA	hallucinogen
Chucks	Hunger following withdrawal from heroin	
Chunky	Marijuana	cannabis
Churus	Marijuana	cannabis
Cid	LSD	hallucinogen
Cigarette paper	Packet of heroin	narcotics
Cigarrode cristal	PCP	hallucinogen
Cinnamon	Methamphetamine	stimulants
Circles	Rohypnol	depressants
Citrol	High potency marijuana from Nepal	cannabis
CJ	PCP	hallucinogen
Clam bake	Sitting inside a car or small enclosed space and smoking marijuana	cannabis
Clarity	MDMA	hallucinogen
Clear	Methamphetamine	stimulants
Clear up	Stop drug use	
Clicker	Crack mixed with PCP; marijuana dipped in formaldehyde and smoked	stim.; halluc.; cannabis
Clickums	A marijuana cigarette laced with PCP	cann.; halluc.

Substance Abuse

Street Name	Definition	Drug Type
Cliffhanger	PCP	hallucinogen
Climax	Crack; heroin; isobutyl nitrite; inhalants	stim.; narc.; inhal.; inhal.
Climb	Marijuana cigarette	cannabis
Clips	Rows of vials heat-sealed together	
Clocker	Entry level crack dealers who sell drugs 24 hours a day	
Clocking paper	Profits from selling drugs	
Closet baser	User of crack who prefers anonymity	stimulants
Cloud	Crack cocaine	stimulants
Cloud nine	Crack cocaine; MDMA	stim.; halluc.
Cluck	Crack smoker	stimulants
Cluckers	Middlemen who facilitate the connection between buyers and sellers	
Co-pilot	Amphetamine	stimulants
Coasting	Under the influence of drugs	
Coasts to coasts	Amphetamine	stimulants
Coca	Cocaine	stimulants
Cocaine blues	Depression after extended cocaine use	stimulants
Cochornis	Marijuana	cannabis
Cocktail	Cigarette laced with cocaine or crack; partially smoked marijuana cigarette inserted in regular cigarette; to smoke cocaine in a cigarette	stim.; cann.; stim.
Coco rocks	Dark brown crack made by adding chocolate pudding during production	stimulants
Coco snow	Banzocaine used as cutting agent for crack	stimulants
Cocoa puff	To smoke cocaine and marijuana	stim.; cann.
Cocofan	Brown Tar Heroin	narcotics
Coconut	Cocaine	stimulants
Cod	Large amount of money	
Coffee	LSD	hallucinogen
Coke	Cocaine; crack	stimulants
Coke bar	A bar where cocaine is openly used	stimulants
Cola	Cocaine	stimulants
Colas	Marijuana	cannabis
Cold turkey	Sudden withdrawal from drugs	
Coli	Marijuana	cannabis
Coliflor tostao	Marijuana	cannabis
Colombian	Marijuana	cannabis
Colorado cocktail	Marijuana	cannabis
Columbo	PCP	hallucinogen
Columbus black	Marijuana	cannabis
Combol	Cocaine	stimulants
Come home	End of a trip from LSD	hallucinogen
Come up	Person who sells drugs for money; to take a small amount of money and increase to a large amount	
Comeback	Benzocaine and mannitol used to adulterate cocaine for conversion to crack	stimulants

Street Name	Definition	Drug Type
Comic book	LSD	hallucinogen
Conductor	LSD	hallucinogen
Connect	Purchase drugs; supplier of illegal drugs	
Contact lens	LSD	hallucinogen
Cook	Drug manufacturer; mix heroin with water; heating heroin to prepare it for injection	narcotics
Cook down	Process in which users liquify heroin in order to inhale it	narcotics
Cooker	To inject a drug; person who manufactures methamphetamine	stimulants
Cookies	Crack cocaine	stimulants
Cooking up	To process powdered cocaine into crack	stimulants
Cooler	Cigarette laced with a drug	
Coolie	Cigarette laced with cocaine	stimulants
Cop	Obtain drugs	
Copping zones	Specific areas where buyers can purchase drugs	
Coral	Depressant	depressants
Coriander seeds	Cash	
Cork the air	To inhale cocaine	stimulants
Corrine	Cocaine	stimulants
Corrinne	Cocaine	stimulants
Cosa	Marijuana	cannabis
Cotics	Heroin	narcotics
Coties	Codeine	narcotics
Cotton	Currency; OxyContin	narcotics
Cotton brothers	Cocaine; heroin; morphine	stim.; narc.
Cotton fever	Critically high temperature associated with accidentally injecting cotton fibers into blood stream	
Courage pills	Heroin; depressants	narc.; deprs.
Course note	Bill large than $2	
Cozmo's	PCP	hallucinogen
CR	Methamphetamine	stimulants
Crack	Cocaine	stimulants
Crack attack	Craving for crack	stimulants
Crack back	Marijuana and crack	cann.; stim.
Crack cooler	Crack soaked in wine cooler	stimulants
Crack gallery	Place where crack is bought and sold	stimulants
Crack house	Place where crack is used	stimulants
Crack kits	Glass pipe and copper mesh	
Crack spot	Area where people can purchase crack; place where crack is sold, but not used	stimulants
Cracker jack/s	Crack smoker	stimulants
Crackers	LSD; injected combination of Talwin and ritalin	hallucinogen
Crank	Crack cocaine; heroin; amphetamine; methamphetamine; methcathinone	stim.; narc.; stimulants
Crap	Low quality heroin	narcotics
Crash	Sleep off effects of drugs	

Street Name	Definition	Drug Type
Crazy coke	PCP	hallucinogen
Crazy Eddie	PCP	hallucinogen
Crazy weed	Marijuana	cannabis
Credit card	Crack stem	stimulants
Crib	Crack cocaine	stimulants
Crimmie	Cigarette laced with crack	stimulants
Crink	Methamphetamine	stimulants
Cripple	Marijuana cigarette	cannabis
Cris	Methamphetamine	stimulants
Crisscross	Amphetamine	stimulants
Crisscrossing	Setting up a line of cocaine next to a line of heroin and snorting both at the same time with two straws	stim.; narc.
Cristal	MDMA	hallucinogen
Cristina	Methamphetamine	stimulants
Cristy	Smokable methamphetamine	stimulants
Croak	Crack mixed with methamphetamine; methamphetamine	stimulants
Crop	Low quality heroin	narcotics
Cross tops	Amphetamine	stimulants
Crossles	Methamphetamine	stimulants
Crossroads	Amphetamine	stimulants
Crown crap	Heroin	narcotics
Crumbs	Tiny pieces of crack	stimulants
Crunch & Munch	Crack cocaine	stimulants
Crush and rush	Method of methamphetamine production in which starch is not filtered out of the ephedrine or pseudoephedrine tablets.	stimulants
Cruz	Opium from Veracruz, Mexico	narcotics
Crying weed	Marijuana	cannabis
Cryppie	Marijuana	cannabis
Crypto	Methamphetamine	stimulants
Cryptonie	Marijuana	cannabis
Crystal	Cocaine; amphetamine; methamphetamine; PCP	stimulants, hallucinogen
Crystal glass	Crystal shards of methamphetamine	stimulants
Crystal joint	PCP	hallucinogen
Crystal meth	Methamphetamine	stimulants
Crystal methadrine	Amphetamine	stimulants
Crystal T	PCP	hallucinogen
Crystal tea	LSD	hallucinogen
Cube	LSD; 1 ounce	hallucinogen
Cubes	Marijuana tablets; crack cocaine	cann.; stim.
Culican	High potency marijuana from Mexico	cannabis
Cupcakes	LSD	hallucinogen
Cura	Heroin	narcotics
Cushion	Vein into which a drug is injected	
Cut	Adulterate drugs	
Cut-deck	Heroin mixed with powdered milk	narcotics

Street Name	Definition	Drug Type
Cycline	PCP	hallucinogen
Cyclones	PCP	hallucinogen
D	LSD; PCP	hallucinogen
Dabble	Use drugs occasionally	
Dagga	Marijuana from South Africa	cannabis
Dama blanca	Cocaine	stimulants
Dance fever	Fentanyl	narcotics
Dank	Marijuana; practice of lacing cigarettes with formaldehyde	cannabis
Dawamesk	Marijuana	cannabis
Dead on arrival	Heroin	narcotics
Dead president	Heroin	narcotics
Dead road	MDMA	hallucinogen
Debs	Amphetamine; MDMA	stim.; halluc.
Deca-Duabolin	Injectable steroids	steroids
Decadence	MDMA	hallucinogen
Deck	1 to 15 grams of heroin, also known as a bag; packet of drugs	narcotics
Deeda	LSD	hallucinogen
Delatestryl	Injectable steroids	steroids
Demo	Crack stem; sample size quantity of crack	stimulants
Demolish	Crack	stimulants
Dep-testosterone	Injectable steroids	steroids
Desocsins	Methamphetamine	stimulants
Desogtion	Methamphetamine	stimulants
DET	Dimethyltryptamine	hallucinogen
Detroit pink	PCP	hallucinogen
Deuce	Heroin; $2 worth of drugs	narcotics
Devil drug	Crack cocaine	stimulants
Devil's dandruff	Crack cocaine; powder cocaine	stimulants
Devil's dick	Crack pipe	stimulants
Devil's dust	PCP	hallucinogen
Devilsmoke	Crack cocaine	stimulants
Dew	Marijuana	cannabis
Dews	$10 worth of drugs	
Dex	Amphetamine; MDMA	stim.; halluc.
Dexedrine	Amphetamine; MDMA	stim.; halluc.
Dexies	Amphetamine	stimulants
Diablito	Crack cocaine and marijuana in a joint	stim.; cann.
Diambista	Marijuana	cannabis
Diamond folds	Folded paper used to package drugs	
Diamonds	Amphetamine; MDMA	stim.; halluc.
Dianabol	Veterinary or oral steroids	steroids
Dice	Crack cocaine	stimulants
Diesel	Heroin	narcotics
Diet pills	Amphetamine	stimulants
Dihydrolone	Injectable steroids	steroids
Dimba	Marijuana from West Africa	cannabis
Dime	Crack cocaine; $10 worth of crack	stimulants

Street Name	Definition	Drug Type
Dime bag	$10 worth of drugs	
Dime special	Crack cocaine	stimulants
Dime's worth	Amount of heroin to cause death	narcotics
Ding	Marijuana	cannabis
Dinkie dow	Marijuana	cannabis
Dinosaurs	Populations of heroin users in their 40s & 50s	narcotics
Dip	Crack cocaine	stimulants
Dipper	PCP	hallucinogen
Dipping out	Crack runners taking a portion of crack from vials	stimulants
Dirt	Heroin	narcotics
Dirt grass	Inferior quality marijuana	cannabis
Dirties	Marijuana cigarettes with powder cocaine	cann.; stim.
Dirty basing	Crack cocaine	stimulants
Dirty joints	Cigarettes with crack cocaine and marijuana	stim.; cann.
Disco biscuit(s)	Depressants; MDMA	deprs; halluc.
Disco pellets	Stimulant	stimulants
Discorama	Inhalants	inhalants
Disease	Drug of choice	
Ditch	Marijuana	cannabis
Ditch weed	Inferior quality marijuana	cannabis
Djamba	Marijuana	cannabis
DMT	Dimethyltryptamine; PCP	hallucinogen
Do a joint	Marijuana	cannabis
Do a line	To inhale cocaine	stimulants
Do it Jack	PCP	hallucinogen
DOA	Crack; heroin; PCP	stim.; narc.; halluc.
Doctor	MDMA	hallucinogen
Doctor shopping	Going from doctor to doctor to obtain prescriptions for pharmaceuticals	
Dog	Good friend	
Dog food	Heroin	narcotics
Dogie	Heroin	narcotics
Dollar	$100 worth of drugs	
Dolls	Amphetamine; depressant; MDMA	stim.; deprs.; halluc.
Domes	LSD	hallucinogen
Domestic	Locally grown marijuana	cannabis
Domex	PCP and MDMA	hallucinogen
Dominican knot	The torn and knotted corner of a baggie containing drugs	
Dominoes	Amphetamine	stimulants
Don jem	Marijuana	cannabis
Don Juan	Marijuana	cannabis
Dona Juana	Marijuana	cannabis
Dona Juanita	Marijuana	cannabis
Donk	Marijuana and PCP combination	cann.; halluc.

Street Name	Definition	Drug Type
Doob	Marijuana	cannabis
Doobee	Marijuana	cannabis
Doobie/dubbe/ duby	Marijuana	cannabis
Doogie/doojee/ dugie	Heroin	narcotics
Dooley	Heroin	narcotics
Doosey	Heroin	narcotics
Dope	Marijuana; heroin; any other drug	cann.; narc.
Dope fiend	Person who is drug dependent; crack addict	stimulants
Dope smoke	To smoke marijuana	cannabis
Dopium	Opium	narcotics
Doradilla	Marijuana	cannabis
Dors and 4's	Combination of Doriden and Tylenol 4	narcotics
Doses	LSD	hallucinogen
Dosure	LSD	hallucinogen
Dots	LSD	hallucinogen
Doub	$20 rock of crack	stimulants
Double breasted dealing	Dealing cocaine and heroin together	stim.; narc.
Double bubble	Cocaine	stimulants
Double cross	Amphetamine	stimulants
Double dome	LSD	hallucinogen
Double rock	Crack diluted in procaine	stimulants
Double trouble	Depressants	depressants
Double up	When a crack dealer delivers an extra rock as a marketing ploy to attract customers	stimulants
Double ups	A $20 rock that can be broken into two $20 rocks	stimulants
Double yoke	Crack cocaine	stimulants
Dove	$35 piece of crack	stimulants
Dover's deck	Opium	narcotics
Dover's powder	Opium	narcotics
Down	Codeine cough syrup	narcotics
Downer	Depressants	depressants
Downie	Depressants	depressants
Dr. Feelgood	Heroin	narcotics
Draf	Marijuana; ecstasy, with cocaine	cann.; halluc., stim.
Draf weed	Marijuana	cannabis
Drag weed	Marijuana	cannabis
Dragon rock	Mixture of heroin and crack	narc.; stim.
Draw up	To inject a drug	
Dream	Cocaine	stimulants
Dream gun	Opium	narcotics
Dream stick	Opium	narcotics
Dreamer	Morphine	narcotics
Dreams	Opium	narcotics
Dreck	Heroin	narcotics
Drink	PCP	hallucinogen

Substance Abuse

Street Name	Definition	Drug Type
Drivers	Amphetamine; MDMA	stim.; halluc.
Drop	To swallow drugs	
Dropper	To inject a drug	
Dropping	Wrapping methamphetamine in bread and then consuming it	stimulants
Drowsy high	Depressants	depressants
Dry high	Marijuana	cannabis
Dry up	To inject drugs	
Dub	When a crack dealer delivers an extra rock as a marketing ploy to attract customers	stimulants
Dube	Marijuana	cannabis
Duby	Marijuana	cannabis
Duct	Cocaine	stimulants
Due	Residue of oils trapped in a pipe after smoking base	
Duji	Heroin	narcotics
Dujra	Heroin	narcotics
Dujre	Heroin	narcotics
Dummy dust	PCP	hallucinogen
Dump	To vomit after taking drugs	
Durabolin	Injectable steroids	steroids
Durong	Marijuana	cannabis
Duros	Marijuana	cannabis
Dust	Marijuana mixed with various chemicals; cocaine; heroin; PCP	cann.; stim.; narc.; halluc.
Dust blunt	Marijuana and PCP combination	cann.; halluc.
Dust joint	PCP	hallucinogen
Dust of angels	PCP	hallucinogen
Dusted parsley	PCP	hallucinogen
Dusting	Adding PCP, heroin, or other drug to marijuana	halluc.; narc.; cann.
Dymethzine	Injectable steroids	steroids
Dynamite	Cocaine mixed with heroin	stim.; narc.
Dyno	Heroin	narcotics
Dyno-pure	Heroin	narcotics
E	Ecstasy; MDMA	hallucinogen
E-bombs	MDMA	hallucinogen
E-puddle	Sleeping due to MDMA use & exhaustion	hallucinogen
E-tard	Person under the influence of MDMA	hallucinogen
Earth	Marijuana cigarette	cannabis
Easing powder	Opium	narcotics
Eastside player	Crack cocaine	stimulants
Easy lay	GHB	depressants
Easy score	Obtaining drugs without difficulty	
Eating	Taking a drug orally	
Ecstasy	MDMA	hallucinogen
Egg	Crack cocaine	stimulants
Eggs	Heroin in rock form	narcotics
Egyptians	MDMA	hallucinogen
Eight ball	1/8 ounce of drugs	

Street Name	Definition	Drug Type
Eightball	Crack mixed with heroin	stim.; narc.
Eighth	Heroin	narcotics
El diablito	Cocaine, marijuana, heroin and PCP	stim.; cann.; narc.; halluc.
El diablo	Cocaine, marijuana and heroin	stim.; cann.; narc.
El gallo	Marijuana	cannabis
El perico	Cocaine	stimulants
Elbows	1 pound of methamphetamine	stimulants
Electric Kool Aid	LSD	hallucinogen
Electric kool-aid	Crack cocaine	stimulants
Elephant	Marijuana; PCP	cann.; halluc.
Elephant flipping	Use of PCP and MDMA	hallucinogen
Elephant trank	PCP	hallucinogen
Elephant tranquilizer	PCP	hallucinogen
Elephants	MDMA	hallucinogen
Elvis	LSD	hallucinogen
Embalming fluid	PCP	hallucinogen
Emergency gun	Instrument used to inject other than a syringe	
Emsel	Morphine	narcotics
Endo	Marijuana	cannabis
Energizer	PCP	hallucinogen
Enoltestovis	Injectable steroids	steroids
Ephedrone	Methcathinone	stimulants
Equipose	Veterinary steroids	steroids
Erth	PCP	hallucinogen
Esnortiar	Cocaine	stimulants
Esra	Marijuana	cannabis
Essence	MDMA	hallucinogen
Estuffa	Heroin	narcotics
ET	Alpha-ethyltryptamine	hallucinogen
Eve	MDMA	hallucinogen
Everclear	Cocaine; GHB	stim.; deprs.
Exiticity	MDMA	hallucinogen
Explorers club	Group of LSD users	hallucinogen
Eye opener	Crack; amphetamine	stimulants
Eye openers	Amphetamine	stimulants
Factory	Place where drugs are packaged, diluted, or manufactured	
Fake STP	PCP	hallucinogen
Fall	Arrested	
Fallbrook redhair	Marijuana, term from Fallbrook, CA	cannabis
Famous dimes	Crack cocaine	stimulants
Fantasia	Dimethyltryptamine	hallucinogen
Fantasy	GHB	depressants
Fast	Methamphetamine	stimulants
Fast white lady	Powder cocaine	stimulants
Fastin	Amphetamine; MDMA	stim.; halluc.

Street Name	Definition	Drug Type
Fat bags	Crack cocaine	stimulants
Fatty	Marijuana cigarette	cannabis
Feed bag	Container for marijuana	cannabis
Feeling	Marijuana	cannabis
Feenin	Behavior associated with a person craving cocaine or other drugs when they're unavailable	stimulants
Felix the Cat	LSD	hallucinogen
Ferry dust	Heroin	narcotics
Fi-do-nie	Opium	narcotics
Fields	LSD	hallucinogen
Fiend	Someone who smokes marijuana alone	cannabis
Fifteen cents	$15 worth of drugs	
Fifty-one	Crack; crack sprinkled on tobacco	stimulants
Finajet/finaject	Veterinary steroids	steroids
Fine stuff	Marijuana	cannabis
Finger	Marijuana cigarette	cannabis
Finger lid	Marijuana	cannabis
Fingers	To cut off fingers of surgical gloves that are then used to package drugs	
Fir	Marijuana	cannabis
Fire	Crack and methamphetamine; to inject a drug	stimulants
Fire it up	To smoke marijuana	cannabis
Firewater	GBL-containing product	depressants
Firewood	Marijuana	cannabis
First line	Morphine	narcotics
Fish scales	Crack cocaine	stimulants
Five C note	$500 bill	
Five cent bag	$5 worth of drugs	
Five dollar bag	$50 worth of drugs	
Five-way	Combines snorting of heroin, cocaine, methamphetamine, ground up flunitrazepam pills, and drinking alcohol	narc.; stim.; stim.; deprs.
Fives	Amphetamine	stimulants
Fix	To inject a drug	
Fizzies	Methadone	hallucinogen
Flag	Appearance of blood in the vein	
Flake	Cocaine	stimulants
Flakes	PCP	hallucinogen
Flame cooking	Smoking cocaine base by putting the pipe over a stove flame	stimulants
Flamethrowers	Cigarette laced with cocaine and heroin; heroin, cocaine and tobacco	stim.; narc.; narc.; stim.
Flash	LSD; the rush of a cocaine injection	halluc.; stim.
Flat blues	LSD	hallucinogen
Flat chunks	Crack cut with benzocaine	stimulants
Flatliners	4-methylthioamphetamine	hallucinogen
Flave	Powder cocaine	stimulants
Flea powder	Low purity heroin	narcotics

Street Name	Definition	Drug Type
Flex	Fake crack (rock cocaine)	stimulants
Flipping	MDMA	hallucinogen
Florida snow	Cocaine	stimulants
Flower	Marijuana	cannabis
Flower flipping	Ecstacy, MDMA mixed with mushrooms	hallucinogen
Flower tops	Marijuana	cannabis
Fly Mexican airlines	To smoke marijuana	cannabis
Flying	Under the influence of drugs	
Foil	Heroin	narcotics
Following that cloud	Searching for drugs	
Foo Foo	Cocaine	stimulants
Foo foo stuff	Heroin; cocaine	narc.; stim.
Foo-foo dust	Cocaine	stimulants
Foolish powder	Cocaine; heroin	stim.; narc.
Footballs	Amphetamine	stimulants
Forget me drug	Rohypnol	depressants
Forget pill	Rohypnol	depressants
Forget-me pill	Rohypnol	depressants
Forwards	Amphetamine	stimulants
Four leaf clover	MDMA	hallucinogen
Fraho/frajo	Marijuana	cannabis
Freebase	To smoke cocaine; crack cocaine	stimulants
Freebasing	Smoking crack cocaine	stimulants
Freeze	Cocaine; renege on a drug deal	stimulants
French blue	Amphetamine	stimulants
French fries	Crack cocaine	stimulants
Fresh	PCP	hallucinogen
Friend	Fentanyl	narcotics
Fries	Crack cocaine	stimulants
Frios	Marijuana laced with PCP	cann.; halluc.
Frisco special	Cocaine, heroin, and LSD	stim.; narc.; halluc.
Frisco speedball	Cocaine, heroin, and a dash of LSD	stim.; narc.; halluc.
Friskie powder	Cocaine	stimulants
Frontloading	Transferring a drug solution from one syringe to another	
Fry	Marijuana cigarettes dipped in embalming fluid, sometimes also laced with PCP; Crack cocaine	cann., halluc.; stim.
Fry daddy	Crack and marijuana; cigarette laced with crack; marijuana joint laced with crack	stim., cann.; stim; cann., stim.
Fry sticks	Marijuana cigarettes dipped in embalming fluid, sometimes also laced with PCP	cann., halluc.
Fu	Marijuana	cannabis
Fuel	Marijuana mixed with insecticides; PCP	cann.; halluc.
Fuete	Hypodermic needle	

Street Name	Definition	Drug Type
Fuma D'Angola	Marijuana	cannabis
Furra	Heroin	narcotics
G	$1000 or 1 gram of drugs; term for an unfamiliar male; GHB	depressants
G-riffic	GHB	depressants
G-rock	1 gram rock cocaine	stimulants
G-shot	Small dose of drugs used to hold off withdrawal symptoms until full dose can be taken	
G.B.	Depressants	depressants
Gaffel	Fake cocaine	stimulants
Gaffus	Hypodermic needle	
Gage/gauge	Marijuana	cannabis
Gagers	Methcathinone	stimulants
Gaggers	Methcathinone	stimulants
Gaggler	Amphetamine; MDMA	stim.; halluc.
Galloping horse	Heroin	narcotics
Gallup	Heroin	narcotics
Gamma Oh	GHB	depressants
Gamot	Heroin	narcotics
Gange	Marijuana	cannabis
Gangster	Marijuana; person who uses or manufactures methamphetamine	cannabis
Gangster pills	Depressants	depressants
Ganja	Marijuana; term from Jamaica	cannabis
Gank	Fake crack	stimulants
Ganoobies	State of being stoned & laughing uncontrollably	
Garbage	Inferior quality marijuana; low quality heroin	cann.; narc.
Garbage heads	Users who buy crack from street dealers instead of cooking it themselves	
Garbage rock	Crack cocaine	stimulants
Gash	Marijuana	cannabis
Gasper	Marijuana cigarette	cannabis
Gasper stick	Marijuana cigarette	cannabis
Gato	Heroin	narcotics
Gauge butt	Marijuana	cannabis
GBH	GHB	depressants
GBL	Gamma butyrolactone; used in making GHB	depressants
Gee	Opium	narcotics
Geek	Crack mixed with marijuana	stim.; cann.
Geek-joints	Cigarettes or cigars filled with tobacco and crack; a marijuana cigarette laced with crack or powdered cocaine	stim.; cann., stim.
Geeker	Crack users	stimulants
Geep	Methamphetamine	stimulants
Geeter	Methamphetamine	stimulants
Geeze	To inhale cocaine	stimulants
Geezer	To inject a drug	

Street Name	Definition	Drug Type
Geezer a bit of dee gee	To inject a drug	
George	Heroin	narcotics
George smack	Heroin	narcotics
Georgia home boy	GHB	depressants
Get a gage up	To smoke marijuana	cannabis
Get a gift	Obtain drugs	
Get high	To smoke marijuana	cannabis
Get lifted	Under the influence of drugs	
Get off	To inject a drug; to get 'high'	
Get off houses	Private places heroin users can purchase and use heroin for a fee	narcotics
Get the wind	To smoke marijuana	cannabis
Get through	Obtain drugs	
Getgo	Methamphetamine	stimulants
Getting roached	Using Rohypnol	depressants
Getting snotty	Using heroin	narcotics
Ghana	Marijuana	cannabis
GHB	Gamma hydroxybutyrate	depressants
Ghost	LSD	hallucinogen
Ghostbusting	Smoking cocaine; searching for white particles in the belief that they are crack	stimulants
Gick monster	Crack smoker	stimulants
Gift-of-the-sun	Cocaine	stimulants
Gift-of-the-sun-god	Cocaine	stimulants
Giggle smoke	Marijuana	cannabis
Giggle weed	Marijuana	cannabis
Gimmick	Drug injection equipment	
Gimmie	Crack and marijuana; marijuana joint laced with crack	stim., cann.; cann.; stim.
Gin	Cocaine	stimulants
Girl	Cocaine; Crack cocaine; heroin	stim.; narc.
Girlfriend	Cocaine	stimulants
Giro house	Non-bank financial institutions for businesses frequently used by drug traffickers to launder drug proceeds	
Give wings	Inject someone or teach someone to inject heroin	narcotics
Glacines	Heroin	narcotics
Glad stuff	Cocaine	stimulants
Glading	Using inhalant	inhalants
Glass	Heroin; amphetamine; hypodermic needle; methamphetamine	narc.; stim.; stim.
Glass gun	Hypodermic needle	
Glo	Crack cocaine	stimulants
Gluey	One who sniffs or inhales glue	inhalants
Go	Amphetamines; MDMA	stim.; halluc.
Go into a sewer	To inject a drug; inject in the vein	

Substance Abuse

Street Name	Definition	Drug Type
Go loco	To smoke marijuana	cannabis
Go on a sleigh ride	To inhale cocaine	stimulants
Go-fast	Methcathinone; crank; methamphetamine	stimulants
Goat	Heroin	narcotics
Goblet of jam	Marijuana	cannabis
God's drug	Morphine	narcotics
God's flesh	LSD; psilocybin/psilocin	hallucinogen
God's medicine	Opium	narcotics
Gold	Marijuana; Crack cocaine; heroin	cann.; stim.; narc.
Gold dust	Cocaine	stimulants
Gold star	Marijuana	cannabis
Golden	Marijuana	cannabis
Golden dragon	LSD	hallucinogen
Golden eagle	4-methylthioamphetamine	hallucinogen
Golden girl	Heroin	narcotics
Golden leaf	Very high quality marijuana	cannabis
Golf ball	Crack cocaine	stimulants
Golf balls	Depressants	depressants
Golpe	Heroin	narcotics
Goma	Black tar heroin; opium	narcotics
Gondola	Opium	narcotics
Gone, Shot to the curb	Lost everything to crack	stimulants
Gong	Marijuana; opium	cann.; narc.
Gonj	Marijuana	cannabis
Goob	Methcathinone	stimulants
Good	PCP; heroin	halluc.; narc.
Good and plenty	Heroin	narcotics
Good butt	Marijuana cigarette	cannabis
Good giggles	Marijuana	cannabis
Good go	Proper amount of drugs for the money paid	
Good H	Heroin	narcotics
Good horse	Heroin	narcotics
Good lick	Good drugs	
Good stuff	High potency drug, especially marijuana	cannabis
Goodfellas	Fentanyl	narcotics
Goody-goody	Marijuana	cannabis
Goof butt	Marijuana cigarette	cannabis
Goofball	Cocaine mixed with heroin; depressants	stim.; narc.; deprs.
Goofers	Depressants	depressants
Goofy's	LSD	hallucinogen
Goon	PCP	hallucinogen
Goon dust	PCP	hallucinogen
Goop	GHB	depressants
Gopher	Person paid to pickup drugs	
Gorge	Marijuana	cannabis
Goric	Opium	narcotics

Street Name	Definition	Drug Type
Gorilla biscuits	PCP	hallucinogen
Gorilla pills	Depressants	depressants
Gorilla tab	PCP	hallucinogen
Got it going on	Fast sale of drugs	
Graduate	Completely stop using drugs; progress to stronger drugs	
Gram	Hashish	cannabis
Granulated orange	Methamphetamine	stimulants
Grape parfait	LSD	hallucinogen
Grass	Marijuana	cannabis
Grass brownies	Marijuana	cannabis
Grasshopper	Marijuana	cannabis
Grata	Marijuana	cannabis
Gravel	Crack cocaine	stimulants
Gravy	Heroin; to inject a drug	narcotics
Grease	Currency	
Great bear	Fentanyl	narcotics
Great hormones at bedtime	GHB	depressants
Great tobacco	Opium	narcotics
Greek	Combination of marijuana and powder cocaine	cann.; stim.
Green	Inferior quality marijuana; ketamine; PCP	cann.; halluc.
Green buds	Marijuana	cannabis
Green double domes	LSD	hallucinogen
Green dragons	Depressants	depressants
Green frog	Depressants	depressants
Green goddess	Marijuana	cannabis
Green goods	Paper currency	
Green leaves	PCP	hallucinogen
Green single dome	LSD	hallucinogen
Green tea	PCP	hallucinogen
Green triangles	MDMA	hallucinogen
Green wedge	LSD	hallucinogen
Greenies	Amphetamine; MDMA	stim.; halluc.
Greens	Marijuana	cannabis
Greens/green stuff	Paper currency	
Greeter	Marijuana	cannabis
Gremmies	Combination of cocaine and marijuana	stim.; cann.
Greta	Marijuana	cannabis
Grey shields	LSD	hallucinogen
Griefo	Marijuana	cannabis
Griefs	Marijuana	cannabis
Grievous bodily harm	GHB	depressants
Grifa	Marijuana	cannabis

Substance Abuse

Street Name	Definition	Drug Type
Griff	Marijuana	cannabis
Griffa	Marijuana	cannabis
Griffo	Marijuana	cannabis
Grit	Crack cocaine	stimulants
Groceries	Crack cocaine	stimulants
Ground control	The guide or caretaker during a hallucinogenic experience	hallucinogen
Grow/s	Marijuana growing operations (indoor & outdoor)	cannabis
Gum	Opium; MDMA	narc.; halluc.
Guma	Opium	narcotics
Gun	To inject a drug; needle; hypodermic needle	
Gunga	Marijuana	cannabis
Gungeon	Marijuana	cannabis
Gungun	Marijuana	cannabis
Gunja	Marijuana	cannabis
Gutter	Vein into which a drug is injected	
Gutter junkie	Addict who relies on others to obtain drugs	
GWM	MDMA	hallucinogen
Gym candy	Steroids	steroids
Gyve	Marijuana cigarette	cannabis
H	Heroin	narcotics
H & C	Heroin and cocaine	narc.; stim.
H Caps	Heroin	narcotics
H-bomb	Ecstasy, MDMA, mixed with heroin	halluc.; narc.
Hache	Heroin	narcotics
Hail	Crack cocaine	stimulants
Haircut	Marijuana	cannabis
Hairy	Heroin	narcotics
Half	½ ounce	
Half a football field	50 rocks of crack	stimulants
Half elbows	½ pound of methamphetamine	stimulants
Half G	$500	
Half load	15 bags (decks) of heroin	narcotics
Half moon	Peyote	hallucinogen
Half piece	½ ounce of heroin or cocaine	narc.; stim.
Half track	Crack cocaine	stimulants
Half-a-C	$50 bill	
Hamburger helper	Crack cocaine	stimulants
Hammerheading	MDMA used with Viagra	hallucinogen
Hand-to-hand	Direct delivery and payment	
Hand-to-hand man	Transient dealers who carry small amounts of crack	stimulants
Hanhich	Marijuana	cannabis
Hanyak	Smokable methamphetamine	stimulants
Happy cigarette	Marijuana cigarette	cannabis
Happy drug	MDMA	hallucinogen
Happy dust	Cocaine	stimulants

Street Name	Definition	Drug Type
Happy pill	MDMA	hallucinogen
Happy powder	Cocaine	stimulants
Happy stick	Marijuana and PCP combination	cann.; halluc.
Happy Sticks	PCP	hallucinogen
Happy trails	Cocaine	stimulants
Hard ball	Crack cocaine	stimulants
Hard candy	Heroin	narcotics
Hard line	Crack cocaine	stimulants
Hard rock	Crack cocaine	stimulants
Hard stuff	Heroin; opium	narcotics
Hardware	Isobutyl nitrite; inhalants	inhalants
Harry	Heroin	narcotics
Harsh	Marijuana	cannabis
Has	Marijuana	cannabis
Hats	LSD	hallucinogen
Have a dust	Cocaine	stimulants
Haven dust	Cocaine	stimulants
Hawaiian	Very high potency marijuana	cannabis
Hawaiian Black	Marijuana	cannabis
Hawaiian homegrown hay	Marijuana	cannabis
Hawaiian sunshine	LSD	hallucinogen
Hawk	LSD	hallucinogen
Hay	Marijuana	cannabis
Hay butt	Marijuana cigarette	cannabis
Hayron	Heroin	narcotics
Haze	LSD	hallucinogen
Hazel	Heroin	narcotics
HCP	PCP	hallucinogen
He-man	Fentanyl	narcotics
Head drugs	Amphetamine	stimulants
Head light	LSD	hallucinogen
Head shop	Store specializing in sale of drug paraphernalia	
Heart-on	Inhalants	inhalants
Hearts	Amphetamine	stimulants
Heat	Police or narcotics officers	
Heaven	Cocaine; heroin	stim.; narc.
Heaven & Hell	PCP	hallucinogen
Heaven dust	Cocaine; heroin	stim.; narc.
Heavenly blue	LSD	hallucinogen
Heeled	Having plenty of money	
Helen	Heroin	narcotics
Hell	Crack cocaine	stimulants
Hell dust	Heroin	narcotics
Henpecking	Searching on hands and knees for crack	stimulants
Henry	Heroin	narcotics
Henry VIII	Cocaine	stimulants

Street Name	Definition	Drug Type
Her	Cocaine	stimulants
Hera	Heroin	narcotics
Herb	Marijuana	cannabis
Herb and Al	Marijuana and alcohol	cannabis
Herba	Marijuana	cannabis
Herbal bliss	MDMA	hallucinogen
Herms	PCP	hallucinogen
Hero	Heroin	narcotics
Hero of the underworld	Heroin	narcotics
Heroina	Heroin	narcotics
Herone	Heroin	narcotics
Hessle	Heroin	narcotics
Hiagra in a bottle	Inhalants	inhalants
Highball	Inhalants	inhalants
Highbeams	The wide eyes of a person on crack	stimulants
Hikori	Peyote	hallucinogen
Hikuli	Peyote	hallucinogen
Hillbilly heroin	OxyContin	narcotics
Him	Heroin	narcotics
Hinkley	PCP	hallucinogen
Hippie crack	Inhalants	inhalants
Hippieflip	Use of mushrooms and MDMA	hallucinogen
Hironpon	Smokable methamphetamine	stimulants
Hiropon	Smokable methamphetamine	stimulants
Hit	To smoke marijuana; marijuana cigarette; crack cocaine	cann.; stim.
Hit house	House where users go to shoot up and leave the owner drugs as payment	
Hit the hay	To smoke marijuana	cannabis
Hit the main line	To inject a drug	
Hit the needle	To inject a drug	
Hit the pit	To inject a drug	
Hitch up the reindeers	To inhale cocaine	stimulants
Hitter	Little pipe designed for only one hit	
Hitters	People who inject others who have hard to find veins in exchange for drugs	
Hitting up	To inject a drug	
Hocus	Marijuana; opium	cann.; narc.
Hog	PCP	hallucinogen
Holding	Possessing drugs	
Holiday meth	Green methamphetamine produced using Drano crystals	stimulants
Holy terror	Heroin	narcotics
Hombre	Heroin	narcotics
Hombrecitos	Psilocybin	hallucinogen
Homegrown	Marijuana	cannabis
Homicide	Heroin cut with scopolamine or strychnine	narcotics
Honey	Currency	

Street Name	Definition	Drug Type
Honey blunts	Marijuana cigars sealed with honey	cannabis
Honey oil	Ketamine; inhalants	deprs.; inhal.
Honeymoon	Early stages of drug use before addiction or dependency develops	
Hong-yen	Heroin in pill form	narcotics
Hooch	Marijuana	cannabis
Hooked	Addicted	
Hooter	Cocaine; marijuana	stim.; cann.
Hop/hops	Opium	narcotics
Hopped up	Under the influence of drugs	
Horn	To inhale cocaine; crack pipe; to inhale a drug	stimulants
Horning	To inhale cocaine; heroin	stim.; narc.
Horse	Heroin	narcotics
Horse heads	Amphetamine	stimulants
Horse tracks	PCP	hallucinogen
Horse tranquilizer	PCP	hallucinogen
Horsebite	Heroin	narcotics
Hospital heroin	Dilaudid	narcotics
Hot dope	Heroin	narcotics
Hot heroin	Heroin poisoned to give to a police informant	narcotics
Hot ice	Smokable methamphetamine	stimulants
Hot load/hot shot	Lethal injection of a narcotic	narcotics
Hot rolling	Liquefying methamphetamine in an eye dropper and then inhaling it	stimulants
Hot stick	Marijuana cigarette	cannabis
Hotcakes	Crack cocaine	stimulants
House fee	Money paid to enter a crack house	stimulants
House piece	Crack given to the owner of a crack house of apartment where crack users congregate	stimulants
How do you like me now?	Crack cocaine	stimulants
Hows	Morphine	narcotics
HRN	Heroin	narcotics
Hubba	Crack cocaine	stimulants
Hubba pigeon	Crack users looking for rocks on the floor after a police raid	stimulants
Hubba, I am back	Crack cocaine	stimulants
Hubbas	Crack	stimulants
Huff	Inhalants	inhalants
Huffer	Inhalant abuser	inhalants
Hug drug	MDMA	hallucinogen
Hugs and Kisses	Combination of methamphetamine and MDMA	stim.; halluc.
Hulling	Using others to get drugs	
Hunter	Cocaine	stimulants
Hustle	Attempt to obtain drug customers	

Street Name	Definition	Drug Type
Hyatari	Peyote	hallucinogen
Hydro	Amphetamine; high quality methamphetamine; marijuana; MDMA; marijuana grown in water	stim.; stim.; cann.; halluc.; cann.
Hype	Heroin addict; an addict; MDMA	hallucinogen
Hype stick	Hypodermic needle	
I am back	Crack	
Iboga	Amphetamine; MDMA	stim.; halluc.
Ice	Cocaine; crack cocaine; smokable methamphetamine; methamphetamine; MDMA; PCP	stim.; halluc.
Ice cream habit	Occasional use of drugs	
Ice cubs	Crack cocaine	stimulants
Icing	Cocaine	stimulants
Idiot pills	Depressants	depressants
Igloo	MDMA	hallucinogen
Ill	PCP	hallucinogen
Illies	Marijuana dipped in PCP	cann.; halluc.
Illing	Marijuana dipped in PCP	cann.; halluc.
Illy	Marijuana cigarettes soaked in embalming fluid and dried	cannabis
Illy momo	PCP	hallucinogen
In	Connected with drug suppliers	
Inbetweens	Amphetamine; depressants	stim.; deprs.
Inca message	Cocaine	stimulants
Indian boy	Marijuana	cannabis
Indian hay	Marijuana from India	cannabis
Indian hemp	Marijuana	cannabis
Indica	Species of cannabis found in hot climate	cannabis
Indo	Marijuana, term from Northern CA	cannabis
Indonesian bud	Marijuana; opium	cann.; narc.
Instaga	Marijuana	cannabis
Instagu	Marijuana	cannabis
Instant zen	LSD	hallucinogen
Interplanetary mission	Travel from one crack house to another to search for crack	stimulants
Isda	Heroin	narcotics
Issues	Crack cocaine	stimulants
J	Marijuana cigarette	cannabis
Jab/job	To inject a drug	
Jackpot	Fentanyl	narcotics
Jag	Keep a high going	
Jam	Cocaine; amphetamine	stimulants
Jam cecil	Amphetamine	stimulants
Jamaican gold	Marijuana	cannabis
Jamaican red hair	Marijuana	cannabis
Jane	Marijuana	cannabis
Jay	Marijuana cigarette	cannabis
Jay smoke	Marijuana	cannabis
Jee gee	Heroin	narcotics

Street Name	Definition	Drug Type
Jefferson airplane	Used match cut in half to hold a partially smoke marijuana cigarette	cannabis
Jejo	Cocaine	stimulants
Jellies	Depressants; MDMA in gel caps	deprs.; halluc.
Jelly	Cocaine	stimulants
Jelly baby	Amphetamine	stimulants
Jelly bean	Amphetamine; depressants	stim.; deprs.
Jelly beans	Crack cocaine	stimulants
Jerry Garcias	MDMA	hallucinogen
Jerry Springer	Heroin	narcotics
Jet	Ketamine	depressants
Jet fuel	PCP; methamphetamine	halluc.; stim.
Jib	GHB	depressants
Jim Jones	Marijuana laced with cocaine and PCP	cann.; stim.; halluc.
Jive	Marijuana; heroin; drugs	cann.; narc.
Jive doo jee	Heroin	narcotics
Jive stick	Marijuana	cannabis
Joharito	Heroin	narcotics
Johnson	Crack cocaine	stimulants
Joint	Marijuana cigarette	cannabis
Jojee	Heroin	narcotics
Jolly bean	Amphetamine	stimulants
Jolly green	Marijuana	cannabis
Jolly pop	Casual user of heroin	narcotics
Jolt	Strong reaction to drugs; to inject a drug	
Jones	Heroin	narcotics
Jonesing	Need for drugs	
Joy	Heroin	narcotics
Joy flakes	Heroin	narcotics
Joy juice	Depressants	depressants
Joy plant	Opium	narcotics
Joy pop	To inject a drug	
Joy popping	Occasional use of drugs	
Joy powder	Cocaine; heroin	stim.; narc.
Joy smoke	Marijuana	cannabis
Joy stick	Marijuana cigarette; marijuana and PCP combination	cann.; halluc.
Ju-ju	Marijuana cigarette	cannabis
Juan Valdez	Marijuana	cannabis
Juanita	Marijuana	cannabis
Juggle	Sell drugs to another addict to support a habit	
Juggler	Teen-aged street dealer	
Jugs	Amphetamine	stimulants
Juice	PCP; steroids	halluc.; ster.
Juice joint	Marijuana cigarette sprinkled with crack	cann.; stim.
Juja	Marijuana	cannabis
Jum	Sealed plastic bag containing crack	stimulants

Substance Abuse

Street Name	Definition	Drug Type
Jumbos	Large vials of crack sold on the streets; marijuana mixed with crack	stim.; cann.; stim.
Junco	Heroin	narcotics
Junk	Cocaine; heroin	stim.; narc.
Junkie	Addict	
Junkie kits	Glass pipe and copper mesh	
K	PCP	hallucinogen
K-blast	PCP	hallucinogen
K-hole	Periods of ketamine-induced confusion; the depressant high associated with ketamine	hallucinogen
Kabak	Marijuana; Turkish marijuana	cannabis
Kabayo	Heroin	narcotics
Kabuki	Crack pipe made from a plastic rum bottle and a rubber sparkplug cover	stimulants
Kaff	Very potent marijuana from Morocco, Lebanon and other Arab/Middle Eastern countries	cannabis
Kaksonjae	Smokable methamphetamine	stimulants
Kalakit	Marijuana	cannabis
Kali	Marijuana	cannabis
Kangaroo	Crack	stimulants
Kansas grass	Marijuana	cannabis
Kaps	PCP	hallucinogen
Karachi	Heroin, phenobarbital, and methaqualone	narc.; deprs.
Karo	Codeine cough syrup	narcotics
Kate bush	Marijuana	cannabis
Kaya	Marijuana	cannabis
KB	Marijuana	cannabis
Kee	Marijuana	cannabis
Kentucky blue	Marijuana	cannabis
Kester plant	Drugs hidden in the rectum	
Ket	Ketamine	depressants
Key	Marijuana	cannabis
KGB (Killer Green Bud)	Marijuana	cannabis
Khat	Amphetamine; methcathinone; MDMA	stim.; halluc.
Khayf	Very potent marijuana from Morocco, Lebanon and other Arab/Middle Eastern countries	cannabis
Ki	Marijuana	cannabis
Kibbles & Bits	Small crumbs of crack	stimulants
Kick	Inhalants; getting off a drug habit	inhalants
Kick stick	Marijuana cigarette	cannabis
Kicker	OxyContin	narcotics
Kiddie dope	Prescription drugs	
Kief	Very potent marijuana from Morocco, Lebanon and other Arab/Middle Eastern countries	cannabis

Street Name	Definition	Drug Type
Kiff	Marijuana cigarette; very potent marijuana from Morocco, Lebanon and other Arab/Middle Eastern countries	cannabis
Killer	Marijuana; PCP	cann.; halluc.
Killer green bud	Marijuana	cannabis
Killer joints	PCP	hallucinogen
Killer weed	Marijuana (in the 1980s: Marijuana and PCP)	cannabis
Kilo	2.2 pounds	
Kilter	Marijuana	cannabis
Kind	Marijuana	cannabis
Kind bug	High quality marijuana	cannabis
King	Cocaine	stimulants
King bud	Marijuana	cannabis
King ivory	Fentanyl	narcotics
King Kong pills	Depressants	depressants
King's habit	Cocaine	stimulants
Kissing	The exchange of plastic wrapped rocks (crack) by kissing or through mouth to mouth transfer	stimulants
Kit	Equipment used to inject drugs	
Kit kat	Ketamine	depressants
Kitty flipping	Ketamine and MDMA	deprs.; halluc.
KJ	PCP	hallucinogen
Kleenex	MDMA	hallucinogen
Klingons	Crack addicts	stimulants
Kokomo	Crack cocaine	stimulants
Kona gold	Marijuana	cannabis
Kools	PCP	hallucinogen
Krippy	Marijuana	cannabis
Kryptonite	Crack cocaine; marijuana	stim.; cann.
Krystal	PCP	hallucinogen
Krystal joint	PCP	hallucinogen
Kumba	Marijuana	cannabis
KW	PCP	hallucinogen
L	LSD	hallucinogen
L.A.	Long-acting amphetamine	stimulants
L.A. glass	Smokable methamphetamine	stimulants
L.A. ice	Smokable methamphetamine	stimulants
L.L.	Marijuana	cannabis
La buena	Heroin	narcotics
La chiva	Heroin	narcotics
La rocha	Rohypnol	depressants
Lace	Cocaine and marijuana	stim.; cann.
Lactone	GBL	depressants
Lady	Cocaine	stimulants
Lady caine	Cocaine	stimulants
Lady snow	Cocaine	stimulants
Lakbay diva	Marijuana	cannabis

Substance Abuse

Street Name	Definition	Drug Type
Lamborghini	Crack pipe made from a plastic rum bottle and a rubber sparkplug cover	stimulants
Las mujercitas	Psilocybin	hallucinogen
Lason sa daga	LSD	hallucinogen
Late night	Cocaine	stimulants
Laugh and scratch	To inject a drug	
Laughing gas	Nitrous oxide	inhalants
Laughing grass	Marijuana	cannabis
Laughing weed	Marijuana	cannabis
Lay back	Depressants	depressants
Lay-out	Equipment for taking drugs	
LBJ	Heroin; LSD; PCP	narc.; halluc.
Leaf	Cocaine; Marijuana	stim.; cann.
Leak	Marijuana and PCP combination	cann.; halluc.
Leaky bolla	PCP	hallucinogen
Leaky leak	PCP	hallucinogen
Lean	Codeine cough syrup	narcotics
Leapers	Amphetamine	stimulants
Leaping	Under the influence of drugs	
Legal speed	Over the counter asthma drug; trade name MiniThin	
Lemon 714	PCP	hallucinogen
Lemon drop	Methamphetamine with a dull yellow tint	stimulants
Lemonade	Heroin; poor quality drugs	narcotics
Leno	Marijuana	cannabis
Lenos	PCP	hallucinogen
Lens	LSD	hallucinogen
Lethal weapon	PCP	hallucinogen
Letter biscuits	MDMA	hallucinogen
Lettuce	Money	
LG (Lime Green)	Marijuana	cannabis
Lib (Librium)	Depressants	depressants
Lid	1 ounce of marijuana	cannabis
Lid poppers	Amphetamine	stimulants
Lid proppers	Amphetamine	stimulants
Light stuff	Marijuana	cannabis
Lightning	Amphetamine	stimulants
Lima	Marijuana	cannabis
Lime acid	LSD	hallucinogen
Line	Cocaine	stimulants
Liprimo	Marijuana and crack rolled in a joint	cann.; stim.
Lipton tea	Poor quality drugs	
Liquid E	GHB	depressants
Liquid ecstasy	GHB	depressants
Liquid G	GHB	depressants
Liquid lady	Cocaine dissolved in water and used as nasal spray	stimulants
Liquid X	GHB	depressants
Lit up	Under the influence of drugs	

Street Name	Definition	Drug Type
Little bomb	Heroin; amphetamine; depressants	narc.; stim.; deprs.
Little ones	PCP	hallucinogen
Little smoke	Marijuana; LSD; psilocybin/psilocin	cann.; halluc.
Live ones	PCP	hallucinogen
Llesca	Marijuana	cannabis
Load	25 bags of heroin	narcotics
Load of laundry	Methamphetamine	stimulants
Loaded	High	
Loaf	Marijuana	cannabis
Lobo	Marijuana	cannabis
Locker room	Isobutyl nitrite; inhalants	inhalants
Loco	Marijuana	cannabis
Loco weed	Marijuana	cannabis
Locoweed	Marijuana	cannabis
Log	Marijuana cigarette; PCP	cann.; halluc.
Logor	LSD	hallucinogen
Loony Toons	LSD	hallucinogen
Loose shank	Marijuana	cannabis
Loused	Covered by sores and abscesses from repeated use of unsterile needles	
Love	Crack cocaine	stimulants
Love affair	Cocaine	stimulants
Love boat	Marijuana dipped in formaldehyde; PCP; blunts mixed with marijuana and heroin; blunts mixed with marijuana and PCP	cann.; halluc.; cann., narc.; cann., halluc.
Love drug	Depressants; MDMA	deprs.; halluc.
Love flipping	Mescaline and MDMA	hallucinogen
Love leaf	Marijuana and PCP combination	cann.; halluc.
Love pearls	Alpha-ethyltryptamine	hallucinogen
Love pill	MDMA	hallucinogen
Love pills	Alpha-ethyltryptamine	hallucinogen
Love trip	Mescaline and MDMA	hallucinogen
Love weed	Marijuana	cannabis
Loveboat	PCP; Marijuana and PCP combination	hallucinogen
Lovelies	Marijuana laced with PCP	cann.; halluc.
Lovely	PCP	hallucinogen
Lover's speed	MDMA	hallucinogen
Lover's special	MDMA	hallucinogen
LSD	Lysergic acid diethylamide	hallucinogen
Lubage	Marijuana	cannabis
Lucy in the sky with diamonds	LSD	hallucinogen
Ludes	Depressants; methaqualone	depressants
Luding out	Depressants	depressants
Luds	Depressants	depressants
Lunch money drug	Rohypnol	depressants
M	Marijuana; morphine	cann.; narc.
M&M	Depressants	depressants

Street Name	Definition	Drug Type
M.J.	Marijuana	cannabis
M.O.	Marijuana	cannabis
M.S.	Morphine	narcotics
M.U.	Marijuana	cannabis
Ma'a	Crack cocaine (Samoan)	stimulants
Macaroni	Marijuana	cannabis
Macaroni and Cheese	$5 pack of marijuana and a dime bag of cocaine	cann.; stim.
Machinery	Marijuana	cannabis
Macon	Marijuana	cannabis
Maconha	Marijuana	cannabis
Mad dog	PCP	hallucinogen
Madman	PCP	hallucinogen
Mafu	Marijuana	cannabis
Magic	PCP	hallucinogen
Magic dust	PCP	hallucinogen
Magic mushroom	Psilocybin/psilocin	hallucinogen
Magic smoke	Marijuana	cannabis
Mainline	To inject a drug	
Mainliner	Person who injects into the vein	
Make up	Need to find more drugs	
Mama coca	Cocaine	stimulants
Manhattan silver	Marijuana	cannabis
Manteca	Heroin	narcotics
MAO	Amphetamine; MDMA	stim.; halluc.
Marathons	Amphetamine	stimulants
Marching dust	Cocaine	stimulants
Marching powder	Cocaine	stimulants
Mari	Marijuana cigarette	cannabis
Maria Pastora	Salvia divinorum	cannabis
Marimba	Marijuana	cannabis
Marshmallow reds	Depressants	depressants
Mary	Marijuana	cannabis
Mary and Johnny	Marijuana	cannabis
Mary Ann	Marijuana	cannabis
Mary Jane	Marijuana	cannabis
Mary Jonas	Marijuana	cannabis
Mary Warner	Marijuana	cannabis
Mary Weaver	Marijuana	cannabis
Maserati	Crack pipe made from a plastic rum bottle and a rubber sparkplug cover	stimulants
Matchbox	¼ ounce of marijuana or 6 marijuana cigarettes	cannabis
Matsakow	Heroin	narcotics
Maui wauie	Marijuana from Hawaii	cannabis
Maui-wowie	Marijuana; methamphetamine	cann.; stim.
Max	GHB dissolved in water and mixed with amphetamines	deprs.; stim.
Maxibolin	Oral steroids	steroids

Street Name	Definition	Drug Type
Mayo	Cocaine; heroin	stim.; narc.
MDM	MDMA	hallucinogen
MDMA	Methylenedioxymethamphetamine	stimulants
Mean green	PCP	hallucinogen
Medusa	Inhalants	inhalants
Meg	Marijuana	cannabis
Megg	Marijuana cigarette	cannabis
Meggie	Marijuana	cannabis
Mellow yellow	LSD	hallucinogen
Mercedes	MDMA	hallucinogen
Merchandise	Drugs	
Merck	Cocaine	stimulants
Merk	Cocaine	stimulants
Mesc	Mescaline	hallucinogen
Mescal	Mescaline	hallucinogen
Mese	Mescaline	hallucinogen
Messorole	Marijuana	cannabis
Meth	Methamphetamine	stimulants
Meth head	Methamphetamine regular user	stimulants
Meth monster	One who has a violent reaction to methamphetamine	stimulants
Meth speed ball	Methamphetamine combined with heroin	stim.; narc.
Methatriol	Injectable steroids	steroids
Methedrine	Amphetamine; MDMA	stim.; halluc.
Methlies Quik	Methamphetamine	stimulants
Methyltesto-sterone	Oral steroids	steroids
Mexican brown	Marijuana; heroin	cann.; narc.
Mexican crack	Methamphetamine with the appearance of crack; methamphetamine	stimulants
Mexican green	Marijuana	cannabis
Mexican horse	Heroin	narcotics
Mexican locoweed	Marijuana	cannabis
Mexican mud	Heroin	narcotics
Mexican mushrooms	Psilocybin/psilocin	hallucinogen
Mexican red	Marijuana	cannabis
Mexican reds	Depressants	depressants
Mexican speedballs	Crack and methamphetamine	stimulants
Mexican valium	Rohypnol	depressants
Mezc	Mescaline	hallucinogen
MFT	Nexus	hallucinogen
Mickey Finn	Depressants	depressants
Mickey's	Depressant; LSD	deprs.; halluc.
Microdot	LSD	hallucinogen
Midnight oil	Opium	narcotics
Mighty Joe Young	Depressants	depressants

Street Name	Definition	Drug Type
Mighty mezz	Marijuana cigarette	cannabis
Mighty Quinn	LSD	hallucinogen
Mighty white	A form of crack cocaine that is hard, white, and pure	stimulants
Mind detergent	LSD	hallucinogen
Mini beans	Amphetamine; MDMA	stim.; halluc.
Minibennie	Amphetamine	stimulants
Mint leaf	PCP	hallucinogen
Mint weed	PCP	hallucinogen
Mira	Opium	narcotics
Miss	To inject a drug	
Miss Emma	Morphine	narcotics
Missile basing	Crack liquid and PCP	stim.; halluc.
Mission	Trip out of the crack house to obtain crack	stimulants
Mist	PCP; crack smoke in the bottom of a glass pipe	hallucinogen
Mister blue	Morphine	narcotics
Mitsubishi	MDMA	hallucinogen
Mix	Cocaine; a drug environment	stimulants
Mixed jive	Crack cocaine	stimulants
Mo	Marijuana	cannabis
Modams	Marijuana	cannabis
Mohasky	Marijuana	cannabis
Mohasty	Marijuana	cannabis
Mojo	Cocaine; heroin	stim.; narc.
Money talks	Heroin	narcotics
Monkey	Cigarette made from cocaine paste and tobacco; drug dependency; heroin	stim.; narc.
Monkey dust	PCP	hallucinogen
Monkey tranquilizer	PCP	hallucinogen
Monoamine oxidase	Amphetamine; MDMA	stim.; halluc.
Monos	Cigarette made from cocaine paste and tobacco	stimulants
Monster	Cocaine	stimulants
Monte	Marijuana from South America	cannabis
Mooca/moocah	Marijuana	cannabis
Moon	Mescaline	hallucinogen
Moon gas	Inhalants	inhalants
Moonrock	Crack mixed with heroin	stim.; narc.
Moonstone	When a dealer shaves a slice of MDMA into a bag of heroin	halluc.; narc.
Mooster	Marijuana	cannabis
Moota/mutah	Marijuana	cannabis
Mooters	Marijuana cigarette	cannabis
Mootie	Marijuana	cannabis
Mootos	Marijuana	cannabis
Mor a grifa	Marijuana	cannabis
More	PCP	hallucinogen

Street Name	Definition	Drug Type
Morf	Morphine	narcotics
Morning shot	Amphetamine; MDMA	stim.; halluc.
Morning wake-up	First black of crack from the pipe	stimulants
Morotgara	Heroin	narcotics
Morpho	Morphine	narcotics
Mortal combat	High potency heroin	narcotics
Mosquitos	Cocaine	stimulants
Mota/moto	Marijuana	cannabis
Mother	Marijuana	cannabis
Mother's little helper	Depressants	depressants
Motorcycle crack	Methamphetamine	stimulants
Mouth worker	One who takes drugs orally	
Movie star drug	Cocaine	stimulants
Mow the grass	To smoke marijuana	cannabis
Mu	Marijuana	cannabis
Mud	Heroin; opium	narcotics
Muggie	Marijuana	cannabis
Muggle	Marijuana	cannabis
Muggles	Marijuana	cannabis
Mujer	Cocaine	stimulants
Mule	Carrier of drugs	
Murder 8	Fentanyl	narcotics
Murder One	Heroin and cocaine	narc.; stim.
Murotugora	Heroin	narcotics
Mushrooms	Psilocybin/psilocin	hallucinogen
Musk	Psilocybin/psilocin	hallucinogen
Muta	Marijuana	cannabis
Mutha	Marijuana	cannabis
Muzzle	Heroin	narcotics
Nail	Marijuana cigarette	cannabis
Nailed	Arrested	
Nanoo	Heroin	narcotics
Nazimeth	Methamphetamine	stimulants
Nebbies	Depressants	depressants
Nemmies	Depressants	depressants
New acid	PCP	hallucinogen
New addition	Crack cocaine	stimulants
New Jack Swing	Heroin and morphine	narcotics
New magic	PCP	hallucinogen
Nexus	2-(4-Bromo-2,5 diethoxy-phenyl)-ethylamine; 2CB	hallucinogen
Nexus flipping	Use of Nexus and MDMA	hallucinogen
Nice and easy	Heroin	narcotics
Nickel bag	$5 worth of drugs; heroin	narcotics
Nickel deck	Heroin	narcotics
Nickel note	$5 bill	
Nickelonians	Crack addicts	stimulants
Niebla	PCP	hallucinogen

Street Name	Definition	Drug Type
Nieve	Cocaine	stimulants
Nigra	Marijuana	cannabis
Nimbies	Depressants	depressants
Nineteen	Amphetamine; MDMA	stim.; halluc.
Nix	Stranger among the group	
No worries	Depressant	depressants
Nod	Effects of heroin	narcotics
Nods	Codeine cough syrup	narcotics
Noise	Heroin	narcotics
Nontoucher	Crack user who doesn't want affection during or after smoking crack	stimulants
Northern lights	Marijuana from Canada	cannabis
Nose	Cocaine; heroin	stim.; narc.
Nose candy	Cocaine	stimulants
Nose drops	Liquified heroin	narcotics
Nose powder	Cocaine	stimulants
Nose stuff	Cocaine	stimulants
NOX	Use of nitrous oxide and MDMA	inhal.; halluc.
Nubs	Peyote	hallucinogen
Nugget	Amphetamine	stimulants
Nuggets	Crack cocaine	stimulants
Number	Marijuana cigarette	cannabis
Number 3	Cocaine; heroin	stim.; narc.
Number 4	Heroin	narcotics
Number 8	Heroin	narcotics
Nurse	Heroin	narcotics
O	Opium	narcotics
O.J.	Marijuana	cannabis
O.P.	Opium	narcotics
O.P.P.	PCP	hallucinogen
O.Z.	1 ounce of a drug substance	
Octane	PCP laced with gasoline	hallucinogen
Ogoy	Heroin	narcotics
Oil	Heroin; PCP	narc.; halluc.
Old garbage	Heroin	narcotics
Old navy	Heroin	narcotics
Old Steve	Heroin	narcotics
On a mission	Searching for crack and/or being high on crack	stimulants
On a trip	Under the influence of drugs	
On ice	In jail	
On the ball	When a dealer shaves a slice of MDMA into a bag of heroin	halluc.; narc.
On the brocks	Walking the streets	
On the nod	Under the influence of narcotics or depressant	narc.; deprs.
One and one	To inhale cocaine	stimulants
One and Ones	Injected combination of Talwin and Ritalin	stimulants
One bomb	100 rocks of crack cocaine	stimulants

Street Name	Definition	Drug Type
One on one house	Where cocaine and heroin can be purchased	stimulants
One plus one sales	Selling cocaine and heroin together	stimulants
One tissue box	1 ounce of crack	stimulants
One way	LSD; heroin	halluc.; narc.
One-fifty-one	Crack; crack sprinkled on tobacco	stimulants
One-stop shop	Place where more than one drug is sold	
Onion	1 ounce of crack cocaine	stimulants
Oolies	Marijuana cigarettes laced with crack	cann.; stim.
Ope	Opium	narcotics
Optical illusions	LSD	hallucinogen
Orange bandits	MDMA	hallucinogen
Orange barrels	LSD	hallucinogen
Orange crystal	PCP	hallucinogen
Orange cubes	LSD	hallucinogen
Orange haze	LSD	hallucinogen
Orange line	Heroin	narcotics
Orange micro	LSD	hallucinogen
Orange wedges	LSD	hallucinogen
Oranges	Amphetamine	stimulants
Organic quaalude	GHB	depressants
Os	OxyContin	narcotics
Outerlimits	Crack and LSD	stim.; halluc.
Owsley	LSD	hallucinogen
Owsley's acid	LSD	hallucinogen
Ox	OxyContin	narcotics
Oxicotten	A semi-synthetic opiate	narcotics
Oxy	OxyContin	narcotics
Oxy 80's	A semi-synthetic opiate	narcotics
Oxycet	A semi-synthetic opiate	narcotics
Oxycotton	OxyContin	narcotics
Oyster stew	Cocaine	stimulants
Oz	Inhalants	inhalants
Ozone	Marijuana, PCP and crack cigarette; marijuana cigarette; PCP	cann.; halluc. stim.; cann.; halluc.
OZs	Methamphetamine	stimulants
P	Peyote; PCP	hallucinogen
P-dogs	Cocaine and marijuana combination	stim.; cann.
P-dope	20-30% pure heroin	narcotics
P-funk	Crack mixed with PCP; heroin	stim.; halluc.; narc.
P.R.	Panama Red	cannabis
Pack	Marijuana; heroin	cann.; narc.
Pack a bowl	Marijuana	cannabis
Pack of rocks	Marijuana cigarette	cannabis
Pakaloco	Marijuana ("crazy tobacco")	cannabis
Pakalolo	Marijuana	cannabis
Pakistani black	Marijuana	cannabis

Street Name	Definition	Drug Type
Panama cut	Marijuana	cannabis
Panama gold	Marijuana	cannabis
Panama red	Marijuana	cannabis
Panatella	Large marijuana cigarette	cannabis
Pancakes and syrup	Combination of glutethimide and codeine cough syrup	deprs.; narc.
Pane	LSD	hallucinogen
Pangonadalot	Heroin	narcotics
Panic	Drugs not available	
Paper	A dosage unit of heroin; 1/10 of a gram or less of the drug ice or methamphetamine	narc.; stim.
Paper acid	LSD	hallucinogen
Paper bag	Container for drugs	
Paper blunts	Marijuana within a paper casing rather than a tobacco leaf casing	cannabis
Paper boy	Heroin peddler	narcotics
Papers	Folded paper used to package drugs	
Parabolin	Oral steroids; veterinary steroid	steroids
Parachute	Crack and PCP smoked; heroin; smokable crack and heroin mixture	stim.; halluc.; narc.; stim.; narc.
Parachute down	Use of MDMA after heroin	halluc.; narc.
Paradise	Cocaine	stimulants
Paradise white	Cocaine	stimulants
Pariba	Powder cocaine	stimulants
Parlay	Crack cocaine	stimulants
Parsley	Marijuana; PCP	cann.; halluc.
Party pack	Combination of 2C-B (Nexus) with other illicit drugs, particularly MDMA	hallucinogen
Paste	Crack cocaine	stimulants
Pasto	Marijuana	cannabis
Pat	Marijuana	cannabis
Patico	Crack cocaine	stimulants
Paz	PCP	hallucinogen
PCPA	PCP	hallucinogen
Peace	PCP; LSD	hallucinogen
Peace pill	PCP	hallucinogen
Peace tablets	LSD	hallucinogen
Peace weed	PCP	hallucinogen
Peaches	Amphetamine	stimulants
Peanut	Depressants	depressants
Peanut butter	Methamphetamine; PCP mixed with peanut butter	stim.; halluc.
Pearl	Cocaine	stimulants
Pearls	Amyl nitrite	inhalants
Pearly gates	LSD	hallucinogen
Pebbles	Crack cocaine	stimulants
Peddlar	Drug supplier	
Pee Wee	Crack cocaine; $5 worth of crack	stimulants
Peep	PCP	hallucinogen

Street Name	Definition	Drug Type
Peeper/s	MDMA user	hallucinogen
Peg	Heroin	narcotics
Pellets	LSD	hallucinogen
Pen yan	Opium	narcotics
Pep pills	Amphetamine	stimulants
Pepsi habit	Occasional use of drugs	
Percia	Cocaine	stimulants
Percio	Cocaine	stimulants
Perfect high	Heroin	narcotics
Perico	Cocaine	stimulants
Perlas	Street dealer, especially heroin	narcotics
Perp	Fake crack made of candle wax and baking soda	stimulants
Peruvian	Cocaine	stimulants
Peruvian flake	Cocaine	stimulants
Peruvian lady	Cocaine	stimulants
Peter	Depressants	depressants
Peter Pan	PCP	hallucinogen
Peth	Depressant	depressants
Peyote	Mescaline	hallucinogen
Pharming	Consuming a mixture of prescription drugs	
Phennies	Depressants	depressants
Phenos	Depressants	depressants
Philly blunts	Marijuana	cannabis
Pianoing	Using the fingers to find lost crack	stimulants
Picking	Searching on hands and knees for cocaine or crack	stimulants
Piece	Cocaine; crack cocaine; 1 ounce	stimulants
Piedra	Crack cocaine	stimulants
Pig killer	PCP	hallucinogen
Piggybacking	Simultaneous injection of 2 drugs; sequential use of more than one MDMA tablet	hallucinogen
Pikachu	Pills containing PCP and Ecstasy	hallucinogen
Piles	Crack cocaine	stimulants
Pill houses	Residences where pills are illicitly sold	
Pill ladies	Female senior citizens who sell OxyContin	narcotics
Pills	OxyContin	narcotics
Pimp	Cocaine	stimulants
Pimp your pipe	Lending or renting crack pipe or stem	stimulants
Pin	Marijuana	cannabis
Pin gon	Opium	narcotics
Pin yen	Opium	narcotics
Ping-in-wing	To inject a drug	
Pingus	Rohypnol	depressants
Pink	Methamphetamine	stimulants
Pink blotters	LSD	hallucinogen
Pink elephants	Methamphetamine	stimulants
Pink hearts	Amphetamine; methamphetamine	stimulants
Pink ladies	Depressants	depressants

Substance Abuse

Street Name	Definition	Drug Type
Pink panther	LSD	hallucinogen
Pink panthers	MDMA	hallucinogen
Pink robots	LSD	hallucinogen
Pink wedges	LSD	hallucinogen
Pink witches	LSD	hallucinogen
Pipe	Crack pipe; marijuana pipe; vein into which a drug is injected; mix drugs with other substances	stim.; cann.
Pipero	Crack user	stimulants
Pit	PCP	hallucinogen
Pits	PCP	hallucinogen
Pixies	Amphetamine	stimulants
Plant	Hiding place for drugs	
Playboy bunnies	MDMA	hallucinogen
Playboys	MDMA	hallucinogen
Pluto	Heroin	narcotics
Pocket rocket	Marijuana; marijuana cigarette	cannabis
Pod	Marijuana	cannabis
Point	A needle	
Poison	Heroin; fentanyl	narcotics
Poke	Marijuana; to smoke marijuana	cannabis
Pollutants	Amphetamine; MDMA	stim.; halluc.
Polo	Mixture of heroin and motion sickness drug	narcotics
Polvo	Heroin; PCP	narc.; halluc.
Polvo blanco	Cocaine	stimulants
Polvo de angel	PCP	hallucinogen
Polvo de estrellas	PCP	hallucinogen
Pony	Crack cocaine	stimulants
Pony packs	Folded paper used to package drugs	
Poor man's coke	Methamphetamine	stimulants
Poor man's heroin	Injected combination of Talwin and Ritalin	stimulants
Poor man's pot	Inhalants	inhalants
Pop	To inhale cocaine	stimulants
Poppers	Isobutyl nitrite; amyl nitrite; methamphetamine	inhalants
Poppy	Heroin	narcotics
Pot	Marijuana	cannabis
Potato	LSD	hallucinogen
Potato chips	Crack cut with benzocaine	stimulants
Potlikker	Marijuana	cannabis
Potten bush	Marijuana	cannabis
Powder	Cocaine HCL; heroin; amphetamine	stim.; narc.; stim.
Powder diamonds	Cocaine	stimulants
Power puller	Rubber piece attached to crack stem	stimulants
Pox	Opium	narcotics
Predator	Heroin	narcotics
Prescription	Marijuana cigarette	cannabis
Press	Cocaine; crack cocaine	stimulants

Street Name	Definition	Drug Type
Pretendica	Marijuana	cannabis
Pretendo	Marijuana	cannabis
Primbolin	Injectable and oral steroids	steroids
Prime time	Crack cocaine	stimulants
Primo	Crack; marijuana mixed with cocaine; crack and heroin; heroin, cocaine and tobacco	stim.; cann.; stim.; stim., narc.; narc., stim.
Primo square	A marijuana joint laced with crack	cann.; stim.
Primobolan	Injectable and oral steroid	steroids
Primos	Cigarette laced with cocaine and heroin	stim.; narc.
Product	Crack cocaine	stimulants
Proviron	Oral steroids	steroids
Pseudocaine	Phenylpropanola-mine, an adulterant for cutting crack	stimulants
Puff the dragon	To smoke marijuana	cannabis
Puffer	Crack smoker	stimulants
Puffy	PCP	hallucinogen
Pulborn	Heroin	narcotics
Pullers	Crack users who pull at parts of their bodies excessively	stimulants
Pumpers	Steroids	steroids
Pumping	Selling crack	stimulants
Pure	Heroin	narcotics
Pure love	LSD	hallucinogen
Purple	Ketamine	depressants
Purple barrels	LSD	hallucinogen
Purple caps	Crack cocaine	stimulants
Purple flats	LSD	hallucinogen
Purple gel tabs	LSD	hallucinogen
Purple haze	LSD; crack cocaine; marijuana	halluc.; stim.; cann.
Purple hearts	LSD; amphetamine; depressants	halluc.; stim.; deprs.
Purple ozoline	LSD	hallucinogen
Purple rain	PCP	hallucinogen
Push	Sell drugs	
Push shorts	To cheat; sell short amounts	
Pusher	Metal hanger or umbrella rod used to scrape residue out of crack stems; one who sells drugs	stimulants
Q	Depressants	depressants
Qat	Methcathinone	stimulants
Quads	Depressants	depressants
Quarter	¼ ounce or $25 worth of drugs	
Quarter bag	$25 worth of drugs	
Quarter moon	Hashish	cannabis
Quarter piece	¼ ounce	
Quartz	Smokable methamphetamine	stimulants
Quas	Depressants	depressants

Street Name	Definition	Drug Type
Queen Ann's lace	Marijuana	cannabis
Quicksilver	Isobutyl nitrite; inhalants	inhalants
Quill	Cocaine; heroin; methamphetamine	stim.; narc.; stim.
Quinolone	Injectable steroids	steroids
R-2	Rohypnol	depressants
Racehorse charlie	Cocaine; heroin	stim.; narc.
Ragweed	Inferior quality marijuana; heroin	cann.; narc.
Railroad weed	Marijuana	cannabis
Rainbow	LSD	hallucinogen
Rainbows	Depressants	depressants
Rainy day woman	Marijuana	cannabis
Rambo	Heroin	narcotics
Rane	Cocaine; heroin	stim.; narc.
Rangood	Marijuana grown wild	cannabis
Rap	Criminally charged; to talk with someone	
Raspberry	Female who trades sex for crack or money to buy crack	stimulants
Rasta weed	Marijuana	cannabis
Rave	All night dance parties frequently designed to enhance a hallucinogenic experience through music and lights	hallucinogen
Rave energy	MDMA	hallucinogen
Raw	Crack cocaine; high purity heroin	stim.; narc.
Raw fusion	Heroin	narcotics
Raw hide	Heroin	narcotics
Razed	Under the influence of drugs	
Ready rock	Cocaine; crack cocaine; heroin	stim.; narc.
Real tops	Crack cocaine	stimulants
Recompress	Change the shape of cocaine flakes to resemble 'rock'	stimulants
Recycle	LSD	hallucinogen
Red	Under the influence of drugs; methamphetamine	stimulants
Red and blue	Depressants	depressants
Red bud	Marijuana	cannabis
Red bullets	Depressants	depressants
Red caps	Crack cocaine	stimulants
Red chicken	Heroin	narcotics
Red cross	Marijuana	cannabis
Red devil	Depressants; PCP; heroin	deprs.; halluc.; narc.
Red devils	MDMA	hallucinogen
Red dirt	Marijuana	cannabis
Red eagle	Heroin	narcotics
Red lips	LSD	hallucinogen
Red phosphorus	Smokable speed	stimulants
Red rock	Heroin	narcotics
Red rock opium	Heroin, barbital, strychnine, and caffeine	narc.; deprs.

Street Name	Definition	Drug Type
Red rum	Heroin, barbital, strychnine, and caffeine	narc.; deprs.
Red stuff	Heroin, barbital, strychnine, and caffeine	narc.; deprs.
Redneck cocaine	Methamphetamine	stimulants
Reds	Depressants	depressants
Reefer	Marijuana	cannabis
Reefers	Marijuana cigarette	cannabis
Regular "P"	Crack cocaine	stimulants
Reindeer dust	Heroin	narcotics
RenewTrient	GBL-containing product	depressants
Res	Potent residue left as a result of smoking crack which is scraped and smoked	stimulants
Rest in peace	Crack cocaine	stimulants
Revivarant	GBL-containing product	depressants
Revivarant-G	GBL-containing product	depressants
Reynolds	Rohypnol	depressants
Rhine	Heroin	narcotics
Rhythm	Amphetamine	stimulants
Rib	Rohypnol; MDMA	deprs.; halluc.
Rider	5 kg of heroin sometimes provided at no cost per 100 kg of cocaine imported from Columbia	narc.; stim.
Riding the wave	Under the influence of drugs	
Rig	Equipment used to inject drugs	
Righteous bush	Marijuana	cannabis
Ringer	Good hit of crack; hear bells	stimulants
Rip	Marijuana	cannabis
Rippers	Amphetamine	stimulants
Ritual spirit	MDMA	hallucinogen
Ritz and Ts	Injected combination of Talwin and Ritalin	stimulants
Roach	Butt of marijuana cigarette	cannabis
Roach clip	Holds partially smoke marijuana cigarette	cannabis
Roach-2	Rohypnol	depressants
Roacha	Marijuana	cannabis
Roaches	Rohypnol	depressants
Roachies	Rohypnol	depressants
Road dope	Amphetamine	stimulants
Roapies	Rohypnol	depressants
Roasting	Smoking marijuana	cannabis
Robin's egg	Stimulant	stimulants
Robutal	Rohypnol	depressants
Roca	Crack cocaine; MDMA	stim.; halluc.
Rochas dos	Rohypnol	depressants
Roche	Rohypnol	depressants
Rock/s	Cocaine; crack; methamphetamine	stimulants
Rock attack	Crack cocaine	stimulants
Rock house	Place where crack is sold and smoked	stimulants
Rock star	Female who trades sex for crack or money to buy crack; a person who uses rock cocaine	stimulants
Rocket caps	Dome-shaped caps on crack vials	stimulants

Substance Abuse

Street Name	Definition	Drug Type
Rocket fuel	PCP	hallucinogen
Rockets	Marijuana cigarette	cannabis
Rockette	Female who uses crack	stimulants
Rocks of hell	Crack cocaine	stimulants
Rocky III	Crack	stimulants
Roid rage	Aggressive behavior cause by excessive steroid use	steroids
Roller	To inject a drug	
Rollers	Police	
Rolling	MDMA	hallucinogen
Rolls Royce	MDMA	hallucinogen
Rompums	Marijuana with horse tranquilizers	cann.; deprs.
Roofies	Rohypnol	depressants
Rooster	Crack cocaine	stimulants
Root	Marijuana	cannabis
Rope	Marijuana; rohypnol	cann.; deprs.
Rophies	Rohypnol	depressants
Rophy	Rohypnol	depressants
Ropies	Rohypnol	depressants
Roples	Rohypnol	depressants
Rosa	Amphetamine	stimulants
Rose marie	Marijuana	cannabis
Roses	Amphetamine	stimulants
Rough stuff	Marijuana	cannabis
Row-shay	Rohypnol	depressants
Rox	Crack cocaine	stimulants
Roxanne	Cocaine; crack	stimulants
Royal blues	LSD	hallucinogen
Roz	Crack cocaine	stimulants
Rubia	Marijuana	cannabis
Ruderalis	Cannabis species found in Russia	cannabis
Ruffies	Rohypnol	depressants
Ruffles	Rohypnol	depressants
Rugs	Marijuana	cannabis
Runners	People who sell drugs for others	
Running	MDMA	hallucinogen
Rush	Cocaine; isobutyl nitrite; inhalants	stim.; inhal.
Rush hour	Heroin	narcotics
Rush Snappers	Isobutyl nitrite	inhalants
Russian sickles	LSD	hallucinogen
Sack	Heroin	narcotics
Sacrament	LSD	hallucinogen
Sacred mushroom	Psilocybin	hallucinogen
Salad	Marijuana	cannabis
Salt	Heroin	narcotics
Salt and pepper	Marijuana	cannabis
Salty water	GHB	depressants
Sam	Federal narcotics agent	

Street Name	Definition	Drug Type
Sancocho	To steal	
Sandoz	LSD	hallucinogen
Sandwich	Two layers of cocaine with a layer of heroin in the middle	stim.; narc.
Sandwich bag	$40 bag of marijuana	cannabis
Santa Marta	Marijuana	cannabis
Sasfras	Marijuana	cannabis
Satan's secret	Inhalants	inhalants
Stach	Papers, letters, cards, clothing, etc., saturated with drug solution - used to smuggle drugs into prisons or hospitals	
Sativa	Species of cannabis, found in cool, damp climates	cannabis
Scaffle	PCP	hallucinogen
Scag	Heroin	narcotics
Scat	Heroin	narcotics
Scate	Heroin	narcotics
Schmeck	Cocaine	stimulants
Schmiz	Methamphetamine	stimulants
Schoolboy	Cocaine; codeine	stim.; narc.
Schoolcraft	Crack cocaine	stimulants
Schwagg	Marijuana	cannabis
Scissors	Marijuana	cannabis
Scooby snacks	MDMA	hallucinogen
Scoop	GHB	depressants
Scootie	Methamphetamine	stimulants
Score	Purchase drugs	
Scorpion	Cocaine	stimulants
Scott	Heroin	narcotics
Scottie	Cocaine	stimulants
Scotty	Cocaine; crack; the high from crack	stimulants
Scrabble	Crack cocaine	stimulants
Scramble	Crack cocaine; low purity, adulterated heroin	stim.; narc.
Scrape and snort	To share crack by scraping off small pieces to snort	stimulants
Scratch	Money	
Scrub	Marijuana	cannabis
Scruples	Crack cocaine	stimulants
Scuffle	PCP	hallucinogen
Seccy	Depressants	depressants
Second to none	Heroin	narcotics
Seconds	Second inhalation of crack from a pipe	stimulants
Seeds	Marijuana	cannabis
Seggy	Depressants	depressants
Sen	Marijuana	cannabis
Seni	Peyote	hallucinogen
Serial speedballing	Sequencing cocaine, cough syrup, and heroin over a 1-2 day period	stim.; narc.
Sernyl	PCP	hallucinogen

Substance Abuse

Street Name	Definition	Drug Type
Serpico 21	Cocaine	stimulants
Server	Crack dealer	stimulants
Sess	Marijuana	cannabis
Set	Place where drugs are sold; Injected combination of Talwin and Ritalin	stimulants
Seven-Up	Crack cocaine	stimulants
Sevenup	Cocaine; crack	stimulants
Sewer	Vein into which a drug is injected	
Sextasy	Ecstasy used with Viagra	hallucinogen
Sezz	Marijuana	cannabis
Sh*t	Heroin	narcotics
Shabu	Ice; crack cocaine; methamphetamine; MDMA	stim.; halluc.
Shake	Marijuana; powder cocaine	cann.; stim.
Shaker/baker/ water	Materials needed to freebase cocaine; shaker bottle, baking soda, water	stimulants
Sharps	Hypodermic needles	
She	Cocaine	stimulants
Shebanging	Mixing cocaine with water and squirting it up nose	stimulants
Sheet rocking	Crack and LSD	stim.; halluc.
Sheets	PCP	hallucinogen
Sherm	Psychedelic mushrooms	hallucinogen
Sherm sticks	PCP	hallucinogen
Sherman stick	Crack cocaine combined with marijuana in a blunt	stim.; cann.
Shermans	PCP	hallucinogen
Sherms	Crack; PCP; cigars dipped in or laced with PCP	stim.; halluc.
Shmeck/ schmeek	Heroin	narcotics
Shoot	Heroin	narcotics
Shoot the breeze	Nitrous oxide	inhalants
Shoot up/Shoot	To inject a drug	
Shooting gallery	Place where drugs are used	
Shoppers	Individuals who buy drugs for others, sometimes keeping some of the drug for themselves	
Shot	To inject a drug; an amount of cocaine; 10 shot or 20 shot	stimulants
Shot down	Under the influence of drugs	
Shot to the curb	A person who has lost it all to crack	stimulants
Shotgun	Inhaling marijuana smoke forced into one's mouth by another's exhaling	cannabis
Shrile	Powder cocaine	stimulants
Shrooms	Psilocybin/psilocin	hallucinogen
Siddi	Marijuana	cannabis
Sightball	Crack cocaine	stimulants
Silk	Heroin	narcotics
Silly putty	Psilocybin/psilocin	hallucinogen
Simple Simon	Psilocybin/psilocin	hallucinogen

Street Name	Definition	Drug Type
Sinse	Marijuana	cannabis
Sinsemilla	Potent variety of marijuana	cannabis
Sixty-two	2 ½ ounces of poor quality crack	stimulants
Skag	Heroin	narcotics
Skee	Opium	narcotics
Skeegers/ skeezers	Crack-smoking prostitute	stimulants
Sketch	Methamphetamine	stimulants
Sketching	Coming down from a speed induced high	
Skid	Heroin	narcotics
Skied	Heroin	narcotics
Skin popping	Injecting drugs under the skin; to inject drugs on any part of the body without hitting a vein	
Skittling	Abuse of cold tablets containing dextromethorphan (a cough suppressant)	stimulants
Skuffle	PCP	hallucinogen
Skunk	Marijuana; heroin	cann.; narc.
Skunkweed	Marijuana	cannabis
Slab	A large piece of crack cocaine the size of a stick of chewing gum	stimulants
Slam	To inject a drug	
Slammin'/ Slamming	Amphetamine; MDMA	stim.; halluc.
Slanging	Selling drugs	
Sleep	GHB	depressants
Sleep-500	GHB	depressants
Sleeper	Heroin; depressants	narc.; deprs.
Sleet	Crack cocaine	stimulants
Sleigh ride	Cocaine	stimulants
Slick superspeed	Methcathinone	stimulants
Slime	Heroin	narcotics
Smack	Heroin	narcotics
Smears	LSD	hallucinogen
Smoke	Marijuana; crack cocaine; heroin and crack	cann.; stim.; narc.
Smoke a bowl	Marijuana	cannabis
Smoke Canada	Marijuana	cannabis
Smoke houses	Crack houses	stimulants
Smoke-out	Under the influence of drugs	
Smoking	PCP	hallucinogen
Smoking gun	Heroin and cocaine	narc.; stim.
Smurf	Cigar dipped in embalming fluid	
Smurfs	MDMA	hallucinogen
Snackies	MDMA adulterated with mescaline	hallucinogen
Snap	Amphetamine	stimulants
Snappers	Isobutyl nitrite	inhalants
Sniff	To inhale cocaine; methcathinone; inhalants	stim.; inhal.
Sniffer bag	$5 bag of heroin intended for inhalation	narcotics

Substance Abuse

Street Name	Definition	Drug Type
Snop	Marijuana	cannabis
Snort	To inhale cocaine; powder cocaine; use inhalant	stimulants
Snorting	Using inhalants	inhalants
Snorts	PCP	hallucinogen
Snot	Residue produced from smoking amphetamine	stimulants
Snotballs	Rubber cement rolled into balls, burned, and then inhaled	inhalants
Snotty	Heroin	narcotics
Snow	Cocaine; heroin; amphetamine	stim.; narc.; stim.
Snow bird	Cocaine user; cocaine	stimulants
Snow coke	Crack	stimulants
Snow pallets	Amphetamine	stimulants
Snow seals	Cocaine and amphetamine	stimulants
Snow white	Cocaine	stimulants
Snowball	Cocaine and heroin	stim.; narc.
Snowcones	Cocaine	stimulants
Snowmen	LSD	hallucinogen
Soap	GHB; crack cocaine; methamphetamine	deprs.; stim.
Soap dope	Methamphetamine with a pinkish tint	stimulants
Society high	Cocaine	stimulants
Soda	Injectable cocaine	stimulants
Soft	Powder cocaine	stimulants
Softballs	Depressants	depressants
Soles	Hashish	cannabis
Soma	PCP	hallucinogen
Somali tea	Methcathinone; khat	stimulants
Somatomax	GHB	depressants
Sopers	Depressants	depressants
Soup	Crack cocaine	stimulants
South parks	LSD	hallucinogen
Space	Crack cocaine	stimulants
Space base	Crack dipped in PCP; hollowed out cigar refilled with PCP and crack	stim.; halluc.
Space cadet	Crack dipped in PCP	stim.; halluc.
Space dust	Crack dipped in PCP	stim.; halluc.
Space ship	Glass pipe used to smoke crack	stimulants
Spaceball	PCP used with crack	halluc.; stim.
Spackle	Methamphetamine	stimulants
Spark it up	To smoke marijuana	cannabis
Sparkle	Methamphetamine that has a somewhat shiny appearance	stimulants
Sparkle plenty	Amphetamine	stimulants
Sparklers	Amphetamine	stimulants
Special "K"	Ketamine	depressants
Weightless	High on crack	stimulants
West Coast	Methylphenidate (Ritalin)	stimulants

Street Name	Definition	Drug Type
West Coast turnarounds	Amphetamine; MDMA	stim.; halluc.
Wet	Blunts mixed with marijuana and PCP; methamphetamine; marijuana cigarettes soaked in PCP ("embalming fluid") and dried	cann.; halluc.; stim.
Whack	Crack cocaine; heroin and PCP; crack and PCP mixture or marijuana laced with insecticides	stim.; narc.; halluc.; cann.
Whackatabacky	Marijuana	cannabis
Wheat	Marijuana	cannabis
Wheels	MDMA	hallucinogen
When-shee	Opium	narcotics
Whiffledust	Amphetamine; MDMA	stim.; halluc.
Whippets	Nitrous oxide	inhalants
White	Heroin; amphetamine	narc.; stim.
White ball	Crack cocaine	stimulants
White boy	Heroin; powder cocaine	narc.; stim.
White cloud	Smoke that collects in bottom of crack pipe; crack smoke	stimulants
White cross	Amphetamine; methamphetamine	stimulants
White diamonds	MDMA	hallucinogen
White dove	MDMA	hallucinogen
White dragon	Powder cocaine; heroin	stim.; narc.
White dust	LSD	hallucinogen
White ghost	Crack cocaine	stimulants
White girl	Cocaine; heroin	stim.; narc.
White horizon	PCP	hallucinogen
White horse	Cocaine; heroin	stim.; narc.
White junk	Heroin	narcotics
White lady	Cocaine; heroin	stim.; narc.
White lightning	LSD	hallucinogen
White mosquito	Cocaine	stimulants
White nurse	Heroin	narcotics
White Owsley's	LSD	hallucinogen
White powder	Cocaine; PCP	stim.; halluc.
White Russian	Marijuana	cannabis
White stuff	Heroin	narcotics
White sugar	Crack cocaine	stimulants
White tornado	Crack cocaine	stimulants
White-haired lady	Marijuana	cannabis
Whiteout	Inhalants; isobutyl nitrite	inhalants
Whites	Amphetamine; folded paper used to package drugs	stimulants
Whiz bang	Cocaine; heroin and cocaine	stim.; narc.
Wicked	A potent brand of heroin	narcotics
Wicky stick	PCP, marijuana, and crack	halluc.; cann.; stim.
Wigging	Odd behavior resulting from the use of mind-altering drugs	

Substance Abuse

Street Name	Definition	Drug Type
Wigits	MDMA	hallucinogen
Wild cat	Methcathinone mixed with cocaine	stimulants
Window glass	LSD	hallucinogen
Window pane	LSD; crack cocaine	halluc.; stim.
Wings	Cocaine; heroin	stim.; narc.
Winstrol	Oral steroids	steroids
Winstrol V	Veterinary steroids	steroids
Witch	Cocaine; heroin	stim.; narc.
Witch hazel	Heroin	narcotics
Wobble weed	PCP	hallucinogen
Wolf	PCP	hallucinogen
Wolfies	Rohypnol	depressants
Wollie	Rocks of crack rolled into a marijuana cigarette or in a cigar	stim.; cann.
Wonder star	Methcathinone	stimulants
Woo blunts	Marijuana; marijuana combined with cocaine	cann.; stim.
Woola blunt	Marijuana and heroin combination	cann.; narc.
Woolah	Hollowed out cigar refilled with marijuana and crack	cann.; stim.
Woolas	Cigarettes laced with cocaine; crack sprinkled on marijuana cigarette	stim.; cann.
Woolies	Marijuana and crack or PCP	cann.; stim.; halluc.
Wooly blunts	Marijuana and crack or PCP	cann.; stim.; halluc.
Wooties	Crack smoked in marijuana joints	stim.; cann
Work	Methamphetamine	stimulants
Working	Selling crack	stimulants
Working bags	Bags containing several small rocks of crack cocaine	stimulants
Working fifty	Crack rock weighing ½ gram or more	stimulants
Working half	Crack rock weighing ½ gram or more	stimulants
Working man's cocaine	Methamphetamine	stimulants
Works	Equipment for injecting drugs	
Worm	PCP	hallucinogen
Wrecking crew	Crack cocaine	stimulants
WTC	Heroin (after September 11)	narcotics
X	Marijuana; amphetamine; MDMA	cann.; stim.; halluc.
X-ing	MDMA	hallucinogen
X-Pills	MDMA	hallucinogen
XTC	MDMA	hallucinogen
Ya Ba	Pure and powerful form of methamphetamine from Thailand; "crazy drug"	stimulants
Yahoo/yeaho	Crack cocaine	stimulants
Yale	Crack cocaine	stimulants
Yam	Crack cocaine	stimulants
Yao	Powder cocaine	stimulants

Street Name	Definition	Drug Type
Yayoo	Crack cocaine	stimulants
Yeah-O	Crack cocaine	stimulants
Yeh	Marijuana	cannabis
Yellow	LSD; depressants	halluc.; deprs.
Yellow bam	Methamphetamine	stimulants
Yellow bullets	Depressants	depressants
Yellow dimples	LSD	hallucinogen
Yellow fever	PCP	hallucinogen
Yellow jackets	Depressants; methamphetamine	deprs.; stim.
Yellow powder	Methamphetamine	stimulants
Yellow submarine	Marijuana	cannabis
Yellow sunshine	LSD	hallucinogen
Yen pop	Marijuana	cannabis
Yen Shee Suey	Opium wine	narcotics
Yen sleep	Restless, drowsy state after LSD use	hallucinogen
Yeo	Crack	stimulants
Yeola	Marijuana and crack	cann.; stim.
Yerba	Marijuana	cannabis
Yerba mala	PCP and marijuana	halluc.; cann.
Yerhia	Marijuana	cannabis
Yesca	Marijuana	cannabis
Yesco	Marijuana	cannabis
Yeyo	Cocaine, Spanish term	stimulants
Yimyom	Crack cocaine	stimulants
Ying Yang	LSD	hallucinogen
Z	1 ounce of heroin	narcotics
Zacatecas purple	Marijuana from Mexico	cannabis
Zambi	Marijuana	cannabis
Zay	Marijuana with other substances in a cigar; blunts	cannabis
Ze	Opium	narcotics
Zen	LSD	hallucinogen
Zero	Opium	narcotics
Zig Zag man	Marijuana; LSD; marijuana rolling papers	cann.; halluc.
Zip	Cocaine	stimulants
Zol	Marijuana cigarette	cannabis
Zombie	PCP; heavy user of drugs	hallucinogen
Zombie weed	PCP	hallucinogen
Zonked	Extremely high on drugs	
Zooie	Holds butt of marijuana cigarette	cannabis
Zoom	Marijuana laced with PCP; PCP	cann.; halluc.
Zoomer	Individual who sells fake crack and then flees	stimulants
Zoquete	Heroin	narcotics
Zulu	Bogus crack	stimulants

Source: Office of National Drug Control Policy ONDCP, *Street Terms: Drugs and the Drug Trade*, February 2004, http://www.whitehousedrugpolicy.gov/streetterms

Substance Abuse

Substance Abuse Estimates by State

Average Monthly Illicit Drug Use (Percentages)

State	Total State Estimate	12-17 yrs	Age Group 18-25 yrs	26+ yrs
Alabama	6.62	11.44	20.24	5.72
Alaska	**12.01**	**13.34**	**27.29**	**9.17**
Arizona	8.87	12.61	18.88	6.53
Arkansas	7.78	11.72	21.05	4.89
California	9.01	11.44	18.83	6.86
Colorado	11.12	13.83	25.52	8.24
Connecticut	8.75	12.43	25.58	5.82
Delaware	8.74	13.54	25.77	5.19
Florida	8.72	11.42	21.32	6.58
Georgia	7.54	10.43	17.51	5.31
Hawaii	8.90	13.97	19.31	6.56
Idaho	7.24	11.02	15.80	4.86
Illinois	7.50	10.83	20.22	4.80
Indiana	8.07	10.15	20.67	5.45
Iowa	6.47	9.22	15.80	4.33
Kansas	6.74	9.33	16.67	4.43
Kentucky	8.33	11.70	18.43	6.15
Louisiana	8.07	10.76	20.54	5.17
Maine	9.31	12.58	25.20	6.52
Maryland	7.57	10.76	22.02	4.85
Massachusetts	9.28	13.94	27.46	5.81
Michigan	9.06	12.80	21.22	6.42
Minnesota	7.59	11.59	19.28	4.91
Mississippi	6.56	10.59	16.33	3.98
Missouri	9.17	10.05	21.37	6.90
Montana	10.58	15.57	22.34	7.77
Nebraska	7.67	12.71	18.91	4.78
Nevada	10.30	12.46	22.02	8.17
New Hampshire	11.15	14.46	29.61	7.82
New Jersey	6.97	10.42	21.36	4.48
New Mexico	10.00	14.16	22.17	7.08
New York	8.90	11.68	23.89	6.07
North Carolina	7.92	13.62	20.35	5.09
North Dakota	7.22	11.64	18.02	4.35
Ohio	8.04	11.39	20.64	5.42
Oklahoma	8.58	12.23	18.97	6.06
Oregon	10.84	12.30	24.72	8.30
Pennsylvania	7.50	11.28	20.54	4.91
Rhode Island	10.95	13.25	32.44	6.75
South Carolina	7.23	11.05	19.54	4.54
South Dakota	7.15	13.26	17.92	4.13
Tennessee	6.70	9.23	16.16	4.78
Texas	6.97	10.18	16.54	4.59
Utah	**6.32**	**8.76**	**12.69**	**4.00**
Vermont	10.96	16.67	29.58	6.99

State	Total State Estimate	12-17 yrs	Age Group 18-25 yrs	26+ yrs
Virginia	7.68	11.88	20.53	5.03
Washington	9.96	13.49	24.65	6.96
Washington, DC	11.59	11.54	26.23	8.71
West Virginia	6.61	11.70	17.37	4.29
Wisconsin	7.48	10.73	18.85	4.98
Wyoming	7.51	10.05	18.36	5.07

Notes: Any Illicit Drug includes marijuana/hashish, cocaine, heroin, hallucinogens, inhalants, or any prescription-type psychotherapeutic used nonmedically.

Source: SAMHSA, Office of Applied Studies, National Survey on Drug Use and Health, 2002 and 2003

RADAR Network State Centers

The RADAR Network is sponsored by the U.S. Department of Health and Human Services and SAMSHA's National Clearinghouse for Alcohol and Drug Information. The numbers listed below are for the central office within each state. The RADAR Network is the largest substance abuse prevention and treatment network with more than 700 centers worldwide encompassing state clearinghouses, prevention resource centers, and groups that focus on substance abuse prevention. For more information go to: http://www.health.org/radar/

Alabama	Drug Education Council	251-433-5456
Alaska	Akeela, Inc	800-478-7738
Am. Samoa	Drugs and Alcohol Program	684-633-2696
Arizona	Arizona Prevention Resource Center	800-432-2772
Arkansas	Office of Alcohol Abuse & Prevention	501-686-9448
California	California Dept of Alcohol & Drug Programs	800-879-2772
Colorado	Dept of Human Services	303-866-7508
Connecticut	Wheeler Clinic Inc	800-232-4424
Delaware	Office of Prevention	302-892-4513
Florida	Florida Alcohol & Drug Abuse Assoc	850-878-2196
Georgia	Dept of Human Resources	404-463-6955
Guam	Dept of Mental Health & Substance Abuse	671-647-5415
Hawaii	Coalition for Drug-Free Hawaii	800-845-1946
Idaho	Boise State University	800-937-2327
Illinois	Prevention First, Inc	800-252-8951
Indiana	Indiana Prevention Resource Center	800-346-3077
Iowa	Iowa Substance Abuse Info Center	866-242-4111

Substance Abuse

Kansas	Dept of Social & Rehabilitation Services	785-291-3326
Kentucky	Cabinet for Health & Family Services	502-564-7996
Louisiana	Office for Addictive Disorders	225-342-5988
Maine	Office of Substance Abuse	800-499-0027
Maryland	Alcohol & Drug Abuse Admin	410-402-8622
Massachusetts	Partnership for Healthy Communities	617-423-4337
Michigan	Michigan Resource Center	800-626-4636
Micronesia	Dept of Health, Education & Social Affairs	691-320-5520
Minnesota	Minnesota Prevention Resource Center	800-782-1878
Mississippi	Dept of Mental Health	601-359-1288
Missouri	Dept of Mental Health	800-575-7480
Montana	Dept of Public Health & Human Services	800-457-2327
Nebraska	Health & Human Services System	402-479-5576
Nevada	Nevada Prevention Resource Center	866-784-6336
New Hampshire	Division of Public Health Services	603-271-4972
New Jersey	Dept of Human Services	609-292-4394
New Mexico	Dept of Health	505-827-2625
New York	New York State Office of Alcoholism and Substance Abuse Services	518-485-1768
North Carolina	Alcohol & Other Drug Resource Center	877-627-2327
North Dakota	Division of Mental Health and Substance Abuse Services	800-642-6774
North Mariana Islands, Community Guidance Center		670-323-6585
Ohio	Prevention & Education Resource Center	800-788-7254
Oklahoma	Prevention Resource Center	405-522-3810
Oregon	Office of Mental Health & Addictive Services	503-945-7814
Palau	Ministry of Health	680-488-1907
Pennsylvania	Bureau of Drug & Alcohol Programs	717-783-8200
Puerto Rico	Substance Abuse & Mental Health Services Administration	787-763-7575
Rhode Island	Dept of MHRH	401-462-4680
South Carolina	Dept of Alcohol & Other Drug Abuse	803-896-1172
South Dakota	Division of Alcohol & Drug Abuse	605-773-3123
Tennessee	TAADAS Clearinghouse	800-889-9789
Texas	Mental Health & Substance Abuse Services	866-378-8440
Utah	Substance Abuse & Mental Health Div	801-538-4684
Vermont	Dept of Health	802-652-4146
Virgin Islands	Division of Mental Health	340-774-7700
Virginia	Dept of Mental Health	800-451-5544
Washington	State Alcohol/Drug Clearinghouse	800-662-9111
Washington, D.C.	Addiction Prevention and Recovery Administration (APRA)	202-727-9075
West Virginia	Library Commission	800-642-9021
Wisconsin	Clearinghouse for Prevention Resources	800-248-9244
Wyoming	Chemical Abuse Research & Education	800-895-1121

Substance Abuse Statistics

- The most common drugs used by people over the age of 12 are marijuana, cocaine, and hallucinogens (PCP, LSD, MDMA).

- Illicit drug use within the past month ranges from 6.32% (in Utah) to 12.01% (in Alaska).

- Approximately 10.8% of the population aged 12 or older in the U.S. has used marijuana in the past year. Ranges per state start at 7.4% (in Tennessee) and go up to 16.7% (in Alaska).

- An estimated 6.2% of the population aged 12 or older has used marijuana in the past month. Ranges per state start at 4.0% (in Utah) and go up to 10.2% (in New Hampshire).

- Cocaine use in the past year among the population aged 12 or older ranges from 1.6% (in Idaho) to 3.9% (in Colorado).

- Illicit drug dependence or abuse in the past year among the population aged 12 or older ranges from 2.5% (in Kansas) to 4.0% (in Washington, D.C.).

- The highest percentage of people 12 or older needing illicit drug abuse treatment and not receiving it is New Mexico (3.5%).

- 53% of seniors in high school have used an illicit drug at least once, 41% have used an illicit drug within the past year, and 25.4% within the past month.

Sources:
SAMHSA, Office of Applied Studies, National Survey on Drug Use and Health, 2002 and 2003

Office of National Drug Control Policy, Drug Data Summary, March 2003, http://www.whitehousedrugpolicy.gov

Substance Abuse

Substance Abuse Resources

Adult Children of Alcoholics (ACA/ACoA) ·················310-534-1815
Alanon/Alateen (literature) ·······································800-356-9996
  meeting referral ···800-344-2666
Alcoholics Anonymous - AA (literature) ·················212-870-3400
  meeting referral ···212-647-1680
American Council for Drug Education·····················800-488-3784
Center for Substance Abuse Prevention (CSAP) ······240-276-2420
Nt'l Clearinghouse for Drug Info ····301-468-2600·····800-729-6686
Cocaine Anonymous···800-347-8998
Families Anonymous···800-736-9805
Marijuana Anonymous ··800-766-6779
Mothers Against Drunk Driving (MADD) ···············214-744-6233
  Victim Hotline···800-438-6233
Nar-Anon Family Group Headquarters ··················310-534-8188
Narcotics Anonymous (NA)··818-773-9999
National Association of Children of Alcoholics···········888-554-2627
National Association of State Alcohol and Drug Abuse
  Directors (NASADAD)··202-293-0090
National Council on Alcoholism and
  Drug Dependence (NCADD) ··································800-622-2255
National Families in Action ······································770-934-6364
Nt'l Inhalant Prevention Coalition ··800-269-4237······512-480-8953
National Institute on Drug Abuse (NIDA) ···············301-443-1124
RADAR Network Center/SAMHSA's National Clearinghouse
  for Alcohol and Drug Information (NCADI) ············800-729-6686
Rational Recovery Systems··530-621-2667
SAMHSA - Substance Abuse & Mental Health
  Services Administration·············202-619-0257······877-696-6775
Secular Organizations for Sobriety (SOS) ···············323-666-4295
Substance Abuse & Mental Health Services Admin.
  National Treatment & Referral Hotline·····················800-662-4357
Women for Sobriety ··215-536-8026

TERRORISM AND COUNTERMEASURES

Terrorism · **462**
  Threats or Warnings · 462
  Early Warning Signs · 464
  Likely Targets for Terrorists · · · · · · · · · · · · · · · · 466
Suspicious Mail · **467**
  Anthrax · 468
  Mail Bombs and Bomb Threats · · · · · · · · · · · · · · 471
Improvised Explosive Devices (IEDs) · · · · · · · · · · **473**
Weapons of Mass Destruction · · · · · · · · · · · · · · · **477**
Biological Weapons · **481**
Chemical Weapons · **490**
  Blister Agents · 491
  Blood Agents · 492
  Choking Agents · 493
  Nerve Agents · 494
  Riot Control Agents · 495
Victim Decontamination · **496**
Nuclear and Radiological Weapons · · · · · · · · · · · **497**
  Radiological Agents · 500
  Pre-Hospital Treatment for Radiation Exposure · · · · · 501
  Radiation Sickness · 501
Federal Response to Terrorism · · · · · · · · · · · · · · · **503**
Role of the Military · **505**
Federal Hotlines for CBR Events · · · · · · · · · · · · · **506**
Department of Homeland Security · · · · · · · · · · · · · **507**
  Border and Transportation Security · · · · · · · · · · · 508
  Emergency Preparedness & Response (EP&R) · · · · · 510
  Information Analysis and Infrastructure Protection · · · 510
  Science and Technology · · · · · · · · · · · · · · · · · · · 511
  Office of Management · 512
  U.S. Coast Guard · 513
  U.S. Secret Service · 514
  Dept. of Homeland Security Organization Chart · · · · · 515
  Homeland Security Advisory System · · · · · · · · · · · 516

Terrorism

Terrorism is the calculated use of violence or the threat of violence to instill fear in order to intimidate governments or societies. They generally have goals and objectives that are political, religious, or ideological. As we have found, small groups of terrorists can inflict significant damage and suffering. Law enforcement officers, firefighters, and other emergency personnel are the first line of defense against these threats.

This chapter is designed to provide "Awareness Level" information only and is not sufficient to allow anyone to function safely and effectively in a real incident. For responders to function properly they need Operations or Technician level training.

Types of Weapons

The primary weapons available to terrorists consist of:
- conventional weapons and explosives
- chemical weapons
- biological weapons
- nuclear or radiological weapons

As shown by the incidents on Sept. 11, 2001, they have also found unique ways to use otherwise innocent, everyday objects (i.e., aircraft) as effective weapons.

Experts still consider explosive devices to be the most likely type of weapon to be used by terrorists. These are covered in the Explosives chapter of this book (see page 109). This chapter will include information on chemical, biological, and nuclear and radiological weapons.

Threats or Warnings

If the threat is credible, your department should contact the nearest FBI office (see pg 992) or Dept. of Homeland Security (202-282-8000) for additional threat assessment and support.

Incident Information Checklist

If someone calls to report an incident, or if you observe what seems to be a terrorist incident, report the following information:
1. The caller's name and phone number.
2. The date and time of incident.
3. Estimated time spent in suspected area.
4. Distance from the point of impact or incident.
5. Reason for report: Unusual liquid droplets, people becoming sick, cloud, people dying, unusual odors, dead or discolored vegetation, other.

6. Location of incident: Street address, city, state.
7. Terrain description: Flat, hills, mountains, desert, urban, suburban, sparse trees, forest, jungle, shore, river, other.
8. Weather: Clear, cloudy, windy, rainy, foggy, snowy, misty, dusty, mild breeze, other.
9. Temperature: Hot, warm, cool, cold.
10. Odor: None, sweet, fruity, irritating, pepper, flower, garlic/horseradish, almond/peach, newly mown hay, forest, rotten eggs, changing, etc.
11. Visible emission: Smoke, mist, none.
12. Unexplained symptoms: None, tightness in chest, stinging of skin, dizziness, blurred vision, reddening of skin, runny nose, fever, welts or blisters on skin, choking, difficulty breathing, nausea and vomiting, cough, diarrhea, headaches, other. Note the time of onset and any changes.
13. Explosion: None, air, ground, structure, underground. Describe location. Describe device: Military munitions, improvised device, other, none. Describe container: condition, size.

Emergency Calls from an Aircraft

Calls from cell phones or from aircrafts can be lost very quickly. It is important to get the following information first, especially what flight is involved. If there is additional time, try to get some of the information listed above in the Incident Information checklist. Note: Cellular calls can bounce around when their systems are overloaded. Be sure not to disregard any calls as hoaxes since they might appear to be coming from someone far away.

1. The name of the airline and flight number (if known).
2. City it departed from and where it's supposed to land.
3. Where the plane is now located.
4. Caller's name and seat number.
5. Calling from a wireless phone or an onboard phone?
   - If a wireless phone, what is their phone number and carrier's name?
6. What is the emergency?
7. Seat number(s) of those creating the emergency.

This information should be forwarded to the Federal Aviation Administration (FAA) at 202-267-3484.

Early Warning Signs

Signs of a Suicide Bomber

External appearance:

- Clothes unsuitable for time of year (i.e. a coat in the summer).
- A person trying to blend in by means of dress and behavior with group of people they don't belong with.
- Anything protruding in a unusual way under the person's clothing.

Suspicious Behavior:

- Nervousness, tension, profuse perspiration.
- Walking slowly while glancing right and left, or running in a suspicious manner.
- Repeated attempts to steer clear of police.
- Repeatedly and nervously reaching for something under one's clothing.
- Nervous, hesitant mumbling.

Suspicious Equipment:

- A suitcase, shoulder/handbag, backpack.
- Electrical wires, switches, or electronic devices sticking out of a bag or pocket.

Suspicious Vehicle:

- License plate looks "improvised" or is mismatched in the front and back.
- A vehicle has been parked suspiciously for a long time in a central place or in a no parking zone.
- The vehicle's back end sags noticeably as if it were loaded down.

Source: Community and Civil Guard Dept., Israel Police

Other Categories of Suspicious Activities

Surveillance:

Someone recording or monitoring activities with cameras, notes, diagrams, notes on maps, or using binoculars.

Elicitation:

People or organizations trying to get information about operations, capabilities, or people.

Tests of Security:

Attempts to measure reaction times to security breaches or to penetrate physical security barriers and procedures to assess strengths and weaknesses.

Acquiring supplies:
  Purchasing or stealing explosives, weapons, ammunition, detonators, times, uniforms, decals, flight manuals, passes or badges, etc.

Suspicious persons out of place:
  People who don't seem to belong where they are.

Practicing:
  Putting people into position and moving them around according to their plan without actually committing the act. This could include mapping routes, timing traffic lights and flow, and people moving from place to place without any apparent reason for doing so, especially if they do it repeatedly.

Getting into position:
  Look for people loading up vehicles with weaponry and explosives, parking the vehicle somewhere, people who seem out of place and seem to be standing around waiting for something to happen, and people in uniform who don't look right (uniform is incomplete, or worn improperly, etc.).

Source: *Eagle Eyes: Categories of Suspicious Activities*, Air Force Office of Special Investigations at www.dtic.mil/afosi/eagle/suspicious_behavior.html

Indicators of Chemical/Biological Agent Manufacturing

The following items may be signs that a person or group has or is interested in establishing a chemical/biological agent manufacturing capability:

- Subject related textbooks.
- People with a high level of university training in organic chemistry, microbiology, aerobiology, pathology and genetics.
- Raw materials.
- Bacteria seed cultures.
- Lab equipment such as beakers, reflux apparatus, centrifuge, petri dishes with culture medium, stirring apparatus, fume hoods, etc.
- Improvised synthesis/culture equipment, such as home brewing equipment, egg incubators, yogurt makers, etc.
- Animals to use as test subjects for determining agent toxicity.
- Personal safety equipment.
- Spraying devices or other improvised dispersal devices for chemical/biological agents.

Source: *Criminal/Terrorist Use of Chemical/Biological Agents*, Royal Canadian Mounted Police Online University, at www.rcmp-learning.org/docs/ecdd1022.htm

Likely Targets for Terrorists

- Government offices
- Military installations
- Landmarks and buildings with symbolic value
- Headquarters of companies dealing with defense, environmentally sensitive products, or that operate in politically sensitive countries
- Transportation system
- Communication systems
- Utilities
- Water supplies
- Sites where explosives or fuel are stored
- Sports arenas
- Schools, hospitals, and shopping centers
- Venues for special events
- Post offices
- Abortion clinics
- Events that attract large crowds

Suspicious Mail

Suspicious Mail Characteristics:

- It has no return address or has one that can't be confirmed as legitimate.
- It is marked with restrictive endorsements, such as "Personal," "Confidential," or "Do Not X-Ray.".
- There is an unusual amount of tape.
- There are misspellings of common words.
- It is from an unknown person or unexpected.
- It is addressed to someone who is no longer at the house or business.
- There are incorrect titles or titles with no name.
- The address is handwritten or poorly typed.
- It has unusual weight for its size, is lopsided, uneven, oddly shaped, rigid, or bulky.
- It has a strange odor.
- It has any powdery substance, crystallization, oily stains, or discolorations on the outside.
- There is excessive postage.

If you receive a suspicious letter or package:

DO NOT shake it, bump it, or sniff it. Handle with care.

1. Notify supervisor (who will in turn contact the US Postal Inspection Service, law enforcement, safety officers, etc.)
2. Isolate the damaged or suspicious packages. Place it carefully in a plastic bag or some other type of container to prevent leakage of contents. If it is too large for a bag, cover it with paper, plastic, or cloth. Also turn off any fans.
3. Anyone who has come in contact with the package should wash their hands with soap and water.
4. List all persons who have touched the mail piece. Include contact information and have the list available for the authorities & US Postal Inspection Service.
5. Place all items worn when in contact with the suspected mail piece into plastic bags and have them available for law enforcement.
6. Shower with soap and water as soon as possible.

7. Notify the Centers for Disease Control and Prevention's Emergency Response line at (770) 488-7100 for answers to any questions.
8. Call a Postal Inspector to report that you have received a letter or parcel in the mail that may contain biological or chemical substances.

If you think the package contains:

A Bomb:
- Evacuate immediately.
- Call police.
- Contact postal inspectors.
- Call local Fire Department/HAZMAT Unit.

A Radiological Threat:
- Limit exposure - don't handle.
- Evacuate area.
- Shield yourself from the object.
- Call police.
- Contact postal inspectors.
- Call local Fire Department/HAZMAT Unit.

A Biological or Chemical Threat:
- Isolate the package - don't handle.
- Evacuate immediate area.
- Wash your hands with soap and warm water.
- Call police.
- Contact postal inspectors.
- Call local Fire Department/HAZMAT Unit.

First Responders:
If you are responding to a call about possible contaminated mail, wear at least Level B PPE. When bagging letters or packages, avoid creating a puff of air that could spread the pathogen. Avoid using a large bag and work very slowly and carefully when putting the object into it.

Anthrax

Anthrax is a bacterial, zoonotic disease caused by *Bacillus (B.) anthracis.* In humans, three types of anthrax infections can occur depending on how it was exposed to the person.

Anthrax Prevention:

- Restrict the number of people working at or near sites where aerosolized particles may be generated (i.e. restrict supporting staff, contractors, business visitors).
- Dry sweep and dusting should be avoided. Instead, it should be jet-cleaned and vacuumed with HEPA-equipped vacuum cleaners.
- Mail sorters and workers should wear protective, impermeable gloves. Workers should avoid touching their skin, eyes, or other mucous membranes since contaminated gloves may transfer the spores. Workers might also consider wearing long-sleeved shirts and long pants.
- Workers should wash their hands with soap and water after handling mail or removing their gloves.
- People working with or near machinery (such as electronic mail sorters) should wear NIOSH-approved respirators that are at least as protective as an N95 respirator. Workers near machinery where oil mist is present should wear P-type filters.
- Workers with beards or large moustaches may want alternative respirators such as powered air-purifying respirators (PAPRs) with loose fitting hoods.
- Locations with high-speed mail sorting machines:
  - An industrial vacuum cleaner equipped with a high-efficiency particulate air (HEPA) filter for cleaning.
  - Local exhaust ventilation at pinch roller areas.
  - HEPA-filtered exhaust hoods installed in areas where dust is generated.
  - Air curtains installed in areas where large amounts of mail are processed. HEPA filters installed in the building's HVAC systems to capture aerosolized spores.

Anthrax Treatment:

- Penicillin, doxycycline, and ciproflaxin are effective against most strains of anthrax.
- A vaccine is available (most effective against cutaneous).
- To decontaminate exposed articles of clothing, boil the article in water for 30 minutes or longer using some form of common disinfectant. Chlorine is effective in destroying spores and vegetative cells.

Types of Anthrax Infections

Type	Exposure	Characteristics	Symptoms
Cutaneous	Skin	• Most common type of infection. • Occurs after skin contact with contaminated meat, wool, hides, or leather from infected animals. • Incubation period is 1 to 12 days. • Infection is introduced through scratches or abrasion of the skin.	• Skin infection starts as a raised bump that looks like a spider bite. After 1-2 days, the infection develops into a blister, followed by a painless ulcer with a black necrotic (dying) area in the center. • The ulcer is painless, but victims may have a fever, malaise, and headache. • Lymph glands in the adjacent may swell.
Inhalation	Inhalation	• Spores must be aerosolized to cause inhalational anthrax. • Contracted by inhalation of spores. Occurs mainly among workers handling infected animal hides, wool, and fur. • Incubation period is not known, but can range from 1-7 days, possibly up to 60 days.	• Resembles a viral respiratory illness. Initial symptoms include sore throat, mild fever, muscle aches, and malaise. • Symptoms may worsen to respiratory failure and shock with meningitis. • After incubation period (possibly 1-7 days) the onset of inhalation anthrax is gradual.
Gastro-intestinal	Ingestion	• Usually followed by consumption of raw or undercooked contaminated meat. • Incubation period is 1 to 7 days.	• Acute inflammation of the intestinal tract. • Initial symptoms include nausea, loss of appetite, vomiting, fever followed by abdominal pain, vomiting of blood, and severe diarrhea.

Mail Bombs and Bomb Threats

It is extremely unlikely that your workplace will ever receive a mail bomb. It is more likely that you will receive a telephoned bomb threat or find a suspicious package placed on the property. Most bombs are sent by people seeking revenge. Mail bombs are usually targeted to specific individuals, whereas bombs placed on the property are generally intended to disrupt the workplace and injure indiscriminately.

Mail Bomb & Bomb Threat Prevention:

Since most bombs are placed, not mailed, security and physical access around the workplace should be a top priority. The following are ways to enhance security:

- Have security guards greet all visitors and examine personal belongings brought into the building or office area.
- Restrict access to the facility through locked or guarded entryways.
- Keep storage rooms, boiler rooms, telephone and utility closets, and similar potential hiding places locked and off-limits to visitors.
- Use easily distinguishable identification badges for staff and visitors.
- Require visitors to be accompanied by staff employees to and from the office or facility entrance.
- Request visitors to display identification to security personnel when they sign in.
- Keep detailed logs on the arrival & departure of visitors.
- Consider using the services of a certified protection professional to evaluate your company's personnel and physical security safeguards.

In addition it may be necessary to have a Bomb Threat Response Plan that would encompass all facilities, outbuildings, parking lots, and garages. This plan should include procedures, provisions, and policies for:

- Ensuring that nonpostal deliveries (except commercial shipments) are channeled through the mail center.
- Operating a command center.
- Channeling all mail and parcels through a mail bomb screening program.
- Defining & maintaining communication channels among the mail center security coordinator, management, and security.
- Responding to written and phoned in bomb threats.

Response to Phoned In Bomb Threats

• Keep the caller on the line, ask them to repeat the message several times, and gather additional information (caller ID etc). Write down the threat verbatim (exactly as the caller states it) and record any additional information or observations. Do not hang up on the caller under any circumstances!

• Evacuate and notify law enforcement and the fire department immediately.

Sample Questions to ask Bomb Threat Caller:

– What kind of bomb is it?
– What does it look like? Please describe it.
– Where is it located? Office, floor, building number
– What will cause it to detonate?
– Many innocent people may be hurt.
– Why are you doing this?
– What is your name and address?

Bomb Threat and Search Procedures:

• Evacuate the building via your company's emergency evacuation and fire prevention plan.

• **DO NOT** use the fire alarms to evacuate the building, the bomber might have targeted routes such as stairwells and emergency exits normally used in an fire alarm.

• Contact law enforcement and fire departments about their bomb search policies. Determine if they will help conduct the search (police agencies often will not conduct searches of private facilities).

• If needed, organize a search team of volunteers. Start with areas of the facility most accessible to the public, then move indoors through the main entrance. The search patterns should overlap somewhat between searchers. Repeat from office to office, floor to floor throughout the entire facility.

• If a suspicious parcel or device is found, evacuate and cordon off the area immediately. Do not touch the object or walk near it as vibrations may cause an explosion. Report the find to the supervisor in charge who will call the police.

• Once the area is cleared, continue a thorough search of the facility as the bomber might have planted more than one device.

Source: United States Postal Service, "Mail Center Security Guidelines", Publication 166, September 2002.
http://www.usps.com/communications/news/security/mailcenter.htm

Improvised Explosive Devices (IEDs)

IED is a term for an explosive device that is constructed in an improvised manner designed to kill, maim, or destroy property. These devices are categorized by their container (i.e. vehicle bombs) and by the way they are initiated. IEDs are usually homemade and constructed for a specific target.

IEDs can be contained in almost anything. It is designed to be carried or driven to where it will be placed, so it is usually disguised in some manner. They can be in trash cans, dumpsters, mailboxes, bushes, storage areas, parked vehicles, and just about anywhere inside a building.

Possible External Appearances of an IED:

- **Pipe Bombs:** Steel or PVC pipe section with end caps in nearly any configuration. These are the most prevalent type of container.
- **Briefcase/Box/Backpack:** Any style, color, or size. It can be as small as a cigarette pack.
- **Postal Service Mail:** A letter or parcel may contain a bomb. Never accept unexpected packages at your home. See page 471 for indicators of suspicious mail.
- **Vehicle Bombs:** By far this is the most devastating as vehicles may hold thousands of pounds of explosives and are often the easiest to conceal. Indicators may include inappropriate decals or an unfamiliar vehicle parked in your area. The device can be placed anywhere in the vehicle. A vehicle bomb is intended to create mass casualties or cause extensive property damage.
- **Existing Objects:** Items that seem to have a purpose can be substituted or used as a bomb container. Examples include fire extinguishers, propane bottles, trash cans, gasoline cans, or books.

Possible Internal Components of an IED:

All devices require a firing train that consists of a fusing system, detonator, and main charge (explosive or incendiary). Any switch that can turn something on or off can be used to activate a device. Fusing systems can be categorized into the following:

- **Time:** Preset to detonate or arm the device at an unknown interval of time. The timer may be mechanical such as a kitchen timer, wind-up wristwatch, pocket watch, or electronic (i.e. digital wristwatches, integrated circuit chips, or solid-state timers).

- **Victim Activated:** These may be designed to function by pressure, pull, movement, vibration, tension release, or tilting the item. Booby-trapped is the common way to describe this type.

- **Command:** These send a signal via radio frequency or through a hidden wire from a remote location.

- **Environmental:** These are designed to function when there is a change in temperature, pressure, light, sound, or magnetic field.

The detonator or blasting cap is a small explosive component, widely available from military and commercial sources, which can be limited by a variety of mechanical and electrical devices. With the increased availability of blasting caps, fabrication and use of improvised detonators are on the decline. However, the possibility of encountering one may still exist.

Main charges can be used to burn or detonate (or both) depending on the bomber's desired effect. Explosives fall into three general categories:

- **Common Explosives:** Used for property demolition, mining, and blasting operations. Commercial explosives come in assorted shapes and consistencies, including binary (two-part), slurries, gels, and standard dynamites.

- **Military Explosives:** These differ from commercial explosives because they must have high rates of detonation, be relatively insensitive, and be usable underwater. Examples include TNT, C-4 plastic explosives, and military dynamite.

- **Improvised Explosives:** When manufactured explosives are not available, it is relatively easy to obtain all of the ingredients necessary to make improvised explosives, such as ammonium nitrate (fertilizer), and potassium/sodium chlorate.

- **Incendiary:** Improvised devises may be designed to burn. Common materials include gasoline, iodine crystals, magnesium, glycerin, and aluminum powder.

Automobile and Vehicle Searches

How to Search for an IED:

- Start with a 360 degree sweep, looking around and under vehicles. Be alert for booby traps and secondary devices. Inspect the area for suspicious items such as wire, tape, or string. You may spot a suspicious object underneath or attached to the vehicle without approaching it.

- Start and finish your search at a predetermined point.
- Look for suspicious packages or items in, on, attached, or under the vehicle.
- Look for tool marks on the vehicle or other indications of forced entry.
- DO NOT sit in or move the vehicle prior to searching the engine and trunk compartments.
- Search the exterior of the car: Exhaust pipe (insure nothing is inside), inspect the gas tank, fuel entry point and neck of fuel tank, underneath the vehicle, wheel wells, tires, and brakes.
- Search the interior of the car: Under the seats (front and rear), under the dashboard (driver's side and passenger side), under the headrest, the sun visor, and any areas where you think a bomb could be concealed.
- Search the engine compartment: Raise the hood slowly while searching for hanging wires, tape, or packages attached to the underside, check the battery and wiring, scan the firewall (rear wall of engine compartment), open the air cleaner, and be familiar with the general appearance of an engine and components.
- Search the trunk or luggage storage area: Slowly raise the trunk while inspecting the underside for suspicious items such as wires, string, or packages, inspect the rear wall of trunk (back or rear seat), inspect wiring on rear light assemblies, and check the spare tire (let a little air out).

Building and Room Searches

- Prior to entering a room and during a search, check for trip wires and possible indications of pressure-sensitive devices.
- Be systematic, thorough, and quick. Use two-person teams, preferably with people familiar with the building or room. Using one's body as a reference, search from floor to waist, from waist to chin, and from chin to ceiling. Don't forget to check false ceiling if applicable. For more search techniques, see page 111.
- Do not alter existing environmental conditions.
- Inspect wall hangings, plants, or other decorations.

- Listen for suspicious or unusual sounds after entering the room. Background noise may mask sounds such as ticking or buzzing.
- Because a radio-controlled device may be present and pick up on stray RF (as well as pose a hazard to electric blasting caps), do not use hand-held radios for communication within 35 feet of the suspicious items or areas not properly searched and cleared.

If an IED is Found

- Notify the proper authorities in accordance with existing bomb threat procedures.
- If necessary, security personnel should initiate and coordinate the evacuation in accordance with existing procedures.
- Using adequate cover (frontal and overhead) get as far away from the device as possible.
- Keep away from glass windows; they can become lethal if the bomb explodes.
- If the device is outside of a building, get low to the floor and go to the other side. Do not look out the window to see what is going on.
- Secondary devices are always a possibility. A common tactic is to detonate a device attracting a crowd, and then detonate a second device to inflict heavy casualties.
- Increasing your distance from a suspicious device increases the chances for survival after a detonation.

Source: US State Department, http://www.state.gov/m/ds/rls/rpt/19726.htm

Weapons of Mass Destruction (WMD)

Incident Handling

The handling of biological, chemical, or radiological terrorist attacks will be similar in many ways to the handling of incidents involving other explosives or hazardous materials. Listed below are several differences between the two:

1. The situation may not be recognizable until there are multiple casualties.
2. There may be multiple events. Be aware of secondary devices designed to kill those responding to the initial attack.
3. First responders are at higher risk of becoming casualties because it may not be possible to detect the presence of biological, chemical, or radioactive agents before being exposed to them.
4. The location of the incident is a crime scene and it is critically important to preserve evidence even while dealing with casualties, decontamination, and other aftermath.
5. Since those who have been contaminated (including first responders) may not be aware of it for some time, they will contaminate a much larger area, including critical facilities.
6. The scope of the incident may expand geographically and affect multiple jurisdictions.
7. There will be a stronger reaction from the public than with other types of incidents.
8. Time is working against responders. The chemical, biological, or radiological agent may expand geometrically and very quickly. The effects of some agents become worse with time.
9. Support facilities, such as utility stations and 911 centers, along with critical infrastructure, may be targets of attack.
10. Specialized state and local response capabilities may be overwhelmed.

Protocol

A first responder's responsibility upon arriving at an incident is to:
- Recognize the presence of dangerous goods.
- Protect him or herself and the public.
- Secure the area.
- Call for help from trained personnel as soon as conditions permit.

Follow the steps outlined in your organization's standard operating procedures and/or local emergency response plan for obtaining qualified assistance.

1. **Approach cautiously from upwind.** Resist the urge to rush in; others cannot be helped until the situation has been fully assessed.
2. **Immediately put on a respiratory mask and protective clothing.** Use the highest level of PPE until notified that the area is safe without it. If PPE is not available, do whatever you can to cover all skin and protect your respiratory system.
3. **Secure the scene.** Without entering the immediate hazard area, isolate the area and assure the safety of people and the environment. Keep people away from the scene and outside the safety perimeter. Allow enough room to move and remove your own equipment.
4. **Identify the hazards.** In most cases you will not have any handy hazmat placards to help you identify any biological, chemical or radiological (CBR) materials that may be present.
   - Deploy CBR detection equipment if available.
   - Look for the following signs of a CBR attack:

Sign	Detailed Explanation	Weapon type(s)
Sick, dying, or dead animals, birds, and fish	Large numbers of different kinds of animals sick or dying in a given area.	Chemical
Unusual number of sick or dying people or animals	May involve any number of symptoms, which may arise any time from hours to weeks after exposure. Length of delay varies by agent used and dose received. Call local hospitals to see if other people with similar symptoms have come in for treatment. Geographic distribution may be widespread due to delay in onset.	Biological, Radiological
Pattern of casualties	All downwind, near ventilation outlet if indoors, or some other pattern that suggests a dissemination method. People working indoors have symptoms while those outdoor do not, or vice versa.	Chemical, Radiological
Lack of insect life	Check ground, air, and water for dead insects.	Chemical

Sign	Detailed Explanation	Weapon type(s)
Dead, withered vegetation	All vegetation within a given area looks dead or withered, and there is no current drought.	Chemical
Blisters and rashes	Blisters, eye irritation, reddening of the skin, and rashes.	Chemical
Other symptoms	Nausea, vomiting, choking, coughing, difficulty breathing, and convulsions.	Biological, Chemical
Unusual or out-of-place odors	Odors that are fruity or flowery, sharp or pungent, garlicky/horseradish, burnt almond, or new-mown hay. Inconsistent with type of surroundings.	Chemical
Strange colored smoke	Smoke that has an unusual color or density.	Chemical
Unusual droplets or liquids	Surfaces within a given area may be coated with an oily film or droplets; no recent rain or other explanation.	Chemical
Low-lying clouds	Fog-like conditions not consistent with surroundings or weather. May appear suddenly.	Chemical
Unusual spraying	Unscheduled or unusual, especially if done at night.	Biological
Abandoned spraying devices	No distinct odor.	Biological
Very small explosions	Explosions seem to do very little damage, release an unusual amount of smoke, leaves droplets in the area, or there are fragments covered with liquid or droplets.	Biological, Chemical, Radiological
Unusual metal debris	Unexplained bomb or munitions-like material, especially if it contains liquid and there has been no recent rain.	Chemical
Heat emitting material	Material may be present that seems to emit heat without any obvious heating source.	Radiological
Glowing material or particles	A strongly radioactive material may emit radio luminescence.	Radiological
Unidentified low flyer aircraft	Especially crop dusters over a populated area.	Biological, Chemical

5. **Assess the situation.** Consider the following:
   - Is there a fire?
   - What are the weather conditions?
   - What is the terrain like?
   - Who or what is at risk?
   - What actions should be taken?
   - Is an evacuation necessary?
   - Should there be a decontamination area?
   - Is diking necessary?
   - What resources (human and equipment) are needed and readily available?
   - What can be done immediately?
6. **Call for help!** Call your organization or agency. Alert other first responders of potentially dangerous conditions. Ensure that local fire and emergency medical departments have been notified. Notify your state emergency management office.
7. **Decide whether or not to enter the site.** Efforts to rescue persons or to protect property or the environment must be weighed against the possibility that you could become part of the problem. Enter the area only when wearing appropriate protective gear.
8. **Respond.** Implement your Incident Command system. Establish a command post and lines of communication. Rescue casualties where possible and evacuate if necessary. Maintain control of the site. Continually reassess the situation and modify the response accordingly. The first duty is to consider the safety of people in the immediate area, including your own.
   - Establish decontamination stations immediately.
   - Contain all runoff from decontamination activities.
   - Be on the alert for structural collapses and secondary devices.
   - Remember that you are in a CRIME SCENE and should preserve all evidence when possible.

ABOVE ALL - Do not walk into or touch spilled material.

Avoid inhaling fumes, smoke, and vapors, even if no dangerous goods are known to be involved. Do not assume that gases or vapors are harmless because of lack of smell; odorless gases or vapors may be harmful.

Biological Weapons

Types: Bacteria, Virus, Toxin

There are three types of biological weapons: Bacteria, Viral, and Toxin. Bacteria and viral cause disease and can multiply and spread beyond the initial attack. Toxins are poisonous substances produced by living things, some of which are extremely lethal. Toxins are not contagious.

Governments have found these agents unsatisfactory as battlefield weapons because they are difficult to deliver efficiently while protecting their own troops. However, they may be attractive to terrorists because they have the potential to cause casualties, and above all, to instill fear and panic in a general population.

Biological attacks using bacteria or viral agents are likely to escape detection for a time period corresponding to the incubation period for the disease they cause, anywhere from hours to weeks. Toxins typically act much faster. Doctor offices and emergency rooms are, therefore, considered most likely to be the "first responders" in case of a bacterial or viral attack.

Law enforcement officers are most likely to encounter attacks with toxins. They will be more at risk of exposure to bacterial or viral agents when investigating suspicious activities or where terrorists were observed or caught in the process of disseminating the agent.

Dissemination
Most likely aerosol; some could also be used as food or water contaminants. Inhalation is the most deadly route of exposure in all cases.

More Information
Biological Hazards fall under DOT Hazmat Guide 153 on page 839.

Key to Biological Weapons Table (page 483):

CDC Category A

These organisms pose a risk to national security because they can be easily disseminated or transmitted from person to person. They result in high mortality rates and have the potential for major public health impact and might cause public panic and social disruption. They require special action for public health preparedness.

CDC Category B

These are moderately easy to disseminate and result in moderate morbidity rates and low mortality rates. They require specific enhancements of CDC's diagnostic capacity and enhanced disease surveillance.

CDC Category C

These agents include emerging pathogens that could be engineered for mass dissemination in the future because of availability, ease of production and dissemination, potential for high morbidity and mortality rates, and major health impact.

Type

B=Bacteria
V=Virus
T=Toxin
R=Rickettsial

Precautions

Standard, Airborne, Droplet, Contact (see page 367) for definitions.

Biological Weapons

Bioagent	CDC Category	Contagious	Type	Incubation period	Symptoms	Untreated Lethality	Treatment	Protection	Persistence
Arboral Encephalitis: Venezuelan, East or West Nile Viruses	B	No	V	2-6 days	Sudden onset with malaise, spiking fever, headache, sensitivity to light, and muscle aches. Nausea, vomiting, cough, sore throat, and diarrhea. Full recover takes 1-2 weeks.	Very low	Supportive	Standard Precautions	Relatively Unstable
Botulism toxin	A	No	T	1-5 days if eaten, several days if inhaled	Drooping eyelids, generalized weakness, dizziness, dry mouth and throat, blurred vision and double vision, disturbed swallowing, difficulty speech and language, and altered voice. Followed by paralysis on both sides of the body that begins at the head and works its way downward leading to respiratory failure.	High without respiratory support	Anti-Toxin and supportive care	Standard Precautions, vaccine available. Wash & water disinfect with bleach solution.	For weeks in nonmoving water or food. Degraded by humidity, high temperatures. Aerosolized form dissipates after 2 days.
Brucellosis	B	No	B	50-60 days/ 1 to 2 months	Fever, headache, weakness, profuse sweating, chills, aching joints, depression, weight loss, and generalized aching.	<5%	Antibiotics	Standard Prec., no vaccine. Contact Prec. if draining lesion is present.	Very stable

Biological Weapons (cont.)

Bioagent	CDC Category	Contagious	Type	Incubation period	Symptoms	Untreated Lethality	Treatment	Protection	Persistence
Cholera	B	Rare; not contagious with proper hygiene	B	4 hours to 5 days - usually 2-3 days	Diarrhea, nausea and vomiting. In untreated cases, rapid dehydration, acidosis, circulatory collapse and renal failure.	High	Hydration antibiotics in serious illness only	Standard Precautions, no vaccine in US	Unstable in aerosols and fresh water; stable in salt water
E.Coli	B	No	B	24-72 hours	Abdominal pain, severe cramps, diarrhea, and vomiting.	Low	Supportive	Thoroughly cook meats, especially ground beef. Proper cleaning of cooking area, utensils, and hands.	Viable for several mo. in grasslands and manure. Will survive freezing but decline in #s when exposed to drying & sunlight. Survival in farm water troughs >4 mo.
Epsilon Toxin of Clostridium perfringens	B	No	T	8-12 hours	Diarrhea with severe abdominal cramping and bloating.	Very low	Supportive	No antidote; decontaminate w/ soap & water. Poisoning clears in 1-2 days (for healthy adults)	Presumed to be indefinitely stable in sewage; insensitive to chlorine.

Glanders	B	Yes	B	10-14 days	Pulmonary: cough, nasal discharge Cutaneous: ulceration of skin, mucous membranes and soft tissues.	High	Antibiotics and supportive	Standard contact, no vaccine.	Can stand drying for 2-3 weeks; killed by sunlight & high temps.
Melioidosis	B	By contact (rare)	B	10-14 days	Effects can range from bronchitis to severe pneumonia accompanied by tissue death. Fever of 102° F (38.9°C) and some chest pain.	Can be lethal	Antibiotics	Standard	Years in soil and water.
Mycotoxins		No	T	Minutes to hours	Skin: burning pain, redness, tenderness, blistering, leather blackening, and sloughing of large area in lethal cases. Nose & Throat: pain, discharge, itching and sneezing, cough wheezing, difficult breathing, chest pain, and bloody sputum. Eyes: tearing, pain, redness, blurred vision. Nausea, vomiting, diarrhea, & abdominal pain. Severe poisoning: weakness, loss of muscle coordination, collapse, shock, and death in minutes, hours or days.	Moderate	Flush out eyes and wash skin w/ soap and water. Super activated charcoal if ingested.	Remove contaminated clothes and place in bags. Clean contaminated surfaces with bleach solution.	Extremely stable in heat and sunlight.

Biological Weapons (cont.)

Bioagent	CDC Category	Contagious	Type	Incubation period	Symptoms	Untreated Lethality	Treatment	Protection	Persistence
Pneumonic Plague	A	Yes	B	2-3 days	High fever, chills, headache, followed by cough (often with blood), difficult and noisy breathing, cyanosis, and death. Enlarged lymph nodes, often turning black. May have gastrointestinal symptoms.	Nearly 100%	Antibiotics No vaccine in US.	Standard Precautions	Sensitive to sunlight and heat. Can live for 1 year in soil; 270 days in live tissue.
Psittacosis	B	Yes	B	4-15 days	Fever, chills, headache, muscle aches, & respiratory tract symptoms. Non-productive cough, bloody sputum, nausea, and vomiting, distended abdomen in severe cases.	About 10%	Antibiotics	Standard Precautions, no vaccine. Airborne and Droplet Prec. in severe cases.	Can survive for many days as a wind-blown aerosol. Susceptible to disinfectants and heat.
Pulmonary Anthrax	A	No	B	2-50 days	Initial Symptoms: fever, malaise, fatigue, cough, mild chest discomfort. Then a short period of improvement follows. Then sudden severe respiratory distress with difficult and noisy breathing, heavy sweating, and cyanosis. Shock/death within 24-36 hrs of severe symptoms.	High	Antibiotics	Standard Precautions, vaccine available to military only.	Very stable, spores remain viable for >40 years.

						Antibiotics no vaccine in US.	Standard Precautions	Months on wood and sand. Susceptible to bleach solution.
Q Fever	B	No	B	10-40 days	Fever, cough, weakness, chest pain, headache, malaise, & severe sweats. In severe cases, inflammation of the brain and tissue surrounding heart.	Very low		
Ricin	B	No	T	A few hours if ingested 18-24 hours if inhaled	Ingestion: nausea, vomiting, diarrhea, bloody diarrhea, abdominal pain, internal bleeding of stomach & intestines, and liver, spleen, & kidney failure. Inhalation: fever, cough, difficult breathing, tightness of chest, nausea, and muscle aches, leading to pulmonary edema.	High	Supportive	Standard Precautions, no vaccine. Use protective mask against aerosol forms.	Stable
Salmonella	B	No	B	6-48 hours	Vomiting and diarrhea	Very low	Antibiotics	Good hygiene; susceptible to chlorine & UV radiation.	29-58 days in soil; 9 days in seawater; 8 days in fresh water; up to 5 months in ice.
Saxitoxin	None	No	T	Minutes	Uncoordinated movement, incoherent speech, light headedness, nausea, vomiting, eye irritation, & respiratory distress. In severe cases, respiratory paralysis results and without treatment will be fatal very quickly.	High, Death usually occurs within 2-12 hours	Supportive	Standard Precautions, no vaccine.	Stable but can be inactivated by strong alkalis.

Biological Weapons (cont.)

Bioagent	CDC Category	Contagious	Type	Incubation period	Symptoms	Untreated Lethality	Treatment	Protection	Persistence
Shigella	B	Yes, via contaminated fingers	B	12 hours to 6 days	Severe diarrhea, abdominal pain, vomiting, and bloody urine.	Very low	Usually resolved in 5-7 dys without treatment.	Cook foods thoroughly. Wash hands often w/ soap and water.	2-3 days in water, susceptible to chlorine & heat (as in cooking).
Smallpox	A	Yes	V	7-17 days - avg. 12 days	Fever, rigors, vomiting, headache, and backache. 2-3 days later rash appears, form pus-filled lesions that crust over (more abundant on face & extremities, developing at same time).	Low	Vaccinate within 4 days of exposure; antiral meds.	Contact Precautions, strictly airborne.	Very stable
Staphylococcal Enterotixin B	B	No	T	3-12 hours after inhalation	Ingested: acute gastrointestinal illness Inhaled: fever, chills, headache, muscle aches, difficult breathing, cough, and ultimately acute pulmonary edema & respiratory failure.	Low (<1%)	Supportive; most symptoms resolve in 24-36 hours.	Standard Precautions no vaccine. Contact Prec. if draining lesion is present.	Easily aerosolized, stable in aersol form. Resistant to freezing.
Trichothecine Mycotoxin (aka T-2 or "yellow rain")	--	No	T	<20 min. for skin irritation 8-12 hours rest of symptoms	Skin pain, redness, itching, blisters, shedding of dead skin. Nose & throat pain, nasal discharge, itching, sneezing, cough, shortness of breath, wheezing, chest pain, spitting blood. Severe poisoning: protration, weakness, jerky movements, collapse, shock, & death.	Moderate	Decontaminate with soap and water. Treat symptoms	No vaccine. Wear protective mask and chemical protective overgarment	Years at room temperature.

Tularemia	A	B	No	2-10 days	Local ulcers, enlarged lymph nodes, fever, chills, headache, chest discomfort, prostration, weight loss, and no productive cough.	Moderate	Antibiotics no vaccine in US.	Standard Precautions	For months in moist soil or other media.
Typhus	B	R	No	6-15 days	Severe headache, chills, high fever that can last up to 2 weeks, general pain, and skin rash that appears 5 days after fever begins. Can effect both circulatory and nervous systems.	Often fatal if untreated.	Antibiotics, supportive	Vaccine available; Standard flea & tick control	Unstable in storage; unlikely bioweapon. Treat affected area for tick infestation; clean surfaces with 0.1% formalin, glutaraldehyde or 0.5% phenol. Can be killed by heat (112°F or 45°C) for 15-30 minutes.
Viral Hemorrhagic Fevers: Ebola, Marburg, et al.	A	V	Yes, through direct contact with bodily fluids or contaminated surfaces	4-21 days	Initial Symptoms: high fever, headache, malaise, weakness, exhaustion, dizziness, nausea, non-bloody diarrhea, and achiness. Later Symptoms: flushing, red itchy eyes, sore throat, edema, low blood pressure, petechiae, and bleeding (with some agents).	Moderate to high	Supportive therapy, aggressive mgmt. of secondary infections and hypotension	Droplet and strict Contact Precautions. Airborne Precautions if victim has prominent cough, vomiting, diarrhea or hemorrhage	Relatively unstable

Chemical Weapons

Types: Blister, Blood, Choking, Nerve, Riot Control

Blister Agents:
Also known as vesicants or mustard agents. Most obvious effect is blistering of skin, however, they also cause serious damage to eyes and internal organs if inhaled or ingested. Initial reaction to the chemicals is delayed, so victims may not immediately realize they've been contaminated. For more information, see Hazmat Guide 153 on page 839.

Blood Agents:
These attack the ability of the blood to carry oxygen and cause death by suffocation. For more information, see Hazmat Guide 117 on page 713 for Hydrogen Cyanide; and Hazmat Guide 125 on page 737 for Cyanogen Chloride (CK).

Choking Agents:
These attack the lungs, causing them to fill with fluid bringing about death by asphyxiation. For more information, see Hazmat Guide 124 on page 734 for Chlorine gas and Hazmat Guide 125 on page 737 for Phosgene.

Nerve Agents:
These are considered the most deadly type by attacking the victim's nervous system. Most are chemically similar to pesticides. For more information, see Hazmat Guide 153 on page 839.

Riot Control:
Also known as "tear gas", they are "non-lethal" agents that have a short-term incapacitating effect. They can be deadly to people with preexisting respiratory or other medical problems. For more information, see Hazmat Guide 159 on page 865 for Riot Control Agents.

Types are abbreviated in the table as follows:
Bs = Blister Agents
Bl = Blood Agents
Ch = Choking Agents
Ne = Nerve Agents
Ri = Riot Control Agents

Chemical Weapons - Blister Agents

Chemical Agents	Type	Symptoms	Time to onset	Distributed by	Description	Treatment	Lethality	Precautions	Detection	Persistence
Lewisite (L)	Bs	Immediate pain in eyes, skin, and respiratory tract. Symptoms like those resulting from Mustard (below).	Immediate	Aerosol Vapor	Colorless oily liquid if pure; usually amber to dark brown. Odor of geranium oil.	No antidote	Low, but damage is long-term. Human carcinogen	Apply British Anti-Lewisite (BAL) to skin. PPE: Level A	M18S2 (yellow band); bubblers (arsenic & GC method); M256A1 kits.	Summer: 1 to 3 days. Winter: Weeks
Nitrogen Mustards HN1, HN2, HN3		Skin: Reddening, burning, itching, stinging pain. Inhalation: Irritates and congests nose, throat, sneezing, coughing, bronchitis, loss of appetite, fever. May be fatal if inhaled. Ingested: Stomach pain, vomiting, bloody stools.	High Exp: Immediate, progressing up to 24 hrs. Mild Exp: 20 minutes progressing for 8-10 hrs		Colorless or yellow oily liquid. Fish or soap odor.			PPE Level A	M8 and M9 Paper; Drager detection tubes; Chemical Agent Monitor; M256A1 kit	Summer: 3 days to 1 week Winter: Weeks
Sulfur Mustard (T)			Delay depends on exposure level. Can be from 2 min. for high exp. to 2-24 hrs for mild exp.		Yellow liquid with garlic odor.					More than H, HD, HS
Sulfur Mustards H, HD, HS					Colorless & odorless if pure; agent grade is usually yellow to black. Garlic or horseradish odor.					Summer: 3 days to 1 week Winter: Weeks

Chemical Weapons - Blood Agents

Chemical Agents	Type	Symptoms	Time to onset	Distributed by	Description	Treatment	Lethality	Precautions	Detection	Persistence
Cyanogen Chloride (CK)	Bl	Nose, throat, & eye irritation, coughing, chest, tearing, tightness, headache, and giddiness. High Exposure: Difficulty breathing, very rapid breathing followed 15-30 seconds later by convulsions. 6-8 min. after heavy exp. breathing and heart stops. Heavier Exp.: result in more rapid death.	Immediate	Aerosol, Gas	Colorless gas; pungent, biting odor (may not be noticed due to nasal irritation caused by the gas).	Aggressive breathing support Administer antidote ASAP.	High in sufficient concentrations	Level B is adequate except Level A should be used in enclosed areas. Do not remove PPE to check for odor	M256A1 Detector kit, or Drager detection tubes	Non-persistent
Hydrogen Cyanide (AC) (HCN)		Rapid heart and breathing rate, difficulty breathing, vomit, giddiness, headache, convulsions, respiratory arrest & death.	Immediate in high concentrations, slower as concentration decreases.	Aerosol, Vapor can also be absorbed through skin.	Colorless liquid; bitter, burnt almond or peach kernel odor.	Aggressive breathing support and correction of acidosis				Summer: 1 to 10 minutes Winter: 10 minutes to 1 hour

Chemical Weapons - Choking Agents

Chemical Agents	Type	Symptoms	Time to onset	Distributed by	Description	Treatment	Lethality	Precautions	Detection	Persistence
Chlorine (cl)	Ch	Inhalation: cough, burning sensation, headache, difficulty breathing, nausea, sore throat. Without treatment may result in pulmonary edema & death. Skin: Painful burning sensation. Eyes: Pain, blurred vision, severe deep burns.	May be delayed	Inhaled vapors or absorbed through skin	Greenish-yellow gas with bleach odor.	Remove victims from area ASAP. No antidote. Treatment is supportive.	High if untreated	Stay out of low lying areas. Contact with liquid can cause frostbite! Level B PPE is adequate, but Level A may be needed in an enclosed space. Do not remove PPE to check for odor.	Drager detection tubes are the most sensitive means. M18A2 Chemical Agent Detector Kit. Chemical Agent Detector (ICAD) can be used as a warning device.	Summer: 1 to 10 minutes Winter: 10 minutes to 1 hour
Phosgene (CG)		Cough, choking, tightness and pain in chest, tears, nausea, vomiting. Latent period of 30 min. to 24 hrs, followed by signs of pulmonary edema. Anoxia, circulatory collapse.	Immediate to 3 hours.		A colorless gas which may form a white cloud. Odor of new-mown hay. Heavier than air.					

Chemical Weapons - Nerve Agents

Chemical Agents	Type	Symptoms	Time to onset	Distributed by	Description	Treatment	Lethality	Precautions	Detection	Persistence
GA (Tabun)	Ne	Pinpoint pupils, excessive secretions, seizures, convulsions, death.	Inhaled: A few minutes. Skin: 20-30 minutes.	Aerosol or mixed with other liquids. Exposure: primarily inhaled but may be through ingestion or absorption through skin or eyes.	Oily liquid; can be released as aerosol or mixed with other liquids.	Antidote available. Must be given immediately!	High	Do not breathe vapor. Avoid skin contact at all times. Level A PPE.	M8 and M9 Paper; Drager detection tubes; M8A1 alarm; Chemical Agent Monitor M256A1 Kit.	Summer: 10 minutes to 24 hours. Winter: 2 hours to 3 days.
GB (Sarin)					Oily liquid, can be released as aerosol or mixed with other liquids. Color ranges from clear to light brown. Essentially odorless and tasteless. Very soluble in water.					
GD (Soman)										
GF										
VX (TX60)					Clear to straw colored oily liquid. Odorless when pure.		Very High			

Chemical Weapons - Riot Control Agents

Chemical Agents	Type	Symptoms	Time to onset	Distributed by	Description	Treatment	Lethality	Precautions	Detection	Persistence
Chloroacetophenone (CN)	Ri	Severe irritation of eyes, nose, throat, and skin. Causes tearing and eyes swell shut. Coughing and choking are common; vomiting is rare. Those with respiratory problems like asthma or bronchitis may be at risk for more serious injury.	Immediate	Fine particulate smoke or vapor; liquid may be dispersed from airplane, spray, or bursting munitions	Solid powder, white to yellow. May also be a liquid.	See decontamination. People with respiratory complications may need medical treatment.	Considered non-lethal, but a few deaths have been reported	SCBA or full-face chemical respirator or with appropriate filter.	No detector available	Non-persistent
o-Chlorobenzylidene Malnonitrile (CS)		Severe irritation of eyes, nose, throat, and skin. Causes tearing and eyes swell shut. Coughing and choking are common; vomiting is rare.		Dispersed by burning, exploding and forming an aerosol.	White crystalline solid, or liquid with a pepper odor. White at point of release.					

Victim Decontamination

For any chemical weapon other than riot control agents, immediate (within 1 minute!) decontamination is essential. Speed is more important than method used.

Caution: Decontamination should only be performed by trained first responders wearing Level A PPE! Secondary contamination is probable with all biological and chemical weapons.

- Spray or douse victims with non-contaminated water; do not wait to remove clothing or for soap arrive.
- If no water is available, use any absorbent material such as earth, talcum powder, flour, sawdust, ashes, or rags to soak up as much of the chemical as possible.
- Flush eyes with large amounts of clean water by tilting the head to the side, pulling eyelids apart with fingers, and pouring water slowly into the eyes.
- Have victims discard all clothing and go through another water spray using soap if available. Move them upwind immediately.
- If standard decontamination equipment is still not available, get victims to a safe area where they can shower with large amounts of warm water and dishwashing liquid or strong bath soap. They must avoid letting contaminated water get into their eyes while showering.
- If standard decontamination is STILL not available, a 5% hypochlorite solution (1 part household bleach to 9 parts water) may be used. Spray or pour the solution over the victims, being careful not to get it into the eyes or into open wounds on the abdomen, chest, brain, or spine.
  NOTE: If biological agents are suspected, bleach solution should remain in contact with skin at least 10-15 minutes.
- No victim should be transported without at least gross decontamination.
- All water that runs off of the decontamination area may still hold casualty producing levels of the agent. It should be treated as contaminated and handled as such.

Nuclear and Radiological Weapons

Nuclear weapons vs. Radiological weapons

A nuclear weapon is one in which the radioactive material is the explosive and creates most of its damage through its thermal radiation and blast wave, and lingering health effects through radioactive fallout, a side effect of the nuclear explosion.

A radiological weapon, on the other hand, uses a conventional explosive to disperse a radioactive material. It involves a smaller explosion and the radioactive material is distributed over a smaller area than with a nuclear weapon.

Potential Types of Attack

Nuclear bomb: Terrorist-built or Black Market/Stolen

According to many authorities these are the least likely options, but the "possibility is not zero." It is seen as being difficult, but not impossible, for terrorists to obtain the radioactive material needed to build a nuclear bomb. Since the highly enriched Uranium needed to build a nuclear bomb is tightly guarded, the most likely source of radioactive ammunition would be the spent fuel rods from a nuclear reactor. However, spent fuel rods are very hot, heavy, and difficult to handle. Getting the bomb built without it killing the builder would be a bigger challenge than obtaining the material.

There is much speculation about the possibility of terrorists purchasing a small nuclear weapon on the black market or stealing one from a country whose security is lax. No one can say just how likely either scenario is, or whether the terrorists would actually be able to detonate one. Some believe that the fail-safe mechanisms built into Russian or American bombs would prevent them from being used.

Both the United States and Russia are known to have built "suitcase bombs" small enough to be carried by one strong person.

The majority of casualties from nuclear bomb detonations result from the blast, with secondary casualties from the radiation.

Attack on Nuclear facility

Terrorists could use conventional weapons (or unconventional weapons, like aircraft) to attack a nuclear power plant in hopes of penetrating the containment structure. The Nuclear Regulatory Commission did not specifically contemplate attacks by large aircraft (Boeing 757 or 767) when developing its design requirements for nuclear reactors or storage for spent fuel. The requirements are designed to withstand extreme events such as hurricanes, tornadoes, and earthquakes. However, a recent study by the Nuclear Energy Institute (the main lobbying group for the US nuclear industry) found that power plant structures that house radioactive materials could withstand a terrorist attack involving a hijacked commercial airliner.

A disaster at a nuclear power plant would not cause a nuclear explosion. The worst case scenario would involve the release of radioactive material which could potentially require evacuation and cause mass casualties needing decontamination and treatment for radiation sickness and trauma.

Radiological Dispersal Device (aka Dirty Bomb or RDD)

Effects would vary greatly depending on the amount and type of radioactive material used, amount of explosive used, and weather conditions. According to the NRC, "immediate deaths or serious injuries would likely result from the explosion itself rather than from radiation exposure. The radioactive material would be dispersed into the air and reduced to relatively low concentrations, resulting in low dosages to people exposed." Its primary impacts are thought to be the psychological effect and the cost and disruption involved in the decontamination process.

Sources of radiological materials

- Hospital Radiation Therapy
- Food irradiation plants
- Radio pharmaceuticals
- Nuclear power plant fuel rods
- Universities, laboratories, radiography and gauging

Most of these uses involve relatively weak radiation. According to the NRC there are about 21,000 licensed organizations in the US that use radiological materials for medical, industrial, and scientific research. (There are others that use materials not subject to NRC licensing.) The NRC receives about 300 reports a year of lost or stolen radioactive material. However, they are very small amounts or very short-lived materials and the losses are not concentrated in one or two locations, so it is unlikely that the substances are being collected for use in a dirty bomb.

Dangers from Radiation

Energy released from radioactive materials can take one of three forms: Gamma rays, alpha particles, and beta particles.

Gamma rays are the most damaging in the short term. They can travel up to a mile at the speed of light and easily penetrate most materials.

Alpha particles are the largest and heaviest of the three. They are the highest energy form of radiation, but lose their energy quickly. They travel only up to six inches and cannot penetrate skin. However, if inhaled or ingested they can do considerable damage inside the body.

Beta particles are smaller than alpha particles and can penetrate skin, but don't usually penetrate as far as muscles or organs. They can cause radiation burns and cataracts.

Radioactive materials can also emit x-rays and neutrons.

Different radiological materials emit different types of radiation. See table on page 500.

Protecting yourself from radiation

To protect yourself from radiation, remember the three basic elements: time, distance, and shielding.

- Minimize the amount of time you are exposed.
- Maximize your distance from the source.
- Use shielding materials to reduce your dosage of radiation received.

Radiation Shielding Efficiencies of materials

1 thickness reduces received radiation by 1/2:

Iron/Steel	0.7 inches
Brick	2.0 inches
Concrete	2.2 inches
Earth	3.3 inches
Cinder block	5.3 inches
Ice	6.8 inches
Wood (soft)	8.8 inches
Snow	20.3 inches

The greatest long term danger of radiation exposure results from inhaling contaminated air or ingesting contaminated food or water. Alpha or beta particles brought into the body can cause cancer 20 to 30 years later.

For your own protection, do not smoke, eat or drink at the incident site, as this will increase the chances of inhaling or ingesting radioactive material.

The following table includes a few of the more commonly used radioactive isotopes out of roughly 2300. For more information on handling radioactive materials, refer to Hazmat Guide 165 on page 882.

Radiological Agents

Radiological Agents	Symbol	Half Life	Radiation Type			Used In	Notes
			Alpha	Beta	Gamma		
Americium 241	Am241	458 years	Yes		Yes	Medical research and diagnostics; smoke detectors; glass industry	
Americium 243	Am243	7,650 years	Yes		Yes	Gauges, distance sensing	
Californium 252	Cf252	2.55 years	Yes		Yes	Cancer treatment	
Cesium 137	Cs137	30 years		Yes	Yes	Cancer treatment, gauges	Chemically binds to glass, concrete and asphalt
Corium	Cm246	5,480 years	Yes			Thermoelectric power generation	
Iodine 131	I131	8 days				Nuclear medicine	
Neptunium	Np237	2.14×10^6 years	Yes		Yes	Research, neutron detection	
Plutonium 238	Pu238	89 years	Yes		Yes	Bombs	
Plutonium 239	Pu239	24,360 years	Yes	Yes	Yes	Bombs	
Plutonium 241	Pu241	13 years	Yes	Yes	Yes	Bombs	
Plutonium 242	Pu242	3.79×10^5 years	Yes		Yes	Bombs	
Thorium	Th232	1.41×10^{10} years	Yes		Yes	Strong alloys, ultraviolet photoelectric cells	
Tritium	(3)H	12.16 years		Yes		Boosted fission bombs and multi-stage thermonuclear weapons	
Uranium 233	U233	1.62×10^5 years	Yes		Yes	Bombs and Nuclear energy	
Uranium 235 including depleted, enriched, normal	U235	7.13×10^8 years	Yes		Yes	Bombs and Nuclear energy	Highly enriched uranium is the best bomb-building material.

Pre-Hospital Treatment for Radiation Exposure

- At a suspected radiological incident site, wear appropriate protective gear and carry a dosimeter if available.
- Attend to life-threatening injuries without stopping to assess contamination status. Routine emergency treatment can be administered while victims are being moved. Expose wounds and cover with sterile dressings.
- Remove victims from radiation hazard area, but keep them within the controlled area if contaminated.
- Monitor victims for contamination only after serious injuries have been addressed. If radiation readings are above background levels, victims will require decontamination.
- Remove contaminated clothing if it can be done without further injuring the victim.
- Put ambulance cot on clean side of control line. Cover it with a clean sheet or blanket, put the victim on top of the sheet or blanket, then wrap the rest around the victim.
- Remove your contaminated protective gear at the control line. If possible, the victim should be transported by a crew that did not enter the controlled area. They should be wearing gloves.
- Make sure the hospital knows they will be expecting radiation victims.
- If necessary, ambulance and crew should be monitored for radiation and decontaminated before returning to service.

Radiation Sickness

Acute Radiation Syndrome (radiation sickness) is caused by the entire body being exposed to a high dose of penetrating radiation in a very short period of time. In order for this syndrome to develop, the radiation:

- dose must be large (> 0.7 Gray).
- source must be outside the patient's body.
- must be able to penetrate all they way to the patient's internal organs (gamma rays, X-rays or neutrons).
- must have been delivered to most or all of the body.
- must have been delivered over short period of time (minutes).

With this type of exposure, three types of illness usually develop: Bone Marrow Syndrome, Gastrointestinal Syndrome, or Cardiovascular Syndrome.

Bone Marrow Syndrome:

- Requires a dose of radiation between 0.7 and 10 Gray.
- Survival rate decreases as dose received increases.
- Radiation destroys the bone marrow, resulting in death from infection and hemorrhage.

Gastrointestinal Syndrome:

- Usually occurs with a radiation dose of 10 to 100 Gray, but some symptoms may occur with doses as low as 6 Gray.
- Survival is extremely unlikely.
- Irreparable damage to the GI tract and bone marrow generally cause death within 2 weeks of exposure.

Cardiovascular Syndrome:

- Usually requires a dose of more than 50 Gray, with some symptoms occurring with as little as 20 Gray.
- Death occurs within 3 days due to collapse of circulatory system along with edema, vasculitis, and meningitis.

Each syndrome has 4 stages:

1. **Prodromal (NVD Stage):** Nausea, vomiting, diarrhea. May last anywhere from minutes to several days.
2. **Latent:** Victim looks and feels generally healthy. May last from a few hours to a few weeks.
3. **Manifest Illness:** Symptoms depend on specific syndrome; may last from hours to several months.
4. **Recovery or death:** Most who do not recover will die within several months of exposure. The recovery process can last anywhere from several weeks to 2 years.

Cutaneous Radiation Syndrome

Results from acute radiation exposure of the skin. Can occur in conjunction with ARS (above) or as a result of exposure to beta or x-ray radiation.

Symptoms:

Within hours after exposure, redness and itching set in. Then there is a period where skin feels and looks normal, followed a few days to weeks later by irritation, redness, shedding of skin cells, hair loss resulting from damage to follicles, blistering, and ulceration. Usually heals by normal regeneration, although very large doses can cause permanent hair loss, damage to sebaceous and sweat glands, atrophy, fibrosis, changes in pigmentation, and ulceration or necrosis of tissue.

Federal Response to Terrorism

As of 2003, a National Incident Management System (NIMS) has been developed to provide a central nationwide template for Federal, State, local, and tribal government responses to domestic incidents (such as terrorism, fires, floods, earthquakes, hurricanes, tornados, typhoons, hazardous material spills, nuclear incidents, aircraft accidents, war-related disasters, etc.) Refer to the Incident Command chapter for organizational information (page 199).

The information below contains brief descriptions of basic roles certain agencies may have within the Incident Command structure. As the National Response Plan (NRP) is ongoing and not yet completed, the roles of these agencies may change, be sure to check with your department as well as current releases of the NRP and Incident Command literature.

Federal Bureau of Investigation - FBI

The FBI is designated as the lead federal agency (LFA) for "crisis management" for terrorist incidents that take place within the United States. In other words, the law enforcement aspect of a terrorist incident, including management of "resources needed to anticipate, prevent and/or resolve an act of terrorism" as well as intelligence, surveillance, tactical operations, negotiations, forensics, and investigations. They will typically respond as soon as the incident occurs, although depending on the location of the "local" field, office there may be a delay in arrival. If they do not do so and you suspect you're dealing with a terrorist event, your first call should be to the local FBI office (see phone numbers on page 992). While local law enforcement, fire, hazmat and emergency medicine agencies will handle initial response, the FBI On-Scene Commander (OSC) will assume the role of Federal On-Scene Commander. The Federal OSC functions as the manager of the multi-agency Joint Operations Command Group (aka Unified Command).

FEMA - Federal Emergency Management Agency - The Department of Homeland Security

FEMA is designated as the LFA for "consequence management", defined as "measures to protect public health and safety, restore essential government services, and provide emergency relief to governments, businesses and individuals." FEMA will coordinate all consequence-related federal assistance to state and local governments.

Other Federal Agencies that may be involved:

Resources provided by the federal government are grouped into 12 Emergency Support Functions (ESFs):

Transportation: Providing civilian & military transportation.
Lead agency: Department of Transportation

Communications: Providing telecommunications support.
Lead agency: National Communications System

Public Works and Engineering: Restoring essential public services and facilities.
Lead agencies: US Army Corps of Engineers, Department of Defense

Fire Fighting: Detecting and suppressing wildland, rural, and urban fires.
Lead agencies: US Forest Service, Dept. of Agriculture

Information and Planning: Collecting, analyzing and disseminating critical information to facilitate the overall federal response and recovery operations.
Lead agency: FEMA

Mass Care: Managing and coordinating food, shelter and first aid for victims; providing bulk distribution of relief supplies; operating a system to assist family reunification.
Lead agency: American Red Cross

Resource Support: Providing equipment, materials, supplies and personnel to federal entities during response operations.
Lead agency: General Services Administration

Health and Medical Services: Providing assistance for public health and medical care needs.
Lead agencies: US Public Health Service, Department of Health & Human Services

Urban Search and Rescue: Locating, extricating and providing initial medical treatment to victims trapped in collapsed structures.
Lead agency: FEMA

Hazardous Materials: Supporting federal response to actual or potential releases of oil and hazardous materials.
Lead agency: Environmental Protection Agency

Food: Identifying food needs; ensuring that food gets to areas affected by disaster.
Lead agencies: Food and Nutrition Service, Department of Agriculture

Energy: Restoring power systems and fuel supplies.
Lead agency: Department of Energy

Role of the Military

Department of Defense: NorthCom

Role is limited to Homeland Defense (meaning "the military protection of a US territory, the domestic population, and critical defense infrastructure against external threat and aggression") and support of civilian agencies due to the Posse Comitatus Act. Homeland Security is the effort to prevent terrorist attacks within the U.S., reduce its vulnerability to terrorism, and mitigate the effects of an attack if it does occur. The mission of the Dept. of Defense is Homeland Defense, as opposed to Homeland Security.

There are three circumstances in which the Dept. of Defense would be involved in Homeland Security activities.

1. Military missions performed inside the United States, such as combat air patrols in which military aircraft might have to shoot down a terrorist controlled airliner before it hits its target.
2. Aid to civilian authorities in emergency circumstances, such as disaster relief efforts or consequence management following a terrorist attack. In these circumstances the military is always in support of a civilian lead agency, such as FEMA.
3. Temporary circumstances, such as when the military provided support to the Olympics.

The National Guard

The Guard has both a federal and state mission. In peacetime, the National Guard is commanded by the governor and may be called to state active duty by the governor during natural disasters, civil disturbances, or other state emergencies. During a war or national emergency, the Air National Guard may be called to federal active duty by the President or Congress. National Guard troops are likely to be the nearest source of equipment and manpower to help with terrorism incidents.

The Guard has already organized Weapons of Mass Destruction Civil Support Teams (WMD-CSTs), which they describe as "a high-priority response unit supporting civil authorities in responding to a weapon of mass destruction situation. The team is formed specifically to provide advice to the Incident Commander to help make assessments of the requirements for follow-on forces." Teams consist of 22 soldiers who are specially trained and are equipped with high-end protective, detection, and communications equipment, including satellite, secure, and cellular telephones so that they can connect with both civil and military forces. These teams can provide assessment of the damage, consultation on logistics, medical, chemical and biological defense, and the ability to transmit information about the situation to higher headquarters and facilitate bringing in additional forces if needed.

Federal Hotlines for CBR Events

Domestic Preparedness Chemical/Biological HelpLine
Phone: 800-368-6498   FAX: 410-612-0715
Provides technical assistance during business hours to eligible State and local emergency responders and their organizations.

National Response Center Hotline
Phone: 800-424-8802
Receives reports of oil, chemical, biological, and radiological releases and actual or potential domestic terrorism. They provide technical assistance to emergency responders and connect callers with appropriate Federal resources.
24 hours/day, 365 days/year

Nuclear Regulatory Commission Operations Center
Phone: 301-816-5100, collect calls accepted.
Accepts reports of accidents involving radiological materials.

Department of Homeland Security

The Department of Homeland Security (DHS) was created as a result of the terrorist attack on the United States in New York City and Washington D.C. on September 11, 2001. President George W. Bush signed into executive order the Homeland Security Act of 2002 (Public Law 107-296) which serves to mobilize and organize our nation's agencies into one unified core with the purpose of preventing and deterring terrorist attacks and protecting and responding to threats and hazards to the United States.

DHS website: http://www.dhs.gov

Phone: 202-282-8000

For detailed DHS contact information see page 959.

DHS has a three part mission:
1. To prevent terrorist attacks within the U.S.
2. To reduce our vulnerability to terrorism.
3. To minimize the damage and recover from attacks that do occur.

DHS goals and objectives:
1. **Awareness:** Identify and understand threats, assess vulnerabilities, determine potential impacts and disseminate timely information to homeland security partners and the American public.
2. **Prevention:** Detect, deter & mitigate threats to the US
3. **Protection:** Safeguard the American people and their freedoms, critical infrastructure, property and the economy from acts of terrorism, natural disasters, or other emergencies.
4. **Response:** Lead, manage, and coordinate the national response to acts of terrorists, natural disasters, or other emergencies.
5. **Recovery:** Lead national, state, local, and private sector efforts to restore services and rebuild communities after acts of terrorism, natural disasters, or other emergencies.
6. **Service:** Serve the public effectively by facilitating lawful trade, travel, and immigration.
7. **Organizational Excellence:** Create a culture that promotes a common identity, innovation, mutual respect, accountability, and teamwork to achieve efficiencies, effectiveness, and operational synergies.

DHS consists of 5 Directorates (Divisions):

- Border and Transportation Security
- Emergency Preparedness and Response
- Science and Technology
- Information Analysis and Infrastructure Protection
- Management

In addition to the five directorates, the Coast Guard and the Secret Service report directly to the Secretary of DHS.

Border and Transportation Security

This directorate is responsible for maintaining the security of borders and transportation systems, including enforcing the nation's immigration laws. Immigration enforcement includes preventing aliens from entering the country unlawfully, detecting and removing those who are living in the U.S. unlawfully, and preventing terrorists and other criminal aliens from entering or residing in the United States.

This directorate encompasses these departments:

- **Animal & Plant Health Inspection Service (APHIS)**
  APHIS assesses the import requirements for plant and animal health and evaluates the risk of wildlife and invasive pests to our nation's ecosystems.

- **Federal Law Enforcement Training Center (FLETC)**
  FLETC offers training for law enforcement professionals who operate in various field positions in law enforcement and government.

- **Office for Domestic Preparedness (ODP)**
  ODP is the primary office that prepares for terrorist attacks. They provide training, equipment, support, and planning to federal, state, and local agencies and jurisdictions.

- **Transportation Security Administration (TSA)**
  TSA works to secure the transportation systems in the United States.

- **U.S. Citizenship & Immigration Service (USCIS)**
  USCIS is responsible for administering the process of immigration and naturalization. They work to resolve issues, establish immigration policies, and oversee naturalization, immigration, and refugee applications.

- **U.S. Customs & Border Protection**
  The agency works with US Customs, US Immigration, APHIS, and the US Border Patrol to manage, monitor, control, and protect our nation's borders & ports of entry.

- **U.S. Immigration & Customs Enforcement (ICE)**
  ICE works to prevent acts of terrorism by identifying, monitoring, and closing vulnerabilities in our nation's borders, economic, transportation, and infrastructure security. They work by identifying suspicious people, financial transactions, and materials that could support criminal, terrorist, or security threats to the U.S.

  - **Detention & Removal Operations (DRO)**
    DRO works with U.S. Customs & Border Protection and USCIS to fairly and safely remove illegal aliens from the United States. They transport aliens, provide a holding center for them during pending cases, and remove unauthorized aliens when necessary.
  - **Federal Air Marshal Service (FAMS)**
    FAMS works to protect air travel security by identifying and defeating acts of terrorism on U.S. air carriers, airline crews, and airports
  - **Federal Protective Service (FPS)**
    FPS provides security and law enforcement to employees and visitors in federally owned and leased facilities.
  - **Office of Intelligence**
    This office collects, analyzes, and coordinates information on security vulnerabilities and communicates it with field agents and enforcement agencies.
  - **Office of Investigations**
    This office focuses on national security related to financial and smuggling crimes. They focus their investigations on protecting critical agencies that are susceptible to exploitation and sabotage, and also investigate crimes such as illegal arms and narcotics trafficking, financial and commercial crimes, human trafficking, immigration crimes, and child pornography.
  - **Students & Exchange Visitor Information Program (SEVIS)**
    This web-based system provides information for and helps international exchange students with the entry and exit process for study in the U.S.
- **U.S. Visit Program (US-VISIT)**
  US-VISIT assists visitors in the entry, exit, and immigration process into the United States. It works to make legitimate travel as smooth as possible while maintaining the visitor's privacy and enhancing security for U.S. citizens.

Emergency Preparedness & Response (EP&R)

This directorate is responsible for the management of our nation's natural disasters and terrorist assaults. They oversee and coordinate the federal government's national preparedness, response, and recovery strategies for terrorist attacks including any sort of biological or radiological attack.

This directorate encompasses these departments:

- **Domestic Emergency Support Teams (DEST)**
  This team is formed during national disasters or hazards, and is composed of specialized agencies brought together for that specific incident.

- **Federal Emergency Management Agency (FEMA)**
  This agency leads preparation, response, and recovery for national disasters and hazards.

- **National Disaster Medical System (NDMS)**
  This agency manages and coordinates the medical responses to national disasters and hazards.

- **Nuclear Incident Response Team (NIRT)**
  This team provides specialized personnel and equipment to deal with nuclear emergencies, terrorism, and accidents.

- **Office for Domestic Preparedness (ODP)**
  This is the primary office that prepares for terrorist attacks. They provide training, equipment, support, and planning to federal, state, and local agencies and jurisdictions.

- **Strategic National Stockpile (SNS)**
  This organization operates with the Center for Disease Control (CDC) and provides medicine and medical supplies in the event of a public health emergency that would deplete local supplies.

Information Analysis and Infrastructure Protection (IAIP)

This directorate deters, prevents, and mitigates acts of terrorism by assessing our nation's vulnerabilities as continuously changing threats occur. With the help of all available intelligence agencies (CIA, FBI, NSA), they identify and assess current and future threats to the United States, compare the threats to our nation's vulnerabilities, and issue timely warnings for preventative and protective action.

This directorate encompasses these departments:

- **Homeland Security Operations Center (HSOC)**
  This is the main center for information and incident management. They work to analyze and distribute relevant incident information through the Homeland Security Information Network (HSIN).

- **Office of Energy Assurance (OEA)**
  This office works to secure, protect, and restore our nation's energy systems from any type of disruption, and also to protect citizens from the use of the infrastructure to carry out acts of terrorism.

- **National Communications System (NCS)**
  This system works to coordinate national security and emergency readiness communications for the federal government.

- **National Infrastructure Coordinating Center (NICC)**
  This center coordinates communications between the HSOC (see above) and other critical agencies and infrastructures during an incident.

- **U.S. Computer Emergency Readiness Team (US-CERT)**
  This team protects and defends the nation's internet infrastructure against cyberattacks.

Science and Technology

This directorate is responsible for research and development. They work to provide scientific and technological resources to federal, state, and local officials to counter catastrophic terrorism.

This directorate encompasses these departments:

- **CBRN Countermeasures Program**
  This program works to research, analyze, and prevent chemical, biological, radiological, and nuclear incidents.

- **Environmental Measurements Laboratory (EML)**
  This federally owned and operated laboratory applies new technologies and science to aid in preventing, protecting, and responding to radiological and nuclear incidents.

- **Homeland Security Advanced Research Projects Agency (HSARPA)**
  This agency works to coordinate research and development projects relating to the Department of Homeland Security.

- **National BW (Bioweapons) Defense Analysis Center**
  This center coordinates countermeasures that would be used on biological weapons of mass destruction.
- **Office of National Laboratories**
  This team of laboratories, scientists, engineers, and academics work to develop testing and research programs, and provide a scientific knowledge base to lead against and prevent acts of terrorism.
- **Plum Island Animal Disease Center**
  This center works to protect the United States from foreign animal disease.

Office of Management

This office is responsible for the budget, accounting, expenditure of funds, finance, procurement, appropriations, information technology systems, property, equipment, and facilities. They also track the performance of the responsibilities of Homeland Security.

Office of the Secretary

This office is responsible for the collaboration of federal, state, local, and private entities. They work to oversee activities and communicate to provide intelligence analysis, improve technology, strengthen our borders, and provide infrastructure protection.

- Office of the Chief Privacy Officer
- Office of Civil Rights and Civil Liberties
- Office of Counter Narcotics
- Office of General Counsel
- Office of the Inspector General
- Office of Legislative Affairs
- Office of National Capital Region Coordination
- Office of the Private Sector
- Office of Public Affairs
- Office of State & Local Government Coordination & Preparedness

U.S. Coast Guard (USCG)

The U.S. Coast Guard is responsible for protecting the public, the environment, and U.S. economic interest by supporting national security in the nation's ports, waterways, coastal and international waters, and any maritime regions.

The Coast Guard's mission includes:

- **Maritime Safety:** Eliminate deaths, injuries and property damage associated with maritime transportation, fishing, and recreational boating. The service is always ready to respond to calls for help at sea.
    - Search & Rescue
    - Marine Safety
    - Recreational Boating Safety
    - International Ice Patrol
    - Port Security
- **Maritime Mobility:** Facilitate maritime commerce and eliminate interruptions and impediments to the efficient and economical movement of goods and people, while maximizing recreational access to and enjoyment of the water.
    - Aids to Navigation
    - Icebreaking Services
    - Vessel Traffic/Waterways Management
    - Bridge Administration
    - Rules of the Road
- **Maritime Security:** Protect America's maritime borders from all intrusions by halting the flow of illegal drugs, aliens, and contraband into the United States through maritime routes, preventing illegal fishing, and suppressing violations of federal law in the maritime arena.
    - Drug Interdiction
    - Alien Migrant Interdiction
    - EEZ & Living Marine Resource
    - General Maritime Law Enforcement
    - Law/Treaty Enforcement
- **National Defense:** Defend the nation as one of the five U.S. armed services. Enhance regional stability in support of the National Security Strategy, utilizing the Coast Guard's unique and relevant maritime capabilities.
    - General Defense and Protection
    - Homeland Security
    - Port and Waterways Security
    - Polar Icebreaking

- **Protection of Natural Resources:** Eliminate environmental damage and the degradation of natural resources associated with maritime transportation, fishing, and recreational boating.
  - Marine Pollution Education, Prevention, Response, and Enforcement
  - Foreign Vessel Inspections
  - Living Marine Resources Protection
  - Marine and Environmental Science

U.S. Secret Service (USSS)

The U.S. Secret Service is responsible for protecting the President, our nation's leaders, the country's financial and critical infrastructures, and provides security for designated national events. They are divided into two components, one focusing on protection of government leaders and foreign dignitaries, and the other focusing on investigations that will safeguard the payment and financial systems of the United States.

Chapter Sources:
Chemical/Biological/Radiological Incident Handbook (October 1998), Central Intelligence Agency at www.cia.gov/cia/publications/cbr_handbook.htm

ConPlan, United State Government Interagency Domestic Terrorism Concept of Operations Plan, January 2001

Criminal/Terrorist Use of Chemical/Biological Agents, Royal Canadian Mounted Police Online University at www.rcmp-learning.org/docs/ecdd1022.htm

Heyser, Robert J., *Introduction to NBC Terrorism: An Awareness Primer and Preparedness Guide for Emergency Responders*, Oct. 15, 2001, The Disaster Preparedness and Emergency Response Association

Kane, Lt. John, *The Incident Command System and the Concept of Unified Command at a Terrorist Incident*, from Community Response to the Threat of Terrorism, A Public Entity Risk Institute Symposium

VDEM Terrorism Information, Virginia Dept. of Emergency Management at www.vaemergency.com/prepare/terrorismtoolkit/

Centers for Disease Control & Prevention, CDC Health Advisory, Oct. 12, 2001

Department of Homeland Security Tree

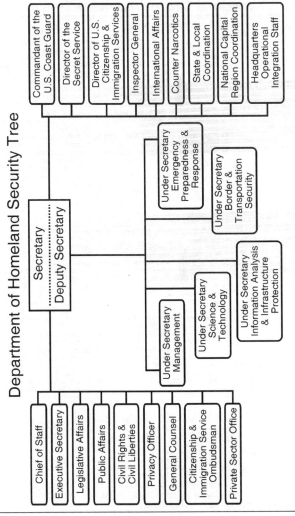

Reporting to Secretary / Deputy Secretary (top row):
- Commandant of the U.S. Coast Guard
- Director of the Secret Service
- Director of U.S. Citizenship & Immigration Services
- Inspector General
- International Affairs
- Counter Narcotics
- State & Local Coordination
- National Capital Region Coordination
- Headquarters Operational Integration Staff

Under Secretaries:
- Under Secretary Emergency Preparedness & Response
- Under Secretary Border & Transportation Security
- Under Secretary Management
- Under Secretary Science & Technology
- Under Secretary Information Analysis & Infrastructure Protection

Offices (left column):
- Chief of Staff
- Executive Secretary
- Legislative Affairs
- Public Affairs
- Civil Rights & Civil Liberties
- Privacy Officer
- General Counsel
- Citizenship & Immigration Service Ombudsman
- Private Sector Office

Homeland Security Advisory System

Code	Risk of Attack	Federal Departments and Agencies	Public
Red	Severe	• Increase or redirect personnel to address critical emergency needs. • Assign emergency response personnel and pre-position and mobilize specially trained teams or resources. • Monitor, redirect or constrain transportation systems. • Close non-critical public and government facilities.	• Avoid sports arenas, holiday gatherings, or other high risk locations. • Follow official restrictions to normal activities. • Contact employer to determine status of work. • Listen to radio and TV for advisories/warnings. • Prepare to evacuate or shelter-in-place if told to do so by public officials.
Orange	High	• Coordinate security efforts with agencies at all levels. • Take extra precautions at public events, such as other sites or cancellation. • Prepare for contingency procedures, such as moving to an alternate site or dispersing the workforce. • Restrict access to a threatened facility to essential personnel only.	• Review preparedness measures for potential terrorist actions. • Avoid high profile or symbolic locations. • Exercise caution when traveling.
Yellow	Elevated	• Increase surveillance of critical locations. • Coordinate emergency plans with nearby jurisdictions. • Assess whether the threat requires refinement of prearranged plans. • Implement appropriate contingency and emergency response plans	• Be alert for suspicious activity and report it to authorities. • Discuss plans and needs with neighbors. • Check with school about emergency procedures to reunite children with parents and care givers. • Update the household communication plan.
Blue	General	• Check communications with designated emergency response or command locations. • Review and update emergency response procedures. • Provide public with information to strengthen its ability to act appropriately.	• Update/review disaster plan. • Develop household communication plan. • Apartment residents discuss emergency procedures with building managers. • People with special needs should discuss their emergency plans with friends, family & employers.
Green	Low	• Refine and exercise planned protective measures. • Train personnel on the Homeland Security Advisory System and specific department or agency protective measures. • Create a plan to regularly check and address facility security weaknesses.	• Develop a household disaster plan and assemble a disaster supply kit.

Source: *Are You Ready? A Guide to Citizen Preparedness,* Federal Emergency Management Agency, 2002

TRANSPORTATION

Military Crash Site Protection Protocol · · · · · · · · · · 518

Civil Air Patrol (CAP) - Search and Rescue · · · · · · · 521

Helicopter Landing Zones · 522

Traffic Formulas · 529

  Grade of Road - Degrees of Slope to Percent Grade· 529
  Automobile Stopping Distances· · · · · · · · · · · · · · · · 529
  Railroad Stopping Distances · · · · · · · · · · · · · · · · · · 530
  Estimated Speed Based on Skid Marks · · · · · · · · · · 530
  Speed Under Dry Conditions· · · · · · · · · · · · · · · · · · 531
  Speed Under Wet Conditions · · · · · · · · · · · · · · · · · 532
  Velocity Conversions· 534

International Driver's License · · · · · · · · · · · · · · · · · 535

Items Permitted/Prohibited on Commercial Aircraft · 536

Transportation

Military Crash Site Protection Protocol

The first officer on scene

- Should request needed assistance and equipment.
- Can provide emergency medical aid.
- Should secure the site.
- Should establish entry and exit corridors.
- Should identify authorized personnel and restrict admission.
- Has the authority to investigate the crash of a military aircraft.

Site Safety

Avoid the instinct to rush to the scene to either help or observe. This attitude, while commendable, is dangerous. Numerous hazards can turn investigators into casualties. Be aware of potential hazards, stay upwind of mishaps, and stay well clear of the wreckage until professional help is available.

Common Hazardous Material Injuries:

- **Chemical Injury:** Occurs when the substance is ingested, inhaled, or comes in contact with the skin.
- **Thermal injury:** Occurs when the substance freezes or burns.
- **Asphyxiation:** Occurs when the substance displaces oxygen needed to breathe.
- **Radiation injury:** Occurs when a radioactive material emits ionizing energy or particles that can harm personnel.
- **Disease:** Can be contracted from microbiological agents.
- **Mechanical injury:** Occurs with explosive fragments, rocketing containers, explosive over pressures, etc.

NOTE: Many normally benign items such as tires, batteries, beryllium mirrors, parachute oxygen bottles, hydraulic accumulators, etc., can become lethal in a post-crash context.

Injury Avoidance

Investigators should follow these four steps to avoid injury.

1. Expect

- Expect hazardous materials to be present until their presence has been ruled out.
- Scan the wreckage to RULE OUT the presence of hazardous materials: assume that they are present until it is conclusively established that they are not.

- Look for hazardous materials such as freight cargo, ejection seats, ordnance, fluids, and propellants. Also be alert to the presence of fuels propelling the vehicles. Hazardous materials may be dangerous whether or not they are still in their containers.
- Search for warning placards or signs, labels on packages, shipping papers, or verbal information from people at the scene.

2. Wait

- Wait until potential energy transfers (such as fires, explosions, vapors, breached radioactive materials containers, etc) have been eliminated if hazardous materials are present. It is almost impossible to tell precisely when they will activate and envelope the danger zone with the investigator in it. Unless there is compelling reason to enter the crash site area while the hazardous material containment systems are under mechanical or thermal stress, wait for those potential energy transfers to be eliminated. Use other ways of collecting evidence in the wreckage.

3. Follow

- Follow, rather than lead, others into the wreckage. Stay away from wreckage containing hazardous material until a competent expert is available. Ask the expert to predict the behavior of the hazardous material in that emergency to be sure he or she is truly knowledgeable. If the expected behavior poses no threat to personal safety, it may be permissible to follow him or her into the wreckage area. If assistance or information is requested, refer the person making the inquiry to emergency response agencies to contact the CHEMTREC emergency toll free telephone number (800-424-9300) for expert advice and assistance. Obey evacuation instructions of EOD, police, and firefighters. Never follow firefighters or other emergency or rescue personnel into the wreckage area. Stay at least 2000 feet upwind from any fires burning in wreckage where hazardous materials are present, and stay out of any plume of smoke from the site.

4. Don't

- DON'T TAKE CHANCES. If uncertain about potentially destructive hazardous material behavior, don't enter the site. The investigator's role is to determine what happened, not to be a part of what is happening. Refer to the HazMat chapter of this book beginning on page 603.

Transportation

Classified Information

Federal law and Executive Order 12065 require military personnel to protect classified information. However, military authority is limited at an off-base mishap site where civil police are responsible for enforcing the law. Military officials must ask local law enforcement officials for help at such sites and must also remind civil officials that unauthorized photography, publication, or possession of classified information may be prosecuted as criminal acts under 18 U.S.C. 793(e), 795, and 797.

Site Security

Prompt posting of guards is important both to protect onlookers from danger and to safeguard evidence, property, and classified information. Security forces working with local law enforcement agencies should quickly define broad limits of the site. A site access roster and security plan for at least 30 days should be prepared. Access to the mishap site should be restricted to essential medical, EOD, Rescue, and firefighting personnel until the site is declared safe.

Response Phase

- Ensure that security police advise state and local law officers when off-base convoy response is required or civil involvement exists.
- Ensure that emergency response agencies initiate mutual support agreements.
- Coordinate with the command post to obtain helicopter support (if available) for airlift to the mishap site.

For more information on Hazardous Materials incidents, see the chapter beginning on page 603.

Civil Air Patrol (CAP) - Search & Rescue

Most commonly associated with the mission of emergency services, Civil Air Patrol (CAP) volunteer pilots fly 85% of all inland search and rescue missions that are directed by the Air Force Rescue Coordination Center at Langely AFB, VA.

- CAP volunteer members provide air and ground transportation and aerial reconnaissance in support of disaster relief efforts on the part of such agencies as the American Red Cross and the Federal Emergency Management Agency (FEMA).
- CAP's extensive communications network is available free to local, state, and national disaster relief agencies.
- CAP also transports time-sensitive medical materials in support of humanitarian organizations. The live organ transplant program is credited with saving an average of 10 lives per year.
- CAP has formal agreements with the US Air Force, US Customs Service, the DEA, and the US Forest Service to support counterdrug operations by providing aerial reconnaissance, airborne communications support, and airlift of law enforcement personnel.

Contact information:
Civil Air Patrol Operations Center: 888-211-1812
Website: http://www.cap.gov

Air Force Rescue Coordination provides federal assistance to local civil search and rescue when the scope of the operation exceeds local SAR capabilities. For more information call 800-851-3051.

Transportation

Guidelines For Use Of Air Transport

Air transport is indicated for the acutely ill patient if time is critical to survival and/or distances are long.

Guidelines for use of air-medical ambulances vary throughout the country and depend on a number of factors including location and number of trauma centers, certification level of pre-hospital care, ground accessibility to trauma centers, and terrain.

Guidelines as defined by the 1983 Conference on Injury Severity Scoring and Triage are as follows:

Anatomic Factors
- Severe penetrating trauma to the head, neck, or torso, with shock
- Major amputation above the ankle or wrist
- Major burns associated with trauma
- Paralysis
- Acute airway obstruction or respiratory system compromise

Medical Conditions
Note: One or more conditions under Situational Factors also must be present.
- Shock
- Unconsciousness or decreasing level of consciousness
- Exposure to deadly chemicals or toxins
- Hypothermia
- Drowning or near drowning
- Electrocution
- Cardiac emergencies

Situational Factors
- Prolonged extrication time (20 minutes or more)
- Increased ground transport time at reduced speed due to snow, ice, construction, traffic gridlock, etc.
- Rural or isolated areas
- Need for specialized equipment and/or personnel at a disaster scene

Mechanism of Injury

- High energy dissipation (rapid deceleration)
- Passenger space invaded by one foot or more
- Ejection
- Death of another passenger
- Deformity of a contact point (steering wheel, etc.)
- Multiple injured passengers
- Falls of 15 feet or more (consider surface, was fall broken?)
- Child under 12 struck by motor vehicle
- Trauma score of 12 or less
- Glascow Coma Score of 10 or less

While treatment and transport decisions in the field vary, the guidelines can assist in making the decision to use air transport.

Helicopter Operations

Authority And Responsibility

In accordance with Federal Aviation Regulations, the Pilot in Command holds final authority and responsibility for decisions or actions which will affect the safety of the flight. These include final selection and acceptance of the landing zone, continuing or canceling any mission due to weather, all loading and unloading of equipment, patients, medical supplies, or anything directly related to the safety operations of the helicopter.

Operational Safety Procedures

From a safety viewpoint, there are separate phases of helicopter operation that may require special attention:

- Selecting a landing zone
- Preparing for arrival
- Contacting the helicopter
- Landing
- Patient loading
- Departure

Selecting The Landing Zone (LZ)

The LZ is an area intended for the purpose of a helicopter landing or taking off. This can be a parking lot, highway, open field, rooftop structure, etc. It may also be called a landing site, helipad, or helistop. In selecting a landing zone, consider the following:

- **Area - Day:** Should be at least 60 feet by 60 feet, free of wires, trees, buildings, and other vertical obstructions. **Night:** Should be at least 100 feet by 100 feet, free of wires, trees, buildings, and other vertical obstructions.

- **Night Landings:** Some special considerations need to be followed at night. The landing area should be identified with some sort of lighting device such as high intensity chemical light sticks or battery powered flashing lights, both of which are good, safe, and inexpensive. If these are not available, headlights from the rescue vehicles will work if pointed at the landing site.

- **Rotorwash:** The main downwash of a helicopter can generate very high winds at the landing site. Flying dirt, dust, and gravel can become a hazard during landing and takeoff. If possible, a dusty area should be wet down just prior to the arrival of the helicopter.

- **Ground Surface:** Should be firm, smooth (no tall shrubs, brush, grass, weeds, etc. higher than 18 inches), and have a slope no greater than 5 degrees. Although some portions of the landing site may have a steeper gradient, the touchdown point cannot exceed this limit.

Maximum safe slope for landing

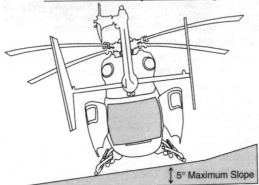

↕ 5° Maximum Slope

- **Safety Precautions:** Ground personnel on the landing site should wear goggles or a face visor to protect their eyes from blowing debris. If these are not available, they should turn their backs to the helicopter until the rotorwash diminishes.

Preparing For Arrival

Prior to the arrival of the helicopter, certain objectives must be accomplished.

- Locate a safe landing zone.
- Designate someone to direct the helicopter landing.
- Give the helicopter service a radio frequency to contact ground units at the landing site.
- If at the scene of an accident, the injured should be protected from rotorwash during landing. Emergency vehicles make a good windbreak if parked between the helicopter and the patient(s).
- Secure loose gear, medic cases, open doors, trunk lids, helmets, hats, etc. to prevent articles from being blown away or blown into the rotor system of the helicopter.
- Arrange for traffic control.
- Permit no one to come closer than 100 feet from the landing site. Designate a landing site manager to keep the landing site secure at all times during the emergency.
- If there is press coverage, be sure no flash photography, flood lights, or other artificial lighting is used while filming the helicopter landing at night, as these can also temporarily blind the pilot.
- During night landings, do not allow spotlights or vehicle headlights to shine directly at the helicopter during final approach and landing, since the glare can temporarily blind the pilot. If vehicle lights are used to mark the landing site, be sure to use low beams.

Illuminating a Night Landing

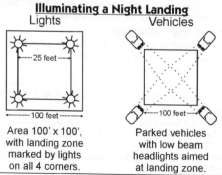

Lights	Vehicles
Area 100' x 100', with landing zone marked by lights on all 4 corners.	Parked vehicles with low beam headlights aimed at landing zone.

Transportation

Contacting the Helicopter

Communicating with the helicopter prior to its arrival is always beneficial for the pilot and medical crew. Use your unit number when contacting the helicopter, and give the following info:

Accident Scene Information
- Location with respect to geographical reference, water tank, antenna, roads, towns, etc.
- Landing zone location with respect to accident scene, roads, etc.
- Location of obstacles that may be around landing zone
- Type of landing surface
- Wind direction
- Hazardous materials, if present

Patient Information
- Mechanism of injury and time of accident
- Number of patients
- Approximate age of patients
- Level of consciousness
- Obvious injuries
- Call back phone number

Landing

As a normal operating procedure, once on the ground the engine is shut off and the rotor system is stopped with the rotor brake. This eliminates the greatest hazard around any helicopter, the rotating blades of the main and tail rotor. In some cases the patient(s) will be loaded with the aircraft running (hot loading or unloading). In such cases, extreme caution should be used and all directions given by the pilot or flight crew should be followed. The following rules should be strictly adhered to.

Approaching the Helicopter
- No one is allowed within the landing zone when the blades are in motion, unless directed by the pilot.
- Stay clear of the tail rotor system.
- Always approach the helicopter from the front, well within the pilot's field of vision and only when eye-to-eye contact is made.
- Gurneys should not have mattress pads, IV poles, sheets, blankets, or other loose articles on them when brought near the helicopter.
- Always approach and depart the helicopter from the downhill side of a slope.

Landing Zone Activity

- No vehicles, including emergency vehicles, are to be driven within 30 feet of the rotor blades.

- There is no smoking within 50 feet of the helicopter because of the presence of oxygen on board and the possibility of flammable liquids at the accident scene.

- Never run or chase after any item that is loose and blowing around in the landing zone. There should be no running or horseplay within 150 feet of the helicopter.

- Never lift any object higher than your head, as a rotor strike is a very expensive and dangerous accident.

- No one other than emergency/rescue personnel should be allowed within 100 feet of the helicopter. They should not be within 20 feet of the helicopter while the blades are in motion unless directed by pilot or flight crew.

- The flight crew will close all doors on the helicopter and will get any equipment out of the helicopter as needed.

Readying The Patient

The flight crew will brief the patient about the procedures of being flown in the helicopter.

Predeparture And Take Off

- The landing site manager should insure that the tail of the helicopter is clear and the landing site as a whole is clear for the aircraft to depart the area. All bystanders are to be kept clear of the landing area.

- It takes about 90 seconds from the time the engine is started until the helicopter can lift off. The noise and blowing dust can cause extreme hazards. Cover your eyes and protect your hearing from the noise.

- No one is allowed within 100 feet of the helicopter during departure.

- At night no spotlights or vehicle headlights should be aimed at the departing helicopter.

Hazardous Material

- Just as accidents involving hazardous materials require special handling by fire and rescue units on the ground, they also require special precautions for helicopter operations.

- Hazardous materials that are the primary concern are those which are toxic, poisonous, flammable, explosive, irritating, or radioactive.

- Helicopter ambulance crews do not normally carry protective suits or breathing apparatus to protect themselves, so they must be told about the presence of hazardous materials on the scene. Patients and victims contaminated by hazardous materials may require special precautions to protect the medical crew during aircraft loading.

- Hazardous gases and chemicals are extremely dangerous to the unprotected person and may be fatal if inhaled or absorbed through the skin.

- Upon initial radio contact, the helicopter crew must be made aware of any hazardous gases in the area. Never assume that the crew has already been informed. If the aircraft were to fly through the hazardous gases, the crew could be poisoned and/or the engines could develop mechanical problems.

- Poisonous or irritating gases may cling to a victim's clothing and go unnoticed until the patient is loaded and the doors of the helicopter are closed and the crew would be compromised.

- Some radioactive materials are more dangerous than others, depending upon the type and amounts of those materials. In general, radioactive materials are difficult to ignite, but will burn and the smoke is toxic.

- Helicopter crews should be advised if victims may be contaminated by radioactivity.

- Helicopter landing zones must be selected to avoid ALL possibility of compromising the safety of the helicopter and its crew.

When explosives, poisonous gases and vapors, or chemicals are on site and in danger of exploding and burning, the helicopter landing zones must be upwind, at least one mile from the accident site, and never in low-lying areas since the toxic gases or vapors may be heavier than air.

For accidents involving radioactive materials, the helicopter landing zone must be upwind, at least one-quarter mile from the accident, unless there are radioactive gases (steam or smoke), in which case the landing zone must be at least one mile upwind of the accident site.

Source: Information courtesy of Aerocare, *Helicopter Utilization and Preparing a Landing Zone.*

Traffic Formulas

Grade of Road

Degrees of Slope	Percent Grade	Degrees of Slope	Percent Grade	Degrees of Slope	Percent Grade
0.1	0.2	10.0	17.6	28.0	53.2
0.2	0.3	11.0	19.4	29.0	55.4
0.3	0.5	12.0	21.3	30.0	57.7
0.4	0.7	13.0	23.1	31.0	60.1
0.5	0.9	14.0	24.9	32.0	62.5
0.6	1.0	15.0	26.8	33.0	64.9
0.7	1.2	16.0	28.7	34.0	67.5
0.8	1.4	17.0	30.6	35.0	70.0
0.9	1.6	18.0	32.5	36.0	72.7
1.0	1.7	19.0	34.4	37.0	75.4
2.0	3.5	20.0	36.4	38.0	78.1
3.0	5.2	21.0	38.4	39.0	81.0
4.0	7.0	22.0	40.4	40.0	83.9
5.0	8.7	23.0	42.4	41.0	86.9
6.0	10.5	24.0	44.5	42.0	90.0
7.0	12.3	25.0	46.6	43.0	93.3
8.0	14.1	26.0	48.8	44.0	96.6
9.0	15.8	27.0	51.0	45.0	100.0

Transportation

Automobile Stopping Distances

Speed (mph)	Stopping Distance (feet)	
	Dry Pavement	Wet Pavement
25	61	65
30	79	85
35	98	107
40	120	131
45	144	157
50	169	186
55	197	217
60	226	250
65	258	286
70	291	324
75	326	364
80	363	406
85	402	451
90	443	498
95	486	547
100	531	598

Assumptions:

A. Stopping distance = Distance covered from the instant a hazard is recognized until the vehicle comes to a complete stop. Car doesn't skid.

B. "Average" passenger vehicle.

C. Reaction time of 1.0 second.

D. Deceleration rates:
Dry = 28.0 feet/second^2 Wet = 23.9 feet/second^2

Estimated Speed based on Skid Marks

The tables on the following pages show the estimated speed of a vehicle prior to braking, based on the length of skid marks. The tables were calculated using the following equation:

$$\text{Speed} = \sqrt{30df}$$

Speed = Miles per hour
d = distance in feet
f = coefficient of friction, ranges from .05 (very slick) to .90 (very high friction)

The source for the equation and the coefficients of drag used in the calculations is *The Traffic Accident Investigation Manual*, by J. Stannard Baker and Lynn B. Fricke.

Note: This formula should be used as a general guide, not for the prosecution of speed offenses.

Railroad Stopping Distances

- A 150 car freight train moving at 60 mph (100 km/hr) needs up to 1.5 miles (2.5 km) to stop.
- At 30 mph (48.28 km/hr), the same freight train needs 0.6 miles (1.06 km) to stop.
- An 8 car passenger train moving at 60 mph (100 km/hr) needs 0.6 miles (1.06 km) to stop.
- At 79 mph (127.13 km/hr), the same passenger train needs 1.125 miles (1.81 km) to stop.

For more information regarding highway and rail grade crossing safety, call Operation Lifesaver, 800-537-6224.

Speed Under **Dry** Conditions (Miles Per Hour)

Road Surface	Length of Skid Marks (feet)					
	10	20	40	60	80	100
Asphalt						
New	15-19	22-27	28-35	34-42	39-49	44-55
Traveled	13-15	19-22	27-29	31-35	36-41	41-46
Traffic Polished	13-15	18-21	26-28	28-34	33-39	37-44
Excess tar	12-13	17-19	24-27	25-33	29-38	32-42
Concrete						
New	15-19	22-27	29-35	35-42	41-49	56-67
Traveled	13-15	19-22	27-30	33-37	38-42	42-47
Traffic Polished	13-15	18-21	26-28	30-34	35-39	39-44
Gravel						
Loose	11-14	15-20	22-29	27-35	31-41	35-46
Packed & Oiled	13-16	18-23	26-31	30-38	35-44	39-49
Cinders, packed	12-14	17-20	24-29	30-35	35-41	39-46
Rock, Crushed	13-15	18-21	26-30	31-37	36-42	41-47
Ice, Smooth	05-09	08-12	11-17	13-21	15-24	17-27
Snow						
Packed	09-13	13-18	19-26	23-31	27-36	32-41
Loose	05-09	08-12	11-17	13-21	15-24	17-27

Road Surface	Length of Skid Marks (feet)					
	150	200	250	300	350	400
Asphalt						
New	54-67	62-77	70-87	76-95	83-102	88-110
Traveled	50-56	57-65	64-72	70-79	76-86	81-92
Traffic Polished	45-54	52-62	58-70	64-76	69-83	73-88
Excess tar	40-52	46-60	51-67	56-73	61-79	65-85
Concrete						
New	56-67	65-77	72-87	79-95	86-102	92-110
Traveled	52-58	60-67	67-75	73-82	79-89	85-95
Traffic Polished	47-54	55-62	61-70	67-76	72-83	77-88
Gravel						
Loose	42-56	49-65	55-72	60-79	65-86	69-92
Packed & Oiled	47-60	55-69	61-77	67-85	72-92	77-98
Cinders, packed	47-56	55-65	61-72	67-79	72-86	77-92
Rock, Crushed	50-58	57-67	64-75	70-82	76-89	81-95
Ice, Smooth	21-30	24-35	27-39	25-42	27-46	29-49
Snow						
Packed	40-50	46-57	51-64	56-70	61-76	65-81
Loose	21-30	24-35	27-39	30-42	32-46	35-49

Note: This formula should be used as a general guide, not for the prosecution of speed offenses.

Speed Under <u>Dry</u> Conditions (mph) cont.

Road Surface	Length of Skid Marks (feet)					
	450	500	550	600	700	800
Asphalt						
New	94-116	99-122	104-128	108-134	117-145	125-155
Traveled	86-97	91-102	95-107	99-112	107-121	115-130
Traffic Polished	78-94	82-99	86-104	90-108	97-117	104-125
Excess tar	69-90	72-95	76-99	79-104	86-112	92-120
Concrete						
New	97-116	102-122	107-128	112-134	121-145	130-155
Traveled	90-101	95-106	99-111	104-116	112-125	120-134
Traffic Polished	82-94	87-99	91-104	95-108	102-117	110-125
Gravel						
Loose	73-97	77-102	81-107	85-112	92-121	98-130
Packed & Oiled	82-104	87-110	91-115	95-120	102-130	110-139
Cinders, packed	82-97	87-102	91-107	95-112	102-121	110-130
Rock, Crushed	86-101	91-106	95-111	99-116	107-125	115-134
Ice, Smooth	31-52	32-55	34-57	35-60	38-65	41-69
Snow						
Packed	69-86	72-91	76-95	79-99	86-107	92-115
Loose	37-52	39-55	41-57	42-60	46-65	49-69

Speed Under <u>Wet</u> Conditions (Miles Per Hour)

Road Surface	Length of Skid Marks (ft)					
	10	20	40	60	80	100
Asphalt						
New	12-15	17-22	23-30	28-37	33-42	37-47
Traveled	12-14	16-20	23-28	27-34	31-39	35-44
Traffic Polished	14-14	20-20	28-27	27-33	31-38	35-42
Excess tar	09-13	13-19	19-27	21-31	24-36	27-41
Concrete						
New	12-15	17-22	22-30	27-37	31-42	35-47
Traveled	12-14	16-20	23-28	28-34	33-39	37-44
Traffic Polished	12-14	16-20	23-27	28-33	33-38	37-42
Gravel						
Loose	12-15	16-21	23-30	28-37	33-42	37-47
Packed & Oiled	11-15	15-22	22-27	27-33	31-38	35-42
Cinders, packed	14-15	20-21	28-30	34-37	39-42	44-47
Rock, Crushed	13-15	18-21	26-30	31-37	36-42	41-47
Ice, Smooth	04-05	05-08	08-11	09-13	11-15	12-17
Snow						
Packed	09-13	13-19	19-27	23-33	27-38	30-42
Loose	09-13	13-19	19-27	23-33	27-38	30-42

Note: This formula should be used as a general guide, not for the prosecution of speed offenses.

Speed Under <u>Wet</u> Conditions (mph) cont.

Road Surface	Length of Skid Marks (feet)					
	150	200	250	300	350	400
Asphalt						
New	45-58	52-67	58-75	64-82	69-89	73-95
Traveled	42-54	49-62	55-70	60-76	65-83	69-88
Traffic Polished	42-52	49-60	55-67	60-73	65-79	69-85
Excess tar	34-50	39-57	43-64	47-70	51-76	55-81
Concrete						
New	42-58	49-67	55-75	60-82	65-89	69-95
Traveled	45-54	52-62	58-70	64-76	69-83	73-88
Traffic Polished	45-52	52-60	58-67	64-73	69-79	73-85
Gravel						
Loose	45-58	52-67	58-75	64-82	69-89	73-95
Packed & Oiled	42-52	49-60	55-67	60-73	65-79	69-85
Cinders, packed	54-58	62-67	70-75	76-82	83-89	88-95
Rock, Crushed	50-58	57-67	64-75	70-82	76-89	81-95
Ice, Smooth	15-21	17-24	19-27	21-30	23-32	24-35
Snow						
Packed	37-52	42-60	47-67	52-73	56-79	60-85
Loose	37-52	42-60	47-67	52-73	56-79	60-85

Road Surface	Length of Skid Marks (feet)					
	450	500	550	600	700	800
Asphalt						
New	78-101	82-106	86-111	90-116	97-125	104-134
Traveled	73-94	77-99	81-104	85-108	92-117	98-125
Traffic Polished	73-90	77-95	81-99	85-104	92-112	98-120
Excess tar	58-86	61-91	64-95	67-99	72-107	77-115
Concrete						
New	73-101	77-106	81-111	85-116	92-125	98-134
Traveled	78-94	82-99	86-104	90-108	97-117	104-125
Traffic Polished	78-90	82-95	86-99	90-104	97-112	104-120
Gravel						
Loose	78-101	82-106	86-111	90-116	97-125	104-134
Packed & Oiled	73-90	77-95	81-99	85-104	92-112	98-120
Cinders, packed	78-101	82-106	86-111	90-116	97-125	104-134
Rock, Crushed	86-101	91-106	95-111	99-116	107-125	115-134
Ice, Smooth	26-37	27-39	29-41	30-42	32-46	35-49
Snow						
Packed	64-90	67-95	70-99	73-104	79-112	85-120
Loose	64-90	67-95	70-99	73-104	79-112	85-120

Note: This formula should be used as a general guide, not for the prosecution of speed offenses.

Velocity Conversions

Miles/ Hour	Feet/ Second	Meters/ Second	Miles/ Hour	Feet/ Second	Meters/ Second
5.0	7.3	2.2	48.0	70.4	21.5
6.0	8.8	2.7	49.0	71.9	21.9
7.0	10.3	3.1	50.0	73.3	22.4
8.0	11.7	3.6	52.0	76.3	23.2
9.0	13.2	4.0	54.0	79.2	24.1
10.0	14.7	4.5	56.0	82.1	25.0
11.0	16.1	4.9	58.0	85.1	25.9
12.0	17.6	5.4	60.0	88.0	26.8
13.0	19.1	5.8	62.0	90.9	27.7
14.0	20.5	6.3	64.0	93.9	28.6
15.0	22.0	6.7	66.0	96.8	29.5
16.0	23.5	7.2	68.0	99.7	30.4
17.0	24.9	7.6	70.0	103.0	31.3
18.0	26.4	8.0	72.0	106.0	32.2
19.0	27.9	8.5	74.0	109.0	33.1
20.0	29.3	8.9	76.0	111.0	34.0
21.0	30.8	9.4	78.0	114.0	34.9
22.0	32.3	9.8	80.0	117.0	35.8
23.0	33.7	10.3	82.0	120.0	36.7
24.0	35.2	10.7	84.0	123.0	37.6
25.0	36.7	11.2	86.0	126.0	38.4
26.0	38.1	11.6	88.0	129.0	39.3
27.0	39.6	12.1	90.0	132.0	40.2
28.0	41.1	12.5	92.0	135.0	41.1
29.0	42.5	13.0	94.0	138.0	42.0
30.0	44.0	13.4	96.0	141.0	42.9
31.0	45.5	13.9	98.0	144.0	43.8
32.0	46.9	14.3	100.0	147.0	44.7
33.0	48.4	14.8	102.0	150.0	45.6
34.0	49.9	15.2	104.0	153.0	46.5
35.0	51.3	15.6	106.0	155.0	47.4
36.0	52.8	16.1	108.0	158.0	48.3
37.0	54.3	16.5	110.0	161.0	49.2
38.0	55.7	17.0	112.0	164.0	50.1
39.0	57.2	17.4	114.0	167.0	51.0
40.0	58.7	17.9	116.0	170.0	51.9
41.0	60.1	18.3	118.0	173.0	52.8
42.0	61.6	18.8	120.0	176.0	53.6
43.0	63.1	19.2	122.0	179.0	54.5
44.0	64.5	19.7	124.0	182.0	55.4
45.0	66.0	20.1	126.0	185.0	56.3
46.0	67.5	20.6	128.0	188.0	57.2
47.0	68.9	21.0	130.0	191.0	58.1

International Driver's License

An International Driver's License, or International Driving Permit (IDP), is issued by the government or by an authorized association in a person's home country (AAA issues such licenses for Americans who want to drive overseas). It certifies in several languages that the holder possesses a valid driver's license in his country of residence.

The purpose of the International Driving Permit is to give the officer who stops a foreign motorist an indication of whether that person's drivers license is valid, nothing more. Some countries require foreign drivers to carry one.

The United States does not require people visiting from most foreign countries to carry an IDP, since we have agreements with them to recognize the validity of driver's licenses issued in those countries. Nevertheless, some tourists will carry one as a precaution.

The document is a booklet about the size of a passport. It contains a passport-sized photograph of the holder, information about the individual and the permit, and is valid for 1 year from the date of issuance. It becomes invalid if the person establishes residency in the U.S.

Transportation

Items Prohibited or Permitted on Commercial Aircraft

You may not bring the listed items to security checkpoints without authorization.

If you bring a prohibited item to the checkpoint, you may be criminally and/or civilly prosecuted or, at the least, asked to rid yourself of the item. A screener and/or Law Enforcement Officer will make this determination, depending on what the item is and the circumstances. Bringing a prohibited item to a security checkpoint, even accidentally, is illegal.

Your prohibited item may be detained for use in an investigation and, if necessary, as evidence in your criminal and/or civil prosecution. If permitted by the screener or Law Enforcement Officer, you may be allowed to: consult with the airlines for possible assistance in placing the prohibited item in checked baggage; withdraw with the item from the screening checkpoint at that time; make other arrangements for the item, such as taking it to your car; or, voluntarily abandon the item. Items that are voluntarily abandoned cannot be recovered and will not be returned to you.

Footnotes at the bottom contain important information about restrictions.

The prohibited and permitted items chart is not intended to be all-inclusive, as regulations change from time to time. Screeners may determine that an item not on the prohibited items chart is prohibited, or that an item on the permitted chart is dangerous and therefore may not be brought through the security checkpoint.

The chart applies to flights originating within the United States. Please check with your airline or travel agent for restrictions at destinations outside of the United States.

This table was compiled with the TSA Rev. 5-16-2005 release. For updates and for more information, call the TSA at 866-289-9673 or check the website: http://www.tsa.gov

Item	Okay for Carry-On?	Okay for Checked Bags?
Aerosols (except personal care)	No	No
Aerosols (personal care or toiletries, such as hair spray, deodorants)[1]	Yes	Yes
Alcoholic Beverages[2]	Yes	Yes
Ammunition[3] (If permitted, it must be declared to the airline at check-in.)	No	Yes
Animal Repellant[4]	No	Yes
Ax or Hatchet[5]	No	Yes
Baseball Bat	No	Yes
BB Gun - *Unloaded*	No	Yes
Billy Club	No	Yes
Black Jacks[5]	No	Yes
Blasting Caps	No	No
Bows and Arrows[5]	No	Yes
Box Cutter[5]	No	Yes
Braille Note-Taker, Slate and Stylus, Augmentation Devices	Yes	Yes
Brass Knuckles[5]	No	Yes
Camcorder	Yes	Yes
Camera Equipment (Note: checked baggage screening equipment will damage undeveloped film in camera equipment. It is recommended to either put it in your carry-on or ask the ticket agent/screener to conduct a hand-inspection.)	Yes	Yes (See note in description to the left)
Camp Stoves[6]	Yes	Yes
Cattle Prod[5]	No	Yes
Cigar Cutter	Yes	Yes
Chlorine for Pools and Spas	No	No
Compressed Air Gun[7] - *Unloaded*	No	Yes
Compressed Gas Cylinders (including fire extinguishers)	No	No
Corkscrew	Yes	Yes
Crematory Container[8]	Yes	Yes
Cricket Bat	No	Yes
Crowbar	No	Yes

Item	Okay for Carry-On?	Okay for Checked Bags?
Cuticle Cutter	Yes	Yes
Diabetes Related Supplies and Equipment[9] (Including: insulin and insulin loaded dispensing products, vials, jet injectors, pens, infusers, preloaded syringes, unused syringes when accompanied by insulin, lancets, blood glucose meters, blood glucose meter test strips, insulin pumps & pump supplies. Insulin and insulin dispensers must be property marked with a professional printed label identifying the medication or manufacturer's name or pharmaceutical label.)	Yes	Yes
Drain Cleaner or Similar Solvent	No	No
Drill[5] (including cordless portable power drills)	No	Yes
Dry Ice[10]	No	Yes
Dynamite	No	No
Explosives	No	No
Explosives, Realistic Replicas	No	No
Eyeglass Repair Tools (including screwdriver)	Yes	Yes
Eyelash Curler	Yes	Yes
Firearm and/or Gun[7] - *Unloaded*	No	Yes
Firearm and/or Gun Parts[7]	No	Yes
Firearm and/or Gun, Realistic Replica	No	Yes
Fireworks	No	No
Fishing Rod or Pole[5]	Yes	Yes
Flare Gun	No	No
Flares (in any form)	No	No
Fuel (Including: cooking fuel and any flammable liquid fuel)	No	No
Gas Torch	No	No
Gasoline	No	No
Golf Clubs	No	Yes
Gun Lighters	No	No
Gun Powder	No	No

Item	Okay for Carry-On?	Okay for Checked Bags?
Hammer	No	Yes
Hand Grenades	No	No
Hockey Stick	No	Yes
Ice Ax/Ice Pick	No	Yes
Ice Skates[5]	No	Yes
Incendiaries, Realistic Replicas	No	No
Knitting and Crochet Needles[11]	Yes	Yes
Knives, round-bladed butter or plastic	Yes	Yes
Knives, all, except for those above[5]	No	Yes
Kubaton[5]	No	Yes
Lacrosse Stick	No	Yes
Laptop Computer	Yes	Yes
Lighter[12]	No	No
Lighter Fluid[12]	No	No
Liquid Bleach	No	No
Mace or Pepper Spray[13] (with safety)	No	Yes
Martial Arts Weapons[5]	No	Yes
Matches, Safety[14] (non-strike anywhere)	Yes	No
Matches, Strike-anywhere	No	No
Meat Cleaver[5]	No	Yes
Mobile Phone	Yes	Yes
Nail Clipper	Yes	Yes
Nail File	Yes	Yes
Night Stick	No	Yes
Nitroglycerine pills or spray (For medical use, must be properly marked with a professionally printed label identifying the medication or manufacturer's name or pharmaceutical label.)	Yes	Yes
Nunchakus[5]	No	Yes
Pager	Yes	Yes
Paint	No	No
Paintball Gun[15]	No	Yes
PDA (Personal Data Assistant)	Yes	Yes

Item	Okay for Carry-On?	Okay for Checked Bags?
Pellet Gun[7] - *Unloaded*	No	Yes
Plastic Explosives	No	No
Poison or Infectious Substance	No	No
Pool Cue	No	Yes
Pressurized Containers (Including: spray cans, CO_2 cartridges, butane fuel, propane tanks, self-inflating rafts)	No	No
Prosthetic Device Tools and Appliances - only if carried by the individual with the prosthetic device or his/her companion. (Tools include: drills, allen wrenches, pullsleeves used to put on or remove prosthetic devices)	Yes	Yes
Razor-Type Blades[5] (such as box cutters, utility knives, razor blades not in a cartridge, *excluding safety razors.*	No	Yes
Razors, Safety (including disposable)	Yes	Yes
Saber[5]	No	Yes
Saw[5] (including cordless portable power saws)	No	Yes
Scissors, plastic or metal with blunt tip	Yes	Yes
Scissors, metal with pointed tips[5]	No	Yes
Screwdriver[5] (except those in eyeglass repair kits)	No	Yes
Ski Poles	No	Yes
Spear Gun[5]	No	Yes
Spillable Batteries (except those in wheelchairs)	No	No
Spray Paint	No	No
Starter Pistol	No	Yes
Stun Gun/Shocking Device[5]	No	Yes
Sword[5]	No	Yes
Tackle Equipment[5]	No	Yes
Tear Gas	No	No
Throwing Stars[5]	No	Yes
Tools[5] (including but not limited to wrenches and pliers)	No	Yes
Toy Transformer Robots	Yes	Yes

Item	Okay for Carry-On?	Okay for Checked Bags?
Toy Weapons (only if not realistic replicas)	Yes	Yes
Turpentine and Paint Thinner	**No**	**No**
Tweezers	Yes	Yes
Umbrellas[9]	Yes	Yes
Walking Canes[9]	Yes	Yes
Wrench and/or Plier[5]	**No**	Yes

Notes:

1: Some personal care items containing aerosol are regulated as hazardous materials (such as flammable perfume). The FAA regulates hazardous materials on aircraft, and states that no more than 70 ounces may be carried onboard, with individual containers holding no more than 16 fluid ounces. For more information contact the FAA at 202-267-7211 or their website http://asi.faa.gov/Passenger.asp

2: Alcoholic beverages with 70% or more alcohol content (or 140 proof), including 95% grain alcohol and 150 proof rum, are <u>prohibited</u> from carry-on and checked luggage. Up to 5 liters of alcohol per person with alcoholic content between 24% and 70% are allowed as carry-on or in checked luggage, but it must be packaged in its retail container. Alcoholic beverages with less than 24% alcoholic content are not subject to hazardous materials regulations. Please verify alcoholic beverage limits and restrictions with your airline.

3: Ammunition regulations vary between airlines, check with your airline or travel agent to see if it is permitted in checked luggage, and what limitations or fees apply. If it is permitted, it must be declared to the airline at check-in. Small arms ammunition for personal use must be securely packed in fiber boxes, wood boxes, metal boxes, or other packaging specifically designed to carry small amounts of ammunition.

4: Animal repellants are only allowed in checked bags if the volume is less than 4 ounces and has less than 2% active ingredient. Most bear repellants exceed these limitations. TSA recommends buying repellants at your destination to avoid complications.

5: Any sharp object in checked luggage should be sheathed or securely wrapped to prevent injury to baggage handlers and inspectors.

6: Camp stoves are only permitted if emptied of **all** fuel and cleaned such that all vapors and residue are absent. Simply emptying the fuel container is not acceptable. TSA recommends shipping stoves ahead of time to avoid complications due to fuel vapors.

7: Firearms in checked baggage **MUST** be unloaded, packed in a locked hard-sided gun case, and declared to the airline at check-in. Only you, the passenger, may have the key or combination for the gun case. See Note 3 for firearm specifications.

8: The TSA provides a list of funeral homes who have agreed to transfer remains from a temporary container to a permanent container free of charge. This complimentary service is provided to that you can pass through TSA screening with a safe container. Once upon your final destination you can have the remains transferred for free to a permanent container. Passengers may transfer remains without these containers, but they are subject to screening. Carry-on containers must pass through the x-ray machine and be must made of a material that can be screened. Any material that prevents the screener from clearly seeing what is inside will not be allowed through the checkpoint. Containers in checked baggage will be checked for explosive materials and devices using a variety of techniques. Once cleared, it will only be permitted as checked baggage. Screeners may not open the container under any circumstance as a respect for the deceased; therefore, it is advisable to use the temporary to permanent container system provided by funeral homes. Some airlines do not allow cremated remains as checked baggage and may also have additional regulations; therefore, always check with your airline before flying. TSA provides a list of funeral homes that provide the complimentary container service at: http://www.tsa.gov/public/interapp/editorial/editorial_1296.xml

9: Items are allowed in carry-on baggage once they have been inspected to ensure that prohibited items are not concealed within them.

10: Up to 4 pounds of dry ice may be carried on board for packaging perishables provided that the container is vented. However, restrictions may apply, please contact your travel agent or airline directly.

11: Knitting needles are permitted in carry-on and checked baggage; however, there is a possibility that the TSA screener might perceive them as a possible weapon and might not allow them to pass through security. To avoid complications bring circular knitting needles less than 31 inches in total length and made of bamboo or plastic (non-metal). Scissors must have blunt points and thread cutters (or any cutter with a blade contained inside) are not permitted as carry-on items. Knitting needles are permitted in checked luggage; however, it is advisable to have them securely wrapped to prevent injury to baggage handlers.

12: <u>All</u> lighters are now prohibited as carry-on items. Lighters without fuel are permitted in checked baggage, but if they contain any fuel they are prohibited. If you are uncertain as to whether your lighter is prohibited or not, please refrain from bringing it to the airport or packing it in your luggage.

13: Mace or pepper spray can be considered a hazardous material. One 118ml or 4 fluid ounce container of mace or pepper spray is permitted in checked baggage. It must be equipped with a safety mechanism to prevent accidental discharge. For more information on hazardous materials go to: http://asi.faa.gov/Passenger.asp

14: <u>All</u> matches are prohibited in checked baggage. Up to 4 books of safety (non-strike anywhere) matches are permitted as carry-on items.

15: Paintball guns may only be checked. They are not considered a firearm and, therefore, may be transported unlocked and in soft or hard sided luggage. Compressed gas cylinders are allowed in carry-on or checked baggage **only** if the regulator valve is completely disconnected from the cylinder and the cylinder is no longer sealed (i.e. has an open end to allow for a visual inspection). TSA screeners will not remove the valve, so if the cylinder is sealed then it will not be permitted through the checkpoint regardless of the reading on the pressure gauge. It is advised to contact the manufacturer for guidance in removing the regulators and seals. Passengers might also want to consider shipping the system to avoid complications during screening.

WEAPONS AND BALLISTICS

Ammunition Specs · 544

  Pistol Ammunition Energy · · · · · · · · · · · · · · · · · · 544
  Pistol Ammunition Velocity · · · · · · · · · · · · · · · · · 545
  Rifle Ammunition Energy · · · · · · · · · · · · · · · · · · · 546
  Rifle Ammunition Trajectory · · · · · · · · · · · · · · · · 547
  Rifle Ammunition Velocity · · · · · · · · · · · · · · · · · 547

Bullet Proof Vests and Body Armor · · · · · · · · · · · · · 549

  Body Armor Standards · 550
  Ammunition Manufacturers · · · · · · · · · · · · · · · · · 551
  U.S. Body Armor Manufacturers · · · · · · · · · · · · · 551
  Weapons Manufacturers · · · · · · · · · · · · · · · · · · · 553

Federal Gun Laws · 554

  Acquiring Firearms · 554
  Age Restrictions · 554
  Ammunition · 555
  Antiques & Replicas · 555
  Gun Length Requirements · · · · · · · · · · · · · · · · · 555
  Ineligible Persons · 555
  Machine Guns · 556
  Sale of Firearms to Aliens · · · · · · · · · · · · · · · · · 556
  Shipping Firearms & Ammunition · · · · · · · · · · · 556
  Silencers · 556

Transportation of Firearms · · · · · · · · · · · · · · · · · · · 557

Gun Laws By State · 561

Canadian Gun Laws · 601

Weapons & Ballistics

Ammunition Specs

Pistol Ammunition Energy

Barrel Length	Caliber	Energy Muzzle	Energy 100 yds
2"	25 Auto, 35 gr. JHP/XTP	63	43
3 ¾"	380 Auto, 90 gr. JHP/XTP	200	135
4"	32 Auto, 71 gr. FMJ	128	100
4"	40 S&W, 155 gr. JHP/XTP	479	331
4"	40 S&W, 180 gr. JHP/XTP	361	297
4"	9 x 18 Makarov, 95 gr. JHP/XTP	211	161
4"	9MM Luger, 90 gr. JHP/XTP	370	191
4"	9MM Luger, 115 gr. FMJ V	341	241
4"	9MM Luger, 115 gr. JHP/XTP	341	241
4"	9MM Luger, 124 gr. JHP/XTP	339	259
4"	9MM Luger, 147 gr. JHP/XTP	310	264
4"V	38 Special, 125 gr. JHP/XTP	225	185
4"V	38 Special, 140 gr. JHP/XTP	252	202
4"V	38 Special, 148 gr. HBWC	210	122
4"V	38 Special, 158 gr. JHP/XTP	225	188
5"	10MM Auto, 155 gr. JHP/XTP	551	358
5"	10MM Auto, 180 gr. JHP/XTP Full	556	403
5"	10MM Auto, 200 gr. JHP/XTP	490	399
5"	45 ACP, 185 gr. JHP/XTP	371	276
5"	45 ACP, 200 gr. JHP/XTP	444	348
5"	45 ACP, 230 gr. FMJ/FP	369	304
5"	45 ACP, 230 gr. FMJ/RN	369	304
5"	45 ACP+P, 200 gr. HP/XTP	494	380
5"	45 ACP+P, 230 gr. HP/XTP	462	382
7 1/2"V	44 Rem. Mag., 180 gr. JHP/XTP	960	550
7 1/2"V	44 Rem. Mag., 200 gr. JHP/XTP	999	565
7 1/2"V	44 Rem. Mag., 240 gr. JHP/XTP	971	619
7 1/2"V	44 Rem. Mag., 300 gr. JHP/XTP	881	708
7 1/2"V	44 Special, 180 gr. JHP/XTP	400	311
8"V	357 Mag., 125 gr. JHP/XTP	624	374
8"V	357 Mag., 125 gr. JHP/XTP	624	377
8"V	357 Mag., 140 gr. JHP/XTP	609	397
8"V	357 Mag., 158 gr. JFP	548	400
8"V	357 Mag., 158 gr. JHP/XTP	548	404

Pistol Ammunition Velocity

Barrel Length	Caliber	Velocity (ft/second) Muzzle	100 yds
2"	.25 Auto, 35 gr. JHP/XTP	900	742
3 ¾"	.380 Auto, 90 gr. JHP/XTP	1000	823
4"	.32 Auto, 71 gr. FMJ	900	797
4"	.40 S&W, 155 gr. JHP/XTP	1180	980
4"	.40 S&W, 180 gr. JHP/XTP	950	862
4"	9 x 18 Makarov, 95 gr. JHP/XTP	1000	874
4"	9MM Luger, 90 gr. JHP/XTP	1360	978
4"	9MM Luger, 115 gr. FMJ V	1155	971
4"	9MM Luger, 115 gr. JHP/XTP	1155	971
4"	9MM Luger, 124 gr. JHP/XTP	1110	971
4"	9MM Luger, 147 gr. JHP/XTP	975	899
4"V	38 Special, 125 gr. JHP/XTP	900	817
4"V	38 Special, 140 gr. JHP/XTP	900	806
4"V	38 Special, 148 gr. HBWC	800	610
4"V	38 Special, 158 gr. JHP/XTP	800	731
5"	10MM Auto, 155 gr. JHP/XTP	1265	1020
5"	10MM Auto, 180 gr. JHP/XTP Full	1180	1004
5"	10MM Auto, 200 gr. JHP/XTP	1050	948
5"	45 ACP, 185 gr. JHP/XTP	950	819
5"	45 ACP, 200 gr. JHP/XTP	900	885
5"	45 ACP, 230 gr. FMJ/FP	850	771
5"	45 ACP, 230 gr. FMJ/RN	850	771
5"	45 ACP+P, 200 gr. HP/XTP	1055	925
5"	45 ACP+P, 230 gr. HP/XTP	950	865
7 1/2"V	44 Rem. Mag., 180 gr. JHP/XTP	1550	1173
7 1/2"V	44 Rem. Mag., 200 gr. JHP/XTP	1500	1128
7 1/2"V	44 Rem. Mag., 240 gr. JHP/XTP	1350	1078
7 1/2"V	44 Rem. Mag., 300 gr. JHP/XTP	1150	1031
7 1/2"V	44 Special, 180 gr. JHP/XTP	1000	882
8"V	357 Mag., 125 gr. JHP/XTP	1500	1161
8"V	357 Mag., 125 gr. JHP/XTP	1500	1166
8"V	357 Mag., 140 gr. JHP/XTP	1400	1130
8"V	357 Mag., 158 gr. JFP	1250	1068
8"V	357 Mag., 158 gr. JHP/XTP	1250	1073

Weapons & Ballistics

Rifle Ammunition Energy

Standard Ammo Rifle Caliber	Energy (Foot-Pounds) Muzzle	100 yds	500 yds
22-250 Rem., 53 gr. HP	1594	1194	319
22-250 Rem., 60 gr. HP	1727	1360	470
220 Swift, 50 gr. SP	1645	1228	327
220 Swift, 60 gr. HP	1727	1364	465
223 Rem., 53 gr. HP	1305	978	356
223 Rem., 60 gr. HP	1322	1031	331
243 Win., 75 gr. HP	1926	1469	425
243 Win., 100 gr. BTSP	1945	1653	810
25-06 117 gr. BTSP	2322	1962	938
257 Roberts,117 gr. BTSP	2007	1689	787
270 Win., 130 gr. SP	2700	2265	1045
270 Win., 140 gr. BTSP	2688	2346	1307
270 Win., 150 gr. SP	2802	2400	1237
30-30 Win., 150 gr. RN	1902	1296	316
30-30 Win., 170 gr. FP	1827	1355	425
30-06 150 gr. BTSP	2820	2397	1177
30-06 150 gr. SP	2820	2281	876
30-06 165 gr. BTSP	2873	2460	1252
30-06 168 gr. BTHP MATCH	2925	2561	1442
30-06 180 gr. SP	2913	2436	1105
300 Wby. Mag., 180 gr. SP	3890	3340	1727
300 Win. Mag., 150 gr. BTSP	3573	2974	1727
300 Win. Mag., 165 gr. BTSP	3522	3033	1592
300 Win. Mag., 180 gr. SP	3501	3011	1565
300 Win. Mag., 190 gr. BTSP	3549	3101	1732
303 British, 150 gr. SP	2401	1984	500
303 British, 175 gr. RN	2414	1837	557
308 Win., 150 gr. BTSP	2648	2183	922
308 Win., 165 gr. BTSP	2670	2283	1148
308 Win., 168 gr BTHP MATCH	2720	2377	1326
6MM Rem., 100 gr. BTSP	2134	1818	904
7 x 57 Mau.,139 gr. BTSP	2251	1936	1002
7mm Rem. Mag.,139 gr BTSP	3063	2656	1440
7mm Rem. Mag.,154 gr. SP	3151	2708	1408
7mm Rem. Mag.,162 gr BTSP	3110	2735	1578
7mm Rem Mag.,175 gr. SP	3180	2720	1370
7mm Wby. Mag.,154 gr. SP	3501	3017	1593
7mm Wby. Mag., 175 gr. SP	3290	2850	1531

Rifle Ammunition Trajectory

Standard Ammo Rifle Caliber	Trajectory Tables 100 yds	500 yds
22-250 Rem., 53 gr. HP	+1.0	-38.8
22-250 Rem., 60 gr. HP	+1.0	-34.8
220 Swift, 50 gr. SP	+0.8	-35.3
220 Swift, 60 gr. HP	+1.0	-34.8
223 Rem., 53 gr. HP	+1.7	-49.1
223 Rem., 60 gr. HP	+1.6	-48.1
243 Win, 75 gr. HP	+1.2	-43.8
243 Win, 100 gr. BTSP	+1.6	-42.8
25-06 117 gr. BTSP	+1.6	-42.2
257 Roberts, 117 gr. BTSP	+1.9	-49.9
270 Win, 130 gr. SP	+1.8	-42.0
270 Win, 140 gr. BTSP	+1.6	-40.3
270 Win, 150 gr. SP	+1.7	-43.9
30-30 Win., 150 gr. RN	0.0	0.0
30-30 Win., 170 gr. FP	0.0	0.0
30-06 150 gr. BTSP	+2.0	-44.9
30-06 150 gr. SP	+2.1	-51.8
30-06 165 gr. BTSP	+1.8	-47.0
30-06 168 gr. BTHP MATCH	+1.7	-44.3
30-06 180 gr. SP	+2.4	-54.9
300 Wby. Mag., 180 gr. SP	+1.3	-36.8
300 Win. Mag., 150 gr. BTSP	+1.2	-36.5
300 Win. Mag., 165 gr. BTSP	+1.3	-37.3
300 Win. Mag., 180 gr. SP	+1.9	-41.9
300 Win. Mag., 190 gr. BTSP	+1.6	-41.0
303 British, 150 gr. SP	+2.2	-56.5
303 British, 175 gr. RN	+2.9	-83.4
308 Win., 150 gr. BTSP	+2.0	-51.8
308 Win., 165 gr. BTSP	+2.0	-51.0
308 Win., 168 gr. BTHP MATCH	+2.0	-48.0
6MM Rem., 100 gr. BTSP	+1.3	-38.5
7 x 57 Mau., 139 gr. BTSP	+2.0	-50.3
7MM Rem. Mag., 139 gr. BTSP	+1.2	-35.5
7MM Rem. Mag., 154 gr. SP	+1.3	-39.3
7MM Rem. Mag., 162 gr. BTSP	+1.6	-39.3
7MM Rem. Mag., 175 gr. SP	+2.0	-45.8
7MM Wby. Mag., 154 gr. SP	+1.2	-34.5
7MM Wby. Mag., 175 gr. SP	+1.6	-41.7

Weapons & Ballistics

Rifle Ammunition Velocity

Standard Ammo Rifle Caliber	Velocity (feet per second) Muzzle	100 yds	500 yds
22-250 Rem., 53 gr. HP	3680	3185	1646
22-250 Rem., 60 gr. HP	3600	3195	1878
220 Swift, 50 gr. SP	3850	3327	1716
220 Swift, 60 gr. HP	3600	3199	1868
223 Rem., 53 gr. HP	3330	2882	1475
223 Rem., 60 gr. HP	3150	2782	1575
243 Win, 75 gr. HP	3400	2970	1595
243 Win, 100 gr. BTSP	2960	2728	1910
25-06 117 gr. BTSP	2990	2749	1900
257 Roberts, 117 gr. BTSP	2780	2550	1740
270 Win, 130 gr. SP	3060	2800	1900
270 Win, 140 gr. BTSP	2940	2747	2050
270 Win, 150 gr. SP	2800	2684	1927
30-06 150 gr. BTSP	2910	2683	1880
30-06 150 gr. SP	2910	2617	1622
30-06 165 gr. BTSP	2800	2591	1848
30-06 168 gr. BTHP MATCH	2790	2620	1966
30-06 180 gr. SP	2700	2469	1663
30-30 Win., 150 gr. RN	2390	1973	974
30-30 Win., 170 gr. FP	2200	1895	1064
300 Wby. Mag., 180 gr. SP	3120	2891	2079
300 Win. Mag., 150 gr. BTSP	3275	2988	1998
300 Win. Mag., 165 gr. BTSP	3100	2877	2084
300 Win. Mag., 180 gr. SP	2960	2745	1979
300 Win. Mag., 190 gr. BTSP	2900	2711	2026
303 British, 150 gr. SP	2685	2441	1598
303 British, 175 gr. RN	2500	2181	1201
308 Win., 150 gr. BTSP	2820	2560	1644
308 Win., 165 gr. BTSP	2700	2496	1770
308 Win., 168 gr. BTHP MATCH	2700	2524	1885
6MM Rem., 100 gr. BTSP	3100	2861	2018
7 x 57 Mau., 139 gr. BTSP	2700	2504	1802
7MM Rem. Mag., 139 gr. BTSP	3150	2933	2160
7MM Rem. Mag., 154 gr. SP	3035	2814	2029
7MM Rem. Mag., 162 gr. BTSP	2940	2757	2094
7MM Rem. Mag., 175 gr. SP	2860	2650	1880
7MM Wby. Mag., 154 gr. SP	3200	2971	2159
7MM Wby. Mag., 175 gr. SP	2910	2709	1985

Bullet Proof Vests and Body Armor

Officers should wear body armor throughout each duty shift. Soft body armor is primarily designed to protect against handgun assault, but it has also prevented serious and potentially fatal injuries from traffic accidents, physical assault with improvised clubs, and to some extent assaults from knives. Officer fatality statistics suggest that a large percentage of the officer fatalities reported each year could have been prevented if the officer had been wearing armor.

Armor should be selected to protect against the type of weapons known to be used in the local area, and the department's service weapons. Over the last ten years, one in six officers killed was shot with his or her own weapon. Full coverage of the torso is critical, because fatalities among officers wearing armor have resulted from bullets entering an officer's side through the opening between the front and rear panels.

Body armor becomes less comfortable as level of protection increases, so these two factors should be weighed against each other in deciding what to buy.

Departments should choose body armor that their officers will wear and that also provides the level of protection needed in their locale. Each officer should be familiar with the degree of safety that the armor delivers.

Author's Note: When I first became a cop, my wife bought me a Second Chance model Y vest. It was comfortable and I wore it religiously, year round. The one call I didn't think I'd need it for was a possible heart attack victim, (I was cross-trained as an EMT.) The guy was simply drunk and had wandered off. I found him lying on a bed, looking dead. When I went to check his pulse, he jumped me and we had a wrestling contest. Turns out the guy had done time for shooting a cop. From that day on, I always wore my vest, and never again assumed that a guy lying on a bed was innocuous. My partner in the highway patrol had a department issued vest that when worn felt like you were sandwiched between two sheets of plywood. He kept it in his trunk, protecting his flares. When you buy a vest, talk to other cops, and find one that is comfortable. You wouldn't think of starting a shift without your weapon, and in some cases your vest is more important. So make a commitment to always wear your vest, and honor it - NO EXCEPTIONS!

Body Armor Standards

Type	Bullet Caliber and Type Protection	Bullet Mass (grains)	Impact Velocity (feet/second)
I	.22 long rifle high velocity	40	1,050
	.38 round nose lead	158	850
II-A	.357 jacketed soft point	158	1,250
	9 mm full metal jacket	124	1,090
II	.357 jacketed soft point	158	1,395
	9 mm full metal jacket	124	1,175
III-A	.44 magnum lead semi wadcutter gas checked	240	1,400
	9 mm full metal jacket	124	1,400
	(Both are used as routine wear in many situations, and provide the max. protection available in soft body armor.)		
III	7.62 mm full metal jacket (Used in tactical situations)	150	2,750
IV	.30-06 armor piercing (Used in tactical situations)	166	2,850

Source: NIJ Standard-0101.03

Ammunition Manufacturers

Ammunitionstore.com···················800-432-0255······330-498-0864
ATK···800-256-8685
Black Hills Ammunition Inc············800-568-6625······605-348-5150
CCI Ammunition···866-286-7436
Cheaper Than Dirt!·····················800-559-0943······817-625-7171
Delta Frangible Ammunition··········800-339-1933······540-720-5778
Federal Cartridge···800-322-2342
Glaser Safety Slug Inc···············800-221-3489······605-347-4544
Hornady Manufacturing Co···········800-338-3220······308-382-1390
Midwall Corp (Outdoor Marksman)····························503-399-5463
PMC Ammunition···800-456-9182
Remington Ammunition···800-243-9700
Sportsman's Guide··888-844-0667
TTI Armory···801-545-0174
Winchester Ammunition···············800-356-2666······203-789-5000
Your American Backyard Ammunition························800-482-2024

U.S. Body Armor Manufacturers

3 TEX (Ballistic & Armor System Division)··············919-481-2500
Alpha Armor America···562-945-8177
Alpine Armoring Inc··················800-992-7667······703-471-0002
American Body Armor & Equip.·····800-347-1200······909-923-7300
Armacel Body Armor Corp····································805-482-0016
Armor Holding··························800-428-0588······904-741-5400
Armor USA Inc···972-315-1750
Armored Steel Co & Technology····························858-359-0222
ArmorShield LLC···866-628-8899
ArmorTech International··425-712-9703
ArmorWorks Inc···480-517-1150
Armour of America···310-532-0690
Astralloy Wear Technology············800-633-6635······205-853-0300
Atlantic Body Armor (Canada)······························450-659-3334
Be Safe International···239-693-7233
Centra Special Materials LLC·······························781-272-7887
Ceramic Protection Corp······································403-250-1007
Custom Armor Technologies··································866-296-1228
DHK Defense & Aerospace Group···························949-588-1170
DiamondBack Tactical··800-735-7030
Dupont Advanced Fibers Systems···························800-931-3456
First Choice Armor & Equipment···800-882-7667······508-559-0777
First Defense International····································714-366-8444
ForceOne·······························800-462-7880······828-766-7675
Front-Line Body Armor··708-479-3436
G.T. Distributors Inc···512-451-8298

Weapons & Ballistics

Gall's Inc.	866-290-3385	859-266-7227
Gator Hawk Armor	866-487-4295	805-639-0841
Guardian Technologies Intl.	800-462-7880	828-766-7675
Intapol Industries		800-631-0480
International Armor Corporation		949-366-9049
JH Design Group (Ligion Brigade Inc)	800-353-1010	213-747-5700
JHRG, Inc	800-849-4997	252-478-4997
Lifetek Armor Inc		252-229-3659
MDT Armor		334-321-0762
Med-Eng Systems Inc (Canada)		613-739-9646
MPS Co.		704-847-8793
Pacific Safety Products (Canada)	800-667-5487	250-491-0911
Paraclete Armor & Equipment		910-865-2425
Park Technology, Inc. (PTI Armor)		804-379-7275
Pan United Inc		703-471-1900
Pinnacle Armor	800-200-0915	559-320-1221
Point Blank Body Armor	800-413-5155	954-630-0900
Prolite Armor Systems		516-795-6543
Protech Armored Products	800-234-3105	413-684-3104
Protective Apparel Corporation of America, Inc (PACA)	800-722-7667	423-562-1115
Protective Armor International (PAI)		305-820-4273
Protective Products International	800-509-9111	954-846-8222
PT Armor Inc		703-560-1020
Public Safety Products (Canadian Body Armor)		905-799-2999
RBR Armor Inc	800-672-7667	804-798-6787
Reliance Armor	800-346-6699	513-742-7100
Safariland Ltd	800-347-1200	909-923-7300
SECO Manufacturing Inc		530-225-8155
Second Chance Body Armor	800-253-7090	231-544-5721
Simula Inc		602-643-7603
Smith & Wesson Body Guard		866-868-0461
Stiletto Industries Inc		800-752-5483
Survival Inc		206-726-9363
Tactical Armor Products		423-563-0069
Taurus Intl. Manufacturing	800-327-3776	305-623-7506
TG FAUST	800-407-8378	610-375-8549
UNICOR (Federal Prison Industries)		800-827-3168
US Armor	800-443-9798	562-949-1733
USA Armoring		559-292-3185
Widder Bolt Vest Inc		800-715-8334

Weapons Manufacturers

ArmaLite Inc	800-336-0184	309-944-6939
Barrett Firearms Manufacturing		615-896-2938
Benelli USA		301-283-6981
Berretta USA Corp		301-283-2191
Browning	800-333-3288	801-876-2711
Cheyenne Tactical		208-527-8614
Colt Manufacturing Co	800-426-8001	860-232-4489
Dakota Arms		605-347-4686
Desert Toys		480-835-6643
Ferret50		407-957-3617
FN Manufacturing Inc		803-736-0522
GastlingGuns.com		928-854-3538
Glock Inc USA		770-432-1202
Heckler & Koch (H&K)		703-450-1900
Kimber	800-880-2418	914-964-0771
Les Baer Custom		309-658-2716
Magnum Research Inc	800-772-6168	763-574-1868
Mossberg & Sons Inc		203-230-5300
Nor-Cal Precision		707-552-3810
Remington Arms Co		800-243-9700
Robinson Armament		801-355-0401
Savage Arms		413-568-7001
Sebru Firearms		813-243-8899
SigArms		603-772-2302
Smith & Wesson		413-781-8300
Springfield Armory	800-680-6866	309-944-5631
Sturm, Ruger & Co		203-256-3860
Tactical Operations Inc		310-275-8797
Taurus International Firearms		305-624-1115
Walther		800-372-6454
Weatherby		805-466-1767
Wilson Combat	800-955-4856	870-545-3635
Winchester Rifles & Shotguns	800-333-3288	801-876-2711
Z-M Weapons		413-648-9501

Weapons & Ballistics

Federal Gun Laws

Gun laws change frequently and are often lengthy and complex. Therefore the following information should be considered an overview, not all-inclusive, and may be outdated; it should not be considered legal advice or a restatement of law. There are also many unique circumstances and exceptions to gun laws for people in law enforcement, the government, or security. Check with local authorities for definitive, current information.

Acquiring Firearms

Firearms From a Dealer:
All federal and state laws should be followed from the dealer's and buyer's states.

- A buyer who is 21 years or older may acquire a handgun from a federally licensed dealer in the buyer's resident state.
- A buyer who is 18 years or older may purchase a rifle or shotgun from a federally licensed dealer in any state.
- The sale of any firearm from a federally licensed dealer requires the federal form 4473 (which includes information on the buyer and records the make, model, and serial number of the firearm.)
- Any sale of one or more handguns within a 5 day period requires the dealer to notify the Federal Bureau of Alcohol, Tobacco and Firearms.

Firearms Between Individuals:
- Any person who does not possess a federal firearms license may not sell a firearm to a resident of another state without first transferring the firearm to a dealer in the buyer's state.

Temporary Use of Someone Else's Firearm:
All state and federal laws must be followed.

- An individual may temporarily borrow or rent a firearm for lawful sporting and recreation purposes.

Age Restrictions

Licensed firearms dealers may not sell or deliver any firearm or ammunition to anyone under 18 years old. Firearms other than shotguns or rifles, and ammunition for such firearms, may not be sold or delivered to anyone under 21 years old. Ammunition interchangeable between rifles and handguns may be sold to those between 18 and 21 years old if the dealer is satisfied that it is being purchased for use in a rifle.

It is illegal to transfer a handgun to anyone less than 18 years old or for anyone under 18 to possess a handgun (with exceptions for employment, ranching, farming, target practice, or hunting).

Ammunition

It is unlawful to manufacture or sell armor-piercing handgun ammunition.

Antiques

Antique and replica firearms are usually exempted from most restrictions. However, laws may vary by state, so check with local authorities on specific state specifications regarding antique and replica firearms. Antique firearms are defined as any firearm with a matchlock, flintlock, percussion cap, or similar type of ignition system, and manufactured before 1898. Replica firearms are defined as not designed or redesigned for using rimfire or conventional centerfire ammunition, or fixed ammunition (which is not readily available or manufactured in the U.S.), any muzzle loading rifle, shotgun, or pistol which is designed to use black powder (or black powder substitute) and which cannot used fixed ammunition.

Gun Length Requirements

The National Firearms Act of 1934 regulates the barrel length of shotguns and rifles. It is unlawful to possess a shotgun whose barrel is less than 18" long (or 26" long overall) or a rifle whose barrel is less than 16" long (or 26" long overall).

Ineligible Persons

It is unlawful to possess, receive, ship, transport, or own firearms or ammunition if:

- Convicted of crimes punishable by imprisonment for over one year, except state misdemeanors punishable by 2 years or less.
- A fugitive from justice.
- A user of certain depressant, narcotic, or stimulant drugs.
- Adjudicated as a mental defective or incompetent.
- Committed to a mental institution.
- An illegal alien.
- U.S. citizenship has been renounced.
- Dishonorably discharged from the U.S. Armed Forces.
- Less than 18 years old (for the purchase of a rifle or shotgun).
- Less than 21 years old (for the purchase of any other firearm).

- Subject to a court order restraining the person from harassing, stalking, or threatening a family member.
- Convicted of a misdemeanor of domestic violence.

Machine Guns

The National Firearms Act of 1934 makes it unlawful for civilians to own or possess machine guns without permission from the Federal Government. In order to own a NFA weapon, the person must present a "reasonable necessity" and be subject to a background investigation.

Sale Of Firearms To Aliens

To purchase firearms in the United States, an alien must:
- Be 18 years of age, or 21 for handguns.
- Provide suitable identification.
- Have lived in the state 90 days when the purchase is made.
- Not be a felon or in any other prohibited category.
- Complete AFT Form 4473, Firearms Transaction Record.

Note: A legal resident alien may have lived in the U.S. much longer than 90 days, but may still have to wait 90 days to purchase a firearm if he/she moves to another state.

Shipping Firearms & Ammunition

It is unlawful to mail or ship a firearm from one non-FFL (Federal Firearms Licensee) to another non-FFL. Rifles and shotguns personally owned may be mailed or shipped to any FFL in any state so long as it is for a lawful purpose such as customizing, repair, or sale. Any FFL may ship or mail a firearm or replacement firearm of the identical style to the person that it was received from. In order to mail a handgun through the U.S. Mail, it must be sent either from one FFL to another, or between authorized government officials.

Anyone may ship a rifle or shotgun to themselves, in care of a person who lives in another state, for the purpose of hunting.

Firearms or ammunition shipped via a common carrier must have an written notice accompanied with the packaging to notify the carrier of the shipment contents.

Silencers

The National Firearms Act of 1934 makes it unlawful to own or possess a silencer without permission from the Federal Government.

Transportation of Firearms

Federal law does not restrict individuals (except convicted felons, persons under indictment for felonies, mental defectives or incompetents, illegal users of controlled drugs, illegal aliens, veterans dishonorably discharged, those who have renounced their U.S. citizenship, fugitives from justice, persons convicted of a misdemeanor crime of domestic violence, and persons subject to domestic violence restraining orders) from transporting firearms across state lines. Thus, there is no federal interstate transportation permit for firearms.

Many states have laws governing the transportation of firearms. Also, many cities and localities have ordinances restricting their transportation. Travelers must be aware of these laws and comply with the legal requirements in each jurisdiction. There is no uniform state transportation procedure for firearms.

Laws

A provision of federal law serves as a defense to state or local laws which would prohibit the passage of persons with firearms in interstate travel.

Notwithstanding any state or local law, a person shall be entitled to transport a firearm from any place where he may lawfully possess and transport such firearm to any other place where he may lawfully possess and transport such firearm if the firearm is unloaded and in the trunk. In vehicles without a trunk, the unloaded firearm shall be in a locked container other than the glove compartment or console. Necessary stops, e.g., gasoline and rest, seem permissible.

Carrying On Or About The Person

It must be stressed that as soon as any firearm (handgun, rifle, or shotgun) is carried on or about the person, or placed in a vehicle where it is readily accessible, state and local firearms laws dealing with carrying come into play. If you seek to transport firearms in such a manner, it is advisable that you determine what the law is by contacting the Attorney General's office in each state through which you may travel or by reviewing an NRA State Firearms Law Digest. You should determine whether a permit is needed and how to obtain one if available. While many states require a permit for this type of carrying, most will not issue such permits to nonresidents, and others prohibit such carrying altogether.

By Motor Vehicle

In most states, personally-owned firearms may be transported legally if they are unloaded, cased, and locked in the automobile trunk. As an additional precaution, firearms may be disassembled and separated from ammunition. The exceptions to this rule deal mainly with interstate transportation of handguns. The myriad and conflicting legal requirements for firearm transportation through the states make caution the key for travelers.

If you travel with a trailer or camper that is hauled by an automobile, it is advisable to transport the firearms unloaded, cased and locked in the automobile trunk. If your vehicle is of the type in which driving and living spaces are not separated, the problem becomes one of access. If the firearm (handgun, rifle or shotgun) is carried on or about the person, or placed in the camper where it is readily accessible to the driver or any passenger, state and local laws dealing with concealed carrying of firearms may come into play. It is suggested, therefore, that the firearm be transported unloaded, cased, and placed in a locked rear compartment of the camper or mobile home, inaccessible to the driver or passenger.

Once you reach your destination, the state or, in some areas, municipal law, will control the ownership, possession, and transportation of your firearms.

Note: Generally, when a mobile home is readily mobile, i.e., when one can simply start its engine or the engine of its towing vehicle and drive away — even if it is capable of being used as a home — a mobile home is considered a vehicle. If a mobile home is not mobile, i.e., it does not have an engine, or is not attached to a towing vehicle, and is on blocks, permanently connected to utilities, it is considered a house, not a vehicle.

Aboard an Aircraft

Federal law prohibits the carrying of any firearm, concealed or unconcealed, on or about the person or in carry-on baggage while aboard an aircraft. Unloaded firearms not accessible to the passenger while aboard the aircraft are permitted when:

- The passenger has notified the airline when checking the baggage that the firearm is in the baggage and that it is unloaded.
- The baggage in which the firearm is carried is locked, and only the passenger checking the baggage retains a key.
- The baggage is carried in an area, other than the flight crew compartment, that is inaccessible to passengers.

Aboard Other Carriers

Any passenger who owns or legally possesses a firearm being transported aboard any common or contract carrier for movement with the passenger in interstate or foreign commerce must deliver the unloaded firearm into the custody of the pilot, captain, conductor, or operator of such common or contract carrier for the duration of the trip. Check with each carrier before your trip to avoid problems.

Bus companies usually refuse to transport firearms. Trains usually allow the transportation of encased long guns, if they are disassembled or the bolt is removed.

National And State Parks

Generally, firearms are prohibited in national parks. If you are transporting firearms, you must notify the ranger or gate attendant of this fact on your arrival, and your firearm must be rendered "inoperable" before you enter the park. The National Park Service defines "inoperable" to mean unloaded, cased, broken down if possible, and out of sight. Individuals in possession of an operable firearm in a national park are subject to arrest. Again, rules in various state park systems vary, so inquiry should be made concerning the manner of legal firearms possession in each particular park system.

Hunters

In many states, game wardens strictly enforce regulations dealing with the transportation of firearms during hunting season. Some states, for instance, prohibit the carrying of uncased long guns in the passenger compartment of a vehicle after dark. For up-to-date information on these regulations, it is advisable to contact local fish and game authorities.

Canada

Canada has very strict laws governing the transport of handguns and "military type" long guns. United States citizens may bring "sporting" rifles and shotguns into Canada. These must be declared to Customs officials when entering Canada. Handguns and other "restricted" weapons may be brought into Canada if a "permit to transport" has first been obtained from Canadian authorities. The permit is issued by a "local registrar of firearms" in a province for a limited period of time. The head of the provincial police can inform you where one is located. Travelers to Alaska should take note.

Conclusion

Common sense and caution are important whenever you are traveling with firearms. Prudence in the way in which your firearms are packed and located in your vehicle are important factors in your compliance with the law.

It should also be remembered that you have constitutional protections both against unreasonable searches and seizures and against compelled self-incrimination. Although the authorities may search anywhere within your reach without a search warrant after a valid stop, they may not open and search closed luggage without probable cause to believe evidence of a crime will be found, particularly when it is in a locked storage area or trunk of a vehicle, unless you consent. You have a right not to consent. Furthermore, although you may be required to produce a driver's license, vehicle registration, and, perhaps, proof of automobile insurance, you have a right to remain silent.

There is no substitute, however, for scrupulous compliance with every requirement of the law in the state or locality through which you are traveling.

Source: National Rifle Association, copyright 1997. Used by Permission.

For more information contact:
NRA Institute for Legislative Action
11250 Waples Mill Road, Fairfax, VA 22030

Gun Laws by State

State laws regarding firearms change frequently and are often lengthy and complex. Therefore, the following information should be considered an overview, not all-inclusive, and may be outdated; it should not be considered legal advice or a restatement of law. Be aware that many cities have more restrictive ordinances than the state. All fifty states have passed sportsmen's protection laws to ease transportation of firearms for hunting, target practice, and competitions; refer to each state for specific information. There are also many unique circumstances and exceptions to gun laws for people in law enforcement, the government, or security. Check with local authorities for definitive, current information.

State	Permit to Buy		Permit to Carry		Registration of Firearms		Owner Licensing		Gun Ban
	R & S	Hand	R & S	Hand	R & S	Hand	R & S	Hand	
Alabama	N	N	N	Y	N	N	N	N	N
Alaska	N	N	N	Y*	N	N	N	N	N
Arizona	N	N	N	Y	N	N	N	N	N
Arkansas	N	N	N	Y	N	N	N	N	N
California	N	N	N	Y*	N	Y*	N	N	Y
Colorado	N	N	N	Y	N	N	N	N	N
Connecticut	N	Y	N	Y	N	N	N	N	Y
Delaware	N	Y	N	N	N	N	N	N	N
Florida	N	N	N	Y	N	N	N	N	N
Georgia	N	N	N	Y	N	N	N	N	N
Hawaii	Y	Y	Y	Y	Y	Y	N	N	Y
Idaho	N	N	N	Y	N	N	N	N	N
Illinois	Y*	Y*	Y*	Y*	N	N	Y*	Y*	Y
Indiana	N	N	N	Y	N	N	N	N	N
Iowa	N	Y	N	Y	N	N	N	N	N
Kansas	N	N	N	N*	N	N	N	N	N
Kentucky	N	N	N	Y	N	N	N	N	N
Louisiana	N	N	N	Y	N	N	N	N	N
Maine	N	N	N	Y	N	N	N	N	N
Maryland	N	N	N	Y	N	N	N	N	Y
Massachusetts	Y	Y	Y	Y	N	N	Y	Y	Y

Weapons & Ballistics

State	Permit to Buy		Permit to Carry		Registration of Firearms		Owner Licensing		Gun Ban
	R & S	Hand	R & S	Hand	R & S	Hand	R & S	Hand	
Michigan	N	Y	N	Y	N	Y	N	N	N
Minnesota	N	Y	N	Y	N	N	N	N	N
Mississippi	N	N	N	Y	N	N	N	N	N
Missouri	N	Y	N	Y	N	N	N	N	N
Montana	N	N	N	Y	N	N	N	N	N
Nebraska	N	Y	N	N*	N	N	N	N	N
Nevada	N	N	N	Y	N	N	N	N	N
New Hampshire	N	N	N	Y	N	N	N	N	N
New Jersey	Y*	Y	Y*	Y	N	N	Y	Y	Y
New Mexico	N	N	N	Y	N	N	N	N	N
New York	Y/N*	Y	Y/N*	Y	Y/N*	Y	Y/N*	Y	Y
North Carolina	N	Y	N	Y	N	N	N	N	N
North Dakota	N	N	N	Y	N	N	N	N	N
Ohio	N	N	N	Y	N	N	N	N	Y*
Oklahoma	N	N	N	Y	N	N	N	N	N
Oregon	N	N	N	Y	N	N	N	N	N
Pennsylvania	N	N	N	Y	N	N	N	N	N
Rhode Island	N	N	N	Y	N	N	N	N	N
South Carolina	N	N	N	Y	N	N	N	N	N
South Dakota	N	N	N	Y	N	N	N	N	N
Tennessee	N	N	N	Y	N	N	N	N	N
Texas	N	N	N	Y	N	N	N	N	N
Utah	N	N	N	Y	N	N	N	N	N
Vermont	N	N	N	N	N	N	N	N	N
Virginia	N	N	N	Y	N	N	N	N	Y
Washington	N	N	N	Y	N	N	N	N	N
Washington, DC	Y	Y*	Y	Y	Y	Y	Y	Y	Y
West Virginia	N	N	N	Y	N	N	N	N	N
Wisconsin	N	N	N	N	N	N	N	N	N
Wyoming	N	N	N	Y	N	N	N	N	N

* Review state gun law information below for a more thorough explanation.

<u>State Laws and Firearm Information</u>

Alabama:

- There is no state mandated waiting period to purchase handguns or longguns.
- No state permit is required to possess a rifle, shotgun, or handgun.
- It is unlawful for a drug addict, habitual drunkard, anyone of unsound mind, anyone convicted of a crime of violence, or anyone under 18 to own, possess, borrow, or purchase a handgun.
- It is unlawful to carry a concealed pistol, firearm, or airgun without a permit.
- A non-resident who is licensed to carry a handgun in another state (whose laws recognize and give effect in that state to a license issued under the laws of Alabama) is allowed to carry a handgun as long as they are in compliance with Alabama law.

Alaska:

- There is no state mandated waiting period to purchase handguns or longguns.
- No state permit is required to purchase or possess a rifle, shotgun, or handgun.
- It is unlawful to sell or transfer a firearm to anyone convicted of a felony (less than 10 years ago), whose physical or mental condition is impaired as a result of liquor or drugs, or to sell a firearm to anyone under 18 years old.
- Loaded firearms may not be possessed in a place where liquor is sold for consumption of the premises (except the owner of the establishment).
- A minor under 16 years may not possess a firearm without parental or guardian consent.
- A person convicted of a felony (or a delinquent minor whose conduct would be a felony if committed as an adult) may not possess or own a "firearm capable of being concealed on his person" unless at least 10 years have elapsed between the date of their unconditional discharge on the prior offense.
- Any person 21 years or older may carry a concealed handgun on their person, as long as they inform police officers when contacted. They must also not carry it into any place prohibited by state or federal law. When entering

the residence of another person, the carrier must notify the resident that they are carrying a concealed handgun.
- A permit to carry a concealed handgun isn't required in Alaska, but permits are made available for those who want to carry a concealed handgun in another state that recognizes Alaska permits.
- A non-resident with a valid permit in another state is considered an Alaska permit holder.

Arizona:
- There is no state mandated waiting period to purchase handguns or longguns.
- No state permit is required to purchase a rifle, shotgun, or handgun.
- It is unlawful to give or sell firearms or ammunition to a minor without written consent of the minor's parent or guardian.
- It is unlawful for prohibited possessors to possess, own, buy, or transfer a firearm. Prohibited possessors include anyone who has been convicted of a felony involving violence or possession and use of a deadly weapon, anyone on probation for a conviction of domestic violence, a felony, etc., or anyone who is found to be a danger to himself or others pursuant to a court order. (Refer to Arizona State law for more information on prohibited possessors.)
- No person may carry a concealed firearm on his person outside of their own dwelling, business premises, or property owned or leased by the carrier. A handgun carried in a belt holster which is wholly or partially visible or carried in luggage is not considered being concealed.

Arkansas:
- There is no state mandated waiting period to purchase handguns or longguns.
- No permit is required to purchase or possess a rifle, shotgun, or handgun.
- It is unlawful to posses or own any firearm if the person has been convicted of a felony, has been adjudicated a mental defective, or has been committed involuntarily to any mental institution.
- It is unlawful to possess a handgun on or about his person, in a vehicle occupied by him, or otherwise readily available

for use with the purpose to employ it as a weapon against another person.

- Arkansas courts have determined that a loaded handgun under the front seat or in the glove compartment of a car driven by a defendant has been placed there as a weapon. Generally an unloaded or cased handgun is not considered carried as a weapon.

- A license is required to carry a concealed handgun. A non-resident must have a license issued by another state in order to carry a concealed firearm.

California:

- There is a 10 day waiting period for the sale, transfer, and loan of handguns and longguns made through a dealer or through the sheriff's office. However, those who have a valid permit to carry are exempt from the waiting period for longguns only.

- California has numerous and complex gun laws, please refer to these laws before visiting or moving to the state or before purchasing or selling a firearm. Contact the California Department of Justice in Sacramento for additional information.

- The state of California bans "assault weapons," .50MG caliber firearms, some .50 caliber ammunition, and "unsafe handguns." (For a complete list of "assault weapons" see Section 12276, more commonly known as the "Roberti-Roos List." There are certain circumstances where an "assault weapon" can be owned, but it must be registered and have a permit from the Department of Justice, refer to California state law for more details.

- It is unlawful to manufacture, import, sell, give, lend, own, or possess any "unsafe handgun" (a firearm capable of being concealed that lacks a safety device, or fails a 600-round firing requirement test or drop test performed by an independent lab certified by the Attorney General.)

- It is unlawful to manufacture, import, sell, give, lend, own, or possess any ammunition magazine that can hold more than 10 rounds (not including .22 tube magazines).

- Transfer or sale of all firearms must be processed with a California gun dealer's license.

- Police recordation is made of handgun purchases from dealers.

- Those purchasing handguns must have a Handgun Safety Certificate receipt.
- Any firearm capable of concealment on a person must present the gun dealer a basic firearms safety certificate approved by the California Department of Justice in order for the gun to be delivered or sold.
- A dealer may not transfer a pistol to anyone under 21 or any other firearm to anyone under 18.
- No person can apply to purchase more than one pistol, revolver, or other concealable firearm within a 30-day period.
- It is unlawful to purchase, receive, or attempt to purchase a firearm if the person is subject to a protective order, temporary restraining order, or injunction.
- It is unlawful to own or possess a firearm if the person has been convicted of a felony, is a drug addict, a present or former mental patient, has ever been committed for mental observation, or been acquitted by reason of insanity. People who have been convicted of certain misdemeanors involving force or violence may not possess or own any firearm for 10 years after conviction. A juvenile offender who has been adjudicated for a crime which would have been a felony or misdemeanor involving force or violence as an adult may not possess or own any firearm until they are at least 30 years of age.
- Within 60 days of entering the state of California from another state, a person must complete and return a Dept. of Justice registration form, or sell or transfer the firearm to a licensed dealer, sheriff, or police department for any pistol, revolver, or firearm capable of being concealed upon the person.
- It is unlawful to carry a loaded rifle, shotgun, or handgun in any public place or street where firing a firearm is prohibited.
- It is unlawful to carry a handgun concealed in a vehicle without a license. A handgun kept under the seat or in the glove box is considered concealed. However, if a handgun is in the trunk or locked in a container that is fully enclosed with a key lock or similar locking device, it is *not* considered concealed.

Colorado:

- There is no state mandated waiting period to purchase handguns or longguns.
- No permit is required to purchase a rifle, shotgun, or handgun.
- Dealers are required to keep a record of the retail sale, rental, or exchange of handguns, including the name of the buyer, their age, occupation, and residence, and the make, caliber, finish, and serial number of the handgun, and the date of the transfer or sale and name of the employee making the transfer or sale.
- Prospective buyers or transferees at gun shows are required to a have a background check and obtain approval of the transfer from CBI (Colorado Bureau of Investigation) through a licensed gun dealer.
- It is unlawful for anyone convicted of a felony, conspiracy, attempt to commit a felony, misdemeanor domestic violence, or adjudicated delinquent for a felony to possess or own a firearm.
- It is unlawful to carry a concealed firearm without a permit unless in his or her own home, place of business, or property owned or controlled by him or her. A permit is not required if carrying a handgun where it is legal to carry one, as long as it is not concealed. A sheriff can issue a permit as long as the person is a legal resident of Colorado, at least 21, has not been convicted of perjury in relation to an application for a concealed weapon permit, is not otherwise ineligible to possess a firearm, is not a habitual alcohol or substance abuser, and is not subject to a restraining order; additionally the person must demonstrate competency with the firearm.
- It is unlawful to have a firearm other than a handgun in or on any vehicle unless the chamber is unloaded.
- It is unlawful to possess a firearm while under the influence of alcohol or controlled substances.

Connecticut:

- There is a 14 day waiting period for the sale, transfer, and loan of handguns and longguns. However, those who have a valid certificate of eligibility are exempt from the waiting period; hunters with a valid hunting license are exempt from the waiting period for longguns only.

- The state of Connecticut bans "assault weapons" (any selective-fire firearm capable of fully automatic, semiautomatic, or burst fire at the option of the user).
- No permit is required to purchase or possess rifles or shotguns. However, to obtain a pistol or revolver, the buyer must have a permit to carry, permit to sell handguns, or handgun eligibility certificate. A certificate of eligibility is obtained by completing a handgun safety course approved by the Commissioner of Public Safety.
- To sell a pistol or revolver, the person, firm, or corporation must have an application filled out (with a full description of the pistol or revolver and the buyer) and have it sent to the Commissioner of Public Safety; it is then held for a two week waiting period.
- No person, firm, or corporation can sell, deliver, or transfer a pistol or revolver at retail unless it is equipped with a reusable trigger lock, gun lock, or gun locking device.
- It is unlawful for a person convicted of a felony, convicted as a delinquent of a serious juvenile offense, discharged from custody within the past 20 years after being acquitted by mental disease or defect, confined by court order for mental illness within the past 12 months, subject to a restraining or protective order involving physical force, or an illegal alien to possess or own a handgun.
- A permit is required to carry a handgun on or about one's person or in a vehicle. Loaded shotguns and rifles may not be carried in vehicles (or snowmobiles).
- A non-resident may carry a handgun in or through Connecticut only if it's for use in a competition, for the purpose of repair, to attend formal pistol or revolver training, meeting, or exhibition of an organized group, as long as the possessor is a resident of the US and has a valid permit to carry the firearm in the state in which the person resides.

Delaware:
- There is no state mandated waiting period to purchase handguns or longguns.
- No permit is required to purchase a rifle, shotgun, or handgun. However, prior to the purchase of a firearm (excluding shotguns and antique firearms) from a licensed dealer, a criminal history record check is required.
- It is unlawful to possess or own a firearm if convicted of a felony, convicted a crime of violence involving bodily injury

to another, convicted of any offense involving narcotics, dangerous drugs, or controlled substances, any person under 16 years old, any adjudicated person if the crime would be a felony if committed by an adult, and anyone who has ever been committed to a mental institution, sanitarium, or hospital for mental disorder, and does not possess a certificate of rehabilitation.

- It is unlawful to carry a loaded or unloaded firearm concealed upon or about a person's body. Handguns must be in open view or in inaccessible areas such as the trunk of a vehicle. Rifles and shotguns must be unloaded while being carried in any vehicle.

Florida:

- There is a 3 day waiting period for handgun purchases from a retail establishment (concealed weapon permit holders and handgun trade-ins are exempt from the waiting period), and no waiting period for longgun purchases.
- No permit is required to purchase a rifle, shotgun, or handgun.
- It is unlawful for drug addicts, alcoholics, mental incompetents, and vagrants to own or posses a firearm.
- It is unlawful to openly carry on or about the person any firearm. It is also unlawful to carry a concealed firearm on or about the person without a license. Exceptions to this are: persons having firearms in their home or business, enrolled members of gun and shooting clubs, persons engaged in hunting or on their way to such an activity, persons engaged in target practice or on the way to such activities, carrying a gun from the place of purchase (as long as it is securely encased), persons engaged in manufacturing, repairing, or dealing firearms, and military or law enforcement personnel while employed.
- It is unlawful to possess a concealed firearm for self defense or other lawful purposes without a license. For more information and license qualifications for a concealed weapon license, contact the Department of Agriculture.
- A non-resident may carry a concealed firearm if they are 21 years or older, has on their person a license to carry a concealed weapon from their state of residence, and obeys Florida laws on carrying a concealed weapon.

Georgia:

- There is no state mandated waiting period to purchase handguns or longguns.
- No permit is required to purchase or possess a rifle, shotgun, or handgun.
- It is unlawful for anyone convicted of a felony to possess, receive, transport, or own any firearm.
- A gun dealer must perform an instant criminal history background check that is conducted and approved by the Georgia Bureau of Investigation whenever selling or delivering a handgun to another person.
- It is unlawful to carry a handgun or concealable firearm, openly or concealed, on or about one's person without a license. Exceptions are: carrying a firearm, openly or concealed, in one's home or business, transporting a firearm (as long as it's separated from ammunition and enclosed in a case), transporting a firearm in a private vehicle (as long as it's in open view or in the glove compartment or similar), and carrying a firearm for hunting or fishing (must be accompanied with a valid hunting license).
- Concealed weapons must be carried in a shoulder holster, waist belt holster, or any other holster, hipgrip, or similar device. Carrying a firearm on the person in a concealed manner not listed above is a violation.
- It is unlawful to point a firearm at another person.
- It is unlawful to carry a concealed firearm, even with a license, to any public gathering.
- A non-resident may carry a handgun in Georgia as long as they are licensed in their own state and comply with Georgia gun laws.

Hawaii:

- There is no state mandated waiting period to purchase handguns or longguns.
- Assault pistols are prohibited in the state of Hawaii. Assault pistols include semiautomatic pistols that accept detachable magazines and has two or more of the following criteria: an ammunition magazine which attaches to the pistol outside the pistol grip; a threaded barrel capable of accepting a barrel extender, flash suppressor, forward hand grip, or silencer; a shroud which is attached to or partially or completely encircles the barrel and which permits the

shooter to hold the firearm with the second hand without being burned; a manufactured weight of fifty ounces or more when the pistol is unloaded; a centerfire pistol with an overall length of 12 inches or more; or is a semiautomatic version of an automatic firearm.

- A permit from the chief of police (in the county of residence or business) is required to purchase, own, inherit, or bequest a firearm or ammunition.
- In order to acquire a permit for a pistol or revolver, the person must complete an approved firearms safety training course.
- Every person arriving to Hawaii must register their firearm within 3 days of arrival of the person or the firearm, whichever occurs later.
- Handguns purchased from licensed dealers must be registered within 5 days.
- It is unlawful for a person to own or posses any firearm or ammunition if they are a fugitive from justice, have been convicted of a felony, convicted of the illegal use, possession, or sale of any drug, are 25 years or younger and has been adjudicated by the family court to have committed a felony, two or more crimes of violence, or illegal sale of drugs, are addicted to alcohol, have been committed to a mental institution or been diagnosed to have mental disorders, or has a restraining order by any court.

Idaho:

- There is no state mandated waiting period to purchase handguns or longguns.
- No permit is required to purchase or possess any rifle, shotgun, or handgun.
- A firearm dealer must submit an application and instant criminal history background check to be conducted and approved by the department of law enforcement before any sale or transfer of any handgun to another person.
- It is unlawful to possess or carry any concealed weapon while intoxicated.
- It is unlawful for a felon to possess, control, or own a firearm.
- Unless in a person's place of residence or business, it is illegal to carry a concealed weapon without a license. Concealed weapon refers to any dirk, dirk knife, bowie knife, dagger, pistol, revolver, or any other dangerous or

deadly weapon. This does not apply to any lawfully possessed shotgun or rifle.
- Non-residents may carry concealed weapons so long as they have a license from the state they reside and have the license in their possession while carrying the concealed weapon.

Illinois:
- There is a 3 day waiting period for handgun purchases and a 2 day waiting period for longguns.
- Handgun possession and licensing can change between municipalities. Some municipalities such as Chicago, Evanston, Oak Park, Morton Grove, Winnetka, Wilmette, and Highland Park have banned handguns, while other cities prohibit other kinds of firearms. Check with each municipality for more information.
- Chicago requires registration of all firearms.
- It is unlawful to carry a concealed firearm (there is no permit for concealed firearm). It is unlawful to possess or carry any firearm in any vehicle or concealed on or about the person except on one's land or in their place of home or business.
- A FOID (Firearms Owner's Identification Card - available from the Illinois State Police 217-782-2980) is required to possess or purchase any firearm or ammunition.
- FOIDs are not given to anyone convicted of a felony, anyone convicted in the past 5 years of battery, assault, aggravated assault, violation of a protection order, or similar offense, narcotic addicts, patients that have been in a mental hospital in the past 5 years, mentally retarded persons, and illegal aliens.
- Non-residents may possess and carry a firearm without a FOID if it is unloaded and enclosed in a case.
- Firearm dealers are required to withhold delivery of any handgun for 72 hours and any rifle or shotgun for 24 hours after the application for purchase has been made. Federally licensed dealers must also contact the Dept. of State Police to conduct a background check.
- It is unlawful to carry or possess a firearm when a person is hooded or masked.
- It is unlawful to possess a silencer.

Indiana:

- There is no state mandated waiting period to purchase handguns or longguns.
- No permit is required to possess a rifle, shotgun, or handgun.
- It is unlawful to possess or own a firearm if the person is convicted of a felony, a drug abuser or under the influence of drugs, is an alcohol abuser or under the influence of alcohol, or is mentally incompetent.
- Firearm dealers must request and receive a criminal history from the state police department for potential buyers.
- It is unlawful to carry a handgun in any vehicle or on or about his person without a license, except in one's home or business.

Iowa:

- There is no state mandated waiting period to purchase handguns or longguns.
- No permit is required to purchase a rifle or shotgun.
- A permit is required to purchase a handgun. Permits are not given if the buyer is under 21 years of age, a convicted felon, addicted to alcohol or controlled substances, has a history of repeated acts of violence, has been adjudged mentally incompetent, or convicted of a wide variety of serious crimes (including, but not limited to: hazing, stalking, disarming a police officer, intimidation with a dangerous weapon, and many types of assaults). Contact the Sheriff of the county of residence for more information.
- No permit is required to possess a rifle, shotgun, or handgun.
- It is unlawful to possess a handgun or handgun ammunition if under 21 years old.
- It is unlawful to be armed with a handgun or loaded firearm within the limits of any city, whether concealed or not.
- It is unlawful to be armed with a handgun or other firearm that is concealed on or about one's person or vehicle, unless in one's residence or business.
- Permits are required to carry any dangerous weapon on or about a person.

Weapons & Ballistics

Kansas:

- There is no state mandated waiting period to purchase handguns or longguns. However some cities and counties may require a waiting period to purchase handguns, or a license to purchase handguns or longguns; check with the city or county of residence.
- No permit is required to purchase or possess a rifle, shotgun, or handgun.
- It is unlawful to possess or own a firearm if addicted to a controlled substance, is a habitual drunkard, or has been convicted of certain types of felonies.
- It is unlawful to carry any pistol, revolver, or other firearm concealed on the person (there is no available permit to civilians), except when in one's own residence or business.

Kentucky:

- There is no state mandated waiting period to purchase handguns or longguns.
- No permit is required to purchase or possess a rifle, shotgun, or handgun.
- It is unlawful to own or possess a firearm if convicted of a felony.
- It is unlawful to carry a concealed firearm on or about one's person without a license. The firearm must be within immediate reach to be considered concealed; therefore, a firearm located in glove compartments (locked or unlocked) are not considered concealed.
- It is unlawful to carry a loaded rifle or shotgun in a vehicle.
- Non-residents may carry concealed firearms with a license from another state, so long as that state grants Kentucky residents reciprocal privilege.

Louisiana:

- There is no state mandated waiting period to purchase handguns or longguns.
- No permit is required to purchase, own, or possess a rifle, shotgun, or handgun.
- It is unlawful for anyone who is a national of a country with whom the U.S. is at war to own or possess a firearm.
- It is unlawful for anyone convicted of certain violent crimes to possess a firearm for 10 years from the date of completion of the sentence, probation, parole, or suspension of the sentence.

- It is unlawful to carry a concealed firearm intentionally without a license.
- It is unlawful to possess a firearm while on the premises of an alcoholic beverage outlet.

Maine:
- There is no state mandated waiting period to purchase handguns or longguns.
- No permit is required to purchase, own, or possess a rifle, shotgun, or handgun.
- Dealers are required to keep a record of all firearm sales, rentals, and loans.
- It is unlawful to possess a firearm in a posted liquor establishment or while under the influence of alcohol.
- It is unlawful to carry a concealed firearm about the person or concealed in a vehicle (glove box) without a permit.
- It is unlawful to have a loaded firearm (a firearm with a cartridge or shell in the chamber or in an attached magazine, clip or cylinder or a muzzle-loading firearm charged with powder, lead, and a primed ignition device or mechanism) while in or on a motor vehicle. A person who has a valid Maine concealed weapon permit may have a loaded pistol or revolver in a vehicle.
- Non-residents may apply to the Chief of the State Police for a concealed weapon permit.

Maryland:
- There is a 7 day waiting period for handgun, longgun, and legal "assault weapon" purchases. In addition, an application must be filled out along with a background check done by State Police.
- Assault pistols are banned from Maryland unless they were registered before Aug. 1, 1994. For a listing of assault pistols, contact the Secretary of the State Police. The sale or manufacture of certain handguns not appearing on the Handgun Roster that were manufactured after Jan. 1, 1985 is also banned.
- It is unlawful for any handgun manufactured after Jan. 1, 2003 to be sold if it is not equipped with an "integrated mechanical safety device."
- No permit is required to purchase, own, or possess a rifle or shotgun.

- The sale, transfer, rent, and possession of regulated firearms (handguns and assault weapons) are regulated by the state of Maryland. Only a dealer can sell, rent, transfer, or purchase any regulated firearm.
- An approved handgun safety course must be taken in order to purchase a handgun.
- It is unlawful to possess or own any regulated firearm, or for a dealer to sell or transfer a regulated firearm to anyone under 21 years old, convicted of a disqualifying crime, who is a fugitive from justice, who is a habitual drunkard, addicted to a controlled substance, who has a mental disorder and has a history of violent behavior against himself or another, committed for more than 30 days for a mental disorder, visibly under the influence of drugs or alcohol, is a participant in a straw purchase, anyone under the age of 30 who has been adjudicated delinquent by a juvenile court for an act that would be a disqualifying crime if committed by an adult, or who is a respondent against whom a current non ex parte civil protective order has been issued.
- Rifles and shotguns being transported in a motor vehicle must be unloaded.
- It is unlawful to carry a handgun, openly or concealed, without a permit. It is unlawful for permit holders to carry a handgun while under the influence of alcohol or drugs.
- A permit is required to acquire another handgun before 30 days of acquisition of a handgun.

Massachusetts:
- There is no state mandated waiting period to purchase handguns or longguns.
- Massachusetts has enacted some of the most restrictive gun laws in the nation. These laws are complex and care should be taken to understand and verify the laws completely when purchasing, possessing, and carrying firearms. Be sure to carry the correct card or license on your person for each firearm.
- Firearms and feeding devices are divided into four classes. Depending on the class of the firearm, a firearm identification card (FID), class A license, or class B license is required to possess, purchase, or carry any firearm, ammunition, or feeding device.

- A FID authorizes a person to possess, purchase, or carry a non-large capacity rifle or shotgun and the feeding devices and ammunition for it.
- FID cards may be denied due to a disqualifying conviction or juvenile adjudication, mental illness confinement, treatment of drug addiction or drunkenness, felony convictions, domestic protective orders, or if they are an alien.
- Class A License: A carry license that is required to possess, purchase, or carry any large capacity firearm (handgun, rifle, or shotgun), large capacity ammunition feeding devices for it, or ammunition for it. The person must be at least 21 years old, demonstrate that they are a "suitable person," and demonstrate a "good reason to fear injury to his person or property, or for any other reason including...sport or target practice only."
- Class B License: A carry license that is required to possess, purchase, or carry any non-large capacity handgun, any large or non-large capacity rifle or shotgun, feeding devices for it, and ammunition for it. Class B licenses also entitles the person to possess a large-capacity handgun under a class A club license or the direct supervision of a class A license holder at an incorporated shooting club or licensed shooting range. The person must be at least 21 years old, demonstrate that they are a "suitable person," and demonstrate a "good reason to fear injury to his person or property, or for any other reason...sport or target practice only."

- It is unlawful to carry a firearm in a vehicle, or in one's possession outside their residence or business, without the required license or card. If properly licensed, it is unlawful to leave the firearm unattended in the vehicle.

- A private individual may not sell more than four firearms per year unless sold to a licensed gun dealer.

- It is unlawful to sell, transfer, or possess "any assault weapon or large capacity feeding device" (more than 10 rounds) that was not legally possessed on Sept. 13, 1994.

- It is unlawful to sell any handgun not on the Firearms Roster.

- The City of Boston has a separate "assault weapons" law. It is unlawful to possess, display, transfer, or receive numerous "assault weapons" without a license granted by the Boston Police Commissioner. Contact the

Commissioner for more information on which weapons are classified as "assault weapons."

- Police records are made of all firearm transfers.
- Any person who inherits a rifle, shotgun, or handgun is required to obtain a FID or license to carry within 180 days in order to retain possession of the firearm.
- Non-residents may be issued a class A or class B temporary license by the colonel of state police. Non-residents may possess a rifle or shotgun in Massachusetts if hunting (and in possession of a valid hunting license), if on a firing or shooting range, while traveling in or through Massachusetts so long as its unloaded and enclosed in a case, if at an official firearms show, or if he has a license or permit to possess any firearm in his home state (so long as the licensing requirements are as stringent as those of Massachusetts; a published list of states is available from the colonel of state police).
- Airguns and BB guns have the same regulations as listed above.

Michigan:

- There is no state mandated waiting period to purchase handguns or longguns.
- No permit is required to purchase or possess a rifle or shotgun.
- To purchase a handgun from a dealer or an individual, the buyer must have a license to purchase from local law enforcement. Licenses are denied if the potential buyer has a felony conviction or been adjudged insane. In addition, the buyer must score 70% on a basic pistol safety review questionnaire.
- Any person who owns or obtains a handgun must have a certificate of safety inspection for the gun (obtained from the chief of police or sheriff where the owner resides) within 10 days of possession of the handgun.
- It is unlawful to carry a handgun concealed on or about one's person or in a vehicle (either openly or concealed) without a license to carry a concealed pistol.
- It is unlawful for a person who has consumed any amount of alcoholic beverage to carry a firearm.
- It is unlawful to intentionally point, even without malice, any firearm at another person.

- Pellet guns are considered firearms and regulated by the above provisions (including obtaining a license).
- Non-residents may carry concealed firearms so long as they have a concealed firearm license from their state of residence and abide by Michigan gun laws for licensed persons.

Minnesota:
- There is a 7 day waiting period (and a required handgun transfer report available from the police chief of the municipality or the county sheriff) for the purchase of handguns or "assault weapons." However, the waiting period may be waived for those who have a valid carrying permit or a handgun transfer permit.
- No permit is required to possess a rifle, shotgun, or handgun.
- It is unlawful to possess a firearm if convicted of a crime of violence and less than 10 years have passed since the sentence expired, committed as mentally ill, convicted of a gross misdemeanor drug violation, in a treatment facility or program for alcohol or drug addiction, and anyone convicted of assault or battery against a family or household member in any state and less that 3 years have passed since the conviction.
- It is unlawful to carry a concealed firearm without a permit, unless inside one's own residence or business. In order to obtain a permit, a basic firearms training course must be taken and taught by a certified instructor.
- Firearms may be transported in a vehicle without a permit if it is unloaded and in a closed fastened case or gun box.
- Except when at an official target range or engaged in lawful hunting, it is unlawful to possess a rifle or shotgun outdoors unless it is unloaded and either cased or broken down.
- Non-residents may carry a concealed weapon after they have applied for a permit from any Minnesota sheriff.

Mississippi:
- There is no state mandated waiting period to purchase handguns or longguns.
- No permit is required to purchase or possess any rifle, shotgun, or handgun.
- It is unlawful to give, lend, or sell any firearm to a minor or anyone under the influence of alcohol.

- It is unlawful to possess a firearm if convicted of a felony, if disability relief (under federal law) has been received, or if a certificate of rehabilitation has been received.
- It is unlawful to carry a pistol, revolver, rifle (with barrel less than 16 inches in length), shotgun (with barrel less than 18 inches in length), machine gun, fully automatic weapon, or any muffler or silencer for firearms if it is concealed in any way (in whole or in part) without a license. An exception is if the person is in their place of residence or business, or in their motor vehicle.
- Concealed firearm permits are denied to people who are less than 21 years of age, those who have not been a resident of Mississippi for over 12 months, anyone with a physical infirmity which would prevent safe handling of a handgun, a drug or alcohol abuser, a convicted felon, a fugitive from justice, anyone with mental problems, or anyone who has a violent misdemeanor conviction within the last 3 years.
- Non-residents may carry a concealed firearm if they have a license from their state of residence and if that state provides a reciprocal privilege.

Missouri:

- There is no state mandated waiting period to purchase handguns or longguns.
- No permit is required to purchase rifles and shotguns.
- It is unlawful to buy, sell, lease, borrow, exchange, receive, loan, give away, deliver, or transfer a handgun without a Permit to Acquire a Concealable Firearm. To obtain a permit the person must be at least 21 years old, not ever been convicted of a crime punishable by imprisonment for a term exceeding one year, not a fugitive from justice, not been dishonorably discharged from the U.S. armed forces, not known to be habitually intoxicated or addicted to drugs, and never been adjudged mentally incompetent or committed to a mental health facility.
- No permit is required to possess a rifle, shotgun, or handgun.
- It is unlawful to possess a loaded or unloaded firearm while intoxicated.
- It is unlawful to carry a concealed firearm on or about one's person without a concealed carry endorsement on the Missouri driver's or non-driver's license, or have a valid

permit to carry concealed firearms issued by another state, unless inside their own residence.

- It is unlawful to exhibit any weapon readily capable of lethal use in an angry or threatening manner.

Montana:

- There is no state mandated waiting period to purchase handguns or longguns.
- No permit is required to purchase or possess any rifle, shotgun, or handgun.
- It is unlawful to carry or bear a concealed handgun without a permit (either wholly or partially). It is not necessary to have a permit when carrying concealed handguns at one's own residence of business, while lawfully engaged in hunting or outdoor activities in which weapons are often carried for recreation or protection, outside of official city or town boundaries, or within the confines of a logging, lumbering, mining or railroad camp.
- Concealed weapon permits are denied to anyone convicted of a state or federal crime that is punishable by one or more years imprisonment, previously convicted of carrying a concealed weapon while under the influence or in a prohibited place, dishonorably discharged from the U.S. armed forces, has a warrant outstanding for their arrest, has been adjudicated to be an unlawful user of an intoxicating substance, or has been adjudicated to be mentally ill.
- Non-residents may carry concealed handguns so long as they carry a concealed firearm permit from the state in which they reside.

Nebraska:

- There is no state mandated waiting period to purchase handguns or longguns.
- A certificate is required to purchase, receive, or sell a handgun unless the transfer occurs between one's spouse, sibling, parent, child, aunt, uncle, niece, nephew, or grandparent (so long as the receiver is 18 years or older).
- No permit is required to possess a rifle or shotgun.
- It is unlawful to possess a firearm if convicted of a felony or a fugitive of justice.
- It is unlawful to carry a concealed weapon on or about one's person (no concealed weapon permit is available).

Nevada:

- There is no state mandated waiting period to purchase handguns or longguns. However, some cities and counties may require a waiting period to purchase handguns; check with the city or county of residence.

- No permit is required to purchase or possess a rifle, shotgun, or handgun.

- It is unlawful to own or possess any firearm if convicted of a felony.

- It is unlawful to control or possess on one's person a firearm while intoxicated or under the influence of a controlled substance.

- It is unlawful to carry a concealed handgun or any other concealed firearm on one's person without a permit. Permits will be denied if under 21 years of age, convicted of a felony, declared incompetent or insane, habitually uses alcohol or a controlled substance, been convicted of a crime involving the use or threatened use of force or violence (punishable as a misdemeanor) within the past 3 years, been convicted of a crime involving domestic violence or stalking, is currently subject to a restraining order, or is currently on parole or probation. In addition, the applicant must present a certificate or other documentation to the sheriff issuing the permit that shows a successful completion of a course in firearm safety offered by an approved agency.

- It is unlawful to carry a loaded rifle or shotgun in a vehicle on a public highway. An individual can carry a firearm in their vehicle so long as it is not actually on the person or in a container carried or held by the person.

New Hampshire:

- There is no state mandated waiting period to purchase handguns or longguns.

- No permit is required to purchase or possess a rifle, shotgun, or handgun.

- It is unlawful to own, possess, or control a firearm if convicted of a felony.

- It is unlawful to carry a concealed loaded handgun on or about one's body or in any vehicle without a license, unless in one's residence or business.

- Non-residents may carry a concealed weapon as long as they have a valid license from their state of residence, and if their state honors a reciprocal privilege.

New Jersey:

- There is no state mandated waiting period to purchase handguns or longguns.
- "Assault Firearms" are banned in New Jersey. "Assault Firearms" not owned and licensed prior to May 1, 1991 are considered contraband. See New Jersey state law as to which semi-automatic and other weapons are classified as "assault firearms."
- It is unlawful to sell, give, transfer, assign, dispose of, receive, purchase, or otherwise acquire a rifle or shotgun (other than an antique) unless the purchase, donee, receiver, or holder is a licensed dealer or possesses a valid Firearms Purchasers Identification Card (FID).
- It is unlawful to sell, give, transfer, assign, dispose of, receive, purchase, or otherwise acquire a handgun unless the purchase, assignee, donee, receiver, or holder is a licensed dealer or has secured a Permit to Purchase a handgun. Only one handgun can be purchased or delivered for each permit.
- It is unlawful to knowingly possess or carry (either openly or concealed) any handgun (including antique handguns) without having a Permit to Carry, unless in one's own residence or business.
- It is unlawful to knowingly possess any rifle or shotgun without having a Firearms Purchaser Identification Card (FID), unless in one's own residence or business.
- Firearms may be transported in a vehicle without a permit so long as it is unloaded and in a closed and fastened case, gunbox, securely tied package, or locked in the trunk.
- A Permit to Purchase or an FID card will be denied if the person has been convicted of a crime, is a drug dependent person, is a habitual drunkard, has ever confined for a mental disorder, has a physical defect or disease that would make it unsafe to handle firearms, is under 21 years old (for handguns or pistols) and under 18 for other firearms, and if the person knowingly falsified information on the application form.
- It is unlawful to possess, own, control, or purchase a firearm if convicted of a crime (aggravated assault, arson,

burglary, escape, extortion, homicide, kidnaping, robbery, sexual assault, bias intimidation, endangering the welfare of a child, any weapons offense, or any domestic violence offense including harassment, stalking, or criminal restraint), if ever convicted of a mental disorder, or ever convicted for the use, possession, or sale of a controlled dangerous substance.

New Mexico:

- There is no state mandated waiting period to purchase handguns or longguns.

- No permit is required to purchase or possess a rifle, shotgun, or handgun. In addition, residents of states contiguous to New Mexico may purchase firearms in New Mexico, and residents of New Mexico may purchase firearms in states contiguous to New Mexico.

- It is unlawful to receive, transport, or own a firearm if convicted of a felony.

- It is unlawful to possess or transport a handgun for anyone less that 19 years old.

- It is unlawful to carry a concealed loaded firearm unless in one's own residence or if in the possession of a valid concealed handgun license.

- Concealed handgun licenses will be denied if the person is not a resident of New Mexico, under 25 years old, a fugitive from justice, convicted of a felony, under indictment for a felony criminal offense, convicted of a misdemeanor offense involving a crime of violence, adjudicated as mentally incompetent, or addicted to alcohol or controlled substances. In addition, the applicant must complete a firearms training course approved by the department for the category and caliber of handgun that they want to be licensed to carry as concealed.

New York:

- There is no state mandated waiting period to purchase handguns or longguns.

- "Assault Weapons" are prohibited in New York state. Those lawfully possessed prior to September 14, 1994 can continue to be lawfully possessed. See New York law for a complete list of firearms that are considered "Assault Weapons."

- No permit is required to purchase a rifle or shotgun, except in New York City.

- No permit is required to possess a rifle or shotgun as long as rifle barrels are at least 16 inches long and shotgun barrels are at least 18 inches long.
- It is unlawful to possess a handgun (even within one's residence or place of business) without a license. A license may be denied if under 21 years old, convicted of a serious offense, ever treated for mental illness, or subject to a protective court order. A license to possess a handgun also counts as a license to carry one unless otherwise restricted. A special permit from the police commissioner of New York City is required in addition to the license to possess or carry a firearm in the city of New York. Additionally, some counties require a handgun safety training course in order to receive a license.
- New York City has a separate city permit that is required for possession and transportation of handguns and longguns. New York State handgun permits are invalid within the city limits; however, New York State residents may transport their licensed handguns unloaded through the city if these are locked in a container and the trip is continuous. Longguns may be kept in the city for only 24 hours while in transit and must be unloaded and stored in a locked container or vehicle trunk for the period.
- It is unlawful for anyone convicted of a felony or mentally incompetent to possess a firearm.
- It is unlawful to possess 20 or more firearms outside of one's home or business.
- It is unlawful to intentionally point or discharge any firearm toward another person (except in self-defense), even if no malice or injury is involved.
- Non-residents may not carry, possess, or transport a handgun in or through the state without a valid New York license, except in the case of target shooters going to a NRA approved competition or IHMSA sanctioned match, and then only within 48 hours of the competition; the gun must be unloaded and transported in a locked opaque container.
- New York is the only state in the Union which prohibits the transportation of handguns without a license. Law-abiding citizens should, therefore, be particularly careful since they face severe consequences should they inadvertently violate the state's myriad, technical, anti-gun provisions.

North Carolina:
- There is no state mandated waiting period to purchase handguns or longguns.
- No permit is required to purchase a rifle or shotgun.
- It is unlawful to purchase, sell, give away, transfer, or receive a handgun without a permit. Permits may be denied if the applicant is a fugitive from justice, an unlawful user of or addicted to a drug, mentally incompetent, an illegal alien, dishonorably discharged from the military, renounced his/her citizenship, or under a court restraining order for harassing, stalking, or threatening an intimate partner or child.
- No permit is required to possess a rifle, shotgun, or handgun.
- It is unlawful to carry a concealed handgun, or any other deadly weapon, on or about his person unless in one's own residence or if they have a concealed handgun permit. Permits may be denied if the applicant is under 21 years old, has suffered from physical or mental infirmity that prevents the safe handling of a handgun, has been dishonorably discharged from the armed forces, has a judgement for a violent misdemeanor, convicted of an impaired driving offense within the past three years, or is an unlawful user of, or addicted to, marijuana, alcohol, depressants, stimulants, or other controlled substances.
- It is unlawful to hunt on Sunday with any rifle, shotgun, or handgun.

North Dakota:
- There is no state mandated waiting period to purchase handguns or longguns.
- It is unlawful to possess a firearm if convicted anywhere of a felony involving violence or intimidation and released in the past ten years, if convicted any other felony or misdemeanor involving violence or intimidation and release in the past five years, or if diagnosed as mentally ill within the past three years.
- It is unlawful to possess a firearm in a liquor establishment or gaming site.
- It is unlawful to carry a concealed firearm on or about one's person without a license.
- It is unlawful to keep or carry a loaded firearm in a vehicle without a license.

- A license to carry a concealed firearm will be reviewed by the chief of the bureau of criminal investigation. The criteria is having a valid reason to carry a firearm in a concealed manner, clearing a background investigation, and is not otherwise prohibited from possessing a firearm. In addition, the applicant must go through a testing procedure including a book test and a proficiency test.
- Handguns may only be carried unloaded and in plain view (or secured) between the hours of one hour before sunrise and one hour after sunset.

Ohio:

- There is no state mandated waiting period to purchase handguns or longguns.
- Caution: Some municipalities control the possession, sale, or transfer of firearms while others do not. Laws regarding handgun registration, identification cards, waiting periods, permits to purchase, or restrictions of handgun specifications may vary. The following information is regarding state-wide laws and regulations; be sure to double check the laws within each municipality.
- While there is no state law preempting the whole field of firearm controls, a recent law preempts any local governing body the ability to restrict or impede the lawful carry of a concealed handgun when carried with a valid permit.
- It is unlawful to knowingly acquire, have, carry, or use any dangerous ordnance (automatic firearms specially adapted to fire a succession of cartridges with a single function of the trigger, semi-automatic firearms, short barreled rifles and shotguns, firearms of crude or extemprized manufacture, devices that are not designed to be firearms but can be adapted for use as firearms, or are capable of being firearms).
- Cincinnati, Cleveland, Columbus, and Dayton (among many other local ordinances not listed here) have special "Assault Weapon" ordinances affecting various types of semi-automatic firearms prohibition. See Ohio state law for more information.
- No state permit is required to purchase a rifle, shotgun, or handgun.
- It is unlawful to have a loaded firearm in a vehicle if it is accessible without leaving the vehicle. The firearm must be in a closed case or box, secured in a rack in plain sight with the action open or the weapon stripped, or in a

compartment that can only be reached by leaving the vehicle.

- It is unlawful to acquire, have, carry, or use a firearm if a fugitive, convicted of a violent felony or adjudicated delinquent child for an offense that if committed as an adult would have been a violent felony, convicted of a drug offense, alcoholics, drug dependency, or adjudicated as mentally incompetent.
- It is unlawful to carry or have a firearm concealed on one's person or ready at hand without a permit. (Note: State law allows handguns to be carried openly, but many municipalities prohibit the carrying of any firearm.) Concealed weapon permits are usually granted if the applicant has been a resident of the county for the past 30 days, a resident of the state for the past 45 days, taken a firearms safety training course within the last 3 years, and at least 21 years of age. Permits might be denied if the applicant is a fugitive from justice, under indictment for or convicted of a felony, under indictment or convicted of a crime involving drugs, convicted of a crime of violence in the past 3 years, convicted of assault or aggravated assault in the past 5 years, convicted of resisting arrest or interfering with the lawful arrest of another person in the past 10 years, or if subject to a protection order.
- It is unlawful to possess a firearm in any room where liquor is being dispensed pursuant to a liquor license.
- It is unlawful to carry or use any firearm while under the influence of alcohol or any drug of abuse.
- Non-residents may carry a concealed firearm so long as they have a concealed firearm permit from their resident state, and so long as their state grants a reciprocal privilege to Ohio licensees.

Oklahoma

- There is no state mandated waiting period to purchase handguns or longguns.
- No permit is required to purchase or possess a rifle, shotgun, or handgun (however, it is unlawful to possess a sawed-off shotgun or rifle without a federal license). Residents may purchase legal firearms and ammunition from contiguous states, and residents of contiguous states may purchase firearms and ammunition in Oklahoma.

- It is unlawful to furnish a firearm to any person who is a felon, delinquent, under the influence of alcohol or drugs, or is mentally or emotionally unbalanced or disturbed.
- A firearm may be transported in a vehicle without a permit so long as it is in plain view and unloaded. A rifle or shotgun without the clip or magazine loaded may be carried with the chamber empty in an exterior locked compartment or trunk, or inside the vehicle if the person has a valid CCL.
- It is unlawful to possess or have in any vehicle any pistol or easily concealable firearm if convicted of a felony or under the supervision of the Department of Corrections.
- It is unlawful for anyone (except peace officers on duty) to carry a firearm upon or about one's person, or in any container, unless the firearm is in plain view while hunting, fishing, or training (education or recreation), or concealed if they have valid Concealed Carry License (CCL). CCLs are usually given to people who are residents of Oklahoma, at least 21 years old, and have completed a safety and training course. CCLs may be denied if convicted of a felony, adjudicated as mentally incompetent, any false statement on the application, convictions of certain misdemeanors, any attempted suicide, habitual misdemeanor criminal activity, an outstanding felony warrant, impatient treatment for substance abuse in the past 3 years, convictions of intoxication or driving under the influence in the past 3 years, or any victim protection order. In addition, the applicant must complete a safety and training course.
- It is unlawful to possess a firearm in any establishment where alcohol is served and consumed, or to carry or use a firearm while under the influence of alcohol, any unprescribed drug, or any prescribed drug that could cause abnormal behavior. A person with a valid CCL may carry a firearm onto the premises where alcohol is sold, provided that the sale of alcohol is not the primary business.
- Non-residents may carry concealed weapons so long as they carry a valid concealed weapon license from their home state.

Oregon:
- There is no state mandated waiting period to purchase handguns or longguns.
- No permit is necessary to purchase or possess rifles, shotguns, or handguns.

- It is unlawful to sell, deliver, or transfer any firearm to anyone convicted of a felony (who has not had his civil rights restored), convicted of a misdemeanor involving violence within the past 4 years, listed in the Health Division Registry, committed to the Department of Human Services, with outstanding felony warrants, or who is free on any form of pretrial release for a felony.
- Dealers must keep a record of every handgun sold and must do a criminal history record check on every purchaser.
- It is unlawful for a felon to possess a firearm (except in a few cases - see Oregon state law).
- It is unlawful to carry a concealed firearm on one's person or in a vehicle without a concealed weapon permit, unless they are in their own residence or business. Firearms carried openly in belt holsters are not considered to be "concealed." A concealed weapon permit may be granted to an applicant who is over 21 years of age, is a resident in the county of application, has no outstanding warrants, and can demonstrate competence with a handgun either from a handgun safety program or certified training in the armed forces. A license may be denied if the applicant is on any form of pretrial release, convicted of a felony, has ever been committed to the Mental Health and Developmental Disability Services Division, has been found mentally ill, has ever been cited for stalking, or has ever been under a protective order.

Pennsylvania:
- There is no state mandated waiting period to purchase handguns or longguns.
- Any individual or dealer selling or transferring a handgun must do it at a place of business licensed by the county sheriff's office. Rifles and shotguns may be sold or transferred without being at a licensed location.
- It is unlawful for a person convicted of drunk driving 3 times within a 5 year period to purchase a firearm. However, they may possess a firearm.
- No permit is required to possess a rifle or shotgun.
- It is unlawful for to possess a firearm if the person is a fugitive, convicted or a crime of violence, convicted of a controlled substance offense punishable by more than 2 years, adjudicated mentally incompetent, is an illegal alien, adjudicated a delinquent for an offense that would

disqualify an adult , or subject to a protection from abuse court order.

- A Sportsman's Firearm Permit is required to carry a handgun on or about one's person or in any vehicle, and is only valid for hunting, fishing, trapping, and dog training. No permit is required to carry a handgun in one's own residence or place of business or while engaged in target shooting. In order to get the permit, the person must not be of a character or reputation that would be dangerous to public safety, currently charged or convicted of certain crimes, a habitual drunkard, abuser of controlled substances, involuntarily committed to a mental institution, or dishonorably discharged from the Armed Forces.
- Handguns transported in a vehicle without a license to carry must be unloaded (and must demonstrate a valid reason allowed under state law for carrying the gun such as going to or from target shooting, hunting, purchase, etc.). Rifles and shotguns may be transported in a vehicle as long as they are unloaded.

Rhode Island:

- There is a 7 day waiting period for handguns and longguns. Private sales can be made through a dealer; otherwise the seller must follow the same guidelines as a sale from a dealer.
- A handgun may only be purchased if the buyer is a resident of Rhode Island, at least 21 years old, and must receive a state-issued handgun safety card. Cards are issued upon completion of a hunter safety course, completion of a pistol safety course, or passage of an objective test on handgun safety.
- No permits are required to possess a rifle, shotgun or handgun.
- It is unlawful to possess, own, or control a firearm if convicted of a crime of violence, a fugitive from justice, an illegal alien, mentally incompetent, or under treatment as a drug addict or habitual drunkard in the previous five years.
- It is unlawful to carry a handgun on or about one's person or in a vehicle without a license unless in one's own residence or business. Licenses may be obtained to any resident who is 21 years or older and takes a qualifying test through the state. In addition, any rifle or shotgun must be unloaded inside a vehicle.

- It is unlawful to carry or transport any firearm while intoxicated or under the influence of narcotic drugs.

South Carolina:
- There is no state mandated waiting period to purchase handguns or longguns.
- Any resident may lawfully purchase and receive delivery of a rifle or shotgun from a contiguous state so long as the seller is a Federal Firearms Licensee (FFL). Non-residents may purchase rifles or shotguns in South Carolina so long as they follow applicable provisions and statutes from South Carolina.
- In order to purchase a handgun, the buyer must complete an application in the dealer's presence.
- No permit is required to possess a rifle, shotgun, or handgun.
- It is unlawful to possess or own a handgun if convicted of a crime of violence, a member of a subversive organization, a fugitive from justice, a habitual drunkard, a drug addict, adjudicated as mentally incompetent, under 21 years of age, or adjudicated as unfit to carry or possess a handgun by a court order.
- It is unlawful to carry a handgun (concealed or openly) unless in one's own residence or business, licensed as a hunter or fisherman and is engaged in that activity, or possesses a valid concealed weapon permit. Handguns (loaded or unloaded) may be transported without a permit in a vehicle so long as it is secured in a closed glove compartment, console, or closed trunk.
- It is unlawful to discharge a firearm while intoxicated or under the influence of a controlled substance.

South Dakota:
- There is a 2 day (48 hour) waiting period for handgun purchases, but no waiting period for longguns. When the handgun is delivered, it must be unloaded and securely wrapped. Permit holders are exempt from the waiting period.
- It is unlawful to possess, carry, transfer, control, or own a firearm if within 15 years of discharge from prison, jail, probation, or parole for convicted violent felonies.
- No permit is required to possess a rifle, shotgun, or handgun.

- It is unlawful to possess a firearm while intoxicated.

- It is unlawful to carry a pistol concealed on or about one's body or vehicle without a license to carry. Licenses may be denied anyone who has been convicted of a felony or crime of violence, is a habitual drunkard, a drug user, a history of repeated acts of violence, adjudged as mentally incompetent, been found in the previous 10 years to be mentally ill, a fugitive from justice, convicted of a misdemeanor or felony offense in the past 5 years, or is not a resident of South Dakota. Those with a license may not carry a concealed pistol into any establishment that makes more than 50% of its sales from alcoholic beverages. A handgun may be transported in a vehicle without a license so long as it is unloaded and in the trunk or any other closed compartment and in a closed container which cannot be concealed on a person.

- It is unlawful to carry a loaded rifle or shotgun in any vehicle.

- "Controlled weapons" (machine guns, silencers, and short shotguns) are banned unless the person is a law enforcement officer, a member of the armed forces or National Guard (acting in the lawful discharge of his duties), has a valid state or federal license, has the weapon registered with the proper authorities, or possesses the machine gun briefly after having found it or taken it from an aggressor.

Tennessee:
- There is no state mandated waiting period to purchase handguns or longguns.

- No permit is required to purchase a rifle, shotgun, or handgun; however background checks are required for handgun purchases.

- It is unlawful to sell or transfer a handgun to anyone who is intoxicated.

- No permit is required to possess a rifle, shotgun, or handgun.

- It is unlawful to possess or own a handgun if convicted of a felony involving the use or attempted use of force, violence, or a deadly weapon, convicted of a felony drug offense, or under 18 years old.

- It is unlawful to carry "with the intent to go armed" a firearm, knife with a blade longer than 4 inches, or a club unless in one's own residence or business. Unloaded rifles, shotguns, and handguns may be carried openly so long as the ammunition is not in the immediate vicinity of the person or weapon.

- A permit to carry a handgun may be denied if under 21 years of age, not a resident of Tennessee, convicted of any offense punishable by imprisonment for a term exceeding 1 year (except in offenses related to business practices), subject to a order of protection, a fugitive from justice, addicted to alcohol or any controlled substance, a patient in a rehabilitation program within the past 10 years, convicted of driving under the influence 2 or more times in the past 10 years, adjudicated as a mental defective, committed to a mental institution, determined to be mentally disabled, an illegal alien, or convicted of domestic violence. In addition, the applicant must successfully complete a handgun safety course.
- It is unlawful to possess a firearm anyplace where alcoholic beverages are served unless in one's own home.
- Non-residents may carry concealed handguns so long as they have a valid license from their state of residence.

Texas:
- There is no state mandated waiting period to purchase handguns or longguns.
- No permit is required to own or possess a rifle, shotgun, or handgun.
- It is unlawful to carry a handgun on or about one's person (openly or concealed), without a license unless in one's own residence or while engaged in lawful hunting. Applicants must be at least 21 years old and have a handgun proficiency certificate from a qualified handgun instructor. Permits may be denied to those with a felony conviction, certain misdemeanors, addiction, mental illness, or delinquency in child support or tax payments.
- It is unlawful to sell, rent, loan, or give a handgun to anyone if it is known that the person intends to use it unlawfully or is intoxicated.
- It is unlawful to carry a handgun, even with a license, on the premises of a business that derives 51% of its income from alcohol for on-premises consumption or if the holder is intoxicated.

Utah:

- There is no state mandated waiting period to purchase handguns or longguns.
- No permit is required to purchase or possess a rifle, shotgun, or handgun. Dealers must run an instant criminal history background check for all sales.
- It is unlawful to possess or own a firearm if convicted of a felony, adjudicated as a delinquent within the past 7 years for an offense which would be a felony if an adult, a user of controlled substances, in possession of a dangerous weapon and a controlled substance, adjudicated as mentally defective, mentally incompetent, on parole or probation for any felony, on parole from a 'secure facility', an illegal alien, dishonorably discharged from the armed forces, or has renounced U.S. citizenship.
- It is unlawful to possess or use a firearm while under the influence of alcohol or a controlled substance.
- It is unlawful to possess a firearm with the intent to assault another person.
- It is unlawful to carry a "concealed dangerous weapon" without a permit unless in one's own residence or business. Weapons are not considered concealed if it is unloaded, or not readily accessible (such as in a gun rack, closed case, or trunk). Weapons kept in the glove box or console box of a vehicle are considered concealed. Permits may be denied if the applicant is under 21 years of age, convicted of a felony or crime of violence, convicted of an offense involving alcohol, narcotics, or other controlled substances, convicted of an offense involving moral turpitude, convicted of any offense involving domestic violence, adjudicated as mentally incompetent, or otherwise not allowed to lawfully possess a firearm.
- It is unlawful for anyone in the presence of two or more persons to exhibit any firearm in an angry and threatening manner unless in a situation of self-defense.
- Non-residents may carry a concealed firearm so long as they have a permit from their state of residence.

Vermont:

- There is no state mandated waiting period to purchase handguns or longguns.
- No permit is required to purchase or possess a rifle, shotgun, or handgun.

- No permit is required to lawfully carry a firearm, openly or concealed. It is unlawful to carry a firearm with the intent or avowed purpose of injuring a fellow man.
- It is unlawful to carry or possess a loaded rifle or shotgun in a vehicle on a public highway.

Virginia:

- There is no state mandated waiting period to purchase handguns or longguns.
- "Street Sweeper" shotguns are banned in Virginia.
- No permit is required to purchase or possess a rifle, shotgun, or handgun. A criminal history record information check is required prior to all purchases.
- It is unlawful to possess a firearm if convicted of a felony, under 29 years old with a juvenile conviction which would have been a felony if convicted as an adult, subject to a protective order for family abuse or stalking, a non-citizen of the U.S., or committed to a mental institution.
- It is unlawful to carry any concealed firearm on or about one's person hidden from common observation without a permit unless in one's own residence . Permits may be denied to anyone under 21 years old, who is a habitual drunkard, addicted to a controlled substance, dishonorably discharged from the armed forces, an illegal alien, convicted of drunkenness or a violent misdemeanor, involuntarily committed in the past 5 years, or otherwise ineligible to purchase or possess a firearm. In addition, the court may require the applicant to demonstrate a competence with the handgun by completing an authorized training course.
- A permit is required to acquire another handgun within a 30 day period of acquisition of a handgun. Those with concealed weapon permits are exempt from acquiring another permit.
- It is unlawful to carry a concealed handgun onto the premises of any restaurant or club that serves alcoholic beverages.
- Non-residents may carry a concealed handgun so long as they are at least 21 years of age and have a valid permit from their home state and the qualifications for the permit are the same as those in Virginia.

Washington:

- There is a 5 day waiting period for handgun purchases, but no waiting period for longguns. The police may require a 30 day waiting period in some cases. Applicants not holding a driver's license or have not been a resident of Washington for the past 90 days, must wait for 60 days. Concealed weapon permit holders are not subject to the 5 day waiting period.

- No permit is required to purchase or possess rifles, shotguns, or handguns. However, in order to purchase a pistol, the applicant must fill out an application which will be kept on file with the police department.

- It is unlawful to own or possess a firearm if convicted of a felony, convicted of a serious offense committed after July 1, 1993 (such as 4th degree assault, coercion, stalking, reckless endangerment, criminal trespass in 1st degree, violating a protective order and/or restraining order), free on bond or personal recognizance pending trial, or committed due to mental illness.

- Canadian citizens from certain providences may possess firearms while hunting or competing in organized shooting contests, so long as the province provides reciprocal agreements with Washington residents.

- It is unlawful to carry a pistol concealed on one's person without a license unless in one's own residence or business. A license may be denied if the applicant is under 21 years old, free on bond of personal recognizance pending trial, has a warrant for a felony or misdemeanor, subject to a restraining order or domestic violence action requiring the surrender of a deadly weapon, or is otherwise ineligible to possess a pistol.

- It is unlawful to carry or place a loaded pistol in a vehicle without a concealed weapon license.

- It is unlawful to carry, transport, convey, possess or control a shotgun or rifle containing shells or cartridges in the magazine or chamber, or a muzzle-loading firearm loaded and capped or primed in any vehicle.

- It is unlawful to possess firearms outside one's own residence or business during a state of emergency.

Weapons & Ballistics

Washington, D.C.:

- There is no state mandated waiting period to purchase longguns. The sale of new handguns is prohibited.

- Washington, D.C. has strict transportation, possession, and ownership laws. Be sure to double check the regulations before bringing a gun into the district.

- The purchase, possession, and carrying of all firearms is regulated in Washington, D.C. All firearms must be registered and licensed.

  - The district prohibits new acquisition of handguns and any semi-automatic firearm capable of using a detachable ammunition magazine of more than 12 rounds capacity and any handgun not registered after February 5, 1977. No one may bring a handgun into the district unless registered prior to Sept. 23, 1976 (and re-registered by Feb. 5, 1977).

  - Rifles and shotguns may be purchased or sold only from a licensed dealer in the district. Delivery will be made upon completion and approval of the registration certificate. Ammunition may be purchased only for the caliber or gauge of the firearm registered to that buyer.

  - It is unlawful to possess a rifle or shotgun if under 21 years old, convicted of a crime of violence, convicted of a weapons offense, under indictment for a crime of violence, convicted of a narcotics or an assault or battery charge within the last 5 years, adjudicated an alcoholic within the last 5 years, committed to a mental hospital within the last 5 years, suffering from a physical defect which might render possession of a gun as unsafe, or found negligent in any firearm mishap.

  - Any person bringing a rifle or shotgun into the district must "immediately" notify the Identification and Records Division, and must fill out an application for registration within 48 hours.

  - No handguns may be legally possessed unless registered. Therefore, it is unlawful to possess, acquire or bring into the district any handgun. Even those which were registered (prior to 1976) may not be carried; they are to be kept at one's residence or business.

  - All firearms must be unloaded and disassembled or locked with a trigger lock except when kept in one's own residence or business.

- Residents and nonresidents may possess firearms while engaged in lawful recreational firearms related activities, so long as the firearm is legally possessed in their place of residence. The carrier must be able to exhibit proof that they are on the way or leaving the recreational activity and the firearm must be unloaded and securely wrapped and carried in open view.
- Non-residents are prohibited from carrying or possessing a firearm while traveling through the district unless it has been registered with the Metropolitan Police. An exception is if passing through the district, so long as the firearm is unloaded, securely wrapped, and carried in the trunk.

West Virginia:

- There is no state mandated waiting period to purchase handguns or longguns.
- No permit is required to purchase or possess a rifle, shotgun, or handgun.
- It is unlawful to purchase or possess a firearm if convicted of a crime punishable by imprisonment for more than one year, dishonorably discharged from the armed forces, adjudged as mentally incompetent, committed to a mental institution, is an illegal alien, uses or is addicted to alcohol or any controlled substance, or subject to a domestic violence protective order.
- It is unlawful to carry a concealed handgun on or about one's person without a license unless in one's own residence. Licenses may be denied if not a citizen and resident of the state, under 21 years old, addicted or an unlawful user of alcohol or controlled substances, convicted of a felony, convicted of an act of violence involving the misuse of firearms or deadly weapons, physically or mentally incompetent, serving a sentence of confinement, on parole or probation on a charge of domestic violence, or on a restraining order as a result of domestic violence. In addition, applicants must complete an approved training course in handling and firing a handgun.
- Non-residents may carry a concealed handgun so long as they possess a permit from their home state and that state has a reciprocity agreement with West Virginia.

Wisconsin:

- There is a 2 day waiting period for handgun purchases, but no waiting period for longguns.
- No permit is required to possess a rifle, shotgun, or handgun.
- It is unlawful to carry a concealed dangerous weapon on one's person. There is no license available to carry a concealed weapon. A person may carry a firearm openly, but should exercise caution when carrying in public.

Wyoming:

- There is no state mandated waiting period to purchase handguns or longguns.
- No permit is required to purchase or possess a rifle, shotgun, or handgun.
- It is unlawful to wear or carry a concealed deadly weapon without a permit. Permits may be denied if he or she is a resident of Wyoming for less than 6 months, under 21 years old, suffers from a physical infirmity which would prevent the safe handling of a firearm, committed to an institution for the abuse of a controlled substance, convicted of a state or federal controlled substance act, chronically or habitually uses alcoholic beverages, convicted of one or more crimes of violence constituting a misdemeanor offense within the last three years, is likely to danger himself or others, or is otherwise ineligible to possess a firearm. In addition the applicant must demonstrate familiarity with a firearm proven by the completion of a firearm safety course.
- Non-residents may carry a concealed weapon so long as they have a valid permit from their home state with laws similar to Wyoming.

Canadian Gun Laws

Canadian law divides firearms into three categories: Prohibited, Restricted, and Longguns.

1. Prohibited Firearms
- Handguns
- Firearms "which have no legitimate sporting or recreational use" such as:
    - Those capable of firing bullets in rapid succession during one pressure of the trigger.
    - A rifle or shotgun which has been modified so that its barrel is less than 46 cm (18 in) long, the total length of which is less than 66 cm (26 in) in overall length.

2. Restricted Firearms
- Any firearm designed, altered, or intended to be aimed and fired by the action of one hand, including handguns.
- Any firearm that has a barrel less than 47 cm (18.5 in) long, capable of discharging center fire ammunition in a semi-automatic manner.
- Any firearm designed or adapted to be fired when reduced to a length of less than 66 cm (26 in) by folding, telescoping, or otherwise.
- Visitors traveling in or through Canada may not import restricted weapons, unless competing in a meet recognized by the Amateur Trap Shooting Association, the Dominion of Canada Rifle Association, or the National Skeet Shooting Association, in which case a permit may be secured in advance in coordination with the host club.

3. Longguns
A regular hunting rifle or shotgun (as described by the manufacturer) may be imported or moved through Canada as long as:

- The visitor is 16 years of age or older.
- The firearm is for sporting or competition use.
- The firearm does not fall into the prohibited or restricted categories as described above.

All firearms must be declared upon arrival at a Canada Customs port. Those attempting to bring restricted weapons into Canada will be given a chance to export them. All weapons not declared will be seized and forfeited, and criminal charges may be brought.

Pellet guns with a muzzle velocity greater than 152.5 meters (500 ft./second) are considered firearms and are covered under the above regulations; those with a lesser muzzle velocity are exempt.

For further information, contact: Ministry of the Solicitor General, Firearms Policy Centre, 340 Laurier Avenue West, 12th floor, Ottawa, Ontario, Canada K1A 0P8.

Hunting In Canada

In general, non-residents are required to get a hunting license from each province or territory in which they plan to hunt. Entry of any type of weapon is prohibited in many Canadian provincial parks and reserves.

Hunting is prohibited in Canada's National Parks and firearms may not be carried into the parks unless:

- The barrel and stock can be separated and the gun is carried in this dismantled condition
- The gun is carried in a closed case, or
- The gun is wrapped and tied securely so that no part of the firearm is exposed.

British Columbia: A non-resident must have either a British Columbia firearms license or hunting license in order to carry a firearm anywhere other than on an arterial or secondary highway.

Source: U.S. Treasury Dept., Bureau of Alcohol, Tobacco and Firearms, General Information, Section 6, Canadian Firearms Information

HAZARDOUS MATERIALS

Hazardous Materials Communication Systems · · · · **604**
  Hazardous Materials Information System (HMIS) · · · · 604
  National Fire Protection Assoc. (NFPA) Diamond · · · 605
  American National Standards Institute ANSI Z1291 · · 606
  European ADR Agreement · 607
  DOT Hazardous Materials Transportation Act (HMTA) 610
Hazardous Materials Incidents · · · · · · · · · · · · · · · · **611**
  US Emergency Contact Numbers · · · · · · · · · · · · · · · 613
  Canadian Emergency Contact Numbers · · · · · · · · · · 614
Shipping Papers · **616**
Isolation and Evacuation · **617**
Fire and Spill Control · **617**
Protective Clothing · **619**
Hazard Classification System · · · · · · · · · · · · · · · · · **621**
Hazmat Placards · **623**
Hazardous Substances by ID Number · · · · · · · · · · · **630**
Hazardous Substances by Name · · · · · · · · · · · · · · · **639**
Guides · **696**
Evacuation Distances · **903**
Water-Reactive Materials that Produce Toxic Gas · · **934**
Hazardous Materials Glossary · · · · · · · · · · · · · · · · · **937**

Hazmat

Hazardous Materials Communication Systems

Four hazardous material warning systems are commonly used in the United States.

- Hazardous Materials Information System (HMIS)
- National Fire Protection Association (NFPA)
- American National Standards Institute (ANSI)
- US Department of Transportation (DOT)

The first three were created to communicate health hazard information to workers in on-site situations; the DOT system is used for materials in transport.

Hazardous Materials Information System (HMIS)

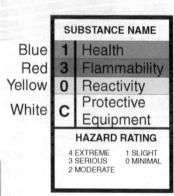

This system was created by the National Paint & Coating Assn. (NPCA) to address the needs of workers in that industry.

Labels and placards include: Manufacturer, name of chemical, and seriousness and type of hazard posed by the substance (communicated by color & number).

- Health hazard - Blue area
- Flammability - Red area
- Reactivity - yellow area
- Personal Protection - white area

Degree of hazard is indicated by a number ranging from 0-4, 4 being the most dangerous and 0 the least.

An alphabetic code is used in the white section to indicate what Personal Protection gear should be worn. The higher the letter, the more gear should be worn.

HMIS now uses an * in the Health block to indicate a material known to be a carcinogen or chronic health hazard.

National Fire Protection Assoc. (NFPA) Diamond

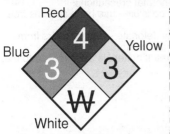

This placarding/labeling system is used on large-capacity storage tanks at chemical manufacturing plants, oil refineries, and other storage facilities. The type of hazard is indicated by color and the degree of hazard is indicated by number (the same colors and numbers as HMIS are used, except that the white area of the diamond indicates special hazards instead of personal protection). The numbers assigned in the NFPA system assume that a fire is present; no such assumption holds in the HMIS system. For this reason, the hazard ratings for the same chemical may differ between the two systems.

Diamond Key:

BLUE: Health (short-term effects that might be experienced in an emergency situation)

0 MINIMAL - ordinary material.
1 SLIGHT - hazard.
2 MODERATE - hazard, use breathing apparatus.
3 SERIOUS - danger, use full protective clothing; toxic, may cause serious temporary or residual injury; small animal carcinogen, mutagen, or teratogen.
4 EXTREME -Too dangerous to enter, vapor or liquid. Highly toxic, very short exposure could cause death or major residual injury; known or suspected human carcinogen.

RED: Flammability

0 Will not burn
1 Must be preheated to burn. Will burn in air after 5 minutes at 1500° F (815.5°C).
2 Ignites when moderately heated; solids which give off flammable vapors. Flash point at or above 100°F (37.8° C).
3 Ignites at normal temperatures - vaporized readily, can ignite under almost all ambient conditions; may form explosive mixtures with or burn rapidly in air; may burn rapidly because of self contained oxygen. Flash point at or above 73°F, but less than 200°F.
4 Extremely flammable - flash point below 73°F (22.8°C).

YELLOW: Reactivity
0 Normally stable.
1 Unstable if heated - use normal precautions.
2 Violent chemical change possible - use hose streams from a distance.
3 Strong shock or heat may detonate - Use monitors from behind explosive-resistant barriers.
4 May detonate - vacate area if materials are exposed to fire.

WHITE: Special hazards
- W̶ = Water Reactive
- Ox = Oxidizing Agent
- Corrosive
- Radioactive

Note difference in use of white area compared to HMIS.

NFPA uses special symbols to indicate flammability, explosivity, corrosivity, or poison.

American National Standards Institute ANSI Z1291

A voluntary labeling standard that was developed by the Chemical Manufacturers Association (CMA) and the American Conference on Chemical Labeling and is used primarily on bottles of chemicals.

Each label should contain the following information:

- Name of chemical.
- Signal word: Danger (most serious), Warning (Moderate hazard), or Caution (lesser hazard).
- Highly toxic materials marked "Poison".
- Hazard Statement: "Flammable" or "Vapor Harmful".
- Statements of precaution to avoid the hazard (i.e., wash thoroughly after handling; avoid contact with eyes).
- First Aid instructions in case of exposure (i.e., move to fresh air, give artificial respiration if not breathing).
- Antidotes if needed or "Notes to Physician" for emergency treatment.
- Instructions in case of fire or chemical spill.
- Instructions for handling and storage.

European ADR Agreement

Hazard identification codes, referred to as "hazard identification numbers" under European and some South American regulations, may be found in the top half of an orange panel on some intermodal bulk containers. The 4-digit identification number is in the bottom half of the orange panel.

The hazard identification code in the top half of the orange panel consists of two or three figures. The hazard identification codes listed below have the following meanings:

- Doubling of a figure indicates an intensification of that particular hazard (i.e. 33, 66, 88).
- Where the hazard associated with a material can be adequately indicated by a single figure, the figure is followed by a zero (i.e. 30).
- A hazard identification code prefixed by the letter "X" indicates that the material will react dangerously with water (i.e. X88).
- Combinations of digits in a hazard identification code indicate multiple hazards (i.e., 23 indicates a gas which is also flammable).

These digits indicate the following hazards:

2 ....Emission of Gas due to pressure or chemical reaction
3 ....Flammability of liquids (vapors) and gases or self-heating liquid
4 ....Flammability of solids or self-heating solid
5 ....Oxidizing (fire-intensifying) effect
6 ....Toxicity or risk of infection
7 ....Radioactivity
8 ....Corrosivity
9 ....Risk of spontaneous violent reaction

Additional Hazard Identification Code Meanings:

20 ....Inert gas
22 ....Refrigerated gas
223 ......Refrigerated gas, flammable
225 ......Refrigerated gas, oxidizing (fire-intensifying)
23 ....Flammable gas
236 ......Flammable gas, toxic
239 ......Flammable gas which can spontaneously lead to a violent reaction
25 ....Oxidizing (fire-intensifying) gas
26 ....Toxic gas

263 ......Toxic gas, flammable
265 ......Toxic gas, oxidizing (fire-intensifying)
266 ......Highly toxic gas
268 ......Toxic gas, corrosive

30 ....Flammable liquid
323 ......Flammable liquid which reacts with water, emitting
          flammable gas
X323 ....Flammable liquid which reacts dangerously with water,
          emitting flammable gas
33 ....Highly flammable liquid
333 ......Pyrophoric liquid
X333 ....Pyrophoric liquid which reacts dangerously w/ water
336 ......Highly flammable liquid, toxic
338 ......Highly flammable liquid, corrosive
X338 ....Highly flammable liquid, corrosive, which reacts
          dangerously with water
339 ......Highly flammable liquid which can spontaneously lead to
          a violent reaction
36 ....Flammable liquid, toxic, or self-heating liquid, toxic
362 ......Flammable liquid, toxic, which reacts with water, emitting
          flammable gas
X362 ....Flammable liquid, toxic, which reacts dangerously with
          water, emitting flammable gas
368 ......Flammable liquid, toxic, corrosive
38 ....Flammable liquid, corrosive
382 ......Flammable liquid, corrosive, which reacts with water,
          emitting flammable gas
X382 ....Flammable liquid, corrosive, which reacts dangerously
          with water emitting flammable gas
39 ....Flammable liquid which can spontaneously lead to a
          violent reaction

40 ....Flammable solid, or self-reactive material, or self heating
          material
423 ......Solid which reacts with water, emitting flammable gas
X423 ....Flammable solid which reacts dangerously with water,
          emitting flammable gas
43 ....Spontaneously flammable (pyrophoric) solid
44 ....Flammable solid, in the molten state at an elevated
          temperature
446 ......Flammable solid, toxic, in the molten state at an elevated
          temperature
46 ....Flammable solid, toxic, or self-heating solid, toxic
462 ......Toxic solid which reacts with water, emitting flammable
          gas
X462 ....Solid which reacts dangerously with water, emitting toxic
          gas
48 ....Flammable or self-heating solid, corrosive

482 ......Corrosive solid which reacts with water, emitting flammable gas

X482 ....Solid which reacts dangerously with water, emitting corrosive gas

50 ....Oxidizing (fire-intensifying) substance
539 ......Flammable organic peroxide
55 ....Strongly oxidizing (fire-intensifying) substance
556 ......Strongly oxidizing (fire-intensifying) substance, toxic
558 ......Strongly oxidizing (fire-intensifying) substance, corrosive
559 ......Strongly oxidizing (fire-intensifying) substance which can spontaneously lead to violent reaction
56 ....Oxidizing (fire-intensifying) substance, toxic
568 ......Oxidizing (fire-intensifying) substance, toxic, corrosive
58 ....Oxidizing (fire-intensifying) substance, corrosive
59 ....Oxidizing (fire-intensifying) substance which can spontaneously lead to a violent reaction

60 ....Toxic material
606 ......Infectious substance
623 ......Toxic liquid which reacts with water, emitting flammable gas
63 ....Toxic liquid, flammable
638 ......Toxic liquid, flammable, corrosive
639 ......Toxic liquid, flammable, which can spontaneously lead to a violent reaction
64 ....Toxic solid, flammable or self-heating
642 ......Toxic solid which reacts with water, emitting flammable gas
65 ....Toxic material, oxidizing (fire-intensifying)
66 ....Highly toxic material
663 ......Highly toxic liquid, flammable
664 ......Highly toxic solid, flammable or self-heating
665 ......Highly toxic material, oxidizing (fire-intensifying)
668 ......Highly toxic material, corrosive
669 ......Highly toxic material which can spontaneously lead to a violent reaction
68 ....Toxic material, corrosive
69 ....Toxic material which can spontaneously lead to a violent reaction

70 ....Radioactive material
72 ....Radioactive gas
723 ......Radioactive gas, flammable
73 ....Radioactive liquid, flammable
74 ....Radioactive solid, flammable
75 ....Radioactive material, oxidizing (fire-intensifying)
76 ....Radioactive material, toxic
78 ....Radioactive material, corrosive

Hazmat

80	Corrosive material
X80	Corrosive material which reacts dangerously w/ water
823	Corrosive liquid which reacts with water, emitting flammable gas
83	Corrosive liquid, flammable
X83	Corrosive liquid, flammable, which reacts dangerously with water
839	Corrosive liquid, flammable, which can spontaneously lead to a violent reaction
X839	Corrosive liquid, flammable, which can spontaneously lead to a violent reaction and which reacts dangerously with water
84	Corrosive solid, flammable or self-heating
85	Corrosive material, oxidizing (fire-intensifying)
856	Corrosive material, oxidizing and toxic
86	Corrosive material, toxic
88	Highly corrosive material
X88	Highly corrosive material which reacts dangerously with water
883	Highly corrosive liquid, flammable
884	Highly corrosive solid, flammable or self-heating
885	Highly corrosive material, oxidizing (fire-intensifying)
886	Highly corrosive material, toxic
X886	Highly corrosive material, toxic, which reacts dangerously with water
89	Corrosive material which can spontaneously lead to a violent reaction
90	Miscellaneous dangerous substance; environmentally hazardous substance
99	Miscellaneous dangerous substance transported at elevated temperature

DOT Hazardous Materials Transportation Act (HMTA)

The rest of this chapter focuses on the guidelines contained in the DOT communication system. It was designed to deal with hazardous materials being transported, usually by truck or train. This system requires information to be communicated in two ways: on the shipping papers (page 616), which contain the most detail, and on labels or placards (page 623).

Hazardous Materials Incidents

A first responder's responsibility upon arriving at an incident is to:

- Recognize the presence of dangerous goods.
- Protect him or herself and the public.
- Secure the area.
- Call for help from trained personnel as soon as conditions permit.

Follow the steps outlined in your organization's standard operating procedures and local emergency response plan for obtaining qualified assistance.

1. Approach Cautiously From Upwind

Resist the urge to rush in, as others cannot be helped until the situation has been fully assessed.

2. Secure the Scene

Without entering the immediate hazard area, isolate the area and assure the safety of people and the environment. Keep people away from the scene and outside the safety perimeter. Allow enough room to move and remove your own equipment.

3. Identify the Hazards

1. Identify The Material
Find one of the following:
- The 4-Digit ID number on a placard, orange panel, shipping document, or package.
- The name of the material on a shipping document, placard, or package.
- If an ID number or the name of the material cannot be found, skip to the note below.

2. Look Up The 3-Digit Guide Number
- The ID number index on page 630.
- The name of material index on page 639.
  - If the guide number contains the letter "P," or is bold-faced, the material may undergo violent polymerization if subjected to heat or contamination.
  - If the index entry is highlighted, the material is a toxic inhalation hazard (TIH), a chemical warfare agent, or a dangerous water reactive material (produces toxic gas on contact with water).
    Look for the ID number or name of the material in the

table of initial isolation and protective action distances.
Then, if necessary, begin protective actions immediately.

- Use Guide 114 (page 704) for Division 1.4 (Explosives C)
- Use Guide 112 (page 699) for all other explosives.

3. Turn to the numbered guide and read carefully

NOTE: If a numbered guide cannot be found by following the above steps and a placard can be seen, find the placard starting on page 623, then go to the 3-digit guide shown next to the sample placard.

If A Guide Number Cannot Be Found, Use Guide 111 Until Additional Information Becomes Available.

4. Assess the Situation

Consider the following:
- Is there a fire, a spill, or a leak?
- What are the weather conditions?
- What is the terrain like?
- Who or what is at risk: people, property, or the environment?
- What actions should be taken:
    - Is an evacuation necessary?
    - Is diking necessary?
    - What resources (human and equipment) are required and readily available?
- What can be done immediately?

5. Call for Help

1. Call your organization/agency.
Ensure that local fire and police departments have been notified.
2. Call the emergency telephone number listed on the shipping document.
3. Get national assistance.
When the emergency response telephone number is not available, the agencies listed below will provide immediate advice on handling the early stages of the incident, contact the shipper or manufacturer of the material for more detailed information, and request on-scene help when necessary.

Collect and provide as much of the following information as can safely be obtained:

- Your name, call back phone number, and FAX number.
- Location and nature of problem.
- Name and identification number of material(s) involved.

- The shipper, consignee, and point of origin.
- Carrier name, rail car or truck number.
- Container type and size.
- Quantity of material being transported and released.
- Conditions (weather, terrain, school proximity, hospitals, etc.).
- Injuries and exposures.
- Local emergency services that have been notified.

United States Assistance:

CHEMTREC®
800-424-9300 (Toll-free in the U.S. and Canada)
703-527-3887 (Calls originating elsewhere; collect calls are accepted)

CHEM-TEL, INC
800-255-3924 (Toll-free in the U.S. and Canada)
813-248-0585 (Calls originating elsewhere; collect calls are accepted)

INFOTRAC
800-535-5053 (Toll-free in the U.S. and Canada)
352-323-3500 (Calls originating elsewhere; collect calls are accepted)

3E Company
800-451-8346 (Toll-free in the U.S. and Canada)
760-602-8703 (Calls originating elsewhere; collect calls are accepted)

The above companies maintain a current list of state and Federal radiation authorities that provide information and technical assistance on handling incidents involving radioactive materials.

National Response Center (NRC)
The NRC, which is operated by the U.S. Coast Guard, receives reports that are required when dangerous goods and hazardous substances are spilled. After receiving notification of an incident, the NRC will immediately notify the appropriate Federal On-Scene Coordinator and concerned Federal agencies. Federal law requires that anyone who releases into the environment a reportable quantity of a hazardous substance (including oil when water is, or may be affected) or a material identified as a marine pollutant, must immediately notify the NRC. When in doubt as to whether the amount released equals the required reporting levels for these materials, the NRC should be notified.
800-424-8802 (Toll-free in the U.S. and Canada)
202-267-2675 (in Washington, D.C.)

Military Shipments

For incidents involving materials being shipped by, for, or to the Department of Defense (DOD), call one of the following numbers:

703-697-0218 (collect) (U.S. Army Operations Center) for incidents involving explosives and ammunition.

800-851-8061 (Defense Logistics Agency) for incidents involving dangerous goods other than explosives and ammunition.

The above numbers are for emergencies only.

Canadian Assistance:

CANUTEC (Canadian Transport Emergency Centre) provides a national bilingual (French and English) advisory service and is staffed by professional chemists experienced and trained in interpreting technical information and providing emergency response advice.

613-996-6666 (24-hour Emergency Phone, call collect)
613-992-4624 (Non-emergency information line)

Provincial Agencies: Federal and provincial regulations require the reporting of dangerous goods incidents to certain authorities. (see phone list on following page)

Canadian Assistance Notes:

• The appropriate federal agency must be notified in the case of rail, air, or marine incidents.

• The nearest police department must be notified in the case of lost, stolen, or misplaced explosives, radioactive materials, or infectious substances.

• CANUTEC must be notified in the case of an incident:
  – involving lost, stolen or misplaced infectious substances.
  – involving infectious substances.
  – where the shipping documents display CANUTEC's telephone number (613-996-6666) as the emergency telephone number.
  – involving a railway vehicle.

Province	Emergency Authority/Phone Number
Alberta	Local Police and Provincial Authorities, 800-272-9600*
British Columbia	Local Police or 800-663-3456

Hazmat

Manitoba	Local Police or fire brigade, as appropriate, or 204-945-4888
New Brunswick	Local Police or 800-565-1633** or 902-426-6030
Newfoundland	Local Police or 709-772-2083
Northwest Territories	867-920-8130
Nova Scotia	Local Police or 800-565-1633** or 902-426-6030
Nunavut	867-920-8130
Ontario	Local Police
Prince Edward Island	Local Police or 800-565-1633** or 902-426-6030
Quebec	Local Police
Saskatchewan	Local Police or 800-667-7525
Yukon Territory	867-667-7244

   * Not accessible from outside Alberta.

  ** Not accessible from outside New Brunswick, Nova Scotia or Prince Edward Island.

Mexican Assistance

SETIQ (Emergency Transportation System for the Chemical Industry), a service of the National Association of Chemical Industries (ANIQ).
01-800-00-214 (in the Mexican Republic)
5559-1588 (Mexico City and the Metropolitan Area)
0-11-52-5-559-1588 (For calls originating elsewhere)

CECOM, the National Center for Communications of the Civil Protection Agency.
1-800-00-413-00 (in the Mexican Republic)
Mexico City and the Metropolitan Area:
5550-1496; 5550-1552; 5550-1485; or 5550-4885
For calls originating elsewhere, call: 0-11-52-5-550-1496;
0-11-52-5-550-1552; 0-11-52-5-550-1485; or
0-11-52-5-550-4885

6. Decide Whether to Enter the Site

Efforts to rescue persons, protect property, or protect the environment must be weighed against the possibility that you could become part of the problem. Enter the area only when wearing appropriate protective gear.

Hazmat

7. Respond

Establish a command post and lines of communication. Rescue casualties where possible and evacuate if necessary. Maintain control of the site. Continually reassess the situation and modify the response accordingly. The first duty is to consider the safety of people in the immediate area, including your own.

ABOVE ALL - Do not walk into or touch spilled material. Avoid inhaling fumes, smoke and vapors, even if no dangerous goods are known to be involved. Do not assume that gases or vapors are harmless because of lack of smell as odorless gases or vapors may be harmful.

Shipping Papers

All hazardous materials in transport MUST be accompanied by shipping papers. The papers fully explain the hazards involved. Shipping documents are usually kept in the cab of the vehicle or in possession of a train crew member, a person on the bridge of a vessel, or an aircraft pilot.

The shipping description must always include:
- Proper shipping name.
- Hazard class or division of the material.
- Identification number.
- Packing group.
- Total quantity of material, including unit of measurement.
- Emergency response number & the shipper's certification.

Sample Shipping Papers:

Emergency Contact 1-800-999-9999

No. & Type of Packages	Description of Articles	Hazard Class or Division Number		Quantity
1 Tank Truck	Isopropanol	3	UN1219 II	3000 liters
	Shipping Name		ID Number Packing Group	

The shipping papers must be in English and be legible. The description may not contain codes or abbreviations. Name of the shipper must be included when transported by water. If there are multiple pages, the first page must show the total number. Names used in this system are based on international agreements.

Isolation and Evacuation

Isolation and evacuation distances are shown in the guides.

Toxic Inhalation Hazards (TIH)

Toxic or Poison Inhalation Hazards are gases and volatile liquids that are toxic when inhaled. It is presumed to be toxic when it has an LC50 value of not more than 5000 ppm when tested on laboratory animals.

Inhalation Hazard Zone (IHZ)

Zones are assigned on the basis of their Lethal Concentration 50 (LC50) not any actual area or distance. For example, IHZ A is more toxic than IHZ D. All distances which are listed in the guides are calculated by the use of mathematical models for each substance.

- IHZ A: Gases: LC50 $\leq$ 200 ppm
  Liquids: V $\geq$ 500 LC50 and LC 50 $\leq$ 200 ppm
- IHZ B: Gases: LC50 > 200 ppm and $\leq$ 1000 ppm
  Liquids: V $\geq$ 10 LC50 and LC50 $\leq$ 1000 ppm
  and criteria for Hazard Zone A are not met.
- IHZ C: LC50 >1000 ppm and $\leq$ 3000 ppm
- IHZ D: LC50 > 3000 ppm and $\leq$ 5000 ppm

Fire and Spill Control

Fire Control

Exercise caution when selecting fire extinguishing methods at an incident. The most common and available form of fire extinguishing agent is water. However, water may be ineffective in fighting fires involving some materials. Therefore, get as much information as possible before choosing a fire extinguishing method.

The selection of an extinguishing agent depends on many factors such as location, exposure hazards, size of the fire, environmental concerns, and available of extinguishing agents at the scene. The first course of action should be to contact the emergency response telephone number on the shipping documents (or an appropriate emergency response team) for guidance on proper fire extinguishing.

Spill fires involving flammable liquids are generally controlled by applying a fire fighting foam to the surface of the burning

Hazmat

material. The foam is made to be chemically compatible with the burning material, and with correct mixing of the foam with water and air, and a careful application it should form a foam blanket over the material. There are two general types of foam: regular and alcohol-resistant.

Regular Foam

- Protein-base
- Fluoroprotein
- Aqueous Film Forming Foam (AFFF)
- Many flammable liquids (including petroleum products) can be controlled by applying regular foam.

Alcohol-Resistant Foam

- Polar Solvents (flammable liquids which are water solvent) such as alcohols and keytones.
- Polar solvents have different chemical properties and cannot be easily controlled with regular foam.
- Polar solvent fires may be difficult to control and require a higher foam application rate.
- Although is it impossible to make specific recommendations for flammable liquids which have subsidiary corrosive or toxic hazards, alcohol-resistant foam may be effective on these types of materials.

Water Reactive Materials

Water is sometimes used to reduce or redirect vapors and flush out spills. However, some materials can react violently or explosively with water. In cases that involve these types of materials, consider letting the fire burn or leaving the spill alone (except to prevent its spread by diking) until additional technical advice can be obtained. The guides will clearly warn you of potentially dangerous reactions, so be sure to refer to them.

Considerations for water reactive materials:

- Conditions such as wind, precipitation, location, accessibility to the incident, and the availability of agents to control the fire or spill.
- If water gets inside a ruptured or leaking container, it may cause an explosion.
- Water may be needed to cool adjoining containers to prevent their rupturing and further spread of the fire.

- Water may be effective in mitigating an incident involving a water-reactive material, but must be applied at a sufficient flooding rate for an extended period.
- Products from the reaction of materials and water might be more toxic or corrosive than the original material without water applied.

Because of these variables, extinguishing fires or spills involving water-reactive materials should be done in conjunction with an authoritative source (a producer of the material or emergency response agency).

Vapor Control

Minimizing the amount of vapor released from a pool of flammable or corrosive liquids might be necessary. However, it requires the use of proper protective clothing, specialized equipment, appropriate chemical agents, and skilled personnel. Before engaging in vapor control, get advice from an authoritative source.

Foams, adsorbing agents, absorbing agents, and neutralizing agents can be effective in minimizing vapors. The type of method will depend on the specific material involved and will be applied in a manner that will not worsen the incident. Since first responders usually only have water and one type of foam in their vehicles, they may not be effective in vapor control. If they do not have the appropriate foam, they are likely to use water spray. Vapors that do not react with water may be directed away from the site using the air currents of water spray. Before using water spray or other methods, obtain technical advice based on the material involved in the incident.

Protective Clothing

Uniforms & Street Clothing

Street clothing and uniforms (such as those worn by law enforcement or emergency medical technicians) provide almost no protection from the harmful effects of dangerous goods.

Structural Fire Fighters' Protective Clothing (SFPC)

This type of clothing (also called turnout or bunker gear) refers to typical protective clothing normally worn by fire fighters during fire fighting operations. It includes a helmet, coat, pants, boots, gloves, and a hood. It may be used with a full-facepiece positive pressure self-contained breathing apparatus (SCBA). This

Hazmat

clothing should at least meet the OSHA Fire Brigades Standard. It will provide limited protection from heat and cold, but may not protect from harmful vapors or liquids encountered during dangerous goods incidents. Each guide will include statements about the use and protection of SFPC during that chemical incident. In cases where the guide states that SFPC provides 'limited protection,' the responder may be able to perform an expedient (quick in-and-out) operation. However, even expedient operations can place the responder at risk of exposure and may result in injury or death. The incident commander will make the decision on whether to allow an expedient operation (usually it will only be made if there is a great overriding benefit, such as to perform an immediate rescue, turn off a valve to control a leak, etc.) The cover-all type protective clothing normally worn to fight wild or forest fires is **not** SFPC and is not recommended for any incidents involving dangerous goods.

Positive Pressure Self-Contained Breathing Apparatus (SCBA)

This apparatus provides a constant, positive pressure flow of air within the facepiece. Use an apparatus certified by NIOSH and the Department of Labor/Mine Safety and Health Administration. Use it in accordance with the requirements for respiratory protection. Chemical-cartridge respirators or other filtering masks are not acceptable substitutes for a positive pressure self-contained breathing apparatus.

Chemical Protective Clothing and Equipment

Safe and effective use of this type of clothing and equipment requires special skills, training, and experience. It is generally not available, or used, by first responders. It is usually designed to protect against a single chemical and, therefore, should not be used unless is was designed to be compatible with the released material. It offers little or no protection against heat and cold. Examples are Vapor Protective Suits (aka Totally-Encapsulating Chemical Protective Suits - TECP), Liquid-Splash Protective Suits (aka Level B or C protection or suits for chemical/biological terrorism incidents). No single protective clothing material will protect from all dangerous goods. Do not assume it is resistant to hot, cold, or flame exposure unless it is certified by the manufacturer.

Hazmat

Hazard Classification System

The hazard class of dangerous goods is indicated either by its class (or division) number or name. For a placard corresponding to the primary hazard class of a material, the hazard class or division number must be displayed in the lower corner of the placard. However, no hazard class or division number may be displayed on a placard representing the subsidiary hazard of a material.

For other than Class 7 or the OXYGEN placard, text indicating a hazard (for example, "CORROSIVE") is not required. Text is shown only in the U.S. The hazard class or division number must appear on the shipping document after each shipping name.

Class 1 - Explosives

Division 1.1   Explosives with a mass explosion hazard
Division 1.2   Explosives with a projection hazard
Division 1.3   Explosives with predominantly a fire hazard
Division 1.4   Explosives with no significant blast hazard
Division 1.5   Very intensive explosives with a mass explosion hazard
Division 1.6   Extremely insensitive articles

Class 2 - Gases

Division 2.1   Flammable gases
Division 2.2   Non-flammable, non-toxic gases
Division 2.3   Toxic gases

Class 3 - Flammable liquids (& Combustible liquids [U.S.])

Class 4 - Flammable solids; Spontaneously combustible materials, and Dangerous when wet materials (Water-reactive substances)

Division 4.1   Flammable solids
Division 4.2   Spontaneously combustible materials
Division 4.3   Water-reactive substances/Dangerous when wet materials

Class 5 - Oxidizing substances and Organic peroxides

Division 5.1   Oxidizing substances
Division 5.2   Organic peroxides

Class 6 - Toxic substances and Infectious substances

Division 6.1   Toxic substances
Division 6.2   Infectious substances

Hazmat

Class 7 - Radioactive materials

Class 8 - Corrosive substances

Class 9 - Miscellaneous hazardous materials, products, substances, or organisms

Compatibility Group Letters

Letters identify Class 1 materials that can be transported together without significantly increasing the probability of an incident or the magnitude of the effects of such an incident.

A   Substances expected to mass detonate very soon after fire reaches them.

B   Articles expected to mass detonate very soon after fire reaches them.

C   Substances or articles may readily ignite and burn violently without necessarily exploding.

D   Substances or articles which may mass detonate with blast and/or fragment hazard when exposed to fire.

E&F   Articles which may mass detonate in a fire.

G   Substances and articles which may mass explode and give off smoke or toxic gases.

H   Articles which in a fire may eject hazardous projectiles and dense white smoke.

J   Articles which may mass explode.

K   Articles which in a fire may eject hazardous projectiles and toxic gases.

L   Substances and articles which present a special risk and could be activated by exposure to air or water.

N   Articles which contain only extremely insensitive detonating substances and are unlikely to accidentally ignite or propagate.

S   Packaged substances or articles which, if accidentally initiated, produce effects that are usually confined to the immediate area.

Placards

The 4-digit ID Number may be shown on the diamond-shaped placard or on an adjacent orange panel displayed on the ends and sides of a cargo tank, vehicle, or rail car.

Examples

A Numbered Placard.   A Placard and an Orange Panel.

Placard Groupings

Use the following placard guide only if materials cannot be specifically identified by using the shipping document, numbered placard, or orange panel number.

- Match the vehicle placard(s) with one of the placards below.
- Consult the numbered guide associated with the sample placard. If multiple placards point to more than one guide, use the most conservative (most protect action) guide until more information becomes available.
- The guides associated with the placards provide the most significant risk and hazard information.
- When specific information (such as ID number) becomes available, use the guide associated with it.
- If Guide 111 is being used because only the Danger/Dangerous placard is displayed or the nature of the spilled, leaking, or burning material is not known, get more specific information concerning the materials involved as soon as possible.
- Asterisks (*) on orange placards represent explosives "Compatibility Group" letters (see previous page).
- Double asterisks (**) on orange placards represent the division of the explosive.

Hazmat

Use Guide 111

Red
White
•DANGER

Red
White
DANGEROUS

Use Guide 112

Orange
1.5
*
1

Orange
1.5
BLASTING
AGENTS
*
1

Orange
BLASTING
AGENTS
*
1

Use Guide 112

Orange
EXPLOSIVE
*
1

Orange
EXPLOSIVES
*
1

Orange
**
*
1

Use Guide 112

Orange
1.6
*
1

Orange
1.6
EXPLOSIVES
*
1

Use Guide 114

Use Guide 118

Use Guide 121

Use Guide 122

Hazmat

Use Guide 123

White

White

White

Use Guide 127

White

Red

White

Red

FLAMMABLE

White

Red

COMBUSTIBLE

Black

Red

Use Guide 128

White

FUEL OIL

Red

Hazmat

Use Guide 134

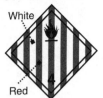

White
Red
4

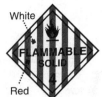

White
FLAMMABLE SOLID
Red
4

Use Guide 136

White
SPONTANEOUSLY COMBUSTIBLE
Red
4

White
Red
4

Use Guide 139

White
Blue
4

White
DANGEROUS WHEN WET
Blue
4

Black
Blue
4

Use Guide 143

Yellow
5.1

OXIDIZER
Yellow
5.1

Hazmat

Yellow — 5.2

ORGANIC PEROXIDE
Yellow — 5.2

Use Guide 153

White

White
CORROSIVE
Black — 8 / Black — 8

Use Guide 153

White

White
TOXIC
6

White
POISON
6

White
INHALATION HAZARD
6

Haznat

Hazardous Materials

Use Guide 158

White

White

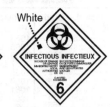
White

Use Guide 163

White

Yellow

Yellow

Yellow

Yellow

Use Guide 171

Black
White

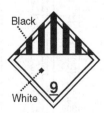
Black
White

Hazmat

Placard No.	Guide No.	Placard No.	Guide No.	Placard No.	Guide No.	Placard No.	Guide No.
——	112	1053	125	1125	132	1189	129
——	158	1055	115	1126	130	1190	129
——	112	1056	121	1127	130	1191	129
——	112	1057	115	1128	129	1192	129
——	112	1058	120	1129	129	1193	127
——	114	**1060**	**116P**	1130	128	1194	131
——	112	1061	118	1131	131	1195	129
——	114	1062	123	1133	128	1196	155
——	153	1063	115	1134	130	1197	127
1001	116	1064	117	1135	131	1198	132
1002	122	1065	121	1136	128	**1199**	**132P**
1003	122	1066	121	1139	127	1201	127
1005	125	1067	124	**1143**	**131P**	1202	128
1006	121	1069	125	1144	128	1203	128
1008	125	1070	122	1145	128	1204	127
1009	126	1071	119	1146	128	1206	128
1010	**116P**	1072	122	1147	130	1207	130
1011	115	1073	122	1148	129	1208	128
1012	115	1075	115	1149	128	1210	129
1013	120	1076	125	**1150**	**130P**	1212	129
1014	122	1077	115	1152	130	1213	129
1015	126	1078	126	1153	127	1214	132
1016	119	1079	125	1154	132	1216	128
1017	124	1080	126	1155	127	**1218**	**130P**
1018	126	**1081**	**116P**	1156	127	1219	129
1020	126	**1082**	**119P**	1157	128	1220	129
1021	126	1083	118	1158	132	1221	132
1022	126	**1085**	**116P**	1159	127	1222	130
1023	119	**1086**	**116P**	1160	132	1223	128
1026	119	**1087**	**116P**	1161	129	1224	127
1027	115	1088	127	1162	155	1226	128
1028	126	1089	129	1163	131	1228	131
1029	126	1090	127	1164	130	1229	129
1030	115	1091	127	1165	127	1230	131
1032	118	**1092**	**131P**	1166	127	1231	129
1033	115	**1093**	**131P**	**1167**	**131P**	1233	130
1035	115	1098	131	1169	127	1234	127
1036	118	1099	131	1170	127	1235	132
1037	115	1100	131	1171	127	1237	129
1038	115	1104	129	1172	129	1238	155
1039	115	1105	129	1173	129	1239	131
1040	**119P**	1106	132	1175	130	1242	139
1041	115	1107	129	1176	129	1243	129
1043	125	1108	128	1177	130	1244	131
1044	126	1109	129	1178	127	1245	127
1045	124	1110	127	1179	127	**1246**	**127P**
1046	121	1111	130	1180	130	**1247**	**129P**
1048	125	1112	140	1181	155	1248	129
1049	115	1113	129	1182	155	1249	127
1050	125	1114	130	1183	139	1250	155
1051	117	1120	129	1184	131	**1251**	**131P**
1052	125	1123	129	**1185**	**131P**	1259	131
				1188	127		

Highlighted = Toxic when inhaled   **Bold = may polymerize & explode.**

Hazmat

Placard No.	Guide No.	Placard No.	Guide No.	Placard No.	Guide No.	Placard No.	Guide No.
1261	129	1330	133	1396	138	1463	141
1262	128	1331	133	1397	139	1465	140
1263	128	1332	133	1398	138	1466	140
1264	129	1333	170	1400	138	1467	143
1265	128	1334	133	1401	138	1469	141
1266	127	1336	113	1402	138	1470	141
1267	128	1337	113	1403	138	1471	140
1268	128	1338	133	1404	138	1472	143
1270	128	1339	139	1405	138	1473	140
1272	129	1340	139	1406	138	1474	140
1274	129	1341	139	1407	138	1475	140
1275	129	1343	139	1408	139	1476	140
1276	129	1344	113	1409	138	1477	140
1277	132	1345	133	1410	138	1479	140
1278	129	1346	170	1411	138	1481	140
1279	130	1347	113	1412	139	1482	140
1280	127P	1348	113	1413	138	1483	140
1281	129	1349	113	1414	138	1484	140
1282	129	1350	133	1415	138	1485	140
1286	127	1352	170	1417	138	1486	140
1287	127	1353	133	1418	138	1487	140
1288	128	1354	113	1419	139	1488	140
1289	132	1355	113	1420	138	1489	140
1292	129	1356	113	1421	138	1490	140
1293	127	1357	113	1422	138	1491	144
1294	130	1358	170	1423	138	1492	140
1295	139	1360	139	1426	138	1493	140
1296	132	1361	133	1427	138	1494	141
1297	132	1362	133	1428	138	1495	140
1298	155	1363	135	1431	138	1496	143
1299	128	1364	133	1432	139	1498	140
1300	128	1365	133	1433	139	1499	140
1301	129P	1366	135	1435	138	1500	140
1302	127P	1369	135	1436	138	1502	140
1303	130P	1370	135	1437	138	1503	140
1304	127P	1372	133	1438	140	1504	144
1305	155P	1373	133	1439	141	1505	140
1306	129	1374	133	1442	143	1506	143
1307	130	1376	135	1444	140	1507	140
1308	170	1378	170	1445	141	1508	140
1309	170	1379	133	1446	141	1509	143
1310	113	1380	135	1447	141	1510	143
1312	133	1381	136	1448	141	1511	140
1313	133	1382	135	1449	141	1512	140
1314	133	1383	135	1450	141	1513	140
1318	133	1384	135	1451	140	1514	140
1320	113	1385	135	1452	140	1515	140
1321	113	1386	135	1453	140	1516	143
1322	113	1387	133	1454	140	1517	113
1323	170	1389	138	1455	140	1541	155
1324	133	1390	139	1456	140	1544	151
1325	133	1391	138	1457	140	1545	155
1326	170	1392	138	1458	140	1546	151
1327	133	1393	138	1459	140	1547	153
1328	133	1394	138	1461	140	1548	153
		1395	139	1462	143	1549	157

Highlighted=Toxic when inhaled   **Bold=may polymerize & explode.**

Hazmat

Placard No.	Guide No.	Placard No.	Guide No.	Placard No.	Guide No.	Placard No.	Guide No.
1550	151	1612	123	1679	157	1744	154
1551	151	1613	154	1680	157	1745	144
1553	154	1614	152	1683	151	1746	144
1554	154	1616	151	1684	151	1747	155
1555	151	1617	151	1685	151	1748	140
1556	152	1618	151	1686	154	1749	124
1557	152	1620	151	1687	153	1750	153
1558	152	1621	151	1688	152	1751	153
1559	151	1622	151	1689	157	1752	156
1560	157	1623	151	1690	154	1753	156
1561	151	1624	154	1691	151	1754	137
1562	152	1625	141	1692	151	1755	154
1564	154	1626	157	1693	159	1756	154
1565	157	1627	141	1694	159	1757	154
1566	154	1629	151	1695	131	1758	137
1567	134	1630	151	1697	153	1759	154
1569	131	1631	154	1698	154	1760	154
1570	152	1634	154	1699	151	1761	154
1571	113	1636	154	1700	159	1762	156
1572	151	1637	151	1701	152	1763	156
1573	151	1638	151	1702	151	1764	153
1574	151	1639	151	1704	153	1765	156
1575	157	1640	151	1707	151	1766	156
1577	153	1641	151	1708	153	1767	155
1578	152	1642	151	1709	151	1768	154
1579	153	1643	151	1710	160	1769	156
1580	154	1644	151	1711	153	1770	153
1581	123	1645	151	1712	151	1771	156
1582	119	1646	151	1713	151	1773	157
1583	154	1647	151	1714	139	1774	154
1585	151	1648	127	1715	137	1775	154
1586	151	1649	131	1716	156	1776	154
1587	151	1650	153	1717	155	1777	137
1588	157	1651	153	1718	153	1778	154
1589	125	1652	153	1719	154	1779	153
1590	153	1653	151	1722	155	1780	156
1591	152	1654	151	1723	132	1781	156
1593	160	1655	151	1724	155	1782	154
1594	152	1656	151	1725	137	1783	153
1595	156	1657	151	1726	137	1784	156
1596	153	1658	151	1727	154	1786	157
1597	152	1659	151	1728	155	1787	154
1598	153	1660	124	1729	156	1788	154
1599	153	1661	153	1730	157	1789	157
1600	152	1662	152	1731	157	1790	157
1601	151	1663	153	1732	157	1791	154
1602	151	1664	152	1733	157	1792	157
1603	155	1665	152	1736	137	1793	153
1604	132	1669	151	1737	156	1794	154
1605	154	1670	157	1738	156	1796	157
1606	151	1671	153	1739	137	1798	157
1607	151	1672	151	1740	154	1799	156
1608	151	1673	153	1741	125	1800	156
1610	159	1674	151	1742	157	1801	156
1611	151	1677	151	1743	157	1802	140
		1678	154				

Highlighted=Toxic when inhaled   **Bold=may polymerize & explode.**

Hazmat

Placard No.	Guide No.	Placard No.	Guide No.	Placard No.	Guide No.	Placard No.	Guide No.
1803	153	1870	138	1957	115	2018	152
1804	156	1871	170	1958	126	2019	152
1805	154	1872	141	**1959**	**116P**	2020	153
1806	137	1873	143	1960	115	2021	153
1807	137	1884	157	1961	115	2022	153
1808	137	1885	153	**1962**	**116P**	2023	131P
1809	137	1886	156	1963	120	2024	151
1810	137	1887	160	1964	115	2025	151
1811	154	1888	151	1965	115	2026	151
1812	154	1889	157	1966	115	2027	151
1813	154	1891	131	1967	123	2028	153
1814	154	1892	151	1968	126	2029	132
1815	132	1894	151	1969	115	2030	153
1816	155	1895	151	1970	120	2031	157
1817	137	1897	160	1971	115	2032	157
1818	157	1898	156	1972	115	2033	154
1819	154	1902	153	1973	126	2034	115
1823	154	1903	153	1974	126	2035	115
1824	154	1905	154	1975	124	2036	121
1825	157	1906	153	1976	126	2037	115
1826	157	1907	154	1977	120	2038	152
1827	137	1908	154	1978	115	2044	115
1828	137	1910	157	1979	121	2045	130
1829	137	1911	119	1980	121	2046	130
1830	137	1912	115	1981	121	2047	129
1831	137	1913	120	1982	126	2048	130
1832	137	1914	130	1983	126	2049	130
1833	154	1915	127	1984	126	2050	128
1834	137	1916	152	1986	131	2051	132
1835	153	**1917**	**129P**	1987	127	2052	128
1836	137	1918	130	1988	131	2053	129
1837	157	**1919**	**129P**	1989	129	2054	132
1838	137	1920	128	1990	129	**2055**	**128P**
1839	153	**1921**	**131P**	**1991**	**131P**	2056	127
1840	154	1922	132	1992	131	2057	128
1841	171	1923	135	1993	128	2058	129
1843	141	1928	135	1994	131	2059	127
1845	120	1929	135	1999	130	2067	140
1846	151	1931	171	2000	133	2068	140
1847	153	1932	135	2001	133	2069	140
1848	132	1935	157	2002	135	2070	143
1849	153	1938	156	2003	135	2071	140
1851	151	1939	137	2004	135	2072	140
1854	135	1940	153	2005	135	2073	125
1855	135	1941	171	2006	135	**2074**	**153P**
1856	133	1942	140	2008	135	2075	153
1858	126	1944	133	2009	135	2076	153
1859	125	1945	133	2010	138	2077	153
1860	**116P**	1950	126	2011	139	2078	156
1862	130	1951	120	2012	139	2079	154
1863	128	1952	126	2013	139	2186	125
1865	131	1953	119	2014	140	2187	120
1866	127	1954	115	2015	143	2188	119
1868	134	1955	123	2016	151	2189	119
1869	138	1956	126	2017	159	2190	124

Highlighted=Toxic when inhaled   **Bold=may polymerize & explode.**

Hazmat

Placard No.	Guide No.	Placard No.	Guide No.	Placard No.	Guide No.	Placard No.	Guide No.
2191	123	2253	153	2312	153	2372	129
2192	119	2254	133	2313	129	2373	127
2193	126	2256	130	2315	171	2374	127
2194	125	2257	138	2316	157	2375	129
2195	125	2258	132	2317	157	2376	127
2196	125	2259	153	2318	135	2377	127
2197	125	2260	132	2319	128	2378	131
2198	125	2261	153	2320	153	2379	132
2199	119	2262	156	2321	153	2380	127
2200	**116P**	2263	128	2322	152	2381	130
2201	122	2264	132	2323	130	2382	131
2202	117	2265	129	2324	128	2383	132
2203	116	2266	132	2325	129	2384	127
2204	119	2267	156	2326	153	2385	129
2205	153	2269	153	2327	153	2386	132
2206	155	2270	132	2328	156	2387	130
2208	140	2271	128	2329	130	2388	130
2209	132	2272	153	2330	128	2389	127
2210	135	2273	153	2331	154	2390	129
2211	133	2274	153	2332	129	2391	129
2212	171	2275	129	2333	131	2392	129
2213	133	2276	132	2334	131	2393	129
2214	156	**2277**	**130P**	2335	131	2394	129
2215	156	2278	128	2336	131	2395	132
2216	171	2279	151	2337	131	**2396**	**131P**
2217	135	2280	153	2338	127	2397	127
2218	**132P**	2281	156	2339	130	2398	127
2219	129	2282	129	2340	130	2399	132
2222	128	**2283**	**130P**	2341	130	2400	130
2224	152	2284	131	2342	130	2401	132
2225	156	2285	156	2343	130	2402	130
2225	156	2286	128	2344	129	**2403**	**129P**
2226	156	2287	128	2345	130	2404	131
2227	**130P**	2288	128	2346	127	2405	129
2232	153	2289	153	2347	130	2406	127
2233	152	2290	156	**2348**	**130P**	2407	155
2234	130	2291	151	2350	127	2409	129
2235	153	2293	128	2351	129	2410	129
2236	156	2294	153	**2352**	**127P**	2411	131
2237	153	2295	155	2353	132	2412	130
2238	129	2296	128	2354	131	2413	128
2239	153	2297	128	2356	129	2414	130
2240	154	2298	128	2357	132	2416	129
2241	128	2299	155	**2358**	**128P**	2417	125
2242	128	2300	153	2359	132	2418	125
2243	130	2301	128	**2360**	**131P**	2419	116
2244	129	2302	127	2361	132	2420	125
2245	128	2303	128	2362	130	2421	124
2246	128	2304	133	2363	129	2422	126
2247	128	2305	153	2364	128	2424	126
2248	132	2306	152	2366	128	2426	140
2249	131	2307	152	2367	130	2427	140
2250	156	2308	157	2368	128	2428	140
2251	**128P**	**2309**	**128P**	2369	152	2429	140
2252	127	2310	131	2370	128	2430	153
		2311	153	2371	128		

Highlighted=Toxic when inhaled   **Bold=may polymerize & explode.**

Hazmat

Placard No.	Guide No.	Placard No.	Guide No.	Placard No.	Guide No.	Placard No.	Guide No.
2431	153	2496	156	2573	141	2649	153
2432	153	2498	129	2574	151	2650	153
2433	152	2501	152	2576	137	2651	153
2434	156	2502	132	2577	156	2653	156
2435	156	2503	137	2578	157	2655	151
2436	129	2504	159	2579	153	2656	154
2438	**132**	2505	154	2580	154	2657	153
2439	154	2506	154	2581	154	2658	152
2440	154	2507	154	2582	154	2659	151
2441	135	2508	156	2583	153	2660	153
2442	156	2509	154	2584	153	2661	153
2443	137	2511	153	2585	153	2662	153
2444	137	2512	152	2586	153	2664	160
2445	135	2513	156	2587	153	2666	156
2446	153	2514	130	2588	151	2667	152
2447	136	2515	159	2589	155	2668	131
2448	133	2516	151	2590	171	2669	152
2451	122	2517	115	2591	120	2670	157
2452	**116P**	2518	153	2599	126	2671	153
2453	115	**2520**	**130P**	2600	119	2672	154
2454	115	**2521**	**131P**	2601	115	2673	151
2455	116	**2522**	**153P**	2602	126	2674	154
2456	**130P**	2524	129	2603	131	2676	119
2457	128	2525	156	2604	132	2677	154
2458	130	2526	132	2605	155	2678	154
2459	128	**2527**	**130P**	2606	155	2679	154
2460	128	2528	130	**2607**	**129P**	2680	154
2461	128	2529	132	2608	129	2681	154
2463	138	2530	132	2609	156	2682	157
2464	141	**2531**	**153P**	2610	132	2683	132
2465	140	2533	156	2611	131	2684	132
2466	143	2534	119	2612	127	2685	132
2467	140	2535	132	2614	129	2686	132
2468	140	2536	127	2615	127	2687	133
2469	140	2538	133	2616	129	2688	159
2470	152	2541	128	2617	129	2689	153
2471	154	2542	153	**2618**	**130P**	2690	152
2473	154	2545	135	2619	132	2691	137
2474	157	2546	135	2620	130	2692	157
2475	157	2547	143	2621	127	2693	154
2477	131	2548	124	**2622**	**131P**	2698	156
2478	155	2552	151	2623	133	2699	154
2480	155	**2554**	**130P**	2624	138	**2705**	**153P**
2481	155	2555	113	2626	140	2707	127
2482	155	2556	113	2627	140	2708	127
2483	155	2557	133	2628	151	2709	128
2484	155	2558	131	2629	151	2710	128
2485	155	2560	129	2630	151	2711	129
2486	155	2561	128	2642	154	2713	153
2487	155	2564	153	2643	155	2714	133
2488	155	2565	153	2644	151	2715	133
2490	153	2567	154	2645	153	2716	153
2491	153	2570	154	2646	151	2717	133
2493	132	2571	156	2647	153	2719	141
2495	144	2572	153	2648	154	2720	141
						2721	141

Highlighted=Toxic when inhaled   Bold=may polymerize & explode.

Hazmat

Placard No.	Guide No.	Placard No.	Guide No.	Placard No.	Guide No.	Placard No.	Guide No.
2722	140	2783	152	2854	151	2936	153
2723	140	2784	131	2855	151	2937	153
2724	140	2785	152	2856	151	2938	152
2725	140	2786	153	2857	126	2940	135
2726	140	2787	131	2858	170	2941	153
2727	141	2788	153	2859	154	2942	153
2728	140	2789	132	2861	151	2943	129
2729	152	2790	153	2862	151	2945	132
2730	152	2793	170	2863	154	2946	153
2732	152	2794	154	2864	151	2947	155
2733	132	2795	154	2865	154	2948	153
2734	132	2796	157	2869	157	2949	154
2735	153	2797	154	2870	135	2950	138
2738	153	2798	137	2871	170	2956	149
2739	156	2799	137	2872	159	2965	139
2740	155	2800	154	2873	153	2966	153
2741	141	2801	154	2874	153	2967	154
2742	155	2802	154	2875	151	2968	135
2743	155	2803	172	2876	153	2969	171
2744	155	2805	138	2878	170	2974	164
2745	157	2806	138	2879	157	2975	162
2746	156	2807	171	2880	140	2976	162
2747	156	2809	172	2881	135	2977	166
2748	156	2810	153	2900	158	2978	166
2749	130	2811	154	2901	124	2979	162
2750	153	2812	154	2902	151	2980	162
2751	155	2813	138	2903	131	2981	162
2752	127	2814	158	2904	154	2982	163
2753	153	2815	153	2905	154	**2983**	**129P**
2754	153	2817	154	2907	133	2984	140
2757	151	2818	154	2908	161	2985	155
2758	131	2819	153	2909	161	2986	155
2759	151	2820	153	2910	161	2987	156
2760	131	2821	153	2911	161	2988	139
2761	151	2822	153	2912	162	2989	133
2762	131	2823	153	2913	162	2990	171
2763	151	2826	155	2915	163	2991	131
2764	131	2829	153	2916	163	2992	151
2765	152	2830	139	2917	163	2993	131
2766	131	2831	160	2918	165	2994	151
2767	151	2834	154	2919	163	2995	131
2768	131	2835	138	2920	132	2996	151
2769	151	2837	154	2921	134	2997	131
2770	131	**2838**	**129P**	2922	154	2998	151
2771	151	2839	153	2923	154	2999	131
2772	131	2840	129	2924	132	3000	152
2773	151	2841	131	2925	134	3001	131
2774	131	2842	129	2926	134	3002	151
2775	151	2844	138	2927	154	3003	131
2776	131	2845	135	2928	154	3004	151
2777	151	2846	135	2929	131	3005	131
2778	131	2849	153	2930	134	3006	151
2779	153	2850	128	2931	151	3007	131
2780	131	2851	157	2933	129	3008	151
2781	151	2852	113	2934	129	3009	131
2782	131	2853	151	2935	129	3010	151

Highlighted=Toxic when inhaled   **Bold=may polymerize & explode.**

Hazmat

Placard No.	Guide No.	Placard No.	Guide No.	Placard No.	Guide No.	Placard No.	Guide No.
3011	131	3097	140	3153	115	3220	126
3012	151	3098	140	3154	115	3221	149
3013	131	3099	142	3155	154	3222	149
3014	153	3100	135	3156	122	3223	149
3015	131	3101	146	3157	122	3224	149
3016	151	3102	146	3158	120	3225	149
3017	131	3103	146	3159	126	3226	149
3018	152	3104	146	3160	119	3227	149
3019	131	3105	145	3161	115	3228	149
3020	153	3106	145	3162	123	3229	149
3021	131	3107	145	3163	126	3230	149
3022	**127P**	3108	145	3164	126	3231	150
3023	131	3109	145	3165	131	3232	150
3024	131	3110	145	3166	128	3233	150
3025	131	3111	148	3167	115	3234	150
3026	151	3112	148	3168	119	3235	150
3027	151	3113	148	3169	123	3236	150
3028	154	3114	148	3170	138	3237	150
3048	157	3115	148	3171	154	3238	150
3049	138	3116	148	3172	153	3239	150
3050	138	3117	148	3174	135	3240	150
3051	135	3118	148	3175	133	3241	133
3052	135	3119	148	3176	133	3242	149
3053	135	3120	148	3178	133	3243	151
3054	129	3121	144	3179	134	3244	154
3055	154	3122	142	3180	134	3245	171
3056	129	3123	139	3181	133	3246	156
3057	125	3124	136	3182	170	3247	140
3064	127	3125	139	3183	135	3248	131
3065	127	3126	136	3184	136	3249	151
3066	153	3127	135	3185	136	3250	153
3070	126	3128	136	3186	135	3251	133
3071	131	3129	138	3187	136	3252	115
3072	171	3130	139	3188	135	3253	154
3073	**131P**	3131	138	3189	135	3254	135
3076	138	3132	138	3190	135	3255	135
3077	171	3133	138	3191	136	3256	128
3078	138	3134	139	3192	136	3257	128
3079	**131P**	3135	138	3194	135	3258	171
3080	155	3136	120	3200	135	3259	154
3082	171	3137	140	3203	135	3260	154
3083	124	3138	115	3205	135	3261	154
3084	140	3139	140	3206	136	3262	154
3085	140	3140	151	3207	138	3263	154
3086	141	3141	157	3208	138	3264	154
3087	141	3142	151	3209	138	3265	153
3088	135	3143	151	3210	140	3266	154
3089	170	3144	151	3211	140	3267	153
3090	138	3145	153	3212	140	3268	171
3091	138	3146	153	3213	140	3269	128
3092	129	3147	154	3214	140	3270	133
3093	140	3148	138	3215	140	3271	127
3094	138	3149	140	3216	140	3272	127
3095	136	3150	115	3217	140	3273	131
3096	138	3151	171	3218	140	3274	132
		3152	171	3219	140	3275	131

Highlighted=Toxic when inhaled   Bold=may polymerize & explode.

Hazmat

Placard No.	Guide No.	Placard No.	Guide No.	Placard No.	Guide No.	Placard No.	Guide No.
3276	151	3331	165	3387	142	3444	151
3277	154	3332	164	3388	142	3445	151
3278	151	3333	165	3389	154	3446	152
3279	131	3334	171	3390	154	3447	152
3280	151	3335	171	3391	135	3448	159
3281	151	3336	130	3392	135	3449	159
3282	151	3337	126	3393	135	3450	151
3283	151	3338	126	3394	135	3451	153
3284	151	3339	126	3395	135	3452	153
3285	151	3340	126	3396	138	3453	154
3286	131	3341	135	3397	138	3454	152
3287	151	3342	135	3398	135	3455	153
3288	151	3343	113	3399	138	3456	157
3289	154	3344	113	3400	138	3457	152
3290	154	3345	153	3401	138	3458	152
3291	158	3346	131	3502	138	3459	152
3292	138	3347	131	3403	138	3460	153
3293	152	3348	153	3404	138	3461	135
3294	131	3349	151	3405	141	3462	153
3295	128	3350	131	3406	141	3464	151
3296	126	3351	131	3407	140	3465	151
3297	126	3352	151	3408	141	3466	151
3298	126	3353	126	3409	152	3467	151
3299	126	3354	115	3410	153	3468	115
3300	**119P**	3355	119	3411	153	8000	171
3301	136	3356	140	3413	157	8013	171
3302	152	3357	113	3414	157	8038	171
3303	124	3358	115	3415	154	9035	123
3304	123	3359	171	3416	153	9163	171
3305	119	3360	133	3417	152	9191	143
3306	124	3361	156	3418	151	9192	167
3307	124	3362	155	3419	157	9195	135
3308	123	3363	171	3420	157	9202	168
3309	119	3364	113	3421	154	9206	137
3310	124	3365	113	3422	154	9260	169
3311	122	3366	113	3423	153	9263	156
3312	115	3367	113	3424	141	9264	151
3313	135	3368	113	3425	156	9269	132
3314	171	3369	113	**3426**	**153P**	9275	158
3315	151	3370	113	3427	153	9279	115
3316	171	3371	129	3428	156		
3317	113	3372	138	3429	153		
3318	125	3373	158	3430	153		
3319	113	3374	116	3431	152		
3320	157	3375	140	3432	171		
3321	162	3376	113	3433	135		
3322	162	3377	140	3434	153		
3323	163	3378	140	3435	153		
3324	165	3379	128	3436	151		
3325	165	3380	133	3437	152		
3326	165	3381	151	3438	153		
3327	165	3382	151	3439	151		
3328	165	3383	131	3440	151		
3329	165	3384	131	3441	153		
3330	165	3385	139	3442	153		
		3386	139	3443	152		

Highlighted=Toxic when inhaled   **Bold=may polymerize & explode.**

Hazardous Materials

Notes for Table & Guides

Sulphur - see Sulfur
Poisonous - see Toxic
n.o.s. = not otherwise specified
> = more than
< = less than
$\leq$ = not more than
$\geq$ = not less than; at least
Bold = Polymerization hazards

Highlighted = Toxic when inhaled

Highlighted & Bold = Toxic when inhaled and a polymerization hazard.

Substance	Guide	ID
AC	117	1051
Accumulators, pressurized, pneumatic or hydraulic	126	1956
Acetal	127	1088
Acetaldehyde	129	1089
Acetaldehyde ammonia	171	1841
Acetaldehyde oxime	129	2332
Acetic acid, glacial	132	2789
Acetic acid, solution, > 10% but $\leq$ 80% acid	153	2790
Acetic acid, solution, > 80% acid	132	2789
Acetic anhydride	137	1715
Acetone	127	1090
Acetone cyanohydrin, stabilized	155	1541
Acetone oils	127	1091
Acetonitrile	127	1648
Acetyl bromide	156	1716
Acetyl chloride	155	1717
Acetylene	116	1001
Acetylene, dissolved	116	1001
Acetylene, solvent free	116	3374
Acetylene, Ethylene and Propylene in mixture, refrigerated liquid containing $\geq$ 71.5% Ethylene with $\leq$ 22.5% Acetylene and $\leq$ 6% Propylene	115	3138
Acetylene tetrabromide	159	2504
Acetyl iodide	156	1898
Acetyl methyl carbinol	127	2621
Acid, sludge	153	1906
Acid butyl phosphate	153	1718
Acridine	153	2713
Acrolein, inhibited	**131P**	**1092**
Acrolein, stabilized	**131P**	**1092**
Acrolein dimer, stabilized	**129P**	**2607**
Acrylamide	**153P**	**2074**
Acrylamide, solid	**153P**	**2074**
Acrylamide, solution	**153P**	**2074**
Acrylic acid, inhibited	**132P**	**2218**
Acrylic acid, stabilized	**132P**	**2218**

Hazmat

Substance	Guide	ID
Acrylonitrile, inhibited	**131P**	**1093**
Acrylonitrile, stabilized	**131P**	**1093**
Adamsite	154	1698
Adhesives (flammable)	128	1133
Adiponitrile	153	2205
Aerosol dispensers	126	1950
Aerosols	126	1950
Air, compressed	122	1002
Air, refrigerated liquid (cryogenic liquid)	122	1003
Air, refrigerated liquid (cryogenic liquid), non-pressurized	122	1003
Air bag inflators	171	3268
Air bag inflators, compressed gas	126	3353
Air bag inflators, pyrotechnic	171	3268
Air bag modules	171	3268
Air bag modules, compressed gas	126	3353
Air bag modules, pyrotechnic	171	3268
Aircraft hydraulic power unit fuel tank	131	3165
Alcoholates solution, n.o.s., in alcohol	132	3274
Alcoholic beverages	127	3065
Alcohols, flammable, toxic, n.o.s.	131	1986
Alcohols, n.o.s.	127	1987
Alcohols, toxic, n.o.s.	131	1986
Aldehydes, flammable, toxic, n.o.s.	131	1988
Aldehydes, n.o.s.	129	1989
Aldehydes, toxic, n.o.s.	131	1988
Aldol	153	2839
Aldrin, liquid	131	2762
Aldrin, solid	151	2761
Alkali metal alcoholates, self-heating, corrosive, n.o.s.	136	3206
Alkali metal alloy, liquid, n.o.s.	138	1421
Alkali metal amalgam	138	1389
Alkali metal amalgam, liquid	138	1389
Alkali metal amalgam, solid	138	1389
Alkali metal amalgam, solid	138	3401
Alkali metal amides	139	1390
Alkali metal dispersion	138	1391
Alkaline earth metal alcoholates, n.o.s.	135	3205
Alkaline earth metal alloy, n.o.s.	138	1393
Alkaline earth metal amalgam	138	1392
Alkaline earth metal amalgam, liquid	138	1392
Alkaline earth metal amalgam, solid	138	3402
Alkaline earth metal dispersion	138	1391
Alkaloids, liquid, n.o.s. (toxic)	151	3140
Alkaloids, solid, n.o.s. (toxic)	151	1544
Alkaloid salts, liquid, n.o.s. (toxic)	151	3140
Alkaloid salts, solid, n.o.s. (toxic)	151	1544
Alkylamines, n.o.s.	132	2733
Alkylamines, n.o.s.	132	2734
Alkylamines, n.o.s.	153	2735
Alkyl phenols, liquid, n.o.s. (including C2-C12 homologues)	153	3145
Alkyl phenols, solid, n.o.s. (including C2-C12 homologues)	153	2430
Alkyl sulfonic acids, liquid, with > 5% free Sulfuric acid	153	2584
Alkyl sulfonic acids, liquid, with $\leq$ 5% free Sulfuric acid	153	2586
Alkyl sulfonic acids, solid, with > 5% free Sulfuric acid	153	2583
Alkyl sulfonic acids, solid, with $\leq$ 5% free Sulfuric acid	153	2585
Alkylsulfuric acids	156	2571
Allyl acetate	131	2333

Substance	Guide	ID
Allyl alcohol	131	1098
Allylamine	131	2334
Allyl bromide	131	1099
Allyl chloride	131	1100
Allyl chlorocarbonate	155	1722
Allyl chloroformate	155	1722
Allyl ethyl ether	131	2335
Allyl formate	131	2336
Allyl glycidyl ether	129	2219
Allyl iodide	132	1723
Allyl isothiocyanate, inhibited	155	1545
Allyl isothiocyanate, stabilized	155	1545
Allyltrichlorosilane, stabilized	155	1724
Aluminum, molten	169	9260
Aluminum alkyl halides	135	3052
Aluminum alkyl halides, liquid	135	3052
Aluminum alkyl halides, solid	135	3052
Aluminum alkyl halides, solid	135	3461
Aluminum alkyl hydrides	138	3076
Aluminum alkyls	135	3051
Aluminum borohydride	135	2870
Aluminum borohydride in devices	135	2870
Aluminum bromide, anhydrous	137	1725
Aluminum bromide, solution	154	2580
Aluminum carbide	138	1394
Aluminum chloride, anhydrous	137	1726
Aluminum chloride, solution	154	2581
Aluminum dross	138	3170
Aluminum ferrosilicon powder	139	1395
Aluminum hydride	138	2463
Aluminum nitrate	140	1438
Aluminum phosphide	139	1397
Aluminum phosphide pesticide	157	3048
Aluminum powder, coated	170	1309
Aluminum powder, pyrophoric	135	1383
Aluminum powder, uncoated	138	1396
Aluminum processing by-products	138	3170
Aluminum remelting by-products	138	3170
Aluminum resinate	133	2715
Aluminum silicon powder, uncoated	138	1398
Aluminum smelting by-products	138	3170
Amines, flammable, corrosive, n.o.s.	132	2733
Amines, liquid, corrosive, flammable, n.o.s.	132	2734
Amines, liquid, corrosive, n.o.s.	153	2735
Amines, solid, corrosive, n.o.s.	154	3259
2-Amino-4-chlorophenol	151	2673
2-Amino-5-diethylaminopentane	153	2946
2-Amino-4,6-dinitrophenol, wetted with $\geq$ 20% water	113	3317
2-(2-Aminoethoxy)ethanol	154	3055
N-Aminoethylpiperazine	153	2815
Aminophenols	152	2512
Aminopyridines	153	2671

Hazmat

Substance	Guide	ID
Ammonia, anhydrous	125	1005
Ammonia, anhydrous, liquefied	125	1005
Ammonia, solution, with > 10% but ≤ 35% Ammonia	154	2672
Ammonia, solution, with > 35% but ≤ 50% Ammonia	125	2073
Ammonia solution, with > 50% Ammonia	125	1005
Ammonia solution, with > 50% Ammonia	125	3318
Ammonium arsenate	151	1546
Ammonium bifluoride, solid	154	1727
Ammonium bifluoride, solution	154	2817
Ammonium dichromate	141	1439
Ammonium dinitro-o-cresolate	141	1843
Ammonium dinitro-o-cresolate, solid	141	1843
Ammonium dinitro-o-cresolate, solution	141	3424
Ammonium fluoride	154	2505
Ammonium fluorosilicate	151	2854
Ammonium hydrogendifluoride, solid	154	1727
Ammonium hydrogendifluoride, solution	154	2817
Ammonium hydrogen fluoride, solid	154	1727
Ammonium hydrogen fluoride, solution	154	2817
Ammonium hydrogen sulfate	154	2506
Ammonium hydroxide	154	2672
Ammonium hydroxide, with > 10% but ≤ 35% Ammonia	154	2672
Ammonium metavanadate	154	2859
Ammonium nitrate, liquid (hot concentrated solution)	140	2426
Ammonium nitrate, with ≤ 0.2% combustible substances	140	1942
Ammonium nitrate emulsion	140	3375
Ammonium nitrate fertilizer, n.o.s.	140	2072
Ammonium nitrate fertilizer, with ≤ 0.4% combustible material	140	2071
Ammonium nitrate fertilizers	140	2067
Ammonium nitrate fertilizers	140	2071
Ammonium nitrate fertilizers	140	2072
Ammonium nitrate fertilizers, with Ammonium sulfate	140	2069
Ammonium nitrate fertilizers, with Calcium carbonate	140	2068
Ammonium nitrate fertilizers, with Phosphate or Potash	143	2070
Ammonium nitrate-fuel oil mixtures	112	----
Ammonium nitrate gel	140	3375
Ammonium nitrate mixed fertilizers	140	2069
Ammonium perchlorate	143	1442
Ammonium persulfate	140	1444
Ammonium picrate, wetted with ≥ 10% water	113	1310
Ammonium polysulfide, solution	154	2818
Ammonium polyvanadate	151	2861
Ammonium silicofluoride	151	2854
Ammonium sulfide, solution	132	2683
Ammunition, poisonous, non-explosive	151	2016
Ammunition, tear-producing, non-explosive	159	2017
Ammunition, toxic, non-explosive	151	2016
Amyl acetates	129	1104
Amyl acid phosphate	153	2819
Amyl alcohols	129	1105
Amylamines	132	1106
Amyl butyrates	130	2620
Amyl chloride	129	1107
n-Amylene	128	1108
Amyl formates	129	1109
Amyl mercaptan	130	1111

Substance	Guide	ID
n-Amyl methyl ketone	127	1110
Amyl methyl ketone	127	1110
Amyl nitrate	140	1112
Amyl nitrite	129	1113
Amyltrichlorosilane	155	1728
Anhydrous ammonia	125	1005
Anhydrous ammonia, liquefied	125	1005
Aniline	153	1547
Aniline hydrochloride	153	1548
Anisidines	153	2431
Anisidines, liquid	153	2431
Anisidines, solid	153	2431
Anisole	128	2222
Anisoyl chloride	156	1729
Antimony compound, inorganic, liquid, n.o.s.	157	3141
Antimony compound, inorganic, n.o.s.	157	1549
Antimony compound, inorganic, solid, n.o.s.	157	1549
Antimony lactate	151	1550
Antimony pentachloride, liquid	157	1730
Antimony pentachloride, solution	157	1731
Antimony pentafluoride	157	1732
Antimony potassium tartrate	151	1551
Antimony powder	170	2871
Antimony tribromide, solid	157	1549
Antimony tribromide, solution	157	1549
Antimony trichloride	157	1733
Antimony trichloride, liquid	157	1733
Antimony trichloride, solid	157	1733
Antimony trichloride, solution	157	1733
Antimony trifluoride, solid	157	1549
Antimony trifluoride, solution	157	1549
Aqua regia	157	1798
Argon	121	1006
Argon, compressed	121	1006
Argon, refrigerated liquid (cryogenic liquid)	120	1951
Arsenic	152	1558
Arsenic acid, liquid	154	1553
Arsenic acid, solid	154	1554
Arsenical dust	152	1562
Arsenical pesticide, liquid, flammable, toxic	131	2760
Arsenical pesticide, liquid, toxic	151	2994
Arsenical pesticide, liquid, toxic, flammable	131	2993
Arsenical pesticide, solid, toxic	151	2759
Arsenic bromide	151	1555
Arsenic chloride	157	1560
Arsenic compound, liquid, n.o.s.	152	1556
Arsenic compound, liquid, n.o.s., inorganic	152	1556
Arsenic compound, solid, n.o.s.	152	1557
Arsenic compound, solid, n.o.s., inorganic	152	1557
Arsenic pentoxide	151	1559
Arsenic sulfide	152	1557
Arsenic trichloride	157	1560
Arsenic trioxide	151	1561
Arsenic trisulfide	152	1557
Arsenic trisulphide	152	1557

Substance	Guide	ID
Arsine	119	2188
Articles containing Polychlorinated biphenyls (PCB)	171	2315
Articles, pressurized, hydraulic (containing non-flammable gas)	126	3164
Articles, pressurized, pneumatic (containing non-flammable gas)	126	3164
Aryl sulfonic acids, liquid, with > 5% free Sulfuric acid	153	2584
Aryl sulfonic acids, liquid, with ≤ 5% free Sulfuric acid	153	2586
Aryl sulfonic acids, solid, with > 5% free Sulfuric acid	153	2583
Aryl sulfonic acids, solid, with ≤ 5% free Sulfuric acid	153	2585
Asbestos	171	2212
Asbestos, blue	171	2212
Asbestos, brown	171	2212
Asbestos, white	171	2590
Asphalt	130	1999
Aviation regulated liquid, n.o.s.	171	3334
Aviation regulated solid, n.o.s.	171	3335
1-Aziridinyl phosphine oxide (Tris)	152	2501
Azodicarbonamide	149	3242
Barium	138	1400
Barium alloys, pyrophoric	135	1854
Barium azide, wetted with ≥ 50% water	113	1571
Barium bromate	141	2719
Barium chlorate, solid	141	1445
Barium chlorate, solid	141	1445
Barium chlorate, solution	141	3405
Barium compound, n.o.s.	154	1564
Barium cyanide	157	1565
Barium hypochlorite, with > 22% available Chlorine	141	2741
Barium nitrate	141	1446
Barium oxide	157	1884
Barium perchlorate	141	1447
Barium perchlorate, solid	141	1447
Barium perchlorate, solution	141	3406
Barium permanganate	141	1448
Barium peroxide	141	1449
Batteries, containing Sodium	138	3292
Batteries, dry, containing Potassium hydroxide, solid	154	3028
Batteries, wet, filled with acid	154	2794
Batteries, wet, filled with alkali	154	2795
Batteries, wet, non-spillable	154	2800
Battery fluid, acid	157	2796
Battery fluid, alkali	154	2797
Battery fluid, alkali, with battery	154	2797
Battery fluid, alkali, with electronic equipment or actuating device	154	2797
Battery-powered equipment (wet battery)	154	3171
Battery-powered vehicle (wet battery)	154	3171
Benzaldehyde	129	1990
Benzene	130	1114
Benzene phosphorus dichloride	137	2798
Benzene phosphorus thiodichloride	137	2799
Benzenesulfonyl chloride	156	2225
Benzidine	153	1885
Benzoic derivative pesticide, liquid, flammable, toxic	131	2770
Benzoic derivative pesticide, liquid, toxic	151	3004
Benzoic derivative pesticide, liquid, toxic, flammable	131	3003
Benzoic derivative pesticide, solid, toxic	151	2769

Substance	Guide	ID
Benzonitrile	152	2224
Benzoquinone	153	2587
Benzotrichloride	156	2226
Benzotrifluoride	127	2338
Benzoyl chloride	137	1736
Benzyl bromide	156	1737
Benzyl chloride	156	1738
Benzyl chloroformate	137	1739
Benzyldimethylamine	132	2619
Benzylidene chloride	156	1886
Benzyl iodide	156	2653
Beryllium compound, n.o.s.	154	1566
Beryllium nitrate	141	2464
Beryllium powder	134	1567
Bhusa, wet, damp or contaminated with oil	133	1327
Bicyclo[2.2.1]hepta-2,5-diene	**128P**	**2251**
Bicyclo[2.2.1]hepta-2,5-diene, inhibited	**128P**	**2251**
Bicyclo[2.2.1]hepta-2,5-diene, stabilized	**128P**	**2251**
Biological agents	158	----
(Bio)Medical waste, n.o.s.	158	3291
Bipyridilium pesticide, liquid, flammable, toxic	131	2782
Bipyridilium pesticide, liquid, toxic	151	3016
Bipyridilium pesticide, liquid, toxic, flammable	131	3015
Bipyridilium pesticide, solid, toxic	151	2781
Bisulfates, aqueous solution	154	2837
Bisulfites, aqueous solution, n.o.s.	154	2693
Bisulfites, inorganic, aqueous solution, n.o.s.	154	2693
Blasting agent, n.o.s.	112	----
Bleaching powder	140	2208
Blue asbestos	171	2212
Bombs, smoke, non-explosive, with corrosive liquid, without initiating device	153	2028
Borate and Chlorate mixtures	140	1458
Borneol	133	1312
Boron tribromide	157	2692
Boron trichloride	125	1741
Boron trifluoride	125	1008
Boron trifluoride, compressed	125	1008
Boron trifluoride, dihydrate	157	2851
Boron trifluoride acetic acid complex	157	1742
Boron trifluoride acetic acid complex, liquid	157	1742
Boron trifluoride acetic acid complex, solid	157	3419
Boron trifluoride diethyl etherate	132	2604
Boron trifluoride dimethyl etherate	139	2965
Boron trifluoride propionic acid complex	157	1743
Boron trifluoride propionic acid complex, liquid	157	1743
Boron trifluoride propionic acid complex, solid	157	3420
Bromates, inorganic, aqueous solution, n.o.s.	140	3213
Bromates, inorganic, n.o.s.	141	1450
Bromine	154	1744
Bromine, solution	154	1744
Bromine chloride	124	2901
Bromine pentafluoride	144	1745
Bromine trifluoride	144	1746
Bromoacetic acid	156	1938

Hazmat

Substance	Guide	ID
Bromoacetic acid, solid	156	3425
Bromoacetic acid, solution	156	1938
Bromoacetone	131	1569
Bromoacetyl bromide	156	2513
Bromobenzene	130	2514
Bromobenzyl cyanides	159	1694
Bromobenzyl cyanides, liquid	159	1694
Bromobenzyl cyanides, solid	159	1694
Bromobenzyl cyanides, solid	159	3449
1-Bromobutane	129	1126
2-Bromobutane	130	2339
Bromochlorodifluoromethane	126	1974
Bromochloromethane	160	1887
1-Bromo-3-chloropropane	159	2688
2-Bromoethyl ethyl ether	130	2340
Bromoform	159	2515
1-Bromo-3-methylbutane	130	2341
Bromomethylpropanes	130	2342
2-Bromo-2-nitropropane-1,3-diol	133	3241
2-Bromopentane	130	2343
2-Bromopropane	130	2344
Bromopropanes	130	2344
3-Bromopropyne	129	2345
Bromotrifluoroethylene	116	2419
Bromotrifluoromethane	126	1009
Brown asbestos	171	2212
Brucine	152	1570
Butadienes, inhibited	**116P**	**1010**
Butadienes, stabilized	**116P**	**1010**
Butadienes and hydrocarbon mixture, stabilized	**116P**	**1010**
Butane	115	1011
Butane	115	1075
Butanedione	127	2346
Butane mixture	115	1011
Butane mixture	115	1075
Butanols	129	1120
Butoxyl	127	2708
Butyl acetates	129	1123
Butyl acid phosphate	153	1718
Butyl acrylate	**130P**	**2348**
Butyl acrylates, inhibited	**130P**	**2348**
Butyl acrylates, stabilized	**130P**	**2348**
n-Butylamine	132	1125
N-Butylaniline	153	2738
Butylbenzenes	128	2709
n-Butyl bromide	130	1126
Butyl chloride	130	1127
n-Butyl chloroformate	155	2743
sec-Butyl chloroformate	155	2742
tert-Butylcyclohexyl chloroformate	156	2747
Butylene	115	1012
Butylene	115	1075
1,2-Butylene oxide, stabilized	**127P**	**3022**
Butyl ethers	128	1149
n-Butyl formate	129	1128
tert-Butyl hypochlorite	135	3255
N,n-Butylimidazole	152	2690

Hazmat

Substance	Guide	ID
n-Butyl isocyanate	155	2485
tert-Butyl isocyanate	155	2484
Butyl mercaptan	130	2347
n-Butyl methacrylate	**130P**	**2227**
n-Butyl methacrylate, inhibited	**130P**	**2227**
n-Butyl methacrylate, stabilized	**130P**	**2227**
Butyl methyl ether	127	2350
Butyl nitrites	129	2351
Butyl propionates	130	1914
Butyltoluenes	152	2667
Butyltrichlorosilane	155	1747
5-tert-Butyl-2,4,6-trinitro-m-xylene	149	2956
Butyl vinyl ether, inhibited	**127P**	**2352**
Butyl vinyl ether, stabilized	**127P**	**2352**
1,4-Butynediol	153	2716
Butyraldehyde	129	1129
Butyraldoxime	129	2840
Butyric acid	153	2820
Butyric anhydride	156	2739
Butyronitrile	131	2411
Butyryl chloride	132	2353
Buzz	153	2810
BZ	153	2810
CA	159	1694
Cacodylic acid	151	1572
Cadmium compound	154	2570
Caesium	138	1407
Caesium hydroxide	157	2682
Caesium hydroxide, solution	154	2681
Caesium nitrate	140	1451
Calcium	138	1401
Calcium, metal and alloys, pyrophoric	135	1855
Calcium, pyrophoric	135	1855
Calcium alloys, pyrophoric	135	1855
Calcium arsenate	151	1573
Calcium arsenate and Calcium arsenite mixture, solid	151	1574
Calcium arsenite, solid	151	1574
Calcium arsenite and Calcium arsenate mixture, solid	151	1574
Calcium carbide	138	1402
Calcium chlorate	140	1452
Calcium chlorate, aqueous solution	140	2429
Calcium chlorate, solution	140	2429
Calcium chlorite	140	1453
Calcium chromate	171	9096
Calcium cyanamide, with > 0.1% Calcium carbide	138	1403
Calcium cyanide	157	1575
Calcium dithionite	135	1923
Calcium hydride	138	1404
Calcium hydrosulfite	135	1923
Calcium hypochlorite, dry	140	1748
Calcium hypochlorite, hydrated, with $\geq$ 5.5% but $\leq$ 16% water	140	2880
Calcium hypochlorite, hydrated mixture, with $\geq$ 5.5% but $\leq$ 16% water	140	2880

Substance	Guide	ID
Calcium hypochlorite mixture, dry, with > 10% but ≤ 39% available Chlorine	140	2208
Calcium hypochlorite mixture, dry, with > 39% available Chlorine (8.8% available Oxygen)	140	1748
Calcium manganese silicon	138	2844
Calcium nitrate	140	1454
Calcium oxide	157	1910
Calcium perchlorate	140	1455
Calcium permanganate	140	1456
Calcium peroxide	140	1457
Calcium phosphide	139	1360
Calcium resinate	133	1313
Calcium resinate, fused	133	1314
Calcium silicide	138	1405
Calcium silicon	138	1406
Camphor	133	2717
Camphor, synthetic	133	2717
Camphor oil	128	1130
Caproic acid	153	2829
Carbamate pesticide, liquid, flammable, toxic	131	2758
Carbamate pesticide, liquid, toxic	151	2992
Carbamate pesticide, liquid, toxic, flammable	131	2991
Carbamate pesticide, solid, toxic	151	2757
Carbon, activated	133	1362
Carbon, animal or vegetable origin	133	1361
Carbon bisulfide	131	1131
Carbon dioxide	120	1013
Carbon dioxide, compressed	120	1013
Carbon dioxide, refrigerated liquid	120	2187
Carbon dioxide, solid	120	1845
Carbon dioxide and Ethylene oxide mixture, < 9% but ≤ 87% Ethylene oxide	115	1041
Carbon dioxide and Ethylene oxide mixture, with > 87% Ethylene oxide	**119P**	**3300**
Carbon dioxide and Ethylene oxide mixtures, with > 6% Ethylene oxide	115	1041
Carbon dioxide and Ethylene oxide mixtures, with ≤ 6% Ethylene oxide	126	1952
Carbon dioxide and Ethylene oxide mixtures, with ≤ 9% Ethylene oxide	126	1952
Carbon dioxide and Nitrous oxide mixture	126	1015
Carbon dioxide and Oxygen mixture	122	1014
Carbon dioxide and Oxygen mixture, compressed	122	1014
Carbon disulfide	131	1131
Carbon monoxide	119	1016
Carbon monoxide, compressed	119	1016
Carbon monoxide, refrigerated liquid (cryogenic liquid)	168	9202
Carbon monoxide and Hydrogen mixture	119	2600
Carbon monoxide and Hydrogen mixture, compressed	119	2600
Carbon tetrabromide	151	2516
Carbon tetrachloride	151	1846
Carbonyl fluoride	125	2417
Carbonyl fluoride, compressed	125	2417
Carbonyl sulfide	119	2204

Hazmat

Substance	Guide	ID
Castor beans, meal, pomace or flake	171	2969
Caustic alkali liquid, n.o.s.	154	1719
Caustic potash, dry, solid	154	1813
Caustic potash, liquid	154	1814
Caustic potash, solution	154	1814
Caustic soda, bead	154	1823
Caustic soda, flake	154	1823
Caustic soda, granular	154	1823
Caustic soda, solid	154	1823
Caustic soda, solution	154	1824
Cells, containing Sodium	138	3292
Celluloid, in blocks, rods, rolls, sheets, tubes, etc., except scrap	133	2000
Celluloid, scrap	135	2002
Cerium, slabs, ingots or rods	170	1333
Cerium, turnings or gritty powder	138	3078
Cesium	138	1407
Cesium hydroxide	157	2682
Cesium hydroxide, solution	154	2681
Cesium nitrate	140	1451
CG	125	1076
Charcoal	133	1361
Chemical kit	154	1760
Chemical kit	171	3316
Chemical sample, toxic	151	3315
Chemical sample, toxic liquid	151	3315
Chemical sample, toxic solid	151	3315
Chloral, anhydrous, inhibited	153	2075
Chloral, anhydrous, stabilized	153	2075
Chlorate and Borate mixtures	140	1458
Chlorate and Magnesium chloride mixture	140	1459
Chlorate and Magnesium chloride mixture, solid	140	1459
Chlorate and Magnesium chloride mixture, solution	140	3407
Chlorates, inorganic, aqueous solution, n.o.s.	140	3210
Chlorates, inorganic, n.o.s.	140	1461
Chloric acid, aqueous solution, with ≤ 10% Chloric acid	140	2626
Chlorine	124	1017
Chlorine dioxide, hydrate, frozen	143	9191
Chlorine pentafluoride	124	2548
Chlorine trifluoride	124	1749
Chlorite solution	154	1908
Chlorite solution, with > 5% available Chlorine	154	1908
Chlorites, inorganic, n.o.s.	143	1462
Chloroacetaldehyde	153	2232
Chloroacetic acid, liquid	153	1750
Chloroacetic acid, molten	153	3250
Chloroacetic acid, solid	153	1751
Chloroacetic acid, solution	153	1750
Chloroacetone, stabilized	131	1695
Chloroacetonitrile	131	2668
Chloroacetophenone	153	1697
Chloroacetophenone, liquid	153	1697
Chloroacetophenone, liquid	153	3416
Chloroacetophenone, solid	153	1697

Hazmat

Substance	Guide	ID
Chloroacetyl chloride	156	1752
Chloroanilines, liquid	152	2019
Chloroanilines, solid	152	2018
Chloroanisidines	152	2233
Chlorobenzene	130	1134
Chlorobenzotrifluorides	130	2234
Chlorobenzyl chlorides	153	2235
Chlorobenzyl chlorides, liquid	153	2235
Chlorobenzyl chlorides, solid	153	3427
1-Chloro-3-bromopropane	159	2688
Chlorobutanes	130	1127
Chlorocresols	152	2669
Chlorocresols, liquid	152	2669
Chlorocresols, solid	152	2669
Chlorocresols, solid	152	3437
Chlorocresols, solution	152	2669
Chlorodifluorobromomethane	126	1974
1-Chloro-1,1-difluoroethane	115	2517
Chlorodifluoroethanes	115	2517
Chlorodifluoromethane	126	1018
Chlorodifluoromethane and Chloropentafluoroethane mixture	126	1973
Chlorodinitrobenzenes	153	1577
Chlorodinitrobenzenes, liquid	153	1577
Chlorodinitrobenzenes, solid	153	1577
Chlorodinitrobenzenes, solid	153P	3441
1-Chloro-2,3-epoxypropane	**131P**	**2023**
2-Chloroethanal	153	2232
Chloroform	151	1888
Chloroformates, n.o.s.	155	2742
Chloroformates, toxic, corrosive, flammable, n.o.s.	155	2742
Chloroformates, toxic, corrosive, n.o.s.	154P	3277
Chloromethyl chloroformate	157	2745
Chloromethyl ethyl ether	131	2354
3-Chloro-4-methylphenyl isocyanate	156	2236
3-Chloro-4-methylphenyl isocyanate, liquid	156	2236
3-Chloro-4-methylphenyl isocyanate, solid	156	3428
Chloronitroanilines	153	2237
Chloronitrobenzenes	152	1578
Chloronitrobenzenes, liquid	152	1578
Chloronitrobenzenes, liquid	152	3409
Chloronitrobenzenes, solid	152	1578
Chloronitrotoluenes	152	2433
Chloronitrotoluenes, liquid	152	2433
Chloronitrotoluenes, solid	152	2433
Chloronitrotoluenes, solid	152	3457
Chloropentafluoroethane	126	1020
Chloropentafluoroethane and Chlorodifluoromethane mixture	126	1973
Chlorophenates, liquid	154	2904
Chlorophenates, solid	154	2905
Chlorophenolates, liquid	154	2904
Chlorophenolates, solid	154	2905
Chlorophenols, liquid	153	2021
Chlorophenols, solid	153	2020
Chlorophenyltrichlorosilane	156	1753
Chloropicrin	154	1580
Chloropicrin and Methyl bromide mixture	123	1581
Chloropicrin and Methyl chloride mixture	119	1582

Substance	Guide	ID
Chloropicrin mixture, n.o.s.	154	1583
Chloropivaloyl chloride	156	9263
Chloroplatinic acid, solid	154	2507
Chloroprene, inhibited	**131P**	**1991**
Chloroprene, stabilized	**131P**	**1991**
1-Chloropropane	129	1278
2-Chloropropane	129	2356
3-Chloropropanol-1	153	2849
2-Chloropropene	**130P**	**2456**
2-Chloropropionic acid	153	2511
2-Chloropropionic acid, solid	153	2511
2-Chloropropionic acid, solution	153	2511
2-Chloropyridine	153	2822
Chlorosilanes, corrosive, flammable, n.o.s.	155	2986
Chlorosilanes, corrosive, n.o.s.	156	2987
Chlorosilanes, flammable, corrosive, n.o.s.	155	2985
Chlorosilanes, n.o.s.	155	2985
Chlorosilanes, n.o.s.	155	2986
Chlorosilanes, n.o.s.	156	2987
Chlorosilanes, n.o.s.	139	2988
Chlorosilanes, toxic, corrosive, flammable, n.o.s.	155	3362
Chlorosilanes, toxic, corrosive, n.o.s.	156	3361
Chlorosilanes, water-reactive, flammable, corrosive, n.o.s.	139	2988
Chlorosulfonic acid	137	1754
Chlorosulfonic acid and Sulfur trioxide mixture	137	1754
1-Chloro-1,2,2,2-tetrafluoroethane	126	1021
Chlorotetrafluoroethane	126	1021
Chlorotetrafluoroethane and Ethylene oxide mixture, with ≤ 8.8% Ethylene oxide	126	3297
Chlorotoluenes	130	2238
4-Chloro-o-toluidine hydrochloride	153	1579
4-Chloro-o-toluidine hydrochloride, solid	153	1579
4-Chloro-o-toluidine hydrochloride, solution	153	3410
Chlorotoluidines	153	2239
Chlorotoluidines, liquid	153	2239
Chlorotoluidines, liquid	153	3429
Chlorotoluidines, solid	153	2239
1-Chloro-2,2,2-trifluoroethane	126	1983
Chlorotrifluoroethane	126	1983
Chlorotrifluoromethane	126	1022
Chlorotrifluoromethane and Trifluoromethane azeotropic mixture with approx. 60% Chlorotrifluoromethane	126	2599
Chromic acid, solid	141	1463
Chromic acid, solution	154	1755
Chromic fluoride, solid	154	1756
Chromic fluoride, solution	154	1757
Chromium nitrate	141	2720
Chromium oxychloride	137	1758
Chromium trioxide, anhydrous	141	1463
Chromosulfuric acid	154	2240
CK	125	1589
Clinical specimens	158	3373
Clinical waste, unspecified, n.o.s.	158	3291

Hazmat

Substance	Guide	ID
CN	153	1697
Coal gas	119	1023
Coal gas, compressed	119	1023
Coal tar distillates, flammable	128	1136
Coating solution	127	1139
Cobalt naphthenates, powder	133	2001
Cobalt resinate, precipitated	133	1318
Combustible liquid, n.o.s.	128	1993
Compound, cleaning liquid (corrosive)	154	1760
Compound, cleaning liquid (flammable)	128	1993
Compound, tree or weed killing, liquid (corrosive)	154	1760
Compound, tree or weed killing, liquid (flammable)	128	1993
Compound, tree or weed killing, liquid (toxic)	153	2810
Compressed gas, flammable, n.o.s.	115	1954
Compressed gas, flammable, n.o.s. (Inhalation Hazard Zone A, B, C, or D)	119	1953
Compressed gas, n.o.s.	126	1956
Compressed gas, oxidizing, n.o.s.	122	3156
Compressed gas, toxic, corrosive, n.o.s.	123	3304
Compressed gas, toxic, corrosive, n.o.s. (Inhalation Hazard Zone A, B , C, or D)	123	3304
Compressed gas, toxic, flammable, corrosive, n.o.s.	119	3305
Compressed gas, toxic, flammable, corrosive, n.o.s. (Inhalation Hazard Zone A, B , C, or D)	119	3305
Compressed gas, toxic, flammable, n.o.s.	119	1953
Compressed gas, toxic, flammable, n.o.s. (Inhalation Hazard Zone A, B, C, or D)	119	1953
Compressed gas, toxic, n.o.s.	123	1955
Compressed gas, toxic, n.o.s. (Inhalation Hazard Zone A, B, C, or D)	123	1955
Compressed gas, toxic, oxidizing, corrosive, n.o.s.	124	3306
Compressed gas, toxic, oxidizing, corrosive, n.o.s. (Inhalation Hazard Zone A, B , C, or D)	124	3306
Compressed gas, toxic, oxidizing, n.o.s.	124	3303
Compressed gas, toxic, oxidizing, n.o.s. (Inhalation Hazard Zone A, B, C, or D)	124	3303
Consumer commodity	171	8000
Copper acetoarsenite	151	1585
Copper arsenite	151	1586
Copper based pesticide, liquid, flammable, toxic	131	2776
Copper based pesticide, liquid, toxic	151	3010
Copper based pesticide, liquid, toxic, flammable	131	3009
Copper based pesticide, solid, toxic	151	2775
Copper chlorate	141	2721
Copper chloride	154	2802
Copper cyanide	151	1587
Copra	135	1363
Corrosive liquid, acidic, inorganic, n.o.s.	154	3264
Corrosive liquid, acidic, organic, n.o.s.	153	3265
Corrosive liquid, basic, inorganic, n.o.s.	154	3266
Corrosive liquid, basic, organic, n.o.s.	153	3267
Corrosive liquid, flammable, n.o.s.	132	2920

Substance	Guide	ID
Corrosive liquid, n.o.s.	154	1760
Corrosive liquid, oxidizing, n.o.s.	140	3093
Corrosive liquid, self-heating, n.o.s.	136	3301
Corrosive liquid, toxic, n.o.s.	154	2922
Corrosive liquid, water-reactive, n.o.s.	138	3094
Corrosive liquid, which in contact with water emits flammable gases, n.o.s.	138	3094
Corrosive solid, acidic, inorganic, n.o.s.	154	3260
Corrosive solid, acidic, organic, n.o.s.	154	3261
Corrosive solid, basic, inorganic, n.o.s.	154	3262
Corrosive solid, basic, organic, n.o.s.	154	3263
Corrosive solid, flammable, n.o.s.	134	2921
Corrosive solid, n.o.s.	154	1759
Corrosive solid, oxidizing, n.o.s.	140	3084
Corrosive solid, self-heating, n.o.s.	136	3095
Corrosive solid, toxic, n.o.s.	154	2923
Corrosive solid, water-reactive, n.o.s.	138	3096
Corrosive solid, which in contact with water emits flammable gases, n.o.s.	138	3096
Cotton	133	1365
Cotton, wet	133	1365
Cotton waste, oily	133	1364
Coumarin derivative pesticide, liquid, flammable, toxic	131	3024
Coumarin derivative pesticide, liquid, toxic	151	3026
Coumarin derivative pesticide, liquid, toxic, flammable	131	3025
Coumarin derivative pesticide, solid, toxic	151	3027
Cresols	153	2076
Cresols, liquid	153	2076
Cresols, solid	153	2076
Cresols, solid	153	3455
Cresylic acid	153	2022
Crotonaldehyde, inhibited	**131P**	**1143**
Crotonaldehyde, stabilized	**131P**	**1143**
Crotonic acid	153	2823
Crotonic acid, liquid	153	2823
Crotonic acid, solid	153	2823
Crotonylene	128	1144
CS	153	2810
Cumene	130	1918
Cupriethylenediamine, solution	154	1761
CX	154	2811
Cyanide solution, n.o.s.	157	1935
Cyanides, inorganic, n.o.s.	157	1588
Cyanides, inorganic, solid, n.o.s.	157	1588
Cyanogen	119	1026
Cyanogen, liquefied	119	1026
Cyanogen bromide	157	1889
Cyanogen chloride, inhibited	125	1589
Cyanogen chloride, stabilized	125	1589
Cyanogen gas	119	1026
Cyanuric chloride	157	2670
Cyclobutane	115	2601
Cyclobutyl chloroformate	155	2744
1,5,9-Cyclododecatriene	153	2518
Cycloheptane	128	2241

Substance	Guide	ID
Cycloheptatriene	131	2603
Cycloheptene	128	2242
Cyclohexane	128	1145
Cyclohexanethiol	129	3054
Cyclohexanone	127	1915
Cyclohexene	130	2256
Cyclohexenyltrichlorosilane	156	1762
Cyclohexyl acetate	130	2243
Cyclohexylamine	132	2357
Cyclohexyl isocyanate	155	2488
Cyclohexyl mercaptan	129	3054
Cyclohexyltrichlorosilane	156	1763
Cyclooctadiene phosphines	135	2940
Cyclooctadienes	**130P**	**2520**
Cyclooctatetraene	**128P**	**2358**
Cyclopentane	128	1146
Cyclopentanol	129	2244
Cyclopentanone	128	2245
Cyclopentene	128	2246
Cyclopropane	115	1027
Cyclopropane, liquefied	115	1027
Cymenes	130	2046
DA	151	1699
Dangerous goods in apparatus	171	3363
Dangerous goods in machinery	171	3363
DC	153	2810
Decaborane	134	1868
Decahydronaphthalene	130	1147
n-Decane	128	2247
Denatured alcohol	127	1987
Denatured alcohol (toxic)	131	1986
Desensitized explosive, liquid, n.o.s.	128	3379
Desensitized explosive, solid, n.o.s.	133	3380
Deuterium	115	1957
Deuterium, compressed	115	1957
Devices, small, hydrocarbon gas powered, with release device	115	3150
Diacetone alcohol	129	1148
Diacetyl	127	2346
Diagnostic specimens	158	3373
Diallylamine	132	2359
Diallyl ether	**131P**	**2360**
4,4'-Diaminodiphenylmethane	153	2651
Di-n-amylamine	131	2841
Dibenzyldichlorosilane	156	2434
Diborane	119	1911
Diborane, compressed	119	1911
Diborane mixtures	119	1911
Dibromobenzene	129	2711
1,2-Dibromobutan-3-one	154	2648
Dibromochloropropanes	159	2872
Dibromodifluoromethane	171	1941
Dibromomethane	160	2664
Di-n-butylamine	132	2248
Dibutylaminoethanol	153	2873

Hazmat

Substance	Guide	ID
Dibutyl ethers	128	1149
Dichloroacetic acid	153	1764
1,3-Dichloroacetone	153	2649
Dichloroacetyl chloride	156	1765
Dichloroanilines	153	1590
Dichloroanilines, liquid	153	1590
Dichloroanilines, solid	153	1590
Dichloroanilines, solid	153	3442
o-Dichlorobenzene	152	1591
Dichlorobutene	132	2920
2,2'-Dichlorodiethyl ether	152	1916
Dichlorodifluoromethane	126	1028
Dichlorodifluoromethane and Difluoroethane azeotropic mixture with approximately 74% Dichlorodifluoromethane	126	2602
Dichlorodifluoromethane and Ethylene oxide mixture, with ≤ 12.5% Ethylene oxide	126	3070
Dichlorodifluoromethane and Ethylene oxide mixtures, with ≤ 12% Ethylene oxide	126	3070
Dichlorodimethyl ether, symmetrical	131	2249
1,1-Dichloroethane	130	2362
1,2-Dichloroethylene	**130P**	**1150**
Dichloroethylene	**130P**	**1150**
Dichloroethyl ether	152	1916
Dichlorofluoromethane	126	1029
Dichloroisocyanuric acid, dry	140	2465
Dichloroisocyanuric acid salts	140	2465
Dichloroisopropyl ether	153	2490
Dichloromethane	160	1593
1,1-Dichloro-1-nitroethane	153	2650
Dichloropentanes	130	1152
Dichlorophenyl isocyanates	156	2250
Dichlorophenyltrichlorosilane	156	1766
1,2-Dichloropropane	130	1279
Dichloropropane	130	1279
1,3-Dichloropropanol-2	153	2750
Dichloropropenes	129	2047
Dichlorosilane	119	2189
1,2-Dichloro-1,1,2,2-tetrafluoroethane	126	1958
Dichlorotetrafluoroethane	126	1958
3,5-Dichloro-2,4,6-trifluoropyridine	151	9264
Dicycloheptadiene	**128P**	**2251**
Dicyclohexylamine	153	2565
Dicyclohexylammonium nitrite	133	2687
Dicyclopentadiene	130	2048
1,2-Di-(dimethylamino)ethane	129	2372
Didymium nitrate	140	1465
Dieldrin	151	2761
Diesel fuel	128	1202
Diesel fuel	128	1993
Diethoxymethane	127	2373
3,3-Diethoxypropene	127	2374
Diethylamine	132	1154
2-Diethylaminoethanol	132	2686
Diethylaminoethanol	132	2686
3-Diethylaminopropylamine	132	2684
Diethylaminopropylamine	132	2684
N,N-Diethylaniline	153	2432

Hazmat

Substance	Guide	ID
Diethylbenzene	130	2049
Diethyl carbonate	128	2366
Diethyldichlorosilane	155	1767
Diethylenetriamine	154	2079
Diethyl ether	127	1155
N,N-Diethylethylenediamine	132	2685
Diethyl ketone	127	1156
Diethyl sulfate	152	1594
Diethyl sulfide	129	2375
Diethylthiophosphoryl chloride	155	2751
Diethylzinc	135	1366
Difluorochloroethanes	115	2517
1,1-Difluoroethane	115	1030
Difluoroethane	115	1030
Difluoroethane and Dichlorodifluoromethane azeotropic mixture with approx. 74% dichlorodifluoromethane	126	2602
1,1-Difluoroethylene	**116P**	**1959**
Difluoromethane	115	3252
Difluorophosphoric acid, anhydrous	154	1768
2,3-Dihydropyran	127	2376
Diisobutylamine	132	2361
Diisobutylene, isomeric compounds	128	2050
Diisobutyl ketone	128	1157
Diisooctyl acid phosphate	153	1902
Diisopropylamine	132	1158
Diisopropyl ether	127	1159
Diketene, inhibited	**131P**	**2521**
Diketene, stabilized	**131P**	**2521**
1,1-Dimethoxyethane	127	2377
1,2-Dimethoxyethane	127	2252
Dimethylamine, anhydrous	118	1032
Dimethylamine, aqueous solution	132	1160
Dimethylamine, solution	132	1160
2-Dimethylaminoacetonitrile	131	2378
2-Dimethylaminoethanol	132	2051
2-Dimethylaminoethyl acrylate	152	3302
2-Dimethylaminoethyl methacrylate	**153P**	**2522**
Dimethylaminoethyl methacrylate	**153P**	**2522**
N,N-Dimethylaniline	153	2253
2,3-Dimethylbutane	128	2457
1,3-Dimethylbutylamine	132	2379
Dimethylcarbamoyl chloride	156	2262
Dimethyl carbonate	129	1161
Dimethylcyclohexanes	128	2263
N,N-Dimethylcyclohexylamine	132	2264
Dimethylcyclohexylamine	132	2264
Dimethyldichlorosilane	155	1162
Dimethyldiethoxysilane	127	2380
Dimethyldioxanes	127	2707
Dimethyl disulfide	130	2381
Dimethylethanolamine	132	2051
Dimethyl ether	115	1033
N,N-Dimethylformamide	129	2265
1,1-Dimethylhydrazine	131	1163
1,2-Dimethylhydrazine	131	2382
Dimethylhydrazine, symmetrical	131	2382

Substance	Guide	ID
Dimethylhydrazine, unsymmetrical	131	1163
2,2-Dimethylpropane	115	2044
Dimethyl-N-propylamine	132	2266
Dimethyl sulfate	156	1595
Dimethyl sulfide	130	1164
Dimethyl thiophosphoryl chloride	156	2267
Dimethylzinc	135	1370
Dinitroanilines	153	1596
Dinitrobenzenes	152	1597
Dinitrobenzenes, liquid	152	1597
Dinitrobenzenes, solid	152	1597
Dinitrobenzenes, solid	152	3443
Dinitrochlorobenzenes	153	1577
Dinitro-o-cresol	153	1598
Dinitrogen tetroxide	124	1067
Dinitrogen tetroxide, liquefied	124	1067
Dinitrogen tetroxide and Nitric oxide mixture	124	1975
Dinitrophenol, solution	153	1599
Dinitrophenol, wetted with $\geq$ 15% water	113	1320
Dinitrophenolates, wetted with $\geq$ 15% water	113	1321
Dinitroresorcinol, wetted with $\geq$ 15% water	113	1322
Dinitrotoluenes	152	2038
Dinitrotoluenes, liquid	152	2038
Dinitrotoluenes, molten	152	1600
Dinitrotoluenes, solid	152	2038
Dinitrotoluenes, solid	152	3454
Dioxane	127	1165
Dioxolane	127	1166
Dipentene	128	2052
Diphenylamine chloroarsine	154	1698
Diphenylchloroarsine	151	1699
Diphenylchloroarsine, liquid	151	1699
Diphenylchloroarsine, solid	151	1699
Diphenylchloroarsine, solid	151	3450
Diphenyldichlorosilane	156	1769
Diphenylmethyl bromide	153	1770
Diphosgene	125	1076
Dipicryl sulfide, wetted with $\geq$ 10% water	113	2852
Dipropylamine	132	2383
Di-n-propyl ether	127	2384
Dipropyl ether	127	2384
Dipropyl ketone	128	2710
Disinfectant, liquid, corrosive, n.o.s.	153	1903
Disinfectant, liquid, toxic, n.o.s.	151	3142
Disinfectant, solid, toxic, n.o.s.	151	1601
Disinfectants, corrosive, liquid, n.o.s.	153	1903
Disodium trioxosilicate	154	3253
Disodium trioxosilicate, pentahydrate	154	3253
Dispersant gas, n.o.s.	126	1078
Dispersant gas, n.o.s. (flammable)	115	1954
Dithiocarbamate pesticide, liquid, flammable, toxic	131	2772
Dithiocarbamate pesticide, liquid, toxic	151	3006
Dithiocarbamate pesticide, liquid, toxic, flammable	131	3005
Dithiocarbamate pesticide, solid, toxic	151	2771
Divinyl ether, inhibited	**128P**	**1167**

Hazmat

Substance	Guide	ID
Divinyl ether, stabilized	**128P**	**1167**
DM	154	1698
Dodecylbenzenesulfonic acid	153	2584
Dodecyltrichlorosilane	156	1771
DP	125	1076
Dry ice	120	1845
Dye, liquid, corrosive, n.o.s.	154	2801
Dye, liquid, toxic, n.o.s.	151	1602
Dye, solid, corrosive, n.o.s.	154	3147
Dye, solid, toxic, n.o.s.	151	3143
Dye intermediate, liquid, corrosive, n.o.s.	154	2801
Dye intermediate, liquid, toxic, n.o.s.	151	1602
Dye intermediate, solid, corrosive, n.o.s.	154	3147
Dye intermediate, solid, toxic, n.o.s.	151	3143
ED	151	1892
Elevated temperature liquid, flammable, n.o.s., with flash point above 37.8°C (100°F), at or above its flash point	128	3256
Elevated temperature liquid, flammable, n.o.s., with flash point above 60.5°C (141°F), at or above its flash point	128	3256
Elevated temperature liquid, n.o.s., at or above 100°C (212°F), and below its flash point	128	3257
Elevated temperature solid, n.o.s., at or above 240°C (464°F)	171	3258
Engine starting fluid	115	1960
Engines, internal combustion, flammable gas powered	128	3166
Engines, internal combustion, flammable liquid powered	128	3166
Engines, internal combustion, including when fitted in machinery or vehicles	128	3166
Environmentally hazardous substances, liquid, n.o.s.	171	3082
Environmentally hazardous substances, solid, n.o.s.	171	3077
Epibromohydrin	131	2558
Epichlorohydrin	**131P**	**2023**
1,2-Epoxy-3-ethoxypropane	127	2752
Esters, n.o.s.	127	3272
Ethane	115	1035
Ethane, compressed	115	1035
Ethane, refrigerated liquid	115	1961
Ethane-Propane mixture, refrigerated liquid	115	1961
Ethanol	127	1170
Ethanol, solution	127	1170
Ethanolamine	153	2491
Ethanolamine, solution	153	2491
Ethers, n.o.s.	127	3271
Ethyl acetate	129	1173
Ethylacetylene, inhibited	**116P**	**2452**
Ethylacetylene, stabilized	**116P**	**2452**
Ethyl acrylate, inhibited	**129P**	**1917**
Ethyl acrylate, stabilized	**129P**	**1917**
Ethyl alcohol	127	1170
Ethyl alcohol, solution	127	1170
Ethylamine	118	1036
Ethylamine, aqueous solution, with $\geq$ 50% but $\leq$ 70% Ethylamine	132	2270
2-Ethylaniline	128	2271
2-Ethylaniline	153	2273
N-Ethylaniline	153	2272
Ethylbenzene	130	1175

Substance	Guide	ID
N-Ethyl-N-benzylaniline	153	2274
N-Ethylbenzyltoluidines	153	2753
N-Ethylbenzyltoluidines, liquid	153	2753
N-Ethylbenzyltoluidines, solid	153	2753
N-Ethylbenzyltoluidines, solid	153	3460
Ethyl borate	129	1176
Ethyl bromide	131	1891
Ethyl bromoacetate	155	1603
2-Ethylbutanol	129	2275
2-Ethylbutyl acetate	130	1177
Ethylbutyl acetate	130	1177
Ethyl butyl ether	127	1179
2-Ethylbutyraldehyde	130	1178
Ethyl butyrate	130	1180
Ethyl chloride	115	1037
Ethyl chloroacetate	155	1181
Ethyl chloroformate	155	1182
Ethyl 2-chloropropionate	129	2935
Ethyl chlorothioformate	155	2826
Ethyl crotonate	130	1862
Ethyl cyanoacetate	156	2666
Ethyldichloroarsine	151	1892
Ethyldichlorosilane	139	1183
Ethylene	**116P**	**1962**
Ethylene, Acetylene and Propylene in mixture, refrigerated liquid containing $\geq$ 71.5% Ethylene, $\leq$ 22.5% Acetylene, and $\leq$ 6% Propylene	115	3138
Ethylene, compressed	**116P**	**1962**
Ethylene, refrigerated liquid (cryogenic liquid)	115	1038
Ethylene chlorohydrin	131	1135
Ethylenediamine	132	1604
Ethylene dibromide	154	1605
Ethylene dibromide and Methyl bromide mixture, liquid	151	1647
Ethylene dichloride	131	1184
Ethylene glycol diethyl ether	127	1153
Ethylene glycol monobutyl ether	152	2369
Ethylene glycol monoethyl ether	127	1171
Ethylene glycol monoethyl ether acetate	129	1172
Ethylene glycol monomethyl ether	127	1188
Ethylene glycol monomethyl ether acetate	129	1189
Ethyleneimine, inhibited	**131P**	**1185**
Ethyleneimine, stabilized	**131P**	**1185**
Ethylene oxide	**119P**	**1040**
Ethylene oxide and Carbon dioxide mixture, with > 9% but $\leq$ 87% Ethylene oxide	115	1041
Ethylene oxide and Carbon dioxide mixture, with > 87% Ethylene oxide	**119P**	**3300**
Ethylene oxide and Carbon dioxide mixtures, with > 6% Ethylene oxide	115	1041
Ethylene oxide and Carbon dioxide mixtures, with $\leq$ 6% Ethylene oxide	126	1952
Ethylene oxide and Carbon dioxide mixtures, with $\leq$ 9% Ethylene oxide	126	1952

Substance	Guide	ID
Ethylene oxide and Chlorotetrafluoroethane mixture, with ≤ 8.8% Ethylene oxide	126	3297
Ethylene oxide and Dichlorodifluoromethane mixture, with ≤ 12.5% Ethylene oxide	126	3070
Ethylene oxide and Dichlorodifluoromethane mixtures, with ≤ 12% Ethylene oxide	126	3070
Ethylene oxide and Pentafluoroethane mixture, with ≤ 7.9% Ethylene oxide	126	3298
Ethylene oxide and Propylene oxide mixture, with ≤ 30% Ethylene oxide	**129P**	**2983**
Ethylene oxide and Tetrafluoroethane mixture, with ≤ 5.6% Ethylene oxide	126	3299
Ethylene oxide with Nitrogen	**119P**	**1040**
Ethyl ether	127	1155
Ethyl fluoride	115	2453
Ethyl formate	129	1190
Ethylhexaldehydes	129	1191
2-Ethylhexylamine	132	2276
2-Ethylhexyl chloroformate	156	2748
Ethyl isobutyrate	129	2385
Ethyl isocyanate	155	2481
Ethyl lactate	129	1192
Ethyl mercaptan	129	2363
Ethyl methacrylate	**130P**	**2277**
Ethyl methacrylate, inhibited	**130P**	**2277**
Ethyl methacrylate, stabilized	**130P**	**2277**
Ethyl methyl ether	115	1039
Ethyl methyl ketone	127	1193
Ethyl nitrite, solution	131	1194
Ethyl orthoformate	129	2524
Ethyl oxalate	156	2525
Ethylphenyldichlorosilane	156	2435
Ethyl phosphonothioic dichloride, anhydrous	154	2927
Ethyl phosphonous dichloride, anhydrous	135	2845
Ethyl phosphorodichloridate	154	2927
1-Ethylpiperidine	132	2386
Ethyl propionate	129	1195
Ethyl propyl ether	127	2615
Ethyl silicate	129	1292
Ethylsulfuric acid	156	2571
N-Ethyltoluidines	153	2754
Ethyltrichlorosilane	155	1196
Explosive A	112	----
Explosive B	112	----
Explosive C	114	----
Explosives, division 1.1, 1.2, 1.3, 1.5 or 1.6	112	----
Explosives, division 1.4	114	----
Extracts, aromatic, liquid	127	1169
Extracts, flavoring, liquid	127	1197
Fabrics, animal, synthetic, or vegetable, n.o.s., with oil	133	1373
Fabrics impregnated with weakly nitrated Nitrocellulose, n.o.s.	133	1353
Ferric arsenate	151	1606
Ferric arsenite	151	1607
Ferric chloride	157	1773
Ferric chloride, anhydrous	157	1773

Substance	Guide	ID
Ferric chloride, solution	154	2582
Ferric nitrate	140	1466
Ferrocerium	170	1323
Ferrosilicon	139	1408
Ferrous arsenate	151	1608
Ferrous chloride, solid	154	1759
Ferrous chloride, solution	154	1760
Ferrous metal borings, shavings, turnings, or cuttings	170	2793
Fertilizer, ammoniating solution, with free Ammonia	125	1043
Fibres, animal, synthetic, or vegetable, n.o.s., with oil	133	1373
Fibres, animal or vegetable, burnt, wet, or damp	133	1372
Fibers, animal or vegetable, n.o.s., burnt, wet, or damp	133	1372
Fibres, vegetable, dry	133	3360
Fibres impregnated with weakly nitrated Nitrocellulose, n.o.s.	133	1353
Films, nitrocellulose base	133	1324
Fire extinguisher charges, corrosive liquid	154	1774
Fire extinguishers with compressed gas	126	1044
Fire extinguishers with liquefied gas	126	1044
Firelighters, solid, with flammable liquid	133	2623
First aid kit	171	3316
Fish meal, stabilized	171	2216
Fish meal, unstabilized	133	1374
Fish scrap, stabilized	171	2216
Fish scrap, unstabilized	133	1374
Flammable liquid, corrosive, n.o.s.	132	2924
Flammable liquid, n.o.s.	128	1993
Flammable liquid, toxic, corrosive, n.o.s.	131	3286
Flammable liquid, toxic, n.o.s.	131	1992
Flammable solid, corrosive, inorganic, n.o.s.	134	3180
Flammable solid, corrosive, n.o.s.	134	2925
Flammable solid, corrosive, organic, n.o.s.	134	2925
Flammable solid, inorganic, n.o.s.	133	3178
Flammable solid, n.o.s.	133	1325
Flammable solid, organic, molten, n.o.s.	133	3176
Flammable solid, organic, n.o.s.	133	1325
Flammable solid, oxidizing, n.o.s.	140	3097
Flammable solid, toxic, inorganic, n.o.s.	134	3179
Flammable solid, toxic, n.o.s.	134	2926
Flammable solid, toxic, organic, n.o.s.	134	2926
Fluoboric acid	154	1775
Fluorine	124	1045
Fluorine, compressed	124	1045
Fluorine, refrigerated liquid (cryogenic liquid)	167	9192
Fluoroacetic acid	154	2642
Fluoroanilines	153	2941
Fluorobenzene	130	2387
Fluoroboric acid	154	1775
Fluorophosphoric acid, anhydrous	154	1776
Fluorosilicates, n.o.s.	151	2856
Fluorosilicic acid	154	1778
Fluorosulfonic acid	137	1777
Fluorotoluenes	130	2388
Fluosilicic acid	154	1778
Formaldehyde, solution, flammable	132	1198
Formaldehyde, solutions (Formalin)	132	1198
Formaldehyde, solutions (Formalin) (corrosive)	132	2209
Formic acid	153	1779

Substance	Guide	ID
Fuel, aviation, turbine engine	128	1863
Fuel oil	128	1202
Fuel oil	128	1993
Fuel oil, no. 1,2,4,5,6	128	1202
Fumaryl chloride	156	1780
Fumigated unit	171	3359
Furaldehydes	**132P**	**1199**
Furan	128	2389
Furfural	**132P**	**1199**
Furfuraldehydes	**132P**	**1199**
Furfuryl alcohol	153	2874
Furfurylamine	132	2526
Fusee (rail or highway)	133	1325
Fusel oil	127	1201
GA	153	2810
Gallium	172	2803
Gas, refrigerated liquid, flammable, n.o.s.	115	3312
Gas, refrigerated liquid, n.o.s.	120	3158
Gas, refrigerated liquid, oxidizing, n.o.s.	122	3311
Gas cartridges	115	2037
Gas generator assemblies	171	8013
Gas identification set	123	9035
Gasohol	128	1203
Gas oil	128	1202
Gasoline	128	1203
Gas sample, non-pressurized, flammable, n.o.s., not refrigerated liquid	115	3167
Gas sample, non-pressurized, toxic, flammable, n.o.s., not refrigerated liquid	119	3168
Gas sample, non-pressurized, toxic, n.o.s., not refrigerated liquid	123	3169
GB	153	2810
GD	153	2810
Genetically modified micro-organisms	171	3245
Germane	119	2192
GF	153	2810
Glycerol alpha-monochlorohydrin	153	2689
Glycidaldehyde	**131P**	**2622**
Guanidine nitrate	143	1467
H	153	2810
Hafnium powder, dry	135	2545
Hafnium powder, wetted with ≥ 25% water	170	1326
Halogenated irritating liquid, n.o.s.	159	1610
Hay, wet, damp or contaminated with oil	133	1327
Hazardous waste, liquid, n.o.s.	171	3082
Hazardous waste, solid, n.o.s.	171	3077
HD	153	2810
Heating oil, light	128	1202
Heat producing article	171	8038
Helium	121	1046
Helium, compressed	121	1046
Helium, refrigerated liquid (cryogenic liquid)	120	1963
Heptafluoropropane	126	3296
n-Heptaldehyde	129	3056
Heptanes	128	1206

Substance	Guide	ID
n-Heptene	128	2278
Hexachloroacetone	153	2661
Hexachlorobenzene	152	2729
Hexachlorobutadiene	151	2279
Hexachlorocyclopentadiene	151	2646
Hexachlorophene	151	2875
Hexadecyltrichlorosilane	156	1781
Hexadiene	130	2458
Hexaethyl tetraphosphate	151	1611
Hexaethyl tetraphosphate, liquid	151	1611
Hexaethyl tetraphosphate, solid	151	1611
Hexaethyl tetraphosphate & compressed gas mixture	123	1612
Hexafluoroacetone	125	2420
Hexafluoroacetone hydrate	151	2552
Hexafluoroacetone hydrate, liquid	151	2552
Hexafluoroacetone hydrate, solid	151	3436
Hexafluoroethane	126	2193
Hexafluoroethane, compressed	126	2193
Hexafluorophosphoric acid	154	1782
Hexafluoropropylene	126	1858
Hexafluoropropylene oxide	126	1956
Hexaldehyde	130	1207
Hexamethylenediamine, solid	153	2280
Hexamethylenediamine, solution	153	1783
Hexamethylene diisocyanate	156	2281
Hexamethyleneimine	132	2493
Hexamethylenetetramine	133	1328
Hexamine	133	1328
Hexanes	128	1208
Hexanoic acid	153	2829
Hexanols	129	2282
1-Hexene	128	2370
Hexyltrichlorosilane	156	1784
HL	153	2810
HN-1	153	2810
HN-2	153	2810
HN-3	153	2810
Hydrazine, anhydrous	132	2029
Hydrazine, aqueous solution, with > 37% Hydrazine	153	2030
Hydrazine, aqueous solution, with ≥ 37% and ≤ 64% Hydrazine	153	2030
Hydrazine, aqueous solutions, with ≤ 37% Hydrazine	152	3293
Hydrazine, aqueous solutions, with ≥ 64% Hydrazine	132	2029
Hydrazine hydrate	153	2030
Hydrides, metal, n.o.s.	138	1409
Hydriodic acid	154	1787
Hydriodic acid, solution	154	1787
Hydrobromic acid	154	1788
Hydrobromic acid, solution	154	1788
Hydrocarbon gas, compressed, n.o.s.	115	1964
Hydrocarbon gas, liquefied, n.o.s.	115	1965
Hydrocarbon gas mixture, compressed, n.o.s.	115	1964
Hydrocarbon gas mixture, liquefied, n.o.s.	115	1965
Hydrocarbon gas refills for small devices, with release device	115	3150
Hydrocarbons, liquid, n.o.s.	128	3295

Hazmat

Substance	Guide	ID
Hydrochloric acid	157	1789
Hydrochloric acid, solution	157	1789
Hydrocyanic acid, aqueous solution, with < 5% Hydrogen cyanide	154	1613
Hydrocyanic acid, aqueous solution, with ≤ 20% Hydrogen cyanide	154	1613
Hydrocyanic acid, aqueous solutions, with > 20% Hydrogen cyanide	117	1051
Hydrocyanic acid, liquefied	117	1051
Hydrofluoric acid	157	1790
Hydrofluoric acid, solution	157	1790
Hydrofluoric acid and Sulfuric acid mixture	157	1786
Hydrofluorosilicic acid	154	1778
Hydrogen	115	1049
Hydrogen, absorbed in metal hydride	115	9279
Hydrogen, compressed	115	1049
Hydrogen, in a metal hydride storage system	115	3468
Hydrogen, refrigerated liquid (cryogenic liquid)	115	1966
Hydrogen and Carbon monoxide mixture	119	2600
Hydrogen and Carbon monoxide mixture, compressed	119	2600
Hydrogen and Methane mixture, compressed	115	2034
Hydrogen bromide, anhydrous	125	1048
Hydrogen chloride, anhydrous	125	1050
Hydrogen chloride, refrigerated liquid	125	2186
Hydrogen cyanide, anhydrous, stabilized	117	1051
Hydrogen cyanide, anhydrous, stabilized (absorbed)	152	1614
Hydrogen cyanide, aqueous solution, with ≤ 20% Hydrogen cyanide	154	1613
Hydrogen cyanide, solution in alcohol, with ≤ 45% Hydrogen cyanide	131	3294
Hydrogen cyanide, stabilized	117	1051
Hydrogen cyanide, stabilized (absorbed)	152	1614
Hydrogendifluorides, n.o.s.	154	1740
Hydrogen fluoride, anhydrous	125	1052
Hydrogen iodide, anhydrous	125	2197
Hydrogen peroxide, aqueous solution, stabilized, with > 60% Hydrogen peroxide	143	2015
Hydrogen peroxide, aqueous solution, with ≥ 8% but < 20% Hydrogen peroxide	140	2984
Hydrogen peroxide, aqueous solution, with ≥ 20% but ≤ 60% Hydrogen peroxide (stabilized as necessary)	140	2014
Hydrogen peroxide, stabilized	143	2015
Hydrogen peroxide and Peroxyacetic acid mixture, with acid(s), water, and ≤ 5% acetic acid, stabilized	140	3149
Hydrogen selenide, anhydrous	117	2202
Hydrogen sulfide	117	1053
Hydrogen sulfide, liquefied	117	1053
Hydroquinone	153	2662
Hydroquinone, solid	153	2662
Hydroquinone, solution	153	3435

Hazmat

Substance	Guide	ID
Hydroxylamine sulfate	154	2865
Hypochlorite solution	154	1791
Hypochlorite solution, with > 5% available Chlorine	154	1791
Hypochlorites, inorganic, n.o.s.	140	3212
3,3'-Iminodipropylamine	153	2269
Infectious substance, affecting animals only	158	2900
Infectious substance, affecting humans	158	2814
Ink, printer's, flammable	129	1210
Insecticide gas, flammable, n.o.s.	115	1954
Insecticide gas, flammable, n.o.s.	115	3354
Insecticide gas, n.o.s.	126	1968
Insecticide gas, toxic, flammable, n.o.s.	119	3355
Insecticide gas, toxic, flammable, n.o.s. (Inhalation Hazard Zone A, B, C, or D)	119	3355
Insecticide gas, toxic, n.o.s.	123	1967
Iodine monochloride	157	1792
Iodine pentafluoride	144	2495
2-Iodobutane	129	2390
Iodomethylpropanes	129	2391
Iodopropanes	129	2392
IPDI	156	2290
Iron oxide, spent	135	1376
Iron pentacarbonyl	131	1994
Iron sponge, spent	135	1376
Isobutane	115	1075
Isobutane	115	1969
Isobutane mixture	115	1075
Isobutane mixture	115	1969
Isobutanol	129	1212
Isobutyl acetate	129	1213
Isobutyl acrylate	**130P**	**2527**
Isobutyl acrylate, inhibited	**130P**	**2527**
Isobutyl acrylate, stabilized	**130P**	**2527**
Isobutyl alcohol	129	1212
Isobutyl aldehyde	129	2045
Isobutylamine	132	1214
Isobutyl chloroformate	155	2742
Isobutylene	115	1055
Isobutylene	115	1075
Isobutyl formate	129	2393
Isobutyl isobutyrate	130	2528
Isobutyl isocyanate	155	2486
Isobutyl methacrylate	**130P**	**2283**
Isobutyl methacrylate, inhibited	**130P**	**2283**
Isobutyl methacrylate, stabilized	**130P**	**2283**
Isobutyl propionate	129	2394
Isobutyraldehyde	130	2045
Isobutyric acid	132	2529
Isobutyric anhydride	132	2530
Isobutyronitrile	131	2284
Isobutyryl chloride	132	2395
Isocyanate solution, flammable, toxic, n.o.s.	155	2478
Isocyanate solution, toxic, flammable, n.o.s.	155	3080
Isocyanate solution, toxic, n.o.s.	155	2206
Isocyanate solutions, n.o.s.	155	2206

Hazmat

Substance	Guide	ID
Isocyanate solutions, n.o.s.	155	2478
Isocyanate solutions, n.o.s.	155	3080
Isocyanates, flammable, toxic, n.o.s.	155	2478
Isocyanates, n.o.s.	155	2206
Isocyanates, n.o.s.	155	2478
Isocyanates, n.o.s.	155	3080
Isocyanates, toxic, flammable, n.o.s.	155	3080
Isocyanates, toxic, n.o.s.	155	2206
Isocyanatobenzotrifluorides	156	2285
Isoheptenes	128	2287
Isohexenes	128	2288
Isooctane	128	1262
Isooctene	128	1216
Isopentane	128	1265
Isopentenes	128	2371
Isophoronediamine	153	2289
Isophorone diisocyanate	156	2290
Isoprene, inhibited	**130P**	**1218**
Isoprene, stabilized	**130P**	**1218**
Isopropanol	129	1219
Isopropenyl acetate	**129P**	**2403**
Isopropenylbenzene	128	2303
Isopropyl acetate	129	1220
Isopropyl acid phosphate	153	1793
Isopropyl alcohol	129	1219
Isopropylamine	132	1221
Isopropylbenzene	130	1918
Isopropyl butyrate	129	2405
Isopropyl chloroacetate	155	2947
Isopropyl chloroformate	155	2407
Isopropyl 2-chloropropionate	129	2934
Isopropyl isobutyrate	127	2406
Isopropyl isocyanate	155	2483
Isopropyl nitrate	130	1222
Isopropyl propionate	129	2409
Isosorbide dinitrate mixture	133	2907
Isosorbide-5-mononitrate	133	3251
Kerosene	128	1223
Ketones, liquid, n.o.s.	127	1224
Krypton	121	1056
Krypton, compressed	121	1056
Krypton, refrigerated liquid (cryogenic liquid)	120	1970
L (Lewisite)	153	2810
Lead acetate	151	1616
Lead arsenates	151	1617
Lead arsenites	151	1618
Lead compound, soluble, n.o.s.	151	2291
Lead cyanide	151	1620
Lead dioxide	141	1872
Lead nitrate	141	1469
Lead perchlorate	141	1470
Lead perchlorate, solid	141	1470
Lead perchlorate, solution	141	1470
Lead perchlorate, solution	141	3408
Lead phosphite, dibasic	133	2989
Lead sulfate, with > 3% free acid	154	1794

Substance	Guide	ID
Lewisite	153	2810
Life-saving appliances, not self-inflating	171	3072
Life-saving appliances, self-inflating	171	2990
Lighter refills (cigarettes) (flammable gas)	115	1057
Lighters (cigarettes) (flammable gas)	115	1057
Lighters for cigars, cigarettes (flammable liquid)	127	1226
Liquefied gas (nonflammable)	120	1058
Liquefied gas, flammable, n.o.s.	115	1954
Liquefied gas, flammable, n.o.s.	115	3161
Liquefied gas, flammable, toxic, n.o.s.	119	1953
Liquefied gas, flammable, toxic, n.o.s. (Inhalation Hazard Zone A, B, C, or D)	119	1953
Liquefied gas, n.o.s.	126	1956
Liquefied gas, n.o.s.	126	3163
Liquefied gas, oxidizing, n.o.s.	122	3157
Liquefied gas, toxic, corrosive, n.o.s.	123	3308
Liquefied gas, toxic, corrosive, n.o.s. (Inhalation Hazard Zone A, B, C, or D)	123	3308
Liquefied gas, toxic, flammable, corrosive, n.o.s.	119	3309
Liquefied gas, toxic, flammable, corrosive, n.o.s. (Inhalation Hazard Zone A, B , C, or D)	119	3309
Liquefied gas, toxic, flammable, n.o.s.	119	3160
Liquefied gas, toxic, flammable, n.o.s. (Inhalation Hazard Zone A, B , C, or D)	119	3160
Liquefied gas, toxic, n.o.s.	123	1955
Liquefied gas, toxic, n.o.s.	123	3162
Liquefied gas, toxic, n.o.s. (Inhalation Hazard Zone A, B, C, or D)	123	1955
Liquefied gas, toxic, n.o.s. (Inhalation Hazard Zone A, B, C, or D)	123	3162
Liquefied gas, toxic, oxidizing, corrosive, n.o.s.	124	3310
Liquefied gas, toxic, oxidizing, corrosive, n.o.s. (Inhalation Hazard Zone A, B, C, or D)	124	3310
Liquefied gas, toxic, oxidizing, n.o.s.	124	3307
Liquefied gas, toxic, oxidizing, n.o.s. (Inhalation Hazard Zone A, B , C, or D)	124	3307
Liquiefied gases, non-flammable, charged with Nitrogen, Carbon dioxide, or Air	120	1058
Liquefied natural gas (cryogenic liquid)	115	1972
Liquefied petroleum gas	115	1075
Lithium	138	1415
Lithium alkyls	135	2445
Lithium alkyls, liquid	135	2445
Lithium alkyls, solid	135	3433
Lithium aluminum hydride	138	1410
Lithium aluminum hydride, ethereal	138	1411
Lithium amide	139	1412
Lithium batteries	138	3090
Lithium batteries, liquid or solid cathode	138	3090
Lithium batteries contained in equipment	138	3091
Lithium batteries packed with equipment	138	3091

Substance	Guide	ID
Lithium borohydride	138	1413
Lithium ferrosilicon	139	2830
Lithium hydride	138	1414
Lithium hydride, fused solid	138	2805
Lithium hydroxide	154	2680
Lithium hydroxide, monohydrate	154	2680
Lithium hydroxide, solid	154	2680
Lithium hydroxide, solution	154	2679
Lithium hypochlorite, dry	140	1471
Lithium hypochlorite mixture	140	1471
Lithium hypochlorite mixtures, dry	140	1471
Lithium nitrate	140	2722
Lithium nitride	138	2806
Lithium peroxide	143	1472
Lithium silicon	138	1417
LNG (cryogenic liquid)	115	1972
London purple	151	1621
LPG	115	1075
Magnesium	138	1869
Magnesium, in pellets, turnings, or ribbons	138	1869
Magnesium alkyls	135	3053
Magnesium alloys, with > 50% Magnesium, in pellets, turnings or ribbons	138	1869
Magnesium alloys powder	138	1418
Magnesium aluminum phosphide	139	1419
Magnesium arsenate	151	1622
Magnesium bromate	140	1473
Magnesium chlorate	140	2723
Magnesium chloride and Chlorate mixture	140	1459
Magnesium chloride and Chlorate mixture, solid	140	1459
Magnesium chloride and Chlorate mixture, solution	140	3407
Magnesium diamide	135	2004
Magnesium diphenyl	135	2005
Magnesium fluorosilicate	151	2853
Magnesium granules, coated	138	2950
Magnesium hydride	138	2010
Magnesium nitrate	140	1474
Magnesium perchlorate	140	1475
Magnesium peroxide	140	1476
Magnesium phosphide	139	2011
Magnesium powder	138	1418
Magnesium silicide	138	2624
Magnesium silicofluoride	151	2853
Magnetized material	171	2807
Maleic acid	156	2215
Maleic anhydride	156	2215
Maleic anhydride, molten	156	2215
Malononitrile	153	2647
Maneb	135	2210
Maneb, stabilized	135	2968
Maneb preparation, stabilized	135	2968
Maneb preparation, with ≥ 60% Maneb	135	2210
Manganese nitrate	140	2724
Manganese resinate	133	1330
Matches, fusee	133	2254
Matches, safety	133	1944

Hadmat

Substance	Guide	ID
Matches, "strike anywhere"	133	1331
Matches, wax "vesta"	133	1945
MD	152	1556
Medical waste, n.o.s.	158	3291
Medicine, liquid, flammable, toxic, n.o.s.	131	3248
Medicine, liquid, toxic, n.o.s.	151	1851
Medicine, solid, toxic, n.o.s.	151	3249
Medicines, corrosive, liquid, n.o.s.	154	1760
Medicines, corrosive, solid, n.o.s.	154	1759
Medicines, flammable, liquid, n.o.s.	128	1993
Medicines, flammable, solid, n.o.s.	133	1325
Medicines, oxidizing substances, solid, n.o.s.	140	1479
Mercaptan mixture, liquid, flammable, n.o.s.	130	3336
Mercaptan mixture, liquid, flammable, toxic, n.o.s.	131	1228
Mercaptan mixture, liquid, toxic, flammable, n.o.s.	131	3071
Mercaptan mixtures, liquid, n.o.s.	131	1228
Mercaptan mixtures, liquid, n.o.s.	131	3071
Mercaptans, liquid, flammable, n.o.s.	130	3336
Mercaptans, liquid, flammable, toxic, n.o.s.	131	1228
Mercaptans, liquid, n.o.s.	131	3071
Mercaptans, liquid, toxic, flammable, n.o.s.	131	3071
Mercuric arsenate	151	1623
Mercuric bromide	154	1634
Mercuric chloride	154	1624
Mercuric cyanide	154	1636
Mercuric nitrate	141	1625
Mercuric oxycyanide	151	1642
Mercuric potassium cyanide	157	1626
Mercuric sulfate	151	1645
Mercurous bromide	154	1634
Mercurous nitrate	141	1627
Mercury	172	2809
Mercury acetate	151	1629
Mercury ammonium chloride	151	1630
Mercury based pesticide, liquid, flammable, toxic	131	2778
Mercury based pesticide, liquid, toxic	151	3012
Mercury based pesticide, liquid, toxic, flammable	131	3011
Mercury based pesticide, solid, toxic	151	2777
Mercury benzoate	154	1631
Mercury bromides	154	1634
Mercury compound, liquid, n.o.s.	151	2024
Mercury compound, solid, n.o.s.	151	2025
Mercury cyanide	154	1636
Mercury gluconate	151	1637
Mercury iodide	151	1638
Mercury metal	172	2809
Mercury nucleate	151	1639
Mercury oleate	151	1640
Mercury oxide	151	1641
Mercury oxycyanide, desensitized	151	1642
Mercury potassium iodide	151	1643
Mercury salicylate	151	1644
Mercury sulfate	151	1645
Mercury thiocyanate	151	1646
Mesityl oxide	129	1229
Metal alkyl, solution, n.o.s.	135	9195
Metal alkyl halides, n.o.s.	138	3049

Substance	Guide	ID
Metal alkyl halides, water-reactive, n.o.s.	138	3049
Metal alkyl hydrides, n.o.s.	138	3050
Metal alkyl hydrides, water-reactive, n.o.s.	138	3050
Metal alkyls, n.o.s.	135	2003
Metal alkyls, water-reactive, n.o.s.	135	2003
Metal aryl halides, n.o.s.	138	3049
Metal aryl halides, water-reactive, n.o.s.	138	3049
Metal aryl hydrides, n.o.s.	138	3050
Metal aryl hydrides, water-reactive, n.o.s.	138	3050
Metal aryls, n.o.s	135	2003
Metal aryls, water-reactive, n.o.s.	135	2003
Metal carbonyls, liquid, n.o.s.	151	3281
Metal carbonyls, n.o.s.	151	3281
Metal carbonyls, solid, n.o.s.	151	3466
Metal catalyst, dry	135	2881
Metal catalyst, wetted	170	1378
Metaldehyde	133	1332
Metal hydrides, flammable, n.o.s.	170	3182
Metal hydrides, water-reactive, n.o.s.	138	1409
Metallic substance, water-reactive, n.o.s.	138	3208
Metallic substance, water-reactive, self-heating, n.o.s.	138	3209
Metal powder, flammable, n.o.s.	170	3089
Metal powder, self-heating, n.o.s.	135	3189
Metal salts of organic compounds, flammable, n.o.s.	133	3181
Methacrylaldehyde	**131P**	**2396**
Methacrylaldehyde, inhibited	**131P**	**2396**
Methacrylaldehyde, stabilized	**131P**	**2396**
Methacrylic acid, inhibited	**153P**	**2531**
Methacrylic acid, stabilized	**153P**	**2531**
Methacrylonitrile, inhibited	**131P**	**3079**
Methacrylonitrile, stabilized	**131P**	**3079**
Methallyl alcohol	129	2614
Methane	115	1971
Methane, compressed	115	1971
Methane, refrigerated liquid (cryogenic liquid)	115	1972
Methane and Hydrogen mixture, compressed	115	2034
Methanesulfonyl chloride	156	3246
Methanol	131	1230
Methoxymethyl isocyanate	155	2605
4-Methoxy-4-methyl-pentan-2-one	128	2293
1-Methoxy-2-propanol	129	3092
Methyl acetate	129	1231
Methylacetylene and Propadiene mixture, stabilized	**116P**	**1060**
Methyl acrylate, inhibited	**129P**	**1919**
Methyl acrylate, stabilized	**129P**	**1919**
Methylal	127	1234
Methyl alcohol	131	1230
Methylallyl chloride	**129P**	**2554**
Methylamine, anhydrous	118	1061
Methylamine, aqueous solution	132	1235
Methylamyl acetate	130	1233
Methylamyl alcohol	129	2053
Methyl amyl ketone	127	1110
N-Methylaniline	153	2294

Substance	Guide	ID
Methyl benzoate	152	2938
alpha-Methylbenzyl alcohol	153	2937
alpha-Methylbenzyl alcohol, liquid	153	2937
alpha-Methylbenzyl alcohol, solid	153	3438
Methylbenzyl alcohol (alpha)	153	2937
Methyl bromide	123	1062
Methyl bromide and Chloropicrin mixtures	123	1581
Methyl bromide and Ethylene dibromide mixture, liquid	151	1647
Methyl bromoacetate	155	2643
2-Methylbutanal	129	3371
3-Methylbutan-2-one	127	2397
2-Methyl-1-butene	128	2459
2-Methyl-2-butene	128	2460
3-Methyl-1-butene	128	2561
N-Methylbutylamine	132	2945
Methyl tert-butyl ether	127	2398
Methyl butyrate	129	1237
Methyl chloride	115	1063
Methyl chloride and Chloropicrin mixtures	119	1582
Methyl chloride and Methylene chloride mixture	115	1912
Methyl chloroacetate	155	2295
Methyl chloroformate	155	1238
Methyl chloromethyl ether	131	1239
Methyl 2-chloropropionate	129	2933
Methylchlorosilane	119	2534
Methyl cyanide	127	1648
Methylcyclohexane	128	2296
Methylcyclohexanols	129	2617
Methylcyclohexanone	128	2297
Methylcyclopentane	128	2298
Methyl dichloroacetate	155	2299
Methyldichloroarsine	152	1556
Methyldichlorosilane	139	1242
Methylene chloride	160	1593
Methylene chloride and Methyl chloride mixture	115	1912
Methyl ethyl ether	115	1039
Methyl ethyl ketone	127	1193
2-Methyl-5-ethylpyridine	153	2300
Methyl fluoride	115	2454
Methyl formate	129	1243
2-Methylfuran	128	2301
2-Methyl-2-hepthanethiol	131	3023
5-Methylhexan-2-one	127	2302
Methylhydrazine	131	1244
Methyl iodide	151	2644
Methyl isobutyl carbinol	129	2053
Methyl isobutyl ketone	127	1245
Methyl isocyanate	155	2480
Methyl isopropenyl ketone, inhibited	**127P**	**1246**
Methyl isopropenyl ketone, stabilized	**127P**	**1246**
Methyl isothiocyanate	131	2477
Methyl isovalerate	130	2400

Hazmat

Substance	Guide	ID
Methyl magnesium bromide in Ethyl ether	135	1928
Methyl mercaptan	117	1064
Methyl methacrylate monomer, inhibited	**129P**	**1247**
Methyl methacrylate monomer, stabilized	**129P**	**1247**
4-Methylmorpholine	132	2535
N-Methylmorpholine	132	2535
Methylmorpholine	132	2535
Methyl nitrite	116	2455
Methyl orthosilicate	155	2606
Methyl parathion, liquid	152	3018
Methyl parathion, solid	152	2783
Methylpentadiene	128	2461
2-Methylpentan-2-ol	129	2560
Methylphenyldichlorosilane	156	2437
Methyl phosphonic dichloride	137	9206
Methyl phosphonous dichloride	135	2845
1-Methylpiperidine	132	2399
Methyl propionate	129	1248
Methyl propyl ether	127	2612
Methyl propyl ketone	127	1249
Methyltetrahydrofuran	127	2536
Methyl trichloroacetate	156	2533
Methyltrichlorosilane	155	1250
alpha-Methylvaleraldehyde	130	2367
Methyl valeraldehyde (alpha)	130	2367
Methyl vinyl ketone	**131P**	**1251**
Methyl vinyl ketone, stabilized	**131P**	**1251**
M.I.B.C.	129	2053
Molybdenum pentachloride	156	2508
Monoethanolamine	153	2491
Mononitrotoluidines	153	2660
Monopropylamine	132	1277
Morpholine	132	2054
Motor fuel anti-knock mixture	131	1649
Motor spirit	128	1203
Muriatic acid	157	1789
Musk xylene	149	2956
Mustard	153	2810
Mustard Lewisite	153	2810
Naphthalene, crude	133	1334
Naphthalene, molten	133	2304
Naphthalene, refined	133	1334
alpha-Naphthylamine	153	2077
Naphthylamine (alpha)	153	2077
beta-Naphthylamine	153	1650
beta-Naphthylamine, solid	153	1650
beta-Naphthylamine, solution	153	3411
Naphthylamine (beta)	153	1650
Naphthylamine (beta), solid	153	1650
Naphthylamine (beta), solution	153	3411
Naphthylthiourea	153	1651
Naphthylurea	153	1652
Natural gas, compressed	115	1971
Natural gas, refrigerated liquid (cryogenic liquid)	115	1972

Substance	Guide	ID
Neohexane	128	1208
Neon	121	1065
Neon, compressed	121	1065
Neon, refrigerated liquid (cryogenic liquid)	120	1913
Nickel carbonyl	131	1259
Nickel catalyst, dry	135	2881
Nickel cyanide	151	1653
Nickel nitrate	140	2725
Nickel nitrite	140	2726
Nicotine	151	1654
Nicotine compound, liquid, n.o.s.	151	3144
Nicotine compound, solid, n.o.s.	151	1655
Nicotine hydrochloride	151	1656
Nicotine hydrochloride, liquid	151	1656
Nicotine hydrochloride, solid	151	1656
Nicotine hydrochloride, solid	151	3444
Nicotine hydrochloride, solution	151	1656
Nicotine preparation, liquid, n.o.s.	151	3144
Nicotine preparation, solid, n.o.s.	151	1655
Nicotine salicylate	151	1657
Nicotine sulfate, solid	151	1658
Nicotine sulfate, solid	151	3445
Nicotine sulfate, solution	151	1658
Nicotine tartrate	151	1659
Nitrates, inorganic, aqueous solution, n.o.s.	140	3218
Nitrates, inorganic, n.o.s.	140	1477
Nitrating acid mixture	157	1796
Nitrating acid mixture, spent	157	1826
Nitric acid, fuming	157	2032
Nitric acid, other than red fuming	157	2031
Nitric acid, red fuming	157	2032
Nitric oxide	124	1660
Nitric oxide, compressed	124	1660
Nitric oxide and Dinitrogen tetroxide mixture	124	1975
Nitric oxide and Nitrogen dioxide mixture	124	1975
Nitric oxide and Nitrogen tetroxide mixture	124	1975
Nitriles, flammable, toxic, n.o.s.	131	3273
Nitriles, toxic, flammable, n.o.s.	131	3275
Nitriles, toxic, liquid, n.o.s.	151	3276
Nitriles, toxic, n.o.s.	151	3276
Nitriles, toxic, solid, n.o.s.	151	3439
Nitrites, inorganic, aqueous solution, n.o.s.	140	3219
Nitrites, inorganic, n.o.s.	140	2627
Nitroanilines	153	1661
Nitroanisole	152	2730
Nitroanisole, liquid	152	2730
Nitroanisole, solid	152	2730
Nitroanisole, solid	152	3458
Nitrobenzene	152	1662
Nitrobenzenesulfonic acid	153	2305
Nitrobenzotrifluorides	152	2306
Nitrobenzotrifluorides, liquid	152	2306
Nitrobenzotrifluorides, solid	152	3431
Nitrobromobenzene	152	2732

Hazmat

Substance	Guide	ID
Nitrobromobenzene, liquid	152	2732
Nitrobromobenzene, solid	152	2732
Nitrobromobenzene, solid	152	3459
Nitrocellulose, solution, flammable	127	2059
Nitrocellulose, solution, in a flammable liquid	127	2059
Nitrocellulose membrane filters	133	3270
Nitrocellulose mixture, without plasticizer, without pigment	133	2557
Nitrocellulose mixture, without plasticizer, with pigment	133	2557
Nitrocellulose mixture, with plasticizer, without pigment	133	2557
Nitrocellulose mixture, with plasticizer, with pigment	133	2557
Nitrocellulose with alcohol	113	2556
Nitrocellulose with ≥ 25% alcohol	113	2556
Nitrocellulose with plasticizing substance	133	2557
Nitrocellulose with water, ≥ 25% water	113	2555
3-Nitro-4-chlorobenzotrifluoride	152	2307
Nitrocresols	153	2446
Nitrocresols, liquid	153	3434
Nitrocresols, solid	153	2446
Nitroethane	129	2842
Nitrogen	121	1066
Nitrogen, compressed	121	1066
Nitrogen, refrigerated liquid (cryogenic liquid)	120	1977
Nitrogen and Rare gases mixture	121	1981
Nitrogen and Rare gases mixture, compressed	121	1981
Nitrogen dioxide	124	1067
Nitrogen dioxide, liquefied	124	1067
Nitrogen dioxide and Nitric oxide mixture	124	1975
Nitrogen trifluoride	122	2451
Nitrogen trifluoride, compressed	122	2451
Nitrogen trioxide	124	2421
Nitroglycerin, solution in alcohol, with > 1%, but ≤ 5% Nitroglycerin	127	3064
Nitroglycerin, solution in alcohol, with ≤ 1% Nitroglycerin	127	1204
Nitroglycerin mixture, desensitized, liquid, flammable, n.o.s., with ≤ 30% Nitroglycerin	113	3343
Nitroglycerin mixture, desensitized, liquid, n.o.s., with ≤ 30% Nitroglycerin	113	3357
Nitroglycerin mixture, desensitized, solid, n.o.s., with > 2% but ≤ 10% Nitroglycerin	113	3319
Nitroglycerin mixture with > 2%, but ≤ 10% Nitroglycerin, desensitized	113	3319
Nitroguanidine (Picrite), wetted with ≥ 20% water	113	1336
Nitroguanidine, wetted with ≥ 20% water	113	1336
Nitrohydrochloric acid	157	1798
Nitromethane	129	1261
Nitronaphthalene	133	2538
Nitrophenols	153	1663
4-Nitrophenylhydrazine, ≥ 30% water	113	3376
Nitropropanes	129	2608
p-Nitrosodimethylaniline	135	1369
Nitrostarch, wetted with ≥ 20% water	113	1337
Nitrostarch, wetted with ≥ 30% solvent	113	1337
Nitrosyl chloride	125	1069
Nitrosylsulfuric acid	157	2308
Nitrosysulfuric acid, liquid	157	2308
Nitrosysulfuric acid, solid	157	2308

Substance	Guide	ID
Nitrosysulfuric acid, solid	157	3456
Nitrotoluenes	152	1664
Nitrotoluenes, liquid	152	1664
Nitrotoluenes, solid	152	1664
Nitrotoluenes, solid	152	3446
Nitrotoluidines (mono)	153	2660
Nitrous oxide	122	1070
Nitrous oxide, compressed	122	1070
Nitrous oxide, refrigerated liquid	122	2201
Nitrous oxide and Carbon dioxide mixture	126	1015
Nitroxylenes	152	1665
Nitroxylenes, liquid	152	1665
Nitroxylenes, solid	152	1665
Nitroxylenes, solid	152	3447
Nonanes	128	1920
Nonyltrichlorosilane	156	1799
2,5-Norbornadiene	**128P**	**2251**
2,5-Norbornadiene, inhibited	**128P**	**2251**
2,5-Norbornadiene, stabilized	**128P**	**2251**
Octadecyltrichlorosilane	156	1800
Octadiene	**128P**	**2309**
Octafluorobut-2-ene	126	2422
Octafluorocyclobutane	126	1976
Octafluoropropane	126	2424
Octanes	128	1262
Octyl aldehydes	129	1191
tert-Octyl mercaptan	131	3023
Octyltrichlorosilane	156	1801
Oil, petroleum	128	1270
Oil gas	119P	1071
Oil gas, compressed	119P	1071
Organic peroxide type B, liquid	146	3101
Organic peroxide type B, liquid, temperature controlled	148	3111
Organic peroxide type B, solid	146	3102
Organic peroxide type B, solid, temperature controlled	148	3112
Organic peroxide type C, liquid	146	3103
Organic peroxide type C, liquid, temperature controlled	148	3113
Organic peroxide type C, solid	146	3104
Organic peroxide type C, solid, temperature controlled	148	3114
Organic peroxide type D, liquid	145	3105
Organic peroxide type D, liquid, temperature controlled	148	3115
Organic peroxide type D, solid	145	3106
Organic peroxide type D, solid, temperature controlled	148	3116
Organic peroxide type E, liquid	145	3107
Organic peroxide type E, liquid, temperature controlled	148	3117
Organic peroxide type E, solid	145	3108
Organic peroxide type E, solid, temperature controlled	148	3118
Organic peroxide type F, liquid	145	3109
Organic peroxide type F, liquid, temperature controlled	148	3119
Organic peroxide type F, solid	145	3110
Organic peroxide type F, solid, temperature controlled	148	3120
Organic phosphate compound mixed with compressed gas	123	1955
Organic phosphate mixed with compressed gas	123	1955
Organic phosphorus compound mixed with compressed gas	123	1955

Hazmat

Substance	Guide	ID
Organic pigments, self-heating	135	3313
Organoarsenic compound, liquid, n.o.s.	151	3280
Organoarsenic compound, n.o.s.	151	3280
Organoarsenic compound, solid, n.o.s.	151	3465
Organochlorine pesticide, liquid, flammable, toxic	131	2762
Organochlorine pesticide, liquid, toxic	151	2996
Organochlorine pesticide, liquid, toxic, flammable	131	2995
Organochlorine pesticide, solid, toxic	151	2761
Organometallic compound, solid water-reactive, flammable, n.o.s.	138	3372
Organometallic compound, toxic,n.o.s.	151	3282
Organometallic compound, toxic, liquid, n.o.s.	151	3282
Organometallic compound, toxic, solid, n.o.s.	151	3467
Organometallic compound, water-reactive, flammable, n.o.s.	138	3207
Organometallic compound dispersion, water-reactive, flammable, n.o.s.	138	3207
Organometallic compound solution, water-reactive, flammable, n.o.s.	138	3207
Organometallic substance, liquid, pyrophoric	135	3392
Organometallic substance, liquid, pyrophoric, water-reactive	135	3394
Organometallic substance, liquid, water-reactive	135	3398
Organometallic substance, liquid, water-reactive, flammable	138	3399
Organometallic substance, solid, pyrophoric	135	3391
Organometallic substance, solid, pyrophoric, water-reactive	135	3393
Organometallic substance, solid, self-heating	138	3400
Organometallic substance, solid, water-reactive	135	3395
Organometallic substance, solid, water-reactive, flammable	138	3396
Organometallic substance, solid, water-reactive,self-heating	138	3397
Organophosphorus compound, toxic, flammable, n.o.s.	131	3279
Organophosphorus compound, toxic, liquid, n.o.s.	151	3278
Organophosphorus compound, toxic, n.o.s.	151	3278
Organophosphorus compound, toxic, solid, n.o.s.	151	3464
Organophosphorus pesticide, liquid, flammable, toxic	131	2784
Organophosphorus pesticide, liquid, toxic	152	3018
Organophosphorus pesticide, liquid, toxic, flammable	131	3017
Organophosphorus pesticide, solid, toxic	152	2783
Organotin compound, liquid, n.o.s.	153	2788
Organotin compound, solid, n.o.s.	153	3146
Organotin pesticide, liquid, flammable, toxic	131	2787
Organotin pesticide, liquid, toxic	153	3020
Organotin pesticide, liquid, toxic, flammable	131	3019
Organotin pesticide, solid, toxic	153	2786
Osmium tetroxide	154	2471
Other regulated substances, liquid, n.o.s.	171	3082
Other regulated substances, solid, n.o.s.	171	3077
Oxidizing liquid, corrosive, n.o.s.	140	3098
Oxidizing liquid, n.o.s.	140	3139
Oxidizing liquid, toxic, n.o.s.	142	3099
Oxidizing solid, corrosive, n.o.s.	140	3085
Oxidizing solid, flammable, n.o.s.	140	3137
Oxidizing solid, n.o.s.	140	1479
Oxidizing solid, self-heating, n.o.s.	135	3100
Oxidizing solid, toxic, n.o.s.	141	3087
Oxidizing solid, water-reactive, n.o.s.	144	3121
Oxidizing substances, liquid, corrosive, n.o.s.	140	3098
Oxidizing substances, liquid, n.o.s.	140	3139

Substance	Guide	ID
Oxidizing substances, liquid, toxic, n.o.s.	142	3099
Oxidizing substances, self-heating, n.o.s.	135	3100
Oxidizing substances, solid, corrosive, n.o.s.	140	3085
Oxidizing substances, solid, flammable, n.o.s.	140	3137
Oxidizing substances, solid, n.o.s.	140	1479
Oxidizing substances, solid, self-heating, n.o.s.	135	3100
Oxidizing substances, solid, toxic, n.o.s.	141	3087
Oxidizing substances, solid, which in contact with water emit flammable gases, n.o.s.	144	3121
Oxygen	122	1072
Oxygen, compressed	122	1072
Oxygen, refrigerated liquid (cryogenic liquid)	122	1073
Oxygen and Carbon dioxide mixture	122	1014
Oxygen and Carbon dioxide mixture, compressed	122	1014
Oxygen and Rare gases mixture	121	1980
Oxygen and Rare gases mixture, compressed	121	1980
Oxygen difluoride	124	2190
Oxygen difluoride, compressed	124	2190
Oxygen generator, chemical	140	3356
Oxygen generator, chemical, spent	140	3356
Oxygen generators, small	140	8037
Paint (corrosive)	153	3066
Paint (flammable)	128	1263
Paint related material (corrosive)	153	3066
Paint related material (flammable)	128	1263
Paper, unsaturated oil treated	133	1379
Paraformaldehyde	133	2213
Paraldehyde	129	1264
Parathion	152	2783
Parathion and compressed gas mixture	123	1967
PCB	171	2315
PD	152	1556
Pentaborane	135	1380
Pentachloroethane	151	1669
Pentachlorophenol	154	3155
Pentaerythrite tetranitrate mixture, desensitized, solid, not otherwise specified, with > 10% but ≤ 20% PETN	113	3344
Pentafluoroethane	126	3220
Pentafluoroethane and Ethylene oxide mixture, with ≤ 7.9% Ethylene oxide	126	3298
Pentamethylheptane	128	2286
Pentan-2,4-dione	131	2310
n-Pentane	128	1265
2,4-Pentanedione	131	2310
Pentane-2,4-dione	131	2310
Pentanes	128	1265
Pentanols	129	1105
1-Pentene	128	1108
1-Pentol	**153P**	**2705**
Percarbonates, inorganic, n.o.s.	140	3217
Perchlorates, inorganic, aqueous solution, n.o.s.	140	3211
Perchlorates, inorganic, n.o.s.	140	1481
Perchloric acid, with > 50% but ≤ 72% acid	143	1873
Perchloric acid, with ≤ 50% acid	140	1802
Perchloroethylene	160	1897
Perchloromethyl mercaptan	157	1670

Hazmat

Substance	Guide	ID
Perchloryl fluoride	124	3083
Perfluoroethyl vinyl ether	115	3154
Perfluoro(ethyl vinyl ether)	115	3154
Perfluoromethyl vinyl ether	115	3153
Perfluoro(methyl vinyl ether)	115	3153
Perfumery products, with flammable solvents	127	1266
Permanganate, n.o.s.	140	1482
Permanganates, inorganic, aqueous solution, n.o.s.	140	3214
Permanganates, inorganic, n.o.s.	140	1482
Peroxides, inorganic, n.o.s.	140	1483
Persulfates, inorganic, aqueous solution, n.o.s.	140	3216
Persulfates, inorganic, n.o.s.	140	3215
Pesticide, liquid, flammable, toxic	131	3021
Pesticide, liquid, toxic, n.o.s.	151	2902
Pesticide, liquid, toxic, flammable, n.o.s.	131	2903
Pesticide, liquid, toxic, n.o.s.	151	2902
Pesticide, solid, toxic, n.o.s.	151	2588
Petrol	128	1203
Petroleum crude oil	128	1267
Petroleum distillates, n.o.s.	128	1268
Petroleum gases, liquefied	115	1075
Petroleum oil	128	1270
Petroleum products, n.o.s.	128	1268
Phenacyl bromide	153	2645
Phenetidines	153	2311
Phenol, molten	153	2312
Phenol, solid	153	1671
Phenol solution	153	2821
Phenolates, liquid	154	2904
Phenolates, solid	154	2905
Phenolsulfonic acid, liquid	153	1803
Phenoxyacetic acid derivative pesticide, liquid, flammable, toxic	131	3346
Phenoxyacetic acid derivative pesticide, liquid, toxic	153	3348
Phenoxyacetic acid derivative pesticide, liquid, toxic, flammable	131	3347
Phenoxyacetic acid derivative pesticide, solid, toxic	153	3345
Phenoxy pesticide, liquid, flammable, toxic	131	2766
Phenoxy pesticide, liquid, toxic	152	3000
Phenoxy pesticide, liquid, toxic, flammable	131	2999
Phenoxy pesticide, solid, toxic	152	2765
Phenylacetonitrile, liquid	152	2470
Phenylacetyl chloride	156	2577
Phenylcarbylamine chloride	151	1672
Phenyl chloroformate	156	2746
Phenylenediamines	153	1673
Phenylhydrazine	153	2572
Phenyl isocyanate	155	2487
Phenyl mercaptan	131	2337
Phenylmercuric acetate	151	1674
Phenylmercuric compound, n.o.s.	151	2026
Phenylmercuric hydroxide	151	1894
Phenylmercuric nitrate	151	1895
Phenylphosphorus dichloride	137	2798
Phenylphosphorus thiodichloride	137	2799
Phenyltrichlorosilane	156	1804
Phenyl urea pesticide, liquid, flammable, toxic	131	2768

Substance	Guide	ID
Phenyl urea pesticide, liquid, toxic	151	3002
Phenyl urea pesticide, liquid, toxic, flammable	131	3001
Phenyl urea pesticide, solid, toxic	151	2767
Phosgene	125	1076
9-Phosphabicyclononanes	135	2940
Phosphine	119	2199
Phosphoric acid	154	1805
Phosphoric acid, liquid	154	1805
Phosphoric acid, solid	154	1805
Phosphoric acid, solid	154	3453
Phosphoric acid, solution	154	1805
Phosphorous acid	154	2834
Phosphorous acid, ortho	154	2834
Phosphorus, amorphous	133	1338
Phosphorus, amorphous, red	133	1338
Phosphorus, white, dry, or under water or in solution	136	1381
Phosphorus, white, molten	136	2447
Phosphorus, yellow, dry, or under water or in solution	136	1381
Phosphorus heptasulfide, free from yellow and white Phosphorus	139	1339
Phosphorus oxybromide	137	1939
Phosphorus oxybromide, molten	137	2576
Phosphorus oxybromide, solid	137	1939
Phosphorus oxychloride	137	1810
Phosphorus pentabromide	137	2691
Phosphorus pentachloride	137	1806
Phosphorus pentafluoride	125	2198
Phosphorus pentafluoride, compressed	125	2198
Phosphorus pentasulfide, free from yellow or white Phosphorus	139	1340
Phosphorus pentoxide	137	1807
Phosphorus sesquisulfide, free from yellow and white Phosphorus	139	1341
Phosphorus tribromide	137	1808
Phosphorus trichloride	137	1809
Phosphorus trioxide	157	2578
Phosphorus trisulfide, free from yellow and white Phosphorus	139	1343
Phthalic anhydride	156	2214
Phthalimide derivative pesticide, liquid, flammable, toxic	131	2774
Phthalimide derivative pesticide, liquid, toxic	151	3008
Phthalimide derivative pesticide, liquid, toxic, flammable	131	3007
Phthalimide derivative pesticide, solid, toxic	151	2773
Picolines	129	2313
Picric acid, wet, with ≥ 10% water	113	1344
Picric acid, wetted with ≥ 10% water	113	3364
Picrite, wetted	113	1336
Picryl chloride, wetted with ≥ 10% water	113	3365
alpha-Pinene	128	2368
Pinene (alpha)	128	2368
Pine oil	129	1272
Piperazine	153	2579
Piperidine	132	2401
Plastic molding compound	171	3314

Substance	Guide	ID
Plastic, nitrocellulose-based, spontaneously combustible, n.o.s.	135	2006
Plastics moulding compound	171	3314
Plastics, nitrocellulose-based, self-heating, n.o.s.	135	2006
Poison B, liquid, n.o.s.	153	2810
Polyalkylamines, n.o.s.	132	2733
Polyalkylamines, n.o.s.	132	2734
Polyalkylamines, n.o.s.	153	2735
Polyamines, flammable, corrosive, n.o.s.	132	2733
Polyamines, liquid, corrosive, flammable, n.o.s.	132	2734
Polyamines, liquid, corrosive, n.o.s.	153	2735
Polyamines, solid, corrosive, n.o.s.	154	3259
Polychlorinated biphenyls	171	2315
Polychlorinated biphenyls, liquid	171	2315
Polychlorinated biphenyls, solid	171	2315
Polychlorinated biphenyls, solid	171	3432
Polyester resin kit	128	3269
Polyhalogenated biphenyls, liquid	171	3151
Polyhalogenated biphenyls, solid	171	3152
Polyhalogenated terphenyls, liquid	171	3151
Polyhalogenated terphenyls, solid	171	3152
Polymeric beads, expandable	133	2211
Polystyrene beads, expandable	133	2211
Potassium	138	2257
Potassium, metal	138	2257
Potassium, metal alloys	138	1420
Potassium, metal alloys, liquid	138	1420
Potassium, metal alloys, solid	138	3403
Potassium arsenate	151	1677
Potassium arsenite	154	1678
Potassium borohydride	138	1870
Potassium bromate	140	1484
Potassium chlorate	140	1485
Potassium chlorate, aqueous solution	140	2427
Potassium chlorate, solution	140	2427
Potassium cuprocyanide	157	1679
Potassium cyanide	157	1680
Potassium cyanide, solid	157	1680
Potassium cyanide, solution	157	3413
Potassium dithionite	135	1929
Potassium fluoride	154	1812
Potassium fluoride, solid	154	1812
Potassium fluoride, solution	154	3422
Potassium fluoroacetate	151	2628
Potassium fluorosilicate	151	2655
Potassium hydrogendifluoride	154	1811
Potassium hydrogen difluoride, solid	154	1811
Potassium hydrogen difluoride, solution	154	3421
Potassium hydrogen sulfate	154	2509
Potassium hydrosulfite	135	1929
Potassium hydroxide, dry, solid	154	1813
Potassium hydroxide, flake	154	1813
Potassium hydroxide, solid	154	1813
Potassium hydroxide, solution	154	1814
Potassium metavanadate	151	2864
Potassium monoxide	154	2033
Potassium nitrate	140	1486

Hazmat

Substance	Guide	ID
Potassium nitrate and Sodium nitrate mixture	140	1499
Potassium nitrate and Sodium nitrite mixture	140	1487
Potassium nitrite	140	1488
Potassium perchlorate	140	1489
Potassium permanganate	140	1490
Potassium peroxide	144	1491
Potassium persulfate	140	1492
Potassium phosphide	139	2012
Potassium silicofluoride	151	2655
Potassium sodium alloys	138	1422
Potassium sodium alloys, liquid	138	1422
Potassium sodium alloys, solid	138	3404
Potassium sulfide, anhydrous	135	1382
Potassium sulfide, hydrated, with $\geq$ 30% water of crystallization	153	1847
Potassium sulfide, hydrated, with $\geq$ 30% water of hydration	153	1847
Potassium sulfide, with < 30% water of crystallization	135	1382
Potassium sulfide, with < 30% water of hydration	135	1382
Potassium superoxide	143	2466
Printing ink, flammable	129	1210
Printing ink related material	129P	1210
Propadiene, inhibited	**116P**	**2200**
Propadiene, stabilized	**116P**	**2200**
Propadiene and Methylacetylene mixture, stabilized	**116P**	**1060**
Propane	115	1075
Propane	115	1978
Propane-Ethane mixture, refrigerated liquid	115	1961
Propane mixture	115	1075
Propane mixture	115	1978
Propanethiols	130	2402
n-Propanol	129	1274
Propargyl alcohol	131	1986
Propionaldehyde	129	1275
Propionic acid	132	1848
Propionic anhydride	156	2496
Propionitrile	131	2404
Propionyl chloride	132	1815
n-Propyl acetate	129	1276
normal Propyl alcohol	129	1274
Propyl alcohol, normal	129	1274
Propylamine	132	1277
n-Propyl benzene	128	2364
Propyl chloride	129	1278
n-Propyl chloroformate	155	2740
Propylene	115	1075
Propylene	115	1077
Propylene, Ethylene and Acetylene in mixture, refrigerated liquid containing $\geq$ 71.5% Ethylene with $\leq$ 22.5% Acetylene and $\leq$ 6% Propylene	115	3138
Propylene chlorohydrin	131	2611
1,2-Propylenediamine	132	2258
1,3-Propylenediamine	132	2258
Propylene dichloride	130	1279
Propyleneimine, inhibited	**131P**	**1921**
Propyleneimine, stabilized	**131P**	**1921**
Propylene oxide	**127P**	**1280**

Hazmat

Substance	Guide	ID
Propylene oxide and Ethylene oxide mixture, with ≤ 30%Ethylene oxide	129P	2983
Propylene tetramer	128	2850
Propyl formates	129	1281
n-Propyl isocyanate	155	2482
n-Propyl nitrate	131	1865
Propyltrichlorosilane	155	1816
Pyrethroid pesticide, liquid, flammable, toxic	131	3350
Pyrethroid pesticide, liquid, toxic	151	3352
Pyrethroid pesticide, liquid, toxic, flammable	131	3351
Pyrethroid pesticide, solid, toxic	151	3349
Pyridine	129	1282
Pyrophoric alloy, n.o.s.	135	1383
Pyrophoric liquid, inorganic, n.o.s.	135	3194
Pyrophoric liquid, n.o.s.	135	2845
Pyrophoric liquid, organic, n.o.s.	135	2845
Pyrophoric metal, n.o.s.	135	1383
Pyrophoric organometallic compound, n.o.s.	135	3203
Pyrophoric organometallic compound, water-reactive, n.o.s.	135	3203
Pyrophoric solid, inorganic, n.o.s.	135	3200
Pyrophoric solid, n.o.s.	135	2846
Pyrophoric solid, organic, n.o.s.	135	2846
Pyrosulfuryl chloride	137	1817
Pyrrolidine	132	1922
Quinoline	154	2656
Radioactive material, articles manufactured from depleted Uranium	161	2909
Radioactive material, articles manufactured from natural Thorium	161	2909
Radioactive material, articles manufactured from natural Uranium	161	2909
Radioactive material, empty packages	161	2908
Radioactive material, excepted package, articles manufactured from depleted Uranium	161	2909
Radioactive material, excepted package, articles manufactured from depleted Uranium	161	2910
Radioactive material, excepted package, articles manufactured from natural Thorium	161	2909
Radioactive material, excepted package, articles manufactured from natural Thorium	161	2910
Radioactive material, excepted package, articles manufactured from natural Uranium	161	2909
Radioactive material, excepted package, articles manufactured from natural Uranium	161	2910
Radioactive material, excepted package, empty packaging	161	2908
Radioactive material, excepted package, empty packaging	161	2910
Radioactive material, excepted package, instruments or articles	161	2910
Radioactive material, excepted package, instruments or articles	161	2911
Radioactive material, excepted package, limited quantity of material	161	2910
Radioactive material, fissile, n.o.s.	165	2918
Radioactive material, instruments or articles	161	2911
Radioactive material, limited quantity, n.o.s.	161	2910
Radioactive material, low specific activity (LSA), n.o.s.	162	2912
Radioactive material, low specific activity (LSA-I)	162	2912

Substance	Guide	ID
Radioactive material, low specific activity (LSA-II)	162	3321
Radioactive material, low specific activity (LSA-II), fissile	165	3324
Radioactive material, low specific activity (LSA-III)	162	3322
Radioactive material, low specific activity (LSA-III), fissile	165	3325
Radioactive material, n.o.s.	163	2982
Radioactive material, special form, n.o.s.	164	2974
Radioactive material, surface contaminated objects (SCO)	162	2913
Radioactive material, surface contaminated objects (SCO-I)	162	2913
Radioactive material, surface contaminated objects (SCO-I), fissile	165	3326
Radioactive material, surface contaminated objects (SCO-II)	162	2913
Radioactive material, surface contaminated objects (SCO-II), fissile	165	3326
Radioactive material, transported under special arrangement	163	2919
Radioactive material, transported under special arrangement, fissile	165	3331
Radioactive material, Type A package	163	2915
Radioactive material, Type A package, fissile	165	3327
Radioactive material, Type A package, special form	164	3332
Radioactive material, Type A package, special form, fissile	165	3333
Radioactive material, Type B(M) package	163	2917
Radioactive material, Type B(M) package, fissile	165	3329
Radioactive material, Type B(U) package	163	2916
Radioactive material, Type B(U) package, fissile	165	3328
Radioactive material, Type C package	163	3323
Radioactive material, Type C package, fissile	165	3330
Radioactive material, Uranium hexafluoride	166	2978
Radioactive material, Uranium hexafluoride, fissile	166	2977
Radioactive material, Uranium hexafluoride, non-fissile or fissile excepted	166	2978
Rags, oily	133	1856
Rare gases and Nitrogen mixture	121	1981
Rare gases and Nitrogen mixture, compressed	121	1981
Rare gases and Oxygen mixture	122	1980
Rare gases and Oxygen mixture, compressed	122	1980
Rare gases mixture	121	1979
Rare gases mixture, compressed	121	1979
Receptacles, small, containing gas	115	2037
Red phosphorus	133	1338
Red phosphorus, amorphous	133	1338
Refrigerant gas, n.o.s.	126	1078
Refrigerant gas, n.o.s. (flammable)	115	1954
Refrigerant gas R-12	126	1028
Refrigerant gas R-12 and Refrigerant gas R-152a azeotropic mixture with 74% Refrigerant gas R-12	126	2602
Refrigerant gas R-12B1	126	1974
Refrigerant gas R-13	126	1022
Refrigerant gas R-13 and Refrigerant gas R-23 azeotropic mixture with 60% Refrigerant gas R-13	126	2599
Refrigerant gas R-13B1	126	1009
Refrigerant gas R-14	126	1982
Refrigerant gas R-14, compressed	126	1982
Refrigerant gas R-21	126	1029
Refrigerant gas R-22	126	1018
Refrigerant gas R-23	126	1984

Hazmat

Substance	Guide	ID
Refrigerant gas R-23 and Refrigerant gas R-13 azeotropic mixture with 60% Refrigerant gas R-13	126	2599
Refrigerant gas R-32	115	3252
Refrigerant gas R-40	115	1063
Refrigerant gas R-41	115	2454
Refrigerant gas R-114	126	1958
Refrigerant gas R-115	126	1020
Refrigerant gas R-116	126	2193
Refrigerant gas R-116, compressed	126	2193
Refrigerant gas R-124	126	1021
Refrigerant gas R-125	126	3220
Refrigerant gas R-133a	126	1983
Refrigerant gas R-134a	126	3159
Refrigerant gas R-143a	115	2035
Refrigerant gas R-142b	115	2517
Refrigerant gas R-152a	115	1030
Refrigerant gas R-152a and Refrigerant gas R-12 azeotropic mixture with 74% Refrigerant gas R-12	126	2602
Refrigerant gas R-161	115	2453
Refrigerant gas R-218	126	2424
Refrigerant gas R-227	126	3296
Refrigerant gas R-404A	126	3337
Refrigerant gas R-407A	126	3338
Refrigerant gas R-407B	126	3339
Refrigerant gas R-407C	126	3340
Refrigerant gas R-500 (azeotropic mixture of Refrigerant gas R-12 and Refrigerant gas R-152a with approximately 74% Refrigerant gas R-12)	126	2602
Refrigerant gas R-502	126	1973
Refrigerant gas R-503 (azeotropic mixture of Refrigerant gas R-13 and Refrigerant gas R-23 with approximately 60% Refrigerant gas R-13)	126P	2599
Refrigerant gas R-1132a	**116P**	**1959**
Refrigerant gas R-1216	126	1858
Refrigerant gas R-1318	126	2422
Refrigerant gas RC-318	126	1976
Refrigerating machine	128	1993
Refrigerating machines, containing Ammonia solutions (UN 2073)	126	2857
Refrigerating machines, containing Ammonia solutions (UN2672)	126	2857
Refrigerating machines, containing flammable, non-toxic, non-corrosive, liquefied gas	115	1954
Refrigerating machines containing flammable, non-toxic, liquefied gas	115	3358
Refrigerating machines, containing non-flammable, liquefied gas	126	2857
Refrigerating machines, containing non-flammable, non-toxic gases	126	2857
Refrigerating machines, containing non-flammable, non-toxic, liquefied gas	126	2857
Refrigerating machines, containing non-flammable, non-toxic, non-corrosive, liquefied gas	126	2857
Regulated medical waste	158	9275
Regulated medical waste, n.o.s.	158	3291
Resin solution	127	1866
Resorcinol	153	2876
Rosin oil	127	1286

Substance	Guide	ID
Rubber scrap, powdered or granulated	133	1345
Rubber shoddy, powdered or granulated	133	1345
Rubber solution	127	1287
Rubidium	138	1423
Rubidium hydroxide	154	2678
Rubidium hydroxide, solid	154	2678
Rubidium hydroxide, solution	154	2677
Rubidium metal	138	1423
SA	119	2188
Sarin	153	2810
Seat-belt modules	171	3268
Seat-belt pre-tensioners	171	3268
Seat-belt pre-tensioners, compressed gas	126	3353
Seat-belt pre-tensioners, pyrotechnic	171	3268
Seed cake, with > 1.5% oil and ≤ 11% moisture	135	1386
Seed cake, with ≤ 1.5% oil and ≤ 11% moisture	135	2217
Selenates	151	2630
Selenic acid	154	1905
Selenites	151	2630
Selenium compound, liquid, n.o.s.	151	3440
Selenium compound, n.o.s.	151	3283
Selenium compound, solid, n.o.s.	151	3283
Selenium disulfide	153	2657
Selenium hexafluoride	125	2194
Selenium oxide	154	2811
Selenium oxychloride	157	2879
Selenium powder	152	2658
Self-defense spray, non-pressurized	171	3334
Self-heating liquid, corrosive, inorganic, n.o.s.	136	3188
Self-heating liquid, corrosive, organic, n.o.s.	136	3185
Self-heating liquid, inorganic, n.o.s.	135	3186
Self-heating liquid, organic, not otherwise specified	135	3183
Self-heating liquid, toxic, inorganic, n.o.s.	136	3187
Self-heating liquid, toxic, organic, n.o.s.	136	3184
Self-heating metal powders, n.o.s.	135	3189
Self-heating solid, corrosive, inorganic, n.o.s.	136	3192
Self-heating solid, corrosive, organic, n.o.s.	136	3126
Self-heating solid, inorganic, n.o.s.	135	3190
Self-heating solid, inorganic, toxic, n.o.s.	136	3191
Self-heating solid, organic, n.o.s.	135	3088
Self-heating solid, organic, toxic, n.o.s.	136	3128
Self-heating solid, oxidizing, n.o.s.	135	3127
Self-heating solid, toxic, inorganic, n.o.s.	136	3191
Self-heating solid, toxic, organic, n.o.s.	136	3128
Self-heating substance, solid, corrosive, n.o.s.	136	3126
Self-heating substances, solid, n.o.s.	135	3088
Self-heating substances, solid, oxidizing, n.o.s.	135	3127
Self-heating substances, solid, toxic, n.o.s.	136	3128
Self-reactive liquid type B	149	3221
Self-reactive liquid type B, temperature controlled	150	3231
Self-reactive liquid type C	149	3223
Self-reactive liquid type C, temperature controlled	150	3233
Self-reactive liquid type D	149	3225
Self-reactive liquid type D, temperature controlled	150	3235
Self-reactive liquid type E	149	3227
Self-reactive liquid type E, temperature controlled	150	3237
Self-reactive liquid type F	149	3229

Hazmat

Substance	Guide	ID
Self-reactive liquid type F, temperature controlled	150	3239
Self-reactive solid type B	149	3222
Self-reactive solid type B, temperature controlled	150	3232
Self-reactive solid type C	149	3224
Self-reactive solid type C, temperature controlled	150	3234
Self-reactive solid type D	149	3226
Self-reactive solid type D, temperature controlled	150	3236
Self-reactive solid type E	149	3228
Self-reactive solid type E, temperature controlled	150	3238
Self-reactive solid type F	149	3230
Self-reactive solid type F, temperature controlled	150	3240
Shale oil	128	1288
Silane	116	2203
Silicofluorides, n.o.s.	151	2856
Silane, compressed	116	2203
Silicon powder, amorphous	170	1346
Silicon tetrachloride	157	1818
Silicon tetrafluoride	125	1859
Silicon tetrafluoride, compressed	125	1859
Silver arsenite	151	1683
Silver cyanide	151	1684
Silver nitrate	140	1493
Silver picrate, wetted with ≥ 30% water	113	1347
Sludge acid	153	1906
Smokeless powder for small arms	133	3178
Soda lime, with > 4% Sodium hydroxide	154	1907
Sodium	138	1428
Sodium aluminate, solid	154	2812
Sodium aluminate, solution	154	1819
Sodium aluminum hydride	138	2835
Sodium ammonium vanadate	154	2863
Sodium arsanilate	154	2473
Sodium arsenate	151	1685
Sodium arsenite, aqueous solution	154	1686
Sodium arsenite, solid	151	2027
Sodium azide	153	1687
Sodium bisulfate, solid	154	1821
Sodium bisulfate, solution	154	2837
Sodium borohydride	138	1426
Sodium borohydride and Sodium hydroxide solution, with ≤12% Sodium borohydride and ≤ 40% Sodium hydroxide	157	3320
Sodium bromate	141	1494
Sodium cacodylate	152	1688
Sodium carbonate peroxyhydrate	140	3378
Sodium chlorate	140	1495
Sodium chlorate, aqueous solution	140	2428
Sodium chlorite	143	1496
Sodium chlorite, solution, with > 5% available Chlorine	154	1908
Sodium chloroacetate	151	2659
Sodium cuprocyanide, solid	157	2316
Sodium cuprocyanide, solution	157	2317
Sodium cyanide	157	1689
Sodium cyanide, solid	157	1689
Sodium cyanide, solution	157	3414
Sodium dichloroisocyanurate	140	2465
Sodium dichloro-s-triazinetrione	140	2465

Substance	Guide	ID
Sodium dinitro-o-cresolate, wetted with ≥ 10% water	113	3369
Sodium dinitro-o-cresolate, wetted with ≥ 15% water	113	1348
Sodium dinitro-ortho-cresolate, wetted	113	1348
Sodium dithionite	135	1384
Sodium fluoride	154	1690
Sodium fluoride, solid	154	1690
Sodium fluoride, solution	154	1690
Sodium fluoroacetate	151	2629
Sodium fluorosilicate	154	2674
Sodium hydride	138	1427
Sodium hydrogendifluoride	154	2439
Sodium hydrogen sulfate, solution	154	2837
Sodium hydrosulfide, solid, with < 25% water of crystallization	135	2318
Sodium hydrosulfide, solution	154	2922
Sodium hydrosulfide, with < 25% water of crystallization	135	2318
Sodium hydrosulfide, with ≥ 25% water of crystallization	154	2949
Sodium hydrosulfite	135	1384
Sodium hydroxide, bead	154	1823
Sodium hydroxide, dry	154	1823
Sodium hydroxide, flake	154	1823
Sodium hydroxide, granular	154	1823
Sodium hydroxide, solid	154	1823
Sodium hydroxide, solution	154	1824
Sodium methylate	138	1431
Sodium methylate, dry	138	1431
Sodium methylate, solution in alcohol	132	1289
Sodium monoxide	157	1825
Sodium nitrate	140	1498
Sodium nitrate and Potassium nitrate mixture	140	1499
Sodium nitrite	140	1500
Sodium nitrite and Potassium nitrate mixtures	140	1487
Sodium pentachlorophenate	154	2567
Sodium perborate monohydrate	140	3377
Sodium percarbonates	140	2467
Sodium perchlorate	140	1502
Sodium permanganate	140	1503
Sodium peroxide	144	1504
Sodium peroxoborate, anhydrous	140	3247
Sodium persulfate	140	1505
Sodium phosphide	139	1432
Sodium picramate, wetted with ≥ 20% water	113	1349
Sodium potassium alloys	138	1422
Sodium potassium alloys, liquid	138	1422
Sodium potassium alloys, solid	138	3404
Sodium selenite	151	2630
Sodium silicofluoride	154	2674
Sodium sulfide, anhydrous	135	1385
Sodium sulfide, hydrated, with ≥ 30% water	153	1849
Sodium sulfide, with < 30% water of crystallization	135	1385
Sodium superoxide	143	2547
Solids containing corrosive liquid, n.o.s.	154	3244
Solids containing flammable liquid, n.o.s.	133	3175
Solids containing toxic liquid, n.o.s.	151	3243
Soman	153	2810
Stannic chloride, anhydrous	137	1827

Substance	Guide	ID
Stannic chloride, pentahydrate	154	2440
Stannic phosphides	139	1433
Stibine	119	2676
Straw, wet, damp, or contaminated with oil	133	1327
Strontium arsenite	151	1691
Strontium chlorate	143	1506
Strontium chlorate, solid	143	1506
Strontium chlorate, solution	143	1506
Strontium nitrate	140	1507
Strontium perchlorate	140	1508
Strontium peroxide	143	1509
Strontium phosphide	139	2013
Strychnine	151	1692
Strychnine salts	151	1692
Styrene monomer, inhibited	**128P**	**2055**
Styrene monomer, stabilized	**128P**	**2055**
Substances, which in contact with water emit flammable gases, liquid, corrosive, n.o.s.	138	3129
Substances, which in contact with water emit flammable gases, liquid, n.o.s.	138	3148
Substances, which in contact with water emit flammable gases, liquid, toxic, n.o.s.	139	3130
Substances, which in contact with water emit flammable gases, solid, corrosive, n.o.s.	138	3131
Substances, which in contact with water emit flammable gases, solid, flammable, n.o.s.	138	3132
Substances, which in contact with water emit flammable gases, solid, n.o.s.	138	2813
Substances, which in contact with water emit flammable gases, solid, oxidizing, n.o.s.	138	3133
Substances, which in contact with water emit flammable gases, solid, self-heating, n.o.s.	138	3135
Substances, which in contact with water emit flammable gases, solid, toxic, n.o.s.	139	3134
Substituted nitrophenol pesticide, liquid, flammable, toxic	131	2780
Substituted nitrophenol pesticide, liquid, toxic	153	3014
Substituted nitrophenol pesticide, liquid, toxic, flammable	131	3013
Substituted nitrophenol pesticide, solid, toxic	153	2779
Sulfamic acid	154	2967
Sulfur	133	1350
Sulfur, molten	133	2448
Sulfur chlorides	137P	1828
Sulfur dioxide	125	1079
Sulfur dioxide, liquefied	125	1079
Sulfur hexafluoride	126	1080
Sulfuric acid	137	1830
Sulfuric acid, fuming	137	1831
Sulfuric acid, fuming, with < 30% free Sulfur trioxide	137	1831
Sulfuric acid, fuming, with ≥ 30% free Sulfur trioxide	137	1831
Sulfuric acid, spent	137	1832
Sulfuric acid, with > 51% acid	137	1830
Sulfuric acid, with < 51% acid	157	2796
Sulfuric acid and Hydrofluoric acid mixtures	157	1786
Sulfurous acid	154	1833

Substance	Guide	ID
Sulfur tetrafluoride	125	2418
Sulfur trioxide	137	1829
Sulfur trioxide, inhibited	137	1829
Sulfur trioxide, stabilized	137	1829
Sulfur trioxide, uninhibited	137	1829
Sulfur trioxide and Chlorosulfonic acid mixture	137	1754
Sulfuryl chloride	137	1834
Sulfuryl fluoride	123	2191
Tabun	153	2810
Tars, liquid	130	1999
Tear gas candles	159	1700
Tear gas devices	159	1693
Tear gas grenades	159	1700
Tear gas substance, liquid, n.o.s.	159	1693
Tear gas substance, solid, n.o.s.	159	1693
Tear gas substance, solid, n.o.s.	159	3448
Tellurium compound, n.o.s.	151	3284
Tellurium hexafluoride	125	2195
Terpene hydrocarbons, n.o.s.	128	2319
Terpinolene	128	2541
Tetrabromoethane	159	2504
1,1,2,2-Tetrachloroethane	151	1702
Tetrachloroethane	151	1702
Tetrachloroethylene	160	1897
Tetraethyl dithiopyrophosphate	153	1704
Tetraethyl dithiopyrophosphate, mixture, dry or liquid	153	1704
Tetraethylenepentamine	153	2320
Tetraethyl lead, liquid	131	1649
Tetraethyl pyrophosphate, liquid	152	3018
Tetraethyl pyrophosphate, solid	152	2783
Tetraethyl silicate	129	1292
1,1,1,2-Tetrafluoroethane	126	3159
Tetrafluoroethane and Ethylene oxide mixture, with $\leq$ 5.6% Ethylene oxide	126	3299
Tetrafluoroethylene, inhibited	**116P**	**1081**
Tetrafluoroethylene, stabilized	**116P**	**1081**
Tetrafluoromethane	126	1982
Tetrafluoromethane, compressed	126	1982
1,2,3,6-Tetrahydro-benzaldehyde	129	2498
Tetrahydrofuran	127	2056
Tetrahydrofurfurylamine	129	2943
Tetrahydrophthalic anhydrides	156	2698
1,2,3,6-Tetrahydropyridine	129	2410
1,2,5,6-Tetrahydropyridine	129	2410
Tetrahydrothiophene	130	2412
Tetramethylammonium hydroxide	153	1835
Tetramethylammonium hydroxide, solid	153	3423
Tetramethylammonium hydroxide, solution	153	1835
Tetramethylsilane	130	2749
Tetranitromethane	143	1510
Tetrapropyl orthotitanate	128	2413
Textile waste, wet	133	1857
Thallium chlorate	141	2573
Thallium compound, n.o.s.	151	1707

Hazmat

Substance	Guide	ID
Thallium nitrate	141	2727
Thallium sulfate, solid	151	1707
4-Thiapentanal	152	2785
Thia-4-pentanal	152	2785
Thickened GD	153	2810
Thioacetic acid	129	2436
Thiocarbamate pesticide, liquid, flammable, toxic	131	2772
Thiocarbamate pesticide, liquid, toxic	151	3006
Thiocarbamate pesticide, liquid, toxic, flammable	131	3005
Thiocarbamate pesticide, solid, toxic	151	2771
Thioglycol	153	2966
Thioglycolic acid	153	1940
Thiolactic acid	153	2936
Thionyl chloride	137	1836
Thiophene	130	2414
Thiophosgene	157	2474
Thiophosphoryl chloride	157	1837
Thiourea dioxide	135	3341
Thorium metal, pyrophoric	162	2975
Thorium nitrate, solid	162	2976
Tinctures, medicinal	127	1293
Tin tetrachloride	137	1827
Tin tetrachloride, pentahydrate	154	2440
Titanium disulfide	135	3174
Titanium hydride	170	1871
Titanium powder, dry	135	2546
Titanium powder, wetted with $\geq$ 25% water	170	1352
Titanium sponge granules	170	2878
Titanium sponge powders	170	2878
Titanium sulfate, solution	154	1760
Titanium tetrachloride	137	1838
Titanium trichloride, pyrophoric	135	2441
Titanium trichloride mixture	157	2869
Titanium trichloride mixture, pyrophoric	135	2441
TNT, wetted with $\geq$ 10% water	113	3366
TNT, wetted with $\geq$ 30% water	113	1356
Toe puffs, nitrocellulose base	133	1353
Toluene	130	1294
2,4-Toluenediamine	151	1709
Toluene diisocyanate	156	2078
Toluene sulfonic acid, liquid, with > 5% free Sulfuric acid	153	2584
Toluene sulfonic acid, liquid, with $\leq$ 5% free Sulfuric acid	153	2586
Toluene sulfonic acid, solid, with > 5% free Sulfuric acid	153	2583
Toluene sulfonic acid, solid, with $\leq$ 5% free Sulfuric acid	153	2583
Toluidines	153	1708
Toluidines, liquid	153	1708
Toluidines, solid	153	1708
Toluidines, solid	153	3451
2,4-Toluylenediamine	151	1709
2,4-Toluylenediamine, solid	151	1709
2,4-Toluylenediamine, solution	151	3418
Toxic by inhalation liquid, corrosive, n.o.s. (Inhalation Hazard Zone A)	154	3389
Toxic by inhalation liquid, corrosive, n.o.s. (Inhalation Hazard Zone B)	154	3390

Substance	Guide	ID
Toxic by inhalation liquid, flammable, n.o.s. (Inhalation Hazard Zone A)	131	3383
Toxic by inhalation liquid, flammable, n.o.s. (Inhalation Hazard Zone B)	131	3384
Toxic by inhalation liquid, n.o.s. (Inhalation Hazard Zone A)	151	3381
Toxic by inhalation liquid, n.o.s. (Inhalation Hazard Zone B)	151	3382
Toxic by inhalation liquid, oxidizing, n.o.s. (Inhalation Hazard Zone A)	142	3387
Toxic by inhalation liquid, oxidizing, n.o.s. (Inhalation Hazard Zone B)	142	3388
Toxic by inhalation liquid, water-reactive, n.o.s. (Inhalation Hazard Zone A)	139	3385
Toxic by inhalation liquid, water-reactive, n.o.s. (Inhalation Hazard Zone B)	139	3386
Toxic liquid, corrosive, inorganic, n.o.s.	154	3289
Toxic liquid, corrosive, inorganic, n.o.s. (Inhalation Hazard Zone A and B)	154	3289
Toxic liquid, corrosive, organic, n.o.s.	154	2927
Toxic liquid, corrosive, organic, n.o.s. (Inhalation Hazard Zone A and B)	154	2927
Toxic liquid, flammable, n.o.s.	131	2929
Toxic liquid, flammable, n.o.s. (Inhalation Hazard Zone A and B)	131	2929
Toxic liquid, flammable, organic, n.o.s.	131	2929
Toxic liquid, flammable, organic, n.o.s. (Inhalation Hazard Zone A and B)	131	2929
Toxic liquid, inorganic, n.o.s.	151	3287
Toxic liquid, inorganic, n.o.s. (Inhalation Hazard Zone A and B)	151	3287
Toxic liquid, n.o.s.	153	2810
Toxic liquid, n.o.s. (Inhalation Hazard Zone A and B)	153	2810
Toxic liquid, organic, n.o.s.	153	2810
Toxic liquid, organic, n.o.s. (Inhalation Hazard Zone A and B)	153	2810
Toxic liquid, oxidizing, n.o.s.	142	3122
Toxic liquid, oxidizing, n.o.s. (Inhalation Hazard Zone A and B)	142	3122
Toxic liquid, water-reactive, n.o.s.	139	3123
Toxic liquid, water-reactive, n.o.s. (Inhalation Hazard Zone A and B)	139	3123
Toxic liquid, which in contact with water emits flammable gases, n.o.s.	139	3123
Toxic liquid, which in contact with water emits flammable gases, n.o.s. (Inhalation Hazard Zone A and B)	139	3123
Toxic solid, corrosive, inorganic, n.o.s.	154	3290
Toxic solid, corrosive, organic, n.o.s.	154	2928
Toxic solid, flammable, n.o.s.	134	2930

Substance	Guide	ID
Toxic solid, flammable, organic, n.o.s.	134	2930
Toxic solid, inorganic, n.o.s.	151	3288
Toxic solid, organic, n.o.s.	154	2811
Toxic solid, oxidizing, n.o.s.	141	3086
Toxic solid, self-heating, n.o.s.	136	3124
Toxic solid, water-reactive, n.o.s.	139	3125
Toxic solid, which in contact with water emits flammable gases, n.o.s.	139	3125
Toxins	153	----
Toxins, extracted from living sources, liquid, n.o.s.	153	3172
Toxins, extracted from living sources, n.o.s.	153	3172
Toxins, extracted from living sources, solid, n.o.s.	153	3172
Toxins, extracted from living sources, solid, n.o.s.	153	3462
Triallylamine	132	2610
Triallyl borate	156	2609
Triazine pesticide, liquid, flammable, toxic	131	2764
Triazine pesticide, liquid, toxic	151	2998
Triazine pesticide, liquid, toxic, flammable	131	2997
Triazine pesticide, solid, toxic	151	2763
Tri-(1-aziridinyl)phosphine oxide, solution	152	2501
Tributylamine	153	2542
Tributylphosphane	135	3254
Tributylphosphine	135	3254
Trichloroacetic acid	153	1839
Trichloroacetic acid, solution	153	2564
Trichloroacetyl chloride	156	2442
Trichlorobenzenes, liquid	153	2321
Trichlorobutene	152	2322
1,1,1-Trichloroethane	160	2831
Trichloroethylene	160	1710
Trichloroisocyanuric acid, dry	140	2468
Trichlorosilane	139	1295
(mono)-(Trichloro)-tetra-(monopotassium dichloro)-penta-s-triazinetrione, dry	140	2468
Tricresyl phosphate	151	2574
Triethylamine	132	1296
Triethylenetetramine	153	2259
Triethyl phosphite	130	2323
Trifluoroacetic acid	154	2699
Trifluoroacetyl chloride	125	3057
Trifluorochloroethylene, inhibited	**119P**	**1082**
Trifluorochloroethylene, inhibited	**119P**	**1082**
Trifluorochloroethylene, stabilized	**119P**	**1082**
1,1,1-Trifluoroethane	115	2035
Trifluoroethane, compressed	115	2035
Trifluoromethane	126	1984
Trifluoromethane, refrigerated liquid	120	3136
Trifluoromethane and Chlorotrifluoromethane azeotropic mixture with approx. 60% Chlorotrifluoromethane	126	2599
2-Trifluoromethylaniline	153	2942
3-Trifluoromethylaniline	153	2948
Triisobutylene	128	2324
Triisopropyl borate	129	2616
Trimethoxysilane	132	9269
Trimethylacetyl chloride	132	2438

Hazmat

Substance	Guide	ID
Trimethylamine, anhydrous	118	1083
Trimethylamine, aqueous solution	132	1297
1,3,5-Trimethylbenzene	129	2325
Trimethyl borate	129	2416
Trimethylchlorosilane	155	1298
Trimethylcyclohexylamine	153	2326
Trimethylhexamethylenediamines	153	2327
Trimethylhexamethylene diisocyanate	156	2328
Trimethyl phosphite	130	2329
Trinitrobenzene, wetted with ≥ 10% water	113	3367
Trinitrobenzene, wetted with ≥ 30% water	113	1354
Trinitrobenzoic acid, wetted with ≥ 10% water	113	3368
Trinitrobenzoic acid, wetted with ≥ 30% water	113	1355
Trinitrochlorobenzene, wetted with ≥ 10% water	113	3365
Trinitrophenol, wetted with ≥ 10% water	113	3364
Trinitrophenol, wetted with ≥ 30% water	113	1344
Trinitrotoluene, wetted with ≥ 10% water	113	3366
Trinitrotoluene, wetted with ≥ 30% water	113	1356
Tripropylamine	132	2260
Tripropylene	128	2057
Tris-(1-aziridinyl)phosphine oxide, solution	152	2501
Tungsten hexafluoride	125	2196
Turpentine	128	1299
Turpentine substitute	128	1300
Undecane	128	2330
Uranium hexafluoride	166	2978
Uranium hexafluoride, fissile containing > 1% Uranium-235	166	2977
Uranium hexafluoride, fissile excepted	166	2978
Uranium hexafluoride, low specific activity	166	2978
Uranium hexafluoride, non-fissile	166	2978
Uranium metal, pyrophoric	162	2979
Uranium nitrate, hexahydrate, solution	162	2980
Uranyl nitrate, hexahydrate, solution	162	2980
Uranyl nitrate, solid	162	2981
Urea hydrogen peroxide	140	1511
Urea nitrate, wetted with ≥ 10% water	113	3370
Urea nitrate, wetted with ≥ 20% water	113	1357
Valeraldehyde	129	2058
Valeryl chloride	132	2502
Vanadium compound, n.o.s.	151	3285
Vanadium oxytrichloride	137	2443
Vanadium pentoxide	151	2862
Vanadium tetrachloride	137	2444
Vanadium trichloride	157	2475
Vanadyl sulfate	151	2931
Vehicle, flammable gas powered	128	3166
Vehicle, flammable liquid powered	128	3166
Vinyl acetate	**129P**	**1301**
Vinyl acetate, inhibited	**129P**	**1301**
Vinyl acetate, stabilized	**129P**	**1301**
Vinyl bromide, inhibited	**116P**	**1085**
Vinyl bromide, stabilized	**116P**	**1085**
Vinyl butyrate, inhibited	**129P**	**2838**
Vinyl butyrate, stabilized	**129P**	**2838**
Vinyl chloride, inhibited	**116P**	**1086**

Hazmat

Pocket Partner   693

Substance	Guide	ID
Vinyl chloride, stabilized	**116P**	**1086**
Vinyl chloroacetate	155	2589
Vinyl ethyl ether	**127P**	**1302**
Vinyl ethyl ether, inhibited	**127P**	**1302**
Vinyl ethyl ether, stabilized	**127P**	**1302**
Vinyl fluoride, inhibited	**116P**	**1860**
Vinyl fluoride, stabilized	**116P**	**1860**
Vinylidene chloride, inhibited	**129P**	**1303**
Vinylidene chloride, stabilized	**130P**	**1303**
Vinyl isobutyl ether	**127P**	**1304**
Vinyl isobutyl ether, inhibited	**127P**	**1304**
Vinyl isobutyl ether, stabilized	**127P**	**1304**
Vinyl methyl ether	**116P**	**1087**
Vinyl methyl ether, inhibited	**116P**	**1087**
Vinyl methyl ether, stabilized	**116P**	**1087**
Vinylpyridines, inhibited	**131P**	**3073**
Vinylpyridines, stabilized	**131P**	**3073**
Vinyltoluenes, inhibited	**130P**	**2618**
Vinyltoluenes, stabilized	**130P**	**2618**
Vinyltrichlorosilane	**155P**	**1305**
Vinyltrichlorosilane, inhibited	**155P**	**1305**
Vinyltrichlorosilane, stabilized	**155P**	**1305**
VX	**153**	**2810**
Water-reactive liquid, corrosive, n.o.s.	138	3129
Water-reactive liquid, n.o.s.	138	3148
Water-reactive liquid, toxic, n.o.s.	139	3130
Water-reactive solid, corrosive, n.o.s.	138	3131
Water-reactive solid, flammable, n.o.s.	138	3132
Water-reactive solid, n.o.s.	138	2813
Water-reactive solid, oxidizing, n.o.s.	138	3133
Water-reactive solid, self-heating, n.o.s.	138	3135
Water-reactive solid, toxic, n.o.s.	139	3134
Water-reactive substances, liquid, corrosive, n.o.s.	138	3129
Water-reactive substances, liquid, n.o.s.	138	3148
Water-reactive substances, liquid, toxic, n.o.s.	139	3130
Water-reactive substances, solid, corrosive, n.o.s.	138	3131
Water-reactive substances, solid, flammable, n.o.s.	138	3132
Water-reactive substances, solid, n.o.s.	138	2813
Water-reactive substances, solid, oxidizing, n.o.s.	138	3133
Water-reactive substances, solid, self-heating, n.o.s.	138	3135
Water-reactive substances, solid, toxic, n.o.s.	139	3134
Wheelchair, electric, with batteries	154	3171
White asbestos	171	2590
White phosphorus, dry	136	1381
White phosphorus, in solution	136	1381
White phosphorus, molten	136	2447
White phosphorus, under water	136	1381
Wood preservatives, liquid	129	1306
Wool waste, wet	133	1387
Xanthates	135	3342
Xenon	121	2036
Xenon, compressed	121	2036
Xenon, refrigerated liquid (cryogenic liquid)	120	2591
Xylenes	130	1307
Xylenols	153	2261
Xylenols, liquid	153	3430
Xylenols, solid	153	2261

Substance	Guide	ID
Xylidines	153	1711
Xylidines, liquid	153	1711
Xylidines, solid	153	1711
Xylidines, solid	153	3452
Xylyl bromide	152	1701
Xylyl bromide, liquid	152	1701
Xylyl bromide, solid	152	3417
Yellow phosphorus, dry	136	1381
Yellow phosphorus, in solution	136	1381
Yellow phosphorus, molten	136	2447
Yellow phosphorus, under water	136	1381
Zinc ammonium nitrite	140	1512
Zinc arsenate	151	1712
Zinc arsenate and Zinc arsenite mixture	151	1712
Zinc arsenite	151	1712
Zinc arsenite and Zinc arsenate mixture	151	1712
Zinc ashes	138	1435
Zinc bromate	140	2469
Zinc chlorate	140	1513
Zinc chloride, anhydrous	154	2331
Zinc chloride, solution	154	1840
Zinc cyanide	151	1713
Zinc dithionite	171	1931
Zinc dross	138	1435
Zinc dust	138	1435
Zinc fluorosilicate	151	2855
Zinc hydrosulfite	171	1931
Zinc nitrate	140	1514
Zinc permanganate	140	1515
Zinc peroxide	143	1516
Zinc phosphide	139	1714
Zinc powder	138	1436
Zinc residue	138	1435
Zinc resinate	133	2714
Zinc silicofluoride	151	2855
Zinc skimmings	138	1435
Zirconium, dry, coiled wire, finished metal sheets or strips	170	2858
Zirconium, dry, finished sheets, strips or coiled wire	135	2009
Zirconium hydride	138	1437
Zirconium metal, liquid, suspension	170	1308
Zirconium metal, powder, wet	170	1358
Zirconium nitrate	140	2728
Zirconium picramate, wetted with ≥ 20% water	113	1517
Zirconium powder, dry	135	2008
Zirconium powder, wetted with ≥ 25% water	170	1358
Zirconium scrap	135	1932
Zirconium sulfate	171	9163
Zirconium suspended in a flammable liquid	170	1308
Zirconium suspended in a liquid (flammable)	170	1308
Zirconium tetrachloride	137	2503

Hazmat

Hazardous Materials Guides

How to Use the Guides Effectively

Each numbered guide is designed to provide first responders who have limited dangerous goods training with the essential information. A numbered guide is assigned to each material listed in the indexes. The titles of the guides identify the general hazards of the dangerous goods covered.

The guides are not applicable when materials of different classes and/or divisions are involved in an incident and are intermingled. Incidents involving more than one class of material require the incident commander to obtain informed advice as soon as the scope of the incident can be determined. Materials involved in an incident may, by themselves, be nonhazardous; however, a combination of several materials or the involvement of a single material in a fire, may still produce serious health, fire or explosion hazards.

Each guide is divided into four main sections:

- The first section recaps the substances covered by that guide.
- The second section describes potential hazards that the material may display in terms of fire, explosion, and health effects upon exposure. This allows the responder to make decisions regarding the protection of the emergency response team as well as the surrounding population.
- The third section outlines suggested public safety measures based on the situation at hand. It provides general information regarding immediate isolation of the incident site, the recommended type of protective clothing and respiratory protection. Suggested evacuation distances are listed for small and large spills and for fire situations. Some chemical warfare agents have been added to the lists, and are included in the Initial Isolation Distances tables where applicable, with the note "Used as a weapon."
- The fourth section covers emergency response actions and first aid. It outlines special precautions for incidents that involve fire, spill, or chemical exposure. The information on first aid is general guidance prior to seeking medical care. Factors such as the extent of the exposure, the material involved, the nature and severity of the injuries, the proximity to emergency, and medical services may vary. When human exposure has occurred, immediate efforts should be made to remove all contaminated clothing and shoes and to get medical help.

Guide 111: Mixed Load/Unidentified Cargo

POTENTIAL HAZARDS

FIRE OR EXPLOSION

- May explode from heat, shock, friction or contamination.
- May react violently or explosively on contact with air, water, or foam.
- May be ignited by heat, sparks or flames.
- Vapors may travel to source of ignition and flash back.
- Containers may explode when heated.
- Ruptured cylinders may rocket.

HEALTH

- Inhalation, ingestion or contact with substance may cause severe injury, infection, disease, or death.
- High concentration of gas may cause asphyxiation without warning.
- Contact may cause burns to skin and eyes.
- Fire or contact with water may produce irritating, toxic and/or corrosive gases.
- Runoff from fire control may cause pollution.

PUBLIC SAFETY

- **CALL Emergency Response Telephone Number on Shipping Paper first. If Shipping Paper is not available or there is no answer, refer to telephone numbers listed on page 613.**
- Isolate spill/ leak area for at least 100 m (330 ft) in all directions.
- Keep unauthorized personnel away.
- Stay upwind.
- Keep out of low areas.

PROTECTIVE CLOTHING

- Wear positive pressure self-contained breathing apparatus (SCBA).
- Structural firefighters' protective clothing provides limited protection in fire situations ONLY; it may not be effective in spill situations.

EVACUATION

Fire

- If tank, rail car, or tank truck is involved in a fire, isolate for 800 m (½ mile) in all directions; also, consider initial evacuation for 800 m (½ mile) in all directions.

EMERGENCY RESPONSE

FIRE

CAUTION: Material may react with extinguishing agent.
Small Fires

- Dry chemical, CO_2, water spray, or regular foam.

Pocket Partner 697

Large Fires
- Water spray, fog or regular foam.
- Move containers from fire area if you can do it without risk.

Fire involving Tanks
- Cool containers with flooding quantities of water until well after fire is out.
- Do not get water inside containers.
- Withdraw immediately in case of rising sound from venting safety devices or discoloration of tank.
- ALWAYS stay away from tanks engulfed in fire.

SPILL OR LEAK

- Do not touch or walk through spilled material.
- ELIMINATE all ignition sources (no smoking, flares, sparks, or flames in immediate area).
- All equipment used when handling the product must be grounded.
- Keep combustibles (wood, paper, oil, etc.) away from spilled material.
- Use water spray to reduce vapors or divert vapor cloud drift. Avoid allowing water runoff to contact spilled material.
- Prevent entry into waterways, sewers, basements, or confined areas.

Small Spills
- Take up with sand or other noncombustible absorbent material and place into containers for later disposal.

Large Spills
- Dike far ahead of liquid spill for later disposal.

FIRST AID

- Move victim to fresh air.
- Call 911 or emergency medical service.
- Give artificial respiration if victim is not breathing.
- Do not use mouth-to-mouth method if the victim has ingested or inhaled the substance; give artificial respiration with the aid of a pocket mask equipped with a one-way valve or other proper respiratory medical device.
- Administer oxygen if breathing is difficult.
- Remove and isolate contaminated clothing and shoes.
- In case of contact with substance, immediately flush skin or eyes with running water for at least 20 minutes.
- Shower and wash with soap and water.
- Keep victim warm and quiet.
- Effects of exposure (inhalation, ingestion, or skin contact) to substance may be delayed.
- Ensure that medical personnel are aware of the material(s) involved, and take precautions to protect themselves.

Guide 112: Explosives - Division 1.1, 1.2, 1.3, 1.5, or 1.6; Class A or B

SUBSTANCES INCLUDED

Ammonium nitrate-fuel oil mixtures
Blasting agent, n.o.s.
Explosive A
Explosive B
Explosives, division 1.1, 1.2, 1.3, 1.5, or 1.6

POTENTIAL HAZARDS

FIRE OR EXPLOSION

- **May explode and throw fragments 1600 meters (1 mile) or more if fire reaches cargo.**

HEALTH

- Fire may produce irritating, corrosive, and/or toxic gases.

PUBLIC SAFETY

- **CALL Emergency Response Telephone Number on Shipping Paper first. If Shipping Paper is not available or there is no answer, refer to telephone numbers listed on page 613.**
- Isolate spill or leak area immediately for at least 500 meters (1/3 mile) in all directions.
- Move people out of line of sight of the scene and away from windows.
- Keep unauthorized personnel away.
- Stay upwind.
- Ventilate closed spaces before entering.

PROTECTIVE CLOTHING

- Wear positive pressure self-contained breathing apparatus (SCBA).
- Structural firefighters' protective clothing will only provide limited protection.

EVACUATION

Large Spill

- Consider evacuation for 800 meters (1/2 mile) in all directions.

Fire

- If rail car or trailer is involved in a fire and heavily encased explosives such as bombs or artillery projectiles are suspected, ISOLATE for 1600 meters (1 mile) in all directions; also, initiate evacuation including emergency responders for 1600 meters (1 mile) in all directions.
- When heavily encased explosives are not involved, evacuate the area for 800 meters (1/2 mile) in all directions.

Hazmat

FIRE

Cargo Fires
- **DO NOT fight fire when fire reaches cargo! Cargo may explode!**
- Stop all traffic and clear the area for at least 1600 meters (1 mile) in all directions and let burn.
- DO NOT move cargo or vehicle if cargo has been exposed to heat.

Tire or Vehicle Fires
- Use plenty of water - FLOOD IT! If water is not available, use CO_2, dry chemical, or dirt.
- If possible, and without risk, use unmanned hose holders or monitor nozzles from maximum distance to prevent fire from spreading to cargo area.
- Pay special attention to tire fires as re-ignition may occur. Stand by with extinguisher ready.

SPILL OR LEAK

- ELIMINATE all ignition sources (no smoking, flares, sparks, or flames in immediate area).
- All Equipment used when handling product must be grounded.
- DO NOT touch or walk through spilled material.
- DO NOT operate radio transmitters within 100 meters (330 feet) of electric detonators.
- **DO NOT clean-up or dispose of, except under supervision of a specialist.**

FIRST AID

- Move victim to fresh air.
- Call 911 or emergency medical service.
- Give artificial respiration if victim is not breathing.
- Administer oxygen if breathing is difficult.
- Remove and isolate contaminated clothing and shoes.
- In case of contact with substance, immediately flush skin or eyes with running water for at least 20 minutes.
- Ensure that medical personnel are aware of the material(s) involved, and take precautions to protect themselves.

Guide 113: Flammable Solids - Toxic
(Wet/Desensitized Explosive)

SUBSTANCES INCLUDED

1310 Ammonium picrate, wetted with $\geq$ 10% water
1320 Dinitrophenol, wetted with $\geq$ 15% water
1321 Dinitrophenolates, wetted with $\geq$ 15% water
1322 Dinitroresorcinol, wetted with $\geq$ 15% water
1336 Nitroguanidine (Picrite), wetted with > 20% water
1336 Picrite, wetted
1337 Nitrostarch, wetted with $\geq$ 20% water
1337 Nitrostarch, wetted with $\geq$ 30% solvent
1344 Picric acid, wet, with > 10% water
1344 Trinitrophenol, wetted with $\geq$ 30% water
1347 Silver picrate, wetted with $\geq$ 30% water
1348 Sodium dinitro-o-cresolate, wetted with $\geq$ 15% water
1348 Sodium dinitro-ortho-cresolate, wetted
1349 Sodium picramate, wetted with $\geq$ 20% water
1354 Trinitrobenzene, wetted with $\geq$ 30% water
1355 Trinitrobenzoic acid, wetted with $\geq$ 30% water
1356 TNT, wetted with $\geq$ 30% water
1356 Trinitrotoluene, wetted with $\geq$ 30% water
1357 Urea nitrate, wetted with $\geq$ 20% water
1517 Zirconium picramate, wetted with $\geq$ 20% water
1571 Barium azide, wetted with $\geq$ 50% water
2555 Nitrocellulose with water, $\geq$ 25% water
2556 Nitrocellulose with $\geq$ 25% alcohol
2556 Nitrocellulose with alcohol
2852 Dipicryl sulfide, wetted with $\geq$ 10% water
3317 2-Amino-4,6-dinitrophenol, wetted with $\geq$ 20% water
3319 Nitroglycerin mixture with > 2%, but $\leq$ 10% Nitroglycerin, desensitized
3319 Nitroglycerin mixture, desensitized, solid, n.o.s.,
  with > 2% but $\leq$ 10% Nitroglycerin
3343 Nitroglycerin mixture, desensitized, liquid, flammable, n.o.s.,
  with $\leq$ 30% Nitroglycerin
3344 Pentaerythrite tetranitrate mixture, desensitized, solid, n.o.s.,
  with > 10% but $\leq$ 20% PETN
3357 Nitroglycerin mixture, desensitized, liquid, n.o.s.,
  with $\leq$ 30% Nitroglycerin
3364 Picric acid, wetted with $\geq$ 10% water
3364 Trinitrophenol, wetted with $\geq$ 10% water
3365 Picryl chloride, wetted with $\geq$ 10% water
3365 Trinitrochlorobenzene, wetted with $\geq$ 10% water
3366 TNT, wetted with $\geq$ 10% water
3366 Trinitrotoluene, wetted with $\geq$ 10% water
3367 Trinitrobenzene, wetted with $\geq$ 10% water
3368 Trinitrobenzoic acid, wetted with $\geq$ 10% water
3369 Sodium dinitro-o-cresolate, wetted with $\geq$ 10% water
3370 Urea nitrate, wetted with $\geq$ 10% water
3376 4-Nitrophenylhydrazine, $\geq$ 30% water

POTENTIAL HAZARDS
FIRE OR EXPLOSION

- Flammable/combustible material.
- May be ignited by heat, sparks, or flames.

Pocket Partner   **701**

- Dried out material may explode if exposed to heat, flame, friction, or shock; treat as an explosive (Guide 112).
- **Keep material wet with water or treat as an explosive (Guide 112).**
- Runoff to sewer may create fire or explosion hazard.

HEALTH

- Some are toxic and may be fatal if inhaled, swallowed or absorbed through skin.
- Contact may cause burns to skin and eyes.
- Fire may produce irritating, corrosive, or toxic gases.
- Runoff from fire control or dilution water may cause pollution.

PUBLIC SAFETY

- **CALL Emergency Response Telephone Number on Shipping Paper first. If Shipping Paper is not available or there is no answer, refer to telephone numbers listed on page 613.**
- Isolate spill or leak area for at least 100 meters (330 feet) in all directions.
- Keep unauthorized personnel away.
- Stay upwind.
- Ventilate closed spaces before entering

PROTECTIVE CLOTHING

- Wear positive pressure self-contained breathing apparatus (SCBA).
- Structural firefighters' protective clothing will only provide limited protection.

EVACUATION

Large Spill
- Consider initial evacuation for 500 meters (1/3 mile) in all directions.

Fire
- If tank, rail car, or tank truck is involved in a fire, ISOLATE for 800 meters (½ mile) in all directions; also, consider initial evacuation for 800 meters(½ mile) in all directions.

EMERGENCY RESPONSE
FIRE

Cargo fires
- **DO NOT fight fire when fire reaches cargo! Cargo may explode!**
- Stop all traffic and clear the area for at least 800 meters (½ mile) in all directions and let burn.
- **DO NOT move cargo or vehicle if cargo has been exposed to heat.**

Tire or Vehicle Fires
- Use plenty of water - FLOOD IT! If water is not available, use CO_2, dry chemical, or dirt.
- If possible, and without risk, use unmanned hose holders or monitor nozzles from maximum distance to prevent fire from spreading to cargo area.
- Pay special attention to tire fires as re-ignition may occur. Stand by with extinguisher ready.

SPILL OR LEAK
- ELIMINATE all ignition sources (no smoking, flares, sparks, or flames in immediate area).
- All equipment used when handling the product must be grounded.
- DO NOT touch or walk through spilled material.

Small Spills
- Flush area with flooding quantities of water.

Large Spills
- Wet down with water and dike for later disposal.
- Keep "wetted" product wet by slowly adding flooding quantities of water.

FIRST AID
- Move victim to fresh air.
- Call 911 or emergency medical service.
- Give artificial respiration if victim is not breathing.
- Administer oxygen if breathing is difficult.
- Remove and isolate contaminated clothing and shoes.
- In case of contact with substance, immediately flush skin or eyes with running water for at least 20 minutes.
- Ensure that medical personnel are aware of the material(s) involved, and take precautions to protect themselves.

Hazmat

Guide 114: Explosives - Division 1.4; Class C

SUBSTANCES INCLUDED

Explosive C
Explosives Division 1.4

POTENTIAL HAZARDS

FIRE OR EXPLOSION

- May explode and throw fragments 500 meters (1/3 mile) or more if fire reaches cargo.

HEALTH

- Fire may produce irritating, corrosive, or toxic gases

PUBLIC SAFETY

- **CALL Emergency Response Telephone Number on Shipping Paper first. If Shipping Paper is not available or there is no answer, refer to telephone numbers listed on page 613.**
- Isolate spill or leak area for at least 100 meters (330 feet) in all directions.
- Move people out of line of sight of the scene and away from windows.
- Keep unauthorized personnel away.
- Stay upwind.
- Ventilate closed spaces before entering.

PROTECTIVE CLOTHING

- Wear positive pressure self-contained breathing apparatus (SCBA).
- Structural firefighters' protective clothing will only provide limited protection.

EVACUATION

Large Spill

- Consider evacuation for 250 meters (800 feet) in all directions.

Fire

- If rail car or trailer is involved in a fire, ISOLATE for 500 meters (1/3 mile) in all directions; also, initiate evacuation including emergency responders for 500 meters (1/3 mile) in all directions.

EMERGENCY RESPONSE

FIRE

Cargo fires

- **DO NOT fight fire when fire reaches cargo! Cargo may explode!**
- Stop all traffic and clear the area for at least 500 meters (1/3 mile) in all directions and let burn.
- **DO NOT move cargo or vehicle if cargo has been exposed to heat.**

Tire or Vehicle Fires

- Use plenty of water - FLOOD IT! If water is not available, use CO_2, dry chemical, or dirt.
- If possible, and without risk, use unmanned hose holders or monitor nozzles from maximum distance to prevent fire from spreading to cargo area.
- Pay special attention to tire fires as re-ignition may occur. Stand by with extinguisher ready.

SPILL OR LEAK

- ELIMINATE all ignition sources (no smoking, flares, sparks, or flames in immediate area).
- All equipment used when handling the product must be grounded.
- DO NOT touch or walk through spilled material.
- DO NOT operate radio transmitters within 100 meters (330 feet) of electric detonators.
- **DO NOT clean-up or dispose of, except under supervision of a specialist.**

FIRST AID

- Move victim to fresh air.
- Call 911 or emergency medical service.
- Give artificial respiration if victim is not breathing.
- Administer oxygen if breathing is difficult.
- Remove and isolate contaminated clothing and shoes.
- In case of contact with substance, immediately flush skin or eyes with running water for at least 20 minutes.
- Ensure that medical personnel are aware of the material(s) involved, and take precautions to protect themselves.

SUPPLEMENTAL INFORMATION

- Packages bearing the 1.4S label or packages containing material classified as 1.4S are designed or packaged in such a manner that when involved in a fire, may burn vigorously with localized detonations and projection of fragments.
- Effects are usually confined to immediate vicinity of packages.
- If fire threatens cargo area containing packages bearing the 1.4S, consider isolating at least 15 meters (50 feet) in all directions. Fight fire with normal precautions from a reasonable distance.

Hazmat

Guide 115: Gases - Flammable
(Including Refrigerated Liquids)

SUBSTANCES INCLUDED

1011	Butane; Butane mixture
1012	Butylene
1027	Cyclopropane; Cyclopropane, liquefied
1030	1,1-Difluoroethane; Difluoroethane
1030	Refrigerant gas R-152a
1033	Dimethyl ether
1035	Ethane; Ethane, compressed
1037	Ethyl chloride
1038	Ethylene, refrigerated liquid (cryogenic liquid)
1039	Ethyl methyl ether; Methyl ethyl ether
1041	Carbon dioxide and Ethylene oxide mixture, with > 9% but ≤ 87% Ethylene oxide
1041	Carbon dioxide and Ethylene oxide mixtures, with > 6% Ethylene oxide
1049	Hydrogen; Hydrogen, compressed
1055	Isobutylene
1057	Lighters (& refills) (cigarettes) (flammable gas)
1063	Methyl chloride
1063	Refrigerant gas R-40
1075	Butane; Butane mixture
1075	Butylene
1075	Isobutane; Isobutane mixture
1075	Isobutylene
1075	Liquefied petroleum gas; LPG; Petroleum gas, liquefied
1075	Propane; Propane mixture
1075	Propylene
1077	Propylene
1912	Methyl chloride and Methylene chloride mixture
1954	Compressed gas, flammable, n.o.s.
1954	Dispersant gas, n.o.s. (flammable)
1954	Insecticide gas, flammable, n.o.s.
1954	Liquefied gas, flammable, n.o.s.
1954	Refrigerant gas, n.o.s. (flammable)
1954	Refrigerating machines, containing flammable, non-toxic, non-corrosive, liquefied gas
1957	Deuterium; Deuterium, compressed
1960	Engine starting fluid
1961	Ethane, refrigerated liquid
1961	Ethane-Propane mixture, refrigerated liquid
1964	Hydrocarbon gas mixture, compressed, n.o.s.
1964	Hydrocarbon gas, compressed, n.o.s.
1965	Hydrocarbon gas mixture, liquefied, n.o.s.
1965	Hydrocarbon gas, liquefied, n.o.s.
1966	Hydrogen, refrigerated liquid (cryogenic liquid)
1969	Isobutane; Isobutane mixture
1971	Methane; Methane, compressed
1971	Natural gas, compressed
1972	Liquefied natural gas (LNG) (cryogenic liquid)
1972	Methane, refrigerated liquid (cryogenic liquid)
1972	Natural gas, refrigerated liquid (cryogenic liquid)
1978	Propane; Propane mixture
2034	Hydrogen and Methane mixture, compressed
2035	1,1,1-Trifluoroethane; Trifluoroethane, compressed

2035	Refrigerant gas R-143a
2037	Gas cartridges
2037	Receptacles, small, containing gas
2044	2,2-Dimethylpropane
2453	Ethyl fluoride
2453	Refrigerant gas R-161
2454	Methyl fluoride
2454	Refrigerant gas R-41
2517	1-Chloro-1,1-difluoroethane; Chlorodifluoroethanes
2517	Difluorochloroethanes
2517	Refrigerant gas R-142b
2601	Cyclobutane
3138	Acetylene, Ethylene and Propylene in mixture, refrigerated liquid containing $\geq$ 71.5% Ethylene with $\leq$ 22.5% Acetylene and $\leq$ 6% Propylene
3150	Devices, small, hydrocarbon gas powered, w/ release device
3150	Hydrocarbon gas refills for small devices, w/ release device
3153	Perfluoro(methyl vinyl ether); Perfluoromethyl vinyl ether
3154	Perfluoro(ethyl vinyl ether); Perfluoroethyl vinyl ether
3161	Liquefied gas, flammable, not otherwise specified
3167	Gas sample, non-pressurized, flammable, not otherwise specified, not refrigerated liquid
3252	Difluoromethane
3252	Refrigerant gas R-32
3312	Gas, refrigerated liquid, flammable, not otherwise specified
3354	Insecticide gas, flammable, not otherwise specified
3358	Refrigerating machines containing flammable, non-toxic, liquefied gas
3468	Hydrogen, in a metal hydride storage system
9279	Hydrogen, absorbed in metal hydride

POTENTIAL HAZARDS

FIRE OR EXPLOSION

- **EXTREMELY FLAMMABLE.**
- Will be easily ignited by heat, sparks, or flames.
- Will form explosive mixtures with air.
- Vapors from liquefied gas are initially heavier than air and spread along the ground.
  CAUTION: Hydrogen (UN1049), Deuterium (UN1957), and Methand (UN1971) are lighter than air and will rise. Hydrogen and Deuterium fires are difficult to detect since they burn with an invisible flame. Use an alternate method of detection (thermal camera, broom handle, etc.)
- Vapors may travel to source of ignition and flash back.
- Cylinders exposed to fire may vent and release flammable gas through pressure relief devices.
- Containers may explode when heated.
- Ruptured cylinders may rocket.

HEALTH

- Vapors may cause dizziness or asphyxiation without warning.
- Some may be irritating if inhaled at high concentrations.
- Contact with gas or liquefied gas may cause burns, severe injury, and/or frostbite.
- Fire may produce irritating or toxic gases.

Hazmat

PUBLIC SAFETY

- **CALL Emergency Response Telephone Number on Shipping Paper first. If Shipping Paper is not available or there is no answer, refer to telephone numbers listed on page 613.**
- As an immediate precautionary measure, isolate spill or leak area for at least 100 m (330 ft) in all directions.
- Keep unauthorized personnel away.
- Stay upwind.
- Many gases are heavier than air and will spread along ground and collect in low or confined areas (sewers, basements, tanks).
- Keep out of low areas.

PROTECTIVE CLOTHING

- Wear positive pressure self-contained breathing apparatus (SCBA).
- Structural firefighters' protective clothing will only provide limited protection.
- Always wear thermal protective clothing when handling refrigerated/cryogenic liquids.

EVACUATION

Large Spill

- Consider evacuation for 800 meters (½ mile) in all directions.

Fire

- If tank, rail car, or tank truck is involved in a fire, ISOLATE for 1600 meters (1 mile) in all directions; also, initiate evacuation including emergency responders for 1600 meters (1 mile) in all directions.

EMERGENCY RESPONSE

FIRE

- **DO NOT extinguish a leaking gas fire unless leak can be stopped.**
  CAUTION: Hydrogen (UN1049) and Deuterium (UN1957) burn with an invisible flame.

Small Fires

- Dry chemical or CO_2.

Large Fires

- Water spray or fog.
- Move containers from fire area if you can do it without risk.

Fire Involving Tanks

- Fight fire from maximum distance or use unmanned hose holders or monitor nozzles.
- Cool containers with flooding quantities of water until well after fire is out.
- DO NOT direct water at source of leak or safety devices; icing may occur.

- Withdraw immediately in case of rising sound from venting safety devices or discoloration of tank.
- ALWAYS stay away from tanks engulfed in fire.
- For massive fire, use unmanned hose holders or monitor nozzles; if this is impossible, withdraw from area and let fire burn.

SPILL OR LEAK

- ELIMINATE all ignition sources (no smoking, flares, sparks, or flames in immediate area).
- All equipment used when handling the product must be grounded.
- DO NOT touch or walk through spilled material.
- Stop leak if you can do it without risk.
- If possible, turn leaking containers so that gas escapes rather than liquid.
- Use water spray to reduce vapors or divert vapor cloud drift. Avoid allowing water runoff to contact spilled material.
- DO NOT direct water at spill or source of leak.
- Prevent spreading of vapors through sewers, ventilation systems, and confined areas.
- Isolate area until gas has dispersed.

CAUTION: When in contact with refrigerated/ cryogenic liquids, many materials become brittle and are likely to break without warning.

FIRST AID

- Move victim to fresh air.
- Call 911 or emergency medical service.
- Give artificial respiration if victim is not breathing.
- Administer oxygen if breathing is difficult.
- Remove and isolate contaminated clothing and shoes.
- Clothing frozen to the skin should be thawed before being removed.
- In case of contact with liquefied gas, thaw frosted parts with lukewarm water.
- In case of burns, immediately cool affected skin for as long as possible with cold water. Do not remove clothing if adhering to skin.
- Keep victim warm and quiet.
- Ensure that medical personnel are aware of the material(s) involved, and take precautions to protect themselves.

Hazmat

Guide 116: Gases - Flammable (Unstable)

SUBSTANCES INCLUDED

1001	Acetylene; Acetylene, dissolved
1010	**Butadienes and hydrocarbon mixture, stabilized**
1010	**Butadienes (, inhibited; & , stabilized)**
1060	**Methylacetylene and Propadiene mixture, stabilized**
1081	**Tetrafluoroethylene, inhibited (& , stabilized)**
1085	**Vinyl bromide, inhibited (& , stabilized)**
1086	**Vinyl chloride, inhibited (& , stabilized)**
1087	**Vinyl methyl ether (& , inhibited; & , stabilized)**
1860	**Vinyl fluoride, inhibited (& , stabilized)**
1959	1,1-Difluoroethylene
1959	Refrigerant gas R-1132a
1962	Ethylene; Ethylene, compressed
2203	Silane; Silane, compressed
2200	**Propadiene, inhibited (& , stabilized)**
2419	Bromotrifluoroethylene
2452	**Ethylacetylene, inhibited (& , stabilized)**
2455	Methyl nitrite
3374	Acetylene, solvent free

POTENTIAL HAZARDS
FIRE OR EXPLOSION

- **EXTREMELY FLAMMABLE**
- Will be easily ignited by heat, sparks, or flames.
- Will form explosive mixtures with air.
- Silane will ignite spontaneously in air.
- Those substances designated with a "**P**" may polymerize explosively when heated or involved in a fire.
- Vapors from liquefied gas are initially heavier than air and spread along ground.
- Vapors may travel to source of ignition and flash back.
- Cylinders exposed to fire may vent and release flammable gas through pressure relief devices.
- Containers may explode when heated.
- Ruptured cylinders may rocket.

HEALTH

- Vapors may cause dizziness or asphyxiation without warning.
- Some may be toxic if inhaled at high concentrations.
- Contact with gas or liquefied gas may cause burns, severe injury and/or frostbite.
- Fire may produce irritating or toxic gases.

PUBLIC SAFETY

- **CALL Emergency Response Telephone Number on Shipping Paper first. If Shipping Paper is not available or there is no answer, refer to telephone numbers listed on page 613.**
- As an immediate precautionary measures, isolate spill or leak area for at least 100 m (330 ft) in all directions.

- Keep unauthorized personnel away.
- Stay upwind.
- Many gases are heavier than air and will spread along ground and collect in low or confined areas (sewers, basements, tanks).
- Keep out of low areas.

PROTECTIVE CLOTHING

- Wear positive pressure self-contained breathing apparatus (SCBA).
- Structural firefighters' protective clothing will only provide limited protection.

EVACUATION

Large Spill

- Consider evacuation for 800 meters (1/2 mile) in all directions.

Fire

- If tank, rail car, or tank truck is involved in a fire, ISOLATE for 1600 meters (1 mile) in all directions; also, initiate evacuation including emergency responders for 1600 meters (1 mile) in all directions.

EMERGENCY RESPONSE

FIRE

- **DO NOT extinguish a leaking gas fire unless leak can be stopped.**

Small Fires

- Dry chemical or CO_2.

Large Fires

- Water spray or fog.
- Move containers from fire area if you can do it without risk.

Fire Involving Tanks

- Fight fire from maximum distance or use unmanned hose holders or monitor nozzles.
- Cool containers with flooding quantities of water until well after fire is out.
- DO NOT direct water at source of leak or safety devices; icing may occur.
- Withdraw immediately in case of rising sound from venting safety devices or discoloration of tank.
- ALWAYS stay away from tanks engulfed in fire.
- For massive fire, use unmanned hose holders or monitor nozzles; if this is impossible, withdraw from area and let fire burn.

SPILL OR LEAK

- ELIMINATE all ignition sources (no smoking, flares, sparks, or flames in immediate area).
- All equipment used when handling the product must be grounded.

Hazmat

- Stop leak if you can do it without risk.
- DO NOT touch or walk through spilled material.
- DO NOT direct water at spill or source of leak.
- Use water spray to reduce vapors or divert vapor cloud drift. Avoid allowing water runoff to contact spilled material.
- If possible, turn leaking containers so that gas escapes rather than liquid.
- Prevent spreading of vapors through sewers, ventilation systems, and confined areas.
- Isolate area until gas has dispersed.

FIRST AID

- Move victim to fresh air.
- Call 911 or emergency medical service.
- Give artificial respiration if victim is not breathing.
- Administer oxygen if breathing is difficult.
- Remove and isolate contaminated clothing and shoes.
- In case of contact with liquefied gas, thaw frosted parts with lukewarm water.
- In case of burns, immediately cool affected skin for as long as possible with cold water. Do not remove clothing if adhering to skin.
- Keep victim warm and quiet.
- Ensure that medical personnel are aware of the material(s) involved, and take precautions to protect themselves.

Hazmat

Guide 117: Gases - Toxic - Flammable (Extreme Hazard)

SUBSTANCES INCLUDED

1051 AC
1051 Hydrocyanic acid, aqueous solutions, with > 20% Hydrogen cyanide
1051 Hydrocyanic acid, liquefied
1051 Hydrogen cyanide, stabilized (& , anhydrous)
1053 Hydrogen sulfide; Hydrogen sulfide, liquefied
1064 Methyl mercaptan
2202 Hydrogen selenide, anhydrous

POTENTIAL HAZARDS

FIRE OR EXPLOSION

- These materials are extremely flammable.
- May form explosive mixtures with air.
- May be ignited by heat, sparks, or flames.
- Vapors from liquefied gas are initially heavier than air and spread along ground.
- Vapors may travel to source of ignition and flash back.
- Runoff may create fire or explosion hazard.
- Cylinders exposed to fire may vent and release toxic and flammable gas through pressure relief devices.
- Containers may explode when heated.
- Ruptured cylinders may rocket.

HEALTH

- **TOXIC; Extremely Hazardous.**
- May be fatal if inhaled or absorbed through skin.
- Initial odor may be irritating or foul and may deaden your sense of smell.
- Contact with gas or liquefied gas may cause burns, severe injury and/or frostbite.
- Fire will produce irritating, corrosive and/or toxic gases.
- Runoff from fire control may cause pollution.

PUBLIC SAFETY

- **CALL Emergency Response Telephone Number on Shipping Paper first. If Shipping Paper is not available or there is no answer, refer to telephone numbers listed on page 613.**
- As an immediate precautionary measure, isolate spill or leak area for at least 100 m (330 ft) in all directions.
- Keep unauthorized personnel away.
- Stay upwind.
- Many gases are heavier than air and will spread along ground and collect in low or confined areas (sewers, basements, tanks).
- Keep out of low areas.
- Ventilate cloased spaces before entering.

Hazmat

PROTECTIVE CLOTHING

- Wear positive pressure self-contained breathing apparatus (SCBA).
- Wear chemical protective clothing that is specifically recommended by the manufacturer. It may provide little or no thermal protection.
- Structural firefighters' protective clothing provides limited protection in fire situations ONLY; it is not effective in spill situations where direct contact with the substance is possible.

EVACUATION

Spill

- See the Table of Initial Isolation and Protective Action Distances (page 908).

Fire

- If tank, rail car, or tank truck is involved in a fire, ISOLATE for 1600 meters (1 mile) in all directions; also, initiate evacuation including emergency responders for 1600 meters (1 mile) in all directions.

EMERGENCY RESPONSE
FIRE

- **DO NOT extinguish a leaking gas fire unless leak can be stopped.**

Small Fires

- Dry chemical or CO_2.

Large Fires

- Water spray or fog.
- Move containers from fire area if you can do it without risk.
- Damaged cylinders should be handled only by specialists.

Fire Involving Tanks

- Fight fire from maximum distance or use unmanned hose holders or monitor nozzles.
- Cool containers with flooding quantities of water until well after fire is out.
- DO NOT direct water at source of leak or safety devices; icing may occur.
- Withdraw immediately in case of rising sound from venting safety devices or discoloration of tank.
- ALWAYS stay away from tanks engulfed in fire.

SPILL OR LEAK

- ELIMINATE all ignition sources (no smoking, flares, sparks, or flames in immediate area).
- All equipment used when handling the product must be grounded.
- Fully encapsulating, vapor protective clothing should be worn for spills and leaks with no fire.

- DO NOT touch or walk through spilled material.
- Stop leak if you can do it without risk.
- Use water spray to reduce vapors or divert vapor cloud drift. Avoid allowing water runoff to contact spilled material.
- DO NOT direct water at spill or source of leak.
- If possible, turn leaking containers so that gas escapes rather than liquid.
- Prevent entry into waterways, sewers, basements, and confined areas.
- Isolate area until gas has dispersed.
- Consider igniting spill or leak to eliminate toxic gas concerns.

FIRST AID

- Move victim to fresh air.
- Call 911 or emergency medical service.
- Give artificial respiration if victim is not breathing.
- **DO NOT use mouth-to-mouth method if victim ingested or inhaled the substance; give artificial respiration with the aid of a pocket mask equipped with a one-way valve or other proper respiratory medical device.**
- Administer oxygen if breathing is difficult.
- Remove and isolate contaminated clothing and shoes.
- In case of contact with substance, immediately flush skin or eyes with running water for at least 20 minutes.
- In case of contact with liquefied gas, thaw frosted parts with lukewarm water.
- In case of burns, immediately cool affected skin for as long as possible with cold water. Do not remove clothing if adhering to skin.
- Keep victim warm and quiet.
- Keep victim under observation.
- Effects of contact or inhalation may be delayed.
- Ensure that medical personnel are aware of the material(s) involved, and take precautions to protect themselves.

Hazmat

Guide 118: Gases - Flammable - Corrosive

SUBSTANCES INCLUDED

1032 Dimethylamine, anhydrous
1036 Ethylamine
1061 Methylamine, anhydrous
1083 Trimethylamine, anhydrous

POTENTIAL HAZARDS

FIRE OR EXPLOSION

- **EXTREMELY FLAMMABLE**
- May be easily ignited by heat, sparks, or flames.
- May form explosive mixtures with air.
- Vapors from liquefied gas are initially heavier than air and spread along ground.
- Vapors may travel to source of ignition and flash back.
- Some of these materials may react violently with water.
- Cylinders exposed to fire may vent and release flammable gas through pressure relief devices.
- Containers may explode when heated.
- Ruptured cylinders may rocket.

HEALTH

- May cause toxic effects if inhaled.
- Vapors are extremely irritating.
- Contact with gas or liquefied gas may cause burns, severe injury and/or frostbite.
- Fire will produce irritating, corrosive and/or toxic gases.
- Runoff from fire control may cause pollution.

PUBLIC SAFETY

- **CALL Emergency Response Telephone Number on Shipping Paper first. If Shipping Paper is not available or there is no answer, refer to telephone numbers listed on page 613.**
- As an immediate precautionary measure, isolate spill or leak area for at least 100 meters (330 feet) in all directions.
- Keep unauthorized personnel away.
- Stay upwind.
- Many gases are heavier than air and will spread along ground and collect in low or confined areas (sewers, basements, tanks).
- Keep out of low areas.
- Ventilate closed spaces before entering.

PROTECTIVE CLOTHING

- Wear positive pressure self-contained breathing apparatus (SCBA).

- Wear chemical protective clothing that is specifically recommended by the manufacturer. It may provide little or no thermal protection.
- Structural firefighters' protective clothing provides limited protection in fire situations ONLY; it is not effective in spill situations where direct contact with the substance is possible.

EVACUATION

Large Spill

- Consider evacuation for 800 meters (1/2 mile) in all directions.

Fire

- If tank, rail car, or tank truck is involved in a fire, ISOLATE for 1600 meters (1 mile) in all directions; also, initiate evacuation including emergency responders for 1600 meters (1 mile) in all directions.

EMERGENCY RESPONSE

FIRE

- **DO NOT extinguish a leaking gas fire unless leak can be stopped.**

Small Fires

- Dry chemical or CO_2.

Large Fires

- Water spray or fog.
- Move containers from fire area if you can do it without risk.
- Damaged cylinders should be handled only by specialists.

Fire Involving Tanks

- Fight fire from maximum distance or use unmanned hose holders or monitor nozzles.
- Cool containers with flooding quantities of water until well after fire is out.
- DO NOT direct water at source of leak or safety devices; icing may occur.
- Withdraw immediately in case of rising sound from venting safety devices or discoloration of tank.
- ALWAYS stay away from tanks engulfed in fire.

SPILL OR LEAK

- ELIMINATE all ignition sources (no smoking, flares, sparks, or flames in immediate area).
- All equipment used when handling the product must be grounded.
- Fully encapsulating, vapor protective clothing should be worn for spills and leaks with no fire.
- DO NOT touch or walk through spilled material.
- Stop leak if you can do it without risk.
- If possible, turn leaking containers so that gas escapes rather than liquid.

Hazmat

- Use water spray to reduce vapors or divert vapor cloud drift. Avoid allowing water runoff to contact spilled material.
- DO NOT direct water at spill or source of leak.
- Isolate area until gas has dispersed.

FIRST AID

- Move victim to fresh air.
- Call 911 or emergency medical service.
- Give artificial respiration if victim is not breathing.
- **DO NOT use mouth-to-mouth method if victim ingested or inhaled the substance; give artificial respiration with the aid of a pocket mask equipped with a one-way valve or other proper respiratory medical device.**
- Administer oxygen if breathing is difficult.
- Remove and isolate contaminated clothing and shoes.
- In case of contact with liquefied gas, thaw frosted parts with lukewarm water.
- In case of burns, immediately cool affected skin for as long as possible with cold water. Do not remove clothing if adhering to skin.
- Keep victim warm and quiet.
- Keep victim under observation.
- Effects of contact or inhalation may be delayed.
- Ensure that medical personnel are aware of the material(s) involved, and take precautions to protect themselves.

Harmat

Guide 119: Gases - Toxic - Flammable

SUBSTANCES INCLUDED

1016	Carbon monoxide; Carbon monoxide, compressed
1023	Coal gas; Coal gas, compressed
1026	Cyanogen; Cyanogen gas; Cyanogen, liquefied
1040	**Ethylene oxide; Ethylene oxide with Nitrogen**
1071	Oil gas; Oil gas, compressed
1082	**Trifluorochloroethylene (& , inhibited; & , stabilized)**
1582	Chloropicrin and Methyl chloride mixture
1911	Diborane; Diborane mixtures; Diborane, compressed
1953	Compressed gas, flammable, toxic, n.o.s. (Inhalation Hazard Zone A, B, C, or D)
1953	Compressed gas, toxic, flammable, n.o.s. (& Inhalation Hazard Zone A, B, C, or D)
1953	Liquefied gas, flammable, toxic, n.o.s. (& Inhalation Hazard Zone A, B, C, or D)
2188	Arsine
2188	SA
2189	Dichlorosilane
2192	Germane
2199	Phosphine
2204	Carbonyl sulfide
2534	Methylchlorosilane
2600	Carbon monoxide and Hydrogen mixture (& , compressed)
2676	Stibine
3160	Liquefied gas, toxic, flammable, n.o.s. (& Inhalation Hazard Zone A, B , C, or D)
3168	Gas sample, non-pressurized, toxic, flammable, n.o.s., not refrigerated liquid
3300	**Carbon dioxide and Ethylene oxide mixture, with > 87% Ethylene oxide**
3305	Compressed gas, toxic, flammable, corrosive, n.o.s. (& Inhalation Hazard Zone A, B , C, or D)
3309	Liquefied gas, toxic, flammable, corrosive, n.o.s. (& Inhalation Hazard Zone A, B , C, or D)
3355	Insecticide gas, toxic, flammable, n.o.s. (& Inhalation Hazard Zone A, B, C, or D)

POTENTIAL HAZARDS

FIRE OR EXPLOSION

- Flammable; easily ignited by heat, sparks, or flames.
- May form explosive mixtures with air.
- Those substances designated with a "**P**" may polymerize explosively when heated or involved in a fire.
- Vapors from liquefied gas are initially heavier than air and spread along ground.
- Vapors may travel to source of ignition and flash back.
- Some of these materials may react violently with water.
- Cylinders exposed to fire may vent and release flammable gas through pressure relief devices.
- Containers may explode when heated.
- Ruptured cylinders may rocket.
- Runoff may create fire or explosion hazard.

HEALTH

- **TOXIC; may be fatal if inhaled or absorbed through skin.**
- Contact with gas or liquefied gas may cause burns, severe injury and/or frostbite.
- Fire will produce irritating, corrosive and/or toxic gases.
- Runoff from fire control may cause pollution.

PUBLIC SAFETY

- **CALL Emergency Response Telephone Number on Shipping Paper first. If Shipping Paper is not available or there is no answer, refer to telephone numbers listed on page 613.**
- As an immediate precautionary measure, isolate spill or leak area for at least 100 meters (330 feet) in all directions.
- Keep unauthorized personnel away.
- Stay upwind.
- Many gases are heavier than air and will spread along ground and collect in low or confined areas (sewers, basements, tanks).
- Keep out of low areas.
- Ventilate closed spaces before entering.

PROTECTIVE CLOTHING

- Wear positive pressure self-contained breathing apparatus (SCBA).
- Wear chemical protective clothing that is specifically recommended by the manufacturer. It may provide little or no thermal protection.
- Structural firefighters' protective clothing provides limited protection in fire situations ONLY; it is not effective in spill situations where direct contact with the substance is possible.

EVACUATION

Spill

- See the Table of Initial Isolation and Protective Action Distances for highlighted substances (page 908). For non-highlighted substances, increase, in the downwind direction, as necessary, the isolation distance shown above under "PUBLIC SAFETY."

Fire

- If tank, rail car, or tank truck is involved in a fire, ISOLATE for 1600 meters (1 mile) in all directions; also, initiate evacuation including emergency responders for 1600 meters (1 mile) in all directions.

EMERGENCY RESPONSE

FIRE

- **DO NOT extinguish a leaking gas fire unless leak can be stopped.**

Small Fires

- Dry chemical, CO_2, water spray, or alcohol-resistant foam.

Large Fires

- Water spray, fog, or alcohol-resistant foam
- **DO NOT use water for chlorosilanes, use AFFF alcohol-resistant medium expansion foam.**
- Move containers from fire area if you can do it without risk.
- Damaged cylinders should be handled only by specialists.

Fire Involving Tanks

- Fight fire from maximum distance or use unmanned hose holders or monitor nozzles.
- Cool containers with flooding quantities of water until well after fire is out.
- DO NOT direct water at source of leak or safety devices; icing may occur.
- Withdraw immediately in case of rising sound from venting safety devices or discoloration of tank.
- ALWAYS stay away from tanks engulfed in fire.

SPILL OR LEAK

- ELIMINATE all ignition sources (no smoking, flares, sparks, or flames in immediate area).
- All equipment used when handling the product must be grounded.
- Fully encapsulating, vapor protective clothing should be worn for spills and leaks with no fire.
- DO NOT touch or walk through spilled material.
- Stop leak if you can do it without risk.
- DO NOT direct water at spill or source of leak.
- Use water spray to reduce vapors or divert vapor cloud drift. Avoid allowing water runoff to contact spilled material.
- For chlorosilanes, use AFFF alcohol-resistant medium expansion foam to reduce vapors.
- If possible, turn leaking containers so that gas escapes rather than liquid.
- Prevent entry into waterways, sewers, basements, or confined areas.
- Isolate area until gas has dispersed.

FIRST AID

- Move victim to fresh air.
- Call 911 or emergency medical service.
- Give artificial respiration if victim is not breathing.
- **DO NOT use mouth-to-mouth method if victim ingested or inhaled the substance; give artificial respiration with the aid of a pocket mask equipped with a one-way valve or other proper respiratory medical device.**
- Administer oxygen if breathing is difficult.
- Remove and isolate contaminated clothing and shoes.

Hazmat

- In case of contact with substance, immediately flush skin or eyes with running water for at least 20 minutes.
- In case of contact with liquefied gas, thaw frosted parts with lukewarm water.
- In case of burns, immediately cool affected skin for as long as possible with cold water. Do not remove clothing if adhering to skin.
- Keep victim warm and quiet.
- Keep victim under observation.
- Effects of contact or inhalation may be delayed.
- Ensure that medical personnel are aware of the material(s) involved, and take precautions to protect themselves.

Hazmat

Guide 120: Gases - Inert
(Including Refrigerated Liquids)

SUBSTANCES INCLUDED

1013	Carbon dioxide; Carbon dioxide, compressed
1058	Liquefied gas (non-flammable)
1058	Liquefied gases, non-flammable, charged with Nitrogen, Carbon dioxide, or Air
1845	Carbon dioxide, solid
1845	Dry ice
1913	Neon, refrigerated liquid (cryogenic liquid)
1951	Argon, refrigerated liquid (cryogenic liquid)
1963	Helium, refrigerated liquid (cryogenic liquid)
1970	Krypton, refrigerated liquid (cryogenic liquid)
1977	Nitrogen, refrigerated liquid (cryogenic liquid)
2187	Carbon dioxide, refrigerated liquid
2591	Xenon, refrigerated liquid (cryogenic liquid)
3136	Trifluoromethane, refrigerated liquid
3158	Gas, refrigerated liquid, n.o.s.

POTENTIAL HAZARDS
FIRE OR EXPLOSION

- **Non-flammable gases.**
- Containers may explode when heated.
- Ruptured cylinders may rocket.

HEALTH

- Vapors may cause dizziness or asphyxiation without warning.
- Vapors from liquefied gas are initially heavier than air and spread along the ground.
- Contact with gas or liquefied gas may cause burns, severe injury and/or frostbite.

PUBLIC SAFETY

- **CALL Emergency Response Telephone Number on Shipping Paper first. If Shipping Paper is not available or there is no answer, refer to telephone numbers listed on page 613.**
- As an immediate precautionary measure, isolate spill or leak area for at least 100 m (330 ft) in all directions.
- Keep unauthorized personnel away.
- Stay upwind.
- Many gases are heavier than air and will spread along ground and collect in low or confined areas (sewers, basements, tanks).
- Keep out of low areas.
- Ventilate closed spaces before entering.

PROTECTIVE CLOTHING

- Wear positive pressure self-contained breathing apparatus (SCBA).

Hazmat

- Structural firefighters' protective clothing will only provide limited protection.
- Always wear thermal protective clothing when handling refrigerated/cryogenic liquids or solids.

EVACUATION

Large Spill
- Consider initial downwind evacuation at least 100 m (330 ft).

Fire
- If tank, rail car, or tank truck is involved in a fire, ISOLATE for 800 meters (½ mile) in all directions; also, initiate evacuation including emergency responders for 800 meters (½ mile) in all directions.

EMERGENCY RESPONSE

FIRE

- Use extinguishing agent suitable for type of surrounding fire.
- Move containers from fire area if you can do it without risk.
- Damaged cylinders should be handled only by specialists.

Fire Involving Tanks
- Fight fire from maximum distance or use unmanned hose holders or monitor nozzles.
- Cool containers with flooding quantities of water until well after fire is out.
- DO NOT direct water at source of leak or safety devices; icing may occur.
- Withdraw immediately in case of rising sound from venting safety devices or discoloration of tank.
- ALWAYS stay away from tanks engulfed in fire.

SPILL OR LEAK

- DO NOT touch or walk through spilled material.
- Stop leak if you can do it without risk.
- DO NOT direct water at spill or source of leak.
- Use water spray to reduce vapors or divert vapor cloud drift. Avoid allowing water runoff to contact spilled material.
- If possible, turn leaking containers so that gas escapes rather than liquid.
- Prevent entry into waterways, sewers, basements, or confined areas.
- Allow substance to evaporate
- Ventilate the area.

CAUTION: When in contact with refrigerated/cryogenic liquids, many materials become brittle and are likely to break without warning.

Hazmat

- Move victim to fresh air.
- Call 911 or emergency medical service.
- Give artificial respiration if victim is not breathing.
- Administer oxygen if breathing is difficult.
- Clothing frozen to the skin should be thawed before being removed.
- In case of contact with liquefied gas, thaw frosted parts with lukewarm water.
- Keep victim warm and quiet.
- Ensure that medical personnel are aware of the material(s) involved, and take precautions to protect themselves.

Hazmat

Guide 121: Gases - Inert

SUBSTANCES INCLUDED

1006 Argon; Argon, compressed
1046 Helium; Helium, compressed
1056 Krypton; Krypton, compressed
1065 Neon; Neon, compressed
1066 Nitrogen; Nitrogen, compressed
1979 Rare gases mixture; Rare gases mixture, compressed
1980 Oxygen and Rare gases mixture (& , compressed)
1981 Nitrogen and Rare gases mixture (& , compressed)
2036 Xenon; Xenon, compressed

POTENTIAL HAZARDS

FIRE OR EXPLOSION

- **Non-flammable gases.**
- Containers may explode when heated.
- Ruptured cylinders may rocket.

HEALTH

- Vapors may cause dizziness or asphyxiation without warning.
- Vapors from liquefied gas are initially heavier than air and spread along the ground.

PUBLIC SAFETY

- **CALL Emergency Response Telephone Number on Shipping Paper first. If Shipping Paper is not available or there is no answer, refer to telephone numbers listed on page 613.**
- As an immediate precautionary measure, isolate spill or leak area for at least 100 m (330 ft) in all directions.
- Keep unauthorized personnel away.
- Stay upwind.
- Many gases are heavier than air and will spread along ground and collect in low or confined areas (sewers, basements, tanks).
- Keep out of low areas.
- Ventilate closed spaces before entering.

PROTECTIVE CLOTHING

- Wear positive pressure self-contained breathing apparatus (SCBA).
- Structural firefighters' protective clothing will only provide limited protection.

EVACUATION

Large Spill
- Consider initial downwind evacuation for at least 100 meters (330 feet).

Fire

- If tank, rail car, or tank truck is involved in a fire, ISOLATE for 800 meters (1/2 mile) in all directions; also, initiate evacuation including emergency responders for 800 meters (1/2 mile) in all directions.

EMERGENCY RESPONSE
FIRE

- Use extinguishing agent suitable for type of surrounding fire.
- Move containers from fire area if you can do it without risk.
- Damaged cylinders should be handled only by specialists.

Fire Involving Tanks

- Fight fire from maximum distance or use unmanned hose holders or monitor nozzles.
- Cool containers with flooding quantities of water until well after fire is out.
- DO NOT direct water at source of leak or safety devices; icing may occur.
- Withdraw immediately in case of rising sound from venting safety devices or discoloration of tank.
- ALWAYS stay away from tanks engulfed in fire.

SPILL OR LEAK

- DO NOT touch or walk through spilled material.
- Stop leak if you can do it without risk.
- Use water spray to reduce vapors or divert vapor cloud drift. Avoid allowing water runoff to contact spilled material.
- DO NOT direct water at spill or source of leak.
- If possible, turn leaking containers so that gas escapes rather than liquid.
- Prevent entry into waterways, sewers, basements, or confined areas.
- Allow substance to evaporate
- Ventilate the area.

FIRST AID

- Move victim to fresh air.
- Call 911 or emergency medical service.
- Give artificial respiration if victim is not breathing.
- Administer oxygen if breathing is difficult.
- Keep victim warm and quiet.
- Ensure that medical personnel are aware of the material(s) involved, and take precautions to protect themselves.

Hazmat

Guide 122: Gases - Oxidizing
(Including Refrigerated Liquids)

SUBSTANCES INCLUDED

1002 Air, compressed
1003 Air, refrigerated liquid (cryogenic liquid)
1003 Air, refrigerated liquid (cryogenic liquid), non-pressurized
1014 Carbon dioxide and Oxygen mixture (& , compressed)
1070 Nitrous oxide; Nitrous oxide, compressed
1072 Oxygen; Oxygen, compressed
1073 Oxygen, refrigerated liquid (cryogenic liquid)
1980 Rare gases and Oxygen mixture (& , compressed)
2201 Nitrous oxide, refrigerated liquid
2451 Nitrogen trifluoride; Nitrogen trifluoride, compressed
3156 Compressed gas, oxidizing, n.o.s.
3157 Liquefied gas, oxidizing, n.o.s.
3311 Gas, refrigerated liquid, oxidizing, n.o.s.

POTENTIAL HAZARDS
FIRE OR EXPLOSION

- Substance does not burn but will support combustion.
- Some may react explosively with fuels.
- May ignite combustibles (wood, paper, oil, clothing, etc.)
- Vapors from liquefied gas are initially heavier than air and spread along ground.
- Runoff may create fire or explosion hazard.
- Containers may explode when heated.
- Ruptured cylinders may rocket.

HEALTH

- Vapors may cause dizziness or asphyxiation without warning.
- Contact with gas or liquefied gas may cause burns, severe injury and/or frostbite.
- Fire may produce irritating or toxic gases.

PUBLIC SAFETY

- **CALL Emergency Response Telephone Number on Shipping Paper first. If Shipping Paper is not available or there is no answer, refer to telephone numbers listed on page 613.**
- As an immediate precautionary measure, isolate spill or leak area for at least 100 meters (330 feet) in all directions.
- Keep unauthorized personnel away.
- Stay upwind.
- Many gases are heavier than air and will spread along ground and collect in low or confined areas (sewers, basements, tanks).
- Keep out of low areas.
- Ventilate closed spaces before entering.

PROTECTIVE CLOTHING

- Wear positive pressure self-contained breathing apparatus (SCBA).
- Wear chemical protective clothing that is specifically recommended by the manufacturer. It may provide little or no thermal protection.
- Structural firefighters' protective clothing provides limited protection in fire situations ONLY; it is not effective in spill situations where direct contact with the substance is possible.
- Always wear thermal protective clothing when handling refrigerated/cryogenic liquids or solids.

EVACUATION

Large Spill

- Consider initial downwind evacuation for at least 500 meters (1/3 mile).

Fire

- If tank, rail car, or tank truck is involved in a fire, ISOLATE for 800 meters (1/2 mile) in all directions; also, initiate evacuation including emergency responders for 800 meters (1/2 mile) in all directions.

EMERGENCY RESPONSE
FIRE

- Use extinguishing agent suitable for type of surrounding fire.

Small Fires

- Dry chemical or CO_2.

Large Fires

- Water spray, fog, or regular foam.
- Move containers from fire area if you can do it without risk.
- Damaged cylinders should be handled only by specialists.

Fire Involving Tanks

- Fight fire from maximum distance or use unmanned hose holders or monitor nozzles.
- Cool containers with flooding quantities of water until well after fire is out.
- DO NOT direct water at source of leak or safety devices; icing may occur.
- Withdraw immediately in case of rising sound from venting safety devices or discoloration of tank.
- ALWAYS stay away from tanks engulfed in fire.
- For massive fire, use unmanned hose holders or monitor nozzles; if this is impossible, withdraw from area and let fire burn.

Hazmat

SPILL OR LEAK

- Keep combustibles (wood, paper, oil, etc.) away from spilled material.
- DO NOT touch or walk through spilled material.
- Stop leak if you can do it without risk.
- If possible, turn leaking containers so that gas escapes rather than liquid.
- DO NOT direct water at spill or source of leak.
- Use water spray to reduce vapors or divert vapor cloud drift. Avoid allowing water runoff to contact spilled material.
- Prevent entry into waterways, sewers, basements, or confined areas.
- Allow substance to evaporate
- Isolate area until gas has dispersed.

CAUTION: When in contact with refrigerated/cryogenic liquids, many materials become brittle and are likely to break without warning.

FIRST AID

- Move victim to fresh air.
- Call 911 or emergency medical service.
- Give artificial respiration if victim is not breathing.
- Administer oxygen if breathing is difficult.
- Remove and isolate contaminated clothing and shoes.
- Clothing frozen to the skin should be thawed before being removed.
- In case of contact with liquefied gas, thaw frosted parts with lukewarm water.
- Keep victim warm and quiet.
- Ensure that medical personnel are aware of the material(s) involved, and take precautions to protect themselves.

Hazmat

Guide 123: Gases - Toxic and/or Corrosive

SUBSTANCES INCLUDED

1062	Methyl bromide
1581	Chloropicrin and Methyl bromide mixture
1612	Hexaethyl tetraphosphate & compressed gas mixture
1955	Compressed gas, toxic, not otherwise specified (& Inhalation Hazard Zone A, B, C, or D)
1955	Liquefied gas, toxic, not otherwise specified (& Inhalation Hazard Zone A, B, C, or D)
1955	Organic phosphate compound mixed with compressed gas
1955	Organic phosphorus compound mixed with compressed gas
1967	Insecticide gas, toxic, not otherwise specified
1967	Parathion and compressed gas mixture
2191	Sulfuryl fluoride
3162	Liquefied gas, toxic, not otherwise specified (& Inhalation Hazard Zone A, B, C, or D)
3169	Gas sample, non-pressurized, toxic, n.o.s., not refrigerated liquid
3304	Compressed gas, toxic, corrosive, n.o.s. (& Inhalation Hazard Zone A, B , C, or D)
3308	Liquefied gas, toxic, corrosive, n.o.s. (& Inhalation Hazard Zone A, B, C, or D)
9035	Gas identification set

POTENTIAL HAZARDS

FIRE OR EXPLOSION

- Some may burn, but none ignite readily.
- Vapors from liquefied gas are initially heavier than air and spread along ground.
- Cylinders exposed to fire may vent and release toxic and/or corrosive gas through pressure relief devices.
- Containers may explode when heated.
- Ruptured cylinders may rocket.

HEALTH

- **TOXIC; may be fatal if inhaled/absorbed through skin.**
- Vapors may be irritating.
- Contact with gas or liquefied gas may cause burns, severe injury and/or frostbite.
- Fire may produce irritating or toxic gases.
- Runoff from fire control may cause problem.

PUBLIC SAFETY

- **CALL Emergency Response Telephone Number on Shipping Paper first. If Shipping Paper is not available or there is no answer, refer to telephone numbers listed on page 613.**
- As an immediate precautionary measure, isolate spill or leak area for at least 100 m (330 ft) in all directions.
- Keep unauthorized personnel away.
- Stay upwind.

Hazmat

- Many gases are heavier than air and will spread along ground and collect in low or confined areas (sewers, basements, tanks).
- Keep out of low areas.
- Ventilate closed spaces before entering.

PROTECTIVE CLOTHING

- Wear positive pressure self-contained breathing apparatus (SCBA).
- Wear chemical protective clothing that is specifically recommended by the manufacturer. It may provide little or no thermal protection.
- Structural firefighters' protective clothing provides limited protection in fire situations ONLY; it is not effective in spill situations where direct contact with the substance is possible.

EVACUATION

Spill
- See the Table of Initial Isolation and Protective Action Distances for highlighted substances (page 908). For non-highlighted substances, increase, in the downwind direction, as necessary, the isolation distance shown above under "PUBLIC SAFETY."

Fire
- If tank, rail car, or tank truck is involved in a fire, ISOLATE for 800 meters (½ mile) in all directions; also, initiate evacuation including emergency responders for 800 meters (½ mile) in all directions.

EMERGENCY RESPONSE
FIRE

Small Fires
- Dry chemical or CO_2.

Large Fires
- Water spray, fog, or regular foam.
- DO NOT get water inside containers.
- Move containers from fire area if you can do it without risk.
- Damaged cylinders should be handled only by specialists.

Fire Involving Tanks
- Fight fire from maximum distance or use unmanned hose holders or monitor nozzles.
- Cool containers with flooding quantities of water until well after fire is out.
- DO NOT direct water at source of leak or safety devices; icing may occur.
- Withdraw immediately in case of rising sound from venting safety devices or discoloration of tank.
- ALWAYS stay away from tanks engulfed in fire.

Hazmat

SPILL OR LEAK

- Fully encapsulating, vapor protective clothing should be worn for spills and leaks with no fire.
- DO NOT touch or walk through spilled material.
- Stop leak if you can do it without risk.
- If possible, turn leaking containers so that gas escapes rather than liquid.
- Prevent entry into waterways, sewers, basements, or confined areas.
- Use water spray to reduce vapors or divert vapor cloud drift. Avoid allowing water runoff to contact spilled material.
- DO NOT direct water at spill or source of leak.
- Isolate area until gas has dispersed.

FIRST AID

- Move victim to fresh air.
- Call 911 or emergency medical service.
- Give artificial respiration if victim is not breathing.
- **DO NOT use mouth-to-mouth method if victim has ingested or inhaled the substance; give artificial respiration with the aid of a pocket mask equipped with a one-way valve or other proper respiratory medical device.**
- Administer oxygen if breathing is difficult.
- Remove and isolate contaminated clothing and shoes.
- In case of contact with liquefied gas, thaw frosted parts with lukewarm water.
- In case of contact with substance, immediately flush skin or eyes with running water for at least 20 minutes.
- Keep victim warm and quiet.
- Keep victim under observation.
- Effects of contact or inhalation may be delayed.
- Ensure that medical personnel are aware of the material(s) involved, and take precautions to protect themselves.

Hazmat

SUBSTANCES INCLUDED

1017	Chlorine
1045	Fluorine; Fluorine, compressed
1067	Dinitrogen tetroxide; Dinitrogen tetroxide, liquefied
1067	Nitrogen dioxide; Nitrogen dioxide, liquefied
1660	Nitric oxide; Nitric oxide, compressed
1749	Chlorine trifluoride
1975	Dinitrogen tetroxide and Nitric oxide mixture
1975	Nitric oxide and Nitrogen dioxide mixture
1975	Nitric oxide and Nitrogen tetroxide mixture
2190	Oxygen difluoride; Oxygen difluoride, compressed
2421	Nitrogen trioxide
2548	Chlorine pentafluoride
2901	Bromine chloride
3083	Perchloryl fluoride
3303	Compressed gas, toxic, oxidizing, n.o.s. (& Inhalation Hazard Zone A, B, C, or D)
3306	Compressed gas, toxic, oxidizing, corrosive, n.o.s. (& Inhalation Hazard Zone A, B , C, or D)
3307	Liquefied gas, toxic, oxidizing, n.o.s. (& Inhalation Hazard Zone A, B, C, or D)
3310	Liquefied gas, toxic, oxidizing, corrosive, n.o.s. (& Inhalation Hazard Zone A, B, C, or D)

POTENTIAL HAZARDS

FIRE OR EXPLOSION

- Substance does not burn but will support combustion.
- Vapors from liquefied gas are initially heavier than air and spread along ground.
- These are strong oxidizers and react vigorously or explosively with many materials including fuels.
- May ignite combustibles (wood, paper, oil, clothing, etc.)
- Some will react violently with air, moist air, and water.
- Cylinders exposed to fire may vent and release toxic and/or corrosive gas through pressure relief devices.
- Containers may explode when heated.
- Ruptured cylinders may rocket.

HEALTH

- **TOXIC; may be fatal if inhaled or absorbed (in skin).**
- Fire may produce irritating or toxic gases.
- Contact with gas or liquefied gas may cause burns, severe injury and/or frostbite.
- Runoff from fire control may cause pollution.

PUBLIC SAFETY

- **CALL Emergency Response Telephone Number on Shipping Paper first. If Shipping Paper is not available or there is no answer, refer to telephone numbers listed on page 613.**

Hazmat

- As an immediate precautionary measure, isolate spill or leak area for at least 100 m (330 ft) in all directions.
- Keep unauthorized personnel away.
- Stay upwind.
- Many gases are heavier than air and will spread along ground and collect in low or confined areas (sewers, basements, tanks).
- Keep out of low areas.
- Ventilate closed spaces before entering.

PROTECTIVE CLOTHING

- Wear positive pressure self-contained breathing apparatus (SCBA).
- Wear chemical protective clothing that is specifically recommended by the manufacturer. It may provide little or no thermal protection.
- Structural firefighters' protective clothing provides limited protection in fire situations ONLY; it is not effective in spill situations where direct contact with the substance is possible.

EVACUATION

Spill
- See the Table of Initial Isolation and Protective Action Distances (page 908).

Fire
- If tank, rail car, or tank truck is involved in a fire, ISOLATE for 800 meters (½ mile) in all directions; also, initiate evacuation including emergency responders for 800 meters (½ mile) in all directions.

EMERGENCY RESPONSE
FIRE

Small Fires
- **Water only; no dry chemical, CO_2, or Halon®.**
- Contain fire and let burn. If fire must be fought, water spray or fog is recommended.
- DO NOT get water inside containers.
- Move containers from fire area if you can do it without risk.
- Damaged cylinders should be handled only by specialists.

Fire Involving Tanks
- Fight fire from maximum distance or use unmanned hose holders or monitor nozzles.
- Cool containers with flooding quantities of water until well after fire is out.
- DO NOT direct water at source of leak or safety devices; icing may occur.
- Withdraw immediately in case of rising sound from venting safety devices or discoloration of tank.
- ALWAYS stay away from tanks engulfed in fire.

Hazmat

- For massive fire, use unmanned hose holders or monitor nozzles; if this is impossible, withdraw from area and let fire burn.

SPILL OR LEAK

- Fully encapsulating, vapor protective clothing should be worn for spills and leaks with no fire.
- DO NOT touch or walk through spilled material.
- Keep combustibles (wood, paper, oil, etc.) away from spilled material.
- Stop leak if you can do it without risk.
- Use water spray to reduce vapors or divert vapor cloud drift. Avoid allowing water runoff to contact spilled material.
- DO NOT direct water at spill or source of leak.
- If possible, turn leaking containers so that gas escapes rather than liquid.
- Prevent entry into waterways, sewers, basements, or confined areas.
- Isolate area until gas has dispersed.
- Ventilate the area.

FIRST AID

- Move victim to fresh air.
- Call 911 or emergency medical service.
- Give artificial respiration if victim is not breathing.
- **DO NOT use mouth-to-mouth method if victim has ingested or inhaled the substance; give artificial respiration with the aid of a pocket mask equipped with a one-way valve or other proper respiratory medical device.**
- Administer oxygen if breathing is difficult.
- Clothing frozen to the skin should be thawed before being removed.
- Remove and isolate contaminated clothing and shoes.
- In case of contact with liquefied gas, thaw frosted parts with lukewarm water.
- In case of contact with substance, immediately flush skin or eyes with running water for at least 20 minutes.
- Keep victim warm and quiet.
- Keep victim under observation.
- Effects of contact or inhalation may be delayed.
- Ensure that medical personnel are aware of the material(s) involved, and take precautions to protect themselves.

Hazmat

Guide 125: Gases - Corrosive

SUBSTANCES INCLUDED

1005	Ammonia solution, with > 50% Ammonia
1005	Ammonia, anhydrous; Ammonia, anhydrous, liquefied
1005	Anhydrous ammonia; Anhydrous ammonia, liquefied
1008	Boron trifluoride; Boron trifluoride, compressed
1043	Fertilizer, ammoniating solution, with free Ammonia
1048	Hydrogen bromide, anhydrous
1050	Hydrogen chloride, anhydrous
1052	Hydrogen fluoride, anhydrous
1069	Nitrosyl chloride
1076	CG
1076	Diphosgene
1076	DP
1076	Phosgene
1079	Sulfur dioxide; Sulfur dioxide, liquefied
1589	CK
1589	Cyanogen chloride (& , inhibited; & , stabilized)
1741	Boron trichloride
1859	Silicon tetrafluoride; Silicon tetrafluoride, compressed
2073	Ammonia, solution, with > 35% but ≤ 50% Ammonia
2186	Hydrogen chloride, refrigerated liquid
2194	Selenium hexafluoride
2195	Tellurium hexafluoride
2196	Tungsten hexafluoride
2197	Hydrogen iodide, anhydrous
2198	Phosphorus pentafluoride (& , compressed)
2417	Carbonyl fluoride; Carbonyl fluoride, compressed
2418	Sulfur tetrafluoride
2420	Hexafluoroacetone
3057	Trifluoroacetyl chloride
3318	Ammonia solution, with > 50% Ammonia

POTENTIAL HAZARDS

FIRE OR EXPLOSION

- Some may burn, but none ignite readily.
- Vapors from liquefied gas are initially heavier than air and spread along ground.
- Some of these materials may react violently with water.
- Cylinders exposed to fire may vent and release toxic and/or corrosive gas through pressure relief devices.
- Containers may explode when heated.
- Ruptured cylinders may rocket.

HEALTH

- **TOXIC; may be fatal if inhaled or absorbed (in skin).**
- Vapors are extremely irritating and corrosive.
- Contact with gas or liquefied gas may cause burns, severe injury and/or frostbite.
- Fire will produce irritating, corrosive, or toxic gases.
- Runoff from fire control may cause pollution.

PUBLIC SAFETY

- **CALL Emergency Response Telephone Number on Shipping Paper first. If Shipping Paper is not available or there is no answer, refer to telephone numbers listed on page 613.**
- As an immediate precautionary measure, isolate spill or leak area for at least 100 m (330 ft) in all directions.
- Keep unauthorized personnel away.
- Stay upwind.
- Many gases are heavier than air and will spread along ground and collect in low or confined areas (sewers, basements, tanks).
- Keep out of low areas.
- Ventilate closed spaces before entering.

PROTECTIVE CLOTHING

- Wear positive pressure self-contained breathing apparatus (SCBA).
- Wear chemical protective clothing that is specifically recommended by the manufacturer. It may provide little or no thermal protection.
- Structural firefighters' protective clothing provides limited protection in fire situations ONLY; it is not effective in spill situations where direct contact with the substance is possible.

EVACUATION

Spill

- See the Table of Initial Isolation and Protective Action Distances for highlighted substances (page 908). For non-highlighted substances, increase, in the downwind direction, as necessary, the isolation distance shown above under "PUBLIC SAFETY."

Fire

- If tank, rail car, or tank truck is involved in a fire, ISOLATE for 1600 meters (1 mile) in all directions; also, initiate evacuation including emergency responders for 1600 meters (1 mile) in all directions.

EMERGENCY RESPONSE
FIRE

Small Fires

- Dry chemical or CO_2.

Large Fires

- Water spray, fog, or regular foam.
- Move containers from fire area if you can do it without risk.
- DO NOT get water inside containers.
- Damaged cylinders should be handled only by specialists.

Fire Involving Tanks

- Fight fire from maximum distance or use unmanned hose holders or monitor nozzles.

- Cool containers with flooding quantities of water until well after fire is out.
- DO NOT direct water at source of leak or safety devices; icing may occur.
- Withdraw immediately in case of rising sound from venting safety devices or discoloration of tank.
- ALWAYS stay away from tanks engulfed in fire.

SPILL OR LEAK

- Fully encapsulating, vapor protective clothing should be worn for spills and leaks with no fire.
- DO NOT touch or walk through spilled material.
- Stop leak if you can do it without risk.
- If possible, turn leaking containers so that gas escapes rather than liquid.
- Prevent entry into waterways, sewers, basements, or confined areas.
- DO NOT direct water at spill or source of leak.
- Use water spray to reduce vapors or divert vapor cloud drift. Avoid allowing water runoff to contact spilled material.
- Isolate area until gas has dispersed.

FIRST AID

- Move victim to fresh air.
- Call 911 or emergency medical service.
- Give artificial respiration if victim is not breathing.
- **DO NOT use mouth-to-mouth method if victim has ingested or inhaled the substance; give artificial respiration with the aid of a pocket mask equipped with a one-way valve or other proper respiratory medical device.**
- Administer oxygen if breathing is difficult.
- Remove and isolate contaminated clothing and shoes.
- In case of contact with liquefied gas, thaw frosted parts with lukewarm water.
- In case of contact with substance, immediately flush skin or eyes with running water for at least 20 minutes.
- In case of contact with Hydrogen fluoride, anhydrous (UN1052), flush skin and eyes with water for 5 minutes; then, for skin exposures rub on a calcium/jelly combination; for eyes, flush with a warm, calcium solution for 15 minutes.
- Keep victim warm and quiet.
- Keep victim under observation.
- Effects of contact or inhalation may be delayed.
- Ensure that medical personnel are aware of the material(s) involved, and take precautions to protect themselves.

Hazmat

Guide 126: Gases - Compressed or Liquefied
(Including Refrigerant Gases)

SUBSTANCES INCLUDED

1009	Bromotrifluoromethane
1009	Refrigerant gas R-13B1
1015	Carbon dioxide and Nitrous oxide mixture
1018	Chlorodifluoromethane
1018	Refrigerant gas R-22
1020	Chloropentafluoroethane
1020	Refrigerant gas R-115
1021	1-Chloro-1,2,2,2-tetrafluoroethane; Chlorotetrafluoroethane
1021	Refrigerant gas R-124
1022	Chlorotrifluoromethane
1022	Refrigerant gas R-13
1028	Dichlorodifluoromethane
1028	Refrigerant gas R-12
1029	Dichlorofluoromethane
1029	Refrigerant gas R-21
1044	Fire extinguishers with compressed gas
1044	Fire extinguishers with liquefied gas
1078	Dispersant gas, n.o.s.
1078	Refrigerant gas, n.o.s.
1080	Sulfur hexafluoride
1858	Hexafluoropropylene
1858	Refrigerant gas R-1216
1950	Aerosol dispensers; Aerosols
1952	Carbon dioxide and Ethylene oxide mixtures, with ≤ 6% Ethylene oxide
1952	Carbon dioxide and Ethylene oxide mixtures, with ≤ 9% Ethylene oxide
1956	Accumulators, pressurized, pneumatic or hydraulic
1956	Compressed gas, n.o.s.
1956	Hexafluoropropylene oxide
1956	Liquefied gas, n.o.s.
1958	1,2-Dichloro-1,1,2,2-tetrafluoroethane
1958	Dichlorotetrafluoroethane
1958	Refrigerant gas R-114
1968	Insecticide gas, not otherwise specified
1973	Chlorodifluoromethane and Chloropentafluoroethane mixture
1973	Refrigerant gas R-502
1974	Bromochlorodifluoromethane
1974	Chlorodifluorobromomethane
1974	Refrigerant gas R-12B1
1976	Octafluorocyclobutane
1976	Refrigerant gas RC-318
1982	Refrigerant gas R-14; Refrigerant gas R-14, compressed
1982	Tetrafluoromethane; Tetrafluoromethane, compressed
1983	1-Chloro-2,2,2-trifluoroethane; Chlorotrifluoroethane
1983	Refrigerant gas R-133a
1984	Refrigerant gas R-23
1984	Trifluoromethane
2193	Hexafluoroethane; Hexafluoroethane, compressed
2193	Refrigerant gas R-116; Refrigerant gas R-116, compressed
2422	Octafluorobut-2-ene
2422	Refrigerant gas R-1318

Hazmat

2424	Octafluoropropane
2424	Refrigerant gas R-218
2599	Chlorotrifluoromethane and Trifluoromethane azeotropic mixture with approx. 60% Chlorotrifluoromethane
2599	Refrigerant gas R-13 and Refrigerant gas R-23 azeotropic mixture with 60% Refrigerant gas R-13
2599	Refrigerant gas R-503 (azeotropic mixture of Refrigerant gas R-13 and Refrigerant gas R-23 with 60% Refrigerant gas R-13)
2602	Dichlorodifluoromethane and Difluoroethane azeotropic mixture with approx. 74% Dichlorodifluoromethane
2602	Refrigerant gas R-12 and Refrigerant gas R-152a azeotropic mixture with 74% Refrigerant gas R-12
2602	Refrigerant gas R-500 (azeotropic mixture of Refrigerant gas R-12 and Refrigerant gas R-152a with approx. 74% Refrigerant gas R-12)
2857	Refrigerating machines, with Ammonia solutions (UN 2073)
2857	Refrigerating machines, with Ammonia solutions (UN2672)
2857	Refrigerating machines, containing non-flammable, liquefied gas
2857	Refrigerating machines, containing non-flammable, non-toxic gases
2857	Refrigerating machines, containing non-flammable, non-toxic, liquefied gas
2857	Refrigerating machines, containing non-flammable, non-toxic, non-corrosive, liquefied gas
3070	Dichlorodifluoromethane and Ethylene oxide mixture, with ≤ 12.5% Ethylene oxide
3070	Dichlorodifluoromethane and Ethylene oxide mixtures, with ≤ 12% Ethylene oxide
3159	1,1,1,2-Tetrafluoroethane
3159	Refrigerant gas R-134a
3163	Liquefied gas, not otherwise specified
3164	Articles, pressurized, hydraulic (containing non-flammable gas)
3164	Articles, pressurized, pneumatic (containing non-flammable gas)
3220	Pentafluoroethane
3220	Refrigerant gas R-125
3296	Heptafluoropropane
3296	Refrigerant gas R-227
3297	Chlorotetrafluoroethane and Ethylene oxide mixture, with ≤ 8.8% Ethylene oxide
3298	Ethylene oxide and Pentafluoroethane mixture, with ≤ 7.9% Ethylene oxide
3299	Ethylene oxide and Tetrafluoroethane mixture, with ≤ 5.6% Ethylene oxide
3337	Refrigerant gas R-404A
3338	Refrigerant gas R-407A
3339	Refrigerant gas R-407B
3340	Refrigerant gas R-407C
3353	Air bag inflators, compressed gas
3353	Air bag modules, compressed gas
3353	Seat-belt pre-tensioners, compressed gas

POTENTIAL HAZARDS
FIRE OR EXPLOSION

- Some may burn, but none ignite readily.
- Containers may explode when heated.
- Ruptured cylinders may rocket.

HEALTH

- Vapors may cause dizziness or asphyxiation without warning.
- Vapors from liquefied gas are initially heavier than air and spread along ground.
- Contact with gas or liquefied gas may cause burns, severe injury and/or frostbite.
- Fire will produce irritating, corrosive, or toxic gases.

PUBLIC SAFETY

- **CALL Emergency Response Telephone Number on Shipping Paper first. If Shipping Paper is not available or there is no answer, refer to telephone numbers listed on page 613.**
- As an immediate precautionary measure, isolate spill or leak area for at least 100 m (330 ft) in all directions.
- Keep unauthorized personnel away.
- Stay upwind.
- Many gases are heavier than air and will spread along ground and collect in low or confined areas (sewers, basements, tanks).
- Keep out of low areas.
- Ventilate closed spaces before entering.

PROTECTIVE CLOTHING

- Wear positive pressure self-contained breathing apparatus (SCBA).
- Wear chemical protective clothing that is specifically recommended by the manufacturer. It may provide little or no thermal protection.
- Structural firefighters' protective clothing will only provide limited protection.

EVACUATION

Large Spill

- Consider initial downwind evacuation for at least 500 meters (1/3 mile).

Fire

- If tank, rail car, or tank truck is involved in a fire, ISOLATE for 800 meters (½ mile) in all directions; also, initiate evacuation including emergency responders for 800 meters (½ mile) in all directions.

EMERGENCY RESPONSE

FIRE

- Use extinguishing agent suitable for type of surrounding fire.

Small Fires

- Dry chemical or CO_2.

Large Fires

- Water spray, fog, or regular foam.

- Move containers from fire area if you can do it without risk.
- Damaged cylinders should be handled only by specialists.

Fire Involving Tanks
- Fight fire from maximum distance or use unmanned hose holders or monitor nozzles.
- Cool containers with flooding quantities of water until well after fire is out.
- DO NOT direct water at source of leak or safety devices; icing may occur.
- Withdraw immediately in case of rising sound from venting safety devices or discoloration of tank.
- ALWAYS stay away from tanks engulfed in fire.
- Some of these materials, if spilled, may evaporate leaving a flammable residue.

SPILL OR LEAK
- DO NOT touch or walk through spilled material.
- Stop leak if you can do it without risk.
- DO NOT direct water at spill or source of leak.
- Use water spray to reduce vapors or divert vapor cloud drift. Avoid allowing water runoff to contact spilled material.
- If possible, turn leaking containers so that gas escapes rather than liquid.
- Prevent entry into waterways, sewers, basements, or confined areas.
- Allow substance to evaporate.
- Ventilate the area.

FIRST AID
- Move victim to fresh air.
- Call 911 or emergency medical service.
- Give artificial respiration if victim is not breathing.
- Administer oxygen if breathing is difficult.
- Remove and isolate contaminated clothing and shoes.
- In case of contact with liquefied gas, thaw frosted parts with lukewarm water.
- Keep victim warm and quiet.
- Ensure that medical personnel are aware of the material(s) involved, and take precautions to protect themselves.

SUBSTANCES INCLUDED

1088	Acetal
1090	Acetone
1091	Acetone oils
1110	Amyl methyl ketone; n-Amyl methyl ketone
1139	Coating solution
1153	Ethylene glycol diethyl ether
1155	Diethyl ether
1155	Ethyl ether
1156	Diethyl ketone
1159	Diisopropyl ether
1165	Dioxane
1166	Dioxolane
1169	Extracts, aromatic, liquid
1170	Ethanol; Ethanol, solution
1170	Ethyl alcohol; Ethyl alcohol, solution
1171	Ethylene glycol monoethyl ether
1179	Ethyl butyl ether
1188	Ethylene glycol monomethyl ether
1193	Ethyl methyl ketone
1197	Extracts, flavoring, liquid
1201	Fusel oil
1204	Nitroglycerin, solution in alcohol, with ≤ 1% Nitroglycerin
1224	Ketones, liquid, not otherwise specified
1226	Lighters for cigars, cigarettes (flammable liquid
1234	Methylal
1245	Methyl isobutyl ketone
1246	**Methyl isopropenyl ketone (, inhibited; & , stabilized)**
1249	Methyl propyl ketone
1266	Perfumery products, with flammable solvents
1280	**Propylene oxide**
1286	Rosin oil
1287	Rubber solution
1293	Tinctures, medicinal
1302	**Vinyl ethyl ether (& , inhibited; & , stabilized)**
1304	**Vinyl isobutyl ether (& , inhibited; & , stabilized)**
1648	Acetonitrile
1648	Methyl cyanide
1866	Resin solution
1915	Cyclohexanone
1987	Alcohols, n.o.s.
1987	Denatured alcohol
2056	Tetrahydrofuran
2059	Nitrocellulose, solution, flammable
2059	Nitrocellulose, solution, in a flammable liquid
2252	1,2-Dimethoxyethane
2302	5-Methylhexan-2-one
2338	Benzotrifluoride
2346	Butanedione
2346	Diacetyl
2350	Butyl methyl ether
2352	**Butyl vinyl ether (, inhibited; & , stabilized)**
2373	Diethoxymethane
2374	3,3-Diethoxypropene
2376	2,3-Dihydropyran
2377	1,1-Dimethoxyethane

2380	Dimethyldiethoxysilane
2384	Di-n-propyl ether; Dipropyl ether
2397	3-Methylbutan-2-one
2398	Methyl tert-butyl ether
2406	Isopropyl isobutyrate
2536	Methyltetrahydrofuran
2612	Methyl propyl ether
2615	Ethyl propyl ether
2621	Acetyl methyl carbinol
2707	Dimethyldioxanes
2708	Butoxyl
2752	1,2-Epoxy-3-ethoxypropane
3022	**1,2-Butylene oxide, stabilized**
3064	Nitroglycerin, solution in alcohol, with > 1%, but $\leq$ 5% Nitroglycerin
3065	Alcoholic beverages
3271	Ethers, n.o.s.
3272	Esters, n.o.s.

POTENTIAL HAZARDS

FIRE OR EXPLOSION

- **HIGHLY FLAMMABLE: Will be easily ignited by heat, sparks, or flames.**
- Vapors may form explosive mixtures with air.
- Vapors may travel to source of ignition and flash back.
- Most vapors are heavier than air. They will spread along the ground and collect in low or confined areas (sewers, basements, tanks).
- Vapor explosion hazard indoors, outdoors, or in sewers.
- Those substances designated with a "**P**" may polymerize explosively when heated or involved in a fire.
- Runoff to sewer may create fire or explosion hazard.
- Containers may explode when heated.
- Many liquids are lighter than water.

HEALTH

- Inhalation or contact with material may irritate or burn skin/eyes.
- Fire may produce irritating, corrosive, or toxic gases.
- Vapors may cause dizziness or suffocation.
- Runoff from fire control may cause pollution.

PUBLIC SAFETY

- **CALL Emergency Response Telephone Number on Shipping Paper first. If Shipping Paper is not available or there is no answer, refer to telephone numbers listed on page 613.**
- As an immediate precautionary measure, isolate spill or leak area for at least 50 meters (150 feet) in all directions.
- Keep unauthorized personnel away.
- Stay upwind.
- Keep out of low areas.
- Ventilate closed spaces before entering.

Hazmat

PROTECTIVE CLOTHING

- Wear positive pressure self-contained breathing apparatus (SCBA).
- Structural firefighters' protective clothing will only provide limited protection.

EVACUATION

Large Spill
- Consider initial downwind evacuation for at least 300 meters (1000 feet).

Fire
- If tank, rail car, or tank truck is involved in a fire, ISOLATE for 800 meters (½ mile) in all directions; also, initiate evacuation including emergency responders for 800 meters (½ mile) in all directions.

EMERGENCY RESPONSE
FIRE

CAUTION: All these products have a very low flash point: Use of water spray when fighting fire may be inefficient.

Small Fires
- Dry chemical, CO_2, water spray, or alcohol-resistant foam.

Large Fires
- Water spray, fog, or alcohol-resistant foam.
- Use water spray or fog; DO NOT use straight streams.
- Move containers from fire area if you can do it without risk.

Fire Involving Tanks of Car/Trailer Loads
- Fight fire from maximum distance or use unmanned hose holders or monitor nozzles.
- Cool containers with flooding quantities of water until well after fire is out.
- Withdraw immediately in case of rising sound from venting safety devices or discoloration of tank.
- ALWAYS stay away from tanks engulfed in fire.
- Some of these materials, if spilled, may evaporate leaving a flammable residue.

SPILL OR LEAK

- Eliminate all ignition sources (no smoking, flares, sparks, or flames in the immediate area).
- All equipment used when handling the product must be grounded.
- DO NOT touch or walk through spilled material.
- Stop leak if you can do it without risk.
- Prevent entry into waterways, sewers, basements, or confined areas.
- A vapor suppressing foam may be used to reduce vapors.

Hazmat

- Absorb or cover with dry earth, sand, or other non-combustible material and transfer to containers.
- Use clean non-sparking tools to collect absorbed material.

Large Spills
- Dike far ahead of liquid spill for later disposal.
- Water spray may reduce vapor; but may not prevent ignition in closed spaces.

FIRST AID

- Move victim to fresh air.
- Call 911 or emergency medical service.
- Give artificial respiration if victim is not breathing.
- Administer oxygen if breathing is difficult.
- Remove and isolate contaminated clothing and shoes.
- In case of contact with substance, immediately flush skin or eyes with running water for at least 20 minutes.
- Wash skin with soap and water.
- In case of burns, immediately cool affected skin for as long as possible with cold water. Do not remove clothing if adhering to skin.
- Keep victim warm and quiet.
- Ensure that medical personnel are aware of the material(s) involved, and take precautions to protect themselves.

Hazmat

Guide 128: Flammable Liquids
(Non-Polar/Water-Immiscible)

SUBSTANCES INCLUDED

1108	1-Pentene
1108	n-Amylene
1130	Camphor oil
1133	Adhesives (flammable)
1136	Coal tar distillates, flammable
1144	Crotonylene
1145	Cyclohexane
1146	Cyclopentane
1149	Butyl ethers
1149	Dibutyl ethers
1157	Diisobutyl ketone
1167	**Divinyl ether, inhibited; Divinyl ether, stabilized**
1202	Diesel fuel
1202	Fuel oil; Fuel oil, no. 1,2,4,5,6
1202	Gas oil
1202	Heating oil, light
1203	Gasohol
1203	Gasoline
1203	Motor spirit
1203	Petrol
1206	Heptanes
1208	Hexanes
1208	Neohexane
1216	Isooctene
1223	Kerosene
1262	Isooctane
1262	Octanes
1263	Paint (flammable)
1263	Paint related material (flammable)
1265	Isopentane; n-Pentane
1265	Pentanes
1267	Petroleum crude oil
1268	Petroleum distillates, n.o.s.
1268	Petroleum products, n.o.s.
1270	Petroleum oil
1288	Shale oil
1299	Turpentine
1300	Turpentine substitute
1863	Fuel, aviation, turbine engine
1920	Nonanes
1993	Combustible liquid, n.o.s.
1993	Compound, cleaning liquid (flammable)
1993	Compound, tree or weed killing, liquid (flammable)
1993	Diesel fuel
1993	Flammable liquid, n.o.s.
1993	Fuel oil
1993	Medicines, flammable, liquid, n.o.s.
1993	Refrigerating machine
2050	Diisobutylene, isomeric compounds
2052	Dipentene
2055	**Styrene monomer (, inhibited; & , stabilized)**
2057	Tripropylene
2222	Anisole

2241	Cycloheptane
2242	Cycloheptene
2245	Cyclopentanone
2246	Cyclopentene
2247	n-Decane
2251	**2,5-Norbornadiene (& , inhibited; & , stabilized)**
2251	**Bicyclo[2.2.1]hepta-2,5-diene (& , inhibited; & , stabilized)**
2251	**Dicycloheptadiene**
2263	Dimethylcyclohexanes
2271	Ethyl amyl ketone
2278	n-Heptene
2286	Pentamethylheptane
2287	Isoheptenes
2288	Isohexenes
2293	4-Methoxy-4-methyl-pentan-2-one
2296	Methylcyclohexane
2297	Methylcyclohexanone
2298	Methylcyclopentane
2301	2-Methylfuran
2303	Isopropenylbenzene
2309	**Octadiene**
2319	Terpene hydrocarbons, not otherwise specified
2324	Triisobutylene
2330	Undecane
2358	**Cyclooctatetraene**
2364	n-Propyl benzene
2366	Diethyl carbonate
2368	alpha-Pinene; Pinene (alpha)
2370	1-Hexene
2371	Isopentenes
2389	Furan
2413	Tetrapropyl orthotitanate
2457	2,3-Dimethylbutane
2459	2-Methyl-1-butene
2460	2-Methyl-2-butene
2461	Methylpentadiene
2541	Terpinolene
2561	3-Methyl-1-butene
2709	Butylbenzenes
2710	Dipropyl ketone
2850	Propylene tetramer
3166	Engines, internal combustion, flammable gas powered
3166	Engines, internal combustion, flammable liquid powered
3166	Engines, internal combustion, including when fitted in machinery or vehicles
3166	Vehicle, flammable gas powered
3166	Vehicle, flammable liquid powered
3256	Elevated temperature liquid, flammable, n.o.s., with flash point above 37.8°C (100°F), at or above its flash point
3256	Elevated temperature liquid, flammable, n.o.s., with flash point above 60.5°C (141°F), at or above its flash point
3257	Elevated temperature liquid, n.o.s., at or above 100°C (212°F), and below its flash point
3269	Polyester resin kit
3295	Hydrocarbons, liquid, n.o.s.
3379	Desensitized explosive, liquid, n.o.s.

Hazmat

POTENTIAL HAZARDS

FIRE OR EXPLOSION

- **HIGHLY FLAMMABLE: Will be easily ignited by heat, sparks, or flames.**
- Vapors may form explosive mixtures with air.
- Vapors may travel to source of ignition and flash back.
- Most vapors are heavier than air. They will spread along the ground and collect in low or confined areas (sewers, basements, tanks).
- Vapor explosion hazard indoors, outdoors, or in sewers.
- Those substances designated with a "**P**" may polymerize explosively when heated or involved in a fire.
- Runoff to sewer may create fire or explosion hazard.
- Containers may explode when heated.
- Many liquids are lighter than water.
- Substance may be transported hot.
- **If molten aluminum is involved, refer to Guide 169.**

HEALTH

- Inhalation or contact with material may irritate or burn skin and eyes.
- Fire may produce irritating, corrosive, or toxic gases.
- Vapors may cause dizziness or suffocation.
- Runoff from fire control may cause pollution.

PUBLIC SAFETY

- **CALL Emergency Response Telephone Number on Shipping Paper first. If Shipping Paper is not available or there is no answer, refer to telephone numbers listed on page 613.**
- As an immediate precautionary measure, isolate spill or leak area for at least 50 m (150 ft) in all directions.
- Keep unauthorized personnel away.
- Stay upwind.
- Keep out of low areas.
- Ventilate closed spaces before entering.

PROTECTIVE CLOTHING

- Wear positive pressure self-contained breathing apparatus (SCBA).
- Structural firefighters' protective clothing will only provide limited protection.

EVACUATION

Large Spill

- Consider initial downwind evacuation for at least 300 meters (1000 feet).

Fire

- If tank, rail car, or tank truck is involved in a fire, ISOLATE for 800 meters (½ mile) in all directions; also, initiate evacuation including emergency responders for 800 meters (½ mile) in all directions.

EMERGENCY RESPONSE

FIRE

CAUTION: All these products have a very low flash point: Use of water spray when fighting fire may be inefficient.

CAUTION: For mixtures containing a high percentage of an alcohol or polar solvent, alcohol-resistant foam may be more effective.

Small Fires

- Dry chemical, CO_2, water spray, or regular foam.

Large Fires

- Water spray, fog, or regular foam.
- Use water spray or fog; DO NOT use straight streams.
- Move containers from fire area if you can do it without risk.

Fire Involving Tanks of Car/Trailer Loads

- Fight fire from maximum distance or use unmanned hose holders or monitor nozzles.
- Cool containers with flooding quantities of water until well after fire is out.
- Withdraw immediately in case of rising sound from venting safety devices or discoloration of tank.
- ALWAYS stay away from tanks engulfed in fire.
- For massive fire, use unmanned hose holders or monitor nozzles; if this is impossible, withdraw from area and let fire burn.

SPILL OR LEAK

- Eliminate all ignition sources (no smoking, flares, sparks, or flames in the immediate area).
- All equipment used when handling the product must be grounded.
- DO NOT touch or walk through spilled material.
- Stop leak if you can do it without risk.
- Prevent entry into waterways, sewers, basements, or confined areas.
- A vapor suppressing foam may be used to reduce vapors.
- Absorb or cover with dry earth, sand, or other non-combustible material and transfer to containers.
- Use clean non-sparking tools to collect absorbed material.

Large Spills

- Dike far ahead of liquid spill for later disposal.
- Water spray may reduce vapor; but may not prevent ignition in closed spaces.

Hazmat

FIRST AID

- Move victim to fresh air.
- Call 911 or emergency medical service.
- Give artificial respiration if victim is not breathing.
- Administer oxygen if breathing is difficult.
- Remove and isolate contaminated clothing and shoes.
- In case of contact with substance, immediately flush skin or eyes with running water for at least 20 minutes.
- Wash skin with soap and water.
- In case of burns, immediately cool affected skin for as long as possible with cold water. Do not remove clothing if adhering to skin.
- Keep victim warm and quiet.
- Ensure that medical personnel are aware of the material(s) involved, and take precautions to protect themselves.

Hazmat

Guide 129: Flammable Liquids
(Polar/Water-Miscible/Noxious)

SUBSTANCES INCLUDED

1089	Acetaldehyde
1104	Amyl acetates
1105	Amyl alcohols
1105	Pentanols
1107	Amyl chloride
1109	Amyl formates
1113	Amyl nitrite
1120	Butanols
1123	Butyl acetates
1126	1-Bromobutane
1128	n-Butyl formate
1129	Butyraldehyde
1148	Diacetone alcohol
1161	Dimethyl carbonate
1172	Ethylene glycol monoethyl ether acetate
1173	Ethyl acetate
1176	Ethyl borate
1189	Ethylene glycol monomethyl ether acetate
1190	Ethyl formate
1191	Ethylhexaldehydes
1191	Octyl aldehydes
1192	Ethyl lactate
1195	Ethyl propionate
1210	Printing ink related material
1210	Printing ink, flammable
1212	Isobutanol; Isobutyl alcohol
1213	Isobutyl acetate
1219	Isopropanol; Isopropyl alcohol
1220	Isopropyl acetate
1229	Mesityl oxide
1231	Methyl acetate
1237	Methyl butyrate
1243	Methyl formate
1247	**Methyl methacrylate monomer(& , inhibited; & , stabilized)**
1248	Methyl propionate
1261	Nitromethane
1264	Paraldehyde
1272	Pine oil
1274	normal Propyl alcohol; n-Propanol
1275	Propionaldehyde
1276	n-Propyl acetate
1278	1-Chloropropane
1278	Propyl chloride
1281	Propyl formates
1282	Pyridine
1292	Ethyl silicate
1292	Tetraethyl silicate
1301	**Vinyl acetate (& , inhibited; & , stabilized)**
1303	**Vinylidene chloride, inhibited**
1306	Wood preservatives, liquid
1917	**Ethyl acrylate (, inhibited; & , stabilized)**
1919	**Methyl acrylate (, inhibited; & , stabilized)**
1989	Aldehydes, not otherwise specified

Hazmat

1990 Benzaldehyde
2045 Isobutyl aldehyde
2047 Dichloropropenes
2053 M.I.B.C.; Methyl isobutyl carbinol
2053 Methylamyl alcohol
2058 Valeraldehyde
2219 Allyl glycidyl ether
2244 Cyclopentanol
2265 N,N-Dimethylformamide
2275 2-Ethylbutanol
2282 Hexanols
2313 Picolines
2325 1,3,5-Trimethylbenzene
2332 Acetaldehyde oxime
2345 3-Bromopropyne
2351 Butyl nitrites
2356 2-Chloropropane
2363 Ethyl mercaptan
2372 1,2-Di-(dimethylamino)ethane
2375 Diethyl sulfide
2385 Ethyl isobutyrate
2390 2-Iodobutane
2391 Iodomethylpropanes
2392 Iodopropanes
2393 Isobutyl formate
2394 Isobutyl propionate
2403 Isopropenyl acetate
2405 Isopropyl butyrate
2409 Isopropyl propionate
2410 1,2,3,6-Tetrahydropyridine; 1,2,5,6-Tetrahydropyridine
2416 Trimethyl borate
2436 Thioacetic acid
2498 1,2,3,6-Tetrahydro-benzaldehyde
2524 Ethyl orthoformate
2554 Methylallyl chloride
2560 2-Methylpentan-2-ol
2607 Acrolein dimer, stabilized
2608 Nitropropanes
2614 Methallyl alcohol
2616 Triisopropyl borate
2617 Methylcyclohexanols
2711 Dibromobenzene
2838 Vinyl butyrate (, inhibited; & , stabilized)
2840 Butyraldoxime
2842 Nitroethane
2933 Methyl 2-chloropropionate
2934 Isopropyl 2-chloropropionate
2935 Ethyl 2-chloropropionate
2943 Tetrahydrofurfurylamine
2983 Ethylene oxide and Propylene oxide mixture, with ≤ 30% Ethylene oxide
3054 Cyclohexanethiol; Cyclohexyl mercaptan
3056 n-Heptaldehyde
3092 1-Methoxy-2-propanol
3371 2-Methylbutanal

Hazmat

POTENTIAL HAZARDS

FIRE OR EXPLOSION

- **HIGHLY FLAMMABLE: Will be easily ignited by heat, sparks, or flames.**
- Vapors may form explosive mixtures with air.
- Vapors may travel to source of ignition and flash back.
- Most vapors are heavier than air. They will spread along the ground and collect in low or confined areas (sewers, basements, tanks).
- Vapor explosion hazard indoors, outdoors, or in sewers.
- Those substances designated with a "**P**" may polymerize explosively when heated or involved in a fire.
- Runoff to sewer may create fire or explosion hazard.
- Containers may explode when heated.
- Many liquids are lighter than water.

HEALTH

- May cause toxic effects if inhaled or absorbed (skin).
- Inhalation or contact with material may irritate or burn skin and eyes.
- Fire may produce irritating, corrosive, or toxic gases.
- Vapors may cause dizziness or suffocation.
- Runoff from fire control may cause pollution.

PUBLIC SAFETY

- **CALL Emergency Response Telephone Number on Shipping Paper first. If Shipping Paper is not available or there is no answer, refer to telephone numbers listed on page 613.**
- As an immediate precautionary measure, isolate spill or leak area for at least 50 m (150 ft) in all directions.
- Keep unauthorized personnel away.
- Stay upwind.
- Keep out of low areas.
- Ventilate closed spaces before entering.

PROTECTIVE CLOTHING

- Wear positive pressure self-contained breathing apparatus (SCBA).
- Structural firefighters' protective clothing will only provide limited protection.

EVACUATION

Large Spill

- Consider initial downwind evacuation for at least 300 meters (1000 feet).

Hazmat

Fire

- If tank, rail car, or tank truck is involved in a fire, ISOLATE for 800 meters (½ mile) in all directions; also, initiate evacuation including emergency responders for 800 meters (½ mile) in all directions.

EMERGENCY RESPONSE
FIRE

CAUTION: All these products have a very low flash point: Use of water spray when fighting fire may be inefficient.

Small Fires

- Dry chemical, CO_2, water spray, or alcohol-resistant foam.

Large Fires

- Water spray, fog, or alcohol-resistant foam.
- DO NOT use straight streams.
- Move containers from fire area if you can do it without risk.

Fire Involving Tanks of Car/Trailer Loads

- Fight fire from maximum distance or use unmanned hose holders or monitor nozzles.
- Cool containers with flooding quantities of water until well after fire is out.
- Withdraw immediately in case of rising sound from venting safety devices or discoloration of tank.
- ALWAYS stay away from tanks engulfed in fire.
- For massive fire, use unmanned hose holders or monitor nozzles; if this is impossible, withdraw from area and let fire burn.

SPILL OR LEAK

- Eliminate all ignition sources (no smoking, flares, sparks, or flames in the immediate area).
- All equipment used when handling the product must be grounded.
- DO NOT touch or walk through spilled material.
- Stop leak if you can do it without risk.
- Prevent entry into waterways, sewers, basements, or confined areas.
- A vapor suppressing foam may be used to reduce vapors.
- Absorb or cover with dry earth, sand, or other non-combustible material and transfer to containers.
- Use clean non-sparking tools to collect absorbed material.

Large Spills

- Dike far ahead of liquid spill for later disposal.
- Water spray may reduce vapor; but may not prevent ignition in closed spaces.

FIRST AID

- Move victim to fresh air.
- Call 911 or emergency medical service.
- Give artificial respiration if victim is not breathing.
- Administer oxygen if breathing is difficult.
- Remove and isolate contaminated clothing and shoes.
- In case of contact with substance, immediately flush skin or eyes with running water for at least 20 minutes.
- Wash skin with soap and water.
- Keep victim warm and quiet.
- In case of burns, immediately cool affected skin for as long as possible with cold water. Do not remove clothing if adhering to skin.
- Effects of exposure (inhalation, ingestion, or skin contact) to substance may be delayed.
- Ensure that medical personnel are aware of the material(s) involved, and take precautions to protect themselves.

Hazmat

SUBSTANCES INCLUDED

1111	Amyl mercaptan
1114	Benzene
1126	n-Butyl bromide
1127	Butyl chloride
1127	Chlorobutanes
1134	Chlorobenzene
1147	Decahydronaphthalene
1150	**1,2-Dichloroethylene; Dichloroethylene**
1152	Dichloropentanes
1164	Dimethyl sulfide
1175	Ethylbenzene
1177	2-Ethylbutyl acetate; Ethylbutyl acetate
1178	2-Ethylbutyraldehyde
1180	Ethyl butyrate
1207	Hexaldehyde
1218	**Isoprene, inhibited; Isoprene, stabilized**
1222	Isopropyl nitrate
1233	Methylamyl acetate
1279	1,2-Dichloropropane; Dichloropropane
1279	Propylene dichloride
1294	Toluene
1303	**Vinylidene chloride, stabilized**
1307	Xylenes
1862	Ethyl crotonate
1914	Butyl propionates
1918	Cumene
1918	Isopropylbenzene
1999	Asphalt
1999	Tars, liquid
2045	Isobutyraldehyde
2046	Cymenes
2048	Dicyclopentadiene
2049	Diethylbenzene
2227	**n-Butyl methacrylate (& , inhibited; & , stabilized)**
2227	**Ethyl methacrylate (& , inhibited; & , stabilized)**
2234	Chlorobenzotrifluorides
2238	Chlorotoluenes
2243	Cyclohexyl acetate
2256	Cyclohexene
2283	**Isobutyl methacrylate (& , inhibited; & , stabilized)**
2323	Triethyl phosphite
2329	Trimethyl phosphite
2339	2-Bromobutane
2340	2-Bromoethyl ethyl ether
2341	1-Bromo-3-methylbutane
2342	Bromomethylpropanes
2343	2-Bromopentane
2344	2-Bromopropane; Bromopropanes
2347	Butyl mercaptan
2348	**Butyl acrylate (& , inhibited; & , stabilized)**
2362	1,1-Dichloroethane
2367	alpha-Methylvaleraldehyde; Methyl valeraldehyde (alpha)
2381	Dimethyl disulfide

2387	Fluorobenzene
2388	Fluorotoluenes
2400	Methyl isovalerate
2402	Propanethiols
2412	Tetrahydrothiophene
2414	Thiophene
2456	**2-Chloropropene**
2458	Hexadiene
2514	Bromobenzene
2520	**Cyclooctadienes**
2527	**Isobutyl acrylate (& , inhibited; & , stabilized)**
2528	Isobutyl isobutyrate
2618	**Vinyltoluenes (, inhibited; & , stabilized)**
2620	Amyl butyrates
2749	Tetramethylsilane
3336	Mercaptan mixture, liquid, flammable, n.o.s.
3336	Mercaptans, liquid, flammable, n.o.s.

POTENTIAL HAZARDS

FIRE OR EXPLOSION

- **HIGHLY FLAMMABLE: Will be easily ignited by heat, sparks, or flames.**
- Vapors may form explosive mixtures with air.
- Vapors may travel to source of ignition and flash back.
- Most vapors are heavier than air. They will spread along the ground and collect in low or confined areas (sewers, basements, tanks).
- Vapor explosion hazard indoors, outdoors, or in sewers.
- Those substances designated with a "**P**" may polymerize explosively when heated or involved in a fire.
- Runoff to sewer may create fire or explosion hazard.
- Containers may explode when heated.
- Many liquids are lighter than water.

HEALTH

- May cause toxic effects if inhaled or absorbed through skin.
- Inhalation or contact with material may irritate or burn skin and eyes.
- Fire may produce irritating, corrosive, or toxic gases.
- Vapors may cause dizziness or suffocation.
- Runoff from fire control may cause pollution.

PUBLIC SAFETY

- **CALL Emergency Response Telephone Number on Shipping Paper first. If Shipping Paper is not available or there is no answer, refer to telephone numbers listed on page 613.**
- As an immediate precautionary measure, isolate spill or leak area for at least 50 meters (150 feet) in all directions.
- Keep unauthorized personnel away.
- Stay upwind.

Hazmat

- Keep out of low areas.
- Ventilate closed spaces before entering.

PROTECTIVE CLOTHING

- Wear positive pressure self-contained breathing apparatus (SCBA).
- Structural firefighters' protective clothing will only provide limited protection.

EVACUATION

Large Spill
- Consider initial downwind evacuation for at least 300 meters (1000 feet).

Fire
- If tank, rail car, or tank truck is involved in a fire, ISOLATE for 800 meters (½ mile) in all directions; also, initiate evacuation including emergency responders for 800 meters (½ mile) in all directions.

EMERGENCY RESPONSE
FIRE

CAUTION: All these products have a very low flash point: Use of water spray when fighting fire may be inefficient.

Small Fires
- Dry chemical, CO_2, water spray, or regular foam.

Large Fires
- Water spray, fog, or regular foam.
- DO NOT use straight streams.
- Move containers from fire area if you can do it without risk.

Fire Involving Tanks of Car/Trailer Loads
- Fight fire from maximum distance or use unmanned hose holders or monitor nozzles.
- Cool containers with flooding quantities of water until well after fire is out.
- Withdraw immediately in case of rising sound from venting safety devices or discoloration of tank.
- ALWAYS stay away from tanks engulfed in fire.
- For massive fire, use unmanned hose holders or monitor nozzles; if this is impossible, withdraw from area and let fire burn.

SPILL OR LEAK

- Eliminate all ignition sources (no smoking, flares, sparks, or flames in the immediate area).
- All equipment used when handling the product must be grounded.
- DO NOT touch or walk through spilled material.
- Stop leak if you can do it without risk.

- Prevent entry into waterways, sewers, basements, or confined areas.
- A vapor suppressing foam may be used to reduce vapors.
- Absorb or cover with dry earth, sand, or other non-combustible material and transfer to containers.
- Use clean non-sparking tools to collect absorbed material.

Large Spills
- Dike far ahead of liquid spill for later disposal.
- Water spray may reduce vapor; but may not prevent ignition in closed spaces.

FIRST AID

- Move victim to fresh air.
- Call 911 or emergency medical service.
- Give artificial respiration if victim is not breathing.
- Administer oxygen if breathing is difficult.
- Remove and isolate contaminated clothing and shoes.
- In case of contact with substance, immediately flush skin or eyes with running water for at least 20 minutes.
- Wash skin with soap and water.
- Keep victim warm and quiet.
- In case of burns, immediately cool affected skin for as long as possible with cold water. Do not remove clothing if adhering to skin.
- Effects of exposure (inhalation, ingestion, or skin contact) to substance may be delayed.
- Ensure that medical personnel are aware of the material(s) involved, and take precautions to protect themselves.

Hazmat

SUBSTANCES INCLUDED

1092 **Acrolein, inhibited; Acrolein, stabilized**
1093 **Acrylonitrile, inhibited; Acrylonitrile, stabilized**
1098 Allyl alcohol
1099 Allyl bromide
1100 Allyl chloride
1131 Carbon bisulfide; Carbon disulfide
1135 Ethylene chlorohydrin
1143 **Crotonaldehyde, inhibited; Crotonaldehyde, stabilized**
1163 1,1-Dimethylhydrazine
1163 Dimethylhydrazine, unsymmetrical
1184 Ethylene dichloride
1185 **Ethyleneimine, inhibited; Ethyleimine, stabilized**
1194 Ethyl nitrite, solution
1228 Mercaptan mixture, liquid, flammable, toxic, n.o.s.
1228 Mercaptan mixtures, liquid, flammable, toxic, n.o.s.
1228 Mercaptans, liquid, flammable, toxic, n.o.s.
1230 Methanol; Methyl alcohol
1239 Methyl chloromethyl ether
1244 Methylhydrazine
1251 **Methyl vinyl ketone; Methyl vinyl ketone, stabilized**
1259 Nickel carbonyl
1569 Bromoacetone
1649 Motor fuel anti-knock mixture
1649 Tetraethyl lead, liquid
1695 Chloroacetone, stabilized
1865 n-Propyl nitrate
1891 Ethyl bromide
1921 **Propyleneimine, inhibited; Propyleneimine, stabilized**
1986 Alcohols, flammable, toxic, n.o.s.
1986 Alcohols, toxic, n.o.s.
1986 Denatured alcohol (toxic)
1986 Propargyl alcohol
1988 Aldehydes, flammable, toxic, n.o.s.
1988 Aldehydes, toxic, n.o.s.
1991 **Chloroprene, inhibited; Chloroprene, stabilized**
1992 Flammable liquid, toxic, not otherwise specified
1994 Iron pentacarbonyl
2023 **1-Chloro-2,3-epoxypropane; Epichlorohydrin**
2249 Dichlorodimethyl ether, symmetrical
2284 Isobutyronitrile
2310 2,4-Pentanedione; Pentan-2,4-dione; Pentane-2,4-dione
2333 Allyl acetate
2334 Allylamine
2335 Allyl ethyl ether
2336 Allyl formate
2337 Phenyl mercaptan
2354 Chloromethyl ethyl ether
2360 **Diallyl ether**
2378 2-Dimethylaminoacetonitrile
2382 1,2-Dimethylhydrazine; Dimethylhydrazine, symmetrical
2396 **Methacrylaldehyde (& , inhibited; & , stabilized)**
2404 Propionitrile
2411 Butyronitrile
2477 Methyl isothiocyanate
2521 **Diketene, inhibited; Diketene, stabilized**

2558	Epibromohydrin
2603	Cycloheptatriene
2611	Propylene chlorohydrin
2622	**Glycidaldehyde**
2668	Chloroacetonitrile
2758	Carbamate pesticide, liquid, flammable, toxic
2760	Arsenical pesticide, liquid, flammable, toxic
2762	Aldrin, liquid
2762	Organochlorine pesticide, liquid, flammable, toxic
2764	Triazine pesticide, liquid, flammable, toxic
2766	Phenoxy pesticide, liquid, flammable, toxic
2768	Phenyl urea pesticide, liquid, flammable, toxic
2770	Benzoic derivative pesticide, liquid, flammable, toxic
2772	Dithiocarbamate pesticide, liquid, flammable, toxic
2772	Thiocarbamate pesticide, liquid, flammable, toxic
2774	Phthalimide derivative pesticide, liquid, flammable, toxic
2776	Copper based pesticide, liquid, flammable, toxic
2778	Mercury based pesticide, liquid, flammable, toxic
2780	Substituted nitrophenol pesticide, liquid, flammable, toxic
2782	Bipyridilium pesticide, liquid, flammable, toxic
2784	Organophosphorus pesticide, liquid, flammable, toxic
2787	Organotin pesticide, liquid, flammable, toxic
2841	Di-n-amylamine
2903	Pesticide, liquid, toxic, flammable, n.o.s.
2929	Toxic liquid, flammable, n.o.s. (& Inhalation Hazard Zone A and B)
2929	Toxic liquid, flammable, organic, n.o.s. (& Inhalation Hazard Zone A and B)
2991	Carbamate pesticide, liquid, toxic, flammable
2993	Arsenical pesticide, liquid, toxic, flammable
2995	Organochlorine pesticide, liquid, toxic, flammable
2997	Triazine pesticide, liquid, toxic, flammable
2999	Phenoxy pesticide, liquid, toxic, flammable
3001	Phenyl urea pesticide, liquid, toxic, flammable
3003	Benzoic derivative pesticide, liquid, toxic, flammable
3005	Dithiocarbamate pesticide, liquid, toxic, flammable
3005	Thiocarbamate pesticide, liquid, toxic, flammable
3007	Phthalimide derivative pesticide, liquid, toxic, flammable
3009	Copper based pesticide, liquid, toxic, flammable
3011	Mercury based pesticide, liquid, toxic, flammable
3013	Substituted nitrophenol pesticide, liquid, toxic, flammable
3015	Bipyridilium pesticide, liquid, toxic, flammable
3017	Organophosphorus pesticide, liquid, toxic, flammable
3019	Organotin pesticide, liquid, toxic, flammable
3021	Pesticide, liquid, flammable, toxic
3023	2-Methyl-2-hepthanethiol
3023	tert-Octyl mercaptan
3024	Coumarin derivative pesticide, liquid, flammable, toxic
3025	Coumarin derivative pesticide, liquid, toxic, flammable
3071	Mercaptan mixture, liquid, toxic, flammable, n.o.s.
3071	Mercaptan mixtures, liquid, n.o.s.
3071	Mercaptans, liquid, n.o.s.
3071	Mercaptans, liquid, toxic, flammable, n.o.s.
3073	**Vinylpyridines, inhibited; Vinylpyridines, stabilized**
3079	**Methacrylonitrile, inhibited; Methacrylonitrile, stabilized**
3165	Aircraft hydraulic power unit fuel tank
3248	Medicine, liquid, flammable, toxic, n.o.s.
3273	Nitriles, flammable, toxic, n.o.s.
3275	Nitriles, toxic, flammable, n.o.s.
3279	Organophosphorus compound, toxic, flammable, n.o.s.

Hazmat

3286 Flammable liquid, toxic, corrosive, n.o.s.
3294 Hydrogen cyanide, solution in alcohol, with $\leq$ 45% Hydrogen cyanide
3346 Phenoxyacetic acid derivative pesticide, liquid, flammable, toxic
3347 Phenoxyacetic acid derivative pesticide, liquid, toxic, flammable
3350 Pyrethroid pesticide, liquid, flammable, toxic
3351 Pyrethroid pesticide, liquid, toxic, flammable
3383 Toxic by inhalation liquid, flammable, n.o.s.
(Inhalation Hazard Zone A)
3384 Toxic by inhalation liquid, flammable, n.o.s.
(Inhalation Hazard Zone B)

POTENTIAL HAZARDS

FIRE OR EXPLOSION

- **HIGHLY FLAMMABLE: Will be easily ignited by heat, sparks, or flames.**
- Vapors may form explosive mixtures with air.
- Vapors may travel to source of ignition and flash back.
- Most vapors are heavier than air. They will spread along the ground and collect in low or confined areas (sewers, basements, tanks).
- Vapor explosion hazard indoors, outdoors, or in sewers.
- Those substances designated with a "**P**" may polymerize explosively when heated or involved in a fire.
- Runoff to sewer may create fire or explosion hazard.
- Containers may explode when heated.
- Many liquids are lighter than water.

HEALTH

- **TOXIC; may be fatal if inhaled, ingested, or absorbed through skin.**
- Inhalation or contact with material may irritate or burn skin and eyes.
- Fire may produce irritating, corrosive, or toxic gases.
- Vapors may cause dizziness or suffocation.
- Runoff from fire control may cause pollution.

PUBLIC SAFETY

- **CALL Emergency Response Telephone Number on Shipping Paper first. If Shipping Paper is not available or there is no answer, refer to telephone numbers listed on page 613.**
- As an immediate precautionary measure, isolate spill or leak area for at least 50 meters (150 feet) in all directions.
- Keep unauthorized personnel away.
- Stay upwind.
- Keep out of low areas.
- Ventilate closed spaces before entering.

PROTECTIVE CLOTHING

- Wear positive pressure self-contained breathing apparatus (SCBA).
- Wear chemical protective clothing that is specifically recommended by the manufacturer. It may provide little or no thermal protection.
- Structural firefighters' protective clothing provides limited protection in fire situations ONLY; it is not effective in spill situations where direct contact with the substance is possible.

EVACUATION

Spill

- See the Table of Initial Isolation and Protective Action Distances for highlighted substances (page 908). For non-highlighted substances, increase, in the downwind direction, as necessary, the isolation distance shown above under "PUBLIC SAFETY."

Fire

- If tank, rail car, or tank truck is involved in a fire, ISOLATE for 800 meters (½ mile) in all directions; also, initiate evacuation including emergency responders for 800 meters (½ mile) in all directions.

EMERGENCY RESPONSE

FIRE

CAUTION: All these products have a very low flash point: Use of water spray when fighting fire may be inefficient.

Small Fires

- Dry chemical, CO_2, water spray, or alcohol-resistant foam.

Large Fires

- Water spray, fog, or alcohol-resistant foam.
- Move containers from fire area if you can do it without risk.
- Dike fire control water for later disposal; do not scatter the material.
- Use water spray or fog; DO NOT use straight streams.

Fire Involving Tanks of Car/Trailer Loads

- Fight fire from maximum distance or use unmanned hose holders or monitor nozzles.
- Cool containers with flooding quantities of water until well after fire is out.
- Withdraw immediately in case of rising sound from venting safety devices or discoloration of tank.
- ALWAYS stay away from tanks engulfed in fire.
- For massive fire, use unmanned hose holders or monitor nozzles; if this is impossible, withdraw from area and let fire burn.

Hazmat

SPILL OR LEAK

- Fully encapsulating, vapor protective clothing should be worn for spills and leaks with no fire.
- Eliminate all ignition sources (no smoking, flares, sparks, or flames in the immediate area).
- All equipment used when handling the product must be grounded.
- DO NOT touch or walk through spilled material.
- Stop leak if you can do it without risk.
- Prevent entry into waterways, sewers, basements, or confined areas.
- A vapor suppressing foam may be used to reduce vapors.

Small Spills

- Absorb or cover with earth, sand, or other non-combustible material and transfer to containers for later disposal.
- Use clean non-sparking tools to collect absorbed material.

Large Spills

- Dike far ahead of liquid spill for later disposal.
- Water spray may reduce vapor; but may not prevent ignition in closed spaces.

FIRST AID

- Move victim to fresh air.
- Call 911 or emergency medical service.
- Give artificial respiration if victim is not breathing.
- **DO NOT use mouth-to-mouth method if victim ingested or inhaled the substance; give artificial respiration with the aid of a pocket mask equipped with a one-way valve or other proper respiratory medical device.**
- Administer oxygen if breathing is difficult.
- Remove and isolate contaminated clothing and shoes.
- In case of contact with substance, immediately flush skin or eyes with running water for at least 20 minutes.
- Wash skin with soap and water.
- Keep victim warm and quiet.
- In case of burns, immediately cool affected skin for as long as possible with cold water. Do not remove clothing if adhering to skin.
- Effects of exposure (inhalation, ingestion, or skin contact) to substance may be delayed.
- Ensure that medical personnel are aware of the material(s) involved, and take precautions to protect themselves.

Hazmat

SUBSTANCES INCLUDED

1106	Amylamines
1125	n-Butylamine
1154	Diethylamine
1158	Diisopropylamine
1160	Dimethylamine, aqueous solution
1160	Dimethylamine, solution
1198	Formaldehyde, solution, flammable
1198	Formaldehyde, solutions (Formalin)
1199	**Furaldehydes; Furfural; Furfuraldehydes**
1214	Isobutylamine
1221	Isopropylamine
1235	Methylamine, aqueous solution
1277	Monopropylamine; Propylamine
1289	Sodium methylate, solution in alcohol
1296	Triethylamine
1297	Trimethylamine, aqueous solution
1604	Ethylenediamine
1723	Allyl iodide
1815	Propionyl chloride
1848	Propionic acid
1922	Pyrrolidine
2029	Hydrazine, anhydrous
2029	Hydrazine, aqueous solutions, with > 64% Hydrazine
2051	2-Dimethylaminoethanol; Dimethylethanolamine
2054	Morpholine
2209	Formaldehyde, solutions (Formalin) (corrosive)
2218	**Acrylic acid, inhibited; Acrylic acid, stabilized**
2248	Di-n-butylamine
2258	1,2-Propylenediamine; 1,3-Propylenediamine
2260	Tripropylamine
2264	Dimethylcyclohexylamine; N,N-Dimethylcyclohexylamine
2266	Dimethyl-N-propylamine
2270	Ethylamine, aqueous solution, with $\geq$ 50% but $\leq$ 70% Ethylamine
2276	2-Ethylhexylamine
2353	Butyryl chloride
2357	Cyclohexylamine
2359	Diallylamine
2361	Diisobutylamine
2379	1,3-Dimethylbutylamine
2383	Dipropylamine
2386	1-Ethylpiperidine
2395	Isobutyryl chloride
2399	1-Methylpiperidine
2401	Piperidine
2438	Trimethylacetyl chloride
2493	Hexamethyleneimine
2502	Valeryl chloride
2526	Furfurylamine
2529	Isobutyric acid
2530	Isobutyric anhydride
2535	4-Methylmorpholine
2535	Methylmorpholine
2535	N-Methylmorpholine
2604	Boron trifluoride diethyl etherate
2610	Triallylamine

Hazmat

2619	Benzyldimethylamine
2683	Ammonium sulfide, solution
2684	3-Diethylaminopropylamine; Diethylaminopropylamine
2685	N,N-Diethylethylenediamine
2686	2-Diethylaminoethanol; Diethylaminoethanol
2733	Alkylamines, n.o.s.
2733	Amines, flammable, corrosive, n.o.s.
2733	Polyalkylamines, n.o.s.
2733	Polyamines, flammable, corrosive, n.o.s.
2734	Alkylamines, n.o.s.
2734	Amines, liquid, corrosive, flammable, n.o.s.
2734	Polyalkylamines, n.o.s.
2734	Polyamines, liquid, corrosive, flammable, n.o.s.
2789	Acetic acid, glacial; Acetic acid, solution, > 80% acid
2920	Corrosive liquid, flammable, n.o.s.
2920	Dichlorobutene
2924	Flammable liquid, corrosive, n.o.s.
2945	N-Methylbutylamine
3274	Alcoholates solution, n.o.s., in alcohol
9269	Trimethoxysilane

POTENTIAL HAZARDS

FIRE OR EXPLOSION

- **Flammable/combustible materials.**
- May be ignited by heat, sparks, or flames.
- Vapors may form explosive mixtures with air.
- Vapors may travel to source of ignition and flash back.
- Most vapors are heavier than air. They will spread along the ground and collect in low or confined areas (sewers, basements, tanks).
- Vapor explosion hazard indoors, outdoors, or in sewers.
- Those substances designated with a "**P**" may polymerize explosively when heated or involved in a fire.
- Runoff to sewer may create fire or explosion hazard.
- Containers may explode when heated.
- Many liquids are lighter than water.

HEALTH

- May cause toxic effects if inhaled or ingested/swallowed.
- Inhalation or contact with material may irritate or burn skin and eyes.
- Fire may produce irritating, corrosive, or toxic gases.
- Vapors may cause dizziness or suffocation.
- Runoff from fire control may cause pollution.

PUBLIC SAFETY

- **CALL Emergency Response Telephone Number on Shipping Paper first. If Shipping Paper is not available or there is no answer, refer to telephone numbers listed on page 613.**
- As an immediate precautionary measure, isolate spill or leak area for at least 50 m (150 ft) in all directions.

Hazmat

- Keep unauthorized personnel away.
- Stay upwind.
- Keep out of low areas.
- Ventilate closed spaces before entering.

PROTECTIVE CLOTHING

- Wear positive pressure self-contained breathing apparatus (SCBA).
- Wear chemical protective clothing that is specifically recommended by the manufacturer. It may provide little or no thermal protection.
- Structural firefighters' protective clothing provides limited protection in fire situations ONLY; it is not effective in spill situations where direct contact with the substance is possible.

EVACUATION

Large Spill

- See the Table of Initial Isolation and Protective Action Distances for highlighted substances (page 908). For non-highlighted substances, increase, in the downwind direction, as necessary, the isolation distance shown above under "PUBLIC SAFETY."

Fire

- If tank, rail car, or tank truck is involved in a fire, ISOLATE for 800 meters (½ mile) in all directions; also, initiate evacuation including emergency responders for 800 meters (½ mile) in all directions.

EMERGENCY RESPONSE

FIRE

- **Some of these materials may react violently with water.**

Small Fires

- Dry chemical, CO_2, water spray, or alcohol-resistant foam.

Large Fires

- Water spray, fog, or alcohol-resistant foam.
- Move containers from fire area if you can do it without risk.
- Dike fire control water for later disposal; DO NOT scatter the material.
- DO NOT get water inside containers.

Fire Involving Tanks of Car/Trailer Loads

- Fight fire from maximum distance or use unmanned hose holders or monitor nozzles.
- Cool containers with flooding quantities of water until well after fire is out.
- Withdraw immediately in case of rising sound from venting safety devices or discoloration of tank.
- ALWAYS stay away from tanks engulfed in fire.

Hazmat

- For massive fire, use unmanned hose holders or monitor nozzles; if this is impossible, withdraw from area and let fire burn.

SPILL OR LEAK

- Fully encapsulating, vapor protective clothing should be worn for spills and leaks with no fire.
- Eliminate all ignition sources (no smoking, flares, sparks, or flames in the immediate area).
- All equipment used when handling the product must be grounded.
- DO NOT touch or walk through spilled material.
- Stop leak if you can do it without risk.
- Prevent entry into waterways, sewers, basements, or confined areas.
- A vapor suppressing foam may be used to reduce vapors.
- Absorb or cover with dry earth, sand, or other non-combustible material and transfer to containers.
- Use clean non-sparking tools to collect absorbed material.

Large Spills

- Dike far ahead of liquid spill for later disposal.
- Water spray may reduce vapor; but may not prevent ignition in closed spaces.

FIRST AID

- Move victim to fresh air.
- Call 911 or emergency medical service.
- Give artificial respiration if victim is not breathing.
- **DO NOT use mouth-to-mouth method if victim ingested or inhaled the substance; give artificial respiration with the aid of a pocket mask equipped with a one-way valve or other proper respiratory medical device.**
- Administer oxygen if breathing is difficult.
- Remove and isolate contaminated clothing and shoes.
- In case of contact with substance, immediately flush skin or eyes with running water for at least 20 minutes.
- In case of burns, immediately cool affected skin for as long as possible with cold water. Do not remove clothing if adhering to skin.
- Keep victim warm and quiet.
- Effects of exposure (inhalation, ingestion, or skin contact) to substance may be delayed.
- Ensure that medical personnel are aware of the material(s) involved, and take precautions to protect themselves.

SUBSTANCES INCLUDED

1312	Borneol
1313	Calcium resinate
1314	Calcium resinate, fused
1318	Cobalt resinate, precipitated
1324	Films, nitrocellulose base
1325	Flammable solid, n.o.s.; Flammable solid, organic, n.o.s.
1325	Fusee (rail or highway)
1325	Medicines, flammable, solid, n.o.s.
1327	Bhusa, wet, damp or contaminated with oil
1327	Hay, wet, damp or contaminated with oil
1327	Straw, wet, damp, or contaminated with oil
1328	Hexamethylenetetramine; Hexamine
1330	Manganese resinate
1331	Matches, "strike anywhere"
1332	Metaldehyde
1334	Naphthalene, crude; Naphthalene, refined
1338	Phosphorus, amorphous; Phosphorus, amorphous, red
1345	Rubber scrap, powdered or granulated
1345	Rubber shoddy, powdered or granulated
1350	Sulfur
1353	Fabrics impregnated with weakly nitrated Nitrocellulose, n.o.s.
1353	Fibres impregnated with weakly nitrated Nitrocellulose, n.o.s.
1353	Toe puffs, nitrocellulose base
1361	Carbon, animal or vegetable origin
1361	Charcoal
1362	Carbon, activated
1364	Cotton waste, oily
1365	Cotton; Cotton, wet
1372	Fibers, animal or vegetable, n.o.s., burnt, wet, or damp
1372	Fibres, animal or vegetable, burnt, wet, or damp
1373	Fabrics, animal, synthetic, or vegetable, n.o.s. with oil
1373	Fibres, animal, synthetic, or vegetable, n.o.s. with oil
1374	Fish meal, unstabilized; Fish scrap, unstabilized
1379	Paper, unsaturated oil treated
1387	Wool waste, wet
1856	Rags, oily
1857	Textile waste, wet
1944	Matches, safety
1945	Matches, wax "vesta"
2000	Celluloid, in blocks, rods, rolls, sheets, tubes, etc., except scrap
2001	Cobalt naphthenates, powder
2211	Polymeric beads, expandable
2211	Polystyrene beads, expandable
2213	Paraformaldehyde
2254	Matches, fusee
2304	Naphthalene, molten
2448	Sulfur, molten
2538	Nitronaphthalene
2557	Nitrocellulose mixture, with plasticizer, with pigment
2557	Nitrocellulose mixture, with plasticizer, without pigment
2557	Nitrocellulose mixture, without plasticizer, with pigment
2557	Nitrocellulose mixture, without plasticizer, without pigment
2557	Nitrocellulose with plasticizing substance
2623	Firelighters, solid, with flammable liquid
2687	Dicyclohexylammonium nitrite

Hazmat

2714	Zinc resinate
2715	Aluminum resinate
2717	Camphor; Camphor, synthetic
2907	Isosorbide dinitrate mixture
2989	Lead phosphite, dibasic
3175	Solids containing flammable liquid, n.o.s.
3176	Flammable solid, organic, molten, n.o.s.
3178	Flammable solid, inorganic, n.o.s.
3178	Smokeless powder for small arms
3181	Metal salts of organic compounds, flammable, n.o.s.
3241	2-Bromo-2-nitropropane-1,3-diol
3251	Isosorbide-5-mononitrate
3270	Nitrocellulose membrane filters
3360	Fibres, vegetable, dry
3380	Desensitized explosive, solid, n.o.s.

POTENTIAL HAZARDS

FIRE OR EXPLOSION

- Flammable/combustible materials.
- May be ignited by friction, heat, sparks, or flames.
- Some may burn rapidly with flare burning effect.
- Powders, dusts, shavings, borings, turnings, or cuttings may explode or burn with explosive violence.
- Substance may be transported in a molten form at a temperature that may be above its flash point.
- May re-ignite after fire is extinguished.

HEALTH

- Fire may produce irritating, or toxic gases.
- Contact may cause burns to skin and eyes.
- Contact w/ molten substance may cause severe burns to skin/eyes.
- Runoff from fire control may cause pollution.

PUBLIC SAFETY

- **CALL Emergency Response Telephone Number on Shipping Paper first. If Shipping Paper is not available or there is no answer, refer to telephone numbers listed on page 613.**
- As an immediate precautionary measure, isolate spill or leak area for at least 25 meters (75 feet) in all directions.
- Keep unauthorized personnel away.
- Stay upwind.
- Keep out of low areas.

PROTECTIVE CLOTHING

- Wear positive pressure self-contained breathing apparatus (SCBA).
- Structural firefighters' protective clothing will only provide limited protection.

EVACUATION

Large Spill

- Consider initial downwind evacuation for at least 100 m (330 ft).

Fire

- If tank, rail car, or tank truck is involved in a fire, ISOLATE for 800 meters (½ mile) in all directions; also, initiate evacuation including emergency responders for 800 meters (½ mile) in all directions.

EMERGENCY RESPONSE
FIRE

Small Fires
- Dry chemical, CO_2, sand, earth, water spray, or regular foam.

Large Fires
- Water spray, fog, or regular foam.
- Move containers from fire area if you can do it without risk.

Fire Involving Tanks of Car/Trailer Loads
- Cool containers with flooding quantities of water until well after fire is out.
- For massive fire, use unmanned hose holders or monitor nozzles; if this is impossible, withdraw from area and let fire burn.
- Withdraw immediately in case of rising sound from venting safety devices or discoloration of tank.
- ALWAYS stay away from tanks engulfed in fire.

SPILL OR LEAK
- Eliminate all ignition sources (no smoking, flares, sparks, or flames in the immediate area).
- DO NOT touch or walk through spilled material.

Small Dry Spills
- With clean shovel place material into clean, dry container and cover loosely; move containers from spill area.

Large Spills
- Wet down with water and dike for later disposal.
- Prevent entry into waterways, sewers, basements, or confined areas.

FIRST AID
- Move victim to fresh air.
- Call 911 or emergency medical service.
- Give artificial respiration if victim is not breathing.
- Administer oxygen if breathing is difficult.
- Remove and isolate contaminated clothing and shoes.
- In case of contact with substance, immediately flush skin or eyes with running water for at least 20 minutes.
- Removal of solidified molten material from skin requires medical assistance.
- Keep victim warm and quiet.
- Ensure that medical personnel are aware of the material(s) involved, and take precautions to protect themselves.

Hazmat

Guide 134: Flammable Solids - Toxic and/or Corrosive

SUBSTANCES INCLUDED

1567	Beryllium powder
1868	Decaborane
2921	Corrosive solid, flammable, n.o.s.
2925	Flammable solid, corrosive, n.o.s.
2925	Flammable solid, corrosive, organic, n.o.s.
2926	Flammable solid, toxic, n.o.s.
2926	Flammable solid, toxic, organic, n.o.s.
2930	Poisonous solid, flammable, n.o.s.
2930	Poisonous solid, flammable, organic, n.o.s.
2930	Toxic solid, flammable, n.o.s.
2930	Toxic solid, flammable, organic, n.o.s.
3179	Flammable solid, toxic, inorganic, n.o.s.
3180	Flammable solid, corrosive, inorganic, n.o.s.

POTENTIAL HAZARDS

FIRE OR EXPLOSION

- Flammable/combustible materials.
- May be ignited by heat, sparks, or flames.
- When heated, vapors may form explosive mixtures with air: indoors, outdoors, and sewers explosion hazards.
- Contact with metals may evolve flammable hydrogen gas.
- Containers may explode when heated.

HEALTH

- **TOXIC; inhalation, ingestion or skin contact with material may cause severe injury or death.**
- Fire may produce irritating or toxic gases.
- Runoff from fire control or dilution water may be corrosive and/or toxic and cause pollution.

PUBLIC SAFETY

- **CALL Emergency Response Telephone Number on Shipping Paper first. If Shipping Paper is not available or there is no answer, refer to telephone numbers listed on page 613.**
- As an immediate precautionary measure, isolate spill or leak area for at least 25 meters (75 feet) in all directions.
- Stay upwind.
- Keep unauthorized personnel away.
- Keep out of low areas.
- Ventilate enclosed areas.

PROTECTIVE CLOTHING

- Wear positive pressure self-contained breathing apparatus (SCBA).

- Wear chemical protective clothing that is specifically recommended by the manufacturer. It may provide little or no thermal protection.
- Structural firefighters' protective clothing provides limited protection in fire situations ONLY; it is not effective in spill situations where direct contact with the substance is possible.

EVACUATION

Large Spill
- Consider initial downwind evacuation for at least 100 m (330 ft).

Fire
- If tank, rail car, or tank truck is involved in a fire, ISOLATE for 800 meters (½ mile) in all directions; also, initiate evacuation including emergency responders for 800 meters (½ mile) in all directions.

EMERGENCY RESPONSE
FIRE

Small Fires
- Dry chemical, CO_2, water spray, or alcohol-resistant foam.

Large Fires
- Water spray, fog, or alcohol-resistant foam.
- Move containers from fire area if you can do it without risk.
- Use water spray or fog; DO NOT use straight streams.
- DO NOT get water inside containers.
- Dike fire control water for later disposal; DO NOT scatter the material.

Fire Involving Tanks of Car/Trailer Loads
- Fight fire from maximum distance or use unmanned hose holders or monitor nozzles.
- Cool containers with flooding quantities of water until well after fire is out.
- Withdraw immediately in case of rising sound from venting safety devices or discoloration of tank.
- ALWAYS stay away from tanks engulfed in fire.

SPILL OR LEAK
- Fully encapsulating, vapor protective clothing should be worn for spills and leaks with no fire.
- Eliminate all ignition sources (no smoking, flares, sparks, or flames in the immediate area).
- Stop leak if you can do it without risk.
- DO NOT touch damaged containers or spilled material unless wearing appropriate protective clothing.
- Prevent entry into waterways, sewers, basements, or confined areas.
- Use clean non-sparking tools to collect material and place it into loosely covered plastic containers for later disposal.

Hazmat

- Move victim to fresh air.
- Call 911 or emergency medical service.
- Give artificial respiration if victim is not breathing.
- **DO NOT use mouth-to-mouth method if victim ingested or inhaled the substance; give artificial respiration with the aid of a pocket mask equipped with a one-way valve or other proper respiratory medical device.**
- Administer oxygen if breathing is difficult.
- Remove and isolate contaminated clothing and shoes.
- In case of contact with substance, immediately flush skin or eyes with running water for at least 20 minutes.
- For minor skin contact, avoid spreading material on unaffected skin.
- Keep victim warm and quiet.
- Effects of exposure (inhalation, ingestion, or skin contact) to substance may be delayed.
- Ensure that medical personnel are aware of the material(s) involved, and take precautions to protect themselves.

Hazmat

SUBSTANCES INCLUDED

1363	Copra
1366	Diethylzinc
1369	p-Nitrosodimethylaniline
1370	Dimethylzinc
1376	Iron oxide, spent; Iron sponge, spent
1380	Pentaborane
1382	Potassium sulfide, anhydrous
1382	Potassium sulfide, with < 30% water of crystallization
1382	Potassium sulfide, with < 30% water of hydration
1383	Aluminum powder, pyrophoric
1383	Pyrophoric alloy, n.o.s.; Pyrophoric metal, n.o.s.
1384	Sodium dithionite; Sodium hydrosulfite
1385	Sodium sulfide, anhydrous
1385	Sodium sulfide, with < 30% water of crystallization
1386	Seed cake, with > 1.5% oil and ≤ 11% moisture
1854	Barium alloys, pyrophoric
1855	Calcium alloys, pyrophoric
1855	Calcium, metal and alloys, pyrophoric
1855	Calcium, pyrophoric
1923	Calcium dithionite; Calcium hydrosulfite
1928	Methyl magnesium bromide in Ethyl ether
1929	Potassium dithionite; Potassium hydrosulfite
1932	Zirconium scrap
2002	Celluloid, scrap
2003	Metal alkyls, n.o.s.; Metal alkyls, water-reactive, n.o.s.
2003	Metal aryls, n.o.s; Metal aryls, water-reactive, n.o.s.
2004	Magnesium diamide
2005	Magnesium diphenyl
2006	Plastic, nitrocellulose-based, spontaneously combustible, n.o.s.
2006	Plastics, nitrocellulose-based, self-heating, n.o.s.
2008	Zirconium powder, dry
2009	Zirconium, dry, finished sheets, strips or coiled wire
2210	Maneb
2210	Maneb preparation, with ≥ 60% Maneb
2217	Seed cake, with ≤ 1.5% oil and ≤ 11% moisture
2318	Sodium hydrosulfide, solid, with < 25% water of crystallization
2318	Sodium hydrosulfide, with < 25% water of crystallization
2441	Titanium trichloride mixture, pyrophoric
2441	Titanium trichloride, pyrophoric
2445	Lithium alkyls; Lithium alkyls, liquid
2545	Hafnium powder, dry
2546	Titanium powder, dry
2845	Ethyl phosphonous dichloride, anhydrous
2845	Methyl phosphonous dichloride
2845	Pyrophoric liquid, n.o.s.
2845	Pyrophoric liquid, organic, n.o.s.
2846	Pyrophoric solid, n.o.s.
2846	Pyrophoric solid, organic, n.o.s.
2870	Aluminum borohydride (& in devices)
2881	Metal catalyst, dry
2881	Nickel catalyst, dry
2940	9-Phosphabicyclononanes; Cyclooctadiene phosphines
2968	Maneb preparation, stabilized; Maneb, stabilized
3051	Aluminum alkyls
3052	Aluminum alkyl halides (& , liquid; & , solid)

Hazmat

3053	Magnesium alkyls
3088	Self-heating solid, organic, n.o.s.
3088	Self-heating substances, solid, n.o.s.
3100	Oxidizing solid, self-heating, n.o.s.
3100	Oxidizing substances, self-heating, n.o.s.
3100	Oxidizing substances, solid, self-heating, n.o.s.
3127	Self-heating solid, oxidizing, n.o.s.
3127	Self-heating substances, solid, oxidizing, n.o.s.
3174	Titanium disulfide
3183	Self-heating liquid, organic, n.o.s.
3186	Self-heating liquid, inorganic, n.o.s.
3189	Metal powder, self-heating, n.o.s.
3189	Self-heating metal powders, n.o.s.
3190	Self-heating solid, inorganic, n.o.s.
3194	Pyrophoric liquid, inorganic, n.o.s.
3200	Pyrophoric solid, inorganic, n.o.s.
3203	Pyrophoric organometallic compound, n.o.s.
3203	Pyrophoric organometallic compound, water-reactive, n.o.s.
3205	Alkaline earth metal alcoholates, n.o.s.
3254	Tributylphosphane; Tributylphosphine
3255	tert-Butyl hypochlorite
3313	Organic pigments, self-heating
3341	Thiourea dioxide
3342	Xanthates
3391	Organometallic substance, solid, pyrophoric
3392	Organometallic substance, liquid, pyrophoric
3393	Organometallic substance, solid, pyrophoric, water-reactive
3394	Organometallic substance, liquid, pyrophoric, water-reactive
3395	Organometallic substance, solid, water-reactive
3398	Organometallic substance, liquid, water-reactive
3433	Lithium alkyls, solid
3461	Aluminum alkyl halides, solid
9195	Metal alkyl, solution, n.o.s.

POTENTIAL HAZARDS

FIRE OR EXPLOSION

- Flammable/combustible material.
- May be ignited on contact with moist air or moisture.
- May burn rapidly with flare-burning effect.
- Some react vigorously/explosively on contact w/ water.
- Some may decompose explosively when heated or involved in a fire.
- May re-ignite after fire is extinguished.
- Runoff may create fire or explosion hazard
- Containers may explode when heated.

HEALTH

- Fire will produce irritating, corrosive, or toxic gases.
- Inhalation of decomposition products may cause severe injury or death.
- Contact with substance may cause severe burns to skin and eyes.
- Runoff from fire control may cause pollution.

PUBLIC SAFETY

- **CALL Emergency Response Telephone Number on Shipping Paper first. If Shipping Paper is not available or there is no answer, refer to telephone numbers listed on page 613.**
- As an immediate precautionary measure, isolate spill or leak area in all directions for at least 50 m (150 ft) for liquids and at least 25 m (75 ft) for solids.
- Stay upwind.
- Keep unauthorized personnel away.
- Keep out of low areas.

PROTECTIVE CLOTHING

- Wear positive pressure self-contained breathing apparatus (SCBA).
- Wear chemical protective clothing that is specifically recommended by the manufacturer. It may provide little or no thermal protection.
- Structural firefighters' protective clothing will only provide limited protection.

EVACUATION

Spill

- See the Table of Initial Isolation and Protective Action Distances for highlighted substances (page 908). For non-highlighted substances, increase, in the downwind direction, as necessary, the isolation distance shown above under "PUBLIC SAFETY."

Fire

- If tank, rail car, or tank truck is involved in a fire, ISOLATE for 800 meters (½ mile) in all directions; also, initiate evacuation including emergency responders for 800 meters (½ mile) in all directions.

EMERGENCY RESPONSE

FIRE

- **DO NOT use water, CO_2, or foam on material itself!**
- Some of these materials may react violently with water. **EXCEPTION:** For Xanthates, UN3342, and for Dithionite (Hydrosulfite) UN1384, UN1923, and UN1929, use flooding amounts of water for small and large fires to stop the reaction. Smothering will not work for these materials; they do not need air to burn.

Small Fires

- Dry chemical, soda ash, lime, or DRY sand, **EXCEPT** for UN1384, UN1923, and UN1929.

Hazmat

Large Fires
- DRY sand, dry chemical, soda ash, or lime, **EXCEPT** for UN1284, UN1923, and UN1929, or withdraw from area and let fire burn.
- Move containers from fire area if you can do it without risk.

Fire Involving Tanks of Car/Trailer Loads
- Fight fire from maximum distance or use unmanned hose holders or monitor nozzles.
- DO NOT get water inside containers or in contact with substance.
- Cool containers with flooding quantities of water until well after fire is out.
- Withdraw immediately in case of rising sound from venting safety devices or discoloration of tank.
- ALWAYS stay away from tanks engulfed in fire.

SPILL OR LEAK
- Fully encapsulating, vapor protective clothing should be worn for spills and leaks with no fire.
- Eliminate all ignition sources (no smoking, flares, sparks, or flames in the immediate area).
- DO NOT touch or walk through spilled material.
- Stop leak if you can do it without risk.

Small Spills
EXCEPTION: For spills of Xanthates, UN3342, and for Dithionite (Hydrosulfite), UN1384, UN1923, and UN1929, dissolve in 5 parts water and collect for proper disposal.
- Cover with DRY earth, DRY sand, or other non-combustible material followed with plastic sheet to minimize spreading or contact with rain.
- Use clean non-sparking tools to collect material and place it into loosely covered plastic containers for later disposal.
- Prevent entry into waterways, sewers, basements, or confined areas.

FIRST AID
- Move victim to fresh air.
- Call 911 or emergency medical service.
- Give artificial respiration if victim is not breathing.
- Administer oxygen if breathing is difficult.
- Remove and isolate contaminated clothing and shoes.
- In case of contact with substance, immediately flush skin or eyes with running water for at least 20 minutes.
- Keep victim warm and quiet.
- Ensure that medical personnel are aware of the material(s) involved, and take precautions to protect themselves.

Guide 136: Substances - Spontaneously Combustible-Toxic and/or Corrosive (Air-Reactive)

SUBSTANCES INCLUDED

1381	Phosphorus, white, dry, or under water or in solution
1381	Phosphorus, yellow, dry, or under water or in solution
2447	Phosphorus, white, molten
2447	Phosphorus, yellow, molten
3095	Corrosive solid, self-heating, n.o.s.
3124	Toxic solid, self-heating, n.o.s.
3126	Self-heating solid, corrosive, organic, n.o.s.
3126	Self-heating substance, solid, corrosive, n.o.s.
3128	Self-heating solid, organic, toxic, n.o.s.
3128	Self-heating solid, toxic, organic, n.o.s.
3128	Self-heating substances, solid, toxic, n.o.s.
3184	Self-heating liquid, toxic, organic, n.o.s.
3185	Self-heating liquid, corrosive, organic, n.o.s.
3187	Self-heating liquid, toxic, inorganic, n.o.s.
3188	Self-heating liquid, corrosive, inorganic, n.o.s.
3191	Self-heating solid, inorganic, toxic, n.o.s.
3191	Self-heating solid, toxic, inorganic, n.o.s.
3192	Self-heating solid, corrosive, inorganic, n.o.s.
3206	Alkali metal alcoholates, self-heating, corrosive, n.o.s.
3301	Corrosive liquid, self-heating, n.o.s.

POTENTIAL HAZARDS

FIRE OR EXPLOSION

- Extremely flammable; will ignite itself if exposed to air.
- Burns rapidly, releasing dense, white, irritating fumes.
- Substance may be transported in a molten form.
- May re-ignite after fire is extinguished.
- Corrosive substances in contact with metals may produce flammable hydrogen gas.
- Containers may explode when heated.

HEALTH

- Fire will produce irritating, corrosive, or toxic gases.
- TOXIC; ingestion of substance or inhalation of decomposition products will cause severe injury or death.
- Contact with substance may cause severe burns to skin and eyes.
- Some effects may be experienced due to skin absorption.
- Runoff from fire control may cause pollution.

PUBLIC SAFETY

- **CALL Emergency Response Telephone Number on Shipping Paper first.   If Shipping Paper is not available or there is no answer, refer to telephone numbers listed on page 613.**
- As an immediate precautionary measure, isolate spill or leak area in all directions for at least 50 meters (150 feet) for liquids and at least 25 meters (75 feet) for solids.

Hazmat

- Stay upwind.
- Keep unauthorized personnel away.
- Keep out of low areas.

PROTECTIVE CLOTHING

- Wear positive pressure self-contained breathing apparatus (SCBA).
- Wear chemical protective clothing that is specifically recommended by the manufacturer. It may provide little or no thermal protection.
- Structural firefighters' protective clothing provides limited protection in fire situations ONLY; it is not effective in spill situations where direct contact with the substance is possible.
- **For Phosphorus (UN1381): Special aluminized protective clothing should be worn when direct contact with the substance is possible.**

EVACUATION

Spill

- Consider initial downwind evacuation for at least 300 meters (1000 feet).

Fire

- If tank, rail car, or tank truck is involved in a fire, ISOLATE for 800 meters (½ mile) in all directions; also, initiate evacuation including emergency responders for 800 meters (½ mile) in all directions.

EMERGENCY RESPONSE
FIRE

Small Fires

- Water spray, wet sand, or wet earth.

Large Fires

- Water spray or fog.
- **DO NOT scatter spilled material with high pressure water systems.**
- Move containers from fire area if you can do it without risk.

Fire Involving Tanks of Car/Trailer Loads

- Fight fire from maximum distance or use unmanned hose holders or monitor nozzles.
- Cool containers with flooding quantities of water until well after fire is out.
- Withdraw immediately in case of rising sound from venting safety devices or discoloration of tank.
- ALWAYS stay away from tanks engulfed in fire.

SPILL OR LEAK

- Fully encapsulating, vapor protective clothing should be worn for spills and leaks with no fire.
- Eliminate all ignition sources (no smoking, flares, sparks, or flames in the immediate area).
- DO NOT touch or walk through spilled material.
- DO NOT touch damaged containers or spilled material unless wearing appropriate protective clothing.
- Stop leak if you can do it without risk.

Small Spills

- Cover with water, sand, or earth. Shovel into metal container and keep material under water.

Large Spills

- Dike for later disposal and cover with wet sand or earth.
- Prevent entry into waterways, sewers, basements, or confined areas.

FIRST AID

- Move victim to fresh air.
- Call 911 or emergency medical service.
- Give artificial respiration if victim is not breathing.
- Administer oxygen if breathing is difficult.
- Remove and isolate contaminated clothing and shoes.
- In case of contact with substance, keep exposed skin areas immersed in water or covered with wet bandages until medical attention is received.
- Removal of solidified molten material from skin requires medical assistance.
- Remove and isolate contaminated clothing and shoes at the site and place in metal container filled with water. Fire hazard if allowed to dry.
- Effects of exposure (inhalation, ingestion, or skin contact) to substance may be delayed.
- Keep victim warm and quiet.
- Ensure that medical personnel are aware of the material(s) involved, and take precautions to protect themselves.

Hazmat

Guide 137: Substances - Water-Reactive - Corrosive

SUBSTANCES INCLUDED

1715	Acetic anhydride
1725	Aluminum bromide, anhydrous
1726	Aluminum chloride, anhydrous
1736	Benzoyl chloride
1739	Benzyl chloroformate
1754	Chlorosulfonic acid
1754	Chlorosulfonic acid and Sulfur trioxide mixture
1758	Chromium oxychloride
1777	Fluorosulfonic acid
1806	Phosphorus pentachloride
1807	Phosphorus pentoxide
1808	Phosphorus tribromide
1809	Phosphorus trichloride
1810	Phosphorus oxychloride
1817	Pyrosulfuryl chloride
1827	Stannic chloride, anhydrous
1827	Tin tetrachloride
1828	Sulfur chlorides
1829	Sulfur trioxide (& , inhibited; & , stabilized; & , uninhibited)
1830	Sulfuric acid
1830	Sulfuric acid, with > 51% acid
1831	Sulfuric acid, fuming
1831	Sulfuric acid, fuming, with < 30% free Sulfur trioxide
1831	Sulfuric acid, fuming, with $\geq$ 30% free Sulfur trioxide
1832	Sulfuric acid, spent
1834	Sulfuryl chloride
1836	Thionyl chloride
1838	Titanium tetrachloride
1939	Phosphorus oxybromide; Phosphorus oxybromide, solid
2443	Vanadium oxytrichloride
2444	Vanadium tetrachloride
2503	Zirconium tetrachloride
2576	Phosphorus oxybromide, molten
2691	Phosphorus pentabromide
2798	Benzene phosphorus dichloride
2798	Phenylphosphorus dichloride
2799	Benzene phosphorus thiodichloride
2799	Phenylphosphorus thiodichloride
9206	Methyl phosphonic dichloride

POTENTIAL HAZARDS

FIRE OR EXPLOSION

- EXCEPT for Acetic Anhydride (UN1715), that is flammable, some of these materials may burn, but none ignite readily.
- May ignite combustibles (wood, paper, oil, clothing, etc.)
- Substance will react with water (some violently), releasing corrosive and/or toxic gases.
- Flammable/toxic gases may accumulate in confined areas (basement, tanks, hopper/tank cars, etc.)
- Contact with metals may evolve flammable hydrogen gas.
- Containers may explode when heated or contaminated with water.
- Substance may be transported in a molten form.

Hazmat

HEALTH

- CORROSIVE and/or TOXIC; inhalation, ingestion, or contact (skin, eyes) with vapors, dusts, or substance may cause severe injury, burns, or death.
- Fire will produce irritating, corrosive, or toxic gases.
- Reaction with water may generate much heat which will increase the concentration of fumes in the air.
- Contact with molten substance may cause severe burns to skin and eyes.
- Runoff from fire control or dilution water may cause pollution.

PUBLIC SAFETY

- **CALL Emergency Response Telephone Number on Shipping Paper first. If Shipping Paper is not available or there is no answer, refer to telephone numbers listed on page 613.**
- As an immediate precautionary measure, isolate spill or leak area in all directions for at least 50 meters (150 feet) for liquids and at least 25 meters (75 feet) for solids.
- Keep unauthorized personnel away.
- Stay upwind.
- Keep out of low areas.
- Ventilate enclosed areas.

PROTECTIVE CLOTHING

- Wear positive pressure self-contained breathing apparatus (SCBA).
- Wear chemical protective clothing that is specifically recommended by the manufacturer. It may provide little or no thermal protection.
- Structural firefighters' protective clothing provides limited protection in fire situations ONLY; it is not effective in spill situations where direct contact with the substance is possible.

EVACUATION

Spill

- See the Table of Initial Isolation and Protective Action Distances for highlighted substances (page 908). For non-highlighted substances, increase, in the downwind direction, as necessary, the isolation distance shown above under "PUBLIC SAFETY."

Fire

- If tank, rail car, or tank truck is involved in a fire, ISOLATE for 800 meters (½ mile) in all directions; also, initiate evacuation including emergency responders for 800 meters (½ mile) in all directions.

Hazmat

FIRE

- **When material is not involved in fire: do not use water on material itself.**

Small Fires

- Dry chemical or CO_2.
- Move containers from fire area if you can do it without risk.

Large Fires

- Flood fire area with large quantities of water, while knocking down vapors with water fog. If insufficient water supply: knock down vapors only.

Fire Involving Tanks of Car/Trailer Loads

- Cool containers with flooding quantities of water until well after fire is out.
- DO NOT get water inside containers.
- Withdraw immediately in case of rising sound from venting safety devices or discoloration of tank.
- ALWAYS stay away from tanks engulfed in fire.

SPILL OR LEAK

- Fully encapsulating, vapor protective clothing should be worn for spills and leaks with no fire.
- DO NOT touch damaged containers or spilled material unless wearing appropriate protective clothing.
- Stop leak if you can do it without risk.
- Eliminate all ignition sources (no smoking, flares, sparks, or flames in the immediate area).
- Use water spray to reduce vapors; do not put water directly on leak, spill area, or inside container.
- Keep combustibles (wood, paper, oil, etc.) away from spilled material.

Small Spills

- Cover with DRY earth, DRY sand, or other non-combustible material followed with plastic sheet to minimize spreading or contact with rain.
- Use clean non-sparking tools to collect material and place it into loosely covered plastic containers for later disposal.
- Prevent entry into waterways, sewers, basements, or confined areas.

FIRST AID

- Move victim to fresh air.
- Call 911 or emergency medical service.
- Give artificial respiration if victim is not breathing.
- **DO NOT use mouth-to-mouth method if victim ingested or inhaled the substance; give artificial respiration with the aid**

of a pocket mask equipped with a one-way valve or other proper respiratory medical device.
- Administer oxygen if breathing is difficult.
- Remove and isolate contaminated clothing and shoes.
- In case of contact with substance, immediately flush skin or eyes with running water for at least 20 minutes.
- For minor skin contact, avoid spreading material on unaffected skin.
- Removal of solidified molten material from skin requires medical assistance.
- Keep victim warm and quiet.
- Effects of exposure (inhalation, ingestion, or skin contact) to substance may be delayed.
- Ensure that medical personnel are aware of the material(s) involved, and take precautions to protect themselves.

Guide 138: Substances - Water-Reactive
(Emitting Flammable Gases)

SUBSTANCES INCLUDED

1389 Alkali metal amalgam (& , liquid; & , solid)
1391 Alkali metal dispersion; Alkaline earth metal dispersion
1392 Alkaline earth metal amalgam (& , liquid)
1393 Alkaline earth metal alloy, n.o.s.
1394 Aluminum carbide
1396 Aluminum powder, uncoated
1398 Aluminum silicon powder, uncoated
1400 Barium
1401 Calcium
1402 Calcium carbide
1403 Calcium cyanamide, with > 0.1% Calcium carbide
1404 Calcium hydride
1405 Calcium silicide
1406 Calcium silicon
1407 Caesium; Cesium
1409 Hydrides, metal, n.o.s.
1409 Metal hydrides, water-reactive, n.o.s.
1410 Lithium aluminum hydride
1411 Lithium aluminum hydride, ethereal
1413 Lithium borohydride
1414 Lithium hydride
1415 Lithium
1417 Lithium silicon
1418 Magnesium alloys powder; Magnesium powder
1420 Potassium, metal alloys; Potassium, metal alloys, liquid
1421 Alkali metal alloy, liquid, not otherwise specified
1422 Potassium sodium alloys (& , liquid)
1423 Rubidium; Rubidium metal
1426 Sodium borohydride
1427 Sodium hydride
1428 Sodium
1431 Sodium methylate; Sodium methylate, dry
1435 Zinc ashes; Zinc dross; Zinc residue; Zinc skimmings
1436 Zinc dust; Zinc powder
1437 Zirconium hydride
1869 Magnesium
1869 Magnesium alloys, with > 50% Magnesium, in pellets,
     turnings or ribbons
1869 Magnesium, in pellets, turnings, or ribbons
1870 Potassium borohydride
2010 Magnesium hydride
2257 Potassium; Potassium, metal
2463 Aluminum hydride
2624 Magnesium silicide
2805 Lithium hydride, fused solid
2806 Lithium nitride
2813 Substances, which in contact with water emit flammable gases,
     solid, n.o.s.
2813 Water-reactive solid, n.o.s.
2813 Water-reactive substances, solid, n.o.s.
2835 Sodium aluminum hydride
2844 Calcium manganese silicon
2950 Magnesium granules, coated

3049	Metal alkyl halides, n.o.s.
3049	Metal alkyl halides, water-reactive, n.o.s.
3049	Metal aryl halides, n.o.s.
3049	Metal aryl halides, water-reactive, n.o.s.
3050	Metal alkyl hydrides, n.o.s.
3050	Metal alkyl hydrides, water-reactive, n.o.s.
3050	Metal aryl hydrides, n.o.s.
3050	Metal aryl hydrides, water-reactive, n.o.s.
3076	Aluminum alkyl hydrides
3078	Cerium, turnings or gritty powder
3090	Lithium batteries
3090	Lithium batteries, liquid or solid cathode
3091	Lithium batteries contained in equipment
3091	Lithium batteries packed with equipment
3094	Corrosive liquid, water-reactive, n.o.s.
3094	Corrosive liquid, which in contact with water emits flammable gases, n.o.s.
3096	Corrosive solid, water-reactive, n.o.s.
3096	Corrosive solid, which in contact with water emits flammable gases, n.o.s.
3129	Substances, which in contact with water emit flammable gases, liquid, corrosive, n.o.s.
3129	Water-reactive liquid, corrosive, n.o.s.
3129	Water-reactive substances, liquid, corrosive, n.o.s.
3131	Substances, which in contact with water emit flammable gases, solid, corrosive, n.o.s.
3131	Water-reactive solid, corrosive, n.o.s.
3131	Water-reactive substances, solid, corrosive, n.o.s.
3132	Substances, which in contact with water emit flammable gases, solid, flammable, n.o.s.
3132	Water-reactive solid, flammable, n.o.s.
3132	Water-reactive substances, solid, flammable, n.o.s.
3133	Substances, which in contact with water emit flammable gases, solid, oxidizing, n.o.s.
3133	Water-reactive solid, oxidizing, n.o.s.
3133	Water-reactive substances, solid, oxidizing, n.o.s.
3135	Substances, which in contact with water emit flammable gases, solid, self-heating, n.o.s.
3135	Water-reactive solid, self-heating, n.o.s.
3135	Water-reactive substances, solid, self-heating, n.o.s.
3148	Substances, which in contact with water emit flammable gases, liquid, n.o.s.
3148	Water-reactive liquid, n.o.s.
3148	Water-reactive substances, liquid, n.o.s.
3170	Aluminum dross
3170	Aluminum processing by-products
3170	Aluminum remelting by-products
3170	Aluminum smelting by-products
3207	Organometallic compound dispersion, water-reactive, flammable, nos
3207	Organometallic compound solution, water-reactive, flammable, n.o.s.
3207	Organometallic compound, water-reactive, flammable, n.o.s.
3208	Metallic substance, water-reactive, n.o.s.
3209	Metallic substance, water-reactive, self-heating, n.o.s.
3292	Batteries, containing Sodium
3292	Cells, containing Sodium
3372	Organometallic compound, solid water-reactive, flammable, n.o.s.
3396	Organometallic substance, solid, water-reactive, flammable
3397	Organometallic substance, solid, water-reactive, self-heating
3399	Organometallic substance, liquid, water-reactive, flammable

Hazmat

3400	Organometallic substance, solid, self-heating
3401	Alkali metal amalgam, solid
3402	Alkaline earth metal amalgam, solid
3403	Potassium, metal alloys, solid
3404	Potassium sodium alloys, solid

POTENTIAL HAZARDS

FIRE OR EXPLOSION

- Produce flammable gases on contact with water.
- May ignite on contact with water or moist air.
- Some react vigorously or explosively on contact with water.
- May be ignited by heat, sparks, or flames.
- May re-ignite after fire is extinguished.
- Some are transported in highly flammable liquids.
- Runoff may create fire or explosion hazard

HEALTH

- Inhalation or contact with vapors, substance, or decomposition products may cause severe injury or death.
- May produce corrosive solutions on contact with water.
- Fire will produce irritating, corrosive, or toxic gases.
- Runoff from fire control may cause pollution.

PUBLIC SAFETY

- **CALL Emergency Response Telephone Number on Shipping Paper first. If Shipping Paper is not available or there is no answer, refer to telephone numbers listed on page 613.**
- As an immediate precautionary measure, isolate spill or leak area in all directions for at least 50 meters (150 feet) for liquids and at least 25 meters (75 feet) for solids.
- Keep unauthorized personnel away.
- Stay upwind.
- Keep out of low areas.
- Ventilate enclosed areas.

PROTECTIVE CLOTHING

- Wear positive pressure self-contained breathing apparatus (SCBA).
- Wear chemical protective clothing that is specifically recommended by the manufacturer. It may provide little or no thermal protection.
- Structural firefighters' protective clothing provides limited protection in fire situations ONLY; it is not effective in spill situations where direct contact with the substance is possible.

EVACUATION

Large Spill

- See the Table of Initial Isolation and Protective Action Distances for highlighted substances (page 908). For non-highlighted substances, increase, in the downwind direction, as necessary, the isolation distance shown above under "PUBLIC SAFETY."

Fire

- If tank, rail car, or tank truck is involved in a fire, ISOLATE for 800 meters (½ mile) in all directions; also, initiate evacuation including emergency responders for 800 meters (½ mile) in all directions.

EMERGENCY RESPONSE

FIRE

- **DO NOT use water or foam!**

Small Fires

- Dry chemical, soda ash, lime, or sand.

Large Fires

- DRY sand, DRY chemical, soda ash, or lime, or withdraw from area and let fire burn.
- Move containers from fire area if you can do it without risk.

Magnesium Fires

- DRY sand, sodium chloride powder, graphite powder, or Met-L-X® powder.

Lithium Fires

- DRY sand, sodium chloride powder, graphite powder, copper powder, or Lith-X® powder.

Fire Involving Tanks of Car/Trailer Loads

- Fight fire from maximum distance or use unmanned hose holders or monitor nozzles.
- DO NOT get water inside containers.
- Cool containers with flooding quantities of water until well after fire is out.
- Withdraw immediately in case of rising sound from venting safety devices or discoloration of tank.
- ALWAYS stay away from tanks engulfed in fire.

SPILL OR LEAK

- Eliminate all ignition sources (no smoking, flares, sparks, or flames in the immediate area).
- DO NOT touch or walk through spilled material.
- Stop leak if you can do it without risk.
- Use water spray to reduce vapors; do not put water directly on leak, spill area, or inside container.
- **DO NOT get water on spilled substance or inside containers.**

Small Spills

- Cover with DRY earth, DRY sand, or other non-combustible material followed with plastic sheet to minimize spreading or contact with rain.

- Dike for later disposal; do not apply water unless directed to do so.

Powder Spills
- Cover powder spill with plastic sheet or tarp to minimize spreading and keep powder dry.
- **DO NOT clean-up or dispose of, except under supervision of a specialist.**

FIRST AID

- Move victim to fresh air.
- Call 911 or emergency medical service.
- Give artificial respiration if victim is not breathing.
- Administer oxygen if breathing is difficult.
- Remove and isolate contaminated clothing and shoes.
- In case of contact with substance, wipe from skin immediately; flush skin or eyes with running water for at least 20 minutes.
- Keep victim warm and quiet.
- Ensure that medical personnel are aware of the material(s) involved, and take precautions to protect themselves.

Hazmat

Guide 139: Substances - Water-Reactive
(Emitting Flammable and Toxic Gases)

SUBSTANCES INCLUDED

1183	Ethyldichlorosilane
1242	Methyldichlorosilane
1295	Trichlorosilane
1339	Phosphorus heptasulfide, free from yellow and white Phosphorus
1340	Phosphorus pentasulfide, free from yellow or white Phosphorus
1341	Phosphorus sesquisulfide, free from yellow and white Phosphorus
1343	Phosphorus trisulfide, free from yellow and white Phosphorus
1360	Calcium phosphide
1390	Alkali metal amides
1395	Aluminum ferrosilicon powder
1397	Aluminum phosphide
1408	Ferrosilicon
1412	Lithium amide
1419	Magnesium aluminum phosphide
1432	Sodium phosphide
1433	Stannic phosphides
1714	Zinc phosphide
2011	Magnesium phosphide
2012	Potassium phosphide
2013	Strontium phosphide
2830	Lithium ferrosilicon
2965	Boron trifluoride dimethyl etherate
2988	Chlorosilanes, n.o.s.
2988	Chlorosilanes, water-reactive, flammable, corrosive, n.o.s.
3123	Toxic liquid, water-reactive, n.o.s. (& Inhalation Hazard Zone A and B)
3123	Toxic liquid, which in contact with water emits flammable gases, n.o.s. (& Inhalation Hazard Zone A and B)
3125	Toxic solid, water-reactive, n.o.s.
3125	Toxic solid, which in contact with water emits flammable gases, n.o.s.
3130	Substances, which in contact with water emit flammable gases, liquid, toxic, n.o.s.
3130	Water-reactive liquid, toxic, n.o.s.
3130	Water-reactive substances, liquid, toxic, n.o.s.
3134	Substances, which in contact with water emit flammable gases, solid, toxic, n.o.s.
3134	Water-reactive solid, toxic, n.o.s.
3134	Water-reactive substances, solid, toxic, n.o.s.
3385	Toxic by inhalation liquid, water-reactive, n.o.s. (Inhalation Hazard Zone A)
3386	Toxic by inhalation liquid, water-reactive, n.o.s. (Inhalation Hazard Zone B)

POTENTIAL HAZARDS
FIRE OR EXPLOSION

- Produce flammable gases on contact with water.
- May ignite on contact with water or moist air.
- Some react vigorously or explosively on contact with water.
- May be ignited by heat, sparks, or flames.
- May re-ignite after fire is extinguished.
- Some are transported in highly flammable liquids.

- Containers may explode when heated.
- Runoff may create fire or explosion hazard

HEALTH

- Highly toxic: contact with water produces toxic gas, may be fatal if inhaled.
- Inhalation or contact with vapors, substance, or decomposition products may cause severe injury or death.
- May produce corrosive solutions on contact with water.
- Fire will produce irritating, corrosive, or toxic gases.
- Runoff from fire control may cause pollution.

PUBLIC SAFETY

- **CALL Emergency Response Telephone Number on Shipping Paper first. If Shipping Paper is not available or there is no answer, refer to telephone numbers listed on page 613.**
- As an immediate precautionary measure, isolate spill or leak area in all directions for at least 50 m (150 ft) for liquids and at least 25 m (75 ft) for solids.
- Keep unauthorized personnel away.
- Stay upwind.
- Keep out of low areas.
- Ventilate enclosed areas.

PROTECTIVE CLOTHING

- Wear positive pressure self-contained breathing apparatus (SCBA).
- Wear chemical protective clothing that is specifically recommended by the manufacturer. It may provide little or no thermal protection.
- Structural firefighters' protective clothing provides limited protection in fire situations ONLY; it is not effective in spill situations where direct contact with the substance is possible.

EVACUATION

Large Spill
- See the Table of Initial Isolation and Protective Action Distances for highlighted substances (page 908). For non-highlighted substances, increase, in the downwind direction, as necessary, the isolation distance shown above under "PUBLIC SAFETY."

Fire
- If tank, rail car, or tank truck is involved in a fire, ISOLATE for 800 meters (½ mile) in all directions; also, initiate evacuation including emergency responders for 800 meters (½ mile) in all directions.

FIRE

- **DO NOT use water or foam! (Foam may be used for chlorosilanes, see below)**

Small Fires

- Dry chemical, soda ash, lime, or sand.

Large Fires

- DRY sand, DRY chemical, soda ash, or lime, or withdraw from area and let fire burn.
- **For chlorosilanes:** DO NOT use water; use AFFF alcohol-resistant medium expansion foam; DO NOT use dry chemicals, soda ash, or lime on chlorosilane fires (large or small) as they may release large quantities of hydrogen gas that may explode.
- Move containers from fire area if you can do it without risk.

Fire Involving Tanks of Car/Trailer Loads

- Fight fire from maximum distance or use unmanned hose holders or monitor nozzles.
- Cool containers with flooding quantities of water until well after fire is out.
- DO NOT get water inside containers.
- Withdraw immediately in case of rising sound from venting safety devices or discoloration of tank.
- ALWAYS stay away from tanks engulfed in fire.

SPILL OR LEAK

- Fully encapsulating, vapor protective clothing should be worn for spills and leaks with no fire.
- Eliminate all ignition sources (no smoking, flares, sparks, or flames in the immediate area).
- DO NOT touch or walk through spilled material.
- Stop leak if you can do it without risk.
- **DO NOT get water on spilled substance or inside containers.**
- Use water spray to reduce vapors; do not put water directly on leak, spill area, or inside container.
- **For chlorosilanes:** use AFFF alcohol-resistant medium expansion foam to reduce vapors.

Small Spills

- Cover with DRY earth, DRY sand, or other non-combustible material followed with plastic sheet to minimize spreading or contact with rain.
- Dike for later disposal; do not apply water unless directed to do so.

Powder Spills

- Cover powder spill with plastic sheet or tarp to minimize spreading and keep powder dry.

- **DO NOT clean-up or dispose of, except under supervision of a specialist.**

FIRST AID

- Move victim to fresh air.
- Call 911 or emergency medical service.
- Give artificial respiration if victim is not breathing.
- **DO NOT use mouth-to-mouth method if victim ingested or inhaled the substance; give artificial respiration with the aid of a pocket mask equipped with a one-way valve or other proper respiratory medical device.**
- Administer oxygen if breathing is difficult.
- Remove and isolate contaminated clothing and shoes.
- In case of contact with substance, wipe from skin immediately; flush skin or eyes with running water for at least 20 minutes.
- Keep victim warm and quiet.
- Ensure that medical personnel are aware of the material(s) involved, and take precautions to protect themselves.

Guide 140: Oxidizers

SUBSTANCES INCLUDED

1112	Amyl nitrate
1438	Aluminum nitrate
1444	Ammonium persulfate
1451	Caesium nitrate; Cesium nitrate
1452	Calcium chlorate
1453	Calcium chlorite
1454	Calcium nitrate
1455	Calcium perchlorate
1456	Calcium permanganate
1457	Calcium peroxide
1458	Borate and Chlorate mixtures
1459	Chlorate and Magnesium chloride mixture (& , solid)
1461	Chlorates, inorganic, n.o.s.
1465	Didymium nitrate
1466	Ferric nitrate
1471	Lithium hypochlorite mixture (& , dry)
1473	Magnesium bromate
1474	Magnesium nitrate
1475	Magnesium perchlorate
1476	Magnesium peroxide
1477	Nitrates, inorganic, n.o.s.
1479	Medicines, oxidizing substances, solid, n.o.s.
1479	Oxidizing solid, n.o.s.
1479	Oxidizing substances, solid, n.o.s.
1481	Perchlorates, inorganic, n.o.s.
1482	Permanganate, n.o.s.
1482	Permanganates, inorganic, n.o.s.
1483	Peroxides, inorganic, n.o.s.
1484	Potassium bromate
1485	Potassium chlorate
1486	Potassium nitrate
1487	Potassium nitrate and Sodium nitrite mixture
1488	Potassium nitrite
1489	Potassium perchlorate
1490	Potassium permanganate
1492	Potassium persulfate
1493	Silver nitrate
1495	Sodium chlorate
1498	Sodium nitrate
1499	Potassium nitrate and Sodium nitrate mixture
1500	Sodium nitrite
1502	Sodium perchlorate
1503	Sodium permanganate
1505	Sodium persulfate
1507	Strontium nitrate
1508	Strontium perchlorate
1511	Urea hydrogen peroxide
1512	Zinc ammonium nitrite
1513	Zinc chlorate
1514	Zinc nitrate
1515	Zinc permanganate
1748	Calcium hypochlorite mixture, dry, with > 39% available Chlorine (8.8% available Oxygen)
1748	Calcium hypochlorite, dry
1802	Perchloric acid, with $\leq$ 50% acid

Hazmat

1942	Ammonium nitrate, with ≤ 0.2% combustible substances
2014	Hydrogen peroxide, aqueous solution, with ≥ 20% but ≤ 60% Hydrogen peroxide (stabilized as necessary)
2067	Ammonium nitrate fertilizers
2068	Ammonium nitrate fertilizers, with Calcium carbonate
2069	Ammonium nitrate fertilizers, with Ammonium sulfate
2069	Ammonium nitrate mixed fertilizers
2071	Ammonium nitrate fertilizer, with ≤ 0.4% combustible material
2071	Ammonium nitrate fertilizers
2072	Ammonium nitrate fertilizer, n.o.s.
2072	Ammonium nitrate fertilizers
2208	Bleaching powder
2208	Calcium hypochlorite mixture, dry, with > 10% but ≤ 39% available Chlorine
2426	Ammonium nitrate, liquid (hot concentrated solution)
2427	Potassium chlorate, aqueous solution
2427	Potassium chlorate, solution
2428	Sodium chlorate, aqueous solution
2429	Calcium chlorate, aqueous solution
2429	Calcium chlorate, solution
2465	Dichloroisocyanuric acid salts
2465	Dichloroisocyanuric acid, dry
2465	Sodium dichloroisocyanurate
2465	Sodium dichloro-s-triazinetrione
2467	Sodium percarbonates
2468	(mono)-(Trichloro)-tetra-(monopotassium dichloro)-penta-s-triazinetrione, dry
2468	Trichloroisocyanuric acid, dry
2469	Zinc bromate
2626	Chloric acid, aqueous solution, with ≤ 10% Chloric acid
2627	Nitrites, inorganic, n.o.s.
2722	Lithium nitrate
2723	Magnesium chlorate
2724	Manganese nitrate
2725	Nickel nitrate
2726	Nickel nitrite
2728	Zirconium nitrate
2880	Calcium hypochlorite, hydrated mixture, with ≥ 5.5% but ≤ 16% water
2984	Hydrogen peroxide, aqueous solution, with ≥ 8% but < 20% Hydrogen peroxide
3084	Corrosive solid, oxidizing, n.o.s.
3085	Oxidizing solid, corrosive, n.o.s.
3085	Oxidizing substances, solid, corrosive, n.o.s.
3093	Corrosive liquid, oxidizing, n.o.s.
3097	Flammable solid, oxidizing, n.o.s.
3098	Oxidizing liquid, corrosive, n.o.s.
3098	Oxidizing substances, liquid, corrosive, n.o.s.
3137	Oxidizing solid, flammable, n.o.s.
3137	Oxidizing substances, solid, flammable, n.o.s.
3139	Oxidizing liquid, n.o.s.
3139	Oxidizing substances, liquid, n.o.s.
3149	Hydrogen peroxide and Peroxyacetic acid mixture, with acid(s), water, and ≤ 5% acetic acid, stabilized
3210	Chlorates, inorganic, aqueous solution, n.o.s.
3211	Perchlorates, inorganic, aqueous solution, n.o.s.
3212	Hypochlorites, inorganic, n.o.s.
3213	Bromates, inorganic, aqueous solution, n.o.s.
3214	Permanganates, inorganic, aqueous solution, n.o.s.
3215	Persulfates, inorganic, n.o.s.

Hazmat

3216	Persulfates, inorganic, aqueous solution, n.o.s.
3217	Percarbonates, inorganic, n.o.s.
3218	Nitrates, inorganic, aqueous solution, n.o.s.
3219	Nitrites, inorganic, aqueous solution, n.o.s.
3247	Sodium peroxoborate, anhydrous
3356	Oxygen generator, chemical (& , spent)
3375	Ammonium nitrate emulsion; Ammonium nitrate gel
3377	Sodium perborate monohydrate
3378	Sodium carbonate peroxyhydrate
3407	Chlorate and Magnesium chloride mixture, solution
8037	Oxygen generators, small

POTENTIAL HAZARDS

FIRE OR EXPLOSION

- These substances will accelerate burning when involved in a fire.
- Some may decompose explosively when heated or involved in a fire.
- May explode from heat or contamination.
- Some will react explosively with hydrocarbons (fuels).
- May ignite combustibles (wood, paper, oil, clothing, etc.)
- Containers may explode when heated.
- Runoff may create fire or explosion hazard

HEALTH

- Inhalation, ingestion, or contact (skin, eyes) with vapors or substance may cause severe injury, burns, or death.
- Fire will produce irritating, corrosive, or toxic gases.
- Runoff from fire control may cause pollution.

PUBLIC SAFETY

- **CALL Emergency Response Telephone Number on Shipping Paper first. If Shipping Paper is not available or there is no answer, refer to telephone numbers listed on page 613.**
- As an immediate precautionary measure, isolate spill or leak area in all directions for at least 50 meters (150 feet) for liquids and at least 25 meters (75 feet) for solids.
- Keep unauthorized personnel away.
- Stay upwind.
- Keep out of low areas.
- Ventilate enclosed areas.

PROTECTIVE CLOTHING

- Wear positive pressure self-contained breathing apparatus (SCBA).
- Wear chemical protective clothing that is specifically recommended by the manufacturer. It may provide little or no thermal protection.
- Structural firefighters' protective clothing will only provide limited protection.

Hazmat

EVACUATION

Large Spill

• Consider initial downwind evacuation for at least 100 meters (330 feet).

Fire

• If tank, rail car, or tank truck is involved in a fire, ISOLATE for 800 meters (½ mile) in all directions; also, initiate evacuation including emergency responders for 800 meters (½ mile) in all directions.

EMERGENCY RESPONSE
FIRE

Small Fires

• Use water. DO NOT use dry chemicals or foams. CO_2 or Halon® may provide limited control.

Large Fires

• Flood fire area with water from a distance.
• Move containers from fire area if you can do it without risk.
• DO NOT move cargo or vehicle if cargo has been exposed to heat.
• Fight fire from maximum distance or use unmanned hose holders or monitor nozzles.
• Cool containers with flooding quantities of water until well after fire is out.
• ALWAYS stay away from tanks engulfed in fire.
• For massive fire, use unmanned hose holders or monitor nozzles; if this is impossible, withdraw from area and let fire burn.

SPILL OR LEAK

• Keep combustibles (wood, paper, oil, etc.) away from spilled material.
• DO NOT touch or walk through spilled material unless wearing appropriate protective clothing.
• Stop leak if you can do it without risk.
• DO NOT get water inside containers.

Small Dry Spills

• With clean shovel place material into clean, dry container and cover loosely; move containers from spill area.

Small Liquid Spills

• Use a non-combustible material like vermiculite or sand to soak up the product and place into a container for later disposal.

Large Spills

• Dike far ahead of liquid spill for later disposal.
• **Following product recovery, flush area with water.**

FIRST AID

- Move victim to fresh air.
- Call 911 or emergency medical service.
- Give artificial respiration if victim is not breathing.
- Administer oxygen if breathing is difficult.
- Remove and isolate contaminated clothing and shoes.
- Contaminated clothing may be a fire risk when dry.
- In case of contact with substance, immediately flush skin or eyes with running water for at least 20 minutes.
- Keep victim warm and quiet.
- Ensure that medical personnel are aware of the material(s) involved, and take precautions to protect themselves.

Hazmat

Guide 141: Oxidizers - Toxic

SUBSTANCES INCLUDED

1439	Ammonium dichromate
1445	Barium chlorate; Barium chlorate, solid
1446	Barium nitrate
1447	Barium perchlorate; Barium perchlorate, solid
1448	Barium permanganate
1449	Barium peroxide
1450	Bromates, inorganic, not otherwise specified
1463	Chromic acid, solid; Chromium trioxide, anhydrous
1469	Lead nitrate
1470	Lead perchlorate (& , solid; & , solution)
1494	Sodium bromate
1625	Mercuric nitrate
1627	Mercurous nitrate
1843	Ammonium dinitro-o-cresolate (& , solid)
1872	Lead dioxide
2464	Beryllium nitrate
2573	Thallium chlorate
2719	Barium bromate
2720	Chromium nitrate
2721	Copper chlorate
2727	Thallium nitrate
2741	Barium hypochlorite, with > 22% available Chlorine
3086	Toxic solid, oxidizing, n.o.s.
3087	Oxidizing solid, toxic, n.o.s.
3087	Oxidizing substances, solid, toxic, n.o.s.
3405	Barium chlorate, solution
3406	Barium perchlorate, solution
3408	Lead perchlorate, solution
3424	Ammonium dinitro-o-cresolate, solution

POTENTIAL HAZARDS

FIRE OR EXPLOSION

- These substances will accelerate burning when involved in a fire.
- May explode from heat or contamination.
- Some may burn rapidly.
- Some will react explosively with hydrocarbons (fuels).
- May ignite combustibles (wood, paper, oil, clothing, etc.)
- Containers may explode when heated.
- Runoff may create fire or explosion hazard

HEALTH

- Toxic by ingestion.
- Inhalation of dust is toxic.
- Fire may produce irritating, corrosive, or toxic gases.
- Contact with substance may cause severe burns to skin and eyes.
- Runoff from fire control may cause pollution.

PUBLIC SAFETY

- CALL Emergency Response Telephone Number on Shipping Paper first. If Shipping Paper is not available or there is no answer, refer to telephone numbers listed on page 613.
- As an immediate precautionary measure, isolate spill or leak area in all directions for at least 50 meters (150 feet) for liquids and at least 25 meters (75 feet) for solids.
- Keep unauthorized personnel away.
- Stay upwind.
- Keep out of low areas.
- Ventilate enclosed areas.

PROTECTIVE CLOTHING

- Wear positive pressure self-contained breathing apparatus (SCBA).
- Wear chemical protective clothing that is specifically recommended by the manufacturer. It may provide little or no thermal protection.
- Structural firefighters' protective clothing will only provide limited protection.

EVACUATION

Large Spill
- Consider initial downwind evacuation for at least 100 meters (330 feet).

Fire
- If tank, rail car, or tank truck is involved in a fire, ISOLATE for 800 meters (½ mile) in all directions; also, initiate evacuation including emergency responders for 800 meters (½ mile) in all directions.

EMERGENCY RESPONSE
FIRE

Small Fires
- Use water. DO NOT use dry chemicals or foams. CO_2 or Halon® may provide limited control.

Large Fires
- Flood fire area with water from a distance.
- Move containers from fire area if you can do it without risk.
- DO NOT move cargo or vehicle if cargo has been exposed to heat.
- Fight fire from maximum distance or use unmanned hose holders or monitor nozzles.
- Cool containers with flooding quantities of water until well after fire is out.
- ALWAYS stay away from tanks engulfed in fire.

- For massive fire, use unmanned hose holders or monitor nozzles; if this is impossible, withdraw from area and let fire burn.

SPILL OR LEAK

- Keep combustibles (wood, paper, oil, etc.) away from spilled material.
- DO NOT touch or walk through spilled material unless wearing appropriate protective clothing.
- Stop leak if you can do it without risk.

Small Dry Spills

- With clean shovel place material into clean, dry container and cover loosely; move containers from spill area.

Large Spills

- Dike far ahead of liquid spill for later disposal.

FIRST AID

- Move victim to fresh air.
- Call 911 or emergency medical service.
- Give artificial respiration if victim is not breathing.
- Administer oxygen if breathing is difficult.
- Remove and isolate contaminated clothing and shoes.
- Contaminated clothing may be a fire risk when dry.
- In case of contact with substance, immediately flush skin or eyes with running water for at least 20 minutes.
- Keep victim warm and quiet.
- Ensure that medical personnel are aware of the material(s) involved, and take precautions to protect themselves.

Guide 142: Oxidizers - Toxic (Liquid)

SUBSTANCES INCLUDED

3099 Oxidizing liquid, toxic, n.o.s.
3099 Oxidizing substances, liquid, toxic, n.o.s.
3122 Toxic liquid, oxidizing, n.o.s.
3122 Toxic liquid, oxidizing, n.o.s. (Inhalation Hazard Zone A and B)
3387 Toxic by inhalation liquid, oxidizing, n.o.s. (Inhalation Hazard Zone A)
3388 Toxic by inhalation liquid, oxidizing, n.o.s. (Inhalation Hazard Zone B)

POTENTIAL HAZARDS

FIRE OR EXPLOSION

- These substances will accelerate burning when involved in a fire.
- May explode from heat or contamination.
- Some will react explosively with hydrocarbons (fuels).
- May ignite combustibles (wood, paper, oil, clothing, etc.)
- Containers may explode when heated.
- Runoff may create fire or explosion hazard

HEALTH

- **Toxic;** inhalation, ingestion or contact (skin, eyes) with vapors or substance may cause severe injury, burns, or death.
- Fire may produce irritating, corrosive, or toxic gases.
- Toxic/flammable fumes may accumulate in confined areas (basement, tanks, tank cars, etc.)
- Runoff from fire control or dilution water may cause pollution.

PUBLIC SAFETY

- **CALL Emergency Response Telephone Number on Shipping Paper first. If Shipping Paper is not available or there is no answer, refer to telephone numbers listed on page 613.**
- As an immediate precautionary measure, isolate spill or leak area for at least 50 meters (150 feet) in all directions.
- Keep unauthorized personnel away.
- Stay upwind.
- Keep out of low areas.
- Ventilate enclosed areas.

PROTECTIVE CLOTHING

- Wear positive pressure self-contained breathing apparatus (SCBA).
- Wear chemical protective clothing that is specifically recommended by the manufacturer. It may provide little or no thermal protection.
- Structural firefighters' protective clothing provides limited protection in fire situations ONLY; it is not effective in spill situations where direct contact with the substance is possible.

EVACUATION

Spill

- See the Table of Initial Isolation and Protective Action Distances for highlighted substances (page 908). For non-highlighted substances, increase, in the downwind direction, as necessary, the isolation distance shown above under "PUBLIC SAFETY."

Fire

- If tank, rail car, or tank truck is involved in a fire, ISOLATE for 800 meters (½ mile) in all directions; also, initiate evacuation including emergency responders for 800 meters (½ mile) in all directions.

EMERGENCY RESPONSE
FIRE

Small Fires

- Use water. DO NOT use dry chemicals or foams. CO_2 or Halon® may provide limited control.

Large Fires

- Flood fire area with water from a distance.
- Move containers from fire area if you can do it without risk.
- DO NOT move cargo or vehicle if cargo has been exposed to heat.
- Fight fire from maximum distance or use unmanned hose holders or monitor nozzles.
- Cool containers with flooding quantities of water until well after fire is out.
- ALWAYS stay away from tanks engulfed in fire.
- For massive fire, use unmanned hose holders or monitor nozzles; if this is impossible, withdraw from area and let fire burn.

SPILL OR LEAK

- Keep combustibles (wood, paper, oil, etc.) away from spilled material.
- Fully encapsulating, vapor protective clothing should be worn for spills and leaks with no fire.
- DO NOT touch damaged containers or spilled material unless wearing appropriate protective clothing.
- Stop leak if you can do it without risk.
- Use water spray to reduce vapors or divert vapor cloud drift.
- DO NOT get water inside containers.

Small Liquid Spills

- Use a non-combustible material like vermiculite or sand to soak up the product and place into a container for later disposal.

Large Spills

- Dike far ahead of liquid spill for later disposal.

- Move victim to fresh air.
- Call 911 or emergency medical service.
- Give artificial respiration if victim is not breathing.
- **DO NOT use mouth-to-mouth method if victim ingested or inhaled the substance; give artificial respiration with the aid of a pocket mask equipped with a one-way valve or other proper respiratory medical device.**
- Administer oxygen if breathing is difficult.
- Remove and isolate contaminated clothing and shoes.
- Contaminated clothing may be a fire risk when dry.
- In case of contact with substance, immediately flush skin or eyes with running water for at least 20 minutes.
- Keep victim warm and quiet.
- Ensure that medical personnel are aware of the material(s) involved, and take precautions to protect themselves.

Hazmat

Guide 143: Oxidizers (Unstable)

SUBSTANCES INCLUDED

1442	Ammonium perchlorate
1462	Chlorites, inorganic, n.o.s.
1467	Guanidine nitrate
1472	Lithium peroxide
1496	Sodium chlorite
1506	Strontium chlorate (& , solid; & , solution)
1509	Strontium peroxide
1510	Tetranitromethane
1516	Zinc peroxide
1873	Perchloric acid, with > 50% but ≤ 72% acid
2015	Hydrogen peroxide, aqueous solution, stabilized, with > 60% Hydrogen peroxide
2015	Hydrogen peroxide, stabilized
2070	Ammonium nitrate fertilizers, with Phosphate or Potash
2466	Potassium superoxide
2547	Sodium superoxide
9191	Chlorine dioxide, hydrate, frozen

POTENTIAL HAZARDS

FIRE OR EXPLOSION

- May explode from friction, heat, or contamination.
- These substances will accelerate burning when involved in a fire.
- May ignite combustibles (wood, paper, oil, clothing, etc.)
- Some will react explosively with hydrocarbons (fuels).
- Containers may explode when heated.
- Runoff may create fire or explosion hazard

HEALTH

- **Toxic;** inhalation, ingestion or contact (skin, eyes) with vapors, dusts, or substance may cause severe injury, burns, or death.
- Fire may produce irritating, corrosive, or toxic gases.
- Toxic fumes may accumulate in confined areas (basement, tanks, hopper/tank cars, etc.)
- Runoff from fire control or dilution water may cause pollution.

PUBLIC SAFETY

- **CALL Emergency Response Telephone Number on Shipping Paper first. If Shipping Paper is not available or there is no answer, refer to telephone numbers listed on page 613.**
- As an immediate precautionary measure, isolate spill or leak area in all directions for at least 50 meters (150 feet) for liquids and at least 25 meters (75 feet) for solids.
- Keep unauthorized personnel away.
- Stay upwind.
- Keep out of low areas.
- Ventilate closed spaces before entering.

PROTECTIVE CLOTHING

- Wear positive pressure self-contained breathing apparatus (SCBA).
- Wear chemical protective clothing that is specifically recommended by the manufacturer. It may provide little or no thermal protection.
- Structural firefighters' protective clothing provides limited protection in fire situations ONLY; it is not effective in spill situations where direct contact with the substance is possible.

EVACUATION

Spill

- See the Table of Initial Isolation and Protective Action Distances for highlighted substances (page 908). For non-highlighted substances, increase, in the downwind direction, as necessary, the isolation distance shown above under "PUBLIC SAFETY."

Fire

- If tank, rail car, or tank truck is involved in a fire, ISOLATE for 800 meters (½ mile) in all directions; also, initiate evacuation including emergency responders for 800 meters (½ mile) in all directions.

EMERGENCY RESPONSE
FIRE

Small Fires

- Use water. DO NOT use dry chemicals or foams. CO_2 or Halon® may provide limited control.

Large Fires

- Flood fire area with water from a distance.
- DO NOT move cargo or vehicle if cargo has been exposed to heat.
- Move containers from fire area if you can do it without risk.
- DO NOT get water inside containers; a violent reaction may occur.
- Cool containers with flooding quantities of water until well after fire is out.
- Dike fire-control water for later disposal.
- ALWAYS stay away from tanks engulfed in fire.
- For massive fire, use unmanned hose holders or monitor nozzles; if this is impossible, withdraw from area and let fire burn.

SPILL OR LEAK

- Keep combustibles (wood, paper, oil, etc.) away from spilled material.
- DO NOT touch damaged containers or spilled material unless wearing appropriate protective clothing.
- Use water spray to reduce vapors or divert vapor cloud drift.

Hazmat

• Prevent entry into waterways, sewers, basements, or confined areas.

Small Spills

• Flush area with flooding quantities of water.

Large Spills

• **DO NOT clean-up or dispose of, except under supervision of a specialist.**

FIRST AID

• Move victim to fresh air.
• Call 911 or emergency medical service.
• Give artificial respiration if victim is not breathing.
• Administer oxygen if breathing is difficult.
• Remove and isolate contaminated clothing and shoes.
• Contaminated clothing may be a fire risk when dry.
• In case of contact with substance, immediately flush skin or eyes with running water for at least 20 minutes.
• Keep victim warm and quiet.
• Ensure that medical personnel are aware of the material(s) involved, and take precautions to protect themselves.

Hazmat

Guide 144: Oxidizers (Water-Reactive)

SUBSTANCES INCLUDED

1491 Potassium peroxide
1504 Sodium peroxide
1745 Bromine pentafluoride
1746 Bromine trifluoride
2495 Iodine pentafluoride
3121 Oxidizing solid, water-reactive, n.o.s.
3121 Oxidizing substances, solid, which in contact with water emit
    flammable gases, n.o.s.

POTENTIAL HAZARDS
FIRE OR EXPLOSION

- May ignite combustibles (wood, paper, oil, clothing, etc.)
- React vigorously and/or explosively with water.
- Produce toxic and/or corrosive substances on contact with water.
- Flammable/toxic gases may accumulate in tanks and hopper cars.
- Some may produce flammable hydrogen gas upon contact with metals.
- Containers may explode when heated.
- Runoff may create fire or explosion hazard

HEALTH

- **Toxic;** inhalation or contact with vapor, substance, or decomposition products may cause severe injury or death.
- Fire may produce irritating, corrosive, or toxic gases.
- Runoff from fire control or dilution water may cause pollution.

PUBLIC SAFETY

- **CALL Emergency Response Telephone Number on Shipping Paper first. If Shipping Paper is not available or there is no answer, refer to telephone numbers listed on page 613.**
- As an immediate precautionary measure, isolate spill or leak area in all directions for at least 50 meters (150 feet) for liquids and at least 25 meters (75 feet) for solids.
- Keep unauthorized personnel away.
- Stay upwind.
- Keep out of low areas.
- Ventilate closed spaces before entering.

PROTECTIVE CLOTHING

- Wear positive pressure self-contained breathing apparatus (SCBA).
- Wear chemical protective clothing that is specifically recommended by the manufacturer. It may provide little or no thermal protection.

Hazmat

- Structural firefighters' protective clothing provides limited protection in fire situations ONLY; it is not effective in spill situations where direct contact with the substance is possible.

EVACUATION

Spill

- See the Table of Initial Isolation and Protective Action Distances for highlighted substances (page 908). For non-highlighted substances, increase, in the downwind direction, as necessary, the isolation distance shown above under "PUBLIC SAFETY."

Fire

- If tank, rail car, or tank truck is involved in a fire, ISOLATE for 800 meters (½ mile) in all directions; also, initiate evacuation including emergency responders for 800 meters (½ mile) in all directions.

EMERGENCY RESPONSE

FIRE

- **DO NOT use water or foam.**

Small Fires

- Dry chemical, soda ash, or lime.

Large Fires

- DRY sand, DRY chemical, soda ash, or lime, or withdraw from area and let fire burn.
- Move containers from fire area if you can do it without risk.

Fire Involving Tanks or Car/Trailer Loads

- Fight fire from maximum distance or use unmanned hose holders or monitor nozzles.
- Cool containers with flooding quantities of water until well after fire is out.
- Withdraw immediately in case of rising sound from venting safety devices or discoloration of tank.
- ALWAYS stay away from tanks engulfed in fire.

SPILL OR LEAK

- Eliminate all ignition sources (no smoking, flares, sparks, or flames in immediate area).
- DO NOT touch damaged containers or spilled material unless wearing appropriate protective clothing.
- Stop leak if you can do it without risk.
- Use water spray to reduce vapors or divert vapor cloud drift. Avoid allowing water runoff to contact spilled material.
- **DO NOT get water on spilled substance or inside containers.**

Small Spills

- Cover with DRY earth, DRY sand, or other non-combustible material followed with plastic sheet to minimize spreading or contact with rain.

Large Spills

- **DO NOT clean-up or dispose of, except under supervision of a specialist.**

FIRST AID

- Move victim to fresh air.
- Call 911 or emergency medical service.
- Give artificial respiration if victim is not breathing.
- **DO NOT use mouth-to-mouth method if victim ingested or inhaled the substance; give artificial respiration with the aid of a pocket mask equipped with a one-way valve or other proper respiratory medical device.**
- Administer oxygen if breathing is difficult.
- Remove and isolate contaminated clothing and shoes.
- Contaminated clothing may be a fire risk when dry.
- In case of contact with substance, immediately flush skin or eyes with running water for at least 20 minutes.
- Keep victim warm and quiet.
- Keep victim under observation.
- Effects of contact or inhalation may be delayed.
- Ensure that medical personnel are aware of the material(s) involved, and take precautions to protect themselves.

Guide 145: Organic Peroxides
(Heat and Contamination Sensitive)

SUBSTANCES INCLUDED

3105 Organic peroxide type D, liquid
3106 Organic peroxide type D, solid
3107 Organic peroxide type E, liquid
3108 Organic peroxide type E, solid
3109 Organic peroxide type F, liquid
3110 Organic peroxide type F, solid

POTENTIAL HAZARDS

FIRE OR EXPLOSION

- May explode from heat or contamination.
- May ignite combustibles (wood, paper, oil, clothing, etc.)
- May be ignited by heat, sparks, or flames.
- May burn rapidly with flare-burning effect.
- Containers may explode when heated.
- Runoff may create fire or explosion hazard

HEALTH

- Fire may produce irritating, corrosive, or toxic gases.
- Ingestion or contact (skin, eyes) with substance may cause severe injury or burns.
- Runoff from fire control or dilution water may cause pollution.

PUBLIC SAFETY

- **CALL Emergency Response Telephone Number on Shipping Paper first. If Shipping Paper is not available or there is no answer, refer to telephone numbers listed on page 613.**
- As an immediate precautionary measure, isolate spill or leak area in all directions for at least 50 meters (150 feet) for liquids and at least 25 meters (75 feet) for solids.
- Keep unauthorized personnel away.
- Stay upwind.
- Keep out of low areas.

PROTECTIVE CLOTHING

- Wear positive pressure self-contained breathing apparatus (SCBA).
- Wear chemical protective clothing that is specifically recommended by the manufacturer. It may provide little or no thermal protection.
- Structural firefighters' protective clothing will only provide limited protection.

EVACUATION

Spill

- Consider initial evacuation for at least 250 meters (800 feet).

Fire

- If tank, rail car, or tank truck is involved in a fire, ISOLATE for 800 meters (½ mile) in all directions; also, initiate evacuation including emergency responders for 800 meters (½ mile) in all directions.

EMERGENCY RESPONSE
FIRE

Small Fires

- Water spray or fog is preferred; if water is not available, use dry chemical, CO_2, or regular foam.

Large Fires

- Flood fire area with water from a distance.
- Use water spray or fog; DO NOT use straight streams.
- Move containers from fire area if you can do it without risk.
- DO NOT move cargo or vehicle if cargo has been exposed to heat.
- Fight fire from maximum distance or use unmanned hose holders or monitor nozzles.
- Cool containers with flooding quantities of water until well after fire is out.
- ALWAYS stay away from tanks engulfed in fire.
- For massive fire, use unmanned hose holders or monitor nozzles; if this is impossible, withdraw from area and let fire burn.

SPILL OR LEAK

- Eliminate all ignition sources (no smoking, flares, sparks, or flames in immediate area).
- Keep combustibles (wood, paper, oil, etc.) away from spilled material.
- DO NOT touch damaged containers or spilled material unless wearing appropriate protective clothing.
- Keep substance wet using water spray.
- Stop leak if you can do it without risk.

Small Spills

- Take up with inert, damp, non-combustible material using clean non-sparking tools and place into loosely covered plastic containers for later disposal.

Large Spills

- Wet down with water and dike for later disposal.
- Prevent entry into waterways, sewers, basements, or confined areas.
- **DO NOT clean-up or dispose of, except under supervision of a specialist.**

Hazmat

- Move victim to fresh air.
- Call 911 or emergency medical service.
- Give artificial respiration if victim is not breathing.
- Administer oxygen if breathing is difficult.
- Remove and isolate contaminated clothing and shoes.
- Contaminated clothing may be a fire risk when dry.
- Remove material from skin immediately.
- In case of contact with substance, immediately flush skin or eyes with running water for at least 20 minutes.
- Keep victim warm and quiet.
- Ensure that medical personnel are aware of the material(s) involved, and take precautions to protect themselves.

Guide 146: Organic Peroxides
(Heat, Contamination, and Friction Sensitive)

SUBSTANCES INCLUDED

3101 Organic peroxide type B, liquid
3102 Organic peroxide type B, solid
3103 Organic peroxide type C, liquid
3104 Organic peroxide type C, solid

POTENTIAL HAZARDS
FIRE OR EXPLOSION

- May explode from heat, shock, friction, or contamination.
- May ignite combustibles (wood, paper, oil, clothing, etc.)
- May be ignited by heat, sparks, or flames.
- May burn rapidly with flare-burning effect.
- Containers may explode when heated.
- Runoff may create fire or explosion hazard

HEALTH

- Fire may produce irritating, corrosive, or toxic gases.
- Ingestion or contact (skin, eyes) with substance may cause severe injury or burns.
- Runoff from fire control or dilution water may cause pollution.

PUBLIC SAFETY

- **CALL Emergency Response Telephone Number on Shipping Paper first. If Shipping Paper is not available or there is no answer, refer to telephone numbers listed on page 613.**
- As an immediate precautionary measure, isolate spill or leak area in all directions for at least 50 meters (150 feet) for liquids and at least 25 meters (75 feet) for solids.
- Keep unauthorized personnel away.
- Stay upwind.
- Keep out of low areas.

PROTECTIVE CLOTHING

- Wear positive pressure self-contained breathing apparatus (SCBA).
- Wear chemical protective clothing that is specifically recommended by the manufacturer. It may provide little or no thermal protection.
- Structural firefighters' protective clothing will only provide limited protection.

EVACUATION

Spill

- Consider initial evacuation for at least 250 meters (800 feet).

Hazmat

Fire

- If tank, rail car, or tank truck is involved in a fire, ISOLATE for 800 meters (½ mile) in all directions; also, initiate evacuation including emergency responders for 800 meters (½ mile) in all directions.

EMERGENCY RESPONSE
FIRE

Small Fires

- Water spray or fog is preferred; if water is not available, use dry chemical, CO_2, or regular foam.

Large Fires

- Flood fire area with water from a distance.
- Use water spray or fog; DO NOT use straight streams.
- Move containers from fire area if you can do it without risk.
- DO NOT move cargo or vehicle if cargo has been exposed to heat.
- Fight fire from maximum distance or use unmanned hose holders or monitor nozzles.
- Cool containers with flooding quantities of water until well after fire is out.
- ALWAYS stay away from tanks engulfed in fire.
- For massive fire, use unmanned hose holders or monitor nozzles; if this is impossible, withdraw from area and let fire burn.

SPILL OR LEAK

- Eliminate all ignition sources (no smoking, flares, sparks, or flames in immediate area).
- Keep combustibles (wood, paper, oil, etc.) away from spilled material.
- DO NOT touch damaged containers or spilled material unless wearing appropriate protective clothing.
- Keep substance wet using water spray.
- Stop leak if you can do it without risk.

Small Spills

- Take up with inert, damp, non-combustible material using clean non-sparking tools and place into loosely covered plastic containers for later disposal.

Large Spills

- Wet down with water and dike for later disposal.
- Prevent entry into waterways, sewers, basements, or confined areas.
- **DO NOT clean-up or dispose of, except under supervision of a specialist.**

FIRST AID

- Move victim to fresh air.
- Call 911 or emergency medical service.
- Give artificial respiration if victim is not breathing.
- Administer oxygen if breathing is difficult.
- Remove and isolate contaminated clothing and shoes.
- Contaminated clothing may be a fire risk when dry.
- Remove material from skin immediately.
- In case of contact with substance, immediately flush skin or eyes with running water for at least 20 minutes.
- Keep victim warm and quiet.
- Ensure that medical personnel are aware of the material(s) involved, and take precautions to protect themselves.

Hazmat

Guide 148: Organic Peroxides (Heat and Contamination Sensitive/ Temperature Controlled)

SUBSTANCES INCLUDED

3111 Organic peroxide type B, liquid, temperature controlled
3112 Organic peroxide type B, solid, temperature controlled
3113 Organic peroxide type C, liquid, temperature controlled
3114 Organic peroxide type C, solid, temperature controlled
3115 Organic peroxide type D, liquid, temperature controlled
3116 Organic peroxide type D, solid, temperature controlled
3117 Organic peroxide type E, liquid, temperature controlled
3118 Organic peroxide type E, solid, temperature controlled
3119 Organic peroxide type F, liquid, temperature controlled
3120 Organic peroxide type F, solid, temperature controlled

POTENTIAL HAZARDS

FIRE OR EXPLOSION

- May explode from heat, contamination, or loss of temperature control.
- These materials are particularly sensitive to temperature issues. Above a given "Control Temperature," they decompose violently and catch fire.
- May ignite combustibles (wood, paper, oil, clothing, etc.)
- May ignite spontaneously if exposed to air.
- May be ignited by heat, sparks, or flames.
- May burn rapidly with flare-burning effect.
- Containers may explode when heated.
- Runoff may create fire or explosion hazard

HEALTH

- Fire may produce irritating, corrosive, or toxic gases.
- Ingestion or contact (skin, eyes) with substance may cause severe injury or burns.
- Runoff from fire control or dilution water may cause pollution.

PUBLIC SAFETY

- **CALL Emergency Response Telephone Number on Shipping Paper first. If Shipping Paper is not available or there is no answer, refer to telephone numbers listed on page 613.**
- As an immediate precautionary measure, isolate spill or leak area in all directions for at least 50 meters (150 feet) for liquids and at least 25 meters (75 feet) for solids.
- Keep unauthorized personnel away.
- Stay upwind.
- Keep out of low areas.
- **DO NOT allow the substance to warm up. Obtain liquid nitrogen, dry ice, or ice for cooling. If none can be obtained, evacuate the area immediately.**

PROTECTIVE CLOTHING

- Wear positive pressure self-contained breathing apparatus (SCBA).
- Wear chemical protective clothing that is specifically recommended by the manufacturer. It may provide little or no thermal protection.
- Structural firefighters' protective clothing will only provide limited protection.

EVACUATION

Spill

- Consider initial evacuation for at least 250 meters (800 feet).

Fire

- If tank, rail car, or tank truck is involved in a fire, ISOLATE for 800 meters (½ mile) in all directions; also, initiate evacuation including emergency responders for 800 meters (½ mile) in all directions.

EMERGENCY RESPONSE

FIRE

- **The temperature of the substance must be maintained at or below the "Control Temperature" at all times.**

Small Fires

- Water spray or fog is preferred; if water is not available, use dry chemical, CO_2, or regular foam.

Large Fires

- Flood fire area with water from a distance.
- Use water spray or fog; DO NOT use straight streams.
- Move containers from fire area if you can do it without risk.
- DO NOT move cargo or vehicle if cargo has been exposed to heat.
- Fight fire from maximum distance or use unmanned hose holders or monitor nozzles.
- Cool containers with flooding quantities of water until well after fire is out.
- **BEWARE of possible container explosion.**
- ALWAYS stay away from tanks engulfed in fire.
- For massive fire, use unmanned hose holders or monitor nozzles; if this is impossible, withdraw from area and let fire burn.

SPILL OR LEAK

- Eliminate all ignition sources (no smoking, flares, sparks, or flames in immediate area).
- Keep combustibles (wood, paper, oil, etc.) away from spilled material.
- DO NOT touch or walk through spilled material.
- Stop leak if you can do it without risk.

Small Spills
- Take up with inert, damp, non-combustible material using clean non-sparking tools and place into loosely covered plastic containers for later disposal.

Large Spills
- Wet down with water and dike for later disposal.
- Prevent entry into waterways, sewers, basements, or confined areas.
- **DO NOT clean-up or dispose of, except under supervision of a specialist.**

FIRST AID
- Move victim to fresh air.
- Call 911 or emergency medical service.
- Give artificial respiration if victim is not breathing.
- Administer oxygen if breathing is difficult.
- Remove and isolate contaminated clothing and shoes.
- Contaminated clothing may be a fire risk when dry.
- Remove material from skin immediately.
- In case of contact with substance, immediately flush skin or eyes with running water for at least 20 minutes.
- Keep victim warm and quiet.
- Ensure that medical personnel are aware of the material(s) involved, and take precautions to protect themselves.

Guide 149: Substances (Self-Reactive)

SUBSTANCES INCLUDED

2956	5-tert-Butyl-2,4,6-trinitro-m-xylene; Musk xylene
3221	Self-reactive liquid type B
3222	Self-reactive solid type B
3223	Self-reactive liquid type C
3224	Self-reactive solid type C
3225	Self-reactive liquid type D
3226	Self-reactive solid type D
3227	Self-reactive liquid type E
3228	Self-reactive solid type E
3229	Self-reactive liquid type F
3230	Self-reactive solid type F
3242	Azodicarbonamide

POTENTIAL HAZARDS

FIRE OR EXPLOSION

- **Self-decomposition or self-ignition may be triggered by heat, chemical reaction, friction, or impact.**
- May be ignited by heat, sparks, or flames.
- Some may decompose explosively when heated or involved in a fire.
- May burn violently. Decomposition may be self-accelerating and produce large amounts of gases.
- Vapors or dust may form explosive mixtures with air.

HEALTH

- Inhalation or contact with vapors, substance, or decomposition products may cause severe injury or death.
- May produce irritating, toxic, and/or corrosive gases.
- Runoff from fire control may cause pollution.

PUBLIC SAFETY

- **CALL Emergency Response Telephone Number on Shipping Paper first. If Shipping Paper is not available or there is no answer, refer to telephone numbers listed on page 613.**
- As an immediate precautionary measure, isolate spill or leak area in all directions for at least 50 meters (150 feet) for liquids and at least 25 meters (75 feet) for solids.
- Keep unauthorized personnel away.
- Stay upwind.
- Keep out of low areas.

PROTECTIVE CLOTHING

- Wear positive pressure self-contained breathing apparatus (SCBA).
- Wear chemical protective clothing that is specifically recommended by the manufacturer. It may provide little or no thermal protection.

Hazmat

• Structural firefighters' protective clothing will only provide limited protection.

EVACUATION

Spill
• Consider initial evacuation for at least 250 meters (800 feet).

Fire
• If tank, rail car, or tank truck is involved in a fire, ISOLATE for 800 meters (½ mile) in all directions; also, initiate evacuation including emergency responders for 800 meters (½ mile) in all directions.

EMERGENCY RESPONSE
FIRE

Small Fires
• Dry chemical, CO_2, water spray, or regular foam.

Large Fires
• Flood fire area with water from a distance.
• Move containers from fire area if you can do it without risk.

Fire Involving Tanks or Car/Trailer Loads
• **BEWARE of possible container explosion.**
• Fight fire from maximum distance or use unmanned hose holders or monitor nozzles.
• Cool containers with flooding quantities of water until well after fire is out.
• Withdraw immediately in case of rising sound from venting safety devices or discoloration of tank.
• ALWAYS stay away from tanks engulfed in fire.

SPILL OR LEAK

• Eliminate all ignition sources (no smoking, flares, sparks, or flames in immediate area).
• Keep combustibles (wood, paper, oil, etc.) away from spilled material.
• DO NOT touch or walk through spilled material.
• Stop leak if you can do it without risk.

Small Spills
• Take up with inert, damp, non-combustible material using clean non-sparking tools and place into loosely covered plastic containers for later disposal.
• Prevent entry into waterways, sewers, basements, or confined areas.

FIRST AID

• Move victim to fresh air.
• Call 911 or emergency medical service.
• Give artificial respiration if victim is not breathing.
• Administer oxygen if breathing is difficult.

- Remove and isolate contaminated clothing and shoes.
- In case of contact with substance, immediately flush skin or eyes with running water for at least 20 minutes.
- Keep victim warm and quiet.
- Ensure that medical personnel are aware of the material(s) involved, and take precautions to protect themselves.

Hazmat

Guide 150: Substances
(Self-Reactive/ Temperature Controlled)

SUBSTANCES INCLUDED

3231	Self-reactive liquid type B, temperature controlled
3232	Self-reactive solid type B, temperature controlled
3233	Self-reactive liquid type C, temperature controlled
3234	Self-reactive solid type C, temperature controlled
3235	Self-reactive liquid type D, temperature controlled
3236	Self-reactive solid type D, temperature controlled
3237	Self-reactive liquid type E, temperature controlled
3238	Self-reactive solid type E, temperature controlled
3239	Self-reactive liquid type F, temperature controlled
3240	Self-reactive solid type F, temperature controlled

POTENTIAL HAZARDS

FIRE OR EXPLOSION

- **Self-decomposition or self-ignition may be triggered by heat, chemical reaction, friction, or impact.**
- Self-accelerating decomposition may occur if the specific control temperature is not maintained.
- These materials are particularly sensitive to temperature rises. Above a given "Control Temperature," they decompose violently and catch fire.
- May be ignited by heat, sparks, or flames.
- Some may decompose explosively when heated or involved in a fire.
- May burn violently. Decomposition may be self-accelerating and produce large amounts of gases.
- Vapors or dust may form explosive mixtures with air.

HEALTH

- Inhalation or contact with vapors, substance, or decomposition products may cause severe injury or death.
- May produce irritating, toxic, and/or corrosive gases.
- Runoff from fire control may cause pollution.

PUBLIC SAFETY

- **CALL Emergency Response Telephone Number on Shipping Paper first. If Shipping Paper is not available or there is no answer, refer to telephone numbers listed on page 613.**
- As an immediate precautionary measure, isolate spill or leak area in all directions for at least 50 meters (150 feet) for liquids and at least 25 meters (75 feet) for solids.
- Keep unauthorized personnel away.
- Stay upwind.
- Keep out of low areas.

- **DO NOT allow the substance to warm up. Obtain liquid nitrogen, dry ice, or ice for cooling. If none can be obtained, evacuate the area immediately.**

PROTECTIVE CLOTHING

- Wear positive pressure self-contained breathing apparatus (SCBA).
- Wear chemical protective clothing that is specifically recommended by the manufacturer. It may provide little or no thermal protection.
- Structural firefighters' protective clothing will only provide limited protection.

EVACUATION

Spill

- Consider initial evacuation for at least 250 meters (800 feet).

Fire

- If tank, rail car, or tank truck is involved in a fire, ISOLATE for 800 meters (½ mile) in all directions; also, initiate evacuation including emergency responders for 800 meters (½ mile) in all directions.

EMERGENCY RESPONSE

FIRE

- **The temperature of the substance must be maintained at or below the "Control Temperature" at all times.**

Small Fires

- Dry chemical, CO_2, water spray, or regular foam.

Large Fires

- Flood fire area with water from a distance.
- Move containers from fire area if you can do it without risk.

Fire Involving Tanks or Car/Trailer Loads

- **BEWARE of possible container explosion.**
- Fight fire from maximum distance or use unmanned hose holders or monitor nozzles.
- Cool containers with flooding quantities of water until well after fire is out.
- Withdraw immediately in case of rising sound from venting safety devices or discoloration of tank.
- ALWAYS stay away from tanks engulfed in fire.

SPILL OR LEAK

- Eliminate all ignition sources (no smoking, flares, sparks, or flames in immediate area).
- DO NOT touch or walk through spilled material.
- Stop leak if you can do it without risk.

Small Spills

- Take up with inert, damp, non-combustible material using clean non-sparking tools and place into loosely covered plastic containers for later disposal.
- Prevent entry into waterways, sewers, basements, or confined areas.
- **DO NOT clean-up or dispose of, except under supervision of a specialist.**

FIRST AID

- Move victim to fresh air.
- Call 911 or emergency medical service.
- Give artificial respiration if victim is not breathing.
- Administer oxygen if breathing is difficult.
- Remove and isolate contaminated clothing and shoes.
- In case of contact with substance, immediately flush skin or eyes with running water for at least 20 minutes.
- Keep victim warm and quiet.
- Ensure that medical personnel are aware of the material(s) involved, and take precautions to protect themselves.

1544	Alkaloid salts, solid, n.o.s. (toxic)
1544	Alkaloids, solid, n.o.s. (toxic)
1546	Ammonium arsenate
1550	Antimony lactate
1551	Antimony potassium tartrate
1555	Arsenic bromide
1559	Arsenic pentoxide
1561	Arsenic trioxide
1572	Cacodylic acid
1573	Calcium arsenate
1574	Calcium arsenate and Calcium arsenite mixture, solid
1574	Calcium arsenite, solid
1585	Copper acetoarsenite
1586	Copper arsenite
1587	Copper cyanide
1601	Disinfectant, solid, toxic, n.o.s.
1602	Dye intermediate, liquid, toxic, n.o.s.
1602	Dye, liquid, toxic, n.o.s.
1606	Ferric arsenate
1607	Ferric arsenite
1608	Ferrous arsenate
1611	Hexaethyl tetraphosphate (& , liquid; & , solid)
1616	Lead acetate
1617	Lead arsenates
1618	Lead arsenites
1620	Lead cyanide
1621	London purple
1622	Magnesium arsenate
1623	Mercuric arsenate
1629	Mercury acetate
1630	Mercury ammonium chloride
1637	Mercury gluconate
1638	Mercury iodide
1639	Mercury nucleate
1640	Mercury oleate
1641	Mercury oxide
1642	Mercuric oxycyanide; Mercury oxycyanide, desensitized
1643	Mercury potassium iodide
1644	Mercury salicylate
1645	Mercuric sulfate; Mercury sulfate
1646	Mercury thiocyanate
1647	Ethylene dibromide and Methyl bromide mixture, liquid
1653	Nickel cyanide
1654	Nicotine
1655	Nicotine compound, solid, n.o.s.
1655	Nicotine preparation, solid, n.o.s.
1656	Nicotine hydrochloride (& , liquid; & , solid; & , solution)
1657	Nicotine salicylate
1658	Nicotine sulfate, solid; Nicotine sulfate, solution
1659	Nicotine tartrate
1669	Pentachloroethane
1672	Phenylcarbylamine chloride
1674	Phenylmercuric acetate
1677	Potassium arsenate
1683	Silver arsenite
1684	Silver cyanide

1685	Sodium arsenate
1691	Strontium arsenite
1692	Strychnine; Strychnine salts
1699	DA; Diphenylchloroarsine (& , liquid; & , solid)
1702	1,1,2,2-Tetrachloroethane; Tetrachloroethane
1707	Thallium compound, n.o.s.; Thallium sulfate, solid
1709	2,4-Toluenediamine; 2,4-Toluylenediamine (& , solid)
1712	Zinc arsenate
1712	Zinc arsenate and Zinc arsenite mixture
1712	Zinc arsenite
1713	Zinc cyanide
1846	Carbon tetrachloride
1851	Medicine, liquid, toxic, n.o.s.
1888	Chloroform
1892	ED; Ethyldichloroarsine
1894	Phenylmercuric hydroxide
1895	Phenylmercuric nitrate
2016	Ammunition, toxic, non-explosive
2024	Mercury compound, liquid, n.o.s.
2025	Mercury compound, solid, n.o.s.
2026	Phenylmercuric compound, n.o.s.
2027	Sodium arsenite, solid
2279	Hexachlorobutadiene
2291	Lead compound, soluble, n.o.s.
2516	Carbon tetrabromide
2552	Hexafluoroacetone hydrate (& , liquid)
2574	Tricresyl phosphate
2588	Pesticide, solid, toxic, n.o.s.
2628	Potassium fluoroacetate
2629	Sodium fluoroacetate
2630	Selenates; Selenites
2630	Sodium selenite
2644	Methyl iodide
2646	Hexachlorocyclopentadiene
2655	Potassium fluorosilicate; Potassium silicofluoride
2659	Sodium chloroacetate
2673	2-Amino-4-chlorophenol
2757	Carbamate pesticide, solid, toxic
2759	Arsenical pesticide, solid, toxic
2761	Aldrin, solid
2761	Dieldrin
2761	Organochlorine pesticide, solid, toxic
2763	Triazine pesticide, solid, toxic
2767	Phenyl urea pesticide, solid, toxic
2769	Benzoic derivative pesticide, solid, toxic
2771	Dithiocarbamate pesticide, solid, toxic
2771	Thiocarbamate pesticide, solid, toxic
2773	Phthalimide derivative pesticide, solid, toxic
2775	Copper based pesticide, solid, toxic
2777	Mercury based pesticide, solid, toxic
2781	Bipyridilium pesticide, solid, toxic
2853	Magnesium fluorosilicate; Magnesium silicofluoride
2854	Ammonium fluorosilicate; Ammonium silicofluoride
2855	Zinc fluorosilicate; Zinc silicofluoride
2856	Fluorosilicates, n.o.s.
2856	Silicofluorides, n.o.s.
2861	Ammonium polyvanadate
2862	Vanadium pentoxide
2864	Potassium metavanadate

2875	Hexachlorophene
2902	Pesticide, liquid, toxic, n.o.s.
2931	Vanadyl sulfate
2992	Carbamate pesticide, liquid, toxic
2994	Arsenical pesticide, liquid, toxic
2996	Organochlorine pesticide, liquid, toxic
2998	Triazine pesticide, liquid, toxic
3002	Phenyl urea pesticide, liquid, toxic
3004	Benzoic derivative pesticide, liquid, toxic
3006	Dithiocarbamate pesticide, liquid, toxic
3006	Thiocarbamate pesticide, liquid, toxic
3008	Phthalimide derivative pesticide, liquid, toxic
3010	Copper based pesticide, liquid, toxic
3012	Mercury based pesticide, liquid, toxic
3016	Bipyridilium pesticide, liquid, toxic
3026	Coumarin derivative pesticide, liquid, toxic
3027	Coumarin derivative pesticide, solid, toxic
3140	Alkaloid salts, liquid, n.o.s. (toxic)
3140	Alkaloids, liquid, n.o.s. (toxic)
3142	Disinfectant, liquid, toxic, n.o.s.
3143	Dye intermediate, solid, toxic, n.o.s.
3143	Dye, solid, toxic, n.o.s.
3144	Nicotine compound, liquid, n.o.s.
3144	Nicotine preparation, liquid, n.o.s.
3243	Solids containing toxic liquid, n.o.s.
3249	Medicine, solid, toxic, n.o.s.
3276	Nitriles, toxic, liquid, n.o.s.
3276	Nitriles, toxic, n.o.s.
3278	Organophosphorus compound, toxic, liquid, n.o.s.
3278	Organophosphorus compound, toxic, n.o.s.
3280	Organoarsenic compound, liquid, n.o.s.
3280	Organoarsenic compound, n.o.s.
3281	Metal carbonyls, liquid, n.o.s.
3281	Metal carbonyls, n.o.s.
3282	Organometallic compound, toxic, liquid, n.o.s.
3282	Organometallic compound, toxic, n.o.s.
3283	Selenium compound, n.o.s.
3283	Selenium compound, solid, n.o.s.
3284	Tellurium compound, n.o.s.
3285	Vanadium compound, n.o.s.
3287	Toxic liquid, inorganic, n.o.s. (& Inhalation Hazard Zone A and B)
3288	Toxic solid, inorganic, n.o.s.
3315	Chemical sample, toxic (& , liquid; & , solid)
3349	Pyrethroid pesticide, solid, toxic
3352	Pyrethroid pesticide, liquid, toxic
3381	Toxic by inhalation liquid, n.o.s. (Inhalation Hazard Zone A)
3382	Toxic by inhalation liquid, n.o.s. (Inhalation Hazard Zone B)
3418	2,4-Toluylenediamine, solution
3436	Hexafluoroacetone hydrate, solid
3439	Nitriles, toxic, solid, n.o.s.
3440	Selenium compound, liquid, n.o.s.
3444	Nicotine hydrochloride, solid
3445	Nicotine sulfate, solid
3450	Diphenylchloroarsine, solid
3464	Organophosphorus compound, toxic, solid, n.o.s.
3465	Organoarsenic compound, solid, n.o.s.
3466	Metal carbonyls, solid, n.o.s.
3467	Organometallic compound, toxic, solid, n.o.s.
9264	3,5-Dichloro-2,4,6-trifluoropyridine

POTENTIAL HAZARDS

FIRE OR EXPLOSION

- Non-combustible, substance itself does not burn, but may decompose upon heating to produce corrosive or toxic fumes.
- Containers may explode when heated.
- Runoff may pollute waterways.

HEALTH

- **Highly Toxic,** may be fatal if inhaled, swallowed, or absorbed through skin.
- Avoid any skin contact.
- Effects of contact or inhalation may be delayed.
- Fire may produce irritating, corrosive, or toxic gases.
- Runoff from fire control or dilution water may be corrosive or toxic and cause pollution.

PUBLIC SAFETY

- **CALL Emergency Response Telephone Number on Shipping Paper first. If Shipping Paper is not available or there is no answer, refer to telephone numbers listed on page 613.**
- As an immediate precautionary measure, isolate spill or leak area in all directions for at least 50 meters (150 feet) for liquids and at least 25 meters (75 feet) for solids.
- Keep unauthorized personnel away.
- Stay upwind.
- Keep out of low areas.

PROTECTIVE CLOTHING

- Wear positive pressure self-contained breathing apparatus (SCBA).
- Wear chemical protective clothing that is specifically recommended by the manufacturer. It may provide little or no thermal protection.
- Structural firefighters' protective clothing provides limited protection in fire situations ONLY; it is not effective in spill situations where direct contact with the substance is possible..

EVACUATION

Spill

- See the Table of Initial Isolation and Protective Action Distances for highlighted substances (page 908). For non-highlighted substances, increase, in the downwind direction, as necessary, the isolation distance shown above under "PUBLIC SAFETY."

Fire

- If tank, rail car, or tank truck is involved in a fire, ISOLATE for 800 meters (½ mile) in all directions; also, initiate evacuation including emergency responders for 800 meters (½ mile) in all directions.

Hazmat

Small Fires
- Dry chemical, CO_2, or water spray.

Large Fires
- Water spray, fog, or regular foam.
- Move containers from fire area if you can do it without risk.
- Dike fire control water for later disposal; DO NOT scatter the material.
- Use water spray or fog; DO NOT use straight streams.

Fire Involving Tanks or Car/Trailer Loads
- Fight fire from maximum distance or use unmanned hose holders or monitor nozzles.
- DO NOT get water inside containers.
- Cool containers with flooding quantities of water until well after fire is out.
- Withdraw immediately in case of rising sound from venting safety devices or discoloration of tank.
- ALWAYS stay away from tanks engulfed in fire.
- For massive fire, use unmanned hose holders or monitor nozzles; if this is impossible, withdraw from area and let fire burn.

SPILL OR LEAK
- DO NOT touch damaged containers or spilled material unless wearing appropriate protective clothing.
- Stop leak if you can do it without risk.
- Prevent entry into waterways, sewers, basements, or confined areas.
- Cover with plastic sheet to prevent spreading.
- Absorb or cover with DRY earth, sand, or other non-combustible material and transfer to containers.
- DO NOT get water inside containers.

FIRST AID
- Move victim to fresh air.
- Call 911 or emergency medical service.
- Give artificial respiration if victim is not breathing.
- **DO NOT use mouth-to-mouth method if victim ingested or inhaled the substance; give artificial respiration with the aid of a pocket mask equipped with a one-way valve or other proper respiratory medical device.**
- Administer oxygen if breathing is difficult.
- Remove and isolate contaminated clothing and shoes.
- In case of contact with substance, immediately flush skin or eyes with running water for at least 20 minutes.

Hazmat

- For minor skin contact, avoid spreading material on unaffected skin.
- Keep victim warm and quiet.
- Effects of exposure (inhalation, ingestion, or skin contact) to substance may be delayed.
- Ensure that medical personnel are aware of the material(s) involved, and take precautions to protect themselves.

SUBSTANCES INCLUDED

1556	Arsenic compound, liquid, n.o.s.
1556	Arsenic compound, liquid, n.o.s., inorganic
1556	MD; Methyldichloroarsine; PD
1557	Arsenic compound, solid, n.o.s.
1557	Arsenic compound, solid, n.o.s., inorganic
1557	Arsenic sulfide; Arsenic trisulfide; Arsenic trisulphide
1558	Arsenic
1562	Arsenical dust
1570	Brucine
1578	Chloronitrobenzenes (& , liquid; & , solid)
1591	o-Dichlorobenzene
1594	Diethyl sulfate
1597	Dinitrobenzenes (& , liquid; & , solid)
1600	Dinitrotoluenes, molten
1614	Hydrogen cyanide, anhydrous, stabilized (absorbed)
1614	Hydrogen cyanide, stabilized (absorbed)
1662	Nitrobenzene
1664	Nitrotoluenes (& , liquid; & , solid)
1665	Nitroxylenes (& , liquid; & , solid)
1688	Sodium cacodylate
1701	Xylyl bromide; Xylyl bromide, liquid
1916	2,2'-Dichlorodiethyl ether; Dichloroethyl ether
2018	Chloroanilines, solid
2019	Chloroanilines, liquid
2038	Dinitrotoluenes (& , liquid; & , solid)
2224	Benzonitrile
2233	Chloroanisidines
2306	Nitrobenzotrifluorides; Nitrobenzotrifluorides, liquid
2307	3-Nitro-4-chlorobenzotrifluoride
2322	Trichlorobutene
2369	Ethylene glycol monobutyl ether
2433	Chloronitrotoluenes (& , liquid; & , solid)
2470	Phenylacetonitrile, liquid
2501	1-Aziridinyl phosphine oxide (Tris)
2501	Tri-(1-aziridinyl)phosphine oxide, solution
2501	Tris-(1-aziridinyl)phosphine oxide, solution
2512	Aminophenols
2658	Selenium powder
2667	Butyltoluenes
2669	Chlorocresols (& , liquid; & , solid; & , solution)
2690	N,n-Butylimidazole
2729	Hexachlorobenzene
2730	Nitroanisole (& , liquid; & , solid)
2732	Nitrobromobenzene (& , liquid; & , solid)
2765	Phenoxy pesticide, solid, toxic
2783	Methyl parathion, solid
2783	Organophosphorus pesticide, solid, toxic
2783	Parathion
2783	Tetraethyl pyrophosphate, solid
2785	4-Thiapentanal; Thia-4-pentanal
2938	Methyl benzoate
3000	Phenoxy pesticide, liquid, toxic
3018	Methyl parathion, liquid
3018	Organophosphorus pesticide, liquid, toxic
3018	Tetraethyl pyrophosphate, liquid

Hazmat

3293	Hydrazine, aqueous solutions, with ≤ 37% Hydrazine
3302	2-Dimethylaminoethyl acrylate
3409	Chloronitrobenzenes, liquid
3417	Xylyl bromide, solid
3431	Nitrobenzotrifluorides, solid
3437	Chlorocresols, solid
3443	Dinitrobenzenes, solid
3446	Nitrotoluenes, solid
3447	Nitroxylenes, solid
3454	Dinitrotoluenes, solid
3457	Chloronitrotoluenes, solid
3458	Nitroanisole, solid
3459	Nitrobromobenzene, solid

POTENTIAL HAZARDS

FIRE OR EXPLOSION

- Combustible material: may burn but does not ignite readily.
- Containers may explode when heated.
- Runoff may pollute waterways.
- Substance may be transported in a molten form.

HEALTH

- **Highly Toxic,** may be fatal if inhaled, swallowed, or absorbed through skin.
- Contact with molten substance may cause severe burns to skin and eyes.
- Avoid any skin contact.
- Effects of contact or inhalation may be delayed.
- Fire may produce irritating, corrosive, or toxic gases.
- Runoff from fire control or dilution water may be corrosive or toxic and cause pollution.

PUBLIC SAFETY

- **CALL Emergency Response Telephone Number on Shipping Paper first. If Shipping Paper is not available or there is no answer, refer to telephone numbers listed on page 613.**
- As an immediate precautionary measure, isolate spill or leak area in all directions for at least 50 meters (150 feet) for liquids and at least 25 meters (75 feet) for solids.
- Keep unauthorized personnel away.
- Stay upwind.
- Keep out of low areas.

PROTECTIVE CLOTHING

- Wear positive pressure self-contained breathing apparatus (SCBA).
- Wear chemical protective clothing that is specifically recommended by the manufacturer. It may provide little or no thermal protection.

- Structural firefighters' protective clothing provides limited protection in fire situations ONLY; it is not effective in spill situations where direct contact with the substance is possible..

EVACUATION

Spill
- See the Table of Initial Isolation and Protective Action Distances for highlighted substances (page 908). For non-highlighted substances, increase, in the downwind direction, as necessary, the isolation distance shown above under "PUBLIC SAFETY."

Fire
- If tank, rail car, or tank truck is involved in a fire, ISOLATE for 800 meters (½ mile) in all directions; also, initiate evacuation including emergency responders for 800 meters (½ mile) in all directions.

EMERGENCY RESPONSE
FIRE

Small Fires
- Dry chemical, CO_2, or water spray.

Large Fires
- Water spray, fog, or regular foam.
- Move containers from fire area if you can do it without risk.
- Dike fire control water for later disposal; DO NOT scatter the material.
- Use water spray or fog; DO NOT use straight streams.

Fire Involving Tanks or Car/Trailer Loads
- Fight fire from maximum distance or use unmanned hose holders or monitor nozzles.
- DO NOT get water inside containers.
- Cool containers with flooding quantities of water until well after fire is out.
- Withdraw immediately in case of rising sound from venting safety devices or discoloration of tank.
- ALWAYS stay away from tanks engulfed in fire.
- For massive fire, use unmanned hose holders or monitor nozzles; if this is impossible, withdraw from area and let fire burn.

SPILL OR LEAK
- Eliminate all ignition sources (no smoking, flares, sparks, or flames in immediate area).
- DO NOT touch damaged containers or spilled material unless wearing appropriate protective clothing.
- Stop leak if you can do it without risk.
- Prevent entry into waterways, sewers, basements, or confined areas.
- Cover with plastic sheet to prevent spreading.

- Absorb or cover with DRY earth, sand, or other non-combustible material and transfer to containers.
- DO NOT get water inside containers.

FIRST AID

- Move victim to fresh air.
- Call 911 or emergency medical service.
- Give artificial respiration if victim is not breathing.
- **DO NOT use mouth-to-mouth method if victim ingested or inhaled the substance; give artificial respiration with the aid of a pocket mask equipped with a one-way valve or other proper respiratory medical device.**
- Administer oxygen if breathing is difficult.
- Remove and isolate contaminated clothing and shoes.
- In case of contact with substance, immediately flush skin or eyes with running water for at least 20 minutes.
- For minor skin contact, avoid spreading material on unaffected skin.
- Keep victim warm and quiet.
- Effects of exposure (inhalation, ingestion, or skin contact) to substance may be delayed.
- Ensure that medical personnel are aware of the material(s) involved, and take precautions to protect themselves.

Guide 153: Substances - Toxic and/or Corrosive (Combustible)

SUBSTANCES INCLUDED

Toxins
1547 Aniline
1548 Aniline hydrochloride
1577 Chlorodinitrobenzenes (& , liquid; & , solid)
1577 Dinitrochlorobenzenes
1579 4-Chloro-o-toluidine hydrochloride (& , solid)
1590 Dichloroanilines (& , liquid; & , solid)
1596 Dinitroanilines
1598 Dinitro-o-cresol
1599 Dinitrophenol, solution
1650 beta-Naphthylamine; beta-Naphthylamine, solid
1650 Naphthylamine (beta); Naphthylamine (beta), solid
1651 Naphthylthiourea
1652 Naphthylurea
1661 Nitroanilines
1663 Nitrophenols
1671 Phenol, solid
1673 Phenylenediamines
1687 Sodium azide
1697 CN; Chloroacetophenone (& , liquid; & , solid)
1704 Tetraethyl dithiopyrophosphate, mixture, dry or liquid
1708 Toluidines; Toluidines, liquid; Toluidines, solid
1711 Xylidines; Xylidines, liquid; Xylidines, solid
1718 Acid butyl phosphate; Butyl acid phosphate
1750 Chloroacetic acid, liquid; Chloroacetic acid, solution
1751 Chloroacetic acid, solid
1764 Dichloroacetic acid
1770 Diphenylmethyl bromide
1779 Formic acid
1783 Hexamethylenediamine, solution
1793 Isopropyl acid phosphate
1803 Phenolsulfonic acid, liquid
1835 Tetramethylammonium hydroxide (& , solution)
1839 Trichloroacetic acid
1847 Potassium sulfide, hydrated, with $\geq$ 30% water of crystallization
1847 Potassium sulfide, hydrated, with $\geq$ 30% water of hydration
1849 Sodium sulfide, hydrated, with $\geq$ 30% water
1885 Benzidine
1902 Diisooctyl acid phosphate
1903 Disinfectant, liquid, corrosive, n.o.s.
1903 Disinfectants, corrosive, liquid, n.o.s.
1906 Acid, sludge; Sludge acid
1940 Thioglycolic acid
2020 Chlorophenols, solid
2021 Chlorophenols, liquid
2022 Cresylic acid
2028 Bombs, smoke, non-explosive, with corrosive liquid, without initiating device
2030 Hydrazine hydrate
2030 Hydrazine, aqueous solution, with $\geq$ 37% and $\leq$ 64% Hydrazine
2030 Hydrazine, aqueous solution, with > 37% Hydrazine
2074 Acrylamide; Acrylamide, solid; Acrylamide, solution
2075 Chloral, anhydrous (, inhibited; & , stabilized)

2076	Cresols; Cresols, liquid; Cresols, solid
2077	alpha-Naphthylamine; Naphthylamine (alpha)
2205	Adiponitrile
2232	2-Chloroethanal; Chloroacetaldehyde
2235	Chlorobenzyl chlorides; Chlorobenzyl chlorides, liquid
2237	Chloronitroanilines
2239	Chlorotoluidines (& , liquid; & , solid)
2253	N,N-Dimethylaniline
2259	Triethylenetetramine
2261	Xylenols; Xylenols, solid
2269	3,3'-Iminodipropylamine
2272	N-Ethylaniline
2273	2-Ethylaniline
2274	N-Ethyl-N-benzylaniline
2280	Hexamethylenediamine, solid
2289	Isophoronediamine
2294	N-Methylaniline
2300	2-Methyl-5-ethylpyridine
2305	Nitrobenzenesulfonic acid
2311	Phenetidines
2312	Phenol, molten
2320	Tetraethylenepentamine
2321	Trichlorobenzenes, liquid
2326	Trimethylcyclohexylamine
2327	Trimethylhexamethylenediamines
2430	Alkyl phenols, solid, not otherwise specified (including C2-C12 homologues)
2431	Anisidines; Anisidines, liquid; Anisidines, solid
2432	N,N-Diethylaniline
2446	Nitrocresols; Nitrocresols, solid
2490	Dichloroisopropyl ether
2491	Ethanolamine; Ethanolamine, solution
2491	Monoethanolamine
2511	2-Chloropropionic acid (& , solid; & , solution)
2518	1,5,9-Cyclododecatriene
2522	**2-Dimethylaminoethyl methacrylate**
2522	**Dimethylaminoethyl methacrylate**
2531	**Methacrylic acid, inhibited; Methacrylic acid, stabilized**
2542	Tributylamine
2564	Trichloroacetic acid, solution
2565	Dicyclohexylamine
2572	Phenylhydrazine
2579	Piperazine
2583	Alkyl sulfonic acids, solid, with > 5% free Sulfuric acid
2583	Aryl sulfonic acids, solid, with > 5% free Sulfuric acid
2583	Toluene sulfonic acid, solid, with ≤ 5% free Sulfuric acid
2583	Toluene sulfonic acid, solid, with > 5% free Sulfuric acid
2584	Alkyl sulfonic acids, liquid, with > 5% free Sulfuric acid
2584	Aryl sulfonic acids, liquid, with > 5% free Sulfuric acid
2584	Dodecylbenzenesulfonic acid
2584	Toluene sulfonic acid, liquid, with > 5% free Sulfuric acid
2585	Alkyl sulfonic acids, solid, with ≤ 5% free Sulfuric acid
2585	Aryl sulfonic acids, solid, with ≤ 5% free Sulfuric acid
2586	Alkyl sulfonic acids, liquid, with ≤ 5% free Sulfuric acid
2586	Aryl sulfonic acids, liquid, with ≤ 5% free Sulfuric acid
2586	Toluene sulfonic acid, liquid, with ≤ 5% free Sulfuric acid
2587	Benzoquinone
2645	Phenacyl bromide
2647	Malononitrile

2649	1,3-Dichloroacetone
2650	1,1-Dichloro-1-nitroethane
2651	4,4'-Diaminodiphenylmethane
2657	Selenium disulfide
2660	Mononitrotoluidines; Nitrotoluidines (mono)
2661	Hexachloroacetone
2662	Hydroquinone; Hydroquinone, solid
2671	Aminopyridines
2689	Glycerol alpha-monochlorohydrin
2705	**1-Pentol**
2713	Acridine
2716	1,4-Butynediol
2735	Alkylamines, n.o.s.
2735	Amines, liquid, corrosive, n.o.s.
2735	Polyalkylamines, n.o.s.
2735	Polyamines, liquid, corrosive, n.o.s.
2738	N-Butylaniline
2750	1,3-Dichloropropanol-2
2753	N-Ethylbenzyltoluidines (& , liquid; & , solid)
2754	N-Ethyltoluidines
2779	Substituted nitrophenol pesticide, solid, toxic
2786	Organotin pesticide, solid, toxic
2788	Organotin compound, liquid, n.o.s.
2790	Acetic acid, solution, > 10% but ≤ 80% acid
2810	Buzz; BZ; CS; DC; GA; GB; GD; GF; H; HD; HL; HN-1; HN-2; HN-3; L (Lewisite): Mustard; Mustard Lewisite; Sarin; Soman; Tabon; Thickened GD; VX
2810	Compound, tree or weed killing, liquid (toxic)
2810	Toxic liquid, n.o.s. (& Inhalation Hazard Zone A and B)
2810	Toxic liquid, organic, n.o.s. (& Inhalation Hazard Zone A and B)
2815	N-Aminoethylpiperazine
2819	Amyl acid phosphate
2820	Butyric acid
2821	Phenol solution
2822	2-Chloropyridine
2823	Crotonic acid; Crotonic acid, liquid; Crotonic acid, solid
2829	Caproic acid
2829	Hexanoic acid
2839	Aldol
2849	3-Chloropropanol-1
2873	Dibutylaminoethanol
2874	Furfuryl alcohol
2876	Resorcinol
2936	Thiolactic acid
2937	alpha-Methylbenzyl alcohol; Methylbenzyl alcohol (alpha)
2937	alpha-Methylbenzyl alcohol, liquid
2941	Fluoroanilines
2942	2-Trifluoromethylaniline
2946	2-Amino-5-diethylaminopentane
2948	3-Trifluoromethylaniline
2966	Thioglycol
3014	Substituted nitrophenol pesticide, liquid, toxic
3020	Organotin pesticide, liquid, toxic
3066	Paint (corrosive); Paint related material (corrosive)
3145	Alkyl phenols, liquid, n.o.s. (including C2-C12 homologues)
3146	Organotin compound, solid, n.o.s.
3172	Toxins, extracted from living sources, liquid, n.o.s.
3172	Toxins, extracted from living sources, n.o.s.
3172	Toxins, extracted from living sources, solid, n.o.s.

3250	Chloroacetic acid, molten
3265	Corrosive liquid, acidic, organic, n.o.s.
3267	Corrosive liquid, basic, organic, n.o.s.
3345	Phenoxyacetic acid derivative pesticide, solid, toxic
3348	Phenoxyacetic acid derivative pesticide, liquid, toxic
3410	4-Chloro-o-toluidine hydrochloride, solution
3411	beta-Naphthylamine, solution
3411	Naphthylamine (beta), solution
3416	Chloroacetophenone, liquid
3423	Tetramethylammonium hydroxide, solid
3427	Chlorobenzyl chlorides, solid
3429	Chlorotoluidines, liquid
3430	Xylenols, liquid
3434	Nitrocresols, liquid
3435	Hydroquinone, solution
3438	alpha-Methylbenzyl alcohol, solid
3441	Chlorodinitrobenzenes, solid
3442	Dichloroanilines, solid
3451	Toluidines, solid
3452	Xylidines, solid
3455	Cresols, solid
3460	N-Ethylbenzyltoluidines, solid
3462	Toxins, extracted from living sources, solid, n.o.s.

POTENTIAL HAZARDS

FIRE OR EXPLOSION

- Combustible material: may burn but doesn't ignite readily.
- When heated, vapors may form explosive mixtures with air: indoors, outdoors, and sewers explosion hazards.
- Those substances designated with a "**P**" may polymerize explosively when heated or involved in a fire.
- Contact with metals may evolve flammable hydrogen gas.
- Containers may explode when heated.
- Runoff may pollute waterways.
- Substance may be transported in molten form.

HEALTH

- **Toxic,** inhalation, ingestion, or skin contact with material may cause severe injury or death.
- Contact with molten substance may cause severe burns to skin and eyes.
- Avoid any skin contact.
- Effects of contact or inhalation may be delayed.
- Fire may produce irritating, corrosive, or toxic gases.
- Runoff from fire control or dilution water may be corrosive or toxic and cause pollution.

PUBLIC SAFETY

- **CALL Emergency Response Telephone Number on Shipping Paper first.   If Shipping Paper is not available or there is no answer, refer to telephone numbers listed on page 613.**

Hazmat

- As an immediate precautionary measure, isolate spill or leak area in all directions for at least 50 m (150 ft) for liquids and at least 25 m (75 ft) for solids.
- Keep unauthorized personnel away.
- Stay upwind.
- Keep out of low areas.
- Ventilate enclosed areas.

PROTECTIVE CLOTHING

- Wear positive pressure self-contained breathing apparatus (SCBA).
- Wear chemical protective clothing that is specifically recommended by the manufacturer. It may provide little or no thermal protection.
- Structural firefighters' protective clothing provides limited protection in fire situations ONLY; it is not effective in spill situations where direct contact with the substance is possible..

EVACUATION

Spill
- See the Table of Initial Isolation and Protective Action Distances for highlighted substances (page 908). For non-highlighted substances, increase, in the downwind direction, as necessary, the isolation distance shown above under "PUBLIC SAFETY."

Fire
- If tank, rail car, or tank truck is involved in a fire, ISOLATE for 800 meters (½ mile) in all directions; also, initiate evacuation including emergency responders for 800 meters (½ mile) in all directions.

EMERGENCY RESPONSE
FIRE

Small Fires
- Dry chemical, CO_2, or water spray.

Large Fires
- Dry chemical, CO_2, alcohol-resistant foam, or water spray.
- Move containers from fire area if you can do it without risk.
- Dike fire control water for later disposal; DO NOT scatter the material.

Fire Involving Tanks or Car/Trailer Loads
- Fight fire from maximum distance or use unmanned hose holders or monitor nozzles.
- DO NOT get water inside containers.
- Cool containers with flooding quantities of water until well after fire is out.
- Withdraw immediately in case of rising sound from venting safety devices or discoloration of tank.
- ALWAYS stay away from tanks engulfed in fire.

Hazmat

SPILL OR LEAK

- Eliminate all ignition sources (no smoking, flares, sparks, or flames in immediate area).
- DO NOT touch damaged containers or spilled material unless wearing appropriate protective clothing.
- Stop leak if you can do it without risk.
- Prevent entry into waterways, sewers, basements, or confined areas.
- Absorb or cover with DRY earth, sand, or other non-combustible material and transfer to containers.
- DO NOT get water inside containers.

FIRST AID

- Move victim to fresh air.
- Call 911 or emergency medical service.
- Give artificial respiration if victim is not breathing.
- **DO NOT use mouth-to-mouth method if victim ingested or inhaled the substance; give artificial respiration with the aid of a pocket mask equipped with a one-way valve or other proper respiratory medical device.**
- Administer oxygen if breathing is difficult.
- Remove and isolate contaminated clothing and shoes.
- In case of contact with substance, immediately flush skin or eyes with running water for at least 20 minutes.
- For minor skin contact, avoid spreading material on unaffected skin.
- Keep victim warm and quiet.
- Effects of exposure (inhalation, ingestion, or skin contact) to substance may be delayed.
- Ensure that medical personnel are aware of the material(s) involved, and take precautions to protect themselves.

Hazmat

SUBSTANCES INCLUDED

1553	Arsenic acid, liquid
1554	Arsenic acid, solid
1564	Barium compound, n.o.s.
1566	Beryllium compound, n.o.s.
1580	Chloropicrin
1583	Chloropicrin mixture, n.o.s.
1605	Ethylene dibromide
1613	Hydrocyanic acid, aqueous solution, with ≤ 20% Hydrogen cyanide
1613	Hydrocyanic acid, aqueous solution, with < 5% Hydrogen cyanide
1613	Hydrogen cyanide, aqueous solution, with ≤ 20% Hydrogen cyanide
1624	Mercuric chloride
1631	Mercuric benzoate
1634	Mercuric bromide; Mercurous bromide; Mercury bromides
1636	Mercuric cyanide; Mercury cyanide
1678	Potassium arsenite
1686	Sodium arsenite, aqueous solution
1690	Sodium fluoride (& , solid; & , solution)
1698	Adamsite
1698	DM; Diphenylamine chloroarsine
1719	Caustic alkali liquid, n.o.s.
1727	Ammonium bifluoride, solid
1727	Ammonium hydrogen fluoride, solid
1727	Ammonium hydrogendifluoride, solid
1740	Hydrogendifluorides, n.o.s.
1744	Bromine; Bromine, solution
1755	Chromic acid, solution
1756	Chromic fluoride, solid
1757	Chromic fluoride, solution
1759	Corrosive solid, n.o.s.
1759	Ferrous chloride, solid
1759	Medicines, corrosive, solid, n.o.s.
1760	Chemical kit
1760	Compound, cleaning liquid (corrosive)
1760	Compound, tree or weed killing, liquid (corrosive)
1760	Corrosive liquid, n.o.s.
1760	Ferrous chloride, solution
1760	Medicines, corrosive, liquid, n.o.s.
1760	Titanium sulfate, solution
1761	Cupriethylenediamine, solution
1768	Difluorophosphoric acid, anhydrous
1774	Fire extinguisher charges, corrosive liquid
1775	Fluoboric acid; Fluoroboric acid
1776	Fluorophosphoric acid, anhydrous
1778	Fluorosilicic acid; Fluosilicic acid; Hydrofluorosilicic acid
1782	Hexafluorophosphoric acid
1787	Hydriodic acid; Hydriodic acid, solution
1788	Hydrobromic acid; Hydrobromic acid, solution
1791	Hypochlorite solution
1791	Hypochlorite solution, with > 5% available Chlorine
1794	Lead sulfate, with > 3% free acid
1805	Phosphoric acid (& , liquid; & , solid; & , solution)
1811	Potassium hydrogen difluoride, solid
1811	Potassium hydrogendifluoride

1812	Potassium fluoride; Potassium fluoride, solid
1813	Caustic potash, dry, solid
1813	Potassium hydroxide(, dry, solid; & , flake; & solid)
1814	Caustic potash, liquid; Caustic potash, solution
1814	Potassium hydroxide, solution
1819	Sodium aluminate, solution
1821	Sodium bisulfate, solid
1823	Caustic soda (, bead; & , flake; & , granular; & , solid)
1823	Sodium hydroxide (, bead; & , flake; & granular; & , solid)
1824	Caustic soda, solution; Sodium hydroxide, solution
1833	Sulfurous acid
1840	Zinc chloride, solution
1905	Selenic acid
1907	Soda lime, with > 4% Sodium hydroxide
1908	Chlorite solution
1908	Chlorite solution, with > 5% available Chlorine
1908	Sodium chlorite, solution, with > 5% available Chlorine
2033	Potassium monoxide
2079	Diethylenetriamine
2240	Chromosulfuric acid
2331	Zinc chloride, anhydrous
2439	Sodium hydrogendifluoride
2440	Stannic chloride, pentahydrate
2440	Tin tetrachloride, pentahydrate
2471	Osmium tetroxide
2473	Sodium arsanilate
2505	Ammonium fluoride
2506	Ammonium hydrogen sulfate
2507	Chloroplatinic acid, solid
2509	Potassium hydrogen sulfate
2567	Sodium pentachlorophenate
2570	Cadmium compound
2580	Aluminum bromide, solution
2581	Aluminum chloride, solution
2582	Ferric chloride, solution
2642	Fluoroacetic acid
2648	1,2-Dibromobutan-3-one
2656	Quinoline
2672	Ammonia, solution, with > 10% but ≤ 35% Ammonia
2672	Ammonium hydroxide
2672	Ammonium hydroxide, with > 10% but ≤ 35% Ammonia
2674	Sodium fluorosilicate; Sodium silicofluoride
2677	Rubidium hydroxide, solution
2678	Rubidium hydroxide; Rubidium hydroxide, solid
2679	Lithium hydroxide, solution
2680	Lithium hydroxide (& , monohydrate; & , solid)
2681	Caesium hydroxide, solution; Cesium hydroxide, solution
2693	Bisulfites, aqueous solution, n.o.s.
2693	Bisulfites, inorganic, aqueous solution, n.o.s.
2699	Trifluoroacetic acid
2794	Batteries, wet, filled with acid
2795	Batteries, wet, filled with alkali
2797	Battery fluid, alkali
2797	Battery fluid, alkali, with battery
2797	Battery fluid, alkali, with electronic equipment or actuating device
2800	Batteries, wet, non-spillable
2801	Dye intermediate, liquid, corrosive, n.o.s.
2801	Dye, liquid, corrosive, n.o.s.
2802	Copper chloride

2811	CX
2811	Selenium oxide
2811	Toxic solid, organic, n.o.s.
2812	Sodium aluminate, solid
2817	Ammonium bifluoride, solution
2817	Ammonium hydrogen fluoride, solution
2817	Ammonium hydrogendifluoride, solution
2818	Ammonium polysulfide, solution
2834	Phosphorous acid; Phosphoric acid, ortho
2837	Sodium bisulfate, solution
2837	Sodium hydrogen sulfate, solution
2859	Ammonium metavanadate
2863	Sodium ammonium vanadate
2865	Hydroxylamine sulfate
2904	Chlorophenates, liquid; Chlorophenolates, liquid
2904	Phenolates, liquid
2905	Chlorophenates, solid; Chlorophenolates, solid
2905	Phenolates, solid
2922	Corrosive liquid, toxic, n.o.s.
2922	Sodium hydrosulfide, solution
2923	Corrosive solid, toxic, n.o.s.
2923	Toxic solid, corrosive, n.o.s.
2927	Ethyl phosphonothioic dichloride, anhydrous
2927	Ethyl phosphorodichloridate
2927	Toxic liquid, corrosive, organic, (& Inhalation Hazard Zone A and B)
2928	Toxic solid, corrosive, organic, n.o.s.
2949	Sodium hydrosulfide, with ≥ 25% water of crystallization
2967	Sulfamic acid
3028	Batteries, dry, containing Potassium hydroxide, solid
3055	2-(2-Aminoethoxy)ethanol
3147	Dye intermediate, solid, corrosive, n.o.s.
3147	Dye, solid, corrosive, n.o.s.
3155	Pentachlorophenol
3171	Battery-powered equipment (wet battery)
3171	Battery-powered vehicle (wet battery)
3171	Wheelchair, electric, with batteries
3244	Solids containing corrosive liquid, n.o.s.
3253	Disodium trioxosilicate (& , pentahydrate)
3259	Amines, solid, corrosive, n.o.s.
3259	Polyamines, solid, corrosive, n.o.s.
3260	Corrosive solid, acidic, inorganic, n.o.s.
3261	Corrosive solid, acidic, organic, n.o.s.
3262	Corrosive solid, basic, inorganic, n.o.s.
3263	Corrosive solid, basic, organic, n.o.s.
3264	Corrosive liquid, acidic, inorganic, n.o.s.
3266	Corrosive liquid, basic, inorganic, n.o.s.
3277	Chloroformates, toxic, corrosive, n.o.s.
3289	Toxic liquid, corrosive, inorganic, n.o.s. (& Inhalation Hazard Zone A and B)
3290	Toxic solid, corrosive, inorganic, n.o.s.
3389	Toxic by inhalation liquid, corrosive, n.o.s. (Inhalation Hazard Zone A)
3390	Toxic by inhalation liquid, corrosive, n.o.s. (Inhalation Hazard Zone B)
3421	Potassium hydrogen difluoride, solution
3422	Potassium fluoride, solution
3453	Phosphoric acid, solid

POTENTIAL HAZARDS

FIRE OR EXPLOSION

- Non-combustible, substance itself does not burn, but may decompose upon heating to product corrosive and/or toxic fumes.
- Some are oxidizers and may ignite combustibles (wood, paper, oil, clothing, etc.).
- Contact with metals may evolve flammable hydrogen gas.
- Containers may explode when heated.

HEALTH

- **Toxic;** inhalation, ingestion, or skin contact with material may cause severe injury or death.
- Contact with molten substance may cause severe burns to skin and eyes.
- Avoid any skin contact.
- Effects of contact or inhalation may be delayed.
- Fire may produce irritating, corrosive, or toxic gases.
- Runoff from fire control or dilution water may be corrosive or toxic and cause pollution.

PUBLIC SAFETY

- **CALL Emergency Response Telephone Number on Shipping Paper first. If Shipping Paper is not available or there is no answer, refer to telephone numbers listed on page 613.**
- As an immediate precautionary measure, isolate spill or leak area in all directions for at least 50 m (150 ft) for liquids and at least 25 m (75 ft) for solids.
- Keep unauthorized personnel away.
- Stay upwind.
- Keep out of low areas.
- Ventilate enclosed areas.

PROTECTIVE CLOTHING

- Wear positive pressure self-contained breathing apparatus (SCBA).
- Wear chemical protective clothing that is specifically recommended by the manufacturer. It may provide little or no thermal protection.
- Structural firefighters' protective clothing provides limited protection in fire situations ONLY; it is not effective in spill situations where direct contact with the substance is possible.

EVACUATION

Spill

- See the Table of Initial Isolation and Protective Action Distances for highlighted substances (page 908). For non-highlighted substances, increase, in the downwind direction, as necessary, the isolation distance shown above under "PUBLIC SAFETY."

Hazmat

Fire

- If tank, rail car, or tank truck is involved in a fire, ISOLATE for 800 meters (½ mile) in all directions; also, initiate evacuation including emergency responders for 800 meters (½ mile) in all directions.

EMERGENCY RESPONSE
FIRE

Small Fires

- Dry chemical, CO_2, or water spray.

Large Fires

- Dry chemical, CO_2, alcohol-resistant form, or water spray.
- Move containers from fire area if you can do it without risk.
- Dike fire control water for later disposal; DO NOT scatter the material.

Fire Involving Tanks or Car/Trailer Loads

- Fight fire from maximum distance or use unmanned hose holders or monitor nozzles.
- DO NOT get water inside containers.
- Cool containers with flooding quantities of water until well after fire is out.
- Withdraw immediately in case of rising sound from venting safety devices or discoloration of tank.
- ALWAYS stay away from tanks engulfed in fire.

SPILL OR LEAK

- Eliminate all ignition sources (no smoking, flares, sparks, or flames in immediate area).
- DO NOT touch damaged containers or spilled material unless wearing appropriate protective clothing.
- Stop leak if you can do it without risk.
- Prevent entry into waterways, sewers, basements, or confined areas.
- Absorb or cover with DRY earth, sand, or other non-combustible material and transfer to containers.
- DO NOT get water inside containers.

FIRST AID

- Move victim to fresh air.
- Call 911 or emergency medical service.
- Give artificial respiration if victim is not breathing.
- **DO NOT use mouth-to-mouth method if victim ingested or inhaled the substance; give artificial respiration with the aid of a pocket mask equipped with a one-way valve or other proper respiratory medical device.**
- Administer oxygen if breathing is difficult.
- Remove and isolate contaminated clothing and shoes.

Hazmat

- In case of contact with substance, immediately flush skin or eyes with running water for at least 20 minutes.
- For minor skin contact, avoid spreading material on unaffected skin.
- Keep victim warm and quiet.
- Effects of exposure (inhalation, ingestion, or skin contact) to substance may be delayed.
- Ensure that medical personnel are aware of the material(s) involved, and take precautions to protect themselves.

Guide 155: Substances - Toxic and/or Corrosive (Flammable/Water-Sensitive)

SUBSTANCES INCLUDED

1162	Dimethyldichlorosilane
1181	Ethyl chloroacetate
1182	Ethyl chloroformate
1196	Ethyltrichlorosilane
1238	Methyl chloroformate
1250	Methyltrichlorosilane
1298	Trimethylchlorosilane
1305	**Vinyltrichlorosilane (& , inhibited; & , stabilized)**
1541	Acetone cyanohydrin, stabilized
1545	Allyl isothiocyanate (, inhibited; & , stabilized)
1603	Ethyl bromoacetate
1717	Acetyl chloride
1722	Allyl chlorocarbonate; Allyl chloroformate
1724	Allyltrichlorosilane, stabilized
1728	Amyltrichlorosilane
1747	Butyltrichlorosilane
1767	Diethyldichlorosilane
1816	Propyltrichlorosilane
2206	Isocyanate solution, toxic, n.o.s.
2206	Isocyanate solutions, n.o.s.
2206	Isocyanates, n.o.s.
2206	Isocyanates, toxic, n.o.s.
2295	Methyl chloroacetate
2299	Methyl dichloroacetate
2407	Isopropyl chloroformate
2478	Isocyanate solution, flammable, toxic, n.o.s.
2478	Isocyanate solutions, n.o.s.
2478	Isocyanates, flammable, toxic, n.o.s.
2478	Isocyanates, n.o.s.
2480	Methyl isocyanate
2481	Ethyl isocyanate
2482	n-Propyl isocyanate
2483	Isopropyl isocyanate
2484	tert-Butyl isocyanate
2485	n-Butyl isocyanate
2486	Isobutyl isocyanate
2487	Phenyl isocyanate
2488	Cyclohexyl isocyanate
2589	Vinyl chloroacetate
2605	Methoxymethyl isocyanate
2606	Methyl orthosilicate
2643	Methyl bromoacetate
2740	n-Propyl chloroformate
2742	Chloroformates, n.o.s.
2742	Chloroformates, toxic, corrosive, flammable, n.o.s.
2742	Isobutyl chloroformate; sec-Butyl chloroformate
2743	n-Butyl chloroformate
2744	Cyclobutyl chloroformate
2751	Diethylthiophosphoryl chloride
2826	Ethyl chlorothioformate
2947	Isopropyl chloroacetate
2985	Chlorosilanes, flammable, corrosive, n.o.s.
2985	Chlorosilanes, n.o.s.

2986	Chlorosilanes, corrosive, flammable, n.o.s.
2986	Chlorosilanes, n.o.s.
3080	Isocyanate solution, toxic, flammable, n.o.s.
3080	Isocyanate solutions, n.o.s.
3080	Isocyanates, n.o.s.
3080	Isocyanates, toxic, flammable, n.o.s.
3362	Chlorosilanes, toxic, corrosive, flammable, n.o.s.

POTENTIAL HAZARDS

FIRE OR EXPLOSION

- **HIGHLY FLAMMABLE: Will be easily ignited by heat, sparks, or flames.**
- Vapors form explosive mixtures with air: indoors, outdoors, and sewers explosion hazards.
- Most vapors are heavier than air. They will spread along ground and collect in low or confined areas (sewers, basements, tanks).
- Vapors may travel to source of ignition and flash back.
- Those substances designated with a "**P**" may polymerize explosively when heated or involved in a fire.
- Substance will react with water (some violently) releasing flammable, toxic, or corrosive gases and runoff.
- Contact with metals may evolve flammable hydrogen gas.
- Containers may explode when heated or if contaminated with water.

HEALTH

- **Toxic;** inhalation, ingestion, or contact (skin, eyes) with vapors, dusts, or substance may cause severe injury, burns, or death.
- **Bromoacetates and chloroacetates are extremely irritating/lachrymators.**
- Reaction with water or moist air will release toxic, corrosive, or flammable gases.
- Reaction with water may generate much heat which will increase the concentration of fumes in the air.
- Fire may produce irritating, corrosive, or toxic gases.
- Runoff from fire control or dilution water may be corrosive or toxic and cause pollution.

PUBLIC SAFETY

- **CALL Emergency Response Telephone Number on Shipping Paper first. If Shipping Paper is not available or there is no answer, refer to telephone numbers listed on page 613.**
- As an immediate precautionary measure, isolate spill or leak area in all directions for at least 50 m (150 ft) for liquids and at least 25 m (75 ft) for solids.
- Keep unauthorized personnel away.
- Stay upwind.
- Keep out of low areas.
- Ventilate enclosed areas.

PROTECTIVE CLOTHING

- Wear positive pressure self-contained breathing apparatus (SCBA).
- Wear chemical protective clothing that is specifically recommended by the manufacturer. It may provide little or no thermal protection.
- Structural firefighters' protective clothing provides limited protection in fire situations ONLY; it is not effective in spill situations where direct contact with the substance is possible.

EVACUATION

Spill

- See the Table of Initial Isolation and Protective Action Distances for highlighted substances (page 908). For non-highlighted substances, increase, in the downwind direction, as necessary, the isolation distance shown above under "PUBLIC SAFETY."

Fire

- If tank, rail car, or tank truck is involved in a fire, ISOLATE for 800 meters (½ mile) in all directions; also, initiate evacuation including emergency responders for 800 meters (½ mile) in all directions.

EMERGENCY RESPONSE
FIRE

- **Note: Most foams will react with the material and release corrosive/toxic gases.**
- **CAUTION: For Acetyl chloride (UN1717), use CO_2 or dry chemical only.**

Small Fires

- CO_2, dry chemical, dry sand, or alcohol-resistant foam.

Large Fires

- Water spray, fog, or alcohol-resistant foam.
- **For chlorosilanes, DO NOT use water**; use AFFF alcohol-resistant medium expansion foam.
- Move containers from fire area if you can do it without risk.
- Use water spray or fog; DO NOT use straight streams.

Fire Involving Tanks or Car/Trailer Loads

- Fight fire from maximum distance or use unmanned hose holders or monitor nozzles.
- DO NOT get water inside containers.
- Cool containers with flooding quantities of water until well after fire is out.
- Withdraw immediately in case of rising sound from venting safety devices or discoloration of tank.
- ALWAYS stay away from tanks engulfed in fire.

Hazmat

SPILL OR LEAK

- Eliminate all ignition sources (no smoking, flares, sparks, or flames in immediate area).
- All equipment used when handling the product must be grounded.
- DO NOT touch damaged containers or spilled material unless wearing appropriate protective clothing.
- Stop leak if you can do it without risk.
- A vapor suppressing foam may be used to reduce vapors.
- **For chlorosilanes,** use AFFF alcohol-resistant medium expansion foam to reduce vapors.
- DO NOT get water on spilled substance or inside containers.
- Use water spray to reduce vapors or divert vapor cloud drift. Avoid allowing water runoff to contact spilled material.
- Prevent entry into waterways, sewers, basements, or confined areas.

Small Spills

- Cover with DRY earth, DRY sand, or other non-combustible material followed with plastic sheet to minimize spreading or contact with rain.
- Use clean non-sparking tools to collect material and place it into loosely covered plastic containers for later disposal.

FIRST AID

- Move victim to fresh air.
- Call 911 or emergency medical service.
- Give artificial respiration if victim is not breathing.
- **DO NOT use mouth-to-mouth method if victim ingested or inhaled the substance; give artificial respiration with the aid of a pocket mask equipped with a one-way valve or other proper respiratory medical device.**
- Administer oxygen if breathing is difficult.
- Remove and isolate contaminated clothing and shoes.
- In case of contact with substance, immediately flush skin or eyes with running water for at least 20 minutes.
- For minor skin contact, avoid spreading material on unaffected skin.
- Keep victim warm and quiet.
- Effects of exposure (inhalation, ingestion, or skin contact) to substance may be delayed.
- Ensure that medical personnel are aware of the material(s) involved, and take precautions to protect themselves.

Hazmat

SUBSTANCES INCLUDED

1595	Dimethyl sulfate
1716	Acetyl bromide
1729	Anisoyl chloride
1737	Benzyl bromide
1738	Benzyl chloride
1752	Chloroacetyl chloride
1753	Chlorophenyltrichlorosilane
1762	Cyclohexenyltrichlorosilane
1763	Cyclohexyltrichlorosilane
1765	Dichloroacetyl chloride
1766	Dichlorophenyltrichlorosilane
1769	Diphenyldichlorosilane
1771	Dodecyltrichlorosilane
1780	Fumaryl chloride
1781	Hexadecyltrichlorosilane
1784	Hexyltrichlorosilane
1799	Nonyltrichlorosilane
1800	Octadecyltrichlorosilane
1801	Octyltrichlorosilane
1804	Phenyltrichlorosilane
1886	Benzylidene chloride
1898	Acetyl iodide
1938	Bromoacetic acid; Bromoacetic acid, solution
2078	Toluene diisocyanate
2214	Phthalic anhydride
2215	Maleic acid; Maleic anhydride; Maleic anhydride, molten
2225	Benzenesulfonyl chloride
2226	Benzotrichloride
2236	3-Chloro-4-methylphenyl isocyanate (& , liquid)
2250	Dichlorophenyl isocyanates
2262	Dimethylcarbamoyl chloride
2267	Dimethyl thiophosphoryl chloride
2281	Hexamethylene diisocyanate
2285	Isocyanatobenzotrifluorides
2290	IPDI; Isophorone diisocyanate
2328	Trimethylhexamethylene diisocyanate
2434	Dibenzyldichlorosilane
2435	Ethylphenyldichlorosilane
2437	Methylphenyldichlorosilane
2442	Trichloroacetyl chloride
2496	Propionic anhydride
2508	Molybdenum pentachloride
2513	Bromoacetyl bromide
2525	Ethyl oxalate
2533	Methyl trichloroacetate
2571	Alkylsulfuric acids
2571	Ethylsulfuric acid
2577	Phenylacetyl chloride
2609	Triallyl borate
2653	Benzyl iodide
2666	Ethyl cyanoacetate
2698	Tetrahydrophthalic anhydrides
2739	Butyric anhydride

Hazmat

2746	Phenyl chloroformate
2747	tert-Butylcyclohexyl chloroformate
2748	2-Ethylhexyl chloroformate
2987	Chlorosilanes, corrosive, n.o.s.
2987	Chlorosilanes, n.o.s.
3246	Methanesulfonyl chloride
3361	Chlorosilanes, toxic, corrosive, n.o.s.
3425	Bromoacetic acid, solid
3428	3-Chloro-4-methylphenyl isocyanate, solid
9263	Chloropivaloyl chloride

POTENTIAL HAZARDS

FIRE OR EXPLOSION

- Combustible material: may burn but does not ignite readily.
- Substance will react with water (some violently) releasing flammable, toxic, or corrosive gases and runoff.
- When heated, vapors may form explosive mixtures with air: indoors, outdoors, and sewers explosion hazards.
- Most vapors are heavier than air. They will spread along ground and collect in low or confined areas (sewers, basements, tanks).
- Vapors may travel to source of ignition and flash back.
- Contact with metals may evolve flammable hydrogen gas.
- Containers may explode when heated or if contaminated with water.

HEALTH

- **Toxic;** inhalation, ingestion, or contact (skin, eyes) with vapors, dusts, or substance may cause severe injury, burns, or death.
- Contact with molten substance may cause severe burns to skin and eyes.
- Reaction with water or moist air will release toxic, corrosive, or flammable gases.
- Reaction with water may generate much heat which will increase the concentration of fumes in the air.
- Fire may produce irritating, corrosive, or toxic gases.
- Runoff from fire control or dilution water may be corrosive or toxic and cause pollution.

PUBLIC SAFETY

- **CALL Emergency Response Telephone Number on Shipping Paper first. If Shipping Paper is not available or there is no answer, refer to telephone numbers listed on page 613.**
- As an immediate precautionary measure, isolate spill or leak area in all directions for at least 50 m (150 ft) for liquids and at least 25 m (75 ft) for solids.
- Keep unauthorized personnel away.
- Stay upwind.
- Keep out of low areas.
- Ventilate enclosed areas.

PROTECTIVE CLOTHING

- Wear positive pressure self-contained breathing apparatus (SCBA).
- Wear chemical protective clothing that is specifically recommended by the manufacturer. It may provide little or no thermal protection.
- Structural firefighters' protective clothing provides limited protection in fire situations ONLY; it is not effective in spill situations where direct contact with the substance is possible.

EVACUATION

Spill

- See the Table of Initial Isolation and Protective Action Distances for highlighted substances (page 908). For non-highlighted substances, increase, in the downwind direction, as necessary, the isolation distance shown above under "PUBLIC SAFETY."

Fire

- If tank, rail car, or tank truck is involved in a fire, ISOLATE for 800 meters (½ mile) in all directions; also, initiate evacuation including emergency responders for 800 meters (½ mile) in all directions.

EMERGENCY RESPONSE
FIRE

- **Note: Most foams will react with the material and release corrosive/toxic gases.**

Small Fires

- CO_2, dry chemical, dry sand, or alcohol-resistant foam.

Large Fires

- Water spray, fog, or alcohol-resistant foam.
- **For chlorosilanes, DO NOT use water**; use AFFF alcohol-resistant medium expansion foam.
- Move containers from fire area if you can do it without risk.
- Use water spray or fog; DO NOT use straight streams.

Fire Involving Tanks or Car/Trailer Loads

- Fight fire from maximum distance or use unmanned hose holders or monitor nozzles.
- DO NOT get water inside containers.
- Cool containers with flooding quantities of water until well after fire is out.
- Withdraw immediately in case of rising sound from venting safety devices or discoloration of tank.
- ALWAYS stay away from tanks engulfed in fire.

Hazmat

SPILL OR LEAK

- Eliminate all ignition sources (no smoking, flares, sparks, or flames in immediate area).
- All equipment used when handling the product must be grounded.
- DO NOT touch damaged containers or spilled material unless wearing appropriate protective clothing.
- Stop leak if you can do it without risk.
- A vapor suppressing foam may be used to reduce vapors.
- **For chlorosilanes,** use AFFF alcohol-resistant medium expansion foam to reduce vapors.
- DO NOT get water on spilled substance or inside containers.
- Use water spray to reduce vapors or divert vapor cloud drift. Avoid allowing water runoff to contact spilled material.
- Prevent entry into waterways, sewers, basements, or confined areas.

Small Spills

- Cover with DRY earth, DRY sand, or other non-combustible material followed with plastic sheet to minimize spreading or contact with rain.
- Use clean non-sparking tools to collect material and place it into loosely covered plastic containers for later disposal.

FIRST AID

- Move victim to fresh air.
- Call 911 or emergency medical service.
- Give artificial respiration if victim is not breathing.
- **DO NOT use mouth-to-mouth method if victim ingested or inhaled the substance; give artificial respiration with the aid of a pocket mask equipped with a one-way valve or other proper respiratory medical device.**
- Administer oxygen if breathing is difficult.
- Remove and isolate contaminated clothing and shoes.
- In case of contact with substance, immediately flush skin or eyes with running water for at least 20 minutes.
- For minor skin contact, avoid spreading material on unaffected skin.
- Keep victim warm and quiet.
- Effects of exposure (inhalation, ingestion, or skin contact) to substance may be delayed.
- Ensure that medical personnel are aware of the material(s) involved, and take precautions to protect themselves.

Hazmat

Guide 157: Substances - Toxic and/or Corrosive (Non-Combustible/ Water-Sensitive)

SUBSTANCES INCLUDED

1549	Antimony compound, inorganic, n.o.s.
1549	Antimony compound, inorganic, solid, n.o.s.
1549	Antimony tribromide (, solid; & , solution)
1549	Antimony trifluoride (, solid; & , solution)
1560	Arsenic chloride; Arsenic trichloride
1565	Barium cyanide
1575	Calcium cyanide
1588	Cyanides, inorganic, n.o.s.
1588	Cyanides, inorganic, solid, n.o.s.
1626	Mercuric potassium cyanide
1670	Perchloromethyl mercaptan
1679	Potassium cuprocyanide
1680	Potassium cyanide; Potassium cyanide, solid
1689	Sodium cyanide; Sodium cyanide, solid
1730	Antimony pentachloride, liquid
1731	Antimony pentachloride, solution
1732	Antimony pentafluoride
1733	Antimony trichloride (& , liquid; & , solid; & , solution)
1742	Boron trifluoride acetic acid complex (& , liquid)
1743	Boron trifluoride propionic acid complex (& , liquid)
1773	Ferric chloride; Ferric chloride, anhydrous
1786	Hydrofluoric acid and Sulfuric acid mixture
1789	Hydrochloric acid; Hydrochloric acid, solution
1789	Muriatic acid
1790	Hydrofluoric acid; Hydrofluoric acid, solution
1792	Iodine monochloride
1796	Nitrating acid mixture
1798	Aqua regia
1798	Nitrohydrochloric acid
1818	Silicon tetrachloride
1825	Sodium monoxide
1826	Nitrating acid mixture, spent
1837	Thiophosphoryl chloride
1884	Barium oxide
1889	Cyanogen bromide
1910	Calcium oxide
1935	Cyanide solution, not otherwise specified
2031	Nitric acid, other than red fuming
2032	Nitric acid, fuming; Nitric acid, red fuming
2308	Nitrosylsulfuric acid (& , liquid; & , solid)
2316	Sodium cuprocyanide, solid
2317	Sodium cuprocyanide, solution
2474	Thiophosgene
2475	Vanadium trichloride
2578	Phosphorus trioxide
2670	Cyanuric chloride
2682	Caesium hydroxide; Cesium hydroxide
2692	Boron tribromide
2745	Chloromethyl chloroformate
2796	Battery fluid, acid
2796	Sulfuric acid, with $\leq$ 51% acid
2851	Boron trifluoride, dihydrate
2869	Titanium trichloride mixture

2879	Selenium oxychloride
3048	Aluminum phosphide pesticide
3141	Antimony compound, inorganic, liquid, n.o.s.
3320	Sodium borohydride and Sodium hydroxide solution, with ≤ 12% Sodium borohydride and ≤ 40% Sodium hydroxide
3413	Potassium cyanide, solution
3414	Sodium cyanide, solution
3419	Boron trifluoride acetic acid complex, solid
3420	Boron trifluoride propionic acid complex, solid
3456	Nitrosysulfuric acid, solid

POTENTIAL HAZARDS
FIRE OR EXPLOSION

- Non-combustible, substance itself does not burn but may decompose upon heating to produce corrosive and/or toxic fumes.
- Vapors may accumulate in confined areas (basement, tanks, hopper/tank cars, etc.).
- Substance will react with water (some violently) releasing toxic or corrosive gases.
- Contact with metals may evolve flammable hydrogen gas.
- Containers may explode when heated or if contaminated with water.

HEALTH

- **Toxic;** inhalation, ingestion, or contact (skin, eyes) with vapors, dusts, or substance may cause severe injury, burns, or death.
- Reaction with water or moist air will release toxic, corrosive, or flammable gases.
- Reaction with water may generate much heat which will increase the concentration of fumes in the air.
- Fire may produce irritating, corrosive, or toxic gases.
- Runoff from fire control or dilution water may be corrosive or toxic and cause pollution.

PUBLIC SAFETY

- **CALL Emergency Response Telephone Number on Shipping Paper first.   If Shipping Paper is not available or there is no answer, refer to telephone numbers listed on page 613.**
- As an immediate precautionary measure, isolate spill or leak area in all directions for at least 50 m (150 ft) for liquids and at least 25 m (75 ft) for solids.
- Keep unauthorized personnel away.
- Stay upwind.
- Keep out of low areas.
- Ventilate enclosed areas.

PROTECTIVE CLOTHING

- Wear positive pressure self-contained breathing apparatus (SCBA).
- Wear chemical protective clothing that is specifically recommended by the manufacturer. It may provide little or no thermal protection.
- Structural firefighters' protective clothing provides limited protection in fire situations ONLY; it is not effective in spill situations where direct contact with the substance is possible.

EVACUATION

Spill

- See the Table of Initial Isolation and Protective Action Distances for highlighted substances (page 908). For non-highlighted substances, increase, in the downwind direction, as necessary, the isolation distance shown above under "PUBLIC SAFETY."

Fire

- If tank, rail car, or tank truck is involved in a fire, ISOLATE for 800 meters (½ mile) in all directions; also, initiate evacuation including emergency responders for 800 meters (½ mile) in all directions.

EMERGENCY RESPONSE

FIRE

- **Note: Most foams will react with the material and release corrosive/toxic gases.**

Small Fires

- CO_2 (except for Cyanides), dry chemical, dry sand, or alcohol-resistant foam.

Large Fires

- Water spray, fog, or alcohol-resistant foam.
- Move containers from fire area if you can do it without risk.
- Use water spray or fog; DO NOT use straight streams.
- Dike fire control water for later disposal; DO NOT scatter the material.

Fire Involving Tanks or Car/Trailer Loads

- Fight fire from maximum distance or use unmanned hose holders or monitor nozzles.
- DO NOT get water inside containers.
- Cool containers with flooding quantities of water until well after fire is out.
- Withdraw immediately in case of rising sound from venting safety devices or discoloration of tank.
- ALWAYS stay away from tanks engulfed in fire.

Hazmat

SPILL OR LEAK

- Eliminate all ignition sources (no smoking, flares, sparks, or flames in immediate area).
- All equipment used when handling the product must be grounded.
- DO NOT touch damaged containers or spilled material unless wearing appropriate protective clothing.
- Stop leak if you can do it without risk.
- A vapor suppressing foam may be used to reduce vapors.
- DO NOT get water on spilled substance or inside containers.
- Use water spray to reduce vapors or divert vapor cloud drift. Avoid allowing water runoff to contact spilled material.
- Prevent entry into waterways, sewers, basements, or confined areas.

Small Spills

- Cover with DRY earth, DRY sand, or other non-combustible material followed with plastic sheet to minimize spreading or contact with rain.
- Use clean non-sparking tools to collect material and place it into loosely covered plastic containers for later disposal.

FIRST AID

- Move victim to fresh air.
- Call 911 or emergency medical service.
- Give artificial respiration if victim is not breathing.
- **DO NOT use mouth-to-mouth method if victim ingested or inhaled the substance; give artificial respiration with the aid of a pocket mask equipped with a one-way valve or other proper respiratory medical device.**
- Administer oxygen if breathing is difficult.
- Remove and isolate contaminated clothing and shoes.
- In case of contact with substance, immediately flush skin or eyes with running water for at least 20 minutes.
- For minor skin contact, avoid spreading material on unaffected skin.
- Keep victim warm and quiet.
- Effects of exposure (inhalation, ingestion, or skin contact) to substance may be delayed.
- Ensure that medical personnel are aware of the material(s) involved, and take precautions to protect themselves.

Guide 158: Infectious Substances

SUBSTANCES INCLUDED

Biological agents
2814 Infectious substance, affecting humans
2900 Infectious substance, affecting animals only
3291 (Bio)Medical waste, n.o.s.
3291 Clinical waste, unspecified, n.o.s.
3291 Medical waste, n.o.s.
3291 Regulated medical waste, n.o.s.
3373 Clinical specimens
3373 Diagnostic specimens
9275 Regulated medical waste

POTENTIAL HAZARDS

FIRE OR EXPLOSION

- Some of these materials may burn, but none ignite readily.
- Some may be transported in flammable liquids.

HEALTH

- Inhalation or contact with substance may cause infection, disease, or death.
- Runoff from fire control may cause pollution.
- **Note:** Damaged packages containing solid CO_2 as a refrigerant may produce water or frost from condensation of air. Do not touch this liquid as it could be contaminated by the contents of the parcel.

PUBLIC SAFETY

- **CALL Emergency Response Telephone Number on Shipping Paper first. If Shipping Paper is not available or there is no answer, refer to telephone numbers listed on page 613.**
- As an immediate precautionary measure, isolate spill or leak area for at least 25 meters (75 feet) in all directions.
- Keep unauthorized personnel away.
- Stay upwind.
- Obtain identity of substance involved.

PROTECTIVE CLOTHING

- Wear positive pressure self-contained breathing apparatus (SCBA).
- Structural firefighters' protective clothing will only provide limited protection.

EMERGENCY RESPONSE

FIRE

Small Fires
- Dry chemical, soda ash, lime, or sand.

Hazmat

Large Fires

- Use extinguishing agent suitable for type of surrounding fire.
- Move containers from fire area if you can do it without risk.
- DO NOT scatter spilled material with high pressure water streams.

SPILL OR LEAK

- DO NOT touch or walk through spilled material.
- DO NOT touch damaged containers or spilled material unless wearing appropriate protective clothing.
- Absorb with earth, sand, or other non-combustible material.
- Cover damaged package or spilled material with damp towel or rag and keep wet with liquid bleach or other disinfectant.
- **DO NOT clean-up or dispose of, except under supervision of a specialist.**

FIRST AID

CAUTION: Victim may be a source of contamination.

- Move victim to a safe isolated area.
- Call 911 or emergency medical service.
- Remove and isolate contaminated clothing and shoes.
- In case of contact with substance, immediately flush skin or eyes with running water for at least 20 minutes.
- Effects of exposure (inhalation, ingestion, or skin contact) to substance may be delayed.
- **For further assistance, contact your local Poison Control Center (page 148).**
- Ensure that medical personnel are aware of the material(s) involved, and take precautions to protect themselves.

Guide 159: Substances (Irritating)

SUBSTANCES INCLUDED

1610	Halogenated irritating liquid, n.o.s.
1693	Tear gas devices
1693	Tear gas substance, liquid, n.o.s.
1693	Tear gas substance, solid, n.o.s.
1694	Bromobenzyl cyanides (& , liquid; & , solid)
1694	CA
1700	Tear gas candles; Tear gas grenades
2017	Ammunition, tear-producing, non-explosive
2504	Acetylene tetrabromide; Tetrabromoethane
2515	Bromoform
2688	1-Bromo-3-chloropropane; 1-Chloro-3-bromopropane
2872	Dibromochloropropanes
3448	Tear gas substance, solid, n.o.s.
3449	Bromobenzyl cyanides, solid

POTENTIAL HAZARDS

FIRE OR EXPLOSION

- Some of these materials may burn, but none ignite readily.
- Containers may explode when heated.

HEALTH

- Inhalation of vapors or dust is extremely irritating.
- May cause burning of eyes and flow of tears.
- May cause coughing, difficult breathing, and nausea.
- Brief exposure effects last only a few minutes.
- Exposure in an enclosed area may be very harmful.
- Fire may produce irritating, corrosive, or toxic gases.
- Runoff from fire control or dilution water may cause pollution.

PUBLIC SAFETY

- **CALL Emergency Response Telephone Number on Shipping Paper first. If Shipping Paper is not available or there is no answer, refer to telephone numbers listed on page 613.**
- As an immediate precautionary measure, isolate spill or leak area in all directions for at least 50 meters (150 feet) for liquids and at least 25 meters (75 feet) for solids.
- Keep unauthorized personnel away.
- Stay upwind.
- Keep out of low areas.
- Ventilate enclosed areas.

PROTECTIVE CLOTHING

- Wear positive pressure self-contained breathing apparatus (SCBA).
- Wear chemical protective clothing that is specifically recommended by the manufacturer. It may provide little or no thermal protection.

Hazmat

- Structural firefighters' protective clothing provides limited protection in fire situations ONLY; it is not effective in spill situations where direct contact with the substance is possible.

EVACUATION

Spill

- See the Table of Initial Isolation and Protective Action Distances for highlighted substances (page 908). For non-highlighted substances, increase, in the downwind direction, as necessary, the isolation distance shown above under "PUBLIC SAFETY."

Fire

- If tank, rail car, or tank truck is involved in a fire, ISOLATE for 800 meters (½ mile) in all directions; also, initiate evacuation including emergency responders for 800 meters (½ mile) in all directions.

EMERGENCY RESPONSE
FIRE

Small Fires

- Dry chemical, CO_2, water spray, or regular foam.

Large Fires

- Water spray, fog, or regular foam.
- Move containers from fire area if you can do it without risk.
- Dike fire control water for later disposal; DO NOT scatter the material.

Fire Involving Tanks or Car/Trailer Loads

- Fight fire from maximum distance or use unmanned hose holders or monitor nozzles.
- DO NOT get water inside containers.
- Cool containers with flooding quantities of water until well after fire is out.
- Withdraw immediately in case of rising sound from venting safety devices or discoloration of tank.
- ALWAYS stay away from tanks engulfed in fire.
- For massive fire, use unmanned hose holders or monitor nozzles; if this is impossible, withdraw from area and let fire burn.

SPILL OR LEAK

- DO NOT touch or walk through spilled material.
- Stop leak if you can do it without risk.
- Fully encapsulating, vapor protective clothing should be worn for spills and leaks with no fire.

Small Spills

- Take up with sand or other non-combustible absorbent material and place into containers for later disposal.

Large Spills
- Dike far ahead of liquid spill for later disposal.
- Prevent entry into waterways, sewers, basements, or confined areas.

FIRST AID

- Move victim to fresh air.
- Call 911 or emergency medical service.
- Give artificial respiration if victim is not breathing.
- **DO NOT use mouth-to-mouth method if victim ingested or inhaled the substance; give artificial respiration with the aid of a pocket mask equipped with a one-way valve or other proper respiratory medical device.**
- Administer oxygen if breathing is difficult.
- Remove and isolate contaminated clothing and shoes.
- In case of contact with substance, immediately flush skin or eyes with running water for at least 20 minutes.
- For minor skin contact, avoid spreading material on unaffected skin.
- Keep victim warm and quiet.
- Effects should disappear after individual has been exposed to fresh air for approximately 10 minutes.
- Ensure that medical personnel are aware of the material(s) involved, and take precautions to protect themselves.

Hazmat

Guide 160: Halogenated Solvents

SUBSTANCES INCLUDED

1593	Dichloromethane; Methylene chloride
1710	Trichloroethylene
1887	Bromochloromethane
1897	Perchloroethylene; Tetrachloroethylene
2664	Dibromomethane
2831	1,1,1-Trichloroethane

POTENTIAL HAZARDS

FIRE OR EXPLOSION

- Some of these materials may burn, but none ignite readily.
- Most vapors are heavier than air.
- Air/vapor mixtures may explode when ignited.
- Containers may explode in heat of fire.

HEALTH

- Toxic by ingestion.
- Vapors may cause dizziness or suffocation.
- Exposure in an enclosed area may be very harmful.
- Contact may irritate or burn skin and eyes.
- Fire may produce irritating or toxic gases.
- Runoff from fire control or dilution water may cause pollution.

PUBLIC SAFETY

- **CALL Emergency Response Telephone Number on Shipping Paper first. If Shipping Paper is not available or there is no answer, refer to telephone numbers listed on page 613.**
- As an immediate precautionary measure, isolate spill or leak area for at least 50 m (150 ft) in all directions.
- Keep unauthorized personnel away.
- Stay upwind.
- Many gases are heavier than air and will spread along ground and collect in low or confined areas (sewers, basements, tanks).
- Keep out of low areas.
- Ventilate enclosed areas.

PROTECTIVE CLOTHING

- Wear positive pressure self-contained breathing apparatus (SCBA).
- Wear chemical protective clothing that is specifically recommended by the manufacturer.
- Structural firefighters' protective clothing will only provide limited protection.

EVACUATION

Spill

- Consider initial downwind evacuation for at least 100 m (330 ft).

Fire

- If tank, rail car, or tank truck is involved in a fire, ISOLATE for 800 meters (½ mile) in all directions; also, initiate evacuation including emergency responders for 800 meters (½ mile) in all directions.

EMERGENCY RESPONSE
FIRE

Small Fires

- Dry chemical, CO_2, or water spray.

Large Fires

- Dry chemical, CO_2, alcohol-resistant form, or water spray.
- Move containers from fire area if you can do it without risk.
- Dike fire control water for later disposal; DO NOT scatter the material.

Fire Involving Tanks or Car/Trailer Loads

- Fight fire from maximum distance or use unmanned hose holders or monitor nozzles.
- Cool containers with flooding quantities of water until well after fire is out.
- Withdraw immediately in case of rising sound from venting safety devices or discoloration of tank.
- ALWAYS stay away from tanks engulfed in fire.

SPILL OR LEAK

- Eliminate all ignition sources (no smoking, flares, sparks, or flames in immediate area).
- Stop leak if you can do it without risk.

Small Spills

- Take up with sand or other non-combustible absorbent material.

Large Spills

- Dike far ahead of liquid spill for later disposal.
- Prevent entry into waterways, sewers, basements, or confined areas.

FIRST AID

- Move victim to fresh air.
- Call 911 or emergency medical service.
- Give artificial respiration if victim is not breathing.
- Administer oxygen if breathing is difficult.
- Remove and isolate contaminated clothing and shoes.
- In case of contact with substance, immediately flush skin or eyes with running water for at least 20 minutes.
- For minor skin contact, avoid spreading material on unaffected skin.
- Keep victim warm and quiet.
- Ensure that medical personnel are aware of the material(s) involved, and take precautions to protect themselves.

Hazmat

Guide 161: Radioactive Materials (Low Level Radiation)

SUBSTANCES INCLUDED

2908	Radioactive material, empty packages
2908	Radioactive material, excepted package, empty packaging
2909	Radioactive material, articles manufactured from depleted Uranium
2909	Radioactive material, articles manufactured from natural Thorium
2909	Radioactive material, articles manufactured from natural Uranium
2909	Radioactive material, excepted package, articles manufactured from depleted Uranium
2909	Radioactive material, excepted package, articles manufactured from natural Thorium
2909	Radioactive material, excepted package, articles manufactured from natural Uranium
2910	Radioactive material, articles manufactured from natural Uranium
2910	Radioactive material, articles manufactured from depleted Uranium
2910	Radioactive material, articles manufactured from natural Thorium
2910	Radioactive material, excepted package, empty packaging
2910	Radioactive material, excepted package, instruments or articles
2910	Radioactive material, excepted package, limited quantity of material
2910	Radioactive material, limited quantity, n.o.s.
2911	Radioactive material, excepted package, instruments or articles
2911	Radioactive material, instruments or articles

POTENTIAL HAZARDS

FIRE OR EXPLOSION

- Some of these materials may burn, but none ignite readily.
- Many have cardboard outer packaging; content (physically large or small) can be of many different physical forms.
- Radioactivity does not change flammability or other properties of materials.

HEALTH

- Radiation presents minimal risk to transport workers, emergency response personnel, and the public during transportation accidents. Packaging durability increases as potential hazard of radioactive content increases.
- Very low levels of contained radioactive materials and low radiation levels outside packages result in low risks to people. Damaged packages may release measurable amounts of radioactive material, but the resulting risks are expected to be low.
- Some radioactive materials cannot be detected by commonly available instruments.
- Packages do not have RADIOACTIVE I, II, or III labels. Some may have EMPTY labels or may have the word "Radioactive" in the package marking.

PUBLIC SAFETY

- **CALL Emergency Response Telephone Number on Shipping Paper first. If Shipping Paper is not available or there is no answer, refer to telephone numbers listed on page 613.**
- **Priorities for rescue, life-saving, first aid, fire control, and other hazards are higher than the priority for measuring radiation levels.**
- Radiation Authority must be notified of accident conditions. Radiation Authority is usually responsible for decisions about radiological consequences and closure of emergencies.
- As an immediate precautionary measure, isolate spill or leak area for at least 25 meters (75 feet) in all directions.
- Stay upwind.
- Keep unauthorized personnel away.
- Detain or isolate uninjured persons or equipment suspected to be contaminated; delay decontamination and cleanup until instructions are received from Radiation Authority.

PROTECTIVE CLOTHING

- Positive pressure self-contained breathing apparatus (SCBA) and structural firefighters' protective clothing will provide adequate protection.

EVACUATION

Large Spill

- Consider initial downwind evacuation for at least 100 meters (330 feet)

Fire

- When a large quantity of this material is involved in a major fire, consider an initial evacuation distance of 300 meters (1000 feet) in all directions.

EMERGENCY RESPONSE
FIRE

- Presence of radioactive material will not influence the fire control processes and should not influence selection of techniques.
- Move containers from fire area if you can do so without risk.
- DO NOT move damaged packages; move undamaged packages out of fire zone.

Small Fires

- Dry chemical, CO_2, water spray, or regular foam.

Large Fires

- Water spray, fog (flooding amounts).

Hazmat

SPILL OR LEAK

- DO NOT touch damaged packages or spilled material.
- Cover liquid with sand, earth, or other non-combustible absorbent material.
- Cover powder spill with plastic sheet or tarp to minimize spreading.

FIRST AID

- Medical problems take priority over radiological concerns.
- Use first aid treatment according to the nature of the injury.
- DO NOT delay care and transport of a seriously injured person.
- Give artificial respiration if victim is not breathing.
- Administer oxygen if breathing is difficult.
- In case of contact with substance, immediately flush skin or eyes with running water for at least 20 minutes.
- Injured persons contaminated by contact with released material are not a serious hazard to health care personnel, equipment, or facilities.
- Ensure that medical personnel are aware of the material(s) involved, take precautions to protect themselves, and prevent spread of contamination.

Guide 162: Radioactive Materials (Low to Moderate Level Radiation)

SUBSTANCES INCLUDED

2912	Radioactive material, low specific activity (LSA), n.o.s.
2912	Radioactive material, low specific activity (LSA-I)
2913	Radioactive material, surface contaminated objects (SCO)
2913	Radioactive material, surface contaminated objects (SCO-I)
2913	Radioactive material, surface contaminated objects (SCO-II)
2975	Thorium metal, pyrophoric
2976	Thorium nitrate, solid
2979	Uranium metal, pyrophoric
2980	Uranium nitrate, hexahydrate, solution
2980	Uranyl nitrate, hexahydrate, solution
2981	Uranyl nitrate, solid
3321	Radioactive material, low specific activity (LSA-II)
3322	Radioactive material, low specific activity (LSA-III)

POTENTIAL HAZARDS

FIRE OR EXPLOSION

- Some of these materials may burn, but none ignite readily.
- Uranium and Thorium metal cuttings may ignite spontaneously if exposed to air (see Guide 136).
- Nitrates are oxidizers and may ignite other combustibles (see Guide 141).

HEALTH

- Radiation presents minimal risk to transport workers, emergency response personnel, and the public during transportation accidents. Packaging durability increases as potential hazard of radioactive content increases.
- Undamaged packages are safe. Contents of damaged packages may cause higher external radiation exposure, or both external and internal radiation exposure if contents are released.
- Low radiation hazard when material is inside container. If material is released from package or bulk container, hazard will vary from low to moderate. Level of hazard will depend on the type and amount of radioactivity, the kind of material it is in, and/or the surfaces it is on.
- Some materials may be released from packages during accidents of moderate severity but risks to people are not great.
- Released radioactive materials or contaminated objects usually will be visible if packaging fails.
- Some exclusive use shipments of bulk and packaged materials will not have "RADIOACTIVE" labels. Placards, markings, and shipping papers provide identification.
- Some packages may have a "RADIOACTIVE" label and a second hazard label. The second hazard is usually greater than the radiation hazard; so follow this GUIDE as well as the response GUIDE for the second hazard class label.

Hazmat

- Some radioactive materials cannot be detected by commonly available instruments.
- Runoff from control of cargo fire may cause low-level pollution.

PUBLIC SAFETY

- **CALL Emergency Response Telephone Number on Shipping Paper first. If Shipping Paper is not available or there is no answer, refer to telephone numbers listed on page 613.**
- **Priorities for rescue, life-saving, first aid, fire control, and other hazards are higher than the priority for measuring radiation levels.**
- Radiation Authority must be notified of accident conditions. Radiation Authority is usually responsible for decisions about radiological consequences and closure of emergencies.
- As an immediate precautionary measure, isolate spill or leak area for at least 25 meters (75 feet) in all directions.
- Stay upwind.
- Keep unauthorized personnel away.
- Detain or isolate uninjured persons or equipment suspected to be contaminated; delay decontamination and cleanup until instructions are received from Radiation Authority.

PROTECTIVE CLOTHING

- Positive pressure self-contained breathing apparatus (SCBA) and structural firefighters' protective clothing will provide adequate protection.

EVACUATION

Large Spill
- Consider initial downwind evacuation for at least 100 m (330 ft).

Fire
- When a large quantity of this material is involved in a major fire, consider an initial evacuation distance of 300 meters (1000 feet) in all directions.

EMERGENCY RESPONSE

FIRE

- Presence of radioactive material will not influence the fire control processes and should not influence selection of techniques.
- Move containers from fire area if you can do so without risk.
- DO NOT move damaged packages; move undamaged packages out of fire zone.

Small Fires
- Dry chemical, CO_2, water spray, or regular foam.

Large Fires
- Water spray, fog (flooding amounts).
- Dike fire-control water for later disposal.

SPILL OR LEAK

- DO NOT touch damaged packages or spilled material.
- Cover liquid with sand, earth, or other non-combustible absorbent material.
- Dike to collect large liquid spills
- Cover powder spill with plastic sheet or tarp to minimize spreading.

FIRST AID

- Medical problems take priority over radiological concerns.
- Use first aid treatment according to the nature of the injury.
- DO NOT delay care and transport of a seriously injured person.
- Give artificial respiration if victim is not breathing.
- Administer oxygen if breathing is difficult.
- In case of contact with substance, immediately flush skin or eyes with running water for at least 20 minutes.
- Injured persons contaminated by contact with released material are not a serious hazard to health care personnel, equipment, or facilities.
- Ensure that medical personnel are aware of the material(s) involved, take precautions to protect themselves, and prevent spread of contamination.

Hazmat

Guide 163: Radioactive Materials (Low to High Level Radiation)

SUBSTANCES INCLUDED

2915 Radioactive material, Type A package
2916 Radioactive material, Type B(U) package
2917 Radioactive material, Type B(M) package
2919 Radioactive material, transported under special arrangement
2982 Radioactive material, n.o.s.
3323 Radioactive material, Type C package

POTENTIAL HAZARDS

FIRE OR EXPLOSION

- Some of these materials may burn, but none ignite readily.
- Radioactivity does not change flammability or other properties of materials.
- Type B packages are designed and evaluated to withstand total engulfment in flames at temperatures of 800°C (1475°F) for a period of 30 minutes.

HEALTH

- Radiation presents minimal risk to transport workers, emergency response personnel, and the public during transportation accidents. Packaging durability increases as potential hazard of radioactive content increases.
- Undamaged packages are safe. Contents of damaged packages may cause higher external radiation exposure, or both external and internal radiation exposure if contents are released.
- Type A packages (cartons, boxes, drums, articles, etc.) identified as "Type A" by marking on packages or by shipping papers contain non-life endangering amounts. Partial releases might be expected if "Type A" packages are damaged in moderately severe accidents.
- Type B packages, and the rarely occurring Type C packages, (large and small, usually metal) contain the most hazardous amounts. They can be identified by package markings or by shipping papers. Life threatening conditions may exist only if contents are released or package shielding fails. Because of design, evaluation and testing of packages, these conditions would be expected only for accidents of utmost severity.
- The rarely occurring "Special Arrangement" shipments may be of Type A, Type B, or Type C packages. Package type will be marked on packages, and shipment details will be on shipping papers.
- Radioactive White-I labels indicate radiation levels outside single, isolated, undamaged packages are very low (less than 0.005 mSv/h (0.5 mrem/h)).
- Radioactive Yellow-II and Yellow-III labeled packages have higher radiation levels. The transport index (TI) on the label

identified the maximum radiation level in mrem/h one meter from a single, isolated, undamaged package.
- Some radioactive materials cannot be detected by commonly available instruments.
- Water from cargo fire control may cause pollution.

PUBLIC SAFETY

- **CALL Emergency Response Telephone Number on Shipping Paper first. If Shipping Paper is not available or there is no answer, refer to telephone numbers listed on page 613.**
- **Priorities for rescue, life-saving, first aid, fire control, and other hazards are higher than the priority for measuring radiation levels.**
- Radiation Authority must be notified of accident conditions. Radiation Authority is usually responsible for decisions about radiological consequences and closure of emergencies.
- As an immediate precautionary measure, isolate spill or leak area for at least 25 meters (75 feet) in all directions.
- Stay upwind.
- Keep unauthorized personnel away.
- Detain or isolate uninjured persons or equipment suspected to be contaminated; delay decontamination and cleanup until instructions are received from Radiation Authority.

PROTECTIVE CLOTHING

- Positive pressure self-contained breathing apparatus (SCBA) and structural firefighters' protective clothing will provide adequate protection against internal radiation exposure, but not external radiation exposure.

EVACUATION

Large Spill
- Consider initial downwind evacuation for at least 100 m (330 ft).

Fire
- When a large quantity of this material is involved in a major fire, consider an initial evacuation distance of 300 meters (1000 feet) in all directions.

EMERGENCY RESPONSE
FIRE

- Presence of radioactive material will not influence the fire control processes and should not influence selection of techniques.
- Move containers from fire area if you can do so without risk.
- DO NOT move damaged packages; move undamaged packages out of fire zone.

Small Fires
- Dry chemical, CO_2, water spray, or regular foam.

Large Fires
- Water spray, fog (flooding amounts).
- Dike fire-control water for later disposal.

SPILL OR LEAK
- DO NOT touch damaged packages or spilled material.
- Damp surfaces on undamaged or slightly damaged packages are seldom an indication of packaging failure. Most packaging for liquid content have inner containers and/or inner absorbent materials.
- Cover liquid spill with sand, earth, or other non-combustible absorbent material.

FIRST AID
- Medical problems take priority over radiological concerns.
- Use first aid treatment according to the nature of the injury.
- DO NOT delay care and transport of a seriously injured person.
- Give artificial respiration if victim is not breathing.
- Administer oxygen if breathing is difficult.
- In case of contact with substance, immediately flush skin or eyes with running water for at least 20 minutes.
- Injured persons contaminated by contact with released material are not a serious hazard to health care personnel, equipment, or facilities.
- Ensure that medical personnel are aware of the material(s) involved, take precautions to protect themselves, and prevent spread of contamination.

Guide 164: Radioactive Materials(Special Form/ Low to High Level Radiation)

SUBSTANCES INCLUDED

2974 Radioactive material, special form, n.o.s.
3332 Radioactive material, Type A package, special form

POTENTIAL HAZARDS

FIRE OR EXPLOSION

- Packaging can burn completely without risk of content loss from sealed source capsule.
- Radioactivity does not change flammability or other properties of materials.
- Radioactive source capsules and Type B packages are designed and evaluated to withstand total engulfment in flames at temperature of 800°C (1475°F).

HEALTH

- Radiation presents minimal risk to transport workers, emergency response personnel, and the public during transportation accidents. Packaging durability increases as potential hazard of radioactive content increases.
- Undamaged packages are safe; contents of damaged packages may cause external radiation exposure, and much higher external exposure if contents (source capsules) are released.
- Contamination and internal radiation hazards are not expected, but not impossible.
- Type A packages (cartons, boxes, drums, articles, etc.) identified as "Type A" by marking on packages or by shipping papers contain non-life endangering amounts. Radioactive sources may be released if "Type A" packages are damaged in moderately severe accidents.
- Type B packages, and the rarely occurring Type C packages, (large and small, usually metal) contain the most hazardous amounts. They can be identified by package markings or by shipping papers. Life threatening conditions may exist only if contents are released or package shielding fails. Because of design, evaluation and testing of packages, these conditions would be expected only for accidents of utmost severity.
- Radioactive White-I labels indicate radiation levels outside single, isolated, undamaged packages are very low (less than 0.005 mSv/h (0.5 mrem/h)).
- Radioactive Yellow-II and Yellow-III labeled packages have higher radiation levels. The transport index (TI) on the label identified the maximum radiation level in mrem/h one meter from a single, isolated, undamaged package.
- Radiation from the package contents, usually in durable metal capsules, can be detected by most radiation instruments.
- Water from cargo fire control is not expected to cause pollution.

PUBLIC SAFETY

- **CALL Emergency Response Telephone Number on Shipping Paper first. If Shipping Paper is not available or there is no answer, refer to telephone numbers listed on page 613.**
- **Priorities for rescue, life-saving, first aid, fire control, and other hazards are higher than the priority for measuring radiation levels.**
- Radiation Authority must be notified of accident conditions. Radiation Authority is usually responsible for decisions about radiological consequences and closure of emergencies.
- As an immediate precautionary measure, isolate spill or leak area for at least 25 meters (75 feet) in all directions.
- Stay upwind.
- Keep unauthorized personnel away.
- Delay final cleanup until instructions or advice is received from Radiation Authority.

PROTECTIVE CLOTHING

- Positive pressure self-contained breathing apparatus (SCBA) and structural firefighters' protective clothing will provide adequate protection against internal radiation exposure, but not external radiation exposure.

EVACUATION

Large Spill

- Consider initial downwind evacuation for at least 100 m (330 ft).

Fire

- When a large quantity of this material is involved in a major fire, consider an initial evacuation distance of 300 meters (1000 feet) in all directions.

EMERGENCY RESPONSE

FIRE

- Presence of radioactive material will not influence the fire control processes and should not influence selection of techniques.
- Move containers from fire area if you can do so without risk.
- DO NOT move damaged packages; move undamaged packages out of fire zone.

Small Fires

- Dry chemical, CO_2, water spray, or regular foam.

Large Fires

- Water spray, fog (flooding amounts).

Hazmat

SPILL OR LEAK

- DO NOT touch damaged packages or spilled material.
- Damp surfaces on undamaged or slightly damaged packages are seldom an indication of packaging failure. Contents are seldom liquid. Content is usually a metal capsule, easily seen if released from package.
- If source capsule is identified as being out of package, **DO NOT TOUCH.** Stay away and await advice from Radiation Authority.

FIRST AID

- Medical problems take priority over radiological concerns.
- Use first aid treatment according to the nature of the injury.
- DO NOT delay care and transport of a seriously injured person.
- Persons exposed to special form sources are not likely to be contaminated with radioactive material.
- Give artificial respiration if victim is not breathing.
- Administer oxygen if breathing is difficult.
- Injured persons contaminated by contact with released material are not a serious hazard to health care personnel, equipment, or facilities.
- Ensure that medical personnel are aware of the material(s) involved, take precautions to protect themselves, and prevent spread of contamination.

Hazmat

Guide 165: Radioactive Materials
(Fissile/Low to High Level Radiation)

SUBSTANCES INCLUDED

2918 Radioactive material, fissile, n.o.s.
3324 Radioactive material, low specific activity (LSA-II), fissile
3325 Radioactive material, low specific activity (LSA-III), fissile
3326 Radioactive material, surface contaminated objects (SCO-I), fissile
3326 Radioactive material, surface contaminated objects (SCO-II), fissile
3327 Radioactive material, Type A package, fissile
3328 Radioactive material, Type B(U) package, fissile
3329 Radioactive material, Type B(M) package, fissile
3330 Radioactive material, Type C package, fissile
3331 Radioactive material, transported under special arrangement, fissile
3333 Radioactive material, Type A package, special form, fissile

POTENTIAL HAZARDS
FIRE OR EXPLOSION

- These materials are seldom flammable. Packages are designed to withstand fires without damage to contents.
- Radioactivity does not change flammability or other properties of materials.
- Type AF, IF, B(U)F, B(M)F, and CF packages are designed and evaluated to withstand total engulfment in flames at temperatures of 800°C (1475°F) for a period of 30 minutes.

HEALTH

- Radiation presents minimal risk to transport workers, emergency response personnel, and the public during transportation accidents. Packaging durability increases as potential hazard of radioactive content increases.
- Undamaged packages are safe. Contents of damaged packages may cause external radiation exposure, or both external and internal radiation exposure if contents are released.
- Type AF or IF packages, identified by package markings, do not contain life-threatening amounts of material. External radiation levels are low and packages are designed, evaluated, and tested to control releases and to prevent a fission chain reaction under severe transport conditions.
- Type B(U)F, B(M)F, and CF packages (identified by markings on packages or shipping papers) contain potentially life endangering amounts. Because of design, evaluation and testing of packages, fission chain reactions are prevented and releases are not expected to be life endangering for all accidents except those of utmost severity.
- The rarely occurring "Special Arrangement" shipments may be of Type AF, BF, or CF packages. Package type will be marked on packages, and shipment details will be on shipping papers.
- The transport index (TI) shown on labels or a shipping paper might not indicate the radiation level at one meter from a single, isolated, undamaged package; instead, it might relate to

controls needed during transport because of the fissile properties of the materials. Alternatively, the fissile nature of the contents may be indicated by a criticality safety index (CSI) on a special FISSILE label or on the shipping paper.
- Some radioactive materials cannot be detected by commonly available instruments.
- Water from cargo fire control is not expected to cause pollution.

PUBLIC SAFETY

- CALL Emergency Response Telephone Number on Shipping Paper first. If Shipping Paper is not available or there is no answer, refer to telephone numbers listed on page 613.
- Priorities for rescue, life-saving, first aid, fire control, and other hazards are higher than the priority for measuring radiation levels.
- Radiation Authority must be notified of accident conditions. Radiation Authority is usually responsible for decisions about radiological consequences and closure of emergencies.
- As an immediate precautionary measure, isolate spill or leak area for at least 25 meters (75 feet) in all directions.
- Stay upwind.
- Keep unauthorized personnel away.
- Delay final cleanup until instructions or advice is received from Radiation Authority.

PROTECTIVE CLOTHING

- Positive pressure self-contained breathing apparatus (SCBA) and structural firefighters' protective clothing will provide adequate protection against internal radiation exposure, but not external radiation exposure.

EVACUATION

Large Spill
- Consider initial downwind evacuation for at least 100 meters (330 feet)

Fire
- When a large quantity of this material is involved in a major fire, consider an initial evacuation distance of 300 meters (1000 feet) in all directions.

EMERGENCY RESPONSE

FIRE

- Presence of radioactive material will not influence the fire control processes and should not influence selection of techniques.
- Move containers from fire area if you can do so without risk.
- DO NOT move damaged packages; move undamaged packages out of fire zone.

Small Fires

• Dry chemical, CO_2, water spray, or regular foam.

Large Fires

• Water spray, fog (flooding amounts).

SPILL OR LEAK

• DO NOT touch damaged packages or spilled material.
• Damp surfaces on undamaged or slightly damaged packages are seldom an indication of packaging failure. Most packaging for liquid content have inner containers and/or inner absorbent materials.

Liquid Spills

• Package contents are seldom liquid. If any radioactive contamination resulting from a liquid release is present, it probably will be low-level.

FIRST AID

• Medical problems take priority over radiological concerns.
• Use first aid treatment according to the nature of the injury.
• DO NOT delay care and transport of a seriously injured person.
• Give artificial respiration if victim is not breathing.
• Administer oxygen if breathing is difficult.
• In case of contact with substance, immediately flush skin or eyes with running water for at least 20 minutes.
• Injured persons contaminated by contact with released material are not a serious hazard to health care personnel, equipment, or facilities.
• Ensure that medical personnel are aware of the material(s) involved, take precautions to protect themselves, and prevent spread of contamination.

Hazmat

Guide 166: Radioactive Materials - Corrosive
(Uranium Hexafluoride/Water-Sensitive)

SUBSTANCES INCLUDED

2977 Radioactive material, Uranium hexafluoride, fissile
2977 Uranium hexafluoride, fissile containing > 1% Uranium-235
2978 Radioactive material, Uranium hexafluoride
2978 Radioactive material, Uranium hexafluoride, non-fissile or fissile excepted
2978 Uranium hexafluoride
2978 Uranium hexafluoride, fissile excepted
2978 Uranium hexafluoride, low specific activity
2978 Uranium hexafluoride, non-fissile

POTENTIAL HAZARDS
FIRE OR EXPLOSION

- Substance does not burn.
- The material may react violently with fuels.
- Containers in protective overpacks (horizontal cylindrical shape with short legs for tie-downs), are identified with "AF", "B(U)F", or "H(U)" on shipping papers or by markings on the overpacks. They are designed and evaluated to withstand severe conditions including total engulfment in flames at temperatures of 800°C (1475°F).
- Bare filled cylinders, identified with UN2978 as part of the marking (may also be marked H(U) or H(M)), may rupture in heat of engulfing fire; bare empty (except for residue) cylinders will not rupture in fires.
- Radioactivity does not change flammability or other properties of materials.

HEALTH

- Radiation presents minimal risk to transport workers, emergency response personnel, and the public during transportation accidents. Packaging durability increases as potential hazard of radioactive content increases.
- Chemical hazard greatly exceeds radiation hazard.
- Substance reacts with water and water vapor in air to form toxic and corrosive hydrogen fluoride gas and an extremely irritating and corrosive, white-colored, water-soluble residue.
- If inhaled, may be fatal.
- Direct contact causes burns to skin, eyes, and respiratory tract.
- Low-level radioactive material; very low radiation hazard to people.
- Runoff from control of cargo fire may cause low-level pollution.

PUBLIC SAFETY

- **CALL Emergency Response Telephone Number on Shipping Paper first. If Shipping Paper is not available or there is no answer, refer to telephone numbers listed on page 613.**

Hazmat

- **Priorities for rescue, life-saving, first aid, fire control, and other hazards are higher than the priority for measuring radiation levels.**
- Radiation Authority must be notified of accident conditions. Radiation Authority is usually responsible for decisions about radiological consequences and closure of emergencies.
- As an immediate precautionary measure, isolate spill or leak area for at least 25 meters (75 feet) in all directions.
- Stay upwind.
- Keep unauthorized personnel away.
- Delay final cleanup until instructions or advice is received from Radiation Authority.

PROTECTIVE CLOTHING

- Wear positive pressure self-contained breathing apparatus (SCBA).
- Wear chemical protective clothing that is specifically recommended by the manufacturer. It may provide little or no thermal protection.
- Structural firefighters' protective clothing provides limited protection in fire situations ONLY; it is not effective in spill situations where direct contact with the substance is possible.

EVACUATION

Large Spill
- See the Table of Initial Isolation and Protective Action Distances (page 908).

Fire
- When a large quantity of this material is involved in a major fire, consider an initial evacuation distance of 300 meters (1000 feet) in all directions.

EMERGENCY RESPONSE
FIRE

- DO NOT use water or foam on the material itself.
- Move containers from fire area if you can do so without risk.

Small Fires
- Dry chemical or CO_2.

Large Fires
- Water spray, fog, or regular foam.
- Cool containers with flooding quantities of water until well after fire is out.
- If this is impossible, withdraw from area and let fire burn.
- Always stay away from tanks engulfed in fire.

SPILL OR LEAK

- DO NOT touch damaged packages or spilled material.
- Without fire or smoke, leak will be evident by visible and irritating vapors and residue forming at the point of release.
- Use fine water spray to reduce vapors; DO NOT put water directly on point of material release from container.
- Residue buildup may self-seal small leaks.
- Dike far ahead of spill to collect runoff water.

Liquid Spills

- Package contents are seldom liquid. If any radioactive contamination resulting from a liquid release is present, it probably will be low-level.

FIRST AID

- Medical problems take priority over radiological concerns.
- Use first aid treatment according to the nature of the injury.
- DO NOT delay care and transport of a seriously injured person.
- Give artificial respiration if victim is not breathing.
- Administer oxygen if breathing is difficult.
- In case of contact with substance, immediately flush skin or eyes with running water for at least 20 minutes.
- Effects of exposure (inhalation, ingestion, or skin contact) to substance may be delayed.
- Injured persons contaminated by contact with released material are not a serious hazard to health care personnel, equipment, or facilities.
- Ensure that medical personnel are aware of the material(s) involved, take precautions to protect themselves, and prevent spread of contamination.

Hazmat

Guide 167: Fluorine (Refrigerated Liquid)

SUBSTANCES INCLUDED

9192 Fluorine, refrigerated liquid (cryogenic liquid)

POTENTIAL HAZARDS

FIRE OR EXPLOSION

- Substance does not burn but will support combustion.
- This is a strong oxidizer and will react vigorously or explosively with many materials including fuels.
- May ignite combustibles (wood, paper, oil, clothing, etc.).
- Vapor explosion and poison hazard indoors, outdoors, or in sewers.
- Containers may explode when heated.
- Ruptured cylinders may rocket.

HEALTH

- **TOXIC; may be fatal if inhaled.**
- Vapors are extremely irritating.
- Contact with gas or liquefied gas will cause burns, severe injury and/or frostbite.
- Vapors from liquefied gas are initially heavier than air and spread along ground.
- Runoff from fire control may cause pollution.

PUBLIC SAFETY

- **CALL Emergency Response Telephone Number on Shipping Paper first. If Shipping Paper is not available or there is no answer, refer to telephone numbers listed on page 613.**
- As an immediate precautionary measure, isolate spill or leak area for at least 100 m (330 ft) in all directions.
- Stay upwind.
- Many gases are heavier than air and will spread along ground and collect in low or confined areas (sewers, basements, tanks).
- Keep out of low areas.
- Ventilate closed spaces before entering.

PROTECTIVE CLOTHING

- Wear positive pressure self-contained breathing apparatus (SCBA).
- Wear chemical protective clothing that is specifically recommended by the manufacturer. It may provide little or no thermal protection.
- Structural firefighters' protective clothing provides limited protection in fire situations ONLY; it is not effective in spill situations where direct contact with the substance is possible.
- Always wear thermal protective clothing when handling refrigerated/cryogenic liquids.

EVACUATION

Large Spill
- See the Table of Initial Isolation and Protective Action Distances (page 908).

Fire
- If tank, rail car, or tank truck is involved in a fire, ISOLATE for 1600 meters (1 mile) in all directions; also, consider initial evacuation for 1600 meters (1 mile) in all directions.

EMERGENCY RESPONSE
FIRE

Small Fires
- Dry chemical, soda ash, lime, or sand.

Large Fires
- Water spray, fog (flooding amounts).
- DO NOT get water inside containers.
- Move containers from fire area if you can do it without risk.

Fire Involving Tanks
- Fight fire from maximum distance or use unmanned hose holders or monitor nozzles.
- Cool containers with flooding quantities of water until well after fire is out.
- DO NOT direct water at source of leak or safety devices; icing may occur.
- Withdraw immediately in case of rising sound from venting safety devices or discoloration of tank.
- Always stay away from tanks engulfed in fire.
- For massive fire, use unmanned hose holders or monitor nozzles; if this is impossible, withdraw from area and let fire burn.

SPILL OR LEAK
- DO NOT touch or walk through spilled material.
- If you have not donned special protective clothing approved for this material, DO NOT expose yourself to any risk of this material touching you.
- DO NOT direct water at spill or source of leak.
- A fine water spray remotely directed to the edge of the spill pool can be used to direct and maintain a hot flare fire which will burn the spilled material in a controlled manner.
- Keep combustibles (wood, paper, oil, etc.) away from spilled material.
- Stop leak if you can do it without risk.
- Use water spray to reduce vapors or divert vapor cloud drift. Avoid allowing water runoff to contact spilled material.
- If possible, turn leaking containers so that gas escapes rather than liquid.

Hazmat

- Prevent entry into waterways, sewers, basements, or confined areas.
- Isolate area until gas has dispersed.
- Ventilate the area.

FIRST AID

- Move victim to fresh air.
- Call 911 or emergency medical service.
- Give artificial respiration if victim is not breathing.
- Administer oxygen if breathing is difficult.
- Clothing frozen to the skin should be thawed before being removed.
- Remove and isolate contaminated clothing and shoes.
- In case of contact with substance, immediately flush skin or eyes with running water for at least 20 minutes.
- Keep victim warm and quiet.
- Keep victim under observation.
- Effects of contact or inhalation may be delayed.
- Ensure that medical personnel are aware of the material(s) involved, and take precautions to protect themselves.

Hazmat

Guide 168: Carbon Monoxide (Refrigerated Liquid)

SUBSTANCES INCLUDED

9202   Carbon monoxide, refrigerated liquid (cryogenic liquid)

POTENTIAL HAZARDS

FIRE OR EXPLOSION

- **EXTREMELY FLAMMABLE.**
- May be ignited by heat, sparks, or flames.
- Flame may be invisible.
- Containers may explode when heated.
- Vapor explosion and poison hazard indoors, outdoors, in sewers.
- Vapors from liquefied gas are initially heavier than air and spread along ground.
- Vapors may travel to source of ignition and flash back.
- Runoff may create fire or explosion hazard.

HEALTH

- **TOXIC; extremely hazardous.**
- Inhalation extremely dangerous; may be fatal.
- Contact with gas or liquefied gas will cause burns, severe injury and/or frostbite.
- Odorless, will not be detected by sense of smell.

PUBLIC SAFETY

- **CALL Emergency Response Telephone Number on Shipping Paper first. If Shipping Paper is not available or there is no answer, refer to telephone numbers listed on page 613.**
- As an immediate precautionary measure, isolate spill or leak area for at least 100 meters (330 feet) in all directions.
- Keep unauthorized personnel away.
- Stay upwind.
- Many gases are heavier than air and will spread along ground and collect in low or confined areas (sewers, basements, tanks).
- Keep out of low areas.
- Ventilate closed spaces before entering.

PROTECTIVE CLOTHING

- Wear positive pressure self-contained breathing apparatus (SCBA).
- Wear chemical protective clothing that is specifically recommended by the manufacturer. It may provide little or no thermal protection.
- Structural firefighters' protective clothing provides limited protection in fire situations ONLY; it is not effective in spill situations where direct contact with the substance is possible.
- Always wear thermal protective clothing when handling refrigerated/cryogenic liquids.

Pocket Partner   891

EVACUATION

Large Spill
- See the Table of Initial Isolation and Protective Action Distances (page 908).

Fire
- If tank, rail car, or tank truck is involved in a fire, ISOLATE for 800 meters (½ mile) in all directions; also, consider initial evacuation for 800 meters (½ mile) in all directions.

EMERGENCY RESPONSE

FIRE

- **DO NOT extinguish a leaking gas fire unless leak can be stopped.**

Small Fires
- Dry chemical, CO_2, or water spray.

Large Fires
- Water spray, fog, or regular foam.
- Move containers from fire area if you can do it without risk.

Fire Involving Tanks
- Fight fire from maximum distance or use unmanned hose holders or monitor nozzles.
- Cool containers with flooding quantities of water until well after fire is out.
- DO NOT direct water at source of leak or safety devices; icing may occur.
- Withdraw immediately in case of rising sound from venting safety devices or discoloration of tank.
- Always stay away from tanks engulfed in fire.

SPILL OR LEAK

- Eliminate all ignition sources (no smoking, flares, sparks, or flames in immediate area).
- All equipment used when handling the product must be grounded.
- Fully encapsulating, vapor protective clothing should be worn for spills and leaks with no fire.
- DO NOT touch or walk through spilled material.
- Stop leak if you can do it without risk.
- Use water spray to reduce vapors or divert vapor cloud drift. Avoid allowing water runoff to contact spilled material.
- DO NOT direct water at spill or source of leak.
- If possible, turn leaking containers so that gas escapes rather than liquid.
- Prevent entry into waterways, sewers, basements, or confined areas.
- Isolate area until gas has dispersed.

Hazmat

FIRST AID

- Move victim to fresh air.
- Call 911 or emergency medical service.
- Give artificial respiration if victim is not breathing.
- Administer oxygen if breathing is difficult.
- Remove and isolate contaminated clothing and shoes.
- In case of contact with substance, immediately flush skin or eyes with running water for at least 20 minutes.
- Keep victim warm and quiet.
- Keep victim under observation.
- Effects of contact or inhalation may be delayed.
- Ensure that medical personnel are aware of the material(s) involved, and take precautions to protect themselves.

Hazmat

Guide 169: Aluminum (Molten)

SUBSTANCES INCLUDED

9260 Aluminum, molten

POTENTIAL HAZARDS

FIRE OR EXPLOSION

- Substance is transported in molten form at a temperature above 705°C (1300°F).
- Violent reaction with water; contact may cause an explosion or may produce a flammable gas.
- Will ignite combustible materials (wood, paper, oil, debris, etc.).
- Contact with nitrates or other oxidizers may cause an explosion.
- Contact with containers or other materials, including cold, wet, or dirty tools, may cause an explosion.
- Contact with concrete will cause spalling and small pops.

HEALTH

- Contact causes severe burns to skin and eyes.
- Fire may produce irritating or toxic gases.

PUBLIC SAFETY

- **CALL Emergency Response Telephone Number on Shipping Paper first. If Shipping Paper is not available or there is no answer, refer to telephone numbers listed on page 613.**
- As an immediate precautionary measure, isolate spill or leak area for at least 50 meters (150 feet) in all directions.
- Keep unauthorized personnel away.
- Ventilate closed spaces before entering.

PROTECTIVE CLOTHING

- Wear positive pressure self-contained breathing apparatus (SCBA).
- Wear flame retardant structural firefighters' protective clothing, including faceshield, helmet, and gloves; this will provide limited thermal protection.

EMERGENCY RESPONSE

FIRE

- **DO NOT use water, except in life threatening situations and then only in a fine spray.**
- **DO NOT use halogenated extinguishing agents or foam.**
- Move combustibles out of path of advancing pool if you can do so without risk.
- Extinguish fires started by molten material by using appropriate method for the burning material; keep water, halogenated extinguishing agents, and foam away from the molten material.

Hazmat

SPILL OR LEAK

- DO NOT touch or walk through spilled material.
- DO NOT attempt to stop leak, due to danger of explosion.
- Keep combustibles (wood, paper, oil, etc.) away from spilled material.
- Substance is very fluid, spreads quickly, and may splash. DO NOT try to stop it with shovels or other objects.
- Dike far ahead of spill; use dry sand to contain the flow of material.
- Where possible, allow molten material to solidify naturally.
- Avoid contact even after material solidifies. Molten, heated and cold aluminum look alike; DO NOT touch unless you know it is cold.
- Clean up under supervision of an expert after material has solidified.

FIRST AID

- Move victim to fresh air.
- Call 911 or emergency medical service.
- Give artificial respiration if victim is not breathing.
- Administer oxygen if breathing is difficult.
- For severe burns, immediate medical attention is required.
- Removal of solidified molten material from skin requires medical assistance.
- Remove and isolate contaminated clothing and shoes.
- In case of contact with substance, immediately flush skin or eyes with running water for at least 20 minutes.
- Keep victim warm and quiet.

Hazmat

Guide 170: Metals (Powders, Dusts, Shavings, Borings, Turnings, or Cuttings, etc.)

SUBSTANCES INCLUDED

1308	Zirconium metal, liquid, suspension
1308	Zirconium suspended in a flammable liquid
1309	Aluminum powder, coated
1323	Ferrocerium
1326	Hafnium powder, wetted with $\geq$ 25% water
1333	Cerium, slabs, ingots or rods
1346	Silicon powder, amorphous
1352	Titanium powder, wetted with $\geq$ 25% water
1358	Zirconium metal, powder, wet
1358	Zirconium powder, wetted with $\geq$ 25% water
1378	Metal catalyst, wetted
1871	Titanium hydride
2793	Ferrous metal borings, shavings, turnings, or cuttings
2858	Zirconium, dry, coiled wire, finished metal sheets or strips
2871	Antimony powder
2878	Titanium sponge granules; Titanium sponge powders
3089	Metal powder, flammable, n.o.s.
3182	Metal hydrides, flammable, n.o.s.

POTENTIAL HAZARDS

FIRE OR EXPLOSION

- May react violently or explosively on contact with water.
- Some are transported in flammable liquids.
- May be ignited by friction, heat, sparks, or flames.
- Some of these materials will burn with intense heat.
- Dusts or fumes may form explosive mixtures in air.
- Containers may explode when heated.
- May re-ignite after fire is extinguished.

HEALTH

- Oxides from metallic fires are a severe health hazard.
- Inhalation or contact with substance or decomposition products may cause severe injury or death.
- Fire may produce irritating, corrosive, or toxic gases.
- Runoff from fire control or dilution water may cause pollution.

PUBLIC SAFETY

- **CALL Emergency Response Telephone Number on Shipping Paper first. If Shipping Paper is not available or there is no answer, refer to telephone numbers listed on page 613.**
- As an immediate precautionary measure, isolate spill or leak area for at least 50 meters (150 feet) in all directions.
- Stay upwind.
- Keep unauthorized personnel away.

PROTECTIVE CLOTHING

- Wear positive pressure self-contained breathing apparatus (SCBA).
- Structural firefighters' protective clothing will only provide limited protection.

EVACUATION

Large Spill
- Consider initial downwind evacuation for at least 50 m (160 ft).

Fire
- If tank, rail car, or tank truck is involved in a fire, ISOLATE for 800 meters (½ mile) in all directions; also, consider initial evacuation for 800 meters (½ mile) in all directions.

EMERGENCY RESPONSE

FIRE

- **DO NOT use water, foam, or CO_2.**
- Dousing metallic fires with water may generate hydrogen gas, an extremely dangerous explosion hazard, particularly if fire is in a confined environment (i.e. building, cargo hold, etc.).
- Use DRY sand, graphite powder, dry sodium chloride based extinguishers, G-1® or Met-L-X® powder.
- Confining and smothering metal fires is preferable rather than applying water.
- Move containers from fire area if you can do it without risk.

Fire Involving Tanks
- If impossible to extinguish, protect surroundings and allow fire to burn itself out.

SPILL OR LEAK

- Eliminate all ignition sources (no smoking, flares, sparks, or flames in immediate area).
- DO NOT touch or walk through spilled material.
- Stop leak if you can do it without risk.
- Prevent entry into waterways, sewers, basements, or confined areas.

FIRST AID

- Move victim to fresh air.
- Call 911 or emergency medical service.
- Give artificial respiration if victim is not breathing.
- Administer oxygen if breathing is difficult.
- Remove and isolate contaminated clothing and shoes.
- In case of contact with substance, immediately flush skin or eyes with running water for at least 20 minutes.
- Keep victim warm and quiet.
- Ensure that medical personnel are aware of the material(s) involved, and take precautions to protect themselves.

Hazmat

SUBSTANCES INCLUDED

1841	Acetaldehyde ammonia
1931	Zinc dithionite; Zinc hydrosulfite
1941	Dibromodifluoromethane
2212	Asbestos; Blue asbestos; Brown asbestos
2216	Fish meal, stabilized; Fish scrap, stabilized
2315	Articles containing Polychlorinated biphenyls (PCB)
2315	PCB; Polychlorinated biphenyls (& , liquid; & , solid)
2590	White asbestos
2807	Magnetized material
2969	Castor beans, meal, pomace or flake
2990	Life-saving appliances, self-inflating
3072	Life-saving appliances, not self-inflating
3077	Environmentally hazardous substances, solid, n.o.s.
3077	Hazardous waste, solid, n.o.s.
3077	Other regulated substances, solid, n.o.s.
3082	Environmentally hazardous substances, liquid, n.o.s.
3082	Hazardous waste, liquid, n.o.s.
3082	Other regulated substances, liquid, n.o.s.
3151	Polyhalogenated biphenyls, liquid
3151	Polyhalogenated terphenyls, liquid
3152	Polyhalogenated biphenyls, solid
3152	Polyhalogenated terphenyls, solid
3245	Genetically modified micro-organisms
3258	Elevated temperature solid, n.o.s., at or above 240°C (464°F)
3268	Air bag inflators; Air bag inflators, pyrotechnic
3268	Air bag modules; Air bag modules, pyrotechnic
3268	Seat-belt modules
3268	Seat-belt pre-tensioners (& , pyrotechnic)
3314	Plastic molding compound; Plastics moulding compound
3316	Chemical kit
3316	First aid kit
3334	Aviation regulated liquid, n.o.s.
3334	Self-defense spray, non-pressurized
3335	Aviation regulated solid, n.o.s.
3359	Fumigated unit
3363	Dangerous goods in apparatus
3363	Dangerous goods in machinery
3432	Polychlorinated biphenyls, solid
8000	Consumer commodity
8013	Gas generator assemblies
8038	Heat producing article
9096	Calcium chromate
9163	Zirconium sulfate

POTENTIAL HAZARDS
FIRE OR EXPLOSION

- **EXTREMELY FLAMMABLE.**
- Some may burn but none ignite readily.
- Containers may explode when heated.
- Some may be transported hot.

HEALTH

- Inhalation of material may be harmful.
- Contact may cause burns to skin and eyes.
- Inhalation of Asbestos dust may have a damaging effect on the lungs.
- Fire may produce irritating, corrosive, or toxic gases.
- Some liquids produce vapors that may cause dizziness or suffocation.
- Runoff from fire control may cause pollution.

PUBLIC SAFETY

- **CALL Emergency Response Telephone Number on Shipping Paper first. If Shipping Paper is not available or there is no answer, refer to telephone numbers listed on page 613.**
- As an immediate precautionary measure, isolate spill or leak area in all directions for at least 50 meters (150 feet) for liquids and at least 25 meters (75 feet) for solids.
- Keep unauthorized personnel away.
- Stay upwind.

PROTECTIVE CLOTHING

- Wear positive pressure self-contained breathing apparatus (SCBA).
- Structural firefighters' protective clothing will only provide limited protection.

EVACUATION

Large Spill
- See the Table of Initial Isolation and Protective Action Distances for highlighted substances (page 908). For non-highlighted substances, increase, in the downwind direction, as necessary, the isolation distance shown above under "PUBLIC SAFETY."

Fire
- If tank, rail car, or tank truck is involved in a fire, ISOLATE for 800 meters (½ mile) in all directions; also, consider initial evacuation for 800 meters (½ mile) in all directions.

EMERGENCY RESPONSE
FIRE

Small Fires
- Dry chemical, CO_2, water spray, or regular foam.

Large Fires
- Water spray, fog, or regular foam.
- Move containers from fire area if you can do it without risk.
- DO NOT scatter spilled material with high pressure water streams.
- Dike fire-control water for later disposal.

Hazmat

Fire Involving Tanks

- Cool containers with flooding quantities of water until well after fire is out.
- Withdraw immediately in case of rising sound from venting safety devices or discoloration of tank.
- Always stay away from tanks engulfed in fire.

SPILL OR LEAK

- DO NOT touch or walk through spilled material.
- Stop leak if you can do it without risk.
- Prevent dust cloud.
- Avoid inhalation of asbestos dust.

Small Dry Spills

- With clean shovel place material into clean, dry container and cover loosely; move containers from spill area.

Small Spills

- Take up with sand or other non-combustible absorbent material and place into containers for later disposal.

Large Spills

- Dike far ahead of liquid spill for later disposal.
- Cover powder spill with plastic sheet or tarp to minimize spreading.
- Prevent entry into waterways, sewers, basements, or confined areas.

FIRST AID

- Move victim to fresh air.
- Call 911 or emergency medical service.
- Give artificial respiration if victim is not breathing.
- Administer oxygen if breathing is difficult.
- Remove and isolate contaminated clothing and shoes.
- In case of contact with substance, immediately flush skin or eyes with running water for at least 20 minutes.
- Ensure that medical personnel are aware of the material(s) involved, and take precautions to protect themselves.

Hazmat

Guide 172: Gallium and Mercury

SUBSTANCES INCLUDED

2803 Gallium
2809 Mercury; Mercury metal

POTENTIAL HAZARDS

FIRE OR EXPLOSION

- Non-combustible, substance itself does not burn, but may react upon heating to produce corrosive or toxic fumes.
- Runoff may pollute waterways.

HEALTH

- Inhalation of vapors or contact with substance will result in contamination and potential harmful effects.
- Fire will produce irritating, corrosive, or toxic gases.

PUBLIC SAFETY

- **CALL Emergency Response Telephone Number on Shipping Paper first. If Shipping Paper is not available or there is no answer, refer to telephone numbers listed on page 613.**
- As an immediate precautionary measure, isolate spill or leak area for at least 50 meters (150 feet) in all directions.
- Stay upwind.
- Keep unauthorized personnel away.

PROTECTIVE CLOTHING

- Wear positive pressure self-contained breathing apparatus (SCBA).
- Structural firefighters' protective clothing will only provide limited protection.

EVACUATION

Large Spill
- Consider initial downwind evacuation for at least 100 m (330 ft).

Fire
- When any large container is involved in a fire, consider an initial evacuation for 500 meters (1/3 mile) in all directions.

EMERGENCY RESPONSE

FIRE

- Use extinguishing agent suitable for type of surrounding fire.
- **DO NOT direct water at the heated metal.**

SPILL OR LEAK

- DO NOT touch or walk through spilled material.
- DO NOT touch damaged containers or spilled material unless wearing appropriate protective clothing.
- Stop leak if you can do it without risk.

Hazmat

- Prevent entry into waterways, sewers, basements, or confined areas.
- DO NOT use steel or aluminum tools or equipment.
- Cover with earth, sand, or other non-combustible material followed with plastic sheet to minimize spreading or contact with rain.
- For mercury, use a mercury spill kit.
- Mercury spill areas may be subsequently treated with calcium sulfide or with sodium thiosulfate wash to neutralize any residual mercury.

FIRST AID

- Move victim to fresh air.
- Call 911 or emergency medical service.
- Give artificial respiration if victim is not breathing.
- Administer oxygen if breathing is difficult.
- Remove and isolate contaminated clothing and shoes.
- In case of contact with substance, immediately flush skin or eyes with running water for at least 20 minutes.
- Keep victim warm and quiet.
- Ensure that medical personnel are aware of the material(s) involved, and take precautions to protect themselves.

Hazmat

Evacuation Distance Table

The Table of Isolation and Protective Action Distances on the following pages suggests distances that would be appropriate to protect people from vapors which are considered toxic by inhalation (TIH) that have resulted from a spill involving dangerous goods, chemical warfare agents, or goods which produce toxic gases upon contact with water. The distances should be used as an initial guide until technically qualified emergency response personnel arrive or become available.

Distances in the table represent areas that are likely to be affected during the first thirty minutes of a material spill; the distance could increase over more time. The Initial Isolation Zone defines an area surrounding the incident in which persons may be exposed to dangerous (upwind) and life threatening (downwind) concentrations of material. The Protective Action Zone defines an area downwind from the incident in which persons may become incapacitated and unable to take protective action and incur serious or irreversible health effects. The table also references small and large spills, as well as whether they occur during the day or night.

Adjusting distances for a specific incident involves many interdependent variables and should be made only by personnel technically qualified to make such adjustments. Therefore, these tables do not provide precise guidance.

Evacuation Terms

Evacuate: Move all people from a threatened area to a safer place. To perform an evacuation, there must be enough time for people to be warned, to get ready, and to leave an area. If there is enough time, evacuation is the best protective action. Begin evacuating people nearby and those outdoors in direct view of the scene. When additional help arrives, expand the area downwind and crosswind to at least the recommendation in the following tables. Even after people move to the recommended distance, they may not be completely safe from harm. The evacuees should not be allowed to congregate at these distances. They should be sent to a definite place, by a specific route, far enough away so they will not have to be moved again if the winds change.

Isolate Hazard Area and Deny Entry: Keep everybody away from the area if they are not directly involved in emergency response operations. Unprotected emergency responders should not be allowed to enter the isolation zone. This is the first step for any protective actions that may follow.

Hazmat

Protective Actions: These are the steps that are taken to preserve the health and safety of emergency responders and the public during an incident involving the release of dangerous goods. The following tables predict the size of downwind areas which could be affected by a cloud of toxic gas. People in this area should be evacuated and/or sheltered in place inside buildings.

Shelter In Place: People should seek shelter inside a building and remain inside until the danger passes. This technique is used when evacuating the public would cause greater risk than staying where they are, or when an evacuation cannot be performed. Direct people inside and have them close all doors and windows and to shut off all ventilating, heating, and cooling systems. People should also be warned to stay clear from windows due to the danger from glass and projected metal fragments in a fire or explosion. Vehicles can offer some protection for a short period if the windows are closed and the ventilating systems are shut off; however, they are not as effective as buildings.

In place protection may not be the best option if:

• The vapors are flammable
• It will take a long time for the gas to clear the area.
• Buildings cannot be closed tightly.

Protective Action Factors to Consider

Every situation has different factors which will lead to protective action choices. For some situations, evacuation may be the best option, for others it may be sheltering in place, or sometimes a combination of the two.

The following indicates what kind of information may be needed to make the initial decision for protective action distances.

• **The Dangerous Goods**
  – Degree of health hazard
  – Chemical and physical properties
  – Amount involved
  – Containment/control of release
  – Rate of vapor movement
• **The Population Threatened**
  – Location
  – Number of people
  – Time available to evacuate or shelter in place
  – Ability to control evacuation or shelter in place
  – Building types and availability

- Special institutions or populations (i.e. nursing homes, hospitals, prisons)
- **Weather Conditions**
  - Effect on vapor and cloud movement
  - Potential for change
  - Effect on evacuation or protection in place

Factors That May Affect Protective Action Distances

- **Fire:** If a material becomes involved in a fire, the toxic hazard may become less important than the fire or explosion hazard. See the guide for the material to see special evacuation and fire notes.
- **Multiple Tanks:** If more than one tank car, cargo tank, portable tank, or large cylinder involved in the incident is leaking, large spill distances may need to be increased.
- **Atmospheric Conditions:** Certain atmospheric conditions may require the distance to be larger for materials with a protective action distance of 11.0+km (7.0+).
  - If the dangerous goods vapor plume is channeled in a valley or between many tall buildings, distances may be larger than shown due to less mixing of the plume with the atmosphere.
  - Daytime spills in regions with known strong inversions or snow cover, or occurring near sunset, accompanied by a steady wind, may require an increase in protective action distance. When these conditions are present, airborne contaminants mix and disperse more slowly and may travel much farther downwind.
  - Protective action distances may be larger for liquid spills when either the material or outdoor temperature exceeds 30°C (86°F).
- **Water-Reactive Materials:** Materials which react with water to produce large amounts of toxic gases are included in the following tables. Some water-reactive materials (WRM) which are also TIH produce additional TIH materials when spilled in water. If it is not clear whether the spill is on land or in water, or in cases where the spill occurs both on land and in water, choose the larger Protective Action Distance.
- **In a River or Stream:** When water-reactive TIH producing material is spilled into a river or stream, the source of the

toxic gas may move with the current and stretch from the spill point downstream for a substantial distance.

- **Chemical Warfare Agents:** Distances may need to be increased when certain chemical warfare agents have been added, These are listed in the table as "when used as a weapon".
- **Instantaneous Release:** For worst case scenarios involving the instantaneous release of the entire contents of a package (i.e. as a result of terrorism, sabotage, or catastrophic accident), the distances may increase. The increase can be estimated by multiplying the distances by a factor of 2.

How to Use the Initial Isolation Table

Call the emergency response telephone number listed on the shipping paper, or the appropriate response agency as soon as possible for additional information on the material, safety precautions, and mitigation procedures!

1. Before using the table, the responder should have:
   - Identified the material by its ID number and Name.
   - Found the three-digit guide for that material in order to consult the emergency actions recommended jointly with this table.
   - Noted the wind direction.

2. Find the ID number and Name in the Isolation table for the material involved. Some ID numbers have more than one shipping name listed - look for the specific name of the material. If the shipping name is not known, use the entry with the largest protective action distance.

3. Determine if the incident involves a small or large spill and whether it is day or night.
   - A small spill involves a single, small package (i.e. a drum containing up to approx. 200 liters), a small cylinder, or a small leak from a large package.
   - A large spill involves a spill from a large package, or multiple spills from many small packages.
   - Day is considered anytime after sunrise and before sunset.
   - Night is considered anytime between sunset and sunrise.

4. Look up the initial ISOLATION distance in the following tables. Direct all persons to move, in a crosswind direction, away from the spill to the distance specified. (see figure to right)

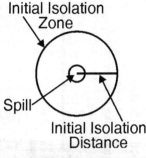

5. Look up the initial PROTECTIVE ACTION DISTANCE in the following tables. For a given material, spill size, and whether it is day or night, the table gives the downwind distance for which protective actions should be considered. For practical purposes, the Protective Action Zone (the area in which people are at risk of harmful exposure) is a square, whose length and width are the same as the downwind distance shown in the table.

6. Initiate Protective Actions to the extent possible, beginning with those closest to the spill site and working away from the site in the downwind direction. When a water-reactive TIH producing material is spilled into a river or stream, the source of the toxic gas may move with the current or stretch from the spill point downstream for a substantial distance. (see figure below)

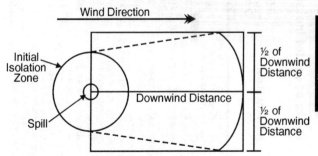

Hazmat

Table of Initial Isolation and Protective Action Distances

ID #	Name of Material	Small Spills (small package or small leak)						Large Spills (large pkg or many small pkgs)					
		Isolate in all Directions		Downwind Protection				Isolate in all Directions		Downwind Protection			
				Day		Night				Day		Night	
		meters	feet	km	miles	km	miles	meters	feet	km	miles	km	miles
1005	Ammonia anhydrous (&, liquefied); Ammonia, solution with > 50% Ammonia; Anhydrous ammonia (&, liquefied)	30	100	0.1	0.1	0.1	0.1	60	200	0.6	0.4	2.2	1.4
1008	Boron trifluoride (&, compressed)	30	100	0.1	0.1	0.6	0.4	180	600	1.8	1.1	4.8	3.0
1016	Carbon monoxide (&, compressed)	30	100	0.1	0.1	0.1	0.1	90	300	0.7	0.4	2.4	1.5
1017	Chlorine	30	100	0.2	0.2	1.2	0.8	240	800	2.4	1.5	7.4	4.6
1023	Coal gas; coal gas, compressed	30	100	0.1	0.1	0.2	0.1	60	200	0.4	0.2	0.5	0.3
1026	Cyanogen (&, liquefied); Cyanogen gas	30	100	0.2	0.2	1.2	0.8	120	400	1.1	0.7	4.3	2.7
1040	Ethylene oxide (& with Nitrogen)	30	100	0.1	0.1	0.2	0.1	90	300	0.8	0.5	2.4	1.5
1045	Fluorine; Fluorine, compressed	30	100	0.2	0.1	0.5	0.3	90	300	0.8	0.5	3.5	2.2
1048	Hydrogen bromide, anhydrous	30	100	0.1	0.1	0.5	0.3	180	600	1.8	1.1	5.7	3.6
1050	Hydrogen chloride, anhydrous	30	100	0.1	0.1	0.4	0.3	360	1200	3.6	2.2	10.4	6.5
1051	AC (when used as a weapon)	60	200	0.2	0.1	0.5	0.3	500	1500	1.7	1.0	3.9	2.4
1051	Hydrocyanic acid, aqueous solutions with ≥ 20% Hydrogen cyanide; Hydrocyanic acid, liquefied; Hydrogen cyanide, anhydrous, stabilized; Hydrogen cyanide, stabilized	30	100	0.1	0.1	0.4	0.3	150	500	1.3	0.8	3.7	2.3
1052	Hydrogen fluoride, anhydrous	30	100	0.1	0.1	0.5	0.3	210	700	1.9	1.2	4.3	2.7

ID & Name												
1053 Hydrogen sulfide (& , liquefied)	30	100	0.1	0.1	0.3	0.2	210	700	2.1	1.3	6.2	3.9
1062 Methyl bromide	30	100	0.1	0.1	0.1	0.1	90	300	0.7	0.5	2.2	1.4
1064 Methyl mercaptan	30	100	0.1	0.1	0.2	0.2	150	500	1.3	0.8	4.5	2.8
1067 Dinitrogen tetroxide (& , liquefied); nitrogen dioxide (& , liquefied)	30	100	0.1	0.1	0.4	0.3	150	500	1.6	1.0	4.1	2.5
1069 Nitrosyl chloride	30	100	0.2	0.1	1.0	0.6	450	1500	4.3	2.7	11.0	6.9
1071 Oil gas; oil gas, compressed	30	100	0.2	0.1	0.2	0.1	60	200	0.4	0.2	0.5	0.3
1076 CG (when used as a weapon)	150	500	1.3	0.8	3.3	2.0	800	2500	7.3	4.5	11.0+	7.0+
1076 Diphosgene	90	300	0.9	0.6	4.1	2.6	800	2500	6.6	4.1	11.0+	7.0+
1076 DP (when used as a weapon)	60	200	0.4	0.2	1.0	0.6	180	600	1.7	1.0	4.6	2.8
1076 Phosgene	90	300	0.9	0.6	4.1	2.6	800	2500	6.6	4.1	11.0+	7.0+
1079 Sulfur dioxide (& , liquefied)	30	100	0.3	0.2	1.2	0.8	210	700	2.0	1.3	6.3	3.9
1082 Trifluorochloroethylene (&,inhibited; &,stabilized)	30	100	0.1	0.1	0.1	0.1	60	200	0.4	0.3	0.8	0.5
1092 Acrolein, inhibited; acrolein, stabilized	60	200	0.5	0.3	1.7	1.1	500	1600	4.8	3.0	10.2	6.3
1098 Allyl alcohol	30	100	0.1	0.1	0.1	0.1	60	200	0.4	0.2	0.6	0.4
1135 Ethylene chlorohydrin	30	100	0.2	0.1	0.3	0.2	90	300	0.8	0.5	1.5	1.0
1143 Crotonaldehyde (., inhibited; &. stabilized)	30	100	0.1	0.2	0.1	0.1	60	200	0.4	0.3	0.8	0.5
1162 Dimethyldichlorosilane (when spilled in water)	30	100	0.2	0.1	1.1	0.7	300	1000	3.0	1.9	7.9	4.9
1163 1,1-Dimethylhydrazine; Dimethylhydrazine, unsymmetrical	30	100	0.1	0.1	0.2	0.1	60	200	0.5	0.4	1.2	0.8
1182 Ethyl chloroformate	30	100	0.2	0.1	0.3	0.2	90	300	0.9	0.6	1.8	1.1
1185 Ethyleneimine (., inhibited; &. stabilized)	30	100	0.2	0.2	0.7	0.5	180	600	1.8	1.2	40	2.5
1196 Ethyltrichlorosilane (when spilled in water)	30	100	0.2	0.2	1.1	0.7	300	1000	3.0	1.9	7.9	4.9

Hazmat

Table of Initial Isolation and Protective Action Distances (cont.)

ID #	Name of Material	Small Spills (small package or small leak)					Large Spills (large pkg or many small pkgs)					
		Isolate in all Directions		Downwind Protection				Isolate in all Directions		Downwind Protection		
				Day		Night				Day		Night	
		meters	feet	km	miles	km	miles	meters	feet	km	miles	km	miles
1238	Methyl chloroformate	30	100	0.3	0.2	0.8	0.5	180	600	1.8	1.1	3.9	2.4
1239	Methyl chloromethyl ether	30	100	0.3	0.2	1.0	0.6	270	900	2.5	1.6	5.6	3.5
1242	Methyldichlorosilane (when spilled in water)	30	100	0.2	0.1	0.7	0.4	180	600	1.6	1.0	4.8	3.0
1244	Methylhydrazine	30	100	0.3	0.2	0.5	0.3	150	500	1.4	0.9	2.9	1.8
1250	Methyltrichlorosilane (when spilled in water)	30	100	0.1	0.1	0.5	0.3	150	500	1.3	0.8	4.0	2.5
1251	Methyl vinyl ketone (& ,stabilized)	150	500	1.3	0.8	3.3	2.1	1000	3000	11.0+	7.0+	11.0+	7.0+
1259	Nickel carbonyl	90	300	0.8	0.5	3.5	2.2	500	1600	4.7	2.9	9.8	6.1
1295	Trichlorosilane (when spilled in water)	30	100	0.2	0.1	1.0	0.6	270	900	2.5	1.6	6.5	4.1
1298	Trimethylchlorosilane (when spilled in water)	30	100	0.1	0.1	0.3	0.2	90	300	0.8	0.5	2.7	1.7
1305	Vinyltrichlorosilane, when spilled in water (& ,inhibited; & ,stabilized)	30	100	0.2	0.1	0.7	0.5	180	600	1.8	1.1	5.0	3.1
1340	Phosphorus pentasulfide, free from yellow or white Phosphorus (when spilled in water)	30	100	0.1	0.1	0.6	0.4	150	500	1.0	0.6	3.9	2.4
1360	Calcium phosphide (when spilled in water)	60	200	0.5	0.3	2.1	1.3	800	2500	6.3	3.9	11.0+	7.0+
1380	Pentaborane	90	300	0.9	0.6	3.3	2.1	600	1800	5.3	3.3	11.0	6.9

Hazmat

ID	Name											
1384	Sodium dithionite (when spilled in water); sodium hydrosulfite (when spilled in water)	30	100	0.1	0.1	0.1	60	200	0.4	0.3	1.3	0.8
1397	Aluminum phosphide (when spilled in water)	90	300	0.4	2.7	1.7	1000	3000	9.0	5.6	11.0+	7.0+
1412	Lithium amide (when spilled in water)	30	100	0.1	0.2	0.2	30	100	0.4	0.2	1.6	1.0
1419	Magnesium aluminum phosphide (spilled in water)	60	200	0.4	2.5	1.6	1000	3000	7.9	4.9	11.0+	7.0+
1432	Sodium phosphide (when spilled in water)	60	200	0.2	1.7	1.1	500	1600	4.7	2.9	11.0+	7.0+
1510	Tetranitromethane	30	100	0.2	0.6	0.4	90	300	0.8	0.5	1.6	1.0
1541	Acetone cyanohydrin, stabilized (when spilled in water)	30	100	0.1	0.3	0.2	240	800	0.8	0.5	3.0	1.9
1556	MD (when used as a weapon)	30	100	0.1	0.4	0.2	60	200	0.5	0.4	1.1	0.7
1556	Methyldichloroarsine	30	100	0.2	0.9	0.5	120	400	1.3	0.8	3.6	2.2
1556	PD (when used as a weapon)	30	100	0.1	0.2	0.1	30	100	0.2	0.1	0.4	0.2
1560	Arsenic chloride; arsenic trichloride	30	100	0.2	0.4	0.2	90	300	0.9	0.6	1.8	1.1
1569	Bromoacetone	30	100	0.2	0.6	0.4	90	300	0.8	0.5	2.3	1.5
1580	Chloropicrin	60	200	0.4	0.8	0.5	210	700	1.9	1.2	3.6	2.2
1581	Chloropicrin and Methyl bromide mixture	30	100	0.1	0.6	0.4	210	700	2.1	1.3	5.9	3.7
1582	Chloropicrin and methyl chloride mixture	30	100	0.1	0.4	0.3	30	100	0.4	0.2	1.7	1.1
1583	Chloropicrin mixture, not otherwise specified	60	200	0.4	0.8	0.5	210	700	1.9	1.2	3.6	2.2
1589	CK (when used as a weapon)	60	200	0.7	2.5	1.5	420	1300	4.1	2.5	8.1	5.0
1589	Cyanogen chloride (, inhibited &, stabilized)	60	200	0.6	2.8	1.8	450	1400	4.3	2.7	10.1	6.3
1595	Dimethyl sulfate	30	100	0.1	0.1	0.1	60	200	0.5	0.3	0.8	0.5

Hazmat

Table of Initial Isolation and Protective Action Distances (cont.)

ID #	Name of Material	Small Spills (small package or small leak)						Large Spills (large pkg or many small pkgs)					
		Isolate in all Directions		Downwind Protection				Isolate in all Directions		Downwind Protection			
				Day		Night				Day		Night	
		meters	feet	km	miles	km	miles	meters	feet	km	miles	km	miles
1605	Ethylene dibromide	30	100	0.1	0.1	0.1	0.1	30	100	0.3	0.2	0.6	0.4
1612	Hexaethyl tetraphosphate and compressed gas mixture	90	300	0.8	0.5	2.7	1.7	360	1200	3.5	2.2	8.1	5.1
1613	Hydrocyanic acid, aqueous solution with ≤ 20% Hydrogen cyanide; Hydrogen cyanide, aqueous solution with ≤ 20% Hydrogen cyanide	30	100	0.2	0.1	0.2	0.1	120	400	0.5	0.3	1.3	0.8
1614	Hydrogen cyanide, anhydrous stabilized (absorbed); Hydrogen cyanide, stabilized (absorbed)	30	100	0.2	0.1	0.6	0.4	60	200	0.5	0.3	1.7	1.1
1647	Ethylene dibromide and Methyl bromide mixture, liquid	30	100	0.1	0.1	0.1	0.1	30	100	0.3	0.2	0.6	0.4
1660	Nitric oxide; nitric oxide, compressed	30	100	0.2	0.1	0.8	0.5	60	200	0.6	0.4	2.7	1.7
1680	Potassium cyanide, spilled in water (& solid)	30	100	0.2	0.1	0.5	0.3	300	1000	1.0	0.6	3.9	2.4
1689	Sodium cyanide, spilled in water (& solid)	60	200	0.2	0.1	0.7	0.4	390	1300	1.3	0.8	4.9	3.0
1694	CA (when used as a weapon)	30	100	0.2	0.1	0.5	0.3	150	500	1.7	1.0	4.2	2.6
1695	Chloroacetone, stabilized	30	100	0.2	0.1	0.3	0.2	90	300	0.7	0.5	1.5	0.9
1697	CN (when used as a weapon)	30	100	0.2	0.1	0.5	0.3	120	400	1.2	0.7	3.3	2.0

ID	Name	60/30	200/100										
1698	Adamisite (when used as a weapon); DM (when used as a weapon)	60	200	0.4	0.2	1.2	0.7	180	600	2.3	1.4	5.2	3.2
1699	DA (when used as a weapon)	60	200	0.4	0.2	1.2	0.7	180	600	2.3	1.4	5.2	3.2
1716	Acetyl bromide (when spilled in water)	30	100	0.1	0.1	0.3	0.2	90	300	0.7	0.5	2.3	1.4
1717	Acetyl chloride (when spilled in water)	30	100	0.1	0.1	0.4	0.3	120	400	1.1	0.7	3.5	2.2
1722	Allyl chlorocarbonate; allyl chloroformate	30	100	0.4	0.2	0.8	0.5	210	700	2.0	1.2	3.8	2.4
1724	Allytrichlorosilane, stabilized (spilled in water)	30	100	0.2	0.1	0.7	0.5	180	600	1.8	1.2	5.4	3.4
1725	Aluminum bromide, anhydrous (spilled in water)	30	100	0.1	0.1	0.5	0.3	90	300	0.7	0.4	2.6	1.6
1726	Aluminum chloride, anhydrous (spilled in water)	30	100	0.2	0.1	0.7	0.5	120	400	1.2	0.7	4.5	2.8
1728	Amyltrichlorosilane (when spilled in water)	30	100	0.1	0.1	0.2	0.1	60	200	0.5	0.3	1.9	1.2
1732	Antimony pentafluoride (spilled in water)	30	100	0.2	0.1	0.9	0.6	180	600	1.9	1.2	5.4	3.4
1741	Boron trichloride	30	100	0.1	0.1	0.3	0.2	60	200	0.6	0.4	1.7	1.1
1744	Bromine; Bromine, solution	60	200	0.5	0.3	1.8	1.1	330	1100	3.3	2.1	7.3	4.6
1745	Bromine pentafluoride (when spilled on land)	30	100	0.4	0.2	1.4	0.9	270	900	2.7	1.7	6.9	4.3
1745	Bromine pentafluoride (when spilled in water)	30	100	0.2	0.1	1.0	0.6	240	800	2.2	1.4	6.6	4.1
1746	Bromine trifluoride (when spilled on land)	30	100	0.1	0.1	0.6	0.4	180	600	1.8	1.1	4.8	3.0
1746	Bromine trifluoride (when spilled in water)	30	100	0.2	0.1	0.9	0.6	210	700	1.9	1.2	5.8	3.6

Hazmat

Table of Initial Isolation and Protective Action Distances (cont.)

ID #	Name of Material	Small Spills (small package or small leak)						Large Spills (large pkg or many small pkgs)					
		Isolate in all Directions		Downwind Protection				Isolate in all Directions		Downwind Protection			
				Day		Night				Day		Night	
		meters	feet	km	miles	km	miles	meters	feet	km	miles	km	miles
1747	Butyltrichlorosilane (when spilled in water)	30	100	0.1	0.1	0.2	0.2	60	200	0.6	0.4	2.0	1.3
1749	Chlorine trifluoride	60	200	0.4	0.3	2.0	1.3	300	1000	2.8	1.8	8.1	5.1
1752	Chloracetyl chloride (when spilled on land)	30	100	0.3	0.2	0.5	0.4	150	500	1.4	0.9	2.6	1.6
1752	Chloracetyl chloride (when spilled in water)	30	100	0.1	0.1	0.2	0.1	60	200	0.4	0.3	1.5	1.0
1754	Chlorosulfonic acid (when spilled on land)	30	100	0.1	0.1	0.1	0.1	30	100	0.3	0.2	0.4	0.3
1754	Chlorosulfonic acid (when spilled in water)	30	100	0.1	0.1	0.6	0.4	90	300	0.7	0.5	2.8	1.7
1754	Chlorosulfonic acid and Sulfur trioxide mixture (when spilled on land)	60	200	0.4	0.2	1.0	0.6	330	1000	2.5	1.5	6.5	4.0
1754	Chlorosulfonic acid and Sulfur trioxide mixture (when spilled in water)	30	100	0.1	0.1	0.6	0.4	90	300	0.7	0.5	2.8	1.7
1758	Chromium oxychloride (spilled in water)	30	100	0.1	0.1	0.2	0.1	30	100	0.3	0.2	1.3	0.8
1763	Cyclohexyltrichlorosilane (spilled in water)	30	100	0.1	0.1	0.3	0.2	90	300	0.8	0.5	3.0	1.9

ID	Name												
1766	Dichlorophenyltrichlorosilane (spilled in water)	30	100	0.2	0.1	0.9	0.6	210	700	2.1	1.3	5.7	3.6
1767	Diethyldichlorosilane (when spilled in water)	30	100	0.1	0.1	0.1	0.1	60	200	0.4	0.3	1.3	0.8
1769	Diphenyldichlorosilane (spilled in water)	30	100	0.1	0.1	0.1	0.1	30	100	0.3	0.2	1.2	0.8
1771	Dodecyltrichlorosilane (when spilled in water)	30	100	0.1	0.1	0.2	0.1	60	200	0.5	0.3	1.8	1.2
1771	Fluorosulfonic acid (when spilled in water)	30	100	0.1	0.1	0.5	0.3	120	400	1.0	0.6	3.4	2.1
1784	Hexyltrichlorosilane (when spilled in water)	30	100	0.1	0.1	0.4	0.3	120	400	1.0	0.7	3.8	2.4
1799	Nonyltrichlorosilane (when spilled in water)	30	100	0.1	0.1	0.3	0.2	60	200	0.6	0.4	2.5	1.6
1800	Octadecyltrichlorosilane (spilled in water)	30	100	0.1	0.1	0.3	0.2	90	300	0.8	0.5	2.9	1.8
1801	Octyltrichlorosilane (when spilled in water)	30	100	0.1	0.1	0.3	0.2	60	200	0.6	0.4	2.5	1.6
1804	Phenyltrichlorosilane (when spilled in water)	30	100	0.2	0.1	0.9	0.6	240	800	2.2	1.4	6.4	4.0
1806	Phosphorus pentachloride (spilled in water)	30	100	0.1	0.1	0.5	0.3	90	300	0.8	0.5	3.1	1.9
1809	Phosphorus trichloride (spilled on land)	30	100	0.2	0.1	0.4	0.3	150	500	1.5	1.0	3.5	2.2
1809	Phosphorus trichloride (spilled in water)	30	100	0.2	0.1	0.7	0.4	180	600	1.6	1.0	4.8	3.0
1810	Phosphorus oxychloride (spilled on land)	30	100	0.2	0.2	0.4	0.3	120	400	1.0	0.7	2.2	1.4
1810	Phosphorus oxychloride (spilled in water)	30	100	0.2	0.1	1.0	0.6	240	800	2.3	1.5	6.3	3.9

Hazmat

Table of Initial Isolation and Protective Action Distances (cont.)

ID #	Name of Material	Small Spills (small package or small leak)						Large Spills (large pkg or many small pkgs)					
		Isolate in all Directions		Downwind Protection				Isolate in all Directions		Downwind Protection			
				Day		Night				Day		Night	
		meters	feet	km	miles	km	miles	meters	feet	km	miles	km	miles
1816	Propyltrichlorosilane (when spilled in water)	30	100	0.1	0.1	0.5	0.3	120	400	1.3	0.8	4.1	2.6
1818	Silicon tetrachloride (when spilled in water)	30	100	0.1	0.1	0.6	0.4	150	500	1.5	1.0	4.6	2.9
1828	Sulfur chlorides (when spilled on land)	30	100	0.1	0.1	0.2	0.1	90	300	0.9	0.6	1.7	1.1
1828	Sulfur chlorides (when spilled in water)	30	100	0.1	0.1	0.6	0.4	150	500	1.4	0.9	4.9	3.0
1829	Sulfur trioxide (& , inhibited; & , stabilized; & , uninhibited)	60	200	0.4	0.2	1.0	0.6	330	1000	2.5	1.5	6.5	4.0
1831	Sulfuric acid fuming; Sulfuric acid fuming, with ≥ 30% free Sulfur trioxide	60	200	0.4	0.2	1.0	0.6	330	1000	2.5	1.5	6.5	4.0
1834	Sulfuryl chloride (when spilled on land)	30	100	0.1	0.1	0.1	0.1	30	100	0.3	0.2	0.7	0.5
1834	Sulfuryl chloride (when spilled in water)	30	100	0.1	0.1	0.4	0.2	90	300	0.8	0.5	2.9	1.8
1836	Thionyl chloride (when spilled on land)	30	100	0.3	0.2	0.8	0.5	90	300	1.0	0.6	2.2	1.4
1836	Thionyl chloride (when spilled in water)	60	200	0.4	0.2	1.7	1.1	450	1500	4.5	2.8	10.5	6.5

ID	Name												
1838	Titanium tetrachloride (spilled on land)	30	100	0.1	0.1	0.1	0.1	60	200	0.5	0.3	0.8	0.5
1838	Titanium tatrachloride (spilled in water)	30	100	0.1	0.1	0.5	0.3	120	400	1.1	0.7	3.7	2.3
1859	Silicon tatrafluoride (&. compressed)	30	100	0.1	0.1	0.1	0.1	60	200	0.5	0.3	0.8	0.5
1892	ED (when used as a weapon)	30	100	0.4	0.2	0.9	0.5	120	400	1.3	0.8	2.6	1.6
1892	Ethyldichloroarsine	30	100	0.2	0.1	0.2	0.2	60	200	0.6	0.4	1.1	0.7
1898	Acetyl iodide (when spilled in water)	30	100	0.1	0.1	0.2	0.2	60	200	0.6	0.4	1.8	1.1
1911	Diborane: Diborane, compressed	60	200	0.4	0.2	1.6	1.0	180	600	1.8	1.1	5.4	3.4
1923	Calcium dithionite (when spilled in water); Calcium hydrosulfite (when spilled in water)	30	100	0.1	0.1	0.1	0.1	60	200	0.4	0.3	1.3	0.8
1931	Zinc dithionite (when spilled in water); Zinc hydrosulfite (when spilled in water)	30	100	0.1	0.1	0.1	0.1	60	200	0.4	0.3	1.3	0.8
1953	Compressed gas, flammable, toxic, n.o.s. (Inhalation Hazard Zone A)	120	400	1.2	0.8	5.1	3.2	1000	3000	8.7	5.4	11.0+	7.0+
1953	Compressed gas, flammable, toxic, n.o.s. (Inhalation Hazard Zone B)	30	100	0.2	0.2	1.2	0.8	420	1400	4.0	2.5	10.8	6.7
1953	Compressed gas, flammable, toxic, n.o.s. (Inhalation Hazard Zone C)	30	100	0.2	0.1	0.8	0.5	240	800	2.4	1.5	6.4	4.0
1953	Compressed gas, flammable, toxic, n.o.s. (Inhalation Hazard Zone D)	30	100	0.1	0.1	0.2	0.1	90	300	0.8	0.5	2.4	1.5
1953	Compressed gas, toxic, flammable, n.o.s. (& Inhalation Hazard Zone A)	120	400	1.2	0.8	5.1	3.2	1000	3000	8.7	5.4	11.0+	7.0+
1953	Compressed gas, toxic, flammable, n.o.s. (Inhalation Hazard Zone B)	30	100	0.2	0.2	1.2	0.8	420	1400	4.0	2.5	10.8	6.7
1953	Compressed gas, toxic, flammable, n.o.s. (Inhalation Hazard Zone C)	30	100	0.2	0.1	0.8	0.5	240	800	2.4	1.5	6.4	4.0

Hazmat

Table of Initial Isolation and Protective Action Distances (cont.)

ID #	Name of Material	Small Spills (small package or small leak)						Large Spills (large pkg or many small pkgs)					
		Isolate in all Directions		Downwind Protection				Isolate in all Directions		Downwind Protection			
				Day		Night				Day		Night	
		meters	feet	km	miles	km	miles	meters	feet	km	miles	km	miles
1953	Compressed gas, toxic, flammable, n.o.s. (Inhalation Hazard Zone D)	30	100	0.1	0.1	0.2	0.1	90	300	0.8	0.5	2.4	1.5
1953	Liquefied gas, flammable, toxic, n.o.s.& Inhalation Hazard Zone A)	120	400	1.2	0.8	5.1	3.2	1000	3000	8.7	5.4	11.0+	7.0+
1953	Liquefied gas, flammable, toxic, n.o.s. (Inhalation Hazard Zone B)	30	100	0.2	0.2	1.2	0.8	420	1400	4.0	2.5	10.8	6.7
1953	Liquefied gas, flammable, toxic, n.o.s. (Inhalation Hazard Zone C)	30	100	0.2	0.1	0.8	0.5	240	800	2.4	1.5	6.4	4.0
1953	Liquefied gas, flammable, toxic, n.o.s. (Inhalation Hazard Zone D)	30	100	0.1	0.1	0.2	0.1	90	300	0.8	0.5	2.4	1.5
1955	Compressed gas, toxic, n.o.s. (& Inhalation Hazard Zone A)	600	2000	5.9	3.7	11.0+	7.0+	1000	3000	11.0+	7.0+	11.0+	7.0+
1955	Compressed gas, toxic, n.o.s. (Inhalation Hazard Zone B)	60	200	0.4	0.3	2.0	1.3	800	2500	7.8	4.9	11.0+	7.0+
1955	Compressed gas, toxic, n.o.s. (Inhalation Hazard Zone C)	30	100	0.3	0.2	1.2	0.8	240	800	2.4	1.5	6.4	4.0
1955	Compressed gas, toxic, n.o.s. (Inhalation Hazard Zone D)	30	100	0.2	0.1	0.7	0.4	120	400	1.2	0.8	3.8	2.4
1955	Liquefied gas, toxic, n.o.s. (& Inhalation Hazard Zone A)	600	2000	5.9	3.7	11.0+	7.0+	1000	3000	11.0+	7.0+	11.0+	7.0+
1955	Liquefied gas, toxic, n.o.s. (Inhalation Hazard Zone B)	60	200	0.4	0.3	2.0	1.3	800	2500	7.8	4.9	11.0+	7.0+

Hazmat

ID	Name												
1955	Liquefied gas, toxic, n.o.s. (Inhalation Hazard Zone C)	30	100	0.3	0.2	1.2	0.8	240	800	2.4	1.5	6.4	4.0
1955	Liquefied gas, toxic, n.o.s. (Inhalation Hazard Zone D)	30	100	0.2	0.1	0.7	0.4	120	400	1.2	0.8	3.8	2.4
1955	Organic phosphate compound mixed with compressed gas; Organic phosphate mixed with compressed gas; Organic phosphorus compound mixed with compressed gas	120	400	1.0	0.7	3.4	2.1	450	1500	4.4	2.7	9.6	6.0
1967	Insecticide gas, toxic, n.o.s.; Parathion and compressed gas mixture	120	400	1.0	0.7	3.4	2.1	450	1500	4.4	2.7	9.6	6.0
1975	Dinitrogen tetroxide and Nitric oxide mixture; Nitric oxide and Nitrogen dioxide mixture; Nitric oxide and Nitrogen tetroxide mixture	30	100	0.2	0.1	0.8	0.5	60	200	0.6	0.4	2.7	1.7
1994	Iron pentacarbonyl	30	100	0.3	0.2	0.6	0.4	150	500	1.6	1.0	3.0	1.9
2004	Magnesium diamide (when spilled in water)	30	100	0.1	0.1	0.4	0.3	90	300	0.7	0.4	2.9	1.8
2011	Magnesium phosphide (spilled in water)	60	200	0.5	0.4	2.4	1.5	800	2500	7.5	4.7	11.0+	7.0+
2012	Potassium phosphide (spilled in water)	60	200	0.4	0.3	1.7	1.1	500	1600	4.7	2.9	11.0+	7.0+
2013	Strontium phosphide (when spilled in water)	60	200	0.4	0.2	1.7	1.1	500	1600	4.6	2.9	11.0+	7.0+
2032	Nitric acid, fuming; Nitric acid, red fuming	30	100	0.1	0.1	0.2	0.2	60	200	0.6	0.4	1.2	0.8
2186	Hydrogen chloride, refrigerated liquid	30	100	0.1	0.1	0.4	0.3	360	1200	3.6	2.2	10.4	6.5
2188	Arsine	60	200	0.6	0.4	3.0	1.9	420	1400	4.1	2.6	9.5	5.9

Hazmat

Table of Initial Isolation and Protective Action Distances (cont.)

ID #	Name of Material	Small Spills (small package or small leak)						Large Spills (large pkg or many small pkgs)					
		Isolate in all Directions		Downwind Protection				Isolate in all Directions		Downwind Protection			
				Day		Night				Day		Night	
		meters	feet	km	miles	km	miles	meters	feet	km	miles	km	miles
2188	SA (when used as a weapon)	60	200	0.9	0.5	2.5	1.5	420	1300	4.1	2.5	8.1	5.0
2189	Dichlorosilane	30	100	0.2	0.1	1.0	0.6	420	1400	4.0	2.5	10.8	6.7
2190	Oxygen difluoride (&, compressed)	600	2000	5.9	3.7	11.0+	7.0+	1000	3000	11.0+	7.0+	11.0+	7.0+
2191	Sulfuryl fluoride	30	100	0.1	0.1	0.3	0.2	120	400	1.2	0.8	3.8	2.4
2192	Germane	30	100	0.2	0.1	1.0	0.6	30	100	0.8	0.5	3.0	1.9
2194	Selenium hexafluoride	90	300	0.7	0.5	3.2	2.0	450	1500	4.4	2.7	9.0	5.6
2195	Tellurium hexafluoride	90	300	1.0	0.6	4.0	2.5	600	2000	6.0	3.7	11.0+	7.0+
2196	Tungsten hexafluoride	30	100	0.2	0.1	1.1	0.7	120	400	1.0	0.6	3.7	2.3
2197	Hydrogen iodide, anhydrous	30	100	0.1	0.1	0.4	0.2	120	400	1.3	0.8	3.7	2.3
2198	Phosphorus pentafluoride (&, compressed)	30	100	0.3	0.2	1.6	1.0	180	600	1.6	1.0	4.6	2.9
2199	Phosphine	60	200	0.7	0.4	3.1	1.9	450	1400	2.7	1.6	9.6	6.0
2202	Hydrogen selenide, anhydrous	120	400	1.2	0.8	5.1	3.2	1000	3000	8.7	5.4	11.0+	7.0+
2204	Carbonyl sulfide	30	100	0.1	0.1	0.6	0.4	300	1000	3.0	1.9	8.1	5.0
2232	Chloroacetaldehyde; 2-Chloroethanal	30	100	0.2	0.1	0.3	0.2	90	300	0.8	0.5	1.6	1.0
2334	Allylamine	30	100	0.1	0.1	0.5	0.3	120	400	1.1	0.7	2.5	1.5
2337	Phenyl mercaptan	30	100	0.1	0.1	0.1	0.1	60	200	0.4	0.2	0.6	0.4
2382	1,2-Dimethylhydrazine; Dimethylhydrazine, symmetrical	30	100	0.2	0.1	0.2	0.1	60	200	0.6	0.4	1.2	0.8
2407	Isopropyl chloroformate	30	100	0.1	0.1	0.3	0.2	90	300	0.7	0.5	1.5	0.9
2417	Carbonyl fluoride (&, compressed)	30	100	0.2	0.1	1.1	0.7	90	300	0.6	0.6	3.6	2.3

ID	Name												
2418	Sulfur tetrafluoride	60	200	0.7	0.4	3.2	2.0	500	1600	4.7	2.9	10.6	6.6
2420	Hexafluoroacetone	30	100	0.3	0.2	1.3	0.8	800	2500	7.2	4.5	11.0+	7.0+
2421	Nitrogen trioxide	30	100	0.1	0.1	0.5	0.3	60	200	0.4	0.3	1.9	1.2
2437	Methylphenyldichlorosilane (spilled in water)	30	100	0.1	0.1	0.1	0.1	30	100	0.3	0.2	1.1	0.7
2438	Trimethylacetyl chloride	30	100	0.1	0.1	0.2	0.1	60	200	0.5	0.3	0.8	0.5
2442	Trichloroacetyl chloride	30	100	0.2	0.2	0.8	0.5	120	400	1.2	0.8	2.2	1.4
2474	Triophosgene	90	300	0.8	0.5	2.4	1.5	360	1200	3.6	2.3	6.8	4.2
2477	Methyl isothiocyanate	30	100	0.1	0.1	0.2	0.1	60	200	0.5	0.3	1.0	0.7
2480	Methyl isocyanate	60	200	0.5	0.3	1.9	1.2	600	1800	5.4	3.3	11.0+	7.0+
2481	Ethyl Isocyanate	60	200	0.6	0.4	2.1	1.3	800	2500	6.2	3.9	11.0+	7.0+
2482	n-Propyl isocyanate	120	400	1.0	0.7	2.5	1.6	1000	3000	9.0	5.6	11.0+	7.0+
2483	Isopropyl isocyanate	120	400	1.1	0.7	2.8	1.8	1000	3000	11.0+	7.0+	11.0+	7.0+
2484	tert-Butyl isocyanate	90	300	1.0	0.6	2.4	1.5	1000	3000	8.4	5.2	11.0+	7.0+
2485	n-Butyl isocyanate	90	300	0.7	0.5	1.6	1.0	500	1600	4.7	2.9	8.0	5.0
2486	Isobutyl isocyanate	90	300	0.7	0.5	1.6	1.0	500	1600	4.7	3.0	7.8	4.8
2487	Phenyl isocyanate	30	100	0.4	0.2	0.5	0.3	180	600	1.6	1.0	2.9	1.8
2488	Cyclohexyl isocyanate	30	100	0.2	0.2	0.3	0.2	90	300	0.9	0.6	1.6	1.0
2495	Iodine pentafluoride (when spilled in water)	30	100	0.2	0.1	1.0	0.6	210	700	1.9	1.2	5.7	3.6
2521	Diketene, inhibited; Diketene, stabilized	30	100	0.1	0.1	0.1	0.1	30	100	0.3	0.2	0.5	0.3
2534	Methylchlorosilane	30	100	0.2	0.1	0.8	0.5	240	800	2.4	1.5	6.4	4.0
2548	Chlorine pentafluoride	30	100	0.3	0.2	1.7	1.1	240	800	2.4	1.5	7.4	4.6
2600	Carbon monoxide and Hydrogen mixture (& ... compressed)	30	100	0.1	0.1	0.1	0.1	90	300	0.7	0.4	2.4	1.5
2605	Methoxymethyl isocyanate	60	200	0.4	0.2	0.6	0.4	180	600	1.6	1.0	2.6	1.6
2606	Methyl orthosilicate	30	100	0.1	0.1	0.1	0.1	60	200	0.4	0.3	0.7	0.4
2644	Methyl iodide	30	100	0.1	0.1	0.2	0.1	30	100	0.3	0.2	0.8	0.5

Table of Initial Isolation and Protective Action Distances (cont.)

ID #	Name of Material	Small Spills (small package or small leak)						Large Spills (large pkg or many small pkgs)					
		Isolate in all Directions		Downwind Protection				Isolate in all Directions		Downwind Protection			
				Day		Night				Day		Night	
		meters	feet	km	miles	km	miles	meters	feet	km	miles	km	miles
2646	Hexachlorocyclopentadiene	30	100	0.1	0.1	0.1	0.1	60	200	0.4	0.3	0.5	0.3
2668	Chloroacetonitrile	30	100	0.1	0.1	0.1	0.1	30	100	0.3	0.2	0.5	0.3
2676	Stibine	60	200	0.4	0.3	2.2	1.4	270	900	2.8	1.7	7.5	4.7
2691	Phosphorus pentabromide (spilled in water)	30	100	0.1	0.1	0.7	0.4	90	300	0.7	0.4	2.8	1.7
2692	Boron tribromide (when spilled on land)	30	100	0.2	0.1	0.5	0.3	60	200	0.5	0.4	1.3	0.8
2692	Boron tribromide (when spilled in water)	30	100	0.1	0.1	0.5	0.3	90	300	0.7	0.5	2.6	1.6
2740	n-Propyl chloroformate	30	100	0.1	0.1	0.3	0.2	90	300	0.7	0.5	1.5	0.9
2742	Sec-Butyl chloroformate	30	100	0.1	0.1	0.1	0.1	60	200	0.4	0.2	0.6	0.4
2742	Isobutyl chloroformate	30	100	0.1	0.1	0.1	0.1	30	100	0.3	0.2	0.5	0.3
2743	n-Butyl chloroformate	30	100	0.1	0.1	0.1	0.1	30	100	0.4	0.2	0.5	0.3
2806	Lithium nitride (when spilled in water)	30	100	0.1	0.1	0.4	0.2	60	200	0.6	0.4	2.6	1.6
2810	Buzz (used as a weapon); BZ (used as a weapon)	30	100	0.2	0.1	0.5	0.3	60	200	0.5	0.3	2.0	1.2
2810	CS (when used as a weapon)	60	200	0.4	0.2	1.2	0.7	240	800	2.6	1.6	5.7	3.5
2810	DC (when used as a weapon)	30	100	0.2	0.1	0.9	0.5	240	800	2.3	1.4	5.4	3.3
2810	GA (when used as a weapon)	30	100	0.4	0.2	0.7	0.4	150	500	1.7	1.0	3.1	1.9
2810	GB (when used as a weapon)	150	500	1.7	1.0	3.4	2.1	1000	3000	11.0+	7.0+	11.0+	7.0+

ID	Name												
2810	GD (when used as a weapon)	90	300	0.9	0.5	1.8	1.1	800	2500	6.8	4.2	10.5	6.5
2810	GF (when used as a weapon)	30	100	0.4	0.2	0.7	0.4	240	800	2.3	1.4	5.2	3.2
2810	H (used as a weapon); HD (used as a weapon)	30	100	0.2	0.1	0.2	0.1	60	200	0.7	0.4	1.2	0.7
2810	HL (when used as a weapon)	30	100	0.2	0.1	0.4	0.2	90	300	1.0	0.6	1.8	1.1
2810	HN-1 (when used as a weapon)	30	100	0.2	0.1	0.2	0.1	90	200	0.7	0.4	1.3	0.8
2810	HN-2 (when used as a weapon)	30	100	0.2	0.1	0.2	0.1	60	200	0.5	0.3	1.2	0.7
2810	HN-3 (when used as a weapon)	30	100	0.2	0.1	0.2	0.1	30	100	0.2	0.1	0.4	0.2
2810	L (Lewisite) (when used as a weapon)	30	100	0.2	0.1	0.4	0.2	90	300	1.0	0.6	1.8	1.1
2810	Mustard (when used as a weapon)	30	100	0.2	0.1	0.2	0.1	30	100	0.2	0.1	0.4	0.2
2810	Mustard Lewisite (when used as a weapon)	30	100	0.2	0.1	0.4	0.2	90	300	1.0	0.6	1.8	1.1
2810	Sarin (when used as a weapon)	150	500	1.7	1.0	3.4	2.1	1000	3000	11.0+	7.0+	11.0+	7.0+
2810	Soman (when used as a weapon)	90	300	0.9	0.5	1.8	1.1	800	2500	6.8	4.2	10.5	6.5
2810	Tabun (when used as a weapon)	30	100	0.4	0.2	0.7	0.4	150	500	1.7	1.0	3.1	1.9
2810	Thickened GD (when used as a weapon)	90	300	0.9	0.5	1.8	1.1	800	2500	6.8	4.2	10.5	6.5
2810	Toxic liquid, n.o.s. (& Inhalation Hazard Zone A)	150	500	1.3	0.8	3.5	2.2	1000	3000	11.0+	7.0+	11.0+	7.0+
2810	Toxic liquid, n.o.s. (Inhalation Hazard Zone B)	60	200	0.5	0.3	1.8	1.1	330	1100	3.3	2.1	7.3	4.6
2810	Toxic liquid, organic, n.o.s. (& Inhalation Hazard Zone A)	150	500	1.3	0.8	3.3	2.1	1000	3000	11.0+	7.0+	11.0+	7.0+
2810	Toxic liquid, organic, n.o.s. (Inhalation Hazard Zone B)	60	200	0.4	0.2	1.0	0.6	270	900	2.5	1.6	5.6	3.5
2810	VX (when used as a weapon)	30	100	0.2	0.1	0.2	0.1	60	200	0.7	0.4	1.0	0.6
2811	CX (when used as a weapon)	30	100	0.2	0.1	0.5	0.3	90	300	1.0	0.6	3.1	1.9
2826	Ethyl chlorothioformate	30	100	0.1	0.1	0.2	0.1	60	200	0.5	0.4	1.0	0.6

Hazmat

Table of Initial Isolation and Protective Action Distances (cont.)

ID #	Name of Material	Small Spills (small package or small leak)						Large Spills (large pkg or many small pkgs)					
		Isolate in all Directions		Downwind Protection				Isolate in all Directions		Downwind Protection			
				Day		Night				Day		Night	
		meters	feet	km	miles	km	miles	meters	feet	km	miles	km	miles
2845	Ethyl phosphonous dichloride, anhydrous	30	100	0.4	0.2	0.8	0.5	210	700	1.9	1.2	3.6	2.2
2845	Methyl phosphonous dichloride	60	200	0.4	0.3	1.2	0.8	330	1000	3.1	1.9	5.9	3.7
2901	Bromine chloride	30	100	0.2	0.2	0.9	0.6	240	800	2.4	1.5	6.3	3.9
2927	Ethyl phosphonothioic dichloride, anhydrous	30	100	0.1	0.1	0.1	0.1	30	100	0.2	0.1	0.3	0.2
2927	Ethyl phosphorodichloridate	30	100	0.1	0.1	0.1	0.1	30	100	0.3	0.2	0.4	0.2
2927	Toxic liquid, corrosive, organic, n.o.s.(& Inhalation Hazard Zone A)	60	200	0.6	0.4	2.1	1.3	800	2500	6.2	3.9	11.0+	7.0+
2927	Toxic liquid, corrosive, organic, n.o.s. (Inhalation Hazard Zone B)	30	100	0.4	0.2	0.5	0.4	180	600	1.6	1.0	2.9	1.8
2929	Toxic liquid, flammable, n.o.s. (& Inhalation Hazard Zone A)	150	500	1.3	0.8	3.5	2.2	1000	3000	11.0+	7.0+	11.0+	7.0+
2929	Toxic liquid, flammable, n.o.s. (Inhalation Hazard Zone B)	60	200	0.4	0.2	1.0	0.6	270	900	2.5	1.6	5.6	3.5
2929	Toxic liquid, flammable, organic, n.o.s. (& Inhalation Hazard Zone A)	150	500	1.3	0.8	3.3	2.1	1000	3000	11.0+	7.0+	11.0+	7.0+
2929	Toxic liquid, flammable, organic, n.o.s. (Inhalation Hazard Zone B)	60	200	0.4	0.2	1.0	0.6	270	900	2.5	1.6	5.6	3.5

ID	Name												
2977	Radioactive material, Uranium hexafluoride, fissile (when spilled in water); Uranium hexafluoride, fissile containing > 1% Uranium-235 (when spilled in water)	30	100	0.1	0.1	0.6	0.4	90	300	0.7	0.5	3.3	2.1
2978	Radioactive material, Uranium hexafluoride, when spilled in water (&, non-fissile or fissile excepted); Uranium haxafluoride, when spilled in water (& fissile- excepted; &, low specific activity; &, non-fissile)	30	100	0.1	0.1	0.6	0.4	90	300	0.7	0.5	3.3	2.1
2985	Chlorosilanes, not otherwise specified, when spilled in water (&, flammable, corrosive)	30	100	0.1	0.1	0.5	0.3	150	500	1.3	0.8	3.9	2.4
2986	Chlorosilanes, not otherwise specified, when spilled in water (&, corrosive, flammable)	30	100	0.1	0.1	0.5	0.3	150	500	1.3	0.8	3.9	2.4
2987	Chlorosilanes, n.o.s., when spilled in water (&, corrosive)	30	100	0.1	0.1	0.5	0.3	150	500	1.3	0.8	3.9	2.4
2988	Chlorosilanes, not otherwise specified, when spilled in water (&, water-reactive, flammable, corrosive)	30	100	0.1	0.1	0.5	0.3	150	500	1.3	0.8	3.9	2.4
3023	2-Methyl2-hepthanethiol; tert-Octyl mercaptan	30	100	0.1	0.1	0.1	0.1	60	200	0.5	0.3	0.8	0.5
3048	Aluminum phosphide pesticide (when spilled in water)	90	300	0.6	0.4	2.7	1.7	1000	3000	9.0	5.6	11.0+	7.0+
3049	Metal alkyl halides, not otherwise specified, when spilled in water (&, water-reactive); Metal aryl halides, not otherwise specified, when spilled in water (&, water-reactive)	30	100	0.1	0.1	0.2	0.1	30	100	0.3	0.2	1.3	0.8

Hazmat

Table of Initial Isolation and Protective Action Distances (cont.)

ID #	Name of Material	Small Spills (small package or small leak)						Large Spills (large pkg or many small pkgs)						
		Isolate in all Directions		Downwind Protection				Isolate in all Directions		Downwind Protection			
				Day		Night				Day		Night	
		meters	feet	km	miles	km	miles	meters	feet	km	miles	km	miles
3052	Aluminum alkyl halides, when spilled in water (& , liquid; & , solid)	30	100	0.1	0.1	0.2	0.1	30	100	0.3	0.2	1.3	0.8
3057	Trifluoroacetyl chloride	30	100	0.3	0.2	1.3	0.8	800	2500	7.8	4.9	11.0+	7.0+
3079	Methacrylonitrile, inhibite (& , stabilized)	30	100	0.1	0.1	0.3	0.2	90	300	0.8	0.5	1.6	1.0
3083	Perchloryl fluoride	30	100	0.2	0.1	0.6	0.4	360	1200	3.5	2.2	8.8	5.5
3122	Toxic liquid, oxidizing, n.o.s. (& Inhalation Hazard Zone A)	150	500	1.3	0.8	3.5	2.2	1000	3000	11.0+	7.0+	11.0+	7.0+
3122	Toxic liquid oxidizing, n.o.s. (Inhalation Hazard Zone B)	30	100	0.4	0.2	1.4	0.9	270	900	2.7	1.7	6.9	4.3
3123	Toxic liquid, water-reactive, n.o.s. (& Inhalation Hazard Zone A)	150	500	1.3	0.8	3.5	2.2	1000	3000	11.0+	7.0+	11.0+	7.0+
3123	Toxic liquid, water-reactive, n.o.s. (Inhalation Hazard Zone B)	60	200	0.5	0.3	1.8	1.1	330	1100	3.3	2.1	7.3	4.6
3123	Toxic liquid, which in contact with water emits flammable gases, n.o.s. (& Inhalation Hazard Zone A)	150	500	1.3	0.8	3.5	2.2	1000	3000	11.0+	7.0+	11.0+	7.0+
3123	Toxic liquid, which in contact with water emits flammable gases, n.o.s.(Inhalation Hazard Zone B)	60	200	0.5	0.3	1.8	1.1	330	1100	3.3	2.1	7.3	4.6
3160	Liquefied gas, toxic, flammable, n.o.s. (& Inhalation Hazard Zone A)	120	400	1.2	0.8	5.1	3.2	1000	3000	8.7	5.4	11.0+	7.0+

ID	Name											
3160	Liquefied gas, toxic, flammable n.o.s. (Inhalation Hazard Zone B)	30	100	0.2	0.2	1.2	0.8	420	1400	4.0	2.5	10.8	6.7
3160	Liquefied gas, toxic, flammable, n.o.s. (Inhalation Hazard Zone C)	30	100	0.2	0.1	0.8	0.5	240	800	2.4	1.5	6.4	4.0
3160	Liquefied gas, toxic, flammable, n.o.s. (Inhalation Hazard Zone D)	30	100	0.1	0.1	0.2	0.1	90	300	0.8	0.5	2.4	1.5
3162	Liquefied gas, toxic, n.o.s. (& Inhalation Zone A)	600	2000	5.9	3.7	11.0+	7.0+	1000	3000	11.0+	7.0+	11.0+	7.0+
3162	Liquefied gas, toxic, n.o.s. (Inhalation Zone B)	60	200	0.4	0.3	2.0	1.3	800	2500	7.8	4.9	11.0+	7.0+
3162	Liquefied gas, toxic, n.o.s. (Inhalation Zone C)	30	100	0.3	0.2	1.2	0.8	240	800	2.4	1.5	6.4	4.0
3162	Liquefied gas, toxic, n.o.s. (Inhalation Zone D)	30	100	0.2	0.1	0.7	0.4	120	400	1.2	0.8	3.8	2.4
3246	Methanesulfonyl chloride	60	200	0.4	0.2	0.5	0.4	150	500	1.6	1.0	2.6	1.6
3275	Nitriles, toxic, flammable, n.o.s.	30	100	0.1	0.1	0.3	0.2	90	300	0.8	0.5	1.6	1.0
3276	Nitriles toxic, n.o.s. (& ,liquid)	30	100	0.1	0.1	0.3	0.2	90	300	0.8	0.5	1.6	1.0
3278	Organophosphorus compound, toxic, n.o.s. (& ,liquid)	60	200	0.4	0.3	1.2	0.8	330	1000	3.1	1.9	5.9	3.7
3279	Organophosphorus compound, toxic, flammable, n.o.s.	60	200	0.4	0.3	1.2	0.8	330	1000	3.1	1.9	5.9	3.7
3280	Organoarsenic compound, n.o.s. (& ,liquid)	30	100	0.2	0.1	0.7	0.4	210	700	2.1	1.3	5.1	3.2
3281	Metal carbonyls, n.o.s. (& ,liquid)	90	300	0.8	0.5	3.5	2.2	500	1600	4.7	2.9	9.8	6.1
3287	Toxic liquid, inorganic, n.o.s. (& Inhalation Hazard Zone A)	90	300	0.9	0.6	3.5	2.2	600	1800	5.3	3.3	11.0	6.9
3287	Toxic liquid, inorganic, n.o.s. (Inhalation Hazard Zone B)	60	200	0.5	0.3	1.8	1.1	330	1100	3.3	2.1	7.3	4.6
3289	Toxic liquid, corrosive, inorganic, n.o.s. (& Inhalation Hazard Zone A)	90	300	0.9	0.6	3.5	2.2	600	1800	5.3	3.3	11.0	6.9

Hazmat

Table of Initial Isolation and Protective Action Distances (cont.)

ID #	Name of Material	Small Spills (small package or small leak)						Large Spills (large pkg or many small pkgs)					
		Isolate in all Directions		Downwind Protection				Isolate in all Directions		Downwind Protection			
				Day		Night				Day		Night	
		meters	feet	km	miles	km	miles	meters	feet	km	miles	km	miles
3289	Toxic liquid, corrosive, inorganic, n.o.s. (Inhalation Hazard Zone B)	60	200	0.5	0.3	1.8	1.1	330	1100	3.3	2.1	7.3	4.6
3294	Hydrogen cyanide, solution in alcohol, < 45% Hydrogen cyanide	30	100	0.2	0.1	0.4	0.2	210	700	0.7	0.4	2.1	1.3
3300	Carbon dioxide and Ethylene oxide mixture with > 87% Ethylene oxide	30	100	0.1	0.1	0.2	0.1	90	300	0.8	0.5	2.4	1.5
3303	Compressed gas, toxic, oxidizing, n.o.s. (& Inhalation Hazard Zone A)	600	2000	5.9	3.7	11.0+	7.0+	1000	3000	11.0+	7.0+	11.0+	7.0+
3303	Compressed gas, toxic, oxidizing, n.o.s. (Inhalation Hazard Zone B)	60	200	0.4	0.3	2.0	1.3	360	1200	3.5	2.2	8.8	5.5
3303	Compressed gas, toxic, oxidizing, n.o.s. (Inhalation Hazard Zone C)	30	100	0.3	0.2	1.2	0.8	240	800	2.4	1.5	6.4	4.0
3303	Compressed gas, toxic, oxidizing, n.o.s. (Inhalation Hazard Zone D)	30	100	0.2	0.1	0.7	0.4	120	400	1.2	0.8	3.8	2.4
3304	Compressed gas, toxic, corrosive, n.o.s. (& Inhalation Hazard Zone A)	600	2000	5.9	3.7	11.0+	7.0+	1000	3000	11.0+	7.0+	11.0+	7.0+
3304	Compressed gas, toxic, corrosive, n.o.s. (Inhalation Hazard Zone B)	60	200	0.4	0.3	2.0	1.3	800	2500	7.2	4.5	11.0+	7.0+
3304	Compressed gas, toxic, corrosive, n.o.s. (Inhalation Hazard Zone C)	30	100	0.3	0.2	1.2	0.8	240	800	2.4	1.5	6.4	4.0
3304	Compressed gas, toxic, corrosive, n.o.s. (Inhalation Hazard Zone D)	30	100	0.2	0.1	0.7	0.4	60	200	0.6	0.4	2.2	1.4

ID	Name												
3305	Compressed gas, toxic, flammable, corrosive, n.o.s. (& Inhalation Hazard Zone A)	600	2000	5.9	3.7	11.0+	7.0+	1000	3000	11.0+	7.0+	11.0+	7.0+
3305	Compressed gas, toxic, flammable, corrosive, n.o.s. (Inhalation Hazard Zone B)	30	100	0.2	0.1	1.0	0.6	420	1400	4.0	2.5	10.8	6.7
3305	Compressed gas, toxic, flammable, corrosive, n.o.s. (Inhalation Hazard Zone C)	30	100	0.2	0.1	0.8	0.5	240	800	2.4	1.5	6.4	4.0
3305	Compressed gas, toxic, flammable, corrosive, n.o.s. (Inhalation Hazard Zone D)	30	100	0.1	0.1	0.2	0.1	90	300	0.8	0.5	2.4	1.5
3306	Compressed gas, toxic, oxidizing, corrosive, n.o.s. (& Inhalation Hazard Zone A)	600	2000	5.9	3.7	11.0+	7.0+	1000	3000	11.0+	7.0+	11.0+	7.0+
3306	Compressed gas, toxic, oxidizing, corrosive, n.o.s. (Inhalation Hazard Zone B)	60	200	0.4	0.3	2.0	1.3	360	1200	3.5	2.2	8.8	5.5
3306	Compressed gas, toxic, oxidizing, corrosive, n.o.s. (Inhalation Hazard Zone C)	30	100	0.3	0.2	1.2	0.8	240	800	2.4	1.5	6.4	4.0
3306	Compressed gas, toxic, oxidizing, corrosive, n.o.s. (Inhalation Hazard Zone D)	30	100	0.2	0.1	0.7	0.4	60	200	0.6	0.4	2.2	1.4
3307	Liquefied gas, toxic, oxidizing, n.o.s. (& Inhalation Hazard Zone A)	600	2000	5.9	3.7	11.0+	7.0+	1000	3000	11.0+	7.0+	11.0+	7.0+
3307	Liquefied gas, toxic, oxidizing, n.o.s. (Inhalation Hazard Zone B)	60	200	0.4	0.3	2.0	1.3	360	1200	3.5	2.2	8.8	5.5
3307	Liquefied gas, toxic, oxidizing, n.o.s. (Inhalation Hazard Zone C)	30	100	0.3	0.2	1.2	0.8	240	800	2.4	1.5	6.4	4.0

Table of Initial Isolation and Protective Action Distances (cont.)

ID #	Name of Material	Small Spills (small package or small leak)						Large Spills (large pkg or many small pkgs)					
		Isolate in all Directions		Downwind Protection				Isolate in all Directions		Downwind Protection			
				Day		Night				Day		Night	
		meters	feet	km	miles	km	miles	meters	feet	km	miles	km	miles
3307	Liquefied gas, toxic, oxidizing, n.o.s. (Inhalation Hazard Zone D)	30	100	0.2	0.1	0.7	0.4	120	400	1.2	0.8	3.8	2.4
3308	Liquefied gas, toxic, corrosive, n.o.s. (& Inhalation Hazard Zone A)	600	2000	5.9	3.7	11.0+	7.0+	1000	3000	11.0+	7.0+	11.0+	7.0+
3308	Liquefied gas, toxic, corrosive, n.o.s. (Inhalation Hazard Zone B)	60	200	0.4	0.3	2.0	1.3	800	2500	7.2	4.5	11.0+	7.0+
3308	Liquefied gas, toxic, corrosive, n.o.s. (Inhalation Hazard Zone C)	30	100	0.3	0.2	1.2	0.8	240	800	2.4	1.5	6.4	4.0
3308	Liquefied gas, toxic, corrosive, n.o.s. (Inhalation Hazard Zone D)	30	100	0.2	0.1	0.7	0.4	60	200	0.6	0.4	2.2	1.4
3309	Liquefied gas, toxic, flammable, corrosive, n.o.s. (& Inhalation Hazard Zone A)	600	2000	5.9	3.7	11.0+	7.0+	1000	3000	11.0+	7.0+	11.0+	7.0+
3309	Liquefied gas, toxic, flammable, corrosive, n.o.s. (Inhalation Hazard Zone B)	30	100	0.2	0.1	1.0	0.6	420	1400	4.0	2.5	10.8	6.7
3309	Liquefied gas, toxic, flammable, corrosive, n.o.s. (Inhalation Hazard Zone C)	30	100	0.2	0.1	0.8	0.5	240	800	2.4	1.5	6.4	4.0
3309	Liquefied gas, toxic, flammable, corrosive, n.o.s. (Inhalation Hazard Zone D)	30	100	0.1	0.1	0.2	0.1	90	300	0.8	0.5	2.4	1.5

ID	Name											
3310	Liquefied gas, toxic, oxidizing, corrosive, n.o.s. (& Inhalation Hazard Zone A)	600	2000	5.9	3.7	11.0+	7.0+	1000	3000	11.0+	7.0+	11.0+	7.0+
3310	Liquefied gas, toxic, oxidizing, corrosive, n.o.s. (Inhalation Hazard Zone B)	60	200	0.4	0.3	2.0	1.3	360	1200	3.5	2.2	8.8	5.5
3310	Liquefied gas, toxic, oxidizing, corrosive, n.o.s. (Inhalation Hazard Zone C)	30	100	0.3	0.2	1.2	0.8	240	800	2.4	1.5	6.4	4.0
3310	Liquefied gas, toxic, oxidizing, corrosive, n.o.s. (Inhalation Hazard Zone D)	30	100	0.2	0.1	0.7	0.4	60	200	0.6	0.4	2.2	1.4
3318	Ammonia solution with > 50% Ammonia	30	100	0.1	0.1	0.1	0.1	60	200	0.6	0.4	2.2	1.4
3355	Insecticide gas, toxic, flammable, n.o.s. (& Inhalation Hazard Zone A)	120	400	1.2	0.8	5.1	3.2	1000	3000	8.7	5.4	11.0+	7.0+
3355	Insecticide gas, toxic, flammable, n.o.s. (Inhalation Hazard Zone B)	30	100	0.2	0.2	1.2	0.8	420	1400	4.0	2.5	10.8	6.7
3355	Insecticide gas, toxic, flammable, n.o.s. (Inhalation Hazard Zone C)	30	100	0.2	0.1	0.8	0.5	240	800	2.4	1.5	6.4	4.0
3355	Insecticide gas, toxic, flammable, n.o.s. (Inhalation Hazard Zone D)	30	100	0.1	0.1	0.2	0.1	90	300	0.8	0.5	2.4	1.5
3381	Toxic by inhalation liquid, n.o.s. (Inhalation Hazard Zone A)	150	500	1.3	0.8	3.5	2.2	1000	3000	11.0+	7.0+	11.0+	7.0+
3382	Toxic by inhalation liquid, n.o.s. (Inhalation Hazard Zone B)	60	200	0.5	0.3	1.8	1.1	330	1100	3.3	2.1	7.3	4.6
3383	Toxic by inhalation liquid, flammable, n.o.s. (Inhalation Hazard Zone A)	150	500	1.3	0.8	3.5	2.2	1000	3000	11.0+	7.0+	11.0+	7.0+

Hazmat

Table of Initial Isolation and Protective Action Distances (cont.)

ID #	Name of Material	Small Spills (small package or small leak)						Large Spills (large pkg or many small pkgs)					
		Isolate in all Directions		Downwind Protection Day		Night		Isolate in all Directions		Downwind Protection Day		Night	
		meters	feet	km	miles	km	miles	meters	feet	km	miles	km	miles
3384	Toxic by inhalation liquid, flammable, n.o.s. (Inhalation Hazard Zone B)	60	200	0.4	0.2	1.0	0.6	270	900	2.5	1.6	5.6	3.5
3385	Toxic by inhalation liquid, water-reactive, n.o.s. (Inhalation Hazard Zone A)	150	500	1.3	0.8	3.5	2.2	1000	3000	11.0+	7.0+	11.0+	7.0+
3386	Toxic by inhalation liquid, water-reactive, n.o.s. (Inhalation Hazard Zone B)	60	200	0.5	0.3	1.8	1.1	330	1100	3.3	2.1	7.3	4.6
3387	Toxic by inhalation liquid, oxidizing, n.o.s. (Inhalation Hazard Zone A)	150	500	1.3	0.8	3.5	2.2	1000	3000	11.0+	7.0+	11.0+	7.0+
3388	Toxic by inhalation liquid, oxidizing, n.o.s. (Inhalation Hazard Zone B)	30	100	0.4	0.2	1.4	0.9	270	900	2.7	1.7	6.9	4.3
3389	Toxic by inhalation liquid, corrosive, n.o.s. (Inhalation Hazard Zone A)	90	300	0.8	0.5	2.4	1.5	800	2500	6.2	3.9	11.0+	7.0+
3390	Toxic by inhalation liquid, corrosive, n.o.s. (Inhalation Hazard Zone B)	60	200	0.5	0.3	1.8	1.1	330	1100	3.3	2.1	7.3	4.6
3461	Aluminum alkyl halides, solid (spilled in water)	30	100	0.1	0.1	0.2	0.1	30	100	0.3	0.2	1.3	0.8
9191	Chlorine dioxide, hydrate, frozen (when spilled in water)	30	100	0.1	0.1	0.1	0.1	30	100	0.2	0.1	0.7	0.4
9192	Fluorine, refrigerated liquid (cryogenic liquid)	30	100	0.2	0.1	0.5	0.3	90	300	0.8	0.5	3.5	2.2

9202	Carbon monoxide, refrigerated liquid (cryogenic liquid)	30	100	0.1	0.1	0.1	90	300	0.7	0.4	2.4	1.5
9206	Methyl phosphonic dichloride	30	100	0.1	0.1	0.1	30	100	0.2	0.1	0.2	0.1
9263	Chloropivaloyl chloride	30	100	0.1	0.1	0.1	30	100	0.3	0.2	0.5	0.3
9264	3,5-Dichloro-2,4,6-trifluoropyridine	30	100	0.1	0.1	0.1	30	100	0.3	0.2	0.4	0.3
9269	Trimethoxysilane	30	100	0.2	0.4	0.3	120	400	1.1	0.7	2.2	1.4

Notes: Similar materials in this table have been combined for space reasons. When you see a "&" in parenthesis, it means a second material with the same name and the following qualifing words is also represented in that group. For example: Boron trifluoride (&, compressed) really stands for two lines, the first is "Boron trifluoride," the second is "Boron trifluoride, compressed). For a complete listing of all materials spelled out, see the Table of Initial Isolation and Protective Action Distances in the 2004 Emergency Response Guide (ERG), by the Department of Transportation.

Hazmat

Water-Reactive Materials That Produce Toxic Gas

Use the following table only when materials are spilled in water!

ID No.	Guide No.	Name of Material	TIH Gas(es) Produced
1162	155	Dimethyldichlorosilane	HCl
1196	155	Ethyltrichlorosilane	HCl
1242	139	Methyldichlorosilane	HCl
1250	155	Methyltrichlorosilane	HCl
1295	139	Trichlorosilane	HCl
1298	155	Trimethylchlorosilane	HCl
1305	155P	Vinyltrichlorosilane	HCl
1305	155P	Vinyltrichlorosilane, inhibited	HCl
1305	155P	Vinyltrichlorosilane, stabilized	HCl
1340	139	Phosphorus pentasulfide, free from yellow and white Phosphorus	H_2S
1360	139	Calcium phosphide	PH_3
1384	135	Sodium dithionite	H_2S; SO_2
1384	135	Sodium hydrosulfite	H_2S; SO_2
1397	139	Aluminum phosphide	PH_3
1412	139	Lithium amide	NH_3
1419	139	Magnesium aluminum phosphide	PH_3
1432	139	Sodium phosphide	PH_3
1541	155	Acetone cyanohydrin, stabilized	HCN
1680	157	Potassium cyanide	HCN
1680	157	Potassium cyanide, solid	HCN
1689	157	Sodium cyanide	HCN
1689	157	Sodium cyanide, solid	HCN
1716	156	Acetyl bromide	HBr
1717	155	Acetyl chloride	HCl
1724	155	Allyltrichlorosilane, stabilized	HCl
1725	137	Aluminum bromide, anhydrous	HBr
1726	137	Aluminum chloride, anhydrous	HCl
1728	155	Amyltrichlorosilane	HCl
1732	157	Antimony pentafluoride	HF
1745	144	Bromine pentafluoride	HF; Br_2
1746	144	Bromine trifluoride	HF; Br_2
1747	155	Butyltrichlorosilane	HCl
1752	156	Chloroacetyl chloride	HCl
1754	137	Chlorosulfonic acid	HCl
1754	137	Chlorosulfonic acid and Sulfur trioxide mixture	HCl
1754	137	Sulfur trioxide and Chlorosulfonic acid	HCl
1758	137	Chromium oxychloride	HCl
1763	156	Cyclohexyltrichlorosilane	HCl
1766	156	Dichlorophenyltrichlorosilane	HCl

ID No.	Guide No.	Name of Material	TIH Gas(es) Produced
1767	155	Dietyldichlorosilane	HCl
1769	156	Diphenyldichlorosilane	HCl
1771	156	Dodecyltrichlorosilane	HCl
1777	137	Fluorosulfonic acid	HF
1784	156	Hexyltrichlorosilane	HCl
1799	156	Nonyltrichlorosilane	HCl
1800	156	Octadecyltrichlorosilane	HCl
1801	156	Octyltrichlorosilane	HCl
1804	156	Phenyltrichlorosilane	HCl
1806	137	Phosphorus pentachloride	HCl
1809	137	Phosphorus trichloride	HCl
1810	137	Phosphorus oxychloride	HCl
1816	155	Propyltrichlorosilane	HCl
1818	157	Silicon tetrachloride	HCl
1828	137	Sulfur chlorides	HCl; SO_2; H_2S
1834	137	Sulfuryl chloride	HCl; SO_3
1836	137	Thionyl chloride	HCl; SO_2
1838	137	Titanium tetrachloride	HCl
1898	156	Acetyl iodide	HI
1923	135	Calcium dithionite	H_2S; SO_2
1923	135	Calcium hydrosulfite	H_2S; SO_2
1931	171	Zinc Dithionite	H_2S; SO_2
1931	171	Zinc hydrosulfite	H_2S; SO_2
2004	135	Magnesium diamide	NH_3
2011	139	Magnesium phosphide	PH_3
2012	139	Potassium phosphide	PH_3
2013	139	Strontium phosphide	PH_3
2437	156	Methylphenyldichlorosilane	HCl
2495	144	Iodine pentafluoride	HF
2691	137	Phosphorus pentabromide	HBr
2692	157	Boron tribromide	HBr
2806	138	Lithium nitride	NH_3
2977	166	Radioactive material, Uranium hexafluoride, fissile	HF
2977	166	Uranium hexafluoride, fissile containing > 1% Uranium-235	HF
2978	166	Radioactive material, Uranium hexafluoride	HF
2978	166	Radioactive material, Uranium hexafluoride, non-fissile or fissile-excepted	HF
2978	166	Uranium hexafluoride	HF
2978	166	Uranium hexafluoride, fissle-excepted	HF
2978	166	Uranium hexafluoride, low specific activity	HF
2978	166	Uranium hexafluoride, non-fissle	HF

Hazmat

ID No.	Guide No.	Name of Material	TIH Gas(es) Produced
2985	155	Chlorosilanes, flammable, corrosive, n.o.s.	HCl
2985	155	Chlorosilanes, n.o.s.	HCl
2986	155	Chlorosilanes, corrosive, flammable, n.o.s.	HCl
2986	155	Chlorosilanes, n.o.s.	HCl
2987	156	Chlorosilanes, corrosive, n.o.s.	HCl
2987	156	Chlorosilanes, n.o.s.	HCl
2988	139	Chlorosilanes, n.o.s.	HCl
2988	139	Chlorosilanes, water-reactive, flammable, corrosive, n.o.s.	HCl
3048	157	Aluminum phosphide pesticide	PH₃
3049	138	Metal alkyl halides, n.o.s.	HCl
3049	138	Metal alkyl halides, water-reactive, n.o.s.	HCl
3049	138	Metal aryl halides, n.o.s.	HCl
3049	138	Metal aryl halides, water-reactive, n.o.s.	HCl
3052	135	Aluminum alkyl halides	HCl
3052	135	Aluminum alkyl halides, liquid	HCl
3052	135	Aluminum alkyl halides, solid	HCl
3461	135	Aluminum alkyl halides, solid	HCl
9191	143	Chlorine dioxide, hydrate, frozen	Cl₂

Chemical Symbols for TIH Gases:

Br₂ ....Bromine
Cl₂ ....Chlorine
HBr ....Hydrogen bromide
HCl ....Hydrogen chloride
HCN ......Hydrogen cyanide
HF ....Hydrogen fluoride
HI ....Hydrogen iodide
H₂S ....Hydrogen sulfide
NH₃ ....Ammonia
PH₃ ....Phosphine
SO₂ ....Sulfur dioxide
SO₃ ....Sulfur trioxide

Hazmat Glossary

Alcohol resistant foam: A foam that is resistant to "polar" chemicals such as ketones and esters which may break down other types of foam.

Biological agents: Living organisms that cause disease, sickness and mortality in humans. Examples: Anthrax and Ebola. See Guide 158.

Blister agents (vesicants): Substances that cause blistering of the skin. Exposure is through liquid or vapor contact with any exposed tissue (eyes, skin, lungs). Examples: Mustard (H), Distilled Mustard (HD), Nitrogen Mustard (HN), and Lewisite (L).
Symptoms: Red eyes, skin irritation, burning of skin, blisters, upper respiratory damage, cough, hoarseness.

Blood agents: Substances that injure a person by interfering with cell respiration (the exchange of oxygen and carbon dioxide between blood and tissues). Examples: Hydrogen cyanide (AC) and Cyanogen chloride (CK). Symptoms: Respiratory distress, headache, unresponsiveness, seizures, coma.

Burn: Refers to either a chemical or thermal burn. Chemical burns may be caused by corrosive substances; thermal burns may be caused by liquefied cryogenic gases, hot molten substances, or flames.

Choking agents: Substances that cause physical injury to the lungs. Exposure is through inhalation. In extreme cases, membranes swell and lungs become filled with liquid (pulmonary edema). Death results from lack of oxygen; hence, the victim is "choked". Example: Phosgene (CG). Symptoms: Irritation to eyes, nose, and throat, respiratory distress, nausea and vomiting, burning of exposed skin.

CO_2: Carbon dioxide gas.

Cold zone: Area where the command post and support functions that are necessary to control the incident are located. This is also referred to as the clean zone, green zone, or support zone.

Combustible liquid: Liquids which have a flash point greater than 60.5°C (141°F) and below 93°C (200°F). US regulations permit a flammable liquid with a flash point between 38°C (100°F) and 60.5°C (114°F) to be reclassed as a combustible liquid.

Compatibility Group: Letters identify explosives that are deemed to be compatible. Class 1 materials are considered to be "compatible" if they can be transported together without significantly increasing either the probability of an incident or, for a given quantity, the magnitude of the effects of such an incident. See page 622 for letter descriptions.

Control zones: Designated areas at dangerous goods incidents, based on safety and the degree of hazard. Many terms are used to describe control zones; however, this material defines them as hot/exclusion/ restricted zone, warm/contamination reduction/limited access zone, and cold/support/clean zone.

Cryogenic liquid: A refrigerated, liquefied gas that has a boiling point colder than -90°C (-130°F) at atmospheric pressure.

Dangerous Water Reactive Material: Produces significant toxic gas when it comes in contact with water.

Decomposition products: Products of a chemical or thermal break-down of a substance.

Decontamination: The removal of dangerous goods from personnel and equipment to the extent necessary to prevent potential adverse health effects. Always avoid direct or indirect contact with dangerous goods, but if contact occurs, personnel should be decontaminated as soon as possible. Since the methods used to decontaminate personnel and equipment differ from one chemical to another, contact the chemical manufacturer to determine the appropriate procedure. Contaminated clothing and equipment should be removed after use and stored in a controlled area (warm/contamination reduction/limited access zone) until cleanup procedures can be initiated. In some cases, protective clothing and equipment cannot be decontaminated and must be disposed of in a proper manner.

Dry chemical: A preparation designed for fighting fires involving flammable liquids, pyrophoric substances and electrical equipment. Common types contain sodium bicarbonate or potassium bicarbonate.

Edema: The accumulation of an excessive amount of watery fluid in cells and tissues. Pulmonary edema is an excessive buildup of water in the lungs, for instance, after inhalation of a gas that is corrosive to lung tissue.

ERPG(s): Emergency Response Planning Guideline(s). Values intended to provide estimates of concentration ranges above which one could reasonably anticipate observing adverse health effects.
ERPG-1: The maximum airborne concentration below which it is believed nearly all individuals could be exposed for up to 1

hour without experiencing more than mild, transient adverse health effects or without perceiving a clearly defined objectionable odor.

ERPG-2: The maximum airborne concentration below which it is believed nearly all individuals could be exposed for up to 1 hour without experiencing or developing irreversible or other serious health effects or symptoms that could impair an individual's ability to take protective action.

ERPG-3: The maximum airborne concentration below which it is believed nearly all individuals could be exposed for up to 1 hour without experiencing or developing life-threatening health effects.

Flammable liquid: A liquid that has a flash point of 60.5°C (114°F) or lower.

Flash point: Lowest temperature at which a liquid or solid gives off vapor in such a concentration that, when the vapor combines with air near the surface of the liquid or solid, a flammable mixture is formed. Hence, the lower the flash point, the more flammable the material.

Hot zone: Area immediately surrounding a dangerous goods incident which extends far enough to prevent adverse effects from released dangerous goods to personnel outside the zone. This zone is also referred to as exclusion zone, red zone, or restricted zone.

Immiscible: In this reference, this refers to a material that does not mix readily with water.

LC50: Lethal concentration 50. The concentration of a material administered by inhalation that is expected to cause the death of 50% of an experimental animal population within a specified time. Concentration is reported in either ppm or mg/m^3.

Mass explosion: Explosion which affects almost the entire load virtually instantaneously.

mg/m^3: Milligrams of material per cubic meter of air.

Miscible: In this reference, this refers to a material that mixes readily with water.

mL/m^3: Milliliters of a material per cubic meter of air.
($1\ mL/m^3$ = 1 ppm)

Nerve agents: Substances that interfere with the central nervous system. Exposure is primarily through contact with the liquid (via skin and eyes) and secondarily through inhalation of the vapor.
Examples: Tabun (GA), Sarin (GB), Soman (GD), VX.
Symptoms: Pinpoint pupils, extreme headache, severe

tightness in the chest, dyspnea, runny nose, coughing, salivation, unresponsiveness, and seizures.

Non-polar: See Immiscible.

Not otherwise specified: The entries which use this means that the actual chemical name for that corrosive liquid is not listed in the regulations. Therefore, a generic name must be used to describe it on shipping papers.

Noxious: In this reference, this refers to a material that may be harmful or injurious to health or physical well-being.

Oxidizer: A chemical which supplies its own oxygen and which helps other combustible material burn more readily.

P: The letter "P" following a guide number identifies a material which may polymerize violently under high temperature conditions or contamination with other products. This polymerization will produce heat and high pressure buildup in containers which may explode or rupture.

pH: pH is a value that represents the acidity or alkalinity of a water solution. Pure water has a pH of 7. A pH value below 7 indicates an acid solution; above 7 indicates an alkaline solution. Acids and alkalies (bases) are commonly referred to as corrosive materials.

PIH: Poison Inhalation Hazard. Describes gases and volatile liquids that are TIH (Toxic When Inhaled).

Polar: See Miscible.

Polymerization: This term describes a chemical reaction which is generally associated with the production of plastic substances. The individual molecules of the chemical (liquid or gas) react with each other to produce what can be described as a long chain.

ppm: Parts per million. (1 ppm = 1 mL/m³)

Protective clothing: Includes both respiratory and physical protection. One cannot assign a level of protection to clothing or respiratory devices separately.
Level A: SCBA plus totally encapsulating chemical resistant clothing (permeation resistant).
Level B: SCBA plus hooded chemical resistant clothing (splash suit).
Level C: Full or half-face respirator plus hooded chemical resistant clothing (splash suit).
Level D: Coverall with no respiratory protection.

Pyrophoric: A material which ignites spontaneously upon exposure to air (or oxygen).

Radioactivity: The property of some substances to emit invisible and potentially harmful radiation.

Radiation Authority: As referred to in Guides 161-166 for radioactive materials, the Radiation Authority is either a Federal, state/provincial agency, or state/ province designated official. Responsibilities include evaluating radiological hazard conditions during normal operations and during emergencies. If the identity and telephone number of the authority are not known by emergency responders, or included in the local response plan, refer to agencies listed on page 613. They maintain a periodically updated list of Radiation Authorities.

Refrigerated liquid: See Cryogenic liquid.

Straight (solid) stream: Method used to apply or distribute water from the end of a hose. The water is delivered under pressure for penetration. In an efficient stream, approximately 90% of the water passes through an imaginary circle 15 inches in diameter at the breaking point. Hose streams are frequently used to cool tanks and other equipment exposed to flammable liquid fires, or for washing burning spills away from danger points. If streams are improperly used, they may cause a spill fire to spread when directed into open containers of flammable and combustible liquids.

TIH: Toxic Inhalation Hazard. Term used to describe gases and volatile liquids that are toxic when inhaled. (Same as PIH)

V: Saturated vapor concentration in air of a material in mL/m^3 (volatility) at 20°C and standard atmospheric pressure.

Vapor density: Weight of a volume of pure vapor or gas (with no air present) compared to the weight of an equal volume of dry air at the same temperature and pressure. A vapor density less than 1 indicates that the vapor is lighter than air and will tend to rise. A vapor density greater than 1 indicates that the vapor is heavier than air and may travel along the ground.

Vapor pressure: Pressure at which a liquid and vapor are in equilibrium at a given temperature. Liquids with high vapor pressures evaporate rapidly.

Viscosity: Measure of a liquid's internal resistance to flow. This property is important because it indicates how fast a material will leak out through holes in containers or tanks.

Warm zone: Area between Hot and Cold zones where personnel and equipment decontamination and hot zone support takes place. It includes control points for the access corridor and thus assists in reducing the spread of contamination. Also referred to as the contamination reduction

Hazmat

corridor (CRC), contamination reduction zone (CRZ), yellow zone, or limited access zone.

Water-sensitive: Substances which may produce flammable and/or toxic decomposition products upon contact with water.

Water spray (fog): Method or way to apply or distribute water. The water is finely divided to provide for high heat absorption. Water spray patterns can range from 10 to 90 degrees. Water spray streams can be used to extinguish or control the burning of a fire or to provide exposure protection for personnel, equipment, buildings, etc. (This method can be used to absorb, knock-down, or disperse vapors.) Water spray is particularly effective on fires of flammable liquids and volatile solids having flash points above 37.8°C (100°F). Water spray can also be used on flammable liquids with low and high flash points. The effectiveness depends on the method of application.

Hazmat

‖ PHONE DIRECTORY

Federal Agencies · **944**
  Bureau of Alcohol, Tobacco & Firearms (ATF) · · · · · · · · · · 944
  Bureau of Indian Affairs (BIA) · 945
  Bureau of Land Management (BLM) · · · · · · · · · · · · · · · · · 945
  Bureau of Reclamation · 948
  Department of Agriculture (USDA) · · · · · · · · · · · · · · · · · · 949
  Department of Commerce (DOC) · · · · · · · · · · · · · · · · · · · 949
  Department of Education (ED) · 949
  Department of Energy (DOE) · 950
  Department for Health & Human Services (HHS) · · · · · · · · · 953
  Department of Homeland Security (DHS) · · · · · · · · · · · · 959
  Department of Housing & Urban Development (HUD) · · · · · · 979
  Department of Interior (DOI) · 979
  Department of Justice (DOJ) · 980
  Department of Labor (DOL) · 981
  Department of State (DOS) · 981
  Department of Transportation (DOT) · · · · · · · · · · · · · · · · · 982
  Department of Treasury · 983
  Department of Veteran Affairs (VA) · · · · · · · · · · · · · · · · · 984
  Drug Enforcement Administration (DEA) · · · · · · · · · · · · · · 984
  Environmental Protection Agency (EPA) · · · · · · · · · · · · · · 986
  Federal Aviation Administration (FAA) · · · · · · · · · · · · · · · · 989
  Federal Bureau of Investigation (FBI) · · · · · · · · · · · · · · · · 992
  Federal Bureau of Prisons (BOP) · · · · · · · · · · · · · · · · · · 993
  Federal Railroad Administration (FRA) · · · · · · · · · · · · · · · 994
  Federal Transit Administration (FTA) · · · · · · · · · · · · · · · · 994
  Internal Revenue Service (IRS) · 995
  Military Law Enforcement · 995
  National Drug Intelligence Center (NDIC) · · · · · · · · · · · · · 997
  National Highway Traffic Safety Administration (NHTSA) · · · · 997
  National Park Service (NPS) · 998
  U.S. Attorneys' Offices · 998
  U.S. Capitol Police · 1000
  U.S. Marshals Service · 1001
  U.S. Fish and Wildlife Service (FWS) · · · · · · · · · · · · · · · 1003
  U.S. Forest Service · 1004
State Agencies · **1005**
  National Guard · 1005
  State Departments of Corrections · · · · · · · · · · · · · · · · · 1008
  State Divisions of Wildlife · 1009
  State Health Departments · 1010
  State Insurance Fraud Reporting · · · · · · · · · · · · · · · · · · 1011
  State Police · 1012
Other Resources · **1014**
  Includes: American Red Cross, Car Rental Co, Credit Card Co, Domestic Violence & Victim Resources, Railroad Law Enforcement, and Law Enforcement Resources (Associations, Magazines, Newsletters, Organizations, & Websites)
Note: See Index (page 1041) for additional phone lists found throughout the book.

Phone Directory

Bureau of Alcohol, Tobacco & Firearms (ATF)

http://www.atf.gov

General Information	202-927-8810
Arson, Explosive & Firearm Questions	eps@atf.gov
Arson Hotline	888-ATF-FIRE
Bomb Hotline	888-ATF-BOMB
Employment · · · http://www.atf.gov/jobs	202-927-5690
Firearms Theft Hotline	800-800-3855
Firearms Tracing Hotline	800-788-7133
Gang Resistance Education & Training (GREAT)	great@atf.gov
Illegal Firearms Hotline	800-ATF-GUNS
Main E-Mail	ATFMail@atf.gov
Other Criminal Activity Hotline	888-ATF-TIPS
Stolen, Hijacked or Seized Cigarettes Hotline	800-659-6242

ATF Enforcement District Offices

Midwest, Chicago	312-353-6935
North Atlantic, New York	718-650-4000
Southeast, Atlanta	404-417-2600
Southwest, Dallas	469-227-4300
Western, San Francisco	925-479-7500

Field Division Offices

Arizona, Phoenix	602-776-5400
California, Los Angeles	213-534-2450
San Francisco	925-479-7500
Florida, Miami	305-597-4800
Tampa	813-202-7300
Georgia, Atlanta	404-417-2600
Illinois, Chicago	312-846-7200
Kentucky, Louisville	502-753-3400
Louisiana, New Orleans	504-841-7000
Maryland, Baltimore	410-779-1700
Massachusetts, Boston	617-557-1200
Michigan, Detroit	313-259-8050
Minnesota, Saint Paul	651-726-0200
Missouri, Kansas City	816-559-0700
New York, New York City	718-650-4000
North Carolina, Charlotte	704-716-1800
Ohio, Columbus	614-827-8400
Pennsylvania, Philadelphia	215-717-4700
Tennessee, Nashville	615-565-1400
Texas, Dallas	469-227-4300
Houston	281-372-2900
Washington, D.C.	202-927-8810
Washington, Seattle	206-389-5800

Bureau of Indian Affairs (BIA)

http://www.doi.gov/bureau-indian-affairs.html

General Information	202-208-3710
Tribal Leaders Directory	202-208-3711

Area Offices

Alaska, Juneau (AK)	907-586-7177
Arizona, Phoenix (AZ, CA, ID, NV, UT)	602-379-6600
California, Sacramento (CA)	916-978-6000
Eastern (AL, CT, FL, LA, ME, MS, NC, NY)	703-235-2571
Minnesota, Fort Snelling (IA, MI, MN, WI)	612-713-4400
Montana, Billings (MT, WY)	406-247-7943
Navajo (Navajo Reservations in AZ, NM, UT)	505-863-8314
New Mexico, Albuquerque (CO, NM)	505-248-7937
Oklahoma, Anadarko (KS, Western OK)	405-247-6673
Oklahoma, Muskogee (Eastern OK)	918-687-2296
Oregon, Portland (ID, OR, WA)	503-231-6702
South Dakota, Aberdeen (NE, ND, SD)	605-226-7343

Bureau of Land Management (BLM)

http://www.blm.gov

General Information	202-452-5125
Employment Webpage	http://www.usajobs.gov
Hazardous Materials	202-452-5087
Main E-Mail	webteam@ios.doi.gov
National Interagency Fire Center, Boise, Idaho	208-387-5512
National Training Center, Phoenix, Arizona	602-906-5500

District & Regional Offices

Desert District Office, Moreno Valley, California	909-697-5200
Eastern Regional Office, Springfield, Virginia	703-440-1600
Idaho, Boise District Office	208-384-3300
Idaho, Coeur D'Alene District Office	208-769-5030
Northern Regional Office, Fairbanks, Alaska	907-474-2200
South Coast Regional Office, Palm Springs, CA	760-251-4800
Western Slope Regional Office, Grand Junction, CO	970-244-3000

Field Offices

Alaska, Anchorage	907-271-1246
Glennallen	907-822-3217
Arizona, Kingman	928-692-4400
Lake Havasu City	928-505-1200
Phoenix	623-580-5500
Safford	928-348-4400

Tucson	520-258-7200
Yuma	928-317-3200
California, Alturas	530-233-4666
Arcata	707-825-2300
Bakersfield	661-391-6000
Barstow	760-252-6000
Bishop	760-872-5000
Eagle Lake (Susanville)	530-257-0456
El Centro	760-337-4400
Folsom	916-985-4474
Hollister	831-630-5000
Needles	760-326-7000
Redding	530-224-2100
Ridgecrest	760-384-5400
Surprise (Cedarville)	530-279-6101
Ukiah	707-468-4000
Colorado, Columbine (Durango)	970-385-1368
Del Norte	719-657-3321
Dolores	970-882-7296
Glenwood Springs	970-947-2800
Grand Junction	970-244-3000
Gunnison	970-641-0471
Kremmling	970-724-3000
La Jara	719-274-8971
Little Snake (Craig)	970-826-5000
Pagosa	970-264-2268
Royal Gorge (Canon City)	719-269-8500
Saguache	719-655-2547
Umcompahgre (Montrose)	970-240-5300
White River (Meeker)	970-878-3800
Idaho, Boise	208-384-3300
Burley	208-677-6641
Challis	208-879-6200
Coeur D'Alene	208-769-5030
Cottonwood	208-962-3245
Idaho Falls	208-524-7500
Jarbidge (Twin Falls)	208-736-2350
Pocatello	208-478-6340
Salmon	208-756-5400
Shoshone	208-732-7200
Twin Falls	208-735-2060
Mississippi, Jackson	601-977-5400
Montana, Billings	406-896-5013
Butte	406-533-7600
Dillon	406-683-2337
Glasgow	406-228-3750

Great Falls	406-791-7700
Havre	406-265-5891
Lewistown	406-538-7461
Malta	406-654-5100
Miles City	406-233-2800
Missoula	406-329-3914
Nevada, Battle Mountain	775-635-4000
Caliente	775-726-8100
Carson City	775-885-6000
Elko	775-753-0200
Ely	775-289-1800
Las Vegas	702-515-5000
Tonopah	775-482-7800
Winnemucca	775-623-1500
New Mexico, Albuquerque	505-761-8700
Carlsbad	505-234-5972
Farmington	505-599-8900
Las Cruces	505-525-4300
Roswell	505-627-0272
Socorro	505-835-0412
Taos	505-758-8851
North Dakota, Dickinson	701-227-7700
Oklahoma, Moore	405-794-9624
Tulsa	918-621-4100
Oregon, Burns	541-573-4400
Coos Bay (North Bend)	541-756-0100
Eugene	541-683-6600
Lakeview	541-947-2177
Medford	541-618-2200
Prineville	541-416-6700
Roseburg	541-440-4930
Salem	503-375-5646
Vale	541-473-3144
South Dakota, Belle Fourche	605-892-7000
Texas, Amarillo	806-356-1000
Utah, Cedar City	435-586-2401
Fillmore	435-743-3100
Henry Mountain (Hanksville)	435-542-3461
Kanab	435-644-4600
Moab	435-259-2100
Monticello	435-587-1500
Price	435-636-3600
Richfield	435-896-1500
Saint George	435-688-3200
Salt Lake City	801-977-4300
Vernal	435-781-4400

Phone Directory

Washington, Spokane	509-536-1200
Wisconsin, Milwaukee	414-297-4400
Wyoming, Buffalo	307-684-1100
Casper	307-261-7600
Cody	307-578-5900
Kemmerer	307-828-4500
Lander	307-332-8400
Newcastle	307-746-6600
Pinedale	307-367-5300
Rawlins	307-328-4200
Rock Springs	307-352-0256
Worland	307-347-5100

Law Enforcement Offices

Alaska, Anchorage	907-271-6622
Arizona, Phoenix	602-417-9339
California, Sacramento	916-978-4457
Colorado, Lakewood	303-239-3803
Idaho, Boise	208-373-4023
Montana, Billings	406-896-5010
Nevada, Reno	775-861-6667
Utah, Salt Lake City	801-539-4085
Wyoming, Cheyenne	307-775-6266

State Offices

Alaska, Anchorage	907-271-5076
Arizona, Phoenix	602-417-9200
California, Sacramento	916-978-4400
Colorado, Lakewood	303-239-3600
Idaho, Boise	208-373-4000
Montana, Billings	406-896-5012
Nevada, Reno	775-861-6400
New Mexico, Santa Fe	505-438-7400
Oregon, Portland	503-808-6026
Utah, Salt Lake City	801-539-4001
Wyoming, Cheyenne	307-775-6256

Bureau of Reclamation

http://www.usbr.gov

General Information	202-513-0501
Great Plains Regional Office, Billings, MT	406-247-7600
Lower Colorado Regional Office, Boulder City, NV	702-293-8411
Mid-Pacific Regional Office, Sacramento, CA	916-978-5000
Pacific Northwest Regional Office, Boise, ID	208-378-5012
Upper Colorado Regional Office, Salt Lake City, UT	801-524-3600

Department of Agriculture (USDA)

http://www.usda.gov

General Information	202-720-2791
Agricultural Research Service	301-504-1638
Animal & Health Plant Inspection Services	202-720-2511
Center for Nutrition Policy & Promotion	202-606-8000
Crisis Planning & Management	877-617-7857
Farm Service Agency	202-720-3269
Food & Nutrition Service	703-305-2281
Food & Safety Inspection Service	202-720-3897
Food Stamp Hotline	800-221-5689
Foreign Agriculture Service	202-720-7115
Forest Service	202-205-8333
Inspector General's Hotline	202-690-1622 · 800-424-9121
Meat & Poultry Hotline	202-720-3333
National Agricultural Library	301-504-5564
National Agriculture Statistics Service Hotline	800-727-9540
Natural Resources Conservation Service	202-720-3210
Rural Development	202-720-1019

Department of Commerce (DOC)

http://www.commerce.gov

General Information	202-482-2000
Employment	202-482-5138
National Institute of Standards & Technology	301-975-6478
National Oceanic & Atmospheric Admin. (NOAA)	301-713-1045
National Telecommunications & Information Admin.	202-482-7002
Technology Administration	202-482-8321

Department of Education (ED)

http://www.ed.gov

General Information	202-401-2000 · 800-872-5327
Civil Rights	800-421-3481
Education Publications Center	877-433-7827
Educational Resources Information Center (ERIC)	800-538-3742
Federal Student Aid Information Center	800-433-3243
National Library of Education	202-205-5015 · 800-424-1616
No Child Left Behind Act Hotline	888-625-2787
Safe & Drug Free Schools Hotline	202-260-3954 · 800-624-0100

Department of Energy (DOE)

http://www.doe.gov

General Information	202-586-5575	800-342-5363
Chief Information Office		202-586-0166
Civilian Radioactive Waste Managment Office		202-586-5842
Congressional & Intergovernmental Affairs Office		202-586-5450
Counterintelligence Office		202-586-5901
Defense Nuclear Facilities Safety Board		202-586-3887
Economic Impact & Diversity Office		202-586-8383
Employment Webpage	http://www.ma.mbe.doe.gov/pers/	
Energy Assurance		202-287-1808
Energy Efficiency & Renewable Energy Office		202-586-9220
Energy Information Administration		202-586-8800
Environment, Safety, and Health Office		202-586-6151
Environmental Management Office		202-586-7709
Fossil Energy Office		202-586-0166
General Counsel Office		202-586-6732
Hearings and Appeals Office		202-287-1400
Independent Oversight & Performance Assurance Ofc		301-903-3777
Inspector General Office		202-586-1924
Intelligence Office		202-586-2610
Management, Budget, and Evaluation Office		202-586-4171
National Nuclear Security Administration		202-586-5555
Nuclear Energy, Science & Technology Office		202-586-6630
Policy & International Affairs Office		202-586-8660
Public Affairs Office		202-586-5806
Science Office		202-586-5437
Secretary of Energy Advisory Board		202-586-8877
Security Office		202-586-3345
Worker & Community Transition Office		202-586-3323

National Labs, Offices, & Technology Centers

Albany Research Center	541-967-5892
Albuquerque Operations Office	505-845-4154
Amarillo Site Operations Office	806-477-3000
Ames Laboratory Area Office	630-252-2096
Ames National Laboratory	515-294-2680
Argonne Area Office (West)	208-526-0111
Argonne National Laboratory & Area Office (East)	630-252-2000
Argonne National Laboratory (West)	208-533-7341
Ashtabula Environmental Management Project	440-993-1914
Berkeley Site Office	510-486-4353
Bettis Atomic Power Laboratory, Bechtel Bettis Inc.	412-476-5000
Bonneville Power Administration, Portland, OR	503-230-3000
Bonneville Power Administration, Walla Walla, WA	509-527-6230

Bonneville Power Administration, Seattle, WA	206-220-6759
Bonneville Power Administration, Spokane, WA	509-358-7400
Bonneville Power Administration, Washington, D.C.	202-586-5640
Boston Regional Office	617-565-9700
Brookhaven Area Office	631-344-3427
Brookhaven National Laboratory	631-344-2123
Carlsbad Field Office	505-234-7200
Center for Molecular Medicine	310-825-6539
Chicago Operations Office	630-252-2000
Chicago Regional Office	312-353-6749
Columbus Closure Project Office	513-246-0021
Denver Regional Office	303-275-4826
Environmental Measures Laboratory	212-620-3607
Fermi National Accelerator Laboratory & Area Office	630-840-3000
Fernald Environmental Management Project	513-648-3000
Golden Field Office	303-275-4700
Grand Junction Office	970-248-6000
Hanford Environmental Health Foundation	509-373-3155
Idaho National Engineering & Environmental Lab.	208-526-0111
Idaho Operations Office	208-526-1322
Kansas City Site Operations Office	816-997-2000
Kirtland Site Operations Office	505-845-4094
Knolls Atomic Power Laboratory	518-395-4000
Lawrence Berkeley National Laboratory	510-486-5111
Lawrence Livermore National Laboratory, CA	925-422-1100
Lawrence Livermore National Laboratory, NV	702-295-4080
Los Alamos National Laboratory	505-667-5061
Los Alamos Site Operations Office	505-667-5491
Miamisburg Closure Project	513-246-0026
National Energy Technology Laboratory, PA	412-386-6000
National Energy Technology Laboratory, WV	304-285-4764
National Petroleum Technology Office	918-699-2000
National Renewable Energy Laboratory	303-275-3000
Naval Petroleum & Oil Shale Reserves in CO,UT,WY	307-261-5161
Naval Petroleum Reserves in CA	661-837-5000
Naval Reactors Facility	208-533-5316
Nevada Operations Office	702-295-1000
New Brunswick Laboratory	630-252-2442
Oak Ridge Institute for Science & Education	865-576-3000
Oak Ridge National Laboratory & Operations Office	865-574-1000
Oakland Operations Office	510-637-1794
Ohio Field Office	513-246-0021
Pacific Northwest National Laboratory	509-375-2121
Paducah Site Office	270-441-6800
Philadelphia Regional Office	215-656-6950
Pittsburgh Naval Reactors (PNR)	412-473-5000

Portsmouth Site Office	740-897-5010
Power Marketing Liaison Office	202-586-5581
Princeton Area Office	609-243-3700
Princeton Plasma Physics Laboratory	609-243-2000
Radiological & Environmental Sciences Laboratory	208-526-6500
Richland Operations Office	509-376-7411
River Protection Office	509-376-7411
Rocky Flats Field Office	303-966-7000
Rocky Mountain Oilfield Testing Center	888-599-2200
Sandia National Laboratories, CA	925-294-3000
Sandia National Laboratories, NM	505-845-0011
Savannah River Ecology Laboratory	803-725-2472
Savannah River Operations Office	803-725-6211
Schenectady Naval Reactors Office	518-395-4000
Science & Technology Information Office	865-576-1188
Seattle Regional Office	206-553-1004
Southeastern Power Administration	706-213-3800
Southwestern Power Administration	918-595-6600
Stanford Linear Accelerator Center	650-926-3300
Stanford Site Office	650-926-3208
Stanford Synchrotron Radiological Laboratory	650-926-3300
Strategic Petroleum Reserve Project Office	504-734-4200
Thomas Jefferson National Accelerator Facility	757-269-7100
Waste Isolation Pilot Plant	800-336-9477
West Valley Demonstration Project	716-942-4313
Western Area Power Administration, AZ	602-352-2525
Western Area Power Administration, CA	916-353-4416
Western Area Power Administration, CO, Loveland	970-461-7200
Western Area Power Administration, CO, Montrose	970-240-6200
Western Area Power Administration, MT	406-247-7405
Western Area Power Administration, UT	801-524-5493
Yucca Mountain Site Characterization Office	800-225-6972

Department for Health & Human Services (HHS)

http://www.hhs.gov

General Information ·············202-619-0257······877-696-6775
Employment Webpage ·······http://www.hhs.gov/careers/index.html/

Administration for Children & Families (ACF)

http://www.acf.hhs.gov

Administration for Native Americans (ANA) ··············877-922-9262
Child Care Aware···800-424-2246
Childhelp's National Child Abuse Hotline··············800-422-4453
National Center for Missing & Exploited Children ······800-843-5678
National Domestic Violence Hotline·····················800-799-7233
National Runaway Switchboard ···························800-621-4000

Regional Offices

Region 1, Boston, MA (CT, MA, ME, NH, RI, VT)······617-565-1020
Region 2, New York, NY (NJ, NY, PR, Virgin Islands) ·212-264-2890
Region 3, Philadelphia, PA (DC,DE,MD,PA,VA,WV) ·215-861-4000
Region 4, Atlanta, GA (AL,FL,GA,KY,MS,NC,SC,TN)404-562-2800
Region 5, Chicago, IL (IL, IN, MI, MN, OH, WI) ·········312-353-4237
Region 6, Dallas, TX (AR, LA, NM, OK, TX)···············214-767-9648
Region 7, Kansas City, MO (IA, KS, MO, NE) ············816-426-3981
Region 8, Denver, CO (CO, MT, ND, SD, UT, WY)····303-844-3100
Region 9, San Francisco, CA (AZ, CA, Guam, HI,
  Pacific Islands, NV) ································415-437-8400
Region 10, Seattle, WA (AK, ID, OR, WA) ···············206-615-2547

Administration on Aging (AoA)

http://www.aoa.gov

General Information ·····································202-619-0724
Eldercare Locator··800-677-1116

Regional Offices

Region 1, Boston, MA (CT, MA, ME, NH, RI, VT)······617-565-1158
Region 2 & 3, New York, NY (Region 2 = NJ, NY, PR,
  Virgin Isl.)/(Region 3 = DC,DE,MD,PA,VA,WV)······212-264-2976
Region 4, Atlanta, GA (AL,FL,GA,KY,MS,NC,SC,TN)404-562-7600
Region 5, Chicago, IL (IL, IN, MI, MN, OH, WI) ·········312-353-3141
Region 6, Dallas, TX (AR, LA, NM, OK, TX)···············214-767-2971
Region 7, Kansas City, MO (IA, KS, MO, NE) ············816-426-3516
Region 8, Denver, CO (CO, MT, ND, SD, UT, WY)····303-844-2951
Region 9, San Francisco, CA (AZ, CA, Guam, HI,
  Pacific Islands, NV) ································415-437-8780
Region 10, Seattle, WA (AK, ID, OR, WA) ···············206-615-2298

Phone Directory

Agency for Healthcare Research & Quality (AHRQ)

http://www.ahrq.gov

General Information ···301-427-1364
Main E-Mail···info@ahrg.gov

Agency for Toxic Substances & Disease Registry (ATSDR)

http://www.atsdr.cdc.gov

General Information··················404-498-0110······888-422-8737

Regional Offices

Region 1, Boston, MA (CT, MA, ME, NH, RI, VT)······617-918-1495
Region 2, New York, NY (NJ, NY, PR, Virgin Islands) ·212-637-4305
Region 3, Philadelphia, PA (DC,DE,MD,PA,VA,WV) ·215-814-3140
Region 4, Atlanta, GA (AL,FL,GA,KY,MS,NC,SC,TN)404-562-1788
Region 5, Chicago, IL (IL, IN, MI, MN, OH, WI) ·········312-886-0840
Region 6, Dallas, TX (AR, LA, NM, OK, TX) ···········214-665-6615
Region 7, Kansas City, MO (IA, KS, MO, NE) ············913-551-1313
Region 8, Denver, CO (CO, MT, ND, SD, UT, WY)····303-312-7010
Region 9, San Francisco, CA (AZ,CA, Guam, HI,
  Pacific Islands, NV) ····································415-947-4323
Region 10, Seattle, WA (AK, ID, OR, WA) ················206-553-1049

Center for Disease Control and Prevention (CDC)

http://www.cdc.gov

General Information ··404-639-3311
Public Inquiries ······················404-639-3534······800-311-3435

Agencies & Programs

Epidemiology Program Office (EPO) Main email: mmwrq@cdc.gov
  Website ································http://www.cdc.gov/epo/index.htm
National Center for Chronic Disease Prevention and
  Health Promotion (NCCDPHP) ·········http://www.cdc.gov/nccdphp/
  Main E-Mail··ccdinfo@cdc.gov
National Center for Environmental Health (NCEH)
  http://www.cdc.gov/nceh/····································888-232-6789
National Center for Health Statistics (NCHS)
  http://www.cdc.gov/nchs/···································301-458-4000
National Center for HIV, STD and TB Prevention (NCHSTP)
  http://www.cdc.gov/nchstp/od/nchstp.html···············404-639-8040
National Center for Infectious Disease (NCID)·www.cdc.gov/ncidod
  Main E-Mail ··ncid@cdc.gov
National Center for Injury Prevention and Control (NCIPC)
  http://www.cdc.gov/ncipc/···································770-488-1506
National Ctr on Birth Defects & Developmental Disabilities (NCBDDD)
  http://www.cdc.gov/ncbddd/···············Main E-Mail: bddi@cdc.gov

National Immunization Program (NIP)
http://www.cdc.gov/nip/ ··800-232-2522
National Institute for Occupational Safety and Health (NIOSH)
http://www.cdc.gov/niosh/homepage.html ···········800-356-4674
Public Health Practice Program Office (PHPPO)
http://www.phppo.cdc.gov/index.asp

Hotlines

National AIDS Hotline ···800-342-2437
National Immunization Hotline ···800-232-2522
National Sexually Transmitted Disease (STD) Hotline ·800-227-8922
Traveler's Health Hotline ···877-394-8747

Centers for Medicare and Medicaid Services (CMS)

http://www.cms.hhs.gov
General Information ··················410-786-3000 ·······877-267-2323

Regional Offices

Region 1, Boston, MA (CT, MA, ME, NH, RI, VT) ······617-565-1188
Region 2, New York, NY (NJ, NY, PR, Virgin Islands) ·212-264-3657
Region 3, Philadelphia, PA (DC,DE,MD,PA,VA,WV) ·215-861-4140
Region 4, Atlanta, GA (AL,FL,GA,KY,MS,NC,SC,TN)404-562-7500
Region 5, Chicago, IL (IL, IN, MI, MN, OH, WI) ·········312-886-6432
Region 6, Dallas, TX (AR, LA, NM, OK, TX) ···············214-767-6423
Region 7, Kansas City, MO (IA, KS, MO, NE) ············816-426-5233
Region 8, Denver, CO (CO, MT, ND, SD, UT, WY) ····303-844-2111
Region 9, San Francisco, CA (AZ, CA, Guam, HI,
Pacific Islands, NV) ···415-744-3501
Region 10, Seattle, WA (AK, ID, OR, WA) ················206-615-2306

Food and Drug Administration (FDA)

http://www.fda.gov
General Information ··888-463-6332
Registration of Food Facilities ··800-216-7331

FDA Consumer Complaint Coordinators

Alabama ··615-781-5385
Alaska, Idaho, Montana, Oregon, Washington ···········425-483-4949
Arizona ··949-798-7701
Arkansas, Oklahoma, Texas ···214-253-5200
California (Northern), Hawaii, Nevada ·························510-337-6741
California (Southern) ···949-608-3530
Colorado, New Mexico, Utah, Wyoming ·····················303-236-3044
Connecticut, Maine, Massachusetts, New Hampshire,
Rhode Island, Vermont ···781-596-7700
Delaware, Pennsylvania ··215-597-9064
Florida (Northern) ··407-475-4717

Florida (Southern)	305-526-2800
Georgia, North Carolina, South Carolina	404-253-1169
Illinois	312-353-7840
Indiana, Michigan	313-393-8100
Iowa, Kansas, Missouri, Nebraska	913-752-2440
Kentucky, Ohio	513-679-2700
Louisiana, Mississippi	504-253-4511
Maryland, Washington D.C., Virginia, West Virginia	410-779-5713
Minnesota, North Dakota, South Dakota, Wisconsin	612-758-7221
New Jersey	973-526-6017
New York (Northern)	716-551-4461
New York (Southern)	718-340-7000
Puerto Rico, Virgin Islands	787-474-9502
Tennessee	615-781-5380

Health Resources & Services Admin. (HRSA)

http://www.hrsa.gov

General Information	301-443-3376
Employment Webpage	http://www.hrsa.gov/jobs/jobs.htm
Main E-Mail	comments@hrsa.gov

Regional Offices

Region 1, Boston, MA (CT, MA, ME, NH, RI, VT)	617-565-1420
Region 2, New York, NY (NJ, NY, PR, Virgin Islands)	212-264-4498
Region 3, Philadelphia, PA (DC,DE,MD,PA,VA,WV)	215-861-4411
Region 4, Atlanta, GA (AL,FL,GA,KY,MS,NC,SC,TN)	404-562-7972
Region 5, Chicago, IL (IL, IN, MI, MN, OH, WI)	312-353-6835
Region 6, Dallas, TX (AR, LA, NM, OK, TX)	214-767-3872
Region 7, Kansas City, MO (IA, KS, MO, NE)	816-426-5226
Region 8, Denver, CO (CO, MT, ND, SD, UT, WY)	303-844-3203
Region 9, San Francisco, CA (AZ, CA, HI, NV)	415-437-8090
Region 10, Seattle, WA (AK, ID, OR, WA)	206-615-2490

Indian Health Service (IHS)

http://www.ihs.gov

| General Information | 301-443-3593 |
| Employment Webpage: | |

www.ihs.gov/JobsCareerDevelop/CareerCenter/Vacancy/Index.cfm

| Main E-Mail | support@ihs.gov |

Area Offices

Aberdeen, SD (IA, ND, NE, SD)	605-226-7581
Anchorage, AK (All Alaskan Tribes & Nations)	907-729-3686
Albuquerque, NM (CO, NM, TX)	505-248-4102
Bemidji, MN (IN, MI, MN, WI)	218-444-0458
Billings, MT (MT, WY)	406-247-7107
Sacramento, CA (All Californian Tribes & Nations)	916-930-3927

Nashville, TN (AL, AR, CT, DE, FL, GA, IL, KY, LA,
  MA, MD, ME, MO, MS, NC, NJ, NY, OH, PA, RI,
  SC, TN, TX, VA, VT, WV)·······················615-467-1500
Navajo (Navajo Nation Reservation)·················928-871-5811
Oklahoma City, OK (KS, OK, TX)······················405-951-3768
Phoenix, AZ (AZ, NV, UT)·······························602-364-4123
Portland, OR (ID, OR, WA) ·····························503-326-2020
Tucson, AZ (Tohono O'odham Nation, and
  Pascua Yaqui Tribe of Arizona) ·················520-295-2405

National Institute of Health (NIH)

http://www.nih.gov

General Information ·································301-496-4000
Employment Webpage ··················http://www.jobs.nih.gov/

Centers & Institutes

Center for Information Technology (CIT) ··············301-594-6248
Center for Scientific Review (CSR)····················301-435-1115
Clinical Center (CC) ····································301-496-4000
John E. Fogerty International Center (FIC)·············301-496-2075
National Cancer Institute (NCI) ·······················800-422-6237
National Center for Complementary and
  Alternative Medicine (NCCAM)·····················888-644-6226
National Center on Minority Health and
  Health Disparities (NCMHD)························301-402-1366
National Center for Research Resources (NCRR) ·····301-435-0888
National Eye Institute (NEI)····························301-496-5248
National Heart, Lung, and Blood Institute (NHLBI) ·····301-592-8573
National Human Genome Research Institute (NHGRI) 301-402-0911
National Institute on Aging (NIA) ······················301-496-1752
National Inst. on Alcohol Abuse & Alcoholism (NIAAA) 301-443-3860
National Inst. of Allergy & Infectious Diseases (NIAID) 301-496-5717
National Institute of Arthritis and Musculoskeletal
  and Skin Diseases (NIAMS) ·······················301-496-8190
National Institute of Biomedical Imaging and
  Bioengineering (NIBIB)·····························301-451-6768
Nat. Inst. of Child Health & Human Develpmt (NICHD) 800-370-2943
National Institute on Deafness & other
  Communication Disorders (NIDCD)················800-241-1044
Nat. Inst. of Environmental Health Sciences (NIEHS) 919-541-3345
Nat. Inst. of General Medical Sciences (NIGMS) ·301-496-7301
National Institute of Mental Health (NIMH) ·············866-615-6464
Nat. Inst. of Neurological Disorders & Stroke (NINDS)·800-352-9424
National Institute of Nursing Research (NINR) ···········301-496-0207
National Library of Medicine (NLM) ·····················888-346-3656

Program Support Center (PSC)

http://www.psc.gov

General Information ··301-443-0034
Main E-Mail ··solutions@psc.gov

Substance Abuse and Mental Health Services Administration (SAMHSA)

http://www.samhsa.gov/index.aspx

General Information ··240-276-2000
Center for Mental Health Services (CMHS) ··············800-789-2647
Center for Substance Abuse Prevention (CSAP) ·······240-276-2420
Center for Substance Abuse Treatment (CSAT) ········800-662-4357
Main E-Mail ··info@samhsa.hhs.gov

Department of Homeland Security (DHS)

On March 1, 2003, 22 agencies merged to create The Department of Homeland Security. This department is now organized into four directorates: **Border and Transportation Security, Emergency Preparedness and Response, Science and Technology, and Information Analysis and Infrastructure Protection**. The 22 agencies are distributed among these directorates as listed below.

http://www.dhs.gov

General Information (Citizen Line)	202-282-8000
Comment Line	202-282-8495
Employment	http://www.usajobs.opm.gov/homeland.asp
Employment Phone (USAJOBS line)	478-757-3000

State Homeland Security Offices

Alabama, Montgomery	334-956-7250
Alaska, Fort Richardson	907-428-6003
American Samoa, Pago Pago	011-684-633-4116
Arizona, Phoenix	602-542-7030
Arkansas, Conway	501-730-9781
California, Sacramento	916-324-8908
Colorado, Denver	303-239-4398
Connecticut, Waterbury	203-805-6600
Delaware, Dover	302-659-2240
Florida, Tallahassee	850-410-7011
Georgia, Atlanta	404-624-7030
Guam, Hagatna	671-475-9600
Hawaii, Honolulu	808-733-4246
Idaho, Boise	208-422-5242
Illinois, Springfield	217-524-1486
Indiana, Indianapolis	317-232-8998
Iowa, Des Moines	515-252-4211
Kansas, Topeka	785-274-1011
Kentucky, Frankfort	502-564-2611
Louisiana, Baton Rouge	504-278-2812
Maine, Augusta	207-626-4205
Maryland, Annapolis	410-974-2389
Massachusetts, Boston	616-727-3200
Michigan, East Lansing	517-336-6157
Minnesota, Saint Paul	651-215-1527
Mississippi, Jackson	601-987-1499
Missouri, Jefferson City	573-522-3007
Montana, Helena	406-841-3911
Nebraska, Lincoln	402-471-2256
Nevada, Carson City	775-684-4556

New Hampshire, Concord	603-271-6911
New Jersey, Trenton	609-341-5050
New Mexico, Santa Fe	505-476-0267
New York, New York City	212-867-7060
North Carolina, Raleigh	919-733-2126
North Dakota, Bismark	701-328-8100
Northern Mariana Islands, Saipan	670-664-2280
Ohio, Columbus	614-466-3383
Oklahoma, Oklahoma City	405-425-7296
Oregon, Salem	503-378-3725
Pennsylvania, Harrisburg	717-651-2715
Puerto Rico, San Juan	787-724-0388
Rhode Island, Providence	401-275-4333
South Carolina, Columbia	803-737-9000
South Dakota, Pierre	605-773-3450
Tennessee, Nashville	615-532-7825
Texas, Austin	512-936-1882
Utah, Salt Lake City	801-538-3400
Vermont, Waterbury	802-244-8718
Virgin Islands, Saint Thomas	340-712-7710
Virginia, Richmond	804-225-3826
Washington, Camp Murray	253-512-8201
Washington, D.C.	202-727-4036
West Virginia, Charleston	304-558-3795
Wisconsin, Madison	608-242-3210
Wyoming, Cheyenne	307-777-8511

Border and Transportation Security (BTS)

This directorate secures our borders and transportation systems, including enforcing the nation's immigration laws.

Animal & Plant Health Inspection Service (APHIS)

http://www.aphis.usda.gov

Agriculture Importation (Information & Permits)	877-770-5990
Agricultural Quarantine and Inspection	301-734-8295
Animal Care Headquarters	301-734-7833
Eastern Region	919-855-7100
Western Region	970-494-7478
Animal Health, Eastern Region	919-716-5570
Western Region	970-494-7385
Animal Products, Imports & Exports	301-734-3277
Biotechnology Regulatory Services (BRS)	301-734-7324
Center for Epidemiology and Animal Health	970-490-8100
Center for Plant Health Science & Technology	919-513-2662
Center for Veterinary Biologics	301-734-8245
Emergency Operations Ctr (AEOC) 800-601-9327 301-436-3101	

Employment ······http://www.aphis.usda.gov/mrpbs/job_search.html
Employment Phone ···202-720-5323
Environmental Assessments······························301-734-8565
Foreign Animal Disease Diagnostic Laboratory·········631-323-3200
International Regulation Retrieval System···············301-734-8364
International Services ·····································301-734-7550
Invasive Species & Pest Management ··················301-734-8247
Investigative and Enforcement Services (IES)···········301-734-8684
   Eastern Region···919-855-7080
   Western Region ··970-494-7485
Legislative and Public Affairs·····························301-734-7799
Main E-Mail ···························APHIS.Web@aphis.usda.gov
National Animal Health Monitoring System ·············970-490-7937
National Biological Controls Institute ···················301-734-4329
National Ctr for Import/Export (NCIE)(animals & birds) 301-734-8364
National Veterinary Services Laboratory (NVSL)·······515-663-7301
Pest Risk Assessments ···································301-734-8896
Plant Exports/Phytosanitary Issues Mgmt. (PIM)·······301-734-8537
Plant Health, Eastern Region ····························919-716-5576
   Western Region ··970-494-7500
Plant Imports/Phytosanitary Issues Mgmt. (PIM)·······301-734-6799
Plant Inspection Stations; Convention on International
   Trade in Endangered Species (CITES) ···············301-734-7839
Plant Permits ···301-734-8896
Plant Protection & Quarantine Program···················301-734-8262
Preclearance Program ·····································301-734-8295
   Antismuggling Hotline·····································800-877-3835
   Permits ···877-770-5990
Veterinary Biologics Consumer Information Hotline ···800-752-6255
Veterinary Services Program·······························301-734-6188
Wildlife Services Program (WS) ····866-487-3297·······301-734-7921

Federal Law Enforcement Training Center (FLETC)

http://www.fletc.gov

General Information, Headquarters, Glynco ··············912-267-2100
General Information, Washington, D.C. Office············202-233-0260
Admissions Coordinator···································912-267-2421
College Intern Program Coordinator ·····················912-267-2844
Directorate of Training ····································912-267-3373
Employment ···············http://jobsearch.usajobs.opm.gov/a9fletc.asp
International Training E-Mail·······················fletc-intlrqst@dhs.gov
Legal Council ··912-267-2441
Management Institute ······································912-267-2988
Office of Compliance·······································912-554-4443
Office of State and Local Training·························800-743-5382
Office of Training··912-267-2991

Phone Directory

Office of Training Support	912-554-4623
Peer Support Program	912-267-2633
Privacy Act Officer	912-267-3103
Public Affairs Office	912-267-2447
State and Local Law Enforcement Agency	
Training E-Mail	stateandlocaltraining@dhs.gov
Student Records	912-280-5409

Divisions

Behavorial Science	912-267-2605
Budget	912-554-4323
Computer & Financial Investigations	912-267-2314
Counter Terrorism	912-267-2354
Driver & Marine	912-267-2646
Equal Employment Opportunity	912-267-3316
Enforcement Operations	912-267-2599
Enforcement Techniques	912-267-2815
Facilities Management	912-267-2778
Finance	912-280-5358
Firearms	912-267-2278
Human Resources	912-267-2289
Information Systems	912-554-4733
International Programs	912-280-5353
Legal	912-267-2179
Physical Techniques	912-267-2405
Procurement	912-267-2243
Property Management	912-267-2937
Training Management & Coordination	912-280-5409

Training Facilities

Artesia Facility	505-748-8016
Charleston Facility	843-743-2858
Cheltenham Facility	301-877-8500
Glynco Facility	912-267-2100
Internat'l Law Enforcement Academy-Gaborone	011-267-533-7666
International Law Enforcement Academy-San Jose	912-267-3241
Washington Facility	202-233-0260

Office for Domestic Preparedness (ODP)

http://www.ojp.usdoj.gov/odp

| General Information | 800-368-6498 |
| Main E-Mail | askcsid@dhs.gov |

Transportation Security Administration (TSA)

http://www.tsa.gov

For emergencies, contact the airport authorities and local law enforcement directly!

| General Information | 866-289-9673 |

Advanced National Law Enforcement
Telecommunications System (NLETS) Notification
for Law Enforcement Officers Flying Armed ·········· 571-227-1560
Briefing & Public Affairs Office ····························· 571-227-2829
Contact Center E-Mail ····················· TSA-ContactCenter@dhs.gov
Employment ·············· http://jobsearch.usajobs.opm.gov/a9tsa.asp
Employment Phone ··· 800-887-1895
Explosives Unit Instructional Materials (for Security
& LE Officers Only), for webpage access,
fax written request to ····································· 703-603-0302
Lost or missing item left at TSA screening area ········ 866-289-9673
Main E-Mail ································· TellTSA@tsa.dot.gov
National Explosives Detection Canine Program ·········· k-9@dhs.gov
National Response Ctr-Suspicious Activity Hotline···· 866-427-3287
Office of Civil Rights····································· 877-366-4872
Security Violations & Concerns······················· 866-289-9673
Transportation Security Coordination Center··········· 703-563-3234
Travel Assistance··· 866-289-9673
Workplace Concerns (for employees)··············· 877-266-2837

U.S. Citizenship & Immigration Services (USCIS)
formerly Immigration and Naturalization Service (INS)
http://www.uscis.gov

National Customer Service Center 800-375-5283······· 503-326-7475
Case Status (Automated Information)···················· 785-330-1048
Employment ·············· http://jobsearch.usajobs.opm.gov/dhscareers/

District Offices
In case of emergency, contact USCIS or Border Patrol through your dispatcher

Alaska, Anchorage···································· 907-271-3104
Arizona, Phoenix····································· 602-379-3116
California, Los Angeles······························ 213-894-0400
San Diego ······································· 619-557-6011
San Francisco ··································· 415-844-5347
Colorado, Denver···································· 303-371-3841
Florida, Miami ····································· 305-762-3610
Georgia, Atlanta···································· 404-331-2762
Hawaii, Honolulu··································· 808-522-5847
Illinois, Chicago···································· 312-353-4465
Louisiana, New Orleans······························ 504-589-6635
Maine, Portland···································· 207-780-3440
Maryland, Baltimore································· 410-962-7449
Massachusetts, Boston······························ 617-565-3100
Michigan, Detroit··································· 313-568-6042
Minnesota, St. Paul································· 612-313-9040
Missouri, Kansas City ······························ 816-891-8350

Montana, Helena	406-449-3991
Nebraska, Omaha	402-697-9154
New Jersey, Newark	973-645-2240
New York, Buffalo	716-551-4741
New York City	212-264-5923
Ohio, Cleveland	216-522-4774
Oregon, Portland	503-326-7475
Pennsylvania, Philadelphia	215-656-7195
Puerto Rico, San Juan	787-706-2309
Texas, Dallas	214-767-7900
El Paso	915-225-1883
Harlingen	956-427-8542
Houston	281-774-4900
San Antonio	210-967-7036
Washington, D.C.	703-578-4900
Washington, Seattle	206-553-7924

U.S. Customs & Border Protection

http://www.cbp.gov *or* http://www.customs.gov

General Information	877-CUSTOMS	202-354-1000
Employment Webpage	http://www.cbp.gov/xp/cgov/careers/	
Suspicious Acitivity Hotline		888-BE-ALERT

Air and Marine Field Offices

Air and Marine Operations Center	951-656-8000
Albuquerque Air Branch (CO, MT, NM, TX, WY)	505-346-6425
Bellingham Air & Marine Branch (ID, OR, WA)	360-734-7557
Caribbean Air & Marine Branch	787-819-5000
Houston Air Branch (AR, IA, MN, MO, OK, TX)	281-257-7400
Jacksonville Air & Marine (FL,GA,NC,MD,SC,VA,WV)	904-680-6794
Miami Air & Marine Branch (FL)	305-258-5550
National Capital Region Air & Marine (DC,MD,VA)	703-417-7181
New Orleans Air & Marine Branch	
(AL, FL, IL, IN, KY, LA, MI, MS, OH, TN)	985-902-2200
Oklahoma City National Aviation Center	405-319-6400
Pittsburgh Air & Marine (CT,MA,ME,NH,NJ,NY,PA,RI,VT)	518-563-6140
San Angelo Air & Marine (KS,ND,NE,OK,SD,TX)	325-224-1400
San Diego Air & Marine Branch (CA)	619-522-6100
Surveillance Support Branch, East (Jacksonville, FL)	907-317-9927
West (Corpus Christie, TX)	361-698-6700
Tucson Air Branch (AZ, NV, UT)	520-670-6546

Border Patrol Sectors

Arizona, Tucson	520-670-6871
Yuma	928-341-6500
California, El Centro	760-352-3241
San Diego	619-216-4000
Florida, Miami	954-963-9807

Louisiana, New Orleans	504-589-6107
Maine, Houlton	207-532-6521
Michigan, Detroit	586-307-2160
Montana, Havre	406-265-6781
New York, Buffalo	716-447-3942
North Dakota, Grand Forks	701-775-6259
Puerto Rico, Ramey	787-882-3560
Texas, Del Rio	830-778-7000
El Paso	915-834-8350
Laredo	956-764-3200
Marfa	432-729-5200
McAllen	956-984-3800
Vermont, Swanton	802-868-3361
Washington, Blaine	360-332-8781
Spokane	509-353-2747

Field Operations Offices

Arizona, Tucson (Arizona)	520-407-2300
California, Los Angeles (South Pacific)	562-980-3100
San Diego (Southern California)	619-652-9966
San Francisco (Mid-Pacific)	415-744-1530
Florida, Miami (Southern Florida)	305-810-5120
Tampa (Northern Florida)	813-228-2381
Georgia, Atlanta (South Atlantic)	770-944-4100
Illinois, Chicago (Mid-America)	312-983-9100
Louisiana, New Orleans (Gulf)	504-670-2404
Maryland, Baltimore (Mid-Atlantic)	410-962-6200
Massachusetts, Boston (North Atlantic)	617-565-6208
Michigan, Detroit (Western Great Lakes)	313-226-2955
New York, Buffalo (Eastern Great Lakes)	716-626-0400
New York City (New York)	646-733-3100
Oregon, Portland (North Pacific)	503-326-7625
Puerto Rico, San Juan (Puerto Rico & Virgin Islands)	787-729-6950
Texas, El Paso (Texas & New Mexico)	915-633-7300
Houston (Eastern Texas)	713-387-7200
Laredo (Southern Texas)	956-753-1700
Washington, Seattle (Northwest Great Plains)	206-553-6944

U.S. Immigration & Customs Enforcement (ICE)

http://www.ice.gov

General Information	866-347-2423
Employment Webpage·http://jobsearch.usajobs.opm.gov/a9ins.asp	
Internal Affairs Headquarters	202-927-1800
Public Affairs Office	202-514-2648
Suspicious Activity Hotline	866-347-2423

Detention and Removal Operations (DRO)

http://www.ice.gov/graphics/dro/index.htm

General Information ··202-305-2734
Fugitive Operations ···202-353-8003

Detention Facilities

Aguadilla Service Processing Center, Puerto Rico ·····787-890-3600
Aurora Contract Detention Facility, Colorado ·············303-361-6612
Buffalo Federal Detention Center, New York················585-343-0814
El Centro Service Processing Center, California ·······760-353-2170
El Paso Service Processing Center, Texas ················915-225-1941
Elizabeth Contract Detention Facility, New Jersey ·····908-352-3776
Eloy Contract Detention Facility, Arizona····················520-466-2000
Florence Service Processing Center, Arizona ············520-868-5862
Houston Contract Detention Facility, Texas················281-449-1481
Krome Service Processing Center, Florida··················305-552-1845
Laredo Contract Detention Facility, Texas··················956-727-4118
Port Isabel Service Processing Center, Texas ············956-547-1700
San Diego Contract Detention Facility, California ·······619-661-9119
San Pedro Service Processing Center, California ·······310-241-2300
Tacoma Contract Detention Facility, Washington·······253-779-6000

Field Offices

Arizona, Phoenix (AZ)···602-379-3426
California, Los Angeles (Los Angeles, Southern NV) ·213-830-7900
California, San Diego (San Diego)·····································619-557-6117
California, San Francisco (Guam, HI, Northern CA,
  Northern NV, UT)···415-844-5512
Colorado, Denver (CO, ID, MT, WY) ·······························303-371-1067
Florida, Miami (FL)···305-762-3622
Georgia, Atlanta (GA, NC, SC, PR, Virgin Islands)····404-331-0253
Illinois, Chicago (IL, IN, KS, KY, MO, WI) ···················312-385-1701
Louisiana, New Orleans (AL, AR, LA, MS, TN) ··········504-599-7785
Maryland, Baltimore (DE, MD, PA, WV) ·······················410-962-2037
Massachusetts, Boston (CT, MA, ME, NH, RI, VT) ·············617-565-3304
Minnesota, Saint Paul (IA, MN, ND, NE, SD) ·············612-313-9078
New Jersey, South Newark (NJ)······································973-645-3666
New York, Buffalo (upstate NY)·······································716-551-4741
New York, New York City (NY City & Long Island) ·····212-264-3972
Texas, Dallas (OK, Northern TX)······································214-905-5887
Texas, El Paso (NM, Western TX)····································915-881-5599
Texas, Houston (Eastern TX) ···281-774-4610
Texas, San Antonio (Central and Southern TX) ·········210-967-7007
Virginia, Arlington (DC, VA) ··202-307-1554
Washington, Seattle (AK, OR, WA) ·······························206-553-4146

Federal Air Marshal Service (FAMS)
http://www.ice.gov/graphics/fams/index.htm
General Information ·································703-487-3100

Federal Protective Service (FPS)
http://www.ice.gov/graphics/fps/index.htm
General Information ·································202-501-0907
Employment Webpage ·············http://www.usajobs.opm.gov

Life-Threatening & Non-Life-Threatening* Emergencies in Federal Buildings
Life-threatening emergency numbers (right column) will result in police response!

Alabama	877-825-9334*	877-852-9334
Alaska		888-280-3405
Arizona		800-487-4158
Arkansas	888-282-7862*	800-767-2756
California		800-487-4158
Colorado	800-487-4158*	888-511-5060
Connecticut		800-525-5726
Delaware		800-525-5726
Florida	877-825-9334*	877-852-9334
Georgia	877-825-9334*	877-852-9334
Hawaii		800-487-4158
Idaho		888-280-3405
Illinois		877-719-4894
Indiana		877-719-4894
Iowa		877-264-7650
Kansas		877-264-7650
Kentucky	877-719-4894*	877-852-9334
Louisiana	888-282-7862*	800-767-2756
Maine		800-525-5726
Maryland		800-525-5726
Massachusetts		800-525-5726
Michigan		877-719-4894
Minnesota		877-719-4894
Mississippi	877-825-9334*	800-852-9334
Missouri		877-264-7650
Montana	800-487-4158*	888-511-5060
Nebraska		877-264-7650
Nevada	888-282-7862*	800-487-4158
New Hampshire		800-525-5726
New Jersey		800-525-5726
New Mexico	888-282-7862*	800-767-2756
New York		800-525-5726
North Carolina	877-825-9334*	877-852-9334
North Dakota	800-487-4158*	888-511-5060

Phone Directory

Ohio		877-719-4894
Oklahoma	888-282-7862*	800-767-2756
Oregon		888-280-3405
Pennsylvania		800-525-5726
Puerto Rico		800-525-5726
Rhode Island		800-525-5726
South Carolina	877-825-9334*	877-852-9334
South Dakota	800-487-4158*	888-511-5060
Tennessee	877-825-9334*	877-852-9334
Texas	888-282-7862*	800-767-2756
Utah	800-487-4158*	888-511-5060
Vermont		800-525-5726
Virgin Islands		800-525-5726
Virginia		800-525-5726
Washington		888-280-3405
Washington, D.C.	202-708-1111	800-325-9034
West Virginia		800-525-5726
Wisconsin		877-719-4894
Wyoming	800-487-4158*	888-511-5060

* Non-Life-Threatening Emergencies - Security Issues

Regional Offices

Region 1, Boston (CT, ME, MA, NH, VT, RI)	617-565-5776
Region 2, New York (NJ, NY, PR, USVI)	212-264-4255
Region 3, Philadelphia (DE, MD, VA, PA, WV)	215-656-6060
Region 4, Atlanta (AL, FL, GA, KY, MS, NC, SC, TN)	404-331-5132
Region 5, Chicago (IL, IN, MI, MN, OH, WI)	312-353-1496
Region 6, Kansas City (IA, KS, MO, NE)	816-926-7025
Region 7, Fort Worth (AR, LA, NM, OK, TX)	817-334-3559
Region 8, Denver (CO, MT, ND, SD, UT, WY)	303-236-7931
Region 9, San Francisco (AZ, CA, HI, NV)	415-522-3440
Region 10, Auburn, WA (AK, ID, OR, WA)	253-931-7638
Region 11, Washington, D.C. (Metro Area)	202-690-9632

Office of Intelligence

http://www.ice.gov/graphics/intel/index.htm

North Central Field Intelligence Unit, Chicago, IL	312-983-1400
Northeast Field Intelligence Unit, New York, NY	646-733-3190
Pacific Field Intelligence Unit, Long Beach, CA	562-980-3255
South Central Field Intelligence Unit, Houston, TX	281-985-0933
Southeast Field Intelligence Unit, Miami, FL	305-810-5252
Southwest Field Intelligence Unit, Tucson, AZ	520-584-4172

Office of Investigations

http://www.ice.gov/graphics/investigations/index.htm

Strategic Investigations Unit ·····································202-927-1540

Special Agent-In-Charge (SAC) Offices

Arizona, Phoenix	602-364-7830
Arizona, Tucson	520-229-5100
California, Los Angeles	562-624-3800
California, San Diego	619-744-4600
California, San Francisco	510-267-3800
Colorado, Denver	303-784-6480
Florida, Miami	305-597-6000
Florida, Tampa	813-348-1881
Georgia, Atlanta	770-994-4200
Hawaii, Honolulu	808-532-3746
Illinois, Chicago	630-574-4600
Louisiana, New Orleans	504-310-8800
Maryland, Baltimore	410-962-2620
Massachusetts, Boston	617-565-7400
Michigan, Detroit	313-226-3166
Minnesota, Minneapolis/Saint Paul	952-853-2940
New Jersey, Newark	973-776-5500
New York, Buffalo	716-565-2039
New York, New York	646-230-3200
Pennsylvania, Philadelphia	215-597-4305
Puerto Rico, San Juan	787-729-5151
Texas, Dallas	972-444-7300
Texas, El Paso	915-231-3200
Texas, Houston	281-985-0500
Texas, San Antonio	310-541-7200
Washington, D.C.	703-709-9700
Washington, Seattle	206-553-7531

Students and Exchange Visitor Info System (SEVIS)

General Information	202-305-2346
Help Desk	800-892-4829
Main E-Mail	SEVIS.Source@dhs.gov

US-VISIT Program

http://www.dhs.gov/us-visit

Main E-Mail ···USVISIT@dhs.gov

Emergency Preparedness & Response (EP&R)

This directorate is responsible for the management of our nation's natural disasters and terrorist assaults. They oversee the federal government's national preparedness, response and recovery strategies.

Domestic Emergency Support Teams (DEST)
Operated by the Department of Justice (DOJ)

Dept of Justice (DOJ)··202-514-2000

Federal Emergency Management Agency (FEMA)
http://www.fema.gov

General Information ···202-566-1600
Case Helpline (Already Registered)·····························800-525-0321
Disaster Registration Helpline·····································800-621-FEMA
Employment Job Vacancy Hotline·································202-646-3244
Employment Webpage ··········http://www.fema.gov/career/index.jsp
FEMA Publications Distribution Center·······················800-480-2520
Main E-Mail ···FEMAopa@dhs.gov
Map Assistance Center···877-336-2627
Map Service Center ···800-358-9616
National Flood Insurance Hotline·································800-427-4661
Online Disaster Registration Helpline ·······················800-745-0243
US Fire Administration (USFA) ···································301-447-1000
Waste, Fraud & Abuse Hotline·····································800-323-8603

Regional Offices

Region 1 (CT, MA, ME, NH, RI, VT) ·····················617-223-9540
Region 2 (NJ, NY, PR, Virgin Islands) ·····················212-680-3600
Region 3 (DE, MD, PA, VA, WV) ·····························215-931-5608
Region 4 (AL, FL, GA, KY, MS, NC, SC, TN) ············770-220-5200
Region 5 (IL, IN, MI, MN, OH, WI) ··························312-408-5500
Region 6 (AR, LA, NM, OK, TX) ······························940-427-4661
Region 7 (IA, KS, MO, NE) ·····································816-283-7061
Region 8 (CO, MT, ND, SD, UT, WY)·······················303-235-4800
Region 9 (AZ, CA, Guam, HI, NV) ···························510-627-7100
Region 10 (AK, ID, OR, WA)·····································425-487-4600

State Offices

Alabama··205-280-2200
Alaska···907-428-7000
American Samoa ···011-684-699-6415
Arizona··602-244-0504
Arkansas··501-730-9750
California··916-845-8510
Colorado ···303-273-1622
Connecticut··860-566-3180
Delaware···302-659-3362
Florida···850-413-9969
Georgia··404-635-7000
Guam ···671-475-9600
Hawaii···808-733-4300
Idaho ···208-334-3460

Illinois	217-782-2700
Indiana	317-232-3986
Iowa	515-281-3231
Kansas	785-274-1401
Kentucky	502-607-1682
Louisiana	225-925-7500
Maine	207-626-4503
Marshall Islands, Republic of	011-692-625-5181
Maryland	410-517-3600
Massachusetts	508-820-2000
Michigan	517-333-5042
Micronesia	011-691-320-8815
Minnesota	651-296-2233
Mississippi	601-352-9100
Missouri	573-526-9100
Montana	406-841-3911
Nebraska	402-471-7410
Nevada	775-687-4240
New Hampshire	603-271-2231
New Jersey	609-882-2000
New Mexico	505-476-9600
New York	518-457-2222
North Carolina	919-733-3867
North Dakota	701-328-8100
Northern Mariana Islands	670-322-9529
Ohio	614-889-7150
Oklahoma	405-521-2481
Oregon	503-378-2911
Palau, Republic of	011-680-488-2422
Pennsylvania	717-651-2001
Puerto Rico	787-724-0124
Rhode Island	401-946-9996
South Carolina	803-737-8500
South Dakota	605-773-3231
Tennessee	615-741-4332
Texas	512-424-2138
Utah	801-538-3400
Vermont	802-244-8721
Virgin Islands	340-774-2244
Virginia	804-897-6502
Washington	253-512-7000
Washington, D.C.	202-727-6161
West Virginia	304-558-5380
Wisconsin	608-242-3232
Wyoming	307-777-4900

Phone Directory

National Disaster Medical System (NDMS)

http://ndms.dhhs.gov

General Information ···800-872-6367

Regional Offices

Region 1 (CT, MA, ME, NH, RI, VT) ·······················617-565-1693
Region 2 (NJ, NY)···212-264-2802
Region 3 (DE, MD, PA, VA, WV) ·······························215-861-4635
Region 4 (AL, FL, GA, KY, MS, NC, SC, TN) ············404-562-7911
Region 5 (IL, IN, MI, MN, OH, WI)······························312-353-4515
Region 6 (AR, LA, NM, OK, TX) ··································214-767-3843
Region 7 (IA, KS, MO, NE) ···816-426-2829
Region 8 (CO, MT, ND, SD, UT, WY) ·························303-844-7855
Region 9 (AZ, CA, HI, NV)···415-437-8071
Region 10 (AK, ID, OR, WA)··206-615-2266

Nuclear Incident Response Team (NIRT)

Operationally controlled by Department of Homeland Security (DHS), resides in the Department of Energy

www.dhs.gov/dhspublic/display?theme=17&content=368
or   www.llnl.gov/nai/rdiv/nucinc.html

Dept of Energy (DOE) ·············202-586-5575·······800-342-5363

Office of Domestic Preparedness (ODP)

http://www.ojp.usdoj.gov/odp/welcome.html

General Information ···800-368-6498
Main E-Mail ···askcsid@dhs.gov

Strategic National Stockpile (SNS)

Managed jointly by Department of Homeland Security (DHS), Department of Health & Human Services (HHS) and the Center for Disease Control (CDC)

http://www.bt.cdc.gov/stockpile

Center for Disease Control (CDC)·404-639-3311·······888-246-2857

Information Analysis and Infrastructure Protection (IAIP)

This directorate deters, prevents and mitigates acts of terrorism by assessing our nation's vulnerabilities as continuously changing threats occur.

Homeland Security Operations Center (HSOC)

General Information ···202-282-8101

Office of Energy Assurance (OEA)

Energy Security and Assurance Program

http://www.ea.doe.gov

General Information ···202-586-1565

Electricity Sector Programs	202-586-1878
Energy Emergencies	202-586-2003
Oil & Gas Sector Programs	202-586-8710
State & Local Support Programs	202-586-9600

National Communications System (NCS)
http://www.ncs.gov

| General Information | 703-607-6211 |
| Main E-Mail | ncsweb@ncs.gov |

National Infrastructure Coordinating Center (NICC)
Formerly the National Infrastructiore Protection Center (NIPC)

| General Information | 202-282-9201 |
| Main E-Mail | nicc@dhs.gov |

U.S. Computer Emergency Readiness Team (US-CERT)
aka Federal Computer Incident Response Center
http://www.us-cert.gov

General Information	703-235-5110
Main E-Mail	info@us-cert.gov
Technical Comments & Questions	888-282-0870

Science and Technology (S&T)

This directorate is responsible for research and development. They work to provide scientific and technological resources to federal, state and local officials to counter catastrophic terrorism.

CBRN Countermeasures Programs
Operated by The Department of Energy (DOE) and The Department of Homeland Security (DHS)

| Dept of Energy (DOE) | 202-586-5575 | 800-342-5363 |

Environmental Measurements Laboratory (EML)
http://www.eml.doe.gov

General Information	212-620-3619
Applied Physics Dept	212-620-3572
Chemical Sciences Dept	212-620-3524
Employment Webpage	http://www.usajobs.com
Engineering & Computer Sciences Dept	212-620-3623

Homeland Security Advanced Research Projects Agency (HSARPA)

| General Information, call DHS General Info line: | 202-282-8000 |
| Small Business Innovation Research (SBIR) | 800-754-3043 |

National BW Defense Analysis Center
Operated by Dept of Defense (DOD) and Dept of Homeland Security (DHS)

| Dept of Defense (DOD) | 703-545-6700 |

Office of National Laboratories

General Information ··202-254-5859

Plum Island Animal Disease Center

http://www.ars.usda.gov/plum

General Information ··301-504-1638

U.S. Secret Service (USSS)

The U.S. Secret Service is responsible for protecting the President, our nation's leaders, and the country's financial and critical infrastrucures.

http://www.secretservice.gov

General Information	202-406-5700
Employment ········http://www.secretservice.gov/opportunities.shtml	
Employment Phone	202-406-5800
Procurement Division	202-406-6940
Public Affairs Office	202-406-5708
Rowley Training Center, Maryland	301-344-8530

Field Offices

Alabama, Birmingham	205-731-1144
Mobile	251-441-5851
Montgomery	334-223-7601
Alaska, Anchorage	907-271-5148
Arizona, Phoenix	602-640-5580
Tucson	520-670-4730
Arkansas, Little Rock	501-324-6241
California, Fresno	209-487-5204
Los Angeles	213-894-4830
Riverside	909-276-6781
Sacramento	916-930-2130
San Diego	619-557-5640
San Francisco	415-744-9026
San Jose	408-535-5288
Santa Ana	714-246-8257
Ventura	805-339-9180
Colorado, Colorado Springs	719-632-3325
Denver	303-866-1010
Connecticut, New Haven	203-865-2449
Delaware, Wilmington	302-573-6188
Florida, Fort Myers	239-334-0660
Jacksonville	904-296-0133
Miami	305-863-5000
Orlando	407-648-6333
Tallahassee	850-942-9523
Tampa	813-228-2636

West Palm Beach	561-659-0184
Georgia, Albany	912-430-8442
Atlanta	404-331-6111
Savannah	912-652-4401
Hawaii, Honolulu	808-541-1912
Idaho, Boise	208-334-1403
Illinois, Chicago	312-353-5431
Springfield	217-726-8453
Indiana, Evansville	812-858-7365
Indianapolis	317-226-6444
South Bend	219-273-3140
Iowa, Des Moines	515-284-4565
Kansas, Wichita	316-269-6694
Kentucky, Lexington	859-223-2358
Louisville	502-582-5171
Louisiana, Baton Rouge	225-389-0763
New Orleans	504-589-4041
Shreveport	318-676-3500
Maine, Portland	207-780-3493
Maryland, Baltimore	443-263-1000
Eastern Shore	410-268-7286
Massachusetts, Boston	617-565-5640
Michigan, Detroit	313-226-6400
Grand Rapids	616-454-4671
Saginaw	989-497-0580
Minnesota, Minneapolis	612-348-1800
Mississippi, Jackson	601-965-4436
Missouri, Kansas City	816-460-0600
Saint Louis	314-539-2238
Springfield	417-864-8340
Montana, Billings	406-245-8585
Nebraska, Omaha	402-965-9670
Nevada, Las Vegas	702-388-6571
Reno	775-784-5354
New Hampshire, Concord	603-626-5631
New Jersey, Atlantic City	609-487-1300
Newark	973-971-3100
Trenton	609-989-2008
New Mexico, Albuquerque	505-248-5290
New York, Albany	518-436-9600
Buffalo	716-551-4401
JFK Airport	718-553-0911
Melville	631-293-4028
New York City	718-840-1000
Rochester	585-232-4160
Syracuse	315-448-0304

White Plains	914-682-6300
North Carolina, Charlotte	704-442-8370
Greensboro	336-547-4180
Raleigh	919-790-2834
Wilmington	910-815-4511
North Dakota, Fargo	701-239-5070
Ohio, Akron	330-761-0544
Cincinnati	513-684-3585
Cleveland	216-706-4365
Columbus	614-469-7370
Dayton	937-225-2900
Toledo	419-259-6434
Oklahoma, Oklahoma City	405-810-3000
Tulsa	918-581-7272
Oregon, Portland	503-326-2162
Pennsylvania, Philadelphia	215-861-3300
Pittsburgh	412-395-6484
Scranton	570-346-5781
Puerto Rico, San Juan	787-277-1515
Rhode Island, Providence	401-331-6456
South Carolina, Charleston	803-772-4015
Columbia	803-765-5446
Greenville	864-233-1490
South Dakota, Sioux Falls	605-330-4565
Tennessee, Chattanooga	423-752-5125
Knoxville	865-545-4627
Memphis	901-544-0333
Nashville	615-736-5841
Texas, Austin	512-916-5103
Dallas	972-868-3200
El Paso	915-533-6950
Houston	713-868-2299
Lubbock	806-472-7347
McAllen	956-630-5811
San Antonio	210-308-6220
Tyler	903-534-2933
Waco	254-741-0576
Utah, Salt Lake City	801-524-5910
Vermont, Burlington	802-651-4091
Virginia, Norfolk	757-441-3200
Richmond	804-771-2274
Roanoke	540-857-2208
Washington, D.C.	202-406-8000
Washington, Seattle	206-220-6800
Spokane	509-353-2532
West Virginia, Charleston	304-347-5188

Wisconsin, Madison	608-264-5191
Milwaukee	414-297-3587
Wyoming, Cheyenne	307-772-2380

U.S. Coast Guard

The U.S. Coast Guard is responsible for protecting the public, the environment and U.S. economic interest by supporting national security in the nation's ports, waterways, coastal and international waters, and any maritime regions.

http://www.uscg.mil

National Response Center	202-267-2675	800-424-8802
Academy, Coast Guard		860-444-8500
Auxiliary Association (Volunteers)		877-875-6296
Boating Safety Information Line		800-368-5647
Command and Control Engineering Center		757-686-2100
Container Inspection Training & Assistance Team		405-954-8983
Employment/Recruiting		http://www.gocoastguard.com
Employment/Recruiting Phone		877-669-8747
Engineering Logistics Center		410-762-6000
Equipment, Compliance, Inspections		800-842-8740
Historian's Office		202-267-1394
Institute, Coast Guard		405-954-0072
Marine Safety Center		202-366-6480
Marine Safety Laboratories		860-441-2645
Maritime Safety Operation Information		800-682-1796
Merchandise (Gift Shop @ The Academy)		860-444-8488
Military Worldwide Personnel Locator		202-493-1697
National Maritime Center		202-493-1000
Navigation Center		703-313-5800
Public Affairs Office (News & Upcoming Events)		202-267-1587
Research & Development Center		860-441-2600
Vessel Documentation	304-271-2400	800-799-8362

Maritime Search & Rescue Emergencies

Atlantic Area Command Center (Great Lakes, Gulf Coast, and East Coast)	757-398-6390
Pacific Area Command Center (Hawaii Coast, Alaska Coast, and Pacific Coast)	510-437-3701

Units

1st District, Boston, Massachusetts	800-848-3942
5th District, Portsmouth, Virginia	757-398-6272
7th District, Miami, Florida	305-415-6683
8th District, New Orleans, Louisiana	504-589-6225
9th District, Cleveland, Ohio	216-902-6020
11th District, Alameda, California	510-437-3968

13th District, Seattle, Washington ································206-220-7237
14th District, Honolulu, Hawaii ·······························808-541-2121
17th District, Juneau, Alaska ·······························907-463-2065
Maintenance & Logistics Command, Atlantic···········757-628-4279
Maintenance & Logistics Command, Pacific···········510-437-3269

Office of Management

This office is responsible for the budget, accounting, expenditure of funds, finance, procurement, appropriations, information technology systems, property, equipment, and facilities. This office also tracks the performance of the responsibilities of Homeland Security.
General Information (DHS Main Line)·······················202-282-8000

Office of the Secretary

This office is responsible for the collaboration of federal, state, local, and private entites. They work to oversee activities and communicate to provide intelligence analysis, improve technology, strengthen our borders, and provide infrastructure protection. Listed below are many of the offices that are within the Office of the Secretary:

Office of the Chief Privacy Officer·····························202-772-9848
Office of Civil Rights and Civil Liberties ····················202-401-1474
Office of Counter Narcotics (DHS Main Line) ···········202-282-8000
Office of General Counsel (DHS Main Line) ··············202-282-8000
Office of the Inspector General ·······························202-254-4100
Office of Legislative Affairs (DHS Main Line)············202-282-8000
Office of National Capital Region Coordination (DHS) ·202-282-8000
Office of the Private Sector (DHS Main Line) ···········202-282-8000
Office of Public Affairs (DHS Main Line) ··················202-282-8000
Office of State & Local Government
  Coordination & Preparedness (DHS Main Line) ······202-282-8000

Department of Housing & Urban Development (HUD)

http://www.hud.gov

General Information	202-708-1112
Employment	202-708-0408
Fair Housing & Equal Opportunity	202-708-4252
Ginnie Mae	202-708-0926
Housing Counseling for Home Buyers & Renters	800-569-4287
Housing Discrimination Hotline	202-755-5033
Public & Indian Housing	202-708-0950

Regional Offices

California, San Francisco	415-489-6400
Colorado, Denver	303-672-5440
Georgia, Atlanta	404-331-4111
Illinois, Chicago	312-353-5680
Kansas, Kansas City	913-551-5462
Masachusetts, Boston	617-994-8200
New York, New York City	212-264-8000
Pennsylvania, Philadelphia	215-656-0500
Texas, Fort Worth	817-978-5965
Washington, Seattle	206-220-5101

Department of Interior (DOI)

http://www.doi.gov

General Information	202-208-3100
Bureau of Indian Affairs (BIA)	202-208-3710
Bureau of Land Management (BLM)	202-452-5125
Bureau of Reclamation (USBR)	202-513-0501
Main E-Mail	webteam@ios.doi.gov
Minerals Management Service (MMS)	202-208-3985
National Park Service (NPS)	202-208-6843
Office of Surface Mining (OSM)	202-208-2719
U.S. Fish & Wildlife (FWS)	800-344-9453
U.S. Geological Survey (USGS)	888-275-8747

Department of Justice (DOJ)

http://www.usdoj.gov

General Information	202-514-2000
Civil Division (CIV)	202-514-3301
Civil Rights Division (CRT)	202-514-2151
Criminal Division (CRM)	202-514-2601
Drug Enforcement Administration (DEA)	202-307-8000
Environment & Natural Resources Division (ENRD)	202-514-2701
Executive Office for Immigration Review (EOIR)	202-305-0169
Executive Office for U.S. Attorneys (EOUSA)	202-514-2121
Federal Bureau of Alcohol, Tobacco, Firearms and Explosives (ATF)	202-927-8700
Federal Bureau of Prisons (BOP)	202-305-2500
INTERPOL/U.S. National Central Bureau (USNCB) http://www.uddoj.gov/usncb	202-616-9000
Justice Management Division (JMD)	202-514-3101
National Drug Intelligence Center (NDIC) http://www.usdoj.gov/ndic/	814-532-4601
Main E-Mail	AskDOJ@usdoj.gov
Office of Tribal Justice (OTJ)	202-514-8812
Office of Violence Against Women	202-307-3913
U.S. Marshals Service (USMS)	202-307-9001
U.S. Parole Commission (USPC)	301-492-5917

National Law Enforcement & Corrections Technology Center (NLECTC)

Border Research & Technology Center	888-656-2782
Law Enforcement Standards	301-975-2757
Law Enforcement Technology Commercialization	888-306-5382
National Center	800-248-2742
Northeast Region	888-338-0584
Northwest Region	866-569-2969
Rocky Mountain Region	800-416-8086
Rural Law Enforcement Technology Center	866-787-2553
Southeast Region	800-292-4385
Western Region	310-336-2222
Office of LE Standards & Technology	301-975-2757
Office of LE Technology Commercialization	888-306-5382

Office of Justice Programs (OJP)

http://www.ojp.usdoj.gov

General Information	202-307-5933
Bureau of Justice Assistance (BJA) http://www.ojp.usdoj.gov/bja	800-688-4252

Bureau of Justice Statistics (BJS)
http://www.ojp.usdoj.gov/bjs ·····················800-732-3277
Juvenile Justice & Delinquency Prevention ·············202-307-5911
Juvenile Justice Clearinghouse ·····························800-638-8736
National Criminal Justice Reference Service (NCJRS)
http://www.ncjrs.org ···································301-519-5500
National Institute of Justice (NIJ)
http://www.ojp.usdoj.gov/nij ·························202-307-2942
National Law Enforcement & Corrections Technology (NLECTC)
http://www.nlectc.org ·································800-248-2742
National Victims Resource Center (OVC)
http://www.ojp.usdoj.gov/ovc ························800-627-6872
Office of Juvenile Delinquency & Prevention (OJDP)
http://ojjdp.ncjrs.org ·································202-307-5911

Department of Labor (DOL)

http://www.dol.gov
General Information ··866-487-2365
Americans with Disabilities Act (ADA) ·····················866-633-7365
Board of Alien Labor Certification Appeals ··············202-693-7542
Bureau of International Labor Affairs (ILAB) ···········202-693-4770
Child Labor, International··································202-693-4843
Drug Free Workplace···202-693-5919
Employment···202-219-6677
Immigrant Labor Certification·····························202-693-3010
Immigration & Nationality Act·····························202-693-4881
Migrant & Seasonal Farm Workers·······················866-487-9243
North American Free Trade Act (NAFTA) ···············202-693-4900
Occupational Safety & Health Administration (OSHA) ·800-321-6742
Safety & Health ···202-693-1999

Department of State (DOS)

http://www.state.gov
General Information ·································202-647-4000
Diplomatic Security···········http://www.state.gov/m/ds·800-979-9331
Emergency Service for U.S. Citizens Overseas ····**202-647-5225**
Employment···202-647-7284
Overseas Travel Advisory·································202-647-5225

Phone Directory

Department of Transportation (DOT)

http://www.dot.gov

General Information	202-366-4000
Bureau of Transportation Statistics	800-853-1351
Employment Webpage	http://careers.dot.gov
Federal Aviation Administration (FAA)	202-267-3484
Federal Highway Administration (FHWA)	202-366-0537
Federal Motor Carrier Safety Association (FMCSA)	800-832-5660
Federal Railroad Administration (FRA)	202-493-6000
Federal Transit Administration (FTA)	202-366-4043
Main E-Mail	dot.comments@ost.dot.gov
Maritime Administration (MARAD)	800-996-2723
National Highway Traffic Safety Admin. (NHTSA)	888-327-4236
Research & Special Programs Administration (RSPA)	202-366-4400
Office of HAZMAT Safety - Central	847-294-8580
Office of HAZMAT Safety - Eastern	609-989-2256
Office of HAZMAT Safety - Southern	404-305-6120
Office of HAZMAT Safety - Southwestern	713-718-3950
Office of HAZMAT Safety - Special Investigations	202-366-4700
Office of HAZMAT Safety - Western	909-937-3279
Saint Lawrence Seaway Development Corp	800-785-2779
Surface Transportation Board	202-565-1500

State Departments of Transportation (DOT)

Alabama	334-242-6358
Alaska	907-465-3900
Arizona	602-712-7355
Arkansas	501-569-2000
California	916-654-5266
Colorado	303-757-9011
Connecticut	860-594-2000
Delaware	302-760-2080
Florida	850-414-4100
Georgia	404-656-5267
Hawaii	808-587-2160
Idaho	208-334-8000
Illinois	217-782-7820
Indiana	317-232-5533
Iowa	515-239-1101
Kansas	785-296-3566
Kentucky	502-564-4890
Louisiana	225-379-1100
Maine	207-624-3000
Maryland	410-865-1142
Massachusetts	617-973-7000

Michigan	517-373-2090
Minnesota	651-296-3000
Mississippi	601-359-7001
Missouri	573-751-2511
Montana	406-444-6200
Nebraska	402-471-4567
Nevada	775-888-7000
New Hampshire	603-271-3734
New Jersey	609-530-8059
New Mexico	505-827-5100
New York	518-457-6195
North Carolina	919-733-2520
North Dakota	701-328-2500
Ohio	614-466-7170
Oklahoma	405-522-8000
Oregon	888-275-6368
Pennsylvania	717-787-2838
Puerto Rico	787-724-1065
Rhode Island	401-222-2481
South Carolina	803-737-2314
South Dakota	605-773-3265
Tennessee	615-741-2848
Texas	215-463-8588
Utah	801-965-4000
Vermont	802-828-2000
Virginia	804-786-2801
Washington	360-705-7000
Washington, D.C.	202-673-6813
West Virginia	304-558-3456
Wisconsin	608-266-3581
Wyoming	307-777-4375

Department of the Treasury

http://www.treas.gov

General Information	202-622-2000
Alcohol and Tobacco Tax and Trade Bureau (TTB)	877-882-3277
Bureau of Engraving & Printing	202-874-3019
Bureau of Public Debt	202-504-3502
Domestic Finance Office	202-622-1703
Economic Policy Office	202-622-2200
Financial Crimes Enforcement Network (FinCEN)	
http://www.fincen.gov	866-566-3974
Internal Revenue Service (IRS)	800-829-1040
Taxpayer Advocacy Panel	888-912-1227

Department of Veteran Affairs (VA)

http://www.va.gov

General Information	800-827-1000
Education Benefits	888-442-4551
Gulf War/Agent Orange Helpline	800-749-8387
Health Care Benefits	877-222-8387
Life Insurance	800-669-8477
Veterans Health Administration	202-273-5400

Drug Enforcement Administration (DEA)

http://www.dea.gov

General Information	202-307-1000
Employment	http://jobsearch.usajobs.opm.gov/a9dea.asp
Employment Phone	800-DEA-4288

Division Offices

Arizona, Phoenix	602-664-5600
California, Los Angeles	213-621-6700
San Diego	858-616-4100
San Francisco	415-436-7900
Caribbean	787-775-1815
Colorado, Englewood	303-705-7300
Florida, Miami	305-994-4870
Georgia, Atlanta	404-893-7000
Illinois, Chicago	312-353-7875
Louisiana, New Orleans	504-840-1100
Massachusetts, Boston	617-557-2100
Michigan, Detroit	313-234-4000
Missouri, St. Louis	314-538-4600
New Jersey, Newark	973-273-5000
New York, New York	212-337-3900
Pennsylvania, Philadelphia	215-861-3474
Puerto Rico	787-775-1815
Texas, Dallas	214-366-6900
El Paso	915-832-6000
Houston	713-693-3000
Washington, D.C.	202-305-8500
Washington, Seattle	206-553-5443

Demand Reduction Coordinators

Headquarters, Arlington, Virginia ················202-307-7936

Division Offices

Atlanta Division (GA, NC, SC, TN)················404-893-7124
Aviation Operations Center················817-837-2028
Caribbean Division (PR, Virgin Islands, Barbados,
    Curacao, Dominican Republic, Haiti, Jamaica,
    Trinidad & Tobago)················787-775-1736
Chicago Division (IL-North & Central, IN, MN, ND, WI) 312-886-5241
Dallas Division (OK, TX-Northern) ················214-366-6970
Detroit Division (KY, MI, OH)················313-234-4310
El Paso Division (NM, TX-Southwestern)················915-832-6233
EPIC - Intelligence Support Worldwide················915-760-2013
Houston Division (TX-Southeastern, South-central) ···713-693-3152
Los Angeles Division (CA-Central, HI, NV)···213-621-6768
Miami Division (Bahamas, FL)················305-994-4604
New England Division - Manchester, NH (ME, NH, VT) 603-225-1574
New England Division - Springfield, MA (CT, MA, RI) 413-785-0284
New Orleans Division (AL, AR, LA, MS)················504-840-1032
New York Division (NY)················212-337-1266
Newark Division (NJ)················973-273-5095
Philadelphia Division (DE, PA)················215-861-3291
Phoenix Division (AZ)················602-664-5657
Rocky Mountain Division (CO, MT, UT, WY)···303-705-7340
Saint Louis Division (IA, IL-South, KS, MO, NE, SD)··314-538-4752
San Diego Division (CA-Southern)················858-616-4410
San Francisco Division (CA-Northern)················415-436-7851
Seattle Division (AK, ID, OR, WA)················206-553-2824
Washington Division (DC, MD, VA, WV)················202-305-8259

District Offices

Albuquerque, NM················505-346-7419
Billings, MT················406-657-6020
Columbia, SC················803-765-5251
Honolulu, HI (Hawaii, Guam, Siapan)················808-541-3053
Las Vegas, NV················702-759-8117
Little Rock, AR················501-312-8613
Louisville, KY················502-582-5908
Kansas City, MO················816-746-4962
Minneapolis/Saint Paul, MN················612-348-1712
Nashville, TN················615-736-2952
Portland, OR················503-326-2466
Sacramento, CA················916-480-7154
Salt Lake City, UT················801-524-4353

Environmental Protection Agency (EPA)

http://www.epa.gov

General Information	202-272-0167
Employment ········http://www.epa.gov/ezhire/	202-564-0300
Environmental Emergencies	**866-372-7745**
Environmental Justice Hotline	800-962-6215
Headquarters	202-260-2090
Information Resources Center	202-260-5922
National Response Center	800-424-8802

Criminal Investigation Division

Atlanta Area Office	404-562-9795
Boston Area Office	617-918-2300
Chicago Area Office	312-886-9872
Cleveland Area Office	440-250-1770
Dallas Area Office	214-665-6600
Denver Area Office	303-312-6134
Houston Area Office	713-209-4900
Jacksonville Area Office	904-398-0162
Kansas City Resident Office	913-551-1470
Los Angeles Area Office	626-583-7528
New York City Area Office	212-637-3610
Philadelphia Area Office	215-814-2360
Portland Resident Office	503-326-3541
Saint Louis Area Office	315-539-3422
San Francisco Area Office	415-947-8713
Seattle Area Office	206-553-8306
Washington, D.C. Area Office	703-235-1113

Hotlines and Clearinghouses

Acid Rain	202-343-9620
Aerometric Info Retrieval System (AIRS - Pollution)	866-411-4EPA
AgSTAR Program	800-952-4782
Antimicrobial Information	703-308-0127
Asbestos Abatenebt/Management Ombudsman	800-368-5888
Best Workplaces for Commuters	888-856-3131
Center for Exposure Assessment Modeling (CEAM)	706-355-8400
Clean Air Technology Center (CATC) Infoline	919-541-0800
Clearinghouse for Inventories and Emission Factors	919-541-1000
Endangered Species Protection Program	800-447-3813
Energy Efficiency & Renewable Energy Clearinghouse	800-363-3732
Energy Star	888-782-7937
Environmental Education Clearinghouse	800-424-4372
Environmental Financing Information Network (EFIN)	202-564-4994
Environmental Justice Hotline	800-962-6215

EPA Enforcement Economic Models	888-326-6778
EPA Grants & Fellowships	800-490-9194
EPA Imported Vehicles and Engines	734-214-4100
EPA Learning Institute	202-564-7562
EPA Test Methods	617-918-1991
Indoor Air Quality Information Clearinghouse	800-438-4318
Inspector General	888-546-8740
Integrated Risk Information System (IRIS)	202-566-1676
Local Government Reimbursement Program	800-431-9209
Lowest Achievable Emission Rate Clrnghse (RBLC)	919-541-0800
Methods Info Communication Exchange Svc (MICE)	703-676-4690
Mexico Border	800-334-0741
National Alternative Fuels	800-423-1363
National Compliance Assistance Clearinghouse	202-564-7071
National Service Center for Environmental Publications (NSCEP) (formerly known as NCEPI)	800-490-9198
National Hispanic Indoor Air Quality	800-725-8312
National Lead Information Center	800-424-LEAD
National Pesticide Information Center	800-858-7378
National Poison Control (Emergencies Only)	800-222-1222
Administrative & Materials Request	202-362-3867
National Radon Hotlines 800-SOS-RADON	800-55-RADON
National Small Flows Clearinghouse	800-624-8301
Office of Water Resource Center	202-566-1729
Ozone Protection	800-296-1996
Pay-As-You-Throw (PAYT) Helpline	888-EPA-PAYT
Pollution Prevention Info Clearinghouse (PPIC)	202-566-0799
Resource Conservation and Recovery Act (RCRA), Superfund, and EPCRA Call Center	800-424-9346
Safe Drinking Water	800-426-4791
Small Business Ombudsman	800-368-5888
Storet Water Quality System	800-424-9067
Subsurface Remediation Information Center (SRIC)	580-436-8651
Superfund Document Center	202-566-0276
Superfund Hotline	800-533-3508
Tools for Schools (IAQ) Technical Assistance	866-837-3721
Toxic Release Inventory - EPCRA Hotline	800-424-9346
User Support Service	202-566-0250
Toxic Substances Control Act (TSCA)	202-554-1404
Water Efficiency Clearinghouse	800-926-7337
WasteWise	800-EPA-WISE
Wetlands Information	800-832-7828

Regional Offices

Region 1, New England (CT, MA, ME, NH, RI, VT) ···· 617-918-1111
Main E-Mail ···· r1web.mail@epamail.epa.gov

Region 2 (NY, NJ, PR, Virgin Islands) ·····················212-637-5000
   Caribbean Division, Puerto Rico·······················787-977-5870
   Communications Division ······························212-637-3660
   Hudson River Field Office······························518-747-4389
   Main E-Mail ··································dubois.katie@epa.gov
   Niagara Falls Public Information Center ···············716-285-8842
   Research & Reference Library ·························212-637-3185
   Virgin Islands Field Office·····························340-714-2333
   World Trade Center, Community Relations ···········212-637-3651
Region 3, Mid-Atlantic (DE, DC, MD, PA, VA, WV) ·············215-814-5000
   Main E-Mail ··r3public@epa.gov
Region 4 (AL, FL, GA, KY, MS, NC, SC, TN) ·············404-562-9900
   24-Hour Spill Reporting for Region 4 ·················404-562-8700
   Alabama Division ···································334-271-7700
   Cleanup Public Information Line for Region 4 ········800-564-7577
   Florida Division ······································850-921-1222
   Georgia Division ·····································404-657-5947
   Kentucky Division ····································502-564-2150
   Main E-Mail ···r4-library@epa.gov
   Mississippi Division··································601-961-5171
   North Carolina Division ·······························919-733-4984
   Science & Ecosystem Support Div. for Region 4·····706-355-8500
   South Carolina Division ······························803-898-3900
   Tennessee Division ··································615-532-0109
   Toll Free for Region 4 Division ·······················800-241-1754
Region 5 (IL, IN, MI, MN, OH, WI) ·······················312-353-2000
   Main E-Mail ··································reshkin.karen@epa.gov
Region 6 (AR, LA, NM, OK, TX) ························214-665-6444
   Border Liaison Office ·································915-533-7273
Region 7 (IA, KS, MO, NE) ····························913-281-0991
   Main E-Mail ··r7actionline@epa.gov
   Office of External Programs····························913-551-7003
Region 8 (CO, MT, ND, SD, UT, WY) ·····················303-312-6312
   Main E-Mail ··r8eisc@epa.gov
Region 9, Pacific Southwest (American Samoa, AZ,
   CA, Guam, HI, Northern Mariana Islands, NV)·······415-947-8000
   24-Hour Environmental Emergencies Region 9 ·····800-300-2193
   Main E-Mail ··r9.info@epa.gov
   Pacific Island Contact Office··························808-541-2710
   San Diego Border Office·······························619-235-4765
   Southern California Field Office························213-244-1800
   Toll Free for Region 9 Division ·······················866-372-9378
Region 10, Pacific Northwest (AK, ID, OR, WA)·········206-553-1200
   Main E-Mail ··philip.jeff@epa.gov
   Toll Free for Region 10 Division ·······················800-424-4EPA

Federal Aviation Administration (FAA)

http://www.faa.gov

General Information	202-267-3484
Accident Investigation Office	202-267-5043
Aeronautical Center (Oklahoma City)	405-954-3583
Employment Main Office (Washington, D.C.)	202-267-8012
Employment Website	http://www.epa.gov/ezhire/
Flight Standards Main Office	202-493-4876
Technical Center (Trenton, NJ)	609-485-4000

Flight Standards Division (FSDO), and International Field Offices (IFO)

Alaska Region (AAL)		**907-271-5514**
Anchorage (ANC)	800-294-5116*	907-271-5514
Fairbanks (FAI)	800-294-5119*	907-474-0276
Juneau (JNU)	800-478-2231	907-586-7532
Central Region (ACE)		**816-329-3050**
Des Moines, IA (DSM)	800-728-7250	515-289-3840
Kansas City, MO (MCI)	800-519-3269	816-891-2100
LIncoln, NE (LNK)		402-475-1738
Saint Louis, MO (STL)		314-429-1006
Wichita, KS (ICT)		316-941-1200
Eastern Region (AEA)		**718-553-3240**
Accident Command Post, Eastern Region		718-553-3100
Albany, NY (ALB)		518-785-5660
Allegheny, PA (AGC)		412-466-5357
Allentown, PA (ABE)		610-264-2888
Baltimore, MD (BAL)		410-787-0040
Brussels, Belgium - IFO		011-32-2-508-2720
Charleston, WV		304-347-5199
Farmingdale, NY (FRG)		631-755-1300
Frankfurt, Germany - IFO		011-49-0-69-69-7050
FSDO Safety Program, Eastern Region		718-553-3235
Harrisburg, PA (HAR)		717-774-8271
London, England - IFO		011-44-208-754-8819
New York City, NY - FSDO		516-228-8029
New York City, NY - IFO		718-553-0986
Philadelphia, PA (PHL)		610-595-1500
Pittsburgh, PA (PIT)		412-262-9034
Richmond, VA (RIC)		804-222-7494
Rochester, NY (ROC)		585-436-3880
Teterboro, NJ (TEB)		201-556-6600
Washington, D.C. (Dulles, VA) (DCA)		703-661-8160
Great Lakes Region (AGL)		**847-294-7252**
Detroit, MI (DTW)		734-487-7222

Chicago, IL (ORD)		847-928-8000
Cincinnati, OH (CVG)		513-979-6400
Cleveland, OH (CLE)		440-686-2001
Columbus, OH (CMH)		614-225-3120
Grand Rapids, MI (GRR)		616-954-6657
Fargo, ND (FAR)		701-232-8949
Indianapolis, IN (IND)		317-487-2400
Milwaukee, WI (MKE)		414-486-2920
Minneapolis, MN (MSP)		612-713-4211
Rapid City, SD (RAP)		605-737-3050
South Bend, IN (SBN)		574-245-4600
Springfield, IL (SPI)		217-744-1910
West Chicago, IL (DPA)		630-443-3100
New England Region (ANE)		**781-238-7200**
Boston, MA		781-274-7130
Portland, ME (PWM)		207-780-3263
Windsor Locks, CT (BDL)		860-654-1000
Northwest Mountain Region (ANM)		**425-227-1028**
Boise, ID (BOI)	800-453-0001	208-387-4000
Denver, CO (DEN)	800-847-3808	303-342-1100
Helena, MT (HLN)	800-457-9917	406-449-5270
Long Beach, CA (AEG)		562-627-5317
Portland, OR (PDX)	800-847-3806	503-615-3200
Salt Lake City, UT (SLC)	800-532-0268	801-257-5020
Seattle, WA (SEA)		425-227-2813
Spokane, WA (SPO)	800-341-2623	509-532-2340
Southern Region (ASO)		**404-305-6000**
Atlanta, GA (ATL)		404-305-7200
Birmingham, AL (BHM)		205-731-1557
Charlotte, NC (CLT)		704-319-7020
Columbia, SC (CAE)		803-765-5931
Fort Lauderdale, FL (FLL)		954-635-1300
Greensboro, NC (GSO)		336-662-1000
Jackson, MS (JAN)		601-664-9800
Louisville, KY (LOU)		502-753-4200
Memphis, TN (MEM)		901-322-8600
Miami, FL (MIA) - FSDO		305-716-3400
Miami, FL (MIA) - IFO		305-716-3500
Nashville, TN (BNA)		615-324-1300
Orlando, FL (ORL)		407-812-7700
San Juan, Puerto Rico (SJU)		787-764-2538
Tampa, FL (TPA)		813-287-4900
Southwest Region (ASW)		**817-222-5270**
Albuquerque, NM (ABQ)		505-764-1200
Alliance/Fort Worth, TX (AFW)		817-491-5000
Baton Rouge, LA (BTR)		225-932-5900

Dallas, TX (DAL)	800-759-4684	214-902-1800
Dallas/Ft Worth, TX(DFW)-FSDO	866-256-1219	817-684-6700
Dallas/Ft Worth, TX (DFW)-IFO		817-684-6700
Houston, TX (HOU)	888-285-2127	281-929-7000
Little Rock, AR (LIT)	800-632-9566*	501-918-4400
Lubbock, TX (LBB)	800-858-4115	806-740-3800
Oklahoma City, OK (OKC)		405-951-4200
San Antonio, TX (SAT)	800-292-2023	210-308-3300
Western Pacific Region (AWP)		**310-725-3300**
Fresno, CA (FAT)		559-487-5306
Honolulu, HI (HNL)		808-837-8300
Las Vegas, NV (LAS)		702-269-1445
Long Beach, CA (LGB)		562-420-1755
Los Angeles, CA (LAX)		310-215-2150
Oakland, CA (OAK)		510-748-0122
Reno, NV (RNO)		775-858-7700
Riverside, CA (RAL)		909-276-6701
Sacramento, CA (SAC)		916-422-0272
San Diego, CA (SAN)		619-557-5281
San Francisco, CA (SFO) - IFO		650-876-2771
San Jose, CA (SJC)		408-291-7681
Scottsdale, AZ (SDL)		480-419-0111
Singapore - IFO		011-65-6545-5822
Van Nuys, CA (VNY)		818-904-6291

* Number can only be dialed within that calling area.

Hotline Numbers

24-Hour Safety & Hazardous Materials Hotline	800-255-1111
Air Travel Service Problems/Consumer Protection	202-366-2220
Consumer Hotline	800-322-7873
Security & Baggage Screener Concerns	866-289-9673
Whistleblower Hotline	800-255-1111

Regional Offices

Alaska (Anchorage)	907-271-5514
Central (Kansas City)	816-329-3200
Eastern (New York)	718-553-3200
Great Lakes (Chicago)	847-294-7252
New England (Burlington, MA)	781-238-7200
Northwestern (Renton, WA)	425-227-2000
Southern (College Park, GA)	404-305-6000
Southwestern (Fort Worth)	817-222-5200
Western Pacific (Lawndale, CA)	310-725-7200

Phone Directory

Federal Bureau Of Investigation (FBI)

http://www.fbi.gov

Headquarters & General Info (Washington, D.C.)	202-324-3000
Employment ········http://fbijobs.com	202-278-2408
FBI Library	703-632-3200

Field Offices

Alabama, Birmingham	205-326-6166
Mobile	334-438-3674
Alaska, Anchorage	907-258-5322
Arizona, Phoenix	602-279-5511
Arkansas, Little Rock	501-221-9100
California, Los Angeles	310-477-6565
Sacramento	916-481-9110
San Diego	858-565-1255
San Francisco	415-553-7400
Colorado, Denver	303-629-7171
Connecticut, New Haven	203-777-6311
Florida, Jacksonville	904-721-1211
North Miami Beach	305-944-9101
Tampa	813-273-4566
Georgia, Atlanta	404-679-9000
Hawaii, Honolulu	808-566-4300
Illinois, Chicago	312-431-1333
Springfield	217-522-9675
Indiana, Indianapolis	317-639-3301
Kentucky, Louisville	502-583-3941
Louisiana, New Orleans	504-816-3000
Maryland, Baltimore	410-265-8080
Massachusetts, Boston	617-742-5533
Michigan, Detroit	313-965-2323
Minnesota, Minneapolis	612-376-3200
Mississippi, Jackson	601-948-5000
Missouri, Kansas City	816-512-8200
St. Louis	314-231-4324
Nebraska, Omaha	402-493-8688
Nevada, Las Vegas	702-385-1281
New Jersey, Newark	973-792-3000
New Mexico, Albuquerque	505-889-1300
New York, Albany	518-465-7551
Buffalo	716-856-7800
New York City	212-384-1000
North Carolina, Charlotte	704-377-9200
Ohio, Cincinnati	513-421-4310
Cleveland	216-522-1400

Oklahoma, Oklahoma City	405-290-7770
Oregon, Portland	503-224-4181
Pennsylvania, Philadelphia	215-418-4000
Pittsburgh	412-432-4000
Puerto Rico, San Juan	787-754-6000
South Carolina, Columbia	803-551-4200
Tennessee, Knoxville	865-544-0751
Memphis	901-747-4300
Texas, Dallas	972-559-5000
El Paso	915-832-5000
Houston	713-693-5000
San Antonio	210-225-6741
Utah, Salt Lake City	801-579-1400
Virginia, Norfolk	757-455-0100
Richmond	804-261-1044
Washington, D.C.	202-278-2000
Washington, Seattle	206-622-0460
Wisconsin, Milwaukee	414-276-4684

Federal Bureau of Prisons (BOP)

http://www.bop.gov

General Information	202-305-2500	888-317-8455
Central Office	202-307-3198
Management & Specialty Training Center	303-340-7800
National Institute of Corrections	202-307-3106
Training Academy (FLETC)	912-267-2711

Regional Offices

Mid-Atlantic, Annapolis Junction, Maryland	301-317-3100
North Central, Kansas City, Kansas	913-621-3939
Northeast, Philadelphia, Pennsylvania	215-521-7300
South Central, Dallas, Texas	214-224-3389
Southeast, Atlanta, Georgia	678-686-1200
Western, Dublin, California	925-803-4700

Federal Emergency Management (FEMA)

see Dept. of Homeland Security

Federal Law Enforcement Training Center (FLETC)

see Dept. of Homeland Security

Phone Directory

Federal Protective Services Police (FPS)

see Dept. of Homeland Security

Federal Railroad Administration (FRA)

http://www.fra.dot.gov

General Information	202-493-6000
Hazardous Materials & Dangerous Goods Division	202-493-6229
Highway-Rail Crossing and Trespasser Division	202-493-6285
Office of Safety Assurance & Compliance	202-493-6247
Railroad Accident Ivestigation	202-493-6209
Signal & Train Control Division	202-493-6203

Regional Offices

Region 1 (CT, MA, ME, NH, NJ, NY, RI, VT)	617-494-2302
Hotline	800-724-5991
Region 2 (DC, DE, MD, OH, PA, VA, WV)	610-521-8200
Hotline	800-724-5992
Region 3 (AL, FL, GA, KY, MS, NC, SC, TN)	404-562-3800
Hotline	800-724-5993
Region 4 (IL, IN, MI, MN, WI)	312-353-6203
Hotline	800-724-5040
Region 5 (AR, LA, NM, OK, TX)	817-862-2200
Hotline	800-724-5995
Region 6 (CO, IA, KS, MO, NE)	816-329-3840
Hotline	800-724-5996
Region 7 (AZ, CA, NV, UT)	916-498-6540
Hotline	800-724-5997
Region 8 (AK,ID,MT,ND,OR,SD,WA,WY)	360-696-7536
Hotline	800-724-5998

Federal Transit Administration (FTA)

http://www.fta.dot.gov

General Information	202-366-4043
Lower Manhattan Recovery Office	212-668-1770

Metropolitan & Regional Offices

Chicago, IL Office	312-353-2789
Los Angeles, CA Office	213-202-3950
New York City, NY Office	212-668-2201
Philadelphia, PA Office	215-656-7070
Washington, D.C. Office	202-219-3562

Region 1 (CT, MA, ME, NH, RI, VT) ···························617-494-2055
Region 2 (NJ, NY, Virgin Islands) ···························212-668-2170
Region 3 (DC, DE, MD, PA, VA, WV) ························215-656-7100
Region 4 (AL, FL, GA, KY, MS, NC, PR, SC, TN) ·······404-562-3500
Region 5 (IL, IN, MI, MN, OH, WI) ··························312-353-2789
Region 6 (AR, LA, NM, OK, TX) ·····························817-978-0550
Region 7 (IA, KS, MO, NE) ··································816-329-3920
Region 8 (CO, MT, ND, SD, UT, WY) ·······················720-963-3300
Region 9 (American Samoa, AZ, CA, Guam, HI,
    Northern Mariana Islands, NV) ·······················415-744-3133
Region 10 (AK, ID, OR, WA)································206-220-7954

Immigration & Naturalization Service (INS)

*see U.S. Citizenship & Immigration Services under the
Dept. of Homeland Security*

Internal Revenue Service (IRS)

http://www.irs.gov

General Information for Business ····························800-829-4933
General Information for Individuals ·························800-829-1040
Employment ···http://jobs.irs.gov
Ordering Forms or Publications ····························800-829-3676
Return or Refund Status ···································800-829-4477
Tax Fraud Hotline ·······································800-829-0433

Criminal Investigations

Atlanta··404-522-0050
New York City ··212-436-1033
San Francisco ··415-522-6008

Military Law Enforcement

Air Force, Office of Special Investigations HQ··········240-857-0989
Army, Law Enf. Div., Criminal Inv. Command HQ·····703-806-0402
    National Guard, see following table for Counterdrug Coordinators
Navy, Law Enf. Div., Naval Criminal Inv. Service HQ ·202-433-8800
Coast Guard
    Law Enforcement Personnel HQ ·····················202-267-0977
    Coast Guard Investigative Services····················202-493-6600
Marine Corps, Law Enf./Physical Security Section····703-614-2500
Defense Criminal Investigative Service ·················703-604-8600

National Guard Counterdrug Coordinators

Alabama	334-213-7658
Alaska	907-428-3617
Arizona	602-267-2623
Arkansas	501-212-5492
California	916-854-3715
Colorado	303-677-8303
Connecticut	860-524-4980
Delaware	302-326-7085
Florida	904-823-0438
Georgia	770-919-3473
Guam	671-647-1972
Hawaii	808-732-0209
Idaho	208-422-3530
Illinois	217-761-3728
Indiana	317-486-8291
Iowa	515-252-4606
Kansas	785-862-0001
Kentucky	859-293-4142
Louisiana	504-278-8491
Maine	207-626-4416
Maryland	410-576-6135
Massachusetts	508-233-6804
Michigan	517-483-5896
Minnesota	651-282-4147
Mississippi	601-313-1670
Missouri	573-638-9599
Montana	406-324-3178
Nebraska	402-458-1132
Nevada	775-348-5110
New Hampshire	603-227-1542
New Jersey	609-562-0812
New Mexico	505-846-1031
New York	518-786-3477
North Carolina	919-664-6322
North Dakota	701-333-2050
Ohio	614-336-6426
Oklahoma	405-228-5688
Oregon	503-584-3938
Pennsylvania	717-861-2482
Puerto Rico	787-977-4867
Rhode Island	401-392-0827
South Carolina	803-806-1559
South Dakota	605-737-6723
Tennessee	615-355-3901

Texas	512-465-5516
Utah	801-523-4150
Vermont	802-338-3350
Virginia	804-292-8529
Virgin Islands	340-774-3066
Washington	253-512-8894
Washington, D.C.	202-685-9726
West Virginia	304-722-7007
Wisconsin	608-242-3540
Wyoming	307-772-5259

National Drug Intelligence Center (NDIC)

http://www.usdoj.gov/ndic

General Information	814-532-4601
Document Exploitation Division	814-532-4515
Intelligence Division	814-532-4036
Liaison Office	703-556-8970
Main E-Mail	NDIC@usdoj.gov
Pennsylvania Office, Johnstown	814-532-4601
Product Requests	814-532-4541
Washington D.C. Office, McLean, Virginia	703-556-8970

National Highway Traffic Safety Administration (NHTSA)

http://www.nhtsa.dot.gov

General Information	202-366-0123	888-327-4236

Regional Offices

Central (IA, KS, MO, NE)	816-329-3900
Eastern (NJ, NY, PR, Virgin Islands)	914-682-6162
Mid-Atlantic (DC, DE, MD, PA, VA, WV)	410-962-0090
New England (CT, ME, MA, NH, RI, VT)	617-494-3427
Northwest (AK, ID, OR, WA)	206-220-7640
Rocky Mountain (CO, ND, SD, UT, WY)	303-279-2232
South Central (AR, Indian Nations, LA, NM, OK, TX)	817-978-3653
Southeast (AL, FL, GA, KY, MS, NC, SC, TN)	404-562-3739
Western (American Samoa, AZ, CA, Guam, HI, Northern Mariana Islands, NV)	415-744-3089

National Oceanic and Atmospheric Administration

Fisheries Office for Law Enforcement

General Information	800-853-1964

National Park Service (NPS)

http://www.nps.gov

General Information ··202-208-6843
Employment (USA Jobs) ···478-757-3000

Regional Offices

Alaska Anchorage ···907-644-3510
Intermountain, Denver, Colorado ·································303-969-2500
Midwest, Omaha, Nebraska ··402-661-1736
National Capital, Washington, D.C. ·····························202-619-7000
Northeast, Philadelphia, Pennsylvania ·······················215-597-7013
Pacific West, Oakland, California ·································510-817-1304
Southeast, Atlanta, Georgia ···404-562-3100

U.S. Park Police

24-Hour Emergency Number (or dial 911) ···············**202-619-7300**
General Information ···202-619-7105
Criminal Investigation Branch ··202-610-8730
Criminal Investigation Branch Tipline ····························202-610-8737
District 1, Central Station, Washington, D.C. ···············202-426-6710
District 2, GWMP Station, McLean, VA ·······················703-285-1000
District 3, Rock Creek Station, Washington, D.C. ···········202-426-7716
District 4, Balto-Wash Station, Greenbelt, MD ···········301-344-4250
District 5, Anacostia Station, Washington, D.C. ···········202-610-8703
New York Field Office ··718-338-4241
New York Field Office, 24 Hour Emergency ···········**718-338-3988**
New York Field Office, 24 Hour Non-Emergency ·······718-338-3993
San Francisco Field Office ···415-561-5185
San Francisco Field Office, 24 Hour Emergency ···**415-561-5656**
San Francisco Field Office, 24 Hour Non-Emergency 415-561-5505
Training Branch, Washington, D.C. ·······························202-610-3525

Transportation Security Administration (TSA)

see Dept. of Homeland Security

U.S. Attorneys' Offices

http://www.usdoj.gov/usao

Alabama, Middle District ··334-223-7280
   Northern District ···205-244-2001
   Southern District ···251-441-5845
Alaska ··907-271-5071
Arizona ···602-514-7500
Arkansas, Eastern District ···501-340-2600

Western District	479-783-5125
California, Central District	213-894-2434
Eastern District	916-554-2700
Northern District	415-436-7200
Southern District	619-557-5610
Colorado	303-454-0100
Connecticut	203-821-3700
Delaware	302-573-6277
Florida, Middle District	813-274-6000
Northern District	850-942-8430
Southern District	305-961-9000
Georgia, Middle District	478-752-3511
Northern District	404-581-6000
Southern District	912-652-4422
Hawaii	808-541-2850
Idaho	208-334-1211
Illinois, Central District	217-492-4450
Northern District	312-353-5300
Southern District	618-439-3808
Indiana, Northern District	219-937-5500
Southern District	317-226-6333
Iowa, Northern District	319-363-6333
Southern District	515-284-6257
Kansas	316-269-6481
Kentucky, Eastern District	859-233-2661
Western District	502-582-5911
Louisiana, Eastern District	504-680-3000
Middle District	225-389-0443
Western District	318-676-3600
Maine	207-780-3257
Maryland	410-209-4800
Massachusetts	617-748-3100
Michigan, Eastern District	313-226-9100
Western District	616-456-2404
Minnesota	612-664-5600
Mississippi, Northern District	662-234-3351
Southern District	601-965-4480
Missouri, Eastern District	314-539-2200
Western District	816-426-4234
Montana	406-657-6101
Nebraska	402-661-3700
Nevada	702-388-6336
New Hampshire	603-225-1552
New Jersey	973-645-2700
New Mexico	505-346-7274
New York, Eastern District	718-254-7000

Northern District	315-448-0672
Western District	716-843-5700
Southern District	212-637-2200
North Carolina, Eastern District	919-856-4530
Middle District	336-333-5351
Western District	704-344-6222
North Dakota	701-297-7400
Ohio, Northern District	216-622-3600
Southern District	614-469-5715
Oklahoma, Eastern District	918-684-5100
Northern District	918-581-7463
Western District	405-553-8700
Oregon	503-727-1000
Pennsylvania, Eastern District	215-861-8200
Middle District	717-221-4482
Western District	412-644-3500
Rhode Island	401-709-5000
South Carolina	803-929-3000
South Dakota	605-330-4400
Tennessee, Eastern District	865-545-4167
Middle District	615-736-5151
Western District	901-544-4231
Texas, Eastern District	409-839-2538
Northern District	214-659-8600
Southern District	713-567-9000
Western District	210-384-7100
Utah	801-524-5682
Vermont	802-951-6725
Virginia, Eastern District	703-299-3700
Western District	540-857-2250
Washington, Eastern District	509-353-2767
Western District	206-553-7970
Washington, D.C.	202-514-7566
West Virginia, Northern District	304-234-0100
Southern District	304-345-2200
Wisconsin, Eastern District	414-297-1700
Western District	608-264-5158
Wyoming	307-772-2124

U.S. Capitol Police

http://www.usacapitolpolice.gov

General Information	202-224-5151
Employment/Recruitment	866-561-8727

U.S. Customs Service

see Dept. of Homeland Security

U.S. Marshals Service

General Information	202-307-9054
Employment	202-307-9048
Investigative Services	202-307-9707
Judicial Services	202-307-9500
Justice Prisoner Alien Transportation System	816-374-6060
Prisoner Services	202-307-5100

District Offices

Alabama, Middle District	334-223-7401
Northern District	205-731-1712
Southern District	251-690-2841
Alaska	907-271-5154
Arizona	602-382-8767
Arkansas, Eastern District	501-324-6256
Western District	479-783-5215
California, Central District	213-894-6820
Eastern District	916-930-2030
Northern District	415-436-7677
Southern District	619-557-6620
Colorado	303-335-3400
Connecticut	203-773-2107
Delaware	302-573-6176
Florida, Middle District	813-274-6401
Northern District	850-942-8400
Southern District	305-536-5346
Georgia, Middle District	478-752-8280
Northern District	404-331-6833
Southern District	912-652-4212
Hawaii	808-541-3000
Idaho	208-334-1298
Illinois, Central District	217-492-4430
Northern District	312-353-5290
Southern District	618-482-9336
Indiana, Northern District	574-236-8291
Southern District	317-226-6566
Iowa, Northern District	319-362-4411
Southern District	515-284-6240
Kansas	785-295-2775
Kentucky, Eastern District	859-233-2513
Western District	502-588-8000
Louisiana, Eastern District	504-589-6079
Middle District	225-382-2010
Western District	318-676-4202

Maine	207-780-3365
Maryland	410-962-2220
Massachusetts	617-748-2500
Michigan, Eastern District	313-234-5600
Western District	616-456-2438
Minnesota	612-664-5900
Mississippi, Northern District	662-234-6661
Southern District	601-965-4444
Missouri, Eastern District	314-539-2212
Western District	816-512-2000
Montana	406-247-7030
Nebraska	402-221-4782
Nevada	702-388-6355
New Hampshire	603-225-1632
New Jersey	973-645-2404
New Mexico	505-346-6400
New York, Eastern District	718-254-6703
Northern District	315-448-0341
Southern District	212-637-6000
Western District	716-551-4851
North Carolina, Eastern District	919-856-4153
Middle District	336-333-5354
Western District	704-344-6234
North Dakota	701-297-7300
Ohio, Northern District	216-522-2150
Southern District	614-469-5540
Oklahoma, Eastern District	918-687-2523
Northern District	918-581-7738
Western District	405-231-4206
Oregon	503-326-2209
Pennsylvania, Eastern District	215-597-8158
Middle District	570-346-7277
Western District	412-644-3351
Rhode Island	401-528-5300
South Carolina	803-765-5821
South Dakota	605-330-4351
Tennessee, Eastern District	865-545-4182
Middle District	615-736-5417
Western District	901-544-3304
Texas, Eastern District	903-590-1370
Northern District	214-767-0836
Southern District	713-718-4800
Western District	210-472-6540
Utah	801-524-5693
Vermont	802-951-6271
Virginia, Eastern District	703-837-5500

Western District	540-857-2230
Washington, Eastern District	509-353-2781
Western District	206-370-8600
Washington, D.C.	202-616-8600
West Virginia, Northern District	304-623-0486
Southern District	304-347-5136
Wisconsin, Eastern District	414-297-3707
Western District	608-264-5161
Wyoming	307-772-2196

U.S. Fish and Wildlife Service (FWS)

http://www.fws.gov

General Information	800-344-9453
Employment Webpage	http://jobs.fws.gov
Fishing Information	800-275-3474
Import/Export Permit Information	800-358-2104
National Conservation Training Center	304-876-7220
National Eagle & Wildlife Repository, Denver, CO	303-287-2110
National Forensics Laboratory, Ashland, OR	541-482-4191
National Wildlife Refuges System	703-358-1744
Refuges & Endangered Species Visitor Guide	800-344-9453
Volunteers	703-358-2029

FWS Law Enforcement Regional Offices

http://www.le.fws.gov

Hotline	703-358-2087
National Law Enforcement Office, Arlington, VA	703-358-1949
Region 1, Pacific (CA, HI, ID, NV, OR, Pacific Trust Territories, WA)	503-231-6125
Region 2, Southwest (AZ, NM, OK, TX)	505-248-7889
Region 3, Great Lakes (IL,IN,IA,MI,MN,MO,OH,WI)	612-713-5320
Region 4, Southeast (AL, AR, FL, GA, KY, LA, MS, NC, PR, SC, TN, Virgin Islands)	404-679-7057
Region 5, Northeast (CT, DE, ME, MD, MA, NH, NJ, NY, PA, RI, VT, VA, WV)	413-253-8274
Region 6, Mountain-Prairie (CO, KS, MT, NE, ND, SD, UT, WY)	303-236-7540
Region 7, Alaska	907-786-3311

FWS Law Enforcement State Offices

Alaska, Anchorage	907-271-6198
Arizona, Nogales	520-287-4633
California, Los Angeles	310-328-3607
San Diego	619-557-5794
San Francisco	650-876-9078

Colorado, Denver	303-342-7430
Florida, Miami	305-526-2610
Tampa	727-570-5398
Georgia, Atlanta	404-763-7959
Guam, Tamuning	671-647-6064
Hawaii, Honolulu	808-861-8525
Illinois, Chicago	847-298-3250
Kentucky, Louisville	502-582-5989
Louisiana, New Orleans	504-219-8870
Maryland, Baltimore	410-865-2127
Michigan, Detroit	734-247-6800
Minnesota, Minneapolis/Saint Paul	612-726-6302
Montana, Great Falls	406-453-5790
New Jersey, Newark	973-645-6171
New York, Buffalo	716-691-3635
Champlain	518-298-4825
New York	516-825-3950
North Dakota, Dunseith	701-263-4462
Oregon, Portland	503-231-6135
Puerto Rico, Guaynabo	787-749-4338
Tennessee, Memphis	901-360-7007
Texas, Brownsville	956-504-2035
Dallas/Fort Worth	972-574-3254
El Paso	915-872-4765
Houston	281-446-1284
Laredo	956-726-2234
Washington, Blaine	360-332-5388
Seattle	206-764-3463

U.S. Forest Service

Law Enforcement & Investigations

Headquarters, Washington, D.C.	703-605-4690
Region 1, Northern	406-329-3590
Region 2, Rocky Mountain	303-275-5253
Region 3, Southwestern	505-842-3104
Region 4, Intermountain	801-625-5324
Region 5, Pacific Southwest	707-562-8649
Region 6, Pacific Northwest	360-891-5270
Region 8, Southern	404-347-4182
Region 9, Eastern	414-297-3841
Region 10, Alaska	907-586-8820

National Guard
Counterdrug Coordinators

Alabama, Montgomery	334-213-7658
Alaska, Fort Richardson	907-428-3617
Arizona, Phoenix	602-267-2623
Arkansas, North Little Rock	501-791-5492
California, Sacramento	916-854-3715
Colorado, Aurora	303-677-8303
Connecticut, Hartford	860-493-2723
Delaware, Wilmington	302-326-7085
Florida, Saint Augustine	904-823-0438
Georgia, Dobbins ARB	678-919-3473
Guam, Tamuning	671-472-7588
Hawaii, Honolulu	808-732-0209
Idaho, Boise	208-422-3530
Illinois, Spingfield	217-761-3728
Indiana, Indianapolis	317-486-8291
Iowa, Johnston	515-252-4606
Kansas, Pauline	785-862-0001
Kentucky, Lexington	859-293-4192
Louisiana, New Orleans	504-278-8556
Maine, Waterville	207-873-4727
Maryland, Baltimore	410-576-6135
Massachusetts, Milford	508-233-6804
Michigan, Lansing	517-483-5896
Minnesota, Saint Paul	651-282-4147
Mississippi, Flowood	601-313-1670
Missouri, Jefferson City	573-638-9599
Montana, Helena	406-324-3177
Nebraska, Lincoln	402-309-1860
Nevada, Reno	775-348-9724
New Hampshire, Concord	603-227-1542
New Jersey, Fort Dix	609-562-0812
New Mexico, Albuquerque	505-846-1031
New York, Scotia	518-786-3477
North Carolina, Raleigh	919-664-6322
North Dakota, Bismarck	701-333-2050
Ohio, Columbus	614-336-6426
Oklahoma, Oklahoma City	405-228-5043
Oregon, Salem	503-584-3938
Pennsylvania, Annville	717-861-2482

Puerto Rico, San Juan ···································787-289-1548
Rhode Island, Coventry ·····························401-392-0827
South Carolina, Columbia ························803-806-1559
South Dakota, Rapid City·························605-737-6723
Tennessee, Smyrna·································615-355-3901
Texas, Austin ···512-782-5154
Utah, Draper ···801-523-4150
Vermont, Colchester ·······························802-338-3350
Virginia, Blackstone ·······························804-292-8529
Virgin Islands, Saint Croix ·······················340-712-7772
Washington, D.C. ····································202-685-9726
Washington, Tacoma·······························253-512-8894
West Virginia, Saint Albans ······················304-727-5068
Wisconsin, Madison·································608-242-3540
Wyoming, Cheyenne································307-772-5259

Drug Demand Reduction Administration

Alabama, Montgomery·······························334-213-7724
Alaska, Fort Richardson····························907-428-3617
Arizona, Phoenix·····································602-267-2901
Arkansas, North Little Rock ·······················501-212-5484
California, Sacramento ····························916-854-3889
Colorado, Aurora····································303-677-8303
Connecticut, Hartford·······························860-493-2724
Delaware, Wilmington·······························302-326-7079
Florida, Saint Augustine····························904-823-0355
Georgia, Dobbins ARB······························770-919-3475
Guam, Tamuning····································671-475-0834
Hawaii, Honolulu····································808-732-0209
Idaho, Boise···208-422-3534
Illinois, Springfield··································773-288-5482
Indiana, Crown Point ·······························219-769-7679
Iowa, Johnston······································515-252-4190
Kansas, Pauline····································785-862-0001
Kentucky, Lexington·································859-293-3900
Louisiana, New Orleans····························504-278-8555
Maine, Waterville ···································207-873-4727
Maryland, Baltimore·································410-576-6137
Massachusetts, Milford ····························508-233-6834
Michigan, Lansing··································517-483-5601
Minnesota, Saint Paul·······························651-282-4149
Mississippi, Flowood·······························601-313-1670
Missouri, Jefferson City····························816-512-4990
Montana, Helena····································406-324-3179
Nebraska, Lincoln··································402-309-1875
Nevada, Reno·······································775-348-9749

New Hampshire, Concord ···603-228-3364
New Jersey, Fort Dix···201-368-0583
New Mexico, Albuquerque ···505-846-7234
New York, Scotia ···518-786-3478
North Carolina, Charlotte ··704-391-4424
North Dakota, Bismarck ··701-333-2054
Ohio, Columbus ··614-336-6432
Oklahoma, Oklahoma City···405-475-1491
Oregon, Salem···503-584-3351
Pennsylvania, Annville ··717-861-2231
Puerto Rico, San Juan ··787-289-1548
Rhode Island, Coventry ···401-392-0830
South Carolina, Columbia ··803-806-2623
South Dakota, Rapid City··605-737-6602
Tennessee, Smyrna···615-355-3902
Texas, Austin ···512-782-5238
Utah, Riverton···801-253-5521
Vermont, Colchester ···802-338-3440
Virginia, Blackstone ···434-292-8522
Virgin Islands, Saint Croix··340-712-7772
Washington, D.C.···202-685-9723
Washington, Tacoma···253-512-8355
West Virginia, Saint Albans ··304-727-5068
Wisconsin, Madison··608-242-3540
Wyoming, Cheyenne··307-772-5959

State Departments of Corrections

State	Phone	Fax
Alabama	334-240-9500	334-353-3891
Alaska	907-269-7400	907-269-7390
Arizona	602-542-5536	602-542-1728
Arkansas	870-267-6999	870-267-6244
California	916-445-7688	916-322-2877
Colorado	719-579-9580	719-540-4755
Connecticut	860-692-7481	860-692-7483
Delaware	302-739-5601	302-739-8221
Florida	850-488-7480	850-922-2848
Georgia	404-656-6002	404-651-6818
Hawaii	808-587-1350	808-587-1282
Idaho	208-658-2000	208-327-7404
Illinois	217-522-2666	217-522-5089
Indiana	317-232-5715	317-232-6798
Iowa	515-242-5703	515-281-7345
Kansas	785-296-3317	785-296-0014
Kentucky	502-564-4726	502-564-5037
Louisiana	225-342-6741	225-342-2486
Maine	207-287-4360	207-287-4370
Maryland	410-585-3300	410-764-4182
Massachusetts	617-727-3300	617-727-7403
Michigan	517-335-1426	517-373-6883
Minnesota	651-642-0282	651-642-0414
Mississippi	601-359-5600	601-359-5680
Missouri	573-751-2389	573-751-4099
Montana	406-444-3930	406-444-4920
Nebraska	402-471-2654	402-479-5623
Nevada	775-887-3285	775-887-3391
New Hampshire	603-271-5600	603-271-5643
New Jersey	609-292-9860	609-777-0445
New Mexico	505-827-8709	505-827-8801
New York	518-457-8126	518-457-7252
North Carolina	919-716-3700	919-716-3794
North Dakota	701-328-6390	701-328-6651
Ohio	614-752-1164	614-752-1171
Oklahoma	405-425-2500	405-425-2578
Oregon	503-945-0920	503-373-1173
Pennsylvania	717-975-4860	717-731-0486
Rhode Island	401-462-2611	401-462-2630
South Carolina	803-896-8500	803-896-1220
South Dakota	605-773-3478	605-773-3194
Tennessee	615-741-1000	615-532-8281
Texas	512-463-9988	512-936-2169

Utah	801-545-5500	801-545-5670
Vermont	802-241-2442	802-241-2565
Virginia	804-674-3119	804-674-3509
Washington	360-753-1573	360-664-4056
Washington, D.C.	202-673-7316	202-332-1470
West Virginia	304-558-2036	304-558-5934
Wisconsin	608-240-5000	608-240-3300
Wyoming	307-777-7208	307-777-7479

State Divisions of Wildlife

Alabama Game & Fish Division	334-242-3467
Alaska Fish & Game Protection	907-269-5509
Arizona Game & Fish	602-789-3303
Arkansas Game & Fish Enforcement	501-223-6381
California Dept of Fish & Game	916-445-0045
Colorado Division of Wildlife	303-291-7223
Connecticut Dept. Of Environmental Protection	860-424-3012
Delaware Division of Fish & Wildlife	302-739-3440
Florida Game & Freshwater Fish, LE	850-488-6251
Georgia Dept Natural Resources, LE	770-918-6408
Hawaii Conservation & Resource Enforcement	808-587-0068
Idaho Fish & Game	208-334-3700
Illinois Dept Natural Resources LE Division	217-782-6431
Indiana Dept Natural Resources	317-232-4080
Iowa Dept Natural Resources, LE Chief	515-281-5919
Kansas Wildlife & Parks	785-296-2281
Kentucky Fish & Wildlife	502-564-3400
Louisiana Wildlife & Fisheries Enforcement	225-765-2469
Maine Dept of Inland Fisheries & Wildlife	207-287-8000
Maryland Dept Natural Resources Communications	410-260-8888
Massachusetts Division of LE, Dir	617-727-3905
Michigan Dept Natural Resources Law Division	517-373-1230
Minnesota Dept Natural Resources, Enf Division Dir	651-297-2368
Mississippi Dept of Wildlife, Fisheries & Parks	601-432-2400
Missouri Dept of Conservation	573-751-4115
Montana Fish Wildlife & Parks HQ	406-444-2535
Nebraska Game & Parks LE	402-471-5534
Nevada Division of Wildlife	775-688-1500
New Hampshire Fish & Game, Public Affairs	603-271-3211
New Jersey Fish & Game	609-292-9430
New Mexico Game & Fish, LE	505-476-8066
New York LE Div	518-457-5681
North Carolina WL Resources Comm	919-733-3391
North Dakota Game & Fish Enforcement	701-328-9921

Ohio Dept Natural Resources, Div of Wildlife HQ	614-265-6300
Oklahoma LE HQ	405-521-3719
Oregon Fish & Wildlife	503-947-6000
Pennsylvania Game Commission, LE Division	717-787-2084
Rhode Island Dept. Of Environmental Management	401-222-6768
South Carolina DNR, LE Div. Maj/Staff Ops	803-734-4021
South Dakota Game Fish and Parks	605-773-3381
Tennessee Wildlife Resources, LE	615-781-6580
Texas Parks & Wildlife, LE	512-389-4703
Utah Wildlife Resources	801-538-4700
Vermont Fish & Wildlife, LE	802-241-3727
Virginia Dept of Game & Inland Fisheries	804-367-1000
Washington Fish & Wildlife, LE	360-902-2936
West Virginia Dept Natural Resources LE	304-558-2784
Wisconsin Dept Natural Resources, LE	608-266-2141
Wyoming Game & Fish	307-777-4600

State Health Departments

Alabama	334-206-5300
Alaska	907-465-3030
Arizona	602-542-1001
Arkansas	501-661-2000
California	916-445-4171
Colorado	303-692-2000
Connecticut	860-509-8000
Delaware	302-744-4700
Florida	850-245-4443
Georgia	404-657-2700
Hawaii	808-586-4400
Idaho	208-334-5500
Illinois	217-782-4977
Indiana	317-233-1325
Iowa	515-281-7689
Kansas	785-296-1500
Kentucky	877-807-4027
Louisiana	225-342-9500
Maine	207-287-8016
Maryland	410-767-6860
Massachusetts	617-624-6000
Michigan	517-373-3740
Minnesota	651-215-5800
Mississippi	601-576-7400
Missouri	573-751-6400
Montana	406-444-5622

Nebraska	402-471-2306
Nevada	775-684-4200
New Hampshire	603-271-4331
New Jersey	609-272-7837
New Mexico	505-827-2613
New York	518-474-2011
North Carolina	919-733-4534
North Dakota	701-328-2372
Ohio	614-466-3543
Oklahoma	405-271-5600
Oregon	800-422-6012
Pennsylvania	877-724-3258
Rhode Island	401-222-2231
South Carolina	803-898-3432
South Dakota	605-773-3361
Tennessee	615-741-3111
Texas	512-458-7111
Utah	801-538-6101
Vermont	802-863-7200
Virginia	804-864-7001
Washington	800-525-0127
Washington, D.C.	202-671-5000
West Virginia	304-558-0684
Wisconsin	608-266-1865
Wyoming	307-777-7656

State Insurance Fraud Reporting

Alabama	334-242-7334	800-392-5658
Alaska	907-465-3600	
Arizona	602-542-3702	800-352-8431*
Arkansas	501-682-7506	800-482-8982
California	916-445-9555	800-952-5225*
Colorado	303-866-5219	800-332-2071
Connecticut	860-808-5318	
Delaware	302-577-8400	
Florida	850-414-3300	
Georgia	404-656-3300	
Hawaii	808-586-2636	
Idaho	208-334-2424	
Illinois	312-814-4714	800-252-8666
Indiana	317-232-6201	800-382-5516
Iowa	515-281-5926	
Kansas	785-296-2215	800-432-2310*
Kentucky	502-696-5389	

Louisiana		800-488-2770
Maine	207-626-8800	
Maryland	410-576-6557	
Massachusetts	617-727-2200	
Michigan	517-373-1140	
Minnesota	651-296-3353	800-366-4812
Mississippi	601-359-4230	800-281-4418
Missouri	816-889-5000	
Montana	406-444-3553	
Nebraska	402-471-2682	
Nevada	702-486-3420	800-266-8688
New Hampshire	603-271-3658	
New Jersey	609-292-8740	
New Mexico	505-827-6060	
New York	212-416-8300	
North Carolina	919-716-6400	
North Dakota	701-328-3404	800-472-2600*
Ohio	614-466-1306	800-282-0515*
Oklahoma	405-521-4274	
Oregon	503-378-4732	
Pennsylvania	717-787-9707	800-441-2555*
Rhode Island	401-274-4400	
South Carolina	803-734-3970	
South Dakota	605-773-4400	800-300-1986*
Tennessee	615-741-1671	
Texas	512-463-2185	
Utah	801-538-9600	800-244-4636*
Vermont	802-828-3171	
Virginia	804-786-2116	
Washington	360-753-6200	800-551-4636
Washington, D.C.	202-727-6248	
West Virginia	304-558-8986	800-368-8808*
Wisconsin	608-267-8901	
Wyoming	307-777-7841	

* Number can only be dialed within that calling area.

State Police

State Agency	Headquarters	Dispatch
Alabama Highway Patrol	334-242-4378	
Alaska State Troopers	907-269-5641	907-428-7200
Arizona Highway Patrol	602-223-2651	602-223-2000
Arkansas State Police	501-618-8800	
California Highway Patrol (CHP)	916-657-7261	

Colorado State Patrol	303-239-4500	303-239-4501
Connecticut State Police	860-685-8190	
Delaware State Police	302-739-5900	
Florida Highway Patrol	850-488-8676	
Georgia State Patrol	404-624-7000	404-624-6077
Hawaii State Sheriff	808-538-5696	
Idaho State Police	208-884-7200	
Illinois State Police	217-782-1320	
Indiana State Police	317-232-8248	
Iowa State Patrol	515-281-5824	
Kansas Highway Patrol	785-296-6800	785-296-3102
KentuckyState Police	502-695-6306	
Louisiana State Police	225-925-6325	
Maine State Police	207-624-7200	207-624-7000
Maryland State Police	410-486-3101	
Massachusetts State Police	508-820-2300	
Michigan State Police	517-332-2521	
Minnesota State Patrol, East	651-582-1500	
Minnesota State Patrol, West	651-582-1511	
Mississippi Highway Safety Patrol	601-987-1212	
Missouri State Highway Patrol	573-751-3313	
Montana Highway Patrol	406-444-3780	402-444-7001
Nebraska State Patrol	402-471-4545	402-479-4921
Nevada Highway Patrol	775-687-5300	
New Hampshire State Police	603-271-2575	
New Jersey State Police	609-882-2000	
New Mexico Dept of Public Safety	505-827-9000	
New York State Police	518-457-6621	
North Carolina State Hwy Patrol	919-733-7952	919-733-3861
North Dakota State Hwy Patrol	701-328-2455	
Ohio Highway Patrol	614-466-2990	614-466-2260
Oklahoma Highway Patrol	405-425-2043	
Oregon State Police	503-378-3720	
Pennsylvania State Police	717-783-5599	
Rhode Island State Police	401-444-1111	401-444-1000
South Carolina State Hwy Patrol	803-896-7920	803-896-9621
South Dakota Hwy Patrol	605-773-3105	605-773-3536
Tennessee Highway Patrol	615-251-5175	615-741-2060
Texas Dept of Public Safety	512-424-2000 or 512-424-2277	
Utah State Highway Patrol	801-965-4518 or 801-576-8606	
Vermont State Police	802-244-8763	802-244-8727
Virginia Dept of State Police	804-674-2000	804-674-2028
Washington State Patrol	206-439-3834	
West Virginia State Police	304-746-2111	304-746-2100
Wisconsin State Patrol	608-266-3212	
Wyoming Highway Patrol	307-777-4301	

Phone Directory

Other Resources

American Red Cross

www.redcross.org

General information, or to find your local chapter ·······202-303-4498
Disaster Assistance Info ···866-438-4636
Donation Information ··800-435-7669

Car Rental Companies

Ace Rent-A-Car ···········800-243-3443 ···www.acerentacar.com
Advantage Rent-A-Car 800-777-5500 ···www.arac.com
Alamo Rent-A-Car ·······800-327-9633 ···www.alamo.com
Avis Rent-A-Car···········800-230-4898 ···www.avis.com
Budget Rent-A-Car ·······800-455-2838 ···www.budget.com
Dollar Rent-A-Car ·······800-800-4000 ···www.dollar.com
Enterprise Rent-A-Car ·800-325-8007 ···www.enterprise.com
Hertz Corporation ·······800-654-3131 ···www.hertz.com
Payless Car Rental ······800-729-5377 ···www.paylesscarrental.com
National Car Rental ·····800-328-4567 ···www.nationalcar.com
Thrifty Rent-A-Car·······800-367-2277 ···www.thrifty.com

Credit Card Companies

Numbers to call for lost or stolen credit cards:

American Express ·······················800-227-2639·······336-393-1111
BP (British Petrolium, also known as Amoco)·············800-333-3991
Chevron Oil···800-243-8766
Conoco··800-242-1567
Dayton-Hudson Dept Stores
  (Dayton's, Hudson's, Marshall Field's, Target) ·······800-659-2396
Mervyn's California ···························800-637-8967·······612-307-5879
Diamond Shamrock ···800-333-3560
Dillard's··800-643-8278
Diner's Club/Carte Blanche ···········800-234-6377·······303-799-1504
Discover···800-347-2683
Exxon··800-344-4355
Federated Department Stores
  Bloomingdale's··800-950-0047
  The Bon Marche··800-542-7704

Burdine's	800-533-2304
Goldsmith's	800-762-5856
Lazarus	800-654-2813
Macy's East	800-972-4243
Macy's West	800-877-2655
Rich's	800-241-0488
Macy's	800-678-3767
K-Mart	800-345-9211
May Dept. Stores Company	
Famous-Barr	800-528-0780
Filene's	800-323-3227
Foley's	800-527-7147
Hecht's	Call local store
Kaufmann's 412-471-2498	800-836-8895
L.S. Ayres	800-528-0781
Lord & Taylor	Call local store
Meier & Frank	800-432-4002
Robinsons-May	Call local store
Strawbridge's	Call local store
Mastercard	800-307-7309
Neiman Marcus	800-685-6695
Nordstrom	800-964-1800
J.C. Penney	800-542-0800
Phillips 66	800-648-4199
Sears Roebuck	800-877-8691
Shell Oil	800-331-3703
Texaco	800-552-7827
Visa Worldwide	800-336-8472

Domestic Violence Resources

Battered Women's Justice Project	800-903-0111
Center for the Prevention of Sexual and Domestic Violence	206-634-1903
Family Violence Prevention Fund	800-313-1310
Health Resource Center on Domestic Violence, Family Violence Prevention Fund	800-313-1310
National Battered Women's Law Project	212-741-9480
Nat'l Clearinghouse for Defense of Battered Women	215-351-0010
National Clearinghouse on Marital and Date Rape	510-524-1582
National Coalition Against Domestic Violence	303-839-1852
National Domestic Violence Advocate	800-799-7233
National Network to End Domestic Violence	202-434-7405
National Resource Center On Domestic Violence	800-537-2238
Rape, Abuse, Incest National Network	800-656-HOPE
Resource Center on Child Protection & Custody	800-527-3223

State Domestic Violence Coalitions

Alabama	800-650-6522*	334-832-4842
Alaska Network		907-586-3650
Arizona	800-782-6400	602-279-2900
Arkansas	800-269-4668	501-812-0571
California	800-524-4765	818-787-0072
Colorado	888-778-7091	303-831-9632
Connecticut	888-774-2900	860-282-7899
Delaware	800-701-0456*	302-658-2958
Florida	800-500-1119	850-425-2749
Georgia	800-33HAVEN*	770-984-0085
Hawaii		808-832-9316
Iowa	800-942-0333*	515-244-8028
Idaho	888-293-6118	208-384-0419
Illinois		217-789-2830
Indiana	800-538-3393	317-917-3685
Kansas	888-END-ABUSE	785-232-9784
Kentucky		502-695-2444
Louisiana	888-411-1333*	225-752-1296
Maine		207-941-1194
Maryland Network	800-MD-HELPS	301-352-4574
Massachusetts Coalition of Battered Women's Service Groups/ Jane Doe Safety Fund	877-785-2020*	617-248-0922
Michigan		517-347-7000
Minnesota		651-646-6177
Mississippi	800-898-3234	601-981-9196
Missouri		573-634-4161
Montana	888-404-7794	406-443-7794

Nebraska		402-476-6256
Nevada	800-500-1556	775-828-1115
New Hampshire	800-277-5570	603-224-8893
New Jersey	800-572-SAFE	609-584-8107
New Mexico	800-773-3645*	505-246-9240
New York	800-942-6906	518-482-5465
North Carolina	888-232-9124	919-956-9124
North Dakota Council on Abused Women's Services		
State Networking Office	800-472-2911*	701-255-6240
Ohio	800-934-9840	614-781-9651
Oklahoma	800-522-SAFE	405-848-1815
Oregon	888-235-5333*	503-365-9644
Pennsylvania	800-932-4632*	717-545-6400
Puerto Rico		787-721-7676
Rhode Island	800-494-8100	401-467-9940
South Carolina	800-260-9293	803-256-2900
South Dakota	800-572-9196	605-945-0869
Tennessee	800-289-9018*	615-386-9406
Texas Council on Family Violence		512-794-1133
Utah	800-897-LINK*	801-538-4100
Vermont	800-228-7395	802-223-1302
Virginia	800-838-VADV	757-221-0990
Washington	800-562-6025	360-586-1022
Washington, D.C.		202-299-1181
West Virginia		304-965-3552
Wisconsin		608-255-0539
Wyoming	800-990-3877	307-755-5481

* Number can only be dialed within that calling area.

Victim Support Resources

The National Organization for Victim Assistance	
24-hour crisis line	202-232-6682
U.S. Dept of Justice, Office for Victims of Crime	800-627-6872

Law Enforcement Magazines & Newsletters

911 Magazine	800-231-8911	714-544-7666
The 1811		607-277-4899
American Police Beat	800-234-0056	617-491-8878
APA Newsletter		800-272-8037
The Backup		800-822-9398
Blue Line Magazine (CAN)		905-640-3048
The Blues		903-643-2131
California Highway Patrolman		916-452-6751
California Peace Officer		916-263-0541
Canadian Police Chief		613-233-1106
Combat Handguns		888-226-6228
Dispatch Monthly		877-370-3477
Driver's License Checking Guide		650-369-4849
Drug Enforcement Report		202-835-1770
FBI Law Enforcement Bulletin		202-512-1800
FDA Enforcement Report		202-512-1800
Fire and Arson Investigator		800-468-4224
Fire and Police Personnel Reporter		800-763-2802
Fire Service Labor Monthly		800-842-5203
Firehouse		303-322-6400
Guns & Weapons for Law Enforcement		888-444-4953
International Drug Report		518-463-6232
Jailer and Prisoner Law Bulletin		800-763-2802
Law and Order		847-444-3300
Law Enforcement Intelligence Report		800-387-9441
Law Enforcement Legal Review		630-858-6392
Law Enforcement Liability Reporter		800-763-2802
Law Enforcement News		212-237-8442
Law Enforcement Product News		303-322-6400
Law Enforcement Technology		303-322-6400
Law Officer's Bulletin		800-255-8131
Michigan Police Chiefs' Newsletter		517-349-9420
Minnesota Police Journal		651-291-1119
Money Laundering Alert		305-530-0500
The Mounted Officer		847-444-3300
Narcotics Law Bulletin		800-229-2084
National Association of Document Examiners Journal		609-452-7030
National Criminal Justice Reference Service Document Database		800-851-3420
National Fraternal Order of Police Journal		615-399-0900
National Institute of Justice Journal		301-519-5500
National Police Review		502-425-9215
News & Views		416-491-4301
Pennsylvania Chiefs of Police Association Bulletin		717-236-1059

Police and Law Enforcement		310-533-2400
Police and Security News		215-538-1240
Police Chief (International Association)		703-836-6767
Police Chief's Intelligence Report		800-387-9441
Police Dept. Disciplinary Bulletin		617-542-0048
Police Fleet Manager		847-444-3300
Police Journal (St. Louis Metro PD)		314-444-5603
Police Labor Monthly		800-842-5203
Police Magazine	888-239-2455	310-533-2400
Police Marksman	800-223-7869	334-271-2010
Police Martial Arts Association News		506-387-5126
Police Officer Grievances Bulletin		800-229-2084
Police Review		800-824-0768
Police Studies		513-421-4142
Police Times		305-573-0070
Prisoners in [year] (USDOJ publication)		202-512-1800
Public Safety News		303-322-6400
RCMP Quarterly/GRC Revue Trimestrielle (CAN)		613-998-6317
Search and Seizure Bulletin	800-229-2084	617-542-0048
Search and Seizure Law Report		800-328-4880
Security Technology and Design		303-322-6400
Sheriff Magazine		703-836-7827
Special Weapons for Military and Police		212-807-7100
Tactical Response		847-444-3300
TechBeat (NLETC Publication)		800-248-2742
Tennessee Law Enforcement Bulletin		800-274-6774
Texas Lawman		512-445-5888
Tracking Offenders [year] (USDOJ publication)		202-512-1800
Trends in Organized Crime		888-999-6778
U.S. Identification Manual		650-369-4849
White Collar Crime Reporter	800-345-1101	610-225-0510
Wisconsin Sheriff & Deputy		715-723-7173

Law Enforcement Organizations & Associations

Airborne Law Enforcement Association (ALEA)	918-599-0705
Alabama Peace Officers Association	800-436-5719
Alabama Sheriffs Association	334-264-7827
Alabama State Police Association	334-277-7900
Alaska Peace Officers Association	907-277-0515
American Academy of Forensic Sciences	800-701-2237
American Association of State Troopers	800-765-5456
American Board of Forensic Science	719-636-1100
American Board of Forensic Odontology	800-701-2237
American Board of Forensic Toxicologists	800-701-2237
American Correctional Assoc. 800-222-5646	301-918-1800
American Federation of Police	321-264-0911
American Jail Association	301-790-3930
American Polygraph Association	800-272-8037
American Society for Industrial Security (ASIS)	703-519-6200
American Society of Crime Laboratory Directors	727-549-6067
American Society of Law Enforcement Trainers (ASLET)	301-668-9466
American Society of Questioned Document Examiners	901-759-0729
Arkansas Sheriffs Association, Inc.	501-758-0020
Arkansas State Police Association	501-666-2772
Associated Highway Patrolmen of Arizona	480-899-4675
Association of Firearm and Toolmark Examiners	919-662-9107
Association of Public-Safety Communications Officials (APCO)	888-272-6911
California Correctional Peace Officer Association 800-821-6443	916-372-6060
California Gang Investigator's Association	888-229-2442
California Peace Officers Association	912-263-0541
California Reserve Peace Officers Association	408-371-8239
Canadian Society of Forensic Science	613-738-0001
Chicago Police Women's Association	312-458-9683
Colorado Association of Chiefs of Police	303-750-9764
Colorado Law Enforcement Officers Association	303-420-4290
Combined Law Enforcement Associations of Texas (CLEAT) (TX only) 800-252-8153	512-495-9111
Commission for Accreditation of Law Enforcement Agencies (CALEA)	703-352-4225
Connecticut Police Chiefs Association	860-586-7506
Correction Captains Association (NY)	212-227-4090
Correctional Association of Massachusetts	413-525-9833
Correctional Association of New York	212-254-5700
Correctional Industries Association	410-837-5036

Delaware State Trooper Association ····················302-736-9958
Disabled Police Officers Assn. *(See American Federation of Police)*
Emerald Society of the Federal Law Enforcement
  Agencies ···585-453-9011
Emergency Response and Research Institute········773-631-3774
FBI National Academy Associates, Inc. ···············703-632-1990
Federal Law Enforcement Officers Association ·······717-938-2300
Federal Wildlife Officers Association ··················603-433-0502
Florida Peace Officers Association ····················850-222-7070
Florida Police Chiefs Association·······················800-332-8117
Florida Sheriffs Association ·····························850-877-2165
Forensic Sciences Foundation, Inc.····················719-636-1100
Fraternal Order of Police National Headquarters·····800-451-2711
Georgia Sheriff Association ······························770-914-1076
Hispanic American Police Command Officers Assn. ··703-534-2895
Idaho Peace Officers Association ·······················208-362-3898
Illinois Auxiliary Police ···································773-646-3570
Illinois Police Association·································708-452-8332
Illinois Police Crime Fighters ···························708-343-2922
Illinois Police Federation ································847-437-1600
Illinois Tactical Officers Association···················847-459-3857
Indiana Troopers Association········800-671-9851······260-624-2926
Int'l Association for Identification ······················651-681-8566
Int'l Association of Bloodstain Pattern Analysts·······520-760-6620
Int'l Association of Bomb Technicians & Investigators ·540-752-4533
Int'l Association of Campus Law Enforcement
  Administrators··860-586-7517
Int'l Association of Chiefs of Police(IACP) ·············703-836-6767
Int'l Association of Directors of Law Enforcement
  Standards and Training (IADLEST)····················503-378-2100
Int'l Assn. of Law Enforcement Firearms Instructors ·603-524-8787
Int'l Assn. of Law Enforcement Intelligence Analysts·520-547-8760
Int'l Assn. of Law Enforcement Planners (IALEP)······310-225-5148
Int'l Association of Railway Police ·····················800-366-6979
Int'l Brotherhood of Police Officers (IBPO) ············617-376-0220
Int'l Union of Police Associations ··800-247-4872······703-549-7473
Iowa Assn. of Chiefs of Police & Peace Officers ······888-732-1313
Iowa State Police Association·····························515-833-5320
Kentucky Sheriffs Association·····························502-454-3325
Kentucky State Police Professional Association·······502-875-1625
Latin American Police Association ·······················773-927-5058
Law Enforcement Alliance, Inc.··························703-847-2677
Law Enforcement Foundation ···························614-761-9479
Law Enforcement Thermographers' Association ·······405-330-6988
Law Enforcement/Emergency Services Video Assn. ··770-277-0310
Louisiana Sheriffs Association ···························225-343-8402

Phone Directory

Maryland Troopers Association	410-653-3885
Massachusetts Auxiliary Police Association	617-774-0108
Massachusetts Police Association	617-720-3477
Michigan Association of Chiefs of Police	517-349-9420
Michigan Association of Police	248-304-8800
Michigan Corrections Organization	517-485-3310
Minnesota Chiefs of Police Association	651-457-0677
Minnesota Police and Peace Officers Association	651-291-1119
Missouri Deputy Sheriffs Association	573-634-2270
Missouri Police Chiefs Association	573-636-5444
Missouri Sheriffs Association	573-635-5925
National Association of Black Law Enforcement Executives (NOBLE)	305-573-0070
National Association of Chiefs of Police (NACOP)	321-264-0911
National Association of Fire Investigators	877-506-6234
National Assn. of Government Employees (NAGE)	703-519-0300
National Association of Police Organizations	202-842-4420
National Association for Search and Rescue	703-222-6277
National Black Police Association (NBPA)	202-986-2070
National Center for Rural Law Enforcement (Part of Criminal Justice Institute) 800-635-6310	501-570-8000
National Center for Women and Policing	323-651-2532
National Constables Assn. (NCA)	800-272-1775
National Crime Prevention Council	202-466-6272
National Criminal Justice Association	202-628-8550
National Emergency Number Association	703-812-4600
National Law Enforcement Council (NLEC)	202-835-8020
National Narcotic Officers' Associations Coalition	626-960-3328
National Organization of Black Law Enforcement	703-658-1529
National Police Defense Foundation	732-446-3360
National Sheriffs' Association	800-424-7827
National Tactical Officers Association	800-279-9127
National Troopers Coalition	800-232-1392
New Jersey State Association of Chiefs of Police	609-637-9300
New Jersey State Law Enforcement Officers Assn.	888-657-5362
New York State Association of Police Chiefs	518-355-3371
New York Veteran Police Association	212-227-0617
North American Police Work Dog Association	888-422-6463
North Carolina Law Enforcement Association	919-876-0687
North Carolina Sheriffs Association	919-783-8899
North Carolina Troopers Association	336-369-1515
Office of Law Enforcement Technology Commercialization	888-306-5382
Ohio DARE Officers Association	614-761-9498
Oregon State Sheriffs Association	503-364-4204
Park Law Enforcement Association	913-438-3314

Peace Officers Association of Georgia, Inc.	912-557-4793
Pennsylvania Chiefs of Police Association	717-236-1059
Pennsylvania Police Officers Association	215-968-3434
Police Conference of New York, Inc.	518-463-3283
Police Executive Research Forum (PERF)	202-466-7820
Police Foundation (PF)	202-833-1460
Police Hall of Fame *(See American Federation of Police)*	
Police Marksman Association (PMA)	800-223-7869
Police Officers Association of Michigan (POAM)	313-937-9000
Police Reserve Association	212-564-0010
Polish-American Police Association	312-409-7878
Portuguese-American Police Association	973-578-8686
Society of Forensic Toxicologists	480-839-9106
South Carolina Law Enforcement Officers	803-781-5913
South Carolina Sheriffs Association	803-772-1101
South Carolina Troopers Association	803-772-1124
Southern States Police Association	800-233-3506
Southwestern Illinois Law Enforcement Commission	618-277-1550
Texas Peace Officers Association	214-941-9295
Texas Police Association	512-458-3140
Texas Police Chiefs Association	512-281-5400
United States Police Canine Association (USPCA)	800-531-1614
Utah Peace Officers Association	801-313-0760
Virginia State Police Association	804-320-6272
Washington State Council of Police Officers	360-352-8224
Washington State Law Enforcement Association	360-943-7566
West Virginia Sheriffs Association	304-345-2232
West Virginia Troopers Association	304-345-9882
Wisconsin Correctional Service	414-271-2512
Wisconsin Law Enforcement Association	920-734-8425
Wisconsin Professional Police Association	608-273-3840
Women Peace Officers Association of California	760-947-6005

Railroad Law Enforcement

Alaska Railroad	907-265-2462
Amtrak Police	800-331-0008
Ann Arbor Railroad System	517-548-3930
Belfast & Moosehead Lake Railroad	207-948-5500
Belt Railway of Chicago	708-496-4000
Bessemer & Lake Erie Railroad	412-829-6600
Boston & Maine Railroad/Maine Central	978-663-1000
Burlington Northern Santa Fe Railroad	800-795-2673
Canadian National Railways	800-465-9239
Canadian Pacific Limited	800-716-9132
Canadian Pacific Railway Police Service	800-551-2553
Central Michigan Railway Co.	517-684-5088
CN Rail	248-691-6974
Conrail Police Dept	800-272-0911
CP Rail System	518-383-7284
CSX Transportation Company	800-232-0144
Duluth Missabe & Iron Range Railway Co.	218-628-4357
East Erie Commercial Railroad	814-875-2188
Elgin Joliet & Eastern Railway	888-883-4202
Florida East Coast Railway Police	305-887-2672
Guilford Transportation-Rail Division	978-663-1005
Houston Belt & Terminal Railroad, Port Terminal Railroad Association	713-673-3584
Illinois & Midland Railroad Inc.	217-788-8640
Kansas City Southern Railway	601-933-4721
Kansas City Terminal Railway Co.	816-245-2297
Lake Superior & Ishpeming Railroad	906-475-3471
Long Island Railroad	718-558-3300
Manufacturers Railway	314-577-1749
Minnesota Dakota & Western Railway	218-285-5290
Montreal Main & Atlantic Railway	800-635-9449
New England Central Railroad	802-527-3500
New York Susquehanna & Western Railway	607-547-2555
Norfolk Southern Railway Police Communications	800-453-2530
Northeast Illinois Railroad Corp.	312-322-2800
Ontario Northland Police	705-472-4500 ex: 289
Peoria & Pekin Union Railway	309-694-8600
Port Authority of NY & NJ Police	201-216-6800
Providence and Worcester Railroad	508-755-4000
Terminal Railroad Association Of St. Louis	314-539-4750
Tuscola & Saginaw Bay Railway	231-775-2182
Union Pacific Railroad Police Dept	402-271-3528
Vermont Railway	802-658-2550
Winston-Salem Southbound Railway	336-859-3565
Wisconsin Central Railroad Ltd	715-274-4300

Phone Directory

Law Enforcement Websites

Associations and Resources

AJAX US & International Government, Military & Intelligence Agencies
http://www.sagal.com/ajax/
American Academy of Forensic Sciences
http://www.aafs.org
American Board of Forensic Document Examiners
http://www.asqde.org/abfde.htm.
American Federation Of Railroad Police
http://home.nyc.rr.com/afrp
American Society of Crime Laboratory Directors
http://www.ascld-lab.org
American Society of Criminology
http://www.asc41.com
Army CID Agents Association
http://www.randomc.com/~german/cidaa.html
ASC's Critical Criminology Division
http://www.critcrim.org
Association of Oregon Corrections Employees
http://www.aoce.org
Cecil Greek   http://www.criminology.fsu.edu/cj.html
CopNet   http://police.sas.ab.ca
Cops Online   http://www.copsonline.com
Drug Statistics Master Page - Indiana Prevention Resource Center
http://www.drugs.indiana.edu/notice.html
Federal Law Enforcement Officers Association
http://www.fleoa.org
Fraternal Order of Police, Grand Lodge
http://www.grandlodgefop.org
High Technology Crime Investigation Association
http://www.htcia.org/
Institute of Police Technology and Management
http://www.iptm.org/index.htm
International Association of Auto Theft Investigators (IAATI)
http://www.iaati.org
International Association of Bloodstain Pattern Analysts
http://www.law-forensic.com/bloodstainlinks.htm
International Association of Chiefs of Police
http://www.theiacp.org/
International Association of Crime Analysts
http://www.iaca.net
International Association for Identification
http://www.theiai.org
International Association of Women Police
http://www.iawp.org
International Police Association
http://www.ipa-usa.org

International Union of Police Associations
http://www.iupa.org

Ira Wilsker's Home Page
http://www.ih2000.net/ira/ira.htm

Italian American Police Association
http://www.ipsn.org/italcop.html

National Association of State Alcohol and Drug Abuse Directors
http://www.nasadad.org/

National Border Patrol Council
http://nbpc.net

National Conference of Law Enforcement Emerald Societies
http://www.fortunecity.com/bally/cork/96/

National Guard Association of the US
http://www.ngaus.org

National Tactical Officers' Association
http://www.ntoa.org

Officer Down Memorial
http://www.odmp.org

Peace Officers for Christ International
www.pofci.org

PIMA, LE Agencies on the Web
http://www.pima.edu/dps

PoliceGuide http://www.policeguide.com

Police Officer's Internet Directory
http://www.officer.com

Reddy's Forensic Page
http://www.forensicpage.com

Virtual Gumshoe, Investigators' Resource Page
http://www.virtualgumshoe.com

Zeno's Forensic Page   http://forensic.to/forensic.html

Certifying Boards (Forensics)

American Board of Criminalistics (ABC)
http://www.criminalistics.com

American Board of Forensic Anthropology
http://www.csuchico.edu/anth

American Board of Forensic Document Examiners (ABFDE)
http://www.asqde.org/abfde.htm

American Board of Forensic Odontology
http://www.abfo.org

American Board of Forensic Toxicology
http://www.abft.org

Emergency Services

CDC Public Health Emergency Preparedness & Response
http://www.bt.cdc.gov

Emergency Preparedness Center
http://www.areyouprepared.com/emergency_guidebook.html

Emergency Preparedness Information Exchange
http://hoshi.cic.sfu.ca/epix/
EmergencyNet
http://www.emergency.com
National Fire & Rescue
http://www.nfrsmag.com

Forensics

California Association of Criminalists
http://www.cacnews.org
California Association of Toxicologists
http://www.Cal-tox.org
California Criminalistics Institute
http://www.cci.ca.gov
Forensic Education and Consulting
http://www.forensicdna.com
Mid-Atlantic Association of Forensic Scientists
http://www.maafs.org
New Jersey Association of Forensic Scientists
http://www.njafs.org
Northeast Assocation of Forensic Scientists
http://www.neafs.org
Northwest Association of Forensic Scientists
http://members.aol.com/ictox/nwafshome.htm

K-9 Information Sites

California Rescue Dog Association (CARDA)
http://www.carda.org
K9 Academy for Law Enforcement
http://www.policek9.com
North American Police Work Dog Association
http://www.napwda.com

Law Enforcement Products & Services

CopMall   http://www.copmall.com
Police Products and Services
http://www.officer.com

National Law Enforcement Agencies and Government Links

Federal Judicial Center
http://www.fjc.gov
Federal Trade Commission
http://www.ftc.gov
National Guard Bureau
http://www.ngb.army.mil
National Security Agency
http://www.nsa.gov

Office of National Drug Control Policy
http://www.whitehousedrugpolicy.gov
Postal Inspection Service
http://www.usps.gov/websites/depart/inspect/welcome2.htm
US Congress Congressional Information
http://www.access.gpo.gov/congress/
US House of Representatives
http://www.house.gov
US Intelligence Community
http://www.intelligence.gov
US Senate   http://www.senate.gov

Online Law Enforcement Magazines & Newsletters

American Police Beat
http://www.apbweb.com
The Blues   http://www.thebluesnews.com
California Highway Patrolman
http://www.chpmagazine.com
Law and Order Magazine
http://www.lawandordermag.com
Police Marksman
http://www.policemarksman.com
Police Review
http://www.police.janes.com
Rescue Magazine
http://www.t-rescue.com
Traffic Accident Reconstruction Origin
http://www.tarorigin.com

CALENDARS AND TIME

2005 Calendar · **1030**
2005 Holidays & Important Dates · · · · · · · · · · · · 1031
2006 Calendar · **1032**
2006 Holidays & Important Dates · · · · · · · · · · · · 1033
2007 Calendar · **1034**
2007 Holidays & Important Dates · · · · · · · · · · · · 1035
2008 Calendar · **1036**
2008 Holidays & Important Dates · · · · · · · · · · · · 1037
Time Zones - Canada, Alaska, Hawaii · · · · · · · · · · **1038**
Time Zones - U.S.A., Mexico, Caribbean · · · · · · · · **1039**
Notes · **1040**

2005

January

S	M	T	W	T	F	S
						1
2	3	4	5	6	7	8
9	10	11	12	13	14	15
16	17	18	19	20	21	22
23	24	25	26	27	28	29
30	31					

February

S	M	T	W	T	F	S
		1	2	3	4	5
6	7	8	9	10	11	12
13	14	15	16	17	18	19
20	21	22	23	24	25	26
27	28					

March

S	M	T	W	T	F	S
		1	2	3	4	5
6	7	8	9	10	11	12
13	14	15	16	17	18	19
20	21	22	23	24	25	26
27	28	29	30	31		

April

S	M	T	W	T	F	S
					1	2
3	4	5	6	7	8	9
10	11	12	13	14	15	16
17	18	19	20	21	22	23
24	25	26	27	28	29	30

May

S	M	T	W	T	F	S
1	2	3	4	5	6	7
8	9	10	11	12	13	14
15	16	17	18	19	20	21
22	23	24	25	26	27	28
29	30	31				

June

S	M	T	W	T	F	S
			1	2	3	4
5	6	7	8	9	10	11
12	13	14	15	16	17	18
19	20	21	22	23	24	25
26	27	28	29	30		

July

S	M	T	W	T	F	S
					1	2
3	4	5	6	7	8	9
10	11	12	13	14	15	16
17	18	19	20	21	22	23
24	25	26	27	28	29	30
31						

August

S	M	T	W	T	F	S
	1	2	3	4	5	6
7	8	9	10	11	12	13
14	15	16	17	18	19	20
21	22	23	24	25	26	27
28	29	30	31			

September

S	M	T	W	T	F	S
				1	2	3
4	5	6	7	8	9	10
11	12	13	14	15	16	17
18	19	20	21	22	23	24
25	26	27	28	29	30	

October

S	M	T	W	T	F	S
						1
2	3	4	5	6	7	8
9	10	11	12	13	14	15
16	17	18	19	20	21	22
23	24	25	26	27	28	29
30	31					

November

S	M	T	W	T	F	S
		1	2	3	4	5
6	7	8	9	10	11	12
13	14	15	16	17	18	19
20	21	22	23	24	25	26
27	28	29	30			

December

S	M	T	W	T	F	S
				1	2	3
4	5	6	7	8	9	10
11	12	13	14	15	16	17
18	19	20	21	22	23	24
25	26	27	28	29	30	31

Shaded dates are observed Federal holidays.

2005 Holidays & Important Dates

January 1	*New Year's Day*
January 17	*Martin Luther King, Jr. Day*
February 2	Groundhog Day
February 8	Mardi Gras
February 9	Chinese New Year (Year of the Rooster)
February 9	Ash Wednesday (Christian)
February 10	Muharramn/New Year (Islamic)
February 14	Valentine's Day
February 21	*President's Day*
March 17	Saint Patrick's Day
March 20	Spring begins (Vernal Equinox)
March 25	Good Friday (Christian)
March 27	Easter Sunday (Christian)
April 3	Daylight savings time begins (spring ahead)
April 21	Prophet's Birthday (Islamic)
April 22	Earth Day (also on March 21)
April 24	First Day of Passover (Jewish)
May 1	Last Day of Passover (Jewish)
May 8	Mother's Day
May 15	National Peace Officers' Memorial Day
May 21	Armed Forces Day
May 30	*Memorial Day*
June 6	D-Day
June 14	Flag Day
June 19	Father's Day
June 19	Juneteenth
June 21	Summer begins (Summer Solstice)
July 4	*Independence Day*
September 5	*Labor Day*
September 11	Patriot Day
September 22	Autumn begins (Autumnal Equinox)
October 4	Rosh Hashana (Jewish)
October 5	Ramadan begins (Islamic)
October 10	*Columbus Day*
October 13	Yom Kippur (Jewish)
October 30	Daylight savings time ends (fall back)
October 31	Halloween
November 8	Election Day
November 11	*Veterans Day*
November 22	National Stop the Violence Day
November 24	*Thanksgiving Day*
December 7	Pearl Harbor Day
December 21	Winter begins (Winter Solstice)
December 25	*Christmas Day*
December 26	First Day of Chanukah (Jewish)
December 26	Kwanza begins
December 26	*Christmas (observed federal holiday)*

Dates in bold-italics are federal holidays

2005 Full Moons

January 25	May 23	September 18
February 24	June 22	October 17
March 25	July 21	November 16
April 24	August 19	December 15

2006

January

S	M	T	W	T	F	S
1	2	3	4	5	6	7
8	9	10	11	12	13	14
15	16	17	18	19	20	21
22	23	24	25	26	27	28
29	30	31				

February

S	M	T	W	T	F	S
			1	2	3	4
5	6	7	8	9	10	11
12	13	14	15	16	17	18
19	20	21	22	23	24	25
26	27	28				

March

S	M	T	W	T	F	S
			1	2	3	4
5	6	7	8	9	10	11
12	13	14	15	16	17	18
19	20	21	22	23	24	25
26	27	28	29	30	31	

April

S	M	T	W	T	F	S
						1
2	3	4	5	6	7	8
9	10	11	12	13	14	15
16	17	18	19	20	21	22
23	24	25	26	27	28	29
30						

May

S	M	T	W	T	F	S
	1	2	3	4	5	6
7	8	9	10	11	12	13
14	15	16	17	18	19	20
21	22	23	24	25	26	27
28	29	30	31			

June

S	M	T	W	T	F	S
				1	2	3
4	5	6	7	8	9	10
11	12	13	14	15	16	17
18	19	20	21	22	23	24
25	26	27	28	29	30	

July

S	M	T	W	T	F	S
						1
2	3	4	5	6	7	8
9	10	11	12	13	14	15
16	17	18	19	20	21	22
23	24	25	26	27	28	29
30	31					

August

S	M	T	W	T	F	S
		1	2	3	4	5
6	7	8	9	10	11	12
13	14	15	16	17	18	19
20	21	22	23	24	25	26
27	28	29	30	31		

September

S	M	T	W	T	F	S
					1	2
3	4	5	6	7	8	9
10	11	12	13	14	15	16
17	18	19	20	21	22	23
24	25	26	27	28	29	30

October

S	M	T	W	T	F	S
1	2	3	4	5	6	7
8	9	10	11	12	13	14
15	16	17	18	19	20	21
22	23	24	25	26	27	28
29	30	31				

November

S	M	T	W	T	F	S
			1	2	3	4
5	6	7	8	9	10	11
12	13	14	15	16	17	18
19	20	21	22	23	24	25
26	27	28	29	30		

December

S	M	T	W	T	F	S
					1	2
3	4	5	6	7	8	9
10	11	12	13	14	15	16
17	18	19	20	21	22	23
24	25	26	27	28	29	30
31						

Shaded dates are observed Federal holidays.

2006 Holidays & Important Dates

January 1	New Year's Day
January 2	Last Day of Chanukah (Jewish)
January 2	*New Year's Day (observed federal holiday)*
January 16	*Martin Luther King, Jr. Day*
January 29	Chinese New Year (Year of the Dog)
January 31	Maharamn/New Year (Islamic)
February 2	Groundhog Day
February 14	Valentine's Day
February 20	*President's Day*
February 28	Mardi Gras
March 1	Ash Wednesday (Christian)
March 17	Saint Patrick's Day
March 20	Spring begins (Vernal Equinox)
April 2	Daylight savings time begins (spring ahead)
April 11	Prophet's Birthday (Islamic)
April 13	First Day of Passover (Jewish)
April 14	Good Friday (Christian)
April 16	Easter Sunday (Christian)
April 20	Last Day of Passover (Jewish)
April 22	Earth Day (also on March 21)
May 14	Mother's Day
May 15	National Peace Officers' Memorial Day
May 20	Armed Forces Day
May 29	*Memorial Day*
June 6	D-Day
June 14	Flag Day
June 18	Father's Day
June 19	Juneteenth
June 21	Summer begins (Summer Solstice)
July 4	*Independence Day*
September 4	*Labor Day*
September 11	Patriot Day
September 23	Autumn begins (Autumnal Equinox)
September 23	Rosh Hashana (Jewish)
September 24	Ramadan begins (Islamic)
October 2	Yom Kippur (Jewish)
October 9	*Columbus Day*
October 29	Daylight savings time ends (fall back)
October 31	Halloween
November 7	Election Day
November 10	*Veterans Day (observed federal holiday)*
November 11	Veterans Day
November 22	National Stop the Violence Day
November 23	*Thanksgiving Day*
December 7	Pearl Harbor Day
December 16-23	Days of Chanukah (Jewish)
December 22	Winter begins (Winter Solstice)
December 25	*Christmas Day*
December 26	Kwanza begins

Dates in bold-italics are federal holidays

2006 Full Moons

January 14	May 13	September 7
February 13	June 11	October 7
March 14	July 11	November 5
April 13	August 9	December 5

2007

January

S	M	T	W	T	F	S
	1	2	3	4	5	6
7	8	9	10	11	12	13
14	15	16	17	18	19	20
21	22	23	24	25	26	27
28	29	30	31			

February

S	M	T	W	T	F	S
				1	2	3
4	5	6	7	8	9	10
11	12	13	14	15	16	17
18	19	20	21	22	23	24
25	26	27	28			

March

S	M	T	W	T	F	S
				1	2	3
4	5	6	7	8	9	10
11	12	13	14	15	16	17
18	19	20	21	22	23	24
25	26	27	28	29	30	31

April

S	M	T	W	T	F	S
1	2	3	4	5	6	7
8	9	10	11	12	13	14
15	16	17	18	19	20	21
22	23	24	25	26	27	28
29	30					

May

S	M	T	W	T	F	S
		1	2	3	4	5
6	7	8	9	10	11	12
13	14	15	16	17	18	19
20	21	22	23	24	25	26
27	28	29	30	31		

June

S	M	T	W	T	F	S
					1	2
3	4	5	6	7	8	9
10	11	12	13	14	15	16
17	18	19	20	21	22	23
24	25	26	27	28	29	30

July

S	M	T	W	T	F	S
1	2	3	4	5	6	7
8	9	10	11	12	13	14
15	16	17	18	19	20	21
22	23	24	25	26	27	28
29	30	31				

August

S	M	T	W	T	F	S
			1	2	3	4
5	6	7	8	9	10	11
12	13	14	15	16	17	18
19	20	21	22	23	24	25
26	27	28	29	30	31	

September

S	M	T	W	T	F	S
						1
2	3	4	5	6	7	8
9	10	11	12	13	14	15
16	17	18	19	20	21	22
23	24	25	26	27	28	29
30						

October

S	M	T	W	T	F	S
	1	2	3	4	5	6
7	8	9	10	11	12	13
14	15	16	17	18	19	20
21	22	23	24	25	26	27
28	29	30	31			

November

S	M	T	W	T	F	S
				1	2	3
4	5	6	7	8	9	10
11	12	13	14	15	16	17
18	19	20	21	22	23	24
25	26	27	28	29	30	

December

S	M	T	W	T	F	S
						1
2	3	4	5	6	7	8
9	10	11	12	13	14	15
16	17	18	19	20	21	22
23	24	25	26	27	28	29
30	31					

Shaded dates are observed Federal holidays.

2007 Holidays & Important Dates

January 1	*New Year's Day*
January 15	*Martin Luther King, Jr. Day*
January 20	Maharramn/New Year (Islamic)
February 2	Groundhog Day
February 14	Valentine's Day
February 18	Chinese New Year (Year of the Pig)
February 19	*President's Day*
February 20	Mardi Gras
February 21	Ash Wednesday (Christian)
March 17	Saint Patrick's Day
March 21	Spring begins (Vernal Equinox)
March 31	Prophet's Birthday (Islamic)
April 1	Daylight savings time begins (spring ahead)
April 3	First Day of Passover (Jewish)
April 6	Good Friday (Christian)
April 8	Easter Sunday (Christian)
April 10	Last Day of Passover (Jewish)
April 22	Earth Day (Also on March 21)
May 13	Mother's Day
May 15	National Peace Officers' Memorial Day
May 19	Armed Forces Day
May 28	*Memorial Day*
June 6	D-Day
June 14	Flag Day
June 17	Father's Day
June 19	Juneteenth
June 21	Summer begins (Summer Solstice)
July 4	*Independence Day*
September 3	*Labor Day*
September 11	Patriot Day
September 13	Rosh Hashana (Jewish)
September 13	Ramadan begins (Islamic)
September 23	Autumn begins (Autumnal Equinox)
September 22	Yom Kippur (Jewish)
October 8	*Columbus Day*
October 28	Daylight savings time ends (fall back)
October 31	Halloween
November 6	Election Day
November 11	Veterans Day
November 12	*Veterans Day (observed federal holiday)*
November 22	National Stop the Violence Day
November 22	*Thanksgiving Day*
December 5	First Day of Chanukah (Jewish)
December 7	Pearl Harbor Day
December 12	Last Day of Chanukah (Jewish)
December 22	Winter begins (Winter Solstice)
December 25	*Christmas Day*
December 26	Kwanza begins

Dates in bold-italics are federal holidays

2007 Full Moons

January 3	May 2	September 26
February 2	June 1, 30	October 26
March 3	July 30	November 24
April 2	August 28	December 24

2008

January

S	M	T	W	T	F	S
		1	2	3	4	5
6	7	8	9	10	11	12
13	14	15	16	17	18	19
20	21	22	23	24	25	26
27	28	29	30	31		

February

S	M	T	W	T	F	S
					1	2
3	4	5	6	7	8	9
10	11	12	13	14	15	16
17	18	19	20	21	22	23
24	25	26	27	28	29	

March

S	M	T	W	T	F	S
						1
2	3	4	5	6	7	8
9	10	11	12	13	14	15
16	17	18	19	20	21	22
23	24	25	26	27	28	29
30	31					

April

S	M	T	W	T	F	S
		1	2	3	4	5
6	7	8	9	10	11	12
13	14	15	16	17	18	19
20	21	22	23	24	25	26
27	28	29	30			

May

S	M	T	W	T	F	S
				1	2	3
4	5	6	7	8	9	10
11	12	13	14	15	16	17
18	19	20	21	22	23	24
25	26	27	28	29	30	31

June

S	M	T	W	T	F	S
1	2	3	4	5	6	7
8	9	10	11	12	13	14
15	16	17	18	19	20	21
22	23	24	25	26	27	28
29	30					

July

S	M	T	W	T	F	S
		1	2	3	4	5
6	7	8	9	10	11	12
13	14	15	16	17	18	19
20	21	22	23	24	25	26
27	28	29	30	31		

August

S	M	T	W	T	F	S
					1	2
3	4	5	6	7	8	9
10	11	12	13	14	15	16
17	18	19	20	21	22	23
24	25	26	27	28	29	30
31						

September

S	M	T	W	T	F	S
	1	2	3	4	5	6
7	8	9	10	11	12	13
14	15	16	17	18	19	20
21	22	23	24	25	26	27
28	29	30				

October

S	M	T	W	T	F	S
			1	2	3	4
5	6	7	8	9	10	11
12	13	14	15	16	17	18
19	20	21	22	23	24	25
26	27	28	29	30	31	

November

S	M	T	W	T	F	S
						1
2	3	4	5	6	7	8
9	10	11	12	13	14	15
16	17	18	19	20	21	22
23	24	25	26	27	28	29
30						

December

S	M	T	W	T	F	S
	1	2	3	4	5	6
7	8	9	10	11	12	13
14	15	16	17	18	19	20
21	22	23	24	25	26	27
28	29	30	31			

Shaded dates are observed Federal holidays.

2008 Holidays & Important Dates

January 1	*New Year's Day*
January 10	Maharramn/New Year (Islamic)
January 21	*Martin Luther King, Jr. Day*
February 2	Groundhog Day
February 5	Mardi Gras
February 6	Ash Wednesday (Christian)
February 7	Chinese New Year (Year of the Rat)
February 14	Valentine's Day
February 18	*President's Day*
March 17	Saint Patrick's Day
March 20	Spring begins (Vernal Equinox)
March 20	Prophet's Birthday (Islamic)
March 21	Good Friday (Christian)
March 23	Easter Sunday (Christian)
April 6	Daylight savings time begins (spring ahead)
April 20	First Day of Passover (Jewish)
April 22	Earth Day (Also on March 21)
April 27	Last Day of Passover (Jewish)
May 11	Mother's Day
May 15	National Peace Officers' Memorial Day
May 17	Armed Forces Day
May 26	*Memorial Day*
June 6	D-Day
June 14	Flag Day
June 15	Father's Day
June 19	Juneteenth
June 21	Summer begins (Summer Solstice)
July 4	*Independence Day*
September 1	*Labor Day*
September 2	Ramadan begins (Islamic)
September 11	Patriot Day
September 22	Autumn begins (Autumnal Equinox)
September 30	Rosh Hashana (Jewish)
October 9	Yom Kippur (Jewish)
October 13	*Columbus Day*
October 26	Daylight savings time ends (fall back)
October 31	Halloween
November 4	Election Day
November 11	*Veterans Day*
November 22	National Stop the Violence Day
November 27	*Thanksgiving Day*
December 7	Pearl Harbor Day
December 21	Winter begins (Winter Solstice)
December 22	First Day of Chanukah (Jewish)
December 25	*Christmas Day*
December 26	Kwanza begins
December 29	Last Day of Chanukah (Jewish)

Dates in bold-italics are federal holidays

2008 Full Moons

January 22	May 20	September 15
February 21	June 18	October 14
March 21	July 18	November 13
April 20	August 16	December 12

Time Zones - Canada, Alaska, Hawaii

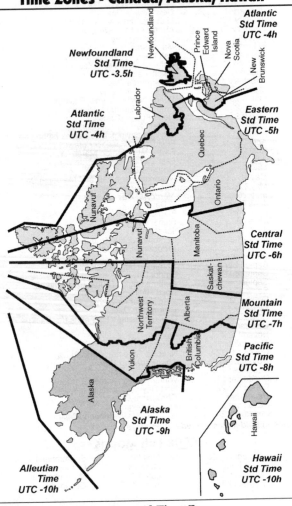

Atlantic
Std Time
UTC -4h

Newfoundland
Std Time
UTC -3.5h

Newfoundland

Prince Edward Island

Nova Scotia

New Brunswick

Atlantic
Std Time
UTC -4h

Labrador

Quebec

Eastern
Std Time
UTC -5h

Ontario

Nunavut

Central
Std Time
UTC -6h

Nunavut

Manitoba

Saskatchewan

Mountain
Std Time
UTC -7h

Northwest Territory

Alberta

British Columbia

Pacific
Std Time
UTC -8h

Yukon

Alaska

Alaska
Std Time
UTC -9h

Hawaii

Alleutian
Time
UTC -10h

Hawaii
Std Time
UTC -10h

Time Zones - U.S.A., Mexico, Caribbean

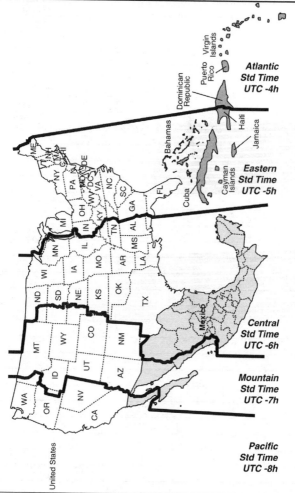

Index

12 keys to a longer career	362
2005 calendar	1030
2005 full moons	1031
2005 holidays & important dates	1031
2006 calendar	1032
2006 full moons	1033
2006 holidays & important dates	1033
2007 calendar	1034
2007 full moons	1035
2007 holidays & important dates	1035
2008 calendar	1036
2008 full moons	1037
2008 holidays & important dates	1037
Abduction	99
By a family member	99
By a non-family member	101
Acronym list	186
NIMS, Incident Management Systems	262
ADR Agreement, European	607
Air Force rank	158
Alaska time zones	1038
Algor mortis	308
Alphabet	29
Braille	31
Phonetic	29
Semaphore	29
Alphabet recitation test	30
AMBER alert plan	104
American National Standards Institute ANSI Z 1291	606
American sign language	28
American time zones	1039
Ammunition manufacturers	551
Ammunition specs	544
Amphetamines	380
Animal & Plant Health Inspection Service (APHIS)	508
Anthrax	468
Area codes	172
By code	178
By state	172
Army rank	162
Arson and fire investigation	264
Assembling emergency supply kits	343
Automobile stopping distances	529
BAC - Blood Alcohol Content	282
Balance test	277
Barbiturates	371
Beaufort wind speed scale	352
Benzodiazepines	372
Biological weapons	481
Bites	135
Bleeding	136
Blister agents	491
Blood agents	492
Blood Alcohol Content (BAC)	282
Female percentages	283
International limits	282
Male percentages	283
Blood exposure	356
Blood stain collection	293
Body armor	549
Body armor manufacturers	551

Body fluid evidence ················· 293
Bomb threats ················· 110
   Checklist ················· 115
   Detecting ················· 116
   Explosive ordnance disposal units ················· 122
   Vehicle bomb explosion hazards and evacuation distance tables ················· 126
Bone marrow syndrome ················· 502
Braille alphabet ················· 31
Broken bones ················· 137
Bullet proof vests ················· 549
Buprenorphine ················· 377
Burns ················· 137
Calendars ················· 1029
   2005 calendar ················· 1030
   2005 full moons ················· 1031
   2005 holidays & important dates ················· 1031
   2006 calendar ················· 1032
   2006 full moons ················· 1033
   2006 holidays & important dates ················· 1033
   2007 calendar ················· 1034
   2007 full moons ················· 1035
   2007 holidays & important dates ················· 1035
   2008 calendar ················· 1036
   2008 full moons ················· 1037
   2008 holidays & important dates ················· 1037
Canadian gun laws ················· 601
Canadian hazardous materials assistance ················· 614
Canadian time zones ················· 1038
Cannabis ················· 370
Cardiovascular syndrome ················· 502
Caribbean time zones ················· 1039
CBR event hotlines ················· 506
CBRN Countermeasures Program ················· 511
Celsius to Fahrenheit conversion ················· 157
Central Index System (CIS) ················· 17
Checklist for emergencies ················· 346
Chemical protective clothing and equipment ················· 620
Chemical weapons ················· 490
Chemical/Biological agent manufacturing signs ················· 465
Chemicals used in the manufacture of drugs ················· 393
Child abuse ················· 70
   Burns ················· 80
   Eye injuries ················· 83
   Head injuries ················· 84
   Homicides ················· 86
   Injuries associated with abuse ················· 79
   Internal injuries ················· 84
   Missing children ················· 93
   Munchausen syndrome by proxy ················· 88
   Poisoning ················· 85
   Regional information sharing systems ················· 108
   Repetitive accidents ················· 85
   Resources ················· 108
   Shaken baby syndrome ················· 87
   Skin (cutaneous) injuries ················· 83
   Sudden Infant Death Syndrome (SIDS) ················· 89
Child homicides ················· 86
   Munchausen syndrome by proxy ················· 88
   Shaken baby syndrome ················· 87
   Sudden Infant Death Syndrome (SIDS) ················· 89
Children, missing ················· 93
Chloral Hydrate ················· 372
Choking ················· 140
Choking agents ················· 493
Circle search pattern ················· 334

CISD - Critical Incident Stress Debriefing····················· 359
Civil Air Patrol (CAP) - Search & Rescue ····················· 521
Classification system for hazardous materials ··············· 621
Clean air for emergencies ··· 342
Clearinghouses, for missing children··························· 106
Coast Guard & Navy rank ··· 160
Cocaine ··· 380
Codeine··· 376
Cold water survival times ··· 350
Command Staff, Incident Command System··················· 206
Commercial aircraft prohibited item list ······················· 536
Communications ··· 9
    American sign language······································· 28
    Braille alphabet··· 31
    Government electronic databases····························· 17
    Ham radio emergency frequencies····························· 33
    Miranda Advisement·· 12
    Morse code··· 28
    Phonetic alphabet·· 29
    Semaphore alphabet·· 30
    Spanish phrase book·· 10
    Swat hand signals·· 25
    Ten radio codes··· 31
Communications systems for hazardous materials ··········· 604
Compatibility group letters for hazardous materials··········· 622
Consular Consolidated Database (CCD)·························· 17
Consular Lookout And Support System (CLASS)··············· 17
Consular Lost & Stolen Passport (CLASP)······················ 17
Controlled substances uses and effects························ 370
Conversion factors ··· 167
    Velocity conversions ·· 534
Counting sequence test·· 277
CPR·· 131
    For dogs and cats··· 152
Crime scene photography ··· 325
Crime scene response ··· 286
    Evidence collection·· 293
    Search procedures··· 288
    Team member responsibilities································· 286
Crimes against children··· 69
    Child abuse resources·· 108
    Child homicides··· 86
    Injuries associated with abuse································· 79
    Missing children·· 93
    Physical abuse·· 70
Critical incident stress debriefing································· 359
Cutaneous radiation syndrome···································· 502
Cypionate·· 379
Dangers from radiation··· 498
Decanoate·· 379
Decontamination ·· 496
Defense Central and Investigations Index (DCII) ·············· 17
Department of Defense (NorthCom)······························ 505
Department of Homeland Security (DHS)························ 507
    Border and Transportation Security····························· 508
    Department diagram·· 515
    Emergency Preparedness & Response (EP&R)·············· 510
    Information Analysis and Infrastructure Protection (IAIP)··· 510
    Office of Management·· 512
    Phone numbers··· 959
    Science and Technology··· 511
    US Coast Guard (USCG) ·· 513
    US Secret Service (USSS)······································ 514
Depressants··· 371
Detecting letter and package bombs····························· 116

Dexterity testing ··· 271
Dextroamphetamine ·· 380
DHS - see Department of Homeland Security ······················ 507
Diabetic emergencies ··· 140
Diamon placard, National Fire Protection Association (NFPA) ···· 605
Diet and eating habits ··· 363
Digital photography ·· 312
    Glossary ·· 316
Dirty bomb ··· 498
Disaster Medical Assistance Team (DMAT), NMIS ··············· 242
Disaster Mortuary Operational Response Team (DMORT), NMIS ·· 242
Documents for shipping hazardous materials ······················ 616
Domestic Emergency Support Teams (DEST) ······················ 510
Domestic preparedness chemical/biological ······················· 506
DOT Hazardous Materials Transportation Act (HMTA) ············ 610
Driving drunk ··· 267
Drug scheduling ··· 382
Drug use by state ·· 456
Drugs ··· 370
    Cannabis ·· 370
    Chemical used in the manufacture of ······························ 393
    Cocaine ·· 380
    Depressants ·· 371
    Hallucinogens ·· 373
    Heroin ··· 377
    Inhalants ·· 375
    Marijuana ··· 370
    Narcotics ·· 376
    Steroids ··· 379
    Stimulants ·· 380
    Street names & terms for drugs ······································ 398
Drunk driving ··· 267
    Alphabet recitation test ··· 276
    Balance test ··· 277
    Blood Alcohol Content (BAC) ··· 282
    Counting sequence test ·· 277
    Dexterity testing ··· 271
    Finger count ··· 276
    Finger to nose test ·· 278
    Horizontal gaze nystagmus test ······································ 273
    One leg stand ·· 275
    Probability value guide ··· 268
    Romberg balance test ·· 277
    Walk and turn test ·· 274
Early warning signs for terrorism ·· 464
Earthquake intensity scales ··· 348
El Paso Intelligence Center (EPIC) ·· 17
Electric shock ·· 141
Electronic Data Gathering, Analysis & Retrieval (EDGAR) ······· 18
Emergency checklist ··· 346
Emergency planning and preparedness ·································· 336
Emergency supplies ·· 338
Emergency supply kit sample contents ··································· 343
Enanthate ··· 379
Environmental Measurements Laboratory (EML) ···················· 511
Estimated speed based on skid marks ··································· 530
European ADR Agreement ··· 607
Evacuation and isolation for hazardous materials ··················· 617
Evacuation distance table ·· 126, 903
Evidence ·· 293
    Algor mortis ··· 308
    Blood stains ··· 293
    Collection ··· 293
    Computers ·· 306
    Documents ··· 304